D. Appleton and Co.

Student's Concordance

To the Revised Version, 1881, of the New Testament of our Lord and Saviour Jesus Christ

D. Appleton and Co.

Student's Concordance
To the Revised Version, 1881, of the New Testament of our Lord and Saviour Jesus Christ

ISBN/EAN: 9783337260576

Printed in Europe, USA, Canada, Australia, Japan

Cover: Foto ©Lupo / pixelio.de

More available books at **www.hansebooks.com**

THE
STUDENT'S CONCORDANCE

TO THE

REVISED VERSION, 1881, OF THE
NEW TESTAMENT OF OUR LORD AND SAVIOUR
JESUS CHRIST.

Compiled upon an Original Plan, shewing the changes in all
Words referred to.

WITH APPENDICES OF THE CHIEF AUTHORISED WORDS AND PASSAGES OMITTED
IN THE REVISION, AND OF NEW AND DISUSED WORDS: A TABLE OF
THE GENEALOGY OF THE ENGLISH NEW TESTAMENT, ETC.

New York:
D. APPLETON & CO., 1, 3, AND 5, BOND STREET.
1882.

COMPILERS' PREFACE.

A CONCORDANCE would seem to be a natural complement of the 1881 Version of the New Testament, and the present volume is an endeavour to supply the want. Its publication was first suggested to one of the compilers by a conversation on the Revised New Testament, during which the need for a Concordance was discussed. A plan of the work was projected, and has been completed by the joint aid of a friend. The object has been to represent every sentence of the New Testament by its principal words, and the texts are given as complete as the space allows, in the very words of the Revised Version, with their capitals and stops, so that they may be taken as quotations without further reference to the Testament itself. Details are given in the "*Plan of the Work*," and it is needless to say more here on that point than to remark on one feature of the book.

The purpose of a Concordance is to enable the student to find any required passage by reference to some principal word in it. But a Concordance of the Revised Version on the old lines would be of comparatively little use, owing to the numerous alterations from the Authorised Version, the familiar words of which are so frequently changed for others. It seemed necessary, therefore, that a Concordance, to answer its end, should in a measure comprise both versions—to the extent, at least, of affording some clue to the changed words. This has been done in the present work, by giving under each word the words which in any text of the New Version are substituted for the same word in the old. And, on the other hand, in every text given, if the word under which it occurs is altered, the reader is referred to the head of the group of texts, where he will find the corresponding word in the Authorized Version. It is hoped that the Concordance will thus not only serve for reference to texts, but that it will aid in an examination of the changes which have been made, and exhibit the uniformity of translation and other features of the New Version.

The time and labour spent upon this work have alike far exceeded what was anticipated. Solicitude for the completeness and accuracy of the book has grown with its progress, and the chief desire of the compilers in its publication is that it may prove a useful and a not unworthy companion to the Holy Scriptures, to the study of which it is intended as an aid.

The compilers began this work, conscious of the defects of the Authorised Version, yet with a predilection for it in the main, and they beheld with some regret the altered character of a version so precious by a thousand associations. But if they may be allowed to judge by the result upon themselves of much examination of the two versions in the course of this work, they venture to express the conviction that the use of the Revised Version will result in a growing appreciation of its value, as carrying within itself the evidence that it is a translation of a purer text, by the hands of a company of devout and more able men than has ever before been joined together for the like purpose.

CONTENTS.

GENEALOGY OF ENGLISH NEW TESTAMENT -   -   viii

NOTES ON ENGLISH BIBLES, REVISED VERSION OF 1881, AND GREEK AND OTHER

    MSS. OF NEW TESTAMENT -   -   -   -   ix

PLAN OF THE WORK -   -   -   -   xii

CONCORDANCE—PART I.—GENERAL.   -   -   1

    PART II.—PROPER NAMES   -   -   391

APPENDIX—OMITTED WORDS OF AUTHORISED VERSION   433

    LIST OF NEW AND DISUSED WORDS AND ALTERED SPELLING   437

THE GENEALOGY OF THE ENGLISH NEW TESTAMENT:

A TABLE SHEWING

The Principal Early Editions of the Greek New Testament and their connection with the English Version of 1611.

ERASMUS, Desiderius, "a great and wonderful light of learning," and reformer. He studied at St. Mary's College, Oxford, 1497-9, and was Professor of Greek at Cambridge from 1509 to 1514. Born at Rotterdam, Oct. 28, 1467, died at Basle, July 12th, 1536.

1516.
The first published edition of the entire Greek Testament. Froben, an eminent printer at Basle, anxious to forestall the Complutensian Bible, (which see,) solicited Erasmus, while in England, in April, 1515, to prepare an Edition of the New Testament, which he undertook to do, and it was printed in ten months' time in a Greek. Erasmus used MSS. at Basle, with one exception, are "neither ancient nor particularly valuable." The last six verses of the Apocalypse which were missing in his mutilated MS. of the Apocalypse, he supplied as he did other parts, by his own translation from the Latin.

1519.
This edition presents a purer text, and more valuable readings than the first edition, which Erasmus here altered in more than four hundred places, being mostly amended readings from a fresh Codex of the Gospels, Acts, and Paul. Of this edition together there were printed 3,300 copies.

1522.
Remarkable chiefly from its containing the controverted clause in 1 Jno. v. The history of its insertion is as follows:— Erasmus had been drawn into controversy by the divines of Louvain, and by Stunica, the most learned of the Complutensian Editors, for not inserting this clause in his first edition. It was not in any of the MSS. he had at that time, but he rashly promised in any subsequent edition, if it could be found in any Greek MS. He redeemed his promise on being directed to a MS. now known as the Codex Montfortianus, in which it appears, "in a form which obviously betrays its origin as a clumsy translation from the Vulgate."—(Westcott). This MS. belonged to Archbishop Ussher, who presented it to Trinity College, Dublin. Erasmus calls it Cod. Britannicus. The MS. made its appearance in 1520, and though some critics have assigned it to the twelfth century, there is indisputable internal evidence, that it was written shortly prior to 1520, and probably for a particular purpose. Tyndale used this edition for his translation. Luther used the 1519 and 1522 editions for his German Bible.

1527.
This edition contains, besides the Greek text and Latin version of Erasmus, the Latin Vulgate, in a third column in each page. The Greek text is partly taken from the third edition and partly from the Complutensian, and it also contains various readings from the Complutensian. Of one hundred alterations ninety are in the Apocalypse. This edition is the most notable of all the editions of Erasmus, from the fact that Stephens adopted it as the basis of his third edition, and was in turn followed by Beza, and by the Elzevir edition of 1624.

1535.
This deviates from the last in four places only, where better readings are substituted.

STEPHENS, or Estienne of Paris. This family whose publications date from 1502 to 1664, was as distinguished for its learning as for its excellence in printing.

1546, 1549.
These two editions are in 12mo. size, beautifully printed by Robert Stephens, from elegant type cast at the King's cost, and as well as the 1550 edition, were printed at the press of Paris. The text was compiled from the Complutensian, the 1535 and 1535 editions of Erasmus, and 15

1550.
Paris, folio. A splendid specimen of typography. This is the Stephens' edition. It contains the first collection of various

1651.
12mo, printed at Geneva, where Stephens took up his residence on professing Protestantism. It is the first edition, which divided the text into verses. Stephens' son tells us that his father marked the divisions during a journey from Paris to Lyons on horseback. The

COMPLUTENSIAN POLYGLOTT BIBLE

The *Complutensian Polyglott*, so called because printed at Complutum (Alcala) in Spain. This splendid Bible, the first executed Polyglot, was due to the able and munificent Cardinal Ximenes, Primate of Spain, at a cost, it is said, of £23,000. It is in six large folio volumes, four of which contain the Old Testament in Hebrew, Greek, and Latin, with the Chaldee Paraphrase. The fifth volume bears the first *printed* Greek Testament, though that of Erasmus was first published. It comprises the New Testament in Greek and the Latin Vulgate, with marginal references to passages in the Old and New Testaments. The sixth volume is an Hebrew and Chaldaic Vocabulary of the Old Testament. The fourth volume was the last printed, in 1517. The Cardinal employed various learned men to compose the work; and though upwards of sixty years of age, undertook to make himself master of the Hebrew tongue, in order to be better acquainted with the more learned parts of it. There is "no cause for believing that any document of high antiquity or first-rate importance was employed by the editors of this Polyglott." (*Scrivener*). This splendid Bible was commenced until 1502, and owing to some doubts of the Church of Rome as to whether it was proper to bring it into general circulation. The Bull of Pope Leo X. giving permission for its publication, was dated March 22nd, 1520, and is affixed to the work, and from which it appears that about 600 copies were printed. By mandate of the Pope, the Polyglot was originally sold at six and a half ducats. Copies of this Bible are in the British Museum, at Oxford and Cambridge, and at Sion College.

ALDUS GREEK BIBLE

1518.
The MS. from which this edition of the Greek Bible was composed were collated by Aldus, the printer of Venice. He died in 1515, and his father-in-law, Andreas Asulanus, undertook the publication of the work.

In the New Testament he closely followed Erasmus. Mill says, "he corrected Erasmus in one hundred places, and vitiated his text in almost as many." He retained even many errors of the press.

MSS. (one of them the **Codex Bezæ**) collated by Stephens' son Henry. They consisted of 10 MSS. of the Gospels, 8 of the Act, 7 of the Catholic Epistles, 8 of Pauline Epistles, 2 of the Apocalypse. The second edition differs from the first in 67 places (*Hill*), and is preferred for its greater rarity and correctness.

BEZA, of the Reformation Party. He fled to Switzerland on account of his religion. Born 1518, died Feb., 1605.

1565, 1576, 1582, 1589, 1598.

Beza's Latin Version was first published at Geneva, in folio, in 1556; and at Basle in 1559, with Stephens' Greek and Latin. His first complete Greek and Latin New Testament was published in 1565. The critical materials at his command were the papers of Stephens; the lately published Syriac Version, with Latin translation, of Tremellius; the Codex Bezæ; and for his third and principal edition, the Codex Claromontanus. All his editions have the Vulgate, and the Latin Version of Beza, with philological,

doctrinal, and practical notes. Beza, being a commentator rather than a critic, did not make the use of his materials which might have been expected; and his various readings rather for polemical purposes in his notes than for emendating the text. His editions do not vary materially from Stephens of 1550, and each other. The 1598 edition is esteemed the most accurate.

ELZEVIR. This family of learned and eminent printers numbered 14 printers in five generations, at Leyden, Amsterdam, etc. Printing the beauty of its types and its finish. 1581-1712.

1624, 1633.

Small 12mo. The Editor is unknown. The text is mainly that of Stephens, 1550, from which it differs in 278 places (many unimportant), and it generally agrees with Beza. In its second edition, the editor in his preface, apparently alludes to Beza, though not by name. The latter of whom he seems to prefer. The preface claims for the 1624 edition, that it has been accepted by all, and the 1633 text that it is "textum ab omnibus receptum," in which is nothing to be amended, or corrupt. From the above expression it has, until a recent date, been generally accepted as the "Received Text" on the Continent, as the 1550 Stephens has been chiefly in England.

| 1641, printed at Leyden. |
| 1652, 1656, 1670, 1678, printed at Amsterdam. |

The edition of 1633 was admirably counterfeited by Arnold Leers, and published by him, 12mo., 1656.

THE KING'S BIBLE, OR AUTHORISED VERSION.

1611.

At a conference held at Hampton Court, in January, 1604, to hear and determine "things pretended to be amiss in the church," Dr. Reynolds, President of Corpus Christi College, Oxford, moved King James, who was present, that there might be a new translation of the Bible. In June, the King appointed fifty-four men to undertake the task; the actual number engaged in it was 1607, when the work was formally undertaken, was forty-seven, and they were men distinguished for their piety and learning. Directions were given to them for their work, which was to be of the nature of revision, rather than translation. As their preface states, "We never thought from the beginning that we should need to make a new translation, nor yet to make of a bad a good one * * but to make a good one out

figures of the verses were printed in the margin, as in the Revised Version of 1881. The paragraphs were first broken up into verses in the Genevan Bible. He probably adopted the plan from two editions of the "Psalterium quincuplex," printed by old Henry Stephens in 1509, and from a book of Psalms printed in 1541. This edition is said to have the Greek of the preceding edition almost unaltered, with the Vulgate and the Latin version of Erasmus, and parallel passages in the margin.

better, or out of many good ones, one principall good one, not justly to be excepted against." The Bishops Bible was to be followed. The work of revision was carried on by six companies, two meeting at each of the three cities of Oxford, Cambridge, and Westminster; and the whole work was revised again in London, by selected members of each company of revisers. This last work of supervision occupied nine months, and the Bible was issued in 1611, in folio. "The revision of the New Testament" may be generally described as a careful examination of the Bishops version, 1572, with the *Greek Text*, and with Beza's, the German, and the Rhemish version. [*Westcott's English Bible.*] The Greek Text they used is substantially that of Beza, 1589. There is no ascertained authority of Convocation, or Parliamentary, or Privy Council, or Royal Proclamation for the words on the title-page. "Appointed to be read in Churches." But, viewing this version as the recognised descendant of Henry VIII.'s "Great Bible," which was unquestionably "authorised" by proclamation of Henry VIII. in 1538, the authority was probably taken for granted without further formality. The 1611 version gradually superseded the Book of Common Prayer, the Psalms intrinsic superiority over its rivals, and are still in use. For details of the general excellencies and defects of the Authorised Version, and for lists of its variations from former versions, its marginal readings, and much deeply interesting information as to it, see Scrivener's Cambridge Paragraph Bible, Canon Westcott's History of the English Bible, and Eadie's History of the English Bible.

ENGLISH BIBLES.

WYCLIFFE'S VERSION—John Wycliffe, born in Yorkshire in 1324, died Dec. 31st, 1384. He was "an able and acute, a zealous and determined man," and without an equal as a Latin Scholar, but of Greek or Hebrew he knew nothing. He finished his translation of the New Testament from the Latin Vulgate in 1380; and his friend, Nicholas de Hereford, translated the greater portion of the Old Testament, which Wycliffe completed. No portion of Wycliffe's version had been printed until 1731, when the Rev. J. Lewis, of London, first printed the New Testament of Wycliffe, and it was re-edited by the Rev. H. H. Baber, M.A., in 1810. It is one of the versions given in Bagster's English Hexapla.

The Registry of Bishop Alnewick, of Norwich, mentions the price of a manuscript copy of the New Testament at a sum equal to forty pounds of our money, in 1429.

TYNDALE'S VERSION.—To William Tyndale the martyr, England owed her first printed English New Testament. Born in Gloucestershire, about 1484, he studied at Oxford and Cambridge, and was well acquainted with the Hebrew, Greek, and after Latin languages, Hebrew, Greek, Latin, Italian, Spanish, English, French." He became a diligent student of Holy Scripture, and says that he was moved to the work of translation, because he "perceived by experience, how that it was impossible to establish the lay people in any truth except the Scripture were plainly laid before their eyes in their mother tongue, that they might see the process, order and meaning of the text." His version is the work of a learned, independent, and original translator, of singular purity of purpose and laborious patience, who "had no man to counterfeit (imitate), neither was helped with English of any that had interpreted the same or such like thing in the Scripture beforetime." [His epilogue to the first Ed.]

He translated about half the Old Testament and the whole of the New, and all subsequent English versions have followed the standard of translation which he laid down, whilst they have for the most part retained his very words. Westcott states as examples, that about nine-tenths of the Authorised Version of the first Epistle of St. John, and five-sixths of that to the Ephesians (which is extremely difficult) are retained from Tyndale. In the New Testament he rendered the Greek Text of Erasmus directly, while still he consulted the Vulgate and the German of Luther. He found he would not be allowed to translate in England, and went to Hamburgh. In 1524, he published the Gospels of SS. Matthew and Mark separately, with notes, and in 1525, went to Cologne to print his complete New Testament Cochlæus, a relentless enemy of the Reformation, obtained from the printers the secret that 3,000 Testaments were being printed for England, and got the Authorities to forbid the work. Tyndale escaped, with his printed sheets, to Worms. He was here in safety, and completed his quarto edition, and also published a new edition without glosses, in octavo. This latter edition was first finished, and both editions reached England in 1526, without any indication of the translator's name. The quarto edition was commenced by Quentel, and was probably completed by Peter Schoeffer, of Worms, who printed the smaller edition. The book was bought up, forbidden, and publicly burnt in England. But these efforts were vain to check its circulation, and indeed led to its careful revision by Tyndale in 1534 (and Ed.) with marginal notes, prologues to the books, and markings of the Church Lessons: and again, while in prison, in 1535 (3rd Ed.) without notes. Three surreptitious editions were printed at Antwerp, in 1534. Tyndale was first strangled and then burned, at Vilvorde, near Antwerp, Oct. 6th, 1536.

COVERDALE'S VERSION.—The first complete English Bible, finished October 4th, 1535, was the work of Myles Coverdale, a Yorkshireman, born 1488, afterwards Bishop of Exeter, a man greatly esteemed for his piety, knowledge of the Scriptures, and diligent preaching. It is now pretty conclusively proved by Mr. H. Stevens, that it was printed at Antwerp, by Jacob van Meteren, ("The Bibles in the Caxton Exhibition, 1878"). The title speaks of it as "faithfully and truly translated out of the Douche (that is, German) and Latin," and though in subsequent editions it is simply "translated in Englishe," it would appear that this is a secondary translation, Coverdale using "five sundry interpreters" as he calls them, of which were the Vulgate, Luther, the Zürich or Swiss German, the Latin of Pagninus, and he certainly consulted Tyndale's Pentateuch and New Testament. In the New Testament, he follows the 1526 and 1534 editions of Tyndale. In 1537, James Nycolson, printer, of St. Thomas' Hospital, Southwark, printed an edition "Set forth with the Kynge's most gracious license." It has been thought that in consequence of a law passed 1534, compelling foreigners to sell their Bibles in sheets to some English stationers, that the whole edition was sold, with the blocks, to Nycolson, who bound and issued them.

MATTHEW'S BIBLE, 1537, though published and known as Matthew's, was the work of John Rogers the Martyr. It has been conjectured that the name of Matthew was assumed by Rogers through prudence or fear. Westcott thinks this most improbable, as the name stands at the end of the dedication, and J. R, at the end of the exhortation, and he suggests that Matthew found money for the work. It is not a new translation, but is made up of the translations of Tyndale and Coverdale. Tyndale had already published the Pentateuch, and it is believed that he had translated to the end of Chronicles. The New Testament is chiefly Tyndale's, and of the whole Bible two-thirds are Tyndale's and one-third Coverdale's. Several revised editions of Matthew's Bible by Richard Taverner and others were published. In Aug. 1537, Cromwell had exhibited the Bible to the king, who ordered that it "shall be allowed by his authority to be bought and read within this realm."

THE GREAT BIBLE, so called from its size, was published owing to the zeal of Lord Cromwell, under the authority of King Henry VIII; the 1539 edition being generally known as Cromwell's Bible; and the second, or 1540 edition, as Cranmer's, from the preface which he wrote for it. This Bible was partly printed in Paris, when the Inquisitor-General forbade the work, and seized the printed sheets. Presses and workmen were brought to England, and the Book was then finished in April, 1539. It is printed in black letter, and is Coverdale's revision of his own translation and of Tyndale's, with the help of Munster and Pagninus for the Old, and the Latin version of Erasmus for the New Testament. This is the first edition of the English Bible with the words on the title-page, "Appoynted in full in the Kalendar. Public copies were sometimes attached by a chain to one of the pillars of the church, with the king's injunction that it should be read with "Discretion, Honest Intent, Charity, Reverence, and Quiet behaviour."

GENEVAN NEW TESTAMENT, OF 1557, printed at Geneva, by Conrad Badius, in 16mo, is a revision of Tyndale's version, collated with the Great Bible, and carefully done, but without due leisure. The influence of Beza is perceptible. The editor was William Whittingham. The chapters are divided into verses and numbered. In 1576, Laurence Tomson, Under-Secretary to Sir F. Walsingham, published a revision professedly from the text of Beza. The variations from the Genevan are few, but the marginal notes differ. This revision was frequently bound up with the Genevan Old Testament.

GENEVAN BIBLE, OF 1560, printed at Geneva, by Hall, an English refugee, was the work of Coverdale, Knox, and other exiles at Geneva. The version of the New Testament is not that of 1557. This version is commonly known as the "Breeches Bible," from the word Breeches in Gen. iii. 7. The same word is used in both the Wycliffite Versions, in Caxton's "Golden Legende," and in Chaucer's Canterbury Tales, 1382. Of this version about 170 editions were printed, in folio, quarto, and octavo. The convenience of the smaller sizes, the division into verses, and the Roman type now first used, with the marginal commentary, "pure and vigorous in style, and, if slightly tinged with Calvinistic doctrine, yet on the whole neither unjust nor illiteral" (*Westcott's English Bible*), at once gave it a place in the English household, and it maintained its position until towards the middle of the seventeenth century.

THE BISHOPS' BIBLE, 1568, was proposed by Archbishop Parker, and the work was allotted by him to various learned men, many of them Bishops. The revision was about four years in hand, and the Great Bible was mainly followed. The New Testament was revised in the editions of 1572. This Bible was published in folio, quarto, and in octavo; but the editions were not so numerous as those of the Genevan.

THE RHEIMS AND DOUAI VERSION.—At Douai, in Flanders, a number of English Roman Catholics settled and founded a Seminary for the training of Priests for England. The Seminary being broken up owing to a Huguenot riot, it was transferred to Rheims, in France, and while there the Rheims version of the New Testament was published, in 1582. In 1593, the Seminary was allowed to return to Douai, and the work of translation was carried on. "For lack of good meanes" the publication of the Old Testament did not take place until 16.9-10. The translation is made from the Latin Vulgate, and may be said to be in Latinized English, almost unintelligible. In the text and the notes the Book is strongly Romish. In after editions of the translation these characteristics have been toned down. This version has been nicknamed "the Rosin Bible," from the reading, Jer. viii. 22, "is there no rosin in Gilead?" The Bishops' and other early versions had "triacle" or "tryacle" and the A.V. "balm."

THE KING'S BIBLE, OR AUTHORISED VERSION, 1611 completes this list of English Bibles. (See above.)

REVISED VERSION OF THE NEW TESTAMENT, 1881.—Reasons in favour of a revision of the 1611 Bible have been forcibly and persistently urged during many years past, by Scholars and Divines of the first rank; while on the other hand, popular instinct seemed to a large extent to support many learned and pious men in their objections to any such work. Nor is a wise jealousy on this head to be wondered at, or to be regretted. An interesting account is given of the opposition which revision has called forth, from the days of Origen and Jerome; and also of works on the revision of the English version in Eadie's English Bible, ch. i., li.

The history of the Bible in Great Britain shows that it has ever been synchronous with the true life and progress of the nation; and the national reverence for the very volume itself—charged upon us as Bibliolatry—is an hereditary quality and trait transmitted to us from the generations to whom that volume was at once the symbol and the guarantee, the weapon and the guerdon, of truth and freedom. The 1611 version, representing all its predecessors—and itself consecrated by the usage of nearly three centuries—written at a time when the English language was in its most perfect state and vigour, has powerfully influenced the literature and the struggles of the Anglo-Saxon race, and has thus grown up with that national greatness of which Queen Victoria, on a memorable occasion, wisely and truthfully declared it to be the source.

Jealousy for the integrity of the Bible, and a desire for its revision, naturally subsist together, and are alike an evidence of the value at which it is estimated. It is too precious to be lightly tampered with—it is so precious that if it can be rendered more pure no cost is too great for that object. Suggestions for a revision of the 1611 version were made not long after its introduction; for as early as 1645, Dr. Lightfoot, in a sermon before the Commons, urged them "to think of a review and survey of the translation of the Bible." In 1653, a Bill was before the Commons for a new translation. The following extract from it contains at once the great reason for revision, and its justification :—"In the original text of the Holy Scriptures there is so great depth, that only by degrees there is progress of light towards the attaining of perfection of the knowledge in the bettering of the translation thereof."

The Table given above shows that the 1527 version of Erasmus has been the basis on which the text of the succession of versions, culminating in the English one of 1611, was formed. The materials which he had, even when supplemented by the additional MSS. used by Stephens and others, were but few in number, and secondary in importance Not one of the four chief MSS. or Codices was then available, nor the host of other MSS. which have since been discovered. And if the materials were but scanty, the labour bestowed on the work was insufficient; and as Erasmus says of his version, "It was rather tumbled headlong into the world than edited." But the appetite of Europe, stimulated by the invention of printing, was keen for the Word of God, and could brook no delay.

As to the fitness of the present time for revision, certainly no age before this has had such ample sources whence to form a text, and none other has had the like wealth of Biblical criticism, which indeed could have no existence until the number of MSS. and the variety of readings furnished material for its exercise, and until the press rendered the labours of each critic available for all engaged in the same work. Not a few of the most important MSS. have been published in their entirety, whilst a large number have been collated by Tregelles, Scrivener, Griesbach, Mill, and others.

An important evidence of the need which is felt for a revised version, and which, perhaps, has been hardly sufficiently noticed, is the number of revised Greek texts, and of commentaries on the whole Bible and certain books of it, which have been published and much read of late years. Many of these latter have, as their special features, improved text or readings, or new translations. It will be sufficient to mention the works of Bengel, Steir, Delitzsch, Lachmann, Tischendorf, Alford, Wordsworth, Ellicott, Lightfoot, the Speaker's Commentary, that of "Five Clergymen," McLellan, Scrivener, Palmer, the just published text of Westcott and Hort, the result of twenty years' labour.

The history of the Revision of 1881, is briefly as follows:—Convocation passed a resolution in favour of a revision of the Authorised Version of the Holy Scriptures, on May 6th, 1870, and a committee of its own members was nominated, with liberty to invite the co-operation of eminent scholars of any nation or religious body. The committee consisted of sixteen members, eight of them being Bishops. At the first meeting of the united committee, twenty-one scholars were elected as members of the New Testament Company.

Half of the added members belonging to the Church of England. In America, in the same year, a Revision Company was formed to co-operate with the English committee, and the members were selected from the larger religious bodies of that country; the New Testament Company consisting of fifteen members. The Principles and Rules laid down for the guidance of the Revisionists by the Committee of Convocation, together with the mode of co-operation with the American Companies, with other information as to the Revised Version, will be found in the Revisers' Preface to that version. The original and invited members of the New Testament Company were the following:—The Bishop of Gloucester and Bristol (Dr. Ellicott), Chairman. The Archbishop of Dublin (Dr. Trench); Bishops of Durham (Dr. J. B. Lightfoot); Salisbury (Dr. Moberley); St. Andrew's (Dr. Wordsworth). The Very Revs. Dr. E. Bickersteth, Dean of Lichfield, and Prolocutor of the Lower House of Convocation; Dr. Arthur P. Stanley, Dean of Westminster; Dr. J. W. Blakesley, Dean of Lincoln; Dr. C. J. Vaughan, Dean of Llandaff and Master of the Temple; Dr. R Scott, Dean of Rochester. The Rev. Canons B. H. Kennedy, Regius Professor of Greek, Cambridge; B. F. Westcott, Regius Professor of Divinity, Cambridge. Prebendary Humphry, St. Paul's, London. The Ven. Archdeacons W. Lee, D.D. (Dublin) and Lecturer in Divinity; E. Palmer (Oxford). Professor of Latin, Oxford. The Rev. Doctors F. H. Scrivener, Regius Professor of Greek at Cambridge; F. J. A. Hort, Fellow of Emmanuel Coll., Cambridge; J. Angus, President of the Baptist College, Regent's Park, London; D. Brown, Professor of Divinity and Principal, Free Church College, Aberdeen; W. Milligan, Professor of Divinity, Aberdeen; W. F. Moulton, Professor of Classics, Wesleyan College, Richmond; S Newth, Principal of New College, London; A. Roberts, Professor of Humanity, St. Andrews; G. Vance Smith, Joint Author of a revised translation of the Scriptures.

The following were also members of the Revision Committee:—The Bishop of Winchester (Dr. Wilberforce) who died 1873; The Dean of Canterbury (Dr. Alford) who died 1871; Dr. Tregelles, who never was able to take part in the revision, and died 1875; Dr. Eadie, who died 1876. The Dean of Ely (Dr. E. Merivale) resigned 1871, and Dr. J. H. Newman (afterwards Cardinal), Rector of the Roman Catholic University, Dublin, declined to act.

GREEK AND OTHER MSS. OF THE NEW TESTAMENT.

GREEK MANUSCRIPTS are known as Uncials (written in capital letters,) and Cursives (written more in common or running hand). The four first named are the most important MSS. and are known as follows, originally each contained the whole Bible :—

CODEX VATICANUS or Codex B., in the Vatican Library, at Rome, is written on parchment, in capital letters, three columns on a page. Of the New Testament, it contains the whole, except the later chapters of Hebrews, the Pastoral Epistles, Philemon, and the Apocalypse. The date assigned to it is the middle of the fourth century.

CODEX SINAITICUS (*Aleph*) contains all the Books entire. This manuscript was discovered by the late Professor Tischendorf, in 1844, when travelling, at the Convent of St. Catherine, on Mount Sinai, where he saw some vellum leaves laid aside for lighting the stove, and these 14 leaves he published. By the favour of the Emperor of Russia, he, in 1859, had obtained possession of the remainder of the manuscript, and it was published in 1862, as a memorial of the thousandth year of the Russian Empire. Supposed date, as (B). It is at St. Petersburgh.

CODEX ALEXANDRINUS, (A) so called from having been sent from Alexandria, in 1628, as a present to King Charles I., by Cyrillus Lucaris, Patriarch of Constantinople. It is in four volumes, and is in the British Museum. The Old Testament is nearly complete. In the New Testament the parts wanting are Matthew to xxv. 6; John from vi. 50 to viii. 52; and 2 Cor. from iv. 13 to xii. 6. Supposed date, the fifth century.

CODEX EPHRAEMI (C) contains about three-fifths of the whole (145 out of 238 leaves), one or more sheets having perished out of almost every quire of four sheets. Fifth century.

CODEX BEZÆ (D), or Cantabrigiensis, or Britannicus. This manuscript was presented by Beza to the University of Cambridge in 1581, he stating that he discovered it about 19 years before, in the Monastery of St. Irenæus, at Lyons. See above, Beza, 1565. It contains, but not complete, in Latin and in Greek, the Gospels and the Acts. Its supposed date is the sixth century.

CODEX CLAROMONTANUS, (Dr.) or Regius, 2245, is a Greek and Latin manuscript of St. Paul's Epistles, found in the Monastery of Clermont, Beauvais. It is one of the most ancient and important in existence, and is of the sixth century. It is Uncial in character, and complete, and is in the Paris Library. See above Beza, 1565.

The following particulars are extracted from the just published vol. 2 (Introduction and Appendix) of Westcott and Hort's "New Testament in the original Greek."—

"The remaining Uncial MSS. (after the four first named above) are all of smaller though wide variable size. None of them show signs of having formed part of a complete Bible, or even of a complete New Testament. The Gospels are contained, in fair completeness, in 19 Uncials, the Acts in 9, Catholic Epistles in 7, Pauline Epistles in 9, and the Apocalypse in 5. The MSS. of the 9th and 10th centuries are about as numerous as those of all the preceding centuries together. With the exception of the Sinaitic, all the more important Uncials, some fragments excepted, have been published in continuous texts. The cursive MSS. range from the 9th to the 16th centuries. About 30 contain the whole New Testament. If each MS. is counted as one, irrespective of the books contained, the total number is between 900 and 1000. Hardly any of these have been printed *in extenso*, but there are complete and trustworthy collations of a select few from Tregelles, and of a large miscellaneous (English) array from Dr. Scrivener, besides collations of other miscellaneous assemblages. About 150 Cursives may be set down as practically known. A larger number are imperfectly known, and many are unknown.

The second class of documents consist of Versions, that is, ancient translations of the whole or parts of the New Testament, made chiefly for the service of churches in which Greek was, at least, not habitually spoken. Besides some outlying Versions, there are three principal classes, the Latin, the Syriac, and the Egyptian, to which may be added two solitary Versions of considerable interest, the Armenian and the Gothic. The other Versions are of comparatively late date, and of little direct value for the Greek text.

The third class of documentary evidence is supplied by the writings of the Fathers, which enables us, with more or less certainty, to discover the readings of the MS. or MSS. of the New Testament which they employed.

For Lists of the Greek MSS. of the New Testament, with detailed description, history, facsimiles, etc., see Scrivener's Plain Introduction to the Criticism of the New Testament for the use of Biblical Students.

PLAN OF THE WORK.

EVERY passage of the Revised Version is represented under its principal words, and the texts are all given in the very words of the Revised Version, with the stops and capitals.

The Concordance consists of two parts :—

I. The General Portion.

II. Proper Names, *i.e.*, of Persons, Places, and Objects personified ; for the most part, all words beginning with capital letters in the Revised Version. Such of these as are not ordinarily treated as proper names, are quoted in the general portion of the work with a note of reference, *e.g.*, "**Christians.**—*see proper names.*"

Order of Words.—The words are arranged in strict alphabetical order, and not in families or groups—as, cry, cried, cries, crying. The latter arrangement was convenient when notes and explanations referring to the whole group were given ; but the present order has been adopted as being natural and better suited for easy reference.

Changed Words.—The instances in which words used in the Authorised Version are replaced by others in the Revised Version, are very numerous. This occurs either when a totally different word is used, as *perceived* for *discovered*, or when one part of a verb is substituted for another, as *stand* for *stood*.

A student looking for a passage under a word familiar to him in the Authorised Version, will very frequently find that the text does not now occur under that word—but that he may nevertheless be able to find the passage, the following plan has been adopted :—

At the foot of the texts given under any word, the Reader is referred to such other words as in the Revised Version are used for the old one—*e.g.*, if the passage sought for is "he which hath begun a good work in you will perform it," a reader looking for it under *perform* will not find it, but he is there referred to *complete*, *perfect ;* and on turning to the texts under *perfect* will find the passage.

At the head of the texts given under any word will be found words of the Authorised Version which have been changed for the word in question ; *e.g.*, if the word referred to is *Perceived*—there will be found at the head five words occurring in the Authorised Version, but which in the texts quoted are all changed in the Revised Version to the word *Perceived*. Such words, and the texts in which the change has been made, are correspondingly numbered.

Omitted Verses and Words.—By the courtesy of the Rev. CANON KENNEDY, D.D., there is inserted, from his "Ely Lectures on the Revised Version of the New Testament" (London : Bentley), a select List of Authorised passages and words which were omitted in the Revision by preponderant authorities.

Disused Words and Altered Spelling.—Words used in the Authorised Version, but now altogether displaced by others, are shewn *in the body of the work* thus—**Perceivest** *A.V.—see considerest*. Where the spelling of words has been altered, the old spelling is given, and the reader is referred to the new, *e.g.*, **Spunge** *A.V.—see spunge*.

Bracketed Words.—To assist in fixing a passage, names of persons or places are inserted in brackets, *e.g.*, Acts 18. 25. "[Apollos] *taught* carefully the things concerning Jesus." Acts 19. 28. "heard this, they [Ephesians] were *filled* with wrath."

A List of New, Disused, and differently spelt Words is given in Appendix II.

THE

STUDENT'S CONCORDANCE

ERRATA.

Page 66. "*In or into City*," Mat. 9. 1, for "Nazareth" read "Capernaum."
,, 84. "*Descending*," Mat. 3. 16, omit "John Baptist."
,, 101. "*Entered*," Acts 28. 8, for "Publius" read "father of Publius."
,, 112. "*Fain*," Philem. 13, read "[Onesimus] whom I would *fain* have kept with me."
,, 116. "*His Father*," Acts 7. 4, read "when *his father* was dead, God removed [Abraham]."
,, 143. "*Go*," for Jno. 7. 6, read Jno. 7. 8.
,, 174. "*Inquired*," for Lu. 18. 26, read Lu. 18. 36.
,, 244. "*Perceived*," Acts 19. 34, for "Paul" read "Alexander."
,, 273. "*Rent*," Mk. 1. 10, for "John" read "Jesus."

Lu. 19. 5. for to-day I must *abide* at thy house
24. 29. *Abide* with us: for it is toward evening—And he went in to ¹*abide* with them
Jno. 4. 40. they besought him to ⁴*a.* with them [disciples
8. 31. If ye ¹*abide* in my word, then are ye truly my
12. 46. believeth on me may not *abide* in the darkness
15. 4. *Abide* in me—except it *abide*—except ye *abide*
6 If a man *abide* not in me
7. If ye *abide* in me, and my words *abide* in you
9. ¹*abide* ye in my love
10. ye shall *abide* in my love ;—*abide* in his love
16. that your fruit should ³*abide*

Abideth.—*A.V.* ¹*dwelleth*, ²*endureth*, ³*remaineth*.
Jno. 3. 36. but the wrath of God *abideth* on him
6. 27. for the meat which ²*abideth* unto eternal life
56. drinketh my blood ¹*abideth* in me
8. 35. the bond servant *a.* not—the son *abideth* for ever
12. 24. a grain of wheat—it *abideth* by itself alone
34. out of the law that the Christ *abideth* for ever
14. 17. he ¹*abideth* with you, and shall be in you
15. 5. He that *abideth* in me, and I in him
1 Cor. 13. 13. now *abideth* faith, hope, love
2 Cor. 9. 9. His righteousness ³*abideth* for ever

ABIDETH

2 Tim. 2. 13. if we are faithless, he *abideth* faithful
Heb. 7. 3. [Melchisedek] *abideth* a priest continually
1 Pet. 1. 23. the word of God, which liveth and *abideth*
  25. But the word of the Lord,²*abideth* for ever
1 Jno. 2. 6. he that saith he *abideth* in him ought
  10. He that loveth his brother *abideth* in the light
  14. young men—the word of God *abideth* in you
  17. he that doeth the will of God *abideth* for ever
  27. the anointing which ye received—*abideth* in you
3. 6. Whosoever *abideth* in him sinneth not
  9. doeth no sin because his seed ³*abideth* in him
  14. He that loveth not *abideth* in death
  24. ¹*abideth* in him—he *abideth* in us
4. 12. if we love one another, God ¹*abideth* in us
  15. Jesus is the Son of God, God ¹*abideth* in him
  16. he that ¹*abideth* in love, ¹*a*. in God, and God *a*. in
2 Jno. 2. for the truth's sake which ¹*abideth* in us [him
  9. Whosoever goeth onward and *abideth* not—he that
    abideth in the teaching

Abiding.—*A.V.* ¹abode, ²continuing, ³dwelleth, ⁴enduring, ⁵present, ⁶remaining.

Lu. 2. 8. shepherds—*abiding* in the field,
Jno. 1. 33. the Spirit descending, and ⁶*abiding* upon him
5. 38. ye have not his word *abiding* in you
14. 10. the Father ³*abiding* in me doeth his works
  25. things have I spoken unto you, while yet ⁵*a*. with you
Acts 1. 13. upper chamber, where they were ¹*a*. (apostles)
Heb. 10. 34. better possession and an ⁴*abiding* one
13. 14. For we have not here an ²*abiding* city
1 Jno. 3. 15. no murderer hath eternal life *abiding* in him
    see tarrying.

Ability.—*A.V.* ¹have.

Mat. 25. 15. to each according to his several *ability*
Acts 11. 29. the disciples, every man according to his *a*.
2 Cor. 8. 11. completion also out of your ¹*ability*
    see strength.

Able.—*A.V.* ¹power.

Mat. 3. 9. God is *able* of these stones to raise. Lu. 3. 8
9. 28. Believe ye that I am *able* to do this [body
  10. 28. fear him which is *able* to destroy both soul and
  19. 12. He that is *able* to receive it, let him receive it
  20. 22. Are ye *able* to drink the cup—We are *able* Mk.
  22. 46. no one was *able* to answer him a word [10. 38, 39
  26. 61. This man said, I am *able* to destroy the temple
Mk. 4. 33. spake he the word—as they were *a*. to hear it
Lu. 14. 31. whether he is *a*. with ten thousand to meet him
Jno. 10. 29. no one is *able* to snatch them out of
Acts 15. 10. neither our fathers nor we were *able* to bear
  20. 32. word of his grace, which is *able* to build you up
Rom. 4. 21. had promised, he was *able* also to perform
8. 39. shall be *able* to separate us from the love of God
11. 23. God is *able* to graft them in again
15. 14. *able* also to admonish one another
16. 25. Now to him that is ¹*able* to stablish you
1 Cor. 5. who shall be *a*. to decide between his brethren
10. 13. tempted above that ye are *a*.—that ye may be *a*.
2 Cor. 1. 4. that we may be *a*. to comfort them [to endure it
9. 8. God is *able* to make all grace abound unto you
Eph. 3. 20. him that is *able* to do exceeding abundantly
6. 11. *able* to stand against the wiles of the devil
  13. that ye may be *able* to withstand in the evil day
  16. wherewith ye shall be *able* to quench all the fiery darts
Phil. 3. 21. he is *a*. even to subject all things unto himself
2 Tim. 1. 12. he is *able* to guard that which I have committed
2. 2. men, who shall be *able* to teach others [mitted
3. 7. never *able* to come to the knowledge of the truth
15. sacred writings which are *able* to make thee wise

ABOMINATION

Tit. 1. 9. be *able* both to exhort in the sound doctrine
Heb. 2. 18. he is *able* to succour them that are tempted
5. 7. unto him that was *able* to save him from death
7. 25. he is *able* to save to the uttermost
11. 19. God is *able* to raise up, even from the dead
Jas. 1. 21. word, which is *able* to save your souls
3. 2. a perfect man, *able* to bridle the whole body
4. 12. lawgiver and judge—*able* to save and to destroy
2 Pet. 1. 15. that—ye may be *able* after my decease
Jude 24. unto him that is *a*. to guard you from stumbling
Rev. 5. 3. no one—was *able* to open the book
6. 17. their wrath is come; and who is *able* to stand
13. 4. the beast? and who is *able* to war with him
15. 8. none was *able* to enter into the temple
    see power, strong, sufficient.

Not Able.

Mat. 10. 28. kill the body, but are *not able* to kill the soul
Lu. 1. 20. thou shalt be silent and *not able* to speak
12. 26. if then ye are *not a*. to do even that which is least
13. 24. seek to enter in, and shall *not be able*
14. 29. laid a foundation, and is *not able* to finish. 30
16. 26. pass from hence to you may *not be able*
21. 15. wisdom—adversaries shall *n*. be *a*. to withstand
Jno. 21. 6. *not able* to draw it for the multitude of fishes
Acts 6. 10. they were *not able* to withstand the wisdom
19. 40. *not be able* to give account of this concourse
1 Cor. 3. 2. *n*. yet *a*. to bear it: nay, *not even* now are ye *a*.

Aboard.

Acts 21. 2. Phœnicia, we went *aboard*, and set sail

Abode.—*A.V.* ¹continued, ²dwelt, ³tarried.

Mat. 17. 22. while they *abode* in Galilee, Jesus said
Lu. 1. 56. Mary *abode* with her about three months
8. 27. *abode* not in any house, but in the tombs
Jno. 1. 32. as a dove out of heaven; and it *abode* upon him
39. saw where he ²*abode*; and they *a*. with him
2. 12. there they ¹*abode* not many days
4. 40. the Samaritans—and he *abode* there two days
7. 9. he *abode* still in Galilee
10. 40. John was at the first baptizing; and there he *a*.
11. 6. he *abode* at that time two days in the place
14. 23. we will come unto him, and make our *abode*
Acts 9. 43. he ²*abode* many days in Joppa
17. 14. Silas and Timothy *abode* there still [Berœa]
18. 3. of the same trade, he *abode* with them
21. 7. saluted the brethren, and *a*. with them one day
8. Philip—one of the seven, we *abode* with him
28. 30. he ²*a*. two whole years in his own hired dwelling
    see abiding, lodged, spent, stood, tarried.

Abolished.—*A.V.* ¹destroyed, ²put down.

1 Cor. 15. 24. when he shall have ²*abolished* all rule
26. last enemy that shall be ¹*abolished* is death
Eph. 2. 15. having *abolished* in his flesh the enmity
2 Tim. 1. 10. Jesus, who *abolished* death, and brought life
    see passing away.

Abominable.

Tit. 1. 16. by their works they deny him, being *a*.
1 Pet. 4. 3. revellings, carousings, and *a*. idolatries
Rev. 21. 8. fearful, and unbelieving, and *abominable*

Abomination—s.

Mat. 24. 15. the *abomination* of desolation. Mk. 13. 14
Lu. 16. 15. that which is exalted among men is an *a*.
Rev. 17. 4. a golden cup full of *abominations*
5. MOTHER OF THE HARLOTS, AND OF THE *A*.
21. 27. or he that maketh an *abomination* and a lie

2

ABOUND

Abound.—*A.V.* ¹*abounded,* ²*abundant,* ³*excel,* ⁴*increase,* ⁵*redound.*

Rom. 5. 15. grace of the one man, Jesus Christ, ¹*a.* unto
20. that the trespass might *a.*—grace did *a.* [the many
6. 1. Shall we continue in sin, that grace may *abound*
15. 13. in believing, that ye may *abound* in hope [church
1 *Cor.* 14. 12. that ye may ³*a.* unto the edifying of the
2 *Cor.* 1. 5. as the sufferings of Christ *abound* unto us
4. 15. cause the thanksgiving to ⁵*abound* unto the glory
8. 7. as ye *abound* in everything, in faith—see that ye *a.*
9. 8. all grace *a.* unto you—may *a.* unto every good work
Eph. 1. 8. grace, which he made to ¹*abound* toward us
Phil. 1. 9. I pray, that your love may *abound* yet more
26. that your glorying may ²*abound* in Christ Jesus
4. 12. I know also how to *a.*—to *a.* and to be in want
18. But I have all things, and *abound*
1 *Th.* 3. 12. the Lord make you to—*abound* in love
4. 1. that ye *abound* more and more. ⁴10
2 *Pet.* 1. 8. For if these things are yours and *abound*
see increaseth, multiplied.

Abounded—eth—ing.—*A.V.* ¹*abundant.*

Rom. 3. 7. if the truth of God through my lie *abounded*
5. 20. where sin *abounded,* grace did *abound* more
1 *Cor.* 15. 58. unmoveable, always *a.* in the work of the
2 *Cor.* 1. 5. so our comfort also *a.* through Christ [Lord
8. 2. deep poverty *a.* unto the riches of their liberality
9. 12. but ¹*aboundeth* also through many thanksgivings
Col. 2. 7. as ye were taught, *abounding* in thanksgiving
2 *Th.* 1. 3. love of—all toward one another *aboundeth*
1 *Tim.* 1. 14. the grace of our Lord ¹*abounded* exceedingly
see abound.

About.—*A.V.* ¹*intend,* ²*meaning,* ³*ready.*

Acts 5. 35. as touching these men, what ye are ¹*about* to do
27. 2. ship of Adramyttium, which was ²*about* to sail
Rev. 12. 4. the woman which was ³*about* to be delivered

Above.

Jno. 8. 23. Ye are from beneath; I am from *above*
Gal. 4. 26. But the Jerusalem that is *above* is free
Col. 3. 1. seek the things that are *above,* where Christ is. 2
Jas. 1. 17. Every good gift and every perfect boon is from *a.*
3. 15. wisdom is not a wisdom that cometh down from *a.*

Abroad.

Rom. 16. 19. your obedience is come *abroad* unto all men
see light.

Absence.

Lu. 22. 6. to deliver him—in the *absence* of the multitude
Phil. 2. 12. much more in my *absence,* work out your own

Absent.

1 *Cor.* 5. 3. being *absent* in body but present in spirit
2 *Cor.* 5. 6. at home in the body, we are *a.* from the Lord
8. willing rather to be *absent* from the body
9. we make it our aim, whether at home or *absent*
10. 1. but being *absent* am of good courage
11. by letters when we are *absent,* such are we also
13. 10. For this cause I write these things while *absent.* 2
Phil. 1. 27. I come and see you or be *absent,* I may hear
Col. 2. 5. For though I am *absent* in the flesh

Abstain.

Acts 15. 20. that they *abstain* from the pollutions of idols
29. that ye *abstain* from things sacrificed to idols
1 *Th.* 4. 3. that ye *abstain* from fornication
5. 22. *abstain* from every form of evil
1 *Tim.* 4. 3. and commanding to *abstain* from meats
1 *Pet.* 2. 11. *abstain* from fleshly lusts, which war

ACCEPTABLE

Abstinence *A.V.*—*see food.*

Abundance.—*A.V.* ¹*abundantly.*

Mat. 12. 34. out of the *a.* of the heart the mouth. *Lu.* 6. 45
13. 12. given, and he shall have *abundance.* 25. 29
Lu. 12. 15. life consisteth not in the *a.* of the things
Rom. 5. 17. much more shall they that receive the *a.* of
2 *Cor.* 8. 2. the *a.* of their joy and their deep poverty [grace
14. your *a.* being a supply—their *a.* also may become
10. 15. according to our province unto further ¹*a.*
see bounty, exceeding, greatness, power, superfluity.

Abundant.

1 *Cor.* 12. 23. more *a.* honour—more *a.* comeliness
24. giving more *abundant* honour to that part
see abound, abounded, aboundeth, abundantly, great, multiplied.

Abundantly.—*A.V.* ¹*abundant,* ²*frequent,* ³*more,* ⁴*much more.*

Jno. 10. 10. may have life, and may have it *abundantly*
1 *Cor.* 15. 10. I laboured more *abundantly* than they all
2 *Cor.* 1. 12. world, and more *abundantly* to you-ward
2. 4. the love which I have more *abundantly* unto you
7. 15. his inward affection is more ¹*a.* toward you
10. 8. glory somewhat ³*a.* concerning our authority
11. 23. in labours more ¹*abundantly,* in prisons more ²*a.*
12 15. If I love you more *abundantly,* am I loved the less
Eph. 3. 20. exceeding *abundantly* above all that we ask
Phil. 1. 14. through my bonds, are more ⁴*a.* bold to speak
Heb. 6. 17. God, being minded to shew more *abundantly*
see abundance, exceedingly, richly.

Abuse *A.V.*—*see use to the full.*

Abusers.—*A.V.* ¹*defile.*

1 *Cor.* 6. 9. nor *abusers* of themselves with men
1 *Tim.* 1. 10. for fornicators, for ¹*abusers* of themselves

Abusing.

1 *Cor.* 7. 31. those that use the world, as not *abusing* it

Abyss.—*A.V.* ¹*bottomless pit,* ²*deep.*

Lu. 8. 31. not command them to depart into the ²*abyss*
Rom. 10. 7. Who shall descend into the ²*abyss*
Rev. 9. 1. given to him the key of the pit of the ¹*abyss*
2. And he opened the pit of the ¹*abyss*
11. They have over them as king the angel of the ¹*abyss*
11. 7. the beast that cometh up out of the ¹*abyss*
17. 8. beast—is about to come up out of the ¹*abyss*
20. 1. I saw an angel—having the key of the ¹*abyss*
3 and cast him [Satan] into the ¹*abyss,* and shut it

Accept.—*A.V.* ¹*accepted,* ²*receive.*

Mk. 4. 20. such as hear the word, and ²*accept* it
Acts 24. 3. we *accept* it in all ways and in all places
2 *Cor.* 11. 4. a different gospel, which ye did not ¹*accept*

Acceptable.—*A.V.* ¹*accepted,* ²*thankworthy.*

Lu. 4. 19. To proclaim the *acceptable* year of the Lord
24. No prophet is ¹*acceptable* in his own country
Acts 10. 35. and worketh righteousness, is ¹*a.* to him
Rom. 12. 1. a living sacrifice, holy, *acceptable* to God
2. the good and *acceptable* and perfect will of God
15. 16. offering up of the Gentiles might be made *a.*
31. ministration—may be ¹*acceptable* to the saints
2 *Cor.* 6. 2. an—¹*a.* time I hearkened—now is the ¹*a.* time
8. 12. readiness—¹*acceptable* according as a man hath
Phil. 4. 18. a sacrifice *acceptable,* well-pleasing to God
1 *Tim.* 2. 3. good and *acceptable* in the sight of God. 5. 4

3

ACCEPTABLE

1 Pet. 2. 5. spiritual sacrifices, *acceptable* to God
19. For this is ²*acceptable*, if for conscience toward God
20. take it patiently, this is *acceptable* with God
see well-pleasing.

Acceptably A.V.—*see well-pleasing.*

Acceptation.
1 Tim. 1. 15. saying, and worthy of all *acceptation.* 4. 9

Accepted.—A.V. ¹*received.*
2 Cor. 8. 17. For indeed he *accepted* our exhortation
1 Th. 2. 13. word of God, ye ¹*a.* it not as the word of men
see accept, acceptable, bestowed, well-pleasing.

Acceptest—eth.
Lu. 20. 21. and *acceptest* not the person of any
Gal. 2. 6. no matter to me: God *accepteth* not man's person)

Accepting.
Heb. 11. 35. were tortured, not *accepting* their deliverance

Access.
Rom. 5. 2. through whom also we have had our *a.* by faith
Eph. 2. 18. through him we both have our *access* in one
3. 12. in whom we have boldness and *a.* in confidence

Accompany—ied.
Acts 10. 23. the brethren from Joppa *accompanied* him
11. 12. these six brethren also *accompanied* me
20. 4. And there *accompanied* him as far as Asia
Heb. 6. 9. and things that *accompany* salvation
see brought.

Accomplish—ed.—A.V. ¹*done,* ²*finish—ed,* ³*fulfilled,* ⁴*performed.*
Mat. 5. 18. pass away from the law, till all things be ³*a.*
24. 34. shall not pass away, till all these things be ³*a.*
Mk. 13. 14. sign when these things shall be about to be ²*a.*
30. until all these things be ¹*accomplished* ˙to the law
Lu. 2. 39. when they had ⁴*a.* all things that were according
9. 31. his decease which he was about to *accomplish*
12. 50. how am I straitened till it be *accomplished*
18. 31. written by the prophets shall be *accomplished*
Jno. 4. 34. will of him—and to ²*accomplish* his work
5. 36. works which the Father hath given me to ²*a.*
17. 4. having ²*a.* the work which thou hast given me
19. 28. scripture might be ³*accomplished,* saith, I thirst
Acts 20. 24. so that I may ²*accomplish* my course
21. 5. when—we had *accomplished* the days, we departed
Rom. 15. 28. When therefore I have ⁴*accomplished* this
1 Pet. 5. 9. the same sufferings are *a.* in your brethren
Rev. 17. 17. until the words of God should be ²*accomplished*
see finished, fulfilled.

Accomplishing.
Heb. 9. 6. into the first tabernacle, *a.* the services

Accomplishment A.V.—*see fulfilment.*

Accord.—A.V. ¹*mind,* ²*willing.*
Acts 1. 14. with one *accord* continued stedfastly in prayer
2. 46. stedfastly with one *accord* in the temple
4. 24. lifted up their voice to God with one *accord*
5. 12. were all with one *accord* in Solomon's porch
7. 57. and rushed upon him with one *accord*
8. 6. the multitudes gave heed with one *accord*
12. 10. iron gate—opened to them of its own *accord*
20. they came with one *accord* to him
15. 25. having come to one *accord,* to choose out men
18. 12. the Jews with one *accord* rose up against Paul
19. 29. they rushed with one *accord* into the theatre

ACCORDING

Rom. 15. 6. with one ¹*a.* ye may with one mouth glorify
2 Cor. 8. 3. beyond their power, they gave of their own ²*a.*
17. [Titus] went forth unto you of his own *accord*
Phil. 2. 2. having the same love, being of one *accord*
see together.

According.—A.V. ¹*pertaining.*
Mat. 2. 16. two years old and under, *according* to the time
9. 29. *According* to your faith be it done unto you
Mk. 7. 5. *according* to the tradition of the elders
Lu. 1. 9. *according* to the custom of the priest's office
2. 22. days of their purification *a.* to the law of Moses
39. accomplished all things that were *a.* to the law
5. 14. offer for thy cleansing, *a.* as Moses commanded
12. 47. made not ready, nor did *according* to his will
23. 56. sabbath they rested *a.* to the commandment
Jno. 7. 24. Judge not *according* to appearance
18. 31. Take him—and judge him *according* to your law
Acts 4. 35. distribution was made unto each, *according* as
7. 44. Moses—should make it *according* to the figure
11. 29. the disciples, every man *according* to his ability
13. 23. Of this man's seed hath God *a.* to promise
22. 12. Ananias, a devout man *according* to the law
Rom. 1. 3. seed of David *according* to the flesh [16. 27
2. 6. who will render to every man *a.* to his works. Mat.
16. judge the secrets of men, *according* to my gospel
4. 1. Abraham, our forefather ¹*according* to the flesh
18. father of many nations, *according* to that which
8. 28. them that are called *according* to his purpose
10. 2. zeal for God, but not *according* to knowledge
11. 5. a remnant *according* to the election of grace
8. were hardened: *according* as it is written
12. 3. think soberly, *according* as God hath dealt
6. gifts differing *according* to the grace that was given
—let us prophecy *according* to the proportion
15. 5. the same mind one with another *a.* to Christ
1 Cor. 1. 31. *according* as it is written, He that glorieth
3. 8. receive his own reward *according* to his own labour
10. A. to the grace of God which was given unto me
15. 3. Christ died for our sins *a.* to the scriptures
4. raised on the third day *according* to the scriptures
2 Cor. 1. 17 do I purpose *according* to the flesh
4. 13. spirit of faith, *according* to that which is written
5. 10. in the body, *according* to what he hath done
8. 12. acceptable *a.* as a man hath, not *a.* as he hath not
9. 7. Let each man do *according* as he hath purposed
10. 2. as if we walked *according* to the flesh [12, 13
11. 15. whose end shall be *a.* to their works. Rev. 20.
13. 10. deal sharply, *according* to the authority
Gal. 1. 4. evil world, *according* to the will of our God
2. 14. not uprightly *according* to the truth of the gospel
3. 29. are ye Abraham's seed, heirs *according* to promise
Eph. 1. 5. unto himself, *according* to the good pleasure
7. forgiveness of our trespasses, *according* to the riches
9. mystery of his will, *according* to his good pleasure
11. foreordained *according* to the purpose of him who
3. 11. *according* to the eternal purpose which he purposed
16. grant you, *according* to the riches of his glory
20. *according* to the power that worketh in us
4. 7. grace given *according* to the measure of the gift
16. every joint supplieth *according* to the working
Phil. 1. 20. *according* to my earnest expectation and hope
3. 21. *according* to the working whereby he is able
4. 19. fulfil every need of yours *a.* to his riches
Col. 1. 11. strengthened with all power, *a.* to the might
29. I labour also, striving *according* to his working
2 Th. 1. 12. ye in him, *according* to the grace of our God
1 Tim. 1. 11. *according* to the gospel of the glory of the
16. Timothy, *according* to the prophecies which went
6. 3. the doctrine which is *according* to godliness

ACCORDING

2 Tim. 1. 8. with the gospel *according* to the power
9. not *a.* to our works, but *a.* to his own purpose
2. 8. of the seed of David, *according* to my gospel
4. 14. Lord will render to him *according* to his works
Tit. 1. 3. I was intrusted *according* to the commandment
3. 5. but *according* to his mercy he saved us
Heb. 8. 9. Not *according* to the covenant that I made
1 Pet. 1. 2. *a.* to the foreknowledge of God the Father
3. who *according* to his great mercy begat us again
4. 6. judged *a.* to men in the flesh, but live *a.* to God
2 Pet. 2. 22. *according* to the true proverb, The dog
3. 13. But, *according* to his promise, we look for new
15. Paul also, *according* to the wisdom given to him
Rev. 2. 23. unto each one of you *according* to your works

Account.—*A.V.* ¹*charge,* ²*consider,* ³*contemptible,*
⁴*count,* ⁵*despised,* ⁶*least,* ⁷*suppose,* ⁸*think.*

Mat. 12. 36. idle word—they shall give *account* thereof
Lu. 16. 2. render the *account* of thy stewardship
Jno. 11. 50. nor do ye take ²*a.* that it is expedient for you
Acts 19. 27. temple of—Diana be made of no ³*account*
40. not be able to give *account* of this concourse
20. 24. But I hold not my life of any ⁴*account*
Rom. 14. 12. each one of us shall give *account* of himself
1 Cor. 4. 1. Let a man so *account* of us, as of ministers
6. 4. set them to judge who are of no ²*a.* in the church
2 Cor. 10. 10. bodily presence is weak, and his speech of
12. 6. lest any man should ⁸*account* of me [no ³*account*
Ph. 4. 17. the fruit that increaseth to your *account*
2 Tim. 4. 16. may it not be laid to their ¹*account*
Philem. 18. oweth thee aught, put that to mine *account*
Heb. 13. 17. your souls, as they that shall give *account*
1 Pet. 4. 5. who shall give *a.* to him that is ready to judge
5. 12. Silvanus, our faithful brother, as I ⁷*account* him
2 Pet. 3. 15. And *a.* that the long-suffering of our Lord
see reckoning.

Accounted—eth—ing.—*A.V.* ¹*esteemeth,* ²*esteeming.*

Mk. 10. 42. which are *accounted* to rule over the Gentiles
Lu. 20. 35. are *accounted* worthy to attain to that world
22. 24. which of them is *accounted* to be greatest
Rom. 8. 36. We were *accounted* as sheep for the slaughter
14. 14. save that to him who ¹*a.* anything to be unclean
Heb. 11. 19. *accounting* that God is able to raise up
26. ²*a.* the reproach of Christ greater riches [Moses]
see prevail, reckoned.

Accursed.—*A.V.* ¹*cursed.*

Jno. 7. 49. multitude which knoweth not the law are ¹*a.*
see anathema.

Accusation.—*A.V.* ¹*object.*

Mat. 27. 37. his *accusation* written, THIS IS JESUS
Mk. 15. his *a.* was written over, THE KING OF THE
Jno. 18. 29. Pilate—saith, What *a.* bring ye [JEWS
Acts 24. 19. to make ¹*a.,* if they had aught against me
1 Tim. 5. 19. Against an elder receive not an *accusation*
see accuse, charge, judgement.

Accuse.—*A.V.* ¹*accusation,* ²*implead,* ³*witness against.*

Mat. 12. 10. they [Pharisees] might *a.* him [Jesus]. Mk. 3. 2
Mk. 15. 4. behold how many things they ³*accuse* thee of
Lu. 6. 7. they [Pharisees] might find how to ¹*accuse*
23. 2. they began to *a.* him, saying, We found this man
14. touching those things whereof ye *accuse* him [Jesus]
Jno. 5. 45. Think not that I will *accuse* you to the Father
8. 6. tempting him, that they might have whereof to *a.*
Acts 19. 38. let them ²*accuse* one another [him
24. 2. Tertullus began to *accuse* him [Paul]

ADD

Acts 24. 8. all these things, whereof we *accuse* him [Paul]
13. the things whereof they now *accuse* me [Paul]
25. 5. amiss in the man, let them *accuse* him [Paul]
11. those things is true, whereof these *accuse* me [Paul]
28. 19. not that I had aught to *accuse* my nation of
see exact, revile.

Accused.—*A.V.* ¹*called in question.*

Mat. 27. 12. when he [Jesus] was *a.* by the chief priests
Mk. 15. 3. the chief priests *accused* him of many things
Lu. 16. 1. the same was *accused* unto him [riot
Acts 19. 40. we are in danger to be ¹*a.* concerning this day's
23. 30. wherefore he [Paul] was *accused* of the Jews
23. 28. the cause wherefore they *accused* him [Paul]
29. whom I found to be *accused* about questions
25. 16. the *accused* have the accusers face to face
26. 2. whereof I [Paul] am *accused* by the Jews
7. I [Paul] am *accused* by the Jews, O king
Tit. 1. 6. who are not *accused* of riot or unruly
see accusing, accuseth.

Accuseth—ing.—*A.V.* ¹*accused.*

Lu. 23. 10. scribes stood, vehemently ¹*a.* him [Jesus]
Jno. 5. 45. there is one that *accuseth* you, even Moses
Rom 2. 15. thoughts—*accusing* or else excusing them
Rev. 12. 10. which ¹*accuseth* them before our God

Accuser—s.

Acts 23. 30. charging his *a.* also—against him [Paul]
25. 16. the accused have the *accusers* face to face
18. Concerning whom, when the *accusers* stood up
Rev. 12. 10. the *accuser* of our brethren is cast down
see slanderers.

Aceldama *A.V.*—*see Akeldama, proper names.*

Acknowledge.

1 Cor. 16. 18. *acknowledge* ye therefore them that are such
2 Cor. 1. 13. ye read or even *a.,* and I hope ye will *a.*
14. as also ye did *acknowledge* us in part
see knowledge.

Acknowledgeth—ing *A.V.*—*see confesseth, knowledge.*

Acknowledgment *A.V.*—*see know.*

Acquaintance.

Lu. 2. 44. they sought for him among their kinsfolk and *a.*
23. 49. all his *acquaintance,* and the women that followed
see friends.

Active.—*A.V.* ¹*powerful.*

Heb. 4. 12. For the word of God is living, and ¹*active*

Act.

Jno. 8. 4. woman hath been taken in adultery, in the very *a.*

Acts.—*A.V.* ¹*judgements.*

Rev. 15. 4. for thy righteous ¹*a.* have been made manifest

Actually.—*A.V.* ¹*commonly.*

1 Cor. 5. 1. It is ¹*actually* reported that there is fornication

Add.—*A.V.* ¹*offer.*

Mat. 6. 27. can *add* one cubit unto his stature. Lu. 12. 25
Rev. 8. 3. that he should ¹*a.* it unto the prayers of all the
22. 18. If any man shall *a.* unto them, God shall *a.* [saints
see raise up, supply.

ADDED

Added.
Mat. 6. 33. all these things shall be *a.* unto you. *Lu.* 12. 31
Lu. 3. 20. [Herod] *added* yet this above all
19. 11. he [Jesus] *added* and spake a parable
Acts 2. 41. there were *a.* unto them in that day about
  47. the Lord *a.* to them day by day [three thousand
  5. 14 believers were the more *added* to the Lord
  11. 24. much people was *added* unto the Lord
Gal. 3. 19. It [the law] was *a.* because of transgressions

Addeth—ing.—*A.V.* ¹*giving*.
Gal. 3. 15. no one maketh it void, or *addeth* thereto
2 *Pet.* 1. 5. for this very cause ¹*a.* on your part all diligence

Addicted *A.V.*—*see set*

Adjure—d.—*A.V.* ¹*charge.*
Mat. 26. 63. I *adjure* thee by the living God
Mk. 5. 7. I *a.* thee by God, torment me not
Acts 19. 13. I *adjure* you by Jesus whom Paul preacheth
1 *Th.* 5. 27. I ¹*a.* you by the Lord that this epistle be read

Administered *A.V.*—*see ministered*.

Administration *A.V.*—*see ministration.*

Admiration *A.V.*—*see respect, wonder.*

Admired *A.V.*—*see marvelled.*

Admonish—ed—ing.—*A.V.* ¹*warn—ing.*
Acts 20. 31. space of three years I cease not to ¹*admonish*
  27. 9. Paul *admonished* them, and said unto them
Rom. 15. 14. able also to *admonish* one another
1 *Cor.* 4. 14. but to ¹*admonish* you as my beloved children
Col. 1. 28. ¹*a.* every man and teaching every man
  3. 16. teaching and *a.* one another with psalms
1 *Th.* 5. 12. are over you in the Lord, and *admonish* you
  14. brethren, ¹*admonish* the disorderly [brother
2 *Th.* 3. 15. not as an enemy, but *admonish* him as a
  see warned.

Admonition.
1 *Cor.* 10. 11. they were written for our *admonition*
Eph. 6. 4. nurture them in the chastening and *a.* of the
Tit. 3. 10. after a first and second *a.* refuse [Lord

Ado.—*A.V.* ¹*trouble.*
Acts 20. 10. Make ye no ¹*ado* ; for his life is in him
  see tumult.

Adoption.
Rom. 8. 15. but ye received the spirit of *adoption*
  23. waiting for our *adoption,* to wit, the redemption
  9. 4. whose is the *adoption,* and the glory
Gal. 4. 5. that we might receive the *adoption* of sons
Eph. 1. 5. having foreordained us unto *adoption* as sons

Adorn—ed—eth.—*A.V.* ¹*garnished.*
Lu. 21. 5. temple, how it was *adorned* with goodly stones
1 *Tim.* 2. 9. that women *a.* themselves in modest apparel
Tit. 2. 10. that they may *adorn* the doctrine of God
1 *Pet.* 3. 5. women also, who hoped in God, *a.* themselves
Rev. 21. 2. as a bride *adorned* for her husband
  19. The foundations of the wall of the city were ¹*a.*

Adorning.
1 *Pet.* 3. 3. Whose *adorning* let it not be the outward *a.*

ADULTERY

Advanced.- *A.V.* ¹*increased,* ²*profited.*
Lu. 2. 52. Jesus ¹*advanced* in wisdom and stature
Gal. 1. 14. I ²*advanced* in the Jews' religion beyond many

Advantage.—*A.V.* ¹*defrauded,* ²*gain.*
Rom. 3. 1. What *advantage* then hath the Jew
2 *Cor.* 2. 11. that no *a.* may be gained over us by Satan
  7. 2. corrupted no man, we took ¹*advantage* of no man
  12. 17. Did I take ²*advantage* of you by any one of them
  18. Did Titus take any ²*advantage* of you
Jude 16. shewing respect of persons for the sake of *a.*

Advantaged—eth *A.V.*—*see profit—ed—eth.*

Adventure.
Acts 19. 31. not to *a.* himself [Paul] into the theatre

Adversary.
Mat. 5. 25. Agree with thine *adversary* quickly,—lest
  haply the *adversary* deliver thee
Lu. 12. 58. going with thine *a.* before the magistrate
  18. 3. Avenge me of mine *adversary*
1 *Tim.* 5. 14. none occasion to the *adversary* for reviling
1 *Pet.* 5. 8. your *adversary* the devil, as a roaring lion

Adversaries.
Lu. 13. 17. all his *adversaries* were put to shame
  21. 15. your *adversaries* shall not be able to withstand
1 *Cor.* 16. 9. and there are many *adversaries*
Phil. 1. 28. in nothing affrighted by the *adversaries*
Heb. 10. 27. fire which shall devour the *adversaries*

Adversity *A.V.*—*see evil entreated.*

Advice *A.V.*—*see judgement.*

Advise—d.
Acts 27. 12. the more part *a.* to put to sea from thence

Adulterer—s.
Lu. 18. 11. unjust, *adulterers,* or even as this publican
1 *Cor.* 6. 9. neither fornicators, nor idolaters, nor *a.*
Heb. 13. 4. fornicators and *adulterers* God will judge

Adulteress—es.—*A.V.* ¹*commit adultery.*
Mat. 5. 32. maketh her an ¹*adulteress*
Rom. 7. 3. she shall be called an *adulteress*—she is no *a.*
Jas. 4. 4. Ye *adulteresses,* know ye not that the friendship

Adulterous.
Mat. 12. 39. *a.* generation seeketh after a sign. 16. 4
Mk. 8. 38. in this *adulterous* and sinful generation

Adultery—ies.
Mat. 5. 27. Thou shalt not commit *adultery.* 19. 18 : *Mk.*
  10. 19 : *Lu.* 18. 20 : *Rom.* 13. 9 : *Jas.* 2. 11
  28. hath committed *adultery* with her already
  32. when she is put away committeth *adultery*
15. 19. Murders, *adulteries,* fornications. *Mk.* 7. 21
Mk. 10. 11. marry another, committeth *a.* against her
  12. and marry another, she committeth *adultery. Mat.*
  19. 9 : *Lu.* 16. 18
Jno. 8. 3. Pharisees bring a woman taken in *adultery.* 4
Rom. 2. 22. should not commit *a.,* dost thou commit *a.*
Jas. 2. 11. Now if thou dost not commit *adultery*
2 *Pet.* 2. 14. having eyes full of *adultery*
Rev. 2. 22. them that commit *adultery* with her
  see adulteress.

ADVOCATE

Advocate.
1 Jno. 2. 1. we have an *a.* with the Father, Jesus Christ

Afar.—*A.V.* ¹*way.*
Mat. 8. 30. there was ¹*afar* off from them a herd
Lu. 15. 20. while he was yet ¹*afar* off, his father saw him
Acts 2. 39. to your children, and to all that are *afar* off
see far.

Affairs.—*A.V.* ¹*state.*
Eph. 6. 21. But that ye also may know my *affairs*
Col. 4. 7. All my ¹*affairs* shall Tychicus make known unto
2 Tim. 2. 4. entangleth himself in the *affairs* of this life
see state.

Affect *A.V.*—*see seek.*

Affected.
Acts 14. 2. made them evil *affected* against the brethren
see sought.

Affection—s.—*A.V.* ¹*bowels.*
Rom. 1. 31. without natural *affection,* unmerciful. 2 Tim.
2 Cor. 6. 12. ye are straitened in your own ¹*affections* [3. 3
7. 15. his inward *affection* is more abundantly toward you
see mind, passion.

Affections *A.V.*—*see passions.*

Affectionately.
1 Th. 2. 8. even so, being *affectionately* desirous of you

Affectioned.
Rom. 12. 10. be tenderly *affectioned* one to another

Affirm—ed.
Lu. 22. 59. another confidently *affirmed,* saying
Acts 12. 15. she [Rhoda] confidently *affirmed* that it was
 25. 19. Jesus, who was dead, whom Paul *a.* to be alive
Rom. 3. 8. reported, and as some *affirm* that we say
1 Tim. 1. 7. nor whereof they confidently *affirm*
Tit. 3. 8. I will that thou *affirm* confidently

Affirming.—*A.V.* ¹*saying.*
Acts 24. 9. Jews also—¹*affirming* that these things were so

Afflict.—*A.V.* ¹*trouble,* ²*vex.*
Acts 12. 1. Herod—to ²*afflict* certain of the church
2 Th. 1. 6. recompense affliction to them that ¹*afflict* you

Afflicted.—*A.V.* ¹*troubled.*
2 Cor. 1. 6. whether we be *afflicted,* it is for your comfort
 7. 5. but we were ¹*afflicted* on every side
2 Th. 1. 7. and to you that are ¹*afflicted* rest with us
1 Tim. 5. 10. if she hath relieved the *afflicted*
Heb. 11. 37. being destitute, *afflicted,* evil entreated
Jas. 4. 9. Be *afflicted,* and mourn, and weep
see suffering, tribulation.

Affliction—s.—*A.V.* ¹*tribulation—s,* ²*trouble.*
Acts 7. 10. delivered him [Joseph] out of all his *afflictions*
 11. great *a.* : and our fathers found no sustenance
 34. I have surely seen the *affliction* of my people
 20. 23. saying that bonds and *afflictions* abide me
2 Cor. 1. 4. who comforteth us in all our ¹*a.*—in any ²*a.*
 8. concerning our ²*affliction* which befell us in Asia
 2. 4. for out of much *affliction* and anguish of heart
 4. 17. For our light *affliction,* which is for the moment
 6. 4. in much patience, in *afflictions,* in necessities

AFRAID

2 Cor. 7. 4. I overflow with joy in all our ¹*affliction*
 8. 2. in much proof of *a.* the abundance of their joy
Phil. 1. 17. to raise up *affliction* for me in my bonds
 4. 14. ye had fellowship with my *affliction*
Col. 1. 24. lacking of the *afflictions* of Christ in my flesh
1 Th. 1. 6. having received the word in much *affliction*
 3. 3. that no man be moved by these *afflictions*
 4. we told you beforehand that we are to suffer ¹*a.*
 7. our distress and *affliction* through your faith
2 Th. 1. 4. all your persecutions and in the ¹*afflictions*
 6. to recompense ¹*affliction* to them that afflict you
Heb. 10. 33. gazingstock both by reproaches and *afflictions*
Jas. 1. 27. fatherless and widows in their *affliction*
see (evil) entreated, hardship, sufferings, tribulation.

Affrighted.—*A.V.* ¹*afraid,* ²*terrified.*
Lu. 24. 5. as they were ¹*a.,* and bowed down their faces
 37. they [the disciples] were terrified and *affrighted*
Acts 10. 4. being ¹*affrighted,* said, What is it, Lord ?
Phil. 1. 28. in nothing ²*affrighted* by the adversaries
Rev. 11. 13. the rest were *affrighted,* and gave glory
see amazed.

Afoot *A.V.*—*see (on) foot, (by) land.*

Aforehand.
Mk. 14. 8. anointed my body *aforehand* for the burying

Aforepromised.—*see promised.*

Aforetime.—*A.V.* ¹*old time,* ²*past,* ³*sometime—s.*
Jno. 9. 13. bring to the Pharisees him that *a.* was blind
Rom. 3. 25. passing over of the sins done ²*aforetime*
 15. 4. whatsoever things were written *aforetime*
Eph. 2. 2. trespasses and sins, wherein ²*a.* ye walked
 11. remember, that ²*a.* ye, the Gentiles in the flesh
Col. 3. 7. disobedience ; in the which ye also walked ³*a.*
Tit. 3. 3. For we also were ³*aforetime* foolish
Philem. 11. Onesimus, who was ³*a.* unprofitable to thee
1 Pet. 3. 5. after this manner ¹*a.* the holy women also
 20. spirits in prison, which ³*aforetime* were disobedient

Afraid.—*A.V.* ¹*feared,* ²*marvelled.*
Mat. 2. 22. [Joseph] was *afraid* to go thither
 9. 8. they were ²*afraid,* and glorified God
 14. 30. when he [Peter] saw the wind, he was *afraid*
 17. 6. they fell on their face, and were sore *a.* Mk 9. 6
 25. 25. I was *afraid,* and went away and hid thy talent
Mk. 5. 15. and they [Gerasenes] were *afraid. Lu.* 8. 35
 9. 32. the saying, and were *afraid* to ask him. *Lu.* 9. ¹45
 10. 32. they [disciples] that followed were *afraid*
 16. 8. for they [the women] were *afraid*
Lu. 2. 9. they [the shepherds] were sore *afraid*
 8. 25. And being *afraid* they [disciples] marvelled
Jno. 6. 19. Jesus walking on the sea—and they were *a.*
 19. 8. he [Pilate] was the more *afraid*
Acts 9. 26. they were all *afraid* of him [Saul]
 22. 29. and the chief captain also was *afraid*
Rom. 13. 4. if thou do that which is evil, be *afraid*
Gal. 4. 11. I am *afraid* of you, lest by any means
see affrighted, fear, fearful.

Not afraid.—*A.V.* ¹*fear not.*
Mat. 10. 28. be ¹*not afraid* of them which kill the body
 14. 27. It is I ; be *not afraid. Mk.* 6. 50 ; Jno. 6. 20 .
 17. 7. touched them and said, Arise, and be *not afraid*
Lu. 2. 10. angel said unto them, Be ¹*not afraid*
 12. 4. Be *not afraid* of them which kill the body
Acts 18. 9. Be not *a.,* but speak, and hold not thy peace
Heb. 11. 23. they were *not a.* of the king's commandment
see fear, fear (with negatives), no fear, tremble.

AFRESH

Afresh.
Heb. 6. 6. crucify to themselves the Son of God *afresh*

After.—*A.V.* ¹*followed.*
Mat. 27. 62. which is the day ¹*after* the Preparation

Against.—*A.V.* ¹*evil.*
Mat. 12. 30. He that is not with me is *a.* me. *Mk.* 10. 40: *Lu.*
Lu. 9. 50. for he that is not *against* you is for you |11. 23
Jas. 4. 11. Speak not one ¹*a.* another—speaketh ¹*a.* a brother, speaketh ¹*against* the law
1 *Pet.* 3. 16. are spoken ¹*against*, they may be put to shame

Age.—*A.V.* ¹*world.*
Lu. 2. 36. she [Anna] was of a great *age*
3. 23. Jesus—was about thirty years of *age*
8. 42. an only daughter, about twelve years of *age*
Jno. 9. 21. ask him; he is of *age.* 23
1 *Cor.* 7. 36. if she be past the flower of her *age*
Heb. 6. 5. the powers of the ¹*age* to come
11. 11. power to conceive seed when she was past *age*
see men, old.

Ages.—*A.V.* ¹*from the beginning,* ²*saints,* ³*world.*
1 *Cor.* 10. 11. upon whom the ends of the ³*ages* are come
Eph. 2. 7. that in the *ages* to come he might shew
3. 9. mystery which from all ¹*a.* hath been hid in God
Col. 1. 26. the mystery which hath been hid from all *ages*
Heb. 9. 26. at the end of the ³*ages* hath he been manifested
Rev. 15. 3. true are thy ways, thou King of the ²*ages*
see generations.

Aged.
Tit. 2. 2. that *aged* men be temperate, grave, sober minded
3. *aged* women likewise be reverent in demeanour
Philem. 9. being such a one as Paul the *aged*

Agony.
Lu. 22. 44. being in an *agony* he prayed more earnestly

Agree—ed.
Mat. 5. 25. *Agree* with thine adversary quickly
18, 19. if two of you shall *agree* on earth as touching
20. 2. when he had *agreed* with the labourers
13. didst not thou *agree* with me for a penny?
Mk. 14. 56. their witness *agreed* not together. 59
Lu. 5. 36. piece from the new will not *agree* with the old
Jno. 9. 22. the Jews had *agreed* already, that if any man
Acts 5. 9. How is it that ye have *agreed* together to tempt
40. And to him [Gamaliel] they *agreed*
15. 15. And to this *agree* the words of the prophets
23. 20. The Jews have *a.* to ask thee to bring down Paul
28. 25. when they *agreed* not among themselves
1 *Jno.* 5. 8. and the three *agree* in one
see (one) mind.

Agreement.
2 *Cor.* 6. 16. what *a.* hath a temple of God with idols?

Aground.
Acts 27. 41. where two seas met, they ran the vessel *a.*

Aim.—*A.V.* ¹*labour,* ²*strived.*
Rom. 15. 20. making it my ²*aim* so to preach the gospel
2 *Cor.* 5. 9. Wherefore also we make it our ¹*aim*

Air.
Acts 22. 23. off their garments, and cast dust into the *air*
1 *Cor.* 9. 26. so fight I, as not beating the *air*
14. 9. for ye will be speaking into the *air*

ALLURE

Eph. 2. 2. according to the prince of the power of the *air*
1 *Th.* 4. 17. to meet the Lord in the *air*
Rev. 9. 2. the sun and the *air* were darkened by reason of
16. 17. the seventh poured out his bowl upon the *air*
see heaven.

Alabaster.
Mat. 26. 7. a woman having an *a.* cruse. *Mk.* 14. 3: *Lu.* 7. 37

Alas *A.V.*—*see woe.*

Aliens.
Heb. 11. 34. turned to flight armies of *aliens*
see alienated.

Alienate—ed.—*A.V.* ¹*aliens.*
Eph. 2. 12. ¹*alienated* from the commonwealth of Israel
4. 18. *a.* from the life of God because of the ignorance
Col. 1. 21. you, being in time past *alienated* and enemies

Alike.
Rom. 14. 5. another esteemeth every day *alike*

Alive.—*A.V.* ¹*life.*
Mat. 27. 63. that deceiver said, while he was yet *alive*
Mk. 16. 11. they heard that he was *a,* and had been seen
Lu. 15 24. my son was dead, and is *alive* again. 32
24. 23. a vision of angels, which said that he was *alive*
Acts 1. 3. he also shewed himself *alive* after his passion
9. 41. he presented her [Dorcas] *alive*
20. 12. And they brought the lad *alive*
25. 19. Jesus—whom Paul affirmed to be *alive*
Rom. 6. 11. but *alive* unto God in Christ Jesus
13. present yourselves unto God, as *a.* from the dead
7. 9. And I was *alive* apart from the law once
1 *Cor.* 15. 22. in Christ shall all be made *alive*
Gal. 3. 21. a law given which could make ¹*alive*
1 *Th.* 4. 15. we that are *alive,* that are left. 17
Rev. 1. 18. and behold, I am *alive* for evermore
19. 20. they twain were cast *alive* into the lake
see lived.

All.—*A V.* ¹*whole.*
Mat. 13. 33. leaven—hid in three measures of meal, till it
56. his sisters, are they not *a.* with us [was ¹*a.* leavened
Mk. 12. 44. of her want did cast in *all. Lu.* 21. 4
Lu. 4. 7. wilt worship before me, it shall *all* be thine
15. 31. Son—*all* that is mine is thine
17. 10. when ye shall have done *all* the things
Jno. 13. 10. ye are clean, but not *all.* 11
1 *Cor.* 2. 22. for *all* things are yours. 23 [be *all in all*
15. 28. when *all* things have been subjected—God may
Eph. 4. 6. Father of *all,* who is over *all,* and through *all,*
Col. 3. 11. Christ is *all,* and in *all*   [and in *all*
Rev. 5. 13. sea, and *all* things that are in them

Alleging.
Acts 17. 3. and *a.* that it behoved the Christ to suffer

Allegory.
Gal 4. 24. Which things contain an *allegory*

Alleluia *A.V.*—*see hallelujah.*

Allow *A.V.*—*see consent, looked for, know, approved, approveth.*

Allure *A.V.*—*see entice.*

ALMIGHTY

Almighty.—*A.V.* ¹*Omnipotent.*
2 *Cor.* 6. 18. saith the Lord *Almighty*
Rev. 1. 8. which was and which is to come, the *Almighty*
4. 8. Holy, holy, holy, is the Lord God, the *Almighty*
11. 17. O Lord God, the *Almighty.* 15. 3 ; 16. 7
16. 14. the great day of God, the *Almighty*
19. 6. the Lord our God, the ¹*Almighty* reigneth
15. the fierceness of the wrath of *Almighty* God
21. 22. the Lord God the *Almighty*, and the Lamb

Almost.
Acts 13. 44. the next sabbath *almost* the whole city
19. 26. but *almost* throughout all Asia
21. 27. when the seven days were *almost* completed
Heb. 9. 22. I may *almost* say, all things are cleansed
see little.

Alms.
Mat. 6. 2. When therefore thou doest *alms.* 3
4. that thine *alms* may be in secret
Lu. 11. 41. Howbeit give for *alms* those things
12. 33. Sell that ye have, and give *alms*
Acts 3. 2. to ask *alms* of them that entered
3. Peter and John—asked to receive an *alms*
10. sat for *alms* at the Beautiful Gate
10. 2. [Cornelius] gave much *alms* to the people
4. Thy prayers and thine *alms* are gone up. 31
24. 17. I came to bring *alms* to my nation
see righteousness.

Almsdeeds.
Acts 9. 36. Dorcas—full of good works and *almsdeeds*

Aloes.
Jno. 19. 39. bringing a mixture of myrrh and *aloes*

Alone.—*A.V.* ¹*only.*
Mat. 4. 4. Man shall not live by bread *alone.* *Lu.* 4. 4
14. 23. even was come, he [Jesus] was there *alone*
18. 15. his fault between thee and him *alone*
Mk. 4. 10. And when he [Jesus] was *alone*
6. 47. and he [Jesus] *alone* on the land
Lu. 5, 21. Who can forgive sins, but God *alone* ?
6. 4. lawful to eat [shewbread] save for the priests *a.*
9. 18. as he was praying *alone*, the disciples
36. when the voice came, Jesus was found *alone*
10. 40. my sister did leave me [Martha] to serve *alone* ?
24. 18. Dost thou ¹*alone* sojourn in Jerusalem
Jno. 6. 15. withdrew again into the mountain himself *a.*
22. his disciples went away *alone*
8. 16. I am not *alone*, but I and the Father
12. 24. it abideth by itself *alone*
16. 32. leave me *alone* : and yet I am not *alone*
Acts 19. 26. that not *alone* at Ephesus
Rom. 4. 23. not written for his sake *alone*
1 *Cor.* 14.36.of God went forth ? or came it unto you ¹*alone*?
Gal. 6. 4. have his glorying in regard of himself *alone*
1 *Th.* 3. 1. thought it good to be left behind at Athens *alone*
Heb. 9. 7. but into the second the high priest *alone*
see privately.

Left alone.
Jno. 8. 9. Jesus was *left alone*, and the woman
29. [the Father] hath not *left* me *alone*
Rom. 11. 3. I am *left alone*, and they seek my life

Let alone.
Mat. 15. 14. *Let* them *alone* : they are blind guides
Mk. 14. 6. Jesus said, *Let* her [Mary] *alone*

AM

Lu. 13. 8. Lord, *let* it *alone* this year also
Jno. 11. 48. If we *let* him [Jesus] thus *alone*, all men
Acts 5. 38. Refrain from these men, and *let* them *alone*

Alpha.—*see proper names.*

Already.—*A.V.* ¹*ready*
Mat. 17. 12. Elijah is come *a.*, and they knew him not
Mk. 15. 44. Pilate marvelled if he were *already* dead
Lu. 12. 49. what will I, if it is *already* kindled ?
Jno. 3. 18. he that believeth not hath been judged *already*
11. 17. [Lazarus] in the tomb four days *already*
19. 33. Jesus, and saw that he was dead *already*
1 *Cor.* 5. 3. present in spirit, have *a.*, as though I were
6 7. Nay, *already* it is altogether a defect
Phil. 3. 16. whereunto we have *already* attained
2 *Th.* 2. 7. mystery of lawlessness doth *already* work
1 *Tim.* 5. 15. *already* some are turned aside after Satan
2 *Tim.* 2. 18. the resurrection is past *already*
4. 6. For I am ¹*already* being offered
1 *Jno.* 4. 3. now it is in the world *already*

Altar.
Mat. 5. 23. offering thy gift at the *altar.* 24
23. 18. Whosoever shall swear by the *a.* 19, 20 [*Lu.* 11. 51
35. Zacharias—ye slew between the sanctuary and the *a.*
Lu. 1. 11. angel—on the right side of the *altar* of incense
Acts 17. 23. I found also an *altar* with this inscription
1 *Cor.* 9. 13. wait upon the *a.* have their portion with the *a.*?
10. 18. eat the sacrifices communion with the *altar* ?
Heb. 7. 13. hath given attendance at the *altar*
13. 10. We have an *altar*, whereof they have no right
Rev. 6. 9. underneath the *altar* the souls of them
8. 3. angel came and stood over the *a.*—upon the golden *a.*
9. 13. a voice from the horns of the golden *altar*
11. 1. Rise and measure the temple of God, and the *a.*
14. 18. angel came out from the *altar*
16. 7. I heard the *altar* saying, Yea, O Lord

Altars.
Rom. 11. 3. they have digged down thine *altars*

Altered.
Lu. 9. 29. the fashion of his countenance was *altered*

Altogether.—*A.V.* ¹*utterly.*
Jno. 9. 34. Thou wast *altogether* born in sins
1 *Cor.* 5. 10. not *altogether* with the fornicators
6 7. already it is ¹*altogether* a defect in you
9. 10. saith he it *altogether* for our sake

Am I—I am.
Mat. 18. 20. there *am I* in the midst of them   [9. 18, 20
Mk. 8. 27. Who do men say that *I am* ? *Mat.* 16. 15 : *Lu.*
14. 62. Jesus said, *I am.* *Lu.* 22. 70
Jno. 7. 33. Yet a little while *am I* with you
8. 58. Before Abraham was, *I am*
12. 26. where *I am*, there shall also my servant be
17. 24. where *I am*, they also may be with me
18. 5. Jesus saith unto them, *I am* he. 6
Acts 26. 29. might become such as *I am*
27. 23. angel of the God whose *I am*
1 *Cor.* 9. 1. *Am I* not free ? *am I* not an apostle ?
15. 10. by the grace of God *I am* what *I am*
Gal. 4. 12. be as *I am*, for *I am* as ye are
Phil. 4. 11. whatsoever state *I am*, therein to be content
Rev. 1 17. *I am* the first and the last
18. *I am* alive for evermore

AMAZED

Amazed.—*A.V.* ¹*affrighted,* ²*astonished,* ³*bewitched,* ⁴*wondered.*
Mat. 12. 23. the multitudes were *amazed. Mk.* 1. 27 : 9. 15
Mk. 2. 12. they were all *amazed,* and glorified God
  5. 42. were ⁴a. straightway with a great amazement
  6. 51. they were sore *amazed* in themselves
  9. 15. when they saw him, [Jesus] were greatly *amazed*
 10. 24. the disciples were ²*amazed* at his words. 32
 14. 33. began to be greatly *amazed,* and sore troubled
 16. 5. young man—arrayed in a white robe; and they
  6. Be not ¹*amazed :* ye seek Jesus [were ¹*amazed*
Lu. 2. 47. all that heard him were ²*amazed*
  5. 9. he was ²*amazed*—at the draught of fishes
  8. 56. And her parents were ²*amazed*
 24. 22. certain women of our company ²*amazed* us
Acts 2. 7. they were all *amazed* and marvelled
  8. 9. used sorcery, and ³*amazed* the people of Samaria. ⁹11
 13. miracles wrought, he [Simon Magus] was ⁴*amazed*
  9. 21. all that heard him [Saul] were *amazed*
 10. 45. they of the circumcision—were ²*amazed*
 12. 16. they saw him, [Peter] and were ²*amazed*
    see amazement, astonished, astonishment.

Amazement.—*A.V.* ¹*amazed,* ²*astonishment.*
Mk. 5. 42. amazed straightway with a great ²*amazement*
Lu. 4. 36. And ¹*amazement* came upon all
  5. 26. And ¹*amazement* took hold on all
Acts 3. 10. were filled with wonder and *a.* at that
    see terror.

Ambassador—s.
2 *Cor.* 5. 20. We are *a.* therefore on behalf of Christ
Eph. 6. 20. for which I am an *ambassador* in chains

Ambassage.—*A.V.* ¹*message.*
Lu. 14. 32. he sendeth an *ambassage,* and asketh
 19. 14. and sent an ¹*ambassage* after him, saying

Amen.
1 *Cor.* 14. 16. unlearned say the *A.* at thy giving of thanks
2 *Cor.* 1. 20. wherefore also through him is the *Amen*
Rev. 3. 14. These things saith the *Amen*
  5. 14. the four living creatures said, *Amen.* 10. 4
  7. 12. and worshipped God, saying, *Amen :* Blessing
 22. 20. *Amen :* Come, Lord Jesus
 21. grace of the Lord Jesus be with the saints, *Amen*

Amend.
Jno. 4. 52. the hour when he began to *amend*

Amethyst.
Rev. 21. 20. the twelfth, *amethyst*

Amiss.—*A.V.* ¹*harm,* ²*wickedness*
Lu. 23. 41. but this man hath done nothing *amiss*
Acts 25. 5. if there is anything ²*a.* in the man, let them
 28. 6. beheld nothing ¹*amiss* come to him
Jas. 4. 3. Ye ask, and receive not, because ye ask *amiss*

Anathema.—*A.V.* ¹*accursed.*
Rom. 9. 3. wish that I myself were ¹*anathema* from Christ
1 *Cor.* 12. 3. no man speaking in the Spirit of God saith,
 16. 22. let him be *anathema.* Maranatha [Jesus is ¹*a.*
Gal. 1. 8. we, or an angel from heaven, should preach—
    let him be ¹*anathema* 9

Anchor—s.
Acts 27. 29. they let go four *anchors* from the stern
 30. they would lay out *anchors* from the foreship
 40. casting off the *anchors,* they left them in the sea
Heb. 6. 19. we have as an *anchor* of the soul, a hope

ANGEL

Ancient.—*A.V.* ¹*old.*
2 *Pet.* 2. 5. God—spared not the ¹*ancient* world

Ancle *A.V.*—*see ankle.*

Anew.—*A.V.* ¹*again.*
Jno. 3. 3. Except a man be born ¹*anew.* ¹7

Angel.
Mat. 28. 5. *angel* answered and said unto the women
Lu. 1. 13. *angel* said unto him, Fear not, Zacharias
 18. Zacharias said unto the *angel*
 19. the *angel* answering said unto him
 26. the *angel* Gabriel was sent from God
 30. the *angel* said unto her, Fear not, Mary
 34. Mary said unto the *angel,* How shall this be
 35. the *angel* answered and said unto her
 38. the *angel* departed from her
 2. 10. the *angel* said unto them [shepherds]
 13. with the *angel* a multitude of the heavenly host
 21. so called by the *angel* before he was conceived
 22. 43. an *angel* from heaven strengthening him
Jno. 5. 4. an *angel*—went down at a certain season [margin]
 12. 29. others said, An *angel* hath spoken to him
Acts 6. 15. as it had been the face of an *angel* [Stephen]
 7. 30. an *angel* appeared—in a flame of fire in a bush
 35. a deliverer with the hand of the *angel* [Moses]
 38. the *angel* which spake to him in the mount Sinai
 10. 7. when the *angel* that spake unto him [Cornelius]
 22. Cornelius—was warned of God by a holy *angel*
 11. 13. he had seen the *angel* standing in his house
 12. 8. *angel* said unto him [Peter], Gird thyself
 9. which was done by the *angel,* but thought
 10. straightway the *angel* departed from him
 11. the Lord hath sent forth his *angel*
 15. and they said, It is his *angel* [Peter]
 23. 8. no resurrection, neither *angel* nor spirit
 9. spirit hath spoken to him, or an *angel ?*
2 *Cor.* 11. 14. Satan fashioneth himself into an *a.* of light
Gal. 1. 8. though we, or an *a.* from heaven, should preach
Rev. 1. 1. signified it by his *angel* unto his servant John
 2. 1. To the *angel* of the church. 8, 12, 18 : 3. 1, 7, 14
 5. 2. I saw a strong *angel* proclaiming
 7. 2. I saw another *angel* ascend
 8. 3. And another *angel* came and stood
 4. went up before God out of the *angel's* hand
 5. And the *angel* taketh the censer
 8. the second *a.* sounded ; 10. third *a.* ; 12. fourth *a.*
 9. 1. fifth *angel* ; 13. sixth *angel* sounded
 11. over them as king, the *angel* of the abyss
 14. the sixth *angel,* which had the trumpet
 10. 1. I saw another strong *a.* coming down. 18. 1 : 20. 1
 5. the *angel* which I saw standing upon the sea
 7. the days of the voice of the seventh *angel*
 8. the book which is open in the hand of the *angel.* 10
 9. I went unto the *angel,* saying unto him
 11. 15. And the seventh *angel* sounded
 14. 6. I saw another *angel* flying in mid heaven
 8. Another, a second *angel,* followed
 9. another *angel,* a third, followed
 15. another *angel* came out from the temple. 17
 18. another *angel* came out from the altar
 19. the *angel* cast his sickle into the earth
 16. 5. I heard the *angel* of the waters saying
 17. 7. the *angel* said unto me, Wherefore didst
 18. 21. a strong *angel* took up a stone
 19. 17. I saw an *angel* standing in the sun
 21. 17. the measure of a man, that is, of an *angel*
 22. 8. to worship before the feet of the *angel*
 16. I Jesus have sent mine *angel* to testify unto you. 6
    see eagle, one.

ANGEL

Angel of God.
Acts 10. 3. an *angel of God* coming in unto him [Cornelius]
27. 23. stood by me this night an *angel of* the *God* [Paul]
Gal. 4. 14. ye received me as an *angel of God*

Angel of the Lord.
Mat. 1. 24. Joseph—did as the *a. of the L.* commanded. 20
2. 13. an *angel of the—Lord* appeareth to Joseph. 19
28. 2. an *angel of the Lord* descended from heaven
Lu. 1. 11. appeared unto him [Zacharias] an *a. of the Lord*
2. 9. *angel of the Lord* stood by them [shepherds]
Acts 5. 19. an *angel of the L.* by night opened the prison
8. 26. an *angel of the Lord* spake unto Philip
12. 7. an *angel of the Lord* stood by him [Peter]
23. an *angel of the Lord* smote him [Herod]

Angels.—*A.V.* ¹*angels of God.*
Mat. 4. 11. *a.* came and ministered unto him. *Mk.* 1. 13
13. 39. the reapers are *angels*
18. 41. Son of man shall send forth his *angels*
49. the *angels* shall come forth, and sever the wicked
18. 10. their *angels* do alway behold the face
22. 30. nor are given in marriage, but are as ¹*a.* in heaven
24. 36. knoweth no one, not even the *angels* of heaven.
25. 31. shall come in his glory, and all the *a.* [*Mk.* 13, 32
26. 53. send me more than twelve legions of *angels?*
Mk. 8. 38. glory of his Father with the holy *a. Lu.* 9. 26
12. 25. but are as *angels* in heaven
13. 27. then shall he send forth the *angels*
Lu. 2. 15. when the *angels* went away from them
16. 22. carried away by the *a.* into Abraham's bosom
20. 36. they are equal unto the angels
24. 23. they had also seen a vision of *angels*
Jno. 20. 12. [Mary] beholdeth two *angels* in white sitting
Acts 7. 53. the law as it was ordained by *angels*
Rom. 8. 38. nor life, nor *angels*, nor principalities
1 *Cor.* 4. 9. unto the world, and to *angels*, and to men
6. 3. know ye not that we shall judge *angels*
11. 10. authority on her head, because of the *angels*
13. 1. with the tongues of men and of *angels*
Gal. 3. 19. [the law] ordained through *a.* by the hand
Col. 2. 18. and worshipping of the *angels*
2 *Th.* 1. 7. Lord Jesus from heaven with the *angels*
1 *Tim.* 3. 16. justified in the spirit; seen of *angels*
5. 21. Christ Jesus, and the elect *angels*
Heb. 1. 4. so much better than the *angels* [Jesus]
5. unto which of the *angels* said he at any time
7 of the *angels* he saith, Who maketh his *angels* winds
2. 2. the word spoken through *angels* proved stedfast
5. For not unto *angels* did he subject the world
7. madest him a little lower than the *angels*. 9
12. 22. to innumerable hosts of *angels*
13. 2. some have entertained *angels* unawares
1 *Pet.* 1. 12. which things *angels* desire to look into
3. 22. *angels* and authorities and powers being made
2 *Pet.* 2. 4. if God spared not *angels* when they sinned
11. whereas *angels*, though greater in might and power
Jude 6. And *angels* which kept not their own principality
Rev. 1. 20. seven stars are the *a.* of the seven churches
5. 11. I saw, and I heard a voice of many *angels*
7. 1. I saw four *angels* standing at the four corners
2. he cried with a great voice to the four *angels*
11. all the *angels* were standing round about the throne
8. 13. the trumpet of the three *a.*, who are yet to sound
9. 14. Loose the four *angels* which are bound
15. And the four *angels* were loosed
14. 10. brimstone in the presence of the holy *angels*
21. 12. having twelve gates, and at the gates twelve *a.*

ANOINTED

Angels of God.
Lu. 12. 8. Son of man also confess before the *a.* of *God*
9. denied in the presence of the *angels of God*
15. 10. joy in the presence of the *angels of God*
Jno. 1. 51. the *angels of God* ascending and descending
Heb. 1. 6. And let all the *angels of God* worship him
see angels.

His Angels.
Mat. 4. 6. He shall give *his angels* charge. *Lu.* 4. 10
13. 41. The Son of man shall send forth *his angels*
16. 27. in the glory of his Father with *his angels*
24. 31. he shall send forth *his angels* with a great sound
25. 41. prepared for the devil and *his angels*
Heb. 1. 7. Who maketh *his angels* winds
Rev. 3. 5. before my Father, and before *his angels*
12. 7. Michael and *his angels* going forth to war—dragon warred and *his angels*
9. and *his angels* were cast down with him

Anger.—*A.V.* ¹*indignation.*
Mk. 3. 5. [Jesus] looked round about on them with *anger*
Rom. 10. 19. nation void of understanding will I *anger* you
Eph. 4. 31. Let all bitterness, and wrath, and *anger*
Col. 3. 8. put ye also away all these; *anger*, wrath, malice
Rev. 14. 10. which is prepared unmixed in the cup of his ¹*a.*

Angry.
Mat. 5. 22. every one who is *angry* with his brother
Lu. 14. 21. the master of the house being *angry* said
15. 28. But he was *angry*, and would not go in
Eph. 4. 26. Be ye *angry*, and sin not
Tit. 1. 7. not self-willed, not soon *angry*
see wroth.

Anguish.—*A.V.* ¹*distress,* ²*tormented.*
Lu. 16. 24. for I [Dives] am in ²*anguish* in this flame
25. he is comforted, and thou art in ²*anguish*
Jno. 16. 21. she remembereth no more the *a.*, for the joy
Rom. 2. 9. tribulation and *anguish*, upon every soul
8. 35. shall tribulation, or ¹*anguish*, or persecution
2 *Cor.* 2. 4. out of much affliction and *anguish* of heart

Animals.—*A.V.* ¹*natural.*
2 *Pet.* 2. 12. born mere ¹*animals* to be taken and destroyed

Anise.
Mat. 23. 23. ye tithe mint and *anise* and cummin

Ankle.
Acts 3. 7. his [lame man] *ankle-*bones received strength

Announce—d.—*A.V.* ¹*declare,* ²*reported.*
1 *Pet.* 1. 12. minister these things which now have been ²*a*
1 *Jno.* 1. 5. and ¹*announce* unto you, that God is light

Anoint.—*A.V.* ¹*anointed.*
Mat. 6. 17. when thou fastest, *anoint* thy head
Mk. 16. 1. might come and *anoint* him [Jesus]
Lu. 7. 46. My head with oil thou didst not *anoint*
Acts 4. 27. thy holy Servant Jesus, whom thou didst ¹*a.*
Rev. 3. 18. and eyesalve to *anoint* thine eyes
see anointed.

Anointed.—*A.V.* ¹*anoint.*
Mk. 6. 13. [apostles] *a.* with oil many that were sick
14. 8. she hath ¹*anointed* my body aforehand

ANOINTED

Lu. 4. 18. he *anointed* me to preach good tidings
7. 36. kissed his feet, and *anointed* them. 46
Jno. 9. 6. and *anointed* his eyes with the clay. 11
11. 2. it was that Mary which *anointed* the Lord
12. 3. Mary—*anointed* the feet of Jesus
Acts 10. 38. Jesus of Nazareth, how that God *a.* him
2 *Cor.* 1. 21. with you in Christ, and *anointed* us, is God
Heb. 1. 9. Therefore God, thy God, hath *anointed* thee
see anoint.

Anointing.—*A.V.* ¹*unction.*
Jas. 5. 14. *a.* him with oil in the name of the Lord
1 *Jno.* 2. 20. ye have an ¹*anointing* from the Holy one
27. the *anointing* which ye received of him—as his *anointing* teacheth you

Another.
Mat. 11. 3. or look we for *another* ? *Lu.* 7. 19
Lu. 16. 7. said he to *another*, And how much owest thou ?
12. not been faithful in that which is *another's*
Acts 1. 20. His office let *another* take
Rom. 15. 20. I might not build upon *a.* man's foundation
2 *Cor.* 11. 4. if he that cometh preacheth *another* Jesus
Gal. 1. 7. which is not *another* gospel
Heb. 4. 8. not have spoken afterward of *another* day
Rev. 6. 4. And *another* horse came forth, a red horse
see different, neighbour, next, second.

One Another.
Mat. 24. 10. shall deliver up *one a.*, and shall hate *one a.*
Jno. 13. 14. ye also ought to wash *one another's* feet
34. that ye love *one another*—ye also love *one a.* 35:
Jno. 15. 12, 17 : *Rom.* 13. 8 : 1 *Th.* 3. 12 : 4. 9 : 1 *Pet.*
1. 22 : 1 *Jno.* 3. 11, 23 : 4. 7, 11, 12 : 2 *Jno.* 5
Rom. 2. 15. their thoughts *one* with *another* accusing
12. 10. tenderly affectioned *one* to *another*—preferring
16. the same mind *one* toward *another.* 15. 5 [*one a.*
14. 13. Let us not therefore judge *one another*
19. whereby we may edify *one another*
15. 7. receive ye *one another*, even as Christ also
14. able also to admonish *one another. Col.* 3. 16
16. 16. Salute *one another* with a holy kiss. 1 *Cor.* 16.
20 : 2 *Cor.* 13. 12 : 1 *Pet.* 5. 14
1 *Cor.* 11. 33. come together to eat, wait *one* for *another*
12. 25. should have the same care *one* for *another*
Gal. 5. 13. through love be servants *one* to *another*
26. provoking *one another*, envying *one another*
6. 2. Bear ye *one another's* burdens
Eph. 4. 2. forbearing *one another* in love. *Col.* 3. 13
32. he ye kind *one* to *another*
1 *Th.* 4. 18. comfort *one another* with these words
Tit. 3. 3. malice and envy, hateful, hating *one another*
Heb. 3. 13. exhort *one another* day by day. 10. 25
10. 24. consider *one another* to provoke unto love
Jas. 5. 9. Murmur not, brethren, *one* against *another*
16. Confess—your sins *one* to *another*, and pray *one* for *a.*
Rev. 6. 4. that they should slay *one another*
see other.

Answer—s.—*A.V.* ¹*answered,* ²*hearken,* ³*sentence,* ⁴*say.*
Mat. 22. 46. And no one was able to *answer* him
25. 37. Then shall the righteous *answer* him. 44
40. the King shall *answer* and say. 45
Mk. 9. 6. he [Peter] wist not what to ⁴*answer*
11 30. from heaven, or from men ? *answer* me
14. 40. and they wist not what to *answer* him
Lu. 2. 47. amazed at his understanding and his *answers*
11. 7. he from within shall *answer* and say
12. 11. be not anxious how or what ye shall *answer*

ANY

Lu. 13. 25. and he shall *answer* and say to you
14. 6. they [Pharisees] could not *answer* again
20. 26. they marvelled at his *a.*, and held their peace
21. 14. not to meditate beforehand how to *answer*
22. 68. if I ask you, ye will not *answer*
Jno. 1. 22. that we may give an *answer* to them
19. 9. Jesus gave him [Pilate] no *answer. Mat.* 27. 114
Acts 12. 13. a maid came to ²*answer*, named Rhoda
Rom. 11. 4. But what saith the *a.* of God unto him
2 *Cor.* 1. 9. have had the ³*a.* of death within ourselves
5. 12. ye may have wherewith to *answer* them
Col. 4. 6. know how ye ought to *answer* each one
1 *Pet.* 3. 15. being ready always to give *answer*
see defence, interrogation, tell.

Answered.—*A.V.* ¹*answering.*
Mat. 15. 23. But he *answered* her not a word
25. 26. his lord *a.* and said unto him, Thou wicked
27. 12. by the chief priests and elders, he *answered* nothing. *Mk.* 14. 61 : 15. 5 : *Lu.* 23. 9.
Mk. 12. 28. knowing that he had *answered* them well
34. Jesus saw that he [scribe] *answered* discreetly
Lu. 10. 28. Thou hast *answered* right : this do
13. 14. ruler of the synagogue—*answered* and said
23. 40. But the other ¹*answered*, and rebuking him said
Acts 15. 13. James *answered*, saying, Brethren
22. 8. I [Saul] *answered*, Who art thou, Lord ?
25. 9. Festus—*answered* Paul, and said, Wilt thou go up
16. To whom I *answered*, that it is not the custom
see answer, answering, defence, said, told.

Answerest—eth.
Mat. 26. 62. said unto him, *Answerest* thou nothing ? *Mk.*
Jno. 18. 22. *Answerest* thou the high priest so ?[14. 60 : 15. 4
Gal. 4. 25. Sinai in Arabia, and *a.* to the Jerusalem

Answering.—*A.V.* ¹*answered.*
Mk. 8. 7. [Jesus] *answering* saith unto him, Thou sayest
Lu. 10. 27. he *answering* said, Thou shalt love the Lord
11. 45. one of the lawyers ¹*answering* saith unto him
see answered, gainsaying.

Antichrist—s.
1 *Jno.* 2. 18. that *a.* cometh—have there arisen many *a.*
22. This is the *antichrist*, even he that denieth
4. 3. this is the spirit of the *a.*, whereof ye have heard
2 *Jno.* 7. This is the deceiver and the *antichrist*

Anxiety.—*A.V.* ¹*care.*
2 *Cor.* 11. 28. presseth upon me daily,¹*a.* for all the churches
1 *Pet.* 5. 7. casting all your ¹*a.* upon him, because he careth

Anxious.—*A.V.* ¹*careful,* ²*take—ing thought.*
Mat. 6. 25. Be not ²*anxious* for your life. *Lu.* 12. ²22 [12. ²25
27. which of you by being ²*a.* can add one cubit. *Lu.*
28. why are ye ²*anxious* concerning raiment. *Lu.* 12. ²26
34. Be not therefore ²*a.*—for the morrow will be ²*a.* ²31
10. 19. be not ²*anxious*—what ye shall speak. *Mk.* 13.
²11 : *Lu.* 12. ²11
Lu. 10. 41. Martha, thou art ¹*anxious* and troubled about
Phil. 4. 6. In nothing be ¹*a.* ; but in everything by prayer

Any one.—*A.V.* ¹*any man.*
Mk. 11. 3. if ¹*any one* say unto you, Why. *Lu.* 19. ¹31
16. 8. they said nothing to ¹*any one* [born blind
Jno. 9. 32. never heard that ¹*a. o.* opened the eyes of a man
Col. 3. 6. lost there shall be ¹*a. o.* that maketh spoil of you
1 *Th.* 5. 15. See that none render unto ¹*any one* evil for evil
1 *Jno.* 2. 27. ye need not that ¹*any one* teach you
see one.

ANYTHING

Anything.—*see (any) thing, p.* 342.

Apart.—*A.V.* ¹*privately,* ²*without.*

Mat. 14. 13. in a boat, to a desert place *apart. Mk.* 6. 31
  23. into the mountain *apart* to pray. 17. 1
  17. 19. came the disciples to Jesus *apart*, and said
  20. 17. he took the twelve disciples a., and in the way
Mk. 6. 32. went away in the boat to a desert place ¹*apart*
Jno. 15. 5. for ²*apart* from me ye can do nothing
Rom. 3. 21. ³*apart* from the law a righteousness of God. ²28
Heb. 11. 40. ²*apart* from us they should not be made perfect
    see putting.

Apiece.

Jno. 2. 6. containing two or three firkins *apiece*

Apostle.

Rom. 1. 1. Paul—called to be an *apostle*. 1 *Cor* 1. 1
  11. 13. Inasmuch then as I am an *apostle* of Gentiles
1 *Cor.* 9. 1. Am I not free ? am I not an *apostle* ?
  2. If to others I am not an a., yet at least I am to you
  15. 9. am not meet to be called an *apostle*, because I
2 *Cor.* 1. 1. Paul, an *apostle* of Christ Jesus. *Gal.* 1. 1:
    Eph. 1. 1: *Col.* 1. 1: 1 *Tim.* 1. 1 : 2 *Tim.* 1. 1: *Tit.* 1. 1
  12. 12. Truly the signs of an *apostle* were wrought
1 *Tim.* 2. 7. appointed a preacher and an a. 2 *Tim.* 1. 11
Heb. 3. 1. the *Apostle* and High Priest of our confession
1 *Pet.* 1. 1. Peter, an *apostle* of Jesus Christ. 2 *Pet.* 1. 1

Apostles.

Mat. 10. 2. the names of the twelve *apostles* are these
Mk. 6. 30. And the *apostles* gather themselves together
Lu. 6. 13. twelve, whom also he named *apostles*
  9. 10. the *apostles*, when they were returned
  11. 49. I will send unto them prophets and *apostles*
  17. 5. And the *apostles* said unto the Lord
  22. 14. he sat down, and the *apostles* with him
  24. 10. women—told these things unto the *apostles*
Acts 1. 2. through the Holy Ghost unto the *apostles*
  26. Matthias—was numbered with the eleven *apostles*
  2. 42. continued stedfastly in the *apostles'* teaching
  43. signs were done by the *apostles*. 5. 12.
  4. 33. with great power gave the *apostles* their witness
  35. laid them at the *apostles'* feet. 37: 5. 2
  5. 18. laid hands on the a., and put them in public ward
  29. Peter and the *apostles* answered and said
  40. called the *apostles* unto them, they beat them
  6. 6. whom they set before the *apostles*
  8. 1. all scattered abroad—except the *apostles*
  14. when the *apostles*—had received the word of God
  18. through the laying on of the *apostles'* hands
  14. 4. with the Jews, and part with the *apostles*
  15. 2. unto the *apostles* and elders. 4, 6, 22, 23
  16. 4. decrees—which had been ordained of the *apostles*
Rom. 16. 7. who are of note among the *apostles*
1 *Cor.* 4. 9. God hath sent forth us the *apostles* last of all
  9. 5. even as the rest of the *apostles*, and the brethren
  12. 28. in the church, first *apostles*, secondly prophets
  29. Are all *apostles* ? are all prophets ?
  15. 7. he appeared to James ; then to all the *apostles*
  9. For I am the least of the *apostles*, that am not meet
2 *Cor.* 11. 5. not a whit behind the very chiefest a. 12. 11
  18. such are false *apostles*—into *apostles* of Christ
Gal. 1. 17. to them which were *apostles* before me
  19. But other of the *apostles* saw I none, save James
Eph. 2. 20. foundation of the *apostles* and prophets
3. 5. revealed unto his holy *apostles* and prophets

APPEARED

Eph. 4. 11. And he gave some to be *apostles*
1 *Th.* 2. 6. burdensome, as *apostles* of Christ
2 *Pet.* 3. 2. Lord and Saviour through your *apostles*
Jude 17. spoken before by the a. of our Lord Jesus Christ
Rev. 2. 2. which call themselves *apostles*, and they are not
  18. 20. Rejoice—and ye saints, and ye *apostles*
  21. 14. twelve names of the twelve a. of the Lamb

Apostleship.

Acts 1. 25. *apostleship*, from which Judas fell
Rom. 1. 5. received grace and *apostleship*, unto obedience
1 *Cor.* 9. 2. for the seal of mine *apostleship* are ye
Gal. 2. 8. he that wrought for Peter unto the *apostleship*

Apparel.—*A.V.* ¹*clothing,* ²*garments,* ³*ornament,* ⁴*robe*

Lu. 23. 11. Herod—arraying him in gorgeous ⁴*apparel*
  24. 4. two men stood by them in dazzling ²*apparel*
Acts 1. 10. two men stood by them in white *apparel*
  10. 30. man stood before me [Cornelius] in bright ¹a.
  12. 21. Herod arrayed himself in royal *apparel*
  20. 33. I coveted no man's silver, or gold, or *apparel*
1 *Tim.* 2. 9. women adorn themselves in modest *apparel*
1 *Pet.* 3. 3. of gold, or of putting on *apparel*
  4. incorruptible ³*apparel* of a meek and quiet spirit
    see clothing.

Apparelled.

Lu. 7. 25. they which are gorgeously *apparelled*

Apparition.—*A.V.* ¹*spirit.*

Mat. 14. 26. It is an ¹*apparition;* and they cried out for fear. *Mk.* 6. ¹49

Appeal—ed.

Acts 25. 11. I [Paul] *appeal* unto Cæsar
  12. Thou hast *appealed* unto Cæsar
  21. when Paul had *appealed* to be kept. 25
  26. 32. if he had not *appealed* unto Cæsar
  28. 19. I was constrained to *appeal* unto Cæsar

Appear.

Mat. 23. 27. sepulchres which outwardly *appear* beautiful
  28. ye [Pharisees] also outwardly a. righteous unto men
  24. 30. then shall *appear* the sign of the Son of man
Lu. 11. 44. ye are as the tombs which *appear* not
  19. 11. kingdom of God was immediately to *appear*
Acts 26. 16. wherein I will *appear* unto thee
2 *Cor.* 13. 7. not that we may *appear* approved
Heb. 9. 24. now to *appear* before the face of God for us
  28. shall *appear* a second time, apart from sin
  11. 3. not been made out of things which do *appear*
1 *Pet.* 4. 18. shall the ungodly and sinner *appear*
    see seen, together, shewn, manifest, manifested.

Appearance.—*A.V.* ¹*countenance,* ²*sight.*

Mat. 28. 3. His [angel] ¹*appearance* was as lightning
Jno. 7. 24. Judge not according to *appearance*
2 *Cor.* 5. 12. answer them that glory in *appearance*
Heb. 12. 21. so fearful was the ²a., that Moses said
    see face, form.

Appeared—eth.—*A.V.* ¹*seemed,* ²*seen,* ³*shewed.*

Mat. 1. 20. angel of the Lord a. unto him in a dream. 2. 13.
  2. 7. learned of them—what time the star *appeared* |19
  13. 26. brought forth fruit, then *appeared* the tares also

APPEARED

Mat. 17. 3. there a. unto them Moses and Elijah. *Mk.* 9. 4
27. 53. entered into the holy city and a. unto many
Mk. 16. 9. he *appeared* first to Mary Magdalene
Lu. 1. 11. there *appeared* unto him [Zacharias] an angel
9. 8. and by some, that Elijah had *appeared*
31. [Moses and Elijah] who *appeared* in glory, and spake
22. 43. there *appeared* unto him [Jesus] an angel
24. 11. these words *appeared* in their sight as idle talk
34. then he *appeared* to above five hundred brethren
Acts 2. 3. And there *appeared* unto them tongues
7. 2. God of glory *appeared* unto our father Abraham
26. day following he [Moses]²a. unto them as they strove
9. 17. Jesus, who *appeared* unto thee in the way
16. 9. And a vision *appeared* to Paul in the night
26. 16. to this end have I *appeared* unto thee
1 *Cor.* 15. 5. and that he [Jesus] ²*appeared* to Cephas
6. then he *appeared* to above five hundred brethren
7. then he ²*appeared* to James
8. one born out of due time, he ²*appeared* to me also
Tit. 2. 11. For the grace of God hath *appeared*
3. 4. our Saviour, and his love toward man, *appeared*
Jas. 4. 14. a vapour, that *appeareth* for a little time
see manifested, seen, shone.

Appearing.—*A.V.* ¹*seen.*

Acts 1. 3 ¹*appearing* unto them by the space of forty days
1 *Tim.* 6. 14. until the *appearing* of our Lord Jesus Christ
2 *Tim.* 1. 10. manifested by the *appearing* of our Saviour
4. 1. and by his *appearing* and his kingdom
8. but also to all them that have loved his *appearing*
Tit. 2. 13. for the blessed hope and appearing of the glory
see revelation.

Appeased *A.V.*—*see quieted.*

Appoint.—*A.V.* ¹*ordain,* ²*make.*

Mat. 24. 51. *appoint* his portion with the hypocrites
Lu. 12. 46. *appoint* his portion with the unfaithful
22. 29. I *appoint* unto you a kingdom
Acts 6. 3. whom we may *appoint* over this business
26. 16. to ²*appoint* thee a minister and a witness
Tit. 1. 5. and ¹*appoint* elders in every city

Appointed—eth—ing.—*A.V.* ¹*chosen,* ²*commanded,* ³*maketh,* ⁴*ordained,* ⁵*preached,* ⁶*putting.*

Mat. 21. 6. disciples went—even as Jesus²a. them. 26. 19: 28.
27. 10. for the potter's field, as the Lord *appointed* me [16
Mk. 3. 14. he ⁴a. twelve, that they might be with him
Lu. 3. 13. Extort no more than that which is a. you
10. 1. the Lord *appointed* seventy others
22. 29. even as my Father *appointed* unto me
Jno. 15. 16. I chose you, and ⁴*appointed* you
Acts 3. 20. may send the Christ who hath been ⁵a. for you
14. 23. they had ⁴a. for them elders in every church
17. 26. having determined their *appointed* seasons
31. he hath *appointed* a day, in the which he will judge
22. 10. told thee of all things which are a. for thee
14. The God of our fathers hath ¹*appointed* thee
28. 23. when they had *appointed* him a day, they came
2 *Cor.* 8. 19. who was also ¹*appointed* by the churches
Gal. 4. 2. stewards until the term *appointed* of the father
1 *Th.* 3. 3. yourselves know that hereunto we are *appointed*
5. 9. For God *appointed* us not unto wrath [his service
1 *Tim.* 1. 12. he counted me faithful, ⁶*appointing* me to
2. 7. whereunto I was ⁴a. a preacher and an apostle. 2
Heb. 1. 2. whom he *appointed* heir of all things [*Tim.* 1. 11
3. 2. who was faithful to him that *appointed* him
5. 1. taken from among men, is ⁴*appointed* for men
7. 28. law ⁴*appointeth* men high priests—²a. a Son

ARISE

Heb. 9. 27. as it is *appointed* unto men once to die
1 *Pet.* 2. 8. whereunto also they were *appointed*
see charge, put (forward).

Apportioned.—*A.V.* ¹*distributed.*

2. *Cor.* 10. 13. measure of the province which God ¹a. to us

Apprehend—ed.—*A.V.* ¹*comprehend*—ed.

Jno. 1. 5. in the darkness; and the darkness ¹a. it not
Eph. 3. 18. may be strong to ¹*apprehend* with all the saints
Phil. 3. 12. that I may a. that for which also I was a.
13. I count not myself yet to have *apprehended*
see take, taken.

Approach—eth—ing. *A.V.*—*see draweth*—ing, *unapproachable.*

Approve—d—est—eth.—*A.V.* ¹*allowed*—eth, ²*tried.*

Acts 2. 22. Jesus of Nazareth, a man *approved* of God
Rom. 2. 18. and *approvest* the things that are excellent
14. 18. well-pleasing to God, and *approved* of men
22. judgeth not himself in that which he ¹*approveth*
16. 10. Salute Apelles the *approved* in Christ
1 *Cor.* 11. 19. they which are a. may be made manifest
16. 3. whomsoever ye shall *approve* by letters
2 *Cor.* 7. 11. in everything ye *approved* yourselves
10. 18. not he that commendeth himself is *approved*
13. 7. not that we may appear *approved*
Phil. 1. 10. may *approve* the things that are excellent
1 *Th.* 2. 4. even as we have been ¹*approved* of God
2 *Tim.* 2. 15. present thyself *approved* unto God
Jas. 1. 12. when he hath been ²a., he shall receive the [crown
see deemed.

Approving *A.V.*—*see commanding.*

Aprons.

Acts 19. 12. sick were carried—handkerchiefs or *aprons*

Apt.

1 *Tim.* 3. 2. bishop therefore must be—*apt* to teach
2 *Tim.* 2. 24. Lord's servant must—be—*apt* to teach

Archangel.

1 *Th.* 4. 16. a shout, with the voice of the *archangel*
Jude 9. Michael the *archangel,* when contending

Aright.—*A.V.* ¹*rightly.*

2 *Tim.* 2. 15. handling ¹*aright* the word of truth

Arise.—*A.V.* ¹*rise.*

Mat. 2. 13. *Arise* and take the young child. 20
9. 5. or to say, *Arise,* and walk? *Mk.* 2. 9: *Lu.* 5. 123
6. *Arise,* and take up thy bed. *Mk.* 2. 11: *Lu.* 5. 24:
17. 7. Jesus—said, *Arise,* and be not afraid [*Jno.* 5. ¹8
24. 11. And many false prophets shall ¹*arise.* 24
26. 46. ¹*Arise,* let us be going. *Mk.* 14. ¹42: *Jno.* 14. 31
Mk. 5. 41. Damsel, I say unto thee, *Arise. Lu.* 8. 54.
Lu. 7. 14. Young man, I say unto thee, *Arise*
15. 18. I will *arise* and go to my father [whole
17. 19. *Arise,* and go thy way: thy faith hath made thee
24. 38. wherefore do reasonings *arise* in your heart?
Acts 9. 34. Æneas—*arise,* and make thy bed
40. Peter—said, Tabitha, *arise*
20. 30. shall men *arise,* speaking perverse things
22. 16. *arise,* and be baptized [Saul]
26. 16. But ¹*arise,* and stand upon thy feet
Eph. 5. 14. *arise* from the dead, and Christ shall shine
Heb. 7. 11. priest should ¹a. after the order of Melchizedek
2 *Pet.* 1. 19. and the day-star *arise* in your hearts
see rise.

ARISEN

Arisen.—*A.V.* ¹*risen.*
Mat. 11. 11. hath not ¹a. a greater than John the Baptist
Lu. 7. 16. A great prophet is ¹*arisen* among us

Ariseth.—*A.V.* ¹*rise,* ²*risen.*
Mat. 13. 21. when tribulation or persecution a. *Mk.* 4. 17
Jno. 7. 52. see that out of Galilee *ariseth* no prophet
Rom. 15. 12. he that ¹*ariseth* to rule over the Gentiles
Heb. 7. 15. of Melchizedek there *ariseth* another priest
Jas. 1. 11. the sun ²*ariseth* with the scorching wind

Arising.—*A.V.* ¹*made.*
Mat. 27. 24. but rather that a tumult was ¹*arising*

Ark.
Mat. 24. 38. day that Noah entered into the a. *Lu.* 17. 27
Heb. 9. 4. and the *ark* of the covenant overlaid
11. 7. Noah—prepared an *ark* to the saving of his house
1 *Pet.* 3. 20. while the *ark* was a preparing
Rev. 11. 19. seen in his temple the *ark* of his covenant

Arm.
Lu. 1. 51. He hath shewed strength with his *arm*
Jno. 12. 38. to whom hath the *arm* of the Lord been
Acts 13. 17. with a high *arm* led he them forth [revealed

Arm—ed.
Lu. 11. 21. When the strong man fully *armed* guardeth
1 *Pet.* 4. 1. arm ye yourselves also with the same mind

Armour.
Lu. 11. 22. taketh from him his whole *armour*
Rom. 13. 12. let us put on the *armour* of light
2 *Cor.* 6. 7. *armour* of righteousness on the right hand
Eph. 6. 11. Put on the whole *armour* of God. 13

Arms.
Mk. 9. 36. a little child—and taking him in his *arms*, he said
10. 16. he took them in his *arms*, and blessed them
Lu. 2. 28. [Simeon] received him into his *arms*

Army—ies.
Mat. 22. 7. and he sent his *armies*, and destroyed those
Lu. 21. 20. when ye see Jerusalem compassed with *armies*
Heb. 11. 34. turned to flight *armies* of aliens
Rev. 9. 16. the number of the *armies* of the horsemen
19. 14. and the *armies* which are in heaven
19. kings of the earth and their a.—against his *army*
see soldiers.

Arose.—*A.V* ¹*raised.*
Mat. 1. 24. And Joseph ¹*arose* from his sleep
2. 14. And he *arose* and took the young child. 21
8. 15. and she [Peter's wife's mother] a., and ministered
24. And behold, there *arose* a great tempest in the sea
26. Then he *arose*, and rebuked the winds
9. 9. [Matthew] *arose*, and followed him. *Mk.* 2. 14
19. And Jesus *arose*, and followed him [Jaïrus]
25. took her by the hand; and the damsel *arose*
Mk. 2. 12. And he *arose*, and straightway took up the bed
9. 27. Jesus—raised him up; and he *arose* [demoniac]
Lu. 6. 48. when a flood *arose*, the stream brake against
15. 20. And he *arose*, and came to his father
Jno. 11. 29. when she [Mary] heard it, *arose* quickly

ASHAMED

Acts 7. 18. till there *arose* another king over Egypt
9. 34. And straightway he *arose* [Æneas]
39. And Peter *arose* and went with them
11. 19. upon the tribulation that *arose* about Stephen
19. 23. And about that time there *arose* no small stir
23. 7. there *arose* a dissension between the Pharisees. 10
9. And there *arose* a great clamour
see awake, raise, raised, rising, rose, stood up.

Array.—*A.V.* ¹*arrayed,* ²*stood up.*
Acts 4. 26. kings of the earth set themselves in ²*array*
Rev. 19. 8. that she should ¹*array* herself in fine linen
see raiment.

Arrayed—ing.—*A.V.* ¹*clothed,* ²*put on.*
Mat. 6. 29. was not *arrayed* like one of these. *Lu.* 12. 27
Mk. 16. 5. young man—¹*arrayed* in a white robe
Lu. 23. 11. Herod—a. him [Jesus] in gorgeous apparel
Jno. 19. 2. ²*arrayed* him [Jesus] in a purple garment
Acts 12. 21. Herod *arrayed* himself in royal apparel
Rev. 3. 5. He that overcometh shall thus be ¹a. in white
4. 4. elders sitting, ¹*arrayed* in white garments
7. 9. great multitude—¹*arrayed* in white robes
13. These which are *arrayed* in the white robes
10. 1. another strong angel—¹*arrayed* with a cloud
12. 1. a woman ¹*arrayed* with the sun
15. 6. seven angels—¹*arrayed* with precious stone
17. 4. the woman was *arrayed* in purple and scarlet
18. 16. she that was ¹*arrayed* in fine linen
19. 13. he is ¹*arrayed* in a garment sprinkled with blood
see array.

Arrive—ed.—*A.V.* ¹*attained.*
Lu. 8. 26. they *arrived* at the country of the Gerasenes
Rom. 9. 31. law of righteousness, did not ¹a. at that law
see touched.

Art—s.
Acts 17. 29. stone, graven by *art* and device of man
19. 19. of them that practised curious *arts* brought

Art (*Verb*).
Mat. 11. 3. *Art* thou he that cometh? *Lu.* 7. 19, 20
Jno. 1. 22. Who *art* thou? 21. 12
19. 9. [Pilate] saith unto Jesus, Whence *art* thou?
Rev. 11. 17. Almighty, which *art* and which wast. 16. 5

Ascend.—*A.V.* ¹*ascending.*
Jno. 20. 17. I *ascend* unto my Father and your Father
Rom. 10. 6. Who shall *ascend* into heaven?
Rev. 7. 2. I saw another angel ¹*ascend* from the sunrising
see ascending, come up.

Ascended.
Jno. 3. 13. no man hath *ascended* into heaven
20. 17. I am not yet *ascended* unto the Father
Acts 2. 34. David *ascended* not into the heavens
Eph. 4. 8. When he *ascended* on high, he led captivity
9. (Now this, He *ascended*, what is it but that he also
10. same also that *ascended* far above all the heavens
see went up.

Ascendeth *A.V.*—*see cometh, goeth.*

Ascending.—*A.V.* ¹*ascend.*
Jno. 1. 51. angels of God a. and descending upon the Son
6. 62. if ye should behold the Son of man ¹*ascending*
see ascend, going.

Ashamed.
Mk. 8. 38. whosoever shall be *ashamed* of me—Son of man
also shall be *ashamed* of him. *Lu.* 9. 26

ASHAMED

Lu. 16. 3. not strength to dig; to beg I am *ashamed*
Rom. 1. 16. For I am not *ashamed* of the gospel
   6. 21. things whereof ye are now *ashamed*
2 *Th.* 3. 14. to the end that he may be *ashamed*
2 *Tim.* 1. 8. Be not *ashamed* therefore of the testimony
   12. yet I am not *ashamed;* for I know him
   16. was not *ashamed* of my chain [Paul]
   2. 15. a workman that needeth not to be *ashamed*
Tit. 2. 8. he that is of the contrary part may be *ashamed*
Heb. 2. 11. he is not *ashamed* to call them brethren
   11. 16. wherefore God is not *ashamed* of them
1 *Pet.* 4. 16. suffer as a Christian, let him not be *ashamed*
1 *Jno.* 2. 28. and not be *ashamed* before him
   see shame.

Ashes.

Mat. 11. 21. long ago in sackcloth and *ashes. Lu.* 10. 13
Heb. 9. 13. the *ashes* of a heifer sprinkling them
2 *Pet.* 2. 6. cities of Sodom and Gomorrah into *ashes*

Aside.—*A. V.* ¹*out of the way.*

Mk. 7. 33. And he took him *aside* from the multitude
Jno. 13. 4. riseth from supper, and layeth a. his garments
Rom. 3. 12. They have all turned ¹*aside*
Heb. 12. 1. cloud of witnesses, lay *aside* every weight

Ask.—*A. V.* ¹*desire,* ²*require.*

Mat. 6. 8. what things ye have need of, before ye *ask* him
   7. 7. *Ask,* and it shall be given you. *Lu.* 11. 9
   9. if his son shall a. him for a loaf. 10: a. for a fish.
   11. give good things to them that *ask* him. | *Lu.*11.11
   14. 7. [Herod] give her whatsoever she should *ask*
   18. 19. anything that they shall *ask* it shall be done
   20. 22. Ye know not what ye *ask. Mk.* 10. 38
   21. 22. whatsoever ye shall *ask* in prayer
   22. 46. from that day forth *ask* him any more questions.
   Mk. 12. 34: *Lu.* 20. 40
Mk. 6. 22. *Ask* of me whatsoever thou wilt. 23
   24. said unto her mother, What shall I *ask?*
   9. 32. [disciples] were afraid to *ask* him. *Lu.* 9. 45
   10. 35. what do for us whatsoever we shall ¹a. of thee
   11. 24. All things whatsoever ye pray and ¹*ask* for
   15. 8. began to ¹*ask* him to do as he was wont to do
Lu. 6. 30. taketh away thy goods *ask* them not again
   11. 12. shall *ask* an egg, will he give him a scorpion?
   13. give the Holy Spirit to them that *ask* him
   12. 48. of him will they *ask* the more
Jno. 1. 19. priests and Levites to *ask* him
   9. 21. *ask* him; he is of age. 23
   11. 22. whatsoever thou shalt *ask* of God   [16. 23, 26
   14. 13. whatsoever ye shall *ask* in my name. 14: 15. 16:
   15. 7. *ask* whatsoever ye will, and it shall be done
   16. 19. they were desirous to *ask* him
   23. in that day ye shall *ask* me nothing
   24. a., and ye shall receive, that your joy may be fulfilled
   30. needest not that any man should *ask* thee
   18. 21. *ask* them that have heard me
Acts 10. 29. I *ask* therefore with what intent ye sent
   23. 20. Jews have agreed to ¹a. thee to bring down Paul
1 *Cor.* 1. 22. Seeing that Jews ²*ask* for signs
   14. 35. let them *ask* their own husbands at home
Eph. 3. 13. Wherefore I ¹*ask* that ye faint not
   20. abundantly above all that we *ask* or think
Jas. 1. 5. lacketh wisdom, let him *ask* of God
   6. let him *ask* in faith, nothing doubting
   4. 2. ye have not, because ye *ask* not
   3. Ye *ask,* and receive not, because ye *ask* amiss

ASKING

1 *Jno.* 3. 22. whatsoever we *ask,* we receive of him
   5. 14. if we *ask* anything according to his will
   15. whatsoever we *ask,* we know that we have
   16. he shall *ask,* and God will give him life
   see inquire, tell.

Asked.—*A.V.* ¹*begged,* ²*besought,* ³*craved,* ⁴*demanded,* ⁵*desired,* ⁶*prayed,* ⁷*required.*

Mat. 16. 1. Sadducees—⁵*asked* him to shew them a sign
   13. Jesus—*asked* his disciples. *Mk.* 8. 27: *Lu.* 9. 18
   22. 23. Sadducees—*asked* him. *Mk.* 12. 18
   35. a lawyer, *asked* him a question   [⁵52: *Jno.* 19. ²38
   27. 58. ¹*asked* for the body of Jesus. *Mk.* 15. ⁸43: *Lu.* 23.
Mk. 9. 11. they *asked* him, saying, The scribes say
   28. his disciples *asked* him privately. 13. 3
   10. 2. came unto him Pharisees, and *asked* him
   14. 61. Again the high priest *asked* him, and saith
   15. 6. release—one prisoner, whom they ⁵*asked* of him
Lu. 3. 10. the multitudes *asked* him, saying, What then
   14. And soldiers also ⁴*asked* him, saying, And we
   5. 3. boats, which was Simon's, and ⁶*asked* him to put out
   8. 37. people of the country of the Gerasenes—²a. him to
   17. 20. And being ⁴*asked* by the Pharisees   [depart
   18. 40. Jesus—when he was come near, he *asked* him
   21. 7. they a. him—when therefore shall those things be?
   22. 31. Simon, Simon, behold, Satan ⁵*asked* to have you
   23. 24. Pilate gave sentence that what they ⁷a. for should
   25. released him—whom they ⁵*asked* for   [be done
Jno. 4. 10. me to drink; thou wouldest have *asked* of him
   12. 21. ⁵*asked* him, saying, Sir, we would see Jesus
   16. 24. Hitherto have ye *asked* nothing in my name
   18. 19. The high priest therefore *asked* Jesus
   19. 31. ²*asked* of Pilate that their legs might be broken
Acts 3. 14. ²*asked* for a murderer to be granted unto you
   7. 46. ⁵*asked* to find a habitation for the God of Jacob
   9. 2. [Saul] ⁵*asked* of him letters to Damascus
   12. 20. they [Tyre and Sidon] ⁵*asked* for peace
   13. 21. afterward they [Israel] ⁵*asked* for a king
   28. yet ⁵*asked* they of Pilate that he should be slain
   16. 39. they ⁵*asked* them to go away from the city
   18. 20. when they ⁵*asked* him to abide a longer time
   23. 18. Paul the prisoner called—and ⁵*asked* me
Rom. 10. 20. manifest unto them that *asked* not of me
1 *Jno.* 5. 15. the petitions which we have ⁵*asked* of him

Askest.

Jno. 4. 9. thou, being a Jew, *askest* drink of me
   18. 21. Why a. thou me? ask them that have heard me

Asketh.—*A.V.* ¹*besought,* ²*desireth.*

Mat. 5. 42. Give to him that *asketh* thee. *Lu.* 6. 30
   7. 8. every one that *asketh* receiveth. *Lu.* 11. 10
Lu. 11. 37. a Pharisee ¹*asketh* him to dine with him
   14. 32. an ambassage, and ²*asketh* conditions of peace
Jno. 16. 5. none of you *asketh* me, Whither goest thou?
1 *Pet.* 3. 15. give answer to every man that *asketh* you

Asking.—*A. V.* ¹*desired,* ²*desiring,* ³*requiring.*

Mat. 20. 20. worshipping him, and ²a. a certain thing of him
Lu. 2. 46. hearing them, and *asking* them questions
   23. 23. loud voices, ³*asking* that he might be crucified
Jno. 8. 7. when they continued *asking* him
Acts 25. 3. ¹a. favour against him, that he would send
   15. ¹*asking* for sentence against him [Paul]
1 *Cor.* 10. 25. sold in the shambles, eat, a. no question. 27

ASLEEP

Asleep.—*A.V.* ¹*sleep—eth,* ²*slept.*
Mat. 8. 24. but he was *asleep.* *Mk.* 4. 38: *Lu.* 9. 23
27. 52. bodies of the saints that had fallen ²*a.* were raised
Jno. 11. 11. Our friend Lazarus is fallen ¹*asleep*
12. Lord, if he is fallen ¹*asleep,* he will recover
Acts 7. 60. when he [Stephen] had said this, he fell *asleep*
1 *Cor.* 15. 6. but some are fallen *asleep*
18. they also which are fallen *asleep* in Christ
20. the firstfruits of them that are ²*asleep*
1 *Th.* 4. 13. concerning them that fall *asleep*
14. them also that are fallen ¹*asleep* in Jesus will God
15. in no wise precede them that are fallen *asleep*
2 *Pet.* 3. 4. from the day that the fathers fell *asleep*
see sleeping.

Asps.
Rom. 3. 13. The poison of *asps* is under their lips

Ass.
Mat. 21. 2. ye shall find an *ass* tied. 7
5. riding upon an *a.,* And upon a colt the foal of an *ass*
Lu. 13. 15. on the sabbath loose his ox or his *ass*
14. 5. have an *ass* or an ox fallen into a well, and will not
Jno. 12. 14. Jesus, having found a young *ass,* sat thereon
15. thy King cometh, sitting on an *ass's* colt
2 *Pet.* 2. 16. a dumb *ass* spake with man's voice

Assassins.—*see proper names.*

Assault—ed *A.V.*—*see onset, assaulting.*

Assaulting.—*A.V.* ¹*assaulted.*
Acts 17. 5. uproar; and ¹*assaulting* the house of Jason

Assayed—ing.—*A.V.* ¹*gone about,* ²*went about.*
Acts 9. 26. [Saul] *assayed* to join himself to the disciples
16. 7. they *assayed* to go into Bithynia
24. 6. who moreover ¹*assayed* to profane the temple
26. 21. Jews seized me—and ²*assayed* to kill me
Heb. 11. 29. Egyptians *assaying* to do were swallowed up

Assemble—ed.—*A.V.* ¹*come.*
Mat. 28. 12. when they were *assembled* with the elders
Acts 1. 4. being *assembled* together with them
1 *Cor.* 11. 20. When therefore ye ¹*a.* yourselves together
15. 23. whole church be¹*assembled* together, and all speak
see come, gathered (together).

Assembling.
Heb. 10. 25. not forsaking the *a.* of ourselves together

Assembly.
Acts 19. 32. for the *assembly* was in confusion
39. it shall be settled in the regular *assembly*
41. he [townclerk] dismissed the *assembly* [firstborn
Heb. 12. 23. to the general *assembly* and church of the
see synagogue.

Assented *A.V.*—*see joined.*

Assist.
Rom. 16. 2. that ye *assist* her in whatsoever matter

Assurance.—*A.V.* ¹*substance.*
Acts 17. 31. whereof he hath given *a.* unto all men
Col. 2. 2. riches of the full *assurance* of understanding
1 *Th.* 1. 5. in the Holy Ghost, and in much *assurance*
Heb. 11. 1. Now faith is the *assurance* of things hoped for
see fulness.

ATTENDANCE

Assure—ed.—*A.V.* ¹*persuaded.*
Rom. 4. 21. being fully ¹*a.* that, what he had promised
14. 5. Let each man be fully ¹*assured* in his own mind
2 *Tim.* 3. 14. thou hast learned and hast been *assured* of
1 *Jno.* 3. 19. and shall *assure* our heart before him

Assuredly.
Acts 2. 36. know *assuredly,* that God hath made him

Astonished.—*A.V.* ¹*amazed.*
Mat. 7. 28. multitudes were *astonished* at his teaching. 13.
54: 22. 33: *Mk.* 1. 22: 6. 2: 11. 18: *Lu.* 4. 32
19. 25. when the disciples heard it, they were ¹*astonished*
Mk. 7. 37. were beyond measure *astonished,* saying
10. 26. they were *astonished* exceedingly
Lu. 2. 48. when they saw him, they were ¹*astonished*
9. 43. they were all ¹*astonished* at the majesty of God
Acts 13. 12. believed, being *a.* at the teaching of the Lord
see amazed.

Astonishment.—*A.V.* ¹*amazed.*
Mk. 16. 8. for trembling and ¹*a.* had come upon them
see amazement.

Astray.—*A.V.* ¹*deceive,* ²*deceived,* ³*deceiveth,* ⁴*erred.*
Mat. 24. 4. Take heed that no man lead you ¹*a.* *Mk.* 13. ¹15
5. I am the Christ; and shall lead many ¹*a.* ¹11: *Mk.*
24. shall arise false Christs—so as to lead ¹*astray* [13. ¹6
Lu. 21. 8. Take heed that ye be not led ²*astray*
Jno. 7. 12. Not so, but he leadeth the multitude ³*astray*
47. Are ye also led ²*astray?*
1 *Tim.* 6. 10. been reaching after have been led ⁴*astray*
1 *Pet.* 2. 25. For ye were going *astray* like sheep
1 *Jno.* 3. 7. let no man lead you ¹*astray*

Asunder.—*A.V.* ¹*sunder.*
Lu. 12. 46. shall cut him ¹*asunder,* and appoint his portion

Ate.—*A.V.* ¹*eat.*
Mk. 6. 44. they that ¹*ate* the loaves were five thousand
Lu. 17. 27. They ¹*ate,* they drank. ¹28 [men
Jno. 6. 26. because ye ¹*ate* of the loaves, and were filled
31. Our fathers ¹*ate* the manna in the wilderness [up
Rev. 10. 10. little book out of the angel's hand, and *ate* it

Athirst.—*A.V.* ¹*thirsty.*
Mat. 25. 44. when saw we thee an hungred, or *athirst.* ¹37
Rev. 21. 6. give unto him that is *athirst* of the fountain
22. 17. And he that is *athirst,* let him come

Atonement *A.V.*—*see reconciliation.*

Attain—ed.—*A.V.* ¹*come,* ²*obtain.*
Lu. 20. 35. are accounted worthy to ²*attain* to that world
Acts 26. 7. serving God night and day, hope to ¹*attain*
Rom. 9. 30. not after righteousness, *a.* to righteousness
1 *Cor.* 9. 24. Even so run, that ye may ²*attain*
Eph. 4. 13. till we all ¹*attain* unto the unity of the faith
Phil. 3. 11. I may *a.* unto the resurrection from the dead
16. whereunto we have already *attained*
see arrived (at), followed, obtained, reach.

Attend.
1 *Cor.* 7. 35. that ye may *attend* upon the Lord
for attended see (give) heed.

Attendance.
Heb. 7. 13. no man hath given *attendance* at the altar
see (give) heed.

ATTENDANT

Attendant.—*A.V.* ¹*minister.*
Lu. 4. 20. closed the book, and gave it back to the ¹*attendant*
Acts 13. 5. they had also John as their ¹*attendant*

Attending.
Rom. 13. 6. ministers of God's service, a. continually

Attentive *A.V.*—*see listening.*

Availeth.
Gal. 5. 6. neither circumcision *availeth* anything
Jas. 5. 16. supplication of a righteous man *availeth* much

Audience.
Acts 22. 22. And they gave him *audience* unto this word
see ears, hearing, hearken.

Aught.—*A.V.* ¹*ought,* ²*anything.*
Mat. 5. 23. that thy brother hath ¹*aught* against thee
21. 3. And if anyone say ¹*aught* unto you, ye shall say
Mk. 7. 12. ye no longer suffer him to do ¹a. for his father
8. 23. he asked him, Seest thou ¹*aught* ?
11. 25. forgive, if ye have ¹*aught* against any one
Lu. 19. 8. if I have wrongfully exacted ²a. of any man
Jno. 4. 33. Hath any man brought him ¹*aught* to eat ?
Acts 4. 32. said that ¹a. of the things which he possessed
24. 19. to make accusation, if they had ¹a. against me
28. 19. not that I had ¹*aught* to accuse my nation of
Philem. 18. if he hath wronged thee at all, or oweth thee ¹a.

Austere.
Lu. 19. 21. because thou art an *austere* man. 22

Author.—*A.V.* ¹*captain.*
Heb. 2. 10. to make the ¹*author* of their salvation perfect
5. 9. obey him the *author* of eternal salvation [faith
12. 2. looking unto Jesus the *author* and perfecter of our
see God, proper names.

Authority—ies.—*A.V.* ¹*power—s,* ²*strength.*
Mat. 7. 29. he taught them as one having a. *Mk.* 1. 22
8. 9. I also am a man under *authority*. *Lu.* 7. 8 [6. 17
10. 1. gave them [disciples] ¹a. over unclean spirits. *Mk.*
20. 25. great ones exercise a. over them. *Mk.* 10. 42
21. 23. By what *authority* doest thou?—who gave thee this *authority* ? *Mk.* 11. 28 : *Lu.* 20. 2
24. I—will tell you by what *authority* I do these things.
27. : *Mk.* 11. 29, 33 ; *Lu.* 20. 8
28. 18. All ¹*authority* hath been given unto me in heaven
Mk. 1. 27. with *authority* he commandeth even the unclean spirits. *Lu.* 4. 36
3. 15. and to have ¹*authority* to cast out devils
13. 34. given a. to his servants, to each one his work
Lu. 4. 6. To thee will I give all this ¹*authority*
32. for his word was with ¹*authority*
9. 1. gave them power and *authority* over all devils
10. 13. I have given you ¹a. to tread upon serpents
12. 11. the rulers, and the ¹*authorities*, be not anxious
19. 17. have thou *authority* over ten cities
20. 20. deliver him—to the *authority* of the governor
22. 25. they that have a. over them are called Benefactors
Jno. 5. 27. he gave him *authority* to execute judgement
17. 2. even as thou gavest him ¹*authority* over all flesh
Acts 1. 7. which the Father hath set within his own ¹a.
8. 27. a eunuch of great *authority* under Candace
9. 14. here he hath a. from the chief priests. 26. 10, 12
1 *Cor.* 11. 10. the woman to have a sign of ¹a. on her head
15. 24. abolished all rule and all *authority* and power

AWE

2 *Cor.* 10. 8. abundantly concerning our *authority*
13. 10. according to the ¹a. which the Lord gave me
Tit. 2. 15. reprove with all *authority*
3 1. to be in subjection to rulers, to ¹*authorities*
1 *Pet.* 3. 22. angels and a. and powers being made subject
Rev. 2. 26. to him will I give ¹*authority* over the nations
6. 8. was given unto them ¹a. over the fourth part
13. 2. dragon gave him—his throne and great a. 14
5. there was given to him ¹*authority* to continue
7. there was given to him ¹*authority* over every tribe
12. exerciseth all the ¹a. of the first beast in his sight
17. 12. they receive ¹*authority* as kings, with the beast
13. give their power and ²*authority* unto the beast
18. 1. angel coming down—having great ¹*authority*
see dominion, high (place).

Avenge.—*A.V.* ¹*revenge.*
Lu. 18. 3. *Avenge* me of mine adversary
5. because this widow troubleth me, I will *avenge* her
7. shall not God *avenge* his elect, which cry to him
8. I say unto you, that he will *avenge* them speedily
Rom. 12. 19. *Avenge* not yourselves, beloved
2 *Cor.* 10. 6. being in readiness to ¹*avenge* all disobedience
Rev. 6. 10. dost thou not judge and a. our blood on them

Avenged.
Acts 7. 24. [Moses] defended him, and *avenged* him
Rev. 19. 2. he hath *avenged* the blood of his servants
see judged.

Avenger.—*A.V.* ¹*revenger.*
Rom. 13. 4. he is a minister of God, an ¹*avenger* for wrath
1 *Th.* 4. 6. because the Lord is an a. in all these things

Avenging.—*A.V.* ¹*revenge.*
2 *Cor.* 7. 11. yea, what zeal, yea, what ¹*avenging* !

Avoid *A.V.*—*see refuse, shun, turn (away).*

Avoiding.
2 *Cor.* 8. 20. *avoiding* this, that any man should blame us
see turning (away).

Awake.
Mk. 4. 38. and they *awake* him, and say unto him
Lu. 9. 32. when they were fully a., they saw his glory
Jno. 11. 11. I go, that I may *awake* him [Lazarus]
Rom. 13. 11. it is high time for you to *awake* out of sleep
1 *Cor.* 15. 34. *Awake* up righteously, and sin not
Eph. 5. 14. *Awake*, thou that sleepest, and arise

Awaking *A.V.* *see (being) roused.*

Aware.—*A.V.* ¹*ware.*
Acts 14. 6. they became ¹*aware* of it, and fled
see know with negatives, knoweth.

Away.—*A.V.* ¹*his way.*
Lu. 23. 18. *A.* with this man, and release unto us Barabbas
Jno. 19. 15. *Away* with him, *away* with him. *Acts* 21. 36
Acts 22. 22. *Away* with such a fellow from the earth
Jas. 1. 24. he beholdeth himself, and goeth ¹*away*

Awe.—*A.V.* ¹*fear.*
Heb. 12. 28. whereby we may offer service well-pleasing to God with reverence and ¹*awe*

AWOKE

Awoke.—*A.V.* ¹*arose,* ³*raised,* ⁸*rose.*
Mat. 8. 25. *awoke* him, saying, Save, Lord. *Lu.* 8. 24
Mk. 4. 39. And he ¹*a.,* and rebuked the wind. *Lu.* 8. ³²4
Acts 12. 7. angel—smote Peter on the side, and ²*a.* him

Axe.
Mat. 3. 10. now is the *axe* laid unto the root. *Lu.* 3. 9

B.

Babbler.
Acts 17. 18. What would this *babbler* say?

Babblings.
1 *Tim.* 6. 20. turning away from the profane *babblings.*
2 *Tim.* 2. 16

Babe.—*A.V.* ¹*child.*
Lu. 1. 41. the *babe* leaped in her womb. 44
2. 12. find a *babe* wrapped in swaddling clothes
16. the *babe* lying in the manger [writings
2 *Tim.* 3. 15. from a ¹*babe* thou hast known the sacred
Heb. 5. 13. word of righteousness; for he is a *babe*

Babes.—*A.V.* ¹*young children,* ²*infants,* ³*children.*
Mat. 11. 25. didst reveal them unto *babes. Lu.* 10. 21
21. 16. Out of the mouth of *babes* and sucklings
Lu. 18. 15. they brought unto him also their ²*babes*
Acts 7. 19. cast out their ¹*b.* to the end they might not live
Rom. 2. 20. a corrector of the foolish, a teacher of *babes*
1 *Cor.* 3. 1. as unto carnal, as unto *babes* in Christ
14. 20. howbeit in malice be ye ³*b.,* but in mind be men
1 *Pet.* 2. 2. as newborn *babes,* long for the spiritual milk

Back.—*A.V.* ¹*backside.*
Rom. 11. 10. And bow thou down their *back* alway
Rev. 5. 1. a book written within and on the ¹*back*

Backbiters.
Rom. 1. 30. *backbiters,* hateful to God

Backbitings.
2 *Cor.* 12. 20. wraths, factions, *backbitings,* whisperings

Backside *A.V.*—*see back.*

Backward.
Jno. 18. 6. they went *backward,* and fell to the ground

Bad.
Mat. 13. 48. good into vessels, but the *b.* they cast away
22. 10. all as many as they found, both *bad* and good
2 *Cor.* 5. 10. what he hath done, whether it be good or *bad*

Bade.
Mat. 16. 12. he *b.* them not beware of the leaven of bread
Lu. 14. 9. he that *bade* thee and him shall come and say
16. made a great supper; and he *bade* many
Acts 11. 12. And the Spirit *bade* me go with them
see bidden, bidding.

Bag.
Jno. 13. 29. because Judas had the *bag.* 12. 6
see purse.

BAPTIZED

Baggage.—*A.V.* ¹*carriages.*
Acts 21. 15. And after these days we took up our ¹*baggage*

Balance.—*A.V.* ¹*balances.*
Rev. 6. 5. he that sat thereon had a ¹*balance* in his hand

Band.
Mat. 27. 27. and gathered unto him the whole *band*
Mk. 15. 16. and they call together the whole *band*
Jno. 18. 3. Judas—having received the *band* of soldiers
12. So the *band* and the chief captain—seized Jesus
Acts 10. 1. Cornelius—a centurion of the *b.*—the Italian *b.*
21. 31. tidings came up to the chief captain of the *band*
27. 1. a centurion named Julius, of the Augustan *band*

Bands.
Lu. 8. 29. and breaking the *bands* asunder, he was driven
Acts 16. 26. and every one's *bands* were loosed
Col. 2. 19. knit together through the joints and *bands*

Banded.
Acts 23. 12. Jews *banded* together, and bound themselves

Bank.—*A.V.* ¹*trench.*
Lu. 19. 23. gavest thou not my money into the *bank*
43. thine enemies shall cast up a ¹*bank* about thee

Bankers.—*A.V.* ¹*exchangers.*
Mat. 25, 27. to have put my money to the ¹*bankers*

Banquetings *A.V.*—*see carousings.*

Baptism—s.
Mat. 3. 7. Sadducees coming to his [John's] *baptism*
21. 25. *b.* of John, whence was it. *Mk.* 11. 30: *Lu.* 20. 4
Mk. 1. 4. the *b.* of repentance. *Lu.* 3. 3: *Acts* 13. 24 : 19. 4
10. 38. baptized with the *b.* that I am baptized with. 39
Lu. 7. 29. being baptized with the *baptism* of John
12. 50. I have a *baptism* to be baptized with
Acts 1. 22. beginning from the *baptism* of John
10. 37. after the *baptism* which John preached
18. 25. knowing only the *baptism* of John
19. 3. And they said, Into John's *baptism*
Rom. 6. 4. buried therefore with him through *b.* into death
Eph. 4. 5. one Lord, one faith, one *baptism*
Col. 2. 12. having been buried with him in *baptism*
Heb. 6. 2. the teaching of *b.,* and of laying on of hands
1 *Pet.* 3. 21. after a true likeness doth now save you, even *b.*

Baptist—*see proper names—John the Baptist.*

Baptize.
Mat. 3. 11. I indeed *b.* you with water—he shall *b.* you with
the Holy Ghost. *Mk.* 1. 8: *Lu.* 3. 16: *Jno.* 1. 26
Jno. 1. 33. he that sent me to *baptize* with water, he said
1 *Cor.* 1. 17. Christ sent me not to *baptize,* but to preach
see baptized.

Baptized.—*A.V.* ¹*baptize.*
Mat. 3. 6. they were *b.* of him in the river Jordan. *Mk.* 1. 5
13. unto John, to be *baptized* of him. *Mk.* 1. 9
14. I have need to be *b.* of thee, and comest thou to me
16. Jesus, when he was *baptized,* went up straightway
Mk. 1. 4. John came, who ¹*baptized* in the wilderness
8. I *baptized* you with water; but he shall baptize [38
10. 39. with the baptism that I am *b.* withal shall ye be *b.*
16. 16. He that believeth and is *baptized* shall be saved

10

BAPTIZED

Lu. 3, 7. the multitudes that went out to be b. of him
12. And there came also publicans to be *baptized*
21. all the people were b.—Jesus also having been b.
7. 29. publicans—being *baptized* with the baptism of John
30. Pharisees and the lawyers—being not b. of him
12. 50. But I have a baptism to be *baptized* with
Jno. 3. 22. and there he tarried with them, and *baptized*
23. and they came, and were *baptized*
4. 2. Jesus himself *baptized* not, but his disciples
Acts 1. 5. John—b. with water; but ye shall be b. 11. 16
2. 39. Repent ye, and be *baptized* every one of you
41. They then that received his word were *baptized*
8. 12. they were *baptized*, both men and women
13. Simon also himself believed: and being *baptized*
16. only they had been *baptized* into the name. 19. 5
36. what doth hinder me to be *baptized* ?
38. both Philip and the eunuch; and he *baptized* him
9. 18. and he [Saul] arose and was *baptized*
10. 47. forbid the water, that these should not be b.
48. commanded them to be b. in the name of Jesus
16. 15. And when she [Lydia] was *baptized*
33. and was *baptized*, he [jailor] and all his
18. 8. the Corinthians hearing believed, and were b.
19. 3. Into what then were ye *baptized*?
4. John *baptized* with the baptism of repentance
22. 16. arise, and be *baptized* [Saul]
Rom. 6. 3. were b. into Christ Jesus were b. into his death ?
1 Cor. 1. 13. were ye *baptized* into the name of Paul?
14. I thank God that I *baptized* none of you
15. should say that ye were *baptized* into my name
16. I b. also the household of Stephanas—I b. any other
10. 2. were all *baptized* unto Moses in the cloud
12. 13. For in one Spirit were we all *baptized*
15. 29. which are b. for the dead—why then are they b.
Gal. 3. 27. *baptized* into Christ did put on Christ
see baptizing.

Baptizest—eth.
Jno. 1. 25. Why then b. thou, if thou art not the Christ
33. same is he that *baptizeth* with the Holy Spirit
3. 26. the same *baptizeth*, and all men come to him

Baptizing.—A.V. ¹baptized.
Mat. 28. 19. *baptizing* them into the name of the Father
Jno. 1. 28. Bethany beyond Jordan, where John was b.
31. for this cause came I *baptizing* with water
3. 23. John also was *baptizing* in Ænon
4. 1. Jesus was making and ¹b. more disciples than John
10. 40. the place where John was at the first ¹*baptizing*

Barbarian—s.—A.V. ¹barbarous people.
Acts 28. 2. the ¹b. showed us no common kindness
4. when the *barbarians* saw the beast
Rom. 1. 14. both to Greeks and to *Barbarians*
1 Cor. 14. 11. be to him that speaketh a *barbarian*, and
he that speaketh will be a *barbarian* unto me
Col. 3. 11. *barbarian*, Scythian, bondman, freeman

Barbarous people A.V.—see barbarian.

Bare.
Mat. 8. 17. took our infirmities, and *bare* our diseases
Lu. 11. 27. Blessed is the womb that *bare* thee
23. 29. Blessed—and the wombs that never *bare*
Jno. 2. 8. bear unto the ruler of the feast. And they *bare* it
1 Cor. 15. 37. but a *bare* grain, it may chance of wheat
1 Pet. 2. 24. who his own self *bare* our sins in his body

BEACH

Bare witness.—A.V. ¹borne witness.
Mk. 14. 56. many *bare* false *witness* against him. 57
Lu. 4. 22. And all *bare* him *witness*, and wondered
Jno. 1. 32. and John *bare witness*, saying
12. 17. multitude—that was with him—*bare witness*
Acts 15. 8. God, which knoweth the heart, *bare* them w.
3 Jno. 6. who ¹*bare witness* to thy love before the church
Rev. 1. 2. John; who *bare witness* of the word of God
see beareth, borne.

Barley.
Jno. 6. 9. There is a lad here, which hath five b. loaves
13. baskets with broken pieces from the five b. loaves
Rev. 6. 6. three measures of *barley* for a penny

Barn—s.
Mat. 6. 26. neither do they reap, nor gather into *barns*.
13. 30. but gather the wheat into my *barn* [Lu. 12. 24
Lu. 12. 18. I will pull down my *barns*, and build greater

Barren.—A.V. ¹dead.
Lu. 1. 7. because that Elisabeth was *barren*
36. the sixth month with her that was called *barren*
23. 29. they shall say, Blessed are the *barren*
Gal. 4. 27. Rejoice, thou *barren* that bearest not
Jas. 2. 20. that faith apart from works is ¹*barren*?
see idle.

Base.
1 Cor. 1. 28. the *base* things of the world
see lowly.

Baser sort A.V.—see rubble.

Basket—s.
Mat.14.20. broken pieces, twelve b. full. Lu. 9. 17: Jno. 6. 13
15. 37. of the broken pieces, seven *baskets* full. Mk. 8. 8
16. 9. how many *baskets* ye took up? 10: Mk. 8. 19
Acts 9. 25. lowering him [Saul] in a *basket*. 2 Cor. 11. 33
see basketfuls.

Basketfuls.—A.V. ¹baskets full.
Mk. 6. 43. took up broken pieces, twelve ¹*basketfuls*. 8. ¹20

Bason.
Jno. 13. 5. [Jesus] poureth water into the *bason*

Bastards.
Heb. 12. 8. then are ye *bastards*, and not sons

Bathed.—A.V. ¹washed.
Jno. 13. 10. He that is ¹b. needeth not save to wash his feet

Battle A.V.—see war.

Bay.—A.V. ¹creek.
Acts 27. 39. they perceived a certain ¹*bay* with a beach

Be.—A.V. ¹abide, ²live.
Jno. 14. 16. Comforter, that he may ¹*be* with you for ever
Rom. 12. 18. as much as in you lieth, ²*be* at peace with all

Beach.—A.V. ¹shore.
Mat. 13. 2. all the multitude stood on the ¹*beach*
48. when it was filled, they drew up on the ¹*beach*
Jno. 21. 4. day was now breaking, Jesus stood on the ¹b.
Acts 21. 5. kneeling down on the ¹*beach*, we prayed
27. 39. perceived a certain bay with a ¹*beach*
40. foresail to the wind, they made for the ¹*beach*

BEAM

Beam.
Mat. 7. 3. considerest not the *beam* that is in thine own eye? 4, 5: Lu. 6. 41, 42

Bear *(animal).*
Rev. 13. 2. and his feet were as the feet of a *bear*

Bear (Verb.)—A.V. ¹borne, ²compassion, ³suffer.
Mat. 3. 11. whose shoes I am not worthy to *bear*
4. 6. on their hands they shall *bear* thee up. Lu. 4. 11
17. 17. how long shall I ³*bear* with you? Lu. 9. ³41
27. 32. that he might *bear* his cross. Mk. 15. 21: Lu. 23. 26
Lu. 14. 27. Whosoever doth not *bear* his own cross
Jno. 2. 8. Draw out now, and *bear* unto the ruler
16. 12. many things to say—but ye cannot *bear* them now
Acts 9. 15. to *bear* my name before the Gentiles and kings
15. 10. neither our fathers nor we were able to *bear* ?
18. 14. reason would that I should *bear* with you
Rom. 15. 1. strong ought to *bear* the infirmities of the weak
1 Cor. 3. 2. for ye were not able to *bear* it
9. 12. we ³*bear* all things, that we may cause no hindrance
10. 13. no temptation taken you but such as man can *bear*
15. 49. we shall also *bear* the image of the heavenly
2 Cor. 11. 1. that ye could *bear* with me—indeed b. with me
4. which ye did not accept, ye do well to *bear* with him
Gal. 5. 10. but he that troubleth you shall b. his judgement
6. 2. *Bear* ye one another's burdens
5. each man shall *bear* his own burden
17. I *bear* branded on my body the marks of Jesus
Heb. 5. 2. who can ²*bear* gently with the ignorant
9. 28. Christ—once offered to *bear* the sins of many
13. 22. brethren, ³*bear* with the word of exhortation
Rev. 2. 2. and that thou canst not *bear* evil men
3. hast patience and didst ¹*bear* for my name's sake
see endure, face, fruit, longsuffering, yield.

Bear record A.V.—see bear witness.

Bear witness—A.V. ¹bear record, ²testify.
Mat. 19. 18. Thou shalt not b. false w. Mk. 10. 19: Lu. 18.
Jno. 1. 7. that he might *bear witness* of the light. 8 [20
3. 28. Ye yourselves *bear* me *witness*
5. 31. If I *bear witness* of myself. 8. ¹14.
36. the very works that I do, *bear witness* of me. 10. 25
39. and these are they which *bear witness* of me
15. 26. Spirit of truth—shall *bear* ²*witness* of me. 27
18. 23. If I have spoken evil, *bear* ²*witness* of the evil
37. that I should *bear witness* unto the truth
Acts 22. 5. As also the high priest doth *bear* me *witness*
23. 11. so must thou *bear witness* also at Rome
Rom. 10. 2. I ¹*bear* them *witness* that they have a zeal
2 Cor. 8. 3. I ¹*bear witness*, yea and beyond their power
Gal. 4. 15. for I ¹*bear* you *witness*, that, if possible
Col. 4. 13. For I ¹*bear* him [Epaphras] *witness*
1 Jno. 1. 2. we have seen, and *bear* w., and declare unto you
5. 6. For there are three who ¹*bear witness*, the Spirit
3 Jno. 12. yea, we also ¹*bear witness*; and thou knowest
see beareth witness.

Bear (bring forth).—A.V. ¹bring forth.
Mk. 4. 20. ¹*bear* fruit, thirtyfold, and sixtyfold
Lu. 1. 13. Elisabeth shall *bear* thee a son
Jno. 15. 2. cleanseth it, that it may ¹*bear* more fruit
16. appointed you, that ye should go and ¹*bear* fruit
1 Tim. 5. 14. that the younger widows marry, b. children

Bearers.—A.V. ¹bare.
Lu. 7. 14. touched the bier: and the ¹*bearers* stood still

BEASTS

Bearest.
Jno. 8. 13. Thou b. witness of thyself; thy witness is not
Rom. 11. 18. it is not thou that *bearest* the root [true
Gal. 4. 27. Rejoice, thou barren that *bearest* not

Beareth.—A.V. ¹bringeth forth.
Mat. 13. 23. who verily *beareth* fruit, and bringeth forth
Mk. 4. 28. The earth ¹*beareth* fruit of herself [fruit
Jno. 15. 2. Every branch in me that b. not fruit—that b.
Rom. 13. 4. he *beareth* not the sword in vain
1 Cor. 13. 7. *beareth* all things, believeth all things
Heb. 6. 8. but if it *beareth* thorns and thistles

Beareth witness.—A.V. ¹bare witness, ²bear witness.
Jno. 1. 15. John ¹*beareth witness* of him [Jesus]
5. 32. another that *beareth witness* of me
8. 18. ²*beareth witness* of myself—*beareth witness* of me
Rom. 8. 16. The Spirit himself *beareth witness*
1 Jno. 5. 7. And it is the Spirit that *beareth witness*

Bearing.—A.V. ¹bare, ²bringeth forth, ³gendereth.
Mk. 14. 13. a man *bearing* a pitcher of water. Lu. 22. 10
Jno. 19. 17. and he went out, b. the cross for himself
Rom. 2. 15. their conscience b. witness therewith. 9. 1
2 Cor. 4. 10. always b. about in the body the dying of Jesus
Gal. 4. 24. ³b. children unto bondage, which is Hagar [ing
Col. 1. 6. as it is also in all the world ²b. fruit and increas-
Heb. 2. 4. God also b. witness with them, both by signs
13. 13. go forth unto him without the camp, b. his reproach
Rev. 22 2. tree of life, ¹*bearing* twelve manner of fruits

Beast.
Lu. 10. 34. and he set him on his own *beast*
Acts 28. 4. when the barbarians saw the *beast*
5. [Paul] shook off the *beast* into the fire
Heb. 12. 20. If even a *beast* touch the mountain
Rev. 11. 7. the *beast* that cometh up out of the abyss
13. 1. I saw a *beast* coming out out of the sea
2. And the *beast* which I saw was like unto a leopard
3. and the whole earth wondered after the *beast*
4. authority unto the *beast*- worshipped the *beast*, say-
    ing, Who is like unto the *beast* ?
11. And I saw another b. coming up out of the earth
12. authority of the first b.—to worship the first *beast*
14. in the sight of the *beast*—image to the *beast*
15. to the image of the *beast*—image of the *beast* should
17. the mark, even the name of the *beast*
18. let him count the number of the *beast*
14. 9. If any man worshippeth the b. and his image. 11
15. 2. and them that come victorious from the *beast*
16. 2. the men which had the mark of the *beast*. 19. 20
10. poured out his bowl upon the throne of the *beast*
13. And I saw coming—out of the mouth of the *beast*
17. 3. a woman sitting upon a scarlet-coloured *beast*
7. the mystery of the woman, and of the *beast*
8. The *beast* that thou sawest—behold the *beast*
11. And the *beast* that was, and is not
12. authority as kings, with the *beast*, for one hour
13. they give their power and authority unto the *beast*
16. the ten horns which thou sawest, and the *beast*
17. and to give their kingdom unto the *beast*
19. 19. And I saw the *beast*, and the kings of the earth
20. And the *beast* was taken, and with him the false
20. 4. and such as worshipped not the *beast*
10. where are also the *beast* and the false prophet
see creature.

Beasts.
Mk. 1. 13. and he [Jesus] was with the wild *beasts*
Acts 7. 42. Did ye offer unto me slain *beasts* and sacrifices

BEASTS

Acts 10. 12. all manner of fourfooted *b.* and creeping things
11. 6. fourfooted *beasts* of the earth and wild *beasts*
23. 24. provide *beasts,* that they might set Paul thereon
Rom. 1. 23. likeness of—birds, and fourfooted *beasts*
1 *Cor.* 15. 32. I fought with *beasts* at Ephesus
39. one flesh of men, and another flesh of *beasts*
Tit. 1. 12. Cretans are alway liars, evil *beasts*
Heb. 13. 11. For the bodies of those *beasts,* whose blood
Jas. 3. 7. For every kind of *beasts* and birds
Rev. 6. 8. with death, and by the wild *beasts* of the earth
see cattle, creatures.

Beat.—*A. V.* ¹*beaten,* ²*smite,* ³*smote,* ⁴*wounded.*
Mat. 7. 25. the winds blew, and *beat* upon that house
21. 35. took his servants, and *beat* one. *Mk.* 12. 3 : *Lu.*
24. 49. shall begin to ²*beat* his fellow-servants [20. 10, 11
Mk. 4. 37. the waves *beat* into the boat
Lu. 10. 30. which both stripped him and ⁴*beat* him
12, 45. and shall begin to *beat* the menservants
22. 63. men that held Jesus mocked him, and ³*beat* him
Acts 5. 40. called the apostles unto them, they ¹*beat* them
16. 22. commanded to *b.* them [Paul and Silas] with rods
18. 17. they all laid hold on Sosthenes—and *beat* him
22. 19. that I imprisoned and *beat* in every synagogue
see brake, smote.

Beaten.
Mk. 13. 9. in synagogues shall ye be *beaten*
Lu. 12. 47. shall be *beaten* with many stripes
48. worthy of stripes, shall be *beaten* with few stripes
Acts 16. 37. They have *beaten* us publicly, uncondemned
2 *Cor.* 11. 25. Thrice was I *beaten* with rods
see beat.

Beateth *A. V.*—*see beating.*
Beating.—*A.V.* ¹*beateth.*
Mk. 12. 5. and many others; *b.* some, and killing some
Acts 21. 32. when they saw—the soldiers, left off *b.* Paul
1 *Cor.* 9. 26. so fight I, as not ¹*beating* the air

Beautiful.
Mat. 23. 27. sepulchres, which outwardly appear *beautiful*
Acts 3. 2. door of the temple which is called *Beautiful*
Rom. 10. 15. How *beautiful* are the feet of them that bring

Became.—*A. V.* ¹*made.*
Mat. 28. 4. the watchers did quake, and *b.* as dead men
Mk. 9. 3. his garments *b.* glistering, exceeding white
Lu. 23. 12. Herod and Pilate ¹*became* friends
Jno. 1. 14. the Word ¹*became* flesh, and dwelt among us
Acts 10. 10. he [Peter] *became* hungry, and desired to eat
Rom. 1. 21. *b.* vain in their reasonings, and their senseless
22. Professing themselves to be wise, they *b.* fools [heart
10, 20. I ¹*became* manifest unto them
1 *Cor.* 9. 20. to the Jews I *became* as a Jew
22. To the weak I *b.* weak, that I might gain [spirit
15, 45. first man Adam ¹*b.* a living soul—¹*b.* a life-giving
2 *Cor.* 8. 9. for your sakes he *became* poor—become rich
Heb. 2. 10. it *became* him, for whom are all things
5. 9. he *b.* unto all them that obey him the author
7. 26. such a high priest *became* us, holy, guileless
11. 7. Noah—*became* heir of the righteousness
Rev. 6. 12. sun *became* black—moon *became* as blood
8. 8. third part of the sea *became* blood
11. and the third part of the waters *became* wormwood
16. 3. bowl into the sea; and it *became* blood, ²*l*
see become, becoming.

Because.—*A.V.* ¹*sake.*
Mat. 17. 20. he saith unto them, *B.* of your little faith
Mk. 4. 17. persecution ariseth ¹*because* of the word

BED

Mk. 9. 41. a cup of water to drink, *because* ye are Christ's
Jno. 6. 26. not *because* ye saw signs, but *because* ye ate
8. 43. Even *because* ye cannot hear my word
44. stood not in the truth, *b.* there is no truth in him
45. But *because* I say the truth, ye believe me not
45. ye hear them not, *because* ye are not of God
10. 13. he fleeth *because* he is a hireling, and careth not
11. 10. he stumbleth, *because* the light is not in him
14. 12. *because* I go unto the Father. 28
19. *because* I live, ye shall live also
15. 19. *because* ye are not of the world, but I chose you
21. *because* they know not him that sent me
Rom. 8. 10. the body is dead *because* of sin; but the spirit
is life *because* of righteousness
Eph. 5. 6. *because* of these things cometh the wrath of God
1 *Jno.* 3. 14. death into life, *because* we love the brethren
4. 19. We love, *because* he first loved us
see sake, since.

Beckoned—**eth.**
Lu. 5. 7. they *beckoned* unto their partners in the other boat
Jno. 13. 24. Simon Peter therefore *beckoneth* to him [John]
Acts 19. 33. Alexander *beckoned* with the hand
21. 40. Paul, standing on the stairs, *beckoned*
24. 10. when the governor had *b.* unto him to speak
see signs.

Beckoning.
Acts 12. 17. [Peter] *beckoning* unto them with the hand
13. 16. And Paul stood up, and *b.* with the hand said

Become—**ing.**—*A.V.* ¹*became,* ²*made,* ³*ordained*
⁴*preferred.*
Mat. 18. 3. Except ye turn, and *become* as little children
23. 15. when he is ²*become* so, ye make him twofold
Lu. 3. 5. And the crooked shall ²*become* straight
Jno. 1. 12. to them gave he the right to *b.* children of God
15. He that cometh after me is ⁴*become* before me
30. After me cometh a man which is ⁴*become* before me
2. 9. ruler of the feast tasted the water now ²*become* wine
9. 39. and that they which see may ²*become* blind
Acts 1. 22. of these must one ³*become* a witness
7. 40. this Moses—we wot not what is *become* of him
52. ye have now *become* betrayers and murderers
12. 18. no small stir—what was *become* of Peter
Rom. 2. 25. thy circumcision is ²*become* uncircumcision
7. 13. Did then that which is good ⁴*b.* death unto me ?
1 *Cor.* 9. 22. I am ²*become* all things to all men
13. 11. now that I am ¹*become* a man, I have put away
2 *Cor.* 5. 17. passed away ; behold, they are *become* new
21. we might ²*become* the righteousness of God in him
Gal. 3. 13. curse of the law, being ¹*become* a curse for us
Phil. 2. 8. humbled himself, ¹*b.* obedient even unto death
20. ²*becoming* conformed unto his death
Heb. 1. 4. having ²*b.* by so much better than the angels
3. 14. we are ²*become* partakers of Christ, if we hold
7. 22. so much also hath Jesus ¹*become* the surety
10. 33. ¹*becoming* partakers with them that were so used
Rev. 11. 15. The kingdom of the world is *b.* the kingdom
see made.

Becometh.
Mat. 3. 15. it *becometh* us to fulfil all righteousness
13. 22. choke the word, and he *b.* unfruitful. *Mk.* 4. 19
32. greater than the herbs, and *b.* a tree. *Mk.* 4. 32.
Eph. 5. 3. not even be named among you, as *b.* saints
1 *Tim.* 2. 10. which *becometh* women professing godliness
see worthily, worthy.

Bed.
Mat. 9. 2. a man sick of the palsy, lying on a *b. Lu.* 5. 18
6. Arise, and take up thy *b. Mk.* 2. 9, 11: *Jno.* 5. 8, 11, 12

BED

Mk. 2. 4. let down the b. whereon the sick
12. And he arose, and straightway took up the bed
4. 21. be put under the bushel, or under the bed. Lu. 8. 16
7. 30. found the child laid upon the bed
Lu. 11. 7. and my children are with me in bed
17. 34. In that night there shall be two men on one bed
Jno. 5. 9. and took up his bed and walked
10. it is not lawful for thee to take up thy bed
Acts 9. 33. Æneas, which had kept his bed eight years
34. Jesus Christ healeth thee: arise, and make thy bed
Heb. 13. 4. let the bed be undefiled
Rev. 2. 22. Behold, I do cast her into a bed

Beds.

Mk. 6. 55. to carry about on their beds those that were sick
Acts 5. 15. laid them on beds and couches, that, as Peter

Been.—A.V. ¹began.
Heb. 2. 3. having at the first ¹b. spoken through the Lord

Befall.—A.V. ¹come.
Jno. 5. 14. sin no more, lest a worse thing ¹befall thee
Acts 20. 22. not knowing the things that shall b. me there

Befallen.—A.V. ¹happened.
Mat. 8. 33. what was b. to them that were possessed
Rom. 11. 25. a hardening in part hath ¹befallen Israel

Befell.—A.V. ¹came.
Mk. 5. 16. how it b. him that was possessed with devils
Acts 20. 19. trials which b. me by the plots of the Jews
2 Cor. 1. 8. concerning our affliction which ¹b. us in Asia
2 Tim. 3. 11. what things ¹befell me at Antioch

Befitting.—A.V. ¹convenient.
Eph. 5. 4. foolish talking, or jesting, which are not ¹b.
Philem. 8. to enjoin thee that which is ¹befitting

Before.—A.V. ¹first, ²presence, ³in the sight.
Acts 7. 10. gave him favour and wisdom ³before Pharaoh
8. 21. [Simon] for thy heart is not right ³before God
1 Cor. 1. 29. that no flesh should glory ³before God
Eph. 1. 12. we who had ¹before hoped in Christ
Col. 1. 22. without blemish and unreproveable ³before him
1 Th. 1. 3. patience of hope in our Lord Jesus Christ, ³b. our
2. 19. even ye, ²b. our Lord Jesus at his coming? God
Heb. 4. 6. they to whom the good tidings were ¹b. preached
see beforehand, presence, sight.

Beforehand.—A.V. ¹before, ²foretell, ³foretold, ⁴premeditate.
Mk. 13. 11. be not anxious ⁴beforehand what ye shall speak
23. behold, I have told you all things ³b. Mat. 24. ¹25
2 Cor. 9. 5. make up beforehand the aforepromised bounty
13. 2. I have said ¹beforehand, and I do say ³beforehand
1 Th. 3. 4. we told you ¹beforehand that we are to suffer
1 Pet. 1. 11. when it testified b. the sufferings of Christ
see evident.

Beforetime.
Acts 8. 9. Simon—which b. in the city used sorcery

Began.—A.V. ¹begun.
Mat. 4. 17. From that time began Jesus to preach
16. 21. From that time b. Jesus to shew unto. Mk. 10. 32
20. 8. and [Jesus] began to be sorrowful. Mk. 14. 33
28. 1. as it b. to dawn toward the first day of the week
Mk. 4. 1. And again he began to teach by the sea side
5. 17. And they began to beseech him to depart
6. 2. he began to teach in the synagogue

BEGINNING

Mk. 6. 7. and began to send them forth by two and two
34. and he began to teach them many things
55. and began to carry about on their beds those
8. 11. Pharisees came forth, and b. to question with him
81. And he began to teach them, that the Son of man
12. 1. he b. to speak unto them in parables. Lu. 20. 9
14. 19. They began to be sorrowful, and to say—Is it I?
Lu. 1. 70. have been since the world b. Jno. 9. 32: Acts 3. 21
3. 23. when he b. to teach, was about thirty years of age
5. 7. filled both the boats, so that they began to sink
21. And the scribes and the Pharisees began to reason
7. 15. And he that was dead sat up, and began to speak
24. began to say unto the multitudes concerning John
9. 12. And the day began to wear away
14. 30. This man b. to build, and was not able to finish
19. 45. he entered into the temple, and began to cast out
22. 23. they began to question among themselves
23. 2. they began to accuse him [Jesus]
Jno. 4. 52. inquired of them the hour when he b. to amend
13. 5. [Jesus] began to wash the disciples' feet
Acts 1. 1. all that Jesus began both to do and to teach
2. 4. and began to speak with other tongues
11. 15. And as I b. to speak, the Holy Ghost fell on them
18. 26. [Apollos] began to speak boldly   [fect it
Phil. 1. 6. he which ¹began a good work in you will perfect
see eternal, beginning, been.

Begat.—A.V. ¹begotten.
Mat. 1. verses 2 to 16, occurs 39 times.
Acts 7. 29. in the land of Midian, where he begat two sons
1 Cor. 4. 15. in Christ Jesus I ¹b. you through the gospel
1 Pet. 1. 3. according to his great mercy ¹begat us again
1 Jno. 5. 1. whosoever loveth him that b. loveth him also
see brought forth.

Beggar.—A.V. ¹begging, ²blind.
Mk. 10. 46. Bartimæus, a blind ¹beggar, was sitting
Lu. 16. 20. a certain beggar named Lazarus
22. And it came to pass, that the beggar died
Jno. 9. 8. saw him aforetime, that he was a ²beggar

Beggarly.
Gal. 4. 9. back again to the weak and b. rudiments

Beg—ged—ging.
Lu. 16. 3. not strength to dig; to beg I am ashamed
18. 35. a certain blind man sat by the wayside begging
Jno. 9. 8. is not this he that sat and begged?
see asked, beggar.

Begin.
Lu. 3. 8. b. not to say within yourselves, We have Abraham
13. 26. then shall ye begin to say, We did eat and drink
21. 28. all that behold begin to mock him
29. when these things begin to come to pass
1 Pet. 4. 17. judgement to begin—if it begin first at us
see beginning.

Beginning.—A.V. ¹began, ²begin, ³begun.
Mat. 14. 30. [Peter] and beginning to sink, he cried out
20. 8. beginning from the last unto the first
24. 8. these things are the b. of travail. Mk. 13. 8
21. tribulation—hath not been from the b. of the world
Mk. 1. 1. The beginning of the gospel of Jesus Christ
Lu. 23. 6. beginning from Galilee. Acts 10. ¹37
24. 27. And b. from Moses and from all the prophets
47. preached—unto all the nations, b. from Jerusalem
Jno. 2. 11. This beginning of his signs did Jesus
8. 9. went out one by one, beginning from the eldest

BEGINNING

Acts 1. 22. *b.* from the baptism of John, unto the day
8. 35. Philip—¹*beginning* from this scripture, preached
11. 15. even as on us at the *beginning*
2 *Cor.* 3. 1. Are we ²*b.* again to commend ourselves?
8. 6. we exhorted Titus, that as he had made a ³*b.* 10
Col. 1. 18. who is the *b.*, the firstborn from the dead
Heb. 3. 14. if we hold fast the *beginning* of our confidence
7 3. having neither *beginning* of days nor end of life
Rev. 3. 14. the *beginning* of the creation of God [22. 13
21. 6. the Alpha and the Omega, the *b.* and the end.
see first.

From the Beginning.—*A. V.* ¹*at the beginning.*

Mat. 19. 4. ¹*from the b.* made them male and female. *Mk.* 10. 6
8. but *from the beginning* it hath not been so
Mk. 13. 19. tribulation—*f. the b.* of the creation. 2 *Pet.* 3. 4
Lu. 1 2. which *from the b.* were eye-witnesses [not
Jno. 6. 64. Jesus knew *f. the b.* who they were that believed
8. 25. that which I have also spoken unto you *f. the b.*
44. He was a murderer *from the beginning*
15. 27. ye have been with me *from the beginning*
16. 4. these things I said not unto you ¹*from the b.*
Acts 15. 18 maketh these things known *from the b.*
2 *Th* 2. 13. God chose you *from the b.* unto salvation
1 *Jno.* 1. 1. That which was *from the beginning*
2. 7 an old commandment which ye had *from the b.*
13. ye know him which is *from the beginning.* 14
24. let that abide in you which ye heard *f. the b.* 3. 11
3. 8. for the devil sinneth *from the beginning*
2 *Jno.* 5. but that which we had *from the beginning*
6. even as ye heard *from the beginning*
see first, from all ages.

In the Beginning.

Jno. 1. 1. *In the b.* was the Word—and the Word was God
2. The same was *in the beginning* with God
Phil. 4. 15 *in the b.* of the gospel, when I departed
Heb 1. 10. Thou, Lord, *in the b.* hast laid the foundation

Begotten.—*A. V.* ¹*born.*

Jno. 1. 14. glory as of the only *begotten* from the Father
18. the only *begotten* Son, which is in the bosom
3. 16. loved the world, that he gave his only *begotten* Son
18. not believed on the name of the only *b.* Son of God
Acts 13. 33. this day have I *begotten* thee. *Heb.* 1. 5: 5. 5
Philem. 10. my child, whom I have *begotten* in my bonds
Heb. 11. 17. Abraham—offering up his only *begotten* son
1 *Pet.* 1. 23. having been ¹*b.* again, not of corruptible seed
1 *Jno.* 2. 29. every one also that doeth righteousness is ¹*b.*
3. 9. Whosoever is ¹*begotten* of God doeth no sin—he
cannot sin, because he is ¹*begotten* of God
4. 7. every one that loveth is ¹*begotten* of God
9. God hath sent his only *begotten* Son into the world
5. 1. believeth that Jesus is the Christ is ¹*begotten* of
God—loveth him also that is *begotten* of him
4. whatsoever is ¹*b.* of God overcometh the world
18. whosoever is ¹*begotten* of God sinneth not; but he
that was *begotten* of God
see beget.

First Begotten *A. V.*—*see firstborn.*

Beguile—d.—*A. V.* ¹*deceive—d.*

Rom. 7. 11. through the commandment ¹*beguiled* me
16. 18. by their smooth and fair speech they ¹*beguile*
2 *Cor.* 11. 3. as the serpent *beguiled* Eve in his craftiness
2 *Th.* 2. 3. let no man ¹*beguile* you in any wise
1 *Tim.* 2. 14. Adam was not ¹*b.*, but the woman being ¹*b.*
see delude, rob.

Beguiling *A. V.*—*see enticing.*

BEHOLD

Begun.

Mat. 18. 24. And when he had *begun* to reckon, one
Gal. 3. 3. Are ye so foolish? having *begun* in the Spirit
see began, beginning.

Behalf.—*A. V.* ¹*sake.*

2 *Cor.* 1. 11. helping together on our *behalf*—on our *behalf*
5. 12. giving you occasion of glorying on our *behalf*
21. Him who knew no sin he made to be sin on our *behalf*
7. 4. great is my glorying on your *behalf.* 8. 24: 9. 2, 3
Phil. 1. 4. on *behalf* of you all making my supplication
7. right for me to be thus minded on your *behalf*
20. granted in the *behalf* of Christ—suffer in his ¹*behalf*
see concerning (you), (in this) name, over you.

Behave—d.—*A. V.* ¹*conversation.*

1 *Cor.* 13 5. love doth not *behave* itself unseemly
2 *Cor.* 1. 12. in the grace of God, we ¹*behaved* ourselves
1 *Th.* 2. 10. unblameably we *behaved* ourselves toward you
2 *Th.* 3. 7. we *behaved* not ourselves disorderly
1 *Tim.* 3 15. how men ought to *behave* themselves

Behaveth.

1 *Cor.* 7. 36. any man thinketh that he *b.* himself unseemly

Behaviour.—*A. V.* ¹*conversation.*

1 *Pet.* 2. 12. having your ¹*b.* seemly among the Gentiles
3. 1. be gained by the ¹*behaviour* of their wives
2. beholding your chaste ¹*behaviour* coupled with fear
see demeanour.

Beheaded.

Mat. 14. 10. *beheaded* John in the prison. *Mk.* 6. 27
Mk. 6. 16. John, whom I *beheaded*, he is risen. *Lu.* 9. 9
Rev. 20. 4. them that had been *b.* for the testimony of Jesus

Beheld.—*A. V.* ¹*beholding,* ²*foresaw,* ³*looked,* ⁴*saw,* ⁵*seen.*

Mk. 15. 47. Mary Magdalene—*b.* where he was. *Lu.* 23. 55
Lu. 10. 18. I *beheld* Satan fallen as lightning from heaven
23. 48. when they ¹*beheld* the things that were done
24. 37. and supposed that they ⁵*beheld* a spirit
Jno. 1. 14. dwelt among us (and we *beheld* his glory
32. I have ⁴*beheld* the Spirit descending as a dove
11. 45. Jews, which came to Mary and ⁵*b.* that which he did
Acts 1. 11. in like manner as ye ⁵*b.* him going into heaven
2. 25. I ²*beheld* the Lord always before my face
4. 13. when they ⁴*b.* the boldness of Peter and John
17. 16. as he [Paul] ⁴*beheld* the city full of idols
22. 9. they that were with me [Paul] ⁴*b.* indeed the light
28. 6. *beheld* nothing amiss come to him [Paul]
1 *Jno.* 1. 1. we have seen with our eyes, that which we ⁵*b.*
4. 12. No man hath ⁵*beheld* God at any time
14. we have ⁵*beheld* and bare witness that the Father
Rev. 11. 12. and their enemies *beheld* them
see saw, seeing, seeth, looking, observed.

Behind.

Mat. 16. 23. said unto Peter, Get thee *b.* me, Satan. *Mk.* 8. 33
Mk. 5. 27. came in the crowd *b.*, and touched. *Mat.* 9. 20
Lu. 2. 43. the boy Jesus tarried *behind* in Jerusalem
1 *Cor.* 1. 7. so that ye come *behind* in no gift
2 *Cor.* 11. 5. I am not a whit *b.* the very chiefest. 12. 11
Phil. 3. 13. forgetting the things which are *behind*
see lacking.

Behold.—*A. V.* ¹*perceive,* ²*see.*

Mat. 11. 7. out into the wilderness to ²*b.? 8. Lu.* 7. ²24
18. 10. in heaven their angels do always *behold* the face
22. 11. when the king came in to ²*behold* the guests

BEHOLD

Mk. 5. 15. come to Jesus, and *²b.* him that was possessed
13. 1. Master, *²behold,* what manner of stones
Lu. 14. 29. all that *behold* begin to mock him
21. 6. As for these things which ye *b.*, the days will come
24. 39. spirit hath not flesh and bones, as ye *²behold* me
Jno. 6. 19. they *²behold* Jesus walking on the sea
62. if ye should *²behold* the Son of man ascending
7. 3. that thy disciples also may *²behold* thy works
12. 19. *¹Behold* how ye prevail nothing
14. 19. world beholdeth me no more; but ye *²behold* me
16. 10. I go to the Father, and ye *²behold* me no more
16. A little while, and ye *²behold* me no more. *²*17, *²*19
17. 24. that they may *behold* my glory
Acts 3. 16. made this man strong, whom ye *²b.* and know
7. 31. Moses—drew near to *behold,* there came a voice
32. And Moses trembled, and durst not *behold*
25. 24. ye *²b.* this man, about whom all the multitude
1 *Cor.* 1. 26. *²b.* your calling, brethren, how that not many
Heb. 2. 9. we *²b.* him who hath been made a little lower
1 *Pet.* 2. 12. by your good works, which they *b.*, glorify God
Rev. 17. 8. shall wonder—when they *behold* the beast
see beholding, look, see.

Beholdest—eth.—*A.V.* *¹saw,* *²seeth.*

Mat. 7. 3. And why *beholdest* thou the mote. *Lu.* 6. 41
Mk. 5. 38. and he *²beholdeth* a tumult, and many weeping
Lu. 6. 42. when thou thyself *b.* not the beam that is in
Jno. 6. 40. every one that *²b.* the Son, and believeth on him
10. 12. whose own sheep are not, *²b.* the wolf coming
12. 45. he that *²beholdeth* me *²b.* him that sent me
14. 17. for it *²beholdeth* him not, neither knoweth him
19. and the world *²beholdeth* me no more
20. 6. Simon Peter—*²beholdeth* the linen clothes lying
12. [Mary] *²beholdeth* two angels in white sitting
14. she turned herself back, and *²b.* Jesus standing
Acts 10. 11. he [Peter] *¹beholdeth* the heaven opened
Jas. 1. 24. for he *beholdeth* himself, and goeth away
1 *Jno.* 3. 17. whoso hath the world's goods, and *²b.* his

Beholding.—*A.V.* *¹behold,* *²looking,* *³saw,* *⁴seeing.*

Mat. 27. 55. women were there *beholding* from afar. *Mk.*
Lu. 23. 35. And the people stood *beholding* [15. *²*40
Jno. 2. 23. many believed on his name, *²beholding* his signs
Acts 8. 13. and *beholding* signs and great miracles wrought
9. 7. hearing the voice, but *⁴beholding* no man
Col. 2. 5. joying and *b.* your order, and the stedfastness
Jas. 1. 23. like unto a man *b.* his natural face in a mirror
1 *Pet.* 3. 2. *¹b.* your chaste behaviour coupled with fear
see behold, fasten—ed—ing (the eyes), looking, reflecting, seeing.

Behoved.—*A.V.* *¹must needs,* *²ought*

Lu. 24. 26. *²Behoved* it not the Christ to suffer
Acts 17. 3. it *¹b.* the Christ to suffer, and to rise again
Heb. 2. 17. Wherefore it *b.* him in all things to be made

Being.—*A.V.* *¹having,* *²waxing.*

Acts 17. 29. for in him we live, and move, and have our *b.*
2 *Cor.* 10. 6. *¹being* in readiness to avenge all disobedience
Phil. 1. 14. *²b.* confident through my bonds, are more—bold

Belief.—*A.V. faith.*

Rom. 10. 17. So *¹b.* cometh of hearing, and hearing by the
2 *Th.* 2. 13. sanctification of the Spirit and *b.* of the truth

Believe.—*A.V.* *¹believed,* *²believers,* *³faithful.*

Mat. 9. 28. *Believe* ye that I am able to do this?
18. 6. one of these little ones which *b.* on me. *Mk.* 9. 42
21. 32. ye—did not even repent—that ye might *b.* him
27. 42. from the cross, and we will *b.* on him. *Mk.* 15. 32

BELIEVE

Mk. 1. 15. repent ye. and *believe* in the gospel
5. 36. Fear not, only *believe.* *Lu.* 8. 50
9. 24. I *believe;* help thou mine unbelief
11. 23. shall *believe* that what he saith cometh to pass
24. whatsoever ye pray and ask for, *believe* that ye
16 17. And these signs shall follow them that *believe*
Lu. 8. 12. that they may not *believe* and be saved
13. have no root, which for a while *believe*
20. 5. From heaven; he will say, Why did ye not *¹b.* him?
24. 25. O foolish men, and slow of heart to *believe*
Jno. 1. 7. that all might *believe* through him
12. even to them that *believe* on his name
3. 12. earthly things, and ye *believe* not, how shall ye *b.*
4 21. Woman, *believe* me, the hour cometh
42. Now we *believe,* not because of thy speaking
48. signs and wonders, ye will in no wise *believe*
5. 44. How can ye *b.,* which receive glory one of another
46. if ye believed Moses, ye would *¹believe* me
47. ye *b.* not his writings, how shall ye *b.* my words?
6. 29. This is the work of God, that ye *believe* on him
30. a sign, that we may see, and *believe* thee?
7. 5. For even his brethren did not *believe* on him
8. 24. except ye *b.* that I am he, ye shall die in your sins
9. 35. Dost thou *believe* on the Son of God?
36. And who is he, Lord, that I may *believe* on him?
38. And he said, Lord, I *believe*
10. 25. Jesus answered them, I told you, and ye *¹b.* not
38. *b.* the works; that ye may know and understand
11. 15. I was not there, to the intent ye may *believe*
42. that they may *believe* that thou didst send me
43. If we let him thus alone, all men will *believe* on him
12. 36. While ye have the light, *believe* on the light
13. 19. when it is come to pass, ye may *b.* that I. 14. 29
14. 1. ye *believe* in God, *believe* also in me
11. *B.* me that I am in the Father—*b.* me for the very
16. 30. we *believe* that thou camest forth from God
31. Jesus answered them, Do ye now *believe?*
17. 20. but for them also that *believe* on me
21. that the world may *believe* that thou didst send me
19. 35. he saith true, that ye also may *believe*
20. 31. that ye may *believe* that Jesus is the Christ
Acts 8. 37. I *b.* that Jesus Christ is the Son of God [margin]
13. 41. A work which ye shall in no wise *believe*
15. 7. should bear the word of the gospel, and *believe*
11. But we *believe* that we shall be saved
16. 31. *B.* on the Lord Jesus, and thou shalt be saved
19. 4. that they should *b.* on him which should come
27. 25. I *believe* God, that it shall be even so
Rom. 3. 22. faith in Jesus Christ unto all them that *believe*
4. 11. that he might be the father of all them that *believe*
24. who *believe* on him that raised Jesus our Lord
6. 8. if we died with Christ, we *b.* that we shall also live
10. 9. and shalt *believe* in thy heart that God raised him
14. how shall they *b.* in him whom they have not heard?
1 *Cor.* 1. 21. of the preaching to save them that *believe*
11. 18. divisions exist among you; and I partly *believe* it
14. 22. for a sign, not to them that *b.*—to them that *b.*
2 *Cor.* 4. 13. we also *believe,* and therefore also we speak
Gal. 3. 22. might be given to them that *believe*
Eph. 1. 19. greatness of his power to us-ward who *believe*
Phil. 1. 29. not only to *believe* on him, but also to suffer
1 *Th.* 1. 7. an ensample to all that *believe* in Macedonia
2. 10. we behaved ourselves toward you that *believe*
13. word of God, which also worketh in you that *believe*
4. 14. For if we *believe* that Jesus died and rose again
2 *Th.* 2. 11. working of error, that they should *b.* a lie
1 *Tim.* 1. 16. should hereafter *b.* on him unto eternal life
4. 3. thanksgiving by them that *b.* and know the truth
10. Saviour of all men, specially of them that *believe*

BELIEVE

1 *Tim.* 4. 12. be thou an ensample to them that ²*believe*
Tit. 1. 6. husband of one wife, having children that ᵇ*b.*
Heb. 11. 6. he that cometh to God must *believe* that he is
Jas. 2. 19. the devils also *believe*, and shudder
1 *Pet.* 2. 7. For you therefore which *b.* is the preciousness
1 *Jno.* 3. 23. that we should *believe* in the name of his Son
5. 13. eternal life, even unto you that *b.* on the name
see believed, believedst, believers, believeth, have faith, keep,
understand.

Believe, *with negatives.*—*A.V.* ¹*believed.*
Mat. 21. 25. did ye *not believe* him ? *Mk.* 11. 31 : *Lu.* 20. 5
24. 23. the Christ, or, Here ; *b.* it *not.* 26 : *Mk.* 13 21
Lu. 22. 67. If I tell you, ye will *not believe*
Jno. 3. 12. If I told you earthly things, and ye *believe not*
4. 48. see signs and wonders, ye will in *no* wise *believe*
5. 38. for whom he sent, him ye *believe not*
47. But if ye *believe not* his writings, how shall ye
6. 36. ye have seen me, and yet *believe not*
64. But there are some of you that *believe not*
8. 45. because I say the truth, ye *believe* me *not*
46. If I say truth, why do ye *not believe* me ?
9. 18. The Jews therefore did *not believe* concerning him
10. 25. I told you, and ye ¹*believe not.* 26
37. If I do not the works of my Father, *believe* me *not*
38. though ye *believe not* me, believe the works
12. 39. For this cause they could *not believe*
16. 9. of sin, because they *believe not* on me
20 25. put my hand into his side, I will *not believe*
1 *Cor.* 10. 27. If one of them that *believe not* biddeth you
1 *Jno.* 4. 1. Beloved, *believe not* every spirit
see believe, disobedient, faithless, (keep) faith, unbelieving.

Believed.—*A.V.* ¹*believe,* ²*believing.*
Mat. 8. 13. Go thy way ; as thou hast *believed,* so be it
21. 32. the publicans and the harlots *believed* him
Mk. 16. 13. told it unto the rest : neither *b.* they them
Lu 1. 45. And blessed is she that *believed*
Jno. 2. 11. and his disciples *believed* on him
22. they *believed* the scripture, and the word
23. many *believed* on his name, beholding his signs
4. 39. many of the Samaritans *believed* on him
41. And many more *believed* because of his word
50. The man *believed* the word that Jesus spake
53. and himself *believed*, and his whole house
5. 46. if ye *believed* Moses, ye would believe me
6. 69 we have ¹*b.* and know that thou art the Holy One
7 31. But of the multitude many *believed* on him
39. which they that ¹*believed* on him were to receive
48 Hath any of the rulers *believed* on him
8. 30. As he spake these things, many *believed* on him
31. said to those Jews which had *believed* him
10 42. And many *believed* on him [Jesus] there
11 27. I have ¹*believed* that thou art the Christ
45. and beheld that which he did, *believed* on him
12. 11. Jews went away, and *believed* on Jesus
38. Lord, who hath *believed* our report? *Rom.* 10. 16
42. even of the rulers many *believed* on him
16. 27. have loved me, and have *b.* that I came forth
17. 8. and they *believed* that thou didst send me
20. 8. to the tomb, and he saw, and *believed*
29. thou hast *believed :* blessed are they that—have *b.*
Acts 2 44 And all that *believed* were together
4 4. But many of them that heard the word *believed*
32. the multitude of them that *believed* were of one
8. 12. But when they *believed* Philip preaching
13. And Simon also himself *believed*
9. 42. and many *believed* on the Lord. 17. 12
10. 45. they of the circumcision which *believed*
11 17. when we *believed* on the Lord Jesus Christ

BELIEVETH

Acts 11 21. number that *believed* turned unto the Lord
13. 12. proconsul, when he saw what was done, *b.*
48. many as were ordained to eternal life *believed*
14. 1. multitude both of Jews and of Greeks *believed*
23. to the Lord, on whom they had *believed*
15. 5. of the sect of the Pharisees who *believed*
16. 1. Timothy, the son of a Jewess which *believed*
34. all his [jailor's] house, having ²*believed* in God
17. 34. certain men clave unto him, and *believed*
18. 8. Crispus, the ruler of the synagogue, *believed—*
many of the Corinthians hearing *believed*
27. helped them much which had *b.* through grace
19. 2. Did ye receive the Holy Ghost when ye *believed ?*
18. Many also of them that had *believed* came
21. 20. among the Jews of them which have ¹*believed*
25. But as touching the Gentiles which have ¹*believed*
22. 19. I [Paul] imprisoned—them that *believed* on thee
28. 24. And some *believed* the things which were spoken
Rom. 4. 3. And Abraham *b.* God. *Gal.* 3. 6 : *Jas.* 2. 23.
17. before him whom he *believed,* even God, who
18. Who in hope *believed* against hope
13. 11. salvation nearer to us than when we first *believed*
1 *Cor.* 3. 5. Ministers through whom ye *believed*
15. 2. if ye hold it fast, except ye *believed* in vain
11. so we preach, and so ye *believed*
2 *Cor.* 4. 13. I *believed,* and therefore did I speak
Gal. 2. 16. even we *b.* on Christ Jesus, that we might
Eph. 1. 13. whom, having also *believed,* ye were sealed
2 *Th.* 1. 10. them that ¹*b.*—our testimony unto you was *b.*
1 *Tim.* 3. 16. among the nations, *believed* on in the world
2 *Tim,* 1. 12. for I know him whom I have *believed*
Tit. 3. 8. they which have *believed* God may be careful
Heb. 4. 3. For we which have *b.* do enter into that rest
1 *Jno.* 4. 16. and have *b.* the love which God hath in us
see believe (with negatives), believing, fulfilled, (gave more) heed,
persuaded.

Believed, *with negatives.*—*A.V.* ¹*believeth.*
Mat. 21. 32. ye *believed* him *not :* but the publicans
Mk. 16. 14. because they *b. not* them which had seen him. 13
Jno. 3. 18. because he hath *not b.* on the name of the only
6. 64. Jesus knew—who they were that *believed not*
12. 37. signs before them, yet they *believed not* on him
Rom. 10. 14. call on him in whom they have *not believed ?*
2 *Th.* 2. 12. all might be judged who *believed not* the truth
1 *Jno.* 5. 10. because he hath *not* ¹*believed* in the witness
Jude 5. afterward destroyed them that *believed not*
see believe, believing, disobedient.

Believer—s.—*A.V.* ¹*believe,* ²*believeth,* ³*sister.*
Acts 5. 14. *believers* were the more added to the Lord
1 *Cor.* 9. 5. no right to lead about a wife that is a ³*b.*
2 *Cor.* 6. 15. what portion hath a ²*b.* with an unbeliever ?
1 *Pet.* 1. 21. who through him are ¹*believers* in God
see believe.

Believest—edst.—*A.V.* ¹*believe.*
Lu. 1. 20. because thou *believedst* not my words
Jno. 1. 50. underneath the fig tree, *b.* thou ? [Nathanael]
11. 26. *Believest* thou this ? [Martha]
40. if thou ¹*b.* thou shouldest see the glory of God ?
14. 10. *Believest* thou not that I am in the Father
Acts 8. 39. Philip said, If thou *b.* with all thy heart [marg.]
26. 27. King Agrippa, *b.* thou—I know that thou *b.*
Jas. 2. 19. Thou *b.* that God is one ; thou doest well

Believeth.—*A.V.* ¹*believe.*
Mk. 9. 23. All things are possible to him that *believeth*
16. 16. He that *believeth* and is baptized shall be saved
Jno. 3. 15. whosoever *b.* may in him have eternal life. 16

BELIEVETH

Jno. 3. 18. He that *believeth* on him—he that *believeth* not
36. He that *believeth* on the Son. 6. 47
5. 24. and *believeth* him that sent me, hath eternal life
6. 35. and he that *believeth* on me shall never thirst
40. every one that beholdeth the Son, and *b*. on him
7. 38. He that *b*. on me. 11. 25, 26: 12. 44, 46: 14. 12
12. 44. *believeth* not on me, but on him that sent me
Acts 10. 43. every one that *believeth* on him shall receive
13. 39. every one that *¹b*. is justified from all things
Rom. 1. 16. of God unto salvation to every one that *b*.
4. 5. worketh not, but *believeth* on him that justifieth
9. 33. *b*.—shall not be put to shame. 10. 11 : 1 *Pet*. 2. 6
10. 4. the law unto righteousness to every one that *b*.
10. with the heart man *believeth* unto righteousness
1 *Cor*. 13. 7. [Love] *believeth* all things, hopeth all things
1 *Tim*. 5. 16. If any woman that *believeth* hath widows
1 *Jno*. 5. 1. Whosoever *believeth* that Jesus is the Christ
5. he that *believeth* that Jesus is the Son of God ?
10. *b*. on the Son of God—he that *believeth* not God
see believed not, believer, disbelieveth, faith, obeyeth, unbelieving.

Believing.—*A. V.* ¹*believed*, ²*faithful*.
Mat. 21. 22. ask in prayer, *believing*, ye shall receive
Jno. 20. 27. be not faithless, but *believing*
31. that *believing* ye may have life in his name
Acts 9. 26. not ¹*believing* that he [Saul] was a disciple
24. 14. *b*. all things which are according to the law
Rom. 15. 13. fill you with all joy and peace in *believing*
1 *Tim*. 6. 2. that have *b*. masters—are ²*b*. and beloved
1 *Pet*. 1. 8. see him not, yet *believing*, ye rejoice greatly
see believed.

Belly.
Mat. 12. 40. Jonah was—in the *belly* of the whale
15. 17. into the mouth passeth into the *belly*. *Mk*. 7. 19
Jno. 7. 38. out of his *belly* shall flow rivers of living water
Rom. 16. 18. serve not our Lord Christ, but their own *b*.
1 *Cor*. 6. 13. Meats for the *belly*, and the *belly* for meats
Phil. 3. 19. whose end is perdition, whose god is the *belly*
Rev. 10. 9. it [little book] shall make thy *belly* bitter. 10

Bellies *A. V.*—*see gluttons.*

Belong—eth.—*A. V.* ¹*pertaineth*.
Lu. 19. 42. the things which *belong* unto peace
Heb. 7. 13. he of whom these things are said ¹*b*. to another
10. 30. Vengeance *belongeth* unto me, I will recompense

Belonging.—*A. V.* ¹*possessions*.
Acts 28. 7. lands ¹*belonging* to the chief man of the island

Beloved.—*A. V.* ¹*well beloved*, ²*dear*, ³*dearly beloved*, ⁴*sanctified*.
Mk. 12. 6. He had yet one, a ¹*beloved* son
Acts 15. 25. them unto you with our *b*. Barnabas and Paul
Rom. 1. 7. all that are in Rome, *b*. of God, called to be
9. 25. And her *beloved*, which was not *beloved*
11. 28. they are *beloved* for the fathers' sake
12. 19. Avenge not yourselves, ³*beloved*
16. 12. Salute Persis, the *beloved*
1 *Cor*. 10. 14. my ³*beloved*. *Phil*. 4. ³1 : 2 *Tim*. 1. ³2
2 *Cor*. 7. 1. promises, ³*beloved*, let us cleanse ourselves
12. 19. all things, ³*beloved*, are for your edifying
Eph. 1. 6. grace, which he freely bestowed on us in the *B*.
5. 1. Be ye therefore imitators of God, as ⁴*b*. children
6. 21. Tychicus, the *beloved* brother. *Col*. 4. 7
Col. 1. 7. Epaphras our ²*beloved* fellow-servant
3. 12. Put on therefore, as God's elect, holy and *beloved*
4. 9. Onesimus, the faithful and *beloved* brother
14. Luke, the *beloved* physician

BESEECH

1 *Th*. 1. 4. brethren *beloved* of God   2 *Th*. 2. 13
1 *Tim*. 6. 2. partake of the benefit are believing and *b*.
Philem. 1. to Philemon our ³*beloved* and fellow-worker
16. more than a servant, a brother *beloved*
Heb. 6. 9. But, *b*., we are persuaded better things of you
1 *Pet*. 2. 11. ³*Beloved*, I beseech you as sojourners
4. 12. *B*., think it not strange concerning the fiery trial
2 *Pet*. 3. 1. This is now, *beloved*, the second epistle
8. forget not this one thing, *beloved*, that one day
14. Wherefore, *b*., seeing that ye look for these things
15. even as our *b*. brother Paul also,—wrote unto you
17. Ye therefore, *b*., knowing these things beforehand
1 *Jno*. 3. 2. *Beloved*, now are we children of God
21. *Beloved*, if our heart condemn us not
4. 1. *Beloved*, believe not every spirit, but prove
7. *Beloved*, let us love one another
11. *Beloved*, if God so loved us, we also ought
3 *Jno*. 1. The elder unto Gaius the ¹*beloved*
2. *B*., I pray that in all things thou mayest prosper
5. *Beloved*, thou doest a faithful work in whatsoever
11. *Beloved*, imitate not that which is evil
Jude 1. to them that are called, ⁴*beloved* in God the Father
3. *Beloved*, while I was giving all diligence to write
17. *b*. remember ye the words which have been spoken
20. But ye, *beloved*, building up yourselves
Rev. 20. 9. the camp of the saints about, and the *b*. city

My Beloved.—*A. V.* ¹*well beloved*.
Mat. 3. 17. This is *my beloved* Son. 17. 5 ; *Mk*. 1. 11 : 9. 7 : *Lu*. 3. 22 : 2 *Pet*. 1. 17
12. 18. *My beloved* in whom my soul is well pleased
Lu. 20. 13. I will send *my beloved* son : it may be they
Rom. 16. 5. Salute Epænetus *my* ¹*beloved*
8. Salute Ampliatus *my beloved* in the Lord
9. Salute—Stachys *my beloved*
1 *Cor*. 4. 14. admonish you as *my beloved* children
17. Timothy, who is *my beloved* and faithful child
15. 58. Wherefore, *my beloved* brethren, be ye stedfast
Phil. 2. 12. So then, *my b*., even as ye have always obeyed
Jas. 1. 16. Be not deceived, *my beloved* brethren
19. Ye know this, *my beloved* brethren
2. 5. Hearken, *my beloved* brethren ; did not God choose

Beneath.
Jno. 8. 23. Ye are from *beneath* ; I am from above

Benefactors.
Lu. 22. 25. that have authority over them are called *B*.

Benefit.
2 *Cor*. 1. 15. that ye might have a second *benefit*
1 *Tim*. 6. 2. they that partake of the *benefit* are believing
see goodness.

Bereaved.—*A. V.* ¹*taken*.
1 *Th*. 2. 17. we, brethren, being ¹*bereaved* of you

Bereft.—*A. V.* ⁴*destitute*.
1 *Tim*. 6. 5. men corrupted in mind and ¹*b*. of the truth

Beryl.
Rev. 21. 20. the eighth, [foundation] *beryl*

Beseech.—*A. V.* ¹*besought*, ²*intreat*, *pray*.
Mat. 26. 53. thinkest thou that I cannot ²*b*. my Father
Mk. 5. 17. they began to ²*beseech* him to depart
7. 32. and they *beseech* him to lay his hand upon him
8. 22. blind man, and ¹*beseech* him to touch him
Lu. 8. 28. I *beseech* thee, torment me not
9. 38. Master, I *beseech* thee to look upon my son

27

BESEECH

Acts 26. 3. wherefore I *beseech* thee to hear me patiently
27 34. Wherefore I *beseech* you to take some food
Rom. 12. 1. I *b.* you therefore. 15. 30; 16. 17 ; 1 *Cor.* 1. 10 : 4. 16 :
2 *Cor.* 2. 8. I *b.* you to confirm your love [16. 15 ; 2 *Cor.* 10. 2
  5. 20. we *²beseech* you on behalf of Christ
Gal. 4. 12. I *beseech* you, brethren, be as I am
Eph. 4. 1. I therefore, the prisoner in the Lord, *b.* you
Phil. 4. 3. I *²beseech* thee also, true yokefellow
1 *Th.* 4. 1. we *beseech* and exhort you. 5. 12 : 2 *Th.* 2. 1
Philem. 9. I rather *b.*, being such a one as Paul the aged
  10. I *beseech* thee for my child—Onesimus
1 *Pet.* 2. 11. Beloved, I *b.* you as sojourners and pilgrims
2 *Jno.* 5. And now I *beseech* thee, lady, not as though
  see exhort, intreat, intreating.

Beseeching—eth.—*A. V.* ¹*besought,* ²*prayed,* ³*praying.*

Mat. 8. 5. there came unto him a centurion, *beseeching* him
Mk. 1. 40. And there cometh to him a leper, *beseeching* him
  5. 23. ¹*beseecheth* him much, saying—lay thy hands
Acts 16. 9. man of Macedonia standing, ²*b.* him, and saying
2 *Cor.* 8. 4. ³*b.* us with much intreaty in regard of this grace

Beset.
Heb. 12. 1. and the sin which doth so easily *beset* us

Beside.—*A. V.* ¹*fool.*
Mk. 3. 21. for they said, He [Jesus] is *beside* himself
2 *Cor.* 5. 13. whether we are *beside* ourselves
  11. 23. (I speak as one ¹*beside* himself) I more
    see mad.

Besought.—*A. V.* ¹*desired,* ²*desiring,* ³*prayed.*

Mat. 8. 31. And the devils *besought* him. *Mk.* 5. 10, 12
  34. they *besought* him that he would depart
  14. 36. they *b.* him that they might only. *Mk.* 6. 56
  15. 23. disciples came and *b.* him, saying, Send her away
  18. 29. *besought* him, saying, Have patience with me
Mk. 5. 18. he that had been possessed with devils ³*b.* him
  7. 26. And she *b.* him that he would cast forth the devil
Lu. 4. 38. Simon's wife's mother—and they *b.* him for her
  5. 12. saw Jesus, he fell on his face, and *besought* him
  7. 4. to Jesus, *b.* him earnestly, saying, He is worthy
  8. 41. Jaïrus—*besought* him to come into his house
  9. 40. And I *besought* thy disciples to cast it out
Jno. 4. 40. Samaritans—*besought* him to abide with them
  47. [nobleman] *besought* him that he would come down
Acts 8. 31. [eunuch] ¹*b.* Philip to come up and sit with him
  13 42. they *besought* that these words might be spoken
  16, 15. [Lydia] *besought* us, saying, If ye have judged
  39. and they came and *besought* them [Paul and Silas]
  19, 31. sent unto him, and ²*besought* him not to adventure
  21. 12. they of that place *besought* him [Paul]
  27. 33. Paul *besought* them all to take some food
1 *Cor.* 16. 12. I ¹*b.* him [Apollos] much to come unto you
2 *Cor.* 12. 8. I *b.* the Lord thrice, that it might depart from
  see asked, asketh, beseech, beseecheth, exhorted, intreated, prayed.

Besoughtest.—*A. V.* ¹*desiredst.*
Mat. 18. 32. I forgave thee all that debt, because thou ¹*b.* me

Best.
Lu. 15. 22. Bring forth quickly the *best* robe
  see greater.

Bestow.
Lu. 12. 17. I have not where to *bestow* my fruits
  18. there will I *bestow* all my corn and my goods
1 *Cor.* 12. 23. upon these we *bestow* more abundant
  13. 3. if I *bestow* all my goods to feed the poor

BEWAILED

Bestowed.—*A. V.* ¹*accepted.*
Rom. 16. 6. Salute Mary, who *bestowed* much labour
1 *Cor.* 15. 10. his grace which was *bestowed* upon me
2 *Cor.* 1. 11. that, for the gift *b.* upon us by means of
Gal. 4. 11. I have *bestowed* labour upon you in vain
Eph. 1. 6. which he freely ¹*bestowed* on us in the Beloved
1 *Jno.* 3. 1. what manner of love the Father hath *b.* upon us
  see given.

Betray.
Mat. 26. 21. of you shall *b.* me   23 : *Mk.* 14. 18 : *Jno.* 13. 21
Jno. 6. 64. who it was that should *b.* him. 71 : 12. 4 : 13. 11
  13. 2. heart of Judas Iscariot, Simon's son, to *b.* him
    see betrayeth, deliver up.

Betrayed.
Mat. 10. 4. Judas Iscariot, who also *b.* him. *Mk.* 3. 19
  26. 24. through whom the Son of man is *b.* ! *Mk.* 14. 21 :
    25. Judas, which *b.* him. 27. 3 : *Jno.* 18. 2, 5 [*Lu.* 22. 22
    45. Son of man is *betrayed* unto the hands. *Mk.* 14. 41
    48. he that *betrayed* him gave them a sign. *Mk.* 14. 44
  27. 4. I have sinned in that I *betrayed* innocent blood
1 *Cor.* 11. 23. in the night in which he was *betrayed*
  see delivered.

Betrayers.
Acts 7. 52. of whom ye have now become *b.* and murderers

Betrayest—eth.—*A. V.* ¹*betray.*
Mat. 26. 46. he is at hand that ¹*betrayeth* me. *Mk.* 14. 42
Lu. 22. 21. the hand of him that *betrayeth* me is with me
  48. Judas, *betrayest* thou the Son of man with a kiss ?
Jno. 21. 20. Lord, who is he that *betrayeth* thee?

Betrothed.—*A. V.* ¹*espoused.*
Mat. 1. 18. When his mother Mary had been ¹*b.* to Joseph
Lu. 1. 27. virgin ¹*b.* to a man whose name was Joseph
  2. 5. enrol himself with Mary, who was ¹*b.* to him

Better.
Mk. 9. 42. it were *better* for him if a great millstone
1 *Cor.* 7. 9. it is *better* to marry than to burn
  38. giveth her not in marriage shall do *better*
  8. 8. nor, if we eat, are we the *better*
  11. 17. come together not for the *b.* but for the worse
Phil. 1. 23. be with Christ; for it is very far *better*
  2. 3. each counting other *better* than himself
Heb. 1. 4. become by so much *better* than the angels
  6. 9. we are persuaded *better* things of you
  7. 7. without any dispute the less is blessed of the *better*
  19. and a bringing in thereupon of a *better* hope
  22. Jesus become the surety of a *better* covenant
  8. 6. the mediator of a *b.* covenant—upon *b.* promises
  9. 23. heavenly things themselves with *better* sacrifices
  10, 34. knowing that ye yourselves have a *b.* possession
  11, 16. now they desire a *b.* country, that is, a heavenly
  35. that they might obtain a *better* resurrection
  40. God having provided some *better* thing
  12. 24. blood of sprinkling that speaketh *better* than that
1 *Pet.* 3. 17. For it is *better,* if the will of God should so will
2 *Pet.* 2. 21. *better* for them not to have known the way
  see good, (*more*) *value, profitable, worse.*

Bettered.
Mk. 5. 26. was nothing *bettered,* but rather grew worse

Bewailed—ing.
Lu. 8. 52. all were weeping, and *bewailing* her [maiden]
  23. 27. women who *bewailed* and lamented him
    see mourn, weep.

BEWARE

Beware.
Mat. 7. 15. *Beware* of false prophets, which come to you
10. 17. But *b.* of men: for they will deliver you [12. 1
16. 6. *b.* of the leaven of the Pharisees. 11 : *Mk.* 8. 15 : *Lu.*
12. bade them not *beware* of the leaven of bread, but
Mk. 12. 38. *Beware* of the scribes. *Lu.* 20. 46
Acts 13. 40. *B.* therefore, lest that come upon you [concision
Phil. 3. 2. *B.* of the dogs, *b.* of the evil workers, *b.* of the
2 *Pet.* 3 17. *beware* lest, being carried away with the error
see keep, take heed.

Bewitch.—*A.V.* ¹*bewitched.*
Gal. 3. 1. O foolish Galatians, who did ¹*bewitch* you
see amazed.

Bewitched *A.V.*—*see bewitch.*

Bewrayeth.
Mat. 26. 73. art one of them; for thy speech *b.* thee

Beyond.—*A.V.* ¹*more,* ²*farther side.*
Mk. 10. 1. borders of Judæa and ²*beyond* Jordan
Philem. 21. thou wilt do even ¹*beyond* what I say

Bid.—*A.V.* ¹*call,* ²*command,* ³*speak to.*
Mat. 14. 28. Lord, if it be thou, *bid* me come unto thee
22. 9. as many as ye shall find, *bid* to the marriage
23. 3. whatsoever they *bid* you, these do and observe
Lu. 9. 54. wilt thou that we ²*bid* fire to come down
61. first suffer me to *bid* farewell to them
10. 40. *bid* her therefore that she help me
12. 13. ³*bid* my brother divide the inheritance with me
14. 12. lest haply they also *bid* thee again
13. But when thou makest a feast, ¹*bid* the poor
see biddeth.

Bidden.—*A.V.* ¹*bade,* ²*called.*
Mat. 22. 3. call them that were *bidden* to the marriage
4. Tell them that are *bidden,* Behold, I have made
8. but they that were *bidden* were not worthy
Lu. 7. 39. when the Pharisee which had *b.* him saw it
14. 7. And he spake a parable unto those which were *b.*
8. When thou art *b.* of any man—than thou be *b.* 10
10. when he that hath ¹*bidden* thee cometh
12. And he said to him also that had ¹*bidden* him
17. to say to them that were *bidden,* Come
24. none of those men which were *bidden* shall taste
Jno. 2. 2. Jesus also was ²*bidden,* and his disciples
Rev. 19. 9. Blessed are they which are ²*bidden*
see commanded.

Biddeth.—*A.V.* ¹*bid.*
1 *Cor.* 10. 27. If one of them that believe not ¹*biddeth* you

Bidding.—*A.V.* ¹*bade.*
Acts 22. 24. ¹*bidding* that he [Paul] should be examined

Bier.
Lu. 7. 14. [Jesus] came nigh and touched the *bier*

Bill.
Mk. 10. 4. Moses suffered to write a *bill* of divorcement
see bond.

Billows.—*A.V.* ¹*waves.*
Lu. 21. 25. perplexity for the roaring of the sea and the ¹*b.*

Bind.
Mat. 12. 29. except he first *b.* the strong man? *Mk.* 3. 27

BITTERNESS

Mat. 13. 30. tares, and *b.* them in bundles to burn them
16. 19. whatsoever thou shalt *bind* on earth. 18. 18
22. 13. *Bind* him hand and foot, and cast him out
23. 4. Yea, they *bind* heavy burdens and grievous
Mk. 5. 3. and no man could any more *bind* him
Acts 9. 14. hath authority from the chief priests to *b.* all
12. 8. Gird thyself, and *bind* on thy sandals
21. 11. So shall the Jews at Jerusalem *bind* the man

Binding.
Acts 22. 4. *binding* and delivering into prisons both men

Bird—s.—*A.V.* ¹*fowls.*
Mat. 6. 26. Behold the ¹*b.* of the heaven, that they sow not
8. 20. the *birds* of the heaven have nests. *Lu.* 9. 58
13. 4. the ¹*b.* came and devoured them. *Mk.* 4. ¹4: *Lu.* 8. ¹5
32. *b.* of the heaven come and lodge. *Mk.* 4. ¹32: *Lu.* 13.
Lu. 12. 24. how much more value are ye than the ¹*b.?* [¹19
Rom. 1. 23. likeness—of *birds,* and fourfooted beasts
1 *Cor.* 15. 39. another flesh of *birds,* and another of fishes
Jas. 3. 7. For every kind of beasts and *birds*
Rev. 18. 2. a hold of every unclean and hateful *bird*
19. 17. saying to all the ¹*birds* that fly in mid heaven
21. and all the ¹*birds* were filled with their flesh

Birth.
Mat. 1. 18. Now the *birth* of Jesus Christ was on this wise
Lu. 1. 14. and many shall rejoice at his *birth*
Jno. 9. 1. as he passed by, he saw a man blind from his *b.*
Rev. 12. 2. and she crieth out, travailing in *birth*

Birthday.
Mat. 14. 6. when Herod's *birthday* came. *Mk.* 6. 21

Birthright.
Heb. 12. 16. Esau—sold his own *birthright*

Bishop—s.—*A.V.* ¹*overseers.*
Acts 20. 28. the Holy Ghost hath made you ¹*bishops*
Phil. 1. 1. which are at Philippi, with the *b.* and deacons
1 *Tim.* 3. 1. If a man seeketh the office of a *bishop*
2. The *bishop* therefore must be without reproach
Tit. 1. 7. For the *b.* must be blameless, as God's steward
1 *Pet.* 2. 25. now returned unto the Shepherd and *Bishop*

Bishoprick *A.V.*—*see office.*

Bite.
Gal. 5. 15. But if ye *bite* and devour one another

Bits *A.V.*—*see bridles.*

Bitter.
Col. 3. 19. love your wives, and be not *bitter* against them
Jas. 3. 11. Doth the fountain send—sweet water and *b.?*
14. if ye have *bitter* jealousy and faction in your heart
Rev. 8. 11. men died of the waters, because they were—*b.*
10. 9. and it [little book] shall make thy belly *bitter.* 10

Bitterly.
Mat. 26. 75. Peter—went out and wept *bitterly.* *Lu.* 22. 62

Bitterness.
Acts 8. 23. thou art in the gall of *bitterness*
Rom. 3. 14. Whose mouth is full of cursing and *bitterness*
Eph. 4. 31. Let all *b.,* and wrath, and anger—be put away
Heb. 12. 15. lest any root of *b.* springing up trouble you

BLACK

Black.
Mat. 5. 36. canst not make one hair white or *black*
Rev. 6. 5. I saw, and behold, a *black* horse
12. the sun became *black* as sackcloth of hair

Blackness.—*A.V.* ¹*mist.*
Heb. 12. 18. unto *blackness*, and darkness, and tempest
2 *Pet.* 2. 17. for whom the ¹*blackness* of darkness. *Jude* 13

Blade.
Mat. 13. 26. But when the *b.* sprang up, and brought forth
Mk. 4. 28. first the *blade*, then the ear, then the full corn

Blame—d.—*A.V.* ¹*blameless.*
2 *Cor.* 6. 3. that our ministration be not *blamed*
8. 20. avoiding this, that any man should *blame* us
1 *Th.* 5. 23. spirit and soul and body—entire, without ¹*b.*
see blemish, condemned.

Blameless.
Lu. 1, 6. walking in—ordinances of the Lord *blameless*
Phil. 2. 15. that ye may be *blameless* and harmless
3. 6. the righteousness which is in the law, found *b.*
1 *Tim.* 3. 10. then let them serve as deacons, if they be *b.*
Tit. 1. 6. if any man is *blameless*, the husband of one wife
7. For the bishop must be *blameless*, as God's steward
2 *Pet.* 3. 14. found in peace, without spot and *b.* in his sight
see blame, guiltless, reproach, unreproachable.

Blaspheme.
Mk. 3. 28. blasphemies wherewith soever they shall *b.*
29. whosoever shall *blaspheme* against the Holy Spirit
Acts 26. 11. I [Paul] strove to make them *blaspheme*
1 *Tim.* 1. 20. that they might be taught not to *blaspheme*
Jas. 2. 7. Do not they *blaspheme* the honourable name
Rev. 13. 6. opened his mouth—against God, to *b.* his name

Blasphemed.—*A.V.* ¹*blaspheming.*
Acts 13. 45. contradicted—Paul, and ¹*blasphemed*
18. 6. And when they opposed themselves, and *b.*
Rom. 2. 24 For the name of God is *b.* among the Gentiles
1 *Tim.* 6. 1. that the name of God and the doctrine be not *b.*
Tit. 2. 5. that the word of God be not *blasphemed*
Rev. 16. 9. and they *blasphemed* the name of the God
11. they *b.* the God of heaven because of their pains
21. and men *b.* God because of the plague of the hail

Blasphemer—s.
Acts 19. 37. neither robbers—nor *b.* of our goddess
1 *Tim.* 1. 13. though I was before a *b.*, and a persecutor
see railers.

Blasphemest—eth.—*A.V.* ¹*blasphemies.*
Mat. 9. 3. the scribes said within themselves, This man *b.*
Mk. 2. 7. Why doth this man thus speak? he ¹*blasphemeth*
Lu. 22. but unto him that *b.* against the Holy Spirit
Jno. 10. 36. whom the Father—sent into the world, Thou *b.*

Blasphemies.—*A.V.* ¹*blasphemy.*
Mk. 3. 28. forgiven unto the sons of men, and their *b.*
Lu. 5. 21. Who is this that speaketh *blasphemies?*
Rev. 13. 5. a mouth speaking great things and *b.*
6. And he opened his mouth for ¹*b.* against God
see blasphemeth.

Blaspheming *A.V.—see blasphemed.*

BLESSED

Blasphemous.
Acts 6. 11. have heard him speak *b.* words against Moses

Blasphemously *A.V.—see reviling.*

Blasphemy.
Mat. 12. 31. Every sin and *b.*—but the *b.* against the Spirit
26. 65. He hath spoken *b.*—ye have heard the *b. Mk.*
Jno. 10. 33. we stone thee not, but for *blasphemy* [14. 64
Rev. 2. 9. and the *b.* of them which say they are Jews
13. 1. and upon his heads names of *blasphemy.* 17. 3
see blasphemies, railing.

Blaze *A.V.—see spread.*

Blemish.—*A.V.* ¹*blame,* ²*fault,* ³*faultless,* ⁴*rebuke,* ⁵*spot,* ⁶*unblameable.*
Eph. 1. 4. that we should be holy and without ¹*blemish*
5. 27. church—should be holy and without ⁶*blemish*
Phil. 2. 15. children of God without ⁴*blemish*
Col. 1. 22. to present you holy and without ⁰*blemish*
Heb. 9. 14. offered himself without ⁵*blemish* unto God
1 *Pet.* 1. 19. with precious blood, as of a lamb without *b.*
Jude 24. set you before the presence of his glory without ³*b.*
Rev. 14. 5. they are without ²*blemish*

Blemishes.
2 *Pet.* 2. 13. spots and *b.*, revelling in their love-feasts

Bless.
Lu. 6. 28. *bless* them that curse you
Acts 3. 26. raised up his Servant, sent him to *bless* you
Rom. 12. 14. *B.* them that persecute you; *b.*, and curse not
1 *Cor.* 4. 12. being reviled, we *bless;* being persecuted, we
10. 16. The cup of blessing which we *bless* [endure
14. 16. Else if thou *bless* with the spirit
Heb. 6. 14. Surely blessing I will *bless* thee
Jas. 3. 9. Therewith *bless* we the Lord

Blessed.—*A.V.* ¹*happy.*
Mat. 5. 3. *Blessed* are the poor in spirit. 4. they that
mourn. 5. the meek. 6. they that hunger and
thirst after righteousness. 7. the merciful. 8. the
pure in heart. 9. the peacemakers. 10. they that
have been persecuted for righteousness' sake.
11. are ye when men shall reproach you
11. 6. *blessed* is he, whosoever shall find none. *Lu.* 7. 23
13. 16. *blessed* are your eyes, for they see. *Lu.* 10. 23
14. 19. [Jesus] *blessed*, and brake. 26. 26; *Mk.* 6. 41:
8. 7: 14. 22: *Lu.* 9. 16; 24. 30
16. 17. *Blessed* art thou, Simon Bar-Jonah
21. 9. *Blessed* is he that cometh in the name of the Lord.
23. 39; *Mk.* 11. 9: *Lu.* 13. 35 [38
24. 26. *Blessed* is that servant, whom his lord. *Lu.* 12. 37,
25. 34. Come, ye *blessed* of my Father, inherit
Mk. 10. 16. took them in his arms, and *blessed* them
11. 10. *Blessed* is the kingdom that cometh
14. 61. Art thou the Christ, the Son of the *Blessed?*
Lu. 1. 42. *B.* art thou among women, and *b.* is the fruit
45. *blessed* is she that believed
48. all generations shall call me *blessed*
68. *Blessed* be the Lord, the God of Israel
2. 28. [Simeon] *blessed* God, and said
34. Simeon *blessed* them, and said unto Mary
6. 20. *Blessed* are ye poor: for yours is the kingdom
21. *Blessed* are ye that hunger now—*B.* are ye that weep
22. *Blessed* are ye, when men shall hate you
11. 27. *Blessed* is the womb that bare thee
28. *blessed* are they that hear the word of God

BLESSED

Lu. 14. 14. and thou shalt be *blessed*—in the resurrection
15. *Blessed* is he that shall eat bread in the kingdom
19. 38. *B.* is the King that cometh in the name of the Lord
23. 39. they shall say, *Blessed* are the barren
24. 50. and he lifted up his hands, and *blessed* them
51. while he *blessed* them, he parted from them
Jno. 12. 13. *B.* is he that cometh in the name of the Lord
13. 17. know these things, *¹blessed* are ye if ye do them
20. 29. *blessed* are they that have not seen
Acts 3. 25. all the families of the earth be *blessed*. *Gal.* 3. 8
20. 35. It is more *blessed* to give than to receive
Rom. 1. 35. than the Creator, who is *blessed* for ever
4. 7. *Blessed* are they whose iniquities are forgiven
8. *B.* is the man to whom the Lord will not reckon sin
9. 5. who is over all, God *blessed* for ever. 2 *Cor.* 11. 31
Gal. 3. 9. So then they which be of faith are *blessed*
Eph. 1. 3. *Blessed* be the God and Father—who hath *blessed*
us with every spiritual blessing. 1 *Pet.* 1. 3
1 *Tim.* 1. 11. the gospel of the glory of the *blessed* God
6. 15. who is the *blessed* and only Potentate
Tit. 2. 13. looking for the *blessed* hope and appearing
Heb. 7. 1. Melchizedek—*blessed* him [Abraham]
6. and hath *blessed* him that hath the promises
7. without any dispute the less is *blessed* of the better
11. 20. By faith Isaac *blessed* Jacob and Esau [Joseph
21. Jacob, when he was a dying, *b.* each of the sons of
Jas. 1. 12. *Blessed* is the man that endureth temptation
25. this man shall be *blessed* in his doing
5. 11. we call them *¹blessed* which endured
1 *Pet.* 3. 14. suffer for righteousness' sake, *¹blessed* are ye
4. 14. reproached for the name of Christ, *¹blessed* are ye
Rev. 1. 3. *Blessed* is he that readeth, and they that hear
14. 13. *Blessed* are the dead which die in the Lord
16 15. *Blessed* is he that watcheth
19. 9. Write, *Blessed* are they which are bidden
20. 6. *Blessed* and holy is he that hath part in the first
22. 7. *Blessed* is he that keepeth the words
14. *Blessed* are they that wash their robes

Blessedness *A.V.—see blessing, gratulation.*

Blessing—s.—*A.V.* ¹*blessedness*, ²*mercies*, ³*praised.*

Lu. 1. 64. he [Zacharias] spake, ³*blessing* God
24. 53. and were continually in the temple, *blessing* God
Acts 13. 34. give you the holy and sure ²*blessings* of David
Rom. 4. 6. as David also pronounceth ¹*b.* upon the man
9. Is this ¹*b.* then pronounced upon the circumcision
15. 29. I shall come in the fulness of the *b.* of Christ
1 *Cor.* 10. 16. The cup of *blessing* which we bless
Gal. 3. 14. upon the Gentiles might come the *blessing*
Eph. 1. 3. who hath blessed us with every spiritual *blessing*
Heb. 6. 7. the land—receiveth *blessing* from God
14. Surely *blessing* I will bless thee
12. 17. [Esau] desired to inherit the *blessing*
Jas. 3. 10. out of the same mouth cometh forth *blessing*
1 *Pet.* 3. 9. contrariwise *blessing*—should inherit a *b.*
Rev. 5. 12. Worthy is the Lamb—honour, and glory, and *b.*
13. and unto the Lamb, be the *blessing*, and the honour
7. 12. *Blessing*, and glory, and wisdom, and thanksgiving

Blew.
Mat. 7. 25. winds *blew*, and beat upon that house. 27
Jno. 6. 18. was rising by reason of a great wind that *blew*
Acts 27. 13. when the south wind *blew* softly
see sprang.

Blind.
Mat. 9. 27. two *blind* men followed him [Jesus]. 28
11. 5. the *blind* receive their sight. *Lu.* 7. 22

BLOOD

Mat. 12. 22. one possessed with a devil, *blind* and dumb
15. 14. if the *blind* guide the *blind*. *Lu.* 6. 39
30. with them the lame, *blind*, dumb, maimed
31. they saw—the lame walking, and the *blind* seeing
20. 30. two *blind* men sitting by the way side
21. 14. And the *blind* and the lame came to him
23. 16. Woe unto you, ye *blind* guides. 24
17. Ye fools and *blind*. 19
26. Thou *blind* Pharisee, cleanse first the inside
Mk. 8. 22. bring to him a *blind* man, and beseech
23. [Jesus] took hold of the *blind* man by the hand
10. 46. Bartimæus, a *blind* beggar, was sitting
49. they call the *blind* man, saying unto him
51. And the *blind* man said unto him, Rabboni
Lu. 4. 18. And recovering of sight to the *blind*
7. 21. on many that were *blind* he bestowed sight
14. 13. the maimed, the lame, the *blind*. 21
18. 35. a certain *blind* man sat by the way side begging
Jno. 5. 3. of them that were sick, *blind*, halt, withered
9. 1. [Jesus] saw a man *blind* from his birth
2. who did sin—should be born *blind*? 19, 20, 32
13. bring to the Pharisees him that aforetime was *b.*
17. They say therefore unto the *blind* man
18. concerning him, that he had been *blind*
24. called a second time the man that was *blind*
25. I know, that, whereas I was *blind*, now I see
39. and that they which see may become *blind*
40. Are we [Pharisees] also *blind*?
41. If ye were *blind*, ye would have no sin
10. 21. Can a devil open the eyes of the *blind*?
11. 37. opened the eyes of him that was *blind*
Acts 13. 11. thou [Elymas] shalt be *b.*, not seeing the sun
Rom. 2. 19. thou thyself art a guide of the *blind*
2 *Pet.* 1. 9. he that lacketh these things is *blind*
Rev. 3. 17. that thou art—poor and *blind* and naked
see beggar.

Blinded—eth.
Jno. 12. 40. He hath *b.* their eyes, and he hardened their
2 *Cor.* 4. 4. the God of this world hath *blinded* the minds
1 *Jno.* 2. 11. because the darkness hath *blinded* his eyes
see hardened.

Blindfolded.
Lu. 22. 64. And they *blindfolded* him [Jesus]

Blindness *A.V.—see hardening.*

Blood.
Mat. 9. 20. issue of *b.* twelve years. *Mk.* 5. 25: *Lu.* 8. 43
16. 17. flesh and *blood* hath not revealed it unto thee
23. 30. partakers with them in the *b.* of the prophets
35. all the righteous *blood*—from the *blood* of Abel—
blood of Zachariah. *Lu.* 11. 51
26. 28. for this is my *blood* of the covenant. *Mk.* 14. 24
27. 4. I have sinned in that I betrayed innocent *blood*
6. into the treasury, since it is the price of *blood*
8. The field of *blood*, unto this day. *Acts* 1. 19
24. I am innocent of the *blood* of this righteous man
25. His *blood* be on us, and on our children
Mk. 5. 29. the fountain of her *b.* was dried up. *Lu.* 8. 44
Lu. 11. 50. the *blood* of all the prophets, which was shed
13. 1. Galilæans, whose *blood* Pilate had mingled
22. 20. the new covenant in my *blood*. 1 *Cor.* 11. 25
44. sweat became as it were great drops of *blood*
Jno. 1. 13. born, not of *blood*, nor of the will of the flesh
6. 54. drinketh my *blood* hath eternal life. 53, 56
55. my *blood* is drink indeed
19. 34. and straightway there came out *blood* and water

31

BLOOD

Acts 2. 19. *Blood*, and fire, and vapour of smoke
20. And the moon into *b*., Before the day of the Lord
5. 28. intend to bring this man's *blood* upon us
15. 20. from what is strangled, and from *blood*. 29: 21. 25
18. 6. Your *blood* be upon your own heads
20. 26. I am pure from the *blood* of all men
28. church of God—purchased with his own *blood*
22. 20. when the *blood* of Stephen thy witness was shed
Rom. 3. 15. Their feet are swift to shed *blood*
25. a propitiation, through faith, by his *blood*
5. 9. being now justified by his *blood*
1 *Cor.* 11. 27. be guilty of the body and the *b*. of the Lord
15. 50. flesh and *blood* cannot inherit the kingdom
Gal. 1. 16. I conferred not with flesh and *blood*
Eph. 1. 7. we have our redemption through his *blood*
6. 12. For our wrestling is not against flesh and *blood*
Col. 1. 20. having made peace through the *b*. of his cross
Heb. 2. 14. children are sharers in flesh and *blood*
9. 7. high priest alone—not without *blood*
12. the *blood* of goats—through his own *blood*
13. For if the *blood* of goats and bulls
14. how much more shall the *blood* of Christ
18. first covenant hath not been dedicated without *b*.
19. he took the *blood* of the calves and the goats
20. This is the *blood* of the covenant
21. sprinkled in like manner with the *blood*
22. cleansed with *blood*, and apart from shedding of *b*.
25. year by year with *blood* not his own
10. 4. impossible that the *blood* of bulls and goats
19. into the holy place by the *blood* of Jesus
11. 28. the passover, and the sprinkling of the *blood*
12. 4. Ye have not yet resisted unto *blood*
24. *blood* of sprinkling that speaketh better than that
13. 11. those beasts, whose *blood* is brought
12. through his own *blood*, suffered without the gate
1 *Pet.* 1. 2. sprinkling of the *blood* of Jesus Christ
1 *Jno.* 5. 6. he that came by water and *blood*—with the *b*.
8. the Spirit, and the water, and the *blood*
Rev. 1. 5. loosed us from our sins by his *blood*
5. 9. didst purchase unto God with thy *blood* men
6. 10. dost thou not judge and avenge our *b*. on them
12. and the whole moon became as *blood*
7. 14. made them white in the *blood* of the Lamb
8. 7. hail and fire, mingled with *blood*
8. third part of the sea became *blood*. 16. 3
11. 6. power over the waters to turn them into *blood*
12. 11. overcame him because of the *blood* of the Lamb
14. 20. and there came out *blood* from the winepress
16. 4. fountains of the waters; and it became *blood*
6. *blood* of saints and prophets, and *b*. hast thou given
17. 6. with the *b*. of the saints,—the *b*. of the martyrs
18. 24. And in her was found the *b*. of prophets and of
19. 2. he hath avenged the *blood* of his servants
13. And he is arrayed in a garment sprinkled with *b*.

Blood *of Christ, or Jesus.*

1 *Cor.* 10. 16. is it not a communion of the *b. of Christ* ?
Eph. 2. 13. far off are made nigh in the *blood of Christ*
Heb. 9. 14. how much more shall the *b. of Christ* – cleanse
1 *Pet.* 1. 19. as of a lamb—without spot, even the *b. of C.*
1 *Jno.* 1. 7. the *b. of J.* his Son cleanseth us from all sin

Blood *of the covenant.*

Heb. 10. 29. the *b. of the c.*, wherewith he was sanctified
13. 20. shepherd of the sheep with the *b. of the* eternal *c.*

Bloody *flux A.V.—see dysentery.*

BOAT

Blot *out*—Blotted *out.—A.V.* ¹*blotting out.*

Acts 3. 19. turn again, that your sins may be *blotted out*
Col. 2. 14. having ¹*b. out* the bond written in ordinances
Rev. 3. 5. I will in no wise *blot* his name *out* of the book

Blotting *out A.V.—see blotted out.*

Blow.

Rev. 7. 1. that no wind should *blow* on the earth
                        see blowing.

Bloweth.

Jno. 3. 8. The wind *bloweth* where it listeth

Blowing.—*A.V.* ¹*blow.*

Lu. 12. 55. when ye see a south wind ¹*blowing*, ye say

Blows.—*A.V.* ¹*palms.*

Mk. 14. 65. officers received him with ¹*b.* of their hands

Boards *A.V.—see planks.*

Boast—ed *A.V.—see gloried, gloriest, glory.*

Boasters *A.V.—see boastful.*

Boasteth.

Jas. 3. 5. tongue also is a little member, and *b.* great things

Boastful.—*A.V.* ¹*boasters.*

Rom. 1. 30. haughty, ¹*boastful*, inventors of evil things
2 *Tim.* 3. 2. lovers of money, *boastful*, haughty, railers

Boasting—s *A.V.—see confidence, giving (out), glorying, vauntings.*

Boat—s.—*A.V.* ¹*ship—s*, ²*shipping.*

Mat. 4. 21. in the ¹*boat* with Zebedee their father
22. they straightway left the ¹*boat. Mk.* 1. ¹20
8. 23. when he was entered into a ¹*boat.* 9. ¹] : 13. ¹²:
    Mk. 4. ¹] : 5. ¹18 : 8. ¹10, ¹13 : *Lu.* 8. ¹22, ¹37
24. insomuch that the ¹*b.* was covered with the waves
14. 13. he withdrew from thence in a ¹*boat* [6. ¹45
22. constrained the disciples to enter into the ¹*b. Mk.*
24. the ¹*b.* was now in the midst of the sea. *Mk.* 6. ¹47
29. Peter went down from the ¹*boat*
32. when they were gone up into the ¹*boat*
33. they that were in the ¹*boat* worshipped him
15. 39. and entered into the ¹*b.*, and came into the borders
Mk. 1. 19. who also were in the ¹*boat* mending the nets
3. 9. spake to his disciples, that a little ¹*boat* should wait
4. 36. even as he was, in the ¹*boat*—And other ¹*boats*
37. waves beat into the ¹*boat*, insomuch that the ¹*boat*
5. 2. when he was come out of the ¹*boat*
21. when Jesus had crossed over again in the ¹*boat*
6. 32. And they went away in the ¹*b.* to a desert place
51. And he went up unto them into the ¹*boat*
54. And when they were come out of the ¹*boat*
8. 14. had not in the ¹*b.* with them more than one loaf
Lu. 5. 2. and he saw two ¹*boats* standing by the lake
3. And he entered into one of the ¹*boats* [both the ¹*b.*
7. beckoned unto their partners in the other ¹*b.*—filled
11. when they had brought their ¹*boats* to land
Jno. 6. 17. and they entered into a ¹*boat*, and were going
19. walking on the sea, and drawing nigh unto the ¹*b.*
21. receive him into the ¹*boat*—the ¹*b.* was at the land
22. none other *boat* there, save one—into the *boat*
23. (howbeit there came *boats* from Tiberias
24. they themselves got into the ²*boats*

BOAT

Jno. 21. 3. They went forth, and entered into the ¹*boat*
6. Cast the net on the right side of the ¹*boat*
8. But the other disciples came in the little ¹*boat*
Acts 27. 16. we were able, with difficulty, to secure the *b.*
30. the sailors—had lowered the *boat* into the sea
32. Then the soldiers cut away the ropes of the *boat*

Bodies.

Mat. 27. 52. many *bodies* of the saints that had fallen asleep
Jno. 19. 31. the *bodies* should not remain on the cross
Rom. 1. 24. that their *bodies* should be dishonoured
8. 11. quicken also your mortal *bodies* through his Spirit
12. 1. to present your *bodies* a living sacrifice, holy
1 *Cor.* 6. 15. Know ye not that your *bodies* are members of Christ?
15. 40. There are also celestial *bodies*, and *b.* terrestrial
Eph. 5. 28. husbands—love their own wives as their own *b.*
Heb. 13. 11. For the *bodies* of those beasts, whose blood
Rev. 11 8. their dead *b.* lie in the street of the great city
9. look upon their dead *bodies*—suffer not their dead *b.*
see body.

Bodily.

Lu. 3. 22. the Holy Ghost descended in a *b.* form, as a dove
2 *Cor.* 10. 10. but his *bodily* presence is weak
Col. 2. 9. in him dwelleth all the fulness of the Godhead *b.*
1 *Tim.* 4. 8. for *bodily* exercise is profitable for a little

Body.—*A.V.* ¹*bodies.*

Mat. 5. 29. and not thy whole *body* be cast into hell
6. 22. of the *b.* is the eye—thy whole *b. Lu.* 11. 34, 36
23. thy whole *b.* shall be full of darkness. *Lu.* 11. 34
25. Be not anxious—for your *body*—the body than the raiment? *Lu.* 12. 22, 23
10. 28. which kill the *b.*—soul and *b.* in hell. *Lu.* 12. 4
26. 12. in that she poured this ointment upon my *body*
26. Take, eat; this is my *body. Mk.* 14. 22: *Lu.* 22. 19:
1 *Cor.* 11. 24
27. 58. [Joseph] asked for the *body* of Jesus. *Mk.* 15. 43: *Lu.* 23. 52: *Jno.* 19. 38
59. And Joseph took the *body*, and wrapped it. *Jno.* 19. 38
Mk. 5. 29. she felt in her *body* that she was healed [38
14. 8. she hath anointed my *body* aforehand
51. a linen cloth cast about him, over his naked *body*
Lu. 17. 37. Where the *b.* is, thither will the eagles also be
24. 3. entered in, and found not the *b.* of the Lord Jesus
Jno. 19. 40. So they took the *body* of Jesus, and bound it
20. 12. sitting—where the *body* of Jesus had lain
Acts 9. 40. Peter—turning to the *body*, he said, Tabitha
Rom. 6. 6. that the *body* of sin might be done away
12. Let not sin therefore reign in your mortal *body*
7. 4. made dead to the law through the *body* of Christ
24. Who shall deliver me out of the *body* of this death?
8. 10. the body is dead because of sin
13. if—ye mortify the deeds of the *body*, ye shall live
23. our adoption, to wit, the redemption of our *body*
1 *Cor.* 5. 3. being absent in *body* but present in spirit
6. 13. the *b.* is not for fornication—the Lord for the *b.*
18. sin—is without the *b.*—sinneth against his own *b.*
19. that your *body* is a temple of the Holy Ghost
20. glorify God therefore in your *body*
7. 4. wife hath not power over her own *body*—husband hath not power over his own *body*
34. unmarried—may be holy both in *body* and in spirit
9. 27. but I buffet my *body*, and bring it into bondage
10. 16. is it not a communion of the *body* of Christ?
11. 27. be guilty of the *body* and the blood of the Lord
29. and drinketh judgement—if he discern not the *b.*
12. 12. as the *body* is one—all the members of the *body*, being many, are one *body*

BODY

1 *Cor.* 12. 14. For the *body* is not one member, but many
15. I am not of the *body*—therefore not of the *body.* 16
17. If the whole *b.* were an eye, where were the hearing?
18. God set the members each one of them in the *body*
19. if they were all one member, where were the *b.*?
20. they are many members, but one *body*
22. members of the *body* which seem to be more. 23
24. but God tempered the *body* together
25. that there should be no schism in the *body*
27. Now ye are the *body* of Christ
13. 3. if I give my *body* to be burned, but have not love
15. 35. and with what manner of *body* do they come?
37. thou sowest not that *body* that shall be
38. God giveth it a *body*—to each seed a body of its own
44. sown a natural *body*; it is raised a spiritual *body.*
If there is a natural *b.*, there is also a spiritual *b.*
2 *Cor.* 4. 10. bearing about in the *body* the dying of Jesus
—life also of Jesus may be manifested in our *b.*
5. 6. whilst we are at home in the *body*, we are absent
8. absent from the *b.*, and to be at home with the Lord
10. may receive the things done in the *body*
12. 3. (whether in the *body*, or apart from the *body.* 2
Gal. 6. 17. bear branded on my *body* the marks of Jesus
Eph. 3. 6. fellow-heirs, and fellow-members of the *body*
4. 12. unto the building up of the *body* of Christ
16. all the *b.* fitly framed—increase of the *b. Col.* 2. 19
5. 23. being himself the saviour of the *body*
Phil. 1. 20. Christ shall be magnified in my *body*
3. 21. *body* of our humiliation—*body* of his glory
Col. 1. 18. And he is the head of the *body*, the church
22. reconciled in the *body* of his flesh through death
2. 11. in the putting off of the *body* of the flesh
17. shadow of the things to come; but the *b.* is Christ's
23. and humility, and severity to the *body*
1 *Th.* 5. 23. spirit and soul and *body* be preserved entire
Heb. 10. 5. But a *body* didst thou prepare for me
10. sanctified through the offering of the *body* of Jesus
22. and our ¹*body* washed with pure water
13. 3. as being yourselves also in the *body*
Jas. 2. 16. ye give them not the things needful to the *body*
26. For as the *body* apart from the spirit is dead
3. 2. a perfect man, able to bridle the whole *body* also
3. we turn about their whole *body* also
6. the tongue, which defileth the whole *body*
Jude 9. Michael—disputed about the *body* of Moses
see corpse.

His Body.

Lu. 23. 55. beheld the tomb, and how *his body* was laid
24. 23. and when they found not *his body*, they came
Jno. 2. 21. But he spake of the temple of *his body*
19. 38. Joseph—came therefore, and took away *his body*
Acts 19. 12. carried away from *his body* handkerchiefs
Rom. 4. 19. *his* [Abraham] own *body* now as good as dead
1 *Cor.* 6. 18. committeth fornication sinneth against *h.* own
7. 4. husband hath not power over *his own body* | *body*
Eph. 1. 23. which is *his b.*, the fulness of him that filleth
Col. 1. 24. afflictions of Christ in my flesh for *his b.'s* sake
1 *Pet.* 2. 24. own self bare our sins in *his b.* upon the tree

One Body.

Rom. 12 4. we have many members in *one body*
5. we, who are many, are *o. b.* in Christ. 1 *Cor.* 10. 17
1 *Cor.* 6. 16. he that is joined to a harlot is *one body*!
12. 12. For as the *body* is *one*—being many, are *one body*
13. in one Spirit were we all baptized into *one body*
20. But now they are many members, but *one body*
Eph. 2. 16. and might reconcile them both in *o. b.* unto God
4. 4. There is *one body*, and one Spirit
Col. 3. 15. peace of Christ rule—ye were called in *one body*

BOLD

Bold.—*A.V.* ¹*dare.*

Rom. 10. 20. And Isaiah is very *bold*, and saith
2 *Cor.* 10. 2. confidence wherewith I count to be *bold*
   12. For we are not ¹*bold* to number or compare ourselves
   11. 21. whereinsoever any is *bold*—I am *bold* also
Phil. 1. 14. *bold* to speak the word of God without fear
1 *Th.* 2. 2. at Philippi, we waxed *bold* in our God to speak
see boldly, boldness, (good) courage, spake.

Boldly.—*A.V.* ¹*bold.*

Mk. 15. 43. Joseph—*boldly* went in unto Pilate
Acts 9. 27. at Damascus he [Paul] had preached *boldly*
   28. [Paul] preaching *boldly* in the name of the Lord
   13. 46. Paul and Barnabas spake out ¹*boldly*
   14. 3. [Paul and Barnabas] tarried there speaking *boldly*
   18. 26. [Apollos] began to speak *boldly* in the synagogue
   19. 8. [Paul] entered into the synagogue, and spake *b.*
Rom. 15. 15. I write the more *b.* unto you in some measure
Eph. 6. 20. that in it I may speak *b.*, as I ought to speak
see boldness, (good) courage, openly.

Boldness.—*A.V.* ¹*bold*, ²*boldly*, ³*confidence*, ⁴*plainness.*

Acts 4. 13. when they beheld the *b.* of Peter and John
   29. thy servants to speak thy word with all *boldness*
   31. and they spake the word of God with *boldness*
   28. 31. concerning the Lord Jesus Christ with all ³*b.*
2 *Cor.* 3. 12. such a hope, we use great ⁴*boldness* of speech
   7. 4. Great is my *boldness* of speech toward you
Eph. 3. 12. in whom we have *b.* and access in confidence
   6. 19. to make known with ¹*b.* the mystery of the gospel
Phil. 1. 20. put to shame, but that with all *b.*, as always
1 *Tim.* 3. 13. deacons gain—great *boldness* in the faith
Philem. 8. though I have all ¹*b.* in Christ to enjoin thee
Heb. 3. 6. if we hold fast our ²*b.* and the glorying of our
   4. 16. draw near with ²*boldness* unto the throne of grace
   10. 19. *boldness* to enter into the holy place by the blood
   35 Cast not away therefore your ²*boldness*
1 *Jno.* 2. 28. if he shall be manifested, we may have ²*b.*
   3. 21. if our heart condemn us not, we have ²*b.* toward
   4. 17. we may have *boldness* in the day of judgement
   5. 14. And this is the ²*b.* which we have toward him

Bond.—*A.V.* ¹*bill*, ²*handwriting*, ³*string.*

Mk. 7. 35. the ³*bond* of his tongue was loosed
Lu. 13. 16. been loosed from this *b.* on the—sabbath?
   16. 6. Take thy ¹*bond*, and sit down quickly. 17
Acts 8. 23. gall of bitterness and in the *bond* of iniquity
1 *Cor.* 12. 13. Jews or Greeks, whether *b.* or free. *Eph.* 6. 8
Gal. 3. 28. there can be neither *bond* nor free
Eph. 4. 3. to keep the unity of the spirit in the *b.* of peace
Col. 2. 14. blotted out the ²*bond* written in ordinances
   3. 14. put on love, which is the *bond* of perfectness
Rev. 13. 16. rich and the poor, and the free and the *bond*
   19. 18. eat—the flesh of all men, both free and *bond*
see bondman.

Bondage.—*A.V.* ¹*servant*, ²*serve*, ³*service*, ⁴*subjection.*

Jno. 8. 33. We [Jews]—have never yet been in *bondage*
Acts 7. 6. they should bring them [Israel] into *bondage*
   7. the nation to which they shall be in *b.* will I judge
Rom. 6. 6. that so we should no longer be in ²*b.* to sin
   8. 15. ye received not the spirit of *bondage* again
   21. delivered from the *b.* of corruption into the liberty
1 *Cor.* 7. 15. brother or the sister is not under *b.* in such cases
   9. 19. I brought myself under ¹*bondage* to all
   27. but I buffet my body, and bring it into ⁴*bondage*
2 *Cor.* 11. 20. ye bear with a man, if he bringeth you into *b.*

BOOK

Gal. 2. 4. that they might bring us into *bondage*
   4. 3. when we were children, were held in *bondage* under
   8. ye were in ²*b.* to them which by nature are no gods
   9. whereunto ye desire to be in *bondage* over again
   24. bearing children unto *bondage*, which is Hagar
   25. Jerusalem—is in *bondage* with her children
   5. 1. be not entangled again in a yoke of *bondage*
Heb. 2. 15. were all their lifetime subject to *bondage*
2 *Pet.* 2. 19. of the same is he also brought into *bondage*

Bondmaid *and* **Bondwoman** *A.V.—see* **handmaid.**

Bondman.—*A.V.* ¹*bond.*

Col. 3. 11. Scythian, ¹*bondman*, freeman : but Christ is all
Rev. 6. 15. *b.* and freeman, hid themselves in the caves

Bonds.—*A.V.* ¹*bound*, ²*chains.*

Acts 20. 23. saying that *bonds* and afflictions abide me [ed
   22. 5. bring them—unto Jerusalem in ¹*b.* for to be punish-
   23. 29. laid to his charge worthy of death or of *b.* 26. 31
   24. 27. to gain favour with the Jews, Felix left Paul in ¹*b.*
   26. 29. become such as I am, except these *bonds*
Phil. 1. 7. both in my *bonds* and in the defence and
   13. so that my *bonds* became manifest in Christ
   14. brethren in the Lord, being confident through my *b.*
   17. thinking to raise up affliction for me in my *bonds*
Col. 4. 3. mystery of Christ, for which I am also in *bonds*
   18. Paul with mine own hand. Remember my *bonds*
2 *Tim* 2. 9. I suffer hardship unto *bonds*, as a malefactor
Philem. 10. my child, whom I have begotten in my *bonds*
   13. minister unto me in the *bonds* of the gospel
Heb 10. 34. both had compassion on them that were in *b.*
   11. 36. yea, moreover of *bonds* and imprisonment
   13. 3. Remember them that are in *bonds*, as bound with
Jude 6. he hath kept in everlasting ²*bonds* under darkness
see prisoner, chains.

Bondservant—s.—*A.V.* ¹*servant—s.*

Jno. 8. 34. Every one that committeth sin is the ¹*b.* of sin
   35. the ¹*bondservant* abideth not in the house for ever
1 *Cor.* 7. 21. Wast thou called being a ¹*bondservant* ?
   22. being a ¹*b.*, is the Lord's freedman—is Christ's ¹*b.*
   23. become not ¹*bondservants* of men
Gal. 4. 1. heir is a child, he differeth nothing from a ¹*b.*
   7. So that thou art no longer a ¹*bondservant*, but a son
1 *Pet.* 2. 16. not using your freedom—but as ¹*b.* of God
2 *Pet.* 2. 19. they themselves are ¹*b.* of corruption

Bone.

Jno. 19. 36. A *bone* of him shall not be broken

Bones.

Mat. 23. 27. but inwardly are full of dead men's *bones*
Lu. 24. 39. a spirit hath not flesh and *b.*, as ye behold me
Heb. 11. 22. Joseph—gave commandment concerning his *b.*

Book.

Mat. 1. 1. The *book* of the generation of Jesus Christ
Mk. 12. 26. have ye not read in the *book* of Moses
Lu. 3. 4. as it is written in the *b.* of the words of Isaiah
Lu. 4. 17. *b.* of the prophet Isaiah. And he opened the *b.*
   20. And he [Jesus] closed the *book*, and gave it back
   20. 42. David—saith in the *book* of Psalms. *Acts* 1. 20
Jno. 20. 30. Many other signs—not written in this *book*
Acts 7. 42. as it is written in the *book* of the prophets
Gal. 3. 10. in all things that are written in the *book*
Phil. 4. 3. fellow-workers, whose names are in the *b.* of life

31

BOOK

Heb. 9. 19. Moses—sprinkled both the *book* itself, and
10. 7. (In the roll of the *book* it is written of me)
Rev. 1. 11. What thou seest, write in a *book*
3. 5. I will in no wise blot his name out of the *book* of life
5. 1. a *book* written within and on the back
2. Who is worthy to open the *book*
3. no one—was able to open the *book*
4. no one was found worthy to open the *book*
5. the Root of David, hath overcome, to open the *book*
8. when he had taken the *b.*, the four living creatures
9. Worthy art thou to take the *book*, and to open
10. 2. and he had in his hand a little *book* open
8. Go, take the *book* which is open in the hand
9. saying—that he should give me the little *book*
10. I took the little *book* out of the angel's hand
13. 8. name hath not been written in the *b.* of life. 17. 8
20. 12. another *book* was opened, which is the *b.* of life
15. And if any was not found written in the *b.* of life
21. 27. only they which are written in the Lamb's *b.* of life
22. 7. keepeth the words of the prophecy of this *book*
9. with them which keep the words of this *book*
18. the prophecy of this *book*—written in this *book*. 19

Books.
see tree.

Jno. 21. 25. even tho world itself would not contain the *b.*
Acts 19. practised curious arts brought their *books*
2 *Tim.* 4. 13. bring—the *books*, especially the parchments
Rev. 20. 12. *b.* were opened—things—were written in the *b.*

Boon.—*A.V.* ¹*gift.*
Jas. 1. 17. good gift and every perfect *boon* is from above

Border.—*A.V.* ¹*hem.*
Mat. 9. 20. touched the ¹*border* of his garment. 14. ¹36
Mk. 6. 56. touch if it were but the *border* of his garment
Lu. 8. 44. behind him, and touched the *b.* of his garment

Borders.—*A.V.* ¹*coasts.*
Mat. 2. 6. Bethlehem, and in all the ¹*borders* thereof
4. 13. Capernaum—in the *b.* of Zebulun and Naphtali
8. 34. besought him that he would depart from their ¹*b.*
15. 22. a Canaanitish woman came out from those ¹*b.*
39. and came into the ¹*borders* of Magadan
23. 5. enlarge the *b.* of their [scribes and P.] garments
Mk. 7. 24. went away into the *borders* of Tyre and Sidon
31. he went out from the ¹*borders* of Tyre, and came—through the midst of the ¹*borders* of Decapolis
10. 1. and cometh into the ¹*borders* of Judæa
Acts 13. 50. Paul and Barnabas, and cast them out of their ¹*b.*

Born.—*A.V.* ¹*made.*
Mat. 1. 16. of whom was *born* Jesus, who is called Christ
2. 1. Now when Jesus was *born* in Bethlehem
4. [Herod] inquired—where the Christ should be *born*
11. 11. *b.* of women there hath not arisen a greater than
19. 12. there are eunuchs, which were so *b.* [John. *Lu.* 7. 28
26. 24. good—for that man if he had not been *b. Mk.* 14. 21
Lu. 1. 35. that which is to be *born* shall be called holy
2. 11. there is *b.* to you this day in the city of David
Jno. 1. 13. which were *born*, not of blood—but of God
3. 3. Except a man be *born* anew, he cannot see
4. How can a man be *b.* when he is old?—and be *b.*?
5. Except a man be *born* of water and the Spirit
6. *born* of the flesh is flesh;—*b.* of the Spirit is spirit
7. I said unto thee, Ye must be *born* anew
8. so is every one that is *born* of the Spirit
8. 41. We [Jews] were not *born* of fornication
9. 2. this man, or his parents, that he should be *b.* blind?
19. Is this your son, who ye say was *born* blind?
20. We know—that he was *born* blind

BOUGHT

Jno. 9. 34. Thou wast altogether *born* in sins
16. 21. for the joy that a man is *born* into the world
18. 37. To this end have I been *born*, and to this end
Acts 2. 8. hear we—our own language, wherein we were *b.*?
7. 20. At which season Moses was *born*
22. 3. I [Paul] am a Jew, *born* in Tarsus of Cilicia.
28. Paul said, But I am a Roman *born*
Rom. 1. 3. his Son, who was ¹*born* of the seed of David
9. 11. for the children being not yet *born*, neither
1 *Cor.* 15. 8. as unto one *b.* out of due time, he appeared
Gal. 4. 4. his Son, ¹*born* of a woman, ¹*born* under the law
23. son by the handmaid is *born* after the flesh; but the son by the freewoman is *born* through promise
29. *born* after the flesh—*born* after the Spirit ⌈months
Heb. 11. 23. By faith Moses, when he was *b.*, was hid three
see begotten, delivered, man, race.

Borne.—*A.V.* ¹*fallen*, ²*sunk.*
Mat. 20. 12. which have *b.* the burden of the day and the
23. 4. heavy burdens and grievous to be *b. Lu.* 11. 46
Mk. 2. 3. unto him a man sick of the palsy, *borne* of four
Jno. 20. 15. Sir, if thou hast *borne* him hence, tell me
Acts 20. 9. Eutychus, ¹*b.* down with deep sleep—being ²*b.*
21. 35. [Paul] was *b.* of the soldiers for the violence of
1 *Cor.* 15. 49. as we have *borne* the image of the earthy
see bear.

Borne witness.—*A.V.* ¹*bare record*, ²*bare witness*, ³*barest witness*, ⁴*gave record*, ⁵*testified.*
Jno. 3. 26. beyond Jordan, to whom thou hast ³*b.* witness
5. 33. he [John] hath ²*borne witness* unto the truth
37. And the Father—hath *borne witness* of me
19. 35. And he that hath seen hath ¹*borne witness*
1 *Jno.* 5. 9. that he hath ⁵*borne w.* concerning his Son. ⁴10
see bare witness.

Borrow.
Mat. 5. 42. him that would *b.* of thee turn not thou away

Bosom.
Lu. 6. 38. good measure—shall they give into your *b.*
16. 22. carried away by the angels into Abraham's *b.*
23. Abraham afar off, and Lazarus in his *bosom*
Jno. 1. 18. only begotten Son, which is in the *b.* of the
13. 28. reclining in Jesus' *bosom* one of his disciples

Both.
Mat. 13. 30. Let *both* grow together until the harvest
15. 14. *both* shall fall into a pit. *Lu.* 6. 39
Lu. 1. 6. [Zacharias and Elisabeth] were *both* righteous
7. 42. had not wherewith to pay, he forgave them *both*
Acts 23. 8. angel, nor spirit: but the Pharisees confess *b.*
Eph. 2. 14. For he is our peace, who made *both* one
16. might reconcile them *both* in one body unto God
2 *Pet.* 3. 1. in *both* of them I stir up your sincere mind
see twain.

Bottles *A.V.—see skins, and wine-skins.*

Bottom.
Mat. 27. 51. rent in twain from the top to the *b. Mk.* 15. 38

Bottomless Pit *A.V.—see abyss.*

Bought.
Mat. 13. 46. pearl—sold all that he had, and *bought* it
21. 12. cast out all them that sold and *bought* in the temple. *Mk.* 11. 15
27. 7. and *b.* with them [thirty pieces] the potter's field
Mk. 15. 46. [Joseph] *bought* a linen cloth
16. 1. [women] *bought* spices that they might come

35

BOUGHT

Lu. 14. 18. I have *bought* a field, and I must needs go out
19. I have *bought* five yoke of oxen
17. 28. they ate, they drank, they *bought*, they sold
Acts 7. 16. laid in the tomb that Abraham *b.* for a price
1 *Cor.* 6. 20. for ye were *bought* with a price. 7. 23
2 *Pet.* 2. 1. denying even the Master that *bought* them

Bound.—*A.V.* ¹*ought*, ²*wound*.

Mat. 14. 3. laid hold on John, and *bound* him. *Mk.* 6. 17
16. 19. shalt bind on earth shall be *b.* in heaven. 18. 18
Mk. 5. 4. been often *b.* with fetters and chains. *Lu.* 8. 29
15. 1. chief priests—*b.* Jesus. *Mat.* 27. 2; *Jno.* 18. 12
7. one called Barabbas, lying *bound* with them
Lu. 10. 34. *b.* up his wounds, pouring on them oil and wine
13. 16. woman—whom Satan had *b.*, lo, these eighteen
Jno. 11. 44. Lazarus—came forth, *bound* hand and foot with grave-clothes; and his face was *bound*
18. 24. Annas therefore sent him *bound* unto Caiaphas
19. 40. took the body of Jesus, and ²*bound* it in linen
Acts 9. 2. Saul—might bring them *bound* to Jerusalem. 21
12. 6. Peter was sleeping between two soldiers, *b.* with
20. 22. I go *bound* in the spirit unto Jerusalem
21. 11. [Agabus] *bound* his own feet and hands
13. I am ready not to be *bound* only, but also to die
33. commanded him [Paul] to be *b.* with two chains
22. 29. chief captain was afraid—because he had *bound*
23. 12. Jews—*bound* themselves under a curse. 14, 21
28. 20. because of the hope of Israel I am *b.* with this
Rom. 7. 2. woman that hath a husband is *b.* 1 *Cor.* 7. 39
1 *Cor.* 7. 27. Art thou *bound* unto a wife? seek not
2 *Th.* 1. 3. We are *bound* to give thanks to God. 2. 13
2 *Tim.* 2. 9. but the word of God is not *bound*
Heb. 5. 3. by reason thereof is ¹*bound*, as for the people
13. 3. Remember them that are in bonds, as *b.* with
Rev. 9. 14. Loose the four angels which are *bound*
20. 2. Satan, and *bound* him for a thousand years
see in bonds, tied.

Bounds.

Acts 17. 26. having determined—the *b.* of their habitation

Bountifully.

2 *Cor.* 9. 6. he that soweth *bountifully* shall reap also *b.*

Bountifulness *A.V.*—*see liberality.*

Bounty.—*A.V.* ¹*abundance*, ²*liberality.*

1 *Cor.* 16. 3. send to carry your ²*bounty* unto Jerusalem
2 *Cor.* 8. 20. should blame us in the matter of this ¹*bounty*
9. 5. your aforepromised *bounty*—as a matter of *bounty*

Bow.

Rev. 6. 2. white horse, and he that sat thereon had a *bow*

Bow.

Rom. 11. 10. And *bow* thou down their back alway
14. 11. saith the Lord, to me every knee shall *bow*
Eph. 3. 14. I *bow* my knees unto the Father
Phil. 2. 10. in the name of Jesus every knee should *bow*

Bowed.

Lu. 13. 11. infirmity eighteen years; and she was *bowed*
24. 5. affrighted, and *b.* down their faces to the earth
Jno. 19. 30. he *bowed* his head, and gave up his spirit
Rom. 11. 4. who have not *bowed* the knee to Baal
see kneeled.

Bowels.

Acts 1. 18. all his [Judas] *bowels* gushed out
see heart, hearts, affections, mercies.

BRANDED

Bowing.

Mk. 15. 19. [soldiers] *bowing* their knees worshipped him

Bowl—s.—*A.V.* ¹*vial—s.*

Rev. 5. 8. having each one a harp and golden ¹*bowls*
15. 7. seven golden ¹*bowls* full of the wrath of God
16. 1. pour out the seven ¹*bowls* of the wrath of God
2. first went, and poured out his ¹*bowl* into the earth
3. second poured out his ¹*bowl* into the sea
4. third poured out his ¹*bowl* into the rivers
8. fourth poured out his ¹*bowl* upon the sun
10. fifth poured out his ¹*bowl* upon the throne
12. sixth poured out his ¹*bowl* upon the great river
17. seventh poured out his ¹*bowl* upon the air
17. 1. one of the seven angels that had the seven ¹*b.* [21. 19

Box *A.V.*—*see cruse*

Boy.—*A.V.* ¹*child.*

Mat. 17. 18. the ¹*boy* was cured from that hour
Lu. 2. 43. the ¹*boy* Jesus tarried behind in Jerusalem
9. 42. healed the ¹*boy*, and gave him back to his father

Braided.—*A.V* ¹*broided.*

1 *Tim.* 2. 9. not with ¹*braided* hair, and gold or pearls

Brake.—*A.V.* ¹*beat*, ²*broken.*

Mat. 14. 19. he blessed, and *brake* and gave. 15 36; 26.
26; *Mk.* 6. 41; 8. 6; 14. 22; *Lu.* 9. 16; 22. 19;
24. 30; 1 *Cor.* 11. 24
Mk. 8. 19. When I *brake* the five loaves
14. 3. and she *brake* the cruse, and poured it
Lu. 6. 48. the stream ¹*brake* against that house. 149
Jno. 5. 18. he not only ²*b.* the sabbath, but also called God
19. 32. soldiers—*brake* the legs of the first [thief]
33. he [Jesus] was dead already, they *brake* not his legs
Acts 27. 35. he [Paul] ²*brake* it, and began to eat
Eph. 2. 14. and ²*brake* down the middle wall of partition
see breaking.

Bramble.

Lu. 6. 44. nor of a *bramble* bush gather they grapes

Branch.

Mat. 24. 32. fig tree—when her *branch* is now become tender. *Mk.* 13. 28
Jno. 15. 2. Every *branch* in me that beareth not—every *branch* that beareth
4. as the *branch* cannot bear fruit of itself
6. abide not in me, he is cast forth as a *branch*

Branches.

Mat. 13. 32. birds of the heaven—lodge in the *b. Lu.* 13. 19
21. 8. others cut *b.* from the trees, and spread. *Mk.* 11. 8
Mk. 4. 32. than all the herbs, and putteth out great *b.*
Jno. 12. 13. took the *branches* of the palm trees
15. 5. I am the vine, ye are the *branches*
Rom. 11. 16. if the root is holy, so are the *branches*
17. But if some of the *branches* were broken off
18. olive tree; glory not over the *branches*
19. Thou wilt say then, *Branches* were broken off
21. for if God spared not the natural *branches*
24. much more shall these, which are the natural *b.*

Branded.—*A.V.* ¹*seared.*

Gal. 6. 17. for I bear *b.* on my body the marks of Jesus
1 *Tim.* 4. 2. ¹*b.* in their own conscience as with a hot iron

BRASEN

Brasen.
Mk. 7. 4. washings of cups, and pots, and *brasen* vessels

Brass.
Mat. 10. 9. no gold, nor silver, nor *brass* in your purses
1 *Cor.* 13. 1. I am become sounding *b.*, or a clanging cymbal
Rev. 1. 15. his feet like unto burnished *brass.* 2. 18
9. 20. idols of gold, and of silver, and of *brass*
18. 12. precious wood, and of *brass*, and iron, and marble

Brawler.—*A.V.* ¹*given to wine.*
1 *Tim.* 3. 3. [bishop] no *brawler*, no striker. *Tit.* 1. ¹⁷
see contentious.

Bread.
Mat. 4. 3. command that these stones become *b. Lu.* 4. 3
4. Man shall not live by *bread* alone. *Lu.* 4. 4
6. 11. Give us this day our daily *bread. Lu.* 11. 3
15. 2. they wash not their hands when they eat *bread*
26. It is not meet to take the children's *bread. Mk.* 7. 27
16. 5. disciples—forgot to take *bread. Mk.* 8. 14
7. saying, We took no *bread.* 6 : *Mk.* 8. 16, 17
11. ye do not perceive that I spake not to you concerning
12. beware of the leaven of *bread* [*bread?*
26. 26. as they were eating, Jesus took *b. Mk.* 14. 22 : *Lu.*
Mk. 3. 20. they could not so much as eat *b.* [22. 19 : 24. 30
6. 8. take nothing for their journey—no *bread*, no wallet
37. Shall we go and buy two hundred pennyworth of *b.*
7. 2. his disciples ate their *bread* with defiled—hands
5. but eat their *bread* with defiled hands?
8. 4. fill these men with *bread* here in a desert place?
Lu. 7. 33. John the Baptist is come eating no *bread*
9. 3. neither staff, nor wallet, nor *bread*, nor money
14. 1. he went—on a sabbath to eat *bread*
15. Blessed is he that shall eat *bread* in the kingdom
15. 17. How many hired servants of my father's have *b.*
24. 35. he was known of them in the breaking of the *b.*
Jno. 6. 5. Whence are we to buy *bread*, that these may eat?
7. Two hundred pennyworth of *bread* is not sufficient
23. nigh unto the place where they ate the *bread*
31. He gave them *bread* out of heaven to eat [*bread*
32. not Moses that gave you the *b.*—but my Father—true
33. For the *bread* of God is that which cometh down
34. Lord, evermore give us this *bread*
35. Jesus said—I am the *bread* of life. 48
41. because he said, I am the *bread* which came. 50, 58
51. I am the living *bread* which came down—eat of
this *bread*—yea and the *bread* which I will give
58. he that eateth this *bread* shall live for ever
13. 18. He that eateth my *b.* lifted up his heel against me
21. 9. and fish laid thereon, and *bread*
13. Jesus cometh, and taketh the *bread*
Acts 2. 42. in the breaking of *bread* and the prayers
46. breaking *bread* at home, they did take their food
20. 7. when we were gathered together to break *bread*
11. when he [Paul]—had broken the *bread*, and eaten
27. 35. when he had said this, and had taken *bread*
1 *Cor.* 10. 16. The *b.* which we break, is it not a communion
17. are one *bread*, one body—all partake of the one *b.*
11. 23. in the night in which he was betrayed took *bread*
26. For as often as ye eat this *bread*
27. whosoever shall eat the *bread* or drink the cup. 28
2 *Cor.* 9. 10. supplieth seed to the sower and *b.* for food
2 *Th.* 3. 8. neither did we eat *bread* for nought
12. with quietness they work, and eat their own *bread*
see eat, loaf, loaves, shewbread.

Loaf or Loaves of **Bread.**—*see loaf, loaves.*

BREATHED

Unleavened **Bread.**
Mat. 26. 17. on the first day of *unl. b. Mk.* 14. 1, 12 : *Lu.*
Acts 12. 3. those were the days of *unl.* bread [22. 1, 7
20. 6. after the days of *unleavened* bread
1 *Cor.* 5. 8. with the *unl.* bread of sincerity and truth

Breadth.
Eph. 3. 18. what is the *b.* and length and height and depth
Rev. 20. 9. they went up over the *breadth* of the earth
21. 16. the length thereof is as great as the *breadth*—
length and *breadth*—thereof are equal

Break.—*A.V.* ¹*broken.*
Mat. 5. 19. whosoever—shall *break* one of these least com-
6. 19. where thieves *b.* through and steal [mandments
20. where thieves do not *break* through nor steal
12. 20. a bruised reed shall he not *break*
Acts 20. 7. gathered together to *b.* bread, Paul discoursed
27. 41. stern began to ¹*b.* up by the violence of the waves
1 *Cor.* 10. 16. bread which we *break*, is it not a communion
Gal. 4. 27. *Break* forth and cry, thou that travailest not
see breaking, burst.

Break *of day.*
Acts 20. 11. even till *break* of *day*, so he [Paul] departed

Break *fast.*—*A.V.* ¹*dine.*
Jno. 21. 12. Jesus saith unto them, Come and ¹*b.* your *fast*

Breaker—s *A.V.*—*see transgressor—s.*

Breaking.—*A.V.* ¹*brake,* ²*break.*
Lu. 5. 6. multitude of fishes ; and their nets were ¹*b.*
8. 29. and ¹*b.* the bands asunder, he was driven of the
24. 35. was known of them in the *breaking* of the bread
Acts 2. 42. in the *breaking* of bread and the prayers
46. *breaking* bread at home, they did take their food
21. 13. What do ye, weeping and ²*breaking* my heart?

Breast—s.—*A.V.* ¹*paps.*
Lu. 11. 27. Blessed is the womb that bare thee, and the ¹*b.*
18. 13. publican—smote his *breast*, saying, God, be
23. 29. Blessed are—the ¹*breasts* that never gave suck
48. multitudes—returned smiting their *breasts*
Jno. 13. 25. He leaning back, as he was, on Jesus' *breast*
21. 20. which also leaned back on his *b.* at the supper
Rev. 15. 6. seven angels—girt about their *b.* with golden

Breastplate—s.
Eph. 6. 14. put on the *breastplate* of righteousness
1 *Th.* 5. 8. putting on the *breastplate* of faith and love
Rev. 9. 9. they had *breastplates*, as it were *b.* of iron
17. having *breastplates* as of fire and of hyacinth

Breath.—*A.V.* ¹*life,* ²*spirit.*
Acts 17. 25. giveth to life, and *breath*, and all things
2 *Th.* 2. 8. Lord Jesus shall slay with the ²*b.* of his mouth
Rev. 11. 11. ¹*breath* of life from God entered into them
13. 15. it was given unto him to give ¹*breath* to it

Breathed.
Jno. 20. 22. he *b.* on them, and saith unto them, Receive

37

BREATHING

Breathing.
Acts 9. 1. Saul, yet *breathing* threatening and slaughter

Brethren.—*A.V.* ¹*men and brethren.*
Mat. 4. 18. Galilee, he saw two *b.*, Simon—and Andrew
21. [Jesus] saw other two *brethren*, James—and John
19. 29. that hath left houses, or *b. Mk.* 10. 29: *Lu.* 18. 29
20. 24. ten—moved with indignation concerning the two
22. 25. were with us seven *b. Mk.* 12. 20; *Lu.* 20. 29 [*b.*
23. 8. one is your teacher, and all ye are *brethren*
Mk. 10. 30. shall receive—houses, and *b.*, and sisters
Lu. 14. 26. hateth not—*b.*, and sisters, yea, and his own
16. 28. for I [Dives] have five *brethren*
21. 16. delivered up even by parents, and *brethren*
Jno. 21. 23. This saying—went forth among the *brethren*
Acts 1. 16. ¹*Brethren*, it was needful that the scripture
2. 29. ¹*B.*, I may say unto you freely of the patriarch
37. [Jews] said unto Peter—*B.*, what shall we do?
3. 17. now, *brethren*, I wot that in ignorance ye did it
6. 3. Look ye out therefore, *brethren*, from among you
7. 2. ¹*Brethren* and fathers, hearken
26. Sirs, ye are *b.*; why do ye wrong one to another?
9. 30. when the *b.* knew it, they brought him down
10. 23. certain of the *b.* from Joppa accompanied him
11. 1. apostles and the *b.*—heard that the Gentiles
12. these six *brethren* also accompanied me [Peter]
29. send relief unto the *brethren* that dwelt in Judæa
12. 17. Tell these things unto James, and to the *b.*
13. 15. ¹*Brethren*, if ye have any word of exhortation
26. ¹*Brethren*, children of the stock of Abraham
38. Be it known unto you therefore, *brethren*
14. 2. and made them evil affected against the *brethren*
15. 1. certain men came—and taught the *brethren*
3. and they caused great joy unto all the *brethren*
7. ¹*Brethren*, ye know how that a good while ago
13. ¹*Brethren*, hearken unto me [James]
22. Barsabbas, and Silas, chief men among the *brethren*
23. The apostles and the elder *b.* unto the *b.* which
32. Judas and Silas—exhorted the *brethren*
33. they were dismissed in peace from the *brethren*
36. Let us return now and visit the *b.* in every city
40. commended by the *b.* to the grace of the Lord
16. 2. [Timothy] well reported of by the *brethren*
40. when they had seen the *b.*, they comforted them
17. 6. dragged Jason and certain *b.* before the rulers
10. And the *brethren* immediately sent away Paul. 14
18. 18. Paul—took his leave of the *brethren*
27. the *b.* encouraged him, and wrote to the disciples
21. 7. we saluted the *brethren*, and abode with them
17. when we were come to Jerusalem, the *b.* received
22. 1. ¹*Brethren* and fathers, hear ye my defence
5. from whom also I received letters unto the *brethren*
23. 1. Paul—said, ¹*Brethren*, I have lived before God
5. Paul said, I wist not, *b.*, that he was high priest
6. Paul—cried—¹*Brethren*, I am a Pharisee
28. 14. Puteoli: where we found *brethren*
15. the *b.*, when they heard of us, came to meet us
17. I, *brethren*, though I had done nothing against
21. nor did any of the *brethren* come hither
Rom. 1. 13. I would not have you ignorant, *brethren*. 11. 25: 1 *Cor.* 10. 1: 12. 1: *Th.* 4. 13
7. 1. Or are ye ignorant, *brethren*—how that the law
8. 12. So then, *brethren*, we are debtors, not to the flesh
29. might be the firstborn among many *brethren*
10. 1. *Brethren*, my heart's desire and my supplication
12. 1. I beseech you therefore, *brethren*. 15. 30: 16. 17: 1 *Cor.* 1. 10: 16. 15: *Gal.* 4. 12
16. 14. Salute—Hermas, and the *brethren*

BRETHREN

1 *Cor.* 1. 26. For behold your calling, *b.*, how that not
2. 1. I, *b.*, when I came unto you, came not with
3. 1. I, *b.*, could not speak unto you as unto spiritual
4. 6. Now these things, *brethren*, I have in a figure
7. 24. *Brethren*, let each man—abide with God
29. But this I say, *brethren*, the time is shortened
8. 12. And thus, sinning against the *brethren*
9. 5. rest of the apostles, and the *brethren* of the Lord
14. 20. *Brethren*, be not children in mind
26. What is it then, *brethren*?
39. Wherefore, my *b.*, desire earnestly to prophesy
15. 1. I make known unto you, *brethren*, the gospel
6. appeared to above five hundred *brethren* at once
50. Now this I say, *brethren*, that flesh and blood
58. Wherefore, my beloved *brethren*, be ye stedfast
16. 11. I expect him [Timothy] with the *brethren*
12. him [Apollos] much to come unto you with the *b.*
20. All the *brethren* salute you. *Phil.* 4. 21
2 *Cor.* 8. 23. or our *b.*, they are the messengers of the
9. 3. But I have sent the *brethren*, that our glorying
5. I thought it necessary therefore to intreat the *b.*
11. 9. for the *b.*, when they came from Macedonia
26. in perils among false *brethren*
13. 11. Finally, *brethren*, farewell
Gal. 1. 2. all the *b.* which are with me, unto the churches
11. I make known to you, *b.*, as touching the gospel
2 4. because of the false *brethren* privily brought in
Eph. 6. 23. Peace be to the *brethren*, and love with faith
Phil. 1. 14. most of the *b.* in the Lord—speak the word
Col. 1. 2. to the saints and faithful *brethren* in Christ
4. 15. Salute the *brethren* that are in Laodicea
1 *Th.* 4. 1. Finally then, *b.*, we beseech. 5. 12: 2 *Th.* 2. 1
10. for indeed ye do it toward all the *brethren*
5. 14. we exhort you, *brethren*. 4. 10: *Heb.* 13. 22
25. *Brethren*, pray for us. 2 *Th.* 3. 1
26. Salute all the *brethren* with a holy kiss
27. that this epistle be read unto all the *brethren*
2 *Th.* 2. 15. So then, *brethren*, stand fast
1 *Tim.* 4. 6. If thou put the *b.* in mind of these things
5. 1. Rebuke—the younger men as *brethren*
6. 2. let them not despise them, because they are *b.*
Heb. 2. 11. he is not ashamed to call them *brethren*
3. 1. Wherefore, holy *b.*, partakers of a heavenly calling
12. Take heed, *b.*, lest haply there shall be in any
7. 5. according to the law, that is, of their *brethren*
Jas. 2. 5. Hearken, my beloved *b.*; did not God choose
4. 11. Speak not one against another, *brethren*
5. 7. Be patient therefore, *b.*, until the coming of the
9. Murmur not, *brethren*, one against another
10. Take, *brethren*, for an example of suffering
1 *Pet.* 1. 22. unto unfeigned love of the *brethren*
3. 8. loving as *b.*, tenderhearted, humbleminded
1 *Jno.* 3. 14. out of death into life, because we love the *b.*
16. we ought to lay down our lives for the *brethren*
3 *Jno.* 3. when he came and bare witness unto thy truth
5. doest toward them that are *brethren* and strangers
10. neither doth he himself receive the *brethren*
Rev. 6. 11. and their *b.*, which should be killed even as
12. 10. for the accuser of our *brethren* is cast down

His **Brethren.**
Mat. 1. 2. Jacob begat Judah and *his brethren*
11. Josiah begat Jechoniah and *his brethren*
12. 46. his mother and *his b.* stood. *Mk.* 3. 31: *Lu.* 8. 19
13. 55. his *brethren*, James, and Joseph. *Acts* 1. 14
Jno. 2. 12. to Capernaum, he, and his mother, and *his b.*
7. 5. his *brethren* did not believe on him [Jesus]
10. when *his brethren* were gone up unto the feast
Acts 7. 13. Joseph was made known to *his brethren*

BRETHREN

Acts 7. 23. [Moses] to visit *his b.* the children of Israel
25. he supposed that *his b.* understood how that God
1 *Cor.* 6. 5. who shall be able to decide between *his b.*
Heb. 2. 17. in all things to be made like unto *his brethren*

Men and Brethren *A.V.—see brethren.*

Love of the Brethren.—*A.V.* ¹*brotherly love,* ²*brotherly kindness.*

Rom. 12 10. In ¹*l. of the b.* be tenderly affectioned one to
1 *Th.* 4. 9. concerning ¹*love of the brethren* ye have no need
Heb. 13. 1. Let ¹*love of the brethren* continue
2 *Pet.* 1. 7. godliness ²*l. of the b.;* and in your ²*l. of the b.*

My Brethren.

Mat. 12. 48. and who are *my brethren? Mk.* 3. 33
49. Behold, my mother and *my brethren! Mk.* 3. 34
25. 40. Inasmuch as ye did it unto one of these *my b.*
28. 10. Fear not: go tell *my brethren* that they depart
Lu. 8. 21. My mother and *my b.* are these which hear the
Jno. 20. 17. go unto *my b.,* and say to them, I ascend
Rom. 7. 4. Wherefore, *my b.,* ye also were made dead
9. 3. anathema from Christ for *my brethren's* sake
15. 14. I myself also am persuaded of you, *my brethren*
Heb. 2. 12. I will declare thy name unto *my brethren*
Jas. 1. 16. Be not deceived, *my beloved brethren*
19. Ye know this, *my beloved brethren*
2. 4. Hearken, *my beloved brethren*
3. 1. Be not many teachers, *my brethren*
5. 12. But above all things, *my brethren,* swear not
19. *My b.,* if any among you do err from the truth

Thy Brethren.

Mat. 12. 47. Behold, thy mother and *thy b.* stand without. *Mk.* 3. 32: *Lu.* 8. 20
Lu. 14. 12. call not thy friends, nor *thy brethren*
22. 32. once thou [Peter] hast turned again, stablish *thy b.*
Rev. 19. 10. with thee and with *thy b.* that hold. 22. 9

Your Brethren.

Mat. 5. 47. if ye salute *your b.* only, what do ye more
Acts 3. 22. A prophet—from among *your b.,* like. 7. 37
1 *Cor.* 6. 8. do wrong, and defraud, and that *your b.*
1 *Pet.* 5. 9. same sufferings are accomplished in *your b*

Bride.

Jno. 3. 29. He that hath the *bride* is the bridegroom
Rev. 18. 23. voice of the bridegroom and of the *bride*
21. 2. new Jerusalem—as a *b.* adorned for her husband
9. I will show thee the *bride,* the wife of the Lamb
22. 17. And the Spirit and the *bride* say, Come

Bride-chamber.

Mat. 9. 15. Can the sons of the *bride-chamber* mourn
Mk. 2. 19. Can the sons of the *bride-chamber* fast. *Lu.* 5. 34

Bridegroom.

Mat. 9. 15. as long as the *bridegroom* is with them ?—*b.* shall be taken away. *Mk.* 2. 19, 20: *Lu.* 5. 34, 35
25. 1 took their lamps, and went forth to meet the
5. while the *bridegroom* tarried, they all slumbered
6. Behold, the *bridegroom!* Come ye forth to meet him
10. while they went away to buy, the *b.* came
Jno. 3. 29. is the *b.*: but the friend of the *b.—of the b.* voice
Rev. 18. 23. voice of the *b.* and of the bride shall be heard

BRING

Bridle—eth.

Jas. 1. 26. thinketh himself to be religious, while he *b.* not
3. 2. a perfect man, able to *bridle* the whole body also

Bridles.—*A.V.* ¹*bits.*

Jas. 3. 3. Now if we put the horses' ¹*b.* into their mouths
Rev. 14. 20. came out blood—even unto the *bridles* of the

Briefly.

1 *Pet.* 5. 12. I have written unto you *briefly,* exhorting
see summed up.

Briers *A.V.—see thistles.*

Bright.—*A.V.* ¹*clean,* ²*clear,* ³*white.*

Mat. 17. 5. behold, a *bright* cloud overshadowed them
Lu. 11. 36. as when the lamp with its *b.* shining doth give
Acts. 10. 30. a man stood before me [Cornelius] in *b.* apparel
Rev. 19. 8. array herself in fine linen, ¹*bright* and pure. 15. 6
22. 1. a river of water of life, ²*bright* as crystal
16. the offspring of David, the *bright,* the morning star

Brightness.

Acts 26. 13. light from heaven, above the *b.* of the sun
see effulgence, manifestation.

Brim.

Jno. 2. 7. And they filled them [waterpots] up to the *brim*

Brimstone.

Lu. 17. 29. rained fire and *b.* from heaven
Rev. 9. 17. breastplates—of *b.*—smoke and *brimstone.* 18
14. 10. he shall be tormented with fire and *brimstone*
19. 20. lake of fire that burneth with *b.* 20. 10: 21. 8

Bring.—*A.V.* ¹*brought,* ²*declare,* ³*fetch,* ⁴*lead,* ⁵*preach,* ⁶*shew.*

Mat. 2. 8. *bring* me word—may come and worship him
6. 13. ⁴*bring* us not into temptation. *Lu.* 11. ⁴4
14. 18. And he said, *Bring* them hither to me
17. 17. *bring* him hither to me. *Mk.* 9. 19: *Lu.* 9. 41.
21. 2. and *bring* them unto me. *Mk.* 11. 2: *Lu.* 19. 30
Mk. 6. 27. and commanded to ⁴*bring* his [John Bap.] head
7. 32. they *bring* unto him one that was deaf
Lu. 1. 19. speak unto thee, and to ⁶*b.* thee—good tidings
2. 10. I *bring* you good tidings of great joy
5. 18. behold, men ¹*bring* on a bed a man that was palsied: and they sought to *bring* him in
not finding by what way they might *bring* him in
8. 14. and *bring* no fruit to perfection
12. 11. when they *bring* you before the synagogues
14. 21. *bring* in hither the poor and maimed
19. 27. *bring* hither, and slay them before me
Jno. 7. 45. Why did ye not ¹*bring* him ? [Jesus]
10. 16. not of this fold: them also must I *bring*
14. 26. Comforter—*bring* to your remembrance all
18. 29. What accusation *bring* ye against this man ?
19. 4. Pilate—saith—Behold, I *bring* him out to you
21. 10. *Bring* of the fish which ye have now taken
Acts 5. 28. intend to *bring* this man's blood upon us
7. 6. that they should *bring* them into bondage
9. 2. [Saul] might *bring* them bound to Jerusalem. 21:
13. 32. we ³*bring* you good tidings of the promise [22. 5
14. 15. and ⁵*bring* you good tidings, that ye should turn
16. 37. let them come themselves and ³*bring* us out
23. 10. and *bring* him [Paul] into the castle
15. chief captain that he *bring* him [Paul] down

BRING

Acts 23. 17. *Bring* this young man unto the chief captain
20. Jews have agreed to ask thee to *bring* down Paul
Rom. 10. 6. Who shall ascend—to *bring* Christ down
7. (that is, to *bring* Christ up from the dead.)
1 *Cor.* 1. 28. that he might *bring* to nought the things
4. 5. who will both *bring* to light the hidden things
9. 27. I buffet my body, and *bring* it into bondage
Gal. 2. 4. that they might *bring* us into bondage
3. 24. law—our tutor to *bring* us unto Christ
1 *Th.* 4. 14. fallen asleep in Jesus will God *bring* with him
2 *Tim.* 4. 11. Take Mark, and *bring* him with thee
1 *Pet.* 3. 18. Christ—that he might *b.* us to God [heresies
2 *Pet.* 2. 1. teachers, who shall privily *bring* in destructive
Rev. 21. 24. kings of the earth do *bring* their glory into it
26. they shall *bring* the glory and the honour
see (bring to) nothing, bringeth, nurture, offering, put, set (forward), tell.

Bring *forth.*—*A.V.* ¹*bring out,* ²*brought forth.*

Mat. 1. 21. And she shall *bring forth* a son. 23 : *Lu.* 1. 31
3. 8. *B.f.* therefore fruit worthy of repentance. *Lu.* 3. 8
7. 18. good tree—*b. f.* evil fruit—corrupt tree *b.f.* good
Lu 8. 15. good heart—*bring f.* fruit with patience [fruit
15. 22. *Bring forth* quickly the best robe
Acts 12. 4. after the Passover to *bring* him [Peter] *forth*
6. when Herod was about to ²*bring* him *forth*
17. 5. sought to ²*b.* them [Paul and Silas] *f.* to the people
Rom. 7. 4. that we might *bring forth* fruit unto God
5. in our members to *bring forth* fruit unto death
see bear, bringeth.

Bring *fruit.*—*see (bear) fruit.*

Bringest.

Acts 17. 20. For thou *bringest*—strange things to our ears

Bringeth.—*A.V.* ¹*bring.* ²*bring forth,* ³*leadeth.*

Mat. 3. 10. every tree—*b.* not forth good fruit. 7. 19: *Lu.* 3. 9.
7. 17. good tree *bringeth* forth good fruit—corrupt tree *bringeth* forth evil fruit. *Lu.* 6. ²43
12. 35. *bringeth* forth good things—*b.* forth evil things.
13. 23. *bringeth* forth, some a hundredfold [*Lu.* 6. 45
52. householder, which *b.* forth out of his treasure
17. 1. Jesus—*b.* them up into a high mountain. *Mk.* 9. ³²
2 *Cor.* 11. 20. a man, if he ¹*bringeth* you into bondage
Heb. 1. 6. *bringeth* in the firstborn into the world
6. 7. *bringeth* forth herbs meet for them for whose sake
Jas. 1. 15. sin, when it is fullgrown, *bringeth* forth death
2 *Jno.* 10. one cometh unto you, and ¹*b.* not this teaching
see beareth, bearing, bearing.

Bringing.—*AV.* ¹*bringeth,* ²*brought,* ³*laid,* ⁴*shewing.*

Mat. 21. 43. to a nation *bringing* forth the fruits thereof
Mk. 2. 3. *bringing* unto him a man sick of the palsy
Lu. 8. 1. preaching and ⁴*b.* the good tidings of the kingdom
21. 12. ²*b.* you before kings and governors for my name's
24. 1. unto the tomb, *b.* the spices which they had ! sake
Acts 5. 16. from the cities round—Jerusalem, *b.* sick folk
25. 7. ³*bringing* against him [Paul] many—charges
Rom. 7. 23. and *b.* me into captivity under the law of sin
2 *Cor.* 10. 5. *bringing* every thought into captivity [men
Tit. 2. 11. grace of God hath appeared, ¹*b.* salvation to all
Heb. 2. 10. in *bringing* many sons unto glory, to make
7. 19. and a *bringing* in thereupon of a better hope
se brought.

Broad.

Mat. 7. 13. wide is the gate, and *broad* is the way
23. 5. [scribes and Pharisees] make *b.* their phylacteries

Broided *A. V.*,—*see braided.*

BROTHER

Broiled.

Lu. 24. 42. they gave him a piece of a *broiled* fish

Broken.

Mat. 21. 44. he that falleth on this stone shall be *b. Lu.*
Mk. 5. 4. and the fetters *broken* in pieces [20. 18
Lu. 12. 39. left his house to be *b.* through. *Mat.* 24. 43
Jno. 7. 23. that the law of Moses may not be *broken*
10. 35. word of God came (and the scripture cannot be *b.*)
19. 31. asked of Pilate that their legs might be *broken*
36. A bone of him [Jesus] shall not be *broken*
Acts 20. 11. [Paul] had *broken* the bread, and eaten
Rom. 11. 17. if some of the branches were *broken* off
19. Thou wilt say then, Branches were *broken* off
20. by their unbelief they were *broken* off
Rev. 2. 27. as the vessels of the potter are *b.* to shivers
see brake, break, rent.

Broken *fast.*—*A.V.* ¹*dined.*

Jno. 21. 15. when they had ¹*broken* their *fast,* Jesus saith

Broken *pieces.*—*A.V.* ¹*broken meat,* ²*fragments.*

Mat. 14. 20. that which remained over of the ²*broken pieces.*
Mat. 15. ¹37; *Mk.* 8. ¹8; *Lu.* 9. ²17
Mk. 6. 43. they took up ²*broken pieces,* twelve basketfuls
8. 19. how many baskets full of ²*broken pieces* took ye up?
Jno. 6. 12. Gather up the ²*broken pieces* which remain over
13. filled twelve baskets with ²*broken pieces*

Broken *up—Broke up.*—*A.V.* ¹*broken up.*

Mk. 2. 4. roof—when they had *broken* it *up,* they let down
Acts 13. 43. Now when the synagogue ¹*broke up*

Brood.

Lu. 13. 34. as a hen gathereth her own *b.* under her wings

Brook.

Jno. 18. 1. Jesus—went—with his disciples over the *brook*

Brother.—*A.V.*—¹*husband.*

Mat. 10. 21. *brother* shall deliver up *b.* to death. *Mk.* 13. 12
Mk. 12. 19. If a man's *b.* die, and leave a wife. *Lu.* 20. 28
Lu. 6. 42. *Brother,* let me cast out the mote that is in
15. 27. Thy *brother* is come; and thy father hath killed
32. this thy *brother* was dead, and is alive again
Jno. 11. 2. Mary—whose *brother* Lazarus was sick
19 Jews—to console them concerning their *brother*
Acts 9. 17 Ananias—said, *Brother* Saul, the Lord. 22. 13
12. 2. [Herod] killed James the *b.* of John with the sword
21. 20. Thou seest, *b.,* how many thousands there are
Rom. 16. 23. Erastus—saluteth you, and Quartus the *b.*
1 *Cor.* 5. 11. if any man that is named a *b.* be a fornicator
6. 6. but *brother* going to law with *brother*
7. 12. If any *brother* hath an unbelieving wife
14. the unbelieving wife is sanctified in the ¹*brother*
15. the *b.* or the sister is not under bondage in such
8. 11. the *brother* for whose sake Christ died
2 *Cor.* 8. 18. the *b.* whose praise in the gospel is spread
12. 18. I exhorted Titus, and I sent the *brother* with him
Gal. 1. 19. saw I none, save James the Lord's *brother*
2 *Th.* 3. 6. withdraw yourselves from every *b.* that walketh
15. not as an enemy, but admonish him as a *brother*
Philem. 7. saints have been refreshed through thee, *b.*
16. more than a servant, a *brother* beloved. *Col.* 4. 9
20. Yea, *brother,* let me have joy of thee in the Lord
Jas. 1. 9. But let the *brother* of low degree glory
2. 15. If a *brother* or sister be naked, and in lack of
4. 11. He that speaketh against a *brother,* or judgeth
Rev. 1. 9. I John, your *brother* and partaker with you

BROTHER

His Brother.
Mat. 5. 22. angry with his b.—shall say to his b., Raca
18. 35. if ye forgive not every one his brother
22. 24. his b. shall marry—seed unto his b. Mk. 12. 19:
25. left his wife unto his brother [Lu. 20. 28
Mk. 6. 17. sake of Herodias, his brother Philip's wife
Jno. 1. 41. [Andrew] findeth first his own brother Simon
Rom. 14. 13. no man put a stumblingblock in his b.'s way
1 Th. 4. 6. transgress, and wrong his brother in the matter
Heb. 8. 11. And every man his b., saying, Know the Lord
Jas. 4. 11. He that—judgeth his brother—judgeth the law
1 Jno. 2. 9. hateth his brother, is in the darkness. 11
10. He that loveth his brother abideth in the light
3. 10. neither he that loveth not his brother. 4. 20
12. Cain was of the evil one, and slew his b.—and his b's.
15. Whosoever hateth his brother. 4. 20 [righteous
17. hath the world's goods, and beholdeth his b. in need
4. 21. that he who loveth God love his brother also
5. 16. If any man see his brother sinning a sin.

My Brother.
Mat. 12. 50. he is my brother, and sister. Mk. 3. 35
18. 21. Lord, how oft shall my brother sin against me
Lu. 12. 13. Master, bid my brother divide the inheritance
Jno. 11. 21. been here, my brother had not died. 32
1 Cor. 8. 13. if meat maketh my b. to stumble—not my b.
2 Cor. 2. 13. I found not Titus my brother [to stumble

Our Brother.
2 Cor. 1. 1. Timothy our brother. Col. 1. 1: 1 Th. 3. 2:
Philem 1: Heb 13. 23
8. 22. And we have sent with them our brother [Titus]
2 Pet 3. 15 even as our beloved brother Paul also

Thy Brother.
Mat. 5. 23. rememberest that thy brother hath aught
24. first be reconciled to thy brother
7. 3. mote that is in thy brother's eye. 5: Lu. 6. 41, 42
4. say to thy b, Let me cast out the mote. Lu. 6. 42
18. 15. if thy b. sin against thee—gained thy b. Lu. 17. 3
Mk. 6. 18. not lawful for thee to have thy brother's wife
Jno 11. 23. Thy brother shall rise again [thy b.?
Rom. 14. 10. why dont thou judge thy b.?—set at nought
15. if because of meat thy brother is grieved
21. nor to do anything whereby thy brother stumbleth

Brotherhood
1 Pet 2. 17. Love the brotherhood. Fear God

Brotherly kindness, love.—see love of the brethren.

Brought.—A.V. ¹accompanied, ²bringing, ³carried, ⁴drew, ⁵led, ⁶made, ⁷raised, ⁸thrust.
Mat. 10. 18. before governors and kings shall ye be b. for
12. 25. divided against itself is b. to desolation. Lu. 11. 17
14. 11. was b. in a charger—gave b. it to her. Mk. 6. 28
17. 16. I b. him to thy disciples, and they could not cure
18. 24. one was brought unto him, which owed him
19. 13. b. unto him little children. Mk. 10. 13: Lu. 18. 15
27. 3. Judas—brought back the thirty pieces of silver
Mk. 4. 21. Is the lamp brought to be put under the bushel
8. 23. blind man—and ⁶brought him out of the village
Lu. 2. 22. they b. him [Jesus] up to Jerusalem, to present
27. and when the parents brought in the child Jesus
3. 5. every mountain and hill shall be brought low
4. 16. Nazareth, where he had been brought up
5. 11. when they had brought their boats to land
7. 37. she [Mary Mag.] b. an alabaster cruse of ointment

BROW

Lu. 10. 15. thou shalt be ⁸brought down unto Hades
34. set him on his own beast, and brought him to an inn
18. 40. Jesus—commanded him to be brought unto him
22. 54. away, and b. him into the high priest's house
23. 1. rose up, and ⁶brought him [Jesus] before Pilate
14. Ye b. unto me this man, as one that perverteth
Jno. 4. 33. Hath any man brought him aught to eat?
Acts 5. 21. to the prison-house to have them brought
7. 45. our fathers, in their turn, brought in with Joshua
9. 8. led him by the hand, and b. him into Damascus
27. Barnabas took him, and brought him to the apostles
30. they brought him [Paul] down to Cæsarea
13. 23. according to promise ⁷b. unto Israel a Saviour
15. 3. being brought on their way by the church
16. 16. maid—which brought her masters much gain
20. had b. them [Paul and Silas] unto the magistrates
19. 19. them that practised curious arts b. their books
24. silver shrines of Diana, brought no little business
33. they ⁴brought Alexander out of the multitude
37. For ye have brought hither these men
20. 12. And they brought the lad [Eutychus] alive
38. they ¹brought him [Paul] on his way unto the ship
21. 5. wives and children, brought us on our way
28. Paul—brought Greeks also into the temple
34. commanded him [Paul] to be ³b. into the castle. 22. 24
37. Paul was about to be ⁶brought into the castle
22. 3. I am a Jew—but brought up in this city
30. and brought Paul down, and set him before them
25. 6. [Festus] commanded Paul to be brought. 17
Rom.15.24. see you in my journey, and to be b. on my way
1 Cor. 6. 12. I will not be brought under the power of any
9. 19. I ⁵brought myself under bondage to all
Gal. 2. 4. because of the false brethren privily brought in
1 Th. 3. 6. Timothy—brought us glad tidings of your faith
1 Tim. 5. 10. if she hath brought up children
6. 7. for we brought nothing into the world
2 Tim. 1. 10. brought life and incorruption to light
Heb. 13. 11. whose blood is brought into the holy place
20. God of peace who brought again from the dead
1 Pet. 1. 13. on the grace that is to be brought unto you
2 Pet. 2. 5. when he ¹brought a flood upon the world
19. of the same is he also brought into bondage
see bring, bringing, came, carried, carrieth, foster brother, go, set, stand.

Brought forth.—A.V. ¹bare, ²begat, ³brought out.
Mat. 1. 25. knew her not till she had b. forth a son. Lu. 2. 7
13. 26. blade sprang up, and brought forth fruit
Mk. 4. 8. and brought forth, thirtyfold, and sixtyfold
Lu. 1. 57. Elisabeth—brought forth a son
8. 8. into the good ground, and grew, and ¹b. forth fruit
12. 16. The ground of a certain rich man b. f. plentifully
Acts 12. 17. how the Lord had ³b. him f. out of the prison
Jas. 1 18. Of his own will he ¹b. us f. by the word of truth
5. 18. and the earth brought forth her fruit
Rev. 12.13. the woman which brought forth the man child
see bring (forth), brought out, delivered, ripe, yielded.

Brought out.—A.V. ¹brought forth.
Jno. 19. 13. Pilate—¹brought Jesus out
Acts 5. 19. opened the prison doors and ¹brought them out
16. 30. and b. them out, and said, Sirs, what must I do
39. when they had b. them out, they asked them to go
see brought forth, led forth.

Brought to pass A.V.—see come to pass.

Brow.
Lu. 4. 29. led him [Jesus] unto the brow of the hill

BRUISE

Bruise—d.
Mat. 12. 20. A *bruised* reed shall he not break
Lu. 4. 18. To set at liberty them that are *bruised*
Rom. 16. 20. the God of peace shall *bruise* Satan

Bruising.
Lu. 9. 39. hardly departeth from him, *bruising* him sorely

Brute A.V.—*see (without) reason.*

Budded.
Heb. 9. 4. holding the manna, and Aaron's rod that *budded*

Buffet.—A.V. ¹*buffeted*, ²*keep under.*
Mat. 26. 27. Then did they spit in his face, and ¹*buffet* him.
   Mk. 14. 65
1 Cor. 9. 27. but I ²b. my body, and bring it into bondage
2 Cor. 12. 7. a messenger of Satan to *buffet* me [Paul]

Buffeted.
1 Cor. 4. 11. hunger, and thirst, and are naked, and are b.
1 Pet. 2. 20. when ye sin, and are *buffeted* for it
   see buffet.

Build—A.V. ¹*edify.*
Mat. 16. 18. upon this rock I will *build* my church
   23. 29. for ye *build* the sepulchres. Lu. 11. 47, 48
   26. 61. temple—and to *build* it in three days. Mk. 14. 58
Lu. 12. 18. I will pull down my barns, and *build* greater
   14. 28. which of you, desiring to *build* a tower
   30. This man began to *build*, and was not able to finish
Acts 7. 49. What manner of house will ye *build* me?
   15. 16. I will ¹b. again the tabernacle—b. again the ruins
   20. 32. word of his grace, which is able to *build* you up
Rom. 15. 20. I might not b. upon another man's foundation
Gal. 2. 18. if I b. up again those things which I destroyed
1 Th. 5. 11. exhort one another, and ¹*build* each other up
   see buildeth.

Builded—A.V. ¹*built*, ²*founded.*
Lu. 6. 48. not shake it: because it had been well ²*builded*
   17. 28. days of Lot—they planted, they *builded*
Eph. 2. 22. in whom ye also are *builded* together
Col. 2. 7. rooted and ¹*builded* up in him
Heb. 3. 4. For every house is *builded* by some one
   see built.

Builder—s.
Mat. 21. 42. The stone which the *builders* rejected. Mk.
   12. 10 : Lu. 20. 17 : 1 Pet. 2. 17
Acts 4. 11. the stone which was set at nought of you the b.
Heb. 11. 10. city—whose *builder* and maker is God

Buildest
Mat. 27. 40. temple, and b. it in three days. Mk. 15. 29

Buildeth.—A.V. ¹*build.*
1 Cor. 3. 10. another b. thereon—heed how he b. thereon
   12. But if any man ¹*buildeth* on the foundation

Building.—A.V. ¹*built*, ²*edification*, ³*edifying.*
Lu. 6. 48. he is like a man ¹*building* a house
Jno. 2. 20. Forty and six years was this temple in *building*
1 Cor. 3. 9. ye are God's husbandry, God's *building*
2 Cor. 5. 1. we have a *building* from God
   10. 8. (which the Lord gave for ²*building* you up. 13. ³10
Eph. 2. 21. in whom each several *building*, fitly framed

BURIED

Eph. 4. 12. unto the ³*building* up of the body of Christ
   16. unto the ³*building* up of itself in love
Jude 20. *building* up yourselves on your most holy faith
Rev. 21. 18. the *building* of the wall thereof was jasper
   see creation.

Buildings.
Mat. 24. 1. disciples—to shew him the b. of the temple
Mk. 13. 1. Master, behold—what manner of *buildings*!
   2. Seest thou these great b? there shall not be left

Built.—A.V. ¹*builded.*
Mat. 7. 24. wise man, which *built* his house upon the rock
   26. man, which b. his house upon the sand. Lu. 6. 49
   21. 33. and *built* a tower. Mk. 12. 1
Lu. 4. 29. the hill whereon their city [Nazareth] was *built*
   7. 5. and himself [centurion] *built* us our synagogue
Acts 7. 47. But Solomon *built* him a house
1 Cor. 3. 14. work shall abide which he *built* thereon
Eph. 2. 20. being *built* upon the foundation of the apostles
Heb. 3. 3. he that ¹*built* the house hath more honour
   4. but he that *built* all things is God
1 Pet. 2. 5. as living stones, are *built* up a spiritual house
   see builded, building.

Bulls.
Heb. 9. 13. if the blood of goats and *bulls*. 10. 4

Bundle—s.
Mat. 13. 10. tares, and bind them in *bundles* to burn them
Acts 28. 3. Paul had gathered a *bundle* of sticks

Burden.—A.V.—¹*burdensome*, ²*chargeable.*
Mat. 11. 30. my yoke is easy, and my *burden* is light
   20. 12. which have borne the *burden* of the day
Acts 15. 28. to lay upon you no greater *burden* than these
   21. 3. there the ship was to unlade her *burden*
2 Cor. 11. 9. I was not a ²*burden* on any man
   12. 16. I myself was not a ¹*burden* to you?
   14. I will not be a ¹*burden* to you: for I seek not yours
Gal. 6. 5. each man shall bear his own *burden*
Rev. 2. 24. I cast upon you none other *burden*

Burden—ed.—A.V. ¹*charged*, ²*chargeable.*
2 Cor. 5. 4. in this tabernacle do groan, being *burdened*
   12. 16. I did not myself *burden* you; but, being crafty
1 Th. 2. 9. that we might not ²*burden* any of you. 2 Th. 3. ²8
1 Tim. 5. 16. let not the church be ¹*burdened*
   see distressed.

Burdens.
Mat. 23. 4. they bind heavy b. and grievous. Lu. 11. 46
Lu. 11. 46. touch not the b. with one of your fingers
Gal. 6. 2. Bear ye one another's *burdens*

Burdensome.
2 Cor. 11. 9. I kept myself from being *burdensome* unto
1 Th. 2. 6. when we might have been b., as apostles of
   see burden.

Burial.
Mat. 26. 12. she [Mary] did it to prepare me for *burial*
   see buried.

Buried.—A.V. ¹*burial.*
Mat. 14. 12. disciples—took up the corpse, and b. [John]
Lu. 16. 22. and the rich man also died, and was *buried*
Acts 2. 29. David, that he both died and was *buried*
   5. 6. young men—carried him [Ananias] out and b. him

BURIED

Acts 5. 9. which have *buried* thy husband are at the door
10. and they carried her [Sapphira] out and *buried* her
8. 2. And devout men ¹*buried* Stephen
Rom. 6. 4. were *b.* therefore with him through baptism
1 *Cor.* 15. 4. that he was *b.*; and that he hath been raised
Col. 2. 12. having been *buried* with him in baptism

Burn.

Mat. 13. 30. bind them [tares] in bundles to *burn* them
Lu. 1. 9. his [Zacharias] lot was to—*burn* incense
3. 17. he will *b.* up with unquenchable fire. *Mat.* 3. 12
1 *Cor.* 7. 9. it is better to marry than to *burn*
2 *Cor.* 11. 29. who is made to stumble, and I *burn* not?
Rev. 17. 16. and shall *burn* her [harlot] utterly with fire
see burning.

Burned.—*A.V.* ¹*burnt.*

Mat. 13. 40. tares are gathered up and ¹*burned* with fire
22. 7. destroyed those murderers, and ¹*b.* their city
Jno. 15. 6. cast them into the fire, and they are *burned*
Acts. 19. 19. brought their books together, and *b.* them
Rom. 1. 27. men—*burned* in their lust one toward another
1 *Cor.* 3. 15. If any man's work shall be ¹*b.*, he shall suffer
13. 3. if I give my body to be *burned*, but have not love
Heb. 6. 8. whose end is to be *burned* [with fire
12. 18. a mount that might be touched, and that *burned*
13. 11. offering for sin, are ¹*burned* without the camp
2 *Pet.* 3 10. earth and the works—shall be ¹*burned* up
Rev. 18. 8. and she shall be utterly ¹*burned* with fire
see refined.

Burneth.—*A.V.* ¹*burning.*

Jno. 5. 35. He was the lamp that ¹*burneth* and shineth
Rev. 19. 20. lake of fire that ¹*burneth* with brimstone
21. 8. part shall be in the lake that *burneth* with fire

Burning.—*A.V.* ¹*burn.*

Lu. 12. 35. loins be girded about, and your lamps *burning*
24. 32. Was not our heart ¹*burning*—while he spake
Rev. 4. 5. seven lamps of fire *burning* before the throne
8. 8. as it were a great mountain *b.* with fire was cast
10. a great star, *burning* as a torch, and it fell
18. 9. look upon the smoke of her *burning.* 18
see burneth, scorching.

Burnished.—*A.V.* ¹*fine.*

Rev. 1. 15. and his feet like unto ¹*burnished* brass

Burnt.

Rev. 8. 7. part of the earth was *burnt* up—part of the trees was *burnt* up, and all green grass was *b.* up
see burned.

Burnt offerings.

Mk. 12. 33. more than all whole *burnt o.* and sacrifices
Heb. 10. 6. In whole *b. offerings* and sacrifices for sin. 8

Burst.—*A.V.* ¹*break.*

Mat. 9. 17. else the skins ¹*burst*, and the wine is spilled
Mk. 2. 22. else the wine will *burst* the skins. *Lu.* 5. 37
Acts 1. 18. and falling headlong, he [Judas] *burst* asunder

Bury.

Mat. 8. 21. suffer me first to go and *b.* my father. *Lu.* 9. 59
22. leave the dead to *bury* their own dead. *Lu.* 9. 60
27. 7. bought—the potter's field, to *bury* strangers in
Jno. 19. 40. as the custom of the Jews is to *bury*

Burying.

Mk. 14. 8. anointed my body aforehand for the *burying*
Jno. 12. 7. Suffer her to keep it against the day of my *b.*

Bush.

Mk. 12. 26. book of Moses—place concerning the *B. Lu.*
Lu. 6. 44. nor of a bramble *b.* gather they grapes ⌊20. 37
Acts 7. 30. Sinai, in a flame of fire in a *bush*
35. angel which appeared to him in the *bush*

Bushel.

Mat. 5. 15. lamp, and put it under the *b. Mk.* 4. 21 : *Lu.* 11. 33

Business.—*A.V.* ¹*craft,* ²*gain.*

Acts 6. 3. seven men—may appoint over this *business*
19. 24. Diana, brought no little ²*b.* unto the craftsmen
25. Sirs, ye know that by this ¹*b.* we have our wealth
1 *Th.* 4. 11. study to be quiet, and to do your own *business*
see house, diligence, matter.

Busybodies.

2 *Th.* 3. 11. some—that work not at all, but are *busybodies*
1 *Tim.* 5. 13. not only idle, but tattlers also and *busybodies*
see meddler.

Buy.

Mat. 14. 15. go into the villages, and *buy*—food. *Mk.* 6. 36
25. 9. go—to them that sell, and *buy* for yourselves
10. while they went away to *buy*, the bridegroom came
Mk. 6. 37. Shall we—*b.* two hundred pennyworth of bread
Lu. 9. 13. except we should go and *buy* food for all this
22. 36. let him sell his cloke, and *buy* a sword [people
Jno. 4. 8. disciples were gone away into the city to *b.* food
6. 5. Whence are we to *buy* bread, that these may eat?
13. 29. *Buy* what things we have need of for the feast
1 *Cor.* 7. 30. those that *buy*, as though they possessed not
Rev. 3. 18. I counsel thee to *buy* of me gold refined
13. 17. no man should be able to *buy* or to sell, save he
see trade.

Buyeth.

Mat. 13. 44. selleth all that he hath, and *buyeth* that field
Rev. 18. 11. no man *buyeth* their merchandise any more

By and by *A.V.*—*see immediately.*

C.

Cage *A.V.*—*see hold.*

Calf.

Lu. 15. 23. and bring the fatted *calf*, and kill it
27. thy father hath killed the fatted *calf*
30. thou killedst for him the fatted *calf*
Acts 7. 41. And they [Israel] made a *calf* in those days
Rev. 4. 7. and the second creature like a *calf*

Call.—*A.V.* ¹*called,* ²*calling,* ³*count,* ⁴*say.*

Mat. 1. 21. thou shalt *call* his name JESUS. *Lu.* 1. 31
23. they shall *call* his name Immanuel
2. 15. Out of Egypt did I ¹*call* my son
9. 13. I came not to *c.* the righteous. *Mk.* 2. 17 : *Lu.* 5. 32
10. 25. much more shall they *c.* them of his household !
11. 16. children—which ²*c.* unto their fellows. *Lu.* 7. ³32
20. 8. *Call* the labourers, and pay them their hire

CALL

Mat. 22. 3. forth his servants to *call* them that were bidden
43. How then doth David in the spirit *call* him Lord
23. 9. *call* no man your father on the earth
Mk. 10. 49. Jesus—said, ¹C. ye him. And they c. the blind
15. 12. do unto him whom ye *call* the King of the Jews?
16. and they *call* together the whole band
Lu. 1. 13. and thou shalt *call* his name John
48. henceforth all generations shall *call* me blessed
6. 46. why *call* ye me, Lord, Lord, and do not the things
14. 12. dinner or a supper, *call* not thy friends
Jno. 4. 16. Jesus said—Go, *call* thy husband, and come
13. 13. Ye *call* me, Master, and, Lord : and ye say well
15. 15. No longer do I *call* you servants
Acts 2. 21. *call* on the name of the Lord shall be saved.
Rom. 10. 13
39. as many as the Lord our God shall *call* unto him
9. 14. authority—to bind all that *call* upon thy name
10. 28. I should not *call* any man common or unclean
32. Send therefore to Joppa, and *call* unto thee Simon
24. 14. after the Way which they *call* a sect, so serve I
25. when I have a convenient season, I will *call* thee
Rom. 9. 25. I will *call* that my people, which was not
10. 12. Lord—is rich unto all that *call* upon him
14. How then shall they *call* on him in whom
1 *Cor.* 1. 2. with all that *call* upon the name of our Lord
2 *Cor.* 1. 23. But I *call* God for a witness upon my soul
2 *Tim.* 2. 22. them that c. on the Lord out of a pure heart
Heb. 2. 11. he is not ashamed to *call* them brethren
10. 32. *call* to remembrance the former days
Jas. 5. 11. Behold, we ²*call* them blessed which endured
14. sick? let him *call* for the elders of the church
1 *Pet.* 1. 17. And if ye *call* on him as Father
Rev. 2. 2. didst try them which ¹*call* themselves apostles
see bid, calleth, fetch, make, name, reminded.

Called. — *A.V.* ¹calleth, ²cried, ³named, ⁴said, ⁵surname—d.

Mat. 1. 16. was born Jesus, who is *called* Christ
2. 7. Herod privily *called* the wise men, and learned
4. 18. Simon who is *called* Peter. 10. 2
21. their nets ; and he *called* them. *Mk.* 1. 20
10. 1. he *called* unto him his twelve disciples. *Mk.* 8. 1
25. If they have c. the master of the house Beelzebub
13. 55. is not his [Jesus] mother *called* Mary?
15. 10. And he c. to him the multitude. *Mk.*7. 14: 8. 34
18. 2. And he [Jesus] *called* to him a little child
20. 32. Jesus stood still, and *called* them [blind men]
22. 14. For many are *called*, but few are chosen
23. 7. and to be *called* of men, Rabbi
8. But be not ye *called* Rabbi
10. Neither be ye *called* masters
26. 3. the high priest, who was *called* Caiaphas
14. one of the twelve, who was *called* Judas Iscariot
27. 8. that field was *called*, The field of blood
16. they had then a notable prisoner, *called* Barabbas
17. Barabbas, or Jesus which is *called* Christ? 22
Mk. 6. 7. he ¹*called* unto him the twelve. 9. 35 : *Lu.* 9. 1
14. 72. And Peter c. to mind the word, how that Jesus
Lu. 1. 36. sixth month with her that was *called* barren
59. they would have *called* him Zacharias
61. none of thy kindred that is *called* by this name
62. signs to his father, what he would have him *called*
2. 21. *called* JESUS, which was so ³*called* by the angel
13. 12. And when Jesus saw her, he *called* her
15. 19. I am no more worthy to be *called* thy son. 21
19. 15. whom he had given the money, to be c. to him
22. 3. Judas who was ⁵*called* Iscariot
23. 13. Pilate *called* together the chief priests
Jno. 1. 48. Before Philip c. thee, when thou wast under

CALLED

Jno. 4. 25. Messiah cometh (which is *called* Christ)
5. 18. but also ¹*called* God his own Father
9. 11. The man that is *called* Jesus made clay
18. until they c. the parents of him that had received
24. So they c. a second time the man that was blind
10. 35. If he c. them gods, unto whom the word of God
11. 28. she went away, and *called* Mary her sister
15. 15. but I have *called* you friends
Acts 4. 18. And they *called* them, and charged them
5. 40. and when they had *called* the apostles unto them
9. 11. go to the street which is *called* Straight
10. 23. So he *called* them in and lodged them
13. 1. Symeon that was *called* Niger
2. for the work whereunto I have *called* them
7. Sergius Paulus—*called* unto him Barnabas and Saul
9. Saul, who is also *called* Paul
14. 12. And they *called* Barnabas, Jupiter
15. 22. Judas ⁵*called* Barsabbas
37. John also, who was ⁵*called* Mark
16. 10. God had *called* us for to preach the gospel
29. [jailor] *called* for lights, and sprang in
20. 17. *called* to him [Paul] the elders of the church
23. 6. resurrection of the dead I am c. in question. 24. 21
18. Paul the prisoner *called* me unto him
23. And he *called* unto him two of the centurions
24. 2. And when he was c., Tertullus began to accuse
26. 1. then we knew that the island was *called* Melita
Rom. 1. 1. Paul—*called* to be an apostle. 1 *Cor.* 1. 1
6. among whom are ye also, *called* to be Jesus Christ's
7. beloved of God, *called* to be saints. 1 *Cor.* 1. 2
8. 28. to them that are *called* according to his purpose
30. whom he foreordained, them he also c.—whom he c.
9. 24. even us, whom he also *called*, not from the Jews
1 *Cor.* 1. 9. through whom ye were c. into the fellowship
24. them that are *called*, both Jews and Greeks
26. not many mighty, not many noble, are *called*
7. 15. but God hath *called* us in peace
17. as God hath *called* each, so let him walk
18. Was any man *called* being circumcised ?—*called* in
20. each man abide in that calling wherein he was c.
21. Wast thou *called* being a bondservant?
22. For he that was c. in the Lord—was c. being free
24. wherein he was *called*, therein abide with God
8. 5. For though there be that are *called* gods
15. 9. that am not meet to be *called* an apostle [Paul]
Gal. 1. 6. from him that *called* you in the grace of Christ
15. God—*called* me through his grace
5. 13. For ye, brethren, were *called* for freedom
Eph. 2. 11. c. Uncircumcision by that which is *called*
4. 1. walk worthily of the calling wherewith ye were c.
4. ye were *called* in one hope of your calling
Col. 3. 15. to the which also ye were *called* in one body
4. 11. Jesus, which is *called* Justus
1 *Th.* 4. 7. God *called* us not for uncleanness, but in
2 *Th.* 2. 4. exalteth himself against all that is *called* God
14. whereunto he *called* you through our gospel
1 *Tim.* 6. 12. life eternal, whereunto thou wast *called*
20. knowledge which is falsely so *called*
2 *Tim.* 1. 9. who saved us, and c. us with a holy calling
Heb. 3. 13. so long as it is *called* To day
5. 4. but when he is *called* of God, even as was Aaron
9. 2. which is *called* the Holy place
3. which is *called* the Holy of holies
15. they that have been c. may receive the promise
11. 8. By faith Abraham, when he was *called*
16. not ashamed of them, to be *called* their God
24. Moses—refused to be *called* the son of Pharaoh's
Jas. 2. 23. Abraham—was *called* the friend of God
1 *Pet.* 1. 15. like as he which *called* you is holy

CALLED

1 Pet. 2. 9. excellencies of him who *called* you out of dark-
21. For hereunto were ye *called*. 3. 9.   [ness
5. 10. the God of all grace, who *c.* you unto his eternal
2 Pet. 1. 3. through the knowledge of him that *called* us
1 Jno. 3. 1. that we should be *called* children of God
Jude 1. to them that are *c.*, beloved in God the Father
Rev. 11. 8. great city, which spiritually is *called* Sodom
12. 9. serpent, he that is *called* the Devil and Satan
14. 18. ²c. with a great voice to him that had the sharp
17. 14. *called* and chosen and faithful
19. 11. he that sat thereon, *called* Faithful and True
see *accused, bidden, call, calleth, calling, gathered, intreat, named, reckoned.*

Called joined with *name*.
Mat. 1. 25. and he *called* his *name* JESUS. Lu. 2. 21
Lu. 1. 6]. none of thy kindred that is *called* by this *name*
Acts 9. 21. havock of them which *called* on this *name*?
15. 17. Gentiles, upon whom my *name* is *called*
Jas. 2. 7. the honourable *name* by the which ye are *called*?
Rev. 8. 11. *name* of the star is *called* Wormwood
19. 13. his *name* is *called* The Word of God

Shall, or *shalt,* or *should be* **Called.**
Mat. 2. 23. that he [Jesus] *should be called* a Nazarene
5. 9. peacemakers: for they *shall be called* sons of God
19. *shall be c.* least—*shall be c.* great in the kingdom
21. 13. My house *s. be c.* a house of prayer. *Mk.* 11. 17
Lu. 1. 32. and *shall be called* the Son of the Most High
35. that which is to be born *shall be called* holy
60. Not so; but he *shall be called* John
76. thou, child, *s. be c.* the prophet of the Most High
2. 23. openeth the womb *s. be called* holy to the Lord)
Jno. 1. 42. Simon—thou *shalt be called* Cephas
Rom. 7. 3. joined to another man, she *s. be c.* an adulteress
9. 7. In Isaac *shall* thy seed *be called*. *Heb.* 11. 18
26. There *shall* they *be called* sons of the living God

Callest.
Mk. 10. 18. Why *callest* thou me good? *Lu.* 18. 19

Calleth.—A. V. ¹*call*, ²*called.*
Mat. 22. 45. David then ¹*c.* him Lord. *Mk.* 12. 37: *Lu.* 20.
27. 47. This man [Jesus] *calleth* Elijah. *Mk.* 15. 35 [44
Mk. 3. 13. And he goeth up into the mountain, and *calleth*
10. 49. Be of good cheer: rise, he *c.* thee [blind man]
Lu. 15. 6. he *calleth* together his friends. 9
20. 37. when he *calleth* the Lord the God of Abraham
Jno. 10. 3. he *calleth* his own sheep by name
11. 28. The Master is here, and *calleth* thee
Rom. 4. 17. *c.* the things that are not, as though they were
9. 11. might stand, not of works, but of him that *calleth*
Gal. 5. 8. persuasion came not of him that *calleth* you
1 Th. 2. 12. God, who ²*calleth* you unto his own kingdom
5. 24. Faithful is he that *calleth* you, who will also do it
Rev. 2. 20. Jezebel, which *calleth* herself a prophetess
see *called, saith.*

Calling.—A. V. ¹*called*, ³*vocation.*
Mk. 3. 31. brethren—sent unto him, *calling* him
11. 21. And Peter *c.* to remembrance saith unto him
15. 44. Pilate—*calling* unto him the centurion
Lu. 7. 19. John *calling* unto him two of his disciples
Acts 7. 59. they stoned Stephen, *calling* upon the Lord
9. 41. [Peter] ¹*calling* the saints and widows
22. 16. wash away thy sins, *calling* on his name
Rom. 11. 29. gifts and the *c.* of God are without repentance
1 Cor. 1. 26. For behold your *calling*, brethren—not many
7. 20. Let each man abide in that *calling* wherein

CAME

Eph. 1. 18. that ye may know what is the hope of his *c.*
4. 1. beseech you to walk worthily of the ²*calling*
4. ye were called in one hope of your *calling*
Phil. 3. 14. the prize of the high *c.* of God in Christ Jesus
2 Th. 1. 11. God may count you worthy of your *calling*
2 Tim. 1. 9. saved us, and called us with a holy *calling*
Heb. 3. 1. brethren, partakers of a heavenly *calling*
1 Pet. 3. 6. Sarah obeyed Abraham, *calling* him lord
2 Pet. 1. 10. diligence to make your *c.* and election sure
see *call.*

Calm.
Mat. 8. 26. and there was a great *c. Mk.* 4. 39: *Lu.* 8. 24

Calves.
Heb. 9. 12. nor yet through the blood of goats and *calves*
19. Moses—took the blood of the *calves* and the goats

Came.—*A.V.* ¹*brought,* ²*came over,* ³*come,* ⁴*cometh,*
⁵*entered,* ⁶*kept,* ⁷*past,* ⁸*proceeded,* ⁹*resorted,*
¹⁰*returned,* ¹¹*sent,* ¹²*went.*
Mat. 1. 18. before they *c.* together she was found with child
2. 1. wise men from the east *came* to Jerusalem
9. star—*came* and stood over where the young child was
5. 17. not that I ³*c.* to destroy the law—I ³*c.* not to destroy,
7. 25. floods *came*, and the winds blew. 27 [but to fulfil
9. 1. crossed over, and *came* into his [Jesus] own city
13. I ³*c.* not to call the righteous, but sinners. *Mk.* 2. 17
20. issue of blood twelve years, *came* behind him.
28. the blind men *came* to him [*Mk.* 5. 27: *Lu.* 8. 44
10. 34. Think not that I ³*c.* to send peace—I *c.* not to send
35. I ⁸*came* to set a man at variance against his father
14. 6. when Herod's birthday ⁶*came*, the daughter
34. *came* to the land, unto Gennesaret. *Mk.* 6. 53
15. 12. Then *came* the disciples, and said. 17. 19
25. she [Canaanitish woman] *c.* and worshipped him
29. Jesus—*came* nigh unto the sea of Galilee
18. 11. Son of man ³*came* to save [margin]. *Lu.* 19. ¹⁰
21. Then *came* Peter, and said to him, Lord, how oft
31. and *came* and told unto their lord. *Lu.* 14. 21
20. 20. *came* to him the mother of the sons of Zebedee
28. even as the Son of man *c.* not to be ministered unto
21. 28. he *c.* to the first, and said, Son, go work to-day
30. And he *came* to the second, and said likewise
32. For John *c.* unto you in the way of righteousness
25. 10. while they went away to buy, the bridegroom *c.*
36. I was in prison, and ye *came* unto me
26. 49. straightway he [Judas] *came* to Jesus
50. Then they *came* and laid hands on Jesus
60. many false witnesses *came*. But afterward *c.* two
73. they that stood by *came* and said to Peter
28. 1. first day of the week, *came* Mary Magdalene
13. His disciples *came* by night, and stole him away
Mk. 1. 29. they ⁵*came* into the house of Simon
45. they *came* to him from every quarter
3. 8. a great multitude—*came* unto him
5. 1. And they ²*came* to the other side of the sea
13. the unclean spirits ¹²*came* out, and entered
14. they ¹²*c.* to see what it was that had come to pass
7. 25. a woman—*came* and fell down at his feet
12. 28. one of the scribes *c.*, and heard them questioning
42. And there *came* a poor widow, and she cast in
14. 40. again he [Jesus] ¹⁰*came*, and found them sleeping
Lu. 2. 16. And they *c.* with haste, and found both Mary
3. 12. there *came* also publicans to be baptized
5. 15. great multitudes *c.* together. *Lu.* 23. 48: *Acts* 2. 6
9. 34. there *came* a cloud, and overshadowed them
35. a voice ⁷*came* out of the cloud, saying. 36
15. 17. But when he [prodigal son] *c.* to himself he said
20. And he arose, and *came* to his father

45

CAME

Lu. 22. 7. And the day of unleavened bread *came*
24. 23. when they found not his body, they *came*, saying
Jno. 1. 7. The same *came* for witness. ¹¹⁸
11. He *came* unto his own, and they that were his own
17. grace and truth *came* by Jesus Christ
31. for this cause ³*came* I baptizing with water
3. 2. [Nicodemus] *came* unto him by night. 7. 50 : 19. 39
23. and they *came*, and were baptized
4. 27. And upon this *came* his disciples
7. 45. The officers therefore *came* to the chief priests
8. 2. *c*. again into the temple, and all the people *c*. unto
14. I know whence I *came*, and whither I go   [him
42. for I ⁸*came* forth, and am come from God
9. 39. For judgement ⁵*came* I into this world
10. 10. I ⁹*came* that they may have life
35. them gods, unto whom the word of God *came*
41. And many ⁰*came* unto him
12. 9. common people—*came*, not for Jesus' sake only
21. these [Greeks] therefore *came* to Philip
27. But for this cause *came* I unto this hour
28. There *came* therefore a voice out of heaven
47. I *came* not to judge the world, but to save
20. 8. other disciple also, which *came* first to the tomb
19. Jesus *came* and stood in the midst   [to nought
Acts 5. 36. obeyed him, [Theudas] were dispersed, and ¹*c*.
8. 36. as they went on the way, they *came* unto a certain
39. when they [Philip and the eunuch] ⁸*c*. up out of the
40. till he [Philip] *came* to Cæsarea
10. 29. wherefore also I *came* without gainsaying
45. were amazed, as many as *came* with Peter
11. 5. by four corners ; and it *came* even unto me
12. 10. they [Peter and angel] *came* unto the iron gate
20. they *came* with one accord to him [Herod]
16. 1. [Paul] *came* also to Derbe and to Lystra
17. 13. Jews—*came* thither likewise, stirring up and
19. 18. Many also of them that had believed *came*
22. 11. being led by the hand—I *came* into Damascus
23. 14. And they [Jews] *came* to the chief priests
27. [Claudius Lysias] when I *came* upon them with the
33. when they [soldiers] *came* to Cæsarea
24. 17. after many years I *c*. to bring alms to my nation
28. 23. they *came* to him [Paul at Rome] into his lodging
Rom. 5. 13. judgement *came* unto all men—free gift *came*
20. the law ⁸*came* in beside, that the trespass might
7. 9. when the commandment *came*, sin revived
1 Cor. 2. 1. when I *c*. unto you, *c*. not with excellency of
14. 36. went forth ? or *came* it unto you alone ?
15. 21. since by man *came* death, by man *came* also the
2 Cor. 3. 7. I wrote this very thing, lest, when I *c*., I should
12. Now when I *came* to Troas for the gospel of Christ
Gal. 1. 21. Then I *came* into the regions of Syria
2. 12. that certain *c*. from James—but when they ⁸*came*
3. 23. But before faith *came*, we were kept in ward
4. 4. when the fulness of the time ⁸*came*, God sent forth
5. 8. This persuasion ⁴*came* not of him that calleth you
Eph. 2. 17. he *c*. and preached peace to you that were far
Phil. 4. 18. received from Epaphroditus the things that ¹¹*c*.
1 Th. 1. 5. how that our gospel *c*. not unto you in word only
1 Tim. 1. 15. Christ Jesus *c*. into the world to save sinners
2 Pet. 1. 17. when there *came* such a voice to him
21. no prophecy ever *came* by the will of man
1 Jno. 5. 6. This is he that *came* by water and blood
3 Jno. 3. when brethren *came* and bare witness   [holy ones
Jude 14. Behold, the Lord ⁴*came* with ten thousand of his
Rev. 7. 13. white robes, who are they, and whence *c*. they ?
   see befell, come, cometh, foot, fulfilled, gathered, returned, went,
      word of God.

Came down.—A.V. ¹*descended.*

Lu. 19. 6. And he [Zacchæus] made haste, and *came down*

CAMEST

Jno. 6. 41. I am the bread which *c. d.* out of heaven. 51, 58
Acts 9. 32. [Peter] *came d.* also to the saints which dwelt
15. 1. certain men *came down* from Judæa
21. 10. there *c. d.* from Judæa a certain prophet—Agabus
24 1. high priest Ananias ¹*came d.* with certain elders
Rev. 20. 9. fire *came d.* out of heaven, and devoured them
   see coming (down), descended, going down, come down.

Came forth.—A.V. ¹*came out*, ²*come*, ⁸*proceeded*, ⁴*went.*

Mk. 1. 38. preach there also; for to this end *came* I *forth*
6. 34. and he ¹*came forth* and saw a great multitude
Lu. 6. 19. for power ⁴*came forth* from him
Jno. 8. 42. for I ⁸*came forth* and am come from God
11. 44. He that was dead *came forth*, bound hand and foot
13. 3. things into his hands, and that he ⁸*c. f.* from God
16. 27. believed that I ¹*came forth* from the Father
17. 8. knew of a truth that I ¹*came forth* from thee
Rev. 19. 5. And a voice ¹*came forth* from the throne
21. even the sword which ⁸*came forth* out of his mouth
   see came out.

Came in.

Mat. 22. 11. But when the king *c. in* to behold the guests
Mk. 6. 25. she *c. in* straightway with haste unto the king
Lu. 1. 28. [Gabriel] *came in* unto her [Mary]
7. 45. since the time I *came in*, hath not ceased to kiss
Acts 5. 7. his [Ananias] wife, not knowing what was done,
10. young men *came in* and found her dead   [*came in*
Gal. 2. 4. who *came in* privily to spy out our liberty
   see went in.

Came near—*nigh A.V.*—*see draw, drew (nigh).*

Came out.—A.V. ¹*came forth*, ²*come out.*

Mat. 8. 32. they ¹*came out*, and went into the swine
34. all the city *came out* to meet Jesus
12. 44. return into my house whence I *c. o.* Lu. 11. 24
27. 32. as they *came out*, they found a man of Cyrene
Mk. 1. 26. unclean spirit, tearing him and crying with a
   loud voice, *came out* of him. Lu. 4. 35
9. 7. there *came* a voice *out* of the cloud, This is my
26. having cried out, and torn him much, he *came out*
Lu. 1. 22. when he [Zacharias] *c. out*, he could not speak
4. 41. devils also *came out* from many. Acts 8. 7
15. 28. and his father *came out*, and intreated him
Jno. 16. 28. I ¹*came out* from the Father
19. 5. Jesus therefore ¹*c. o.*, wearing the crown of thorns
34. and straightway there *came out* blood and water
Acts 7. 4. Then *came* he *out* of the land of the Chaldeans
16. 18. And it *came out* that very hour
Heb. 3. 16. did not all that *c. o.* of Egypt by Moses ?
Rev. 14. 15. another angel *came out* from the temple. 17
18. another angel *came out* from the temple
15. 6. there *came out* from the temple the seven angels
   see coming forth, come out, coming, went forth.

Came over A.V.—*see came.*

Came to pass.—A.V. ¹*done.*

Lu. 24. 21. is now the third day since these things ¹*c. to p.*
Jno. 19. 36. For these things ¹*c. to p.*, that the scripture
Acts 9. 3. it *came to pass* that he drew nigh unto Damascus
1 Th. 3. 4. even as it *came to pass*, and ye know

Camel.

Mat. 3. 4. John—had his raiment of *camel's* hair. Mk. 1. 6
19. 24. It is easier for a *c.* to go. Mk. 10. 25 : Lu. 18. 25
23. 24. which strain out the gnat, and swallow the *camel*

Camest.

Mat. 22. 12. Friend, how *camest* thou in hither

46

CAMEST

Jno. 6. 25. Rabbi, when *camest* thou hither?
16. 30. we believe that thou *camest* forth from God
Acts 9. 17. appeared unto thee in the way which thou c.

Camp.
Heb. 13. 11. an offering for sin, are burned without the *c.*
13. Let us therefore go forth unto him without the *c.*
Rev. 20. 9. and compassed the *camp* of the saints about

Candle *A.V.—see lamp.*

Candlestick—s.
Heb. 9. 2. wherein were the *candlestick*, and the table
Rev. 1. 12. I saw seven golden *candlesticks.* 13, 20 : 2. 1
2. 5. and will move thy *candlestick* out of its place
11. 4. the two olive trees and the two *candlesticks*
see stand.

Canker *A.V.—see gangrene.*

Cankered *A.V.—see rusted.*

Captain.
Jno. 18. 12. band and the chief *captain*, and the officers
Acts 4. 1. the *captain* of the temple. 5. 24
5. 26. Then went the *captain* with the officers. [28, 29
21. 31. tidings came up to the chief *c.* of the band. 22. 26,
32. when they saw the chief *captain.* 33, 37.
23. 17. Bring this young man unto the chief *captain.* 22.
24 : 23, 10, 18, 19, 22
24. 22. When Lysias the chief *captain* shall come down
see author.

Captains.
Mk. 6. 21. Herod—made a supper to his lords, and the high *c.*
Lu. 22. 4. Judas—communed with the chief priests and *c.*
52. Jesus said unto the chief priests, and *captains*
Acts 25. 23. Agrippa was come—with the chief *captains*
Rev. 6. 15. the princes, and the chief *c.*, and the rich
19. 18. that ye may eat—the flesh of *captains*

Captive.—*A.V.* ¹*take of you.*
Lu. 21. 24. shall be led *captive* into all the nations
2 *Cor.* 11. 20. if he devoureth you, if he taketh you ¹*captive*
Eph. 4. 8. he led captivity *captive*, And gave gifts
2 *Tim.* 2. 26. been taken *captive* by the Lord's servant
3. 6. take *captive* silly women laden with sins

Captives.
Lu. 4. 18. sent me to proclaim release to the *captives*

Captivity.
Rom. 7. 23. bringing me into *c.* under the law of sin
2 *Cor.* 10. 5. bringing every thought into *captivity*
Eph. 4. 8. he led *captivity* captive, And gave gifts
Rev. 13. 10. If any man is for *c.*, into *captivity* he goeth

Carcase—s.
Mat. 24. 28. Wheresoever the *c.* is, there will the eagles be
Heb. 3. 17. whose *carcases* fell in the wilderness ?

Care.—*A.V.* ¹*carefulness.*
Mat. 10. 34. the *care* of the world, and the deceitfulness
Lu. 10. 34. and brought him to an inn, and took *c.* of him
35. Take *care* of him ; and whatsoever thou spendest
1 *Cor.* 12. 25. the members should have the same *care* one
2 *Cor.* 7. 11. what earnest ¹*care* it wrought in you

CARRIED

2 *Cor.* 7. 12. your earnest *c.* for us might be made manifest
8. 16. God, which putteth the same earnest *care* for you
1 *Tim.* 3. 5. how shall he take *care* of the church of God ?)
see anxiety, careth, thought.

Care—d.
Lu. 10. 40. dost thou not *care* that my sister did leave me
Jno. 12. 6. not because he [Judas] *cared* for the poor
Acts 18. 17. Gallio *cared* for none of these things
1 *Cor.* 7. 21. called being a bondservant ? *care* not for it
Phil. 2. 20. no man likeminded, who will *care* truly

Careful—*A.V.* ¹*careth.*
1 *Cor.* 7. 32. unmarried is ¹*c.* for the things of the Lord. ¹34
33. that is married is ¹*c.* for the things of the world. ¹34
Tit. 3. 8. may be *careful* to maintain good works
see anxious, thought.

Carefully.—*A.V.* ¹*circumspectly,* ²*diligently,* ³*perfectly.*
Mat. 2. 7. Herod—wise men, and learned of them ²*c.* ²16
8. search out ²*carefully* concerning the young child
Acts 18. 25. he spake and taught ²*c.* the things concerning
26. unto him [Apollos] the way of God more ³*carefully*
Eph. 5. 15. Look therefore ¹*carefully* how ye walk
Heb. 12. 15. looking ²*c.* lest there be any man that falleth
see diligently.

Carefulness *A.V.—see care, cares.*

Cares.—*A.V.* ¹*carefulness.*
Mk 4. 19. *c.* of the world, and the deceitfulness. *Lu.* 8. 14
Lu. 21. 34. with surfeiting, and drunkenness, and *cares*
1 *Cor.* 7. 32. I would have you to be free from ¹*cares*

Carest—eth.—*A.V.* ¹*care.*
Mat. 22. 16. God in truth, and *c.* not for anyone. *Mk.* 12. 14
Mk. 4. 38. Master, *carest* thou not that we perish ?
Jno. 10. 13. is a hireling, and *careth* not for the sheep
1 *Cor.* 9. 9. Is it for the oxen that God ¹*careth*
1 *Pet.* 5. 7. anxiety upon him, because he *careth* for you
see careful.

Carnal.
Rom. 7. 14. but I am *carnal*, sold under sin
15. 27. also to minister unto them in *carnal* things
1 *Cor.* 3. 1. but as unto *carnal*, as unto babes in Christ
3. ye are yet *carnal*—are ye not *carnal*
9. 11. is it a greater matter if we shall reap your *c.* things ?
Heb. 7. 16. not after the law of a *carnal* commandment
9. 10. *c.* ordinances, imposed until a time of reformation
see flesh.

Carnally *A.V.—see flesh.*

Carousings.—*A.V.* ¹*banquetings.*
1 *Pet.* 4. 3. revellings, ¹*c.*, and abominable idolatries

Carpenter.
Mat. 13. 55. Is not this the *carpenter's* son ?
Mk. 6. 3. Is not this the *carpenter*, the son of Mary

Carriage *A.V.—see baggage.*

Carried.—*A.V.* ¹*brought,* ²*carrying,* ³*led.*
Mk. 15. 1. bound Jesus, and *carried* him away
Lu. 7. 12. there was *c.* out one that was dead [widow's son]
16. 22. beggar—he was *carried* away by the angels
24. 51. and was *carried* up into heaven [Jesus]

CARRIED

Acts 3. 2. certain man—was *carried*, whom they laid daily
5. 6. they *carried* him [Ananias] out and buried him
10. they ²*carried* her [Sapphira] out and buried her
15. that they even ¹*carried* out the sick into the streets
7. 16. they were *carried* over unto Shechem
19. 12. unto the sick were ¹c. away from his [Paul] body
Gal. 2. 13. Barnabas was *c.* away with their dissimulation
Eph. 4. 14. children, tossed to and fro and *carried* about
Heb. 13. 9. Be not *carried* away by divers—teachings
2 *Pet.* 3. 17. being ²c. away with the error of the wicked
Jude 12. clouds without water, *carried* along by winds
Rev. 12. 15. cause her to be *carried* away by the stream
17. 3. And he *carried* me away in the Spirit. 21. 10
see brought, carrying, driven, led.

Carrieth—ying.—*A.V.* ¹*brought*, ²*carried away.*
Mat. 1. 11. at the time of the ²c. away to Babylon. 12. ¹17
Rev. 17. 7. of the woman, and of the beast that *carrieth* her
see carried.

Carry.
Mk. 6. 55. to *c.* about on their beds those that were sick
11. 16. any man should *carry* a vessel through the temple
Lu. 10. 4. *Carry* no purse, no wallet, no shoes
Jno. 21. 18. and another shall gird thee, and *carry* thee
Acts 5. 9. they shall *carry* thee [Sapphira] out
7. 43. I will *carry* you away beyond Babylon
1 *Tim.* 6. 7. world, for neither can we *carry* anything out
see take (up).

Case—s.—*A.V.* ¹*cause.*
Mat. 19. 10. If the *case* of the man is so with his wife
Jno. 5. 6. knew that he had been now a long time in that *c.*
Acts 25. 14. Festus laid Paul's ¹*case* before the king
1 *Cor.* 7. 15. sister is not under bondage in such *cases*
see wise.

Cast.—*A.V.* ¹*drove*, ²*fallen*, ³*put*, ⁴*send*, ⁵*threw*, ⁶*thrust.*
Mat. 3. 10. hewn down, and *c.* into the fire. 7. 19; *Lu.* 3. 9
5. 25. to the officer, and thou be *c.* into prison. *Lu.* 12. 58
29. pluck it out, and *cast* it from thee—and not thy whole body be *cast* into hell. 30: 18. 8, 9
6. 30. and to-morrow is *cast* into the oven. *Lu.* 12. 28
7. 6. neither *cast* your pearls before the swine
13. 42. shall *cast* them into the furnace of fire. 50: *Jno.*15.6
47. like unto a net, that was *cast* into the sea
48. good into vessels, but the bad they *cast* away
15. 26. children's bread and *cast* it to the dogs. *Mk.* 7. 27
17. 27. [Peter] *cast* a hook, and take up the fish
18. 30. but went and *cast* him into prison
21. 21. Be thou taken up and *c.* into the sea. *Mk.* 11. 23
22. 13. *cast* him out into the outer darkness
25. 30. *cast* ye out the unprofitable servant
27. 44. were crucified with him *c.* upon him—reproach
Mk. 4. 26. as if a man should *cast* seed upon the earth
9. 22. oft-times it hath *cast* him both into the fire
42. about his neck, and he were *cast* into the sea
45. two feet to be *cast* into hell. 47: *Mat.* 18. 8, 9
11. 7. colt unto Jesus, and *cast* on him their garments
12. 41. multitude *cast* money—rich *cast* in much
42. a poor widow, and she ²*cast* in two mites
43. This poor widow *cast* in more than all. *Lu.* 21. 3
44. they all did *c.* in—she for her want did *c.* in. *Lu.* 21. 4
Lu. 1. 29. [Mary] *cast* in her mind what—salutation
12. 5. after he hath killed hath power to *cast* into hell
49. I came to ⁴*cast* fire upon the earth
13. 19. which a man took, and *cast* into his own garden
19. 43. thine enemies shall *cast* up a bank about thee
22. 41. was parted from them about a stone's *cast*
23. 19. [Barabbas] for murder, was *cast* into prison. 25

CAST

Lu. 23. 34. parting his garments—they *c.* lots. *Jno.* 19. 24
Jno. 2. 15. and ¹*cast* all out of the temple
3. 24. For John was not yet *cast* into prison
8. 7. without sin among you, let him first *cast* a stone
59. They took up stones therefore to *cast* at him
21. 6. *Cast* the net on the right side of the boat—They *c.*
7. Simon Peter—*cast* himself into the sea
Acts 12. 8. *Cast* thy [Peter] garment about thee
16. 23. they *cast* them [Paul and Silas] into prison
24. ⁶*cast* them into the inner prison
37. and have *cast* us into prison
22. 23. thew off their garments, and ⁵*cast* dust into the air
27. 17. fearing lest they should be ²*cast* upon the Syrtis
26. Howbeit we must be *cast* upon a certain island
29. lest haply we should be ²*cast* ashore   [board
43. they which could swim should *cast* themselves over-
1 *Cor.* 7. 35. not that I may *cast* a snare upon you
Heb. 10. 35. *Cast* not away therefore your boldness
Rev. 2. 10. the devil is about to *cast* some of you into prison
14. Balaam, who taught Balak to *cast* a stumblingblock
22. Behold, I do *cast* her into a bed
24. I ¹*cast* upon you none other burden
4. 10. elders—shall *cast* their crowns before the throne
8. 5. fire of the altar, and *cast* it upon the earth
7. and they were *cast* upon the earth
8. a great mountain burning with fire was *c.* into the sea
12. 4. the stars of heaven, and did *cast* them to the earth
13. when the dragon saw that he was *cast* down
14. 16. he that sat on the cloud ⁶*c.* his sickle upon the earth
19. angel ⁶*c.* his sickle into the earth—*c.* it into the wine-
18. 19. they *cast* dust on their heads, and cried   [press
21. as it were a great millstone, and *cast* it into the sea
19. 20. they twain were *cast* alive into the lake of fire
20. 3. and *cast* him [devil] into the abyss
10. the devil that deceived them was *cast* into the lake
14. death and Hades were *cast* into the lake of fire
15. written in the book of life, he was *cast* into the lake
see cast off, delivered, threw, thrown.

Cast down.—*A.V.* ¹*cast out*, ²*thrown.*
Mat. 4. 6. If thou art the son of God, *c.* thyself *d.* *Lu.* 4. 9
15. 30. blind, dumb—they *cast* them *down* at his feet
27. 5. [Judas] *cast down* the pieces of silver
2 *Pet.* 2. 4. angels when they sinned, but *c.* them *d.* to hell
Rev. 12. 9. dragon was ¹*c. d.*—¹*c. d.* to the earth—¹*c. d.* with
10. the accuser of our brethren is *cast down*   [him
18. 21. Babylon, the great city, be ²*cast down*
see lowly, smitten, throw, thrown.

Cast forth.—*A.V.* ¹*cast out*, ²*thrust out.*
Mat. 8. 12. but the sons of the kingdom shall be ¹*c. forth*
21. 39. *c.* him *f.* out of the vineyard. *Mk.* 12. 8; *Lu.*20.15
Mk. 7. 26. that he would *c. f.* the devil out of her daughter
Lu. 4. 29. rose up, and ²*c.* him [Jesus] *forth* out of the city
13. 28. kingdom of God, and yourselves ²*cast f.* without
20. 12. him also they wounded, and ¹*cast* him *forth*
Jno. 15. 6. abide not in me, he is *cast forth* as a branch

Cast off.—*A.V.* ¹*cast away.*
Rom. 11. 1. Did God ¹*cast off* his people?
2. God did not ¹*cast off* his people which he foreknew
13. 12. let us therefore *cast off* the works of darkness
see rejected, threw (off).

Cast out.—*A.V.* ¹*expelled*, ²*pull out.*
Mat. 5. 13. to be *c. out* and trodden under foot. *Lu.* 14. 35
7. 4. Let me ²*c. out* the mote out of thine eye. *Lu.* 6. ²42
5. Thou hypocrite, *cast out* first the beam—clearly to *cast out* the mote. *Lu.* 6. ²42

48

CAST

Mat. 7. 22. did we not—by thy name *cast out* devils
8. 16. he *cast out* the spirit with a word
31. If thou c. us o., send us away into the herd of swine
9. 33. when the devil was *cast out*, the dumb man spake
10. 1. over unclean spirits, to *cast* them *out*. *Mk.* 3. 15
8. raise the dead, cleanse the lepers, *cast out* devils
12. 24. This man doth not *c. out* devils, but by Beelzebub
27. by Beelzebub *c. o.* devils—sons *c.* them *o? Lu.* 11. 19
28. But if I by the Spirit of God *c. out* devils. *Lu.* 11. 20
15. 17. into the belly, and is *cast out* into the draught?
17. 19. Why could not we *c.* it *o.? Mk.* 9. 28 [*Lu.* 19. 45
21. 12. *c. out* all them that sold and bought. *Mk.* 11. 15:
39. *c.* him forth *o.* of the vineyard. *Mk.* 12. 8: *Lu.* 20. 15
Mk. 1. 34. and *cast out* many devils. 6. 13
3. 23. How can Satan *cast out* Satan?
9. 18. that they should *cast* it *out. Lu.* 9. 40
16. 9. Mary—from whom he had *cast out* seven devils
17. in my name shall they *cast out* devils
Lu. 6. 22. reproach you, and *cast out* your name as evil
11. 18. ye say that I *cast out* devils by Beelzebub
20. But if I by the finger of God *cast out* devils. 19
13. 32. Behold, I *cast out* devils and perform cures
Jno. 6. 37. him that cometh to me I will in no wise *c. out*
9. 34. dost thou teach us? And they *cast* him *out*
35. Jesus heard that they had *cast* him *out*
12. 31. now shall the prince of this world be *cast out*
Acts 7. 19. our fathers, that they should *c. out* their babes
21. when he was *cast out*, Pharaoh's daughter took him
58. and they *c.* him [Stephen] *out* of the city
13. 50. against Paul and Barnabas, and ¹*cast* them *out*
27. 19. third day they *cast out* with their own hands
Gal. 4. 30. *Cast out* the handmaid and her son
Rev. 12. 15. the serpent *cast out* of his mouth—water
16. the river which the dragon *cast out* of his mouth
see cast down, cast forth, throwing.

Castaway *A.V.—see rejected.*

Casteth.

Mat. 9. 34. By the prince of the devils *c.* he out devils. 12. 26.
1 *Jno.* 4. 18. perfect love *c.* out fear [*Mk.* 3. 22 : *Lu.* 11. 15
3 *Jno.* 10. he forbiddeth, and *c.* them out of the church
Rev. 6. 13. as a fig tree *casteth* her unripe figs

Casting.—*A.V.* ¹*cast*, ²*destruction*, ³*pulling.*

Mat. 4. 18. Peter, and Andrew—*c.* a net into. *Mk.* 1. 16
27. 35. his garments among them, *casting* lots. *Mk.* 15. 24
Mk. 1. 39. throughout all Galilee, preaching and ¹*c.* out devils
9. 38. we saw one *c.* out devils in thy name. *Lu.* 9. 49
10. 50. And he, *casting* away his garment, sprang up
Lu. 11. 14. he was *casting* out a devil which was dumb
21. 1. that were *c.* their gifts into the treasury. *Mk.* 12. ¹43
2. a certain poor widow *casting* in thither two mites
Rom. 11. 15. the *c.* away of them is the reconciling of the
2 *Cor.* 10. 4. before God to the ³*c.* down of strong holds]
5. *casting* down imaginations, and every high thing
8. for building you up, and not for ²*c.* you down]. 13. ¹¹⁰
1 *Pet.* 5. 7. *casting* all your anxiety upon him

Castle.

Acts 21. 34. him [Paul] to be brought into the *castle.* 22. 24
37. Paul was about to be brought into the *castle*
23. 10. bring him [Paul] into the *castle*
16. entered into the *castle*, and told Paul
32. [So the soldiers] returned to the *castle*

Castor and Pollux *A.V.—see The Twin Brothers,*
proper names.

CAUSED

Catch.

Mk. 12. 13. Herodians, that they might *catch* him in talk
Lu. 5. 10. Fear not; from henceforth thou shalt *c.* men
11. 54. wait for him, to *c.* something out of his mouth

Catcheth *A.V.—see snatcheth.*

Cattle.—*A.V.* ¹*beasts.*

Jno. 4. 12. [Jacob] drank—and his sons, and his *cattle?*
Rev. 18. 13. wheat, and ¹*c.*, and sheep; and merchandise
see sheep.

Caught.

Acts 8. 39. the Spirit of the Lord *caught* away Philip
27. 15. the ship was *caught*, and could not face the wind
2 *Cor.* 12. 2. one *caught* up even to the third heaven [Paul]
4. how that he was *caught* up into Paradise
16. being crafty, I *caught* you with guile
1 *Th.* 4 17. we that are alive—be *caught* up in the clouds
Rev. 12. 5. her child was *caught* up unto God
see (laid) hold, seized, taken, took, they took.

Cause.

Mat. 5. 32. saving for the *cause* of fornication [21. 16
10. 21. and *c.* them to be put to death. *Mk.* 18. 12: *Lu.*
19. 3. lawful for a man to put away his wife for every *c?*
Lu. 8. 47. women—declared—for what *c.* she touched him
23. 22. I have found no *c.* of death in him. *Acts* 13. 28
Jno. 15. 25. They hated me without a *cause* [come?
Acts 10. 21. Peter—said—what is the *c.* wherefore ye are
19. 40. this day's riot, there being no *cause* for it
23. 28. to know the *cause* wherefore they accused him
28. 18. there was no *cause* of death in me [Paul]
2 *Cor.* 7. 12. I wrote not for his *cause*—nor for his *cause*
Col 4. 16. this epistle—*c.* that it be read also in the church
2 *Tim.* 1. 12. For the which *cause* I suffer also [brethren
Heb. 2. 11. for which *cause* he is not ashamed to call them
see cause, causing, manner.

For this Cause.—*A.V.* ¹*besides,* ²*therefore,* ³*these causes.*

Mat. 19. 5. *For this cause* shall a man leave his father and
mother. *Mk.* 10. 7.: *Eph.* 5. 31
Jno. 6. 51. ²*For this c.* have I said unto you, that no man
12. 18. *F. t. c.* also the multitude went and met him
27. But *for this cause* came I unto this hour
30. ²*F. t. c.* they could not believe, for that Isaiah said
Acts 26. 21. ³*F. t. c.* the Jews seized me [Paul] in the temple
28. 20. *For this cause* therefore did I intreat you to see
Rom. 1. 26. *F. t. c.* God gave them up unto vile passions
4. 16. ²*For this cause* it is of faith, that it may be
13. 6. For *for this cause* ye pay tribute also
1 *Cor.* 4. 17. *For this cause* have I sent unto you Timothy
11. 10. *f. t. c.* ought the woman to have a sign of authority
30. *For this cause* many among you are weak
2 *Cor.* 13. 10. ²*For this c.* I write these things while absent
Eph. 3. 1. *For this c.* I Paul, the prisoner of Christ Jesus
14. *For this cause* I bow my knees unto the Father
Col. 1. 9. *For this cause* we also—do not cease to pray
1. *Th.* 2. 13. And *f. t. c.* we also thank God without ceasing.
3. 5. *For this cause* I also—sent that I might know [³. ²⁷
2 *Th.* 2 11. *for this c.* God sendeth them a working of error
1 *Tim.* 1. 16. howbeit *for this cause* I obtained mercy
Tit 1. 5. *For this cause* left I thee in Crete
Heb. 9. 15. *f. t. c.* he is the mediator of a new covenant
2 *Pet.* 1. 5. *for this* very *cause* adding—all diligence
see end.

Caused.—*A.V.* ¹*grieved me.*

Jno. 11. 37. have *caused* that this man also should not die?
Acts 15. 3. [Paul and Barnabas] *c.* great joy unto all the
2 *Cor.* 2. 5. if any hath *c.* sorrow, he hath ¹*c.* sorrow [brethren

CAUSETH

Causeth.
Rev. 13. 16. he *causeth* all, the small and the great
  see leadeth, maketh, worketh.
Causes A.V.—*see for this cause.*
Causing.—A.V. ¹*cause.*
Rom. 16. 17. mark them which are ¹*causing* the divisions
Cave—s.—A.V. ¹*dens.*
Jno. 11. 38. Now it was a *cave*, and a stone lay against it
Heb. 11. 38. wandering in—¹*c.*, and the holes of the earth
Rev. 6. 15. every—freeman, hid themselves in the ¹*caves*
  see holes.
Cease.—A.V. ¹*leaving.*
Acts 13. 10. wilt thou not *c.* to pervert [Saul to Elymas]
1 Cor. 13. 8. whether there be tongues, they shall *cease*
Eph. 1. 16. *c.* not to give thanks for you, making mention
Col. 1. 9. we also—do not *cease* to pray and make request
Heb. 6. 1. Wherefore let us ¹*c.* to speak of the first principles
2 Pet. 2. 14. having eyes—that cannot *cease* from sin
Ceased.
Mat. 14. 32. the wind *ceased*. Mk. 4. 39: 6. 51
Lu. 7. 45. I came in, hath not *ceased* to kiss my feet
  8. 24. they *ceased*, and there was a calm
  11. 1. when he *ceased*, one of his disciples said
Acts 5. 42. they *ceased* not to teach and to preach Jesus
  20. 1. after the uproar was *ceased*, Paul having sent
  31. by the space of three years I *c.* not to admonish
  21. 14. we *ceased*, saying, The will of the Lord be done
Heb. 10. 2. Else would they not have *ceased* to be offered
1 Pet. 4. 1. hath suffered in the flesh hath *ceased* from sin
  see done (away), rested.
Ceaseth—ing.
Acts 6. 13. This man *ceaseth* not to speak words
1 Th. 1. 3. remembering without *c.* your work of faith
  2. 13. we also thank God without *ceasing*
  5. 17. pray without *ceasing*
  see earnestly, unceasing.
Celestial.
1 Cor. 15. 40. There are also *c.* bodies—glory of the *c.* is one
Cell.—A.V. ¹*prison.*
Acts 12. 7. a light shined in the ¹*cell*—smote Peter
Cellar.—A.V. ¹*secret place.*
Lu. 11. 33. lighted a lamp, putteth it in a ¹*cellar*
Censer.
Heb. 9. 4. Holy of holies; having a golden *censer*
Rev. 8. 3. another angel—having a golden *censer*
  5. And the angel taketh the *censer*
Centurion—s.
Mat. 8. 5. there came unto him a *centurion*, beseeching
  8. the *centurion* answered and said. 13
  27. 54. Now the *centurion*, and they that were with him
Mk. 15. 39. when the *c.*, which stood by over against him
  44. Pilate—calling unto him the *centurion*
  45. learned it of the *c.*, he granted the corpse to Joseph
Lu. 7. 2. a certain *centurion's* servant—was sick
  23. 47. when the *centurion* saw what was done
Acts 10. 1. Cornelius by name, a *centurion* of the band
  22. Cornelius a *centurion*, a righteous man
  21. 32. took soldiers, and *centurions*, and ran down
  22. 26. when the *c.* heard it, he went to the chief captain.
  23. 17. Paul called unto him one of the *centurions* [25
  23. [chief captain] called unto him two of the *c.*
  24. 23. [Felix] gave order to the *centurion*
  27. 1. delivered Paul—to a *centurion* named Julius. 6

CHAMBERS

Acts 27. 11. the *centurion* gave more heed to the master
  43. But the *centurion*, desiring to save Paul
Certain.
Mat 18. 23. of heaven likened unto a *certain* king. 22. 2
  20. 20. [Zebedee's wife] asking a *certain* thing of him
Mk. 14. 57. there stood up *certain*, and bare false witness
Lu. 10. 38. he entered into a *certain* village. 17. 12
  11. 27. a *certain* woman—lifted up her voice
  18. 9. this parable unto *c.* which trusted in themselves
  21. 2. a *certain* poor widow casting in thither two mites
  23. 19. Barabbas: one who for a *certain* insurrection
  24. 22. *certain* women of our company amazed us
  24. *certain* of them that were with us went to the tomb
Jno. 5. 4. an angel—went down at *certain* seasons [margin]
Acts 9. 19. [Saul] was *certain* days with the disciples
  10. 48. prayed they him [Peter] to tarry *certain* days
  12. 1. Herod—put forth his hands to afflict *certain*
  15. 24. have heard that *certain* which went out from us
  17. 28. *certain* even of your own poets have said
  25. 26. Of whom I [Festus] have no *certain* thing to write
Rom. 15. 26. and Achaia to make a *certain* contribution
1 Cor. 4. 11. buffeted, and have no *certain* dwelling-place
Gal. 2. 12. For before that *certain* came from James
Heb. 4. 7. he again defineth a *certain* day, saying in David
  10. 27. a *certain* fearful expectation of judgement
Jude 4. there are *certain* men crept in privily
  see one, somewhere.
Certainly.
Lu. 23. 47. *Certainly* this was a righteous man
Certainty.
Lu. 1. 4. mightest know the *c.* concerning the things
Acts 21. 34. could not know the *certainty* for the uproar
  22. 30. desiring to know the *c.*, wherefore he was accused
Certify A.V.—*see (make) known.*
Chaff.
Mat. 3. 12. the *chaff* he will burn up. Lu. 3. 17
Chain—s—A.V. ¹*bonds.*
Mk. 5. 3. no man—bind him, no, not with a *chain* ²rent
  4. [demoniac] bound with fetters and *c.*—*c.* had been
Acts 12. 7. his [Peter's] *chains* fell off from his hands
  28. 20. of the hope of Israel I am bound with this *chain*
Eph. 6. 20. for which I am an ambassador in ¹*chains*
2 Tim. 1. 16. Onesiphorus—was not ashamed of my *chain*
Rev. 20. 1. angel coming—and a great *chain* in his hand
  see pits, bonds.
Bound with Chains.—*see bound.*
Chalcedony.
Rev. 21. 19. the third, *chalcedony*
Chamber.—A.V. ¹*closet*, ²*room.*
Mat. 6. 6. when thou prayest, enter into thine inner ¹*c.*
Acts 1. 13. into the upper ²*c.*, where they were abiding
  9. 37. they laid her [Dorcas] in an upper *chamber*
  39. brought him [Peter] into the upper *chamber*
  20. 8. there were many lights in the upper *chamber*
Chambering.
Rom. 13. 13. not in *chambering* and wantonness
Chambers.—A.V. ¹*closets.*
Mat. 24. 26. Behold, he is in the inner *chambers*
Lu. 12. 3. spoken in the ear in the inner ¹*chambers*

CHAMBERLAIN

Chamberlain.
Acts 12. 20. made Blastus the king's *c.* their friend
   see treasurer.

Chance.
Lu. 10. 31. by *chance* a certain priest was going down
1 *Cor.* 15. 37. but a bare grain, it may *chance* of wheat

Change—d.
Acts 6. 14. shall *change* the customs which Moses delivered
29. 6. *c.* their minds, and said that he [Paul] was a god
Rom. 1. 23. *changed* the glory of the incorruptible God
26. their women *changed* the natural use into that
1 *Cor.* 15. 51. not all sleep, but we shall all be *changed.* 52
Gal. 4. 20. to *change* my voice; for I am perplexed
Heb. 1. 12. As a garment, and they shall be *changed*
7. 12. For the priesthood being *c.*—a *c.* also of the law
   see exchange, fashion, transformed.

Changers.
Jno. 2. 14. and the *changers* of money sitting
15. [Jesus] poured out the *changers'* money

Charge.—*A.V.*—[1]*accusation*, [2]*appointed*, [3]*command*,
[4]*commandment*—*s*, [5]*declare*, [6]*heritage.*

Mat. 4. 6. He shall give his angels *c.* concerning thee. *Lu.*
Acts 7. 60. Lord, lay not this sin to their *charge* {4. 10
15. 5. and to [2]*charge* them to keep the law of Moses
16. 18. I [3]*charge* thee in the name of Jesus Christ
24. [jailor] having received such a *charge*, cast them into
23. 29. nothing laid to his [Paul's] *c.* worthy of death
25. 18. accusers stood up, they brought no [1]*c.* of such evil
Rom. 8. 33. Who shall lay anything to the *c.* of God's elect?
1 *Cor.* 7. 10. the married I give [3]*c.*, yea not I, but the Lord
9. 18. That—I may make the gospel without *charge*
11. 17. But in giving you this [5]*charge*, I praise you not
1 *Th.* 4. 2. For ye know what [4]*charge* we gave you
1 *Tim.* 1. 3. that thou mightest *c.* certain men not to teach
5. But the end of the [4]*charge* is love
18. This *charge* I commit unto thee, my child Timothy
5. 21. I *charge* thee in the sight of God. 6. 13: 2 *Tim.* 4. 1
6. 17. *Charge* them that are rich in this present world
Tit. 1. 5. appoint elders in every city, as I gave thee [2]*charge*
1 *Pet.* 5. 3. neither as lording it over the [6]*c.* allotted to you
   see account, adjure, command, over.

Chargeable *A.V.*—*see burden.*

Charged—*A.V.*—[1]*command*—*ed.*
Mat. 9. 30. Jesus strictly *charged* them. *Mk.* 1. 43
10. 5. These twelve Jesus sent forth, and [1]*c.* them. *Mk.* 6. 18
12. 16. and *c.* them that they should not make. *Mk.* 3. 12
16. 20. Then *c.* he the disciples that they should tell no
Mk. 5. 43. And he *c.* them much that no man. 7. 36 |man
7. 36. but the more he *charged* them, so much the more
8. 15. and he *c.* them, saying, Take heed, beware of the
30. he *charged* them that they should tell. 9. 9
Lu. 5. 14. And he *charged* him to tell no man. *Lu.* 8. 56
9. 21. But he *charged* them, and commanded them
Acts 1. 4. he [1]*c.* them not to depart from Jerusalem
5. 28. We straitly [1]*c.* you not to teach in this name. 140
10. 42. and he [1]*charged* us to preach unto the people
1 *Th.* 4. 11. work with your hands, even as we [1]*c.* you
   see burdened, charging, commanded, dealt (with), rebuked, testifying.

Charger.
Mat. 14. 8. Give me here in a *c.* the head of John. *Mk.* 6. 25
11. his head was brought in a *charger*. *Mk.* 6. 28

CHEER

Charges.—*A.V.* [1]*complaints*, [2]*crimes.*
Acts 21. 24. and be at *charges* for them
25. 7. bringing against him [Paul] many and grievous [1]*c.*
27. not withal to signify the [2]*charges* against him
1 *Cor.* 9. 7. What soldier ever serveth at his own *charges* ?

Charging.—*A.V.* [1]*charged*, [2]*commandment.*
Acts 16. 23. *c.* the jailor to keep them [Paul and Silas]
23. 22. captain let the young man go, [1]*charging* him
30. [2]*charging* his accusers also to speak against him
2 *Tim.* 2. 14. *charging* them in the sight of the Lord

Chariot—*s.*
Acts 8. 28. [eunuch] sitting in his *chariot*, and was reading
29. unto Philip, Go near, and join thyself to this *chariot*
38 [eunuch] commanded the *chariot* to stand still
Rev. 9. 9. sound of their wings was as the sound of *chariots*
18. 13. merchandise of horses and *chariots* and slaves

Charitably *A.V.*—*see in love.*

Charity *A.V.*—*see love.*

Feasts of **Charity** *A.V.*—*see love feasts.*

Chaste.
Tit. 2. 5. to be soberminded, *chaste*, workers at home
1 *Pet.* 3. 2. beholding your *c.* behaviour coupled with fear
   see pure.

Chasten.—*A.V.* [1]*corrected.*
Heb. 12. 9. we had the fathers of our flesh to [1]*chasten* us
Rev. 3. 19. As many as I love, I reprove and *chasten*

Chastened.
1 *Cor.* 11. 32. when we are judged, we are *c.* of the Lord
2 *Cor.* 6. 9. as *chastened*, and not killed
Heb. 12. 10. for a few days *c.* us as seemed good to them

Chasteneth.
Heb. 12. 6. whom the Lord loveth he *chasteneth*
7. what son is there whom his father *chasteneth* not ?

Chastening.—*A.V.* [1]*chastisement*, [2]*nurture.*
Eph. 6. 4. nurture them in the [2]*chastening*—of the Lord
Heb. 12. 5. regard not lightly the *chastening* of the Lord
7. It is for *chastening* that ye endure
8. But if ye are without [1]*chastening*—not sons
11. All *c.* seemeth for the present to be not joyous

Chastise
Lu. 23. 16. I will therefore *c.* him, and release him. 22.

Chastisement *A.V.*—*see chastening.*

Cheek.
Mat. 5. 39. whosoever smiteth thee on thy right *c.*, turn
Lu. 6. 29. him that smiteth thee on the one *cheek* offer

Cheer.—*A.V.* [1]*comfort.*
Mat. 9. 2. Son, be of good *cheer*; thy sins are forgiven
22. Daughter, be of good [1]*cheer*; thy faith hath
14. 27. Be of good *cheer*; it is I. *Mk.* 6. 50
Mk. 10. 49. Be of good [1]*cheer* : rise, he calleth thee
Jno. 16. 33. be of good *c.*; I have overcome the world
Acts 23. 11. the Lord stood by him, and said, Be of good *cheer*
27. 22. [Paul said] be of good *c.*: for there shall be no
25. Wherefore, sirs, be of good *cheer* : for I believe God
36. Then were they all of good *cheer*

51

CHEERFUL

Cheerful.—*A.V.* ¹*merry.*

2 *Cor.* 9. 7. God loveth a *cheerful* giver
Jas. 5. 13. Is any ¹*cheerful*? let him sing praise

Cheerfully.

Acts 24. 10. I [Paul] do *cheerfully* make my defence

Cheerfulness.

Rom. 12. 8. he that sheweth mercy, with *cheerfulness*

Cherisheth.

Eph. 5. 29. nourisheth and c. it, even as Christ also the
1 *Th.* 2. 7. as when a nurse c. her own children [church

Cherubim.—*A.V.* ¹*Cherubims.*

Heb. 9. 5. ¹*cherubim* of glory overshadowing the mercy-seat

Chickens.

Mat. 23. 37. even as a hen gathereth her *chickens*

Chief.—*A.V.* ¹*first*, ²*highest*, ³*uppermost*

Mat. 23. 6. ³*chief* place at feasts—*chief* seats in the synagogues. *Mk.* 12. ³39 : *Lu.* 20. ²46
Mk. 6. 21. Herod—made a supper to—the c. men of Galilee
Lu. 14. 7. he marked how they chose out the *chief* seats
       8. sit not down in the ²*chief* seat; lost haply a more
   19. 2. Zaccheus; and he was a *chief* publican
   22. 26. he that is *chief*, as he that doth serve
Acts 13. 50. and the *chief* men of the city, and stirred up
   14. 12. Paul, Mercury, because he was the *chief* speaker
   15. 22. Judas—and Silas, *chief* men among the brethren
   17. 4. and of the *chief* women not a few
   19. 31. certain also of the *chief* officers of Asia
   21. 31. *chief* captain of the band. 32, 33, 37 : 22. 24, 26, 27, 28 : 23. 10, 17, 18, 19, 22
   24. 7. *chief* captain Lysias came [margin]. 22
   28. 7. *chief* man of the island, named Publius
   17. called together those that were the *chief* of the Jews
Eph. 2. 20. himself being the c. corner stone. 1 *Pet.* 2. 6
1 *Tim.* 1. 15. to save sinners; of whom I am *chief*
   16. that in me as ¹*chief* might Jesus Christ shew forth
1 *Pet.* 5. 4. when the *chief* Shepherd shall be manifested
see first, prince, principal.

Chief priests.—*A.V.* ¹*high priest.*

Mat. 2. 4. [Herod] gathering—*chief priests* and scribes
   16. 21. many things of the elders and *chief priests*
   20. 18. delivered unto the *chief priests* and scribes
   26. 14. Judas—went unto the *chief priests*. *Mk.* 14. 10
   47. swords and staves, from the *chief priests*. *Mk.* 14. 43
   59. c. p. and the whole council sought false. *Mk.* 14.55
   27. 12. accused by the *chief priests*. *Mk.* 15. 3 : *Lu.* 23. 10
   41. *chief priests* mocking him. *Mk.* 15. 31
   62. c. *priests* were gathered together
Mk. 8. 31. rejected by—the *chief priests*. *Lu.* 9. 22
   14. 1. *chief priests*—sought how they might take him
Lu. 19. 47. *chief priests*—sought to destroy him
   22. 2. c. p.—sought how they might put him to death
   23. 4. Pilate said unto the *chief priests*—I find no fault
Jn. 7. 32. *chief priests*—sent officers to take him
   18. 3. received—soldiers, and officers from the *chief p.*
   35. Thine own nation and the *chief priests* delivered
   19. 15. *chief p.* answered, We have no king but Cæsar
Acts 9. 14. hath authority from the *chief p.* to bind. 26. 10
   22. 30. commanded the c. p. and all the council to come
   25. 2. ¹*chief priests* and the principal men of the Jews

Also *Mat.* 21. 15, 23, 45 : 26. 3 : 27. 1, 3, 6 : 27. 20 : 28. 11.
       Mk. 10. 33 : 11. 18, 27 : 14. 53 : 15. 1, 10, 11. *Lu.*
       20. 19 : 22. 4, 52, 66 : 23.13 : 21.20. *Jno.* 11. 47, 57 :
       12. 10 : 19. 6, 21. *Acts* 4. 23 : 5. 24.

CHILDLESS

Chiefest.

2 *Cor.* 11. 5. not a whit behind the very c. apostles. 12. 11
see first.

Chiefly.

2 *Pet.* 2. 10. *chiefly* them that walk after the flesh
see especially, first (of all).

Child.—*A.V.* ¹*children*, ²*damsel*, ³*son.*

Mat. 1. 18. she was found with *child* of the Holy Ghost
   23. Behold, the virgin shall be with *child*
   2. 8. Go [wise men] and search out—the young *child*
   9. star—stood over where the young *child* was
   11. [wise men] saw the young *child* with Mary
   13. Arise and take the young *child* and his mother—
       seek the young *child* to destroy him. 20.
   14. he [Joseph] arose and took the young *child*. 21
   20. they are dead that sought the young *child's* life
   10. 21. to death, and the father his *child*. *Mk.* 13. ³12
   18. 2. [Jesus] called to him a little *child*, and set him
   4. therefore shall humble himself as this little *child*
   5. whoso shall receive one such little *child*
   24. 19. them that are with *child*. *Mk.* 13. 17 : *Lu.* 21. 23
Mk. 5. 39. the ²*child* is not dead, but sleepeth. 26
   40. the father of the ²*child*—goeth in where the ²c. was
   41. taking the ²*child* by the hand, he saith unto her
   9. 21. come unto him? And he said, From a *child*
   36. a little *child*, and set him in the midst. *Lu.* 9. 47
   10. 15. the kingdom of God as a little *child*. *Lu.* 18. 17
   12. 19. leave a wife behind him, and leave no ¹*child*
Lu. 1. 7. they had no c., because that Elisabeth was barren
   59. they came to circumcise the *child* [John Baptist]
   66. What then shall this *child* be?
   76. Yea and thou, *child*, shalt be called the prophet
   80. And the *child* grew, and waxed strong. 2. 40
   2. 5. with Mary—being great with *child*
   17. which was spoken to them about this *child* [Jesus]
   27. when the parents brought in the *child* Jesus
   34. Behold, this *child* is set for the falling and rising
   9.38. look upon my son; for he is mine only *child*
   48. Whosoever shall receive this little *child*
Jno. 4.49. Sir, come down ere my *child* die [nobleman]
   16. 21. delivered of the *child*, she remembereth no more
Acts 7. 5. when as yet he [Abraham] had no *child*
1 *Cor.* 13. 11. When I was a *child*, I spake as a *child*, I felt
       as a *child*, I thought as a *child*
Gal. 4. 1. so long as the heir is a *child*, he differeth nothing
Phil. 2. 22. as a ³*child* serveth a father, so he served with me
1 *Th.* 5. 3. as travail upon a woman with *child*
1 *Tim.* 1. 2. unto Timothy, my true ³*child* in faith
   18. This charge I commit unto thee, my ³*child* Timothy
2 *Tim.* 1. 2. to Timothy, my beloved ³*child*
   2. 1. therefore, my ³*child*, be strengthened in the grace
Tit. 1. 4. Titus, my true ³*child* after a common faith
Philem. 10. I beseech thee for my ³*child*—Onesimus
Heb. 11. 23. Moses—they saw he was a goodly *child*
Rev. 12. 2. she was with *child*: and she crieth out
   4. dragon stood—he might devour her *child*
   5. man *child*—her *child* was caught up unto God
see babe, boy, servant, son.

Childbearing.

1 *Tim.* 2. 15. she shall be saved through the *childbearing*

Childish.

1 *Cor.* 13. 11. I am become a man, I have put away c. things

Childless.—*A.V.* ¹*without children.*

Lu. 20. 29. the first took a wife, and died ¹*childless.* ¹28

CHILDREN

Children.—*A.V.* ¹*daughters*, ²*sons*.
Mat. 2. 16. Herod—slew all the male *c*.—in Bethlehem
18. Rachel weeping for her *children*
3. 9. stones to raise up *children* unto Abraham. *Lu.* 3. 8
7. 11. know how to give good gifts unto your *c*. *Lu.* 11. 13
10. 21. *children* shall rise up against parents. *Mk.* 13. 12
11. 16. *children* sitting in the market-places. *Lu.* 7. 32
14. 21. five thousand men, beside women and *children*
15. 26. not meet to take the *children's* bread. *Mk.* 7. 22
38. four thousand men, beside women and *children*
18. 25. commanded him to be sold, and his wife, and *c*.
19. 20. that hath left—mother, or *c. Mk.* 10. 29; *Lu.* 18. 29
21. 15. saw—the *children* that were crying in the temple
22. 24. If a man die, having no *children*, his brother
23. 37. how often would I have gathered thy *c. Lu.* 13. 34
27. 25. His blood be on us, and on our *children*
Mk. 7. 27. And he said—Let the *children* first be filled
28. dogs under the table eat of the *children's* crumbs
9. 37. shall receive one of such little *c*. in my name
10. 24. *C*., how hard is it for them that trust in riches
30. shall receive a hundredfold—mothers, and *children*
Lu. 1. 17. turn the hearts of the fathers to the *children*
7. 35. And wisdom is justified of all her *children*
11. 7. my *children* are with me in bed [brethren
14. 26. any man—hateth not his—wife, and *children*, and
19. 44. dash thee to the ground, and thy *children*
20. 31. the seven also left no *children*, and died
23. 28. weep for yourselves, and for your *children*
Jno. 8. 39. If ye were Abraham's *children*, ye would do
21. 5. Jesus—saith—*Children*, have ye aught to eat?
Acts 13. Brethren, *children* of the stock of Abraham
33. God hath fulfilled the same unto our *children*
21. 5. with wives and *children*, brought us on our way
21. telling them not to circumcise their *children*
Rom. 8. 17. if *children*, then heirs; heirs of God [all *c*.
9. 7. neither, because they are Abraham's seed, are they
8. *c*. of the flesh that are *c*. of God; but the *c*. of the
11. the *children* being not yet born [promise
1 *Cor.* 4. 14. to admonish you as my beloved ²*children*
14. 20. Brethren, be not *children* in mind
2 *Cor.* 6. 13. (I speak as unto my *children*)
12. 14. *c*. ought not to lay up—parents for the *children*
Gal. 4. 3. when we were *children*, were held in bondage
25. for she is in bondage with her *children*
27. For more are the *c*. of the desolate than of her
28. we, brethren, as Isaac was, are *children* of promise
31. we are not *children* of a handmaid
Eph. 2. 3. and were by nature *children* of wrath
4. 14. that we may be no longer *children*, tossed to and fro
5. 1. Be ye therefore imitators of God, as beloved *children*
8. walk as *children* of light
6. 1. *Children*, obey your parents in the Lord. *Col.* 3. 20
Phil. 2. 15. harmless, ²*children* of God without blemish
Col. 3. 21. Fathers, provoke not your *children*
1 *Th.* 2. 7. as when a nurse cherisheth her own *children*
11. we dealt—as a father with his own *children*
1 *Tim.* 3. 4. having his [bishop] *children* in subjection
12. deacons—ruling their *children* and their own houses
5. 4. if any widow hath *children* or grandchildren
10. if she hath brought up *children*
14. younger widows marry, bear *children*
Tit. 1. 6. husband of one wife, having *children* that believe
2. 4. young women—to love their *children*
Heb. 2. 13. I and the *children* which God hath given me
14. Since then the *children* are sharers in flesh
1 *Pet.* 1. 14. as *c*. of obedience, not fashioning yourselves
3. 6. whose ¹*children* ye now are, if ye do well
2 *Pet.* 2. 14. in covetousness; *children* of cursing
1 *Jno.* 3. 1. we should be called ²*children* of God

CHOSE

1 *Jno.* 3. 2. now are we ²*children* of God
10. *children* of God are manifest, and the *c*. of the devil
2 *Jno.* 1. unto the elect lady and her *children*
4. found certain of thy *children* walking in truth
13. The *children* of thine elect sister salute thee
3 *Jno.* 4. to hear of my *children* walking in the truth
Rev. 2. 23. I will kill her *children* with death
see babes, child, childless, sons, works.

Children of God.—*A.V.* ¹*sons* of God.
Jno. 1. 12. gave he the right to become ¹*children of God*
11. 52. gather together into one the *children of God*
Rom. 8. 16. that we are *children of God.* 1 *Jno.* 3. ¹²
21. liberty of the glory of the *children of God*
9. 8. children of the flesh that are *children of God*
1 *Jno.* 3. 1. we should be called ¹*children of God*
10. In this the *children of God* are manifest
5. 2. we love the *children of God*, when we love God
see sons of God.

Children of Israel.
Mat. 27. 9. whom certain of the *children of Israel* did price
Lu. 1. 16. many of the *c. of I.* shall he [John Bap.] turn
Acts 7. 23. to visit his [Moses] brethren the *c. of Israel*
37. Moses, which said unto the *children of Israel*
9. 15. [Saul] bear my name before—*children of Israel*
10. 36. word which he [God] sent unto the *c. of Israel*
Rom. 9. 27. If the number of the *c. of Israel* be as the sand
2 *Cor.* 3. 7. *c. of I.* could not look—upon the face of Moses. 13
Heb. 11. 22. made mention of the departure of the *c. of I.*
Rev. 2. 14. Balak to cast a stumblingblock before the *c. of*
7. 4. sealed out of every tribe of the *c. of Israel* [*Israel*

Little Children.—*A.V.* ¹*young children*.
Mat. 18. 3. become as little *c*., ye shall in no wise enter
19. 13. Then were there brought unto him *l. c. Mk.* 10. ¹¹³
14. Suffer the *l. c.*, and forbid them not. *Mk.* 10. 14: *Lu.*
Jno. 13. 33. *Little c.*, yet a little while I am with you [18. 16
Gal. 4. 19. My *little children*, of whom I am again in travail
1 *Jno.* 2. 1. *little c.*, these things write I unto you. 12
13. I have written unto you, *little children*
18. *Little children*, it is the last hour
28. And now, my *little children*, abide in him
3. 7. My *little children*, let no man lead you astray
18. My *little children*, let us not love in word
4. 4. Ye are of God, my *little children*
5. 21. My *little children*, guard yourselves from idols

Choice.
Acts 15. 7. Brethren, ye know how—God made *c*. among you

Choke—d.
Mat. 13. 7. thorns grew up, and *c*. them. *Mk.* 4. 7: *Lu.* 8. 7
22. deceitfulness of riches, *choke* the word. *Mk.* 4. 19
Mk. 5. 13. swine—were *choked* in the sea. *Lu.* 8. 33
Lu. 8. 14. as they go on their way they are *c*. with cares

Choose.—*A.V.* ¹*chosen*.
Jno. 6. 70. Did not I ¹*choose* you the twelve
15. 16. ye did not ¹*choose* me, but I chose you
Acts 15. 22. to ¹*choose* men out of their company. ¹²⁵
1 *Cor.* 1. 28. and the things that are despised, did God ¹*c*.
Phil. 1. 22. then what I shall *choose* I wot not
Jas. 2. 5. did not God ¹*choose* them that are poor

Choosing.
Heb. 11. 25. [Moses] *choosing* rather to be evil entreated

Chose.—*A.V.* ¹*chosen*.
Mk. 13. 20. but for the elect's sake, whom he ¹*chose*, he
Lu. 6. 13. [Jesus] *c*. from them twelve—named apostles
14. 7. when he marked how they *c*. out the chief seats

CHOSE

Jno. 15. 16. Ye did not choose me, but I ¹*chose* you
19. I ¹*c*. you out of the world, therefore the world hateth
Acts 6. 5. they *chose* Stephen, a man full of faith
13. 17. The God of this people Israel *chose* our fathers
15. 40. Paul *chose* Silas, and went forth   [things
1 *Cor.* 1. 27. God ¹*c*. the foolish things—God ¹*c*. the weak
Eph. 1. 4. ¹*c*. us in him before the foundation of the world
2 *Th.* 2. 13. for that God ¹*chose* you from the beginning

Chosen.

Mat. 12. 18. Behold, my servant whom I have *chosen*
22. 14. For many are called, but few *chosen*
Lu. 10. 42. Mary hath *chosen* the good part
23. 35. if this is the Christ of God, his *chosen*
Jno. 13. 18. I know whom I have *chosen*
Acts 1. 2. Holy Ghost unto the apostles whom he had *c.*
24. shew of these two the one whom thou hast *chosen*
9. 15. for he [Saul] is a *chosen* vessel unto me
10. 41. unto witnesses that were *chosen* before of God
Rom. 16. 13. Salute Rufus the *chosen* in the Lord
Rev. 17. 14. called and *chosen* and faithful
see choose, chose, appointed, enrolled, elect.

Christ, *Jesus Christ.—see proper names.*
also blood, grace, preach.

Christian—s.—*see proper names.*

Christs.—*see proper names.*

Chrysolite.

Rev. 21. 20. the seventh, *chrysolite*

Chrysoprase.—*A.V.* ¹*chrysoprasus.*

Rev. 21. 20. the tenth, ¹*chrysoprase*

Church.—*A.V.* ¹*churches.*

Mat. 16. 18. upon this rock I will build my *church*
18. 17. tell it unto the *c.:* and if he refuse to hear the *c.*
Acts 5. 11. great fear came upon the whole *church*
8. 1. a great persecution against the *c.*—in Jerusalem
3. Saul laid waste the *church*, entering into every house
9. 31. So the ¹*church* throughout all Judæa—had peace
11. 26. they [Saul and Barnabas] were gathered together with the *church*
14. 23. when they had appointed for them elders in every *c.*
27. and [Saul and Barnabas] had gathered the *c.* together
15. 3. therefore, being brought on their way by the *c.*
22. to the apostles and the elders, with the whole *c.*
18. 22. [Paul] went up and saluted the *church*
Rom. 16. 5. salute the *church* that is in their [Aquila and Priscilla] house. 1 *Cor.* 16. 19
1 *Cor.* 4. 17. I teach everywhere in every *church*
14. 4. he that prophesieth edifieth the *church*
5. except he interpret, that the *c.* may receive edifying
23. If therefore the whole *church* be assembled together
Eph. 1. 22. gave him to be head over all things to the *c.*
3. 10. made known through the *c.* the manifold wisdom
5. 24. as the *church* is subject to Christ, so let the wives
25. even as Christ also loved the *church*
27. might present the *church* to himself a glorious *c.*
29. and cherisheth it, even as Christ also the *church*
32. I speak in regard of Christ and of the *church*
Phil. 3. 6. as touching zeal, persecuting the *church*
4. 15. from Macedonia, no *c.* had fellowship with me
Col. 1. 18. he is the head of the body, the *church*
24. for his body's sake, which is the *church*
4. 15. Nymphas, and the *church* that is in their house
16. this epistle—be read also in the *c.* of the Laodiceans

CHURCHES

1 *Th.* 1. 1. Paul, and Silvanus, and Timothy, unto the *church* of the Thessalonians. 2 *Th.* 1. 1
1 *Tim.* 5. 16. and let not the *church* be burdened
Philem. 2. to Archippus—and to the *church* in thy house
Heb. 12. 23. *c.* of the first born who are enrolled in heaven
3 *Jno.* 6. who bare witness to thy love before the *church*
9. I wrote somewhat unto the *church*

In the Church.

Acts 7. 38. [Moses] was *in the church* in the wilderness
13. 1. at Antioch, *in the church* that was there
1 *Cor.* 6. 4. to judge who are of no account *in the church*?
11. 18. first of all, when ye come together *in the church*
12. 28. God hath set some *in the church*, first apostles
14. 19. howbeit *in the c.* I had rather speak five words
28. no interpreter, let him keep silence *in the church*
35. it is shameful for a woman to speak *in the church*
Eph. 3. 21. unto him be the glory *in t. c.* and in Christ Jesus
Col. 4. 16. that it be read also *in the c.* of the Laodiceans

Of the Church.

Acts 11. 22. concerning them came to the ears *of the church*
12. 1. Herod—put forth his hands to afflict certain *of t. c.*
5. but prayer was made earnestly *of the c.* unto God
15. 4. they [Paul and Barnabas] were received *of the c.*
20. 17. [Paul] called to him elders *of the church*
Rom. 16. 1. Phœbe our sister, who is a servant *of the church*
23. Gaius—and *of the* whole *church*, saluteth you
1 *Cor.* 12. that ye may abound unto the edifying *of t. c.*
Eph. 5. 23. as Christ also is the head *of the church*
32. I speak in regard of Christ and *of the church*
Jas. 5. 14. Is any—sick? let him call for the elders *of t. c.*
3 *Jno.* 10. he forbiddeth, and casteth them out *of the c.*
Rev. 2. 1. To the angel *of the church* in Ephesus write
8. to the angel *of the church* in Smyrna write
12. to the angel *of the church* in Pergamum write
18. to the angel *of the church* in Thyatira write
3. 1. to the angel *of the church* in Sardis write
7. to the angel *of the church* in Philadelphia write
14. to the angel *of the church* in Laodicea write
see congregation.

Church of God.

Acts 20. 28. hath made you bishops, to feed the *c. of God*
1 *Cor.* 1. 2. unto the *c. of God* which is at Corinth. 2 *Cor.* 1. 1
10. 32. or to Greeks, or to the *church of God*
11. 22. or despise ye the *church of God*
15. 9. because I [Paul] persecuted the *c. of G. Gal.* 1. 13
1 *Tim.* 3. 5. how shall he take care of the *church of God*?
15. house of God, which is the *church of* the living God

Churches.

Acts 15. 41. Cilicia, confirming the *c.* [Paul and Silas]
16. 5. the *churches* were strengthened in the faith
Rom. 16. 4. but also all the *churches* of the Gentiles
16. All the *churches* of Christ salute you
1 *Cor.* 7. 17. so ordain I in all the *churches*
11. 16. we have no such custom, neither the *c.* of God
14. 33. as in all the *churches* of the saints
34. Let the women keep silence in the *churches*
16. 1. I gave order to the *churches* of Galatia
19. The *churches* of Asia salute you
2 *Cor.* 8. 1. grace of God which hath been given in the *c.*
18. brother whose praise—is spread through all the *c.*
19. but who was also appointed by the *churches* to travel
23. our brethren, they are the messengers of the *c.*
24. in the face of the *churches* the proof of your love
11. 8. I robbed other *churches*, taking wages of them
28. presseth upon me daily, anxiety for all the *churches*
12. 13. ye were made inferior to the rest of the *churches*
Gal. 1. 2. all the brethren—unto the *churches* of Galatia

54

CHURCHES

Gal. 1. 22. I was still unknown by face unto the *c.* of Judæa
1 *Th.* 2. 14. ye, brethren, became imitators of the *c.* of God
2 *Th.* 1. 4. we ourselves glory in you in the *churches* of God
Rev. 1. 4. John to the seven *churches* which are in Asia
   11. write in a book, and send it to the seven *churches*
   20. seven stars are the angels of the seven *churches;*
      and the seven candlesticks are seven *churches*
2. 7. hear what the Spirit saith to the *c.* 11, 17, 29; 3. 6, 13, 22
   23. and all the *churches* shall know that I am he which
22. 16. to testify unto you these things for the *churches*
      see church, temples.

Cinnamon.

Rev. 18. 13. *cinnamon,* and spice, and incense, and ointment

Circuit.—*A.V.* ¹*compass.*

Acts 28. 13. thence we made a ¹*c.,* and arrived at Rhegium

Circumcise.

Lu. 1. 59. eighth day, that they came to *c.* the child [J. Bap.]
Jno. 7. 22. on the sabbath ye *circumcise* a man
Acts 15. 5. It is needful to *circumcise* them
21. 21. telling them not to *circumcise* their children

Circumcised.

Acts 7. 8. Abraham begat Isaac, and *c.* him the eighth day
15. 1. Except ye be *circumcised* after the custom of Moses
16. 3. Paul—took and *circumcised* him [Timothy]
1 *Cor.* 7. 18. Was any man called being *c.?*—let him not be *c.*
Gal. 2. 3. not even Titus—was compelled to be *circumcised*
6. 12. they compel you to be *circumcised*
   13. but they desire to have you *circumcised*
Phil. 3. 5. *c.* the eighth day, of the stock of Israel [Paul]
Col. 2. 11. in whom ye were also *c.* with a circumcision
      see circumcision, uncircumcision.

Circumcising.

Lu. 2. 21. eight days were fulfilled for *c.* him [Jesus]

Circumcision.—*A.V.* ¹*circumcised.*

Jno. 7. 22. For this cause hath Moses given you *c.*
   23. If a man receiveth *circumcision* on the sabbath
Acts 7. 8. he gave him [Abraham] the covenant of *c.*
10. 45. they of the *c.* which believed were amazed
11. 2. they that were of the *circumcision* contended
Rom. 2. 25. For *c.*—profiteth—thy *c.* is—uncircumcision
   26 shall not his uncircumcision be reckoned for *c.?*
   27. who with the letter and *c.* art a transgressor
   28. neither is that *c.,* which is outward in the flesh
   29. *circumcision* is that of the heart, in the spirit
3. 1. what is the profit of *circumcision?*
30. and he shall justify the *circumcision* by faith
4. 9. Is this blessing then pronounced upon the *c.*
   10. reckoned? when he was in *c.*—Not in *circumcision*
   11. and he received the sign of *circumcision,* a seal of
   12. father of *circumcision*—only are of the *circumcision*
15. 8. Christ hath been made a minister of the *c.*
1 *Cor.* 7. 19. *C.* is nothing, and uncircumcision is nothing
Gal. 2. 8. for Peter unto the apostleship of the *circumcision*
9. go unto the Gentiles, and they unto the *circumcision*
12. fearing them that were of the *circumcision*
5. 2. if ye receive ¹*c.,* Christ will profit you nothing
3. every man that receiveth ¹*c.,* that he is a debtor
6. in Christ Jesus neither *c.* availeth anything. 6. 15
11. if I still preach *c.,* why am I still persecuted?
6. 13. not even they who receive ¹*c.*—keep the law
Eph. 2. 11. by that which is called *Circumcision,* in the flesh
Phil. 3. 3. we are the *c.,* who worship by the Spirit of God

CITY

Col. 2. 11. a *c.* not made with hands—in the *c.* of Christ
3. 11. Greek and Jew, *circumcision* and uncircumcision
4. 11. called Justus, who are of the *circumcision*
Tit. 1. 10 talkers and deceivers, specially they of the *c.*

Circumspectly *A.V.*—*see carefully.*

Cities.—*A.V.* ¹*every city.*

Mat. 9. 35. Jesus went about all the *cities.* *Lu.* 13. 22.
10. 23. Ye shall not have gone through the *c.* of Israel
11. 1. he departed thence to teach and preach in their *c.*
20. Then began he to upbraid the *cities*
14. 13. They followed him on foot from the *c. Mk.* 6. 33
Mk. 6. 56. wheresoever he entered, into villages, or into *c.*
Lu. 4. 43. I must preach—to the other *cities* also
8. 1. he went about through ¹*c.* and villages, preaching
19. 17. have thou authority over ten *cities*
19. Be thou also over five *cities*
Acts 5. 16. there also came together the multitude from the *c.*
8. 40. Philip—preached the gospel to all the *cities*
16. 4. as they went on their way through the *cities*
26. 11. I persecuted them even unto foreign *cities* [ashes
2 *Pet.* 2. 6. turning the *c.* of Sodom and Gomorrah into
Jude 7. as Sodom and Gomorrah, and the *c.* about them
Rev. 16. 19. and the *cities* of the nations fell

Citizen—s.

Lu. 15. 15. went and joined himself to one of the *citizens*
19. 14. But his *citizens* hated him, and sent
Acts 21. 39. Paul—of Tarsus in Cilicia, a *c.* of no mean city
Eph. 2. 19. ye are fellow-*citizens* with the saints

Citizenship.—*A.V.* ¹*conversation,* ²*freedom.*

Acts 22. 28. With a great sum obtained I this ²*citizenship*
Phil. 3. 20. For our ¹*citizenship* is in heaven

City.

Mat. 5. 14. A city set on a hill cannot be hid
35. Jerusalem, for it is the *city* of the great King
8. 34. And behold, all the *city* came out to meet Jesus
10. 11. into whatsoever *city* or village ye shall enter
14. that house or that *city,* shake off the dust. *Lu.* 9. 5
15. the day of judgement, than for that *city.* *Lu.* 10. 12
23. when they persecute you in this *city,* flee into the
21. 10. come into Jerusalem, all the *city* was stirred
18. as he returned to the *city,* he hungered
22. 7. destroyed those murderers, and burned their *city*
23 34. and persecute from *city* to *city*
Mk. 1. 33. all the *city* was gathered together at the door
Lu. 2. 3. to enrol themselves, every one to his own *city*
4. out of the *city* of Nazareth—to the *city* of David
11. born to you this day in the *city* of David a Saviour
7. 11. [Jesus] he went to a *city* called Nain
12. when he [Jesus] drew near to the gate of the *city*
—much people of the *city* was with her
19. 41. when he drew nigh, he saw the *city* and wept
23. 51. a man of Arimathæa, a *city* of the Jews
Jno. 4. 39. from that *c.* many of the Samaritans believed
19. 20. where Jesus was crucified was nigh to the *city*
Acts 13. 44. the whole *city* was gathered together
14. 21. when they had preached the gospel to that *city*
16. 12. Philippi, which is a *city* of Macedonia
14. woman named Lydia—of the *city* of Thyatira
20. [Paul and Silas] do exceedingly trouble our *city*
39. asked them [Paul and Silas] to go away from the *c.*
17. 5. Jews—set the *city* [Thessalonica] on an uproar
16. Paul—beheld the *city* [Athens] full of idols
18. 10. for I have much people in this *city* [Corinth]

65

CITY

Acts 19. 29. the *city* [Ephesus] was filled with the confusion
21. 30. all the *city* [Jerusalem] was moved
  30. Paul said, I am a Jew—a citizen of no mean *city*
22. 3. I am a Jew—brought up in this *city* at the feet of
Heb. 11.10. looked for the *city*—whose builder and maker
  16. their God · for he hath prepared for them a *city*
12. 22. mount Zion, and unto the *city* of the living God
13. 14 an abiding *city*, but we seek after the *city*
Rev. 3. 12. name of the *c.* of my God, the new Jerusalem
11. 13. and the tenth part of the *city* fell
14. 20. And the winepress was trodden without the *city*
18. 18. What *city* is like the great *city*?
20. 9. camp of the saints about, and the beloved *city*
21. 14. the wall of the *city* had twelve foundations
15. for a measure a golden reed to measure the *city*
16. the *city* lieth foursquare—he measured the *city*
18. and the *city* was pure gold, like unto pure glass
19. wall of the *city* were adorned with—precious
21. and the street of the *city* was pure gold
23. And the *city* hath no need of the sun
    see built, into city.

Every City.

Mat. 12. 25. *every city* or house divided against itself shall
Lu. 8. 4. and they of *every city* resorted unto him
  10. 1. Lord appointed seventy—into *every c.* and place
Acts 15. 21. Moses—hath in *every city* them that preach
  36. Paul said—Let us—visit the brethren in *every city*
20. 23. the Holy Ghost testifieth unto me in *every city*
Tit. 1. 5. and appoint elders in *every city*
    see cities.

Great City.

Rev. 11. 8. dead bodies lie in the street of the *great city*
16. 19. the *great city* was divided into three parts
17. 18. And the woman whom thou sawest is the *g. city*
18. 10. Woe, woe, the *g. c.*, Babylon, the strong city! 16,
18. What city is like the *great city?*   [19, 21
    see holy city.

Holy City.—*A.V.* ¹great city.

Mat. 4. 5. Then the devil taketh him into the *holy city*
27. 53. after his resurrection they entered into the *h. c.*
Rev. 11. 2. and the *holy city* shall they tread under foot
21. 2. I saw the *holy city*, new Jerusalem, coming down
10. and shewed me the ¹*holy city* Jerusalem
22. 19. shall take away his part—out of the *holy city*

In or Into City.—*A.V.* ¹unto city.

Mat. 8. 33. went away *into* the *city*. *Mk.* 5. 14 : *Lu.* 8. 34
9. 1. [Jesus] came *into* his own *city* [Nazareth]
10. 5. enter not *into* any *city* of the Samaritans
26. 18. Go *into* the *city* to such a man. *Mk.* 14. 23
28. 11. some of the guard came *into* the *city*
Mk. 1. 45. Jesus could no more openly enter *into* a *city*
14. 16. disciples went forth, and came *into* the *city*
Lu. 7. 37. a woman which was *in* the *city*, a sinner
10. 8. *into* whatsoever *city* ye enter. 10: *Mat.* 10. 11
18. 2. There was *in* a *city* a judge, which feared not God
3. and there was a widow *in* that *city*
22. 10. Behold, when ye are entered *into* the *city*
24. 49. tarry ye *in* the *city*, until ye be clothed
Jno. 4. 8. disciples were gone away ¹*into* the *c.* to buy food
28. woman left her waterpot, and went away *into* the *city*
Acts 8. 8. there was much joy in that *city* [Samaria]
9. 6. rise, and enter *into* the *city* [Saul]
11. 5. [Peter] I was *in* the *city* of Joppa praying
14. 20. [Paul] rose up, and entered *into* the *city*
16. 12. we were *in* this *c.* tarrying certain days [Philippi]
21. 29. seen with him *in* the *c.* Trophimus the Ephesian

CLEANSED

Acts 24. 12. nor in the synagogues, nor *in* the *city*
2 *Cor.* 11. 26. in perils *in* the *c.*, in perils in the wilderness
Jas. 4. 13. To-day or to-morrow we will go *into* this *city*
Rev. 22. 14. and may enter in by the gates *into* the *city*

Out of City.

Mat. 21. 17. went forth *out of* the *c.* to Bethany. *Mk.* 11. 19
Lu. 4. 29. rose up, and cast him forth *out of* the *city*
8. 27. met him a certain man *out of* the *c.*, who had devils
Jno. 4. 30. They [Samaritans] went *out of* the *city*
Acts 7. 58. and they cast him [Stephen] *out of* the *city*
14. 19. they stoned Paul, and dragged him *out of* the *c.*
21. 5. brought us on our way, till we were *out of* the *city*
    see gate.

Clamour.—*A.V.* ¹cry.

Acts 23. 9. there arose a great ¹*c.* : and some of the scribes
Eph. 4. 31. Let all bitterness—*c.*, and railing, be put away

Clanging.—*A.V.* ¹tinkling.

1 *Cor.* 13. 1. sounding brass, or a ¹*clanging* cymbal

Clave.

Acts 17. 31. certain men *clave* unto him, [Paul] and believed

Clay.

Jno. 9. 6. he [Jesus] spat on the ground, and made *c.* of the
  spittle, and anointed his eyes with the *clay*
11. Jesus made *clay*, and anointed mine eyes
14. when Jesus made the *clay*, and opened his eyes
15. He put *c.* upon mine eyes, and I washed, and do see
Rom. 9. 21. hath not the potter a right over the *clay*

Clean.—*A.V.* ¹cleansed, ²pure, ³purging.

Mat. 8. 2. Lord, if thou wilt, thou canst make me *clean*.
    Mk. 1. 40 : *Lu.* 5. 12
3. I will ; be thou made *clean*. *Mk.* 1. 41: *Lu.* 5. 13
23. 26. that the outside thereof may become *clean* also
Mk. 1. 42. leprosy departed from him, and he was made ¹*c.*
7. 19. This he said, making all meats ³*clean*
Lu. 11. 41. and behold, all things are *clean* unto you
Jno. 13. 10. but is *c.* every whit: and ye are *c.*, but not all
11. therefore said he, Ye are not all *clean*
15. 3. Already ye are *clean* because of the word
Acts 18. 6. I [Paul] am *c.* : from henceforth I will go unto
Rom. 14. 20. All things indeed are ²*c.* ; howbeit it is evil
    see bright, cleanse, pure.

Cleanness.—*A.V.* ¹purifying.

Heb. 9. 13. sanctify unto the ¹*cleanness* of the flesh

Cleanse.—*A.V.* ¹make clean, ²purge.

Mat. 3. 12. throughly ²*cleanse* his threshing-floor. *Lu.* 3. 17
10. 8. Heal the sick—*cleanse* the lepers
23. 25. ye ¹*cleanse* the outside of the cup. *Lu.* 11. ¹39
26. Thou blind Pharisee, *c.* first the inside of the cup
2 *Cor.* 7. 1. let us *cleanse* ourselves from all defilement
Heb. 9. 14. ²*cleanse* your conscience from dead works
Jas. 4. 8. *Cleanse* your hands, ye sinners
1 *Jno.* 1. 9. and to *cleanse* us from all unrighteousness
    see cleansed.

Cleansed.—*A.V.* ¹cleanse, ²purged, ³purified.

Mat. 8. 3. straightway his leprosy was *cleansed*
11. 5. the lame walk, the lepers are *cleansed*. *Lu.* 7. 22
Lu. 4. 27. none of them was *cleansed*, but only Naaman
17. 14. as they [ten lepers] went, they were *cleansed*

CLEANSED

Lu. 17. 17. Were not the ten *c.?* but where are the nine?
Acts 10. 16. What God hath *c.*, make not thou common. 11. 9
Eph. 5. 26. having ¹*cleansed* it by the washing of water
Heb. 9. 22. all things are ²*cleansed* with blood
    23. copies of the things in the heavens should be ²*c.*
10. 2. the worshippers, having been once ²*cleansed*
         see (made) clean.

Cleanseth—ing.—*A. V.* ¹*purged—eth—ing,* ²*purifying.*

Mk. 1. 44. thy *c.* the things—Moses commanded. *Lu.* 5. 14
Jno. 15. 2. every branch that beareth fruit, he ¹*cleanseth* it
Acts 15. 9. ²*cleansing* their hearts by faith
2 *Pet.* 1. 9. having forgotten the ¹*cleansing* from his old sins
1 *Jno.* 1. 7. blood of Jesus his Son *cleanseth* us from all sin

Clear.

Rev. 21. 11. as it were a jasper stone, *clear* as crystal
         see bright, pure.

Clearing.

2 *Cor.* 7. 11. yea, what *clearing* of yourselves

Clearly.

Mat. 7. 5. shalt thou see *c.* to cast out the mote. *Lu.* 6. 42
Mk. 8. 25. and was restored, and saw all things *clearly*
Rom. 1 20. invisible things—of the world are *clearly* seen

Cleave.—*A. V.* ¹*joined.*

Mat. 19. 5. mother, and shall *cleave* to his wife. *Mk.* 10. 7
Acts 11. 23. purpose of heart they would *c.* unto the Lord
Rom. 12. 9. Abhor that which is evil; *cleave* to that which
Eph. 5. 31 his father and mother, and shall ¹*c.* to his wife

Cleaveth.

Lu. 10. 11. Even the dust from your city, that *c.* to our

Clemency

Acts 24. 4. I intreat thee to hear us of thy *clemency*

Clerk.—*see town clerk.*

Climbed—eth.

Lu. 19. 4. [Zacchæus] *climbed* up into a sycamore tree
Jno. 10. 1. the fold of the sheep, but *c.* up some other way

Cloke.—*A. V.* ¹*clothes,* ²*garment.*

Mat. 5. 40. take away thy coat, let him have thy *cloke* also
    24. 18. not return back to take his ¹*cloke. Mk.* 13. ²16
Lu. 6. 29. taketh away thy *c.* withhold not thy coat also
    22. 36. let him sell his ²*cloke,* and buy a sword
1 *Th.* 2. 5. nor a *cloke* of covetousness, God is witness
2 *Tim.* 4. 13. The *cloke* that I left at Troas with Carpus
1 *Pet.* 2. 16. using your freedom for a *cloke* of wickedness
         see excuse.

Close.

Acts 27. 13. sailed along Crete, *close* in shore
         see (held) peace.

Closed.

Mat. 13. 15. their eyes they have *closed. Acts* 28. 27
Lu. 4. 20. And he [Jesus] *closed* the book

Closet—s *A. V.—see chamber—s.*

COALS

Cloth—s.—*A. V.* ¹*clothes.*

Mat. 9. 16. a piece of undressed *c.* upon an old. *Mk.* 2. 21
    27. 59. took the body, and wrapped it in a clean linen *c.*
Mk. 14. 51. young man followed—a linen *c.* cast about him
    52. he left the linen *cloth,* and fled naked
Lu. 24. 12. seeth the linen ¹*c.* by themselves. *Jno.* 20. ¹5, ¹6
Jno. 19. 40. body of Jesus, and bound it in linen ¹*cloths*
20. 7. not lying with the linen ¹*cloths,* but rolled up

Clothe—d.—*A. V.* ¹*endued.*

Mat. 6. 30. God doth so *c.* the grass of the field—*c.* you
    31. Wherewithal shall we be *clothed?* [*Lu.* 12. 28
11. 8. a man *clothed* in soft raiment? *Lu.* 7. 25
25. 36. naked, and ye *clothed* me. 38
    43. naked, and ye *clothed* me not
Mk. 1. 6. John was *clothed* with camels' hair
5. 15. devils sitting, *c.* and in his right mind. *Lu.* 8. 35
15. 17. And they *clothe* him with purple
Lu. 16. 19. rich man—*clothed* in purple and fine linen
24. 49. until ye be ¹*clothed* with power from on high
2 *Cor.* 5. 2. For verily in this we groan, longing to be *c.*
    3. if so be that being *c.* we shall not be found naked
    4. we would be *clothed* upon, that what is mortal
Rev. 1. 13. like unto a son of man, *clothed* with a garment
3. 18. white garments, that thou mayest *clothe* thyself
11. 3. a thousand two hundred and threescore days, *c.* in
19. 14. armies—in heaven—*c.* in fine linen [sackcloth
         see arrayed, gird.

Clothes.

Mk. 14. 63. the high priest rent his *clothes*
Lu. 2. 7. she wrapped him in swaddling *clothes.* 12
8. 27. long time he [demoniac] had worn no *clothes*
         see cloke, cloth, garments.

Clothing.—*A. V.* ¹*apparel,* ²*raiment.*

Mat. 7. 15. false prophets, which come to you in sheep's *c.*
Jas. 2. 2. synagogue a man—fine ¹*clothing*—vile ²*clothing*
    3. ye have regard to him that weareth the fine *clothing*
         see raiment, robes, apparel.

Cloud

Mat. 17. 5. a bright *c.*—voice out of the *c. Mk.* 9. 7; *Lu.* 9.
Lu. 9. 34. and they feared as they entered into the *cloud* [35
12. 54. When ye see a *cloud* rising in the west
21. 27. see the Son of man coming in a *cloud* with power
Acts 1. 9. a *cloud* received him out of their sight
1 *Cor.* 10. 1. our fathers were all under the *cloud*
    2. baptized unto Moses in the *cloud* and in the sea
Heb. 12. 1. compassed about with so great a *c.* of witnesses
Rev. 10. 1. strong angel—arrayed with a *cloud*
11. 12. And they went up into heaven in the *cloud*
14. 14. a white *c.;* and on the *c.* I saw one sitting. 15, 16

Clouds.

Mat. 24. 30. Son of man—on the *c.* 26. 64; *Mk.* 13. 26: 14. 62
1 *Th.* 4. 17. caught up in the *c.,* to meet the Lord in the air
Jude 12. *clouds* without water, carried along by winds
Rev. 1. 7. Behold, he cometh with the *clouds*
         see mists.

Cloven *A. V.—see parting (asunder).*

Clusters.

Rev. 14. 18. Send—thy—sickle, and gather the *c.* of the vine

Coals.

Jno. 18. 18. officers were standing—made a fire of *coals*
21. 9. [disciples] see a fire of *coals* there, and fish laid
Rom. 12. 20. thou shalt heap *coals* of fire upon his head

COAST

Coast.—A.V. ¹*coasts*.
Lu. 6. 17. people from all Judæa—and the sea c. of Tyre
Acts 27. 2. about to sail unto the places on the ¹c. of Asia
  see parts.

Coasting.—A.V. ¹*passing*.
Acts 27. 8. with difficulty ¹c. along it we came unto a—place

Coasts A.V.—*see borders, country*.

Coat.
Mat. 5. 40. take away thy *coat*, let him have thy cloke also
Lu. 6. 29. taketh away thy cloke withhold not thy *coat* also
Jno. 19. 23. also the *coat* : now the *coat* was without seam
21. 7. Simon Peter—girt his *coat* about him

Coats.
Mk 6. 9. put not on two *coats*. Mat. 10. 10 : Lu. 9. 3
Lu. 3. 11. He that hath two *coats*, let him impart to him
Acts 9. 39. the *coats* and garments which Dorcas made

Cock
Mat 26. 34. before the *cock* crow, thou shalt deny. 75 :
  Mk. 14 30, 72 : Lu. 22. 34, 61 : Jno. 13. 38
Mk. 14. 68. the c. crew. 72 : Mat. 26. 74 : Lu. 22. 60 : Jno. 18. 27

Cockcrowing.
Mk. 13. 35. midnight, or at *cockcrowing*, or in the morning

Cold
Mat. 10. 42. unto one of these little ones a cup of c. water
24. 12. the love of the many shall wax *cold*
Jno. 18. 18. having made a fire of coals; for it was *cold*
Acts 28 2. kindled a fire—because of the *cold*
2 Cor. 11. 27. in fastings often, in *cold* and nakedness
Rev. 3. 15. neither c. nor hot : I would thou wert c. or hot. 16

Collection—s.—A.V. ¹*gatherings*.
1 Cor. 16. 1 Now concerning the *collection* for the saints
2. that no ¹*collections* be made when I come

Colony.
Acts 16. 12. Philippi—a Roman *colony*

Colour—ed.
Acts 27. 30. under c. as though they would lay out anchors
Rev. 17 3. woman sitting upon a scarlet-*coloured* beast

Colt
Mat. 21. 2. find an ass tied, and a *colt* with her. Mk. 11.
  2, 4 ; Lu. 19. 30
5. And upon a *colt* the foal of an ass
7. and brought the ass, and the *colt*. Mk. 11. 7
Mk. 11. 5. What do ye, loosing the *colt* ? Lu. 19. 33
Lu. 19. 35. and they threw their garments upon the *colt*
Jno. 12. 15. thy King cometh, sitting on an ass's *colt*

Come.—A.V. ¹*assembled*, ²*came*, ³*cometh*, ⁴*go*, ⁵*gotten*,
  ⁶*at hand*, ⁷*proceed*, ⁸*resort*—ed, ⁹*returned*.
Mat. 2. 6. For out of thee shall *come* forth a governor
8. that I [Herod] also may *come* and worship him
3. 7. from the wrath to *come* ? Lu. 3. 7 : 1 Th. 1. 10
5. 24. first be reconciled to thy brother, and then *come*
6. 10. Thy kingdom *come*. Lu. 11. 2
7. 15. false prophets, which c. to you in sheep's clothing
8. 7. I will *come* and heal him [centurion's servant]
8. not worthy that thou shouldest *come* under my roof
9. and to another, *Come*, and he cometh. Lu. 7. 8

COME

Mat. 8. 11. many shall c. from the east and the west. Lu.
9. 14. Then ²*come* to him the disciples of John [13. 29
10. 13. if the house be worthy, let your peace c. upon it
11. 28. C. unto me, all ye that labour and are heavy laden
12. 28. is the kingdom of God *come* upon you. Lu. 11. 20
44. when he is *come*, he findeth it empty, swept
14. 28. bid me [Peter] *come* unto thee upon the waters
29. And he said, *Come*—to ⁴*come* to Jesus
15. 1. there ²c. to Jesus from Jerusalem Pharisees. Mk. 7. ¹1
19. For out of the heart ⁷*come* forth evil thoughts
16. 24. If any man would c. after me. Mk. 8. 34 : Lu. 9. 23
27. Son of man shall *come* in the glory of his Father
17. 10. say the scribes that Elijah must first c. ? Mk. 9. 11
12. that Elijah is *come* already Mk. 9. 13
18. 7. it must needs be that the occasions *come*. Lu. 17. 1
19. 21. treasure in heaven : and c., follow me. Lu. 10. 21 :
22. 4. *come* to the marriage feast. 3   [Lu. 18. 22
23. 35. that upon you may c. all the righteous blood shed
24. 5. many shall c. in my name. Mk. 13. 6 : Lu. 21 8
14. and then shall the end *come*
50. the lord of that servant shall c. in a day. Lu. 12 46
25. 31. when the Son of man shall *come* in his glory
34. *Come*, ye blessed of my Father, inherit the kingdom
26. 50. Friend, do that for which thou [Judas] art *come*
Mk. 1. 17. C. ye after me, and I will make you to become
24. art thou *come* to destroy us ? Lu. 4. 34
4. 22. made secret, but that it should c. to light. Lu. 8 17
29. putteth forth the sickle, because the harvest is *come*
6. 31. *Come* ye yourselves apart into a desert place
8. 3. and some of them are ²*come* from far
9. 1. till they see the kingdom of God *come* with power
21. How long time is it since this hath ²*come* unto him ?
10. 1. multitudes ⁸*come* together unto him [Lu. 18. 16
14. Suffer the little children to c. unto me. Mat. 19 14.
12. 7. This is the heir ; *come*, let us kill him
14. 41. hour is *come* ; behold, the Son of man is betrayed
Lu. 1. 35. The Holy Ghost shall *come* upon thee [Mary]
5. 32. I am not ²*come* to call the righteous but sinners
7. 7. neither thought I myself worthy to *come* unto thee
34. The Son of man is *come* eating and drinking
9. 51. when the days were well nigh c. that he should be
10. 1. whither he himself was about to *come*
9. The kingdom of God is *come* nigh unto you 11
11. 25. when he is ²c., he findeth it swept and garnished
12. 37. sit down to meat, and shall *come* and serve them
38. And if he shall *come* in the second watch
51. Think ye that I am *come* to give peace in the earth ?
13. 7. these three years I c. seeking fruit on this fig tree
14. in them therefore *come* and be healed
14. 17. *Come* ; for all things are now ready
27. doth not bear his own cross, and *come* after me
15. 27. Thy brother is *come* ; and thy father hath killed
19. 9. To-day is salvation *come* to this house [Zacchæus]
13. Trade ye herewith till I *come*
15. it came to pass, when he was ²*come* back again
20. 16. He will *come* and destroy these husbandmen
21. 34. and that day *come* on you suddenly. 35
22. 18. fruit of the vine, until the kingdom of God shall c.
Jno. 1. 39. He saith unto them, *Come*, and ye shall see
46 Can any good thing *come* out of Nazareth ? Philip
  saith—*Come* and see. 11. 34
2. 4. mine hour is not yet *come*. 7. 30 : 8. 20
3. 26. the same baptizeth, and all men *come* to him
4. 25 Christ). when he is *come*, he will declare
5. 43. I am c. in my Father's name—shall c. in his own
6. 37. which the Father giveth me shall c. unto me [name
can no man *come* to me, except. 65
7. 6. My time is not yet c. ; but your time is alway ready
34. and where I am, ye cannot *come*

58

COME

Jno. 7. 37. If any man thirst, let him *c.* unto me, and drink
8. 14. ye know not whence I *come*, or whither I go
42. am *come* from God ; for neither have I ²*c.* of myself
11. 30. Jesus was not yet *come* into the village
12. 23. hour is *c.*, that the Son of man should be glorified
30. This voice hath not ²*come* for my sake
46. I am *come* a light into the world
13. 1. Jesus knowing that his hour was *come*
19. that, when it is *come* to pass, ye may believe
14 18. I will not leave you desolate : I *come* unto you
23. we will *c.* unto him, and make our abode with him
28. I said to you, I go away, and I *come* unto you
15. 26. But when the Comforter is *c.*, whom I will send
16. 4. when their hour is *come*, ye may remember them
8. he, when he is *come*, will convict the world
13. when he, the Spirit of truth, is *come*, he shall guide
21. in travail hath sorrow, because her hour is *come*
28. I came out from the Father, and am *c.* into the world
17. 1. Father, the hour is *come* ; glorify thy Son
11. these are in the world, and I *come* to thee. 13
18. 20. in the temple, where all the Jews ⁶*come* together
21. 3. I [Peter] go a fishing—We also ⁴*come* with thee
22. If I will that he tarry till I *come*. 23
Acts 1. 8. when the Holy Ghost is *come* upon you
11. this Jesus—shall so *come* in like manner
2. 1. And when the day of Pentecost was now *come*
20. Before the day of the Lord *come*
3. 19. may *come* seasons of refreshing from the presence
7. 34. their groaning, and I am *come* down—and now *c.*
8. 24. Of the things which ye have spoken *come* upon me
27. eunuch—who had *come* to Jerusalem for to worship
31. he [eunuch] besought Philip to *come* up and sit
9. 21. and he had ²*come* hither for this intent
38. Delay not to *come* on unto us [nation
10. 28. Jew to join himself or *come* unto one of another
11. 23. when he was ²*come*, and had seen the grace of God
13. 40. Beware therefore, lest that *come* upon you
15. 25. seemed good unto us, having ¹*come* to one accord
16. 9. *Come* over into Macedonia, and help us
13. spake unto the women which were ⁶*come* together
19. 4. him which should *come* after him, that is, on Jesus
23. 15. we, or ever he *come* near, are ready to slay him
26. 22. the prophets and Moses did say should *come*
28. 21. nor did any of the brethren ²*come* hither
Rom. 3. 8. Let us do evil, that good may *come* ?
9. 9. to this season will I *c.*, and Sarah shall have a son
11. 11. salvation is *come* unto the Gentiles
15. 29. when I *come* unto you, I shall *come* in the fulness
16. 19. For your obedience is *come* abroad unto all men
1 *Cor.* 1. 7. so that ye *come* behind in no gift
4. 5. judge nothing before the time, until the Lord *come*
21. shall I *come* unto you with a rod, or in love
10. 11. upon whom the ends of the ages are *come*
11. 26. ye proclaim the Lord's death till he *come*
34. And the rest will I set in order whensoever I *come*
13. 10. but when that which is perfect is *come*
14. 6. if I *come* unto you speaking with tongues
15. 35. and with what manner of body do they *come* ?
16. 2. that no collections be made when I *come*
10. if Timothy *come*, see that he be with you
11. set him forward—that he may *come* unto you
12. Apollos—I besought him much to *come* unto you—not at all his will to *come* now ; but he will *come*
2 *Cor.* 1. 15. I was minded to *come* before unto you. 16
23. to spare you I forbare to ²*come* unto Corinth
12. 20. when I *come*, I should find you not such as I would
Gal. 3. 14. that upon the Gentiles might *come* the blessing
19. till the seed should *come* to whom the promise
25. But now that faith is *come*, we are no longer

COME

Col. 1. 6. [truth of the gospel] which is *come* unto you
1 *Th.* 2. 16. the wrath is *come* upon them to the uttermost
2 *Th.* 1. 10. when he shall *come* to be glorified in his saints
2. 3. will not be, except the falling away *come* first
1 *Tim.* 2. 4. all men—*come* to the knowledge. 2 *Tim.* 3. 7
4. 8. life which now is, and of that which is to *come*
13. Till I *come*, give heed to reading, to exhortation
6. 19. a good foundation against the time to *come*
2 *Tim.* 3. 1. in the last days grievous times shall *come*
4. 3. For the time will *come* when they will not endure
6. being offered, and the time of my departure is ⁶*come*
21. Do thy diligence to *come* before winter. 9
Tit. 3. 12. give diligence to *come* unto me to Nicopolis
Heb. 4. 1. any one of you should seem to have *c.* short of it
9. 11. Christ having *come* a high priest—good things to *c.*
10. 7. Then said I, Lo, I am *come*. 9
37. He that cometh shall *come*, and shall not tarry
12. 22. but ye are *come* unto mount Zion
Jas. 2. 2. if there *c.* into your synagogue—there *c.* in also
4. 1. Whence *come* wars—*c.* fightings—*c.* hence
1 *Pet.* 1. 10. prophesied of the grace that should *c.* unto you
4. 17. For the time is come for judgement to begin
2 *Pet.* 1. 18. this voice we ourselves heard ²*c.* out of heaven
3. 9. but that all should *come* to repentance
10. But the day of the Lord will *come* as a thief
1 *Jno.* 4. 2. confesseth that Jesus Christ is *come* in the flesh
5. 20. we know that the Son of God is *come*
3 *Jno.* 10. if I *come*, I will bring to remembrance his works
Rev. 2. 5. I *come* to thee, and will move thy candlestick
25. Howbeit that which ye have, hold fast till I *come*
3. 3. I will *come* as a thief—I will *come* upon thee. 16. 15
10. that hour which is to *come* upon the whole world
11. I *come* quickly. 22. 7, 12, 20
4. 1. a voice—saying, *Come* up hither. 11. 12
6. 1. four living creatures saying—*Come*. 3, 5, 7
17. for the great day of their wrath is *come*
12. 10. Now is *come* the salvation, and the power
14. 7. for the hour of his judgement is *come*
15. 2. that were ⁶*come* victorious from the beast
4. all the nations shall *come* and worship before thee
17. 10. seven kings—the other is not yet *come*
18. 10. for in one hour is thy judgement *come*
19. 7. for the marriage of the Lamb is *come*
22. 17. Spirit and the bride say, *Come*. And he that heareth, let him say, *Come*

see assemble, attain, befall, came, came forth, come, cometh, coming, days, draw (near), enter, fall, gone, overtake, proceed, resorted.

Come after.—*A.V.* ¹*follow.*

Mat. 4. 19. he saith unto them, ¹*Come* ye *after* me

Come again.

Lu. 10. 35. I, when I *come* back *again*, will repay thee
Jno. 14. 3. I *come again*, and will receive you unto myself
2 *Cor.* 2. 1. I would not *come again* to you with sorrow
12. 21. when I *come again*, my God should humble me
13. 2. if I *come again*, I will not spare

Come down.—*A.V.* ¹*come down*, ²*descend.*

Mat. 27. 40. *come down* from the cross. 42: *Mk.* 15. 30
Mk. 15. 32. Let the Christ, the King of Israel, now ²*c. d.*
Lu. 9. 54. wilt thou that we bid fire to *c. d.* from heaven
19. 5. Zacchæus, make haste, and *come down*
Jno. 4. 49. Sir, *come down* ere my child die. 47
6. 38. I am *c. d.* from heaven, not to do mine own will
42. how doth he now say, I am ¹*c. down* out of heaven ?
Acts 7. 34. and I am *come down* to deliver them
8. 15. who, when they were *come down*, prayed for them

COME

Acts 14. 11. The gods are *c. d.* to us in the likeness of men
Rev. 13. 13. even make fire to *come down* out of heaven
    see coming, go (down), gone (down).

Come forth.—*A.V.* ¹*go out.*

Mat. 13. 49. angels shall *come forth*, and sever the wicked
15. 18. proceed out of the mouth *come f.* out of the heart
25. 6. the bridegroom! ¹*Come* ye *forth* to meet him
Jno. 5. 29. and shall *come f.* ; they that have done good
11. 43. he cried with a loud voice, Lazarus, *come forth*
Acts 7. 7. after that shall they *c. f.*, and serve me [Israel]
Rev. 20. 8. [Satan] shall ¹*come forth* to deceive the nations

Come hither.

Mat. 8. 29. art thou *come hither* to torment us before
Jno. 4. 16. I thirst not, neither *c.* all the way *hither* to draw
16. Go, call thy husband, and *come hither*
Acts 17. 6. have turned the world upside down are *come h.*
Rev. 17. 1. *Come hither*, I will shew thee the judgement
21. 9. *Come hither*, I will shew thee the bride

Come in or into.

Lu. 8. 41. Ja'irus—besought him to *come into* his house
14. 23. them to *come in*, that my house may be filled
16. 28. lest they also come into this place of torment
Jno. 3. 19. that the light is *come into* the world
Acts 7. 3. *come into* the land which I will shew thee
16. 15. *come into* my [Lydia] house, and abide there
Rom. 11. 25. until the fulness of the Gentiles be *come in*
1 *Cor.* 14. 23. there *c. in* men unlearned or unbelieving. 24
Jas. 2. 2. there *c. into* your synagogue—*c. in* also a poor man
Rev. 3. 20. I will *come in* to him, and will sup with him
    see cometh, enter, went away.

Come with negatives.

Mat. 22. 3. to the marriage feast : and they would *not come*
Mk. 2. 4. could *not c.* nigh unto him for the crowd. *Lu.*8.19
Lu. 14. 20. married a wife, and therefore I *cannot come*
Jno. 5. 40. ye will *not come* to me, that ye may have life
7. 28. I am *not come* of myself, but he that sent me is true
34. where I am, ye *cannot come.* 36
8. 21. whither I go, ye *cannot come.* 22 : 13. 33
11. 56. What think ye ? That he will *not c.* to the feast ?
15. 22. If I had *not come*—they had not had sin
16. 7. if I go not away, the Comforter will *not c.* unto you
    see came (not), cometh, coming.

Come out.—*A.V.* ¹*came out,* ²*depart.*

Mat. 5. 26. no means *come out* thence, till thou have paid
26. 45. Are ye *c. o.* as against a robber. *Mk.* 14. 48 : *Lu.*
Mk. 5. 8. *C.* forth, thou unclean spirit, *o.* of the man |22.52
9. 29. This kind can *c. out* by nothing, save by prayer
Lu. 4. 35. Hold thy peace, and *come out* of him. *Mk.*
    1. 25 ; 9. 25 : *Lu.* 8. 29
36. unclean spirits, and they *come out*
12. 59. Thou shalt by no means ¹*come out* thence
Jno. 1. 46. Can any good thing *come out* of Nazareth ?
7. 41. What, doth the Christ *come out* of Galilee ?
Acts 16. 18. in the name of Jesus Christ to *come out* of her
Rom. 11. 26. There shall *come out* of Zion the Deliverer
2 *Cor.* 6. 17. *C.* ye *out* from among them—saith the Lord
Heb. 7. 5. those have *come out* of the loins of Abraham
Rev 7. 14. These are they which¹*c. o.* of the great tribulation
18. 4. voice—saying—*Come* forth, my people, *out* of her
    see came out, proceed.

Come to pass.—*A.V.* ¹*brought to pass,* ²*done,* ³*performed.*

Mat. 1. 22. all this is ²*c. to p.*, that it might be fulfilled.21.²⁴
24. 6. these things must needs *come to pass. Lu.* 21. 9

COMETH

Mk. 5. 14. came to see what it was that had ²*come to pass*
Lu. 1. 20. until the day that these things shall ²*c. to pass*
2. 15. Bethlehem, and see this thing that is *come to pass*
21. 7. sign when these things are about to *come to pass* ?
36. escape all these things that shall *come to pass*
24. 12. wondering at that which was *come to pass*
18. the things which are *c. to pass* there in these days?
Jno. 13. 19. before it *c. to p.*, that, when it is *c. to p.* 14. 29
Acts 4. 28. thy counsel foreordained to ²*come to pass*
1 *Cor.* 15 54. then shall ¹*come to pass* the saying that is
Rev. 1. 1. things which must shortly *come to pass.* 22. ²⁶
21. 6. he said unto me, They are ¹*come to pass*
    see cometh, coming.

Come together.

Mk. 14. 53. there *c. together* with him all the chief priests
Acts 1. 6. when they were *come together*, asked him. 28. 17
10. 27. [Peter] went in, and findeth many *come together*
19. 32. the more part knew not wherefore they were *c. t.*
1 *Cor.* 11. 17. ye *c. t.* not for the better but for the worse
18. first of all, when ye *come together* in the church
33. when ye *come together* to eat, wait one for another
14. 26. When ye *come together*, each one hath a psalm

Come up.—*A.V.* ¹*ascend.*

Rev. 17. 8. The beast—is about to ¹*come up* out of the abyss

Comeliness.

1 *Cor.* 12. 23. uncomely parts have more abundant *c.*

Comely.

1 *Cor.* 12. 24. whereas our *comely* parts have no need
    see seemly.

Comers *A.V.*—*see (them that) draw (nigh).*

Comest.

Mat. 3. 14. to be baptized of thee, and *c.* thou to me ?
*Lu.*23.42. Jesus, remember me when thou *c.* in thy kingdom

Cometh.—*A.V.* ¹*ascendeth,* ²*came,* ³*come,* ⁴*coming,*
    ⁵*proceedeth.*

Mat. 8. 1. in those days ²*cometh* John the Baptist
11. he that *cometh* after me. *Mk.* 1. 7 : *Lu.* 3. 16 : *Jno.*
    1. ⁴27 : *Acts* 13. 25
8. 9. and to another, Come, and he *cometh. Lu.* 7. 8
11. 3. Art thou he that ³*cometh*, or look we for another ?
13. 19. then *cometh* the evil one, and snatcheth away that
17. 27. hook, and take up the fish that first *cometh* up
18. 7. woe to that man through whom the occasion *c. !*
21. 5. Behold, thy King *cometh* unto thee. *Jno.* 12. 15
9. Blessed is he that *cometh* in the name of the Lord.
    23. 39 ; *Mk.* 11. 9, 10 : *Lu.* 13. 35 : *Jno.* 12. 13
24. 27. For as the lightning *cometh* forth from the east
42. ye know not on what day your Lord ⁴*cometh*
44. hour that ye think not the Son of man *c. Lu.* 12. 40
46. whom his lord when he *c.* shall find. *Lu.* 12. 37, 43
25. 19. after a long time the lord of those servants *c.*
26. 40. he *c.* unto the disciples, and. 45 : *Mk.* 14. 37, 41
27. 49. let us see whether Elijah ⁴*cometh* to save him
Mk. 3. 20. And the multitude *cometh* together again
4. 15. they have heard, straightway *c.* Satan. *Lu.* 8. 12
6. 1. and he ²*cometh* into his own country
48. fourth watch of the night he *cometh* unto them
8. 38. shall be ashamed of him, when he *c.* in the glory
9. 12. Elijah indeed *cometh* first, and restoreth all things
13. 35. shall believe that what he saith ⁴*cometh* to pass
13. 35. ye know not when the lord of the house *cometh*
14. 43. straightway, while he yet spake, *cometh* Judas

60

COMETH

Lu. 6. 47. Every one that *cometh* unto me, and heareth
9. 26. of him shall the Son of man be ashamed, when he *c.
12. 54. There *cometh* a shower; and so it *c* to pass. 55
15. 6. when he *c.* home, he calleth together his friends
17. 20. by the Pharisees, when the kingdom of God *c.*
21. The kingdom of God *cometh* not with observation
18. 8. when the Son of man *cometh,* shall he find faith
19. 38. Blessed is the King that *cometh* in the name
Jno. 1. 15. He that *cometh* after me is become before me. 30
3. 8. The wind bloweth—knowest not whence it *cometh*
20. For every one that—*cometh* not to the light
21. he that doeth the truth *cometh* to the light
31. He that *c.* from above is above all—*c.* from heaven
4. 21. Woman, believe me, the hour *c.* 23 : 5. ¹25, ¹28; 16.32
25. I know that Messiah *cometh* (which is called Christ)
5. 24. hath eternal life, and ²*cometh* not into judgement
44. the glory that *c.* from the only God ye seek not?
6. 14. of a truth the prophet that ²*cometh* into the world
35. he that *cometh* to me shall not hunger
37. him that *cometh* to me I will in no wise cast out
45. Every one that—hath learned, *cometh* unto me
7. 27. when the Christ *c.*, no one knoweth whence he is
42. scripture said that the Christ *c.* of the seed of David
9. 4. the night *cometh,* when no man can work
11. 27. Son of God, even he that ²*cometh* into the world
14. 6 no one *cometh* unto the Father, but by me
30. prince of the world *c.* : and he hath nothing in me
16. 2. yea, the hour *cometh,* that whosoever killeth you
25. the hour *cometh,* when I shall no more speak
20. 26. Jesus ²*cometh,* the doors being shut, and stood
Rom. 10. 17. belief *c.* of hearing, and hearing by the word
1 *Cor.* 15. 24. Then *c.* the end, when he shall deliver up
2 *Cor.* 11. 4. if he that *cometh* preacheth another Jesus
Eph. 5. 6. *c.* the wrath of God upon the sons of. *Col.* 3. 6
1 *Th.* 5. 2. the day of the Lord so *c.* as a thief in the night
3. then sudden destruction *cometh* upon them
1 *Tim.* 6. 4. whereof *cometh* envy, strife, railings, evil
Heb. 10. 5. when he *c.* into the world, he saith, Sacrifice
11. 6. he that *cometh* to God must believe that he is
*Jas.*3.10. out of the same mouth⁵*c.* forth blessing and cursing
1 *Jno.* 2. 18. as ye heard that antichrist ²*cometh,* even now
2 *Jno.* 7. that confess not that Jesus Christ ²*c.* in the flesh
Rev. 1. 7. Behold, he *cometh* with the clouds
11. 7. the beast that ¹*cometh* up out of the abyss
14. second Woe is past—the third Woe *cometh* quickly
17. 10. when he *cometh,* he [seventh king] must continue
see came, come, coming, presseth, proceedeth.

Cometh down.—*A.V.* ¹*descendeth.*

Jno. 6. 33. bread of God is that which *c. d.* out of heaven. 50
Jas. 3. 15. This wisdom is not a wisdom that ¹*cometh down*
Rev. 3. 12. new Jerusalem, which *cometh d.* out of heaven

Cometh out *A.V.*—*see proceedeth out.*

Comfort.—*A.V.* ¹*consolation,* ²*exhortation.*

Acts 9. 31. fear of the Lord and in the *c.* of the Holy Ghost
*Rom.*15.4. through *c.* of the scriptures we might have hope
5. Now the God of patience and of ¹*c.* grant you to be
1 *Cor.* 1. 3. speaketh unto men—²*comfort,* and consolation
2 *Cor.* 1. 3. the Father of mercies and God of all *comfort*
4. able to *comfort* them—through the *c.* wherewith
5. even so our ¹*comfort* also aboundeth through Christ
6. whether we be afflicted, it is for your ¹*c.*—whether
we be comforted, it is for your ¹*comfort*
7. partakers of the sufferings, so also are ye of the ¹*c.*
2. 7. ye should rather forgive him and *comfort* him

COMING

2 *Cor.* 7. 4. I am filled with *comfort,* I overflow with joy
7. but also by the ¹*c.* wherewith he was comforted in you
13. in our *comfort* we joyed the more exceedingly
Eph. 6. 22. that bo may *comfort* your hearts. *Col.* 4. 8
Phil. 2. 1. If there is therefore any ¹*comfort* in Christ
19. that I also may be of good *comfort,* when I know
Col. 4. 11. fellow-workers—men that have been a *c.* unto me
1 *Th.* 3. 2. and to *comfort* you concerning your faith
4. 18. Wherefore *comfort* one another with these words
2 *Th.* 2. 16. God our Father—gave us eternal ¹*comfort*
17. *comfort* your hearts and stablish them in every good
Philem. 7. For I had much joy and ¹*comfort* in thy love
see cheer, comforted, console, encourage, exhort.

Comforted.—*A.V.* ¹*comfort.*

Mat. 2. 18. Rachel—would not be *c.,* because they are not
5. 4. Blessed are they that mourn : for they shall be *c.*
Lu. 16. 25. Lazarus—is *comforted,* and thou art in anguish
Acts 16. 40. when they [Paul and Silas] had seen the
brethren, they *comforted* them
20. 12. brought the lad alive, and were not a little *c.*
Rom. 1. 12. that I with you may be *comforted* in you
1 *Cor.* 14. 31. that all may learn, and all may be *comforted*
2 *Cor.* 1. 4. the comfort wherewith we ourselves are *c.* 6
7. 6. even God, *comforted* us by the coming of Titus
7. also by the comfort wherewith he was *c.* in you
13. Therefore we have been *comforted*
13. 11. be ¹*comforted ;* be of the same mind
Col. 2. 2. that their hearts may be *comforted*
1 *Th.* 3. 7. we were *comforted* over you in all our distress
see comforting, encouraging.

Comforter.

Jno. 14. 16. the Father, and he shall give you another *C.*
26. But the *Comforter,* even the Holy Spirit
15. 26. when the *Comforter* is come, whom I will send
16. 7. if I go not away, the *Comforter* will not come

Comforteth.

2 *Cor.* 1. 4. [God] who *comforteth* us in all our afflictions
7. 6. he that *comforteth* the lowly, even God

Comforting.- *A.V.* ¹*comforted.*

Jno. 11. 31. and were ¹*comforting* her, when they saw Mary

Comfortless *A V.*—*see desolate.*

Coming.—*A.V.* ¹*came,* ²*come,* ³*cometh,* ⁴*descending,*
⁵*lighting,* ⁶*rise.*

Mat. 3. 16. descending as a dove, and ⁵*coming* upon him
16. 28. see the Son of man *coming* in his kingdom
17. 9. as they were ¹*c.* down from the mountain. *Mk.* 9. 9
24. 3. what shall be the sign of thy *c.,* and of the end
27. so shall be the *coming* of the Son of man. 37, 39
30. Son of man *coming* on the clouds of heaven. 26. 64:
Mk. 13. 26 ; 14. 62 : *Lu.* 21. 27
25. 27. at my *c.* I should have received back. *Lu.* 19. 23
27. 53. ¹*c.* forth out of the tombs after his resurrection
Mk. 6. 31. For there were many *coming* and going
13. 29. when ye see these things ²*coming* to pass
36. lest *coming* suddenly he find you sleeping
Lu. 2. 38. And *coming* up at that very hour [Anna]
9. 42. as he was yet a *coming,* the devil dashed him down
12. 45. say in his heart, My lord delayeth his *coming*
18. 5. widow—wear me out by her coutinual *coming*
21. 26. expectation of the things which are *c.* on the world
23. 29. For behold, the days are *coming*

COMING

Jno. 1. 9. the light which lighteth every man, ³*coming* into
5. 7. while I am *coming*, another steppeth down before
10. 12. beholdeth the wolf *coming*, and leaveth the sheep
18. 4. Jesus—knowing all the things that were ²*c*. upon
Acts 7. 52. before of the *coming* of the Righteous One
10. 3. angel of God *coming* in unto him [Cornelius]
13. 24. before his *coming* the baptism of repentance
1 *Cor.* 4. 18. some are puffed up, as though I were not ²*c*. to
11. 34. that your ²*coming* together be not unto judgement
15. 23. then they that are Christ's, at his *coming*
16. 17. I rejoice at the *coming* of Stephanas
2 *Cor.* 7. 6. God, comforted us by the *coming* of Titus
7. not by his *coming* only, but also by the comfort
13. 1. This is the third time I am *coming* to you
1 *Th.* 2. 19. even ye, before our Lord Jesus at his *coming*?
3. 13. at the *coming* of our Lord Jesus. 5. 23
4. 15. that are left unto the *coming* of the Lord
2 *Th.* 2. 1. touching the *coming* of our Lord Jesus Christ
8. bring to nought by the manifestation of his *coming*
9. whose *coming* is according to the working of Satan
Jas. 1. 17 Every good gift—²*coming* down from the Father
5. 1. howl for your miseries that are ²*coming* upon you
7. Be patient therefore—until the *coming* of the Lord
8. for the *coming* of the Lord is at hand
1 *Pet.* 2. 4. unto whom *coming*, a living stone, rejected
2 *Pet.* 1. 16. power and *coming* of our Lord Jesus Christ
3. 4. Where is the promise of his *coming* ?
12. earnestly desiring the *coming* of the day of God
1 *Jno.* 2. 28. not be ashamed before him at his *coming*
Rev. 10. 1. I saw another strong angel ²*coming* down out
13. 1. I saw a beast ⁶*coming* up out of the sea
11. I saw another beast *coming* up out of the earth
16. 13. I saw ²*coming* out of the mouth of the dragon
21. 2. new Jerusalem, *coming* down out of heaven. ⁴10
see cometh, going, presence, revelation.

Command.—*A.V.* ¹*charge*, ²*commanded*, ³*commandment*, ⁴*grant.*
Mat. 4. 3. *c.* that these stones become bread. *Lu.* 4. 3
19. 7. Why then did Moses *command* to give a bill of
20. 21. ⁴*C.* that these my two sons may sit, one on thy
27. 64. *C.* therefore that the sepulchre be made sure
Mk. 9. 25. Thou dumb and deaf spirit, I ¹*command* thee
10. 3. What did Moses *command* you ?
Lu. 8. 31. *command* them [devils] to depart into the abyss
14. 22. Lord, what thou didst ²*command* is done
Jno. 15. 14. if ye do the things which I *command* you
17. These things I *command* you, that ye may love
Acts 25. 23. at the ¹*command* of Festus Paul was brought in
2 *Th.* 3. 4. ye—will do the things which we *command*
6. Now we *command* you, brethren, in the name of our
12. such we *c.* and exhort in the Lord Jesus Christ
1 *Tim.* 4. 11. These things *command* and teach
5. 7. These things also ¹*c*. that they may be without
see bid, charge, charged.

Commanded.—*A.V.* ¹*bidden*, ²*charged*, ³*enjoined.*
Mat. 1. 24. Joseph—did as the angel of the Lord ¹*c.* him
8. 4. Moses *c.*, for a testimony. *Mk.* 1. 44 : *Lu.* 5. 14
14. 9. he *c.* it [head of John Baptist] to be given. *Mk.* 6. 27
19. he *c.* the multitudes to sit down. 15. 35 : *Mk.* 6. 39
17. 9. Jesus ²*c*. them, saying, Tell the vision to no man
18. 25. his lord *commanded* him to be sold, and his wife
28. 20. observe all things whatsoever I *commanded* you
Lu. 9. 21. and *commanded* them to tell this to no man
17. 10. done all the things that are *commanded* you. 9
Jno. 8. 5. in the law Moses *commanded* us to stone such
Acts 15. when they had *commanded* them to go aside
10. 33. to hear all things that have been *c.* thee of
48. he *c.* them to be baptized in the name of Jesus

COMMANDMENT

Acts 13. 47. For so hath the Lord *commanded* us, saying
23. 10. *c.* the soldiers to go down and take him [Paul]
25. 6. [Festus] *commanded* Paul to be brought
2 *Th.* 3. 10. this we *commanded* you, If any will not work
Heb. 9. 20. blood of the covenant which God ³*c.* to you-ward
see appointed, charged, command, enjoined, said.

Commandest.
Acts 23. 3. said Paul—*c.* me to be smitten contrary to the

Commandeth.
Mk. 1. 27. he *c.* even the unclean spirits. *Lu.* 4. 36
Lu. 8. 25. he *commandeth* even the winds and the water
Acts 17. 30. he *commandeth* men that they should—repent

Commanding.
Mat. 11. 1. Jesus had made an end of *c.* his twelve disciples
Acts 24. 8. *c.* his accusers to come before thee [margin]
1 *Tim.* 4. 3. and *commanding* to abstain from meats

Commandment.—*A. V.* ¹*commandments*, ²*precept.*
Mat. 8. 18. Jesus—gave *c.* to depart unto the other side
22. 36. which is the great *c.* in the law ? *Mk.* 12. 28
38. This is the great and first *commandment*
Mk. 10. 5. For your hardness of heart he wrote you this ¹*c*.
12. 31. There is none other *c.* greater than these
Lu. 15. 29. I never transgressed a *commandment* of thine
23. 56. on the sabbath they rested according to the *c.*
Jno. 10. 18. This *commandment* received I from my Father
11. 57. the chief priests and the Pharisees had given *c.*
12. 49. but the Father—given me a *commandment*
50. I know that his *commandment* is life eternal
13. 34. A new *commandment* I give unto you
14. 31. as the Father gave me *commandment*, even so I do
15. 12. This is my *c.*, that ye love one another. 1 *Jno.* 3.23
Acts 1. 2. after that he had given ¹*commandment*
15. 24. to whom we gave no *commandment*
17. 15. and receiving a *c.* unto Silas and Timothy
Rom. 7. 8. wrought in me through the *c.*—coveting
9. but when the *c.* came, sin revived, and I died
10. and the *c.*, which was unto life, this I found to be
11. sin, finding occasion, through the *c.* beguiled me
12. law is holy, and the *c.* holy, and righteous, and good
13. through the *c.* sin might become exceeding sinful
13. 9. if there be any other *c.*, it is summed up in this
1 *Cor.* 7. 6. But this I say by way of permission, not of *c.*
2 *Cor.* 8. 8. I speak not by way of *c.*, but as proving
Eph. 6. 2. (which is the first *commandment* with promise)
Heb. 7. 16. not after the law of a carnal *commandment*
18. there is a disannulling of a foregoing *commandment*
9. 19. For when every ²*c.* had been spoken by Moses
11. 22. Joseph—gave *commandment* concerning his bones
23. [Moses' parents] were not afraid of the king's *c.*
2 *Pet.* 2. 21. after knowing it, to turn back from the holy *c.*
3. 2. ye should remember—the *c.* of the Lord and Saviour
1 *Jno.* 2. 7. no new *c.*—an old *c.*—old *c.* is the word
8. Again, a new *commandment* write I unto you
3. 23. this is his *commandment*—as he gave us *c.*
4. 21. And this *commandment* have we from him
2 *Jno* 4. even as we received *c.* from the Father
5. not as though I wrote to thee a new *commandment*
6. This is the *commandment*, even as ye heard
see charge, charging, command, commandments.

Commandment of God, or of the Lord.—*A.V.* ¹*commandments.*
Mat. 15. 3. Why do ye also transgress the *c.* of God
Mk. 7. 8. Ye leave the *c.* of God, and hold fast the tradition
9. Full well do ye reject the *commandment* of God

COMMANDMENT

Rom. 16. 26. according to the *c.* of the eternal God
1 *Cor.* 7. 25. concerning virgins I have no *c. of the Lord*
14. 37. that they are the ¹*commandment of the Lord*
1 *Tim.* 1. 1. according to the *c. of G.* our Saviour. *Tit.* 1. 3
   see word of God.

Commandments.—*A. V.* ¹*commandment.*

Mat. 5. 19. shall break one of these least *commandments*
19. 17. if thou wouldest enter into life, keep the *c.*
22. 40. On these two *c.* hangeth the whole law
Mk. 10. 19. Thou knowest the *c.*, Do not kill. *Lu.* 18. 20
Lu. 1. 6. [Zacharias and Elisabeth] walking in all the *c.*
Jno. 14. 15. If ye love me, ye will keep my *commandments*
21. He that hath my *commandments*, and keepeth them
15. 10. If ye keep my *c.*—as I have kept my Father's *c.*
1 *Cor.* 7. 19. but the keeping of the *commandments* of God
Eph. 2. 15. the law of *c.* contained in ordinances
1 *Jno.* 2. 3. we know him, if we keep his *commandments*
4. and keepeth not his *commandments*, is a liar
3. 22. we keep his ¹*c.*, and do the things that are pleasing
24. he that keepeth his *commandments* abideth in him
5. 2. when we love God, and do his *commandments*
3. this is the love of God, that we keep his *commandments* : and his *commandments* are not grievous
2 *Jno.* 6. love, that we should walk after his *commandments*
Rev. 14. 12. the patience of the saints, they that keep the *c.*
   see commandment, commandment of God, precepts, robes.

Commend- ed—eth—ing.—*A. V.* ¹*approving,* ²*recommended.*

Lu. 16. 8. his lord *commended* the unrighteous steward
23. 46. Father, into thy hands I *commend* my spirit
Acts 14. 23. appointed for them elders—*c.* them to the Lord
15. 40. ²*c.* by the brethren to the grace of the Lord
20. 32. now I *c.* you to God, and to the word of his grace
Rom. 3. 5. our unrighteousness *c.* the righteousness of God
5. 8. But God *commendeth* his own love toward us
16. 1. I *commend* unto you Phœbe our sister
1 *Cor.* 8. 8. But meat will not *commend* us to God
2 *Cor.* 3. 1. Are we beginning again to *commend* ourselves ?
4. 2. of the truth *c.* ourselves to every man's conscience
5. 12. We are not again *commending* ourselves unto you
6. 4. in everything ¹*c.* ourselves, as ministers of God
10. 12. with certain of them that *commend* themselves
18. not he that *c.* himself—but whom the Lord *c.*
12. 11. I ought to have been *commended* of you

Commendation.

2 *Cor.* 3. 1. epistles of *commendation* to you or from you?

Commission.

Acts 26. 12. with the authority and *c.* of the chief priests

Commit.—*A. V.* ¹*committed.*

Mat. 19. 18. Thou shalt not *commit* adultery. *Mk.* 10. 19:
   Lu. 18. 20 ; *Rom.* 13. 9
Lu. 12. 48. to whom they ¹*c.* much, of him will they ask the
16. 11. who will *c.* to your trust the true riches ? ¦more
Rom. 2. 22. thou that sayest a man should not *commit* adultery, dost thou *commit* adultery ?
1 *Cor.* 10. 8. Neither let us *commit* fornication
2 *Cor.* 11, 7. Or did I ¹*commit* a sin in abasing myself
1 *Tim.* 1. 18. This charge I *c.* unto thee, my child Timothy
2 *Tim.* 2. 2. the same *commit* thou to faithful men
Jas. 2. 9. if ye have respect of persons, ye *commit* sin
1 *Pet.* 4. 19. *c.* their souls in well-doing unto a faithful
Rev. 2. 14. children of Israel—to *c.* fornication [Creator
20. seduceth my servants to *commit* fornication
   see adultery, practice, trust.

COMMUNION

Committed.—*A. V.* ¹*delivered,* ²*recommended.*

Mk. 15. 7. Barabbas—had *committed* murder
Acts 8. 3. Saul—haling men and women *c.* them to prison
14. 26. from whence they had been ²*c.* to the grace of God
25. 11. and have *c.* anything worthy of death [Paul]
25. I found that he had *c.* nothing worthy of death
1 *Cor.* 10. 8. commit fornication as some of them *committed*
2 *Cor.* 5. 19. having *c.* unto us the word of reconciliation
12. 21. repented not of the—lasciviousness which they *c.*
1 *Tim.* 1. 11. gospel—which was *committed* to my trust
6. 20. Timothy, guard that which is *committed* unto thee
2 *Tim.* 1. 12. guard that which I have *committed* unto him
14. good thing which was *committed* unto thee guard
Jas. 5. 15. if he have *committed* sins, it shall be forgiven him
1 *Pet.* 2. 23. *c.* himself to him that judgeth righteously
2 *Pet.* 2. 4. down to hell, and ¹*c.* them to pits of darkness
Rev. 17. 2. the kings of the earth *c.* fornication. 18. 3, 9
   see adultery, commit, done, given, intrusted, wrought.

Committeth.

Jno. 8. 34. Every one that *c.* sin is the bondservant of sin
1 *Cor.* 6. 18. he that *committeth* fornication sinneth against
   see adultery, doeth.

Commodious.

Acts 27. 12. because the haven was not *c.* to winter in

Common

Mk. 12. 37. And the *common* people heard him gladly
Acts 2. 44. were together, and had all things *c.* 4. 32
10. 14. never eaten anything that is *c.* and unclean   11 8
15. What God hath cleansed, make not thou *c.* 11. 9
28. that I should not call any man *common* or unclean
Tit. 1. 4. Titus, my true child after a *common* faith
Jude 3. to write unto you of our *common* salvation
   see public.

Commonly *A. V.*—*see actually.*

Commonwealth.

Eph. 2. 12. alienated from the *commonwealth* of Israel

Commotion *A. V.*—*see tumults.*

Communed.—*A. V.* ¹*talked.*

Lu. 6. 11. and *c.* one with another what they might do
22. 4. [Judas] *communed* with the chief priests
24. 14. they ¹*communed* with each other of all these things
15. while they [disciples] *c.* and questioned together
Acts 24. 26. [Felix] *communed* with him [Paul]

Communicate.

Gal. 6. 6. taught in the word *c.* unto him that teacheth
1 *Tim.* 6. 18. ready to distribute, willing to *communicate*
Heb. 13. 16 to do good and to *communicate* forget not
   see laid before, fellowship.

Communicating.—*A. V.* ¹*distributing.*

Rom 12. 13. ¹*communicating* to the necessities of the saints

Communications.

Lu. 24. 17. What *c.* are these that ye have one with another
   see speech, company, fellowship.

Communion.—*A. V.* ¹*fellowship,* ²*partakers.*

1 *Cor.* 10. 16. a *c.* of the blood of Christ ?—*c.* of the body
18. they which eat the sacrifices, ²*c.* with the altar ?
20. not that ye should have ¹*communion* with devils
2 *Cor.* 6. 14. what *communion* hath light with darkness ?
13. 14. the love of God, and the *c.* of the Holy Ghost

COMPACTED

Compacted.—*A.V.* ¹*standing.*
2 *Pet.* 3. 5. and an earth ¹*compacted* out of water

Companied.
Acts 1. 21. men therefore which have *companied* with us

Companies.—*A.V.* ¹*company.*
Mk. 6. 39. all should sit down by c. upon the green grass
Lu. 9. 14. Make them sit down in ¹c., about fifty each

Companions.
Acts 19. 29. men of Macedonia, Paul's *companions* in travel
see fellow-worker, partaker—s.

Company.—*A.V.* ¹*communications,* ²*multitude.*
Lu. 2. 44. supposing him [Jesus] to be in the *company*
6. 22. when they shall separate you from their *company*
23. 1. the whole ²*company* of them rose up
24. 22. certain women of our *company* amazed us
Acts 4. 23. they [Peter and John] came to their own c.
6. 7. great c. of the priests were obedient to the faith
15. 22. to choose men out of their c., and send them
Rom. 15. 24. I shall have been satisfied with your *company*
1 *Cor.* 5. 9. I wrote unto you—to have no c. with fornicators
11. you not to keep *company*—fornicator, or covetous
15. 33. Evil ¹*company* doth corrupt good manners
2 *Th.* 3. 14. note that man, that ye have no c. with him
see crowd, companies, hosts, multitude, join, saileth.

Compare—ed—ing.
Rom. 8. 18. not worthy to be *compared* with the glory
1 *Cor.* 2. 13. *comparing* spiritual things with spiritual
2 *Cor.* 10. 12. are not bold to—¹c. ourselves—c. themselves

Comparison *A.V.*—*see parable.*

Compass.
Mat. 23. 15. for ye c. sea and land to make one proselyte
Lu. 19. 43. cast up a bank about thee, and c. thee round
see circuit.

Compassed.
Lu. 21. 20. ye see Jerusalem *compassed* with armies
Heb. 5. 2. he himself also is *compassed* with infirmity
11. 30. after they had been c. about for seven days
12. 1. are c. about with so great a cloud of witnesses
Rev. 20. 9. and *compassed* the camp of the saints about

Compassion—s—ate.—*A.V.* ¹*mercy—ies.*
Mat. 9. 36. moved with c. for them. 14. 14: *Mk.* 6. 34
15. 32. I have *compassion* on the multitude. *Mk.* 8. 2
18. 27. being moved with c., released him, and forgave
20. 34. Jesus, being moved with c., touched their eyes
Mk. 1. 41. moved with c., he stretched forth his hand
9. 22. have *compassion* on us, and help us
Lu. 7. 13. he had *compassion* on her [widow of Nain]
10. 33. when he saw him, he was moved with *compassion*
15. 20. moved with c., and ran, and fell on his neck
Rom. 9. 15. I will have *compassion* on whom I have c.
Phil. 2. 1. if any tender mercies and ¹*compassions*
Col. 3. 12. a heart of ¹*compassion,* kindness, humility
Heb. 10. 28. set at nought Moses' law dieth without ¹c.
34. ye both had *compassion* on them that were in bonds
1 *Pet.*3.8. *compassionate,* loving as brethren, tenderhearted
1 *Jno.* 3. 17. in need, and shutteth up his c. from him
see bear, mercy.

Compel.—*A.V.* ¹*constrain.*
Mat. 5. 41. *compel* thee to go one mile, go with him twain
Mk. 15. 21. c. one passing by, Simon of Cyrene—bear his
Gal. 6. 12. to make a fair show in the flesh, they ¹c. you to
see constrain.

CONCERNING

Compelled—est.
Mat. 27. 32. Simon by name: him they *compelled* to go
2 *Cor.* 12. 11. I am become foolish : ye *compelled* me
Gal. 2. 3. being a Greek, was *compelled* to be circumcised
14. how c. thou the Gentiles to live as do the Jews ?

Complainers.
Jude 16. These are murmurers, c., walking after their lusts

Complaint.—*A.V.* ¹*quarrel.*
Col. 3. 13. if any man have a ¹*complaint* against any
see charges.

Complete—ly.—*A.V.* ¹*finish,* ²*perfect,* ³*perform,*
⁴*throughly.*
Lu. 14. 28. whether he have wherewith to ¹*complete* it?
2 *Cor.* 8. 6. he would also ¹*complete* in you this grace
11. But now ³*complete* the doing also
2 *Tim.* 3. 17. that the man of God may be ²*complete,*
furnished ⁴*completely* unto every good work
see full, fully.

Completed.—*A.V.* ¹*ended.*
Lu. 4. 2. when they were ¹*completed,* he hungered
13. when the devil had ¹*completed* every temptation
Acts 21. 27. when the seven days were almost ¹*completed*

Completion.—*A.V.* ¹*performance.*
2 *Cor.* 8. 11. there may be the ¹c. also out of your ability

Comprehend—ed *A.V.*—*apprehend—ed, summed.*

Concealed.—*A.V.* ¹*hid.*
Lu. 9. 45. it was ¹c. from them, that they should not

Conceits.
Rom. 11.25. lest ye be wise in your own *conceits.* 12. 16

Conceive—d.
Mat. 1. 20. that which is c. in her is of the Holy Ghost
Lu. 1. 24. after these days Elisabeth his wife *conceived*
31. behold, thou [Mary] shalt *conceive* in thy womb
36. she also hath *conceived* a son in her old age
2. 21. by the angel before he was *conceived* in the womb
Acts 5. 4. How is it that thou hast c. this thing in thy
Rom. 9. 10. Rebecca also having *conceived* by one
Heb. 11. 11. Sarah herself received power to *conceive* seed
*Jas.*1. 15.Then the lust, when it hath *conceived,* beareth sin

Concern.
2 *Cor.* 11.30. I will glory of the things that c. my weakness
see concerning.

Concerning.—*A.V.* ¹*behalf,* ²*concern,* ³*over,* ⁴*pertaining to,* ⁵*sake,* ⁶*touching.*
Mat. 16. 11. that I spake not to you *concerning* bread ?
19. 17. Why askest thou me c. that which is good ?
Mk. 5. 16. declared unto them—*concerning* the swine
6. 52. they understood not *concerning* the loaves
Lu. 4. 10. He shall give his angels charge ³*concerning* thee
24. 27. in all the scriptures the things c. himself
Acts 1. 3. the things ⁴*concerning* the kingdom of God
4. 9. if we this day are examined *concerning* a good deed
8. 12. good tidings *concerning* the kingdom of God
13. 34. as c. that he raised him up from the dead
19. 40. we are in danger to be accused, c. this day's riot
26. 7. And ⁵*concerning* this hope I am accused by the Jews
28. 22. for as c. this sect—everywhere it is spoken against
31. teaching the things ²c. the Lord Jesus Christ

CONCERNING

Rom. 9. 5. of whom is Christ as *concerning* the flesh
1 *Cor.* 1. 4. I thank my God always ¹*concerning* you
    8. 1. Now ⁶*concerning* things sacrificed to idols
1 *Th.* 4. 9. But ⁶*concerning* love of the brethren ye have
1 *Tim.* 6. 21. some professing have erred c. the faith
2 *Tim.* 2. 18. men who *concerning* the truth have erred
    3. 8. reprobate *concerning* the faith
Tit. 3. 8. *concerning* these things I will that thou affirm
Heb. 11. 7. Noah, being warned of God c. things not seen
    20. blessed Jacob and Esau, even c. things to come
1 *Pet.* 4. 12. think it not strange *concerning* the fiery trial
2 *Pet.* 3. 9. The Lord is not slack *concerning* his promise
      see matter, regard, touching, way.

Concision.
Phil. 3. 2. beware of the evil workers, beware of the c.

Conclude A.V.—see reckon.

Concluded A.V.—see shut (up).

Concluding.—A.V. ¹gathering.
Acts 16. 10. ¹*concluding* that God had called us for to preach

Concord.
2 *Cor.* 6. 15. what *concord* hath Christ with Belial ?

Concourse.
Acts 19. 40. shall not be able to give account of this *concourse*

Concupiscence A.V.—see coveting, passion.

Condemn.—A.V. ¹condemned—eth.
Mat. 12. 41. this generation, and shall *condemn* it. 42:
    Lu. 11. 31, 32
    20. 18. and they shall *condemn* him to death. *Mk.* 10. 33
Lu. 6. 37. *condemn* not, and ye shall not be condemned
Jno. 8. 10. did no man ¹*condemn* thee ?
    11. Neither do I *condemn* thee ; go thy way
Rom. 8. 34. who is he that shall ¹*condemn* ?
2 *Cor.* 7. 3. I say it not to *condemn* you
1 *Jno.* 3. 20. whereinsoever our heart *condemn* us
    21. if our heart c. us not, we have boldness toward God
      see judge.

Condemnation.—A.V. ¹damnation.
Mat. 23. 14. ye shall receive greater¹*condemnation*[margin]
    Mk. 12. ¹⁴⁰ : *Lu.* 20. ¹⁴⁷
Lu. 23. 40. seeing thou art in the same *condemnation* ?
Rom. 3. 8. whose ¹*condemnation* is just
    5. 16. for the judgement came of one unto *condemnation*
    18. one trespass the judgement came unto all men to c.
    8. 1. now no c. to them that are in Christ Jesus
2 *Cor.* 3. 9. For if the ministration of *condemnation* is glory
1 *Tim.* 3. 6. lest being puffed up he fall into the c. of the devil
    5. 12. having ¹c., because they have rejected their first
Jude 4. who were of old set forth unto this *condemnation*
      see judgement.

Condemned.—A.V. ¹blamed, ²damned.
Mat. 12. 7. ye would not have *condemned* the guiltless
    37. by thy words thou shalt be *condemned*
    27. 3. Judas—when he saw that he was c., repented
Mk. 14. 64. they all *condemned* him to be worthy of death
    16. 16. he that disbelieveth shall be ²*condemned*
Lu. 6. 37. condemn not, and ye shall not be *condemned*
    24. 20. our rulers delivered him up to be c. to death
Rom. 8. 3. as an offering for sin, *condemned* sin in the flesh
    14. 23. he that doubteth is ²*condemned* if he eat

CONFIDENCE

1 *Cor.* 11. 32. that we may not be c. with the world
Gal. 2. 11. to the face, because he [Peter] stood ¹*condemned*
Tit. 2. 8. sound speech, that cannot be *condemned*
    3. 11. is perverted, and sinneth, being self-*condemned*
Heb. 11. 7. through which he [Noah] *condemned* the world
Jas. 5. 6. Ye have *condemned*, ye have killed the righteous
2 *Pet.* 2. 6. into ashes *condemned* them with an overthrow
      see condemn, judged.

Condemnest—ing.
Acts 13. 27. fulfilled them by *condemning* him
Rom. 2. 1. wherein thou judgest another, thou c. thyself
      see judgeth.

Condemneth A.V.—see condemn, judgeth.

Condescend.
Rom. 12. 16. but *condescend* to things that are lowly

Conditions.
Lu. 14. 32. an ambassage, and asketh *conditions* of peace

Conduct—ed.—A.V. ¹manner of life.
Acts 17. 15. But they that *conducted* Paul brought him
2 *Tim.* 3. 10. follow my teaching, ¹*conduct*, purpose, faith
      see set.

Conferred.
Acts 4. 15. they *conferred* among themselves, saying
    25. 12. Festus, when he had *conferred* with the council
Gal. 1. 16. immediately I c. not with flesh and blood

Confess.—A.V. ¹professed.
Mat. 10. 32. who shall *confess* me before men, him will I
    also *confess* before my Father. *Lu.* 12. 8
Jno. 9. 22. if any man should *confess* him to be Christ
    12. 42. because of the Pharisees they did not *confess* it
Acts 23. 8. neither angel, nor spirit—Pharisees c. both
    24. 14. But this I *confess* unto thee, that after the Way
Rom. 10. 9. shalt *confess* with thy mouth Jesus as Lord
    14. 11. And every tongue shall *confess* to God [Lord
Phil. 2. 11. every tongue should c. that Jesus Christ is
1 *Tim.* 6. 12. and didst ¹*confess* the good confession
Jas. 5. 16. *Confess* therefore your sins one to another
1 *Jno.* 1. 9. If we *confess* our sins, he is faithful
    4. 15. Whosoever shall c. that Jesus is the Son of God
2 *Jno.* 7. *confess* not that Jesus Christ cometh in the flesh
Rev. 3. 5. and I will *confess* his name before my Father
      see praise.

Confessed—eth—ing.—A.V. ¹acknowledgeth
Mat. 3. 6. baptized of him in—Jordan c. their sins. *Mk.* 1. 5.
Jno. 1. 20. And he c., and denied not ; and he c., I am not
Acts 19. 18. came, c., and declaring their deeds | the Christ
Heb. 11. 18. c. that they were strangers and pilgrims
1 *Jno.* 2. 23. he that ¹c. the Son hath the Father also
    4. 2. every spirit which c. that Jesus Christ is come
    3. every spirit which *confesseth* not Jesus is not of God

Confession.—A.V. ¹profession, ²thanks.
Rom. 10. 10. and with the mouth c. is made unto salvation
1 *Tim.* 6. 12. didst confess the good ¹c. in the sight of many
    13. before Pontius Pilate witnessed the good *confession*
Heb. 3. 1. Apostle and High Priest of our ¹*confession*
    4. 14. let us hold fast our ¹*confession*
    10. 23. let us hold fast the ¹c. of our hope that it waver not
    13. 15. fruit of lips which make ²*confession* to his name

Confidence.—A.V. ¹confident boasting, ²trust.
2 *Cor.* 1. 15. And in this c. I was minded to come before
    2. 3. having *confidence* in you all, that my joy is the joy

CONFIDENCE

Cor. 3. 4. such ²c. have we through Christ to God-ward
8. 22. by reason of the great c. which he hath in you
9. 4. should be put to shame in this ¹confidence
10. 2. with the confidence wherewith I count to be bold
11. 17. in foolishness, in this confidence of glorying
Gal. 5. 10. I have confidence to you-ward in the Lord
Eph. 3. 12. and access in c. through our faith in him
Phil. 1. 25. And having this c., I know that I shall abide
3. 3. glory in Christ Jesus, and have no c. in the flesh
4. have c. even in the flesh—to have ²c in the flesh
2 *Th.* 3. 4. And we have confidence in the Lord touching you
Philem. 21. Having confidence in thine obedience
Heb. 3. 14. if we hold fast the beginning of our c. firm
see boldness, courage.

Confident—ly.—*A.V.* ¹*constantly.*
Lu. 22. 59. another confidently affirmed, saying, Of a truth
Acts 12. 15. But she [Rhoda] ¹c.affirmed that it was even so
Rom. 2. 19. confident that thou thyself art a guide
Phil. 1. 6. being confident of this very thing
14. being confident through my bonds
Tit. 3. 8. these things I will that thou affirm ¹confidently
see confidence, courage.

Confirm.
Rom. 15. 8. he might c. the promises given unto the fathers
1 *Cor.* 1. 8. who shall also confirm you unto the end
2 *Cor.* 2. 8. I beseech you to confirm your love toward him

Confirmation.
Phil. 1. 7. in the defence and confirmation of the gospel
Heb. 6. 16. every dispute of theirs the oath is final for c.

Confirmed.
Acts 15. 32. brethren with many words, and c. them
1 *Cor.* 1. 6. testimony of Christ was confirmed in you
Gal. 3. 15. when it hath been c., no one maketh it void. 17
Heb. 2. 3. was confirmed unto us by them that heard
see interposed.

Confirming.
Mk. 16. 20. confirming the word by the signs that followed
Acts 14. 22. confirming the souls of the disciples / churches
15. 41. [Paul] through Syria and Cilicia, confirming the

Conflict.—*A.V.* ¹*contention,* ²*fight.*
Phil. 1. 30. having the same conflict which ye saw in me
1 *Th.* 2. 2. speak unto you the gospel of God in much ¹c.
Heb. 10. 32. ye endured a great ²conflict of sufferings
see strive.

Conformable.—*A.V. see conformed.*

Conformed.—*A.V.* ¹*conformable,* ²*fashioned.*
Rom. 8. 29. foreordained to be c. to the image of his Son
Phil. 3. 10. becoming ¹conformed unto his death
21. that it may be ²conformed to the body of his glory
see fashioned.

Confound.—*A.V. see put to shame.*

Confounded.
Acts 2. 6. the multitude came together,and were confounded
9. 22. Saul—c. the Jews which dwelt at Damascus
see shame.

Confused.—*A.V. see confusion.*

Confusion.—*A.V.* ¹*confused,* ²*uproar.*
Acts 19. 29. And the city was filled with the confusion
32. for the assembly was in ¹confusion
21. 31. all Jerusalem was in ²confusion
1 *Cor.* 14. 33. for God is not a God of confusion
Jas. 3. 16. there is confusion and every vile deed

CONSIDER

Confuted.—*A.V.* ¹*convinced.*
Acts 18. 28. for he [Apollos] powerfully ¹confuted the Jews

Congregation.—*A.V.* ¹*church.*
Heb. 2. 12. in the midst of the ¹c. will I sing thy praise
see synagogue.

Conquer—ing.
Rev. 6. 2. and he came forth conquering, and to conquer

Conquerors.
Rom. 8. 37. more than c. through him that loved us

Conscience—s.
Acts 23. 1. I have lived before God in all good conscience
24. 16. to have a conscience void of offence toward God
Rom. 2. 15. their conscience bearing witness therewith
9. 1. my c. bearing witness with me in the Holy Ghost
13. 5. because of the wrath, but also for conscience sake
1 *Cor.* 8. 7. and their conscience being weak is defiled
10. will not his c., if he is weak, be emboldened to eat
12. and wounding their conscience when it is weak
10. 25. eat, asking no questions for conscience sake. 27
28. for his sake that shewed it, and for conscience sake
29. conscience, I say, not thine own, but the other's. 30
2 *Cor.* 1. 12. our glorying is this, the testimony of our c.
4. 2. commending ourselves to every man's conscience
5. 11. we are made manifest also in your consciences
1 *Tim.* 1. 5. out of a pure heart and a good conscience
19. holding faith and a good conscience
3. 9. holding the mystery of the faith in a pure c.
4. 2. branded in their own conscience as with a hot iron
2 *Tim.* 1. 3. whom I serve from my forefathers in a pure c.
Tit. 1. 15. their mind and their conscience are defiled
Heb. 9. 9. as touching the c., make the worshipper perfect
14. cleanse your conscience from dead works to serve
10. 2. cleansed,would have had no more conscience of sins?
22. having our hearts sprinkled from an evil conscience
13. 18. for we are persuaded that we have a good conscience
1 *Pet.* 2. 19. if for c. toward God a man endureth griefs
3. 16. having a good conscience; that wherein ye are
21. the interrogation of a good conscience toward God
see used.

Consecrated. *A.V.*—*see dedicated, perfected.*

Consent—ed—eth—ing.—*A.V.* ¹*allow,* ²*pleasure,* ³*promised.*
Lu. 11. 48. ¹consent unto the works of your fathers
14. 18. they all with one consent began to make excuse
22. 6. he ²c., and sought opportunity to deliver him
23. 51. (he had not consented to their counsel and deed)
Acts 8. 1. And Saul was consenting unto his death
18. 20. to abide a longer time, he [Paul] c. not [by, and c.
22. 20. blood of Stephen—was shed, I also was standing
Rom. 1. 32. but also ²consent with them that practise them
7. 16. I consent unto the law that it is good
1 *Cor.* 7. 5. except it be by consent for a season
1 *Tim.* 6. 3. and consenteth not to sound words

Consider *A.V.*—¹*think.*
Mat. 6. 28. Consider the lilies of the field. *Lu.* 12. 27
Lu. 12. 24. Consider the ravens, that they sow not
Acts 15. 6. elders were gathered together to c. of this matter
2 *Cor.* 10. 7. is Christ's, let him ¹c. this again with himself
2 *Tim.* 2. 7. C. what I say; for the Lord shall give thee
Heb. 3. 1. c. the Apostle and High Priest of our confession
7. 4. Now consider how great this man was
10. 24. let us consider one another to provoke unto love
12. 3. For c. him that hath endured such gainsaying
see account.

CONSIDERED

Considered—est.—*A.V.* ¹*perceivest.*
Mat. 7. 3. but c. not the beam that is in thine own eye? *Lu.*
Acts 11. 6. I c., and saw the four-footed beasts [6. ¹4¹
12. 12. And when he [Peter] had *considered* the thing
Rom. 4. 19. he c. his own body now as good as dead

Considering.
Heb. 13. 7. and *considering* the issue of their life
see looking.

Consist—eth.
Lu. 12. 15. for a man's life *consisteth* not in the abundance
Col. 1. 17. and in him all things *consist*

Consolation.—*A.V.* ¹*exhortation.*
Lu. 2. 25. looking for the *consolation* of Israel
6. 24. that are rich! for ye have received your *consolation*
Acts 15. 31. read it, they rejoiced for the *consolation* [and ¹c.
1 *Cor.* 14. 3. speaketh unto men edification, and comfort,
Phil. 2. 1. if any *consolation* of love, if any fellowship
see exhortation, comfort, encouragement.

Console.—*A.V.* ¹*comfort.*
Jno. 11. 19. to Martha and Mary, to ¹*console* them

Consorted.
Acts 17. 4. were persuaded, and c. with Paul and Silas

Conspiracy.
Acts 23. 13. more than forty which made this *conspiracy*

Constantly *A.V.*—*see confidently.*

Constrain—ed—eth.—*A.V.* ¹*compel,* ²*needful,* ³*pressed.*
Mat. 14. 22. And straightway he c. his disciples. *Mk.* 6. 45
Lu. 14 23. highways and hedges, and ¹c. them to come in
24. 29. they *constrained* him, saying, Abide with us
Acts 16. 15. and abide there. And she *constrained* us
18. 5. Paul was ³*constrained* by the word, testifying
28. 19, I was *constrained* to appeal unto Cæsar
2 *Cor.* 5. 14. For the love of Christ *constraineth* us
Jude 3. I was ²*constrained* to write unto you exhorting
see compel.

Constraint.
1 *Pet.* 5. 2. exercising the oversight, not of *constraint*

Consult—ed—eth *A.V.*—*see counsel.*

Consultation.
Mk. 15. 1. and the whole council, held a *consultation*

Consume.—*A.V.* ¹*corrupt.*
Mat. 6. 19. where moth and rust doth ¹*consume.* ¹20)
Lu. 9. 54. that we bid fire to come down—and c. them?
see slay, spend.

Consumed.
Gal. 5. 15. take heed that ye be not c. one of another

Consuming.
Heb. 12. 29. for our God is a *consuming* fire

Contain—ed—ing.
Jno. 2. 6. *containing* two or three firkins apiece
21. 25. the world itself would not *contain* the books
Eph. 2. 15. law of commandments *contained* in ordinances
1 *Pet.* 2. 6. Because it is *contained* in scripture
see continency.

Contemptible *A.V.*—*see (of no) account.*

CONTINUE

Contend.—*A.V.* ¹*strive.*
2 *Tim.* 2. 5. if also a man ¹*contend* in the games
Jude 3. exhorting you to *contend* earnestly for the faith

Contended—ing.—*A.V.* ¹*strive.*
Acts. 11. 2. of the circumcision *contended* with him [Peter]
2 *Tim.* 2. 5. not crowned, except he have ¹*contended* lawfully
Jude 9. Michael the Archangel, when c. with the devil

Content.—*A.V.* ¹*pleased.*
Mk. 15. 15. And Pilate, wishing to *content* the multitude
Lu. 3. 14. and be *content* with your wages
1 *Cor.* 7. 12. unbelieving wife, and she is ¹c. to dwell with
13. unbelieving husband, and he is ¹c. to dwell [him
Phil. 4. 11. in whatsoever state I am, therein to be *content*
1 *Tim.* 6. 8. food and covering we shall be therewith c.
Heb. 13. 5. *content* with such things as ye have
3 *Jno.* 10. wicked words ; and not *content* therewith

Contention—s.—*A.V.* ¹*strife.*
Lu. 22. 24. there arose also a ¹c. among them [disciples]
Acts 15. 39. And there arose a sharp *contention*
1 *Cor.* 1. 11. that there are *contentions* among you
see conflict, faction.

Contentious.—*A.V.* ¹*brawler—s.*
1 *Cor.* 11. 16. But if any man seemeth to be *contentious*
1 *Tim.* 3. 3. gentle, not ¹*contentious,* no lover of money
Tit. 3. 2 speak evil of no man, not to be ¹c., to be gentle
see factious.

Contentment.
1 *Tim.* 6. 6. But godliness with *contentment* is great gain

Continency.—*A.V.* ¹*contain.*
1 *Cor.* 7. 9. But if they have not ¹*continency,* let them marry

Continuance *A.V.*—*see patience.*

Continual.
Lu 18. 5. lest she wear me out by her *continual* coming
see importunity, unceasing.

Continually.—*A.V.* ¹*always.*
Lu. 24. 53. and were c. in the temple, blessing God
Acts 10. 7. a devout soldier of them that waited on him c.
Rom. 13. 6. attending *continually* upon this very thing
Heb. 7. 3. like unto the Son of God), abideth a priest c.
9. 6. the priests go in ¹c. into the first tabernacle
10. 1. sacrifices year by year, which they offer c.
13. 15. let us offer up a sacrifice of praise to God c.
see continue.

Continue.—*A.V.* ¹*been,* ²*bide,* ³*continually.*
Mat. 15. 32. because they c. with me now three days. *Mk.*
Acts 6. 4. But we will ³*continue* stedfastly in prayer. [8. ¹2
13. 43. Paul and Barnabas—urged them to c. in the grace
14. 22. exhorting them to *continue* in the faith
Rom. 6. 1. Shall we *continue* in sin, that grace may abound?
11. 22. God's goodness, if thou *continue* in his goodness
23. if they ²c. not in their unbelief, shall be grafted
Gal. 2. 5. the truth of the gospel might *continue* with you
Col. 1. 23. if so be that ye *continue* in the faith
4. 2. *Continue* stedfastly in prayer
1 *Tim.* 2. 15. saved through the childbearing, if they c. in
4. 16. to they teaching. *Continue* in these things
Heb. 13. 1. Let love of the brethren *continue*
2 *Pet.* 3. 4. fell asleep, all things *continue* as they were
Rev. 13. 5. authority to *continue* forty and two months
17. 10. when he cometh, he must *continue* a little while
see abide, continuing, spend, stand.

CONTINUED

Continued.
Lu. 6. 12. he [Jesus] *continued* all night in prayer to God
22. 28. which have c. with me in my temptations
Jno. 8. 7. when they c. asking him, he lifted up himself
Acts 1. 14. These all with one accord *continued* stedfastly
2. 42. And they c. stedfastly in the apostles' teaching
8. 13. and being baptized, he *continued* with Philip
12. 16. But Peter *continued* knocking
19. 10. And this *continued* for the space of two years
Heb. 8. 9. For they *continued* not in my covenant
1 *Jno.* 2. 19. they had been of us, they would have c. with us
see abode, dwelt, prolonged, tarried.

Continuest.—*A.V.* ¹*remainest.*
Heb. 1. 11. They shall perish; but thou ¹*continuest*

Continueth—ing.—*A.V.* ¹*continue.*
Acts 2. 46. *continuing* stedfastly with one accord in the
Rom. 12. 12. *continuing* stedfastly in prayer
Gal. 3. 10. Cursed is every one which c. not in all things
1 *Tim.* 5. 5. and *continueth* in supplications and prayers
Heb. 7. 23. that by death they are hindered from ¹*continuing*
Jas. 1. 25. the law of liberty, and so *continueth*
see abiding.

Contradicted.—*A.V* ¹*spake against.*
Acts 13. 45. and ¹*contradicted* the things which were spoken

Contradiction *A.V.*—*see dispute, gainsaying.*

Contrariwise.
2 *Cor* 2. 7. so that *contrariwise* ye should rather forgive
Gal. 2. 7. but o., when they saw that I had been intrusted
1 *Pet.* 3. 9. reviling for reviling; but *contrariwise* blessing

Contrary.
Mat. 14. 24. the wind was *contrary. Mk.* 6. 48: *Acts* 27. 4
Acts 17 7. these all act *contrary* to the decrees of Cæsar
18. 13. persuadeth men to worship God c. to the law
23. 3. commandest me to be smitten c. to the law ?
26. 9. do many things *contrary* to the name of Jesus
Rom. 11. 24. grafted *contrary* to nature into a good olive
16. 17. *contrary* to the doctrine which ye learned
Gal. 5. 17 Spirit against the flesh; for these are *contrary*
Col. 2 14. which was c. to us: and he hath taken it out
1 *Th.* 2. 15. please not God, and are *contrary* to all men
1 *Tim.* 1. 10. any other thing *contrary* to the sound doctrine
Tit. 2. 8. that is of the *contrary* part may be ashamed

Contribution.—*A.V.* ¹*distribution.*
Rom. 15. 26. a certain c. for the poor among the saints
2 *Cor.* 9. 13. the liberality of your ¹*contribution* unto them

Controversy.
1 *Tim.* 3. 16. And without c. great is the mystery of

Convenient.
Mk. 6. 21. And when a *convenient* day was come
Acts 24. 25. when I have a c. season, I will call thee unto me
see fitting, opportunity, befitting.

Conveniently.
Mk. 14. 11. sought how he might *conveniently* deliver him

Conversation *A.V.*—*see behaved, behaviour, citizenship, (good) life, (manner of) life, living.*

CORNFIELDS

Conversion.
Acts 15. 3. declaring the *conversion* of the Gentiles

Convert—eth.
Jas. 5. 19. do err from the truth, and one *convert* him
20. that he which *converteth* a sinner from the error
see turn.

Converted *A V*—*see turned.*

Conveyed.
Jno. 5. 13. for Jesus had *conveyed* himself away

Convict.—*A.V.* ¹*convince,* ²*reprove.*
Jno. 16. 8. when he is come, will ²*convict* the world
Tit. 1. 9. both to exhort—and to ¹*convict* the gainsayers
Jude 15. to ¹*convict* all the ungodly of all their works

Convicted—*A.V.* ¹*convinced.*
Jas. 2. 9. being ¹*convicted* by the law as transgressors

Convicteth.—*A.V.* ¹*convinceth.*
Jno. 8. 46. Which of you ¹*convicteth* me of sin ?

Convince—ed—eth *A.V.*—*see confuted, convict, convicted, convicteth, reproved.*

Cool.
Lu. 16. 24. his finger in water, and *cool* my tongue

Coppersmith.
2 *Tim.* 4. 14. Alexander the *coppersmith* did me much evil

Copy—ies.—*A.V.* ¹*example,* ²*patterns.*
Heb. 9. 23. that which is a ¹c. and shadow of the heavenly
9. 23. the ²*copies* of the things in the heavens should be

Corban.
Mk. 7. 11. *Corban,* that is to say, Given to God

Cords.
Jno. 2. 15. he made a scourge of *cords,* and cast all out

Corn.—*A.V.* ¹*fruits.*
Mat. 12. 1. began to pluck ears of c. *Mk.* 2. 23: *Lu.* 6. 1
Mk. 4. 28. first the blade, then the ear, then the full *corn*
Lu. 12. 18. there will I bestow all my ¹*corn* and my goods
Acts 7. 12. When Jacob heard that there was c. in Egypt
1 *Cor.* 9. 9. Thou shalt not muzzle the ox when he
treadeth out the *corn.* 1 *Tim.* 5. 18
see cornfields, grain.

Corner.
Mat. 21. 42. The same was made the head of the *corner.*
Mk. 12. 10: *Lu.* 20. 17: *Acts* 4. 11: 1 *Pet.* 2. 7
Acts 26. 26. for this hath not been done in a *corner*

Corner stone.
Eph. 2. 20. Christ Jesus himself being the chief *corner s.*
1 *Pet.* 2. 6. I lay in Zion a chief *corner s.,* elect, precious

Corners.—*A.V.* ¹*quarters.*
Mat. 6. 5. synagogues and in the *corners* of the streets
Acts 10. 11. let down by four *corners* upon the earth. 11. 5
Rev. 7. 1. angels standing at the four *corners* of the earth
20. 8. deceive the nations which are in the four ¹*corners*

Cornfields.—*A.V.* ¹*corn.*
Mat. 12. 1. went on the sabbath day through the ¹*cornfields. Mk.* 2. 23: *Lu.* 6. 1

CORPSE

Corpse.—*A.V.* ¹*body.*
Mat. 14. 12. his disciples—took up the ¹*corpse* [John Baptist]
Mk. 6. 29. took up his *corpse,* and laid it in a tomb
15. 45. he [Pilate] granted the ¹*corpse* to Joseph

Corrected *A.V.—see chasten.*

Correcting—*.A.V.* ¹*instructing.*
2 *Tim.* 2. 25. ¹*correcting* them that oppose themselves

Correction.
2 *Tim.* 3. 16. for reproof, for *correction,* for instruction

Corrector.—*A.V.* ¹*instructor.*
Rom. 2. 20. a ¹*corrector* of the foolish, a teacher of babes

Corrupt.
Mat. 7. 17. the *c.* tree bringeth forth evil fruit. *Lu.* 6. 43
18. neither can a *c.* tree bring forth good fruit. *Lu.* 6. 43
12. 33. or make the tree *corrupt,* and its fruit *corrupt*
1 *Cor.* 15. 33. Evil company doth *corrupt* good manners
Eph. 4. 22. which waxeth *corrupt* after the lusts of deceit
29. Let no *corrupt* speech proceed out of your mouth
Rev. 19. 2. the great harlot, which did *corrupt* the earth
see consume, corrupted, corrupting, destroyed.

Corrupted.—*A.V.* ¹*corrupt.*
2 *Cor.* 7. 2. we wronged no man, we *corrupted* no man
11. 3. your minds should be *corrupted* from the simplicity
1 *Tim.* 6. 5. wranglings of men ¹*c* in mind. 2. *Tim.* 3. ¹⁶
Jas. 5. 2. Your riches are *corrupted,* and your garments
see destroyeth.

Corruptible.
Rom. 1. 23. for the likeness of an image of *corruptible* man
1 *Cor.* 9. 25. Now they do it to receive a *corruptible* crown
15. 54. But when this *corruptible* shall have put on. 53
1 *Pet.* 1. 18. were redeemed, not with *corruptible* things
23. begotten again, not of *corruptible* seed, but of
see incorruptible.

Corrupting.—*A.V.* ¹*corrupt.*
2 *Cor.* 2. 17. we are not as the many, ¹*c.* the word of God

Corruption.
Acts 2. 27. Neither wilt thou give thy Holy One to see *c.*
31. nor did his flesh see *corruption* [13. 35
13. 34. now no more to return to *corruption*
36. was laid unto his fathers, and saw *corruption*
37. but he whom God raised up saw no *corruption*
Rom. 8. 21. shall be delivered from the bondage of *c.*
1 *Cor.* 15. 42. It is sown in *corruption ;* it is raised in
50. neither doth *corruption* inherit incorruption
Gal. 6. 8. soweth unto his own flesh shall of the flesh reap *c.*
2 *Pet.* 1. 4. having escaped from the *c.* that is in the world
2. 19. while they themselves are bondservants of *c.*
see destroying.

Cost—ly.
Lu. 14. 28. doth not first sit down and count the *cost*
1 *Tim.* 2. 9. and gold or pearls or *costly* raiment
see precious.

Costliness.
Rev. 18. 19. had their ships in the sea by reason of her *c.*

Couch.
Lu. 5. 19. with his *couch* into the midst before Jesus
24. take up thy *couch,* and go into thy house
Acts 5. 15. and laid them on beds and *couches*

COUNT

Council.
Mat. 5. 22. Raca, shall be in danger of the *council*
26. 59. the whole *council* sought false witness. *Mk.* 14. 55
Lu. 22. 66. and they led him away into their *c. Mk.* 15. 1
Jno. 11. 47. and the Pharisees gathered a *council*
Acts 4. 15. commanded them to go aside out of the *council*
5. 21. and called the *council* together, and all the senate
27. had brought them, they set them before the *council*
34. But there stood up one in the *council,* a Pharisee
41. departed from the presence of the *council,* rejoicing
6. 12. seized him, and brought him into the *council*
15. And all that sat in the *council,* fastening their eyes
22. 30. all the *c.* to come together, and brought Paul down
23. 6. Paul—cried out in the *council,* Brethren, I am
15. do ye with the *council* signify to the chief captain
24. 20. wrong-doing they found, when I stood before the *c.*
25. 12. Festus, when he had conferred with the *council*
see counsel.

Councillor.—*A. V.* ¹*counsellor.*
Mk. 15. 43. Joseph of Arimathæa, a ¹*councillor. Lu.* 23. ¹⁵⁰

Councils.
Mat. 10. 17. for they will deliver you up to *c. Mk.* 13. 9

Counsel—s.—*A.V.* ¹*consult—ed—eth,* ²*council,* ³*minded,* ⁴*will.*
Mat. 12. 14. Pharisees went out, and took ²*c.* against him
22. 15. and took *counsel* how they might ensnare him
26. 4. took ¹*counsel* together that they might take Jesus
27. 1. took *counsel* against Jesus to put him to death
7. they took *c.,* and bought with them the potter's field
28. 12. had taken *counsel,* they gave large money
Mk. 3. 6. with the Herodians took *counsel* against him
Lu. 7. 30. lawyers rejected for themselves the *c.* of God
14. 31. what king—will not sit down first and take ¹*c.*
23. 51. (he had not consented to their *counsel* and deed)
Jno. 11. 53. took *counsel* that they might put him to death
12. 10. took ¹*counsel* that they might put Lazarus also
18. 14. Now Caiaphas was he which gave *c.* to the Jews
Acts 2. 23. determinate *counsel* and foreknowledge of God
4. 28. thy hand and thy *c.* foreordained to come to pass
5. 38. this *c.* or this work be of men, it will be overthrown
9. 23. the Jews took *counsel* together to kill him
13. 36. David—served the ⁴*counsel* of God
20. 27. from declaring unto you the whole *counsel* of God
27. 29. they took ³*c.* whether they would drive the ship
42. And the soldiers' *counsel* was to kill the prisoners
1 *Cor.* 4. 5. and make manifest the *counsels* of the hearts
Eph. 1. 11. who worketh all things after the *c.* of his will
Heb. 6. 17. immutability of his *c.,* interposed with an oath
Rev. 3. 18. I *counsel* of thee to buy of me gold refined by fire
see minded.

Counsellor.
Rom. 11. 34. the Lord ? or who hath been his *counsellor ?*
see councillor.

Count.—*A.V.* ¹*counteth,* ²*think.*
Lu. 14. 28. doth not first sit down and ¹*count* the cost
2 *Cor.* 10. 2. I ²*count* to be bold against some, which ²*c.* of us
Phil. 3. 8. I *c.* all things to be loss—do *c.* them but dung
13. I *count* not myself yet to have apprehended
2 *Th.* 1. 11. that our God may *c.* you worthy of your calling
3. 15. And yet *count* him not as an enemy
1 *Tim.* 6. 1. *count* their own masters worthy of all honour
Jas. 1. 2. *Count* it all joy, my brethren, when ye fall into
2 *Pet.* 2. 13. men that *c.* it pleasure to revel in the day-time
3. 9. concerning his promise, as some *count* slackness
Rev. 13. 18. let him *count* the number of the beast
see account, call, countest.

COUNTED

Counted.—*A.V.* ¹*judged*, ²*supposed*, ³*thought*.
Mat. 14. 5. because they *counted* him as a prophet
Acts 5. 41. were *c*. worthy to suffer dishonour for the Name
19. 19. and they *counted* the price of them, and found it
Phil. 2. 6. ³*c.* it not a prize to be on an equality with God
25. I ²*counted* it necessary to send to you Epaphroditus
3. 7. gain to me, those have I *counted* loss for Christ
2 *Th.* 1. 5. that ye may be *c.* worthy of the kingdom of God
1 *Tim.* 1. 12. he *c.* me faithful, appointing me to his service
5. 17. that rule well be *counted* worthy of double honour
Heb. 3. 3. hath been *c.* worthy of more glory than Moses
7. 6. whose genealogy is not *c*. from them hath taken tithes
10. 29. and hath *counted* the blood of the covenant
11. 11. since she ¹*counted* him faithful who had promised
see reckoned.

Countenance.
Mat. 6. 16. be not, as the hypocrites, of a sad *countenance*
Mk. 10. 22. his *c.* fell—and he went away sorrowful
Lu. 9. 29. the fashion of his *countenance* was altered
Acts 2. 28. Thou shalt make me full of gladness with thy *c.*
Rev. 1. 16. and his *c.* was as the sun shineth in his strength
see appearance, face.

Countest.—*A.V.* ¹*count*.
Philem. 17. If then thou ¹*countest* me a partner

Counteth *A.V.*—*see count.*

Counting.—*A.V.* ¹*esteem*.
Phil. 2. 3. each ¹*counting* other better than himself

Countries *A.V.*—*see country.*

Country.—*A.V.* ¹*coasts*, ²*countries*, ³*land*.
Mat. 2. 12. they departed into their own *c.* another way
13. 54. And coming into his own *country* he taught them
57. without honour, save in his own *c. Mk.* 6. 4 : *Jno.* 4. 44
21. 33. and went into another *c. Mk.* 12. 1. : *Lu.* 20. 9.
25. 14. as when a man, going into another *country*
Mk. 5. 10. would not send them away out of the *country*
14. told it in the city, and in the *country. Lu.* 8. 34
6. 1. and he cometh into his own *country*
10. 12. walked, on their way into the *country*
Lu. 2. 8. were shepherds in the same *country* abiding
4. 23. do also here in thine own *country*
4. No prophet is acceptable in his own *country*
8. 37. the people of the *c.* of the Gerasenes—asked him
15. 13. and took his [prodigal] journey into a far *country*
14. arose a mighty famine in that ²*country*
15. joined himself to one of the citizens of that *country*
19. 12. A certain nobleman went into a far *c. Mk.* 13. 34
21. 21. let not them that are in the ²*country* enter therein
23. 26. Simon of Cyrene, coming from the *c. Mk.* 15. 21
Jno. 11. 54. departed thence into the *country* near to the
Acts 12. 20. because their *country* was fed from the king's *c.*
19. 1. Paul having passed through the upper ¹*country*
27. 27. surmised they were drawing near to some *country*
Heb. 11. 14. they are seeking after a *country* of their own
15. if indeed they had been mindful of that *country*
16. But now they desire a better *country*
see land, region.

Countrymen.—*A.V.* ¹*nation*.
2 *Cor.* 11. 26. in perils from my *countrymen*
Gal. 1. 14. among my ¹*c*., being more exceedingly zealous
1 *Th.* 2. 14. also suffered the same things of your own *c.*

COVENANT

Coupled.
1 *Pet.* 3. 2. beholding your chaste behaviour *c.* with fear

Courage.—*A.V.* ¹*bold*, ²*boldly*, ³*confidence*, ⁴*confident*.
Acts 28. 15. when Paul saw, he thanked God, and took *c.*
2 *Cor.* 5. 6. Being therefore always of good ⁴*courage*
8. we are of good ⁴*courage*, I say, and are willing
7. 16. I am of good ³*courage* concerning you
10. 1. being absent am of good ¹*courage* toward you
2. that I may not when present shew ¹*courage*
Heb. 13. 6. So that with good ²*c.* we say, The Lord is my

Course.—*A.V.* ¹*place*.
Lu. 1. 5. priest named Zacharias, of the *course* of Abijah
8. priest's office before God in the order of his *course*
Jno. 8. 37. my word hath not free ¹*course* in you
Acts 13. 25. And as John was fulfilling his *course*
16. 11. we made a straight *course* to Samothrace. 21. 1
20. 24. so that I may accomplish my *course*
Eph. 2. 2. ye walked according to the *course* of this world
2 *Tim.* 4. 7. I have finished the *c.*, I have kept the faith
see run, turn, voyage, wheel.

Court—s.—*A.V.* ¹*hall*, ²*law*, ³*palace*.
Mat. 26. 3 elders of the people, unto the ³*c.* of the high priest
58. Peter followed him afar off, unto the ³*court* of the
high priest. 369 : *Mk.* 14. ³54, ³66 : *Jno.* 18. ³15
Mk. 15. 16. soldiers led him away within the ¹*court*
Lu. 7. 25. and live delicately, are in kings' *courts*
11. 21. strong man fully armed guardeth his own ³*court*
22. 55. they had kindled a fire in the midst of the ¹*court*
Acts 19. 38. the ²*courts* are open, and there are proconsuls
Rev. 11. 2. And the *court* which is without the temple

Courteous *A.V.*—*see humbleminded.*

Courteously.
Acts 28. 7. Publius—entertained us three days *courteously*
see kindly.

Cousin.—*A.V.* ¹*sister's son*.
Col. 4. 10. saluteth you, and Mark, the ¹*cousin* of Barnabas
see kinsfolk, kinswoman.

Covenant—s.—*A.V.* ¹*testament*.
Mat. 26. 28. for this is my blood of the ¹*c. Mk.* 14. ¹24
Lu. 1. 72. And to remember his holy *covenant*
22. 20. This cup is the new ¹*c.* in my blood. 1 *Cor.* 11. ¹25
Acts 3. 25. Ye are the sons of the prophets, and of the *c.*
7. 8. And he gave him [Abraham] the *c.* of circumcision
Rom. 9. 4. Whose is—the glory, and the *covenants*
11. 27. And this is my *covenant* unto them, When I
2 *Cor.* 3. 6. sufficient as ministers of a new ¹*covenant*
14. at the reading of the old ¹*covenant* the same veil
Gal. 3. 15. Though it be but a man's *covenant*, yet when
17. A *covenant* confirmed beforehand by God, the law
4. 24. for these women are two *covenants*
Eph. 2. 12. strangers from the *covenants* of the promise
Heb. 7. 22. hath Jesus become the surety of a better ¹*c.*
8. 6. he is the mediator of a better *covenant*
7. For if that first *covenant* had been faultless
8. That I will make a new *covenant* with the house
9. Not according to the *covenant* that I made with
their fathers—they continued not in my *covenant*
10. For this is the *c.* that I will make with the house
13. In that he saith, A new *covenant*
9. 1. even the first *covenant* had ordinances of divine
4. the ark of the *covenant* overlaid round about with
gold—and the tables of the *covenant*
15. he is the mediator of a new ¹*c.*—the redemption of
the transgressions that were under the first ¹*c.*

COVENANT

Heb. 9. 18. first ¹c. hath not been dedicated without blood
20. This is the blood of the ¹c. which God commanded
10. 16. This is the *covenant* that I will make with them
20. and hath counted the blood of the *covenant*
12. 24. and to Jesus the mediator of a new *covenant*
13. 20. the sheep with the blood of the eternal *covenant*
Rev. 11. 19. seen in his temple the ark of his ¹*covenant*

Covenant-breakers.
Rom. 1. 31. without understanding, *covenant-breakers*

Covenanted.
Lu. 22. 5. were glad, and *covenanted* to give him money
see weighed.

Cover—ed.—*A.V.* ¹*hide.*
Mat. 8. 24. the boat was *covered* with the waves
10. 26. nothing c., that shall not be revealed. *Lu.* 12. 2
Mk. 14. 65. began to spit on him, and to *cover* his face
Lu. 23. 30. Fall on us; and to the hills, *Cover* us
Rom. 4. 7. iniquities are forgiven, And whose sins are c.
1 *Cor.* 11. 4. praying or prophesying, having his head c.
Jas. 5. 20. and shall ¹*cover* a multitude of sins
see covereth, veiled.

Covereth.—*A.V.* ¹*cover.*
Lu. 8. 16. lighted a lamp, *covereth* it with a vessel
1 *Pet.* 4. 8. for love ¹*covereth* a multitude of sins

Covering.—*A.V.* ¹*raiment.*
1 *Cor.* 11. 15. for her hair is given her for a *covering*
1 *Tim.* 6. 8. having food and ¹*covering* we shall be—content

Covet—ed.—*A.V.* ¹*desire.*
Acts 20. 33. I *coveted* no man's silver, or gold
Rom. 7. 7. Thou shalt not *covet.* 13. 9
Jas. 4. 2. ye kill, and ¹*covet*, and cannot obtain
see coveting, desire, reaching.

Coveting—s.—*A.V.* ¹*concupiscence*, ²*covetousness*, ³*lust.*
Mk. 7. 22. adulteries, ²*covetings*, wickednesses
Rom. 7. 7. for I had not known ³*coveting*, except the law
8. in me through the commandment all manner of ¹c.

Covetous.
1 *Cor.* 5. 10. or with the *covetous* and extortioners
11. named a brother be a fornicator, or *covetous*
6. 10. nor thieves, nor *covetous*, nor drunkards
Eph. 5. 5. nor *covetous* man, which is an idolator
see covetousness, lovers (of money).

Covetousness.—*A.V.* ¹*covetous practices.*
Lu. 12. 15. and keep yourselves from all *covetousness*
Rom. 1. 29. wickedness, *covetousness*, maliciousness
Eph. 5. 3. or c., let it not even be named among you
Col. 3. 5. and *covetousness*, the which is idolatry
1 *Th.* 2. 5. nor a cloke of *covetousness*, God is witness
2 *Pet.* 2. 3. And in c. shall they with feigned words
14. having a heart exercised in ¹*covetousness*
see coveting, extortion, love (of money).

Craft.
Rev. 18. 22. and no craftsman, of whatsoever *craft*
see business, subtilty, trade.

Craftiness.—*A.V.* ¹*subtilty.*
Lu. 20. 23. But he perceived their *craftiness*
1 *Cor.* 3. 19. He that taketh the wise in their *craftiness*

CREATURE

2 *Cor.* 4. 2. not walking in *craftiness*, nor handling
11. 3. serpent beguiled Eve in his ¹*craftiness*
Eph. 4. 14. by the sleight of men, in *craftiness*

Craftsman—men.
Acts 19. 24. brought no little business unto the *craftsmen*
38. and the *craftsmen* that are with him
Rev 18. 22. and no *craftsman*, of whatsoever craft

Crafty.
2 *Cor.* 12. 16. being *crafty*, I caught you with guile

Craved *A.V.*—*see asked.*

Create.—*A.V.* ¹*created*, ²*make.*
Eph. 2. 15. ²*create* in himself of the twain one new man
Rev. 4. 11. for thou didst ¹*create* all things

Created.—*A.V.* ¹*creature.*
Mk. 13. 19. beginning of the creation which God *created*
1 *Cor.* 11. 9. for neither was the man c. for the woman
Eph. 2. 10. *created* in Christ Jesus for good works
3. 9. ages hath been hid in God who *created* all things
4. 24. which after God hath been c. in righteousness
Col. 1. 16. for in him were all things *created*—all things have been *created* through him
3. 10. after the image of him that *created* him
1 *Tim.* 4. 3. which God c. to be received with thanksgiving
Rev. 4. 11. because of thy will they were, and were *created*
5. 13. And every ¹*created* thing which is in the heaven
10. 6. who *created* the heaven and the things that are
see create.

Creation.—*A.V.* ¹*building*, ²*creature.*
Mk. 10. 6. But from the beginning of the *creation*
13. 19. hath not been the like from the beginning of the c.
16. 15. and preach the gospel to the whole ²*creation*
Rom. 1. 20. For the invisible things of him since the c.
8. 19. For the earnest expectation of the ²c. waiteth
20. For the ²*creation* was subjected to vanity
21. the ²*creation* itself also shall be delivered from the
22. For we know that the whole *creation* groaneth
Col. 1. 15. of the invisible God, the first-born of all ²c.
Heb. 9. 11. not made with hands—not of this ¹*creation*
2 *Pet.* 3. 4. as they were from the beginning of the c.
Rev. 3. 14. true witness, the beginning of the c. of God

Creator.
Rom. 1. 25. served the creature rather than the *Creator*
1 *Pet.* 4. 19. their souls in well-doing unto a faithful *C.*

Creature—s.—*A.V.* ¹*beast—s*, ² *beasts*
Rom. 1. 25. served the *creature* rather than the Creator
8. 39. nor any other c., shall be able to separate us from
2 *Cor.* 5. 17. if any man is in Christ, he is a new *creature*
Gal. 6. 15. nor uncircumcision, but a new *creature*
1 *Tim.* 4. 4. For every *creature* of God is good
Heb. 4. 13. And there is no c. that is not manifest in his
Jas. 1. 18. should be a kind of firstfruits of his c. [sight
2 *Pet.* 2. 12. But these, as ²*creatures* without reason
Jude 10. naturally, like the ²*creatures* without reason
Rev. 4. 6. four living ¹c. full of eyes before and behind
7. first ¹*creature* was—second ¹c.—third ¹c.—fourth ¹c.
8. the four living ¹c., having each one of them six wings
9. And when the living ¹*creatures* shall give glory
5. 6. midst of the throne and of the four living ¹*creatures*
8. when he had taken the book, the four living ¹*creatures*
11. about the throne and the living ¹c. and the elders

71

CREATURES

Rev. 5. 14. the four living ¹*creatures* said, Amen
6. 1. I heard one of the four living ¹c. saying. 13, 15, 17
   6. as it were a voice in the midst of the four ¹living c.
7. 11. about the elders and the four living ¹*creatures*
8. 9. there died the third part of the c. which were in the sea
14. 3. song before the throne, and before the four living ¹c.
15. 7. one of the four living ¹c. gave unto the seven
19. 4. the four living ¹c. fell down and worshipped God
   see creation, created.

Creditor *A.V.—see lender.*

Creek *A.V.—see bay.*

Creep.
2 *Tim.* 3. 6. For of these are they that *creep* into houses

Creeping *things.—A.V.* ¹*serpents.*
Acts 10. 12. c. t. of the earth and fowls of the heaven. 11. 6
Rom. 1. 23. four-footed beasts, and *creeping things*
Jas. 3. 7. kind of beasts and birds, of ¹*creeping things*

Crept.
Jude 4. For there are certain men *crept* in privily

Crew.
Mat. 26. 74. the cock c. *Mk.* 14. 68: 72. *Lu.* 22. 60: *Jno.* 18. 27

Cried, cried out.—*A.V.* ¹*cried mightily.*
Mat. 8. 29. And behold, they [Gadarenes demoniacs] c. *out*
14. 26. an apparition, and they c. out for fear. *Mk.* 6. 49
   30. he [Peter] *cried out,* saying, Lord, save me
20. 30. *cried out,* saying, Lord, have mercy on us. 31
21. 9. c., saying, Hosanna to the son of David. *Mk.* 11. 9:
Mk. 1. 23. an unclean spirit; and he *cried out* [*Jno.* 12. 13
3. 11. unclean spirits—c., saying, Thou art the Son of God
9. 24. Straightway the father of the child *cried out*
26. and having *cried out*, and torn him much
15. 13. And they *cried out* again, Crucify him. 14: *Mat.*
   27. 23: *Jno.* 19. 6, 15
Lu. 8. 8. he *cried*, He that hath ears to hear, let him hear
28. And when he saw Jesus, he *cried out*
9. 39. a man from the multitude *cried*, saying, Master
18. 38. And he c., saying, Jesus, thou son of David. 39:
23. 18. But they *cried out* all together, saying [*Mk.* 10. 48
Jno. 7. 28. Jesus therefore *cried* in the temple, teaching
37. *cried*, saying, If any man thirst, let him come
12. 44. Jesus *cried* and said, He that believeth on me
18. 40. They c. out therefore again, saying, Not this man
19. 12. Jews *cried out*, saying, If thou release this man
Acts 19. 28. *cried out*, saying, Great is Diana. 34
   32. Some therefore *cried* one thing, and some another
22. 23. as they *cried out*, and threw off their garments
23. 6. he [Paul] *cried out* in the council, Brethren, I am
Rev. 10. 3. and he *cried* with a great voice—and when he c.
18. 2. And he ¹*cried* with a mighty voice [burning
18. and *cried out* as they looked upon the smoke of her
19. *cried*, weeping and mourning, saying, Woe, woe
   see called, crieth, cry, crying, shouted.

Cried *with a loud voice, or great voice.*
Mat. 27. 46. about the ninth hour Jesus *cried* with a loud
   voice. 50: *Mk.* 15. 34: *Lu.* 23. 46
Lu. 4. 33. unclean devil; and he *cried out* with a loud voice
Jno. 11. 43. he *cried* with a loud voice, Lazarus, come forth
Acts 7. 57. But they *cried out* with a loud voice
60. he kneeled down, and *cried* with a loud voice
16. 28. Paul c. with a loud voice, saying, Do thyself [long
Rev. 6. 10. and they *cried* with a great voice, saying, How
7. 2. he c. with a great voice to the four angels. 10. 3: 19. 17
   see uttered.

CROWING

Cries—eth.—*A.V.* ¹*cried.*
Mat. 15. 23. Send her away; for she *crieth* after us
Lu. 9. 39. spirit taketh him, and he suddenly *crieth* out
Rom. 9. 27. And Isaiah *crieth* concerning Israel
Jas. 5. 4. which is of you kept back by fraud, *crieth* out
   and the *cries* of them that reaped have entered
Rev. 12. 2. and she ¹*crieth* out, travailing in birth

Crime.—*A.V.* ¹*fault.*
Jno. 18. 38. Pilate saith—I find no ¹c. in him. 19. 14, ¹6
   see matter.

Crimes *A.V.—see charges.*

Cripple.
Acts 14. 8. [at Lystra] a *cripple* from his mother's womb

Crooked.—*A.V.* ¹*untoward.*
Lu. 3. 5. And the *crooked* shall become straight
Acts 2. 40. Save yourselves from this ¹*crooked* generation
Phil. 2. 15. in the midst of a c. and perverse generation

Cross.—*A.V.* ¹ *pass over.*
Mat. 10. 38. he that doth not take his *cross* and follow
16. 24. let him deny himself, and take up his *cross* and
   follow me. *Mk.* 8. 34: *Lu.* 9. 23
27. 32. that he might bear his *cross.* *Mk.* 15. 21: *Lu.* 23. 26
   42. King of Israel; let him now come down from the c. 40:
Lu. 14. 27. Whosoever doth not bear his own c. [*Mk.* 15. 30, 32
15. 26. none may ¹*cross* over from thence to us
Jno. 19. 17. he went out, bearing the *cross* for himself
19. Pilate wrote a title also, and put it on the *cross*
25. there were standing by the *cross* of Jesus his mother
31. bodies should not remain on the c. upon the sabbath
1 *Cor.* 1. 17. lest the *cross* of Christ should be made void
18. word of the *cross* is to them that are perishing
Gal. 5. 11. the stumblingblock of the *cross* been done away
6. 12. may not be persecuted for the *cross* of Christ
14. to glory, save in the *cross* of our Lord Jesus Christ
Eph. 2. 16. both in one body unto God through the *cross*
Phil. 2. 8. obedient even unto death, yea, the death of the c.
3. 18. that they are the enemies of the *cross* of Christ
Col. 1. 20. having made peace through the blood of his c.
2. 14. taken it out of the way, nailing it to the *cross*
Heb. 12. 2. the joy that was set before him endured the c.

Crossed.—*A.V.* ¹*gone over,* ²*passed over.*
Mat. 14. 34. when they had ¹*crossed* over. *Mat.* 9. ²1
Mk. 5. 21. when Jesus had ²c. over again in the boat. 6. ²53

Crossing.—*A.V.* ¹*sailing.*
Acts 21. 2. having found a ship ¹c. over unto Phœnicia

Crow.
Mat. 26. 34. the cock *crow*, thou shalt deny me thrice. 75:
   Mk. 14. 30, 72: *Lu.* 22. 34, 61: *Jno.* 13. 38

Crowd.—*A.V.* ¹*company,* ²*multitude,* ³*people,* ⁴*press.*
Mat. 9. 24. flute-players, and the ²*crowd* making a tumult
25. But when the ²*crowd* was put forth
Mk. 2. 4. could not come nigh unto him for the ⁴c. *Lu.* 8. ⁴19
3. 9. boat should wait on him because of the ²*crowd*
5. 27. came in the ⁴c. behind, and touched his garment
30. Jesus—turned him about in the ⁴*crowd*
Lu. 19. 3. [Zachæus] to see Jesus—and could not for the ⁴c.
Acts 17. 5. Jews—gathering a ¹c., set the city on an uproar
21. 34. shouted one thing, some another, among the ²c. ³35
24. 18. with no ²*crowd*, nor yet with tumult

Crowing *A.V.—see cockcrowing.*

CROWN

Crown.
Mat. 27. 29. c. of thorns, and put it upon his head. Mk. 15. 17;
Jno. 19. 5. Jesus—wearing the *crown* of thorns. [Jno. 19. 2
1 Cor. 9. 25. Now they do it to receive a corruptible *crown*
Phil. 4. 1. beloved and longed for, my joy and *crown*
1 Th. 2. 19. our hope, or joy, or *crown* of glorying ?
2 Tim. 4. 8. there is laid up for me the c. of righteousness
Jas. 1. 12. he shall receive the *crown* of life which the Lord
1 Pet. 5. 4. shall receive the *crown* of glory that fadeth not
Rev. 2. 10. and I will give thee the *crown* of life
3. 11. fast that which thou hast, that no one take thy *crown*
6. 2. and there was given unto him a *crown*
12. 1. upon her head a *crown* of twelve stars
14. 14. having on his head a golden *crown*

Crowned—st.
2 Tim. 2. 5. he is not *crowned*, except he have contended
Heb. 2. 7. Thou *crownedst* him with glory and honour
9. suffering of death *crowned* with glory and honour

Crowns.
Rev. 4. 4. and on their heads *crowns* of gold
10. shall cast their *crowns* before the throne
9. 7. upon their heads as it were *crowns* like unto gold
see diadems.

Crucified.
Mat. 20. 2. Son of man is delivered up to be c. Lu. 24. 7
27. 22. They all say, Let him be *crucified*. 23: Lu. 23. 23
26. scourged and delivered to be c. Mk. 15. 15: Jno. 19. 16
35. had c. him, they parted his garments. Jno. 19. 23
38. c. with him two robbers. Lu. 23. 33: Jno. 19. 18, 32
28. 5. ye seek Jesus, which hath been *crucified*. Mk. 16. 6
Mk. 15. 25. third hour, and they *crucified* him [27. 44
32. they that were c. with him reproached him. Mat.
Lu. 24. 20. condemned to death, and *crucified* him
Jno. 19. 20. for the place where Jesus was *crucified*. 41
Acts 2. 36. both Lord and Christ, this Jesus whom ye c.
4. 10. Jesus Christ of Nazareth, whom ye *crucified*
Rom. 6. 6. that our old man was *crucified* with him
1 Cor. 1. 13. Is Christ divided? was Paul *crucified* for you?
23. but we preach Christ *crucified*
2. 2. save Jesus Christ, and him *crucified*
8. they would not have *crucified* the Lord of glory
2 Cor. 13. 4. for he was *crucified* through weakness
Gal. 2. 20. I have been *crucified* with Christ
3. 1. Jesus Christ was openly set forth *crucified* ?
5. 24. And they that are of Christ Jesus have c. the flesh
6. 14. through which the world hath been c. unto me
Rev. 11. 8. where also their Lord was *crucified*
see crucify.

Crucify.—A.V. ¹*crucified.*
Mat. 20. 19. to mock, and to scourge, and to *crucify*
23. 34. some of them shall ye kill and *crucify*
27. 31. and led him away to *crucify* him. Mk. 15. 20
Mk. 15. 13. *Crucify* him. 14 : Lu. 23. 21 : Jno. 19. 15
24. they ¹*crucify* him, and part his garments
27. And with him they *crucify* two robbers
Jno. 19. 6. they cried out, saying, *Crucify* him, *crucify*
him—Take him yourselves, and *crucify* him
10. power to release thee, and have power to c. thee?
15. Shall I *crucify* your King?
Acts 2. 23. by the hand of lawless men did ¹*crucify*
Heb. 6. 6. they *crucify* to themselves the Son of God afresh

Crumbs.
Mat. 15. 27. even the dogs eat of the c. which fall. Mk. 7. 28
Lu. 16. 21. *crumbs* that fell from the rich man's table

11

CUP

Cruse.—A.V. ¹*box.*
Mat. 26. 7. an alabaster ¹c. of—ointment. Mk. 14. ¹³: Lu. 7. ¹³⁷
Mk. 14. 3. she brake the ¹*cruse*, and poured it over his head

Crush.—A.V. ¹*throng.*
Lu. 8. 45. the multitudes press thee and ¹*crush* thee

Cry.—A.V. ¹*cried.*
Mat. 12. 19. He shall not strive, nor *cry* aloud
25. 6. But at midnight there is a *cry*, Behold
Mk. 10. 47. he began to *cry* out, and say, Jesus, thou son
Lu. 18. 7. his elect, which *cry* to him day and night [out
19. 14. if these shall hold their peace, the stones will *cry*
Rom. 8. 15. the spirit of adoption, whereby we *cry*, Abba
Gal. 4. 27. Break forth and *cry*, thou that travailest not
Rev. 7. 10. and they ¹*cry* with a great voice, saying
see clamour, voice.

Crying.—A.V. ¹*cried.*
Mat. 3. 3. The voice of one *crying* in the wilderness. Mk.
1. 3 : Lu. 3. 4 : Jno. 1. 23
21. 15. children that were *crying* in the temple
Mk. 1. 26. tearing him and ¹*crying* with a loud voice
5. 5. *crying* out, and cutting himself with stones. ¹⁷
Lu. 4. 41. *crying* out, and saying, Thou art the Son of God
Acts 8. 7. they came out, *crying* with a loud voice
14. 14. and sprang forth among the multitude, *crying* out
21. 28. *crying* out, Men of Israel, help
36. the people followed after, *crying* out, Away with him
25. 24. *crying* that he ought not to live any longer
Gal. 4. 6. into our hearts, *crying*, Abba, Father
Heb. 5. 7. with strong *crying* and tears unto him
Rev. 14. 15. c. with a great voice to him that sat on the cloud
21. 4. nor *crying*, nor pain, any more

Crystal.
Rev. 4. 6. as it were a glassy sea like unto *crystal*
21. 11. as it were a jasper stone, clear as *crystal* [as c.
22. 1. And he showed me a river of water of life, bright

Cubit—s.
Mat. 6. 27. which of you by being anxious can add one
cubit unto his stature? Lu. 12. 25
Jno. 21. 8. about two hundred *cubits* off), dragging the net
Rev. 21. 17. wall thereof, a hundred and forty and four c.

Cumber—ed.—A.V. ¹*cumbereth.*
Lu. 10. 40. But Martha was *cumbered* about much serving
13. 7. why doth it [fig tree] also ¹*cumber* the ground ?

Cumbereth A.V.—*see cumber.*

Cummin.
Mat. 23. 23. for ye tithe mint and anise and *cummin*

Cunningly.
2 Pet. 1. 16. For we did not follow *cunningly* devised fables

Cup—s.
Mat. 10. 42. one of those little ones a *cup* of cold water only
20. 22. Are ye able to drink the *cup*. Mk. 10. 38
23. My *cup* indeed ye shall drink. Mk. 10. 39
23. 25. for ye cleanse the outside of the *cup*. Lu. 11. 39
26. cleanse first the inside of the *cup* [Lu. 22. 17
26. 27. And he took a *cup*, and gave thanks. Mk. 14. 23;
39. O my Father, if it be possible, let this *cup* pass
away from me. Mk. 14. 36 : Lu. 22. 42
Mk. 7. 4. washings of *cups*, and pots, and brasen [drink
9. 41. For whosoever shall give you a *cup* of water to
Lu. 22. 20. And the *cup* in like manner after supper—
This *cup* is the new covenant. 1 Cor. 11. 25
Jno. 18. 11. the *cup* which the Father hath given me

73

CUP

1 Cor. 10. 16. The *cup* of blessing which we bless [devils
21. Ye cannot drink the *cup* of the Lord, and the *cup* of
11. 26. and drink the *cup*, ye proclaim the Lord's death
27. or drink the *cup* of the Lord unworthily [till he come
28. so let him eat of the bread, and drink of the *cup*
Rev. 14. 10. which is prepared unmixed in the *c.* of his anger
16. 19. the *cup* of the wine of the fierceness of his wrath
17. 4. having in her hand a golden *cup* full of abominations
18. 6. in the *c.* which she mingled, mingle unto her double

Cure—s—ed.—*A.V.* ¹*healed.*

Mat. 17. 16. to thy disciples, and they could not *cure* him
18. and the boy was *cured* from that hour
Lu. 7. 21. In that hour he *cured* many of diseases
9. 1. authority over all devils, and to *cure* diseases
13. 32. and perform *cures* to-day and to-morrow
Jno. 5. 10. So the Jews said unto him that was *cured*
Acts 28. 9. diseases in the island came, and were ¹*cured*

Curious.

Acts 19. 19. that practised *curious* arts brought their books

Curse.—*A.V.* ¹*cursing*, ²*oath.*

Mat. 26. 74. Then began he to *c.* and to swear. Mk. 14. 71
Lu. 6. 28. bless them that *curse* you
Acts 23. 12. and bound themselves under a *curse*. 14, ²21
Rom. 12. 14. Bless them that persecute you—and *curse* not
Gal. 3. 10. as are of the works of the law are under a *curse*
13. from the *curse* of the law, having become a *c.* for us
Heb. 6. 8. it is rejected and nigh unto a ¹*curse* [we men
Jas. 3. 9. bless we the Lord and Father; and therewith *c.*
Rev. 22. 3. And there shall be no *curse* any more

Cursed—st.

Mat. 25. 41. Depart from me, ye *cursed*
Mk. 11. 21. the fig tree which thou *cursedst* is withered
Gal. 3. 10. C. is every one which continueth not in all things
13. *Cursed* is every one that hangeth on a tree
see accursed, cursing.

Curseth *A.V.*—*see evil.*

Cursing.—*A.V.* ¹*cursed.*

Rom. 3. 14. Whose mouth is full of *cursing* and bitterness
Jas. 3. 10. same mouth cometh forth blessing and *cursing*
2 Pet. 2. 14. children of ¹*cursing*; forsaking the right way
see curse.

Cushion.—*A.V.* ¹*pillow.*

Mk. 4. 38. himself [Jesus] was in the stern asleep on the ¹*c.*

Custom.—*A.V.* ¹*manner*, ²*wont.*

Lu. 1. 9. according to the *custom* of the priests' office
2. 27. might do concerning him after the *c.* of the law
42. they went up after the *custom* of the feast
4. 16. entered, as his *custom* was, into the synagogue
22. 39. went, as his ²*c.* was, unto the mount of Olives
Jno. 18. 39. But ye have a *custom*, that I should release
19. 40. as the ¹*custom* of the Jews is to bury
Acts 15. 1. circumcised after the ¹*custom* of Moses
17. 2. Paul, as his ¹*custom* was, went in unto them
25. 16. it is not the ¹*c.* of the Romans to give up any man
Rom. 13. 7. tribute is due; *custom* to whom *custom*
1 Cor. 11. 16. we have no such *c.*, neither the churches
Heb. 10. 25. as the ¹*custom* of some is, but exhorting
see toll.

DAMSEL

Customs.

Acts 6. 14. shall change the *c.* which Moses delivered
16. 21. set forth *c.* which it is not lawful for us to receive
21. 21. neither to walk after the *customs*
26. 3. especially because thou art expert in all *customs*
28. 17. done nothing against the people, or the *customs*

Cut.

Mat. 18. 8. thee to stumble, *cut* it off. 5. 30; Mk. 9. 43, 45
21. 8. and others *cut* branches from the trees. Mk. 11. 8
24. 51. and shall *cut* him asunder. Lu. 12. 46
Lu. 13. 7. fruit on this fig tree, and find none: *cut* it down
9. bear fruit—well; but if not, thou shalt *cut* it down
Jno. 18. 10. high priest's servant, and *cut* off his right ear
26. a kinsman of him whose ear Peter *cut* off
Acts 5. 33. they heard this, were *cut* to the heart. 7. 54
27. 32. Then the soldiers *cut* away the ropes of the boat
Rom. 11. 22. otherwise thou also shalt be *cut* off
24. thou wast *cut* out of that which is by nature a wild
2 Cor. 11. 12. that I may *cut* off occasion from them
Gal. 5. 12. which unsettle you would even *cut* themselves off
see struck, cutting.

Cutting.—*A.V.* ¹*cut.*

Mk. 5. 5. and *cutting* himself with stones
Rom. 9. 28. finishing it and ¹*cutting* it short

Cymbal.

1 Cor. 13. 1. I am become sounding brass, or a clanging *c.*

D.

Daily.

Mat. 6. 11. Give us this day our *daily* bread. Lu. 11. 3
26. 55. I sat *d.* in the temple. Mk. 14. 49; Lu. 19. 47; 22. 53
Lu. 9. 23. take up his cross *daily*, and follow me
Acts 3. 2. whom they laid *daily* at the door of the temple
6. 1. widows were neglected in the *daily* ministration
16. 5. in the faith, and increased in number *daily*
17. 11. examining the scriptures *daily*
19. 9. reasoning *daily* in the school of Tyrannus
1 Cor. 15. 31. I [Paul] die *daily*   [churches
2 Cor. 11. 28. presseth upon me *daily*, anxiety for all the
Heb. 7. 27. who needeth not *daily*, like those high priests
Jas. 2. 15. brother or sister be naked, and in lack of *d.* food
see every day, day by day.

Dainty

Rev. 18. 14. things that were *dainty* and sumptuous

Damage *A.V.*—*see loss.*

Damnable *A.V.*—*see destructive.*

Damnation *A.V.*—*see condemnation, judgement, destruction, eternal sin.*

Damned *A.V.*—*see condemned, judged.*

Damsel.—*A.V.* ¹*maid.*

Mat. 9. 24. the ¹*damsel* is not dead, but sleepeth
25. took her by the hand; and the ¹*damsel* arose
14. 11. his head was brought in a charger, and given to
the *damsel*. Mk. 6. 28

DAMSEL

Mk. 5. 41. D., I say unto thee [Jairus' daughter], Arise
42. And straightway the *damsel* rose up
6. 22. and the king said unto the *damsel*, Ask of me
see maid, child.

Dance—d.
Mat. 11. 17. We piped unto you, and ye did not d. *Lu.* 7. 32
14. 6. the daughter of Herodias d. in the midst. *Mk.* 6. 22

Dancing.
Lu. 15. 25. drew nigh to the house, he heard music and d.

Danger.
Mat. 5. 21. shall be in *danger* of the judgement. 22
22. be in d. of the council—shall be in d. of the hell of fire
Acts 19. 27. not only is there d. that this our trade come
40. we are in d. to be accused concerning this day's riot
see guilty.

Dangerous.
Acts 27. 9. and the voyage was now *dangerous*

Dare.
Rom. 5. 7. for the good man some one would even d. to die
15. 18. For I will not *dare* to speak of any things
1 *Cor.* 6. 1. Dare any of you, having a matter against his
see bold.

Daring.—A.V. ¹presumptuous.
2 *Pet.* 2. 10. ¹*Daring*, selfwilled, they tremble not to rail

Dark.
Lu. 11. 36. body be full of light, having no part *dark*
Jno. 6. 17. it was now *dark*, and Jesus had not yet come
20. 1. cometh Mary Magdalene early, while it was yet d.
2 *Pet.* 1. 19. as unto a lamp shining in a *dark* place

Darken—ed.—A.V. ¹darkness.
Mat. 24. 29. the sun shall be *darkened*. *Mk.* 13. 24
Rom. 1. 21. and their senseless heart was *darkened*
11. 10. Let their eyes be *darkened*, that they may not see
Eph. 4. 18. being *darkened* in their understanding
Rev. 8. 12. that the third part of them should be *darkened*
9. 2. and the sun and the air were *darkened* by reason
16. 10. and his kingdom was ¹*darkened*
see light, failing.

Darkly.
1 *Cor.* 13. 12. For now we see in a mirror, *darkly*

Darkness.
Mat. 6. 23. thy whole body shall be full of *darkness*—be
darkness, how great is the *darkness!* *Lu.* 11. 34
8. 12. shall be cast forth into the outer *darkness*
22. 13. and cast him out into the outer *darkness*
25. 30. the unprofitable servant into the outer *darkness*
27. 45. from the sixth hour there was *darkness* over all
the land. *Mk.* 15. 33; *Lu.* 23. 44
Lu. 1. 79. To shine upon them that sit in *darkness*
22. 53. but this is your hour, and the power of *darkness*
Jno. 1. 5. shineth in the d.; and the d. apprehended it not
8. 12. he that followeth me shall not walk in the d.
12. 35. walketh in the d. knoweth not whither he goeth
46. believeth on me may not abide in the *darkness*
Acts 2. 20. The sun shall be turned into *darkness*
13. 11. there fell on him [Elymas] a mist and a *darkness*
Eph. 5. 8. for ye were once *darkness*, but are now light
11. have no fellowship with the unfruitful works of d.
6. 12. against the world-rulers of this *darkness*

DAUGHTERS

Col. 1. 13. who delivered us out of the power of *darkness*
1 *Th.* 5. 4. But ye, brethren, are not in *darkness*
5. we are not of the night, nor of *darkness*
Heb. 12. 18. and unto blackness, and *darkness*, and tempest
2 *Pet.* 2. 4. and committed them to pits of *darkness*
17. for whom the blackness of *darkness* hath been reserved. *Jude* 13
1 *Jno.* 1. 6. and walk in the *darkness*, we lie
2. 11. is in the *darkness*, and walketh in the *darkness*—because the *darkness* hath blinded his eyes. 9
Jude 6. he hath kept in everlasting bonds under *darkness*
see darkened.

Darkness *with light*.
Mat. 4. 16. people which sat in *darkness* Saw a great *light*
6. 23. If—the *l.* that is in thee be d., how great is the d
10. 27. What I tell you in the d., speak ye in the *light*
Lu. 11. 35. whether the *light* that is in thee be not d.
12. 3. have said in the *darkness* shall be heard in the *l.*
Jno. 1. 5. And the *light* shineth in the *darkness*
3. 19. and men loved the *darkness* rather than the *light*
12. 35. Walk while ye have the *l.*, that d. overtake you not
Acts 26. 18. that they may turn from *darkness* to *light*
Rom. 13. 12. works of d., and let us put on the armour of *l.*
1 *Cor.* 4. 5. bring to *light* the hidden things of *darkness*
2. *Cor.* 4. 6. *Light* shall shine out of *darkness*
6. 14. or what communion hath *light* with *darkness?*
1 *Pet.* 2. 9. called you out of d. into his marvellous *light*
1 *Jno.* 1. 5. God is *light*, and in him is no *darkness* at all
2. 8. the d. is passing away, and the true *l.* already shineth

Darts.
Eph. 6. 16. to quench all the fiery *darts* of the evil one

Dash—ed.—A.V. ¹lay, ²threw.
Mat. 4. 6. Lest haply thou d. thy foot against a stone. *Lu.*
Lu. 9. 42. the devil ²*dashed* him down, and tare him [4. 11
19. 44. shall ¹*dash* thee to the ground, and thy children

Dasheth.—A.V. ¹teareth.
Mk. 9. 18. [dumb spirit] it ¹d. him down: and he foameth

Daughter.
Mat. 9. 18. saying, My *daughter* is even now dead
22. D., be of good cheer; thy faith. *Mk.* 5. 34; *Lu.* 8. 48
10. 35. the *daughter* against her mother, and the *daughter* in law against her mother in law. *Lu.* 12. 53
37. he that loveth son or *daughter* more than me
14. 6. the *daughter* of Herodias danced. *Mk.* 6. 22
15. 22. my *daughter* is grievously vexed with a devil
28. And her *daughter* was healed from that hour
21. 5. Tell ye the d. of Zion; Behold, thy King cometh
Mk. 5. 23. My little *daughter* is at the point of death [19
35. Thy d. is dead: why troublest thou the Master. *Lu.* 8.
7. 25. a woman, whose little d. had an unclean spirit
26. would cast forth the devil out of her *daughter*
29. the devil is gone out of thy *daughter*
Lu. 8. 42. for he [Jairus] had an only *daughter*, about twelve years of ago
13. 16. And ought not this woman, being a d. of Abraham
Jno. 12. 15. Fear not, d. of Zion: behold, thy King cometh
Acts 7. 21. Pharaoh's d. took him up and nourished him
Heb. 11. 24. refused to be called the son of Pharaoh's d.

Daughters.
Lu. 1. 5. he had a wife of the *daughters* of Aaron
23. 28. *Daughters* of Jerusalem, weep not for me

DAUGHTERS

Acts 2. 17. And your sons and your *d.* shall prophesy
21. 9. Now this man had four *daughters,* virgins
2 *Cor.* 6. 18. And ye shall be to me sons and *daughters*
see children.

Dawn.—A.V. ¹*morning,* ²*shine.*

Mat. 28. 1. as it began to *dawn* toward the first day of
Lu. 24. 1. at early ¹*d.,* they came unto the tomb [upon them
2 *Cor.* 4. 4. Christ, who is the image of God, should not ²*d.*
2 *Pet.* 1. 19. until the day *dawn,* and the day-star arise

Day.—A.V. ¹*daily,* ²*hour,* ³*morning,* ⁴*time.*

Mat. 10. 15. and Gomorrah in the *day* of judgement. 11. 24
11. 22. Tyre and Sidon in the *day* of judgement
12. 36. shall give account thereof in the *day* of judgement
16. 21. and the third *day* be raised up. 17. 23 : 20. 19 :
 Lu. 9. 22 ; 18. 33 : 24. 7, 46
20. 2. agreed with the labourers for a penny a *day*
6. Why stand ye here all the *day* idle ?
12. borne the burden of the *day* and the scorching heat
24. 38. the *day* that Noah entered into the ark. *Lu.* 17. 27
42. ye know not on what ²*day* your Lord cometh
50. shall come in a *day* when he expecteth. *Lu.* 12. 46
25. 13. for ye know not the *day* nor the hour
26. 17. on the first *day* of unleavened bread. *Mk.* 14. 12
27. 64. sepulchre be made sure until the third *day*
28. 1. the first *day* of the week. *Mk.* 16. 2, 9 : *Lu.* 24. 1 :
 Jno. 20. 1, 19 ; *Acts* 20. 7 : 1 *Cor.* 16. 2
Mk. 1. 35. a great while before *day* he rose up and went
4. 27. and should sleep and rise night and *day*
6. 35. when the ⁴*day* was now far spent—and the ⁴*day*
Lu. 1. 20. not able to speak, until the *day* that these
59. And it came to pass on the eighth *day*
80. in the deserts till the *d.* of his shewing unto Israel
4. 42. when it was *day,* he came out. 6. 13
13. 32. and the third *day* I am perfected
16. 19. faring sumptuously every *day* [Dives]
17. 4. And if he sin against thee seven times in the *day*
24. so shall the Son of man be in his *day*
29. but in the *day* that Lot went out from Sodom
30. in the *day* that the Son of man is revealed
21. 37. And every *day* he was teaching in the temple
23. 12. Herod and Pilate became friends with each other
54. it was the *d.* of the Preparation. *Mk.* 15. 42 [that very *d.*
24. 21. it is now the third *day* since these things came
29. evening, and the *day* is now far spent
Jno. 2. 1. And the third *day* there was a marriage in Cana
7. 37. on the last *day,* the great *day* of the feast
8. 56. Your father Abraham rejoiced to see my *day*
9. 4. the works of him that sent me, while it is *day*
11. 9. Are there not twelve hours in the *day* ? If a
 man walk in the *day,* he stumbleth not
19. 31. (for the *day* of that sabbath was a high *day*)
21. 4. But when ²*day* was now breaking, Jesus stood
Acts 1. 2. until the *day* in which he was received up. 22
2. 1. And when the *day* of Pentecost was now come
20. the *day* of the Lord come, That great and notable *day*
5. 42. And every ¹*day,* in the temple and at home
7. 8. and circumcised him the eighth *day.* *Phil.* 3. 5
8. 1. there arose on that ⁴*day* a great persecution
12. 21. And upon a set *day* Herod arrayed himself
16. 35. But when it was *day.* 23. 12 : 27. 39
17. 31. inasmuch as he hath appointed a *day*
20. 16. to be at Jerusalem the *day* of Pentecost
18. from the first *day* that I set foot in Asia
21. 7. saluted the brethren, and abode with them one *day*
27. 19. third *day* they cast out with their own hands
29. anchors from the stern, and wished for the *day*
33. This *day* is the fourteenth *day* that ye wait
28. 13. and after one *day* a south wind sprang up, and
 on the second *day* we came to Puteoli

DAY

Rom. 2. 5. treasurest up for thyself wrath in the *day* of
16. in the *day* when God shall judge the secrets of men
8. 36. For thy sake we are killed all the *day* long
Rom. 10. 21. All the *day* long did I spread out my hands
13. 12. The night is far spent, and the *day* is at hand
13. Let us walk honestly, as in the *day*
14. 5. One man esteemeth one *day* above another :
 another esteemeth every *day* alike
6. He that regardeth the *d.,* regardeth it unto the Lord
1 *Cor.* 1. 8. that ye be unreproveable in the *day* of our Lord
3. 13. made manifest : for the *day* shall declare it
5. 5. spirit may be saved in the *day* of the Lord Jesus
10. 8. and fell in one *day* three and twenty thousand
15. 4. and be that hath been raised on the third *day*
2 *Cor.* 1. 14. as ye also are ours, in the *d.* of our Lord Jesus
6. 2. And in a *day* of salvation did I succour thee—
 behold, now is the *day* of salvation
Eph. 4. 30. ye were sealed unto the *day* of redemption
Phil. 1. 5. of the gospel from the first *day* until now
6. you will perfect it until the *day* of Jesus Christ
10. sincere and void of offence unto the *day* of Christ
2. 16. I may have whereof to glory in the *day* of Christ
Col. 1. 6. since the *day* ye heard and knew the grace
9. since the *day* we heard it, do not cease to pray
2. 16. or in respect of a feast *day* or a new moon
1 *Th.* 5. 2. that the *day* of the Lord so cometh as a thief
 in the night. 2 *Pet.* 3. 10
5. for ye are all sons of light, and sons of the *day*
8. But let us, since we are of the *day,* be sober
2 *Th.* 2. 2. as that the *day* of the Lord is now present
Heb. 3. 8. Like as in the *day* of the temptation
4. 4. seventh *day* on this wise, And God rested on the
 seventh *day* from all his works
7. he again defineth a certain *day,* saying in David
8. he would not have spoken afterward of another *day*
8. 9. In the *day* that I took them by the hand
10. 25. as ye see the *day* drawing nigh
1 *Pet.* 2. 12. glorify God in the *day* of visitation
2 *Pet.* 1. 19. until the *day* dawn, and the day-star arise
2. 8. vexed his righteous soul from *day* to *day*
9. under punishment unto the *day* of judgement
3. 7. being reserved against the *day* of judgement
8. that one *day* is with the Lord as a thousand
 years, and a thousand years as one *day*
12. earnestly desiring the coming of the *day* of God
1 *Jno.* 4. 17. we may have boldness in the *day* of judgement
Jude 6. darkness unto the judgement of the great *day*
Rev. 1. 10. I was in the Spirit on the Lord's *day*
6. 17. for the great *day* of their wrath is come
9. 15. which had been prepared for the hour and *day*
16. 14. them together unto the war of the great *day* of God
18. 8. Therefore in one *day* shall her plagues come
21. 25. the gates thereof shall in no wise be shut by *day*
 see evil, journey, last day, morrow.

Day joined with night.

Mk. 4. 27. and should sleep and rise *night* and *day*
5. 5. And always, *night* and *day,* in the tombs
14. 30. that thou to-day, even this *night*—shalt deny
Lu. 2. 37. with fastings and supplications *night* and *day*
18. 7. his elect, which cry to him *day* and *night*
Acts 9. 24. watched the gates also *day* and *night*
20. 31. I ceased not to admonish every one *night* and *day*
26. 7. earnestly serving God *night* and *day*
2 *Cor.* 11. 25. a *night* and *day* have I been in the deep
1 *Th.* 2. 9. working *n.* and *d.,* that we might not burden.
3. 10. *night* and *day* praying exceedingly [2 *Th.* 3. 8
1 *Tim.* 5. 5. in supplications and prayers *night* and *day*
2 *Tim.* 1. 3. remembrance of thee—*night* and *day*
Rev. 4. 8. and they have no rest *day* and *night*

DAY

Rev. 7. 15. and they serve him *day* and *night* in his temple
8. 12. the *day* should not shine for the third part of it, and the *night* in like manner
12. 10. which accuseth them before our God *day* and *night*
14. 11. no rest *day* and *n.*, they that worship the beast
20. 10. be tormented *day* and *night* for ever and ever

Feast Day.—*see day.*

Sabbath Day.—*A.V.* ¹*sabbath days,* ²*sabbath.*

Mat. 12. 1. Jesus went on the *s. day* through. *Mk.* 2. 23
6. how that on the ¹*sabbath day* the priests—profane
10. Is it lawful to heal on the ¹*sabbath day* ?
11. and if this fall into a pit on the *sabbath d. Lu.* 14. 5
12. Wherefore it is lawful to do good on the ¹*sabbath d.*
28. 1. late on the ²*sabbath day*, as it began to dawn
Mk. 2. 24. on the *s. d.* that which is not lawful? *Lu.* 6. ¹²
3. 2. whether he would heal him on the *sabbath day*
4. Is it lawful on the ¹*sabbath day* to do good, or to do
Lu. 4. 16. into the synagogue on the *s. d. Mk.* 1. 21: *Acts*
31. And he was teaching them on the ¹*s. day.* [13. 14
13. 10. teaching in one of the synagogues on the ²*s. day*
16. loosed from this bond on the *day* of the *sabbath* ?
Jno. 5. 9. Now it was the *sabbath* on that *day*
9. 14. it was the *s.* on the *day* when Jesus made the clay
19. 31. (for the *day* of that *sabbath* was a high day)
Acts 16. 13. on the ²*sabbath day* we went forth without
Col. 2. 16. feast day or a new moon or a ¹*sabbath day*
see journey, sabbath.

Same Day *A.V.*—*see (very) hour, that day.*

That Day.—*A.V.* ¹*same day.*

Mat. 7. 22. Many will say to me in *that day*, Lord, Lord
24. 36. But of *t. d.* and hour knoweth no one. *Mk.* 13. 32
26. 29. until *that day* when I drink it new. *Mk.* 14. 25
Lu. 6. 23. Rejoice in *that day*, and leap for joy
10. 12. It shall be more tolerable in *that day* for Sodom
21. 34. and *that day* come on you suddenly
Jno. 1. 39. and they abode with him *that day*
15. 53. So from *that day* forth they took counsel
14. 20. In *that day* ye shall know that I am in my Father
16. 23. And in *that day* ye shall ask me nothing
26. In *that day* ye shall ask in my name
20. 19. When therefore it was evening, on ¹*that day*
Acts 2. 41. unto them in ¹*t. d.* about three thousand souls
1 *Th.* 5. 4. that *that day* should overtake you as a thief
2 *Th.* 1. 10. our testimony unto you was believed) in *t. day*
2 *Tim.* 1. 12. committed unto him against *that day*
18. grant unto him to find mercy of the Lord in *t. day*)
4. 8. the righteous judge, shall give to me at *that day*

This Day.

Mat. 6. 11. Give us *this day* our daily bread
11. 23. it would have remained until *this day*
27. 8. was called, The field of blood, unto *this day*
19. I have suffered many things *this day* in a dream
28. 15. among the Jews, and continueth until *this day*
Lu. 2. 11. for there is born to you *t. d.* in the city of David
19. 42. If thou hadst known in *this day*, even thou
22. 34. I tell thee, Peter, the cock shall not crow *t. day*
Acts 2. 29. and his tomb is with us unto *this day*
13. 33. my Son, *t. d.* have I begotten thee. *Heb.* 1. 5: 5. 5
20. 26. Wherefore I testify unto you *this day*
22. 3. zealous for God, even as ye all are *this day*
23. 1. lived before God in all good conscience until *this d.*
24. 21. I am called in question before you *this day*
26. 2. that I am to make my defence before thee *this d.*
22. I stand unto *this day* testifying both to small and
29. not thou only, but also all that hear me *this day*

DAYS

Rom. 11. 8. that they should not hear, unto *this very day*
2 *Cor.* 3. 14. for until *this very day* at the reading. 15
see to-day.

To-Day.—*A.V.* ¹*this day.*

Mat. 6. 30. grass of the field, which *to-day* is. *Lu.* 12. 28
16. 3. It will be foul weather *to-day* : for the heaven is
21. 28. Son, go work *to-day* in the vineyard
Mk. 14. 30. thou ¹*to-day*, even this night—shalt deny
Lu. 4. 21. ¹*To-day* hath this scripture been fulfilled in
5. 26. We have seen strange things *to-day*
13. 32. and perform cures *to-day* and to-morrow
33. Howbeit I must go on my way *to-day* and to-morrow
19. 5. for *to-day* I must abide at thy house
9. ¹*To-day* is salvation come to this house
23. 43. *To-day* shalt thou be with me in Paradise
Heb. 3. 7. *To-day* if ye shall hear his voice. 15 : 4. 7
13. so long as it is called *To-day*
4. 7. *To-day*, as it hath been before said
13. 8. Jesus Christ is the same yesterday and *to-day*
Jas. 4. 13. *To-day* or to-morrow we will go into this city

Daybreak.—*A.V.* ¹*morning.*

Acts 5. 21. they entered into the temple about ¹*daybreak*

Day by Day.—*A.V.* ¹*daily.*

Lu. 11. 3. Give us *day by day* our daily bread
Acts 2. 46. And ¹*day by day*, continuing stedfastly with
47. added to them ¹*day by day* those that were being
2 *Cor.* 4. 16. our inward man is renewed *day by day*
Heb. 3. 13. but exhort one another ¹*day by day*
10. 11. And every priest indeed standeth ¹*day by day*

Days.—*A.V.* ¹*time.*

Mat. 2. 1. Bethlehem of Judæa in the *days* of Herod
3. 1. And in those *days* cometh John the Baptist
4. 2. when he had fasted forty *days* and forty nights
9. 15. but the *days* will come, when the bridegroom shall be taken away. *Mk.* 2. 20 : *Lu.* 5. 35
11. 12. And from the *days* of John the Baptist
12. 40. as Jonah was three *days* and three nights—so shall the Son of man be three *d.* and three nights
15. 32. with me now three *d.* and have nothing to. *Mk.* 8. 2
17. 1. after six *d.* Jesus taketh with him Peter. *Mk.* 9. 2
23. 30. If we had been in the *days* of our fathers
24. 19. give suck in those *days* ! *Mk.* 13. 17 : *Lu.* 21. 23
22. except those *days* had been shortened. *Mk.* 13. 20
29. after the tribulation of those *days*, the sun shall be
37. were the *d.* of Noah, so shall be the coming. *Lu.* 17. 26,
38. For as in those *d.* which were before the flood [29
26. 2. after two *days* the passover cometh. *Mk.* 14. 1
61. temple of God, and to build it in three *days*. 27. 40 :
Mk. 14. 58 : 15. 29 : *Jno.* 2. 19, 20 [10. 34
27. 63. After three *d.* I will rise again. *Mk.* 8. 31 : 9. 31 :
Mk. 1. 13. in the wilderness forty *days* tempted. *Lu.* 4. 2
13. 19. for those *days* shall be tribulation, such as there
Lu. 1. 24. after these *days* Elisabeth his wife conceived
25. Thus hath the Lord done unto me in the *days*
39. Mary arose in those *days* and went into the hill
75. holiness and righteousness before him all our *days*
2. 21. eight *days* were fulfilled for circumcising him
46. after three *days* they found him in the temple
4. 25. many widows in Israel in the *days* of Elijah
9. 28. it came to pass about eight *days* after these sayings
14. 14. There are six *days* in which men ought to work
15. 13. And not many *days* after the younger son
17. 22. The *days* will come, when ye shall desire to see one of the *days* of the Son of man
19. 43. the *d.* shall come upon thee, when thine enemies
20. 1. And it came to pass, on one of the *days*

DAYS

Lu. 21. 6. the *days* will come, in which there shall not be
22. For these are *days* of vengeance
23. 7. himself also was at Jerusalem in these ¹*days*
24. 18. things which are come to pass there in these *d.* ?
Jno. 2. 12. and there they abode not many *days*
4. 40. to abide with them: and he abode there two *days*
43. after the two *days* he went forth from thence into
11. 6. he abode at that time two *days* in the place
17. he had been in the tomb four *days* already
12. 1. Jesus—six *d.* before the passover came to Bethany
20. 26. after eight *days* again his disciples were within
Acts 1. 3. appearing unto them by the space of forty *days*
5. with the Holy Ghost not many *days* hence
2. 17. And it shall be in the last *days*, saith God
18. on my handmaidens in those *days* Will I pour
3. 24. many as have spoken, they also told of these *days*
5. 36. For before these *days* rose up Theudas
37. Judas of Galilee in the *days* of the enrolment
7. 41. And they made a calf in those *days*
9. 9. And he was three *days* without sight
10. 30. Cornelius said, Four *days* ago, until this hour
11. 27. Now in these *days* there came down prophets
28. which came to pass in the *days* of Claudius
12. 3. those were the *days* of unleavened bread. 20. 6
13. 31. he was seen for many *days* of them that came
41. For I work a work in your *days*, A work which ye
16. 18. And this she did for many *days*
17. 2. for three sabbath *days* reasoned with them
20. 6. Troas in five *d.*; where we tarried seven *d.* 21. 4
21. 38. which before these *days* stirred up to sedition
24. 1. And after five *days* the high priest Ananias came
11. not more than twelve *days* since I went up to worship
25. 6. tarried among them not more than eight or ten *days*
27. 20. neither sun nor stars shone upon us for many *d.*
28. 7. and entertained us three *days* courteously
17. after three *days* he called together those that were
Gal. 1. 18. to visit Cephas, and tarried with him fifteen *d.*
4. 10. Ye observe *days*, and months, and seasons
Eph. 5. 16. And this she did for many *days* are evil
2 *Tim.* 3. 1. in the last *days* grievous times shall come
Heb. 1. 2. hath at the end of these *days* spoken unto us
5. 7. in the *days* of his flesh, having offered up prayers
7. 3. having neither beginning of *days* nor end of life
8. 8. Behold, the *days* come, saith the Lord
10. 32. But call to remembrance the former *days*
11. 30. after they had been compassed about for seven *d.*
12. 10. For they verily for a few *days* chastened us
Jas. 5. 3. Ye have laid up your treasure in the last *days*
1 *Pet.* 3. 10. He that would love life, And see good *days*
20. longsuffering of God waited in the *days* of Noah
2 *Pet.* 3. 3. that in the last *days* mockers shall come
Rev. 2. 10 and ye shall have tribulation ten *days*
13. even in the *days* of Antipas my witness
9. 6. And in those *days* men shall seek death
10. 7. but in the *days* of the voice of the seventh angel
11. 3. prophesy a thousand two hundred and threescore *d.*
6. that it rain not during the *days* of their prophecy
9. look upon their dead bodies three *days* and a half
11. And after the three *d.* and a half the breath of life
12. 6. may nourish her a thousand two hundred and threescore *days*
see sabbath day.

Dayspring.
Lu. 1. 78. Whereby the *dayspring* from on high shall visit

Day-star.
2 *Pet.* 1. 19. and the *day-star* arise in your hearts

Day-time.
2 *Pet.* 2. 13. count it pleasure to revel in the *day-time*

DEAD

Dazzling.—*A.V.* ¹*glistening*, ²*shining*.
Lu. 9. 29. his raiment became white and ¹*dazzling*
24. 4. two men stood by them in ²*dazzling* apparel

Deacons.—*A.V.* ¹*deacon*.
Phil. 1. 1. the saints—at Philippi, with the bishops and *d.*
1 *Tim.* 3. 8. *Deacons* in like manner must be grave
10. then let them serve as ¹*deacons*. ¹13
12. Let *deacons* be husbands of one wife

Dead.
Mat. 2. 20. for they are *d.* that sought the young child's life
8. 22. leave the *dead* to bury their own *dead*. *Lu.* 9. 60
9. 18. My daughter is even now *d.* *Mk.* 5. 35; *Lu.* 8. 49
24. for the damsel is not *dead*, but sleepeth. *Mk.* 5. 39:
10. 8. raise the *dead*, cleanse the lepers [*Lu.* 8. 52, 53
11. 5. the deaf hear, and the *dead* are raised up. *Lu.* 7. 22
22. 32. God is not the God of the *d.* *Mk.* 12. 27: *Lu.* 20. 38
23. 27. but inwardly are full of *dead* men's bones
28. 4. the watchers did quake, and became as *dead* men
Mk. 9. 26. he came out; and the child became as one *dead*
12. 26. But as touching the *dead*, that they are raised
15. 44. And Pilate marvelled if he were already *dead*— whether he had been any while *dead*
Lu. 10. 30. and departed, leaving him half *dead*
20. 37. But that the *dead* are raised, even Moses shewed
24. 5. Why seek ye the living among the *dead* ? [them
Jno. 5. 21. For as the Father raiseth the *d.* and quickeneth
25. when the *dead* shall hear the voice of the Son of God
11. 39. for he hath been *dead* four days
Acts 5. 10. and the young men came in and found her *dead*
10. 42. God to be the Judge of quick and *dead*. 2 *Tim.* 4. 1
20. 9. from the third story, and was taken up *dead*
26. 8. incredible with you, if God doth raise the *dead* ?
23. how that he first by the resurrection of the *dead*
28. 6. have swollen, or fallen down *dead* suddenly
Rom. 4. 17. even God, who quickeneth the *dead*
19. considered his own body now as good as *dead*
6. 11. Even so reckon ye also yourselves to be *d.* unto sin
7. 4. ye also were made *d.* to the law through the body
14. 9. that he might be Lord of both the *d.* and the living
1 *Cor.* 7. 39. if the husband be *d.*, she is free to be married
15. 13. But if there is no resurrection of the *dead*
15. if so be that the *dead* are not raised [29, 32
16. For if the *d.* are not raised, neither hath Christ been
29. Else what shall they do which are baptized for the *d.*?
35. But some one will say, How are the *dead* raised ?
52. and the *dead* shall be raised incorruptible
2 *Cor.* 1. 9. but in God which raiseth the *dead* [2. 13
Eph. 2. 1. when ye were *dead* through your—sins. 5: *Col.*
1 *Th.* 4. 16. and the *dead* in Christ shall rise first
Heb. 6. 1. laying—a foundation of repentance from *d.* works
9. 14. cleanse your conscience from *dead* works
11. 4. through it he being *dead* yet speaketh
12. there sprang of one, and him as good as *dead*
35. Women received their *dead* by a resurrection
1 *Pet.* 4. 5. ready to judge the quick and the *dead*
6. this end was the gospel preached even to the *dead*
Jude 12. twice *dead*, plucked up by the roots
Rev. 1. 5. faithful witness, the firstborn of the *dead*
17. I [John] fell at his feet as one *dead*
3. 1. thou hast a name that thou livest, and thou art *d.*
11. 18. and the time of the *dead* to be judged
14. 13. Blessed are the *dead* which die in the Lord
16. 3. and it became blood as of a *dead* man
20. 5. The rest of the *dead* lived not until the [judged
12. I saw the *d.*, the great and the small—and the *d.* were
13. the sea gave up the *dead*—and Hades gave up the *d.*
see bodies, death, die, died, resurrection, was dead.

DEAD

From the Dead.
Mat. 14. 2. John the Baptist; he is risen *from the dead.*
 Mk. 6. 14: Lu. 9. 7
17. 9. Son of man be risen *f. the d.* Mk. 9. 9: Jno. 21. 14
27. 64. He is risen *from the dead.* 28. 7
Mk. 9. 10. what the rising again *from the d.* should mean
Lu. 16. 31. be persuaded, if one rise *from the dead.* 30
24. 46. rise again *from the d.* the third day. Jno. 20. 9
Jno. 2. 22. When therefore he was raised *from the dead*
12. 1. whom Jesus raised *from the dead*
Acts 3. 15. whom God raised *from the dead.* 4. 10: 13. 30,
 34: Rom. 10. 9: Gal. 1. 1: Col. 2. 12: 1 Th. 1. 10:
 1 Pet. 1. 21
10. 41. eat and drink with him after he rose *from the dead*
17. 31. in that he hath raised him *from the dead*
Rom. 4. 24. that raised Jesus our Lord *from the dead.* 8. 11
6. 4. like as Christ was raised *from the dead*
 9. Christ being raised *from the dead* dieth no more
13. present yourselves unto God, as alive *from the dead*
7. 4. to another, even to him who was raised *from the d.*
10. 7. (that is, to bring Christ up *from the dead*)
11. 15. receiving of them be, but life *from the dead?*
1 Cor. 15. 12. preached that he hath been raised *from the d.*
20. But now hath Christ been raised *from the dead*
Eph. 1, 20. in Christ, when he raised him *from the dead*
5. 14. *from the dead,* and Christ shall shine upon thee
Col. 1. 18. the beginning, the firstborn *from the dead*
2 Tim. 2. 8. risen *from the dead,* of the seed of David
Heb. 11. 19. God is able to raise up, even *from the dead*
13, 20. brought again *from the dead* the great shepherd
 see raised.

Is Dead.—A.V. ¹*was dead.*
Mat. 9. 18. My daughter is even now *dead.* Mk. 5. 35:
 Lu. 8. 49.
Mk. 9. 26. insomuch that the more part said, He *is dead*
Jno. 8. 52. Abraham *is dead,* and the prophets. 53
11, 14. said unto them plainly, Lazarus *is dead*
Rom. 7. 8. apart from the law sin ¹*is dead*
 8. 10. if Christ is in you, the body *is dead* because of sin
1 Tim. 5. 6. herself to pleasure *is dead* while she liveth
Jas. 2. 17. Even so faith, if it have not works, *is d.* in itself
 26. For as the body apart from the spirit *is dead,* even
 so faith apart from works *is dead.*
 see barren, died.

Was Dead.—A.V. ¹*had been dead.*
Mat. 2. 19. But when Herod *was dead,* behold, an angel
Lu. 7. 12. one that *was dead,* the only son of his mother
15. And he [widow's son] that *was dead* sat up
8. 35. laughed him to scorn, knowing that *was dead*
15. 24. for this my son *was dead,* and is alive again. 32
Jno. 11. 39. Martha, the sister of him that *was dead*
44. that *was dead* came forth, bound hand and foot
19. 33. came to Jesus, and saw that he *was dead* already
Acts 14. 19. out of the city, supposing that he ¹*was dead*
25. 19. and of one Jesus, who *was dead*
Rev. 1. 18. I *was dead,* and behold, I am alive. 2. 8.
 see is dead.

Deadly.
Mk. 16. 18. and if they drink any *deadly* thing
Jas. 3. 8. it is a restless evil, it is full of *deadly* poison
 see death-stroke.

Deadness.
Rom. 4. 19. and the *deadness* of Sarah's womb

Deaf.
Mat. 11. 5. the *deaf* hear, and the dead are raised. Lu. 7. 22

DEATH

Mk. 7. 32. And they bring unto him one that was *deaf*
 37. maketh even the *d.* to hear, and the dumb to speak
9. 25. Thou dumb and *deaf* spirit, I command thee

Deal.—A.V. ¹*use.*
Mk. 7. 36. so much the more a great *deal* they published
10. 48. but he cried out the more a great *deal,* Thou son
2 Cor. 13. 10. that I may not when present ¹*deal* sharply

Dealeth.
Heb. 12. 7. God *dealeth* with you as with sons

Dealings.
Jno. 4. 9. (For Jews have no *dealings* with Samaritans)

Dealt.—A.V. ¹*charged.*
Lu. 2. 48. Son, why hast thou thus *dealt* with us?
Acts 7. 19. The same *dealt* subtilly with our race
Rom. 12. 3. according as God hath *dealt* to each man
1 Th. 2. 11. as ye know how we ¹*d.* with each one of you
 see done, made suit.

Dear.
Lu. 7. 2. centurion's servant, who was *dear* unto him
Acts 20. 24. But I hold not my life of any account, as *dear*
1 Th. 2. 8. because ye were become very *dear* to us
 see beloved, love.

Dearly beloved A.V.—*see beloved.*

Dearth A.V.—*see famine.*

Death.—A.V. ¹*dead,* ²*die,* ³*grave.*
Mat. 2. 15. and was there until the *death* of Herod
4. 16. sat in the region and shadow of *death.* Lu. 1. 79
10. 21. brother shall deliver up brother to *d.* Mk. 13. 12
15. 4. evil of father or mother, let him die the *death.*
 Mk. 7. 10 [Lu. 9. 27
16. 28. which shall in no wise taste of *death.* Mk. 9. 1:
20. 18. and they shall condemn him to *death.* Mk. 10. 33
26. 38. is exceeding sorrowful, even unto *d.* Mk. 14. 34
 66. said, He is worthy of *death.* Mk. 14. 64.
Mk. 5. 23. My little daughter is at the point of *death*
Lu. 2. 26. by the Holy Spirit, that he should not see *death*
7. 2. centurion's servant—at the point of ²*death*
22. 33. with thee I am ready to go both to prison and to *d.*
23. 15. nothing worthy of *death* hath been done by him
22. I have found no cause of *death* in him
24. 20. delivered him up to be condemned to *death*
Jno. 4. 47. heal his son ; for he was at the point of *death*
5. 24. passed out of *death* into life. 1 Jno. 3. 14
8. 51. If a man keep my word, he shall never see *d.* 52
11. 4. This sickness is not unto *death*
13. Now Jesus had spoken of his *death* [18. 32
12. 33. signifying by what manner of *d.* he should die.
21. 19. by what manner of *death* he should glorify God
Acts 2. 24. God raised up, having loosed the pangs of *death*
8. 1. And Saul was consenting unto his *death*
13. 28. And though they found no cause of *death* in him
22. 4. and I persecuted this Way unto the *death*
26. 31. doeth nothing worthy of *d.* 23. 29: 25. 11, 25
28. 18. because there was no cause of *death* in me
Rom. 1. 32. they which practise such things are worthy of *d.*
5. 10. reconciled to God through the *death* of his Son
12. and *d.* through sin ; and so *d.* passed unto all men
14. Nevertheless *death* reigned from Adam until Moses
17. by the trespass of the one, *d.* reigned through the one
21. as sin reigned in *death,* even so might grace reign

DEATH

Rom. 6. 3. into Christ Jesus were baptized unto his *death*?
4. buried therefore with him through baptism into *d.*
5. united with him by the likeness of his *death*
9. *death* no more hath dominion over him
10. For the *death* that he died, he died unto sin
16. whom ye obey; whether of sin unto *death*
21. for the end of those things is *death*
23. For the wages of sin is *death*
7. 5. wrought in our members to bring forth fruit unto *d.*
10. this I found to be unto *death*
13. Did then that which is good become *death* unto me?
24. who shall deliver me out of the body of this *death*?
8. 2. free from the law of sin and of *death*
6. For the mind of the flesh is *death*
38. For I am persuaded, that neither *death*, nor life
1 *Cor.* 3. 22. or life, or *death*, or things present
4. 9. apostles last of all, as men doomed to *death*
11. 26. ye proclaim the Lord's *death* till he come
15. 21. For since by man came *death*
26. The last enemy that shall be abolished is *death*
54. *Death* is swallowed up in victory
55. O ¹*d.*, where is thy victory? O *d.*, where is thy sting?
56. The sting of *death* is sin
2 *Cor.* 1. 9. have had the answer of *death* within ourselves
10. who delivered us out of so great a *death*
2. 16. to the one a savour from *death* unto *death*
3. 7. But if the ministration of *death*, written and
4. 11. are alway delivered unto *death* for Jesus' sake
12. So then *death* worketh in us, but life in you
7. 10. but the sorrow of the world worketh *death*
Phil. 1. 20. magnified in my body, whether by life, or by *d.*
2. 8. obedient even unto *death*, yea, the *d.* of the cross
27. for indeed he was sick nigh unto *death*
30. because for the work of Christ he came nigh unto *d.*
3 10. becoming conformed unto his *death*
Col. 1. 22. reconciled in the body of his flesh through *d.*
2 *Tim.* 1. 10. Saviour Christ Jesus, who abolished *death*
Heb. 2. 9. suffering of *d.* crowned—taste *d.* for every man
14. through *death* he might bring to nought him that had the power of *death*
15. and might deliver all them who through fear of *d.*
5. 7. unto him that was able to save him from *death*
7. 23 that by *death* they are hindered from continuing
9. 15. that a *d.* having taken place for the redemption
16 must of necessity be the *death* of him that made it
17. a testament is of force where there hath been ¹*d.*
11 5. Enoch was translated that he should not see *d.*
Jas. 1. 15 sin, when it is fullgrown, bringeth forth *death*
5. 20. error of his way shall save a soul from *death*
1 *Jno.* 3. 14. He that loveth not abideth in *death*
5. 16. his brother sinning a sin not unto *d.*—for them that sin not unto *d.* There is a sin unto *death*
17. there is a sin not unto *death*
Rev. 1. 18. and I have the keys of *death* and of Hades
2. 10. Be thou faithful unto *death* [*death*
11. He that overcometh shall not be hurt of the second
23. And I will kill her children with *death*
6. 8. sat upon him, his name was *D.*—famine, and with *d.*
9. 6. in those days men shall seek *d.*—*d.* fleeth from them
12. 11. and they loved not their life even unto *death*
13. 3. his heads as though it had been smitten unto *d.*
18. 8. in one day shall her plagues come, *d.*, and mourning
20. 6. over these the second *death* hath no power
. 13. and *death* and Hades gave up the dead [second *d.*
14. *death* and Hades were cast into the lake—This is the
21. 4. and *death* shall be no more

Put to **Death.**—*A.V.* ¹*kill.*
Mat. 10. 21. and cause them to be *put to death. Mk.* 13. 12

Mat. 14. 5. And when he would have *put* him *to death*
Lu. 21. 16. And some of you shall they cause to be *put to d.*
22. 2. scribes sought how they might ¹*put* him *to death*
23. 32. malefactors, led with him to be *put to death*
Jno. 11. 53. they took counsel that they might *put* him *to death. Mat.* 26. 59: 27. 1: *Mk.* 14. 55
12 10. that they might *put* Lazarus also *to death*
18. 31. It is not lawful for us to *put* any man *to death*
Acts 12. 19. commanded that they should be *put to death*
26. 10. and when they were *put to death*, I gave my vote
1 *Pet.* 3. 18. being *put to death* in the flesh, but quickened in *see kill.*

Deaths.

2. *Cor.* 11. 23. in stripes above measure, in *deaths* oft

Death-stroke.—*A.V.* ¹*deadly wound.*
Rev. 13. 3. and his ¹*death-stroke* was healed. ¹12

Debate.—*A.V. see strife.*

Debt—s.
Mat. 6. 12. And forgive us our *debts*
18. 32. Thou wicked servant, I forgave thee all that *d.* 27
Rom. 4. 4. the reward is not reckoned as of grace, but as of *d. see due.*

Debtor—s.—*A.V.* ¹*guilty.*
Mat. 6. 12. as we also have forgiven our *debtors*
23. 16. shall swear by the gold of the temple, he is a *d.*
18. swear by the gift that is upon it he is a ¹*debtor*
Lu. 7. 41. A certain lender had two *debtors*
16. 5. And called to him each one of his lord's *debtors*
Rom. 1. 14. I am *debtor* both to Greeks and Barbarians
8. 12. So then, brethren, we are *debtors*, not to the flesh
15. 27. been their good pleasure; and their *d.* they are
Gal. 5. 3. that he is a *debtor* to do the whole law

Decayed—eth.—*A.V. see old.*

Decaying.—*A.V.* ¹*perish.*
2 *Cor.* 4. 16. though our outward man is ¹*decaying*

Decease—d.
Mat. 22. 25. and the first married and *deceased*
Lu. 9. 31. who appeared in glory, and spake of his *decease*
2 *Pet.* 1. 15. after my *d.* to call these things to remembrance

Deceit.—*A.V.* ¹*deceitful,* ²*deceivableness.*
Mk. 7. 22. wickednesses, *deceit*, lasciviousness, an evil eye
Rom. 1. 29. full of envy, murder, strife, *deceit*
3. 13. With their tongues they have used *deceit*
Eph. 4. 22. which waxeth corrupt after the lusts of ¹*deceit*
Col. 2. 8. spoil of you through his philosophy and vain *d.*
2 *Th.* 2. 10. with all ²*deceit* of unrighteousness for them *see error.*

Deceitful—ly.
2 *Cor.* 4. 2. nor handling the word of God *deceitfully*
11. 13. For such men are false apostles, *d.* workers *see deceit.*

Deceitfulness.
Mat. 13. 22. and the *d.* of riches, choke the word. *Mk.* 4. 19
Heb. 3. 13. lest any one of you be hardened by the *d.* of sin

Deceivableness—*A.V. see deceit.*

Deceive.
1. *Cor.* 3. 18. Let no man *deceive* himself
Eph. 5. 6. Let no man *deceive* you with empty words

DECEIVE

1 Jno. 1. 8. If we say that we have no sin, we d. ourselves
Rev. 20. 3. that he should deceive the nations no more
8. to d. the nations—in the four corners of the earth
see astray, beguile, error.

Deceived.—A.V. ¹err.

1 Cor. 6. 9. Be not d. : neither fornicators. 15. 33 : Gal. 6. 7
2 Tim. 3. 13. wax worse and worse, deceiving and being d.
Tit. 3. 3. deceived, serving divers lusts and pleasures
Jas. 1. 16. Be not ¹deceived, my beloved brethren
Rev. 18. 23. for with thy sorcery were all the nations d.
19. 20. wherewith he d. them that had received the mark
20. 10. the devil that d. them was cast into the lake of fire
see astray, beguiled.

Deceiver—s.—A.V. ¹deceiveth.

Mat. 27. 63. Sir, we remember that that deceiver said
2 Cor. 6. 8. as deceivers, and yet true
Tit. 1. 10. many unruly men, vain talkers and deceive rs
2 Jno. 7. For many deceivers are gone forth into the world—This is the deceiver and the antichrist
Rev. 12. 9. Satan, the ¹deceiver of the whole world

Deceiveth.

Gal. 6. 3. when he is nothing, he deceiveth himself
Jas. 1. 26. but d. his heart, this man's religion is vain
Rev. 13. 14. And he deceiveth them that dwell on the earth
see astray, deceiver.

Deceiving.

2 Tim. 3. 13. wax worse and worse, d. and being deceived
see deluding.

Deceivings A.V.—see love-feasts.

Decently.

1 Cor. 14. 40. But let all things be done decently and in order

Decide.—A.V. ¹judge.

1 Cor. 6. 5. who shall be able to ¹d. between his brethren

Decision.—A.V. ¹hearing.

Acts 25. 21. Paul had appealed to—the ¹d. of the emperor

Decked.

Rev. 17. 4. and d. with gold and precious stone. 18. 16

Declaration A.V —see narrative, shew.

Declare.—A.V. ¹shew, ²tell.

Mat. 12. 18. he shall ¹declare judgement to the Gentiles
15. 15. Declare unto us the parable
Lu. 8. 39. Return to thy house, and ¹d. how great things God
Jno. 4. 25. when he is come, he will ²d. unto us all things
16. 13. he shall ¹d. unto you the things that are to come
14. he shall take of mine, and shall ¹declare it unto you.
Acts 25. 21. His generation who shall declare ? ⌈15
13. 41. in no wise believe, if one declare it unto you
1 Cor. 3. 13. be made manifest : for the day shall declare it
Heb. 2. 12. I will declare thy name unto my brethren
1 Jno. 1. 2. and ¹declare unto you the life, the eternal life
3. that which we have seen and heard d. we unto you
see announce, bring, charge, declaring, explain, (make) known, make manifest, manifest, set (forth), shew.

Declared.—A.V. ¹shewed.

Lu. 8. 47. and falling down before him d. in the presence
Jno. 1. 18. bosom of the Father, he hath declared him

DEEPLY

Acts 9. 27. and d. unto them how he had seen the Lord
12. 17. d. unto them how the Lord had brought him 'lem
26. 20. ¹d. both to them of Damascus first, and at Jerusa-
Rom. 1. 4. who was declared to be the Son of God
Col. 1. 8. who also declared unto us your love in the Spirit
Rev. 10. 7. the good tidings which he d. to his servants
see (made) known, laid, manifest, published, rehearsed, signified.

Declaring.—A.V. ¹declare, ²report, ³shewed, ⁴signify.

Acts 15. 3. declaring the conversion of the Gentiles
19. 18. came, confessing, and ⁴declaring their deeds
20. 20. I shrank not from ³declaring unto you anything
27. I shrank not from ¹d. unto you the—counsel of God
21. 26. ⁴declaring the fulfilment of the days of purification
1 Cor. 14. 25. ²declaring that God is among you indeed
see rehearsing, proclaiming.

Decrease.

Jno. 3. 30. He must increase, but I must decrease

Decree—s.

Lu. 2. 1. there went out a decree from Cæsar Augustus
Acts 16. 4. they delivered them the decrees for to keep
17. 7. and these all act contrary to the decrees of Cæsar

Decreed A.V.—see determined.

Dedicated.—A.V. ¹consecrated.

Heb. 9. 18. the first covenant hath not been d. without blood
10. 20. the way which he ¹d. for us, a new and living way

Dedication.

Jno. 10. 22. And it was the feast of the d. at Jerusalem

Deed.

Lu. 23. 51. not consented to their counsel and deed)
24. 19. a prophet mighty in deed and word before God
Acts 4. 9. if we this day are examined concerning a good d.
Rom. 15. 18. the obedience of the Gentiles, by word and d.
1 Cor. 5. 2. that he that had done this deed might be taken
2 Cor. 10. 11. such are we also in d. when we are present
Col. 3. 17. And whatsoever ye do, in word or in deed
1 Jno. 3. 18. neither with the tongue ; but in d. and truth
see doing, thing.

Deeds.—A.V. ¹works.

Mat. 16. 27. render unto every man according to his ¹deeds
Lu. 23. 41. for we receive the due reward of our deeds
Acts 19. 18. came, confessing, and declaring their deeds
Rom. 8. 13. ye mortify the deeds of the body, ye shall live
2 Pet. 2. 8. vexed his righteous soul—with their lawless d.)
see doings, evils, works.

Deemed A.V.—see surmised.

Deep.—A.V. ¹depths.

Lu. 5. 4. Put out into the deep, and let down your nets
6. 48. building a house, who digged and went deep
Jno. 4. 11. nothing to draw with, and the well is deep
Acts 20. 9. Eutychus, borne down with deep sleep
1 Cor. 2. 10. searcheth all things, yea, the d. things of God
2 Cor. 8. 2. their deep poverty abounded unto the riches
11. 25. a night and a day have I been in the deep
Rev. 2. 24. which know not the ¹deep things of Satan
see abyss.

Deeply.

Mk. 8. 12. And he sighed deeply in his spirit

DEEPNESS

Deepness.—*A.V.* ¹*depth.*
Mat. 18. 5. because they had no *deepness* of earth
Mk. 4. 5. sprang up, because it had no ¹*deepness* of earth

Defamed.
1 *Cor.* 4. 13. being *defamed*, we intreat: we are made as

Defect.—*A.V.* ¹*fault.*
1 *Cor.* 6. 7. already it is altogether a ¹*defect* in you

Defence.—*A.V.* ¹*answer,* ²*answered,* ³*spake for himself.*
Acts 19. 33. and would have made a *d.* unto the people
22. 1. hear ye the *defence* which I now make unto you
24. 10. I do cheerfully make my ¹*defence.* 26. ²1, ¹², ³24
25. 8. while Paul said in his ³*defence,* Neither against
1 *Cor.* 9. 3. My ¹*defence* to them that examine me is this
Phil. 1. 7. in the *defence* and confirmation of the gospel
16. knowing that I am set for the *defence* of the gospel
2 *Tim.* 4. 16. At my first ¹*defence* no one took my part

Defended.
Acts 7. 24. And seeing one of them suffer wrong, he *d.* him

Deferred.
Acts 24. 22. exact knowledge concerning the Way, *d.* them

Defile.—*A.V.* ¹*defiled.*
Mat. 15. 18. and they *defile* the man. 20; *Mk.* 7. 15, 23
Mk. 7. 18. goeth into the man, it cannot *defile* him. 15
Jude 8. these also in their dreamings *defile* the flesh
Rev. 3. 4. names in Sardis which did not ¹*d.* their garments
see abusers, destroyeth.

Defiled.—*A.V.* ¹*polluted,* ²*unclean,* ³*unwashen.*
Mk. 7. 2. disciples ate their bread with *defiled,* that is
5. eat their bread with ³*defiled* hands?
Jno. 18. 28. that they might not be *defiled,* but might eat
Acts 21. 28. the temple, and hath ¹*defiled* this holy place
1 *Cor.* 8. 7. and their conscience being weak is *defiled*
Tit. 1. 15. *defiled* and unbelieving nothing is pure: but
both their mind and their conscience are *defiled*
Heb. 9. 13. sprinkling them that have been ²*defiled*
12. 15. trouble you, and thereby the many be *defiled*
Rev. 14. 4. These are they which were not *d.* with women
see defile.

Defilement—s.—*A.V.* ¹*filthiness,* ²*pollutions,* ³*uncleanness.*
2 *Cor.* 7. 1. from all ¹*defilement* of flesh and spirit
2 *Pet.* 2. 10. walk after the flesh in the lust of ³*defilement*
20. after they have escaped the ²*defilements* of the world

Defileth.
Mat. 15. 11. entereth into the mouth *defileth* the man—
out of the mouth, this *defileth* the man. *Mk.* 7. 20
20. to eat with unwashen hands *defileth* not the man
Jas. 3. 6. the tongue, which *defileth* the whole body
see unclean.

Definite.—*A.V.* ¹*limiteth.*
Heb. 4. 7. he again ¹*defineth* a certain day, saying

Defraud—**ed.**
Mk. 10. 19. Do not *defraud,* Honour thy father and mother
1 *Cor.* 6. 7. why not rather be *defrauded?*
8. do wrong, and *defraud,* and that your brethren
7. 5. *D.* ye not one the other, except it be by consent
see advantage.

DELIVERED

Degree.
Lu. 1. 52. And hath exalted them of low *degree*
Jas. 1. 9. brother of low *degree* glory in his high estate
see standing.

Delay—eth.
Lu. 12. 45. My lord *delayeth* his coming
Acts 9. 33. intreating him, *Delay* not to come on unto us
25. 17. I made no *delay,* but on the next day sat down
see tarrieth.

Delicacies *A.V.*—*see wantonness.*

Delicately.—*A.V.* ¹*pleasure.*
Lu. 7. 25. and live *delicately,* are in kings' courts [sure
Jas. 5. 5. Ye have lived ¹*d.* on the earth, and taken your pleasure.

Deliciously *A.V.*—*see wanton, wantonly.*

Delight.
Rom. 7. 22. For I *d.* in the law of God after the inward man

Deliver.—*A.V.* ¹*betray,* ²*delivered.*
Mat. 5. 25. adversary *deliver* thee—judge *d.* thee. *Lu.* 12. 58
6. 13. but *deliver* us from the evil one
10. 17. for they will *deliver* you up to councils. *Mk.* 13. 9
19. But when they *deliver* you up. *Mk.* 13. 11
21. And brother shall *d.* up brother to death. *Mk.* 13. ¹12
20. 19. shall *d.* him unto the Gentiles. *Mk.* 10. 33; *Acts* 21.
24. 9. Then shall they *d.* you up unto tribulation [11
10. shall ¹*d.* up one another, and shall hate one another
26. 15. and I will *deliver* him unto you? [*Lu.* 22. ¹6
16. sought opportunity to ¹*d.* him unto them. *Mk.* 14. ¹11;
27. 43. let him *deliver* him now, if he desireth him
Mk. 14. 10. priests, that he might ¹*deliver* him. *Lu.* 22. ¹4
Lu. 20. 20. his speech, so as to *deliver* him up to the rule
Acts 7. 34. and I am come down to *deliver* them
Rom. 7. 24. who shall *d.* me out of the body of this death?
1 *Cor.* 5. 5. to *deliver* such a one unto Satan
15. 24. when he shall ²*deliver* up the kingdom to God
2 *Cor.* 1. 10. and will *deliver:* on whom we have set our
hope that he will also still *deliver* us
Gal. 1. 4. that he might *d.* us out of this present evil world
2 *Tim.* 4. 18. The Lord will *deliver* me from every evil work
Heb. 2. 15. might *d.* all them who through fear of death
2 *Pet.* 2. 9. the Lord knoweth how to *deliver* the godly
see deliverance, give.

Deliverance.—*A.V.* ¹*deliver.*
Acts 7. 25. how that God by his hand was giving them ¹*d.*
Heb. 11. 35. were tortured, not accepting their *deliverance*
see release.

Delivered.—*A.V.* ¹*betrayed,* ²*born,* ³*brought forth,* ⁴*cast into prison,* ⁵*put.*
Mat. 4. 12. Now when he heard that John was ⁴*delivered* up
11. 27. have been *d.* unto me of my Father. *Lu.* 10. 22
17. 22. Son of man shall be ¹*d.* up into the hands of men.
18. 34. and *delivered* him to the tormentors [26. ¹2
20. 18. Son of man shall be *d. Mk.* 9. 31; 10. 33: *Lu.* 9. 44:
25. 14. and *delivered* unto them his goods [24. 7
27. 2. and *d.* him up to Pilate the governor. *Mk.* 15. 1
18. that for envy they had *delivered* him up. *Jno.* 19. 16
26. Jesus he scourged and *d.* to be crucified. *Jno.* 19. 16
Mk. 1. 14. after that John was ⁵*delivered* up, Jesus came
7. 13. by your tradition, which ye have *delivered*
15. 15. released unto them Barabbas, and *delivered* Jesus
Lu. 1. 2. even as they *delivered* them unto us
57. time was fulfilled that she should be *delivered.* 2. 6
74. that we being *d.* out of the hand of our enemies

DELIVERED

Lu. 4. 6. *d.* unto me; and to whomsoever I will I give it
17. there was *d.* unto him the book of the prophet Isaiah
18. 32. For he shall be *delivered* up unto the Gentiles
21. 16. ye shall be ¹*delivered* up even by parents
23. 25. but Jesus he *delivered* up to their will
24. 20. and our rulers *delivered* him up to be condemned
Jno. 16. 21. but when she is *delivered* of the child
18. 30. we should not have *delivered* him up unto thee
35. and the chief priests *delivered* thee unto me
36. That I should not be *delivered* to the Jews
19. 11. he that *delivered* me unto thee hath greater sin
16. he *delivered* him unto them to be crucified
Acts 2. 23. him, being *d.* up by the determinate counsel
3. 13. glorified his servant Jesus; whom ye *delivered* up
6. 14. change the customs which Moses *d.* unto us
7. 10. and *delivered* him out of all his afflictions
12. 4. and *delivered* him to four quaternions of soldiers
11. his angel and *d.* me out of the hand of Herod
15. 30. multitude together, they *delivered* the epistle
16. 4. they *delivered* them the decrees for to keep
23. 33. and *delivered* the letter to the governor
27. 1. they *delivered* Paul and certain other prisoners
28. 17. yet was *d.* prisoner from Jerusalem into the hands
Rom. 4. 25. who was *delivered* up for our trespasses
6. 17. form of teaching whereunto ye were *delivered*
8. 21. creation itself also shall be *d.* from the bondage
32. spared not his own Son, but *d.* him up for us all
15. 31. that I may be *d.* from them that are disobedient
1 *Cor.* 11. 2. the traditions, even as I *d.* them to you
23. I received—that which also I *delivered* unto you
15. 3. I *d.* unto you first of all that which also I received
2 *Cor.* 1. 10. who *delivered* us out of so great a death
4. 11. are alway *delivered* unto death for Jesus' sake
Col. 1. 13. who *delivered* us out of the power of darkness
2 *Th.* 3. 2. that we may be *d.* from unreasonable and evil men
1 *Tim.* 1. 20. Hymenæus and Alexander; whom I *d.* unto
2 *Tim.* 3. 11. and out of them all the Lord *d.* me [Satan
4. 17. and I was *delivered* out of the mouth of the lion
2 *Pet.* 2. 7. and *delivered* righteous Lot ⸢them
21. to turn back from the holy commandment *d.* unto
Jude 3. once for all *delivered* unto the saints
Rev. 12. 2. travailing in birth, and in pain to be *delivered*
4. before the woman which was about to be *delivered*,
that when she was ²*delivered*, he might devour
5. she was ³*delivered* of a son, a man child
see committed, deliver, delivereth, discharged, gave, given (up), quit.

Deliveredst.

Mat. 25. 20. Lord, thou *deliveredst* unto me five talents
22. and said, Lord, thou *d.* unto me two talents

Deliverer.

Acts 7. 35. him hath God sent to be both a ruler and a *d.*
Rom. 11. 26. There shall come out of Zion the *Deliverer*

Delivereth—ing.—*A.V.* ¹*delivered*.

Lu. 21. 12. *d.* you up to the synagogues and prisons
Acts 22. 4. binding and *delivering* into prisons both men
26. 17. *delivering* thee from the people
1 *Th.* 1. 10. which ¹*delivereth* us from the wrath to come

Delude.—*A.V.* ¹*beguile*.

Col. 2. 4. that no one may ¹*d.* you with persuasiveness

Deluding.—*A.V.* ¹*deceiving*.

Jas. 1. 22. doers of the word, and not hearers only, ¹*d.* your

Delusion *A.V.*—*see error*.

DEPART

Demanded *A.V.*—*see inquired, asked*.

Demeanour.—*A.V.* ¹*behaviour*.

Tit. 2. 3. aged women be likewise reverent in ¹*demeanour*

Demonstration.

1 *Cor.* 2. 4. but in *demonstration* of the Spirit and of power

Den.

Mat. 21. 13. house of prayer: but ye make it a *den* of
robbers. *Mk.* 11. 17: *Lu.* 19. 46
see caves.

Denied.—*A.V.* ¹*denying*.

Mat. 26. 70. But he *denied* before them all, saying, I know
not. 72: *Mk.* 14. 68, 70: *Lu.* 22. 57: *Jno.* 18. 25, 27
Lu. 8. 45. Who is it that touched me? And when all *d.*
12. 9. shall be *d.* in the presence of the angels of God
Jno. 1. 20. and *denied* not; and he confessed, I am not
13. 38. shall not crow, till thou hast *denied* me thrice
Acts 3. 13. and *denied* before the face of Pilate
14. But ye *denied* the Holy and Righteous One
1 *Tim.* 5. 8. he hath *denied* the faith, and is worse than
2 *Tim.* 3. 5. form of godliness, but having ¹*d.* the power
see deny.

Denieth.

Lu. 12. 9. but he that *denieth* me in the presence of men
1 *Jno.* 2. 22. liar but he that *d.* that Jesus is the Christ?—
antichrist, even he that *d.* the Father and the Son
23. Whosoever *d.* the Son, the same hath not the Father

Deny.—*A.V.* ¹*denied*.

Mat. 10. 33. But whosoever shall *deny* me before men, him
will I also *deny* before my Father [*Lu.* 9. 23
13. 24. let him *d.* himself, and take up his cross. *Mk.* 8. 34:
26. 34. before the cock crow, thou shalt *deny* me thrice.
75: *Mk.* 14. 30, 72: *Lu.* 22. 34, 61 [14. 31
35. if I must die with thee, yet will I not *deny* thee. *Mk.*
Acts 4. 16. manifest—in Jerusalem; and we cannot *d.* it
2 *Tim.* 2. 12. if we shall *deny* him, he also will *deny* us
13. he abideth faithful; for he cannot *deny* himself
Tit. 1. 16. they know God; but by their works they *d.* him
Rev. 2. 13. and didst not ¹*deny* my faith ·
3. 8. didst keep my word, and didst not ¹*deny* my name
see say.

Denying.

Tit. 2. 12. *denying* ungodliness and worldly lusts
2 *Pet.* 2. 1. *denying* even the Master that bought them
Jude 4. and *d.* our only Master and Lord, Jesus Christ
see denied.

Depart.—*A.V.* ¹*go*.

Mat. 7. 23. *d.* from me, ye that work iniquity. *Lu.* 13. 27
8. 18. gave commandment to *d.* unto the other side
34. that he would *depart* from their borders. *Mk.* 5. 17
25. 41. *Depart* from me, ye cursed, into the eternal fire
28. 10. go tell my brethren that they ¹*depart* into Galilee
Mk. 6. 10. there abide till ye *depart* thence
Lu. 2. 29. Now lettest thou thy servant *depart*, O Lord
5. 8. *Depart* from me; for I am a sinful man, O Lord
8. 31. not command them to ¹*depart* into the abyss
37. round about asked him to *depart* from them
9. 4. house ye enter, there abide, and thence *depart*
5. when ye ¹*depart* from that city, shake off the dust
21. 21. and let them that are in the midst of her *d.* out
Jno. 7. 3. *Depart* hence, and go into Judæa ⸢world
13. 1. his hour was come that he should *d.* out of this

DEPART

Acts 1, 4. he charged them not to *depart* from Jerusalem
16. 2. had commanded all the Jews to *depart* from Rome
20. 7. Paul discoursed—intending to *d.* on the morrow
22. 21. *Depart :* for I will send thee forth far hence
25. 4. he himself was about to *depart* thither shortly
1 *Cor.* 7. 10. That the wife *depart* not from her husband
11. (but and if she *depart*, let her remain unmarried
15. Yet if the unbelieving departeth, let him *depart*
2 *Cor.* 12. 8. the Lord thrice, that it might *depart* from me
Phil. 1. 23. having the desire to *depart* and be with Christ
2 *Tim.* 2. 19. nameth the—Lord *d.* from unrighteousness
see come out, departeth, fall (away), go, go away, put.

Departed.—*A.V.* ¹*went his way,* ²*departing.*
Mat. 2. 12. they *d.* into their own country another way. 13
14. and his mother by night, and *departed* into Egypt
9. 7. And he arose, and *d.* to his house. *Lu.* 1, 23: 5, 25
11. 1. Jesus—*departed.* 12. 9: 13. 53: 16. 4: 19. 15: *Mk.*
1. 35 : 8. 13 : *Jno.* 4. 3: 12. 36 [Galilee
15. 29. Jesus *d.* thence, and came nigh unto the sea of
19. 1. Jesus had finished these words, he *d.* from Galilee
27. 5. cast down the pieces of silver—and *departed*
60. a great stone to the door of the tomb, and *departed*
28. 8. they *d.* quickly from the tomb with fear. *Lu.* 24. 12
Mk. 1. 42. And—the leprosy *departed* from him. *Lu.* 5. 13
Lu. 1. 38. And the angel *departed* from her
2. 37. which *departed* not from the temple
4. 13. completed every temptation, he *departed* from him
7. 24. And when the messengers of John were *departed*
9. 6. they *departed*, and went throughout the villages
10. 30. and *departed*, leaving him half dead
Acts 5. 31. They therefore *d.* from the presence of the council
9. 17. Ananias ¹*departed*, and entered into the house
10. 7. And when the angel that spake unto him was *d.*
12. 10. straightway the angel *departed* from him [Peter]
17. And he *departed*, and went to another place
13. 13. and John ²*d.* from them and returned to Jerusalem
16. 40. they comforted them, and *departed*
18. 1. After these things he *departed* from Athens
19. 9. he *d.* from them, and separated the disciples
12. and the diseases *departed* from them
20. 1. and *departed* for to go into Macedonia. 11
21. 8. And on the morrow we *departed.* 5 : 18. 7, 23
22. 29. *departed* from him: and the chief captain also
28. 29. the Jews *d.*, having much disputing (margin)
Phil. 4. 15. when I *departed* from Macedonia, no church
see gone, parted, passed (forth), passing, perished, removed, sailed, went, went away, went forth, went out, withdrew.

Departeth.—*A.V.* ¹*depart.*
Lu. 9. 39. and it hardly *departeth* from him
1 *Cor.* 7. 15. Yet if the unbelieving ¹*d.*, let him depart

Departing.
Acts 20. 29. I know that after my *d.* grievous wolves
see departed, falling (away), going, went out.

Departure.
2 *Tim.* 4. 6. and the time of my ʻPaul' *departure* is come
Heb. 11. 22. made mention of the *d.* of the children of Israel

Deposed.—*A.V.* ¹*destroyed.*
Acts 19. 27. Diana—should even be ¹*deposed* from her

Depth.
Mat. 13. 6. that he should be sunk in the *depth* of the sea
Rom. 8. 39. nor *depth*, nor any other creature, shall be able
11. 33. O the *depth* of the riches both of the wisdom
Eph. 3. 18. the breadth and length and height and *depth*
see deepness.

DESIRE

Depths *A.V.*—*see deep.*

Deputy—ies *A.V.*—*see Proconsul—s.*

Derided *A.V.*—*see scoffed.*

Descend.
Rom. 10. 7. or, Who shall *descend* into the abyss ?
1 *Th.* 4. 16. For the Lord himself shall *descend* from heaven
see come down, descending.

Descended.—*A.V.* ¹*came down.*
Mat. 7. 25. and the rain *descended*, and the floods came. 27
28. 2. for an angel of the Lord *descended* from heaven
Lu. 3. 22. and the Holy Ghost *descended* in a bodily form
Jno. 3. 13. no man hath ascended into heaven, but he
that ¹*descended* out of heaven
Eph. 4. 9. *descended* into the lower parts of the earth ?
10. He that *descended* is the same also that ascended
see came down.

Descendeth *A.V.*—*see cometh down.*

Descending.—*A.V.* ¹*descend.*
Mat. 3. 16. and he [John Baptist] saw the Spirit of God
descending as a dove. *Mk.* 1, 10 ; *Jno.* 1. 32
Jno. 1. 33. whomsoever thou shalt see the Spirit *descending*
51. angels of God ascending and *descending* upon the
Acts. 10. 11. certain vessel *d.*, as it were a great sheet. 11. 15
see coming (down.)

Descent.
Lu. 19. 37. even at the *descent* of the mount of Olives
see genealogy.

Describeth *A.V.*—*see pronounceth, writeth.*

Desert.—*A.V.* ¹*solitary,* ²*wilderness.*
Mat. 14. 15. The place is *desert*. *Mk.* 6. 35: *Lu.* 9.12 ; *Lu.* 9. 1
15. 33. we have so many loaves in a ²*desert* place. *Mk.* 8. 4 ;
Mk. 1. 35. departed into a ¹*desert* place, and there prayed
45. but was without in *desert* places
6. 31. Come ye yourselves apart into a *desert* place
32. in the boat to a *d.* place apart. *Mat.* 14. 13 ; *Lu.* 4. 42
Acts 8. 26. from Jerusalem unto Gaza : the same is *desert*
see wilderness.

Deserts.—*A.V.* ¹*wilderness.*
Lu. 1. 80. the child grew—was in the *deserts* till the day
of his shewing unto Israel [John Baptist]
5. 16. he withdrew himself in the ¹*deserts*, and prayed
8. 29. he was driven of the devil into the ¹*deserts*
Heb. 11. 38. wandering in *deserts* and mountains and caves

Desire—s.—*A.V.* ¹*covet,* ²*pleasure,* ³*will,* ⁴*will have.*
Mat. 9. 13. I *desire* mercy and not sacrifice
Mk. 12. 38. scribes, which *d.* to walk in long robes. *Lu.* 20. 46
Lu. 17. 22. when ye shall *desire* to see one of the days
22. 15. With *desire* I have desired to eat this passover
Acts 28. 22. But we *d.* to hear of thee what thou thinkest
Rom. 10. 1. my heart's *desire* and my supplication to God
1 *Cor.* 12. 31. But *desire* earnestly the greater gifts
14. 1. Follow after love ; yet *desire* earnestly spiritual
39. Wherefore, my brethren, ¹*d.* earnestly to prophesy
2 *Cor.* 11. 12. cut off occasion from them which *desire* an
12. 6. For if I should *d.* to glory, I shall not be foolish
Gal. 4. 21. Tell me, ye that *desire* to be under the law
6. 12. As many as *desire* to make a fair show in the flesh
13. but they *desire* to have you circumcised
Eph. 2. 3. doing the *desires* of the flesh and of the mind
Phil. 1. 23. having the *desire* to depart and be with Christ
1 *Th.* 2. 17. to see your face with great *desire*

84

DESIRE

2 *Th.* 1. 11. fulfil every ²*desire* of goodness and every work
1 *Tim.* 2. 8. I ³*desire* therefore that the men pray
5. 14. I ³*d.* therefore that the younger widows marry
6. 9. But they that ⁴*d.* to be rich fall into a temptation
Heb. 6. 11. we *d.* that each one of you may shew the same
11. 16. But now they *desire* a better country, that is
1 *Pet.* 1. 12. which things angels *desire* to look into
4. 3. to have wrought the ³*desire* of the Gentiles
Rev. 9. 6. and they shall *desire* to die, and death fleeth
11. 6. with every plague, as often as they shall ³*desire*
see ask, covet, long, longing, request, seek, wish, would.

Desired.—*A.V.* ¹*would.*

Mat. 13. 17. righteous men *desired* to see the things which
Lu. 7. 36. one of the Pharisees *desired* him that he would
10. 24. prophets and kings *d.* to see the things which ye
22. 15. I have *d.* to eat this passover with you before
Heb. 12. 17. ¹*desired* to inherit the blessing, he was rejected
see asked, besought, exhorted, intreated, sought.

Desiredst—est *A.V.—see besoughtest.*

Desireth.—*A.V.* ¹*have.*

Mat. 27. 43. let him deliver him now, if he ¹*desireth* him
Lu. 5. 39. no man having drunk old wine *desireth* new
1 *Tim.* 3. 1. the office of a bishop, he *desireth* a good work
see asketh.

Desiring.—*A.V.* ¹*hasting,* ²*intending,* ³*willing.*

Lu. 8. 20. brethren stand without, *desiring* to see thee
10. 29. he, ²*desiring* to justify himself, said unto Jesus
14. 28. which of you, ²*desiring* to build a tower
16. 21. *desiring* to be fed with the crumbs that fell
23. 20. Pilate spake—³*desiring* to release Jesus
Acts 24. 27. Felix—²*desiring* to gain favour with the Jews
27. 43. the centurion, ²*desiring* to save Paul
1 *Tim.* 1. 7. *desiring* to be teachers of the law
Heb. 13. 18. ²*desiring* to live honestly in all things
2 *Pet.* 3. 12. and earnestly ¹*d.* the coming of the day of God
see asking, besought, intreating, longing, seeking.

Desirous.

Lu. 23. 8. Herod—of a long time *desirous* to see him
Jno. 16. 19. Jesus perceived that they were *d.* to ask him
1 *Th.* 2. 8. being affectionately *desirous* of you

Desolate.—*A.V.* ¹*comfortless,* ²*nought.*

Mat. 23. 38. your house is left unto you *d. Lu.* 13. 35
Jno. 14. 18. I will not leave you ¹*d.*: I come unto you
Acts 1. 20. Let his habitation be made *desolate*
Gal. 4. 27. For more are the children of the *desolate*
1 *Tim.* 5. 5. she that is a widow indeed, and *desolate*
Rev. 17. 16. and shall make her *desolate* and naked
18. 17. in one hour so great riches is made ²*desolate*
19. for in one hour is she made *desolate*

Desolation.

Mat. 12. 25. divided against itself is brought to *d. Lu.* 11
24. 15. the abomination of *desolation. Mk.* 13. 14 . 17
Lu. 21. 20. then know that her *desolation* is at hand

Despair—ed—ing.—*A.V.* ¹*hoping for nothing.*

Lu. 6. 35. do them good, and lend, never ¹*despairing*
2 *Cor.* 1. 8. insomuch that we *despaired* even of life
4. 8. perplexed, yet not unto *despair*

Despise.

Mat. 6. 24. hold to one, and *despise* the other. *Lu.* 16. 13
18. 10. See that ye *despise* not one of these little ones
1 *Cor.* 11. 22. or *despise* ye the church of God
16. 11. let no man therefore *despise* him [Timothy]

DESTROYED

1 *Th.* 5. 20. *despise* not prophesyings
1 *Tim.* 4. 12. Let no man *despise* thy youth [Timothy]
6. 2. believing masters, let them not *despise* them
Tit. 2. 15. all authority. Let no man *despise* thee
2 *Pet.* 2. 10. in the lust of defilement, and *d.* dominion
see regard, set at nought.

Despised.

1 *Cor.* 1. 28. and the things that are *d.*, did God choose
Gal. 4. 14. temptation to you in my flesh ye *despised* not
see account, dishonour—ed, set at nought.

Despisers.

Acts 13. 41. Behold, ye *despisers,* and wonder, and perish
see lovers.

Despisest.

Rom. 2. 4. *despisest* thou the riches of his goodness

Despiseth *A.V.—see rejecteth.*

Despising.

Heb. 12. 2. endured the cross, *d.* shame, and hath sat down

Despite.

Heb. 10. 29. hath done *despite* unto the Spirit of grace?

Despiteful *A.V.—see insolent.*

Despitefully.

Lu. 6. 28. pray for them that *despitefully* use you
see shamefully.

Destitute.

Heb. 11. 37. being *destitute,* afflicted, evil entreated
see bereft, lack.

Destroy.

Mat. 2. 13. Herod will seek the young child to *destroy* him
5. 17. Think not that I came to *destroy* the law or the prophets: I came not to *destroy,* but to fulfil
10. 28. fear him which is able to *destroy* both soul
12. 14. how they might *destroy* him. *Mk.* 3. 6: 11. 18
21. 41. He will miserably *destroy* those miserable men
26. 61. I am able to *destroy* the temple of God
27. 20. should ask for Barabbas, and *destroy* Jesus
Mk. 1. 24. art thou come to *destroy* us? *Lu.* 4. 34
9. 22. into the fire and into the waters, to *destroy* him
12. 9. he will come and *d.* the husbandmen. *Lu.* 20. 16
14. 58. I will *d.* this temple that is made with hands
Lu. 6. 9. to save a life, or to *destroy* it?
19. 47. principal men of the people sought to *d.* him
Jno. 2. 19. *Destroy* this temple, and in three days I will
10. 10. but that he may steal, and kill, and *destroy*
Acts 6. 14. Jesus of Nazareth shall *destroy* this place
Rom. 14. 15. *D.* not with thy meat him for whom Christ
1 *Cor.* 1. 19. I will *destroy* the wisdom of the wise ¹died
3. 17. *destroyeth* the temple of God, him shall God *d.*
Jas. 4. 12. judge, even he who is able to save and to *destroy*
1 *Jno.* 3. 8. that he might *destroy* the works of the devil
Rev. 11. 18. and to *destroy* them that *destroy* the earth
see (bring to) nought, overthrow.

Destroyed.—*A.V.* ¹*corrupt,* ²*perish.*

Mat. 22. 7. and he sent his armies, and *d.* those murderers
Lu. 17. 27. and the flood came, and *destroyed* them all
29. fire and brimstone from heaven, and *d.* them all
Acts 3. 23. not hearken to that prophet, shall be utterly *d.*
13. 19. had *d.* seven nations in the land of Canaan
2 *Cor.* 4. 9. yet not forsaken; smitten down, yet not *d.*
Gal. 2. 18. if I build up again those things which I *d.*

85

DESTROYED

2 *Pet.* 2. 12. born mere animals to be taken and *destroyed*—
   in their destroying surely be ²*destroyed*
Jude 5. afterward *destroyed* them that believed not
   10. creatures without reason, in these things are they ¹*d.*
Rev. 8. 9. and the third part of the ships was *destroyed*
   see abolished, deposed, destroyer, done (away), (made) havoc, perished.

Destroyer.—*A.V.* ¹*destroyed.*

1 *Cor.* 10. 10. murmured, and perished by the *destroyer*
Heb. 11. 28. that the ¹*d.* of the firstborn should not touch

Destroyest—eth.—*A.V.* ¹*corrupteth,* ²*defile.*

Mat. 27. 40. Thou that *destroyest* the temple. *Mk.* 15. 29
Lu. 12. 33. where no thief draweth near, neither moth ¹*d.*
1 *Cor.* 3. 17. If any man ²*destroyeth* the temple of God

Destroying.—*A.V.* ¹*corruption.*

2 *Pet.* 2. 12. shall in their ¹*destroying* surely be destroyed

Destruction.—*A.V.* ¹*damnation,* ²*perdition.*

Mat. 7. 13. broad is the way, that leadeth to *destruction*
Rom. 3. 16. *Destruction* and misery are in their ways
   9. 22. much longsuffering vessels of wrath fitted unto *d.*
1 *Cor.* 5. 5. unto Satan for the *destruction* of the flesh
1 *Th.* 5. 3. Peace and safety, then sudden *destruction* cometh
2 *Th.* 1. 9. who shall suffer punishment, even eternal *d.*
1 *Tim.* 6. 9. lusts, such as drown men in *d.* and perdition
2 *Pet.* 2. 1. bringing upon themselves swift *destruction*
   3. lingereth not, and their ¹*destruction* slumbereth not
   3. 7. the day of judgement and ²*destruction* of ungodly men
   16. also the other scriptures, unto their own *destruction*
   see casting (down), perdition.

Destructive.—*A.V.* ¹*damnable.*

2 *Pet.* 2. 1. who shall privily bring in ¹*destructive* heresies

Determinate.

Acts 2. 23. him, being delivered up by the *d.* counsel

Determine—d.—*A.V.* ¹*decreed,* ²*know,* ³*proposed.*

Lu. 22. 22. Son of man indeed goeth, as it hath been *d.*
Acts 3. 13. Pilate, when he had *determined* to release him
   11. 29. *determined* to send relief unto the brethren
   17. 26. having *determined* their appointed seasons
   20. 16. For Paul had *determined* to sail past Ephesus. ³3
   24. 22. captain shall come down, I will ¹*d.* your matter
   25. 25. appealed to the emperor I *determined* to send him
   27. 1. when it was *determined* that we should sail for Italy
1 *Cor.* 2. 2. I *determined* not to know anything among you
   7. 37. hath ¹*determined* this in his own heart, to keep
2 *Cor.* 2. 1. I *d.* this for myself, that I would not come
Tit. 3. 12. for there I have *determined* to winter
   see forcordained, minded, settled.

Device—s.

Acts 17. 29. or stone, graven by art and *device* of man
2 *Cor.* 2. 11. Satan: for we are not ignorant of his *devices*

Devil.

Mat. 4. 1. into the wilderness to be tempted of the *devil*
   5. Then the *devil* taketh him [Jesus]. 8
   11. the *devil* leaveth him; and behold, angels came
   9. 32. a dumb man possessed with a *devil.* 12. 22
   33. when the *devil* was cast out, the dumb man spake
   11. 18. and they say, He hath a *devil. Lu.* 7. 33
   13. 39. and the enemy that sowed them is the *devil*
   15. 22. my daughter is grievously vexed with a *devil*

DEVISED

Mat. 17. 18. Jesus rebuked him; and the *devil* went out
   25. 41. eternal fire which is prepared for the *devil*
Mk. 7. 29. the *devil* is gone out of thy daughter. 26, 30
Lu. 4. 2. forty days, being tempted of the *devil*
   3. And the *devil* said unto him. 6
   13. when the *devil* had completed every temptation
   33. a man, which had a spirit of an unclean *devil*
   35. when the *devil* had thrown him down in the midst
   8. 12. then cometh the *devil,* and taketh away the word
   29. he was driven of the *devil* into the deserts
   9. 42. as he was yet a coming, the *d.* dashed him down
   11. 14. casting out a *devil*—when the *devil* was gone out
Jno. 6. 70. choose you the twelve, and one of you is a *d.?*
   7. 20. Thou hast a *devil.* 8. 48, 52
   8. 44. Ye are of your father the *devil*
   49. Jesus answered, I have not a *devil*
   10. 20. many of them said, He hath a *devil,* and is mad
   21. possessed with a *devil.* Can a *devil* open the eyes
   13. 2. the *d.* having already put into the heart of Judas
Acts 10. 38. healing all that were oppressed of the *devil*
   13. 10. thou son of the *d.,* thou enemy of all righteousness
Eph. 4. 27. neither give place to the *devil*
   6. 11. may be able to stand against the wiles of the *devil*
1 *Tim.* 3. 6. he fall into the condemnation of the *devil*
   7. lest he fall into reproach and the snare of the *devil*
2 *Tim.* 2. 26. recover themselves out of the snare of the *d.*
Heb. 2. 14. had the power of death, that is, the *devil*
Jas. 4. 7. resist the *devil,* and he will flee from you
1 *Pet.* 5. 8. the *devil,* as a roaring lion, walketh about
1 *Jno.* 3. 8. is of the *d.;* for the *d.* sinneth—destroy the
   10. manifest, and the children of the *d.* ¦works of the *d.*
Jude 9. the archangel, when contending with the *devil*
Rev. 2. 10. the *d.* is about to cast some of you into prison
   12. 9. old serpent, he that is called the *D.* and Satan. 20. 2
   12. the *devil* is gone down unto you, having great wrath
   20. 10. the *d.* that deceived them was cast into the lake
   see devils.

Devilish.

Jas. 3. 15. from above, but is earthly, sensual, *devilish*

Devils.—*A.V.* ¹*devil.*

Mat. 4. 24. possessed with *devils.* 8. 16, 28, 33: *Mk.* 1. 32:
   5. ¹15, ¹16, ¹18: *Lu.* 8. 36
   8. 13. the *devils* besought him, saying, If thou cast us out
   9. 34. By the prince of the *devils* casteth he out *devils.*
   12. 24: *Mk.* 3. 22: *Lu.* 11. 15
Mk. 1. 34. and he suffered not the *devils* to speak
   9. 38. one casting out *devils* in thy name. *Lu.* 9. 49
Lu. 4. 41. And *devils* also came out from many, cry¹ng out
   8. 2. Magdalene, from whom seven *devils* had gone out
   27. a certain man out of the city, who had *devils*
   30. for many *devils* were entered into him
   33. And the *devils* came out from the man
   35. the man, from whom the *devils* were gone out. 38
   9. 1. gave them power and authority over all *devils*
   10. 17. Lord, even the *devils* are subject unto us
1 *Cor.* 10. 20. they sacrifice to *devils*—I would not that ye
   should have communion with *devils*
   21. Ye cannot drink the cup of the Lord, and the cup
   of *devils*—table of the Lord, and of the table of *d.*
1 *Tim.* 4. 1. heed to seducing spirits and doctrines of *d.*
Jas. 2. 19. the *devils* also believe, and shudder
Rev. 9. 20. that they should not worship *d.,* and the idols
   16. 14. for they are spirits of *devils,* working signs
   18. 2. and is become a habitation of *devils*
   see cast out.

Devised.

2 *Pet.* 1. 16. For we did not follow cunningly *devised* fables

DEVOTIONS

Devotions *A.V.—see worship.*

Devour.
Mk. 12. 40. they which *devour* widows' houses. *Lu.* 20. 47
Gal. 5. 16. if ye bite and *devour* one another, take heed
Heb. 10. 27. fierceness of fire which shall *d.* the adversaries
1 *Pet.* 5. 8. walketh about, seeking whom he may *devour*
Rev. 12. 4. when she was delivered, he might *d.* her child
see devoureth.

Devoured.
Mat. 13. 4. birds came and *d.* them. *Mk.* 4. 4: *Lu.* 8. 5.
Lu. 15. 30. which hath *devoured* thy living with harlots
Rev. 20. 9. fire came down out of heaven, and *d.* them

Devoureth.—*A.V.* ¹*devour.*
2 *Cor.* 11. 20. if he ¹*devoureth* you, if he taketh you captive
Rev. 11. 5. out of their mouth, and *devoureth* their enemies

Devout.—*A.V.* ¹*religious.*
Lu. 2. 25. Simeon; and this man was righteous and *devout*
Acts 2. 5. dwelling at Jerusalem Jews, *devout* men
8. 2. And *devout* men buried Stephen
10. 2. a *devout* man, and one that feared God
7. and a *devout* soldier of them that waited on him
13. 43. Jews and of the ¹*devout* proselytes followed Paul
50. But the Jews urged on the *devout* women
17. 4. and of the *devout* Greeks a great multitude
17. 4. reasoned—with the Jews and the *devout* persons
22. 12. Ananias, a *devout* man according to the law

Diadems.—*A.V.* ¹*crowns.*
Rev. 12. 3. upon his [dragon] heads seven ¹*diadems*
19. 12. [faithful and true] head are many ¹*diadems*

Did.—*A.V.* ¹*done.*
Mat. 12. 3. have ye not read what David *did. Lu.* 6. 3.
13. 58. And he *did* not many mighty works there
17. 12. but ¹*did* unto him [Elijah] whatsoever they listed
21. 15. saw the wonderful things that he *did* [me. ¹40
25. 45. ye *d.* it not unto one of these least, ye *d.* it not unto
Lu. 6. 10. Stretch forth thy hand. And he *did* so
26. manner *did* their fathers to the false prophets
Jno. 4. 29. which told me all things that ever I *did.* 39
7. 21. I ¹*did* one work, and ye all marvel
8. 40. which I heard from God: this *did* not Abraham
9. 26. What *did* he to thee? how opened he thine eyes?
15. 24. done among them the works which none other *did*
Acts 2. 22. which God *did* by him in the midst of you
3. 17. in ignorance ye *did* it, as *did* also your rulers
7. 51. resist the Holy Ghost: as your fathers *did*, so do ye
9. 13. how much evil he ¹*did* to thy saints at Jerusalem
11. 17. gave unto them the like gift as he *did* also unto us
30. which also they *did*, sending it to the elders
16. 18. this she [damsel at Philippi] *did* for many days
26. 10. And this I also *d.* in Jerusalem: and I both shut up
2 *Cor.* 7. 12. I wrote not for his cause that ¹*did* the wrong
Phil. 4. 14. Howbeit ye ¹*did* well, that ye had fellowship
2 *Tim.* 4. 14. Alexander the coppersmith *did* me much evil
Heb. 4. 10. rested from his works, as God *did* from his
7. 27. this he *did* once for all, when he offered up himself
1 *Pet.* 2. 22. who *did* no sin, neither was guile found

Die.—*A.V.* ¹*dead,* ²*died.*
Mat. 15. 4. evil of father or mother, let him *die. Mk.* 7. 10
22. 24. If a man *die,* having no children. *Mk.* 12. 19: *Lu.*
26. 35. Even if I must *die* with thee. *Mk.* 14. 31 [20. 28
Lu. 20. 36. for neither can they *die* any more
Jno. 4. 49. Sir, come down ere my child *die*
6. 50. that a man may eat thereof, and not *die*
8. 24. ye shall *die* in your sins. 21
11. 16. Let us also go, that we may *die* with him

DIETH

Jno. 11. 25. believeth on me, though he ¹*d.*, yet shall he live
26. liveth and believeth on me shall never *die*
37. caused that this man also should not ²*die?*
50. that one man should *die* for the people. 18. 14.
51. prophesied that Jesus should *die* for the nation
12. 24. wheat fall into the earth and *die*—but if it *die*
33. by what manner of death he should *die.* 18. 32.
19. 7. We have a law, and by that law he ought to *die*
21. 23. that that disciple should not *d.*—he should not *d.*
Acts 21. 13. to *die* at Jerusalem for the name of the Lord
25. 11. anything worthy of death, I refuse not to *die*
Rom. 5. 7. for a righteous man will one *die*—even dare to *d.*
7. 2. if the husband ¹*d.,* she is discharged from the law. ¹3
8. 13. for if ye live after the flesh, ye must *die*
14. 8. or whether we *die,* we *die* unto—we live—or *die*
1 *Cor.* 9. 15. it were good for me rather to *die,* than that
15. 22. For as in Adam all *die,* so also in Christ shall all
31. have in Christ Jesus our Lord, I [Paul] *die* daily
36. thou thyself sowest is not quickened, except it *die*
2 *Cor.* 7. 3. ye are in our hearts to *d.* together and live together
Phil. 1. 21. For to me to live is Christ, and to *die* is gain
Heb. 7. 8. And here men that *die* receive tithes
9. 27. it is appointed unto men once to *die*
Rev. 3. 2. things that remain, which were ready to *die*
9. 6. they shall desire to *die,* and death fleeth from them
14. 13. Blessed are the dead which *die* in the Lord
see (point of) death.

Died.—*A.V.* ¹*dead.*
*Mat.*22.27. after them all the woman *d. Mk.*12. 22: *Lu.*20.32
Mk. 12. 21. and the second took her, and *died*
Lu. 16. 22. the beggar *died*—the rich man also *died*
20. 29. took a wife, and *died* childless. 31
Jno. 6. 49. did eat the manna in the wilderness, and they ¹*d.*
11. 21. been here, my brother had not *died.* 32 [¹58
Acts 2. 29. David, that he both ¹*died* and was buried
7. 15. into Egypt; and he *died,* himself, and our fathers
9. 37. in those days, that she [Dorcas] fell sick, and *died*
Rom. 5. 6. in due season Christ *died* for the ungodly
8. while we were yet sinners, Christ *died* for us
15. if by the trespass of the one the many ¹*died*
6. 2. We who ¹*died* to sin, how shall we—live therein?
7. he that hath ¹*died* is justified from sin
8. we ¹*died* with Christ, we believe that we shall also live
10. the death that he *died,* he *died* unto sin once
7. 6. discharged from the law, having ¹*died* to that
9. commandment came, sin revived, and I *died*
8. 34. It is Christ Jesus that *died,* yea rather
14. 9. For to this end Christ *died,* and lived again
15. him for whom Christ *died.* 1 *Cor.* 8. 11
1 *Cor.* 15. 3. how that Christ *died* for our sins
2 *Cor.* 5. 14. that one *died* for all, therefore all ¹*died*
15. *died* for all—for their sakes *died* and rose again
Gal. 2. 21. through the law, then Christ ¹*died* for nought
Col. 2. 20. If ye ¹*died* with Christ. 2 *Tim.* 2. ¹11
3. 3. For ye ¹*died,* and your life is hid with Christ in God
1 *Th.* 4. 14. if we believe that Jesus *died* and rose again
5. 10. who *died* for us, that, whether we wake or sleep
Heb. 11. 13. *died* in faith, not having received the promises
1 *Pet.* 2. 24. we, having ¹*died* unto sins, might live unto
Rev. 8. 9. there *died* the third part of the creatures
11. wormwood; and many men *died* of the waters
16. 3. and every living soul *died,* even the things
see die, death, end.

Dieth.—*A.V.* ¹*died.*

Mk. 9. 48. where there worm *dieth* not, and the fire
Rom. 6. 9. Christ being raised from the dead *d.* no more
14. 7. liveth to himself, and none *dieth* to himself
Heb. 10. 28. A man that hath set at nought Moses' law ¹*d.*

87

DIFFER

Differ—eth—ing.
Rom. 12. 6. having gifts *differing* according to the grace
1 Cor. 4. 7. For who maketh thee to *differ?*
15. 41. one star *differeth* from another star in glory
Gal. 4. 1. *d.* nothing from a bondservant, though he is lord

Difference.
1 Cor. 7. 34. *difference* also between the wife and the virgin
   see distinction, diversities, doubt.

Different.—*A. V.* ¹*another,* ²*otherwise.*
2 Cor. 11. 4. if ye receive a ¹*different* spirit—a ¹*d.* gospel
Gal. 1. 6. called you in the grace of Christ unto a ¹*d.* gospel
1 Tim. 6. 3. If any man teacheth a ²*different* doctrine

Difficulty.—*A. V.* ¹*hardly,* ²*much work,* ³*scarce.*
Acts 27. 8. with ¹*d.* coasting along it we came unto a certain.
16. we were able, with ²*difficulty*, to secure the boat ³⁷

Dig.
Lu. 13. 8. till I shall *dig* about it, [fig tree] and dung it
16. 3. I have not strength to *dig;* to beg I am ashamed

Digged.
Mat. 21. 33. *d.* a winepress in it, and built a tower. Mk. 12. 1
25. 18. *digged* in the earth, and hid his lord's money
Lu. 6. 48. *digged* and went deep, and laid a foundation
Rom. 11. 3. they have *digged* down thine altars

Dignities.
2 Pet. 2. 10. rail at *dignities.* Jude 8

Diligence.—*A. V.* ¹*business,* ²*diligent,* ³*endeavour—ing.*
   ⁴*labour,* ⁵*study.*
Lu. 12. 58. on the way give *diligence* to be quit of him
Rom. 12. 8. he that ruleth, with *diligence*
11. in ¹*diligence* not slothful; fervent in spirit
Eph. 4. 3. giving *diligence* to keep the unity of the Spirit
2 Tim. 2. 15. Give ⁵*d.* to present thyself approved unto God
4. 9. Do thy *diligence* to come shortly. 21; Tit. 3. ²12
Heb. 4. 11. Let us therefore give ⁴*d.* to enter into that rest
6. 11. desire that each one of you may shew the same *d.*
2 Pet. 1. 5. on your part all *d.*, in your faith supply virtue
10. more *diligence* to make your calling and election
15. I will give ⁵*d.* that at every time ye may be able
3. 14. give ⁴*diligence* that ye may be found in peace
Jude 3. I was giving all *diligence* to write unto you
   see earnestness.

Diligent—ly.—*A. V.* ¹*carefully,* ²*meditate,* ³*oft.*
Mk. 7. 3. except they wash their hands ³*diligently*, eat not
Lu. 15. 8. sweep the house, and seek *d.* until she find it?
Phil. 2. 28. I have sent him [Epaphroditus]—the more ¹*d.*
1 Tim. 4. 15. Be ²*diligent* in these things
5. 10. if she hath *diligently* followed every good work
2 Tim. 1. 17. in Rome, he [Onesiphorus] sought me *d.*
Tit. 3. 13. forward Zenas—and Apollos on their journey *d.*
Heb. 12. 17. [Esau] found no place of repentance), though
   he sought it ¹*diligently* with tears
1 Pet. 1. 10. prophets sought and searched *diligently*
   see carefully, diligence, earnest.

Diminishing *A. V.*—*see loss.*

Dine.
Lu. 11. 37. a Pharisee asketh him [Jesus] to *d.* with him
   see breakfast.

Dined *A. V.*—*see broken fast.*

DISCIPLE

Dinner.
Mat. 22. 4. Behold, I have made ready my *dinner*
Lu. 11. 38. that he had not first washed before *dinner*
14. 12. makest a *dinner* or a supper, call not thy friends

Dip.—*A. V.* ¹*dipped.*
Lu. 16. 24. Lazarus, that he may *dip* the tip of his finger
Jno. 13. 26. He it is, for whom I shall ¹*dip* the sop

Dipped—eth.
Mat. 26. 23. *d.* his hand with me in the dish. Mk. 14. 20
Jno. 13. 26. when he had *d.* the sop, he—giveth it to Judas
   see dip, sprinkled.

Direct.
1 Th. 3. 11. and our Lord Jesus, *direct* our way unto you
2 Th. 3. 5. Lord *direct* your hearts into the love of God

Disallow—ed *A. V.*—*see rejected.*

Disannul.
Gal. 3. 17. not *d.*, so as to make the promise of none effect
   see void.

Disanulling.
Heb. 7. 18. there is a *d.* of a foregoing commandment

Disbelieve—d—eth.—*A. V.* ¹*believed—eth not,* ²*disobedient.*
Mk. 16. 11. alive, and had been seen of her, ¹*d.* Lu. 24. ¹11
16. but he that ¹*disbelieveth* shall be condemned
Lu. 24. 41. while they still ¹*disbelieved* for joy
Acts 28. 24. some believed—some ²*disbelieved*
1 Pet. 2. 7. for such as ²*d.*, The stone which the builders

Discern—ed—ings.—*A. V.* ¹*discerning,* ²*discerner,* ³*judge.*
Mat. 16. 3. Ye know how to *discern* the face of the heaven;
   but ye cannot *discern* the signs of the times
1 Cor. 11. 29. judgement unto himself, if he ¹*d.* not the body
31. But if we ²*d.* ourselves, we should not be judged
12. 10. and to another ¹*discernings* of spirits
14. 29. let the prophets speak—and let the others ³*d.*
Heb. 4. 12. quick to ²*discern* the thoughts—of the heart
5. 14. their senses exercised to *discern* good and evil
   see interpret, judged, know with negatives.

Discerner *A. V.*—*see discern.*

Discernment.—*A. V.* ¹*judgement.*
Phil. 1. 9. abound yet more—in knowledge and all ¹*d.*

Discharged.—*A. V.* ¹*delivered,* ²*loosed.*
Rom. 7. 2. if the husband die, she is ²*d.* from the law
6. But now we have been ¹*discharged* from the law

Disciple.—*A. V.* ¹*instructed.*
Mat. 10. 24. A *disciple* is not above his master. Lu. 6. 40
25. enough for the *disciple* that he be as his master
42. cup of cold water only, in the name of a *disciple*
13. 52. every scribe who hath been made a ¹*disciple*
27. 57. Joseph, who also himself was Jesus' *disciple*
14. 26. he cannot be my *disciple.* 27, 33
Jno. 9. 28. Thou art his *d.*; but we are disciples of Moses
18. 15. so did another *d.* Now that *disciple* was known
16. the other *disciple*, which was known—went out
19. 26. and the *disciple* standing by, whom he loved
27. saith he to the *d.*—from that hour the *d.* took her
38. being a *disciple* of Jesus, but secretly for fear
20. 2. the other *disciple*, whom Jesus loved. 21. 7, 20
3. Peter therefore went forth, and the other *disciple*
4. and the other *disciple* outran Peter

DISCIPLE

Jno. 20. 8. Then entered in therefore the other *disciple* also
21. 23. that that *disciple* should not die
24. This is the *d.* which beareth witness of these things
Acts 9. 10. certain *disciple* at Damascus, named Ananias
26. afraid of him, not believing that he was a *disciple*
36. was at Joppa a certain *disciple* named Tabitha
16. 1. a certain *disciple* was there, named Timothy
21. 16. one Mnason of Cyprus, an early *disciple*

Disciples.—*A.V.* ¹*teach.*

Mat. 9. 14. the *d.* of John—but thy *d.* fast not? *Mk.* 2. 18
19. and followed him, and so did his *disciples*
10. 1. And he called unto him his twelve *disciples*
11. 1. had made an end of commanding his twelve *d.*
2. works of the Christ, he sent by his *disciples. Lu.* 7. 19
12. 2. Behold, thy *disciples* do that which it is not lawful
14. 12. *disciples* came, and took up the corpse. *Mk.* 6 29
19. the *d.*, and the *d.* to the multitudes. 15. 36: *Lu.* 9. 16
26. And when the *disciples* saw him walking on the sea
15. 2. Why do thy *d.* transgress the tradition. *Mk.* 7. 5
17. 6. when the *disciples* heard it, they fell on their face
16. to thy *d.*, and they could not cure him. *Mk.* 9. 18:
19. Then came the *d.* to Jesus. 18. 1: 26 17 [*Lu.* 9. 40
19. 10. The *d.* say unto him, If the case of a man is so
13. and the *disciples* rebuked them *Mk* 10. 13
20. 17. took the twelve *disciples* apart, and in the way
21. 1. then Jesus sent two *d. Mk.* 11. 1: 14 13: *Lu.* 19. 29
22. 16. they send to him their *d.*, with the Herodians
24. 1. his *disciples* came to him to shew him the buildings
26. 8. But when the *disciples* saw it, they had indignation
18. passover at thy house with my *d. Mk.* 14. 14 *Lu.* 22. 11
26. and he gave to the *disciples*, and said, Take, eat
35. not deny thee. Likewise also said all the *disciples*
40. he cometh unto the *d.*, and findeth them sleeping
56. Then all the *disciples* left him, and fled
27. 64. lest haply his *d.* come and steal him away. 28. 13
28. 7. tell his *disciples*, He is risen. 8 : *Mk.* 16. 7
16. But the eleven *disciples* went into Galilee
19. Go ye therefore, and make ¹*d* of all the nations
Mk. 4. 34. privately to his own *d.* he expounded all things
6. 41. he gave to the *disciples* to set before them. 8. 6
7. 2. seen that some of his *d.* ate their bread with defiled
10. 24. And the *d.* were amazed at his words. *Mat.* 19. 25
Lu. 5. 30. murmured against his *disciples. Mat.* 9. 11
33. *disciples* of John fast often—the *d.* of the Pharisees
6. 1. and his *d.* plucked the ears of corn. *Mat* 12. 1. *Mk.* 2. 23
20. And he lifted up his eyes on his *disciples*, and said
7. 18. the *disciples* of John told him of all these things
10. 23. And turning to the *disciples*, he said privately
11. 1. one of his *disciples* said unto him, Lord, teach us
to pray, even as John also taught his *disciples*
19. 37. whole multitude of the *disciples* began to rejoice
39. said unto him, Master, rebuke thy *disciples*
John 2. 11. and his *disciples* believed on him
17. His *disciples* remembered. 22
3. 25. questioning on the part of John's *d.* with a Jew
4. 1. Jesus was making and baptizing more *d.* than John
2. (although Jesus himself baptized not, but his *d.*)
27. his *d.;* and they marvelled that he was speaking
6. 3. into the mountain, and there he sat with his *d.*
22. Jesus entered not with his *disciples* into the boat,
but that his *disciples* went away alone
24. saw that Jesus was not there, neither his *disciples*
61. knowing in himself that his *disciples* murmured
66. Upon this many of his *disciples* went back
7. 3. thy *d.* also may behold thy works which thou doest
8. 31. If ye abide in my word, then are ye truly my *d.*
9. 27. would ye also become his *disciples?*
28. Thou art his disciple; but we are *disciples* of Moses

DISHONOUR

Jno. 11. 12. *d.*—said unto him, Lord, if he is fallen asleep
54 Ephraim; and there he tarried with the *disciples*
13. 5. and began to wash the *disciples'* feet
23. reclining in Jesus' bosom one of his *disciples*
35. By this shall all men know that ye are my *disciples*
15. 8. bear much fruit; and so shall ye be my *disciples*
18 1. his *d.* over the brook Kidron—himself and his *d.*
2. for Jesus oft-times resorted thither with his *disciples*
17. Art thou also one of this man's *disciples* ? 25
19. asked Jesus of his *disciples*, and of his teaching
20. 18. and telleth the *disciples*, I have seen the Lord
20. The *d.* therefore were glad, when they saw the Lord
26. again his *d.* were within, and Thomas with them. 19
21. 12. none of the *d.* durst inquire of him, Who art thou?
14. third time that Jesus was manifested to the *disciples*
Acts 6. 1. when the number of the *d.* was multiplying. 7
9. 1. threatening and slaughter against the *disciples*
25. but his *d.* took him by night, and let him down
26. he [Saul] assayed to join himself to the *disciples*
11. 26. the *d.* were called Christians first in Antioch
29. And the *disciples*, every man according to his ability
13. 52. And the *disciples* were filled with joy
15. 10. should put a yoke upon the neck of the *disciples*
18. 23. stablishing all the *disciples.* 14. 22
27. and wrote to the *disciples* to receive him
19. 1. came to Ephesus, and found certain *disciples*
9. departed from them, and separated the *disciples*
30. unto the people, the *disciples* suffered him not
20. 80. perverse things, to draw away the *d.* after them

Discipline.—*A.V.* ¹*sound mind.*

2 *Tim.* 1. 7. but of power and love and ¹*discipline*

Discouraged.

Col. 3. 21. provoke not your children, that they be not *d.*

Discoursed.—*A.V.* ¹*preached—ing.*

Acts 20. 7. Paul ¹*discoursed* with them
9. as Paul ¹*d.* yet longer, being borne down by his sleep

Discovered *A.V.*—*see perceived, sight.*

Discreetly.

Mk. 12. 34. when Jesus saw that he answered *discreetly*

Disease—s.—*A.V.* ¹*infirmities*, ²*sicknesses.*

Mat. 4. 23. healing all manner of *disease.* 9. 35: 10. 1
24. with divers *diseases. Mk.* 1. 34 : *Lu.* 4. 40
8. 17. took our infirmities, and bare our ²*diseases*
Lu. 6. 17. to hear him, and to be healed of their *diseases*
7. 21. cured many of ¹*d.*, and plagues and evil spirits
9. 1. authority over all devils, and to cure *diseases*
Acts 19. 12. and the *diseases* departed from them
28. 9. rest also which had *diseases* in the island came

Diseased *A.V.*—*see sick.*

Disfigure.

Mat. 6. 16. they *disfigure* their faces, that they may be seen

Dish.

Mat. 26. 23. dipped—with me in the *dish*. *Mk.* 14. 20

Dishonesty *A.V.*—*see shame.*

Dishonour.—*A.V.* ¹*despised*, ²*shame.*

Jno. 8. 49. I honour my Father, and ye *dishonour* me
Acts 5. 41. were counted worthy to suffer ²*d.* for the Name

DISHONOUR

Rom. 9. 21. a vessel unto honour, and another unto *d.*?
1 *Cor.* 4. 10. ye have glory, but we have ¹*dishonour*
11. 14. if a man have long hair, it is a ²*d.* to him?
15. 43. it is sown in *dishonour*; it is raised in glory
2 *Cor.* 6. 8. by glory and *dishonour*, by evil report and good
2 *Tim.* 2. 20. some unto honour, and some unto *dishonour*
see dishonoured.

Dishonoured—est—eth.—*A.V.* ¹*despised*, ²*dishonour.*
Rom. 1. 24. that their bodies should be ²*dishonoured*
2. 23. transgression of the law *dishonourest* thou God?
1 *Cor.* 11. 4. having his head covered, *dishonoureth* his head
5. her head unveiled *dishonoureth* her head
Jas. 2. 6. But ye have ¹*dishonoured* the poor man

Dismissed.—*A.V.* ¹*let go.*
Acts 15. 30. when they were *d.*, came down to Antioch
38. they were ¹*dismissed* in peace from the brethren
19. 41. when he had thus spoken, he *d.* the assembly

Disobedience.—*A.V.* ¹*unbelief.*
Rom. 5. 19. through the one man's *d.* the many were made
11. 30. now have obtained mercy by their ¹*disobedience*
32. God hath shut up all unto ¹*disobedience*
2 *Cor.* 10. 6. being in readiness to avenge all *disobedience*
Eph. 2. 2. spirit that now worketh in the sons of *d.*
5. 6. wrath of God upon the sons of *disobedience. Col.* 3. 6
Heb. 2. 2. *disobedience* received a just recompense of reward
4. 11. fall after the same example of ¹*disobedience.* 16

Disobedient.—*A.V.* ¹*believed not*, ²*not believe—d*, ³*unbelieving.*
Lu. 1. 17. and the *d.* to walk in the wisdom of the just
Acts 14. 2. the Jews that were ²*d.* stirred up—the Gentiles
19. 9. when some were hardened and ²*disobedient*
26. 19. I was not *disobedient* unto the heavenly vision
Rom. 1. 30. *disobedient* to parents. 2 *Tim.* 3. 2
10. 21. my hands unto a *d.* and gainsaying people
11. 30. For as ye in time past were ¹*disobedient* to God
31. so have these also now been ¹*disobedient* [Judma
15. 31. I may be delivered from them that are ¹*d.* in
Tit. 1. 16. they deny him, being abominable, and *d.*
3. 3. For we also were aforetime foolish, *disobedient*
Heb. 3. 18. not enter into his rest, but to them that were ²*d.*?
11. 31. Rahab the harlot perished not with them that
1 *Pet.* 2. 8. for they stumble at the word, being *d.* [were ²*d.*
3. 20. spirits in prison, which aforetime were *disobedient*
see disbelieve, unruly.

Disorderly.—*A.V.* ¹*unruly.*
1 *Th.* 5. 14. admonish the ¹*disorderly.*
2 *Th.* 3. 6. from every brother that walketh *disorderly*
7. for we behaved not ourselves *disorderly* among you
11. we hear of some that walk among you *disorderly*

Disparagement.—*A.V.* ¹*reproach.*
2 *Cor.* 11. 21. I speak by way of ¹*disparagement*

Dispensation.—*A.V.* ¹*edifying*, ²*fellowship.*
Eph. 1. 10. unto a *d.* of the fulness of the times, to sum up
3. 2. that ye have heard of the *d.* of that grace of God
9. to make all men see what is the ²*dispensation*
Col. 1. 25. made a minister, according to the *d.* of God
1. *Tim.* 1. 4. minister questionings, rather than a ¹*d.* of God
see stewardship.

Dispersed.—*A.V.* ¹*scattered.*
Acts 5. 36. as many as obeyed him [Theudas] were ¹*d.*
see dispersion, scattered.

DISTINCTION

Dispersion.—*A.V.* ¹*dispersed*, ²*scattered*, ³*scattered abroad.*
Jno. 7. 35. will he go unto the ¹*D.* among the Greeks
Jas. 1. 1. James—to the twelve tribes which are of the ³*D.*
1 *Pet.* 1. 1. Peter—to the elect who are sojourners of the ²*D.*

Displeased.—*A.V.* ¹*grieved.*
Acts 12. 20. he was highly *d.* with them of Tyre and Sidon
Heb. 3. 10. Wherefore I was ¹*d.* with this generation
17. And with whom was he ¹*displeased* forty years?
see indignation.

Disposed.
1 *Cor.* 10. 27. biddeth you to a feast, and ye are *d.* to go
see minded.

Disposition *A.V.*—*see ordained.*

Disputations.
Rom. 14. 1. receive ye, yet not to doubtful *disputations*
see questioning.

Dispute—s.—*A.V.* ¹*contradiction*, ²*strife—s.*
1 *Tim.* 6. 4. doting about questionings and ²*disputes*
Heb. 6. 16. in every ²*dispute* of theirs the oath is final
7. 7. without any ¹*d.* the less is blessed of the better

Disputed.
Mk. 9. 34. they had *disputed* one with another in the way
Acts 9. 29. he spake and *disputed* against the Grecian Jews
Jude 9. with the devil he *d.* about the body of Moses
see reasoned, reasoning.

Disputer.
1 *Cor.* 1. 20. where is the *disputer* of this world?

Disputing—s.—*A.V.* ¹*doubting.*
Acts 6. 9. them of Cilicia and Asia, *d.* with Stephen
24. 12. neither in the temple did they find me *disputing*
Phil. 2. 14. Do all things without murmurings and *d.*
1 *Tim.* 2. 8. holy hands, without wrath and ¹*disputing*
see questioning, reasoning, wranglings.

Disrepute.—*A.V.* ¹*nought.*
Acts 19. 27. danger that this our trade come into ¹*disrepute*

Dissembled.
Gal. 2. 13. the rest of the Jews *d.* likewise with him [Peter]

Dissension.
Acts 15. 2. Paul and Barnabas had no small *dissension*
23. 7. a *dissension* between the Pharisees and Sadducees
10. And when there arose a great *dissension*

Dissimulation.
Gal. 2. 13. even Barnabas was carried away with their *d.*
see hypocrisy.

Dissolved.—*A.V.* ¹*melt.*
2 *Cor.* 5. 1. if the earthly house of our tabernacle be *d.*
2 *Pet.* 3. 10. the elements shall be ¹*d.* with fervent heat
11. Seeing that these things are thus all to be *d.*
12. the heavens being on fire shall be *dissolved*

Distinction.—*A.V.* ¹*difference—s*, ²*doubting.*
Acts 11. 12. Spirit bade me go with them, making no ²*d.*
15. 9. he made no ¹*distinction* between us and them
Rom. 3. 22. them that believe; for there is no ¹*distinction*
10. 12. For there is no ¹*d.* between Jew and Greek
1 *Cor.* 14. 7. if they give not a *distinction* in the sounds

DISTRACTION

Distraction.
1 *Cor.* 7. 35. ye may attend upon the Lord without *d.*

Distress—ed—es.—*A.V.* ¹*burdened*, ²*fainted*, ³*toiling*, ⁴*tossed*, ⁵*vexed.*
Mat. 9. 36. with compassion for them, because they were ²*d.*
14. 24. was now in the midst of the sea, ⁴*d.* by the waves
Mk. 6. 48. seeing them ³*distressed* in rowing—he cometh
Lu. 21. 23. for there shall be great *distress* upon the land
25. and upon the earth *d.* of nations, in perplexity
1 *Cor.* 7. 26. this is good by reason of the present *distress*
2 *Cor.* 6. 4. in afflictions, in necessities, in *distresses*
8. 13. that others may be eased, and ye ¹*distressed*
12. 10. in persecutions, in *distresses*, for Christ's sake
1 *Th.* 3. 7. comforted over you in all our *d.* and affliction
2 *Pet.* 2. 7. delivered righteous Lot, sore ⁵*distressed*
see anguish, straitened.

Distribute—d.
Lu. 18. 22. sell all that thou hast, and *d.* unto the poor
Jno. 6. 11. he *distributed* to them that were set down
1 *Cor.* 7. 17. as the Lord hath *distributed* to each man
1 *Tim.* 6. 18. ready to *distribute*, willing to communicate
see apportioned.

Distributing *A.V.*—*see communicating.*

Distribution.
Acts 4. 35. and *distribution* was made unto each
see contribution.

Ditch *A.V.*—*see pit.*

Divers.—*A.V.* ¹*diversities*, ²*sundry.*
Mat. 4. 24. with *divers* diseases. *Mk.* 1. 34: *Lu.* 4. 40
24. 7. earthquakes in *d.* places. *Mk.* 13. 8: *Lu.* 21. 11
1 *Cor.* 12. 10. to another *divers* kinds of tongues. ¹28
2 *Tim.* 3. 6. silly women laden with sins, led away by *d.* lusts
Tit. 3. 3. were—deceived, serving *d.* lusts and pleasures
Heb. 1. 1. spoken—by ²*d.* portions and in *divers* manners
9. 10. (with meats and drinks and *divers* washings)
13. 9. Be not carried away by *d.* and strange teachings
see manifold, some.

Diversities.—*A.V.* ¹*differences.*
1 *Cor.* 12. 4. there are *d.* of gifts, but the same Spirit
5. there are ¹*d.* of ministrations, and the same Lord
6. there are *diversities* of workings, but the same God
see divers.

Divide—d.—*A.V.* ¹*partial.*
Mat. 12. 25. kingdom *divided* against itself—every city or house *d.* against itself. *Mk.* 3. 24, 25: *Lu.* 11. 17
26. he is *divided* against himself. *Mk.* 3. 26: *Lu.* 11. 18
Mk. 6. 41. and the two fishes *divided* he among them all
Lu. 12. 13. bid my brother *divide* the inheritance with me
52. be from henceforth five in one house *divided*
53. They shall be *divided*, father against son
15. 12. And he *divided* unto them his living
22. 17. Take this, [the cup] and *d.* it among yourselves
Acts 14. 4. the multitude of the city was *divided*
23. 7. and the assembly was *divided*
1 *Cor.* 1. 13. Is Christ *d.*? was Paul crucified for you?
Jas. 2. 4. are ye not ¹*divided* in your own mind
Rev. 16. 19. And the great city was *d.* into three parts
see gave.

DO

Divider.
Lu. 12. 14. who made me a judge or a *divider* over you?

Divideth—ing.
Lu. 11. 22. wherein he trusted, and *divideth* his spoils
1 *Cor.* 12. 11. *dividing* to each one severally even as he will
Heb. 4. 12. piercing even to the *dividing* of soul and spirit
see handling, separateth.

Divination.
Acts 16. 16. certain maid having a spirit of *divination*

Divine.
Heb. 9. 1. first covenant had ordinances of *divine* service
2 *Pet.* 1. 3. his *d.* power hath granted unto us all things
4. ye may become partakers of the *divine* nature

Divinity.—*A.V.* ¹*godhead.*
Rom. 1. 20. even his everlasting power and ¹*divinity*

Division—s.—*A.V.* ¹*seditions.*
Lu. 12. 51. I tell you, Nay; but rather *division*
Jno. 7. 43. there arose a *division* in the multitude
9. 16. there was a *division* among them. 10. 19
Rom. 16. 17. mark them which are causing the *divisions*
1 *Cor.* 1. 10. and that there be no *divisions* among you
11. 18. I hear that *divisions* exist among you
Gal. 5. 20. wraths, factions, ¹*divisions*, heresies

Divorced *A.V.*—*see put away.*

Divorcement.
Mat. 5. 31. let him give her a writing of *divorcement*
19. 7. Moses command to give a bill of *d. Mk.* 10. 4

Do.—*A.V.* ¹*doest*, ²*done*, ³*fulfil*, ⁴*manner*, ⁵*mean.*
Mat. 5. 19. but whosoever shall *do* and teach them
47. brethren only, what *do* ye more than others?
8. 29. What have we to *do* with thee. *Mk.* 1. 24: *Lu.* 4. 34
20. 15. lawful for me to *do* what I will with mine own?
32. What will ye that I should *do* unto you? *Mk.* 10.51
21. 21. ye shall not only *do* what is done to the fig tree
23. 3. whatsoever they bid you, these *do* and observe
26. 50. Jesus said, ¹*Friend*, *do* that for which thou art come
27. 19. Have thou nothing to *do* with that righteous man
Mk. 3. 4. the sabbath day to *do* good, or to *do* harm? *Lu.* 6. 9
5. 7. What have I to *do* with thee. *Lu.* 8. 28: *Jno.* 2. 4
7. 12. suffer him to *do* aught for his father or his mother
13. and many such like things ye [Pharisees] *do*
9. 22. if thou canst *do* anything, have compassion on us
10. 35. shouldest *do* for us whatsoever we shall ask
36. What would ye that I should *do* for you?
15. 8. began to ask him to *do* as he [Pilate] was wont to ²*do*
12. What then shall I *do* unto him whom ye call the King
4. 23. at Capernaum, *do* also here in thine own country
6. 2. Why *do* ye that which it is not lawful to *do*
11. one with another what they might *do* to Jesus
31. should *do* to you, *do* ye—to them likewise. *Mat.* 7. 12
12. 4. after that have no more that they can *do*
16. 4. I am resolved what to *do*, that, when I am put out
19. 48. and they could not find what they might *do*
23. 31. forgive them; for they know not what they *do*
Jno. 2. 5. Whatsoever he saith unto you, *do* it
5. 19. The Son can *do* nothing of himself. 30
6. 6. for he himself knew what he would *do*
8. 29. for I *do* always the things that are pleasing to him
9. 31. worshipper of God, and *do* his will, him he heareth
33. If this man were not from God, he could *do* nothing

DO

Jno. 11. 47. What *do* we? for this man doeth many signs
13. 7. What I *do* thou knowest not now
15. that ye also should *do* as I have done to you
17. know these things, blessed are ye if ye *do* them
14. 12. I *do* shall he *do* also—greater works than these
15. 5. for apart from me ye can *do* nothing [shall he *do*
21. But all these things will they *do* unto you. 16. 3
21. 21. Lord, and what shall this man *do*?
Acts. 1. 1. all that Jesus began both to *do* and to teach
4. 28. to *do* whatsoever thy hand and thy counsel
9. 6. it shall he told thee what thou must *do*
13. 22. a man after my heart, who shall *¹do* all my will
14. 15. and saying, Sirs, why *do* ye these things?
16. 30. and said, Sirs, what must I *do* to be saved?
21. 13. What *¹do* ye, weeping and breaking my heart
22. 26. What art thou about to *¹do*? for this man is
Rom. 1. 32. not only *do* the same, but also consent
2. 14. have no law *do* by nature the things of the law
3. 8. Let us *do* evil, that good may come?
7. 15. that which I *do* I know not: for not what I would,
that *do* I practise; but what I hate, that I *do*.
16. But if what I would not, that I *do*. 20.
20. no more I that *do* it, but sin which dwelleth in me
13. 4. But if thou *do* that which is evil, be afraid [17
1 *Cor.* 5. 12. For what have I to *do* with judging them
7. 36. let him *do* what he will; he sinneth not
9. 23. And I *do* all things for the gospel's sake
10. 31. whatsoever ye *do*, *do* all to the glory of God
2 *Cor.* 8. 10. not only to *do*, but also to will
13. 7. do no evil—may *do* that which is honourable
8. For we can *do* nothing against the truth
Gal. 2. 10. which very thing I was also zealous to *do*
14. livest as *¹do* the Gentiles, and not as *do* the Jews
5. 17. that ye may not *do* the things that ye would
Eph. 6. 9. And, ye masters, *do* the same things unto them
21. But that ye also may know my affairs, how I *do*
Phil. 4. 9. and heard and saw in me, these things *do*
13. I can *do* all things in him that strengtheneth me
Col. 3. 17. ye *do*, in word or in deed, *do* all in the name
23. whatsoever ye *do*, work heartily
1. *Th.* 3. 12. toward all men, even as we also *do* toward you
4. 10. for indeed ye *do* it toward all the brethren
5. 24. Faithful is he that calleth you, who will also *do* it
2 *Th.* 3. 4. that ye both *do* and will *do* the things
Philem. 14. but without thy mind I would *do* nothing
21. that thou wilt *do* even beyond what I say
Heb. 4. 13. the eyes of him with whom we have to *do*
13. 6. I will not fear: What shall man *do* unto me?
1 *Pet.* 3. 12. face of the Lord is upon them that *do* evil
2 *Pet.* 1. 10. if ye *do* these things, ye shall never stumble
Rev. 17. 17. God did put in their hearts to *¹do* his mind
see doest, fare, perform, practise, work.

Do with good.—A.V. *¹do well.*

Mat. 12. 12. lawful to *¹do g.* on the sabbath day. *Mk.* 3. 4:
Mk. 14. 17. whensoever ye will ye can *do* them *g.* [*Lu.* 6. 9
Lu. 6. 27. *do good* to them that hate you
33. if ye *do good* to them that *do good* to you
35. *do* them *good*, and lend, never despairing
Rom. 7. 18. but to *do* that which is *good* is not
19. For the *good* which I would I *do* not
21. to me who would *do good*, evil is present
13. 3. *do* that which is *good*, and thou shalt have praise
1 *Tim.* 6. 18. that they *do good*, that they be rich in good
Heb. 13. 16. to *do good* and to communicate forget not
Jas. 4. 17. that knoweth to *do good*, and doeth it not
1 *Pet.* 3. 11. And let him turn away from evil, and *do good*

DOCTRINE

Do with not.

Mat. 5. 46. *do not* even the publicans the same? 47
23. 3. *do not* ye after their works; for they say, and *do not*
Lu. 6. 46. Lord, Lord, and *do not* the things which I say?
Rom. 7. 19. For the good which I would I *do not*
8. 3. For what the law could *not do*, in that it was weak
1 *Jno.* 1. 6. we lie, and *do not* the truth
Rev. 19. 10. saith unto me, See thou *do* it *not*. 22. 9

Shall or will Do.—A.V. *¹doeth well.*

Mat. 19. 16. Master, what good thing *s.* I *do*. *Mk.* 10. 17.
27. 22. What then *shall I do* unto Jesus [*Lu.* 10. 25
Lu. 12. 17. What *s. I do*, because I have not where to bestow
16. 3. steward said within himself, What *shall I do*
20. 13. What *shall I do*? I will send my beloved son
Jno. 14. 13. shall ask in my name, that *will I do*. 14
Acts 2. 37. Brethren, what *shall* we *do*?
4. 16. saying, What *shall* we *do* to these men?
22. 10. And I said, What *shall I do*, Lord?
1 *Cor.* 7. 37. keep his own virgin daughter, *¹shall do* well
2 *Cor.* 11. 12. But what I do, that I *will do*

Do with so.

Mat. 7. 12. do unto you, even *so do* ye also unto them
18. 35. *So* shall also my heavenly Father *do* unto you
Jno. 14. 31. gave me commandment, even *so I do*
Acts 7. 51. as your fathers did, *so do* ye
1 *Cor.* 16. 1. to the churches of Galatia, *so also do* ye
Col. 3. 13. even as the Lord forgave you, *so also do* ye
1 *Tim.* 1. 4. dispensation of God which is in faith; *so do* I now
Jas. 2. 12. and *so do*, as men that are to be judged

Do this, this Do.

Mat. 8. 9. to my servant, *Do this*, and he doeth it. *Lu.* 7. 8
9. 28. Believe ye that I am able to *do this*?
Mk. 11. 3. if any one say unto you, Why *do* ye *this*?
Lu. 7. 4. He is worthy that thou shouldest *do this*
10. 28. hast answered right: *this do*, and thou shalt live
12. 18. *This* will I *do*: I will pull down my barns
22. 19. *this do* in remembrance of me. 1 *Cor.* 11. 24, 25
Acts 21. 23. *Do* therefore *this* that we say to thee
Heb. 6. 3. And *this* will we *do*, if God permit
18. 19. exhort you the more exceedingly to *do this*
Jas. 4. 15. If the Lord will, we shall both live, and *do this*

Do well.—A.V. *¹doeth well.*

1 *Cor.* 7. 37. keep his own virgin daughter, shall *¹do well*
Jas. 2. 8. love thy neighbour as thyself, ye *do well*
1 *Pet.* 2. 14. and for praise to them that *do well*
20. but if, when ye *do well*, and suffer for it
3. 6. whose children ye now are, if ye *do well*
2 *Pet.* 1. 19. whereunto ye *do well* that ye take heed
3 *Jno.* 6. whom thou wilt *do well* to set forward
see do good, recover.

Doctor—s.

Lu. 2. 46. [Jesus] sitting in the midst of the *doctors*
5. 17. there were Pharisees and *d.* of the law sitting
Acts. 5. 34. Gamaliel, a *doctor* of the law

Doctrine.—A.V. *¹otherwise.*

Rom. 16. 17. contrary to the *doctrine* which ye learned
Eph. 4. 14. carried about with every wind of *doctrine*
1 *Tim.* 1. 3. men not to teach a different *doctrine*
10. any other thing contrary to the sound *doctrine*
4. 6. words of the faith, and of the good *doctrine*
6. 1. name of God and the *doctrine* be not blasphemed
3. If any man teacheth a different *¹d.*—to the *d.* which

DOCTRINE

2 *Tim.* 4. 3. when they will not endure the sound *doctrine*
Tit. 1. 9. both to exhort in the sound *d.*, and to convict
2. 1. speak thou the things which befit the sound *d.*
7. in thy *doctrine* shewing uncorruptness
10. adorn the *doctrine* of God our Saviour in all things
see teaching.

Doctrines.
Mat 15. 9. Teaching as their *d.* the precepts of men. *Mk.* 7.7
Col. 2. 22. after the precepts and *doctrines* of men?
1 *Tim.* 4. 1. to seducing spirits and *doctrines* of devils
see teachings.

Doer—s.—*A.V.* ¹*keep.*
Rom. 2. 13. but the *doers* of a law shall be justified
25. circumcision—profiteth, if thou be a ¹*doer* of the law
Jas. 1. 22. be ye *doers* of the word, and not hearers only
23. if any one is a hearer of the word, and not a *doer*
25. not a hearer that forgetteth, but a *d.* that worketh
4. 11. thou art not a *doer* of the law, but a judge

Doest.—*A.V.* ¹*do.*
Mat. 6. 2. When therefore thou *doest* alms. 3
21. 23. By what authority *d.* thou these things? *Mk.* 11.
Jno. 2. 18. seeing that thou *d.* these things? [23: *Lu.* 20.2
3. 2. no man can do these signs that thou *doest*
7. 3. disciples also may behold thy works which thou *d.*
4. If thou ¹*doest* these things, manifest thyself
13. 27. That thou *doest*, do quickly [Jesus to Judas]
Rom. 2. 3. practise such things, and *doest* the same
Jas. 2. 19. Thou believest that God is one; thou *d.* well
3 *Jno.* 5. *doest* a faithful work in whatsoever thou *doest*
see do, practise.

Doeth.—*A.V.* ¹*committeth,* ²*keepeth,* ³*transgresseth.*
Mat. 6. 3. left hand know what thy right hand *doeth*
7. 21. but he that *doeth* the will of my Father
24. heareth these words of mine, and *doeth* them. *Lu.*
26. and *doeth* them not. *Lu.* 6. 49 [6. 47
8. 9. to my servant, Do this, and he *doeth* it. *Lu.* 7. 8
Jno. 3. 20. For every one that *doeth* ill hateth the light
21. But he that *doeth* the truth cometh to the light
5. 19. what things soever he *doeth*, these the Son also *d.*
20. and sheweth him all things that himself *doeth*
7. 4. For no man *doeth* anything in secret
19. give you the law, and yet none of you ³*doeth* the law?
51. hear from himself and know what he *doeth*?
14. 10. the Father abiding in me *doeth* his works
15. 15. for the servant knoweth not what his lord *doeth*
Rom. 3. 12. There is none that *doeth* good
10. 5. *d.* the righteousness which is of the law shall live
13. 4. an avenger for wrath to him that *doeth* evil
1 *Cor.* 6. 18. Every sin that a man *d.* is without the body
7. 38. virgin daughter in marriage *doeth* well
Gal. 3. 5. *doeth* he it by the works of the law, or by the
12. He that *doeth* them shall live in them
Eph. 6. 8. that whatsoever good thing each one *doeth*
Col. 3. 25. he that *d.* wrong shall receive again for the wrong
Jas. 4. 17. that knoweth to do good, and *doeth* it not
1 *Jno.* 2. 17. he that *doeth* the will of God abideth for ever
29. every one—that *d.* righteousness is begotten of him
3. 4. Every one that ¹*doeth* sin ³*doeth* also lawlessness
(7. he that *doeth* righteousness is righteous
8. he that ¹*doeth* sin is of the devil
3. *Jno.* 10. bring to remembrance his works which he *d.*
11. He that *doeth* good is of God; he that *doeth* evil
Rev. 13. 13. And he [beast out of the earth] *d.* great signs
see do well, shall do, maketh, offereth, worketh.

DONE

Dog—s.
Mat. 7. 6. Give not that which is holy unto the *dogs*
15. 26. children's bread and cast it to the *dogs*. *Mk.* 7. 27
27. even the *dogs* eat of the crumbs. *Mk.* 7. 28
Lu. 16. 21. even the *dogs* came and licked his sores
Phil. 3. 2. Beware of the *dogs*, beware of the evil workers
2. *Pet.* 2. 22. The *dog* turning to his own vomit again
Rev. 22. 15. Without are the *dogs*, and the sorcerors

Doing—s.—*A.V.* ¹*deed—s,* ²*done,* ³*fulfilling,* ⁴*ways.*
Mat. 24. 46. whom he cometh shall find so *doing.* *Lu.* 12. 43
Acts 10. 38. who went about *doing* good, and healing
14. 18. multitudes from ²*doing* sacrifice unto them
Rom. 12. 20. for in so *doing* thou shalt heap coals of fire
2 *Cor.* 8. 11. But now complete the *doing* also
Eph. 2. 3. ²*doing* the desires of the flesh and of the mind
6. 6. *doing* the will of God from the heart
Phil. 2. 3. ²*d.* nothing through faction or through vainglory
Col. 3. 9. ye have put off the old man with his ¹*doings*
1 *Tim.* 4. 16. in *doing* this thou shalt save both thyself and
5. 21. *doing* nothing by partiality [them
Jas. 1. 25. this man shall be blessed in his ¹*doing*
2 *Pet.* 2. 2. many shall follow their lascivious ⁴*doings*
see well-doing, wrong-doing.

Dominion—s.—*A.V.* ¹*authority,* ²*government,* ³*power.*
Rom. 6. 9. death no more hath *dominion* over him
14. For sin shall not have *dominion* over you
7. 1. how that the law hath *dominion* over a man
Eph. 1. 21. rule, and authority, and power, and *dominion*
Col. 1. 16. whether thrones or *dominions* or principalities
1 *Tim.* 2. 12. permit not a woman to—have ¹*d.* over a man
1 *Pet.* 4. 11. *d.* for ever and ever. 5. ²11 : *Rev.* 1. 6 : 5. ³13
2 *Pet.* 2. 10. lust of defilement, and despise ²*dominion*
Jude 8. set at nought *dominion*, and rail at dignities
25. *dominion* and power, before all time, and now
see lord, lordship.

Done.—*A.V.* ¹*ceased,* ²*committed,* ³*dealt,* ⁴*destroyed,*
⁵*vanish.*
Mat. 6. 10. Thy will be *done.* 26. 42
8. 13. as thou hast believed, so be it *done* unto thee. 9. 29
11. 21. *done* in Tyre and Sidon which were *done* in you.
23. *done* in Sodom which were *done* in thee [*Lu.* 10. 13
13. 28. An enemy hath *done* this
18. 19. shall ask, it shall be *done* for them of my Father
31. saw what was *done*—their lord all that was *done*
21. 21. not only do what is *done*—it shall be *done*
23. 23. but these ye ought to have *done. Lu.* 11. 42
25. 21. Well *done*, good and faithful servant. 23
26. 13. which this woman hath *done* shall be spoken of
27. 23. Why, what evil hath he *d. Mk.* 15. 14 : *Lu.* 23. 22
54. saw the earthquake, and the things that were *done*
Mk. 5. 19. how great things the Lord hath *done* for thee
20. how great things Jesus had *done* for him. *Lu.* 8. 39
32. looked round about to see her that had *d.* this thing
33. knowing what had been *d.* to her, came and fell down
6. 30. told him all things, whatsoever they had *done*
7. 37. He hath *done* all things well
9. 13. have also *done* unto him whatsoever they listed
14. 8. She hath *done* what she could
Lu. 1. 25. Thus hath the Lord ³*done* unto me
49. he that is mighty hath *done* to me great things
3. 19. for all the things which Herod had *done*
5. 6. had this *d.*, they inclosed a great multitude of fishes
8. 56. charged them to tell no man what had been *done*
9. 10. declared unto him what things they had *done*
14. 22. Lord, what thou didst command is *done*
17. 10. have *d.* all—have *d.* that which it was our duty

93

DONE

Lu. 22. 42. nevertheless not my will, but thine, be *done*
23. 31. in the green tree, what shall be *done* in the dry?
41. but this man hath *done* nothing amiss
47. And when the centurion saw what was *done*
Jno. 5. 29. they that have *done* good—have *done* ill
13. 12. Know ye what I have *done* to you?
15. ye also should do as I have *done* to you
15. 7. ask whatsoever ye will, and it shall be *done*
24. If I had not *done* among them the works
Acts 2. 43. wonders and signs were *done* by the apostles
4. 7. By what power, or in what name, have ye *d.* this?
9. concerning a good deed *done* to an impotent man
21. all men glorified God for that which was *done*
5. 7. his wife, not knowing what was *done*, came in
10. 16. And this was *done* thrice. 11. 10
33. and thou hast well *done* that thou art come
12. 9. it was true which was *done* by the angel   [15. 4
14. 27 rehearsed all things that God had *d.* with them.
21. 14. we ceased, saying, The will of the Lord be *done*
33. inquired who he [Paul] was, and what he had *done*
25. 10. to the Jews have I *done* no wrong
26. 26. for this hath not been *done* in a corner
28. 9. And when this was *done*, the rest also—came
17. though I [Paul] had *²d.* nothing against the people
Rom. 6. 6. that the body of sin might be ¹*done* away
9. 11. neither having *done* anything good or bad
1 *Cor.* 5. 2. he that had *d.* this deed might be taken away
9. 15. that it may be so *done* in my case
13. 8. whether there be knowledge, it shall be *²d.* away
10. that which is in part shall be *done* away
14. 26. Let all things be *done* unto edifying
40. let all things be *done* decently and in order
16. 14. Let all that ye do be *done* in love
2 *Cor.* 3. 14. which veil is *done* away in Christ
5. 10. things *done* in the body—what he hath *done*
Gal. 5. 11. the stumblingblock of the cross been ¹*d.* away
Eph. 5, 12. things which are *done* by them in secret
6. 13. and, having *done* all, to stand
Col. 3. 25. receive again for the wrong that he hath *done*
4. 9. make known unto you all things that are *done* here
Tit. 3. 5. not by works *done* in righteousness
Heb. 10. 29. hath *done* despite unto the Spirit of grace?
Rev. 16. 17. from the throne, saying, It is *done*
see accomplished, came to pass, did, do, doing, happened, passing, passeth, wrought.

Doomed. —*A.V.* ¹*approved.*

1 *Cor.* 4. 9. us the apostles last of all, as men ¹*d.* to death

Door. —*A.V.* ¹*gate.*

Mat. 6. 6. and having shut thy *door*, pray to thy Father
25. 10. and the *door* was shut
27. 60. a great stone to the *door* of the tomb. *Mk.* 15. 46
Mk. 1. 33. all the city was gathered together at the *door*
2. 2. room for them, no, not even about the *door*
11. 4. away, and found a colt tied at the *door* without
16. 3. roll us away the stone from the *door* of the tomb?
Lu. 11. 7. Trouble me not: the *door* is now shut
13. 24. Strive to enter in by the narrow ¹*door*
25. and hath shut to the *door*—knock at the *door*
John 10. 1. He that entereth not by the *door* into the fold
2. But he that entereth in by the *door* is the shepherd
7. I am the *door*. 9
18. 16. Peter was standing at the *door* without
17. The maid therefore that kept the *door* saith. 16
Acts 3. 2. whom they laid daily at the ¹*door* of the temple
5. 9. are at the *door*, and they shall carry thee out
12. 6. and guards before the *door* kept the prison
13. And when he knocked at the *door* of the gate

DOVE

Acts 14. 27. opened a *door* of faith unto the Gentiles
1 *Cor.* 16. 9. a great *door* and effectual is opened unto me
2 *Cor.* 2. 12. a *door* was opened unto me in the Lord
Col. 4. 3. God may open unto us a *door* for the word
Rev. 3. 8. I have set before thee a *door* opened
20. Behold, I stand at the *door* and knock: if any man hear my voice and open the *door*
4. 1. I saw, and behold, a *door* opened in heaven
    see doors.

Doors. —*A.V.* ¹*door.*

Mat. 24. 33. know ye that he is nigh, even at the *d. Mk.*
Jno. 20. 26. Jesus cometh, the *doors* being shut. 19 |13. 29
Acts 5. 19. the Lord by night opened the prison *doors*
23. and the keepers standing at the *doors*
16. 26. and immediately all the *doors* were opened
27. seeing the prison *doors* open, drew his sword
21. 30. and straightway the *doors* were shut
Jas. 5. 9. behold, the judge standeth before the ¹*doors*

Doting.

1 *Tim.* 6. 4. *d.* about questionings and disputes of words

Double.

1 *Tim.* 5. 17. rule well be counted worthy of *d.* honour
Rev. 18. 6. and *d.* unto her the *d.* according to her works

Doubleminded.

Jas. 1. 8. a *doubleminded* man, unstable in all his ways
4. 8. and purify your hearts, ye *doubleminded*

Doubletongued.

1 *Tim.* 3. 8. Deacons—must be grave, not *doubletongued*

Doubt. —*A.V.* ¹*difference.*

Mat. 14. 31. of little faith, wherefore didst thou *doubt?*
21. 21. If ye have faith, and *d.* not, ye shall not only do
Mk. 11. 23. not *doubt* in his heart, but shall believe
Acts 28. 4. No *doubt* this man [Paul] is a murderer
Jude 22. on some have mercy, who are in ¹*doubt*
    see perplexed, suspense.

Doubted—eth. —*A.V.* ¹*wavereth.*

Mat. 28. 17. they worshipped him; but some *doubted*
Rom. 14. 23. he that *doubteth* is condemned if he eat
Jas. 1. 6. he that ¹*doubteth* is like the surge of the sea
    see perplexed.

Doubtful.

Lu. 12. 29. neither be ye of *doubtful* mind
Rom. 14. 1. receive ye, yet not to *doubtful* disputations

Doubting. —*A.V.* ¹*wavering.*

Jno. 13. 22. one on another, *doubting* of whom he spake
Acts 10. 20. and go with them, nothing *doubting* [Peter]
Jas. 1. 6. But let him ask in faith, nothing ¹*doubting*
    see disputing, distinction.

Doubtless *A.V.—see least, needs, verily.*

Dove-s.

Mat. 3. 16. God descending as a *d. Mk.* 1. 10: *Lu.* 3. 22:
10. 16. wise as serpents, and harmless as *d.* [*Jno.* 1. 32
21. 12. seats of them that sold the *doves. Mk.* 11. 15
Jno. 2. 14. those that sold oxen and sheep and *doves*
16. sold the *doves* he said, Take these things hence
    see turtle doves.

DRAG

Drag—ging.—*A.V.* ¹*draw*.
Jno. 21. 8. *dragging* the net full of fishes
Jas. 2. 6. themselves ¹*d*. you before the judgement-seats?

Dragged.—*A.V.* ¹*drew*.
Acts 14. 19. stoned Paul, and ¹*dragged* him out of the city
16. 19. and ¹*d*. them [Paul and Silas] into the marketplace
17. 6. ¹*d*. Jason and certain brethren before the rulers
21. 30. laid hold on Paul, and ¹*d*. him out of the temple

Dragon
Rev. 12. 3. behold, a great red *dragon*, having seven heads
4. and the *dragon* stood before the woman
7. to war with the *dragon* ; and the *dragon* warred
9. And the great *dragon* was cast down
13. when the *dragon* saw that he was cast down
16. river which the *dragon* cast out of his mouth
17. And the *dragon* waxed wroth with the woman
13. 2. the *dragon* gave him his power, and his throne
4. and they worshipped the *dragon*
11. horns like unto a lamb, and he spake as a *dragon*
16. 13. I saw coming out of the mouth of the *dragon*
20. 2. And he laid hold on the *dragon*, the old serpent

Drank
Mk. 14. 23. he gave to them : and they all *drank* of it
Lu. 17. 27. They ate, they *drank*, they married. 28
Jno. 4. 12. gave us the well, and *d*. thereof himself [Jacob]
1 *Cor.* 10. 4. they *d.* of a spiritual rock that followed them

Draught.
Mat. 15. 17. and is cast out into the *draught* ? *Mk.* 7. 19
Lu. 5. 4. and let down your nets for a *draught*
9. at the *draught* of the fishes which they had taken

Drave.—*A.V.* ¹*persecuted*.
Acts 18. 16. And he *drave* them from the judgement-seat
1 *Th.* 2. 15. killed the Lord Jesus and the prophets, and ¹*d.*

Draw.—*A.V.* ¹*came nigh*, ²*come*, ³*comers*, ⁴*pull*.
Mk. 11. 1. And when they ¹*draw* nigh unto Jerusalem
Lu. 14. 5. ox fallen into a well, and will not—⁴*draw* him up
Jno. 2. 8. *Draw* out now, and bear unto the ruler of the feast
4. 7. There cometh a woman of Samaria to *draw* water
11. nothing to *draw* with, and the well is deep
15. neither come all the way hither to *draw*
6. 44. except the Father which sent me *draw* him
12. 32. I, if I be lifted up from the earth, will *d*. all men
Acts 20. 30. to *draw* away the disciples after them
Heb. 4. 16. Let us therefore ²*draw* near with boldness
7. 19. better hope, through which we *draw* nigh unto God
25. save to the uttermost them that ²*draw* near
10. 1. make perfect them that ³*draw* nigh
22. let us *draw* near with a true heart
Jas. 4. 8. *Draw* nigh to God, and he will *draw* nigh to you
see drag.

Draw back *A.V.*—*see shrink*.

Draweth—ing. — *A. V.* ¹*approacheth*, ²*approaching*, ³*drew*.
Lu. 12. 33. treasure in the heavens—where no thief ¹*d.* near
15. 1. were ²*drawing* near unto him for to hear him
21. 28. lift up your heads—your redemption *d.* nigh
Jno. 6. 19. walking on the sea, and *d.* nigh to the boat
Acts 27. 27. surmised—they were ²*d.* near to some country
Heb. 10. 25. as ye see the day ²*drawing* nigh
Rev. 12. 4. And his tail ³*draweth* the third part of the stars
see (at) hand, honoureth.

DRINK

Drawn.—*A.V.* ¹*drew*.
Jno. 2. 9. the servants which had ¹*drawn* the water knew
Acts 11. 10. and all were *drawn* up again into heaven
Jas. 1. 14. when he is *drawn* away by his own lust

Dream—s.
Mat. 2. 12. being warned of God in a *dream*. 22
13. appeareth to Joseph in a *dream*. 1. 20; 2. 19
27. 19. I have suffered many things this day in a *dream*
Acts 2. 17. And your old men shall *dream dreams*

Dreamers *A.V.*—*see dreamings*.

Dreamings——*A.V.* ¹*filthy dreamers*.
Jude 8. these also in their ¹*dreamings* defile the flesh

Dressed *A.V.*—*see tilled*.

Dresser *A.V.*—*see vinedresser*.

Drew.—*A.V.* ¹*came*, ²*come*, ³*withdrew*.
Mat. 13. 48. when it was filled, they *drew* up on the beach
21. 1. And when they *drew* nigh unto Jerusalem
34. And when the season of the fruits *drew* near
26. 51. *d.* his sword, and smote the servant. *Mk.* 14. 47
Lu. 7. 12. Now when he ¹*drew* near to the gate of the city
15. 25. and as he came and *drew* nigh to the house
19. 41. when he ²*drew* nigh, he saw the city and wept
22. 1. Now the feast of unleavened bread *drew* nigh
47. and he [Judas] *drew* near unto Jesus to kiss him
23. 54. the Preparation, and the sabbath *drew* on
24. 15. Jesus himself *drew* near, and went with them
28. *drew* nigh unto the village, whither they were going
Jno. 18. 10. Simon Peter therefore having a sword *drew* it
21. 11. and *drew* the net to land, full of great fishes
Acts 5. 37. *d.* away some of the people after him [Judas of
7. 17. But as the time of the promise *d.* near [Galilee]
31. as he [Moses] *d.* near to behold, there came a voice
9. 3. as he [Saul] journeyed—he ¹*d.* nigh unto Damascus
10. 9. on their journey, and *drew* nigh unto the city
16. 27. *d.* his sword, and was about to kill himself [jailor]
Gal. 2. 12. he ³*drew* back and separated himself
see brought, drugged, draweth, drawn, moored.

Dried.
Mk. 5. 29. the fountain of her blood was *dried* up
Rev. 16. 12. Euphrates ; and the water thereof was *d.* up
see withered.

Drift.—*A.V.* ¹*slip*.
Heb. 2. 1. lest haply we ¹*drift* away from them

Drink—s.
Mat. 25. 35. I was thirsty, and ye gave me *drink*
37. or athirst, and gave thee *drink* ?
42. I was thirsty, and ye gave me no *drink*
Lu. 1. 15. he [John Bap.] shall drink no wine nor strong *d.*
Jno. 4. 9. that thou, being a Jew, askest *drink* of me
6. 55. my flesh is meat indeed, and my blood is *d.* indeed
1 *Cor.* 10. 4. and did all drink the same spiritual *drink*
Col. 2. 16. no man therefore judge you in meat, or in *drink*
Heb. 9. 10. (with meats and *drinks* and divers washings)
see drinking.

Drink (Verb).—*A.V.* ¹*drunk*.
Mat. 6. 31. What shall we eat ? or, What shall we *drink* ?
10. 42. shall give to *drink* unto one of these little ones
20. 22. able to *d.* the cup that I am about to *d.* ? *Mk.* 10. 38
23. My cup indeed ye [James and John] shall *drink*

DRINK

Mat. 24. 49. and shall eat and *drink* with the drunken
26. 27. and gave to them, saying, *Drink* ye all of it
29. I will not *drink* henceforth—until that day when I *drink* it new. *Mk.* 14. 25 ; *Lu.* 22. 18
42. pass away, except I *drink* it, thy will be done
27. 34. they gave him wine to *drink*—he would not *drink*
48. put it on a reed, and gave him to *drink*. *Mk.* 15. 36
Mk. 9. 41. cup of water to *drink*, because ye are Christ's
10. 39. The cup that I *drink*, ye shall *drink*
16. 18. and if they *drink* any deadly thing
Lu. 1. 15. he shall *drink* no wine nor strong drink
12. 45. and to eat and *drink*, and to be drunken
13. 26. We did eat and ¹*drink* in thy presence
17. 8. and afterward thou shalt eat and *drink* ?
Jno. 4. 7. Jesus saith unto her, Give me to *drink*. 10
6. 53. Except ye eat—and d. his blood, ye have not life
7. 37. If any man thirst, let him come unto me, and d.
18. 11. the Father hath given me, shall I not *drink* it ?
Rom. 12. 20. if he thirst, give him to *drink*
14. 21. It is good not to eat flesh, nor to *drink* wine
1 *Cor.* 10. 4. and did all *drink* the same spiritual drink
21. cannot d. the cup of the Lord, and the cup of devils
11. 25. as oft as ye *drink* it, in remembrance of me
28. so let him eat of the bread, and *drink* of the cup
12. 13. and were all made to *drink* of one Spirit
Rev. 14. 8. hath made all the nations to *drink* of the wine
10. he also shall *drink* of the wine of the wrath of God
16. 6. and blood hast thou given them to *drink*
see drinker, eat with drink, offered.

Drinker.—*A.V.* ¹*drink.*

1 *Tim.* 5. 23. Be no longer a ¹*drinker* of water [Timothy]

Drinketh.

Mk. 2. 16. He eateth and d. with publicans and sinners
Jno. 4. 13. Every one that d. of this water shall thirst
14. whosoever d. of the water that I shall give him
6. 54. and *drinketh* my blood hath eternal life
56. and *drinketh* my blood abideth in me, and I in him
1 *Cor.* 11. 29. and d., eateth and d. judgement unto himself
see drunk.

Drinking.—*A.V.* ¹*drink.*

Mat. 11. 18. John came neither eating nor d. *Lu.* 7. 33
19. The Son of man came eating and *drinking*. *Lu.* 7. 34
24. 38. before the flood they were eating and *drinking*
Lu. 10. 7. eating and *drinking* such things as they give
Rom. 14. 17. the kingdom of God is not eating and ¹*drinking*

Drive.—*A.V.* ¹*thrust.*

Acts 27. 39. whether they could ¹*drive* the ship upon it
see driven.

Driven.—*A.V.* ¹*carried,* ²*drive.*

Lu. 8. 29. he was *driven* of the devil into the deserts
Acts 27. 15. the wind, we gave way to it, and were ²*driven*
17. they lowered the gear, and so were *driven*
27. as we were *driven* to and fro in the sea of Adria
Jas. 1. 6. is like the surge of the sea *driven* by the wind
3. 4. are *driven* by rough winds, are yet turned about
2 *Pet.* 2. 17. without water, and mists ¹*driven* by a storm

Driveth.

Mk. 1. 12. the Spirit *driveth* him forth into the wilderness

Drops.

Lu. 22. 44. his sweat became as it were great d. of blood

DUMB

Dropsy.

Lu. 14. 2. before him a certain man which had the *dropsy*

Drove *A.V.*—*see cast.*

Drown.

1 *Tim.* 6. 9. foolish and hurtful lusts, such as *drown* men

Drowned *A.V.*—*see sunk, swallowed.*

Drunk.—en.—*A.V.* ¹*drinketh.*

Mat. 24. 49. and shall eat and drink with the *drunken*
Lu. 5. 39. no man having *drunk* old wine desireth new
12. 45. to eat and drink, and to be *drunken*
17. 8. serve me, till I have eaten and *drunken*
Jno. 2. 10. when men have *drunk* freely, then that which
Acts 2. 15. these are not d., as ye suppose ; seeing it is but
1 *Cor.* 11. 21. one is hungry, and another is *drunken*
Eph. 5. 18. be not *drunken* with wine, wherein is riot
1 *Th.* 5. 7. they that be *drunken* are *drunken* in the night
Heb. 6. 7. land which hath ¹*drunk* the rain that cometh
Rev. 17. 2. made *drunken* with the wine of her fornication
6. woman *drunken* with the blood of the saints
see drink.

Drunkard—s.

1 *Cor.* 5. 11. an idolater, or a reviler, or a *drunkard*
6. 10. nor thieves, nor covetous, nor *drunkards*

Drunkenness.

Lu. 21. 34. overcharged with surfeiting, and *drunkenness*
Rom. 13. 13. not in revelling and *drunkenness*
Gal. 5. 21. envyings, *drunkenness*, revellings, and such like

Dry.

Lu. 23. 31. in the green tree, what shall be done in the d. ?
see waterless, land.

Due.—*A.V.* ¹*debt,* ²*meet.*

Mat. 18. 30. prison, till he should pay that which was ¹*due*
34. to the tormentors, till he should pay all that was *due*
24. 45. give them their food in *due* season ? *Lu.* 12. 42
Lu. 23. 41. for we receive the *due* reward of our deeds
Rom. 1. 27. recompense of their error which was ²*due*
5. 6. in *due* season Christ died for the ungodly
13. 7. tribute to whom tribute is *due*
1 *Cor.* 7. 3. Let the husband render unto the wife her *due*
15. 8. last of all, as unto one born out of *due* time
Gal. 6. 9. in *due* season we shall reap, if we faint not
1 *Pet.* 5. 6. that he may exalt you in *due* time
see own.

Dues.

Rom. 13. 7. Render to all their *dues*

Dull.

Mat. 13. 15. And their ears are *dull* of hearing. *Acts* 28. 27
Heb. 5. 11. seeing ye are become *dull* of hearing

Dumb.—*A.V.* ¹*speechless.*

Mat. 9. 32. brought to him a d. man possessed with a devil
33. when the devil was cast out the *dumb* man spake.
Lu. 11. 14
12. 22. blind and d.—insomuch that the d. man spake
15. 30. having with them the lame, blind, d., maimed
31. wondered, when they saw the d. speaking [speak
Mk. 7. 37. maketh even the deaf to hear, and the *dumb* to
9. 17. brought unto thee my son, which hath a d. spirit

DUMB

Mk. 9. 25. Thou *dumb* and deaf spirit, I command thee
Lu. 1. 22. making signs unto them, and remained ¹*dumb*
11. 14. And he was casting out a devil which was *dumb*
1 *Cor.* 12. 2. ye were led away unto those *dumb* idols
2 *Pet.* 2. 16. a *dumb* ass spake with man's voice
see silent

Dung.

Lu. 13. 8. till I shall dig about it, and *dung* it
Phil. 3. 8. do count them but *dung*, that I may gain Christ

Dunghill.

Lu. 14. 35. fit neither for the land nor for the *dunghill*

Dureth *A.V.*—¹*endureth*.

Durst.

Mat. 22. 46 neither *durst* any man from that day forth ask him any more questions. *Mk.* 12. 34: *Lu.* 20. 40
Jno. 21. 12. none of the disciples *durst* inquire of him
Acts 5. 13. of the rest *durst* no man join himself to them
7. 32. And Moses trembled, and *durst* not behold
Jude 9. *durst* not bring against him a railing judgement

Dust.—*A.V.* ¹*powder*.

Mat. 10. 14. shake off the *d.* of your feet. *Mk.* 6. 11 : *Lu.* 9. 5
21. 44. stone—shall fall, it will scatter him as ¹*d. Lu.* 20.¹18
Lu. 10. 11. Even the *dust* from your city, that cleaveth
Acts 13. 51. [Paul and Barnabas] shook off the *d.* of their feet
22. 23. threw off their garments, and cast *d.* into the air
Rev. 18. 19. And they cast *dust* on their heads, and cried

Duty.

Lu. 17. 10. we have done that which it was our *duty* to do
see once.

Dwell.—*A.V.* ¹*dwelleth*, ²*dwelt*, ³*inhabiters*, ⁴*rest*.

Mat. 12. 45. and they enter in and *dwell* there. *Lu.* 11. 26
Lu. 13. 4. offenders above all the men that ²*d.* in Jerusalem?
21. 35. upon all them that *d.* on the face of all the earth
Acts 1. 20. desolate, And let no man *dwell* therein
2. 14. of Judæa, and all ye that *dwell* at Jerusalem
26. Moreover my flesh also shall ⁴*dwell* in hope
4. 16. is manifest to all that *dwell* in Jerusalem
7. 4. removed him into this land, wherein ye now *dwell*
13. 27. For they that *d.* in Jerusalem, and their rulers
17. 26. of men for to *dwell* on all the face of the earth
1 *Cor.* 7. 12. wife, and she is content to *dwell* with him
13. husband, and he is content to *dwell* with her
2 *Cor.* 6. 16. even as God said, I will *dwell* in them
Eph. 3. 17. that Christ may *d.* in your hearts through faith
Col. 1. 19. that in him should all the fulness *dwell*
3. 16. Let the word of Christ *dwell* in you richly in all
Jas. 4. 5. Doth the spirit which he made to ¹*d.* in us long
1 *Pet.* 3. 7. Ye husbands, in like manner, *d.* with your wives
Rev. 3. 10. to try them that *dwell* upon the earth
6. 10. avenge our blood on them that *dwell* on the earth?
8. 13. Woe, woe, woe, for them that ³*dwell* on the earth
11. 10. they that *dwell* on the earth rejoice—tormented them that ³*dwell* on the earth
12. 12. rejoice, O heavens, and ye that *dwell* in them
13. 6. his tabernacle, even them that ³*dwell* in the heaven
8. all that *dwell* on the earth shall worship him
12. them that *dwell* thereiu to worship the first beast
14. he deceiveth them that *dwell* on the earth—saying to them that *dwell* on the earth
14. 6. to proclaim unto them that *dwell* on the earth

14

DYSENTERY

Rev. 17. 2. they that ²*d.* in the earth were made drunken
8. And they that *dwell* on the earth shall wonder
21. 3. he shall *d.* with them, and they shall be his peoples
see abide, dwelleth, spread, tabernacle.

Dwellers.

Acts 1. 19. it became known to all the *d.* at Jerusalem
2. 9. and the *dwellers* in Mesopotamia, in Judæa and

Dwellest.

Rev. 2. 13. I know where thou *d.*, even where Satan's
see abidest.

Dwelleth.—*A.V.* ¹*dwell*.

Mat. 23. 21. sweareth by it, and by him that *d.* therein
Acts 7. 48. *dwelleth* not in houses made with hands. 17. 24
Rom. 7. 17. no more I that do it, but sin which *d.* in me. 20
18. in me, that is, in my flesh, *dwelleth* no good thing
8. 9. if so be that the Spirit of God ¹*dwelleth* in you
11. ¹*d.* in you—through his Spirit that *dwelleth* in you
1 *Cor.* 3. 16. and that the Spirit of God *dwelleth* in you ?
Col. 2. 9. in him *dwelleth* all the fulness of the Godhead
2 *Tim.* 1. 14. guard through the Holy Ghost which *d.* in us
2 *Pet.* 3. 13. a new earth, wherein *dwelleth* righteousness
Rev. 2. 13. killed among you, where Satan *dwelleth*
see abideth, abiding, dwell.

Dwelling.—*A.V.* ¹*house*, ²*intruding*.

Mk. 5. 3. who had his *dwelling* in the tombs
Acts 2. 5. were *dwelling* at Jerusalem Jews, devout men
28. 30. abode two whole years in his own hired ¹*dwelling*
Col. 2. 18. ²*dwelling* in the things which he hath seen
1 *Tim.* 6. 16. *dwelling* in light unapproachable
Heb. 11. 9. *dwelling* in tents, with Isaac and Jacob
2 *Pet.* 2. 8. (for that righteous man *dwelling* among them
see dwell.

Dwellingplace.

1 *Cor.* 4. 11. buffeted, and have no certain *dwellingplace*

Dwelt.—*A.V.* ¹*continued*, ²*dwelling*.

Mat. 2. 23. came and *dwelt* in a city called Nazareth
4. 13. leaving Nazareth, he came and *d.* in Capernaum
Lu. 1. 65. fear came on all that *dwelt* round about them
Jno. 1. 14. the Word became flesh, and *dwelt* among us
Acts 7. 2. in Mesopotamia, before he *dwelt* in Haran
4. and *d.* in Haran : and from thence, when his father
9. 22. confounded the Jews which *dwelt* at Damascus
32. the saints which *dwelt* at Lydda. 35
11. 29. relief unto the brethren that *dwelt* in Judæa
16. 11. he ¹*dwelt* there a year and six months
19. 10. all they which *dwelt* in Asia heard the word
17. both Jews and Greeks, that ²*dwelt* at Ephesus
22. 12. well reported of by all the Jews that *dwelt* there
2 *Tim.* 1. 5. which *dwelt* first in thy grandmother Lois
see abode, dwell, sojourned.

Dying.

Mk. 12. 20. the first took a wife, and *dying* left no seed
Lu. 8. 42. twelve years of age, and she lay a *dying*
2 *Cor.* 4. 10. bearing about in the body the *dying* of Jesus
6. 9. as *dying*, and behold, we live
Heb. 11. 21. By faith Jacob, when he was a *dying*, blessed

Dysentery.—*A.V.* ¹*bloody flux*.

Acts 28. 8. father of Publius lay sick of fever and ¹*dysentery*

97

EAGLE

E.

Eagle—s.—*A.V.* ¹*angel.*
Mat. 24. 28. there will the *eagles* be gathered. Lu. 17. 37
Rev. 4. 7. the fourth creature was like a flying *eagle*
8. 13. I saw, and I heard an ¹*eagle* flying in mid-heaven
12. 14. given to the woman the two wings of the great *e.*

Ear.—*A.V.* ¹*hearken.*
Mat. 10. 27. what ye hear in the *ear*, proclaim upon
26. 51. struck off his *ear*. Mk. 14. 47: Lu. 22. 50: Jno. 18. 10
Lu. 12. 3. and what ye have spoken in the *ear*
22. 51. And he touched his *ear*, and healed him
Jno. 18. 26. being a kinsman of him whose *ear* Peter cut off
Acts 2. 14. Peter—spake forth—give ¹*ear* unto my words
1 Cor. 2. 9. Things which eye saw not, and *ear* heard not
12. 16. if the *ear* shall say, Because I am not the eye
Rev. 2. 7. He that hath an *ear*, let him hear. 11, 17, 29: 3.
13. 9. If any man hath an *ear*, let him hear. [6, 13, 22

Ear—s *of corn.*
Mat. 12. 1. began to pluck *e. of corn*. Mk. 2. 23: Lu. 6. 1
Mk. 4. 28. then the *ear*, then the full *corn* in the *ear*

Early.—*A.V.* ¹*old.*
Mk. 16. 9. he was risen *early* on the first day of the week
Lu. 24. 22. amazed us, having been *early* at the tomb
John 18. 28. lead Jesus—into the palace: and it was *early*
20. 1. cometh Mary Magdalene *e.*, while it was yet dark
Acts 21. 16. Mnason of Cyprus, an ¹*early* disciple
Jas. 5. 7. until it receive the *early* and the latter rain
see morning.

Earnest.—*A.V.* ¹*diligent,* ²*forward.*
Rom. 8. 19. For the *earnest* expectation of the creation
2 Cor. 1. 22. and gave us the *earnest* of the Spirit. 5. 5
8. 16. the same *earnest* care for you into the heart of Titus
17. being himself very ²*earnest*, he went forth
22. proved ¹*earnest* in many things—much more ¹*e.*
Eph. 1. 14. which is an *earnest* of our inheritance
Phil. 1. 20. according to my *earnest* expectation and hope
Heb. 2. 1. Therefore we ought to give the more *e.* heed

Earnestly.—*A.V.* ¹*instantly,* ²*without ceasing.*
Lu. 7. 4. besought him ¹*earnestly*, saying, He is worthy
22. 44. And being in an agony he prayed more *earnestly*
Acts 12. 5. prayer was made ²*e.* of the church unto God
26. 7. twelve tribes, ¹*e.* serving God night and day
1 Cor. 12. 31. But desire *earnestly* the greater gifts
Jude 3. exhorting you to contend *earnestly* for the faith
see fasten, fervently, stedfastly.

Earnestness.—*A.V.* ¹*diligence,* ²*forwardness.*
2 Cor. 8. 7. in all ¹*earnestness*, and in your love to us
8. as proving through the ²*e.* of others the sincerity

Ears.—*A.V.* ¹*audience.*
Mat. 11. 15. He that hath *ears* to hear, let him hear. 13.
9, 43 : Mk. 4. 9, 23 : Lu. 8. 8 : 14. 35 [28. 27
13. 15. *ears* are dull of hearing—hear with their *e. Acts*
16. But blessed are—your *ears*, for they hear
28. 14. if this come to the governor's *e.*, we will persuade
Mk. 7. 33. put his fingers into his *ears*, and he spat
35. And his *ears* were opened
8. 18. having *e.*, hear ye not ? and do ye not remember ?
Lu. 1. 44. thy salutation came into mine *e.*, the babe leaped
4. 21. To-day hath this scripture been fulfilled in your *e.*

EARTH

Lu. 7. 1. ended all his sayings in the ¹*ears* of the people
9. 44. Let these words sink into your *ears*
Acts 7. 51. uncircumcised in heart and *ears*, ye do always
57. cried out with a loud voice, and stopped their *ears*
11. 22. concerning them came to the *ears* of the church
17. 20. thou bringest certain strange things to our *ears*
Rom. 11. 8. not see, and *ears* that they should not hear
2 Tim. 4. 3. having itching *ears*, will heap to themselves
4. and will turn away their *ears* from the truth
Jas. 5. 4. entered into the *ears* of the Lord of Sabaoth
1 Pet. 3. 12. And his *ears* unto their supplication

Earth.—*A.V.* ¹*earthly,* ²*ground,* ³*inhabiters of the earth,* ⁴*world.*
Mat. 5. 5. Blessed are the meek : for they shall inherit the
13. Ye are the salt of the *earth* : but if the salt [*earth*
35. nor by the *earth*, for it is the footstool of his feet
12. 40. three days and three nights in the heart of the *e.*
42. she came from the ends of the *e.* to hear—Solomon
13. 5. not much *earth*—no deepness of *earth*. Mk. 4. 5
25. 18. digged in the *earth*, and hid his lord's money
25. went away and hid thy talent in the *earth*
27. 51. the *earth* did quake ; and the rocks were rent
Mk. 4. 28. The *earth* beareth fruit of herself
Lu. 12. 51. that I am come to give peace in the *earth* ?
24. 5. affrighted, and bowed down their faces to the *e.*
Jno. 3. 31. he that is of the *earth* is of the ¹*earth*, and of
the *earth* he speaketh
12. 24. Except a grain of wheat fall into the ²*earth* and die
32. I, if I be lifted up from the *earth*, will draw all men
Acts 2. 19. And signs on the *earth* beneath ; Blood, and fire
7. 49. And the *earth* the footstool of my feet
8. 33. For his life is taken from the *earth*
9. 8. And Saul arose from the *e.* ; and when his eyes were
13. 47. for salvation unto the uttermost part of the *earth*
22. 22. Away with such a fellow from the *earth*
26. 14. when we were all fallen to the *earth*, I heard
Rom. 9. 17. my name might be published—in all the *earth*
10. 18. Their sound went out into all the *earth*
1 Cor. 10. 26. the *e.* is the Lord's, and the fulness thereof
15. 47. The first man is of the *earth*, earthy
Phil. 2. 10. things on *earth* and things under the *earth*
2 Tim. 2. 20. of silver, but also of wood and of *earth*
Heb. 1. 10. hast laid the foundation of the *earth*
12. 26. whose voice then shook the *earth*—Yet once
more will I make to tremble not the *earth* only
Jas. 5. 7. waiteth for the precious fruit of the *earth*
18. gave rain, and the *earth* brought forth her fruit
2 Pet. 3. 5. and an *earth* compacted out of water
7. heavens that now are, and the *e.*, by the same word
10. the *e.* and the works that are therein shall be burned
Rev. 5. 6. Spirits of God, sent forth into all the *earth*
6. 4. it was given to take peace from the *earth*
13. and the stars of the heaven fell unto the *earth*
7. 1. four corners of the *e.*, holding the four winds of the *e.*
3. Hurt not the *earth*, neither the sea, nor the trees
8. 7. cast upon the *e.*—the third part of the *e.* was burnt
9. 1. I saw a star from heaven fallen unto the *earth*
11. 4. candlesticks, standing before the Lord of the *earth*
12. 4. stars of heaven, and did cast them to the *earth*
12. 12. Woe for the ³*earth* and for the sea
13. dragon saw that he was cast down to the *earth*
16. the *e.* helped the woman—the *e.* opened her mouth
13. 3. and the whole ⁴*earth* wondered after the beast
11. I saw another beast coming up out of the *earth*
12. he maketh the *earth*—to worship the first beast
14. 3. they that had been purchased out of the *earth*
16. sickle upon the *earth* ; and the earth was reaped
16. 2. first went, and poured out his bowl into the *earth*

98

EARTH

Rev. 18. 1. and the *earth* was lightened with his glory
19. 2. the great harlot, which did corrupt the *earth*
20. 9. they went up over the breadth of the *earth*
11. from whose face the *earth* and the heaven fled away
21. 1. new *earth*—and the first *earth* are passed away
  see upon the earth, heaven, land, world.

On or upon the **Earth.**—*A.V.* ¹*ground,* ²*in earth,* ³*to the earth.*

Mat. 6. 10. Thy will be done, as in heaven, so ²*on earth*
19. Lay not up for yourselves treasures *upon the earth*
9. 6. may know that the Son of man hath power *on earth* to forgive sins. *Mk.* 2. 10: *Lu.* 5. 24
10. 34. Think not that I came to send peace *on the earth*
16. 19. bind *on e.*—loose *on e.* shall be loosed in. 18. 18.
18. 19. if two of you shall agree *on earth* as touching
23. 9. And call no man your father *on the earth*
35. may come all the righteous blood shed *on the earth*
Mk. 4. 26. as if a man should cast seed *upon the* ¹*earth*
31. mustard seed, which, when it is sown *upon the earth*—than all the seeds that are *upon the earth*
9. 3. so as no fuller *on earth* can whiten them
Lu. 2. 14. Glory to God in the highest, And *on earth* peace
6. 49. built a house *upon the earth* without a foundation
12. 49. I came to cast fire *upon the earth*
18. 8. Son of man cometh, shall he find faith *on the e.?*
Jno. 17. 4. I glorified thee *on the earth*
Acts 9. 4. he [Saul] fell ³*upon the earth*, and heard a voice
10. 11. sheet, let down by four corners ³*upon the earth*
Rom. 9. 28. the Lord will execute his word *upon the earth*
Phil. 2. 10. of things in heaven and things ²*on e. Col.* 1. ²20
Col. 3. 2. above, not on the things that are *upon the earth*
5. Mortify—your members which are *upon the earth*
Heb. 8. 4. Now if he were *on e.,* he would not be a priest
11. 13. they were strangers and pilgrims *on the earth*
12. 25. when they refused him that warned them *on e.*
Jas. 5. 5. Ye have lived delicately *on the earth*
17. it rained not *on the e.* for three years and six months
Rev. 3. 10. to try them that dwell *upon the earth*
5. 10. kingdom and priests; and they reign *upon the e.*
6. 10. avenge our blood on them that dwell *on the earth?*
7. 1. that no wind should blow *on the earth*
8. 7. and they were cast *upon the earth*
10. 8. angel that standeth *upon the sea and upon the e.*
11. 10. dwell *on the earth.* 13. 8; 14. 6: 17. 8
13. 13. fire to come down out of heaven *upon the earth*
14. 16. sat on the cloud cast his sickle *upon the earth*
18. 24. of all that have been slain *upon the earth*

Earthen.

2 *Cor.* 4. 7. we have this treasure in *earthen* vessels

Earthly.

Jno. 3. 12. If I told you *earthly* things, and ye believe not
2 *Cor.* 5. 1. if the *e.* house of our tabernacle be dissolved
Phil. 3. 19. glory is in their shame, who mind *e.* things
Jas. 3. 15. but is *earthly,* sensual, devilish
  see earth.

Earthquake—s.

Mat. 24. 7. *e.* in divers places. *Mk.* 13. 8 : *Lu.* 21. 11
27. 54. watching Jesus, when they saw the *earthquake*
28. 2. there was a great *e. Acts* 16. 26: *Rev.* 6. 12: 11. 13:
Rev. 8. 5. voices, and lightnings, and an *e.* 11. 19 [16. 18
16. 18. so great an *earthquake,* so mighty

Earthy.

1 *Cor.* 15. 47. The first man is of the earth, *earthy*
48. As is the *earthy,* such are they also that are *earthy*
49. And as we have borne the image of the *earthy*

EAT

Ease—d.

Lu. 12. 19. take thine *ease,* drink, be merry
2 *Cor.* 8. 13. that others may be *eased,* and ye distressed

Easier.

Mat. 9. 5. whether is *e.,* to say, Thy. *Mk.* 2. 9: *Lu.* 5. 23
19. 24. It is *e.* for a camel to go through. *Mk.* 10. 25: *Lu.* 18.
Lu. 16. 17. it is *e.* for heaven and earth to pass away [25

Easily.

Heb. 12. 1. and the sin which doth so *easily* beset us

East.

Mat. 2. 1. wise men from the *east* came to Jerusalem
2. for we saw his star in the *east.* 9
8. 11. many shall come from the *east. Lu.* 13. 29
24. 27. as the lightning cometh forth from the *east*
Rev. 21. 13. on the *east* were three gates
  see south-east, sunrising, west.

Easter.—*A.V.* see *Passover.*

Easy.

Mat. 11. 30. For my yoke is *easy,* and my burden is light
1 *Cor.* 14. 9. utter by the tongue speech *e.* to be understood
Jas. 3. 17. then peaceable, gentle, *easy* to be intreated

Eat.—*A.V.* ¹*bread,* ²*eaten,* ³*live.*

Mat. 12 4. [David] did *e.* the shewbread. *Mk.* 2. 26: *Lu.* 6. 4
14. 20. did all *eat,* and were filled. 15. 37: *Mk.* 6. 42: 8. 8 :
21. they that did ²*eat* were about five thousand ¹*Lu.* 9. 17
15. 27. for even the dogs *eat* of the crumbs. *Mk.* 7. 28
88. that did *eat* were four thousand men, beside women
26. 26. Take, *eat* ; this is my body
Mk. 1. 6. and did *eat* locusts and wild honey [John]
3. 20. so that they could not so much as *eat* bread
6. 36. and buy themselves somewhat to ¹*eat*
7. 3. except they wash their hands diligently, *eat* not. 4, 5
11. 14. No man *e.* fruit from thee henceforward for ever
14. 12. mayest *e.* the passover? 14: *Lu.* 22. 8, 11: *Jno.* 18. 28
Lu. 4. 2. And he did *eat* nothing in those days
6. 1. plucked the ears of corn, and did *eat*
7. 36. the Pharisees desired him that he would *e.* with him
10. 8. *eat* such things as are set before you
12. 22. Be not anxious for your life, what ye shall *eat*
13. 26. We did ²*eat* and drink in thy presence
15. 23. kill it, let us *eat,* and make merry
22. 16. I will not *eat* it, until it be fulfilled
24. 43. And he took it, and did *eat* before them
Jno. 2. 17. The zeal of thine house shall ²*eat* me up
4. 31. the disciples prayed him, saying, Rabbi, *eat*
6. 49. your fathers did *eat* the manna. 58
50. that a man may *eat* thereof, and not die. 51
53. Except ye *eat* the flesh of the Son of man
Acts 10. 13. Rise, Peter; kill and *eat.* 11. 7
11. 3. to men uncircumcised, and didst *eat* with them
Rom. 14. 23. But he that doubteth is condemned if he *eat*
1 *Cor.* 5. 11. an extortioner; with such a one no, not to *eat*
8. 7. some—*eat* as of a thing sacrificed to an idol
8. if we *eat* not, are we the worse ; nor, if we *eat*
13. I will *eat* no flesh for evermore
9. 13. sacred things ³*eat* of the things of the temple
10. 3. and did *eat* the same spiritual meat
18. which *eat* the sacrifices communion with the altar?
25. *eat,* asking no question for conscience sake. 27
28. in sacrifice, *eat* not, for his sake that shewed it
11. 34. If any man is hungry, let him *eat* at home
Gal. 2. 12. [Cephas] from James, he did *e.* with the Gentiles
2 *Th.* 3. 10. If any will not work, neither let him *eat*

EAT

2 Tim. 2. 17. their word will *eat* as doth a gangrene
Jas. 5. 3. their rust—shall *eat* your flesh as fire
Rev. 10. 9. And he saith unto me, Take it, and *eat* it up
17. 16. shall *eat* her flesh, and shall burn her
19. 18. that ye may *eat* the flesh of kings, and the flesh
are ate, eating, taste.

Eat *with drink.*

Mat. 6. 25. ye shall *eat*, or what ye shall d. 31: Lu. 12. 29
24. 49. shall *eat* and *drink* with the drunken. Lu. 12. 45
Lu. 5. 30. Why do ye *eat* and *drink* with the publicans
33. disciples of the Pharisees; but thine *eat* and *drink*
12. 19. Soul—take thine ease, *eat*, *drink*, be merry
17. 8. and afterward thou shalt *eat* and *drink* ?
22. 30. that ye may *eat* and *drink* at my table
Acts 9. 9. [Saul] and did neither *eat* nor *drink*
10. 41. who did *eat* and *drink* with him after he rose
23. 12. *eat* nor *drink* till they had killed Paul. 21
Rom. 14. 21. good not to *eat* flesh, nor to *drink* wine
1 Cor. 9. 4. Have we no right to *eat*, and to *drink* ?
10. 7. The people sat down to *eat* and *drink*
31. therefore you *eat*, or *drink*, or whatsoever ye do
11. 22. have ye not houses to *eat* and to *drink* in ?
26. *eat* this bread, and *drink* the cup. 27, 28
15. 32. let us *eat* and *drink*, for to-morrow we die

To Eat.—A.V. ¹*eaten*, ²*meat.*

Mat. 12. 1. began to pluck ears of corn, and *to eat*
4. not lawful for him *to eat*. Mk. 2. 26 : Lu. 6. 4
14. 16. give ye them *to eat*, Mk. 6. 37 : Lu. 9. 13
15. 20. but *to eat* with unwashen hands defileth not
32. three days and have nothing *to eat*. Mk. 8. 1, 2
26. 17. we make ready for thee *to eat* the passover ?
Mk. 5. 43. that something should be given her *to eat*. Lu.
6. 31. and they had no leisure so much as *to eat* [8. ²55
Lu. 22. 15. I have desired *to eat* this passover with you
24. 41. Have ye here anything ²*to eat* ? Jno. 21. ²5
Jno. 4. 32. I have meat *to eat* that ye know not
33. Hath any man brought him aught *to eat* ?
6. 52. How can this man give us his flesh *to eat* ?
Acts 10. 10. became hungry, and desired ¹*to eat* [Peter]
27. 35. and he brake it, and began *to eat*
Rom. 14. 2. One man hath faith *to eat* all things
1 Cor. 8. 10. be emboldened *to eat* things
11. 20. it is not possible *to eat* the Lord's supper
33. when ye come together *to eat*, wait one for another
Heb. 13. 10. they have no right *to eat* which serve
Rev. 2. 7. to him will I give *to eat* of the tree of life
14. *to eat* things sacrificed to idols. 20

Eaten.

Lu. 17. 8. serve me, till I have *eaten* and drunken
Jno. 6. 13. remained over unto them that had *eaten*
Acts 10. 14. I have never *eaten* any thing that is common
12. 23. [Herod] was *e.* of worms, and gave up the ghost
20. 11. [Paul] had broken the bread, and *eaten*
27. 38. when they had *e.* enough, they lightened the ship
Rev. 10. 10. when I had *eaten* it, my belly was made bitter
see eat, to eat.

Eateth.

Mat. 9. 11. Why *eateth* your Master with the publicans
and sinners ? Mk. 2. 16; Lu. 15, 2
Mk. 14. 18. shall betray me, even he that *eateth* with me
Jno. 6. 54. He that *eateth* my flesh and drinketh my blood.
57. so he that *eateth* me, he also shall live [56
58. he that *eateth* this bread shall live for ever
13. 18. He that *e.* my bread lifted up his heel against me
Rom. 14. 2. but he that is weak *eateth* herbs

EGG

Rom. 14. 3. him that *e.*—*e.* not—not him that *e.*—him that *e.*
6. he that *e.*, *e.* unto the Lord—*e.* not—Lord he *e.* not
20. it is evil for that man who *eateth* with offence
23. condemned if he eat, because he *eateth* not of faith
1 Cor. 9. 7. *e.* not the fruit—*e.* not of the milk of the flock ?
11. 29. For he that *eateth*—*e* and drinketh judgement

Eating.—A.V. ¹*eat*, ²*meat.*

Mat. 11. 18 John came neither *e.* nor drinking. Lu. 7. 33
19. Son of man came *eating* and drinking. Lu. 7. 34
24. 38. before the flood they were *eating* and drinking
26. 21. as they were ¹*e.*, he said, Verily I say. Mk. 14. ¹18
26. as they were *eating*, Jesus took bread. Mk. 14.¹²²
Mk. 2. 16. when they saw that he was ¹*e.* with the sinners
Lu. 10. 7. *eating* and drinking such things as they give
Rom. 14. 17. kingdom of God is not ²*eating* and drinking
1 Cor. 8. 4. Concerning therefore the *e.* of things sacrificed
11. 21. for in your *eating* each one taketh before other

Edge.

Lu. 21. 24. And they shall fall by the *edge* of the sword
Heb. 11. 34. escaped the *edge* of the sword

Edges A.V.—*see two-edged.*

Edification.

1 Cor. 14. 3. he that prophesieth speaketh unto men *e.*
see building, edifying.

Edified—eth.

Acts 9. 31. Galilee and Samaria had peace, being *edified*
1 Cor. 8. 1. Knowledge puffeth up, but love *edifieth*
14. 4. He that speaketh in a tongue *e.* himself—*e.* the
17. givest thanks well, but the other is not *e.* [church

Edify.

Rom. 14. 19. things whereby we may *edify* one another
1 Cor. 10. 23. All things are lawful; but all things *edify* not
see build.

Edifying.—A.V. ¹*edification.*

Rom. 15. 2. his neighbour for that which is good, unto ¹*e.*
1 Cor. 14. 5. that the church may receive *edifying*
12. seek that ye may abound unto the *e.* of the church
26. Let all things be done unto *edifying*
2 Cor. 12. 19. all things, beloved, are for your *edifying*
Eph. 4. 29. but such as is good for *e.* as the need may be
see building, dispensation.

Effect.—A.V. ¹*void.*

¹om. 3. 3. make of none *effect* the faithfulness of God ?
31. make the law of none ¹*effect* through faith ?
4. 14. the promise is made of none *effect*. Gal. 3. 17
see nought, severed, void.

Effectual.

1 Cor. 16. 9. for a great door and *e.* is opened unto me
Philem. 6. the fellowship of thy faith may become *e.*
see worketh.

Effeminate.

1 Cor. 6. 9. nor *effeminate*, nor abusers of themselves

Effulgence.—A.V. ¹*brightness.*

Heb. 1. 3. who being the ¹*e.* of his glory, and the very image

Egg.

Lu. 11. 12. Or if he shall ask an *egg*, will he give him

100

EIGHT

Eight.
Lu. 2. 21. when *eight* days were fulfilled for circumcising
9. 28. it came to pass about *e*. days after these sayings
Jno. 20. 26. after *e*. days again his disciples were within
Acts 9. 38. Æneas, which had kept his bed *eight* years
1 *Pet.* 3. 20. few, that is, *e*. souls, were saved through water

Eighteen.
Lu. 13. 4. Or those *e*., upon whom the tower in Siloam fell
11. a woman which had a spirit of infirmity *e*. years
16. whom Satan had bound, lo, these *eighteen* years

Eighth.
Rev. 17. 11. that was, and is not, is himself also an *eighth*
21. 20. the *eighth*, beryl; the ninth, topaz
see day.

Either.
Mat. 6. 24. No man can serve two masters: for *either* he
will hate the one. *Lu.* 16. 13
12. 33. *Either* make the tree good, and its fruit good
Jno. 19. 18. crucified him, and with him two others, on *e*.
1 *Cor.* 14. 6. I speak to you *e*. by way of revelation [side one

Elder.—*A.V.* ¹*elders.*
Lu. 15. 25. Now his *elder* son was in the field
Acts 15. 23. The apostles and the ¹*elder* brethren
Rom. 9. 12. The *elder* shall serve the younger
1 *Tim.* 5.1. Rebuke not an *e*., but exhort him as a father. 19
2. the *elder* women as mothers; the younger
1 *Pet.* 5. 5. Likewise, ye younger, be subject unto the *elder*
2 *Jno.* 1. The *elder* unto the elect lady and her children
3 *Jno.* 1. The *elder* unto Gaius the beloved

Elders.
Mat. 15. 2. disciples transgress the tradition of the *elders*?
16. 21. suffer many things of the *elders* and chief priests
21. 23. and the *elders* of the people came unto him
26. 3. and the *elders* of the people, unto the court
47. from the chief priests and *elders* of the people
57. the scribes and the *elders* were gathered together
27. 1. the *elders* of the people took counsel against Jesus
12. when he was accused by the chief priests and *elders*
20. the chief priests and the *e*. persuaded the multitudes
41. mocking him, with the scribes and *elders*, said
28. 12. And when they were assembled with the *elders*
Mk. 7. 3. holding the tradition of the *elders*. 5
8. 31. and be rejected by the *elders*. *Lu.* 9. 22
15. 1. the chief priests with the *elders* and scribes
Lu. 7. 3. he sent unto him *elders* of the Jews, asking him
20. 1. him the chief priests and the scribes with the *elders*
22. 52. and *elders*, which were come against him
66. the assembly of the *e*. of the people was gathered
Acts 4. 5. that their rulers and *elders* and scribes were
8. Ye rulers of the people, and *elders*, if we this day
23. reported all that the chief priests and the *e*. had said
6. 12. they stirred up the people, and the *elders*
11. 30. sending it to the *elders* by the hand of Barnabas
14. 23. they had appointed for them *e*. in every church
15. 2 unto the apostles and *elders* about this question
4. of the church and the apostles and the *elders*
⁾ 6. the apostles and the *elders* were gathered together
22. it seemed good to the apostles and the *elders*
16. 4. which had been ordained of the apostles and *elders*

ELI

Acts 20. 17. Ephesus, and called to him the *e*. of the church
21. 18. with us unto James; and all the *e*. were present
22. 5. bear me witness, and all the estate of the *elders*
24. 1. high priest Ananias came down with certain *elders*
25. 15. chief priests and the *e*. of the Jews informed me
1 *Tim.* 5. 17. Let the *e*. that rule well be counted worthy
Tit. 1. 5. and appoint *elders* in every city
Heb. 11. 2. For therein the *elders* had witness borne to them
Jas. 5. 14. let him call for the *elders* of the church
1 *Pet.* 5. 1. The *elders* therefore among you I exhort
Rev. 4. 4. the thrones I saw four and twenty *elders* sitting
10. four and twenty *e*. shall fall down. 5. 8, 14:11.16:19.4
5. 5. and one of the *elders* saith unto me, Weep not
6. in the midst of the *elders*, a Lamb standing
11. the throne and the living creatures and the *e*. 7. 11
7. 13. And one of the *elders* answered, saying unto me
14. 3. before the four living creatures and the *elders*
see chief priests, elder.

Eldest.
Jno. 8. 9. went out one by one, beginning from the *eldest*

Elect.—*A.V.* ¹*chosen,* ²*elected,* ³*strangers.*
Mat. 24. 22. have been saved: but for the *e*.'s sake. *Mk.*13.20
31. gather together his *e*. from the four winds. *Mk.*13.27
Mk. 13. 22. may lead astray, if possible, the *e*. *Mat.* 24. 24
Lu. 18. 7. And shall not God avenge his *elect*, which cry
Rom. 8. 33. lay anything to the charge of God's *elect*?
Col. 3. 12. Put on therefore, as God's *e*., holy and beloved
1 *Tim.* 5. 21. and Christ Jesus, and the *elect* angels
2 *Tim.* 2. 10. I endure all things for the *elect's* sake
Tit. 1. 1. according to the faith of God's *elect*
1 *Pet.* 1. 1. the ³*elect* who are sojourners of the Dispersion
2. 4. rejected indeed of men, but with God ¹*elect*
6. I lay in Zion a chief corner stone, *elect*, precious
9. But ye are an ¹*elect* race, a royal priesthood
5. 13. [church] ²*elect* together with you, saluteth you
2 *Jno.* 1. The *elect* unto the *elect* lady and her children
13. The children of thine *elect* sister salute thee

Elected *A.V.*—*see elect.*

Election.
Rom. 9. 11. purpose of God according to *e*. might stand
11. 5. there is a remnant according to the *e*. of grace
7. but the *e*. obtained it, and the rest were hardened
28. but as touching the *election*, they are beloved
1 *Th.* 1. 4. knowing, brethren beloved of God, your *e*.
2 *Pet.* 1. 10. diligence to make your calling and *e*. sure

Elements.
2 *Pet.* 3. 10. the *e*. shall be dissolved with fervent heat. 12
see rudiments.

Eleven.
Mat. 28. 16. But the *eleven* disciples went into Galilee
Mk. 16. 14. afterward he was manifested unto the *eleven*
Lu. 24. 9. the tomb, and told all these things to the *eleven*
33. to Jerusalem, and found the *e*. gathered together
Acts 1. 26. he was numbered with the *eleven* apostles
2. 14. But Peter, standing up with the *eleven*

Eleventh.
Mat. 20. 6. about the *eleventh* hour he went out. 9
Rev. 21. 20. the *eleventh*, jacinth; the twelfth, amethyst

Eli, Eloi.
Mat. 27. 46. *Eli, Eli*, lama sabachthani? *Mk.* 15. 34

ELOQUENT

Eloquent *A.V.—see learned.*

Embarking.—*A.V.* ¹*entering.*
Acts 27. 2. And ¹*embarking* in a ship of Adramyttium

Emboldened.
1 *Cor.* 8. 10. will not his conscience, if he is weak, be *e.*

Embraced *A.V.—see exhorted, greeted, took leave.*

Embracing.
Acts 20. 10. Paul went down, and fell on him, and *e.* him

Emerald.
Rev. 4. 3. a rainbow—like an *emerald* to look upon
21. 19. the third, chalcedony; the fourth, *emerald*

Emperor.—*A.V.* ¹*Augustus.*
Acts 25. 21. But when Paul had appealed to be kept for the decision of the ¹*emperor.* ¹25

Emptied.—*A.V.* ¹*no reputation.*
Phil. 2. 7. but ¹*e.* himself, taking the form of a servant

Empty.—*A.V.* ¹*vain.*
Mat. 12. 44. he findeth it *empty*, swept, and garnished
Mk. 12. 3. beat him, and sent him away *e. Lu.* 20. 10, 11
Lu. 1. 53. And the rich he hath sent *empty* away
Eph. 5. 6. Let no man deceive you with ¹*empty* words

Emulation—s *A.V.—see jealousy—ies.*

Enabled.
1 *Tim.* 1. 12. I thank him that *enabled* me, even Christ

Enacted.—*A.V.* ¹*established.*
Heb. 8. 6. covenant, which hath been ¹*enacted* upon better

Encounter—ed.—*A.V.* ¹*war.*
Lu. 14. 31. what king, as he goeth to ¹*e.* another king in
Acts 17. 18. Stoic philosophers *encountered* him [war

Encourage—d.—*A.V.* ¹*comfort,* ²*exhorting.*
Acts 18. 27. the brethren ²*encouraged* him, and wrote
1 *Th.* 5. 14. admonish the disorderly; ¹*e.* the faint-hearted

Encouragement.—*A.V.* ¹*consolation.*
Heb. 6. 18. we may have a strong ¹*e.*, who have fled for

Encouraging.—*A.V.* ¹*comforted.*
1 *Th.* 2. 11. his own children, exhorting you, and ¹*e.* you

End.—*A.V.* ¹*cause,* ²*died,* ³*last,* ⁴*purpose,* ⁵*therefore.*
Mat. 10. 22. he that endureth to the *e.* 24. 13: *Mk.* 13. 13
11. 1. when Jesus had made an *end* of commanding
13. 39. the harvest is the *end* of the world; the
40. so shall it be in the *end* of the world. 49 [reapers
24. 3. sign of thy coming, and of the *end* of the world?
6. but the *end* is not yet. *Mk.* 13. 7: *Lu.* 21. 9
14. and then shall the *end* come
31. the four winds, from one *end* of heaven to the other
26. 58. and sat with the officers, to see the *end*
28. 20. with you alway, even unto the *end* of the world
Mk. 1. 38. preach there also; for to this ⁵*end* came I
3. 26. Satan—is divided, he cannot stand, but hath an *e.*
Lu. 1. 33. and of his kingdom there shall be no *end*
18. 1. spake a parable unto them to the *e.* that they ought

ENDURE

Jno. 13. 1. he [Jesus] loved them [disciples] unto the *end*
18. 37. To this *e.* have I been born—to this ¹*e.* am I come
Acts 26. 16. for to this ⁴*e.* have I appeared unto thee [Paul]
Rom. 4. 16. to the *end* that the promise may be sure
18. to the *end* that he might become a father
6. 21. for the *end* of those things is death
22. unto sanctification, and the *end* eternal life
10. 4. Christ is the *end* of the law unto righteousness
14. 9. For to this *end* Christ died, and lived again
1 *Cor.* 1. 8. who shall also confirm you unto the *end*
2 *Cor.* 1. 13. and I hope ye will acknowledge unto the *end*
2. 9. For to this *end* also did I write, that I might know
3. 13. not look stedfastly on the *end* of that—passing away
11. 15. whose *end* shall be according to their works
Phil. 3. 19. whose *end* is perdition, whose god is the belly
1 *Tim.* 1. 5. the *end* of the charge is love out of a pure heart
Heb. 1. 2. hath at the ³*end* of these days spoken
3. 6. and the glorying of our hope firm unto the *end*
14. beginning of our confidence firm unto the *end*
6. 8. nigh unto a curse; whose *end* is to be burned
11. diligence unto the fulness of hope even to the *end*
7. 3. having neither beginning of days nor *end* of life
9. 26. once at the *end* of the ages hath he been manifested
11. 22. By faith Joseph, when his ²*end* was nigh
Jas. 5. 11. and have seen the *end* of the Lord, how that
1 *Pet.* 1. 9. receiving the *e.* of your faith, even the salvation
20. was manifested at the ³*end* of the times for your sake
4. 6. For unto this ¹*end* was the gospel preached
7. But the *end* of all things is at hand   [gospel
17. what shall be the *end* of them that obey not the
1 *Jno.* 3. 8. To this ⁴*end* was the Son of God manifested
Rev. 2. 26. he that keepeth my works unto the *end*
21. 6. the beginning and the *end.* 22. 13
see ever and ever, final, fulfilment, issue, late, perfectly.

Latter End *A.V.—see (last) state.*

Endeavour—ing *A.V.—see diligence.*

Endeavoured.
1 *Th.* 2. 17. *endeavoured* the more—to see your face
see sought.

Ended.
Mat. 7. 28. when Jesus *ended* these words. *Lu.* 7. 1
Acts 19. 21. Now after these things were *ended*
see completed.

Endless.
1 *Tim.* 1. 4. neither to give heed to—*endless* genealogies
Heb. 7. 16. but after the power of an *endless* life

Ends.—*A.V.* ¹*uttermost parts.*
Mat. 12. 42. she came from the ¹*e.* of the earth. *Lu.* 11. ¹31
Rom. 10. 18. And their words unto the *ends* of the world
1 *Cor.* 10. 11. upon whom the *ends* of the ages are come
see uttermost (part).

Endued *A.V.—see clothed, understanding.*

Endure.—*A.V.* ¹*bear,* ²*suffer.*
Mk. 4. 17. no root in themselves, but *endure* for a while
1 *Cor.* 4. 12. being persecuted, we ²*endure*
10. 13. way of escape, that ye may be able to ¹*endure* it
2 *Th.* 1. 4. and in the afflictions which ye *endure*
2 *Tim.* 2. 10. I *endure* all things for the elect's sake
12. if we ²*endure*, we shall also reign with him
4. 3. time will come when they will not *e.* the sound doc-
Heb. 12. 7. It is for chastening that ye *endure*   true
20. for they could not *endure* that which was enjoined
see endured, endureth, suffer.

ENDURED

Endured.—*A. V.* ¹*endure.*
Rom. 9. 22. *e.* with much longsuffering vessels of wrath
2 *Tim.* 3. 11. what persecutions I *endured*
Heb. 6. 15. having patiently *e.*, he obtained the promise
10. 32. ye *endured* a great conflict of sufferings
11. 27. for he *endured*, as seeing him who is invisible
12. 2. *endured* the cross, despising shame, and hath sat
3. *e.* such gainsaying of sinners against themselves
Jas. 5. 11. Behold, we call them blessed which ¹*endured*

Endureth.—*A. V.* ¹*dureth,* ²*endure.*
Mat. 10. 22. but he that *e.* to the end. 24. ²13; *Mk.* 13. ²13
13. 21. not root in himself, but ¹*endureth* for a while
1 *Cor.* 13. 7. hopeth all things, *endureth* all things
Jas. 1. 12. Blessed is the man that *endureth* temptation
1 *Pet.* 2. 19. for conscience toward God a man ²*e.* griefs
see abideth.

Enduring.
2 *Cor.* 1. 6. worketh in the patient *e.* of the same sufferings
see abiding.

Enemies.—*A. V.* ¹*foes.*
Mat. 5. 44. Love your *enemies. Lu.* 6. 27, 35
22. 44. put thine *enemies* underneath. *Mk.* 12. 36: *Lu.* 20. 43: *Acts* 2. ¹35; *Heb.* 1. 13: 10. 13
Lu. 1. 71. from our *enemies,* and from the hand
74. being delivered out of the hand of our *enemies*
19. 27. Howbeit these mine *enemies,* which would not
43. when thine *enemies* shall cast up a bank about thee
Rom. 5. 10. For if, while we were *e.,* we were reconciled
11. 28. touching the gospel, they are *e.* for your sake
1 *Cor.* 15. 25. till he hath put all his *enemies* under his feet
Phil. 3. 18. that they are the *enemies* of the cross of Christ
Col. 1. 21. time past alienated and *enemies* in your mind
Rev. 11. 5. fire proceedeth—and devoureth their *enemies*
12. in the cloud; and their *enemies* beheld them

Enemy.
Mat. 5. 43. love thy neighbour, and hate thine *enemy*
13. 25. while men slept, his *enemy* came and sowed tares
28. And he said unto them, An *enemy* hath done this
39. the *enemy* that sowed them is the devil
Lu. 10. 19. authority—and over all the power of the *enemy*
Acts 13. 10. thou *enemy* of all righteousness, wilt thou not
Rom. 12. 20. But if thine *enemy* hunger, feed him
1 *Cor.* 15. 26. The last *e.* that shall be abolished is death
Gal. 4. 16. become your *enemy,* because I tell you the truth
2 *Th.* 3. 15. yet count him not as an *enemy,* but admonish
Jas. 4. 4. friend of the world maketh himself an *e.* of God

Engrafted *A. V.*—*see implanted.*

Engraven.
2 *Cor.* 3. 7. written, and *e.* on stones, came with glory

Enjoin—ed.—*A. V.* ¹*commanded.*
Philem. 8. to *enjoin* thee that which is befitting
Heb. 12. 20. they could not endure that which was ¹*enjoined*
see commanded.

Enjoy.
Acts 24. 2. Seeing that by thee we *enjoy* much peace
1 *Tim.* 6. 17. who giveth us richly all things to *enjoy*
Heb. 11. 25. than to *enjoy* the pleasures of sin for a season

ENSUE

Enlarge—d.
Mat. 23. 5. and *enlarge* the borders of their garments
2 *Cor.* 6. 11. unto you, O Corinthians, our heart is *enlarged*
13. for a recompense in like kind—be ye also *enlarged*
see magnified.

Enlightened.—*A. V.* ¹*illuminated.*
Eph. 1. 18. having the eyes of your heart *enlightened*
Heb. 6. 4. For as touching those who were once *enlightened*
10. 32. after ye were ¹*enlightened,* ye endured a great

Enmities.—*A. V.* ¹*hatred.*
Gal. 5. 20. idolatry, sorcery, ¹*enmities,* strife

Enmity.
Lu. 23. 12. for before they were at *e.* between themselves
Rom. 8. 7. the mind of the flesh is *enmity* against God
Eph. 2. 15. having abolished in his flesh the *enmity*
16. through the cross, having slain the *enmity* thereby
Jas. 4. 4. the friendship of the world is *enmity* with God?

Enough.
Mat. 10. 25. It is *e.* for the disciple that he be as his master
25. 9. Peradventure there will not be *e.* for us and you
Mk. 14. 41. Sleep on now, and take your rest : it is *enough*
Lu. 15. 17. servants of my father's have bread *enough*
22. 38. And he said unto them, It is *enough*
Acts 27. 38. they had eaten *enough,* they lightened the ship

Enquire *A. V.*—*see inquire, search, question, seek, judge.*

Enquired *A. V.*—*see learned, inquired, sought.*

Enquiry *A. V.*—*see inquiry.*

Enriched.
1 *Cor.* 1. 5. that in everything ye were *enriched* in him
2 *Cor.* 9. 11. ye being *e.* in everything unto all liberality

Enrol—led.—*A. V.* ¹*chosen,* ²*taken into the number,* ³*taxed,* ⁴*written.*
Lu. 2. 1. that all the world should be ³*enrolled*
3. And all went to ³*enrol* themselves, every one to his
5. to ³*e.* himself [Joseph] with Mary, who was betrothed
1 *Tim.* 5. 9. Let none be ²*e.* as a widow under threescore
2 *Tim.* 2. 4. please him who ¹*enrolled* him as a soldier
Heb. 12. 23. of the firstborn who are ⁴*enrolled* in heaven

Enrolment.—*A. V.* ¹*taxing.*
Lu. 2. 2. This was the first ¹*enrolment* made
Acts 5. 37. rose up Judas of Galilee in the days of the ¹*e.*

Ensample—s.—*A. V.* ¹*example,* ²*pattern.*
Phil. 3. 17. which so walk even as ye have us for an *e.*
1 *Th.* 1. 7. so that ye became an *e.* to all that believe
2 *Th.* 3. 9. but to make ourselves an *ensample* unto you
1 *Tim.* 1. 16. an ²*e.* of them which should hereafter believe
4. 12. be thou an ¹*ensample* to them that believe
Tit. 2. 7. showing thyself an ²*ensample* of good works
1 *Pet.* 5. 3. but making yourselves *ensamples* to the flock

Enslaved.—*A. V.* ¹*given.*
Tit. 2. 3. not slanderers, nor ¹*enslaved* to much wine

Ensnare.—*A. V.* ¹*entangle.*
Mat. 22. 15. took counsel how they might ¹*ensnare* him

Ensue *A. V.*—*see pursue.*

ENTANGLE

Entangle *A.V.—see ensnare.*

Entangled—eth.

Gal. 5. 1. and be not *entangled* again in a yoke of bondage
2 Tim. 2. 4. *entangleth* himself in the affairs of this life
2 Pet. 2. 20. they are again *entangled* therein and overcome

Enter.—*A.V.* ¹*come,* ²*entered,* ³*entering,* ⁴*get,* ⁵*go,* ⁶*went.*

Mat. 5. 20. in no wise *enter* into the kingdom of heaven
6. 6. when thou prayest, *enter* into thine inner chamber
7. 13. *Enter* ye in by the narrow gate—many be they that ⁵*enter* in thereby. *Lu.* 13. 24
21. Lord, Lord, shall *enter* into the kingdom of heaven
10. 5. and *enter* not into any city of the Samaritans
11. into whatsoever city or village ye shall *enter*
12. as ye ¹*enter* into the house, salute it. *Lu.* 10. 8, 10
12. 29. *enter* into the house of the strong man. *Mk.* 3. 27
45. and they *enter* in and dwell there. *Lu.* 11. 26
14. 22. constrained the disciples to ⁴*enter* into the boat
18. 3. shall in no wise *enter* into the kingdom of heaven
8. good for thee to *e.* into life maimed. *Mk.* 9. 43, 45, 47
9. *enter* into life with one eye, rather than having two
19. 17. thou wouldest *e.* into life, keep the commandments
23. It is hard for a rich man to *enter* into the kingdom of heaven. 24; *Mk.* 10. 23, 24, 25; *Lu.* 18. 24, 25
23. 13. ye ⁵*enter* not in yourselves, neither suffer ye them that are entering in to ⁵*enter*
25. 21. *enter* thou into the joy of thy lord. 23
26. 41. pray, that ye *enter* not into temptation. *Mk.* 14. 38; *Lu.* 22. 46

Mk. 1. 45. Jesus could no more openly *enter* into a city
5. 12. into the swine, that we may *e.* into them. *Lu.* 8. 32
8. 26. Do not even ⁵*enter* into the village
9. 25. come out of him, and *enter* no more into him
10. 15. little child, he shall in no wise *e.* therein. *Lu.* 18. 17
11. 2. as ye ²*enter* into it, ye shall find. *Lu.* 19. ³³⁰
13. 15. nor *enter* in, to take anything out of his house
14. 14. wheresoever he shall ⁵*e.* in, say to the goodman
Lu. 1. 9. his [Zacharias] lot was to ⁶*enter* into the temple
8. 16. that they which *enter* in may see the light. 11. ¹³³
51. he suffered not any man to ⁵*enter* in with him, save
9. 4. into whatsoever house ye *e.,* there. 10. 5; *Mk.* 6. 10
21. 21. let not them that are in the country *enter* therein
24. 26. suffer these things, and to *enter* into his glory?
Jno. 3. 4. can he *e.* a second time into his mother's womb
5. the Spirit, he cannot *enter* into the kingdom of God
10. 9. by me if any man *enter* in, he shall be saved
Acts 9. 6. rise, and ⁵*enter* into the city [Saul]
14. 22. through many tribulations we must *enter* into the
19. 30. when Paul was minded to ²*e.* in unto the people
20. 29. grievous wolves shall *enter* in among you
Heb. 3. 11. They [Israel] shall not *enter* into my rest. 18
19. they were not able to *enter* in because of unbelief
4. 3. For we which have believed do *enter* into that rest
—They shall not *enter* into my rest. 5
6. it remaineth that some should *enter* thereinto—failed to ²*enter* in because of disobedience
11. Let us therefore give diligence to *enter* into that rest
10. 19. boldness to *enter* into the holy place by the blood
Rev. 15. 8. none was able to *enter* into the temple
21. 27. shall in no wise *enter* into anything unclean
22. 14. and may *enter* in by the gates into the city

Entered.—*A.V.* ¹*went.*

Mat. 8. 5. *entered* into Capernaum. *Mk.* 2. 1; *Lu.* 7. 1
9. 1. And he *entered* into a boat. 8. 23; *Mk.* 4. 1; 8. 10; *Lu.* 5. 3; *Jno.* 6. 17; 21. 3

ENTERING

Mat. 12. 4. how he [David] *entered* into the house of God, and did eat. *Mk.* 2. ¹²⁶
13. 2. great multitudes, so that he ¹*e.* into a boat, and sat
24. 38. until the day that Noah *e.* into the ark. *Lu.* 17. 27
27. 53. they ¹*e.* into the holy city [*Lu.* 6. 6; *Acts* 18. 19
Mk. 1. 21. sabbath day he *entered* into the synagogue. 3. 1:
5. 13. came out, and *entered* into the swine. *Lu.* 8. 33
6. 56. wheresoever he *entered,* into villages, or into cities
7. 17. And when he [Jesus] was *entered* into the house. 24
11. 11. And he *entered* into Jerusalem, into the temple
Lu. 1. 40. and [Mary] *entered* into the house of Zacharias
4. 38. and [Jesus] *entered* into the house of Simon
7. 44. I *entered* into thine house, thou gavest me no water
8. 30. Legion; for many devils were *entered* into him
9. 34. and they feared as they *entered* into the cloud
10. 38. he *entered* into a certain village. 9. 52: 17. 12
11. 52. ye *e.* not in yourselves, and them that were—ye
22. 3. And Satan *e.* into Judas. *Jno.* 13. 27 [hindered
10. when ye are *c.* into the city, there shall meet you a
24. 3. And they *entered* in, and found not the body [man
Jno. 4. 38. and ye are *entered* into their labour
6. 22. that Jesus ¹*e.* not with his disciples into the boat
18. 1. where was a garden, into the which he *entered*
15. Peter—¹*entered* in with Jesus into the court
33. Pilate therefore *entered* again into the palace
20. 5. linen clothes lying; yet ¹*entered* he [John] not in
8. Then ¹*entered* in therefore the other disciple also
Acts 3. 2. *entered* into the temple. 8: 5. 21
7. 45. with Joshua when they *entered* on the possession
9. 17. Ananias departed, and *entered* into the house
10. 24. And on the morrow they *entered* into Cæsarea
11. 8. nothing common or unclean—ever *e.*—my mouth
12. and we *entered* into the man's house
14. 1. ¹*entered* together into the synagogue. 19. ¹⁸
16. 40. and [Paul and Silas] *e.* into the house of Lydia
23. 16. he came and *entered* into the castle, and told Paul
25. 23. and they were *entered* into the place of hearing
28. 8. unto whom [Publius] Paul *entered* in, and prayed
Rom. 5. 12. through one man sin *entered* into the world
1 Cor. 2. 9. And which *entered* not into the heart of man
Heb. 4. 10. For he that is *e.* into his rest hath—also rested
6. 20. whither as a forerunner Jesus *entered* for us
9. 12. *entered* in once for all into the holy place
24. Christ *e.* not into a holy place made with hands
Jas. 5. 4. have *entered* into the ears of the Lord of Sabaoth
Rev. 11. 11. the breath of life from God *entered* into them
see came, enter, entering, failed, gone, went, went in.

Entereth.—*A.V.* ¹*goeth,* ²*presseth.*

Mat. 15. 11. Not that which ¹*e.* into the mouth defileth
Lu. 16. 16. every man ²*entereth* violently into it
Jno. 10. 1. He that *entereth* not by the door into the fold
2. But he that *entereth* in by the door is the shepherd
Heb. 9. 25. as the high priest *entereth* into the holy place
see entering, goeth.

Entering.—*A.V.* ¹*entered—eth,* ²*entrance.*

Mat. 23. 13. neither suffer ye them that are *e.* *Lu.* 11. 52
Mk. 4. 19. the lusts of other things *e.* in, choke the word
8. 13. and again *entering* into the boat departed
16. 5. And *e.* into the tomb, they saw a young man
Acts 8. 3. Saul laid waste the church, *e.* into every house
21. 8. [Paul's company] ¹*e.* into the house of Philip
1 Th. 1. 9. what manner of *entering* in we had unto you
2. 1. yourselves, brethren, know our ²*entering* in
Heb. 4. 1. a promise being left of *entering* into his rest
6. 19. stedfast and ¹*e.* into that which is within the veil
see embarking, enter.

ENTERTAIN

Entertain *A V.—see love.*

Entertained.—*A.V.* ¹*lodged.*
Acts. 28. 7. Publius—received us, and ¹*entertained* us
Heb. 13. 2. some have *entertained* angels unawares

Entice—d.—*A V.* ¹*allure.*
Jas. 1. 14. drawn away by his own lust, and *enticed*
2 *Pet.* 2. 18. they ¹*entice* in the lusts of the flesh

Enticing.—*A. V.* ¹*beguiling.*
2 *Pet.* 2. 14. eyes full of adultery—¹*e.* unstedfast souls
see persuasiveness.

Entire.
Jas. 1. 4. that ye may be perfect and *entire*

Entrance.
2 *Pet.* 1. 11. unto you the *e.* into the eternal kingdom
see entering.

Entreat—ed.—*A.V* ¹*suffer adversity,* ²*suffer affliction,* ³*tormented,* ⁴*use.*
Acts 7. 19. with our race, and evil *entreated* our fathers
14. 5. to ⁴*entreat* them shamefully, and to stone them
Heb. 11. 25. choosing rather to be evil ²*entreated* [Moses]
37. being destitute, afflicted, evil ³*entreated*
13. 3. them that are evil ¹*entreated.*
see intreat—ed.

Envies.
1 *Pet.* 2. 1. hypocrisies, and *envies,* and all evil speakings

Envieth.
1 *Cor.* 13. 4. love *envieth* not ; love vaunteth not itself

Envy.
Mat. 27. 18. for *envy* they had delivered him up. *Mk.* 15. 10
Rom. 1. 29. full of *envy,* murder, strife, deceit, maligulty
Phil. 1. 15. Some indeed preach Christ even of *e.* and strife
1 *Tim.* 6. 4. whereof cometh *envy,* strife, railings
Tit. 3. 3. in malice and *envy,* hateful, hating one another
see envying, jealousy.

Envying—s.—*A.V.* ¹*envy.*
Gal. 5. 21. *e.,* drunkenness, revellings, and such like
26. provoking one another, *envying* one another
Jas. 4. 5. which he made to dwell in us long unto ¹*envying* ?
see jealousy, jealousies.

Ephphatha.
Mk. 7. 34. saith unto him, *Ephphatha,* that is, Be opened

Epileptic.—*A.V.* ¹*lunatick.*
Mat. 4. 24. possessed with devils, and ¹*epileptic*
17. 15. have mercy on my son: for he is ¹*epileptic*

Epistle.—*A.V.* ¹*letter.*
Acts 15. 30. the multitude together, they delivered the *e.*
Rom. 16. 22. I Tertius, who write the *epistle,* salute you
1 *Cor.* 5. 9. I wrote unto you in my *e* to have no company
2 *Cor.* 3. 2. Ye are our *epistle,* written in our hearts
3. being made manifest that ye are an *epistle* of Christ
7. 8. made you sorry with my ¹*e.*—that *e.* made you sorry
Col. 4. 16. when this *e.* hath been read—ye also read the *e.*
1 *Th.* 5. 27. that this *epistle* be read unto all the brethren
2 *Th.* 2. 2. by spirit, or by word, or by ¹*epistle* as from us
15. taught, whether by word, or by *epistle* of ours
3. 14. And if any man obeyeth not our word by this *e.*
17. mine own hand, which is the token in every *epistle*
2 *Pet.* 3. 1. the second *epistle* that I write unto you
see letter.

15

ESCHEWED

Epistles.
2 *Cor.* 3. 1. need we, as do some, *epistles* of commendation
2 *Pet.* 3. 16. as also in all his *epistles,* speaking in them

Equal.
Mat. 20. 12. thou hast made them *equal* unto us
Lu. 20. 36. for they are *equal* unto the angels
Jno. 5. 18. his own Father, making himself *equal* with God
Col. 4. 1. unto your servants that which is just and *equal*
Rev. 21. 16. the breadth and the height thereof are *equal*
see equality.

Equality.—*A. V.* ¹*equal.*
2 *Cor.* 8. 14. but by *equality*—there may be *equality*
Phil. 2. 6. not a prize to be on an ¹*equality* with God

Equals *A.V.— see own (age).*

Err.
Mat. 22. 29. Ye do *err,* not knowing the scriptures. *Mk.*
Heb. 3. 10. They do alway *err* in their heart [12. 24, 27
Jas. 5. 19. brethren, if any among you do *err* from the
see deceived.

Erred—ing.—*A.V.* ¹*out of the way.*
1 *Tim.* 6. 21. professing have *erred* concerning the faith
2 *Tim.* 2. 18. men who concerning the truth have *erred*
Heb. 5. 2. bear gently with the ignorant and ¹*erring*
see astray.

Error.—*A.V.* ¹*deceit,* ²*deceive,* ³*delusion.*
Mat. 27. 64. the last *error* will be worse than the first
Rom. 1. 27. that recompense of their *error* which was due
Eph. 4. 14. in craftiness, after the wiles of ²*error*
1 *Th.* 2. 3 For our exhortation is not of ¹*error*
2 *Th.* 2. 11. God sendeth them a working of ³*error*
Jas. 5. 20. which converteth a sinner from the *e.* of his way
2 *Pet* 2. 18. are just escaping from them that live in *error*
3. 17. being carried away with the *error* of the wicked
1 *Jno.* 4. 6 the spirit of truth, and the spirit of *error*
Jude 11. ran riotously in the *error* of Balaam for hire

Errors.
Heb. 9. 7. offereth for himself, and for the *errors* of the

Escape.
Mat. 23. 33. how shall ye *escape* the judgement of hell ?
Lu. 21. 36. that ye may prevail to *escape* all these things
Acts 27. 42. lest any of them should swim out, and *escape*
Rom. 2. 3. that thou shalt *escape* the judgement of God ?
1 *Cor.* 10 13. will with the temptation make also the way
1 *Th.* 5. 3. and they shall in no wise *escape*   [of *escape*
Heb. 2. 3. how shall we *escape,* if we neglect so great
12. 25. much more shall not we *escape,* who turn away

Escaped.—*A.V.* ¹*fled.*
Acts 16. 27. supposing that the prisoners had ¹*escaped*
27. 44. that they all *escaped* safe to the land
28. 1. And when we were *escaped,* then we knew
4. whom, though he hath *escaped* from the sea
2 *Cor.* 11. 33. in a basket by the wall, and *e.* his hands
Heb. 11. 34. *escaped* the edge of the sword
12. 25. For if they *escaped* not, when they refused
2 *Pet.* 1. 4. having *e.* from the corruption that is in the
2. 20. after they have *e.* the defilements of the world
see escaping, went forth.

Escaping.—*A. V.* ¹*escaped.*
2 *Pet.* 2. 18. those who are just ¹*e.* from them that live in

Eschewed—eth *A.V.—see turn (away).*

105

ESPECIALLY

Especially.—*A.V.* ¹*chiefly.*
Acts 26. 3. e. because thou art expert in all customs
Gal. 6. 10. e. toward them that are of the household of
Phil. 4. 22. ¹*especially* they that are of Cæsar's household
1 *Tim.* 5. 17. e. those who labour in the word and in teaching
2 *Tim.* 4. 13. and the books, *especially* the parchments
  see specially.

Espoused.
2 *Cor.* 11. 2. I *espoused* you to one husband, that I might
  see betrothed.

Establish.
Rom. 3. 31. God forbid: nay, we *establish* the law
  10. 3. righteousness, and seeking to *establish* their own
1 *Th.* 3. 2. to *establish* you, and to comfort you
Heb. 10. 9. taketh away the first, that he may e. the second
  see stablish.

Established.
Mat. 18. 16. at the mouth of two witnesses or three every word may be *established.* 2 *Cor.* 13. 1
Rom. 1. 11. some spiritual gift, to the end ye may be *e.*
2 *Pet.* 1. 12. and are *e.* in the truth which is with you
  see enacted, stablished, strengthened.

Estate.—*A.V.* ¹*exalted.*
Mk. 15. 43. a councillor of honourable *estate*
Lu. 1. 48. looked upon the low *estate* of his handmaiden
Acts. 22. 5. doth bear me witness, and all the e. of the elders
Col. 4. 8. that ye may know our *e.*, and that he may comfort
Jas. 1. 9. the brother of low degree glory in his high ¹*e.*
  see principality.

Estates *A.V.*—*see men.*

Esteem.
1 *Th.* 5. 13. and to *esteem* them exceeding highly in love
  see counting.

Esteemed—**ing** *A.V.*—*see account, accounting, exalted.*

Esteemeth.
Rom. 14. 5. One man *e.* one day—another *e.* every day alike
  see accounteth.

Eternal.—*A.V.* ¹*everlasting,* ²*world began.*
Mat. 18. 8. cast into the ¹*eternal* fire. 25. ¹41
  25. 46. these shall go away into ¹*eternal* punishment
Mk. 3. 29. never forgiveness, but is guilty of an *eternal* sin
Lu. 16. 9. they may receive you into the ¹*e.* tabernacles
Rom. 16. 25. the mystery—kept in silence through times ²*e.*
  26. according to the commandment of the ¹*eternal* God
2 *Cor.* 4. 17. more exceedingly an *eternal* weight of glory
  18. the things which are not seen are *eternal*
Eph. 3. 11. according to the *e.* purpose which he purposed
2 *Th.* 1. 9. suffer punishment, even ¹*eternal* destruction
  2. 16. loved us and gave us ¹*e.* comfort and good hope
1 *Tim.* 1. 17. Now unto the King *eternal,* incorruptible
  6. 16. to whom be honour and power ¹*eternal*
2 *Tim.* 1. 9. given us in Christ Jesus before times ²*eternal*
  2. 10. which is in Christ Jesus with *eternal* glory
Tit. 1. 2. God, who cannot lie, promised before times ²*e.*
Heb. 5. 9. them that obey him the author of *e.* salvation
  6. 2. resurrection of the dead, and of *eternal* judgement
  9. 12. the holy place, having obtained *eternal* redemption
  14. who through the *eternal* Spirit offered himself
  15. may receive the promise of the *eternal* inheritance
1 *Pet.* 5. 10. who called you unto his *e.* glory in Christ
2 *Pet.* 1. 11. the entrance into the ¹*eternal* kingdom
Jude 7. suffering the punishment of *eternal* fire
Rev. 14. 6. having an ¹*eternal* gospel to proclaim
  see covenant, everlasting.

EVEN

Eternal *life.*—*A.V.* ¹*everlasting life.*
Mat. 19. 16. thing shall I do, that I may have *eternal life*?
  29. a hundredfold, and shall inherit ¹*eternal life*
  25. 46. eternal punishment: but the righteous into *e. life*
Mk. 10. 30. and in the world to come *e. life. Lu.* 18. ¹30
Lu. 10. 25. what shall I do to inherit *e. l.* ? 18. 18 : *Mk.* 10. 17
Jno. 3. 15. believeth may in him have *eternal life*
  16. should not perish, but have ¹*eternal life*
  36. That believeth on the Son hath ¹*e. life.* 6. ¹40
  4. 14. a well of water springing up unto ¹*eternal life*
  36. and gathereth fruit unto *life eternal*
  5. 24. him that sent me, hath ¹*eternal life* ʳhave *e. life*
  39. the scriptures, because ye think that in them ye
  6. 27. but for the meat which abideth unto ¹*eternal life*
  47. He that believeth hath ¹*eternal life*
  54. and drinketh my blood hath *eternal life*
  68. shall we go? thou hast the words of *eternal life*
  10. 28. I give unto them *e. life*; and they shall never perish
  12. 25. life in this world shall keep it until *life eternal*
  50. I know that his commandment is ¹*life eternal*
  17. 2. to them he should give *eternal life*
  3. And this is *life eternal,* that they should know thee
Acts 13. 46. judge yourselves unworthy of ¹*eternal life*
  48. as many as were ordained to *eternal life* believed
Rom. 2. 7. glory and honour and incorruption, *eternal life*
  5. 21. grace reign through righteousness unto *eternal life*
  6. 22. fruit unto sanctification, and the end ¹*eternal life*
  23. gift of God is *eternal life* in Christ Jesus our Lord
Gal. 6. 8. shall of the Spirit reap ¹*eternal life*
1 *Tim.* 1. 16. should hereafter believe on him unto ¹*e. life*
  6. 12. lay hold on the *life eternal,* whereunto thou wast
Tit. 1. 2. hope of *eternal life,* which God, who cannot lie
  3. 7. heirs according to the hope of *eternal life*
1 *Jno.* 1. 2. declare unto you the life, the *eternal life*
  2. 25. which he promised us, even the *life eternal*
  3. 15. no murderer hath *eternal life* abiding in him
  5. 11. witness is this, that God gave unto us *eternal life*
  13. that ye may know that ye have *eternal life*
  20. This is the true God, and *eternal life*
Jude 21. the mercy of our Lord Jesus Christ unto *e. life*

Eunuch—**s.**
Mat. 19. 12. are *eunuchs,* which were so born—*e.,* which were made *e.* by men—*e.,* which made themselves *e.*
Acts 8. 27. a *eunuch* of great authority under Candace
  34. And the *eunuch* answered Philip, and said
  36. and the *eunuch* saith, Behold, here is water
  38. down into the water, both Philip and the *eunuch*
  39. caught away Philip; and the *e.* saw him no more

Evangelist—**s.**
Acts 21. 8. entering into the house of Philip the *evangelist*
Eph. 4. 11. and some, *e.*; and some, pastors and teachers
2 *Tim.* 4. 5. suffer hardship, do the work of an *evangelist*

Even.
Mat. 24. 36. knoweth no one, not *even* the angels
Rom. 8. 23. *even* we ourselves groan within ourselves
1 *Cor.* 11. 14. Doth not *even* nature itself teach you
  14. 7. *Even* things without life, giving a voice
  15. 24. shall deliver up the kingdom to God, *e.* the Father
2 *Cor.* 10. 13. to us as a measure, to reach *even* unto you
Phil. 2. 8. humbled himself, becoming obedient *e.* unto death

Even.—*A.V.* ¹*evening.*
Mat. 8. 16. when *e.* was come. 14. ¹15; 20. 8; 26. 20; 27. 57;
  Mk. 4. 35; 6. 47; 15. 42
  14. 23. and when ¹*even* was come, he was there alone
Mk. 1. 32. And at *even,* when the sun did set, they brought
  13. 35. whether at *e.,* or at midnight, or at cockcrowing
  see evening.

EVENING

Evening.—*A.V.* ¹*even.*
Mat. 16. 2. When it is e., ye say, It will be fair weather
Mk. 11. 19. every ¹*evening* he went forth out of the city
  14. 17. And when it was e. he cometh with the twelve
Lu. 24. 29. Abide with us: for it is toward *evening*
Jno. 6. 16. And when ¹*evening* came, his disciples went down
  20. 19. When therefore it was *evening*, on that day
Acts 28. 23. from the prophets, from morning till *evening*
  see even.

Eventide.
Mk. 11. 11. it being now e., he went out unto Bethany
Acts 4. 3. unto the morrow: for it was now *eventide*

Ever.—*A.V.* ¹*any time*, ²*old time.*
Mat. 24. 21. until now, no, nor *ever* shall be
Lu. 15. 31. Son, thou art *ever* with me, and all that is mine
Jno. 4. 29. which told me all things that *ever* I did. 39
  6. 51. eat of this bread, he shall live for *ever*
Acts 15. 8. nothing common or unclean hath ¹e. entered
1 *Cor.* 9. 7. What soldier ¹*ever* serveth at his own charges?
1 *Th.* 4. 17. so shall we *ever* be with the Lord
2 *Pet.* 1. 21. no prophecy ²*ever* came by the will of man
  see wont.

For Ever and ever.—*A.V.* ¹*world without end.*
Gal. 1. 5. be the glory *for ever and ever.* *Phil.* 4. 20:
  1 *Tim.* 1. 17; 2 *Tim.* 4. 18; *Heb.* 13. 21
Eph. 3. 21. unto all generations *for* ¹*ever and ever*
Heb. 1. 8. Thy throne, O God, is *for ever and ever* [5. 13
1 *Pet.* 4. 11. dominion *for ever and ever.* 5. 11; *Rev.* 1. 6;
Rev. 4. 9. to him that liveth *for ever and* e. 10; 10. 6; 15. 7
  7. 12. and might, be unto our God *for ever and ever*
  11. 15. and he shall reign *for ever and ever*
  14. 11. smoke of their torment goeth up *for ever and ever*
  19. 3. And her smoke goeth up *for ever and ever*
  20. 10. tormented day and night *for ever and ever*
  22. 5. and they shall reign *for ever and ever*

Everlasting.—*A.V.* ¹*eternal (life).*
Rom. 1. 20. even his ¹*everlasting* power and divinity
Jude 6. he hath kept in *everlasting* bonds under darkness
  see eternal.

Everlasting life *A.V.*—*see eternal (life).*

Evermore—*A.V.* ¹*world standeth.*
1 *Cor.* 6. 13. I will eat no flesh for ¹*evermore*
Rev. 1. 18. I am alive for *evermore*

Every—*A.V.* ¹*all manner.*
Mat. 12. 31. ¹*Every* sin and blasphemy shall be forgiven

Evidence *A.V.*—*see proving.*

Evident.—*A.V.* ¹*manifest*, ²*open beforehand.*
1 *Cor.* 15. 27. it is ¹e. that he is excepted who did subject
Gal. 3. 11. is justified by the law in the sight of God, is e.
Phil. 1. 28. which is for them an *evident* token of perdition
1 *Tim.* 5. 24. Some men's sins are ²*evident*
  25. also there are good works that are ¹*evident*
2 *Tim.* 3. 9. their folly shall be ¹*evident* unto all men
Heb. 7. 14. it is e. that our Lord hath sprung out of Judah
  15. is yet more abundantly *evident*, if after the likeness

Evidently *A.V.*—*see openly.*

Evil.—*A.V.* ¹*adversity*, ²*affliction*, ³*curseth*, ⁴*tormented*,
  ⁵*wicked.*
Mat. 5. 11. say all manner of *evil* against you falsely
  5. 39. but I say unto you, Resist not him that is *evil*

EVIL

Mat. 6. 23. But if thine eye be *evil*, thy whole body
  34. Sufficient unto the day is the *evil* thereof
7. 11. If ye then, being *evil*, know how. *Lu.* 11. 13
  17. but the corrupt tree bringeth forth *evil* fruit
  18. A good tree cannot bring forth *evil* fruit
9. 4. Wherefore think ye *evil* in your hearts?
12. 34. how can ye, being *evil*, speak good things?
  35. e. man out of his e. treasure bringeth forth e. *Lu.* 6. 45
  39. An *evil* and adulterous generation. 16. ⁵4; *Lu.* 11. 29
  45. seven other spirits more ⁵e. than himself. *Lu.* 11. 526
15. 4. He that speaketh ³e. of father or mother. *Mk.* 7. ⁵10
  19. out of the heart come forth *evil* thoughts. *Mk.* 7. 21
20. 15. or is thine eye *evil*, because I am good?
24. 48. But if that *evil* servant shall say in his heart
27. 23. what *evil* hath he done? *Mk.* 15. 14; *Lu.* 23. 22
Mk. 7. 22. an *evil* eye, railing, pride, foolishness
9. 39. and be able quickly to speak *evil* of me
Lu. 6. 22. reproach you, and cast out your name as *evil*
  35. for he is kind toward the unthankful and *evil*
3. 19. rather than the light; for their works were *evil*
7. 7. I testify of it, that its works are *evil*
18. 23. If I have spoken *evil*, bear witness of the *evil*
Acts 7. 6. and entreat them *evil*, four hundred years
  19. with our race, and *evil* entreated our fathers
9. 13. how much e. he [Saul] did to thy saints at Jerusalem
14. 2. and made them *evil* affected against the brethren
19. 9. speaking *evil* of the Way before the multitude
23. 5. Thou shalt not speak *evil* of a ruler of thy people
9. We find no *evil* in this man [Paul]
Rom. 2. 9. upon every soul of man that worketh *evil*
7. 19. but the *evil* which I would not, that I practise
12. 17. Render to no man *evil* for *evil*
13. 3. are not a terror to the good work, but to the *evil*
4. which is *evil*, be afraid—for wrath to him that doeth e.
14. 16. Let not then your good be *evil* spoken of
20. howbeit it is e. for that man who eateth with offence
1 *Cor.* 10. 30. why am I *evil* spoken of for that for which
13. 5. [love] is not provoked, taketh not account of *evil*
15. 33. *Evil* company doth corrupt good manners
Gal. 1. 4. might deliver us out of this present *evil* world
Eph. 5. 16. redeeming the time, because the days are *evil*
6. 13. ye may be able to withstand in the *evil* day
Phil. 3. 2. Beware of the dogs, beware of the *evil* workers
Col. 1. 21. enemies in your mind in your ⁵*evil* works
3. 5. uncleanness, passion, *evil* desire, and covetousness
1 *Th.* 5. 15. See that none render unto any one *evil* for *evil*
22. abstain from every form of *evil*
1 *Tim.* 6. 4. envy, strife, railings, *evil* surmisings
6. 10. the love of money is a root of all kinds of *evil*
2 *Tim.* 3. 13. But *evil* men and impostors shall wax worse
4. 14. Alexander the coppersmith did me much *evil*
18. The Lord will deliver me from every *evil* work
Tit. 1. 12. Cretians are alway liars, *evil* beasts, idle gluttons
3. 8. speak *evil* of no man, not to be contentious
Heb. 3. 12. be in any one of you an *evil* heart of unbelief
10. 22. our hearts sprinkled from an *evil* conscience
11. 25. rather to be ²*evil* entreated with the people of God
37. being destitute, afflicted, ⁴*evil* entreated
13. 3. them that are *evil* entreated, as being yourselves
Jas. 2. 4. and become judges with *evil* thoughts?
3. 2. the tongue—a restless *evil*, it is full of deadly poison
4. 16. glory in your vauntings: all such glorying is *evil*
1 *Pet.* 2. 1. Putting away—envies, and all *evil* speakings
3. 9. not rendering *evil* for *evil*, or reviling for reviling
10. Let him refrain his tongue from *evil*
2 *Pet.* 2. 2. the way of the truth shall be *evil* spoken of
1 *Jno.* 3. 12. wherefore slew he him?—his works were *evil*
2 *Jno.* 11. giveth him greeting partaketh in his *evil* works

EVIL

3 *Jno.* 11. not that which is *e.*—doeth *e.* hath not seen God
Rev. 2. 2. patience, and that thou canst not bear *evil men*
see against, evil one, eye, ill, rail, railing.

Evil with good.

Mat. 5. 45. maketh his sun to rise on the *e.* and the *good*
Rom. 7. 21. to me who would do *good, evil* is present
12. 9. that which is *evil;* cleave to that which is *good*
21. Be not overcome of *evil*, but overcome *e.* with *good*
16. 19. I would have you wise unto that which is *good*, and simple unto that which is *evil*
Heb. 5. 14. their senses exercised to discern *good* and *evil*
1 *Pet.* 3. 11. let him turn away from *evil,* and do *good*
3 *Jno.* 11. imitate not that which is *e.*, but that which is *g.*

Evil one.—*A.V.* ¹*evil,* ²*wicked,* ³*wickedness,* ⁴*wicked one.*

Mat. 5. 37. whatsoever is more than these is of the ¹*evil one*
6. 13. but deliver us from the ¹*evil one*
13. 19. then cometh the ⁴*evil one*, and snatcheth away
38. the tares are the sons of the ⁴*evil one*
Jno. 17. 15. that thou shouldest keep them from the ¹*evil one*
Eph. 6. 16. quench all the fiery darts of the ²*evil one*
2 *Th.* 3. 3. stablish you, and guard you from the ¹*evil one*
1 *Jno.* 2. 13. because ye have overcome the ⁴*evil one*
3. 12. not as Cain was of the ⁴*e. one,* and slew his brother
5. 18. God keepeth him, and the ⁴*e. one* toucheth him not
19. and the whole world lieth in the ³*evil one*

Evil spirit—s.

Lu. 7. 21. cured—diseases and plagues and *evil spirits*
8. 2. certain women which had been healed of *evil spirits*
Acts 19. 12. and the *evil spirits* went out
13. to name over them which had the *evil s.* the name
15. And the *evil spirits* answered and said unto them
16. the man in whom the *evil spirit* was leaped on them

Evil thing—s.—*A.V.* ¹*evils.*

Mat. 12. 35. out of his evil treasure bringeth forth *e. things*
Mk. 7. 23. all these *evil things* proceed from within
Lu. 3. 19. and for all the ¹*evil things* which Herod had done
16. 25. thy good things, and Lazarus in like manner *e. t.*
Rom. 1. 30. haughty, boastful, inventors of *evil things*
1 *Cor.* 10. 6. the intent we should not lust after *evil things*
Tit. 2. 8. having no *evil thing* to say of us

Evil-doer—s.—*A.V.* ¹*malefactor.*

Jno. 18. 30. If this man were not an ¹*evil-doer*
1 *Pet.* 2. 12. wherein they speak against you as *evil-doers*
14. as sent by him for vengeance on *evil-doers*
4. 15. as a murderer, or a thief, or an *evil-doer*
see malefactor.

Evil-doing.

1 *Pet.* 3. 17. that ye suffer for well-doing than for *evil-doing*
see wrong-doing.

Evils.—*A.V.* ¹*worthy deeds.*

Acts 24. 12. by thy providence ¹*evils* are corrected
see evil things.

Exact—ed.—*A.V.* ¹*accuse,* ²*perfect,* ³*taken.*

Lu. 3. 14. neither ¹*exact* anything wrongfully
19. 8. if I have wrongfully ³*exacted* aught of any man
Acts 24. 22. Felix, having more ²*exact* knowledge
see extort.

Exactly.—*A.V.* ¹*perfectly.*

Acts 23. 15. though ye would judge his case more ¹*e.* ¹20

Exalt.—*A.V.* ¹*exalted,* ²*lift up.*

Mat. 23. 12. whosoever shall *e.* himself shall be humbled

EXCEEDING

Acts 5. 31. Him did God ¹*exalt* with his right hand to be
Jas. 4. 10. sight of the Lord, and he shall ²*exalt* you
1 *Pet.* 5. 6. that he may *exalt* you in due time
see exalteth.

Exalted.—*A.V.* ¹*exalteth,* ²*highly esteemed.*

Mat. 11. 23. shalt thou be *exalted* unto heaven? *Lu.* 10. 15
23. 12. shall humble himself shall be *e. Lu.* 14. 11; 18. 14
Lu. 1. 52. And hath *exalted* them of low degree
16. 15. that which is ²*e.* among men is an abomination
Acts 2. 23. Being therefore by the right hand of God *e.*
13. 17. and *exalted* the people when they sojourned
2 *Cor.* 10. 5. every high thing—¹*e.* against the knowledge of
11. 7. abasing myself that ye might be *exalted* [God
12. 7. that I should not be *exalted* overmuch
Phil. 2. 9. Wherefore also God highly *exalted* him
see estate, exalt.

Exalteth.—*A.V.* ¹*exalt.*

Lu. 14. 11. every one that *e.* himself shall be humbled. 18. 14
2 *Cor.* 11. 20. if he ¹*exalteth* himself, if he smiteth you
2 *Th.* 2. 4. that opposeth and *e.* himself against all that is
see exalted.

Examination.

Acts 25. 26. that, after *e.* had, I may have somewhat to write

Examine.—*A.V.* ¹*examined.*

Acts 22. 29. They then which were about to ¹*examine* him
1 *Cor.* 9. 3. My defence to them that *examine* me is this
see prove, try.

Examined.

Lu. 23. 14. behold, I, having *examined* him before you
Acts 4. 9. if we this day are *e.* concerning a good deed
12. 19. he *examined* the guards, and commanded
22. 24. bidding that he should be *examined* by scourging
28. 18. when they had *e.* me, desired to set me at liberty
see examine.

Examining.—*A.V.* ¹*searched.*

Acts 17. 11. ¹*examining* the scriptures daily
24. 8. by *examining* him thyself, to take knowledge

Example—s.—*A.V.* ¹*ensample—s,* ²*shewed.*

Mat. 1. 19. not willing to make her a public *example*
Jno. 13. 15. For I have given you an *example*
Acts 20. 35. In all things I gave you an ²*example*
1 *Cor.* 10. 6. Now these things were our *examples*
11. things happened unto them by way of ¹*example*
Heb. 4. 11. fall after the same *example* of disobedience
Jas. 5. 10. an *example* of suffering and of patience [steps
1 *Pet.* 2. 21. leaving you an *e.,* that ye should follow his
2 *Pet.* 2. 6. made them an ¹*e.* unto those that should live
Jude 7. are set forth as an *e.,* suffering the punishment
see copy, ensample.

Exceed.

Mat. 5. 20. except your righteousness shall *e.* the righteous-
2 *Cor.* 3. 9. ministration of righteousness *e.* in glory [ness

Exceeding.—*A.V.* ¹*abundance.*

Matt. 2. 10. they rejoiced with *exceeding* great joy
16. was *exceeding* wroth, and sent forth, and slow
4. 8. taketh him unto an *exceeding* high mountain
5. 12. Rejoice, and be *exceeding* glad: for great is your
8. 28. coming forth out of the tombs, *exceeding* fierce
17. 23. And they [disciples] were *exceeding* sorry
26. 22. And they were *exceeding* sorrowful

EXCEEDING

Mat. 26. 38. My soul is *exceeding* sorrowful. *Mk.* 14. 34
Mk. 6. 26. And the king [Herod] was *exceeding* sorry
  9. 3. his garments became glistering, *exceeding* white
Lu. 23. 8. when Herod saw Jesus, he was *exceeding* glad
Acts 7. 20. Moses was born, and was *exceeding* fair
Rom. 7. 13. through the commandment sin might become *e.*
2 Cor. 9. 14. by reason of the *e.* grace of God in you ¦ sinful
  12. 7. by reason of the ¹*e.* greatness of the revelations
Eph. 1. 19. what the *exceeding* greatness of his power
  2. 7. he might shew the *exceeding* riches of his grace
  3. 20. unto him that is able to do *exceeding* abundantly
1 Pet. 4. 13. ye may rejoice with *exceeding* joy
2 Pet. 1. 4. unto us his precious and *exceeding* great promises
Jude 24. before the presence of his glory—in *exceeding* joy
Rev. 16. 21. for the plague thereof is *exceeding* great
    see exceedingly, overflow.

Exceedingly.—*A.V.* ¹*abundantly,* ²*exceeding,* ³*greatly,*
   ⁴*more,* ⁵*much,* ⁶*out of measure,* ⁷*rather.*
Mat. 19. 25. they were astonished ⁶*exceedingly,* saying
  27. 23. cried out ⁴*e.,* saying, Let him be crucified. *Mk.* 15
  54. feared ³*e.,* saying, Truly this was the Son of God ¦ 14
Mk. 4. 41. And they feared *e.,* and said one to another
  10. 26. And they were astonished ⁶*exceedingly,* saying
Acts 26. 7. number of the disciples multiplied—³*exceedingly*
  16. 20. being Jews, do *exceedingly* trouble our city
  26. 11. and being *e.* mad against them, I persecuted them
  27. 18. And as we laboured *exceedingly* with the storm
Rom. 5. 20. grace did abound more ⁵*exceedingly*
2 Cor. 1. 8. that we were weighed down ⁶*exceedingly*
  4. 17. worketh for us more and more ³*exceedingly*
  7. 13. we joyed the more *exceedingly* for the joy of Titus
Gal. 1. 14. being more *exceedingly* zealous for the traditions
1 Th. 2. 17. endeavoured the more ¹*e.* to see your face
  3. 10. praying *exceedingly* that we may see your face
2 Th. 1. 3. for that your faith groweth *exceedingly*
1 Tim. 1. 14. grace of our Lord abounded ²*e.* with faith
Heb. 12. 21. Moses said, I *exceedingly* fear and quake
  13. 19. I exhort you the more ⁷*exceedingly* to do this

Excel *A.V.—see abound.*

Excellency—ies.—*A.V.* ¹*praises.*
1 Cor. 2. 1. came not with *excellency* of speech or of wisdom
Phil. 3. 8. for the *e.* of the knowledge of Christ Jesus
1 Pet. 2. 9. that ye may shew forth the ¹*excellencies* of him
    see greatness.

Excellent.—*A.V.* ¹*noble.*
Lu. 1. 3. write unto thee in order, most *e.* Theophilus
Acts 23. 26. Claudius Lysias unto the most *e.* governor Felix
  24. 3. most ¹*excellent* Felix, with all thankfulness
  26. 25. But Paul saith, I am not mad, most ¹*e.* Festus
Rom. 2. 18. approvest the things that are *e.,* being instructed
1 Cor. 12. 13. a still more *excellent* way shew I unto you
Phil. 1. 10. that ye may approve the things that are *excellent*
Heb. 1. 4. hath inherited a more *excellent* name than they
  8. 6. now hath he obtained a ministry the more *excellent*
  11. 4. Abel offered unto God a more *excellent* sacrifice
2 Pet. 1. 17. came such a voice to him from the *e.* glory

Excelleth *A.V.—see surpasseth.*

Except.
Mat. 5. 20. *except* your righteousness shall exceed the
  12. 29. spoil his goods, *e.* he first bind the strong man ?
  18. 3. *E.* ye turn, and become as little children [*Mk.* 3. 27
  19. 9. shall put away his wife, *except* for fornication
  24. 22. and *e.* those days had been shortened. *Mk.* 13. 20
  26. 42. O my Father—*except* I drink it, thy will be done
Mk. 7. 3. *except* they wash their hands diligently. 4
Lu. 9. 13. five loaves and two fishes; *except* we should go

EXERCISE

Lu. 13. 3. *e.* ye repent, ye shall all in like manner perish. 5
Jno. 3. 2. do these signs that thou doest, *e.* God be with him
  3. Jesus answered—*Except* a man be born anew
  5. *E.* a man be born of water and the Spirit ¦given him
  27. John—said, A man can receive nothing, *e.* it have been
  4. 48. *Except* ye see signs—ye will in no wise believe
  6. 44. No man can come to me, *e.* the Father—draw him
  53. *Except* ye eat the flesh of the Son of man and drink
  65. no man can come unto me, *e.* it be given unto him
  12. 24. *Except* a grain of wheat fall into the earth and die
  15. 4. branch cannot bear fruit—*e.* it abide in the vine
  19. 11. no power against me, *e.* it were given thee [Pilate]
  20. 25. *Except* I shall see in his hands the print
Acts 8. 1. they were all scattered abroad—*e.* the apostles
  31. [eunuch] said, How can I, *e.* some one shall guide me ?
  15. 1. *E.* ye be circumcised after the custom of Moses
  24. 21. *e.* it be for this one voice, that I [Paul] cried
  26. 29. might become such as I [Paul] am, *e.* these bonds
  27. 31. Paul said—*Except* these abide in the ship
Rom. 7. 7. I had not known coveting, *e.* the law had said
  10. 15. how shall they preach, *except* they be sent ? [pret
1 Cor. 14. 5. he that speaketh with tongues, *e.* he inter-
  15. 36. thyself sowest is not quickened, *except* it die
2 Cor. 12. 13. *except* it be that I—was not a burden to you ?
2 Th. 2. 3. it will not be, *except* the falling away come first
2 Tim. 2. 5. not crowned, *e.* he have contended lawfully
Rev. 2. 5. move thy candlestick out of its place, *e.* thou
  22. into great tribulation, *except* they repent [repent

Excepted.
1 Cor. 15. 27. he is *e.* who did subject all things unto him

Excess.
Mat. 23. 25. within they are full from extortion and *excess*
1 Pet. 4. 4. ye run not with them into the same *excess* of riot
    see riot, winebibbings.

Exchange—d.—*A.V.* ¹*changed.*
Mat. 16. 26. shall a man give in *e.* for his life ? *Mk.* 8. 37
Rom. 1. 25. for that they ¹*e.* the truth of God for a lie

Exchangers *A.V.—see bankers.*

Exclude *A.V.—see shut.*

Excluded.
Rom. 3. 27. Where then is the glorying ? It is *excluded*

Excuse—d.—*A.V.* ¹*cloke,* ²*inexcusable.*
Lu. 14. 18. all—began to make *excuse*—have me *excused.* 19
Jno. 15. 22. but now they have no ¹*excuse* for their sin
Rom. 1. 20. that they may be without *excuse*
  2. 1. Wherefore thou art without ²*excuse,* O man
    see excusing.

Excusing.—*A.V.* ¹*excuse.*
Rom. 2. 15. accusing or else *excusing* them
2 Cor. 12. 19. think all this time that we are ¹*e.* ourselves

Execute—d.—*A.V.* ¹*make.*
Lu. 1. 8. while he executed the priest's office before God
Jno. 5. 27. gave him authority to *execute* judgement
Rom. 9. 28. the Lord will ¹*execute* his word upon the earth
Jude 15. to *execute* judgement upon all, and to convict all

Executioner *A.V.—see soldier.*

Exercise.
Mat. 20. 25. great ones, *e.* authority over them. *Mk.* 10. 42
Acts 24. 16. Herein do I also *e.* myself to have a conscience
1 Tim. 4. 7. And *exercise* thyself unto godliness
  8. for bodily *exercise* is profitable for a little

EXERCISED

Exercised—eth.
Heb. 5. 14. their senses *exercised* to discern good and evil
12. 11. becu *e.* thereby, even the fruit of righteousness
2 *Pet.* 2. 14. having a heart *exercised* in covetousness
Rev. 13. 12. And he *e.* all the authority of the first beast

Exercising.—A.V. ¹*taking.*
1 *Pet.* 5. 2. ¹*exercising* the oversight, not of constraint

Exhort.—A.V. ¹*beseech,* ²*comfort,* ³*intreat.*
Acts 27. 22. And now I *exhort* you to be of good cheer
1 *Th.* 4. 1. we beseech and *exhort* you in the Lord Jesus
10. we ¹*e.* you, brethren, that ye abound more and more
5. 11. Wherefore ²*e.* one another, and build each other up
14. we *exhort* you, brethren, admonish the disorderly
2 *Th.* 3. 12. such we command and *e.* in the Lord Jesus
1 *Tim.* 2. 1. I *e.* therefore, first of all, that supplications
5. 1. Rebuke not an elder, but ³*exhort* him as a father
6. 2. These things teach and *exhort*
2 *Tim.* 4. 2. *exhort,* with all longsuffering and teaching
Tit. 1. 9. able both to *exhort* in the sound doctrine
2, 6. younger men likewise *exhort* to be soberminded
9. *E.* servants to be in subjection to their own masters
15. speak and *exhort* and reprove with all authority
Heb. 3. 13. but *exhort* one another day by day
13. 19. I ¹*exhort* you the more exceedingly to do this
22. I ¹*e.* you, brethren, bear with the word of exhorta-
1 *Pet.* 5. 1. The elders therefore among you I *exhort* [tion
see entreat, exhorted, exhorting.

Exhortation—s.—A.V. ¹*consolation.*
Lu. 3. 18. many other *exhortations* therefore preached he
Acts 4. 36. Barnabas (which is, being interpreted, Son of ¹*e.*)
13. 15. if ye have any word of *exhortation* for the people
20. 2. and had given them much *exhortation* [Paul]
2 *Cor.* 8. 17. For indeed he [Titus] accepted our *exhortation*
1 *Th.* 2. 3. For our *exhortation* is not of error
1 *Tim.* 4. 13. give heed to reading, to *e.,* to teaching
Heb. 12. 5. ye have forgotten the *e.,* which reasoneth with
13. 22. brethren, bear with the word of *exhortation* [you
see comfort, consolation, exhortation.

Exhorted.—A.V. ¹*besought,* ²*desired,* ³*embraced,* ⁴*exhort.*
Acts 2. 40. he [Peter] testified, and ⁴*exhorted* them
11. 23. and he [Barnabas] *e.* them all, that with purpose
15. 32. *exhorted* the brethren with many words ¹ of heart
20. 1. Paul-sent for the disciples and ³*exhorted* them
2 *Cor.* 8. 6. insomuch that we ²*exhorted* Titus
12. 18. I ¹*exhorted* Titus, and I sent the brother with him
1 *Tim.* 1. 3. As I ¹*exhorted* thee to tarry at Ephesus
see exhorting.

Exhorteth.
Rom. 12. 8. or he that *exhorteth,* to his exhorting

Exhorting.—A.V. ¹*exhort,* ²*exhortation,* ³*exhorted.*
Acts 14. 22. *exhorting* them to continue in the faith
Rom. 12. 8. he that *exhorteth,* to his ²*exhorting*
1 *Th.* 2. 11. ³*exhorting* you, and encouraging you
Heb. 10. 25. *exhorting* one another; and so much the more
1 *Pet.*5.12. I have written unto you briefly, *e.,* and testifying
Jude 3. ¹*exhorting* you to contend earnestly for the faith
see encouraged.

Exorcists.
Acts 19. 13. strolling Jews, *e.,* took upon them to name

Expect.—A.V. ¹*look for.*
1 *Cor.* 16. 11. for I ¹*e.* him [Timothy] with the brethren

EXTORTIONER

Expectation.—A.V. ¹*looked,* ²*looking.*
Lu. 3. 15. And as the people were in *expectation*
21. 26. men fainting for fear, and for ²*e.* of the things
Acts 12. 11. and from all the *e.* of the people of the Jews
28. 6. when they were long in ¹*expectation*
Rom. 8. 19. For the earnest *expectation* of the creation
Phil. 1. 20. according to my earnest *expectation* and hope
Heb. 10. 27. but a certain fearful ²*expectation* of judgement

Expected—ing.—A.V. ¹*looked.*
Acts 3. 5. *expecting* to receive something from them
28. 6. they ¹*expected* that he [Paul] would have swollen
Heb. 10 13. *expecting* till his enemies be made the footstool

Expecteth.—A.V. ¹*looketh.*
Mat. 24. 50. the lord of that servant shall come in a day
when he ¹*expecteth* not. *Lu.* 12. ¹46

Expedient.—A.V. ¹*good.*
Mat. 19.10. is so with his wife, it is not ¹*expedient* to marry
Jno. 11. 50. it is *e.* for you that one man should die. 18. 14
16. 7. it is *expedient* for you that I go away
1 *Cor.* 6. 12. lawful for me; but not all things are *expedient*
2 *Cor.* 8. 10. for this is *expedient* for you, who were the first
12. 1. I must needs glory, though it is not *expedient*

Expelled A.V.—*see cast out.*

Experience.—A.V. ¹*unskilful.*
Heb. 5. 13. every one that partaketh of milk is without ¹*e.*
see probation.

Experiment A.V.—*see proving.*

Expert.
Acts 26. 3. because thou art *expert* in all customs

Expired A.V.—*see fulfilled, finished.*

Explain.—A.V. ¹*declare.*
Mat. 13. 36. ¹*Explain* unto us the parable of the tares

Expounded.
Mk. 4. 34. to his own disciples he *expounded* all things
Acts 11. 4. Peter began, and *e.* the matter unto them
18. 26. and *e.* unto him the way of God more carefully
28. 23. he *expounded* the matter, testifying the kingdom
see interpreted.

Express A.V.—*see very.*

Expressly.
1 *Tim.* 4. 1. the Spirit saith *expressly,* that in later times

Extort.—A.V. ¹*exact.*
Lu. 3. 13. ¹*E.* no more than that which is appointed you

Extortion.—A.V. ¹*covetousness,* ²*ravening.*
Mat. 23. 25. they are full from *extortion* and excess
Lu. 11. 39. your inward part is full of ²*e.* and wickedness
2 *Cor.* 9. 5. as a matter of bounty, and not of ¹*extortion*

Extortioner—s.
Lu. 18. 11. am not as the rest of men, *extortioners,* unjust
1 *Cor.* 5. 10. or with the covetous and *e.,* or with idolaters
11. a drunkard, or an *extortioner;* with such a one no
6.10. nor revilers, nor *e.,* shall inherit the kingdom of God

EYE

Eye.
Mat. 5. 29. if thy right *eye* causeth thee to stumble. 18. 9:
38. An *eye* for an *eye*, and a tooth for a tooth [*Mk.* 9. 47
6. 22. The lamp of the body is the *eye* : if therefore thine *eye* be single. *Lu.* 11. 43.
23. But if thine *eye* be evil, thy whole body. *Lu.* 11. 34
7. 3. mote that is in thy brother's *eye*—beam that is in thine own *eye* ? 5 : *Lu.* 6. 41, 42
4. Let me cast out the mote out of thine *eye*—beam is in thine own *eye* ? 5 : *Lu.* 6. 24
18. 9. enter into life with one *eye*, rather than. *Mk.* 9. 47
19. 24. to go through a needle's *eye*. *Mk.* 10. 25 : *Lu.* 18. 25
20. 15. or is thine *eye* evil, because I am good ?
Mk. 7. 22. an evil *eye*, railing, pride, foolishness
1 *Cor.* 2. 9. Things which *eye* saw not, and ear heard not
12. 16. Because I am not the *eye*, I am not of the body
17. If the whole body were an *eye*, where were the
21. the *eye* cannot say to the hand, I have no need of
15. 52. in a moment, in the twinkling of an *eye*
Rev. 1. 7. every *eye* shall see him, and they which pierced

Eyes.
Mat. 9. 29. Then touched he their *eyes.* 20. 34
30. And their *eyes* were opened
13. 15. their *e.* they have closed ; Lest haply they should perceive with their *eyes*. *Jno.* 12. 40 : *Acts* 28. 27
16. blessed are your *eyes*, for they see
17. 8. lifting up their *e.*, they saw no one, save Jesus
18. 9. having two *eyes* to be cast into the hell of fire. *Mk.*
20. 33. Lord, that our *eyes* may be opened [9. 47
21. 42. and it is marvellous in our *eyes* ? *Mk.* 12. 11
26. 43. for their *eyes* were heavy. *Mk.* 14. 40
Mk. 8. 18. Having *eyes*, see ye not ?
23. when he [Jesus] had spit on his *e.*, and laid his hands
25. Then again he laid his hands upon his *eyes*
Lu. 2. 30. For mine *eyes* have seen thy salvation
4. 20. the *eyes* of all in the synagogue were fastened
10. 23. Blessed are the *eyes* which see the things
16. 23. he [Dives] lifted up his *eyes*, being in torments
18. 13. would not lift up so much as his *e.* unto heaven
19. 42. but now they are hid from thine *eyes*
24. 16. their *eyes* were holden that they should not know him
31. their *eyes* were opened, and they knew him
Jno. 4. 35. Lift up your *eyes*, and look on the fields
6. 5. therefore lifting up his *eyes*. 11. 41 : 17. 1 : *Lu.* 6. 20
9. 7. and anointed his *eyes* with the clay. 15
10. How then were thine *eyes* opened ? 26
11. Jesus made clay, and anointed mine *eyes*
14. Jesus made the clay, and opened his *eyes*
17. sayest thou of him, in that he opened thine *eyes* ?
21. or who opened his *eyes*, we know not
30. whence he is, and yet he opened mine *eyes*
32. that any one opened the *eyes* of a man born blind
10. 21. can a devil open the *eyes* of the blind ?
11. 37. which opened the *eyes* of him that was blind
Acts 3. 4. Peter, fastening his *eyes* upon him [lame man]
9. 8. when his *eyes* were opened, he saw nothing
18. there fell from his *eyes* as it were scales
Acts 9. 40. And she opened her *e.* ; and when she saw Peter
11. 6. upon the which when I had fastened mine *eyes*
13. 9. Paul, filled with the Holy Ghost ; fastened his *eyes*
26. 18. to open their *eyes*, that they may turn
Rom. 3. 18 There is no fear of God before their *eyes*
11. 8. a spirit of stupor, *eyes* that they should not see
10. Let their *eyes* be darkened, that they may not see
Gal. 3. 1. before whose *eyes* Jesus Christ was openly set
4. 15. have plucked out your *eyes* and given them to me
Eph. 1. 18. having the *eyes* of your heart enlightened
Heb. 4. 13. before the *e.* of him with whom we have to to

FACE

1 *Pet.* 3. 12. For the *eyes* of the Lord are upon the righteous
2 *Pet.* 2. 14. having *eyes* full of adultery
1 *Jno.* 1. 1. that which we have seen with our *eyes*
2. 11. because the darkness hath blinded his *eyes*
16. lust of the *eyes*, and the vainglory of life
Rev. 1. 14. his *eyes* were as a flame of fire. 2. 18 : 19. 12
3. 18. and eyesalve to anoint thine *eyes*
4. 6. four living creatures full of *eyes*. 8
5. 6. and seven *eyes*, which are the seven Spirits of God
7. 17. God shall wipe away every tear from their *e.* 21. 4

Eyesalve.
Rev. 3. 18. and *eyesalve* to anoint thine eyes

Eyeservice.
Eph. 6. 6. not in the way of *eyeservice*. *Col.* 3. 22

Eyewitnesses.
Lu. 1. 2. from the beginning were *eyewitnesses*
2 *Pet.* 1. 16. but we were *eyewitnesses* of his majesty

F.

Fables.
1 *Tim.* 1. 4. to give heed to *fables* and endless genealogies
4. 7. But refuse profane and old wives' *fables*
2 *Tim.* 4. 4. from the truth, and turn aside unto *fables*
Tit. 1. 14. not giving heed to Jewish *fables*
2 *Pet.* 1. 16. For we did not follow cunningly devised *f.*

Face.—A.V. ¹bear, ²before, ³countenance, ⁴outward appearance, ⁵presence.
Mat. 6. 17. anoint thy head and wash thy *face*
11. 10. messenger before thy *face*. *Mk.* 1. 2. : *Lu.* 7. 27
17. 2. his [Jesus] *face* did shine as the sun
6. they fell on their *face*, and were sore afraid
18. 10. do always behold the *face* of my Father
26. 39. he went forward a little, and fell on his *face*
67. Then did they spit in his *face* and buffet him
Mk. 14. 65. began to spit on him, and to cover his *face*
Lu. 1. 76. For thou shalt go before the *face* of the Lord. 17
2. 31. thou hast prepared before the *face* of all peoples
5. 12. when he [leper] saw Jesus, he fell on his *face*
9. 51. stedfastly set his *face* to go to Jerusalem
52. and sent messengers before his *face*
53. his *face* was as though he were going to Jerusalem
10. 1. them two and two before his *face* into every city
12. 56. ye know how to interpret the *face* of the earth.
17. 16. fell upon his *face* at his feet [*Mat.* 16. 3
21. 35. all them that dwell on the *face* of all the earth
Jno. 11. 44. his *face* was bound about with a napkin
Acts 2. 25. I beheld the Lord always before my *face*
3. 13. delivered up, and denied before the ⁵*face* of Pilate
6. 15. saw his *face* as it had been the *face* of an angel
7. 45. God thrust out before the *face* of our fathers
17. 26. men for to dwell on all the *face* of the earth
20. 25. ye all³ shall see my *face* no more. 38
25. 16. that the accused have the accusers *face* to *face*
27. 15. the ship was caught and could not ¹*face* the wind
1 *Cor.* 13. 12. now we see in a mirror, darkly ; but then *f.* to *f.*
14. 25. he will fall down on his *face* and worship God
2 *Cor.* 3. 7. look—upon the *f.* of Moses for the glory of his ⁴*f.*
13. not as Moses, who put a veil upon his *face*
18. But we all, with unveiled *face* reflecting as a mirror
4. 6. the glory of God in the ²*face* of Jesus Christ
8. 24. Shew ye—unto them in the ²*face* of the churches
10. 7. Ye look at the things which are before your ⁴*face*

FACE.

2 Cor. 11. 20. ye bear with a man--if he smiteth you on the *f*.
Gal. 1. 22. unknown by *face* unto the churches of Judæa
2. 11. I resisted him [Cephas] to the *face*
Col. 2. 1. as many as have not seen my *face* in the flesh
1 Th. 2. 17. exceedingly to see your *face* with great desire
3. 10. praying exceedingly that we may see your *face*
2 Th. 1. 9. eternal destruction from the ²*face* of the Lord
Heb. 9. 24. now to appear before the ²*face* of God for us
Jas. 1. 23. a man beholding his natural *face* in a mirror
1 Pet. 3. 12. the *face* of the Lord is upon them that do evil
2 Jno. 12. I hope to come unto you, and to speak *face* to *f.*
3 Jno. 14. I hope shortly to see thee, and—speak *face* to *f.*
Rev. 4. 7. the third creature had a *face* as of a man
6. 16. and hide us from the *face* of him that sitteth
10. 1. his *face* was as the sun, and his feet as pillars of fire
12. 14. and half a time, from the *face* of the serpent
20. 11. from whose *face* the earth and the heaven fled
22. 4. and they shall see his *face* ; and his name shall be

Faces.

Mat. 6. 16. they disfigure their *faces*, that they may be seen
Lu. 24. 5. affrighted, and bowed down their *f.* to the earth
Rev. 7. 11. they fell before the throne on their *faces*
9. 7. and their *faces* were as men's *faces*
11. 16. fell upon their *faces*, and worshipped God

Faction—s.—*A.V.* ¹*contention*, ²*strife*—s.

2 Cor. 12. 20. there should be strife, jealousy, wraths, ²*f.*
Phil. 1. 17. the other proclaim Christ of ¹*faction*
2. 3. doing nothing through ²*f.* or through vainglory
Jas. 3. 14. bitter jealousy and ²*faction* in your heart
16. where jealousy and ²*faction* are, there is confusion

Factious.—*A.V.* ¹*contentious*.

Rom. 2. 8. them that are ¹*factious*, and obey not the truth

Fade—eth.

Jas. 1. 11. so also shall the rich man *fade* away
1 Pet. 1. 4. incorruptible and undefiled, and—*f.* not away
5. 4. receive the crown of glory that *fadeth* not away

Fail—ed.—*A.V.*—¹*entered not*, ²*leave*, ³*wanted*.

Lu. 16. 9. when it shall *fail* ; they may receive you
22. 32. supplication for thee, that thy faith *fail* not
Jno. 2. 3. when the wine ²*failed*, the mother of Jesus saith
Heb. 1. 12. thou art the same, And thy years shall not *fail*
4. 6. ¹*failed* to enter in because of disobedience
11. 32. for the time will *fail* me if I tell of Gideon
13. 5. himself hath said, I will in no wise ²*fail* thee
see fall, falleth.

Faileth.

Lu. 12. 33. a treasure in the heavens that *faileth* not
1 Cor. 13. 8. Love never *faileth* ; but whether there be

Failing.—*A.V.* ¹*darkened.*

Lu. 23. 45. the sun's light ¹*f.* : and the veil of the temple
see fainting.

Fain.

Lu. 15. 16. he would *fain* have filled with the husks
Acts 26. 28. thou wouldest *fain* make me a Christian
1 Th. 2. 18. because he would *fain* have come unto you
Philem. 13. whom I would *f.* have kept with me [Onesimus]

Faint.

Mat. 15. 32. away fasting, lest haply they *faint*. Mk. 8. 3.
Lu. 18. 1. that they ought always to pray, and not to *faint*
2 Cor. 4. 1. as we obtained mercy, we *faint* not
4. 16. Wherefore we *f.* not; but though our outward man

FAITH

Gal. 6. 9. in due season we shall reap, if we *faint* not
Eph. 3. 13. I ask that ye *faint* not at my tribulations
Heb. 12. 5. Nor *faint* when thou art reproved of him
see fainting.

Fainted *A.V.*—*see weary, distressed.*

Fainthearted.—*A.V.* ¹*feeble-minded.*

1 Th. 5. 14. encourage the ¹*fainthearted*, support the weak

Fainting.—*A.V.* ¹*failing*, ²*faint*.

Lu. 21. 26. men ¹*fainting* for fear, and for expectation
Heb. 12. 3. wax not weary, ²*fainting* in your souls

Fair.

Mat. 16. 2. It will be *fair* weather: for the heaven is red
Acts 7. 20. Moses was born, and was exceeding *fair*
Rom. 16. 18. by their smooth and *fair* speech they beguile
Gal. 6. 12. As many as desire to make a *fair* show in the

Faith.—*A.V.* ¹*believe*, ²*believeth*, ³*unbelief.*

Mat. 6. 30. O ye of little *faith ?* 8. 26 : 14. 31 : 16. 8 : Lu. 12. 28
8. 10. found so great *faith*, no, not in Israel. Lu. 7. 9
9. 2. Jesus seeing their *faith*. Mk. 2. 5 : Lu. 5. 20
22. thy *faith* hath made thee whole. Mk. 5. 34 : 10. 52 :
Lu. 8. 48 : 17. 19 : 18. 42
15. 28. O woman, great is thy *faith*
17. 20. Because of your little ²*faith*—If ye have *faith* as
a grain of mustard seed. Lu. 17. 6.
21. 21. If ye have *faith*, and doubt not, ye shall not only
23. 23. matters of the law—and mercy, and *faith*
Mk. 4. 40. Why are ye fearful ? have ye not yet *faith ?*
11. 22. Jesus—saith unto them, Have *faith* in God
Lu. 7. 50. Thy *faith* hath saved thee ; go in peace
17. 5. apostles said unto the Lord, Increase our *faith*
18. 8. Son of man cometh, shall he find *f.* on the earth ?
22. 32. made supplication for thee, that thy *f.* fail not
Acts 3. 16. And by *faith* in his name—the *faith* which is
through him hath given him this perfect soundness
6. 5. and they chose Stephen, a man full of *faith*
7. a great company of the priests were obedient to the *f.*
11. 24. [Barnabas] full of the Holy Ghost and of *faith*
13. 8. seeking to turn aside the proconsul from the *faith*
14. 9. seeing that he [cripple] had *f.* to be made whole
27. had opened a door of *faith* unto the Gentiles
20. 21. and *faith* toward our Lord Jesus Christ
24. 24. Paul, and heard him concerning the *faith* in Christ
Rom. 1. 5. obedience of *faith* among all the nations. 16. 25
17. righteousness of God by *faith* unto *faith* : as it is
written, But the righteous shall live by *faith*
3. 3. what if some were without ¹*f.* ? shall their want of ³*f.*
26. and the justifier of him that hath ²*faith* in Jesus
27. of works ? Nay : but by a law of *faith*
4. 5. his *faith* is reckoned for righteousness. 9
11. circumcision, a seal of the righteousness of the *f.*
12. walk in the steps of that *faith* of our father
13. heir of the world, but through the righteousness of *f.*
14. *f.* is made void, and the promise is made of none
16. it is of *faith*—which is of the *faith* of Abraham
9. 30. the righteousness which is of *faith*. 10. 6
10. 8. that is, the word of *faith*, which we preach
12. 3. God hath dealt to each man a measure of *faith*
6. prophesy according to the proportion of our *faith*
14. 2. One man hath ²*faith* to eat all things
22. The *faith* which thou hast, have thou—before God
23. not of *faith* ; and whatsoever is not of *faith* is sin
1 Cor. 12. 9. to another *faith*, in the same Spirit
13. 2. if I have all *faith*, so as to remove mountains
13. But now abideth *faith*, hope, love, these three

FAITH

2 Cor. 4. 13. having the same spirit of *f.*, according to that
Gal. 1. 23. preacheth the *f.* of which he once made havock
2. 20. I live in *faith*, the *faith* which is in the Son of God
3. 2. by the works of the law, or by the hearing of *faith?*
7. Know therefore that they which be of *faith.* 9
11. The righteous shall live by *faith*
12. the law is not of *faith;* but, He that doeth them
23. before *faith* came—shut up unto the *faith*
25. now that *f.* is come, we are no longer under a tutor
5. 6. nor uncircumcision; but *f.* working through love
6. 10. them that are of the household of the *faith*
Eph. 1. 15. having heard of the *faith* in the Lord Jesus
4. 5. one Lord, one *faith*, one baptism
13. till we all attain unto the unity of the *faith*
6. 16. withal taking up the shield of *faith*
23. Peace be to the brethren, and love with *faith*
Phil. 1. 25. for your progress and joy in the *faith*
27. with one soul striving for the *faith* of the gospel
1 Th. 1. 3. your work of *faith* and labour of love
5. 8. putting on the breastplate of *faith* and love
2 Th. 1. 4. your patience and *f.* in all your persecutions
11. desire of goodness and every work of *f.*, with power
3. 2. unreasonable and evil men; for all have not *faith*
1 Tim. 1. 5. a good conscience and *faith* unfeigned
14. grace of our Lord abounded exceedingly with *f.* and
19. holding *faith*—shipwreck concerning the *f.* [love
3. 9. holding the mystery of the *f.* in a pure conscience
4. 1. in later times some shall fall away from the *faith*
6. nourished in the words of the *faith* [believer
5. 8. he hath denied the *faith*, and is worse than an un-
12. because they have rejected their first *faith*
6. 10. reaching after have been led astray from the *faith*
11. follow after—godliness, *faith*, love, patience
12. Fight the good fight of the *faith*
21. some professing have erred concerning the *faith*
2 Tim. 1. 5. the unfeigned *faith* that is in thee
2. 18. and overthrow the *faith* of some
22. follow righteousness, *faith*, love, peace
3. 8. reprobate concerning the *faith*
10. follow my teaching, conduct, purpose, *faith*
4. 7. I have finished the course, I have kept the *faith*
Tit. 1. 1. according to the *faith* of God's elect
4. to Titus, my true child after a common *faith*
Philem. 5. hearing of thy love, and of the *f.* which thou hast
6. the fellowship of thy *faith* may become effectual
Heb. 4. 2. profit them, because they were not united by *f.*
6. 1. repentance from dead works, and of *f.* toward God
10. 22. draw near with a true heart in fulness of *faith*
39. but of them that have 1*f.* unto the saving of the soul
11. 1. Now *faith* is the assurance of things hoped for
6. without *faith* it is impossible to be well-pleasing
7. heir of the righteousness which is according to *faith*
12. 2. Jesus the author and perfecter of our *faith*
13. 7. considering the issue of their life, imitate their *f.*
Jas. 2. 1. hold not the *faith* of our Lord Jesus Christ
14. hath *f.*, but have not works? can that *f.* save him?
17. Even so *faith*, if it have not works, 20. 26
18. a man will say, Thou hast *faith*, and I have works:
shew me thy *faith*—will shew thee my *faith*
22. *f.* wrought with his works, and by works was *faith*
5. 15. the prayer of *faith* shall save him that is sick
2 Pet. 1. 1. that have obtained a like precious *faith*
1 Jno. 5. 4. that hath overcome the world, even our *faith*
Jude 3. exhorting you to contend earnestly for the *faith*
Rev. 2. 13. boldest fast my name, and didst not deny my *f.*
19. I know thy works, and thy love and *faith*
13. 10. Here is the patience and the *faith* of the saints
14. 12. keep the commandments of God, and the *f.* of Jesus
see belief, faithfulness, hope.

FAITH

By **Faith.**—*A. V.* 1*through faith.*
Acts 3. 16. 1*by faith* in his name hath his name made
15. 9. cleansing their hearts *by faith*
26. 18. them that are sanctified *by faith* in me
Rom. 1. 12. *by* the other's *faith*, both yours and mine
17. righteousness of God *by faith*—shall live *by faith*
3. 28. a man is justified *by faith.* 5. 1: Gal. 2. 16: 3. 24
30. he shall justify the circumcision *by faith*
5. 2. through whom also we have had our access *by faith*
9. 32. Because they sought it not *by faith*
11. 20. thou standest *by* thy *faith.* 2 Cor. 1. 24
2 Cor. 5. 7. (for we walk *by faith*, not by sight)
Gal. 3. 8. foreseeing that God would justify the Gentiles
11. The righteous shall live *by faith* [1*by faith*
22. that the promise *by faith* in Jesus Christ might
5. 5. *by faith* wait for the hope of righteousness
Phil. 3. 9. the righteousness which is of God *by faith*
Heb. 10. 38. But my righteous one shall live *by faith*
11. 3. 1*By faith* we understand that the worlds have been
4. *By faith* Abel. 5. *By faith* Enoch. 7. *By faith* Noah.
8. *By faith* Abraham. 9, 17. 20. *By faith* Isaac
blessed Jacob. 21. *By faith* Jacob. 22. *By faith*
Joseph. 23. *By faith* Moses. 24, 27, 128. 31. *By*
faith Rahab the harlot.
11. *By f.* even Sarah herself received power to conceive
29. *By faith* they [Israel] passed through the Red Sea
30. *By faith* the walls of Jericho fell down
Jas. 2. 24. by works a man is justified, and not only *by faith*
see in faith, through faith, your faith.

In **Faith.**—*A.V.* 1*by faith.*
Acts 14. 22. exhorting them to continue *in* the *faith*
16. 5. So the churches were strengthened *in* the *faith*
Rom. 4. 19. without being weakened *in faith* he considered
14. 1. But him that is weak *in faith* receive ye
1 Cor. 16. 13. Watch ye, stand fast *in* the *faith*
2. Cor. 8. 7. But as ye abound in everything, *in faith*
13. 5. Try your own selves, whether ye be *in* the *faith*
Gal. 2. 20. I live 1*in f.*, the faith which is in the Son of God
Col. 1. 23. if so be that ye continue *in* the *faith*, grounded
2. 7. builded up in him, and stablished *in* your *faith*
1 Tim. 1. 2. unto Timothy, my true child *in faith*
4. rather than a dispensation of God which is *in faith*
2. 7. a teacher of the Gentiles *in faith* and truth
15. if they continue *in faith* and love and sanctification
3. 13. great boldness *in* the *f.* which is in Christ Jesus
4. 12. in manner of life, in love, *in faith*, in purity
2 Tim. 1. 13. which thou hast heard from me, *in f.* and love
Tit. 1. 13. that they may be sound *in* the *faith.* 2. 2
3. 15. Salute them that love us *in faith*
Heb. 11. 13. These all died *in faith*, not having received
Jas. 1. 6. But let him ask *in faith*, nothing doubting
2. 5. them that are poor as to the world to be rich *in f*
see through faith.

Through **Faith.**—*A.V.* 1*by faith,* 2*in faith.*
Rom. 3. 22. even the righteousness of God 1*t. f.* in Jesus
25. to be propitiation, *through faith*, by his blood
30. shall justify—the uncircumcision *through faith*
31. make the law of none effect *through faith?*
4. 20. but waxed strong 2*through f.*, giving glory to God
Gal. 2. 16. works of the law, save 1*t. faith* in Jesus Christ
3. 14. receive the promise of the Spirit *through faith*
26. ye are all sons of God, 1*t. faith*, in Christ Jesus
Eph. 2. 8. for by grace have ye been saved *through faith*
3. 12. access in confidence 1*through* our *faith* in him
17. that Christ may dwell in your hearts 1*through faith*
Phil. 3. 9. that which is *through faith* in Christ

FAITH

Col. 2. 12. ye were also raised with him *through faith*
2 Tim. 3. 15. make thee wise unto salvation *through faith*
Heb. 6. 12. *through faith* and patience inherit the promises
11. 33. who *through faith* subdued kingdoms
39. had witness borne to them *through* their *faith*
1 Pet. 1. 5. by the power of God are guarded *through faith*

Your Faith.

Mat. 9. 29. According to *your faith* be it done unto you
Lu. 8. 25. he said unto them, Where is *your faith*?
Rom. 1. 8. that *your f.* is proclaimed throughout the whole
1 Cor. 2. 5. *your f.* should not stand in the wisdom of men
15. 17. if Christ hath not been raised, *your f.* is vain. 14
2 Cor. 1. 24. Not that we have lordship over *your faith*
10. 15. having hope that, as *your faith* groweth
Phil. 2. 17. offered upon the sacrifice and service of *your f.*
Col. 1. 4. having heard of *your faith* in Christ Jesus
2. 5. order, and the stedfastness of *your faith* in Christ
7. stablished in *your faith*, even as ye were taught
1 Th. 1. 8. in every place *your f.* to God-ward is gone forth
3. 2. and to comfort you concerning *your faith*
5. sent that I might know *your faith*
6. brought us glad tidings of *your faith* and love
7. in all our distress and affliction through *your faith*
10. may perfect that which is lacking in *your faith*?
2 Th. 1. 3. for that *your faith* groweth exceedingly
Jas. 1. 3. that the proof of *your faith* worketh patience
1 Pet. 1. 7. the proof of *your faith*, being more precious
9. receiving the end of *your faith*, even the salvation
21. so that *your faith* and hope might be in God
5. 9. whom withstand stedfast in *your faith*
2 Pet. 1. 5. in *your faith* supply virtue
Jude 20. building up yourselves on *your* most holy *faith*

Faithful.—A.V. ¹*faithfully,* ²*true.*

Mat. 24. 45. Who then is the *faithful* and wise. Lu. 12. 42
25. 21. Well done, good and *faithful* servant: thou hast been *faithful.* 23
Lu. 16. 10. He that is *faithful* in a very little is *faithful*
11. have not been *faithful* in the unrighteous mammon
12. have not been *faithful* in that which is another's
19. 17. because thou wast found *faithful* in a very little
Acts 16. 15. have judged me to be *faithful* to the Lord
1 Cor. 1. 9. God is *f.*, through whom ye were called. 10. 13
4. 2. required in stewards, that a man be found *faithful*
17. Timothy, who is my beloved and *faithful* child
7. 25. hath obtained mercy of the Lord to be *faithful*
2 Cor. 1. 18. But as God is *¹f.*, our word toward you is not
Gal. 3. 9. be of faith are blessed with the *faithful* Abraham
Eph. 1. 1. and the *faithful* in Christ Jesus [4. 7
6. 21. Tychicus, the beloved brother and *f.* minister. Col.
Col. 1. 2. to the saints and *faithful* brethren in Christ
7. who is a *faithful* minister of Christ on our behalf
4. 9. Onesimus, the *faithful* and beloved brother
1 Th. 5. 24. *Faithful* is he that calleth you, who will also
2 Th. 3. 3. the Lord is *faithful*, who shall stablish you
1 Tim. 1. 12. counted me *f.*, appointing me to his service
15. F. is the saying. 3. 11: 4. 9: 2 Tim. 2. 11: Tit. 3. 8
3. 11. not slanderers, temperate, *faithful* in all things
2 Tim. 2. 2. the same commit thou to *faithful* men
13. if we are faithless, he abideth *faithful*
Tit. 1. 9. holding to the *faithful* word which is according
Heb. 2. 17. might be a merciful and *faithful* high priest
3. 2. who was *faithful* to him that appointed him
5. Moses indeed was *faithful* in all his house
10. 23. for he is *faithful* that promised. 11. 11
1 Pet. 4. 19. their souls in well-doing unto a *faithful* Creator
5. 12. Silvanus, our *faithful* brother
1 Jno. 1. 9. he is *f.* and righteous to forgive us our sins

FALLEN

3 Jno. 5. doest a ¹*faithful* work in whatsoever thou doest
Rev. 1. 5. Jesus Christ, who is the *faithful* witness. 3. 14
2. 10. Be thou *faithful* unto death
13. Antipas my witness, my *f.* one, who was killed
17. 14. are with him, called and chosen and *faithful*
19. 11. he that sat thereon, called *Faithful* and *True*
21. 5. these words are *faithful* and true. 22. 6
see believe, believing.

Faithfully A.V.—see *faithful.*

Faithfulness.—A.V. ¹*faith.*

Rom. 3. 3. make of none effect the ¹*faithfulness* of God?
Gal. 5. 22. goodness, ¹*faithfulness*, meekness, temperance

Faithless.—A.V. ¹*believe not.*

Mat. 17. 17. O *f.* and perverse generation. Mk. 9. 19: Lu.
Jno. 20. 27. be not ¹*faithless*, but believing [9. 41
2 Tim. 2. 13. if we are ¹*faithless*, he abideth faithful

Fall.—A.V. ¹*come,* ²*depart,* ³*fail,* ⁴*falling.*

Mat. 4. 9. if thou wilt *fall* down and worship me
7. 27. and it fell: and great was the *fall* thereof
10. 29. not one of them [sparrows] shall *f.* on the ground
12. 11. if this *fall* into a pit on the sabbath day
15. 14. blind, both shall *fall* into a pit. Lu. 6. 39 [table
27. dogs eat of the crumbs which *f.* from their masters'
21. 44. whomsoever it shall *f.*, it will scatter. Lu. 20. 18
24. 29. and the stars shall *fall* from heaven
Lu. 8. 13. a while believe, and in time of temptation *f.* away
16. 17. than for one tittle of the law to ³*fall*
21. 24. they shall *fall* by the edge of the sword
23. 30. begin to say to the mountains, *Fall* on us
Jno. 12. 24. a grain of wheat *fall* into the earth and die
Acts 27. 32. cut away the ropes of the boat, and let her *f.* off
Rom. 3. 23. all have sinned, and ³*f.* short of the glory of God
11. 11. stumble that they might ³*f.*?—by their *f.* salvation
12. Now if their *fall* is the riches of the world
1 Cor. 10. 12. thinketh he standeth take heed lest he *fall*
14. 25. he will *fall* down on his face and worship God
1 Tim. 3. 6. he *fall* into the condemnation of the devil
7. lest he *fall* into reproach and the snare of the devil
4. 1. in later times some shall ¹*fall* away from the faith
6. 9. they that desire to be rich *fall* into a temptation
Heb. 4. 11. no man *f.* after the same example of disobedience
10. 31. a fearful thing to *f.* into the hands of the living God
Jas. 1. 2. my brethren, when ye *f.* into manifold temptations
5. 12. your nay, nay; that ye *fall* not under judgement
2 Pet. 3. 17. error of the wicked, ye *fall* from your own
Rev. 4. 10. four and twenty elders shall *f.* down before him
6. 16. say to the mountains and to the rocks, *Fall* on us
see fallen, falling-eth, fell, perish, stumble.

Fallen.—A.V. ¹*fall.*

Lu. 10. 18. I beheld Satan ¹*fallen* as lightning from heaven
14. 5. have an ass or an ox *fallen* into a well
Acts 8. 16. *fallen* upon none of them: only they had been
26. 14. when we were all *fallen* to the earth [baptized
28. 6. have swollen, or *fallen* down dead suddenly
1 Cor. 15. 6. but some are *fallen* asleep. 18
Gal. 5. 4. justified by the law; ye are *f.* away from grace
Phil. 1. 12. *f.* out rather unto the progress of the gospel
Rev. 2. 5. Remember therefore from whence thou art *fallen*
9. 1. I saw a star from heaven ¹*fallen* unto the earth
14. 8. *Fallen, fallen* is Babylon the great. 18. 2
17. 10. seven kings; the five are *fallen*, the one is
see borne, cast.

FALLETH

Falleth.—*A.V.* ¹*fail,* ²*fall,* ³*fell.*
Mat. 17. 15. oft-times he [demoniac] *falleth* into the fire
Mk. 5. 22. seeing him, he [Jaīrus] ²*falleth* at his feet
Lu. 11. 17. a house divided against a house *falleth*
15. 12. give me the portion of thy substance that *f.* to me
20. 18. Every one that ²*f.* on that stone shall be broken to
Rom. 14. 4. to his own lord he standeth or *falleth* | pieces
Heb. 12. 15. lest there be any man that ¹*f.* short of the grace
Jas. 1. 11. the flower thereof *falleth.* 1 *Pet.* 1. 24 [of God

Falling.—*A.V.* ¹*departing,* ²*fall.*
Mk. 13. 25. and the stars shall be ²*falling* from heaven
Lu. 2. 34. this child is set for the ²*falling* and rising up
8. 47. she came trembling, and *falling* down before him
22. 44. as it were great drops of blood *falling* down
Acts 1. 18. and *falling* headlong, he [Judas] burst asunder
2 *Th.* 2. 3. except the *falling* away come first
Heb. 3. 12. unbelief, in ¹*falling* away from the living God
see fall, lighting, stumbling.

False.—*A.V.* ¹*liars.*
Mat. 7. 15. Beware of *false* prophets, which come to you
15. 19. out of the heart come—*false* witness, railings
19, 18. Thou shalt not bear *f.* witness. *Mk.* 10. 19: *Lu.* 18.
24. 11. many *f.* prophets shall arise. 24 : *Mk.* 13. 22 [20
24. there shall arise *false* Christs. *Mk.* 13. 22
26. 59. the whole council sought *f.* witness against Jesus
60. though many *false* witnesses came
Mk. 14. 56. For many bare *false* witness against him. 57
Lu. 6. 26. same manner did their fathers to the *f.* prophets
Acts 6. 13. and set up *false* witnesses, which said
13. 6. they found a certain sorcerer, a *false* prophet
1 *Cor.* 15. 15. and we are found *false* witnesses of God
2 *Cor.* 11. 13. For such men are *false* apostles
26. in perils in the sea, in perils among *false* brethren
Gal. 2. 4. because of the *false* brethren privily brought in
2 *Pet.* 2. 1. arose *false* prophets—shall be *false* teachers
1 *Jno.* 4. 1. many *f.* prophets are gone out into the world
Rev. 2. 2. they are not, and didst find them ¹*false*
16. 13. out of the mouth of the *false* prophet
19. 20. the beast was taken, and with him the *f.* prophet
20. 10. where are also the beast and the *false* prophet
see wrongfully.

Falsehood.—*A.V.* ¹*lying.*
Eph. 4. 25. putting away ¹*falsehood,* speak ye truth

Falsely.
Mat. 5. 11. say all manner of evil against you *falsely*
1 *Tim.* 6. 20. of the knowledge which is *falsely* so called
see wrongfully.

Fame.
Mat. 9. 26. the *f.* hereof went forth into all that land. 31
Lu. 4. 14. and a *fame* went out concerning him [Jesus]
see report, rumour.

Families.—*A.V.* ¹*kindreds.*
Acts 3. 25. in thy seed shall all the ¹*f.* of the earth be blessed

Family.—*A.V.* ¹*home,* ²*lineage.*
Lu. 2. 4. he was of the house and ²*family* of David
Eph. 3. 15. every *family* in heaven and on earth is named
1 *Tim.* 5. 4. learn first to shew piety towards their own ¹*f.*

FASHION

Famine.—*A.V.* ¹*dearth,* ²*hunger.*
Lu. 4. 25. there came a great *famine* over all the land
15. 14. there arose a mighty *famine* in that country
Acts 7. 11. there came a ¹*f.* over all Egypt and Canaan [¹*f.*
11. 28. signified by the Spirit that there should be a great
Rom. 8. 35. tribulation, or anguish, or persecution, or *f.*
Rev. 6. 8. to kill with sword, and with ²*f.,* and with death
18. 8. shall her plagues come, death, and mourning, and *f.*

Famines.
Mat. 24. 7. shall be *f.* and earthquakes. *Mk.* 13. 8 : *Lu.* 21. 11

Fan.
Mat. 3. 12. whose *fan* is in his hand. *Lu.* 3. 17

Far.—*A.V.* ¹*afar,* ²*by the space.*
Mat. 15. 8. But their heart is *far* from me. *Mk.* 7. 6
16. 22. saying, Be it *far* from thee, Lord
Mk. 6. 35. when the day was now *far* spent, his disciples
8. 3. and some of them are come from *far*
12. 34. Thou art not *far* from the kingdom of God
Lu. 7. 6. when he was now not *far* from the house
22. 51. Jesus answered and said, Suffer ye thus *far*
24. 29. toward evening, and the day is now *far* spent
Acts 11. 19. travelled as *far* as Phœnicia, and Cyprus
22. sent forth Barnabas as *far* as Antioch
17. 27. though he is not *far* from each one of us
28. 15. came to meet us as *far* as The Market of Appius
Rom. 13. 12. The night is *far* spent, and the day is at hand
2 *Cor.* 10. 14. as *far* as unto you in the gospel of Christ
Eph. 1. 21. *far* above all rule, and authority, and power
2. 13. that once were *far* off are made nigh in the blood.
4. 10. that ascended *far* above all the heavens [¹17
Phil. 1. 23. and be with Christ; for it is very *far* better
Rev. 14. 20. bridles of the horses, as ²*far* as a thousand
see country, more, over (against).

Fare.—*A.V.* ¹*do.*
Acts 15. 36. the word of the Lord, and see how they ¹*fare*

Fared *A.V.*—*see faring.*

Farewell, or **Fare ye well.**—*A.V.* ¹*taken leave.*
Lu. 9. 61. to bid *farewell* to them that are at my house
Acts 15. 29. it shall be well with you. *Fare ye well*
21. 6. bade each other ¹*farewell ;* and we went on board
2 *Cor.* 13. 11. Finally, brethren, *farewell.* Be perfected
see leave.

Faring.—*A.V.* ¹*fared.*
Lu. 16. 19. rich man—¹*faring* sumptuously every day

Farm.
Mat. 22. 5. went their ways, one to his own *farm*

Farthing—s.
Mk. 5. 26. till thou have paid the last *farthing*
10. 29. Are not two sparrows sold for a *farthing ?*
Mk. 12. 42. she cast in two mites, which make a *farthing*
Lu. 12. 6. Are not five sparrows sold for two *farthings ?*

Fashion—ed.—*A.V.* ¹*change,* ²*conformed,* ³*transformed.*
Mk. 2. 12. We never saw it on this *fashion*
Lu. 9. 29. the *fashion* of his countenance was altered
Rom. 12. 2. be not ²*fashioned* according to this world
1 *Cor.* 7. 31. for the *fashion* of this world passeth away

115

FASHION

2 Cor. 11. 15. his ministers—*f.* themselves as ministers of
Phil. 2. 8. being found in *fashion* as a man [righteousness
3. 21. who shall *¹f.* anew the body of our humiliation
Jas. 1. 11. the grace of the *fashion* of it perisheth
    see conformed figure.

Fashioneth—ing.—*A.V.* ¹*transformed—ing.*
2 Cor. 11. 13. ¹*fashioning* themselves into apostles of Christ
14. Satan ¹*fashioneth* himself into an angel of light
1 Pet. 1. 14. not *f.* yourselves according to your—lusts

Fast.
Mat. 6. 16. ye *fast*, be not, as the hypocrites—seen of men
18. not seen of men to *fast*, but of thy Father [to *f.*
9. 14. *f.* oft, but thy disciples *f.* not? *Mk.* 2 18: *Lu.* 5. 33
15. then will they *fast*. *Mk.* 2. 20: *Lu.* 5. 35
Mk. 2. 19. Can the sons of the bridechamber *fast*—they
    cannot *fast*. *Lu.* 5. 34
Lu. 18 12. I *fast* twice in the week ; I give tithes of all
Acts 27. 9. the *F.* was now—gone by, Paul admonished them
    see fasting.

Fasted.
Mat. 4. 2. when he had *fasted* forty days and forty nights
Acts 13. 2. as they ministered to the Lord, and *fasted*
3. when they had *f.* and prayed and laid their hands

Fasten—ed.—*A.V.* ¹*look earnestly,* ²*set.*
Lu. 4. 20. eyes of all in the synagogue were *fastened* on him
Acts 3. 12. Ye men of Israel—why ¹*f.* ye your eyes on us
11. 6. upon the which when I had *fastened* mine eyes
13. 9. Saul—²*fastened* his eyes on him [Elymas]
28. 3. a viper came out—and *fastened* on his hand

Fastening.—*A.V.* ¹*beholding,* ²*looked,* ³*looking.*
Acts 3. 4. Peter, *fastening* his eyes upon him, with John
6. 15. sat in the council, ²*f.* their eyes on him [Stephen]
10. 4. he, ³*fastening* his eyes upon him
14. 9. The same heard Paul speaking : who, ¹*f.* his eyes

Fastest.
Mat. 6. 17. when thou *fastest*, anoint thy head, and wash

Fasting.—*A.V* ¹*fast.*
Mat. 15. 32. I would not send them away *fasting*. *Mk.* 8. 3
17. 21. not out save by prayer and *f.* [margin]
Mk. 2. 18. John's disciples and the Pharisees were ¹*fasting*
Acts 14. 23. with *f.*, they commended them to the Lord
27. 33. fourteenth day that ye wait and continue *fasting*

Fastings.
Lu. 2. 37. worshipping with *fastings* and supplications
2 Cor. 6. 5. in labours. in watchings, in *fastings*
11. 27. in *fastings* often, in cold and nakedness

Father, *relating to God.*—*see proper names.*
Father.
Mat. 4. 21. in the boat with Zebedee their *father*
22. they straightway left the boat and their *f. Mk.* 1. 20
8. 21. suffer me first to go and bury my *father*. *Lu.* 9. 59
10. 21. brother to death, and the *f.* his child. *Mk.* 13. 12
37. He that loveth *father* or mother more than me
15. 4. Honour thy *father* and thy mother. 19. 19 : *Mk.*
    7. 10 : 10. 19 : *Lu.* 18. 20 : *Eph.* 6. 2
19. 5. his *father* and mother, and shall cleave to his wife
29. or brethren, or sisters, or *f.*, or mother. *Mk.* 10. 29
23. 9. call no man your *father* on the earth
Mk. 5. 40. the *f.* of the child and her mother. *Lu.* 8. 51

FATHER

Mk. 9. 24. the *father* of the child cried out, and said
15. 21. *father* of Alexander and Rufus, to go with them
Lu. 2. 48. behold, thy *father* and I sought thee sorrowing
11. 11. which of you that is a *f.* shall his son ask a loaf
12. 53. *father* against son, and son against *father*
15. 17. How many hired servants of my *father's*
18. I will arise and go to my *father*, and will say unto
    him, *Father*, I have sinned against heaven. 21
22. the *father* said to his servants, Bring forth quickly
27. thy *father* hath killed the fatted calf
16. 24. *Father* Abraham, have mercy on me, and send
27. I pray thee therefore, *f.*—send him to my *f.'s* house
30. Nay, *father* Abraham : but if one go to them
Jno. 4. 53. the *father* knew that it was at that hour
6. 42. son of Joseph, whose *father* and mother we know ?
8. 38. do the things which ye heard from your *father*
41. Ye do the works of your *father*
44. Ye are of your *father* the devil, and the lusts of your
    father—for he is a liar, and the *father* thereof
56. your *father* Abraham rejoiced to see my day
Acts 28. 8. the *f.* of Publius lay sick of fever and dysentery
Rom. 4. 11. he might be the *f.* of all them that believe
12. the *f.* of circumcision—faith of our *father* Abraham
16. faith of Abraham, who is the *father* of us all
17. A *father* of many nations have I made thee). 18
Gal. 4 2. stewards until the term appointed of the *father*
Phil. 2. 22. as a child serveth a *f.*, so he served with me
1 Th. 2. 11. dealt with each one of you, as a *father*
1 Tim. 5. 1. Rebuke not an elder, but exhort him as a *f.*
Heb. 7. 3. without *f.*, without mother, without genealogy

His **Father.**
Mat. 2. 22. Archelaus was reigning over Judæa in the
    room of *his father* Herod
10. 35. came to set a man at variance against *his father*
15. 5. Whosoever shall say to *his father*. *Mk.* 7. 11
6. he that not honour *his father*
21 31. Whether of the twain did the will of *his father?*
Mk. 7. 12. no longer suffer him to do aught for *his father*
9. 21. And he asked *his father*, How long time is it
10. 7. For this cause shall a man leave *his f.* and mother
Lu. 1. 32. give unto him the throne of *his father* David
59. called him Zacharias, after the name of *his father*
62. signs to *his father*, what he would have him called
67. *his father* Zacharias was filled with the Holy Ghost
9. 42. healed the boy, and gave him back to *his father*
14. 26. cometh unto me, and hateth not *his* own *father*
15. 12. and the younger of them said to *his f., Father*
20. came to *his father*—afar off, *his father* saw him
28. and *his father* came out and intreated him
29. said to *his f.*, Lo, these many years do I serve thee
Acts 7. 4. when *his f.* [Abraham] was dead, God removed
14. Joseph sent, and called to him Jacob *his father*
16. 1. but *his* [Timothy] *father* was a Greek. 3
1 Cor. 5. 1. that one of you hath *his father's* wife
Eph. 5. 31. For this cause shall a man leave *his father*
Heb. 7. 10. for he was yet in the loins of *his father*
12. 7. what son is there whom *his father* chasteneth not

Our **Father.**

Mat. 3. 9. We have Abraham to *our father*. *Lu.* 3. 8 : *Jno.*
Mk. 11. 10. the kingdom of *our father* David [8. 39
Lu. 1. 73. The oath which he sware unto Abraham *our f.*
Jno. 4. 12. Art thou greater than *our father* Jacob
8. 53. Art thou greater than *our father* Abraham
Acts 7. 2. The God of glory appeared unto *our f.* Abraham
Rom. 4. 12. steps of that faith of *our f.* Abraham which he
9. 10. conceived by one, even by *our father* Isaac [had
Jas. 2. 21. Was not Abraham *our father* justified by works
    see forefather.

Father in law.
Jno. 18. 13. for he was *father in law* to Caiaphas

Fatherless.
Jas. 1. 27. to visit the *f.* and widows in their affliction

Fathers.
Lu. 1. 17. turn the hearts of the *fathers* to the children
6. 23. same manner did their *f.* unto the prophets. 26
Jno. 6. 58. not as the *fathers* did eat, and died
7. 22. (not that it is of Moses, but of the *fathers*)
Acts 7. 2. Brethren and *fathers*, hearken. 22. 1
32. the God of thy *fathers*, the God of Abraham
13. 32. promise made unto the *fathers*. Rom. 15. 8
36. laid unto his *fathers*, and saw corruption
22. 3. strict manner of the law of our *fathers*
Rom. 9. 5. whose are the *fathers*, and of whom is Christ
11. 28. they are beloved for the *fathers'* sake
1 Cor. 4. 15. yet have ye not many *fathers*
Gal. 1. 14. zealous for the traditions of my *fathers*
Eph. 6. 4. ye *fathers*, provoke not your children. Col. 3. 21
1 Tim. 1. 9. unholy and profane, for murderers of *fathers*
Heb. 1. 1. God, having of old times spoken unto the *fathers*
8. 9. to the covenant that I made with their *fathers*
12. 9. we had the *fathers* of our flesh to chasten us
2 Pet. 3. 4. from the day that the *fathers* fell asleep
1 Jno. 2. 13. I write unto you, *f.*, because ye know him. 14
see our fathers.

Our **Fathers.**—*A.V.* ¹*my fathers.*
Mat. 23. 30. If we had been in the days of *our fathers*
Lu. 1. 55. (As he spake unto *our fathers*)
72. To shew mercy towards *our fathers*
Jno. 4. 20. *Our fathers* worshipped in this mountain
6. 31. *Our fathers* ate the manna in the wilderness
Acts 3. 13. the God of *our f.*, hath glorified his Servant Jesus
5. 30. The God of *our f.* raised up Jesus, whom ye slew
7. 11. and *our fathers* found no sustenance
12. he sent forth *our fathers* the first time
15. he [Jacob] died, himself, and *our fathers*
19. subtilly with our race, and evil entreated *our fathers*
38. in the mount Sinai, and with *our fathers*
39. to whom *our fathers* would not be obedient
44. *Our fathers* had the tabernacle of the testimony
45. *our fathers*—thrust out before the face of *our fathers*
13. 17. God of this people Israel chose *our fathers*
15. 10. neither *our fathers* nor we were able to bear?
22. 14. The God of *our fathers* hath appointed thee
24. 14. so serve I the God of ¹*our fathers*, believing all
26. 6. promise made of God unto *our fathers*
28. 17. the people, or the customs of *our fathers*
1 Cor. 10. 1. that *our fathers* were all under the cloud
see your fathers.

Your **Fathers.**—*A.V.* ¹*our fathers.*
Mat. 23. 32. Fill ye up then the measure of *your fathers*
Lu. 11. 47. of the prophets, and *your fathers* killed them
48. and consent unto the works of *your fathers*
Jno. 6. 49. *Your f.* did eat the manna in the wilderness
Acts 3. 25. covenant which God made with ¹*your fathers*
7. 51. as *your fathers* did, so do ye
52. Which of the prophets did not *your f.* persecute?
28. 25. Isaiah the prophet unto ¹*your fathers*, saying
Heb. 3. 9. Wherewith *your f.* tempted me by proving me
1 Pet. 1. 18. manner of life handed down from *your fathers*

Fathoms.
Acts 27. 28. found twenty *fathoms*—found fifteen *fathoms*

Fatlings.
Mat. 22. 4. my oxen and my *fatlings* are killed

Fatness.
Rom. 11. 17. of the root of the *fatness* of the olive tree

Fatted.
Lu. 15. 27. thy father hath killed the *fatted* calf. 23

Fault.
Mat. 18. 15. shew him his *f.* between thee and him alone
Lu. 23. 4. I find no *fault* in this man. 14
Rom. 9. 19. Why doth he still find *fault* ?
Heb. 8. 8. For finding *fault* with them, he saith, Behold
see blemish, crime, defect, sins, trespass.

Faults *A.V.*—*see sins.*

Faultless.
Heb. 8. 7. For if that first covenant had been *faultless*
see blemish.

Favour.—*A.V.* ¹*pleasure.*
Lu. 1. 30. Mary: for thou hast found *favour* with God
2. 52. and in *favour* with God and men
Acts 2. 47. and having *f.* with all the people [disciples]
7. 10. gave him *favour* and wisdom before Pharaoh
46. who found *favour* in the sight of God   [in bonds
24. 27. desiring to gain ¹*f.* with the Jews, Felix left Paul
25. 3. asking *f.* against him, that he would send for him

Favoured.
Lu. 1. 28. thou that art highly *f.*, the Lord is with thee

Fear.—*A.V.* ¹*afraid,* ²*feared,* ³*feareth,* ⁴*reverence,* ⁵*terror.*
Mat. 10. 28. but rather *fear* him which is able to destroy
14. 26. an apparition; and they cried out for *fear*
21. 26. if we shall say, From men; we *f.* the multitude
28. 4. and for *fear* of him the watchers did quake
8. quickly from the tomb with *fear* and great joy
Lu. 1. 12. troubled when he saw him, and *f.* fell upon him
50. And his mercy—On them that *fear* him
65. *fear* came on all that dwelt round about them.
7. 16 : Acts 2. 43 : 5. 5, 11 : 19. 17 : Rev. 11. 11
74. Should serve him without *fear*
5. 26. they were filled with *fear*, saying, We have seen
8. 37. for they were holden with great *fear*
12. 5. I will warn you whom ye shall *fear* : *Fear* him—
I say unto you, *Fear* him
21. 26. men fainting for *fear*, and for expectation
23. 40. Dost thou not even *fear* God, seeing thou art
Jno. 7. 13. no man spake openly of him for *fear* of the Jews
19. 38. because for *fear* of the Jews, asked of Pilate
20. 19. where the disciples were, for *fear* of the Jews
Acts 9. 31. being edified; and, walking in the *f.* of the Lord
13. 16. Men of Israel, and ye that *fear* God
26. Brethren—those among you that ³*fear* God
Rom. 3. 18. There is no *fear* of God before their eyes
8. 15. received not the spirit of bondage again unto *fear*
11. 20. Be not highminded, but *fear*
13. 7. *fear* to whom *fear* ; honour to whom honour
1 Cor. 2. 3. I was with you in weakness, and in *fear*
16. 10. if Timothy come—be with you without *fear*
2 Cor. 5. 11. Knowing therefore the ⁵*fear* of the Lord
7. 1. perfecting holiness in the *fear* of God
11. what *fear*, yea, what longing, yea, what zeal
15. how with *fear* and trembling ye received him
11. 3. But I *fear*, lest by any means. 12. 20   [of Christ
Eph. 5. 21. subjecting yourselves one to another in the *f.*
33. and let the wife see that she ⁴*fear* her husband

FEAR

Eph. 6. 5. with *fear* and trembling, in singleness
Phil. 1. 14. bold to speak the word of God without *fear*
  2. 12. work out your own salvation with *f.* and trembling
1 Tim. 5. 20. that the rest also may be in *fear*
Heb. 2. 12. who through *f.* of death were all their lifetime
  4. 1. Let us *fear* therefore, lest haply, a promise
  5. 7. and having been heard for his godly ²*fear*
  11. 7. Noah—moved with godly *fear*, prepared an ark
  12. 21. Moses said, I exceedingly *fear* and quake
1 Pet. 1. 17. pass the time of your sojourning in *fear*
  2. 17. *Fear* God. Honour the king
  18. be in subjection to your masters with all *fear*
  3. 2. beholding your chaste behaviour coupled with *fear*
  14. ¹*fear* not their ⁵*fear*, neither be troubled
  15. give answer—yet with meekness, and *fear*
1 Jno. 4. 18. no *f.* in love—casteth out *f.*, because *f.* hath
Jude 12 that without *fear* feed themselves [punishment
  23. and on some hath mercy with *fear*
Rev. 11. 18. the saints, and to them that *fear* thy name
  14. 7. *Fear* God, and give him glory
  18. 10. standing afar off for the *fear* of her torment. 15
  19. 5. ye that *fear* him, the small and the great
  see awe, fearfulness.

Fear (with negatives).—A.V. ¹not afraid.

Mat. 1. 20. *fear* not to take unto thee Mary thy wife
  10. 26. *Fear* them *not* therefore: for there is nothing
  31. *Fear not* therefore; ye are of more value. Lu. 12. 7
  28. 5. angel—said unto the women, *Fear not* ye. ¹10
Mk. 5. 36. unto the ruler—*F not*, only believe. Lu. 8. 50
Lu. 1. 13. *Fear not*, Zacharias: because thy supplication
  30. *Fear not*, Mary: for thou hast found favour with God
  5. 10. Simon, *Fear not;* from henceforth thou shalt
  12. 32. *Fear not*, little flock; for it is your Father's
  18. 4. Though I *fear* not God, nor regard man
Jno. 12. 15. *Fear not*, daughter of Zion: behold, thy King
Acts 27. 24. *F. not*, Paul; thou must stand before Cæsar
Rom. 13. 3. wouldest thou have ¹*no fear* of the power?
Heb. 13. 6. The Lord is my helper; I will *not fear*
1 Pet. 3. 6. and are ¹*not* put in *fear* by any terror
  14. ¹*fear not* their fear, neither be troubled
Rev. 1. 17. *Fear not;* I am the first and the last
  2. 10. *Fear not* the things which thou art about to suffer
  15. 4. Who shall *not f.*, O Lord, and glorify thy name?
  see not afraid.

Feared.

Mat. 14. 5. *feared* the multitude. 21. 46
  27. 54. when they saw the earthquake—*f.* exceedingly
Mk. 4. 41. and they [disciples] *f.* exceedingly, and said
  6. 20. Herod *f.* John, knowing that he was a righteous
  11. 18. might destroy him: for they *f.* him [Acts 5. 26
  32. they *feared* the people. 12. 12; Lu. 20. 19: 22, 2;
Lu. 9. 34. they *feared* as they entered into the cloud
  18. 2. There was in a city a judge, which *feared* not God
  19. 21. for I *feared* thee, because thou art an austere man
Jno. 9. 22. said his parents, because they *feared* the Jews
Acts 10. 2. one that *feared* God with all his house
  16. 38. they *f.*, when they heard that they were Romans
  see afraid, fear.

Feareth.

Acts 10. 22. a righteous man and one that *feareth* God
  35. but in every nation he that *feareth* him
1 Jno. 4. 18. he that *feareth* is not made perfect in love
  see fear.

Fearful.—A.V. ¹afraid, ²terrible.

Mat. 8. 26. Why are ye *f.*, O ye of little faith? Mk. 4. 40
Jno. 14. 27. not your heart be troubled, neither let it be ¹*f.*

Heb. 10. 27. a certain *fearful* expectation of judgement
  31. It is a *fearful* thing to fall into the hands of the
  12. 21. and so ²*fearful* was the appearance [living God
Rev. 21. 8. for the *f.*, and unbelieving, and abominable
  see terror.

Fearfulness.—A.V. ¹fear.

2 Tim. 1. 7. For God gave us not a spirit of ¹*fearfulness.*

Fearing.

Mk. 5. 33. But the woman *fearing* and trembling, knowing
Acts 23. 10. chief captain, *fearing* lest Paul should be torn
  27. 17. *fearing* lest they should be cast upon the Syrtis
  29. And *fearing* lest haply we should be cast ashore
Gal. 2. 12. *fearing* them that were of the circumcision
Col. 3. 22. in singleness of heart, *fearing* the Lord
Heb. 11. 27. forsook Egypt, not *f.* the wrath of the king

Fears.

2 Cor. 7. 5. without were fightings, within were *fears*

Feast–s.—A.V. ¹feast day.

Mat. 23. 6. love the chief place at *f.* Mk. 12. 39; Lu. 20. 46
  26. 5. they said, Not during the ¹*feast.* Mk. 14. ¹2
Mk. 14. 1. after two days was the *feast* of the passover
  15. 6. at the *f.* he used to release unto them one prisoner.
  Mat. 27. 15; Lu. 23. 17 [margin]
Lu. 2. 41. every year to Jerusalem at the *f.* of the passover
  42. they went up after the custom of the *feast*
  5. 29. Levi made him a great *feast* in his house
  14. 13. But when thou makest a *feast*, bid the poor
  22. 1. Now the *feast* of unleavened bread drew nigh
Jno. 2. 8. Draw out now, and bear unto the ruler of the *f.*
  9. ruler of the *feast* tasted the water—the ruler of the
  feast calleth the bridegroom
  23. during the ¹*feast*, many believed on his name
  4. 45. he did in Jerusalem at the *f.*—went unto the *feast*
  5. 1. After these things there was a *feast* of the Jews
  6. 4. the *feast* of the Jews, was at hand. 7. 2
  7. 8. Go ye up unto the *f.:* I go not up yet unto this *f.*
  10. But when his brethren were gone up unto the *feast*
  11. The Jews therefore sought him at the *feast*
  14. But when it was now the midst of the *feast*
  37. on the last day, the great day of the *f.*, Jesus stood
  10. 22. it was the *feast* of the dedication at Jerusalem
  11. 56. What think ye? That he will not come to the *f.*
  12. 12. a great multitude that had come to the *feast*
  20. among those that went up to worship at the *feast*
  13. 1. before the *feast* of the passover, Jesus knowing
  29. Buy what things we have need of for the *feast*
1 Cor. 5. 8. wherefore let us keep the *f.*, not with old leaven
  10. 27. of them that believe not biddeth you to a *feast*
2 Pet. 2. 13. in their love-feasts while they *feast.* Jude 12
  see love-feasts.

Fed.—A.V. ¹kept, ²nourished.

Mat. 8. 33. they that ¹*fed* them fled. Mk. 5. 14; Lu. 8. 34
  25. 37. when saw we thee an hungred, and *fed* thee?
Lu. 16. 21. desiring to be *fed* with the crumbs [country
Acts 12. 20. because their country was ²*fed* from the king's
1 Cor. 3. 2. I *fed* you with milk, not with meat

Feeble

1 Cor. 12. 22. which seem to be more *feeble* are necessary
  see palsied.

Feebleminded A.V.—see fainthearted.

Feed.—A.V. ¹feeding.

Lu. 15. 15. sent him into his fields to *feed* swine
Jno. 21. 15. *Feed* my lambs. 17
Acts 20. 28. made you bishops, to *feed* the church of God

FEED

Rom. 12. 20. But if thine enemy hunger, *feed* him
1 *Cor.* 13. 3. if I bestow all my goods to *feed* the poor
Jude 12. shepherds that without fear ¹*feed* themselves
    see nourish, tend.

Feedeth.
Mat. 6. 26. your heavenly Father *feedeth* them. *Lu.* 12, 24
1 *Cor.* 9. 7. or who *feedeth* a flock, and eateth not

Feeding.
Mat. 8. 30. herd of many swine *f. Mk.* 5. 11 : *Lu.* 8. 32
    see feed.

Feel—ing.
Acts 17. 27. if haply they might *feel* after him, and find him
Eph. 4. 19. past *f.* gave themselves up to lasciviousness
Heb. 4. 15. be touched with the *feeling* of our infirmities

Feet.—*A.V.* ¹*footstool.*
Mat. 7. 6. lest haply they trample them under their *feet*
10. 14. shake off the dust of your *feet. Mk.* 6. 11 : *Lu.* 9. 5
15. 30. and they cast them down at his [Jesus] *feet*
18. 8. two hands or two *f.* to be cast into—fire. *Mk.* 9. 45
22. 44. Till I put thine enemies underneath thy ¹*feet*?
28. 9. And they came and took hold of his *feet*
Mk. 5. 22. and seeing him, he falleth at his *feet*
7. 25. heard of him, came and fell down at his *feet*
Lu. 1. 79. To guide our *feet* into the way of peace
7. 38. standing—at his *feet*—wet his *f.*—kissed his *f.* 46
44. no water for my *feet* : but she hath wetted my *feet*
45. since—I came in, hath not ceased to kiss my *feet*
8. 35. clothed and in his right mind, at the *feet* of Jesus
41. he fell down at Jesus' *feet*, and besought him to come
10. 39. Mary, which also sat at the Lord's *feet*
15. 22. put a ring on his hand, and shoes on his *feet*
17. 16. he fell upon his face at his *feet*, giving him thanks
24. 39. See my hands and my *feet*, that it is I myself
40. he shewed them his hands and his *feet*
Jno. 11. 32. fell down at his *feet*, saying unto him, Lord
12. 3. anointed the *feet* of Jesus, and wiped his *f.* 11. 2
13. 5. began to wash the disciples' *feet*, and to wipe them
6. he saith unto him, Lord, dost thou wash my *feet*?
8. Thou shalt never wash my [Peter] *feet* [head
9. Lord, not my *feet* only, but also my hands and my
10. He that is bathed needeth not save to wash his *feet*
12. So when he had washed their *feet* [another's?
14. the Lord and the Master—washed your *f.*—wash one
20. 12. one at the *feet*, where the body of Jesus had lain
Acts 3. 7. his *feet* and his ankle-bones received strength
4. 35. laid them at the apostles' *feet.* 37 : 5. 2
5. 9. the *feet* of them which have buried thy husband
10. she [Sapphira] fell down immediately at his *feet*
7. 33. Loose the shoes from thy *feet* : for the place
58. laid down their garments at the *feet* of a young man
10. 25. fell down at his *feet*, and worshipped him
13. 25. the shoes of whose *f.* I am not worthy to unloose
51. they shook off the dust of their *feet* against them
14. 8. at Lystra there sat a certain man, impotent in his *f.*
10. said with a loud voice, Stand upright on thy *feet*
16. 24. and made their *feet* fast in the stocks
21. 11. he [Agabus] bound his own *feet* and hands
22. 3. brought up in this city, at the *feet* of Gamaliel
26. 16. stand upon thy *f.* : for to this end have I appeared
Rom. 3. 15. Their *feet* are swift to shed blood [tidings
10. 15. beautiful are the *feet* of them that bring glad
16. 20. shall bruise Satan under your *feet* shortly
1 *Cor.* 12. 21. the head to the *feet*, I have no need of you
15. 25. till he hath put all his enemies under his *feet*
Eph. 1. 22. all things in subjection under his *feet. Heb.* 2. 8

FELL

Eph. 6. 15. having shod your *f.* with the preparation of the
1 *Tim.* 5. 10. if she hath washed the saints' *feet* [gospel
Heb. 12. 13. make straight paths for your *feet*
Rev. 1. 15. and his *feet* like unto burnished brass. 2. 18
17. I [John] fell at his *feet* as one dead
3. 9. make them to come and worship before thy *feet*
10. 1. his face was as the sun, and his *feet* as pillars of fire
11. 11. they stood upon their *feet* ; and great fear fell
12. 1. with the sun, and the moon under her *feet*
13. 2. his *feet* were as the *feet* of a bear
19. 10. And I fell down before his *feet* to worship him
22. 8. I fell down to worship before the *feet* of the angel

Feigned.—*A.V.* ¹*feign.*
Lu. 20. 20. spies, which ¹*feigned* themselves to be righteous
2 *Pet.* 2. 3. with *feigned* words make merchandise of you

Fell.—*A.V.* ¹*fall.*
Mat. 7. 25. winds blew—upon that house ; and it *fell* not
27. and it *fell* : and great was the fall thereof. *Lu.* 6. 49
13. 4. seeds *fell* by the way side. *Mk.* 4. 4 : *Lu.* 8. 5
5. others *fell* upon the rocky places. *Mat.* 4. 5 : *Lu.* 8. 6
7. others *fell* upon the thorns. *Mk.* 4. 7 : *Lu.* 8. 7, 14
8. others *fell* upon the good gound. *Mk.* 4. 8 : *Lu.* 8. 8
Mk. 9. 20. and he *f.* on the ground, and wallowed foaming
14. 35. *fell* on the ground, and prayed that, if it were
Lu. 1. 12. Zacharias was troubled—and fear *fell* upon him
8. 23. But as they sailed he [Jesus] *fell* asleep
10. 30. he *fell* among robbers, which both stripped him
36. neighbour unto him that *fell* among the robbers?
13. 4. those eighteen, upon whom the tower in Siloam *f.*
15. 20. and ran, and *fell* on his neck, and kissed him
16. 21. crumbs that *fell* from the rich man's table
17. 16. *fell* upon his face at his *feet*, giving him thanks
Jno. 18. 6. they went backward, and *fell* to the ground
Acts 1. 25. apostleship, from which Judas *fell* away
26. and the lot *fell* upon Matthias
7. 60. And when he had said this, he [Stephen] *f.* asleep
9. 4. *fell* upon the earth, and heard a voice. 22. 7
18. there *fell* from his [Saul] eyes as it were scales
10. 10. while they made ready, he *fell* into a trance
44. the Holy Ghost *fell* ou all them which heard. 11. 15
12. 7. And his [Peter] chains *fell* off from his hands
13. 11. there *fell* on him a mist and a darkness
36. *fell* on sleep, and was laid unto his fathers
19. 17. at Ephesus ; and fear *fell* upon them all
20. 10. Paul went down, and *fell* on him [Eutychus]
37. all wept sore, and *fell* on Paul's neck, and kissed
Rom. 11. 22. severity of God : toward them that *fell*
15. 3. reproaches of them that reproached thee *f.* upon me
1 *Cor.* 10. 8. *fell* in one day three and twenty thousand
Heb. 3. 17. whose carcases *fell* in the wilderness?
6. 6. and then ¹*fell* away, it is impossible to renew
2 *Pet.* 3. 4. from the day the fathers *fell* asleep
Rev. 1. 17. when I saw him, I *fell* at his feet as one dead
6. 13. and the stars of the heaven *fell* unto the earth
8. 10. there *fell* from heaven a great star—*fell* upon the
11. 11. great fear *fell* upon them which beheld them
13. a great earthquake, and the tenth part of the city *fell*
16. 19. into three parts, and the cities of the nations *fell*
    see falleth.

Fell down.
Mat. 2. 11. and they *fell down* and worshipped him
18. 26. servant therefore *fell down* and worshipped. 29
Mk. 3. 11. *fell down* before him, and cried, saying
5. 33. the woman fearing—came and *f. down* before him
7. 25. heard of him, came and *fell down* at his feet
Lu. 5. 8. Peter, when he saw it, *fell down* at Jesus' knees

FELL

Lu. 8. 28. he cried out, and *fell down* before him
41. *fell down* at Jesus' feet, and besought him
Jno. 11. 32. Mary—*fell down* at his feet, saying unto him
Acts 5. 5. Ananias hearing these words *fell down*
10. And she *fell down* immediately at his feet
10. 25. Cornelius met him, and *fell down* at his feet
16. 29. *fell down* before Paul and Silas [jailor]
19. 35. the image which *fell down* from Jupiter?
20. 9. Eutychus—*fell down* from the third story
Heb. 11. 30. By faith the walls of Jericho *fell down*
Rev. 5. 8. elders *fell down*. 14 : 19. 4
19. 10. I *fell down* before his feet to worship him. 22. 8

Fellow.

Acts 22. 22. Away with such a *fellow* from the earth
24. 5. For we have found this man a pestilent *fellow*
   see man.

Fellow-citizen—s.—*A.V.* ¹*neighbour*.

Eph. 2. 19. but ye are *fellow-citizens* with the saints
Heb. 8. 11. shall not teach every man his ¹*fellow-citizen*

Fellow-disciples.

Jno. 11. 16. called Didymus, said unto his *fellow-disciples*

Fellow-elder.

1 *Pet.* 5. 1. I exhort, who am a *fellow-elder*, and a witness

Fellow-heirs.

Eph. 3. 6. Gentiles are *fellow-heirs*, and fellow-members

Fellow-helpers *A.V.—see fellow-workers*.

Fellow-labourer *A.V.—see fellow-worker, minister*.

Fellow-members.

Eph. 3. 6. Gentiles are fellow-heirs, and *fellow-members*

Fellow-partakers.

Eph. 3. 6. *fellow-partakers* of the promise in Christ Jesus

Fellow-prisoner—s.

Rom. 16. 7. Junius, my kinsmen, and my *fellow-prisoners*
Col. 4. 10. Aristarchus my *fellow-prisoner* saluteth you
Philem. 23. Epaphras, my *fellow-prisoner* in Christ Jesus

Fellows.

Mat. 11. 16. like unto children—which call unto their *f*.
Heb. 1. 9. With the oil of gladness above thy *fellows*

Fellow-servant—s.

Mat. 18. 28. found one of his *f.-servants*, which owed him
29. his *fellow-servant* fell down and besought him
31. when his *fellow-servants* saw what was done
33. not thou also have had mercy on thy *fellow-servant*
24. 49. shall begin to beat his *fellow-servants*
Col. 1. 7. learned of Epaphras our beloved *fellow-servant*
4. 7. faithful minister and *fellow-servant* in the Lord
Rev. 6. 11. until their *f.-servants* also and their brethren
19. 10. I am a *fellow-servant* with thee. 22. 9

Fellowship.—*A.V.* ¹*communicate—d*, ²*communication*, ³*partakers*.

Acts 2. 42. stedfastly in the apostles' teaching and *fellow-*
1 *Cor.* 1. 9. called into the *f*. of his Son Jesus Christ [*ship*
2 *Cor.* 6. 14. what *f*. have righteousness and iniquity?
8. 4. and the *fellowship* in the ministering to the saints

FEW

Gal. 2. 9. to me and Barnabas the right hands of *fellowship*
Eph. 5. 11. no *f*. with the unfruitful works of darkness
Phil. 1. 5. your *fellowship* in furtherance of the gospel
2. 1. consolation of love, if any *fellowship* of the Spirit
3. 10. resurrection, and the *fellowship* of his sufferings
4. 14. ye did well, that ye had ¹*f*. with my affliction
15. no church had ¹*fellowship* with me in the matter
Philem. 6. the ²*fellowship* of thy faith may become effectual
1 *Jno.* 1. 3. also may have *f*. with us—*f*. is with the Father
6. If we say that ye have *fellowship* with him, and walk
7. as he is in the light, we have *f*. one with another
Rev. 18. 4. that ye have no ³*fellowship* with her sins
   see communion, dispensation.

Fellow-soldier.

Phil. 2. 25. Epaphroditus, my—*fellow*-worker and *fellow-*
Philem. 2. and to Archippus our *fellow-soldier* [*soldier*

Fellow-worker—s.—*A.V.* ¹*companion in labour*, ²*fellow-helper—s*, ³*fellow-labourer—s*, ⁴*helper—s*, ⁵*labourers*.

Rom. 16. 3. Salute Prisca and Aquila my ⁴*fellow-workers*
9. Salute Urbanus our ⁴*fellow-worker*. 21. [in Christ
1 *Cor.* 3. 9. For we are God's ⁵*fellow-workers*
2 *Cor.* 8. 23. Titus, he is my partner and my ²*fellow-worker*
Phil. 2. 25. Epaphroditus, my brother and ¹*fellow-worker*
4. 3. Clement also, and the rest of my ³*fellow-workers*
Col. 4 11. these only are my *fellow-workers*
Philem. 1. Philemon our beloved and ³*fellow-worker*
24. Demas, Luke, my ³*fellow-workers*
3 *Jno.* 8. that we may be ⁵*fellow-workers* with the truth

Felt.

Mk. 5. 29. she *felt* in her body that she was healed
   see took.

Female.

Mat. 19. 4. made them male and *female*. *Mk.* 10. 6
Gal. 3. 28. no male and *female* : for ye all are one man

Fervent.

Acts 18. 25. and being *fervent* in spirit, he spake and taught
Rom. 12. 11. *fervent* in spirit; serving the Lord
1 *Pet.* 4. 8. above all things being *fervent* in your love
2 *Pet.* 3. 10. the elements shall be dissolved with *f*. heat. 12
   see supplication, zeal.

Fervently.—*A.V.* ¹*earnestly*.

Jas. 5. 17. Elijah—prayed ¹*fervently* that it might not rain
1 *Pet.* 1. 22. love one another from the heart *fervently*

Fetch.—*A.V.* ¹*call*.

Acts 10. 5. send men to Joppa, and ¹*f*. one Simon. 11. ¹13
   see bring.

Fetters.

Mk. 5. 4. bound with *fetters—f*. broken in pieces. *Lu.* 8. 29

Fever.

Mat. 8. 14. saw his wife's mother lying sick of a *fever*.
   Mk. 1. 30 : *Lu.* 4. 38   [*Mk.* 1. 31
Lu. 4. 39. he stood over her and rebuked the *f*. *Mat.* 8. 15 :
Jno. 4. 52. the seventh hour the *fever* left him
Acts 28. 8. father of Publius lay sick of *fever* and dysentery

Few.

Mat. 7. 14. unto life, and *few* be they that find it
9. 37. plenteous, but the labourers are *few*. *Lu.* 10. 2
15. 34. Seven, and a *few* small fishes. *Mk.* 8. 7.
22. 14. For many are called, but *few* chosen
25. 21. thou hast been faithful over a *few* things. 23

FEW

Mk. 6. 5. laid his hands upon a *few* sick folk, and healed
Lu. 12. 48. shall be beaten with *few* stripes
13. 23. Lord, are they *few* that be saved ?
Acts 17. 4. and of the chief women not a *few*
12. also of the Greek women—and of men, not a *few*
24. 4. to hear us of thy clemency a *few* words
Eph. 3. 3. mystery, as I wrote afore in *few* words
Heb. 12. 10. they verily for a *few* days chastened us
13. 22. I have written unto you in *few* words
1 Pet. 3. 20. wherein *few*, that is, eight souls, were saved
Rev. 2. 14. But I have a *few* things against thee
3. 4. thou hast a *few* names in Sardis which did not defile

Fickleness.—A.V. ¹lightness.

2 Cor. 1. 17. thus minded, did I shew ¹*fickleness* ?

Fidelity.

Tit. 2. 10. not purloining, but shewing all good *fidelity*

Field.—A.V. ¹piece of ground, ²land.

Mat. 6. 28. Consider the lilies of the *field*, how they grow
30. if God doth so clothe the grass of the *field*, Lu. 12. 28
13. 31. a man took, and sowed in his *field*. 24, 27
36. Explain unto us the parable of the tares of the *field*
38. the *field* is the world ; and the good seed, these are
44. treasure hidden in the *field*—and buyeth that *field*
24. 18. let him that is in the *field* not return back. Mk.
13. 16 ; Lu. 17. 31
40. Then shall two men be in the *f*. Lu. 17. 36 [margin]
27. 7. bought with them the potter's *field*. 10
8. that *field* was called, The *field* of blood. Acts 1. 19
Lu. 2. 8. there were shepherds—abiding in the *field*
14. 18. I have bought a ¹*field*, and I must needs go out
15. 25. Now his elder son was in the *field*
17. 7. in from the *field*, Come straightway and sit down
Acts 1. 18. Now this man obtained a *field* with the reward
4. 37. [Barnabas] having a ²*field*, sold it

Fields.—A.V. ¹trees.

Mk. 11. 8. branches, which they had cut from the ¹*fields*
Lu. 15. 15. he sent him into his *fields* to feed swine
Jno. 4. 35. Lift up your eyes, and look on the *fields*
Jas. 5. 4. hire of the labourers who mowed your *fields*
see cornfields.

Fierce.

Mat. 8. 28. devils, coming forth out of the tombs, exceeding *fierce*
2 Tim. 3. 3. without self-control, *fierce*, no lovers of good
see rough, urgent.

Fierceness.—A.V. ¹fiery indignation.

Heb. 10. 27. a ¹*f.* of fire which shall devour the adversaries
Rev. 16. 19. the cup of the wine of the *fierceness* of his wrath
19. 15. treadeth the winepress of the *f.* of the wrath

Fiery.

Eph. 6. 16. quench all the *fiery* darts of the evil one"
1 Pet. 4. 12. think it not strange concerning the *fiery* trial
see fierceness.

Fifteen.

Jno. 11. 18. nigh unto Jerusalem, about *fifteen* furlongs
Acts 27. 28. sounded again, and found *fifteen* fathoms
Gal. 1. 18. Jerusalem to visit Cephas, and tarried—*f.* days

Fifteenth.

Lu. 3. 1. the *fifteenth* year of the reign of Tiberius Cæsar

FILL

Fifth.

Rev. 6. 9. when he opened the *fifth* seal, I saw
9. 1. the *fifth* angel sounded, and I saw a star
16. 10. the *fifth* poured out his bowl upon the throne
21. 20. the *fifth*, sardonyx ; the sixth, sardius

Fifties.

Mk. 6. 40. sat down in ranks, by hundreds, and by *fifties*
see fifty.

Fifty.—A.V. ¹fifties.

Lu. 7. 41. owed five hundred pence, and the other *fifty*
9. 14. Make them sit down in companies, about ¹*f.* each
16. 6. sit down quickly and write *fifty*   [ham ?
Jno. 8. 57. not yet *fifty* years old, and hast thou seen Abra-

Fig—s.

Mat. 7. 16. gather grapes of thorns, or *figs* of thistles ?
Mk. 11. 13. for it was not the season of *figs*
Lu. 6. 44. For of thorns men do not gather *figs*
Jas. 3. 12. can a fig tree—yield olives, or a vine *figs* ?
Rev. 6. 13. as a fig tree casteth her unripe *figs*

Fig tree.

Mat. 21. 19. seeing a *fig tree* by the way side—the *fig tree*
withered. 20 ; Mk. 11. 13, 20, 21
21. ye shall not only do what is done to the *fig tree*
24. 32. from the *fig tree* learn her parable. Mk. 13. 28
Lu. 13. 6. A certain man had a *fig tree* planted
7. I come seeking fruit on this *fig tree*, and find none
21. 29. Behold the *fig tree*, and all the trees
Jno. 1. 48. when thou wast under the *fig t.*, I saw thee. 50
Jas. 3. 12. can a *fig tree*, my brethren, yield olives
Rev. 6. 13. as a *fig tree* casteth her unripe figs

Fight.

Jno. 18. 36. of this world, then would my servants *fight*
1 Cor. 9. 26. so *fight* I, as not beating the air
1 Tim. 6. 12. Fight the good *fight* of the faith, lay hold
2 Tim. 4. 7. I have fought the good *fight*, I have finished
Jas. 4. 2. ye *f.* and war ; ye have not, because ye ask not
see conflict, fighting, war.

Fighting—s.—A.V. ¹fight, ²strivings.

Acts 5. 39. lest haply ye be found even to be ¹*f.* against God
2 Cor. 7. 5. without were *fightings*, within were fears
Tit. 3. 9. shun foolish questionings—and ²*f.* about the law
Jas. 4. 1. Whence come wars and whence come *fightings*

Figure—s.—A.V. ¹fashion.

Acts 7. 43. The *figures* which ye made to worship them
44. Moses—make it according to the ¹*f.* that he had seen
Rom. 5. 14. who is a *figure* of him that was to come
1 Cor. 4. 6. in a *figure* transferred to myself and Apollos
see likeness, parable, pattern.

Fill.—A.V. ¹filled, ²satisfy.

Mat. 9. 16. which should *fill* it up taketh from the garment
15. 33. so many loaves—as to *fill* so great a multitude ?
23. 32. *Fill* ye up then the measure of your fathers
Mk. 2. 21. else that which should ¹*fill* it up taketh from it
8. 4. Whence shall one be able to ²*fill* these men
Jno. 2. 7. *Fill* the waterpots with water
Rom. 15. 13. Now the God of hope *fill* you with all joy
Eph. 4. 10. all the heavens, that he might *fill* all things

FILL

Col. 1. 24. *fill* up on my part that which is lacking
1 *Th.* 2. 16. to *f.* up their sins alway: but the wrath is come
    see mingled.
Filled.—*A.V.* ¹*full,* ²*furnished.*
Mat. 5. 6. after righteousness: for they shall be *filled*
 13. 48. when it was ¹*fill-d,* they drew up on the beach ⁷9. 17
 14. 19. they did all eat, and were *f. Mk.* 6. 43 : 8. 8 : *Lu.*
 22. 10. and the wedding was ²*filled* with guests
 27. 48. took a sponge, and *filled* it with vinegar
Mk. 7. 27. he said unto her, Let the children first be *filled*
Lu. 1. 15. he shall be *filled* with the Holy Ghost
 41. Elisabeth was *filled* with the Holy Ghost
 53. The hungry he hath *filled* with good things
 67. Zacharias was *filled* with the Holy Ghost
 2. 40. the child grew, and waxed strong, *f.* with wisdom
 3. 5. Every valley shall be *filled,* And every mountain
 4. 28. they were all *filled* with wrath in the synagogue
 5. 7. *filled* both the boats, so that they began to sink
 26. they were *filled* with fear, saying, We have seen
 6. 11. they were *filled* with madness; and communed
 21. Blessed are ye that hunger now: for ye shall be *f.*
 14. 23. them to come in, that my house may be *filled*
 15. 16. And he would fain have been *f.* with the husks
Jno. 2. 7. And they *filled* them up to the brim
 6 12. when they were *filled,* he saith unto his disciples
 13. and *filled* twelve baskets with broken pieces
 12. 3. house was *filled* with the odour of the ointment
 16. 6. these things unto you, sorrow hath *filled* your heart
Acts 2. 2. it *filled* all the house where they were sitting
 4. And they were all *filled* with the Holy Spirit. 4. 31
 13. mocking said, They are ¹*filled* with new wine
 3. 10. they were *filled* with wonder and amazement
 4. 8. Peter, *filled* with the Holy Ghost, said unto them
 5. 3. Ananias, why hath Satan *filled* thy heart to lie
 17. and they were *filled* with jealousy. 13. 45
 28. ye have *filled* Jerusalem with your teaching
 9. 17. receive thy sight, and be *f.* with the Holy Ghost
 13. 9. Paul, *filled* with the Holy Ghost, fastened his eyes
 52. And the disciples were *filled* with joy
 19. 28. heard this, they ⁷Ephesians) were ¹*f.* with wrath
 29. And the city was *filled* with the confusion
Rom. 1. 29. being *f.* with all unrighteousness, wickedness
 15. 14. full of goodness, *filled* with all knowledge
1 *Cor.* 4. 8. Already are ye ¹*f.,* already ye are become rich
2 *Cor.* 7. 4. I am *filled* with comfort, I overflow with joy
Eph. 3. 19. that ye may be *filled* unto all the fulness of God
 5. 18. but be *filled* with the Spirit
Phil. 1. 11. being *filled* with the fruits of righteousness
 4. 12. learned the secret both to be ¹*f.* and to be hungry
 18. I am ¹*filled,* having received from Epaphroditus
Col. 1. 9. ye may be *filled* with the knowledge of his will
2 *Tim.* 1. 4. thy tears, that I may be *filled* with joy
Jas. 2. 16. Go in peace, be ye warmed and *filled*
Rev. 8. 5 he *filled* it with the fire of the altar
 15. 8. And the temple was *filled* with smoke
 19. 21 and all the birds were *filled* with their flesh
 see fill, filling, finished, full, mingled, satisfied.

Filleth—ing.—*A.V.* ¹*filled,* ²*full,* ³*occupieth,* ⁴*supplieth.*

Mk. 4. 37. insomuch that the boat was now ²*filling*
 15. 36. one ran, and ¹*filling* a sponge full of vinegar
Lu. 8. 23. they were ¹*f.* with water, and were in jeopardy
Acts 14. 17. *filling* your hearts with food and gladness
1 *Cor.* 14. 16. he that ³*filleth* the place of the unlearned
2 *Cor.* 9. 12. not only ¹*filleth* up the measure of the wants
Eph. 1. 23. his body, the fulness of him that *filleth* all in all

Filth.

1 *Cor.* 4. 13. we are made as the *filth* of the world
1 *Pet.* 3. 21. not the putting away of the *filth* of the flesh

FINDETH

Filthiness.
Eph. 5. 4 nor *filthiness,* nor foolish talking, or jesting
Jas. 1. 21. Wherefore putting away all *f.* and overflowing
   see defilement, unclean.

Filthy.
1 *Tim.* 3. 8. given to much wine, not greedy of *filthy* lucre
Tit. 1. 7. no striker, not greedy of *filthy* lucre
 11. things which they ought not, for *filthy* lucre's sake
1 *Pet.* 5. 2. nor yet for *filthy* lucre, but of a ready mind
Rev. 22. 11. he that is *filthy,* let him be made *filthy* still
   see lascivious.

Final.—*A.V.* ¹*end.*
Heb. 6. 16. in every dispute of theirs the oath is ¹*final*

Find.—*A.V.* ¹*found.*
Mat. 7. 7. seek, and ye shall *find. Lu.* 11. 9
 14. leadeth unto life, and few be they that *find* it
 10. 39. loseth his life for my sake shall *find* it. 16. 25
 11. 29. and ye shall *find* rest unto your souls
 17. 27. opened his mouth, thou shalt *find* a shekel
 18. 13. if so be that he *find* it, verily I say unto you
 21. 2. ye shall *find* an ass tied. *Mk.* 11. 2; *Lu.* 19. 30
 22. 9. as many as ye shall *find,* bid to the marriage
 24. 46. when he cometh shall *find* so doing. *Lu.* 12. 43
Mk. 11. 13. if haply he might *find* anything thereon
 13. 36. lest coming suddenly he *find* you sleeping
Lu. 2. 12. Ye shall *f.* a babe wrapped in swaddling clothes
 6. 7. that they might *find* how to accuse him
 12. 37. the lord when he cometh shall *find* watching
 38. and *find* them so, blessed are those servants
 13. 7. seeking fruit on this fig tree, and *find* none
 15. 4. go after that which is lost, until he *find* it ?
 8. sweep the house, and seek diligently until she *f.* it ?
 18. 8. Son of man cometh, shall he *f.* faith on the earth ?
 19. 48. they could not *find* what they might do
 23. 4. And Pilate said—I *find* no fault in this man [Jesus]
Jno. 7. 34. Ye shall seek me, and shall not *find* me. 36
 35. will this man go that we shall not *find* him ?
 10. 9. go in and go out, and shall *find* pasture
 18. 38. I *find* no crime in him. 19. 4, 6
 21. 6. on the right side of the boat, and ye shall *find*
Acts 7. 46. to *find* a habitation for the God of Jacob
 17. 27. they might feel after him, and *find* him
 23. 9. saying, We *find* no evil in this man [Paul]
 24. 12. neither in the temple did they ¹*find* me disputing
Rom. 7. 21. I *find* then the law, that, to me who would
 9. 19. Why doth he still *find* fault ?
2 *Cor.* 9. 4. any of Macedonia, and *find* you unprepared
 12. 20. I should *find* you not such as I would
2 *Tim.* 1. 18. grant unto him to *find* mercy of the Lord
Heb. 4. 16. may *find* grace to help us in time of need
Rev. 2. 2. they are not, and didst ¹*find* them false
 9. 6. men shall seek death, and shall in no wise *find* it
 18. 14. and men shall *find* them no more at all
   see finding.

Findeth.—*A.V.* ¹*found.*
Mat. 7. 8. and he that seeketh *findeth. Lu.* 11. 10
 10. 39. He that *findeth* his life shall lose it
 12 43. seeking rest, and *findeth* it not
 44 when he is come, he *findeth* it empty, *Lu.* 11. 25
 26 40. the disciples, and *f.* them sleeping. *Mk.* 14. 37
Jno. 1. 41. He *findeth* first his own brother Simon
 43. On the morrow—he [Jesus] *findeth* Philip
 45. Philip *findeth* Nathanael, and saith unto him
 5. 14. Afterward Jesus *findeth* him in the temple
Acts 10. 27. he went in, and ¹*findeth* many come together

FINDING

Finding.—*A.V.* ¹*find,* ²*found,* ³*taking.*
Lu. 5. 19. not ¹*finding* by what way they might bring him
11. 24. seeking rest; and *f.* none, he saith, I will turn
Jno. 9. 35. and ²*finding* him, he said, Dost thou believe
Acts 4. 21. *finding* nothing how they might punish them
Rom. 7. 8. but sin, ³*finding* occasion, wrought in me
Heb. 8. 8. *finding* fault with them, he saith, Behold
see found, tracing (out).

Fine.—*A.V.* ¹*gay,* ²*goodly.*
Lu. 16. 19. and he was clothed in purple and *fine* linen
Jas. 2. 2. a man with a gold ring, in ²*fine* clothing
3. regard to him that weareth the ¹*fine* clothing
Rev. 18. 12. pearls, and *fine* linen, and purple, and silk
13. *fine* flour, and wheat, and cattle, and sheep
16. she that was arrayed in *fine* linen and purple
19. 8. that she should array herself in *fine* linen—for the *fine* linen is the righteous acts of the saints
14. clothed in *fine* linen, white and pure
see burnished.

Finger.—*A.V.* ¹*fingers.*
Mat. 23. 4. will not move them with their ¹*finger*
Lu. 11. 20. But if I by the *finger* of God cast out devils
16. 24. Lazarus—may dip the tip of his *finger* in water
Jno. 8. 6. Jesus—with his *finger* wrote on the ground.
8 20. 25. and put my *finger* into the print of the nails
27. Reach hither thy *finger,* and see my hands

Fingers
Mk. 7. 33. and put his *fingers* into his ears, and he spat
Lu. 11. 46. touch not the burdens with one of your *fingers*
see finger.

Finish.
Lu. 14. 29. laid a foundation, and is not able to *finish*
30. This man began to build, and was not able to *finish*
see accomplish, complete, finishing.

Finished—ing.—*A.V.* ¹*accomplished,* ²*expired,* ³*finish.*
⁴*fulfilled,* ⁵*filled up.*
Mat. 13. 53. when Jesus had *finished* these parables
19. 1. when Jesus had *finished* these words. 26. 1
Jno. 19. 28. Jesus, knowing that all things are now ¹*finished*
30. received the vinegar, he said, It is *finished*
Acts 21. 7. when we had *finished* the voyage from Tyre
Rom. 9. 28. upon the earth, ³*f.* it and cutting it short
2 *Tim.* 4. 7. *finished* the course, I have kept the faith
Heb. 4. 3. were *finished* from the foundation of the world
Rev. 10. 7. then is *finished* the mystery of God
11. 7. when they shall have *finished* their testimony
15. 1. for in them is ⁵*finished* the wrath of God
8. the seven plagues of the seven angels should be *f.*
20. 3. no more, until the thousand years should be ⁴*f.*
5. lived not until the thousand years should be *f.*
7. when the thousand years are ²*finished,* Satan shall
see accomplished, fullgrown.

Finisher *A.V.*—*see perfecter.*

Fire.
Mat. 3. 10. hewn down, and cast into the *f.* 7. 19 ; *Lu.* 3. 9
11. with the Holy Ghost and with *fire. Lu.* 3. 16
5. 22. Thou fool, shall be in danger of the hell of *fire*
13. 42. and shall cast them into the furnace of *fire.* 50
17. 15. he falleth into the *f.,* and oft-times into the water.
18. 8. or two feet to be cast into the eternal *f.* [*Mk.* 9. 22
9. than having two eyes to be cast into the hell of *fire*
25. 41. depart from me, ye cursed, into the eternal *fire*
Mk. 9. 43. hands to go into hell, into the unquenchable *f.*
48. their worm dieth not, and the *fire* is not quenched
49. For every one shall be salted with *fire*

FIRST

Lu. 3. 17. the chaff he will burn up with unquenchable *f.*
9. 54. wilt thou that we bid *f.* to come down from heaven
12. 49. I came to cast *fire* upon the earth
17. 29. it rained *fire* and brimstone from heaven [court
22. 55. when they had kindled a *fire* in the midst of the
56. maid seeing him as he sat in the light of the *f. Mk.* 14.
Jno. 15. 6. gather them, and cast them into the *fire* [54
Acts 2. 3. tongues parting asunder, like as of *fire*
19. Blood, and *fire,* and vapour of smoke
28. 2. they kindled a *fire,* and received us all
3. a bundle of sticks, and laid them on the *fire*
5. he shook off the beast into the *f.,* and took no harm
1 *Cor.* 3. 13. because it is revealed in *fire ;* and the *fire* itself
15. shall be saved ; yet so as through *fire*
2 *Th.* 1. 8. in flaming *f.,* rendering vengeance 'the sword
Heb. 11. 34. quenched the power of *f.,* escaped the edge of
12. 18. a mount that might be touched, and that burned
29. for our God is a consuming *fire* [with *fire*
Jas. 3. 5. how much wood is kindled by how small a *fire !*
6. the tongue is a *fire*—setteth on *fire* the wheel of nature, and is set on *fire* by hell
5. 3. and shall eat your flesh as *fire*
1 *Pet.* 1. 7. gold that perisheth though it is proved by *fire*
2 *Pet.* 3. 7. by the same word have been stored up for *fire*
12. the heavens being on *fire* shall be dissolved
Jude 7. suffering the punishment of eternal *fire*
23. some save, snatching them out of the *fire*
Rev. 3. 18. I counsel thee to buy of me gold refined by *fire*
4. 5. seven lamps of *fire* burning before the throne
8. 5. the censer ; and he filled it with the *fire* of the altar
7. there followed hail and *fire,* mingled with blood
8. a great mountain burning with *fire* was cast
9. 17 breastplates as of *f.*—mouths proceedeth *f.* 11. 5
18 the third part of men killed, by the *f* and the smoke
10. 1. his face was as the sun, and his feet as pillars of *f.*
13. 13. even make *fire* to come down out of heaven
14. 10. he shall be tormented with *fire* and brimstone
18. another angel—he that hath power over *fire*
15. 2. as it were a glassy sea mingled with *fire*
16. 8. was given unto it to scorch men with *fire*
19 20. into the lake of *fire* that burneth. 20. 10: 21. 8
20. 9. *fire* came down out of heaven, and devoured them
14. were cast into the lake of *fire*—even the lake of *fire*
15. he was cast into the lake of *fire*
see burned, coals, flame.

Firkins.
Jno. 2. 6. waterpots—containing two or three *f.* apiece

Firm.—*A.V.* ¹*stedfast,* ²*sure.*
2 *Tim.* 2. 19. Howbeit the ²*firm* foundation of God standeth
Heb. 3. 6. and the glorying of our hope *firm* unto the end
14. beginning of our confidence ¹*firm* unto the end

First.—*A.V.* ¹*beginning,* ²*chief,* ³*chiefest,* ⁴*chiefly,* ⁵*former,* ⁶*forward,* ⁷*one.*
Mat. 5. 24. *first* be reconciled to thy brother, and then come
6. 33. seek ye *first* his kingdom, and his righteousness
7. 5. cast out *f.* the beam out of thine own eye. *Lu.* 6. 42
8. 21. suffer me *first* to go and bury my father. *Lu.* 9. 59
12. 29. except he *first* bind the strong man ? *Mk.* 3. 27
13. 30. Gather up *f.* the tares, and bind them in bundles
17. 10. that Elijah must *first* come ? *Mk.* 9. 11, 12
27. cast a hook, and take up the fish that *f.* cometh up
20. 8. their hire, beginning from the last unto the *first*
10. when the *f.* came, they supposed that they would
16. the last shall be *first,* and the *first* last. 19. 30:
Mk. 10. 31 : *Lu.* 13. 30 [servant
27. whosoever would be ²*first* among you shall be your
21. 28. he came to the *first,* and said, Son, go work
31. twain did the will of his father? They say, The *f.*

123

FIRST

Mat. 21. 36. Again, he sent other servants more than the *f.*
22. 25. seven brethren: and the *f.* married and deceased
23. 26. blind Pharisee, cleanse *first* the inside of the cup
Mk. 4. 28. *first* the blade, then the ear, then the full corn
7. 27. said unto her, Let the children *first* be filled
10. 44. whosoever would be ²*first* among you, shall be
12. 20. *f.* took a wife, and dying left no seed. *Lu.* 20. 29
28. What commandment is the *first* of all? *Mat.* 22. 38
13. 10. the gospel must *first* be preached unto all
16. 9. *first* day of the week, he appeared *first* to Mary
Lu. 1. 3. the course of all things accurately from the *first*
2. 2. This was the *first* enrolment made when Quirinius
9. 61. *first* suffer me to bid farewell to them that are at
10. 5. ye shall enter, *first* say, Peace be to this house
11. 38. marvelled that he had not *f.* washed before dinner
14. 18. The *first* said unto him, I have bought a field
28. a tower, doth not *first* sit down and count the cost
31. will not sit down *first* and take counsel
16 5. said to the *f.*, How much owest thou unto my lord?
17. 25. But *first* must he suffer many things
19. 16. And the *first* came before him, saying, Lord
21. 9. for these things must needs come to pass *first*
Jno. 1. 41. He findeth *first* his own brother Simon
2. 10. Every man setteth on ¹*first* the good wine
5. 4. *first* after the troubling of the water [margin]
8. 7. without sin among you, let him *first* cast a stone
10. 40. the place where John was at the *first* baptizing
18. 13. led him to Annas *first* ; for he was father in law
19. 32. soldiers therefore came, and brake the legs of the *f.*
20. 4. followed Peter, and came *first* to the tomb. 8
Acts 3. 26. Unto you *f.* God, having raised up his Servant
7. 12. he sent forth our fathers the *first* time
11. 26. disciples were called Christians *first* in Antioch
12. 10. when they were past the *first* and the second ward
13. 24. John had *first* preached before his coming the
46. that the word of God should *first* be spoken to you
26. 5. the Jews; having knowledge of me from the ¹*first*
20. but declared both to them of Damascus *first*
23. how that he *first* by the resurrection of the dead
27. 43. cast themselves overboard, and get *f.* to the land
Rom. 1. 8. *First*, I thank my God through Jesus Christ
2. 9. of the Jew *first*, and also of the Greek. 10
3. 2. ¹*f.* of all, that they were intrusted with the oracles
10. 19. *First* Moses saith, I will provoke you to jealousy
11. 35. or who hath *first* given to him, and it shall be
15. 24. if *first* in some measure I shall have been
1 *Cor.* 12. 28. *first* apostles, secondly prophets, thirdly
14. 30. revelation be made to another—let the *first* keep
15. 3. I delivered unto you *first* of all that which also
45. The *first* man Adam became a living soul
46. Howbeit that is not *first* which is spiritual
47. The *first* man is of the earth, earthy
2 *Cor.* 8. 5. but *f.* they gave their own selves to the Lord
10. for you, who were the ²*first* to make a beginning
Eph. 6. 2. (which is the *first* commandment with promise)
1 *Th.* 4. 16. the dead in Christ shall rise *first*
2 *Th.* 2. 3. except the falling away come *first*
1 *Tim.* 2. 1. exhort therefore, *first* of all, that supplications
13. For Adam was *first* formed, then Eve
3. 10. let these also *first* be proved; then let them serve
5. 4. learn *first* to shew piety towards their own family
12. because they have rejected their *first* faith
2 *Tim.* 1. 5. which dwelt *first* in thy grandmother Lois
2. 6. labourer must be the *first* to partake of the fruit
4. 16. At my *first* defence no one took my part
Tit. 3. 10. after a *first* and second admonition refuse
Heb. 5. 12. teach you the rudiments of the *first* principles
7. 2. being *first*, by interpretation, King of righteousness
27. offer up sacrifices, *f.* for his own sins, and then for

FISHES

Heb. 8. 7. For if that *f.* covenant had been faultless. 13: 9.1
9. 2. a tabernacle prepared, the *first*, wherein were the
6. go in continually into the *first* tabernacle. 8
15. that were under the *first* covenant. 18
10. 9. He taketh away the ¹*first*, that he may establish
Jas. 3. 17. the wisdom that is from above is *first* pure
1 *Pet.* 4. 17. if it begin *first* at us, what shall be the end
2 *Pet.* 1. 20. knowing this *first*, that no prophecy. 3. 3
2. 20. last state is become worse with them than the ¹*f.*
1 *Jno.* 4. 19. We love, because he *first* loved us
Rev. 2. 4. this against thee, that thou didst leave thy *f.* love
5. and repent, and do the *first* works
8. These things saith the *first* and the last [heard
4. 1. a door opened in heaven, and the *first* voice which I
7. And the *first* creature was like a lion
8. 7. the *first* [angel] sounded, and there followed hail
13. 12. authority of the *first* beast—worship the *f.* beast
16. 2. And the *first* went, and poured out his bowl
20. 5. This is the *first* resurrection
6. holy is he that hath part in the *first* resurrection
21. 1. the *f.* heaven and the *first* earth are passed away
4. the ²*first* things are passed away
19. The *f.* foundation was jasper ; the second, sapphire
see before, chief, day, last.

First begotten *A.V.*—see firstborn.

Firstborn.—*A.V.* ¹*first begotten.*

Lu. 2. 7. And she brought forth her *firstborn* son
Rom. 8. 29. that he might be the *f.* among many brethren
Col. 1. 15. image of the invisible God, the *f.* of all creation
18. who is the beginning, the *firstborn* from the dead
Heb. 1. 6. when he again bringeth in the ¹*f.* into the world
11. 28. the destroyer of the *f.* should not touch them
12. 23. church of the *firstborn* who are enrolled in heaven
Rev. 1. 5. the faithful witness, the ¹*firstborn* of the dead

Firstfruit—s.

Rom. 8. 23. which have the *firstfruits* of the Spirit
11. 16. if the *firstfruit* is holy, so is the lump
16. 5. who is the *firstfruits* of Asia unto Christ
1 *Cor.* 15. 20. the *firstfruits* of them that are asleep
23. Christ the *firstfruits*; then they that are Christ's
16. 15. Stephanas, that it is the *firstfruits* of Achaia
Jas. 1. 18. we should be a kind of *firstfruits* of his creatures
Rev. 14. 4. among men, to be the *firstfruits* unto God

Fish.

Mat. 7. 10. ask for a *f.*, will give him a serpent ? *Lu.* 11. 11
17. 27. take up the *fish* that first cometh up
Lu. 24. 42. they gave him a piece of a broiled *fish*
Jno. 21. 9. a fire of coals there, and *fish* laid thereon
16. 15. Stephanas, that it is the *firstfruits* of Achaia
13. the bread, and giveth them, and the *fish* likewise

Fishermen.

Lu. 5. 2. but the *fishermen* had gone out of them [boats]

Fishers.

Mat. 4. 18. casting a net into the sea ; for they were *f. Mk.*
19. I will make you *fishers* of men. *Mk.* 1. 17 [1. 16

Fishes.

Mat. 14. 17. We have here but five loaves, and two *fishes*.
19 : *Mk.* 6. 38, 41, 43 : *Lu.* 9. 13, 16 : *Jno.* 6. 9, 11
15. 34. Seven, and a few small *fishes*. 36 : *Mk.* 8. 7
Lu. 5. 6. they inclosed a great multitude of *fishes*

FISHES

Lu. 5. 9. at the draught of the *fishes* which they had taken
Jno. 21. 6. not able to draw it for the multitude of *fishes*
    11. drew the net to land, full of great *fishes*, 8
1 *Cor.* 15. 39. another flesh of birds, and another of *fishes*

Fishing.
Jno. 21. 3. Simon Peter saith unto them, I go a *fishing*

Fit.—*A.V.* ¹*reason*.
Lu. 9. 62. looking back, is *fit* for the kingdom of God
14. 35. *fit* neither for the land nor for the dunghill
Acts 6. 2. It is not *fit* that we should forsake the word of
22. 22. for it is not *fit* that he should live   [God
                         see fitting.

Fitly.
Eph. 2. 21. *f.* framed together, groweth into a holy temple
4. 16. all the body *fitly* framed and knit together

Fitted—ing.—*A. V.* ¹*convenient*, ²*fit*.
Rom. 1. 28. God gave them up unto a reprobate mind, to do
    those things which are not ¹*fitting*
9. 22. vessels of wrath *fitted* unto destruction
Col. 3. 18. to your husbands, as is ²*fitting* in the Lord

Five.
Mat. 14. 17. We have here but *five* loaves, and two fishes.
    19: *Mk.* 6. 38, 41: *Lu.* 9. 13, 16   [*Mk.* 8. 19
16. 9. remember the *five* loaves of the *five* thousand.
25. 2. *five* of them were foolish, and *five* were wise
15. unto one he gave *five* talents. 16, 20
Mk. 6. 44. they that ate the loaves were *five* thousand. *Lu.*
    9. 14: *Jno.* 6. 10
Lu. 1. 24. she hid herself *five* months, saying
12. 6. Are not *five* sparrows sold for two farthings?
52. shall be from henceforth *five* in one house divided
14. 19. I have bought *five* yoke of oxen, and I go to prove
16. 28. for I have *five* brethren; that he may testify
19. 18. thy pound, Lord, hath made *five* pounds
19. Be thou also over *five* cities
Jno. 4. 18. for thou hast had *five* husbands
5. 2. called in Hebrew Bethesda, having *five* porches
6. 13. broken pieces from the *five* barley loaves. 9
Acts 20. 6. came unto them to Troas in *five* days
24. 1. after *five* days the high priest Ananias came down
1 *Cor.* 14. 19. rather speak *f.* words with my understanding
2 *Cor.* 11. 24. Of the Jews *f.* times received I forty stripes
Rev. 9. 5. but that they should be tormented *five* months
10. in their tails is their power to hurt men *five* months
17. 10. *five* are fallen, the one is, the other is not yet

Fixed.
Lu. 16. 26. between us and you there is a great gulf *fixed*

Flame.
Lu. 16. 24. for I am in anguish in this *flame*
Acts 7. 30. mount Sinai, in a *flame* of fire in a bush
Heb. 1. 7. angels winds, And his ministers a *flame* of fire
Rev. 1. 14. his eyes were as a *flame* of fire. 2. 18: 19. 12

Flaming.
2 *Th.* 1. 8. in *flaming* fire, rendering vengeance to them

Flattering *A. V.*—*see flattery*.

Flattery.—*A.V.* ¹*flattering*.
1 *Th.* 2. 5. neither at any time—using words of ¹*flattery*

Flax.
Mat. 12. 20. And smoking *flax* shall he not quench

FLESH

Fled.
Mat. 8. 33. And they that fed them *f. Mk.* 5. 14: *Lu.* 8. 34
26. 56. Then all the disciples left him, and *fled. Mk.*
Mk. 14. 52. he left the linen cloth, and *fled* naked [14. 50
16. 8. they went out, and *fled* from the tomb
Acts 7. 29. And Moses *fled* at this saying, and became
14. 6. they [Paul and Barnabas]—*fled* unto the cities of
19. 16. they *fled* out of that house naked and wounded
Heb. 6. 18. *f.* for refuge to lay hold of the hope set before us
Rev. 12. 6. the woman *fled* into the wilderness
16. 20. And every island *fled* away, and the mountains
20. 11. from whose face the earth and the heaven *f.* away
                      see escaped.

Flee.
Mat.. 2. 13. *flee* into Egypt, and be thou there
3. 7. warned you to *f.* from the wrath to come? *Lu.* 3. 7
10. 23. when they persecute you in this city, *f.* into the
24. 16. let them that are in Judæa *f. Mk.* 13. 14: *Lu.* 21. 21
Jno. 10. 5. And a stranger will they not follow, but will *flee*
Acts 27. 30. as the sailors were seeking to *f.* out of the ship
1 *Cor.* 6. 18. *Flee* fornication
10. 14. Wherefore, my beloved, *flee* from idolatry
1 *Tim.* 6. 11. But thou, O man of God, *flee* these things
2 *Tim.* 2. 22. But *flee* youthful lusts, and follow after
Jas. 4. 7. resist the devil, and he will *flee* from you
                      see fleeth, fly.

Fleeth.—*A.V.* ¹*flee*.
Jno. 10. 12. hireling—leaveth the sheep, and *fleeth*
13. he *fleeth* because he is a hireling, and careth not
Rev. 9. 6. desire to die, and death ¹*fleeth* from them

Flesh.—*A.V.* ¹*fleshy*.
Mat. 16. 17. for *f.* and blood hath not revealed it unto thee
19. 5. the twain shall become one *flesh? Mk.* 10. 8
6. they are no more twain, but one *flesh. Mk.* 10. 8
24. 22. no *flesh* would have been saved. *Mk.* 13. 20
26. 41. indeed is willing, but the *f.* is weak. *Mk.* 14. 38
Lu. 24. 39. for a spirit hath not *flesh* and bones
Jno. 1. 14. the Word became *flesh*, and dwelt among us
6. 63. spirit that quickeneth; the *f.* profiteth nothing
Rom. 1. 3. born of the seed of David according to the *flesh*
3. 20. works of the law shall no *f.* be justified. *Gal.* 2. 16
4. 1. Abraham, our forefather according to the *flesh*
6. 19. manner of men because of the infirmity of your *f.*
7. 25. the law of God; but with the *flesh* the law of sin
8. 3. it was weak through the *flesh*—likeness of sinful *f.*
12. we are debtors, not to the *f.*, to live after the *flesh*
9. 3. my kinsmen according to the *flesh*
5. and of whom is Christ as concerning the *flesh*
13. 14. make not provision for the *flesh*, to fulfil the lusts
1 *Cor.* 1. 29. that no *flesh* should glory before God [thereof
6. 16. The twain, saith he, shall become one *f. Eph.* 5. 31
15. 39. All *flesh* is not the same *flesh*—one *flesh* of men,
    and another *flesh* of beasts, and another *f.* of birds
50. *flesh* and blood cannot inherit the kingdom of God
2 *Cor.* 1. 17. do I purpose according to the *flesh*
3. 3. but in tables that are hearts of ¹*flesh*
4. 11. also of Jesus may be manifested in our mortal *f.*
7. 1. cleanse ourselves from all defilement of *flesh*
5. our *flesh* had no relief, but we were afflicted
10. 2. count of us as if we walked according to the *flesh*
Gal. 1. 16. immediately I conferred not with *f.* and blood
3. 3. begun in the Spirit, are ye now perfected in the *f.?*
5. 13. use not your freedom for an occasion to the *flesh*
17. For the *flesh* lusteth against the Spirit, and the
    Spirit against the *flesh*
24. they that are of Christ Jesus have crucified the *flesh*
6. 13. circumcised, that they may glory in your *flesh*

FLESH   FLOW

Eph. 2. 3. we also all once lived in the lusts of our *flesh*,
   doing the desires of the *f.* and of the mind [3. 22
6. 5. them that according to the *f.* are your masters. *Col.*
12. For our wrestling is not against *flesh* and blood
Col. 2. 13. dead through—the uncircumcision of your *flesh*
Heb. 2. 14. the children are sharers in *flesh* and blood
12. 9. we had the fathers of our *flesh* to chasten us
1 *Pet.* 1. 24. All *flesh* is as grass, And all the glory thereof
Jude 7. gone after strange *f.*, are set forth as an example
8. these also in their dreamings defile the *flesh*
23. hating even the garment spotted by the *flesh*
Rev. 19. 18. *flesh* of kings—*flesh* of captains—*flesh* of
   mighty men—*flesh* of horses—*flesh* of all men
21. and all the birds were filled with their *flesh*

After the Flesh.

Jno. 8. 15. Ye judge *after the flesh*; I judge no man
Rom. 8. 4. who walk not *after the flesh*, but after the spirit
5. they that are *after the flesh* do mind the things
12. not to the flesh, to live *after the flesh*
13. for if ye live *after the flesh*, ye must die
1 *Cor.* 1. 26. how that not many wise *after the flesh*
10. 18. Behold Israel *after the flesh*
2 *Cor.* 5. 16. henceforth know no man *after the flesh*: even
   though we have known Christ *after the flesh*
11. 18. Seeing that many glory *after the flesh*
Gal. 4. 23. the son by the handmaid is born *after the flesh*
29. But as then he that was born *after the flesh*
2 *Pet.* 2. 10. but chiefly them that walk *after the flesh*

All Flesh.

Lu. 3. 6. And *all flesh* shall see the salvation of God
Jno. 17. 2. thou gavest him authority over *all flesh*
Acts 2. 17. I will pour forth of my Spirit upon *all flesh*
1 *Cor.* 15. 39. *All flesh* is not the same flesh
1 *Pet.* 1. 24. *All flesh* is as grass, And all the glory thereof

His Flesh.

Acts 2. 31. was he left in Hades, nor did *his f.* see corruption
Gal. 6. 8. For he that soweth unto *his* own *flesh* shall
Eph. 2. 15. having abolished in *his flesh* the enmity
5. 29. for no man ever hated *his* own *flesh*
Col. 1. 22. hath he reconciled in the body of *his flesh*
Heb. 5. 7. in the days of *his flesh*, having offered up prayers
10. 20. through the veil, that is to say, *his flesh*

In Flesh, or in the Flesh.

Rom. 2. 28. circumcision, which is outward *in the flesh*
7. 5. For when we were *in the flesh*, the sinful passions
8. 3. as an offering for sin, condemned sin *in the flesh*
8. they that are *in the flesh* cannot please God
9. But ye are not *in the flesh*, but in the spirit
1 *Cor.* 7. 28. Yet such shall have tribulation *in the flesh*
2 *Cor.* 10. 3. For though we walk *in the flesh*
12. 7. there was given to me a thorn *in the flesh*
Gal. 2. 20. that life which I now live *in the flesh* I live
6. 12. As many as desire to make a fair show *in the flesh*
Eph. 2. 11. the Gentiles *in the flesh—in the flesh*, made by
Phil. 1. 22. But if to live *in the flesh*,—if this is the fruit
24. to abide *in the flesh* is more needful for your sake
3. 3. and have no confidence *in the flesh*   [*the flesh*
4. have confidence even *in the flesh*—have confidence in
Col. 2. 1. as many as have not seen my face *in the flesh*
5. though I am absent *in the flesh* yet am I with you
1 *Tim.* 3. 16. He who was manifested *in the flesh*
Philem. 16. brother beloved—both *in the f.* and in the Lord
1 *Pet.* 3. 18. being put to death *in the flesh*, but quickened
4. 1. Christ suffered *in the flesh—*that hath suffered *in t.f.*

1 *Pet.* 4. 2. live the rest of your time *in the flesh*
6. might be judged according to men *in the flesh*
1 *Jno.* 4. 2. that Jesus Christ is come *in the flesh*. 2 *Jno.* 7

My Flesh.

Jno. 6. 51. the bread which I will give is *my flesh*
54. He that eateth *my flesh*. 56
55. For *my flesh* is meat indeed, and my blood is drink
Acts 2. 26. *my flesh* also shall dwell in hope
Rom. 7. 18. in me, that is, in *my f.*, dwelleth no good thing
11. 14. provoke to jealousy them that are *my flesh*
Gal. 4. 14. which was a temptation to you in *my flesh*
Col. 1. 24. lacking of the afflictions of Christ in *my flesh*

Of the Flesh.—*A.V.* ¹carnal, ²carnally.

Jno. 1. 13. not of blood, nor of the will *of the flesh*
3. 6. That which is born *of the flesh* is flesh
Rom. 8. 5. after the flesh do mind the things *of the flesh*
6. for the mind ²*of the flesh* is death
7. because the mind ¹*of the flesh* is enmity against God
9. 8. the children *of the flesh* that are children of God
1 *Cor.* 5. 5. unto Satan for the destruction *of the flesh*
2 *Cor.* 10. 4. weapons of our warfare are not ¹*of the flesh*
Gal. 4. 13. because of an infirmity *of the flesh* I preached
5. 16. and ye shall not fulfil the lust *of the flesh*
19. Now the works *of the flesh* are manifest
6. 8. unto his own flesh shall *of the flesh* reap corruption
Eph. 2. 3. doing the desires *of the flesh* and of the mind
Col. 2. 11. in the putting off of the body *of the flesh*
23. not of any value against the indulgence *of the flesh*
Heb. 9. 13. sanctify unto the cleanness *of the flesh*
1 *Pet.* 3. 21. not the putting away of the filth *of the flesh*
2 *Pet.* 2. 18. they entice in the lusts *of the flesh*
1 *Jno.* 2. 16. the lust *of the flesh*, and the lust of the eyes

Fleshly.

2 *Cor.* 1. 12. not in *fleshly* wisdom but in the grace of God
Col. 2. 18. vainly puffed up by his *fleshly* mind
1 *Pet.* 2. 11. to abstain from *fleshly* lusts, which war

Fleshy *A.V.—see flesh.*

Flight.

Mat. 24. 20. pray ye that your *flight* be not in the winter
Heb. 11. 34. turned to *flight* armies of aliens

Flock.

Mat. 26. 31. the sheep of the *flock* shall be scattered
Lu. 2. 8. keeping watch by night over their *flock*
12. 32. Fear not, little *f.*; for it is your Father's good
Jno. 10. 16. they shall become one *flock*, one shepherd
Acts 20. 28. unto yourselves, and to all the *flock*
29. enter in among you, not sparing the *flock*
1 *Cor.* 9. 7. a *flock*, and eateth not of the milk of the *f.*?
1 *Pet.* 5. 2. Tend the *flock* of God which is among you
3. making yourselves ensamples to the *flock*

Flood—s.

Mat. 7. 25. the *floods* came, and the winds blew. 27
24. 39. those days which were before the *flood*
39. they knew not until the *flood* came. *Lu.* 17. 27
Lu. 6. 48. when a *f.* arose, the stream brake against that
2 *Pet.* 2. 5. when he brought a *f.* upon the world [house
   see river, stream.

Floor *A.V.—see threshing-floor.*

Flourished *A.V.—see revived.*

Flow.

Jno. 7. 38. out of his belly shall *flow* rivers of living water

FLOWER

Flower.
1 *Cor.* 7. 36. if she be past the *flower* of her age
Jas. 1. 10. as the *flower* of the grass he shall pass away
  11. withereth the grass; and the *flower* thereof falleth
1 *Pet.* 1. 24. as the *flower* of the grass—and the *f.* falleth

Flute-players.—*A.V.* ¹*minstrels*, ²*pipers.*
Mat. 9. 23. Jesus came—and saw the ¹*f.-p.* and the crowd
Rev. 18. 22. the voice of harpers and minstrels and ²*f.-p*

Flux *A.V.*—*see dysentery.*

Fly.—*A.V.* ¹*flee.*
Rev. 12. 14. that she might ¹*fly* into the wilderness
  19. 17. saying to all the birds that *fly* in mid heaven
  see flying.

Flying.—*A.V.* ¹*fly.*
Rev. 4. 7. the fourth creature was like a *flying* eagle
  8. 13. I heard an eagle, *flying* in mid heaven
  14. 6. I saw another angel ¹*flying* in mid heaven

Foal.
Mat. 21. 5. And upon a colt the *foal* of an ass

Foameth—ing.
Mk. 9. 18. he *f.*, and grindeth his teeth, and pineth away.
  20. fell on the ground, and wallowed *foaming.* [*Lu.* 9. 39
Jude 13. wild waves of the sea, *f.* out their own shame

Foes.
Mat. 10. 36. a man's *foes* shall be they of his own household
  see enemies.

Fold.—*A.V.* ¹*sheepfold.*
Jno. 10. 1. entereth not by the door into the ¹*f.* of the sheep
  16. other sheep I have, which are not of this *fold*
  see roll.

Folk.
Mk. 6. 5. laid his hands upon a few sick *f.*, and healed them
Acts 5. 16. cities round about Jerusalem, bringing sick *folk*
  see sick.

Follow.—*A.V.* ¹*followed,* ²*followeth,* ³*fully known.*
Mat. 8. 19. I will *f.* thee whithersoever thou goest. *Lu.* 9
  10. 38. not take his cross and ²*follow* after me [57. 61
Mk. 5. 37. he suffered no man to *follow* with him
  6. 1. cometh into his own country; and his disciples *f.* him
  16. 17. these signs shall *follow* them that believe
Lu. 17. 23. go not away, nor *follow* after them
  22. 10. bearing a pitcher of water; *f.* him. *Mk.* 14. 13
  49. they that were about him saw what would *follow*
Jno. 10. 4. the sheep *follow* him: for they know his voice
  5. a stranger will they not *follow*, but will flee from him
  13. 36. but thou shalt *follow* afterwards
  37. Lord, why cannot I *follow* thee even now?
Rom. 14. 19. let us *f.* after things which make for peace
1 *Cor.* 14. 1. *Follow* after love; yet desire—spiritual gifts
1 *Th.* 5. 15. but alway *follow* after that which is good
1 *Tim.* 5. 24. and some men also they *follow* after
  6. 11. flee these things; and *follow* after righteousness.
2 *Tim.* 3. 10. But thou didst ³*f.* my teaching [2 *Tim.* 2. 22
Heb. 12. 14. *Follow* after peace with all men
1 *Pet.* 1. 11. of Christ, and the glories that should *f.* them
  2. 21. an example, that ye should *follow* his steps
2 *Pet.* 1. 16. For we did not ¹*follow* cunningly devised fables
  2. 2. many shall *follow* their lascivious doings
Rev. 14. 4. These are they which *follow* the Lamb
  13. their labours; for their works *follow* with them
  see followed, imitate, press.

FOLLOWED

Follow *me.*
Mat. 8. 22. *Follow me ;* and leave the dead to bury their
  9. 9. he saith unto him, *F. me. Mk.* 2. 14: *Lu.* 5. 27: 9. 59
  16. 24. let him deny himself, and take up his cross, and
  follow me. Mk. 8. 34: 10. 21: *Lu.* 9. 23
  19. 21. treasures in heaven: and come, *f. me. Lu.* 18. 22
Jno. 1. 43. findeth Philip: and Jesus saith unto him, *F. me*
  10. 27. I know them, and they *follow me*
  12. 26. If any man serve me, let him *follow me*
  13. 36. Whither I go, thou canst not *follow me* now
  21. 19. he [Jesus] saith unto him, [¹*eter*] *Follow me*
  22. what is that to thee? *follow* thou *me*
Acts 12. 8. Cast thy garment about thee, and *follow me*
  see come after, followed.

Followed.—*A.V.* ¹*attained,* ²*follow,* ³*followeth,*
  ⁴*following.*
Mat. 8. 10. marvelled, and said to them that *followed*
  19. 27. left all, and *followed* thee. *Mk.* 10. 28: *Lu.* 18. 28
  28. that ye which have *followed* me, in the regeneration
  21. 9. that *followed*, cried, saying, Hosanna. *Mk.* 11. 9.
  27. 55. women—which had *followed* Jesus from Galilee
Mk. 3. 7. a great multitude from Galilee *followed*
  9. 38. we forbade him, because he ³*followed* not us
  10. 32. and they that *followed* were afraid
  52. received his sight, and *followed* him in the way
  16. 20. confirming the word by the signs that *followed*
Lu. 22. 54. high priest's house. But Peter *followed* afar off
  23. 55. the women—*followed* after, and beheld the tomb
Jno. 1. 37. two disciples heard him speak, and they *f.*
  11. 31. *f.* her, supposing that she was going unto the
  18. 15. Simon Peter *followed* Jesus, and so did another
Acts 3. 24. from Samuel and them that ²*followed* after
  12. 9. [¹*eter*] went out, and *followed;* and he wist not
  13. 43. devout proselytes *followed* Paul and Barnabas
  21. 36. *followed* after, crying out, Away with him
Rom. 9. 30. Gentiles, which *f.* not after righteousness
1 *Cor.* 10. 4. drank of a spiritual rock that *followed* them
1 *Tim.* 4. 6. good doctrine which thou hast ¹*followed*
  5. 10. she hath diligently *followed* every good work
2 *Pet.* 2. 15. having ²*followed* the way of Balaam
Rev. 6. 8. was Death; and Hades *followed* with him
  8. 7. there *followed* hail and fire, mingled with blood
  14. 8. a second angel *followed*, saying, Fallen, fallen
  9. another angel, a third, *followed* them
  see after, follow, following.

Followed *him.*
Mat. 4. 20. left the nets, and *followed him. Mk.* 1. 18
  22. left the boat and their father, and *followed him*
  25. *followed him* great multitudes from Galilee. 8. 1:
  12. 15: 14. 13: 19. 2: 20. 29: 23. 27: *Mk.* 2. 15:
  5. 24: *Lu.* 9. 11: 23. 27: *Jno.* 6. 2
  8. 23. he was entered into a boat, his disciples *f.* him.
  9. 9. And he arose, and *followed him. Mk.* 2. 14 |*Lu.* 22. 39
  19. Jesus arose, and *f. him*, and so did his disciples
  27. two blind men *followed him*, crying out, and saying
  20. 34. they received their sight, and *f. him, Lu.* 18. 43
  26. 58. Peter *followed him* afar off. *Mk.* 14. 54
Mk. 1. 36. they that were with him *followed* after *him*
  14. 51. a certain young man *followed* with *him*
  15. 41. women—*followed him*, and ministered unto him
Lu. 5. 11. their boats to land, they left all, and *f. him,* 28
  7. 9. turned and said unto the multitude that *f. him*
  23. 49. the women that *followed* with *him* from Galilee
Jno. 1. 40. *f. him*, was Andrew, Simon Peter's brother
Rev. 19. 14. the armies which are in heaven *followed* him

127

FOLLOWERS   FORBID

Followers *A.V.—see imitators, zealous.*
Followeth.
Lu. 9. 49. we forbade him, because he *followeth* not with us
Jno. 8. 12. he that *f.* me shall not walk in the darkness
    see follow, followed.

Following.—*A.V.* ¹*followed.*
Lu. 13. 33. to-day and to-morrow and the day *following*
Jno. 1. 38. Jesus turned, and beheld them *following*
20. 6. Simon Peter therefore also cometh, *following* him
21. 20. seeth the disciple whom Jesus loved *following*
Acts 16. 17. The same ¹*following* after Paul and us cried out
21. 18. the day *f.* Paul went in with us unto James
23. 11. the night *following* the Lord stood by him
Rom. 9. 31. Israel, ¹*following* after a law of righteousness
    see followed.

Folly.
2 Tim. 3. 9. for their *folly* shall be evident unto all men
    see foolishness.

Food.—*A.V.* ¹*abstinence,* ²*meat—s,* ³*victuals.*
Mat. 3. 4. his ²*food* was locusts and wild honey
6. 25. Is not the life more than the ²*food.* Lu. 12. ²23
10. 10. the labourer is worthy of his ²*food*
14. 15. go into the villages, and buy themselves ³*food*
Lu. 3. 11. he that hath ²*food,* let him do likewise
9. 13. except we should go and buy ²*f.* for all this people
12. 42. them their portion of ²*f.* in due season? Mat. 24. ²45
Jno. 4. 8. disciples were gone away into the city to buy ²*f.*
Acts 2. 46. they did take their ²*food* with gladness
9. 19. he [Saul] took ²*food* and was strengthened
14. 17. fruitful seasons, filling your hearts with *food*
27. 21. they had been long without ¹*f.,* then Paul stood
33. Paul besought them all to take some ²*f.* ³34 [forth
36. were—all of good cheer, and themselves also took ²*f.*
2 Cor. 9. 10. seed to the sower and bread for *food* [content
1 Tim. 6. 8. having *f.* and covering we shall be therewith
Heb. 5. 12. have need of milk, and not of solid ²*food*
14. But solid ²*food* is for fullgrown men
Jas. 2. 15. brother or sister be naked, and in lack of daily *f.*

Fool.
Mat. 5. 22. whosoever shall say, Thou *f.,* shall be in danger
1 Cor. 3. 18. let him become a *f.,* that he may become wise
    see beside myself, foolish.

Foolish.—*A.V.* ¹*fool—s,* ²*unwise.*
Mat. 7. 26. a *f.* man, which built his house upon the sand
25. 2. five of them [virgins] were *foolish*
3. For the *foolish,* when they took their lamps
8. the *foolish* said unto the wise, Give us of your oil
Lu. 11. 40. Ye ¹*foolish* ones, did not he that made the outside
12. 20. Thou ¹*foolish* one, this night is thy soul required
24. 25. O ¹*foolish* men, and slow of heart to believe in all
Rom. 1. 14. I am a debtor—both to the wise and to the ²*f.*
2. 20. a corrector of the *foolish,* a teacher of babes
1 Cor. 1. 20. hath not God made *f.* the wisdom of the world?
27. but God chose the *foolish* things of the world
1. 36. Thou ¹*foolish* one, that which thou thyself sowest
2 Cor. 11. 16. Let no man think me ¹*foolish*—*f.* receive me
19. For ye bear with the ¹*foolish* gladly
12. 6. if I should desire to glory, I shall not be ¹*foolish*
11. I am become ¹*foolish :* ye compelled me
Gal. 3. 1. O *foolish* Galatians, who did bewitch you
3. Are ye so *foolish ?* having begun in the Spirit
Eph. 5. 4. nor filthiness, nor *foolish* talking, or jesting
17. Wherefore be ye not ²*foolish,* but understand
1 Tim. 6. 9. a snare and many *foolish* and hurtful lusts

2. Tim. 2. 23. *foolish* and ignorant questionings refuse
Tit. 3. 3. For we also were aforetime *foolish,* disobedient
9. shun *foolish* questionings, and genealogies
1 Pet. 2. 15. put to silence the ignorance of *foolish* men
    see senseless, void of understanding.

Foolishly *A.V.—see foolishness.*
Foolishness.—*A.V.* ¹*folly,* ²*foolishly.*
Mk. 7. 22. an evil eye, pride, *foolishness:* *foolishness*
1 Cor. 1. 18. word of the cross is to them that are perishing
21. God's good pleasure through the *f.* of the preaching
23. a stumblingblock, and unto Gentiles *foolishness*
25. Because the *foolishness* of God is wiser than men
2. 14. for they are *f.* unto him ; and he cannot know
3. 19. wisdom of this world is *foolishness* with God
2 Cor. 11. 1. ye could bear with me in a little ¹*foolishness*
17. speak not after the Lord, but as in ²*foolishness*
21. any is bold (I speak in ²*foolishness*), I am bold also

Fools.
Mat. 23. 17. Ye *fools* and blind : for whether is greater
Rom. 1. 22. Professing themselves to be wise, they became *f.*
1 Cor. 4. 10. We are *fools* for Christ's sake
    see foolish, unwise.

Foot.—*A.V.* ¹*afoot,* ²*came,* ³*down.*
Mat. 4. 6. haply thou dash thy *f.* against a stone. Lu. 4. 11
5. 13. cast out and trodden under *foot* of men. Ju. 8. ³5
14. 13. they followed him on *foot* from the cities [9. 45
18. 8. if thy hand or thy *f.* causeth thee to stumble. Mk.
22. 13. Bind him hand and *foot,* and cast him out
Mk. 6. 33. there were together on ¹*f.* from all the cities
Jno. 11. 44. was dead came forth, bound hand and *foot*
Acts 7. 5. no, not so much as to set his *foot* on
20. 16. from the first day that I set ²*foot* in Asia
1 Cor. 12. 15. If the *f.* shall say, Because I am not the hand
Heb. 10. 29. who hath trodden under *foot* the Son of God
Rev. 1. 13. clothed with a garment down to the *foot*
10. 2. he [angel] set his right *foot* upon the sea
11. 2. shall they tread under *foot* forty and two months

Footstool.
Mat. 5. 35. the earth, for it is the *f.* of his feet. Acts 7. 49
Mk. 12. 36. make thine enemies the *footstool* of thy feet.
    Lu. 20. 43 : Acts 2. 35: Heb. 1. 13: 10. 13
Jas. 2. 3. Stand thou there, or sit under my *footstool*
    see feet.

Forbade.
Lu. 9. 49. we *f.* him, because he followeth not. Mk. 9. 38
    see hindered, stayed.

Forbear.—*A.V.* ¹*forbearing.*
1 Cor. 9. 6. have we not a right to *forbear* working ?
2 Cor. 12. 6. I *forbear,* lest any man should account of me
Eph. 6. 9. same things unto them, and ¹*forbear* threatening
1 Th. 3. 1. Wherefore when we could no longer *forbear*

Forbearance.—*A.V.* ¹*moderation.*
Rom. 2. 4. despisest thou the riches of his goodness and *f.*
3. 25. sins done aforetime, in the *forbearance* of God
Phil. 4. 5. Let your ¹*forbearance* be known unto all men

Forbearing.—*A.V.* ¹*patient.*
Eph. 4. 2. *forbearing* one another in love. Col. 3. 13
2 Tim. 2. 24. gentle towards all, apt to teach, ¹*forbearing*
    see forbear.

Forbid.
Mk. 9. 39. Jesus said, *Forbid* him not. Lu. 9. 50 [Lu. 18. 16
10. 14. *f.* them not : for of such is the kingdom. Mat. 19. 14:

FORBID

Lu. 20. 16. God *forbid. Rom.* 3. 4, 6, 31 : 6. 2, 15 : 7. 7, 13 :
9. 14 ; 11. 1, 11 : 1 *Cor.* 6. 15 : *Gal.* 2. 17   3. 21
Acts 10. 47. Can any man *forbid* the water, that these
24. 23. not to *f.* any of his [Paul] friends to minister
1 *Cor.* 14. 39. *forbid* not to speak with tongues
see withhold.

Forbidden.
Acts 16. 6. having been *forbidden* of the Holy Ghost to speak

Forbiddeth.
3 *Jno.* 10. receive the brethren, and them that would he *f.*

Forbidding.
Lu. 23. 2. and *forbidding* to give tribute to Cæsar
Acts 28. 31. Christ with all boldness, none *forbidding* him
1 *Th.* 2. 16. *forbidding* us to speak to the Gentiles
1 *Tim.* 4. 3. *f.* to marry, and commanding to abstain

Force.
Mat. 11. 12. and men of violence take it by *force*
Jno. 6. 15. they were about to come and take him by *force*
Acts 23. 10. take him [Paul] by *force* from among them
Heb. 9. 17. For a testament is of *force* where there hath

Forefather—s.—*A.V.* ¹*father.*
Rom. 4. 1. Abraham, our ¹*forefather* according to the flesh
2 *Tim.* 1. 3. I thank God whom I serve from my *forefathers*

Foregoing.—*A.V.* ¹*going before.*
Heb. 7. 18. disannulling of a ¹*foregoing* commandment

Forehead—s.
Rev. 7. 3. sealed the servants of our God on their *forehead*
9. 4. have not the seal of God on their *forehead*
13. 16. mark on their right hand, or upon their *forehead*
14. 1. the name of his Father, written on their *foreheads*
9. receiveth a mark on his *forehead*, or upon his hand
17. 5. and upon her *forehead* a name written, MYSTERY
20. 4. received not the mark upon their *forehead*
22. 4. his name shall be on their *foreheads*

Foreign.—*A.V.* ¹*strange.*
Acts 26. 11. I persecuted them even unto ¹*foreign* cities

Foreigners *A.V.*—*see sojourners.*

Foreknew.—*A.V.* ¹*foreknow.*
Rom. 8. 29. whom he ¹*foreknew*, he also foreordained
11. 2. God did not cast off his people which he *foreknew*

Foreknow *A.V.*—*see foreknew.*

Foreknowledge.
Acts 2. 23. determinate counsel and *foreknowledge* of God
1 *Pet.* 1. 2. according to the *foreknowledge* of God the Father

Foreknown.—*A.V.* ¹*foreordained.*
1 *Pet.* 1. 20. who was ¹*f.* indeed before the foundation

Foreordained.—*A.V.* ¹*determined*, ²*ordained*, ³*pre-destinate—d.*
Acts 4. 28. thy hand and thy counsel ¹*f.* to come to pass
Rom. 8. 29. whom he foreknew, he also³ *foreordained.* ³30
1 *Cor.* 2. 7. wisdom—which God ²*f.* before the worlds
Eph. 1. 5. having ³*foreordained* us unto adoption as sons
11. having been *f.* according to the purpose of him
see foreknown.

Forepart *A.V.*—*foreship.*

FORGIVE

Forerunner.
Heb. 6. 20. whither as a *forerunner* Jesus entered for us

Foresail.—*A.V.* ¹*mainsail.*
Acts 27. 40. hoisting up the ¹*foresail* to the wind, they made

Foresaw *A.V.*—*see beheld.*

Foreseeing.—*A.V.* ¹*seeing.*
Acts 2. 31. he ¹*f.* this spake of the resurrection of the Christ
Gal. 3. 8. scripture, *f.* that God would justify the Gentiles

Foreshewed.—*A.V.* ¹*shewed.*
Acts 3. 18. things which God ¹*f.* by the mouth of all the

Foreship.—*A.V.* ¹*forepart.*
Acts 27. 30. though they would lay out anchors from the *f.*
41. the ¹*foreship* struck and remained unmoveable

Foretell *A.V.*—*see beforehand.*

Foretold *A.V.*—*see beforehand, told.*

Forewarn—ed.—*A.V.* ¹*tell before,* ²*told you in time past*
Gal. 5. 21. I ¹*forewarn* you, even as I did ²*forewarn* you
1 *Th.* 4. 6. these things, as also we *f.* you and testified
see warn.

Forfeit.—*A.V.* ¹*lose.*
Mat. 16. 26. gain the whole world and ¹*f. Mk.* 8.¹36 : *Lu.* 9.¹25

Forgave.—*A.V.* ¹*forgiven.*
Mat. 18. 27. released him, and *forgave* him the debt
32. wicked servant, I *forgave* thee all that debt
Lu. 7. 42. not wherewith to pay, he *forgave* them both
43. I suppose, to whom he *forgave* the most
Eph. 4. 32. each other, even as God also in Christ ¹*f.* you
Col. 3. 13. even as the Lord *forgave* you, so also do ye
see forgiven.

Forget.—*A.V.* ¹*forgetful,* ²*ignorant.*
Heb. 6. 10. God is not unrighteous to *forget* your work
13. 2 ¹*Forget* not to show love unto strangers
16. to do good and to communicate *forget* not
2 *Pet.* 3. 5. they wilfully ²*forget* that there were heavens
8. But *forget* not this one thing, beloved

Forgetful *A.V.*—*see forget, forgetteth.*

Forgetteth—ing.—*A.V.* ¹*forgetful.*
Phil. 3. 13. *forgetting* the things which are behind
Jas. 1. 24. straightway *f.* what manner of man he was
25. being not a hearer that ¹*f.*, but a doer that worketh

Forgive.—*A.V.* ¹*remit.*
Mat. 6. 12. and *f.* us our debts, as we also have forgiven
14. if ye *f.* men their trespasses—Father will also *f.* you
15. if ye *forgive* not—neither will your Father *forgive*
9. 6. the Son of man hath power on earth to *forgive* sins.
Mk. 2. 10 : *Lu.* 5. 24
18. 21. and I *forgive* him ? until seven times ?
35. if ye *f.* not every one his brother from your hearts
Mk. 2. 7. Who can *f.* sins but one, even God ? *Lu.* 5. 21
11. 25. *forgive*, if ye have aught against any one ; that
your Father—*f.* you your trespasses. 26 [margin]
Lu. 11. 4. *f.* us our sins ; for we ourselves also *f.* every one
17. 3. rebuke him ; and if he repent, *forgive* him. 4
23. 34. Father, *f.* them ; for they know not what they do
Jno. 20. 23. whose soever sins ye ¹*f.*, they are forgiven

FORGIVE

2 *Cor.* 2. 7. rather *f.* him and comfort him, lest by any means
  10. to whom ye *forgive* anything, I *forgive* also
  12. 13. not a burden to you? *forgive* me this wrong
1 *Jno.* 1. 9. he is faithful and righteous to *f.* us our sins
    see forgiven, release.

Forgiven.—*A.V.* ¹*forgave,* ²*forgive,* ³*remitted.*
Mat. 6. 12. forgive us our debts, as we also have ²*forgiven*
  9. 2. be of good cheer; thy sins are *forgiven.* 5: *Mk.* 2.
    5, 9: *Lu.* 5. 20, 23: 7. 48
  12. 31. blasphemy shall be *forgiven*—against the Spirit
    shall not be *forgiven.* 32; *Mk.* 3. 28; *Lu.* 12. 10
Mk. 4. 12. should turn again, and it should be *f.* them
Lu. 7. 47. Her sins, which are many, are *f.*—little is *f.*
  48. And he [Jesus] said unto her, Thy sins are *forgiven*
Jno. 20. 23. whose soever sins ye forgive, they are ²*forgiven*
Acts 8. 22. the thought of thy heart shall be *forgiven* thee
Rom. 4. 7. Blessed are they whose iniquities are *forgiven*
2 *Cor.* 2. 10. I also have ¹*f.*—I have ¹*f.*—sakes have I ¹*f.* it
Col. 2. 13. quicken together with him, having *forgiven* us
Jas. 5. 15. if he have committed sins, it shall be *f.* him
1 *Jno.* 2. 12. your sins are *forgiven* you for his name's sake
    see forgave, released.

Forgiveness.
Mk. 3. 29. against the Holy Spirit hath never *forgiveness*
Eph. 1. 7. his blood, the *f.* of our trespasses. *Col.* 1. 14
    see remission.

Forgiveth—ing.
Lu. 7. 49. Who is this that even *forgiveth* sins?
Eph. 4. 32. tenderhearted, *forgiving* each other. *Col.* 3. 13

Forgot.—*A.V.* ¹*forgotten.*
Mat. 16. 5. disciples—*forgot* to take bread. *Mk.* 8. 14

Forgotten.
Lu. 12. 6. not one of them is *forgotten* in the sight of God
Heb. 12. 5. ye have *f.* the exhortation, which reasoneth
2 *Pet.* 1. 9. having *forgotten* the cleansing from his old sins
    see forgot.

Form.—*A.V.* ¹*appearance,* ²*shape.*
Mk. 16. 12. he was manifested in another *form* unto two
Lu. 3. 22. the Holy Ghost descended in a bodily ²*form*
Jno. 5. 37. heard his voice at any time, nor seen his ²*form*
Rom. 2. 20. having in the law the *form* of knowledge
  6. 17. obedient from the heart to that *form* of teaching
Phil. 2. 6. being in the *f.* of God, counted it not a prize
  7. taking the *f.* of a servant, being made in the likeness
1 *Th.* 5. 22. abstain from every ¹*form* of evil [the power
2 *Tim.* 3. 5. holding a *f.* of godliness, but having denied
    see pattern.

Formed.
Rom. 9. 20. Shall the thing *formed* say to him that *f.* it
Gal. 4. 19. I am again in travail until Christ be *f.* in you
1 *Tim.* 2. 13. For Adam was first *formed,* then Eve

Former.
Acts 1. 1. The *former* treatise I made, O Theophilus
Eph. 4. 22. as concerning your *former* manner of life
Heb. 10. 32. But call to remembrance the *former* days
1 *Pet.* 1. 14. according to your *f.* lusts in the time of your
    see first.

Fornication—s.
Mat. 5. 32. saving for the cause of *fornication.* 19. 9
  15. 19. murders, adulteries, *fornications. Mk.* 7. 21
Jno. 8. 41. They said unto him, We were not born of *f.*
Acts 15. 20. *f.,* and from what is strangled. 29; 21. 25

FORTY

1 *Cor.* 5. 1. there is *f.* among you, and such *f.* as is not even
  6. 13. the body is not for *fornication,* but for the Lord
  18. Flee *fornication*—committeth *fornication* sinneth
  7. 2. because of *f.,* let each man have his own wife
  10. 8. commit *fornication,* as some of them committed
2 *Cor.* 12. 21. repented not of the uncleanness and *f.*
Gal. 5. 19. which are these, *fornication,* uncleanness
Eph. 5. 3. *fornication,* and all uncleanness, or covetousness
Col. 3. 5. *fornication,* uncleanness, passion, evil desire
1 *Th.* 4. 3. that ye abstain from *fornication*
Jude 7. like manner with these given themselves over to *f.*
Rev. 2. 14. sacrificed to idols, and to commit *fornication.* 20
  21. and she willeth not to repent of her *fornication*
  9. 21. nor of their *fornication,* nor of their thefts
  14. 8. to drink of the wine of the wrath of her *fornication*
  17. 2. kings of the earth committed *f.*—wine of her *f.*
  4. even the unclean things of her *fornication* [18. 3. 9
  19. 2. which did corrupt the earth with her *fornication*

Fornicator—s.—*A.V.* ¹*whoremonger*—s.
1 *Cor.* 5. 9. in my epistle to have no company with *f.*
  10. not altogether with the *fornicators* of this world
  11. any man that is named a brother be a *fornicator*
  6. 9. neither *fornicators,* nor idolaters, nor adulterers
Eph. 5. 5. that no ¹*fornicator*—hath any inheritance
1 *Tim.* 1. 10. for ¹*fornicators,* for abusers of themselves
Heb. 12. 16. lest their be any *f.,* or profane person, as Esau
  13. 4. for ¹*fornicators* and adulterers God will judge
Rev. 21. 8. murderers, and ¹*fornicators,* and sorcerers. 22. ¹15

Forsake.—*A.V.* ¹*leave.*
Acts 6. 2. not fit that we should ¹*forsake* the word of God
  21. 21. which are among the Gentiles to *forsake* Moses
Heb. 13. 5. neither will I in any wise *forsake* thee

Forsaken.
Mat. 27. 46. My God, my God, why hast thou *f.* me? *Mk.* 15. 34
2 *Cor.* 4. 9. pursued, yet not *forsaken;* smitten down
    see forsaking, forsook, left.

Forsaking.—*A.V.* ¹*forsaken.*
Heb. 10. 25. not *f.* the assembling of ourselves together
2 *Pet.* 2. 15. ¹*forsaking* the right way, they went astray

Forsaketh *A.V.—see renounceth.*

Forsook.—*A.V.* ¹*forsaken,* ²*left.*
Lu. 5. 28. he [Levi] ²*f.* all, and rose up and followed him
2 *Tim.* 4. 10. Demas ¹*f.* me, having loved this present world
  16. no one took my part; but all *forsook* me
Heb. 11. 27. By faith he *f.* Egypt, not fearing the wrath
    see left.

Forswear.
Mat. 5. 33. Thou shalt not *forswear* thyself

Forthwith.—*A.V.* ¹*presently.*
Phil. 2. 23. Him [Timothy] therefore I hope to send ¹*f.*

Forty.
Jno. 2. 20. *Forty* and six years was this temple in building
Acts 4. 22. For the man was more than *forty* years old
  7. 23. when he was well-nigh *forty* years old
  30. And when *f.* years were fulfilled, an angel appeared
  36. in the Red Sea, and in the wilderness *forty* years
  42. offer unto me slain beasts and sacrifices *Forty* years
  13. 18. the time of *forty* years suffered he their manners
  21. the tribe of Benjamin, for the space of *forty* years
  23. 13. were more than *forty* which made this conspiracy

FORTY

Acts. 23. 21. lie in wait for him—more than *forty* men
2 *Cor.* 11. 24. five times received I *forty* stripes save one
Heb. 3. 9. proving me, And saw my works *forty* years
    17. with whom was he displeased *forty* years?
Rev. 11. 2 tread under foot *forty* and two months [months
13. 5. giveu to him authority to continue *forty* and two
    see days.

Forward-ness. *A.V.—see earnest—ness, first, readiness, zealous.*

Foster-brother.—*A.V.* ¹*brought up.*
Acts 13. 1. Manaen the ¹*foster-brother* of Herod the tetrarch

Fought.
1 *Cor.* 15. 32. I *fought* with beasts at Ephesus
2 *Tim.* 4. 7. I have *fought* the good fight, I have finished
    see war, warred.

Foul.
Mat. 16. 3. It will be *f.* weather to-day: for the heaven is
    see unclean spirit.

Found.—*A.V.* ¹*finding,* ²*perceived.*
Mat. 2. 8. when ye have *found* him, bring me word
13. 44. hidden in the field; which a man *found,* and hid
    46. having *found* one pearl of great price, he went
18. 28. *found* one of his fellow-servants, which owed him
20. 6. he went out, and *found* others standing [13. 6
21. 19. came to it, and *f.* nothing thereon. *Mk.* 11. 13: *Lu.*
22. 10. all as many as they *found,* both bad and good
26. 43. *found* them sleeping. *Mk.* 14. 40: *Lu.* 22. 46
27. 32. they *found* a man of Cyrene, Simon by name
Mk. 1. 37. they *f.* him, and say unto him, All are seeking
7. 30. *f.* the child laid upon the bed, and the devil gone
11. 4. *jound* a colt tied at the door without in the open
14. 16. *f.* as he had said unto them. *Lu.* 19. 32: 22. 13
Lu. 2. 46. *f.* both Mary and Joseph, and the babe lying in
    46. after three days they *found* him in the temple
4. 17. the book, and *found* the place where it was written
7. 10. returning to the house, *found* the servant whole
8. 35. *found* the man, from whom the devils were gone
15. 5. when he hath *found* it, he layeth it on his shoulders
    6. Rejoice with me, for I have *found* my sheep
    9. when she hath *found* it, she calleth together her
    friends—I have *found* the piece which I had lost
24. is alive again; he was lost, and is *found.* 32 [God
17. 18. Were there none *f.* that returued to give glory to
23. 2. We *found* this man perverting our nation
14. *found* no fault in this man touching those things
22. I have *found* no cause of death in him
24. 2. they *found* the stone rolled away from the tomb
33. and *found* the eleven gathered together
Jno. 1. 41. We have *found* the Messiah
    45. We have *found* him, of whom Moses in the law
2. 14. he *f.* in the temple those that sold oxen and sheep
6. 25. when they *found* him on the other side of the sea
11. 17. Jesus came, he *f.* that he had been in the tomb
12. 14. Jesus, having *found* a young ass, sat thereon
Acts 5. 10. the young men came in and *found* her dead
    23. The prison-house we *found* shut—but when we
    had opened, we *found* no man within
7. 11. and our fathers *found* no sustenance
9. 2. that if he [Saul] *found* any that were of the Way
11. 26. *found* him, he brought him [Saul] unto Antioch
13. 6. they *found* a certain sorcerer, a false prophet
22. I have *found* David the son of Jesse
28. though they *found* no cause of death in him
17. 23. I *found* also an altar with this inscription
18. 2. And he [Paul] *found* a certain Jew named Aquila
19. 1. came to Ephesus, and *found* certain disciples
    19. and *found* it fifty thousand pieces of silver
21. 2. having ¹*found* a ship crossing over unto Phœnicia

FOUNDATION

Acts 23. 29. whom I ²*found* to be accused about questions
24. 5. For we have *found* this man a pestilent fellow
    18. amidst which they *found* me purified in the temple
    26. men themselves say what wrong-doing they *found*
25. 25. I *f.* that he had committed nothing worthy of death
27. 6. centurion *f.* a ship of Alexandria sailing for Italy
    28. *found* twenty fathoms—*found* fifteen fathoms
    28. 14. where we *f.* brethren, and were intreated to tarry
Rom. 4. 1. our forefather according to the flesh, hath *f.?*
7. 10. which was unto life, this I *found* to be unto death
1 *Cor.* 6. 5. that there cannot be *f.* among you one wise man
15. 15. Yea, and we are *found* false witnesses of God
Gal. 2. 17. we ourselves also were *found* sinners
Phil. 2. 8. *found* in fashion as a man, he humbled himself
2 *Tim.* 1. 17. he sought me diligently, and *found* me
Heb. 12. 17. (for he *found* no place of repentance)
1 *Pet.* 1. 7. proved by fire, might be *found* unto praise
2. 22. neither was guile *found* in his mouth
2 *Jno.* 4. I have *f.* certain of thy children walking in truth
Rev. 3. 2. I have *f.* no works of thine fulfilled before my
5. 4. no one was *found* worthy to open the book [God
12. 8. neither was their place *found* any more in heaven
14. 5. And in their mouth was *found* no lie
18. 21. cast down, and shall be *found* no more at all
22. no craftsman—shall be *found* any more at all in thee
20. 11. and there was *found* no place for them
    see favour, find, findeth, finding.

Be Found.
Acts 5. 39. ye be *found* even to be fighting against God
1 *Cor.* 4. 2. required in stewards, that a man be *f.* faithful
2 *Cor.* 11. 12. wherein they glory, they may be *f.* even as
    12. 20. be *found* of you such as ye would not [own
Phil. 3. 9. be *f.* in him, not having a righteousness of mine
2 *Pet.* 3. 14. give diligence that ye may be *found* in peace
    see true.

Was Found.
Mat. 1. 18. she *was found* with child of the Holy Ghost
Lu. 9. 36. when the voice came, Jesus *was found* alone
Acts 8. 40. But Philip *was found* at Azotus
Rom. 10. 20. I *was found* of them that sought me not
2 *Cor.* 7. 14. which I made before Titus, was *f.* to be truth
Rev. 18. 24. And in her *was found* the blood of prophets

Found, with not.
Mat. 8. 10. not *f.* so great faith, no, not in Israel. *Lu.* 7. 9
26. 60. *f.* it not, though many false witnesses. *Mk.* 14. 55
Lu. 2. 45. when they *f.* him *not,* they returned to Jerusalem
24. 3. entered in, and *f. not* the body of the Lord Jesus
    23. when they *found not* his body, they came, saying
Acts 5. 22. officers that came *f.* them *not* in the prison. 23
12. 19. Herod had sought for him, and *found* him *not*
17. 6. when they *found* them *not,* they dragged Jason
2 *Cor.* 2. 13. because I *found not* Titus my brother
5. 3. that being clothed we shall *not* be *found* naked
Heb. 11. 5. he was *not found,* because God translated him
Rev. 16. 20. island fled away, and the mountains were *not f.*
20. 15. if any was *not found* written in the book of life

Foundation.
Lu. 6. 48. digged and went deep, and laid a *f.* upon the rock
    49. like a man that built a house upon the earth with-
14. 29. but haply, when he hath laid a *f.* [out a *f.*
Rom. 15. 20. that I might not build upon another's man's *f.*
1 *Cor.* 3. 10. as a wise masterbuilder I have laid a *foundation*
    11. For other *f.* can no man lay than that which is laid
    12. if any man buildeth on the *foundation* gold, silver
Eph. 2. 20. being built upon the *f.* of the apostles and
1 *Tim.* 6. 19. laying up in store for themselves a good *f.*

FOUNDATION

2 *Tim.* 2. 19. Howbeit the firm *foundation* of God standeth
Heb. 1. 10. in the beginning hast laid the *f.* of the earth
6. 1. not laying again a *foundation* of repentance
Rev. 21. 19. The first *f.* was jasper; the second, sapphire

Foundation *of the world.*

Mat. 13. 35. things hidden from the *f. of the world*
25. 34. prepared for you from the *foundation of the w.*
Lu. 11. 50. which was shed from the *f. of the world*
Jno. 17. 24. thou lovedst me before the *f. of the world*
Eph. 1. 4. chose us in him before the *f. of the world*
Heb 4. 3. works were finished from the *f. of the world*
9. 26. often have suffered since the *f. of the world*
1 *Pet* 1. 20. foreknown indeed before the *f. of the world*
Rev. 13. 8. Lamb that hath been slain from the *f. of the w.*
17. 8. written in the book of life from the *f. of the world*

Foundations.

Acts 16. 26. the *foundations* of the prison-house were shaken
Heb. 11. 10. he looked for the city which hath the *f.*
Rev. 21. 14. the wall of the city had twelve *foundations*
19. The *foundations* of the wall of the city were adorned

Founded.

Mat. 7. 25. it fell not: for it was *founded* upon the rock
see builded.

Fountain.

Mk. 5. 29. straightway the *f.* of her blood was dried up
Jas. 3. 11. Doth the *f.* send forth from the same opening
Rev. 21. 6. give unto him that is athirst of the *f.* of the

Fountains.

Rev. 7. 17. shall guide them unto *fountains* of waters of life
8. 10. the third part of the rivers, and upon the *f.* of the
14. 7. the earth and sea and *fountains* of waters
16. 4. out his bowl into the rivers and the *f.* of the waters

Four.

Mat. 24. 31. together his elect from the *f.* winds. *Mk.* 13. 27
Mk. 2. 3. unto him a man sick of the palsy, borne of *four*
Lu. 2. 37. a widow even for fourscore and *four* years
Jno. 4. 35. Say not ye, There are yet *four* months [39
11. 17. found that he had been in the tomb *f.* days already.
19. 23. his garments, and made *f.* parts. to every soldier
Acts 10. 11. descending, as it were a great sheet, let down
by *four* corners. 11. 5
30. *Four* days ago, until this hour, I was keeping the
12. 4. delivered him to *four* quaternions of soldiers
21. 9. Now this man had *four* daughters, virgins
23. We have *four* men which have a vow on them
27. 29. they let go *four* anchors from the stern
Rev. 4. 6. *four* living creatures. 8: 5. 6, 8, 14: 6. 1, 6:
7. 11 : 14. 3 : 15, 7 : 19. 4
7. 1. I saw *four* angels—*four* corners of the earth, holding the *four* winds. 2: 9. 14, 15 [of the earth
20. 8. to deceive the nations which are in the *f.* corners

Fourfold.

Lu. 19. 8. wrongfully exacted aught of any man, I restore *f.*

Fourfooted.

Acts 10. 12. wherein were all manner of *fourfooted* beasts.
Rom. 1. 23. *fourfooted* beasts, and creeping things [11. 6

Fourscore.

Lu. 2. 37. she had been a widow even for *f.* and four years
16. 7. He saith unto him, Take thy bond, and write *f.*

FREE

Foursquare.

Rev. 21. 16. And the city lieth *foursquare*

Fourteen.

Mat. 1. 17. from Abraham unto David are *f.* generations—
to Babylon *f.* generations—Christ *f.* generations
2 *Cor.* 12. 2. I know a man in Christ, *fourteen* years ago
Gal. 2. 1. *fourteen* years I went up again to Jerusalem

Fourteenth.

Acts 27. 27. But when the *fourteenth* night was come
see day.

Fourth.

Mat. 14. 25. in the *f.* watch of the night he came unto them.
Rev. 4. 7. the *f.* creature was like a flying eagle [*Mk.* 6. 48
6. 7. the *f.* seal, I heard the voice of the *f.* living creature
8. 12. the *fourth* angel sounded, and the third part
16. 8. the *fourth* poured out his bowl upon the sun
21. 19. the third, chalcedony; the *fourth*, emerald

Fowls.

Acts 10. 12. things of the earth and *f.* of the heaven. 11. 6
see birds.

Fox—es.

Mat. 8. 20. The *foxes* have holes, and the birds of the
heavens have nests. *Lu.* 9. 58
Lu. 13. 32. Go and say to that *f.*, Behold, I cast out devils

Fragments *A.V.—see broken pieces.*

Framed.—*A.V.* ¹*joined.*

Eph. 2. 21. in whom each several building, fitly *f.* together
4. 16. from whom all the body fitly ¹*f.* and knit together
Heb. 11, 3. the worlds have been *f.* by the word of God

Frankincense.

Mat. 2. 11. offered unto him gifts, gold and *f.* and myrrh
Rev. 18. 13. *frankincense*, and wine, and oil, and fine flour

Fraud.

Jas. 5. 4. which is of you kept back by *fraud*, crieth out

Free.—*A.V.* ¹*liberty,* ²*without.*

Mat. 17. 26. Therefore the sons are *free* | make you *free*
Jno. 8. 32. ye shall know the truth, and the truth shall
33. how sayest thou, Ye shall be made *free* ?
36. Son shall make you *free*, ye shall be *free* indeed
Rom. 5. 15. But not as the trespass, so also is the *free* gift
16. but the *free* gift came of many trespasses
18. the *free* gift came unto all men to justification of life
6. 18. being made *free* from sin, ye became servants. 22
20. ye were *free* in regard of righteousness
7. 3. if the husband die, she is *free* from the law
8. 2. Jesus made me *free* from the law of sin and death
1 *Cor.* 7. 21. if thou canst become *free*, use it rather
22. he that was called, being *f.*, is Christ's bondservant
32. But I would have you to be ²*free* from care
39. if the husband be dead, she is ¹*free* to be married
9. 1. Am I not *free* ? am I not an apostle?
19. For though I was *free* from all men, I brought myself
12. 13. whether Jews or Greeks, whether bond or *free*
Gal. 3. 28. there can be neither bond nor *free*
4. 26. But the Jerusalem that is above is *free*
5. 1. With freedom did Christ set us *free*
Eph. 6. 8. from the Lord, whether he be bond or *free*
1 *Pet.* 2. 16. *free*, and not using your freedom for a cloke
Rev. 13. 16. the rich and the poor, and the *free* and the bond
19. 18. the flesh of all men, both *free* and bond
see freeman, freewoman, Roman, run.

FREED

Freed *A.V.—see justified.*

Freedom.—*A.V. ¹liberty.*
Gal. 5. 1. With ¹*freedom* did Christ set us free
13. called for ¹*f.*; only use not your ¹*f.* for an occasion
1 Pet. 2. 16. as free, and not using your ¹*freedom* for a cloke
see citizenship.

Freedman, Freeman.—*A.V. ¹free.*
1 Cor. 7. 22. being a bondservant, is the Lord's *freedman*
Col. 3. 11. barbarian, Scythian, bondman, ¹*freeman*
Rev. 6. 15. every bondman and *freeman*, hid themselves

Freely.
Mat. 10. 8. *freely* ye received, *freely* give
Acts 2. 29. I may say unto you *f.* of the patriarch David
26. unto whom also I speak *f.* : for I am persuaded
Rom. 3. 24. being justified *freely* by his grace
8. 32. shall he not also with him *f.* give us all things?
1 Cor. 2. 12. things that are *freely* given to us by God
Rev. 21. 6. fountain of the water of life *freely*. 22. 17
see nought.

Freewoman.—*A.V. ¹free.*
Gal. 4. 22. one by the handmaid, and one by the *freewoman*
23. the son by the *freewoman* is born through promise
30. not inherit with the son of the *freewoman*
31. not children of a handmaid, but of the ¹*freewoman*

Freight.—*A.V. ¹lightened.*
Acts 27. 18. next day they began to throw the ¹*f.* overboard

Frequent *A.V.—see abundantly.*

Fresh *A.V.—see sweet.*

Friend.
Mat. 11. 19. a *friend* of publicans and sinners! Lu. 7. 34
20. 13. said to one of them, *Friend*, I do thee no wrong
22. 12. saith unto him, *Friend*, how camest thou in hither
26. 50. Jesus said unto him, *F.*, do that for which thou art
Lu. 11. 5. have a *friend*—*Friend*, lend me three loaves
6. for a *friend* of mine is come to me from a journey
8. will not rise and give him, because he is his *friend*
14. 10. may say to thee, *Friend*, go up higher
Jno. 3. 29. the *friend* of the bridegroom, which standeth
11. 11. saith unto them, Our *f.* Lazarus is fallen asleep
19. 12. thou release this man, thou art not Cæsar's *friend*
Acts 12. 20. made Blastus the king's chamberlain their *f.*
Jas. 2. 23. and he was called the *friend* of God
4. 4. a *f.* of the world maketh himself an enemy of God

Friends.—*A.V. ¹acquaintance.*
Mk. 3. 21. when his *f.* heard it, they went out to lay hold
5. 19. Go to thy house unto thy *friends*, and tell them
Lu. 7. 6. the centurion sent *friends* to him, saying
12. 4. my *f.*, Be not afraid of them which kill the body
14. 12. makest a dinner or a supper, call not thy *friends*
15. 6. he calleth together his *friends* and his neighbours
9. she calleth together her *friends* and neighbours
29. a kid, that I might make merry with my *friends*
16. 9. Make to yourselves *f.* by means of the mammon
21. 16. by parents, and brethren, and kinsfolk, and *f.*
23. 12. Herod and Pilate became *friends* with each other
Jno. 15. 13. that a man lay down his life for his *friends*
14. Ye are my *f.*, if ye do the things which I command
15. I have called you *f.* ; for all things that I heard
Acts 10. 24. called together his kinsmen and his near *f.*

FRUIT

Acts 19. 31. chief officers of Asia, being his *f.*, sent unto him
24. 23. not to forbid any of his [Paul] ¹*friends* to minister
27. 3. gave him leave to go unto his *friends* and refresh
3 Jno. 14. The *friends* salute thee. Salute the *f.* by name

Friendship.
Jas. 4. 4. the *friendship* of the world is enmity with God?

Frogs.
Rev. 16. 13. three unclean spirits, as it were *frogs*

Froward.
1 Pet. 2. 18. not only to the good—but also to the *froward*

Fruit.—*A.V. ¹fruits.*
Mat. 3. 8. Bring forth—¹*fruit* worthy of repentance
12. 33. the tree good, and its *fruit* good—tree corrupt,
and its *fruit* corrupt—known by its *fruit*. Lu. 6. 44
13. 8. others fell upon the good ground, and yielded *fruit*
21. 19. Let there be no *fruit* from thee henceforward [19
26. 29. not drink—of this *f.* of the vine. Mk. 14. 25 : Lu. 22.
Mk. 4. 7. grow up. and choked it, and it yielded no *fruit*
8. others fell into the good ground, and yielded *fruit*
Lu. 1. 42. blessed is the *fruit* of thy womb
13. 6. came seeking *fruit* thereon, and found none
7. these three years I come seeking *fruit* on this tree
20. 10. they should give him of the *fruit* of the vineyard
Jno. 4. 36. receiveth wages, and gathereth *fruit* unto life
15. 16. bear *fruit*, and that your *f.* should abide [eternal
Acts 2. 30. of the *fruit* of his loins he would set one upon
Rom. 1. 13. that I might have some *fruit* in you also
6. 21. What *fruit* then had ye at that time in the things
22. your *f.* unto sanctification, and the end eternal life
15. 28. accomplished this, and have sealed to them this *f.*
1 Cor. 9. 7. who planteth a vineyard, and eateth not the *f.*
Gal. 5. 22. But the *fruit* of the Spirit is love, joy [ness
Eph. 5. 9. the *f.* of the light is in all goodness and righteous-
Phil. 1. 22. to live in the flesh,—if this is the *f.* of my work
4. 17. I seek for the *f.* that increaseth to your account
Heb. 12. 11. yieldeth peaceable *f.*—the *f.* of righteousness
13. 15. praise to God continually, that is, the *f.* of lips
Jas. 3. 18. And the *fruit* of righteousness is sown in peace
5. 7. the husbandman waiteth for the precious *fruit*
Jude 12. autumn trees without *fruit*, twice dead
Rev. 22. 2. tree of life,—yielding its *fruit* every month
see fruits.

Bear, or beareth Fruit; also bearing Fruit.--*A.V.*
¹*bring, bringeth, or brought fruit, ²fruitful.*
Mat. 13. 23. beareth *fruit*, and bringeth forth,—a hundred-
Mk. 4. 20. hear the word, and accept it, and ¹*bear f.* [fold
28. The earth ¹*beareth fruit* of herself
Lu. 13. 9. if it bear *fruit* thenceforth, well ; but if not
Jno. 12. 24. but if it die. it ¹*beareth* much *fruit*
15. 2. *beareth* not *fruit*, he taketh—*beareth fruit*, he
cleanseth it, that it may ¹*bear* more *fruit*
4. the branch cannot *bear fruit* of itself, except it abide
5. in me, and I in him, the same ¹*beareth* much *fruit*
8. is my Father glorified, that ye *bear* much *fruit*
16. appointed you, that ye should go and ¹*bear fruit*
Col. 1 6. ¹*bearing f.* and increasing, as it doth in you also
10. ²*bearing fruit* in every good work, and increasing
see brought (forth) fruit.

Bring, bringeth, or brought Fruit.—*A.V. ¹bare fruit,*
²*fruits.*
Mat. 3. 8. *Bring* forth therefore ²*fruit* worthy of repentance
10. *bringeth* not forth good *fruit*. 7. 19 : Lu. 3. 9
7. 17. *bringeth* forth good *fruit*—*bringeth* forth evil *fruit*

133

FRUIT

Mat. 7. 18. good tree cannot *bring* forth evil *fruit*, neither
    can a corrupt tree *bring* forth good *fruit*. *Lu.* 6. 43
13. 26. the blade sprang up, and *brought* forth *fruit*
Lu. 8. 8. good ground, and grew, and ¹*brought* forth *fruit*
14. pleasures of this life, and *bring* no *f.* to perfection
15. hold it fast, and *bring* forth *fruit* with patience
Rom. 7. 4. that we might *bring* forth *fruit* unto God
5. wrought in our members to *b.* forth *fruit* unto death
Jas. 5. 18. gave rain, and the earth *brought* forth her *fruit*
    see bear, bearest, beareth, bearing, ripe.

Fruitful.
Acts 14. 17. gave you from heaven rains and *f.* seasons
    see bearing fruit.

Fruits.—*A.V.* ¹*fruit.*
Mat. 7. 16. By their *fruits* ye shall know them. 20
21. 34. when the season of the ¹*f.* drew near, he sent his
    servants to the husbandmen, to receive his *fruits*
41. which shall render him the *fruits* in their seasons
43. given to a nation bringing forth the *fruits* thereof
Mk. 12. 2. receive from the husbandmen of the ¹*f.* of the
Lu. 3. 8. Bring forth therefore *f.* worthy of repentance
12. 17. because I have not where to bestow my *fruits* ?
2 *Cor.* 9. 10. and increase the *fruits* of your righteousness
Phil. 1. 11. being filled with the *fruits* of righteousness
2 *Tim.* 2. 6. laboureth must be the first to partake of the *f.*
Jas. 3. 17. easy to be intreated, full of mercy and good *f.*
Rev. 18. 14. the *fruits* which thy soul lusted after are gone
22. 2. tree of life, bearing twelve manner of *fruits*
    see corn, fruit, bring forth fruit.

Frustrate *A.V.*—*see void.*

Fulfil.—*A.V.* ¹*make full proof,* ²*supply.*
Mat. 3. 15. thus it becometh us to *fulfil* all righteousness
5. 17. I came not to destroy, but to *fulfil*
Rom. 2. 27. by nature, if it *fulfil* the law, judge thee
13. 14. provision for the flesh, to *fulfil* the lusts thereof
Gal. 5. 16. ye shall not *fulfil* the lust of the flesh
6. 2. one another's burdens, and so *f.* the law of Christ
Phil. 2. 2. *fulfil* ye my joy, that ye be of the same mind
4 19. And my God shall ²*fulfil* every need of yours
Col. 1. 25. given me to you-ward, to *fulfil* the word of God
4 17. thou hast received in the Lord, that thou *fulfil* it
2 *Th* 1. 11. *fulfil* every desire of goodness and every work
2 *Tim.* 4. 5. do the work of an evangelist, ¹*f.* thy ministry
Jas. 2. 8. ye *fulfil* the royal law, according to the scripture
    see do.

Fulfilled.—*A.V.* ¹*accomplished,* ²*believed,* ³*came,*
    ⁴*expired,* ⁵*full,* ⁶*perfect.*
Mat. 1. 22. *fulfilled* which was spoken by the Lord through
    the prophet. 2. 15, 17, 23 : 4. 14 : 8. 17 : 12. 17 :
    13. 35 : 21. 4 : 26. 56 : 27. 9 : *Mk.* 14. 49 : *Jno.* 12. 38
13. 14. unto them is *fulfilled* the prophecy of Isaiah
Mk. 1. 15. The time is *f.*, and the kingdom of God is at
Lu. 1. 1. concerning those matters which have been ²*f.*
20. not my words, which shall be *fulfilled* in their season
23. when the days of his [Zacharias] ministration were ⁴*f.*
57. Elisabeth's time was ⁵*f.* that she should be delivered
2. 6. the days were ¹*f.* that she [Mary] should be delivered
21. when eight days were ²*fulfilled* for circumcising
22. days of their purification.—were ¹*fulfilled*
43. had *f.* the days, as they were returning, the boy
21. 22. all things which are written may be *fulfilled*
24. until the times of the Gentiles be *fulfilled*
22. 16. not eat it, until it be *f.* in the kingdom of God
37. this which is written must be ¹*fulfilled* in me
24. 44. needs be *fulfilled*, which are written in the law

FULL

Jno. 3. 29. this my joy therefore is *fulfilled*
7. 8. because my time is not yet ⁵*fulfilled*
15. 11. and that your joy may be ⁵*fulfilled.* 16. ⁵24
25. may be *fulfilled* that is written in their law
17. 12. that the scripture might be *fulfilled*
13. that they may have my joy *fulfilled* in themselves
18. 9. that the word might be *fulfilled* which he spake
32. that the word of Jesus might be *fulfilled*
Acts 3. 18. his Christ should suffer, he thus *fulfilled*
7. 30. when forty years were ⁴*f.*, an angel appeared to
9. 23. when many days were *f.*, the Jews took counsel
12. 25. when they had *fulfilled* their ministration
13. 27. read every sabbath, *f.* them by condemning him
29. had *fulfilled* all things that were written of him
33. how that God hath *f.* the same unto our children
14. 26. grace of God for the work which they had *f.*
Rom. 8. 4. ordinance of the law might be *fulfilled* in us
13. 8. he that loveth his neighbour hath *fulfilled* the law
2 *Cor.* 10. 6. when your obedience shall be *fulfilled*
Gal. 5. 14. the whole law is *fulfilled* in one word, even in
1 *Jno.* 1. 4. these things we write, that our joy may be ³*f.*
2 *Jno.* 12. speak face to face, that your joy may be ⁵*fulfilled*
Rev. 3. 2. I have found no works of thine ⁶*f.* before my God
6. 11. killed even as they were, should be *fulfilled*
    see accomplished, finished, fulfilling.

Fulfilling.—*A.V.* ¹*fulfilled.*
Acts 13. 25. as John was ¹*fulfilling* his course, he said
    see doing, fulfilment.

Fulfilment.—*A.V.* ¹*accomplishment,* ²*end,* ³*fulfilling,*
    ⁴*performance.*
Lu. 1. 45. there shall be a ⁴*fulfilment* of the things
22. 37. that which concerneth me hath ²*fulfilment*
Acts 21. 26. the ¹*fulfilment* of the days of purification
Rom. 13. 10. love therefore is the ³*fulfilment* of the law

Full.—*A.V.* ¹*complete,* ²*filled,* ³*wholly.*
Mat. 6. 22. thy whole body shall be *full* of light. *Lu.* 11. 36
23. thy whole body shall be *full* of darkness
14. 20. over of the broken pieces, twelve baskets *full*
15. 37. broken pieces, seven baskets *full. Mk.* 8. 19
23. 25. within they are *f.* from extortion and excess. *Lu.*
27. but inwardly are *full* of dead men's bones [11. 39
28. inwardly are *full* of hypocrisy and iniquity
Mk. 7. 9. *Full* well do ye reject the commandment of God
15. 36. filling a sponge *full* of vinegar. *Jno.* 19. 2).
Lu. 4. 1. Jesus, *full* of the Holy Spirit, returned from
5. 12. in one of the cities, behold, a man *full* of leprosy
6. 25. Woe unto you, ye that are *full* now!
11. 34. whole body also is *f.* of light;—*full* of darkness. 36
16. 20. Lazarus was laid at his gate, *full* of sores
Jno. 1. 14. from the Father), *full* of grace and truth
19. 29. set there a vessel *full* of vinegar: so they put a
    sponge ²*full* of the vinegar upon hyssop
21. 11. drew the net to land, *full* of great fishes
Acts 2. 28. make me *full* of gladness with thy countenance
6. 3. seven men of good report, *full* of the Spirit
5. they chose Stephen, a man *full* of faith. 8 [11. 24
7. 55. being *full* of the Holy Ghost, looked up stedfastly.
9. 36. Dorcas: this woman was *full* of good works
13. 10. and said. O *full* of all guile and all villany
17. 16. Paul—beheld the city [Athens] ³*full* of idols
Rom. 1. 29. *full* of envy, murder, strife, deceit
3. 14. Whose mouth is *full* of cursing and bitterness
15. 14. that ye yourselves are *full* of goodness
Col. 2. 10. in him ye are made ¹*full*, who is the head
Jas. 3. 8. it is a restless evil, it is *full* of deadly poison
17. easy to be intreated, *full* of mercy and good fruits

FULL

1 *Pet.* 1. 8. rejoice greatly with joy unspeakable and *full*
2 *Pet.* 2. 14. having eyes *full* of adultery [of glory
2 *Jno.* 8. but that ye receive a *full* reward
Rev. 4. 6. four living creatures *full* of eyes before. 8
5. 8. golden bowls *full* of incense, which are the prayers
15. 7. seven golden bowls *full* of the wrath of God
17. 3. scarlet-coloured beast, *full* of names of blasphemy
4. in her hand a golden cup *full* of abominations
see basketfuls, *filled, filling, fulfil, fulfilled, laden.*

Fuller.

Mk. 9. 3. so as no *fuller* on earth can whiten them

Fullgrown.—*A.V.* ¹*finished,* ²*perfect.*

Eph. 4. 13. knowledge of the Son of God, unto a ²*f.* man
Jas. 1. 15. sin, when it is ¹*fullgrown*, bringeth forth death

Fully.—*A. V.* ¹*complete.*

Rom. 4. 21. *fully* assured that, what he had promised
14. 5. Let each man be *fully* assured in his own mind
15. 19. I have *fully* preached the gospel of Christ
Col. 4. 12. that ye may stand perfect and ¹*fully* assured
2 *Tim.* 4. 17. through me the message might be *f.* proclaimed
Rev. 14. 18. vine of the earth; for her grapes are *fully* ripe
see follow.

Fulness.—*A.V.* ¹*assurance.*

Jno. 1. 16. his *fulness* we all received, and grace for grace
Rom. 11. 12. of the Gentiles; how much more their *f.?*
25. until the *fulness* of the Gentiles be come in
15. 29. I shall come in the *f.* of the blessing of Christ
1 *Cor.* 10. 26. the earth is the Lord's, and the *f.* thereof
Gal. 4. 4. when the *fulness* of the time came, God sent
Eph. 1. 10. of the *f.* of the times, to sum up all things
23. his body, the *fulness* of him that filleth all in all
3. 19. ye may be filled unto all the *fulness* of God
4. 13. measure of the stature of the *fulness* of Christ
Col. 1. 19. that in him should all the *fulness* dwell
2. 9. in him dwelleth all the *fulness* of the Godhead
Heb. 6. 11. unto the ¹*fulness* of hope even to the end
10. 22. draw near with a true heart in ¹*fulness* of faith

Furlongs.

Lu. 24. 13. which was threescore *furlongs* from Jerusalem
Jno. 6. 19. rowed about five and twenty or thirty *furlongs*
11. 18. nigh unto Jerusalem, about fifteen *furlongs* off
Rev. 14. 20. as far as a thousand and six hundred *furlongs*
21. 16. the city with the reed, twelve thousand *furlongs*

Furnace.

Mat. 13. 42. shall cast them into the *furnace* of fire. 50
Rev. 1. 15. as if it had been refined in a *furnace*
9. 2. out of the pit, as the smoke of a great *furnace*

Furnished.

Mk. 14. 15. a large upper room *f.* and ready *Lu.* 22. 12
2 *Tim.* 3. 17. *furnished* completely unto every good work
see filled.

Furtherance *A.V.—see progress.*

G.

Gain.—*A.V.* ¹*gains,* ²*purchase,* ³*trade,* ⁴*win.*

Mat. 16. 26. be profited, if he shall *g. Mk.* 8. 36: *Lu.* 9. 25
Acts 6. 16. brought her masters much *g.* by soothsaying
19. hope of their ¹*g.* was gone, they laid hold on Paul
1 *Cor.* 9. 19. bondage to all, that I might *gain* the more
20. *gain* Jews—*gain* them that are under the law

GARMENT

1 *Cor.* 9. 21. that I might *gain* them that are without the law
22. became weak, that I might *gain* the weak
Phil. 1. 21. For to me to live is Christ, and to die is *gain*
3. 7. were *g.* to me, these have I counted loss for Christ
8. count them but dung, that I may ⁴*gain* Christ
1 *Tim.* 3. 13. deacons ²*gain* to themselves a good standing
6. 5. supposing that godliness is a way of *gain*
6. But godliness with contentment is great *gain*
Jas. 4. 13. spend a year there, and trade, and get *gain*
Rev. 18. 17. as many as ³*gain* their living by sea
see advantage, business.

Gained.—*A.V.* ¹*get,* ²*won.*

Mk. 19. 15. if he hear thee, thou hast *gained* thy brother
25. 17. he also that received the two *gained* other two. 22
20. five talents: lo, I have *gained* other five talents
Lu. 19. 15. might know what they had *gained* by trading
2 *Cor.* 2. 11. no advantage may be ¹*gained* over us by Satan
1 *Pet.* 3. 1. be ²*gained* by the behaviour of their wives
see gotten, made.

Gains *A.V.—see gain.*

Gainsaid.—*A.V.* ¹*spoken against.*

Acts 19. 36. Seeing then that these things cannot be ¹*g.*

Gainsay-ers-ing—*A.V.* ¹*answering,* ²*contradiction.*

Lu. 21. 15. shall not be able to withstand or to *gainsay*
Acts 10. 29. wherefore also I came without *gainsaying*
Rom. 10. 21. unto a disobedient and *gainsaying* people
Tit. 1. 9. and to convict the *gainsayers*
2. 9. well-pleasing to them in all things; not ¹*gainsaying*
Heb. 12. 3. consider him that hath endured such ²*gainsaying*
Jude 11. and perished in the *gainsaying* of Korah

Gall.

Mat. 27. 34. gave him wine to drink mingled with *gall*
Acts 8. 23. I see that thou art in the *gall* of bitterness

Games.—*A.V.* ¹*mastery—ies.*

1 *Cor* 9. 25. every man that striveth in the ¹*games*
2 *Tim.* 2. 5. if also a man contend in the ¹*games*

Gangrene.—*A.V.* ¹*canker.*

2 *Tim.* 2. 17. their word will eat as doth a ¹*gangrene*

Garden.

Lu. 13. 19. cast into his own *g.;* and it—became a tree
Jno. 18. 1. over the brook Kidron, where was a *garden*
26. Did not I see thee in the *g.* with him? [new tomb
19. 41. where he was crucified there was a *g.;*—in the *g.* a

Gardener.

Jno. 20. 15. She, [Mary] supposing him [Jesus] to be the *g.*

Garlands.

Acts 14. 13. brought oxen and *garlands* unto the gates

Garment.—*A.V.* ¹*robe,* ²*vesture.*

Mat. 9. 16. cloth upon an old *g.;*—from the *g. Mk.* 2. 21
20. touched the border of his *g. Mk.* 5. 27: *Lu.* 8. 44
21. touch his *garment*, I shall be made whole [6. 56
14. 36. they might only touch the border of his *g. Mk.*
22. 11. saw—a man which had not on a wedding-*g.* 12
Mk. 10. 50. casting away his *g.*, sprang up, and came to Jesus
Lu 5. 36. piece from a new *garment*—upon an old *garment*
Jno. 19. 2 and arrayed him [Jesus] in a purple ¹*garment*
Acts 12. 8. Cast thy *garment* about thee, and follow me
Heb. 1. 11. they all shall wax old as doth a *garment*
12. As a *garment*, and they shall be changed
Jude 23. hating even the *garment* spotted by the flesh

135

GARMENT

Rev. 1. 13. like unto a son of man, clothed with a *garment*
19. 13. And he is arrayed in a ²*g.* sprinkled with blood
16. And he hath on his ²*garment*—a name written
   see cloke, robe.

Garments.—*A.V.* ¹*clothes,* ²*raiment.*

Mat. 17. 2. his ²*g.* became white as the light. *Mk.* 9. ²⁶
21. 7. put on them their ¹*garments;* and he sat thereon
8. part of the multitude spread their *garments. Mk.* 11. 8
23. 5. and enlarge the borders of their *garments*
26. 65. Then the high priest rent his ¹*garments* [him
27. 31. put on him his ²*g.,* and led him away to crucify
35. parted his *g.* among them. *Mk.* 15. 24 : *Lu.* 23. ²³⁴
Mk. 5. 28. If I touch but his ¹*g.* I shall be made whole. ¹³⁰
15. 20. from him the purple, and put on him his ¹*g.*
Lu. 19. 35. they threw their *g.* upon the colt. *Mk.* 11. 7
36. they spread their ¹*garments* in the way
Jno. 13. 4. riseth from supper, and layeth aside his *g.*
12. he had washed their feet, and taken his *garments*
19. 23. crucified Jesus, took his *g.,* and made four parts
24. They parted my ¹*garments* among them
Acts 7. 58. witnesses laid down their ¹*g.* at the feet of—Saul
9. 39. shewing the coats and *g.* which Dorcas made
14. 14. Barnabas and Paul, heard of it, they rent their ¹*g.*
16. 22. the magistrates rent their ¹*garments* off them
22. 20. keeping the ²*g.* of them that slew him [Stephen]
23. as they cried out, and threw off their ¹*garments*
Jas. 5. 2. and your *garments* are moth-eaten
Rev. 3. 4. in Sardis which did not defile their *garments*
5. He that overcometh shall thus be arrayed in white ²*g.*
18. white ²*garments,* that thou mayest clothe thyself
4. 4. four and twenty elders—arrayed in white ²*garments*
16. 15. Blessed is he that watcheth, and keepeth his *g.*
   see apparel.

Garner.

Mat. 3. 12. he will gather his wheat into the *g. Lu.* 3. 17

Garnish—ed.

Mat. 12. 44. findeth it empty, swept, and *g. Lu.* 11. 25
23. 29. and *garnish* the tombs of the righteous
   see adorned.

Gate.—*A.V.* ¹*city,* ²*market.*

Mat. 7. 13. Enter ye in by the narrow *g. :*—wide is the *g.* 14
Lu. 7. 12. Now when he drew near to the *gate* of the city
16. 20. Lazarus was laid at his *gate,* full of sores
Jno. 5. 2. in Jerusalem by the sheep ²*gate* a pool
Acts 10. 17. inquiry for Simon's house, stood before the *gate*
12. 10. they came unto the iron *gate* that leadeth into
13. knocked at the door of the *gate,* a maid came [*gate*
14. she opened not the *g.* for joy,—Peter stood before the
16. 13. on the sabbath day we went forth without the ¹*g.*
Heb. 13. 12. through his own blood, suffered without the *g.*
   see door, gates; also Beautiful Gate, in proper names.

Gates.—*A.V.* ¹*gate.*

Mat. 16. 18. the *gates* of Hades shall not prevail against it
Acts 9. 24. they watched the *gates* also day and night
14. 13. brought oxen and garlands unto the *gates*
Rev. 21. 12. having twelve *g.,* and at the *g.* twelve angels
13. the east were three *gates*—north three *gates*—south three *gates*—west three *gates*
15. the *gates* thereof, and the wall thereof
21. twelve *g.* were twelve pearls; —several ¹*g.* was of one
25. the *gates* thereof shall in no wise be shut [pearl
22. 14. and may enter in by the *gates* into the city

Gather.

Mat. 3. 12. he will *g.* his wheat into the garner. *Lu.* 3. 17
6. 26. neither do they reap, nor *gather* into barns

GAVE

Mat. 7. 16. Do men *gather* grapes of thorns, or figs of thistles?
13. 28. Wilt thou then that we go and *gather* them up?
29. lest haply while ye *gather* up the tares, ye root up
30. *Gather* up first the tares—*g.* the wheat into my barn
41. they shall *gather* out of his kingdom all things
24. 31. they shall *gather* together his elect. *Mk.* 13. 27
25. 26. where I sowed not, and *g.* where I did not scatter
Lu. 6. 44. men do not *g.* figs—bramble bush *g.* they grapes
Jno. 6. 12. *Gather* up the broken pieces which remain over
11. 52. might also *g.* together into one the children of God
15. 6. and they *gather* them, and cast them into the fire
Rev. 14. 18. *gather* the clusters of the vine of the earth
16. 14. *g.* them together unto the war of the great day
20. 8. Gog and Magog, to *gather* them together to the war
   see gathered, gathereth, sum.

Gathered.—*A.V.* ¹*assembled,* ²*called,* ³*came,* ⁴*gather.*

Mat. 13. 40. the tares are *gathered* up and burned with fire
47. cast into the sea, and *gathered* of every kind. 48
18. 20. where two or three are *g.* together in my name
22. 10. went out into the highways, and *gathered* together
34. Pharisees—*gathered* themselves together. 41
23. 37. how often would I have *g.* thy children. *Lu.* 13. 34
24. 28. there will the eagles be *g.* together. *Lu.* 17. 37
25. 32. before him shall be *gathered* all the nations
26. 3. were ¹*gathered* together the chief priests. 27. 62
57. the scribes and the elders were ¹*g.* together. *Lu.* 22. 66
27. 17. were *gathered* together, Pilate said unto them
27. and *gathered* unto him the whole band
Mk. 1. 33. all the city was *g.* together. 2. 2 : *Acts* 13. ⁴⁴
4. 1. there is *g.* unto him a very great multitude. 5. 21: *Lu.*
7. 1. Are *gathered* together unto him the Pharisees [12. 1
Lu. 15. 13. many days after the younger son *g.* all together
24. 33. Jerusalem, and found the eleven *g.* together
Jno. 6. 13. they *g.* them up, and filled twelve baskets
11. 47. priests—and the Pharisees *gathered* a council
Acts 4. 26. And the rulers were *gathered* together
31. the place was shaken wherein they were ¹*g.* together
11. 26. whole year they were *g.* together with the church
12. 12. where many were *g.* together and were praying
14. 27. and had *gathered* the church together
19. 25. whom he [Demetrius] ²*gathered* together
20. 7. first day of the week, when we were ³*g.* together. 8
28. 3. when Paul had *gathered* a bundle of sticks
1 *Cor.* 5. 4. ye being *gathered* together, and my spirit
Rev. 14. 19. *gathered* the vintage of the earth, and cast it
16. 16. they *gathered* them together into the place
19. 17. Come and be ⁴*g.* together unto the great supper
19. their armies, *gathered* together to make war
   see gathering.

Gathereth.—*A.V.* ¹*gather.*

Mat. 12. 30. he that *g.* not with me scattereth. *Lu.* 11. 2
23. 37. as a hen *gathereth* her chickens under her wing
Lu. 13. 34. even as a hen ¹*gathereth* her own brood
Jno. 4. 36. wages, and *gathereth* fruit unto life eternal

Gathering.—*A.V.* ¹*gathered.*

Mat. 2. 4. And ¹*gathering* together all the chief priests
25. 24. and *gathering* where thou didst not scatter [30
Lu. 11. 29. when the multitudes were ¹*g.* together. *Acts* 15.
Acts 17. 5. ¹*gathering* a crowd, set the city on an uproar
2 *Th.* 2. 1. Christ, and our *gathering* together unto him
   see concluding.

Gatherings *A.V.*—*see collections.*

Gave.—*A.V.* ¹*delivered,* ²*divided,* ³*given,* ⁴*willing,* ⁵*yielded.*

Mat. 10. 1. *gave* them authority over unclean spirits. *Mk.* 6. 7 : *Lu.* 9. 1   [*Mk.* 6. 41 ; 8. 6 ; *Lu.* 9. 16
14. 19. brake and *gave* the loaves to the disciples. 15. 36 :

GAVE

Mat. 21. 23. who *g*. thee this authority? *Mk.* 11. 28: *Lu.* 20. 2
25. 15. unto one he *gave* five talents, to another two
35. ye *gave* me meat—thirsty, and ye *gave* me drink. 37
42. ye *gave* me no meat—and ye *gave* me no drink
26. 26. *g*. to the disciples, and said. *Mk.* 14. 22: *Lu.* 22.
27. took a cup, and *gave* thanks, and *gave* to them [19
Lu. 4. 20. he closed the book, and *g*. it back to the attendant.
7. 15. (Jesus) ^{1}gave him (widow's son) to his mother
9. 42. healed the boy, and ^{1}gave him back to his father
15. 16. swine did eat : and no man *gave* unto him
19. 13. ^{1}gave them ten pounds, and said unto them
24. 30. blessed it, and brake, and *gave* to them
Jno. 1. 12. to them *gave* he the right to become children
3. 16. loved the world, that he *g*. his only begotten Son
5. 26. Father hath life—even so ^{3}gave he to the Son
27. he ^{3}gave him authority to execute judgement
6. 31. *gave* them bread out of heaven to eat
32. not Moses that *gave* you the bread out of heaven
14. 31. as the Father *gave* me commandment
Acts 2. 4. other tongues, as the Spirit *g*. them utterance
5. 10. she [Sapphira] fell down—and ^2g. up the ghost
7. 5. and he *gave* him none inheritance in it
10. *gave* him favour and wisdom before Pharaoh
42. God turned, and *g*. them up to serve the host of
10. 2. *gave* much alms to the people, and prayed heaven
11. 17. If then God *gave* unto them the like gift
12. 23. smote him, because he *g*. not God—*g*. up the ghost
13. 19. he ^{2}gave them their land for an inheritance
20. after these things he *gave* them [Israelites] judges
21. God *gave* unto them Saul the son of Kish
14. 17. *gave* you from heaven rains and fruitful seasons
15. 24. your souls; to whom we *gave* no commandment
26. 10. put to death, I *gave* my vote against them
Rom. 1. 24. God *gave* them up in the lusts of their hearts
26. For this cause God *gave* them up unto vile passions
28. God *gave* them up unto a reprobate mind
11. 8. God ^{8}gave them a spirit of stupor
1 *Cor.* 3. 5. and each as the Lord *gave* to him
6. I planted, Apollos watered ; but God *gave* the increase
16. 1. I ^{2}gave order to the churches of Galatia
2 *Cor.* 5. 5. who ^{3}gave unto us the earnest of the Spirit
8. 3. beyond their power, they ^{4}gave of their own accord
5. first they *gave* their own selves to the Lord
10. 5. which the Lord ^{3}gave for building you up
Gal. 1. 4. who *gave* himself for our sins. *Tit.* 2. 14
2. 20. who loved me, and *gave* himself up for me
Eph. 1. 22. and *gave* him to be head over all things
4. 8. led captivity captive, And *gave* gifts unto man
11. he *gave* some to be apostles ; and some, prophets
19. past feeling ^{2}gave themselves up to lasciviousness
5. 2. ^{3}gave himself up for us, an offering and a sacrifice
25. also loved the church, and *gave* himself up for it
Phil. 2. 9. ^8g. unto him the name which is above every name
1 *Th.* 4. 2. who know what charge we *g*. you through the Lord
1 *Tim.* 2. 6. who *gave* himself a ransom for all [Jesus
2 *Tim.* 1. 7. For God ^{8}gave us not a spirit of fearfulness
Heb. 7. 4. Abraham—*gave* a tenth out of the chief spoils
12. 9. to chasten us, and we *gave* them reverence
Jas. 5. 18. [Elijah] prayed again ; and the heaven *g*. rain
1 *Pet.* 1. 21. raised him from the dead, and *gave* him glory
1 *Jno.* 3. 23. love one another, even as he *g*. us commandment
24. abideth in us, by the Spirit which he ^{2}gave us
5. 11. the witness is this, that God ^3g. unto us eternal life
Rev. 1. 1. Revelation of Jesus Christ, which God *gave* him
2 *Jno.* 1. And *gave* her time that she should repent
11. 13. were affrighted, and *g*. glory to the God of heaven
13. 2. the dragon *gave* him his power, and his throne
4. because he *gave* his authority unto the beast [dead
20. 13. sea *g*. the dead—death and Hades ^{1}gave up the
see burne witness, given, granted.

GENTILES

Gavest.
Lu. 7. 44. thou [Simon] *gavest* me no water for my feet
45. Thou *gavest* me no kiss
15. 29. never *gavest* me a kid, that I might make merry
19. 23. then wherefore *gavest* thou not my money into
Jno. 17. 6. manifested thy name unto the men whom thou
gavest—and thou *gavest* them to me
8. the words which thou *gavest* me I have given unto
see given.

Gay *A.V.*—*see fine.*

Gazing *A.V.*—*see looking.*

Gazingstock.
Heb. 10. 33. being made a *gazingstock* both by reproaches

Gear.—*A.V.* ^{1}sail.
Acts 27. 17. they lowered the ^{1}gear, and so were driven

Gender.
2 *Tim.* 2. 23. questionings refuse, knowing that they *g*.

Gendereth *A.V.*—*see bearing.*

Genealogy—ies.—*A.V.* ^{1}descent.
1 *Tim.* 1. 4. neither to give heed to fables and endless *g*.
Tit. 3. 9. shun foolish questionings, and *genealogies*
Heb. 7. 3. without ^1g., having neither beginning of days
6. he whose ^{1}genealogy is not counted from them

General.
Heb. 12. 23. to the *g*. assembly and church of the firstborn

Generation.—*A.V.* ^{1}nation.
Mat. 1. 1. The book of the *generation* of Jesus Christ
11. 16. whereunto shall I liken this *generation* ? *Lu.* 7. 31
12. 39. An evil and adulterous *generation* seeketh. 16. 4
41. men of Nineveh—judgement with this *g*. 42. *Lu.* 11.
45. so shall it be also unto this evil *generation* [31, 32
17. 17. O faithless and perverse *g*. *Mk.* 9. 19 : *Lu.* 9. 41
23. 36. All these things shall come upon this *generation*
24. 34. This *g*. shall not pass away. *Mk.* 13. 30 : *Lu.* 21. 32
Mk. 8. 12. Why doth this *g*. seek a sign ?—this *generation*
33. of my words in this adulterous and sinful *generation*
Lu. 11. 29. This *generation* is an evil *generation*
30. so shall also the Son of man be to this *generation*
50. blood of all the prophets—required of this *g*. 51
16. 8. own *generation* wiser than the sons of light
17. 25. he suffer many things and be rejected of this *g*.
Acts 2. 40. Save yourselves from this crooked *generation*
8. 33. His *generation* who shall declare ?
13. 36. David—in his own *g*. served the counsel of God
Phil. 2. 15. midst of a crooked and perverse ^{1}generation
Heb. 3. 10. I was displeased with this *generation*
see generations, offspring, race.

Generations.—*A.V.* ^{1}ages, ^{2}generation, ^{8}time.
Mat. 1. 17. all the *generations* from Abraham—are fourteen *generations*—to Babylon fourteen *generations*—unto the Christ fourteen *generations*
Lu. 1. 48. henceforth all *generations* shall call me blessed
50. And his mercy is unto ^{2}generations and ^{2}generations
Acts 14. 16. who in the ^8g. gone by suffered all the nations
15. 21. Moses from ^{2}generations of old hath in every city
Eph. 3. 5. which in other ^1g. was not made known
21. in Christ Jesus unto all ^{1}generations for ever and ever
Col. 1. 26. mystery which hath been hid from all ages and *g*.

Gentiles *A.V.*—*see Greeks (proper names), nations.*

Gentle.—*A.V.* ^{1}patient.
1 *Th.* 2. 7. But we were *gentle* in the midst of you
1 *Tim.* 3. 3. but ^{1}gentle, not contentious, no lover of money

GENTLE

2 Tim. 2. 24. must not strive, but be *gentle* towards all
Tit. 3. 2. to be contentious, to be *g.*, shewing all meekness
Jas. 3. 17. then peaceable, *gentle*, easy to be intreated
1 Pet. 2. 18. not only to the good and *gentle*, but also to the

Gentleness.
2 Cor. 10. 1. by the meekness and *gentleness* of Christ
see kindness.

Gently.—*A.V.* ¹*compassion.*
Heb. 5. 2. who can bear ¹*gently* with the ignorant

Get.—*A.V.* ¹*possess,* ²*provide.*
Mat. 4. 10. *Get* thee hence, Satan: for it is written
10. 9. ²*Get* you no gold, nor silver, nor brass
16. 23. *Get* thee behind me, Satan. *Mk.* 8. 33
Lu. 9. 12. round about, and lodge, and *get* victuals
. 13. 31. *Get* thee [Jesus] out, and go hence: for Herod
18. 12. fast twice in the week; I give tithes of all that I¹*g.*
Acts 7. 3. *Get* thee out of thy land, and from thy kindred
10. 20. But arise, and *get* thee down, and go with them
22. 18. Make haste, and *get* thee quickly out of Jerusalem
27. 43. cast themselves overboard, and *get* first to the land
Jas. 4. 13. and spend a year there, and trade, and *get* gain
see enter, gained.

Ghost
Mk. 15. 37. Jesus uttered a loud voice, and gave up the
ghost. 39. *Lu.* 23. 46
Acts 5. [Ananias] fell down and gave up the *ghost.* 10
12. 23. he was eaten of worms, and gave up the *ghost*
see Holy Ghost (proper names); spirit.

Gift.
Mat. 5 23. If therefore thou art offering thy *gift* at the altar
24. leave there thy *gift* before the altar—offer thy *gift*
8. 4. and offer the *gift* that Moses commanded
23. 18. whosoever shall swear by the *gift* that is upon it
19. greater, the *gift*, or the altar that sanctifieth the *g.*?
Jno. 4. 10. If thou [woman of Samaria] knewest the *g.* of God
Acts 2. 38. ye shall receive the *gift* of the Holy Ghost
8. 20. hast thought to obtain the *gift* of God with money
10. 45. was poured out the *gift* of the Holy Ghost
11. 17. God gave unto them the like *gift* as he did also unto
Rom. 1. 11. I may impart unto you some spiritual *gift* [us
5. 15. is the free *gift*—*gift* by the grace of the one man
16. so is the *gift*—the free *gift* came of many trespasses
17. the *gift* of righteousness reign in life through the one
18. the free *gift* came unto all men to justification
6. 23. the free *gift* of God is eternal life in Christ Jesus
1 Cor. 1. 7. so that ye come behind in no *gift*
7. 7. Howbeit each man hath his own *gift* from God
13. 2. if I have the *gift* of prophecy, and know all
2 Cor. 1. 11. for the *g.* bestowed upon us by means of many
9. 15 Thanks be to God for his unspeakable *gift*
Eph. 2. 8. that not of yourselves; it is the *gift* of God
3. 7. made a minister, according to the *gift* of that grace
4 7 according to the measure of the *gift* of Christ
Phil. 4. 17 Not that I seek for the *gift*, but I seek for the
1 Tim. 4. 14. Neglect not the *gift* that is in thee [fruit
2 Tim. 1. 6. stir up the *gift* of God, which is in thee
Heb. 6. 4. once enlightened and tasted of the heavenly *gift*
Jas. 1. 17. Every good *gift* and every—boon is from above
1 Pet. 4. 10. as each hath received a *gift*, ministering it
see boon, given, grace.

Gifts.—*A.V.* ¹*offerings.*
Mat. 2. 11. they offered unto him *g.*, gold and frankincense
7 11. how to give good *g.* unto your children. *Lu* 11. 13
Lu. 21. 1. rich men—casting their *gifts* into the treasury
4. did of their superfluity cast in unto the ¹*gifts*

GIVE

Rom. 11. 29. the *g.* and the calling of God are without re-
12. 6. having *g.* differing according to the grace [pentance
1 Cor. 12. 1. Now concerning spiritual *gifts*, brethren
4. Now there are diversities of *gifts*, but the same Spirit
9. to another *gifts* of healings, in the one Spirit. 28. 30
31. But desire earnestly the greater *gifts*
14. 1. yet desire earnestly spiritual *gifts*
12. since ye are zealous of spiritual *g.*, seek that ye may
Eph. 4. 8. he led captivity captive, And gave *gifts* unto men
Heb. 2. 4. manifold powers, and by *g.* of the Holy Ghost
5. 1 that he may offer both *g.* and sacrifices. 9. 9 [fices
8. 3. every high priest is appointed to offer—*g.* and sacri-
4. there are those who offer the *g.* according to the law
11. 4. God bearing witness in respect of his *gifts*
Rev. 11. 10, and they shall send *gifts* one to another
see offerings.

Gird—ed.—*A.V.* ¹*clothed.*
Lu. 12. 37 he shall *gird* himself, and make them sit down
17 8. and *gird* thyself, and serve me, till I have eaten
Jno. 13. 4. he took a towel, and *girded* himself 5
21. 18. another shall *gird* thee, and carry thee [Peter]
Acts 12. 8. *Gird* thyself, and bind on thy sandals
1 Pet. 5. 5. Yea, all of you ¹*gird* yourselves with humility
see loins.

Girdedst.
Jno. 21. 18. When thou wast young, thou *girdedst* thyself

Girdle—s.
Mat. 3. 4. a leathern *girdle* about his loins. *Mk.* 1. 6
Acts 21. 11. Paul's *g.*—bind the man that owneth this *g.*
Rev. 1, 13. girt about at the breasts with a golden *girdle*
15. 6. girt about their breasts with golden *girdles*

Girt.
Jno. 21. 7. that it was the Lord, he *girt* his coat about him
Rev. 1. 18. *g.* about at the breasts with a golden girdle. 15. 6

Give.—*A.V.* ¹*deliver,* ²*giveth,* ³*minister,* ⁴*offer.*
Mat. 4. 6. He shall *give* his angels charge. *Lu.* 4. 10
9. All these things will I *give* thee, if thou wilt fall down
5. 42. *Give* to him that asketh thee. *Lu.* 6. 30
6. 11 *Give* us this day our daily bread. *Lu.* 11. 3
7. 6. *Give* not that which is holy unto the dogs
9 ask him for a loaf, will *give* him a stone. *Lu.* 11. 11
10. ask for a fish, will *give* him a serpent? *Lu.* 11. 11
11. how to *give* good gifts unto your children—*give* good
things to them that ask him? *Lu.* 11. 13
9. 24. *Give* place: for the damsel is not dead
10. 8 freely ye received, freely *give* [9. 41
42. whosoever shall *give* to drink unto one of these. *Mk.*
14. 7. with an oath to *g.* her whatsoever she should ask
16. *give* ye them to eat. *Mk.* 6. 37: *Lu.* 9. 13
16. 26. shall a man *g.* in exchange for his life? *Mk.* 8. 37
17. 27. that take, and *give* unto them for me and thee
19. 7. Why then did Moses command to *give* a bill
21. sell that thou hast, and *give* to the poor. *Mk.* 10. 21
20 14. my will to *give* unto this last, even as unto thee
23. on my left hand, is not mine to *give*. *Mk.* 10. 40
28. to *g.* his life a ransom for many. *Mk.* 10. 45 [23. 2
22. 17. to *g.* tribute unto Cæsar. *Mk.* 12. 14: *Lu.* 20. 22:
24. 29. the moon shall not *give* her light. *Mk.* 13. 24
25. 8. *Give* us of your oil; for our lamps are going out
.26. *g.* it unto him that hath the ten talents. *Lu.* 19. 24
26. 15. What are ye willing to *give* me, and I will deliver
Mk. 6. 25. *give* me in a charger the head of John the Baptist
12. 9. and will *g.* the vineyard unto others. *Lu.* 20. 16
15. Shall we *give*, or shall we not *give*?

GIVE

Lu. 1. 32. the Lord God shall *give* unto him the throne
77. To *give* knowledge of salvation unto his people
4. 6. I *give* all this authority—whomsoever I will I *g.* it
6. 38. *give*, and it shall be given unto you; good measure—shall they *give* into your bosom
11. 7. I cannot rise and *give* thee?
8. will not rise and *g.* him—he will arise and *give* him
12. ask an egg, will he ¹*give* him a scorpion?
41. Howbeit *give* for alms those things which are within
12. 33. Sell that ye have, and *give* alms
51. Think ye that I am come to *give* peace in the earth
58. before the magistrate, on the way *give* diligence
14. 9. shall come and say to thee, *Give* this man place
15. 12. Father, *give* me the portion of thy substance
16. 12. who will *give* you that which is your own?
18. 12. I [Pharisee] *give* tithes of all that I get
19. 8. Lord, the half of my goods I *give* to the poor
22. 5. they were glad, and covenanted to *give* him money
Jno. 4. 7. Jesus saith unto her, *Give* me to drink. 10
14. water that I shall *give* him—*give* him shall become
15. *Sir, give* me this water, that I thirst not
6. 27. eternal life, which the Son of man shall *g.* unto you
34. Lord, evermore *give* us this bread
52. How can this man *give* us his flesh to eat?
9. 24. and said unto him, *Give* glory to God
10. 28. and I *give* unto them eternal life
11. 22. whatsoever thou shalt ask of God, God will *g.* thee
13. 26. for whom I shall dip the sop, and *give* it him
29. or, that he [Judas] should *give* something to the poor
34. A new commandment I *give* unto you
14. 16. he shall *give* you another Comforter
27. my peace I *g.* unto you: not as the world giveth, *y.* I
16. 23. ask anything of the Father, he will *g.* it you. 15. 16
17. 2. to them he should *give* eternal life
Acts 3. 6. but what I have, that *give* I thee
5. 31. and a Saviour, for to *give* repentance to Israel
7. 5. promised that he would *give* it to him in possession
8. 19. *Give* me also this power, that on whomsoever I lay
20. 35. It is more blessed to *give* than to receive
25. 11. no man can ¹*give* me up unto them
Rom. not the custom of the Romans to ¹*give* up any man
8. 32. shall he not also with him freely *g.* us all things?
12. 19. but *give* place unto wrath: for it is written
20. enemy hunger, feed him; if he thirst, *g.* him to drink
1 *Cor.* 7. 5. that ye may *give* yourselves unto prayer
10. 32. *Give* no occasion of stumbling, either to Jews
13. 3. and if I *give* my body to be burned
2 *Cor.* 4. 6. to *give* the light of the knowledge of the glory
Eph. 1. 17. may *give* unto you a spirit of wisdom
4. 27. neither *give* place to the devil
28. may have whereof to *give* to him that hath need
29. that it may ³*give* grace to them that hear
2 *Th.* 3. 16. Now the Lord of peace himself *give* you peace
1 *Tim.* 4. 13. Till I come, *give* attendance to reading
15. Be diligent in these things; *g.* thyself wholly to them
5. 14. *give* none occasion to the adversary for reviling
2 *Tim.* 4. 8. the righteous judge, shall *g.* to me at that day
Heb. 2. 1. Therefore we ought to *g.* the more earnest heed
Jas. 2. 16. and yet ye *give* them not the things needful
1 *Pet.* 3. 15. being ready always to *g.* answer to every man
2 *Pet.* 1. 10. *give* the more diligence to make your calling
1 *Jno.* 5. 16. will *g.* him life for them that sin not unto death
Rev. 2. 7. that overcometh, to him will I *give* to eat. 17, 26
10. 9. that he should *give* me the little book
11. 18. the time to *give* their reward to thy servants
13. 15. it was given unto him to *give* breath to it
16. 19. to *g.* unto her the cup of the wine of the fierceness
18. 7. so much *give* her of torment and mourning
19. 7. and let us *give* the glory unto him
22. 5. for the Lord God shall ²*give* them light
see diligence, grant, heed, render.

GIVEN

I will **Give**.—*A.V.* ¹*grant.*

Mat. 11. 28. labour and are heavy laden, and *I will g.* you rest
16. 19. *I will give* unto thee the keys of the kingdom
20. 4. and whatsoever is right *I will give* you
Mk. 6. 22. whatsoever thou wilt, and *I will give* it thee. 23
Lu. 21. 15. for *I will give* you a mouth and wisdom
Jno. 6. 51. the bread which *I will give* is my flesh [David
Acts 13. 34. *I will give* you the holy and sure blessings of
Rev. 2. 10. faithful unto death, and *I will g.* thee the crown
23. *I will give* unto each one of you according to your
28. will *I will give* him the morning star   [works
3. 21. He that overcometh, *I will*¹*give* to him to sit down
11. 3. *I will give* unto my two witnesses—prophesy
21. 6. *I will give* unto him that is athirst of the fountain

Give thanks.

Rom. 16. 4. unto whom not only I *give thanks*, but also
1 *Cor.* 16. 30. spoken of for that for which I *give thanks?*
Eph. 1. 16. cease not to *g. thanks* for you, making mention
Col. 1. 3. We *give thanks* to God the Father of our Lord
1 *Th.* 1. 2. We *give thanks* to God always for you all
5. 18. in every thing *g. thanks:* for this is the will of God
2 *Th.* 2. 13. we are bound to *give thanks* to God alway
Rev. 11. 17. We *give* thee *t.*, O Lord God, the Almighty

Given.—*A.V.* ¹*bestowed,* ²*committed,* ³*delivered,* ⁴*gave,* ⁵*gavest,* ⁶*gift,* ⁷*giving,* ⁸*granted,* ⁹*made,* ¹⁰*receive.*

Mat. 9. 8. God, which had *given* such power unto men
13. 11. it is *given* to know—to them it is not *g. Mk.* 4. 11:
19. 11. this saying, but they to whom it is *g.* | *Lu.* 8. 10
21. 43. shall be *g.* to a nation bringing forth the fruits
22. 30. nor are *given* in marriage. *Mk.* 12. 25: *Lu.* 20. 34
26. 9. sold for much, and *given* to the poor. *Mk.* 14. 5.
27. 58. Then Pilate commanded it [body] to be ³*given* up
28. 18. All authority hath been *given* unto me in heaven
Mk. 4. 24. unto you: and more shall be *given* unto you
6. 2. What is the wisdom that is *given* unto this man
7. 11. Corban, that is to say, ⁶*Given* to God. *Mat.* 15. ⁶5
13. 34. left his house, and ⁸*given* authority to his servants
Lu. 6. 38. give, and it shall be *given* unto you
12. 48. to whomsoever much is *given*, of him shall
22. 19. This is my body which is *given* for you
Jno. 3. 27. except it have been *given* him from heaven
4. 10. he would have *given* thee living water
5. 22. but he hath ⁹*given* all judgement unto the Son
36. works which the Father hath *g.* me to accomplish
6. 23. ate the bread after the Lord had *given* thanks
39. all that which he hath *g.* me I should lose nothing
65. except it be *given* unto him of the Father
7. 39. were to receive: for the Spirit was not yet *given*
10. 29. My Father, which hath ⁴*given* them unto me
12. 49. which sent me, he hath ⁴*g.* me a commandment
13. 15. I have *given* you an example, that ye also should do
17. 2. thou hast *given* him, to them he should give
4. accomplished the work which thou hast ⁸*g.* me to do
7. whatsoever thou hast *given* me have I *given* them
8. the words which thou gavest me I have *g.* unto them
9. I pray not—but for those whom thou hast *given* me
11. keep them in thy name which thou hast *given* me
12. kept them in thy name which thou hast ⁵*given* me
14. I have *g.* them thy word; and the world hated them
22. glory which thou hast ⁵*g.* me I have *g.* unto them
19. 11. no power—except it were *given* thee from above
Acts 3. 16. hath *given* him this perfect soundness
4. 12. name under heaven, that is *given* among men
5. 32. whom God hath *given* to them that obey him
17. 31. whereof he hath *given* assurance unto all men
24. 26. He hoped—that money would be *given* him of Paul
Rom. 5. 5. through the Holy Ghost which was *g.* unto us

GIVEN

Rom. 11. 35. or who hath first *given* to him, and it shall be
12. 3. grace that was *given*. 6: 15. 15: 1 *Cor.* 1. 4:
    3. 10: *Gal.* 2. 9: *Eph.* 3. 2, 7: 4. 7.
13. *given* to hospitality. 1 *Tim.* 3. 2
15. 8. he might confirm the promises ⁰*g.* unto the fathers
1 *Cor.* 2. 12. the things that are freely *given* to us by God
12. 7. to each one is *given* the manifestation of the Spirit
2 *Cor.* 1. 11. may be *given* by many persons on our behalf
8. 1. the grace of God which hath been ¹*g.* in the churches
12. 7. there was *given* to me [Paul] a thorn in the flesh
Gal. 3. 21. had been a law *given* which could make alive
22. that the promise—might be *given* to them that believe
Eph. 3. 8. than the least of all saints, was this grace *given*
6. 19. that utterance may be *given* unto me in opening
1 *Tim.* 3. 8. not *g.* to much wine, not greedy of filthy lucre
4. 14. gift that is in thee, which was *g.* thee by prophecy
2 *Tim.* 1. 9. was *given* us in Christ Jesus before times
Heb. 2. 13. I and the children which God hath *given* me
4. 8. Joshua had *g.* them rest, he would not have spoken
1 *Jno.* 4. 13. because he hath *given* us of his Spirit
5. 20. hath *given* us an understanding, that we know him
Jude 7. with these ⁷*given* themselves over to fornication
Rev. 6. 2. and there was *given* unto him a crown
4. *given* to take peace—*given* unto him a great sword
6. And there was *given* unto them authority
11. And there were *given* them to each one a white robe
7. 2. to whom it was *given* to hurt the earth and the sea
8. 2. and there were *given* unto them seven trumpets
3. another angel—was *given* unto him much incense
9. 1. there was *g.* to him the key of the pit of the abyss
3. locusts upon the earth; and power was *given* them
11. 2. for it hath been *given* unto the nations
12. 14. *g.* to the woman the two wings of the great eagle
13. 5. there was *g.* to him a mouth speaking great things
7. *given* unto him to make war—*given* to him authority
16. there be ¹⁰*given* them a mark on their right hand
16. 6. and blood hast thou *given* them to drink
8. sun ; and it was *given* unto it to scorch men with fire
19. 8. it was ⁸*given* unto her that she should array herself
20. 4. and judgement was *given* unto them
   see enslaved, gave, give, giveth, granted, greedy.

Shall be Given.

Mat. 7. 7. Ask, and it *shall be given* you. *Lu.* 11. 9
10. 19. it *shall be given* you in that hour. *Mk.* 13. 11
12. 39. *shall* no sign *be g.* it. 16. 4: *Mk.* 8. 12: *Lu.* 11. 29
13. 12. whosoever hath, to him *shall be given.* 25. 29:
    Mk. 4. 25: *Lu.* 6. 18: 19. 26
Lu. 6. 38. give, and it *shall be given* unto you
Jas. 1. 5. upbraideth not; and it *shall be given* him

Givest—eth.—A.V. ¹given, ²liveth.

Jno. 3. 34. for he *giveth* not the Spirit by measure
6. 32. but my Father *giveth* you the true bread
33. out of heaven, and *giveth* life unto the world
37. which the Father *giveth* me shall come unto me
14. 27. not as the world *giveth*, give I unto you
Acts 17. 25. himself *g.* to all life, and breath, and all things
Rom. 12. 8. he that *giveth*, let him do it with liberality
14. 6. for he *giveth* God thanks—and *giveth* God thanks
1 *Cor.* 3. 7. but God that *giveth* the increase
7. 38. *g.* his own virgin daughter—*g.* her not in marriage
14. 17. For thou verily *givest* thanks well, but the other
15. 38. God *giveth* it a body even as it pleased him
57. which *giveth* us the victory through our Lord
2 *Cor.* 3. 6. the letter killeth, but the spirit *giveth* life
1 *Th.* 4. 8. God, who ¹*giveth* his Holy Spirit unto you
1 *Tim.* 5. 6. But she that ²*giveth* herself to pleasure is dead
6. 17. God, who *giveth* us richly all things to enjoy

GLISTERING

Jas. 1. 5. let him ask of God, who *giveth* to all liberally
4. 6. he *giveth* more grace—*giveth* grace to the humble.
   1 *Pet.* 5. 5
   see give, layeth down, shineth, suppliteth.

Giver.

2 *Cor.* 9. 7. of necessity : for God loveth a cheerful *giver*

Giving.—A.V. ¹boasting.

Mat. 24. 38. marrying and *g.* in marriage, until the day
Acts 5. 36. rose up Theudas, ¹*g.* himself out to be somebody
8. 9. *g.* out that himself [Simon Magus] was some great one
15. 8. *g.* them the Holy Ghost, even as he did unto us
Rom. 4. 20. strong through faith, *giving* glory to God
9. 4. and the *giving* of the law, and the service of God
1 *Cor.* 14. 7. Even things without life, *giving* a voice
2 *Cor.* 6. 3. *giving* no occasion of stumbling in anything
Phil. 4. 15. in the matter of *giving* and receiving
1 *Tim.* 4. 1. from the faith, *giving* heed to seducing spirits
Tit. 1. 14. not *g.* heed to Jewish fables, and commandments
1 *Pet.* 3. 7. *g.* honour unto the woman, as unto the weaker
   see adding, given, thanks, thanksgivings.

Glad.—A.V. ¹good.

Mat. 5. 12. Rejoice, and be exceedingly *glad :* for great is
Mk. 14. 11. when they heard it, were *glad*. *Lu.* 22. 5
Lu. 15. 32. it was meet to make merry and be *glad*
23. 8. when Herod saw Jesus, he was exceeding *glad*
Jno. 8. 56. day ; and he [Abraham] saw it, and was *glad*
11. 15. I am *glad* for your sakes that I was not there
20. 20. disciples—were *glad*, when they saw the Lord
Acts 2. 26. my heart was *glad*, and my tongue rejoiced
11. 23. and had seen the grace of God, was *glad*
13. 48. as the Gentiles heard this, they were *glad*
Rom. 10. 15. that bring *glad* tidings of good things !
2 *Cor.* 2. 2. who then is he that maketh me *glad*
1 *Th.* 3. 6. when Timothy came—brought us ¹*glad* tidings
Rev. 19. 7. Let us rejoice and be exceeding *glad*
   see good, rejoice.

Gladly.

Mk. 6. 20. much perplexed ; and he heard him *gladly*
12. 37. And the common people heard him *gladly*
Acts 21. 17. the brethren received us *gladly*
2 *Cor.* 11. 19. For ye bear with the foolish *gladly*
12. 9. Most *gladly* therefore will I rather glory
15. I will most *gladly* spend and be spent for your souls
   see welcomed.

Gladness.—A.V. ¹joy.

Lu. 1. 14. And thou shalt have joy and *gladness*
Acts 2. 28. shalt make me full of ¹*g.* with thy countenance
46. they [disciples] did take their food with *gladness*
14. 17. filling your hearts with food and *gladness*
Heb. 1. 9. With the oil of *gladness* above thy fellows
   see joy.

Glass—y.—A.V. ¹glass.

Rev. 4. 6. as it were a ¹*glassy* sea like unto crystal
15. 2. as it were a ¹*g.* sea mingled with fire—by the ¹*g.* sea
21. 18. and the city was pure gold, like unto pure *glass*
21. the street—was pure gold, as it were transparent *g.*
   see mirror.

Glistering.—A.V. ¹shining.

Mk. 9. 3. his garments became ¹*glistering*, exceeding white
   see dazzling.

GLORIED

Gloried.—*A. V.* ¹*boasted.*
2 Cor. 7. 14. I have ¹*gloried* to him [Titus] on your behalf

Glories.—*A. V.* ¹*glory.*
1 Pet. 1. 11. of Christ, and the ¹*g.* that should follow them

Gloriest.—*A. V.* ¹*makest thy boast,* ²*boast.*
Rom. 2. 17. a Jew, and restest upon the law, and ¹*g.* in God
23. thou who ¹*g.* in the law, through thy transgression
11. 18. if thou ²*gloriest,* it is not thou that bearest

Glorieth.—*A. V.* ¹*rejoiceth.*
1 Cor. 1. 31. He that *g.*, let him glory in the Lord. 2 Cor.
Jas. 2. 13. mercy ¹*glorieth* against judgement [10. 17

Glorified.
Mat. 9. 8. multitudes saw it, they were afraid, and *g.* God
15. 31. and they *glorified* the God of Israel
Mk. 2. 12. they were all amazed, and *g.* God, saying. Lu. 5. 26
Lu. 4. 15. he taught in their synagogues, being *g.* of all
7. 16. they *g.* God, saying, A great prophet is arisen
13. 13. she was made straight, and *glorified* God
23. 47. centurion saw what was done, he *glorified* God
Jno. 7. 39. because Jesus was not yet *glorified*
11. 4. that the Son of God may be *glorified* thereby
12. 16. but when Jesus was *glorified,* then remembered
23. that the Son of man should be *glorified*
28. I have both *glorified* it, and will glorify it again
13. 31. Now is the Son of man *g.,* and God is *g.* in him
14. 13. that the Father may be *glorified* in the Son
15. 8. Herein is my Father *g.,* that ye bear much fruit
17. 4. I *glorified* thee on the earth, having accomplished
10. and thine are mine: and I am *glorified* in them
Acts 3. 13. God of our fathers, hath *g.* his Servant Jesus
4. 21. for all men *glorified* God for that which was done
11. 18. they held their peace, and *glorified* God, saying
13. 48. Gentiles—were glad, and *glorified* the word of God
21. 20. they, when they heard it, *glorified* God
Rom. 1. 21. knowing God, they *glorified* him not as God
8. 17. suffer with him, that we may be also *g.* with him
30. whom he justified, them he also *glorified*
Gal. 1. 24. and they *glorified* God in me
2 Th. 1. 10. when he shall come to be *glorified* in his saints
12. name of our Lord Jesus may be *glorified* in you
3. 1. the word of the Lord may run and be *glorified*
Heb. 5. 5. So Christ also *glorified* not himself [Christ
1 Pet. 4. 11. that in all things God may be *g.* through Jesus
Rev. 18. 7. How much soever she [Babylon] *g.* herself
see glorifying.

Glorifieth—ying.—*A V.* ¹*glorified,* ²*honoureth.*
Lu. 2. 20. shepherds returned, *glorifying* and praising God
5. 25. and departed to his house, *glorifying* God
17. 15. turned back, with a loud voice ¹*y.* God [leper]
18. 43. he received his sight, and followed him, *g.* God
Jno. 8. 54. it is my Father that ²*glorifieth* me

Glorify.—*A. V.* ¹*honour,* ²*magnify.*
Mat. 5. 16. *glorify* your Father which is in heaven
Jno. 8. 54. If I ¹*glorify* myself, my glory is nothing
12. 28. Father, *glorify* thy name—will *glorify* it again
13. 32. God shall *glorify* him in himself—*glorify* him
16. 14. He shall *glorify* me: for he shall take of mine
17. 1. *glorify* thy Son, that the Son may *glorify* thee
5. O Father, *glorify* thou me with thine own self [God
21. 19. signifying by what manner of death he should *g.*

GLORY

Rom. 11. 13. I ²*glorify* my ministry
15. 6. ye may with one mouth *glorify* the God and Father
9. that the Gentiles might *glorify* God for his mercy
1 Cor. 6. 20. *glorify* God therefore in your body
2 Cor. 9. 13. by this ministration they *glorify* God
1 Pet. 2. 12. *glorify* God in the day of visitation
4. 16. but let him *glorify* God in this name
Rev. 15. 4. Who shall not fear, O Lord, and *g.* thy name?

Glorious.—*A. V.* ¹*glory.*
Lu. 13. 17. rejoiced for all the *glorious* things that were done
2 Cor. 3. 10. which hath been made *g.* hath not been made ¹*g.*
Eph. 5. 27. present the church to himself a *glorious* church
see glory.

Glory.—*A. V.* ¹*boast,* ²*glorious,* ³*honour,* ⁴*honourable,* ⁵*praise,* ⁶*rejoice,* ⁷*worship.*
Mat. 4. 8. kingdoms of the world, and the *glory* of them
6. 2. in the streets, that they may have *glory* of men
16. 27. shall come in the *glory* of his Father. *Mk.* 8. 38
24. 30. Son of man coming on the clouds of heaven with
power and great *glory.* *Mk.* 13. 26 : *Lu.* 21. 27
Mk. 10. 37. right hand, and one on thy left hand, in thy *g.*
Lu. 2. 14. *Glory* to God in the highest. 19. 38
32. And the *glory* of thy people Israel
4. 6. will I give all this authority, and the *glory* of them
9. 31. who appeared in *glory,* and spake of his decease
14. 10. then shalt thou have ⁷*glory* in the presence of all
Jno. 1. 14. *glory* as of the only begotten from the Father)
5. 41. I receive not ³*glory* from men
44. How can ye believe, which receive ³*glory* one of
another, and the ³*glory* that cometh from the
7. 18. he that seeketh the *glory* of him that sent him
8. 50. But I seek not mine own *g.* : there is one that seek-
54. If I glorify myself, my ³*glory* is nothing |eth
12. 43. they loved the ⁵*g.* of men more than the ⁵*g.* of God
17. 5. the *glory* which I had with thee before the world was
22. the *glory* which thou hast given me I have given
24. behold my *g.,* which thou hast given
Acts 7. 2. The God of *g.* appeared unto our father Abraham
22. 11. I [Paul] could not see for the *glory* of that light
Rom. 4. 2. Abraham—he hath whereof to *glory*
20. waxed strong through faith, giving *glory* to God
6. 4. Christ was raised from the dead through the *glory*
8. 18. not worthy to be compared with the *g.* which shall
21. into the liberty of the ²*glory* of the children of God
9. 4. whose is the adoption, and the *glory*
23. which he afore prepared unto *glory,* even us
11. 18. ¹*glory* not over the branches
36. To him be the *glory* for ever
16. 27. to whom be the *glory* for ever. *Gal.* 1. 5: 1 *Tim.*
1. 17: 2 *Tim.* 4. 18: *Heb.* 13. 21
1 Cor. 1. 29. that no flesh should *glory* before God [10. 17
31. He that *glorieth,* let him *glory* in the Lord. 2 *Cor.*
2. 7. God foreordained before the worlds unto our *glory*
8. they would not have crucified the Lord of *glory*
3. 21. Wherefore let no one *glory* in men
4. 7. why dost thou *g.* as if thou hadst not received it?
10. ye have ²*glory,* but we have dishonour
9. 16. if I preach the gospel, I have nothing to *glory* of
11. 7. forasmuch as he is the image and *glory* of God:
but the woman is the *glory* of the man
15. if a woman have long hair, it is a *glory* to her
15. 40. *glory* of the celestial is one, and the *glory* of the
41. *glory* of the sun—*glory* of the moon—*glory* of the
stars—differeth from another star in *glory*
43. the [body] is sown in dishonour; it is raised in *glory*
2 Cor. 3. 7. written, and engraven on stones, came with
²*glory*—*g.* of his face; which *g.* was passing away
8. rather the ministration of the spirit be with ²*glory?*

GLORY

2 Cor. 3. 9. condemnation is *glory*—righteousness exceed
10. by reason of the *glory* that surpasseth [in *g*.
11. if that which passeth away was with ²*glory*, much more that which remaineth is in ²*glory*
18. transformed into the same image from *glory* to *g.*
4. 4. light of the gospel of the ²*glory* of Christ
17. more exceedingly an eternal weight of *glory*
5. 12. wherewith to answer them that *g.* in appearance
6. 8. by ²*glory* and dishonour, by evil report
8. 23. or our brethren they are the *glory* of Christ
9. 2. which I ¹*g.* on your behalf to them of Macedonia
10. 8. I should ¹*glory* somewhat abundantly concerning
13. But we will not ¹*glory* beyond our measure
16. not to ¹*g.* in another's province in regard of things
11. 12. wherein they *g.*, they may be found even as we
16. as foolish receive me, that I also may ¹*glory* a little
18. Seeing that many *g.* after the flesh, I will *g.* also
30. If I must needs *glory*, I will *glory* of the things
12. 1. I must needs *glory*, though it is not expedient
5. On behalf of such a one will I *glory :* but on mine own behalf I will not *glory*, save in my weaknesses
6. For if I should desire to *glory*, I shall not be foolish
9. Most gladly therefore will I rather *g.* in my weaknesses
Gal. 6. 13. circumcised, that they may *glory* in your flesh
14. But far be it from me to *glory*, save in the cross
Eph. 1. 6. to the praise of the *glory* of his grace
17. Father of *g.*, may give unto you a spirit of wisdom
18. riches of the *glory* of his inheritance in the saints
2. 9. not of works, that no man should ¹*glory*
3. 13. my tribulations for you, which are your *glory*
21. unto him be the *glory* in the church and in Christ
Phil. 2. 16. I may have whereof to °*g.* in the day of Christ
3. 3. worship by the Spirit of God, and °*g.* in Christ Jesus
19. whose *g.* is in their shame, who mind earthly things
4. 19. according to his riches in *glory* in Christ Jesus
20. Now unto our God and Father be the *glory* for ever
Col. 1. 11. according to the might of his ²*glory*
27. riches of the *glory*—Christ in you, the hope of *glory*
3. 4. then shall ye also with him be manifested in *glory*
1 Th. 2. 6. nor seeking *glory* of men, neither from you
12. God, who calleth you into his own kingdom and *g.*
20. For ye are our *glory* and our joy
2 Th. 1. 4. we ourselves *g.* in you in the churches of God
9. from the face of the Lord and from the *glory* of his
2. 14. to the obtaining of the *g.* of our Lord Jesus Christ
1 Tim. 1. 11. according to the gospel of the ²*glory* of the
3. 16. believed on in the world, received up in *glory*
2 Tim. 2. 10. which is in Christ Jesus with eternal *glory*
Tit. 2. 13. blessed hope and appearing of the ²*glory* of our
Heb. 2. 10. in bringing many sons unto *glory*
3. 3. he hath been counted worthy of more *g.* than Moses
9. 5. cherubim of *glory* overshadowing the mercy-seat
Jas. 1. 9. let the brother of low degree °*glory* in his high
2. 1. the faith of our Lord Jesus Christ, the Lord of *g.*
3. 14. *glory* not and lie not against the truth
4. 16. But now ye °*glory* in your vauntings
1 Pet. 1. 8. with joy unspeakable and full of *glory*
24. And all the *glory* thereof as the flower of grass
2. 20. For what *g.* is it, if, when ye sin, and are buffeted
4. 11. whose is the ²*glory* and the dominion for ever
14. because the Spirit of *glory*—resteth upon you
5. 1. a partaker of the *glory* that shall be revealed
10. who called you unto his eternal *glory* in Christ
2 Pet. 1. 3. knowledge of him that called us by his own *g.*
17. from God the Father honour and *g.*—excellent *g.*
3. 18. To him be the *glory* both now and for ever
Jude 25. Jesus Christ our Lord, be *g.*, majesty, dominion
Rev. 7. 12. Blessing, and *g.*, and wisdom, and thanksgiving
see crown, glories, glorious, glorying, honour, rejoice, vain.

GNASHING

Gave or give Glory.—A.V. ¹praise.
Lu. 17. 18. none found—to *give glory* to God, save this
Jno. 9. 24. ¹*Give glory* to God [not God;the *glory*
Acts 12. 23. angel—smote him, [Herod] because he *gave*
1 Pet. 1. 21. raised him from the dead, and *gave* him *glory*
Rev. 11 13. affrighted, and *gave glory* to the God of heaven
14. 7. Fear God, and *give* him *glory*
16. 9. and they repented not to *give* him *glory*

Glory of God—Lord.—see God—Lord (proper names).

His Glory.
Mat. 6. 29. Solomon in all his *g.* was not arrayed. Lu. 12. 27
19. 28. the Son of man shall sit on the throne of *his glory*
25. 31. when the Son of man shall come in *his glory*— then shall he sit on the throne of *his glory*
Lu. 9. 26. be ashamed, when he cometh in *his own glory*
32. when they were fully awake, they saw *his glory*
24. 26. Christ to suffer—and to enter into *his glory ?*
Jno. 1. 14. flesh, and dwelt among us (and we beheld *his g.*
2. 11. did Jesus in Cana of Galilee, and manifested *his g.*
7. 18. He that speaketh from himself seeketh *his own g.*
12. 41. These things said Isaiah, because he saw *his glory*
Rom. 3. 7. abounded unto *his g.*, why am I also still judged
9. 23. might make known the riches of *his glory*
Eph. 1. 12. we should be unto the praise of *his glory.* 14
3. 16. grant you, according to the riches of *his glory*
Heb. 1. 3. who being the effulgence of *his glory*
1 Pet. 4. 13. at the revelation of *his g.* also ye may rejoice
Jude 24. and to set you before the presence of *his glory*
Rev. 18. 1. and the earth was lightened with *his glory*

Glorying.—A.V. ¹boasting, ²ylory, ³rejoicing.
Rom. 3. 27. Where then is the *glorying ?* It is excluded
15. 17. my ²*g.* in Christ Jesus in things pertaining to God
1 Cor. 5. 6. Your *glorying* is not good
9. 15. than that any man should make my *glorying* void
15. 31. I protest by that ³*g.* in you, brethren, which I have
2 Cor. 1. 12. our ²*g.* is this, the testimony of our conscience
14. we are your ³*glorying*, even as ye also are ours
5. 12. speak as giving you occasion of ²*g.* on our behalf
7. 4. great is my *glorying* on your behalf
14. our ¹*glorying* also, which I made before Titus
8. 24. your love, and of our ¹*glorying* on your behalf
9. 3. that our ¹*g.* on your behalf may not be made void
10.15. not ¹*g.* beyond our measure—in other men's labours
11. 10. no man shall stop me of this ¹*glorying*
17. as in foolishness, in this confidence of ¹*glorying*
Gal. 6. 4. then shall he have his ²*g.* in regard of himself
Phil. 1. 26. that your ²*g.* may abound in Christ Jesus in me
1 Th. 2. 19. what is our hope, or joy, or crown of ²*glorying ?*
Heb. 3. 6. the °*glorying* of our hope firm unto the end
Jas. 4. 16. ye glory in your vauntings : all such ²*g.* is evil

Gluttons.—A.V. ¹slow bellies.
Tit. 1. 12. Cretans are alway liars, wild beasts, idle ¹*gluttons*

Gluttonous.
Mat. 11. 19. Behold, a *g.* man, and a winebibber. Lu. 7. 34

Gnashed.
Acts 7. 54. And they *g.* on him [Stephen] with their teeth see grindeth.

Gnashing.
Mat. 8.12. there shall be the weeping and *gnashing* of teeth. 13. 42, 50 : 22. 13 : 24. 51 : 25. 30 : Lu. 13. 28

GNAT

Gnat.
Mat. 23. 24. Ye blind guides, which strain out the *gnat*, and swallow the camel

Gnawed.
Rev. 16. 10. and they *gnawed* their tongues for pain

Goad.—*A.V.* ¹*pricks.*
Acts 26. 14. it is hard for thee to kick against the ¹*goad*

Go.—*A.V.* ¹*brought,* ²*come,* ³*depart,* ⁴*gone,* ⁵*journey,* ⁶*pass,* ⁷*went.*
Mat. 2. 22. of his father Herod, he was afraid to *go* thither
5. 41. compel thee to *go* one mile, *go* with him twain
8. 9. I say to this one, *Go,* and he goeth. *Lu.* 7. 8 [swine
32. And he said unto them, *Go*—they went into the
9. 6. take up thy bed, and *go* unto thy house. *Mk.* 2. 11
13. But *go* ye and learn what this meaneth, I desire
10. 5. *Go* not into any way of the Gentiles
6. but *go* rather to the lost sheep of the house of Israel
7. And as ye *go*, preach, saying, The kingdom [6. ³11
14. as ye ⁸*go* forth out of that house or that city. 11 : *Mk.*
11. 23. thou shalt ¹*go* down unto Hades [him. *Mk.* 6. 45
14. 22. disciples to enter into the boat, and to *go* before
21. 30. And he answered and said, I *go*, sir: and went not
22. 9. *Go* ye therefore unto the partings of the highways
24. 17. him that is on the housetop not ²*go* down. *Mk.* 13. 15
26. Behold, he is in the wilderness ; *go* not forth
25. 9. *go* ye—to them that sell, and buy for yourselves
26. 36. Sit ye here, while I *go* yonder and pray
28. 19. *Go* ye—and make disciples of all the nations
Mk. 1. 38. Let us *go* elsewhere into the next towns
5. 34. *go* in peace, and be whole of thy plague
6. 38. How many loaves have ye ? *go* and see
10. 21. *go*, sell whatsoever thou hast, and give to the poor
11. 6. unto them even as Jesus—said : and they let them *go*
16. 7. But *go*, tell his disciples and Peter, He goeth before
Lu. 1. 17. he shall *go* before his face in the spirit
76. For thou shalt *go* before the face of the Lord
2. 15. Let us [shepherds] now *go* even unto Bethlehem
4. 42. stay him, that he should not ⁵*go* from them
7. 50. Thy faith hath saved thee ; *go* in peace [4. ⁶35
8. 22. Let us *go* over unto the other side of the lake. *Mk.*
9. 51. he stedfastly set his face to *go* to Jerusalem
59. Lord, suffer me first to *go* and bury my father
60. *go* thou and publish abroad the kingdom of God
10. 3. *Go* your ways : behold I send you forth as lambs
7. *Go* not from house to house
10. they receive you not, *go* out into the streets thereof
37. Jesus said—*Go,* and do thou likewise [kill thee
13. 31. *Get* thee out, and ⁸*go* hence : for Herod would fain
14. 10. bidden, *go* and sit down in the lowest place
18. I have bought a field, and I must needs *go* out and
19. five yoke of oxen, and I *go* to prove them [see it
21. *Go* out quickly into the streets and lanes of the city
23. *Go* out into the highways and hedges, and constrain
15. 18. I will arise and *go* to my father
28. But he[elder brother]was angry, and would not *go* in
16. 30. if one ⁶*go* to them from the dead, they will repent
17. 23. Lo, here ! *go* not away, nor follow after them
21. 8. time is at hand : *go* ye not after them [and to death
22. 33. Lord, with thee I am ready to *go* both to prison
24. 28. and he made as though he would ⁴*go* further
Jno. 6. 68. Lord, to whom shall we *go?* thou hast the words
7. 6. *Go* ye up unto the feast : I [Jesus] *go* not up yet
33. I *go* unto him that sent me. 16. 5 [Dispersion
35. Whither will this man *go*—will he *go* unto the
8. 14. whence I came, and whither I *go*—or whither I *go*
21. I *go* away—whither I *go,* ye cannot come. 22 : 13. 33

GO

Jno. 11. 7. Let us *go* into Judæa again
15. nevertheless let us *go* unto him [Lazarus]
16. Let us also *go*, that we may die with him
44. Loose him, [Lazarus] and let him *go*
13. 36. Whither I *go*, thou canst not follow me now
14. 2. I *go* to prepare a place for you. 3
4. And whither I *go,* ye know the way
12. because I *go* unto the Father. 28 : 16. 10, 17, 28
31. Arise, let us *go* hence [fruit should abide
15. 16. that ye should *go* and bear fruit, and that your
16. 7. but if I ⁸*go,* I will send him unto you
21. 3. Simon Peter saith unto them, I *go* a fishing
Acts 1. 25. Judas fell—that he might *go* to his own place
4. 15. commanded them to *go* aside out of the council
21. when they had further threatened them, let them *go*
23. being let *go,* they came to their own company
5. 40. not to speak in the name of Jesus, and let them *go*
7. 40. Make us gods which shall *go* before us
8. 26. Arise, and *go* toward the south unto the way
29. *Go* near, and join thyself [Philip] to this chariot
9. 11. Arise, and *go* to the street which is called Straight
10. 20. get thee [Peter] down, and *go* with them 11 12
16. 3. him [Timothy] would Paul have to *go* forth with
35. Let those men [Paul and Silas] *go*
36. let you *go* : now therefore come forth, and *go* in peace
39. asked them[Paul and Silas] to ⁸*go* away from the city
17. 9. security from Jason and the rest, they let them *go*
18. 6. from henceforth I will *go* unto the Gentiles
20. 13. intending himself [Paul] to *go* by land
22. I *go* bound in the spirit unto Jerusalem. 19. 21
21. 12. besought him [Paul] not to *go* up to Jerusalem
23. 22. So the chief captain let the young man ⁸*go*
25. 5. Let thee—of power among you, *go* down with me
12. hast appealed unto Cæsar : unto Cæsar shalt thou *go*
28. 26. *Go* thou unto this people, and say, By hearing
Rom. 15. 24. whensoever I ⁵*go* unto Spain
25. I *go* unto Jerusalem, ministering unto the saints
1 *Cor.* 5. 10. for then must ye needs *go* out of the world
6. 1. his neighbour, *go* to law before the unrighteous
7. 20. biddeth you to a feast, and ye are disposed to *go*
16. 4. meet for me to *go* also, they shall *go* with me
6. set me forward on my journey whithersoever I *go*
2 *Cor.* 9. 5. that they would *go* before unto you
Gal. 2. 9. that we should *go* unto the Gentiles
Eph. 4. 26. let not the sun *go* down upon your wrath
Phil. 2. 23. so soon as I shall see how it will *go* with me
Heb. 11. 8 Abraham, when he was called, obeyed to *go* out
13. 13. Let us—*go* forth unto him without the camp
Jas. 2. 16. ⁸*Go* in peace, be ye warmed and filled
4. 13 *Go* to now, ye that say, To-day or to-morrow
5. 1. *Go* to now, ye rich, weep and howl for your miseries
Rev. 3. 12. and he shall *go* out thence no more
16. 1. *Go* ye, and pour out the seven bowls of the wrath
14. spirits of devils, working signs ; which *go* forth
see come, come forth, dismissed, do their way, going, liberty, pass, press, release, return, seek, strangers, transgress.

Go away.—*A.V.* ¹*depart.*
Mat. 14. 16. They have no need to ¹*go away* ; give ye them
25. 46. these shall *go away* into eternal punishment
Jno. 6. 67. Would ye [the twelve] also *go away?*
14. 28. I *go away,* and I come unto you
16. 7. expedient for you that I *go away* : for if I *go* not *a.*
see send.

Go in, or into.
Mat. 2. 20. *go into* the land of Israel : for they are dead
20. 4. *Go* ye [labourers] also *into* the vineyard. 7
21. 2. *Go i.* the village that is over against you. *Lu.* 19. 30
31. publicans and the harlots *go into* the kingdom of God

GO

Mat. 26. 18. Go *into* the city to such a man. *Mk.* 14. 13
32. I will *go* before you *into* Galilee. *Mk.* 14. 28
Mk. 6. 36. *go into* the country and villages. *Lu.* 9. 12
9. 43. rather than having thy two hands to *go into* hell
16. 15. Go ye *into* all the world, and preach the gospel
Jno. 7. 3. Depart hence, and *go into* Judœa [Jesus]
10. 9. shall *go in* and go out, and shall find pasture
Acts 3. 3. seeing Peter and John about to *go into* the temple
16. 7. they [Paul and Silas] assayed to *go into* Bithynia
Jas. 4. 13. we will *go into* this city, and spend a year there
Rev. 17. 8. out of the abyss, and to *go into* perdition
see depart, enter, going.

Go *up.*
Mat. 20. 18. we *go up* to Jerusalem. *Mk.* 10. 33 : *Lu.* 18. 31
Lu. 14. 10. he may say to thee, Friend, *go up* higher
Jno. 7. 8. Go ye *up* unto the feast : I *go* not *up* yet
Acts 15. 2. Paul and Barnabas—should *go up* to Jerusalem
25. 9. Wilt thou *go up* to Jerusalem, and there be judged
see set.

Go *their, thy,* or *your way.—A.V. ¹go and shew.*
Mat. 5. 24. leave there thy gift before the altar, and *go t. w.*
2. 4. but *go thy way*, shew thyself to the priest. *Mk.* 1. 44
13. Go *thy way* ; as thou hast believed, so be it done
20. 14. Take up that which is thine, and *go thy way*
27. 65. Ye have a guard : *go your way*, make it as sure
Mk. 7. 29. For this saying *go thy way* ; the devil is gone out
10. 52. *Go thy way* ; thy faith hath made thee. *Lu.* 17. 19
11. 2. *Go your w.* into the village that is over against you
Lu. 7. 22. Go *y. w.*, and tell John what things ye have. *Mat.*
Jno. 4. 50. *Go thy way*; thy [nobleman] son liveth. [11. 14
18. 8. if therefore ye seek me, let these *go their way*
Acts 9. 15. Go *thy way* : for he is a chosen vessel unto me
24. 25. Felix was terrified, and answered, Go *thy way*
see go.

Goal.—*A. V. ¹mark.*
Phil. 3. 14. I press on toward the *¹goal* unto the prize

Goats.
Mat. 25. 32. the shepherd separateth the sheep from the *g.*
33. sheep on his right hand, but the *goats* on his left
Heb. 9. 12. nor yet through the blood of *goats* and calves
13. For if the blood of *goats* and bulls—sanctify unto
19. he took the blood of the calves and the *goats*
10. 4. that the blood of bulls and *g.* should take away sins

Goatskins.
Heb. 11. 37. they went about in sheepskins, in *goatskins*

God.—*Against God, before God, high God, God of heaven, God is or is not, God of Israel, living God, my God, of God, our God, their God, thy God, to or unto God, with God, your God*
see proper names.

God *for idol.*
Acts 7. 43. And the star of the *god* Rephan
12. 22. The voice of a *god*, and not of a man
28. 6. changed their minds, and said that he was a *god*
Phil. 3. 19. whose end is perdition, whose *god* is the belly

God *of this world.*
2 *Cor.* 4. 4. whom the *god of t. w.* hath blinded the minds

Goddess.
Acts 19. 27. the temple of the great *goddess* Diana he made
37. robbers of temples nor blasphemers of our *goddess*

GOETH

Godhead.
Acts 17. 29. to think that the *G.* is like unto gold, or silver
Col. 2. 9. in him dwelleth all the fulness of the *G.* bodily
see Divinity.

Godliness.—*A. V. ¹holiness.*
Acts 3. 12. our own power or *¹g.* we had made him to walk ?
1 *Tim.* 2. 2. lead a tranquil and quiet life in all *godliness*
10. (which becometh women professing *godliness*)
3. 16. great is the mystery of *g.* ; He who was manifested
4. 7. And exercise thyself unto *godliness*
8. but *godliness* is profitable for all things
6. 3. to the doctrine which is according to *godliness*
5. supposing that *godliness* is a way of gain
6. But *godliness* with contentment is great gain
11. follow after righteousness, *godliness*, faith, love
2 *Tim.* 3. 5. holding a form of *godliness*, but having denied
Tit. 1. 1. knowledge of the truth which is according to *g.*
2 *Pet.* 1. 3. all things that pertain unto life and *godliness*
6. in your temperance patience ; and in your patience *g.*
7. and in your *godliness* love of the brethren
3. 11. ought ye to be in all holy living and *godliness*

Godly.
2 *Cor.* 7. 9. for ye were made sorry after a *godly* sort. 11
10. For *godly* sorrow worketh repentance unto salvation
11. 2. For I am jealous over you with a *godly* jealousy
2 *Tim.* 3. 12. would live *godly* in Christ Jesus shall suffer
Tit. 2. 12. should live soberly and righteously and *godly*
2 *Pet.* 2. 9. the Lord knoweth how to deliver the *godly*
see worthily.

Gods.
Jno. 10. 34. written in your law, I said, Ye are *gods* ?
35. If he called them *gods*, unto whom the word of God
Acts 7. 40. saying unto Aaron, Make us *g.* which shall go
14. 11. *gods* are come down to us in the likeness of men
17. 18. He seemeth to be a setter forth of strange *gods*
19. 26. that they be no *gods*, which are made with hands
1 *Cor.* 8. 5. be that are called *gods*—as there are *gods* many
Gal. 4. 8. in bondage to them which by nature are no *gods*

God-ward. '
2 *Cor.* 3. 4. such confidence have we through Christ to *G.*
1 *Th.* 1. 8. every place your faith to *God-ward* is gone forth

Goest.
Mat. 8. 19. I will follow thee whithersoever thou *g. Lu.* 9. 57
Jno. 11. 8. Jews—to stone thee ; and *g.* thou thither again ?
14. 5. Lord, we know not whither thou *goest*
16. 5. none of you asketh me, Whither *goest* thou ?
see going.

Goeth.—*A. V. ¹ascendeth, ²entereth, ³gone, ⁴going, ⁵rose, ⁶went.*
Mat. 8. 9. I say to this one, Go, and he *goeth. Lu.* 7. 8
12. 45. *g.* he, and taketh with himself seven. *Lu.* 11. 26
13. 44. in his joy he *goeth* and selleth all that he hath
15. 17. whatsoever *²goeth* into the mouth passeth into the belly. *Mk.* 7. ²18
17. 21. this kind *g.* not out save by prayer [margin]
18. 12. the mountains, and seek that which *³goeth* astray ?
26. 24. The Son of man *goeth. Mk.* 14. 21 : *Lu.* 22. 22
28. 7. lo, he *goeth* before you into Galilee. *Mk.* 16. 7
Mk. 5. 40. [Jesus] ²*goeth* in where the child was
7. 19. ²*goeth* not into his heart—*g.* out into the draught ?
Lu. 14. 31. Or what king, as he *⁴g.* to encounter another king
22. 10. follow him into the house whereinto he ²*goeth*
Jno. 3. 8. knowest not whence it cometh, and whither it *g.*
10. 4. he *goeth* before them, and the sheep follow him

144

GOETH

Jno. 12. 35. in the darkness knoweth not whither he *goeth*
13. 3. came forth from God, and *goeth* unto God
1 *Cor.* 6. 6. but brother *goeth* to law with brother
Jas. 1. 24. and *goeth* away, and straightway forgetteth
Rev. 14. 4. which follow the Lamb whithersoever he *goeth*
17. 11. and he *goeth* into perdition
19. 3. her smoke ⁵*goeth* up for ever and ever. 14. ¹11
see entereth, proceedeth, seeketh, serveth.

Going.—*A.V.* ¹*ascending,* ²*came,* ³*coming,* ⁴*departing,* ⁵*go,* ⁶*goest,* ⁷*goeth,* ⁸*gone,* ⁹*pass,* ¹⁰*travelling,* ¹¹*wandering,* ¹²*went.*

Mat. 4. 21. *g.* on from thence he saw other two brethren
24. 1. Jesus went out from the temple, and was *going* on
25. 8. Give us of your oil; for our lamps are ⁸*going* out
14. as when a man, ¹⁰*going* into another country
26. 46. let us be *g.*—he is at hand that betrayeth. *Mk.* 14. ⁵42
28. 11. Now while they were *g.,* behold, some of the guard
Mk. 1. 19. And ⁸*going* on a little further, he saw James
6. 33. the people saw them ⁴*going,* and many knew them
10. 17. as he was ⁷*going* forth into the way, there ran one
Lu. 10. 31. by chance a certain priest was ²*g.* down that way
12. 58. For as thou art ⁶*going* with thine adversary
18. 36. and hearing a multitude ⁹*going* by, he inquired
19. 28. he [Jesus] went on before, ¹*g.* up to Jerusalem
Jno. 4. 51. as he was now *going* down, his servants met him
11. 31. supposing that she was ⁷*g.* unto the tomb to weep
Acts 1. 11. like manner as ye beheld him ⁵*g.* into heaven
8. 1. Now Peter and John were ¹*going* up into the temple
9. 28. he was with them ⁸*g.* in and *going* out at Jerusalem
16. 16. as we were ¹²*going* to the place of prayer ₁salem
23. 19. and ¹²*going* aside asked him privately
1 *Tim.* 5. 13. learn—to be idle, ¹¹*g.* about from house to house
5. 24 sins are evident, *going* before unto judgement
1 *Pet.* 2. 25. For ye were *going* astray like sheep
see coming, foregoing, gone, seeking.

Goings.—*A.V.* ¹*ways.*

Jas. 1. 11. shall the rich man fade away in his ¹*goings*

Gold.

Mat. 2. 11. offered unto him gifts, *gold* and frankincense
10. 9. Get you no *gold,* nor silver, nor brass in your purses
23. 16. whosoever shall swear by the *gold* of the temple
17. the *g.,* or the temple that hath sanctified the *gold?*
Acts 3. 6. Peter said, Silver and *gold* have I none
17. 29. think that the Godhead is like unto *gold,* or silver
20. 33. I coveted no man's silver, or *gold,* or apparel
1 *Cor.* 3. 12. any man buildeth on the foundation *g.,* silver
1 *Tim.* 2. 9. not with braided hair, and *gold.* 1 *Pet.* 3. 3
2 *Tim.* 2. 20. are not only vessels of *gold* and of silver
Heb. 9. 4. of the covenant overlaid round about with *gold*
Jas. 2. 2. into your synagogue a man with a *gold* ring
5. 3. Your *gold* and your silver is rusted
1 *Pet.* 1. 7. your faith, being more precious than *gold*
18. not with corruptible things, with silver or *gold*
Rev. 3. 18. I counsel thee to buy of me *gold* refined by fire
4. 4. and on their heads crowns of *gold*
9. 7. upon their heads as it were crowns like unto *gold*
20. not worship devils, and the idols of *g.,* and of silver
17. 4. purple and scarlet, and decked with *gold.* 18. 16
18. 12. merchandise of *gold,* and silver, and precious stone
21. 18. and the city was pure *gold.* 21

GOOD

Golden.

Heb. 9. 4. having a *golden* censer—wherein was a *golden* pot
Rev. 1. 12. having turned I saw seven *g.* candlesticks. 20
13. girt about at the breasts with a *golden* girdle. 15. 6
2. 1. walketh in the midst of the seven *g.* candlesticks
5. 8. and *golden* bowls full of incense
8. 3. having a *golden* censer—upon the *golden* altar
14. 14. a son of man, having on his head a *golden* crown
15. 7. seven *golden* bowls full of the wrath of God
17. 4. in her hand a *golden* cup full of abominations
21. 15. for a measure a *golden* reed to measure the city

Gone.—*A.V.* ¹*come down,* ²*come up,* ³*departed,* ⁴*entered,* ⁵*going,* ⁶*past,* ⁷*spread,* ⁸*went.*

Mat. 10. 23. Ye shall not have *g.* through the cities of Israel
12. 43. unclean spirit, when he is *gone* out. *Lu.* 11. 24
18. 12. a hundred sheep, and one of them be *g.* astray
13. over the ninety and nine which have not ⁸*g.* astray
26. 71. *gone* out into the porch, another maid saw him
Mk. 5. 30. power proceeding from him had *gone. Lu.* 8. 46
7. 29. the devil is *gone* out of thy daughter. 30
Lu. 5. 2. boats standing—fishermen had *gone* out of them
8. 35. the man, from whom the devils were ⁸*gone* out
11. 14. when the devil was *g.* out, the dumb man spake
19. 7. He is *gone* in to lodge with a man that is a sinner
Jno. 4. 8. disciples were *gone* away into the city to buy food
7. 10. when his brethren were *gone* up unto the feast
12. 19. ye prevail nothing; lo, the world is *gone* after him
13. 31. When therefore he was *gone* out, Jesus saith
Acts 10. 4. Thy prayers and thine alms are ²*gone* up for
14. 16. in the generations ⁵*gone* by suffered all the nations
16. 19. masters saw that the hope of their gain was *gone*
20. 2. when he had *gone* through those parts
5. these had ³*g.* before, and were waiting for us at Troas
27. 9. dangerous, because the Fast was now—⁸*gone* by
1 *Th.* 1. 8. your faith to God-ward is ⁷*gone* forth
1 *Pet.* 3. 22. the right hand of God, having *g.* into heaven
1 *Jno.* 4. 1. many false prophets are ⁸*g.* out into the world
2 *Jno.* 7. For many deceivers are *gone* forth into the world
Jude 7. Sodom and Gomorrah—⁵*gone* after strange flesh
Rev. 12. 12. because the devil is ¹*gone* down unto you
18. 14. fruits which thy soul lusted after are ⁸*g.* from thee
see assayed, crossed, go, goeth, going, turned, went, went away, went in, went up, withdrawn.

Good.—*A.V.* ¹*better,* ²*glad,* ³*honest,* ⁴*pleasure,* ⁵*wealth.*

Mat. 3. 10. not forth *good* fruit. 7. 18, 19; *Lu.* 3. 9
7. 11. know how to give *good* gifts. *Lu.* 11. 13
17. every *good* tree bringeth forth *good* fruit
18. A *good* tree cannot bring forth evil fruit
12. 33. Either make the tree *good,* and its fruit *good*
13. 8. upon the *g.* ground. 23; *Mk.* 4. 8, 20; *Lu.* 8. 8, 15
24. a man that soweth *good* seed. 27, 37, 38
48. and gathered the *good* into vessels, but the bad
20. 15. or is thine eye evil, because I am *good?*
25. 21. done, *good,* and faithful servant. 23; *Lu.* 19. 17
26. 24. *g.* were it for that man if he had not. *Mk.* 14. 21
Mk. 9. 45. it is ¹*good* for thee to enter into life halt. ¹47
Lu. 1. 3. it seemed *good* to me also, having traced
19. I was sent—to bring thee these ²*good* tidings
6. 38. *good* measure, pressed down, shaken together
43. no *good* tree that bringeth forth corrupt fruit; nor again a corrupt tree that bringeth forth *good* fruit
8. 1. bringing the ²*good* tidings of the kingdom of God
15. these are such as in an honest and *good* heart
12. 32. Father's *good* pleasure to give you the kingdom
18. 18. *G.* Master, what shall I do to inherit eternal life?
19. Why callest thou me *g.?* none is *g.,* save one. *Rom.* 3. 12
Jno. 2. 10. setteth on first the *good* wine—kept the *g.* wine

GOOD

Jno. 5. 29. have done *good*, unto the resurrection of life
10. 11. the *g.* shepherd: the *g.* shepherd layeth down. 14
Acts 6. 3. from among you seven men of ²*good* report
10. 38. who went about doing *good*, and healing
13. 32. And we bring you ²*good* tidings of the promise
14. 17. in that he did *good*, and gave you—rains
15. 7. a *good* while ago God made choice among you
25. it seemed *good* unto us, having come to one
28. it seemed *good* to the Holy Ghost, and to us, to lay
33. Paul thought not *good* to take with them [Mark]
Rom. 2. 10. and peace to every man that worketh *good*
3. 8. that *good* may come? whose condemnation is just
7. 12. the commandment holy, and righteous, and *good*
8. 28. that love God all things work together for *good*
11. 24. grafted contrary to nature into a *good* olive tree
12. 2. the *good* and acceptable and perfect will of God
13. 4. for he is a minister of God to thee for *good*
14. 16. Let not then your *good* be evil spoken of
15. 2. please his neighbour for that which is *good*
1 *Cor.* 5. 6. Your glorying is not *good*
9. 15. it were ¹*good* for me rather to die
10. 24. man seek his own, but each his neighbour's ¹*good*
15. 33. Evil company doth corrupt *good* manners
Gal. 4. 18. it is *good* to be zealously sought in a *g.* matter
Eph. 1. 5. according to the *good* pleasure of his will
6. 7. with *good* will doing service, as unto the Lord
Phil. 1. 15. Some indeed preach—and some also of *good* will
1 *Th.* 3. 1. we thought it *good* to be left behind at Athens
6. that ye have *good* remembrance of us always
2 *Th.* 2. 16. eternal comfort and *good* hope through grace
1 *Tim.* 6. 18. that they do *g.*, that they be rich in *g.* works
2 *Tim.* 3. 3. without self-control, fierce, no lovers of *good*
Tit. 1. 8. a lover of *good*, soberminded, just, holy, temperate
Heb. 6. 5. and tasted the *good* word of God
11. 12. sprang of one, and him as *good* as dead
12. 10. few days chastened us as seemed ¹*good* to them
Jas. 1. 17. *good* gift and every perfect boon is from above
2. 3. Sit thou here in a *good* place
3. 13. let him shew by his *good* life his works
1 *Pet.* 2. 18. not only to the *good* and gentle, but also
3. 10. He that would love life, And see *good* days
see bad, cheer, comfort, conscience, courage, doeth, evil, expedient, glad, goods, do with good, kind, report, smooth, well-pleasing.

Is Good.—*A.V.* ¹*better.*
Mat. 5. 13. it be salted? it *is* thenceforth *good* for nothing
17. 4. it *is good* for us to be here. *Mk.* 9. 5: *Lu.* 9. 33
18. 8. it *is* ¹*good* for thee to enter into life maimed or halt
19. 17. concerning that which *is g.?* One there is who *is g.*
Mk. 9. 50. Salt *is good*: but if the salt have lost. *Lu.* 14. 34
Lu. 5. 39. old wine desireth new: for he saith, The old *is* ¹*g.*
6. 45. treasure of his heart bringeth forth that which *is g.*
18. 19. none *is good*, save one, even God
Rom. 7. 13. Did then that which *is good* become death—
working death to me through that which *is good*
16. I consent unto the law that it *is good*   [is not
18. will is present with me, but to do that which *is good*
12. 9. Abhor that which is evil; cleave to that which *is g.*
14. 21. It *is good* not to eat flesh, nor to drink wine
16. 19. I would have you wise unto that which *is good*
1 *Cor.* 7. 1. It *is good* for a man not to touch a woman
8. It *is good* for them if they abide even as I
26. this *is good* by reason of the present distress—it *is good* for a man to be as he is
Gal. 4. 18. It *is g.* to be zealously sought in a good matter
Eph. 4. 28. working with his hands the thing that is *good*
29. but such as *is good* for edifying as the need may be
1 *Th.* 5. 15. follow after that which *is good.* 3 *Jno.* 11
21. prove all things; hold fast that which *is good*

GOOD

1 *Tim.* 1. 8. the law *is good*, if a man use it lawfully
2. 3. This *is good* and acceptable in the sight of God
4. 4. For every creature of God *is good*
Tit. 2. 3. teachers of that which *is good*
Heb. 13. 9. it *is good* that the heart be stablished by grace
1 *Pet.* 3. 13. if ye be zealous of that which *is good?*

Good *man.*
Mat. 12. 35. The *g. man* out of his good treasure. *Lu.* 6. 45
Lu. 23. 50. Joseph, who was a councillor, a *good man*
Jno. 7. 12. some said, He is a *g. man*; others said, Not so
Acts 11. 24. he was a *good man*, and full of the Holy Ghost
Rom. 5. 7. for the *g. man* some one would even dare to die

Good *thing.*
Mat. 19. 16. what *good thing* shall I do, that I may have
Jno. 1. 46. Can any *good thing* come out of Nazareth?
Rom. 7. 19. that is, in my flesh, dwelleth no *good thing*
Eph. 4. 28. knowing with his hands the *thing* that is *good*
6. 8. knowing that whatsoever *good thing* each one doeth
2 *Tim.* 1. 14. That *g. thing* which was committed unto thee
Philem. 6. knowledge of every *good thing* which is in you
Heb. 13. 21. make you perfect in every *g. t.* to do his will
see matter.

Good *things.*
Mat. 7. 11. give *good things* to them that ask him?
12. 34. how can ye, being evil, speak *good things?*
35. out of his good treasure bringeth forth *good things*
Lu. 1. 53. The hungry he hath filled with *good things*
16. 25. in thy lifetime receivedst thy *good things*
Rom. 10. 15. them that bring glad tidings of *good things!*
Gal. 6. 6. communicate unto him that teacheth in all *g. t.*
Tit. 3. 8. These *things* are *good* and profitable unto men
Heb. 9. 11. Christ having come a high priest of the *good t.*
10. 1. the law having a shadow of the *good things* to come

Good *tidings.*—*A.V.* ¹*Gospel.*
Mat. 11. 5. the poor have ¹*g. t.* preached to them. *Lu.* 7. 122
Lu. 2. 10. behold, I bring you *good tidings* of great joy
3. 18. preached he [John] *good tidings* unto the people
4. 18. he anointed me to preach ¹*good tidings* to the poor
Acts 10. 36. preaching *g. tidings* of peace by Jesus Christ
14. 15. men of like passions with you, and bring you *g. t.*
Heb. 4. 2. we have had ¹*good tidings* preached unto us
6. they to whom the *good tidings* were before preached
1 *Pet.* 1. 25. this is the word of ¹*good t.* which was preached
Rev. 10. 7. God, according to the *good t.* which he declared
see glad.

Good *work.*—*A.V.* ¹*good works.*
Mat. 26. 10. she hath wrought a *good work. Mk.* 14. 6
Jno. 10. 33. For a *good work* we stone thee [Jesus] not
Rom. 13. 3. For rulers are not a terror to the ¹*good work*
2 *Cor.* 9. 8. may abound unto every *good work*
Phil. 1. 6. he which began a *g. work* in you will perfect it
Col. 1. 10. bearing fruit in every *good work*, and increasing
2 *Th.* 2. 17. stablish them in every *good work* and word
1 *Tim.* 3. 1. office of a bishop, he desireth a *good work*
5. 10. if she hath diligently followed every *good work*
2 *Tim.* 2. 21. master's use, prepared unto every *good work*
3. 17. furnished completely unto every ¹*good work*
Tit. 1. 16. and unto every *good work* reprobate
3. 1. to be obedient, to be ready unto every *good work*

Good *works.*
Mat. 5. 16. that they may see your *good works*
Jno. 10. 32. Many *good works* have I shewed you

GOOD

Acts 9. 36. Dorcas : this woman was full of *good works*
Eph. 2. 10. created in Christ Jesus for *good works*
1 *Tim.* 2. 10. professing godliness) through *good works*
 5. 10. well reported of for *g. w.;* if she hath brought up
 25. there are *good works* that are evident
 6. 18. they do good, that they be rich in *good works*
Tit. 2. 7. shewing thyself an ensample of *good works*
 14. purify unto himself a people—zealous of *good works*
3 8. may be careful to maintain *good works.* 14
Heb. 10. 24. to provoke unto love and *good works*
1 *Pet.* 2. 12. by your *g. w.*, which they behold, glorify God
 see good work.

Goodly.—*A V.* ¹*proper.*

Mat. 13. 45. a merchant seeking *goodly* pearls
Lu. 21. 5 the temple—adorned with *goodly* stones
Heb. 11. 23. because they saw he [Moses] was a ¹*g.* child
 see fine, sumptuous.

Goodman.

Mk. 14. 14. say to the *goodman* of the house. *Lu.* 22. 11
 see householder, master.

Goodness.—*A V.* ¹*benefit.*

Rom. 2. 4. of his *g.*—*g.* of God leadeth thee to repentance
 11. 22. the *goodness* and severity of God—toward thee,
  God's *goodness,* if thou continue in his *goodness*
 15. 14. full of *goodness,* filled with all knowledge
Gal. 5. 22. the fruit of the Spirit is love, joy—*goodness*
Eph. 5. 9. the fruit of the light is in all *goodness*
2 *Th* 1. 11. fulfil every desire of *goodness* and every work
Philem 14. that thy ¹*goodness* should not be as of necessity

Goods.—*A V.* ¹*good,* ²*stuff.*

*Mat.*12.29.house of the strong man,and spoil his *g. Mk.*3.27
 25. 14. own servants, and delivered unto them his *goods*
Lu. 6. 30. of him that taketh away thy *goods* ask them not
 11. 21. guardeth his own court, his *goods* are in peace
 12. 18. there will I bestow all my corn and my *goods*
 19. Soul, thou hast much *goods* laid up for many years
 16. 1. was accused unto him that he was wasting his *g.*
 17. 31. his ²*goods* in the house, let him not go down
 19. 8 Lord, the half of my *goods* I give to the poor
Acts 2. 45. sold their possessions and *g.,* and parted them
1 *Cor.* 13. 3. And if I bestow all my *goods* to feed the poor
1 *Jno.* 3. 17. But whoso hath the world's ¹*g.,* and beholdeth
 see possession, riches, substance.

Gorgeous—ly.

Lu. 7. 25. Behold, they which are *gorgeously* apparelled
 23. 11. and arraying him in *gorgeous* apparel sent him

Gospel.

Mk. 1. 1. The beginning of the *gospel* of Jesus Christ
 15. repent ye, and believe in the *gospel*
 8. 35. shall lose his life for my sake and the *gospel's*
 10. 29. or lands, for my sake, and for the *gospel's* sake
Acts 15 7. Gentiles should hear the word of the *g.,* and
 20. 24. to testify the *gospel* of the grace of God (believe
Rom 1. 1. an apostle, separated unto the *gospel* of God
 9. whom I serve in my spirit in the *gospel* of his Son
 16. I am not ashamed of the *gospel :* for it is the power
 2. 16. judge the secrets of men, according to my *gospel*
 11. 28. As touching the *gospel,* they are enemies
 15. 16. unto the Gentiles, ministering the *gospel* of God
 16. 25. is able to stablish you according to my *gospel*

GOSPEL

1 *Cor.* 4. 15. for in Christ Jesus I begat you through the *g.*
 9. 12. that we may cause no hindrance to the *g.* of Christ
 14. they which proclaim the *g.* should live of the *gospel*
 18. I may make the *gospel* without charge, so as not to
  use to the full my right in the *gospel*
 23. And I do all things for the *gospel's* sake, that I may be
2 *Cor.* 2. 12. when I came to Troas for the *gospel* of Christ
4 3. if our *g.* is veiled, it is veiled in them that are perishing
 4. the light of the *gospel* of the glory of Christ
 8. 18. the brother whose praise in the *gospel* is spread
 9. 13. obedience of your confession unto the *gospel*
 10. 14. we came even as far as unto you in the *g.* of Christ
 11. 4. or a different *gospel,* which ye did not accept
Gal. 1. 6. grace of Christ unto a different *gospel*
 7. trouble you, and would pervert the *gospel* of Christ
 2 5. that the truth of the *gospel* might continue with you
 7. *gospel* of the uncircumcision—*g.* of the circumcision
 14. not uprightly according to the truth of the *gospel*
Eph. 1. 13. word of the truth, the *gospel* of your salvation
 3. 6. of the promise in Christ Jesus through the *gospel*
 6. 15. shod your feet with the preparation of the *g.* of peace
 19. to make known with boldness the mystery of the *g.*
Phil. 1. 5. your fellowship in furtherance of the *gospel*
 7. in the defence and confirmation of the *gospel.* 17
 12. fallen out rather unto the progress of the *gospel*
 27. worthy of the *gospel*—for the faith of the *gospel*
 2. 22. he served with me in furtherance of the *gospel*
 4 3. women, for they laboured with me in the *gospel*
 15. in the beginning of the *g.*—no church had fellowship
Col. 1. 5. heard before in the word of the truth of the *gospel*
 23. and not moved away from the hope of the *gospel*
1 *Th.* 1. 5. our *gospel* came not unto you in word only
 2. 2. bold in our God to speak unto you the *gospel*
 4. approved of God to be intrusted with the *gospel*
 8. pleased to impart unto you, not the *g.* of God only
 3. 2 Timothy—God's minister in the *gospel* of Christ
2 *Th.* 1. 8. them that obey not the *gospel.* 1 *Pet.* 4. 17
 2. 14. whereunto he called you through our *gospel*
1 *Tim.* 1. 11. the *gospel* of the glory of the blessed God
2 *Tim* 1. 8. but suffer hardship with the *gospel*
 10. life and incorruption to light through the *gospel*
 2 8. risen from the dead—according to my *gospel*
Philem. 13. might minister unto me in the bonds of the *g.*
Rev. 14. 6. having an eternal *gospel* to proclaim unto them
 see tidings, (good) tidings, stewardship.

Gospel *with preach—ed—eth—ing.*

Mat. 4. 23 and preaching the *gospel,* 9. 35 : *Mk.* 1. 14
 26. 13. this *gospel* shall be *preached.* 24. 14 : *Mk.* 14. 9
Mk. 13. 10. the *g.* must first be *preached* unto all the nations
 16. 15. and *preach* the *gospel* to the whole creation
Lu. 9. 6. villages, *preaching* the *g.,* and healing everywhere
 20. 1. teaching—in the temple, and *preaching* the *gospel*
Acts. 8. 25 *p.* the *g.* to many villages of the Samaritans. 40
 14. 7. [Lystra and Derbe] and there they *preached* the *g.*
 21. when they had *preached* the *gospel* to that city
 16. 10. God had called us for to *preach* the *g.* unto them
Rom. 1. 15. I am ready to *preach* the *gospel* to you also
 15. 19. I have fully *preached* the *gospel* of Christ
 20. making it my aim so to *preach* the *gospel,* not where
1 *Cor.* 1. 17. sent me not to baptize, but to *preach* the *gospel*
 9. 16. if I *preach* the *gospel*—woe is unto me, if I *preach*
 18. when I *preach* the *gospel,* I may [not the *gospel*
 11. 1. make known unto you—the *gospel* which I *preached*
2 *Cor.* 10. 16. so as to *preach* the *g.* even unto the parts
 11. 7. I *preached* to you the *gospel* of God for nought ?
Gal. 1. 8. *preach* unto you any *gospel* other than that
 9. If any man *preacheth* unto you any *gospel* other than
 11. *gospel* which was *preached* by me—is not after man

GOSPEL

Gal. 2. 2. and I laid before them the *g.* which I *preach*
3. 8. *preached* the *gospel* beforehand unto Abraham
4. 13. infirmity of the flesh I *preached* the *g.* unto you
1 *Th.* 2. 9. we *preached* unto you the *gospel* of God
1 *Pet.* 1. 12. through them that *preached* the *g.* unto you
4. 6. unto this end was the *g. preached* even to the dead

Gotten.—A.V. ¹*gained*, ²*increased*.

Acts 27. 21. from Crete, and have ¹*g.* this injury and loss
Rev. 3. 17. thou sayest, I am rich, and have ²*gotten* riches
see come, parted.

Governments.

1 *Cor.* 12. 28. helps, *governments*, divers kinds of tongues
see dominion.

Governor.

Mat. 2. 6. For out of thee shall come forth a *governor*
27. 2. and delivered him up to Pilate the *governor*
11. Jesus stood before the *g.*: and the *g.* asked him, say-
14. insomuch that the *governor* marvelled greatly ¦ing
15. the *governor* was wont to release—one prisoner
21. the *governor* answered and said unto them
28. 14. come to the *governor's* ears, we will persuade him
Acts 24. 1. they informed the *governor* against Paul
2 *Cor.* 11. 32. the *g.* under Aretas the king guarded the city
see ruler, steersman.

Governors.—A.V. ¹*rulers*.

Mat. 10. 18. before *g.*—shall ye be brought, *Lu.* 21. ¹12
Mk. 13. 9. before ¹*g.* and kings shall ye stand for my sake
1 *Pet.* 2. 14. or unto *g.*, as sent by him for vengeance
see stewards.

Grace.—A.V. ¹*gift*, ²*gracious*.

Lu. 4. 22. wondered at the words of ²*g.* which proceeded
Jno. 1. 14. begotten from the Father), full of *g.* and truth
16. of his fulness we all received, and *grace* for *grace*
17. *grace* and truth came by Jesus Christ
Acts 4. 33. and great *grace* was upon them [apostles], all
14. 3. which bare witness unto the word of his *grace*
15. 40. commended by the brethren to the *g.* of the Lord
18. 27. helped them much which had believed through *g.*
20. 32. I commend you to God, and to the word of his *g.*
Rom. 1. 5. through whom we received *g.* and apostleship
7. *Grace* to you and peace. 1 *Cor.* 1. 3: 2 *Cor.* 1. 2:
Gal. 1. 3: *Eph.* 1. 2: *Phil.* 1. 2: *Col.* 1. 2: 1 *Th.*
1. 1: 2 *Th.* 1. 2: *Tit.* 1. 4: *Philem.* 3: 1 *Pet.* 1. 2:
2 *Pet.* 1. 2; *Rev.* 1. 4
3. 24. being justified freely by his *grace*
4. 4. reward is not reckoned as of *grace*, but as of debt
16. it is of faith, that it may be according to *grace*
5. 2. we have had our access by faith into this *grace*
17. they that receive the abundance of *grace*
20. where sin abounded, *grace* did abound more
21. even so might *grace* reign through righteousness
6. 1. Shall we continue in sin, that *grace* may abound?
14. ye are not under the law, but under *grace*. 15
11. 5. a remnant according to the election of *grace*
6. by *grace*, it is no more of works—*grace* is no more *g.*
12. 3. For I say, through the *grace* that was given me
6. gifts differing according to the *grace* that was given
15. 15. because of the *grace* that was given me of God
1 *Cor.* 10. 30. If I by *g.* partake, why am I evil spoken of
15. 10. his *grace* which was bestowed upon me was not
2 *Cor.* 4. 15. that the *g.*, being multiplied through the many
8. 4. us with much intreaty in regard of this ¹*grace*
6. so he would also complete in you this *grace* also

GRACE

2 *Cor.* 8. 7. see that ye abound in this *grace* also
19. churches to travel with us in the matter of this *g.*
9. 8. God is able to make all *grace* abound unto you
12. 9. said unto me, My *grace* is sufficient for thee
Gal. 1. 6. removing from him that called you in the *grace*
15. God, who separated me—and called me through his *g.*
2. 9. they perceived the *grace* that was given unto me
5. 4. justified by the law; ye are fallen away from *grace*
Eph. 1. 6. to the praise of the glory of his *grace*
7. according to the riches of his *grace*
2. 7. might shew the exceeding riches of his *grace*
8. for by *grace* have ye been saved through faith. 5
3. 8. than the least of all saints, was this *grace* given
4. 7. unto each one of us was the *grace* given according
29. that it may give *grace* to them that hear
6. 24. *G.* be with all them that love our Lord Jesus Christ
Phil. 1. 7. ye all are partakers with me of *grace*
Col. 3. 16. singing with *grace* in your hearts unto God
4. 6. Let your speech be always with *grace*, seasoned
18. *G.* be with you. 1 *Tim.* 6. 21: 2 *Tim.* 4. 22: *Tit.* 3. 15:
2 *Th.* 2. 16. comfort and good hope through *g.* [*Heb.* 13. 25
1 *Tim.* 1. 2. *Grace*, mercy, peace. 2 *Tim.* 1. 2: 2 *Jno.* 3
1. 14. the *grace* of our Lord abounded exceedingly
2 *Tim.* 1. 9. according to his own purpose and *grace*
2. 1. be strengthened in the *grace* that is in Christ Jesus
Tit. 3. 7. justified by his *grace*, we might be made heirs
Heb. 4. 16. unto the throne of *grace*—find *grace* to help us
10. 29. and hath done despite unto the Spirit of *grace*?
12. 28. let us have *grace*, whereby we may offer service
13. 9. it is good that the heart be stablished by *grace*
Jas. 1. 11. and the *grace* of the fashion of it perisheth
4. 6. he giveth more *grace*—*g.* to the humble. 1 *Pet.* 5. 5
1 *Pet.* 1. 10. who prophesied of the *grace* that should come
13. be sober and set your hope perfectly on the *grace*
3. 7. as being also joint-heirs of the *grace* of life
5. 10. And the God of all *grace*, who called you unto
2 *Pet.* 3. 18. grow in the *grace* and knowledge of our Lord
see find.

Grace of God.

Lu. 2. 40. and the *grace* of God was upon him
Acts 11. 23. and had seen the *grace* of God, was glad
13. 43. urged them to continue in the *grace* of God
14. 26. been committed to the *grace* of God for the work
20. 24. to testify the gospel of the *grace* of God
Rom. 5. 15. much more did the *grace* of God, and the gift
1 *Cor.* 1. 4. *g.* of God which was given you in Christ Jesus
3. 10. *grace* of God which was given unto me, as a wise
15. 10. by the *grace* of God I am what I am—yet not I,
but the *grace* of God which was with me
2 *Cor.* 1. 12. not in fleshly wisdom but in the *grace* of God
6. 1. that ye receive not the *grace* of God in vain
8. 1. *g.* of God which hath been given in the churches
9. 14. by reason of the exceeding *grace* of God in you
Gal. 2. 21. I do not make void the *grace* of God
Eph. 3. 2. heard of the dispensation of that *grace* of God
7. according to the gift of that *grace* of God
Col. 1. 6. ye heard and knew the *grace* of God in truth
2 *Th.* 1. 12. and ye in him, according to the *g.* of our God
Tit. 2. 11. *grace* of God hath appeared, bringing salvation
Heb. 2. 9. that by the *grace* of God he should taste death
12. 15. be any man that falleth short of the *grace* of God
1 *Pet.* 4. 10. as good stewards of the manifold *grace* of God
5. 12. testifying that this is the true *grace* of God
Jude 4. turning the *grace* of our God into lasciviousness

Grace of the Lord Jesus—Christ.

Acts 15. 11. shall be saved through the *g.* of the Lord Jesus
Rom. 5. 15. gift by the *grace* of the one man, Jesus Christ

GRACE

Rom. 16. 20. The *grace* of our Lord Jesus Christ be with you. 1 *Cor.* 16. 23: 2 *Cor.* 13, 14: *Phil.* 4. 23: 1 *Th.* 5. 28: 2 *Th.* 3. 18: *Rev.* 22. 21
2 *Cor.* 8. 9. ye know the *grace* of our Lord Jesus Christ
Gal. 6. 18. *g.* of our *L. J. C.* be with your spirit. *Philem.* 25

Gracious.
1 *Pet.* 2. 3. if ye have tasted that the Lord is *gracious*
see grace.

Graft—ed.—*A. V.* ¹*graff—ed.*
Rom. 11. 17. thou, being a wild olive, wast ¹*grafted* in
19. Branches were broken off, that I might be ¹*g.* in
23. shall be ¹*grafted* in: for God is able to ¹*graft* them in
24. ¹*grafted* contrary to nature—natural branches, be ¹*g.*

Grain.—*A. V.* ¹*corn.*
Mat. 13. 31. is like unto a *g.* of mustard. *Mk.* 4. 31 : *Lu.* 13. 19
17. 20. If ye have faith as a *g.* of mustard seed. *Lu.* 17. 6
Jno. 12. 24. Except a ¹*grain* of wheat fall into the earth
1 *Cor.* 15. 37. not the body that shall be, but a bare *grain*
see kind.

Grandchildren.—*A. V.* ¹*nephews.*
1 *Tim.* 5. 4. if any widow hath children or ¹*grandchildren*

Grandmother.
2 *Tim.* 1. 5. which dwelt first in thy *grandmother* Lois

Grant.—*A. V.* ¹*give.*
Mk. 10. 37. *G.* unto us that we may sit, one on thy right
Lu. 1. 74. To *grant* unto us that we being delivered out of
Acts 4. 29. and *grant* unto thy servants to speak thy word
Rom. 15. 5. *g.* you to be of the same mind one with another
Eph. 3. 16. *grant* you, according to the riches of his glory
2 *Tim.* 1. 16. The Lord ¹*g.* mercy unto the house of Onesi-
18. *grant* unto him to find mercy of the Lord [phorous
see command, (I will) give.

Granted—ing.—*A. V.* ¹*gave,* ²*given.*
Acts 3. 14. asked for a murderer to be *granted* unto you
11. 18. to the Gentiles also hath God *granted* repentance
14. 3. *g.* signs and wonders to be done by their hands
27. 24. God hath ²*g.* thee all them that sail with thee
Gal. 3. 18. God hath ¹*granted* it to Abraham by promise
Phil. 1. 29. to you it hath been ²*g.* in the behalf of Christ
Philem. 22. through your prayers I shall be ²*g.* unto you
2 *Pet.* 1. 3. seeing that his divine power hath ²*g.* unto us. ²⁴
see given.

Grapes.
Mat. 7. 16. Do men gather *g.* of thorns, or figs of thistles?
Lu. 6. 44. nor of a bramble bush gather they *grapes*
Rev. 14. 18. vine of the earth; for her *grapes* are fully ripe

Grass.
Mat. 6. 30. if God doth so clothe the *grass. Lu.* 12. 28
14. 19. multitudes to sit down on the *grass. Mk.* 6. 39
Jno. 6. 10. much *grass* in the place. So the men sat
Jas. 1. 10. as the flower of the *grass* he shall pass away
11. with the scorching wind, and withereth the *grass*
1 *Pet.* 1. 24. All flesh is as *grass,* And all the glory thereof
as the flower of *grass.* The *grass* withereth
Rev. 8. 7. and all green *grass* was burnt up
9. 4. that they should not hurt the *grass* of the earth

Gratulation.—*A. V.* ¹*blessedness*
Gal. 4. 15. Where then is that ¹*gratulation* of yourselves?

Grave—s *A. V.—see death, tomb, tombs.*

GREAT

Grave (*Adjective*).
1 *Tim.* 3. 8. Deacons in like manner must be *grave*
11. Women in like manner must be *grave*
Tit. 2. 2. that aged men be temperate, *g.,* soberminded

Grave-clothes
Jno. 11. 44. bound hand and foot with *grave-clothes*

Graven.
Acts 17. 29. like unto gold, or silver, or stone, *graven* by art

Gravity.—*A. V.* ¹*honesty.*
1 *Tim.* 2. 2. quiet life in all godliness and ¹*gravity*
3. 4. having his children in subjection with all *gravity*
Tit. 2. 7. in thy doctrine shewing uncorruptness, *gravity*

Great.—*A. V.* ¹*abundant,* ²*continual,* ³*loud,* ⁴*mighty.*
Mat. 4. 16. people which sat in darkness Saw a *great* light
25. followed him *great* multitudes. 8. 1 : 13. 2 ; 19. 2 :
20. 29 : *Mk.* 3. 7, 8 : 4. 1 : *Lv.* 14. 25 : *Jno.* 6. 2
5. 12. for *great* is your reward. *Lu.* 6. 23, 35
19. shall be called *great* in the kingdom of heaven
35. Jerusalem, for it is the city of the *great* King
6. 23. in thee be darkness, how *great* is the darkness!
7. 27. it fell : and *great* was the fall thereof. *Lu.* 6. 49
8. 10. I have not found so *great* faith. *Lu.* 7. 9
18. when Jesus saw *great* multitudes. 14. 14 : *Mk.* 9. 14
13. 46. and having found one pearl of *great* price
15. 28. O woman, *great* is thy faith : be it done unto thee
33. a desert place, as to fill so *great* a multitude? *Mk.* 8. 1
19. 22. for he was one that had *g.* possessions. *Mk.* 10. 22
20. 25. their *g.* ones exercise authority over them. *Mk.* 10. 42
26. whosoever would become *great* among you
22. 36. Master, which is the *great* commandment. 38
26. 47. with him [Judas] a *great* multitude with swords
27. 60. rolled a *great* stone to the door of the tomb
Mk. 1. 35. a *great* while before day, he rose up and went out
3. 8. hearing what *great* things he did, came unto him
5. 19. how *great* things the Lord hath done. 20 : *Lu.* 8. 39
10. 43. whosoever would become *great* among you
13. 26. Son of man coming in clouds with *great* power
16. 4. stone is rolled back : for it was exceeding *great*
Lu. 1 15. For he shall be *great* in the sight of the Lord
32. *great,* and shall be called the Son of the Most High
49. he that is mighty hath done to me *great* things
5. 6. they inclosed a *great* multitude of fishes [15. 30
15. and *g.* multitudes came together to hear. 6. 17 : *Mat.*
8. 39. declare how *great* things God hath done—how *great* things Jesus had done
9 48. he that is least among you all, the same is *great*
16. 26. between us and you there is a *great* gulf fixed
Acts 4. 33. with *great* power gave—and *great* grace
8. 9. giving out that himself was some *great* one
10. This man is that power of God which is called *Great*
14. 1. *great* multitude both of Jews and Greeks believed
17. 4. and of the devout Greeks a *great* multitude
19. 28. *Great* is Diana of the Ephesians. 34
26. 22. this day testifying both to small and *great*
Rom. 9. 2. I have ²*g.* sorrow and unceasing pain in my heart
1 *Cor.* 9. 11. is it a *great* matter if we shall reap your carnal
2 *Cor.* 1. 10. who delivered us out of so *g.* a death [things?
7. 4. *Great* is my boldness of speech—*g.* is my glorying
11. 15. It is no *g.* thing therefore if his ministers also
1 *Tim.* 3. 16. without controversy *great* is the mystery of
2 *Tim* 2. 20. in a *g.* house there are not only vessels of gold
Tit. 2. 13. and appearing of the glory of our *great* God
Heb. 2. 3. how shall we escape, if we neglect so *g.* salvation?
7. 4. Now consider how *great* this man was, unto whom
12. 1. compassed about with so *g.* a cloud of witnesses

149

GREAT

Jas. 3. 4. Behold, the ships also, though they are so great
 5. tongue also is a little member, and boasteth g. things
1 Pet. 1. 3. who according to his ¹g. mercy begat us again
 3, 4. quiet spirit, which is in the sight of God of g. price
Rev. 5. 2. a strong angel proclaiming with a ²great voice
 12. saying with a ²great voice. 8. ²/3 : 14, ²⁷, ²⁹
 6. 13. her unripe figs, when she is shaken of a ⁴g. wind
 7. 9. a great multitude, which no man could number
 11. 17. thou hast taken thy great power, and didst reign
 18. to them that fear thy name, the small and the great
 12. 10. I heard a ²great voice in heaven, saying
 13. 5. a mouth speaking great things and blasphemies
 16. And he causeth all, the small and the great
 14. 15. crying with a ²great voice to him that sat [sickle
 18. he called with a ²g. voice to him that had the sharp
 15. 1. another sign in heaven, great and marvellous
 3. Great and marvellous are thy works, O Lord God
 16. 18. and there was a g. earthquake—so ⁴y. an earthquake
 19. the great city was divided—Babylon the great was
       remembered in the sight of God
 17. 5. MYSTERY, BABYLON THE GREAT, THE MOTHER OF
     THE HARLOTS   [authority
 18. 1. angel coming down out of heaven, having great
 2. Fallen, fallen is Babylon the great
 17. for in one hour so great riches is made desolate
 19. 5. ye that fear him, the small and the great
 6. heard as it were the voice of a great multitude
 17. be gathered together unto the great supper of God
 18. the flesh of all men—small and great
 20. 12. I saw the dead, the great and the small
  see exceeding, first, many, much, plenteous.

Great men A.V.—see princes.

Greater.—A. V. ¹best, ²greatest.
Mat. 11. 11. a greater than John the Baptist—little in the
       kingdom of heaven is greater. Lu. 7, 28
 12. 6. unto you, that in this place is one greater than the temple is here
 41. behold, a greater than Jonah is here. Lu. 11. 32
 42. behold, a greater than Solomon is here. Lu. 11, 31
 13. 32. is ²greater than the herbs, and becometh. Mk. 4. 32
 23. 14. receive g. condemnation [margin]. Mk. 12. 40: Lu.
 17. for whether is greater, the gold, or the temple [20. 47
 19. greater, the gift, or the altar that sanctifieth
Mk. 12. 31. none other commandment greater than these
Lu. 12. 18. I will pull down my barns, and build greater
 22. 26. ²greater among you, let him become as the younger
 27. whether is greater, he that sitteth at meat
Jno. 1. 50. thou shalt see greater things than these
 4 12. Art thou greater than our father Jacob
 5 20. and greater works than these will he shew. 14. 12
 36. witness which I have is greater than that of John
 8. 53. Art thou greater than our father Abraham
 10. 29. My Father, which hath given them unto me, is
       greater than all. 14. 28
 13. 16 A servant is not greater than his lord, neither
       one that is sent g. than he that sent him. 15. 20
 15. 13. Greater love hath no man than this, that a man
 19. 11 he that delivered me unto thee hath greater sin
Acts 15 28. to lay upon you no greater burden than these
1 Cor. 12. 31. desire earnestly the ¹greater gifts [speaketh
 14. 5. and greater is he that prophesieth than he that
 15. 6. of whom the greater part remain until now
Heb. 6. 13. could swear by none g., he sware by himself
 16. For men swear by the greater : and in every dispute
 9 11. through the greater and more perfect tabernacle
 11. 26. accounting the reproach of Christ greater riches
 2 Pet. 2. 11, whereas angels, though g. in might and power

GREW

1 Jno. 3. 20. God is greater than our heart, and knoweth
 4. 4. g. is he that is in you than he that is in the world
 5. 9. the witness of men, the witness of God is greater
3 Jno. 4. Greater joy have I none than this, to hear of my
  see heavier.

Greatest.
Mat. 18. 1. Who then is g. in the kingdom of heaven ?
 4. humble himself as this little child, the same is the g.
 23. 11. that is greatest among you shall be your servant
Mk. 9. 34. disputed—who was the g Lu. 9. 46 : 22. 24
Acts 8. 10. all gave heed, from the least to the greatest
1 Cor. 13. 13. these three ; and the greatest of these is love
Heb. 8. 11. know me, From the least to the greatest
  see greater.

Greatly.
Mat. 27. 14. insomuch that the governor marvelled greatly
Mk. 5. 38. tumult, and many weeping and wailing greatly
 9. 15. greatly amazed, and running to him saluted him
 12. 27. God of the dead, but of the living : ye do g. err
Jno. 3. 29. rejoiceth g. because of the bridegroom's voice
Acts 3. 11. porch that is called Solomon's, g. wondering
Phil. 4. 10. I rejoice in the Lord g., that now at length
2 Tim. 4. 15. for he greatly withstood our words
1 Pet. 1. 6. ye greatly rejoice, though now for a little while
2 Jno. 4. I rejoice greatly that I have found certain of thy
3 Jno. 3 I rejoiced g., when brethren came and bare witness
  we exceedingly, much.

Greatness.—A.V. ¹abundance, ²excellency.
2 Cor. 4. 7. that the exceeding ²g. of the power may be of
 12. 7 by reason of the exceeding ¹g. of the revelations
Eph. 1. 19. exceeding greatness of his power to us-ward

Greedy.—A.V. ¹given.
1 Tim. 3. 8. not given to much wine, not g. of filthy. Tit. 1. ¹⁷

Greedily A V.—see riotously.

Greediness.
Eph. 4 19. to work all uncleanness with greediness

Greek.—see proper names.

Green.
Mk. 6, 39. sit down by companies upon the green grass
Lu. 23. 31. if they do these things in the green tree, what
Rev. 8. 7. and all green grass was burnt up
 9 4 hurt the grass of the earth, neither any green thing

Greet A.V.—see salute.

Greeteth A.V.—see saluteth.

Greeted.—A.V ¹embraced.
Heb. 11 13. having seen them and ¹greeted them from afar

Greeting.—A V. ¹God speed.
Acts 15. 23. elder brethren unto the brethren—greeting
 23. 26. unto the most excellent governor Felix, greeting
Jas. 1, 1. twelve tribes which are of the Dispersion, g.
2 Jno. 10. bringeth not this teaching—give him no ¹g.
 11. he that giveth him ¹g. partaketh in his evil works
  see salutations.

Grew.—A.V. ¹sprang up, ²sprung.
Mat. 13. 7. thorns ²grew up, and choked them. Mk. 4. 7
Mk. 5. 26. was nothing bettered, but rather grew worse

150

GREW

Lu. 1. 80. child *grew,* and waxed strong in spirit. 2. 40
6. 6. as soon as it ²*grew,* it withered away. 8
13. 19. and it *grew,* and became a tree; and the birds
Acts 7. 17. the people *grew* and multiplied in Egypt
12. 24. But the word of God *grew* and multiplied
19. 20. So mightily *g.* the word of the Lord and prevailed

Grief—s.—*A.V.* ¹*heaviness.*
Heb. 13. 17. may do this with joy, and not with *grief*
1 *Pet.* 1. 6. ye have been put to ¹*g.* in manifold temptations
2. 19. a man endureth *griefs,* suffering wrongfully
see sorrow.

Grieve.
Eph. 4. 30. And *grieve* not the Holy Spirit of God

Grieved.—*A.V.* ¹*sorry.*
Mat. 14. 9. And the king [Herod] was ¹*grieved*
Mk. 3. 5. being *grieved* at the hardening of their heart
Jno. 21. 17. Peter was *grieved* because he said unto him
Rom. 14. 15. For if because of meat thy brother is *grieved*
see displeased, sorrow, sorrowful, sorry, troubled.

Grievous.—*A.V.* ¹*perilous.*
Mat. 23. 4. bind heavy burdens and *grievous. Lu.* 11. 46
Acts 20. 29. after my departing *g.* wolves shall enter in
25. 7. bringing against him many and *grievous* charges
2 *Tim.* 3. 1. in the last days ¹*grievous* times shall come
Heb. 12. 11. for the present to be not joyous, but *grievous*
1 *Jno.* 5. 3. and his commandments are not *grievous*
Rev. 16. 2. *grievous* sore upon the men which had the mark
see irksome.

Grievously.—*A.V.* ¹*sore.*
Mat. 8. 6. sick of the palsy, *grievously* tormented
15. 22. my daughter is *grievously* vexed with a devil
17. 15. he is epileptic, and suffereth ¹*g. Mk.* 9. 20: *Lu.* 9. 40

Grind *A.V.—see scatter.*

Grindeth.—*A.V.* ¹*gnasheth.*
Mk. 9. 18. he foameth, and ¹*grindeth* his teeth, and pineth

Grinding.
Mat. 24. 41. women shall be *grinding* at the mill. *Lu.* 17. 35

Groan—ed.
Jno. 11. 33. he *groaned* in the spirit, and was troubled
Rom. 8. 23. even we ourselves *groan* within ourselves
2 *Cor.* 5. 2. in this we *groan,* longing to be clothed upon
4. in this tabernacle do *groan,* being burdened

Groaneth—ing—s.
Jno. 11. 38. Jesus—*groaning* in himself cometh to the tomb
Acts 7. 34. heard their *groaning,* and I am come down
Rom. 8. 22. we know that the whole creation *groaneth*
26. for us with *groanings* which cannot be uttered

Gross.
Mat. 13. 15. this people's heart is waxed *gross. Acts* 28. 27

Ground.
Mat. 10. 29. not one of them shall fall on the *g.* ˙*Lu.* 8. 8
13. 8. and others fell upon the good *ground. Mk.* 4. 8:
23. he that was sown upon the good *g. Mk.* 4. 20: *Lu.* 8. 15
15. 35. multitude to sit down on the *ground. Mk.* 8. 6
Mk. 4. 6. And other fell on the rocky *ground*
9. 20. he fell on the *ground,* and wallowed foaming
14. 35. fell on the *g.,* and prayed that, if it were possible

GUARDIANS

Lu. 12. 16. The *g.* of a certain rich man brought forth
13. 7. cut it down; why doth it also cumber the *ground?*
19. 44. and shall dash thee to the *ground* [the *ground*
22. 44. sweat—great drops of blood falling down upon
Jno. 4. 5. parcel of *g.* that Jacob gave to his son Joseph
8. 6. and with his finger wrote on the *ground.* 8
9. 6. he spat on the *ground,* and made clay
18. 6. I am he, they went backward, and fell to the *g.*
Acts 7. 33. place whereon thou standest is holy *ground*
22. 7. I fell unto the *ground,* and heard a voice
1 *Tim.* 3. 15. the pillar and *ground* of the truth
see earth, on earth, field, places.

Grounded.
Eph. 3. 17. that ye, being rooted and *grounded* in love
Col. 1. 23. ye continue in the faith, *grounded* and stedfast

Grow.
Mat. 6. 28. lilies of the field, how they *grow. Lu.* 12. 27
13. 30. Let both *grow* together until the harvest
Mk. 4. 27. spring up and *grow,* he knoweth not how
concerning them whereunto this would *grow*
Eph. 4. 15. may *grow* up in all things into him
1 *Pet.* 2. 2. spiritual milk—that ye may *grow* thereby
2 *Pet.* 3. 18. *grow* in the grace and knowledge of our Lord

Groweth.—*A.V.* ¹*increased.*
Mk. 4. 32. *g.* up, and becometh greater than all the herbs
2 *Cor.* 10. 15. having hope that, as your faith ¹*groweth*
Eph. 2. 21. *groweth* into a holy temple in the Lord
2 *Th.* 1. 3. for that your faith *groweth* exceedingly

Grown.—*A.V.* ¹*come to years.*
Mat. 13. 32. when it is *grown,* it is greater than the herbs
Heb. 11. 24. By faith Moses, when he was ¹*g.* up, refused

Grudge—ing *A.V.—see murmur, murmuring.*

Grudgingly.
2 *Cor.* 9. 7. purposed in his heart; not *g.,* or of necessity

Guard.—*A.V.* ¹*keep,* ²*watch.*
Mat. 27. 65. Pilate said—Ye have a ²*guard:* go your way
66. sealing the stone, the ²*guard* being with them
28. 11. behold, some of the ²*guard* came into the city
Lu. 4. 10. angels charge concerning thee, to ¹*guard* thee
8. 29. he was kept under *g.,* and bound with chains
Acts 12. 4. four quaternions of soldiers to ¹*g.* him [Peter]
Phil. 4. 7. passeth all understanding, shall ¹*g.* your hearts
2 *Th.* 3. 3. who shall stablish you, and ¹*guard* you ˙thee
1 *Tim.* 6. 20. O Timothy, ¹*g.* that which is committed unto
2 *Tim.* 1. 12. I am persuaded that he is able to ¹*guard* that
14. committed unto thee ¹*g.* through the Holy Ghost
1 *Jno.* 5. 21. little children, ¹*guard* yourselves from idols
Jude 24. unto him that is able to ¹*g.* you from stumbling

Guarded.—*A.V.* ¹*kept.*
Jno. 17. 12. and I ¹*g.* them, and not one of them perished
Acts 28. 16. abide by himself with the soldier that ¹*g.* him
2 *Cor.* 11. 32. the king ¹*guarded* the city of the Damascenes
1 *Pet.* 1. 5. who by the power of God are ¹*g.* through faith

Guardeth.—*A.V.* ¹*keepeth.*
Lu. 11. 21 the strong man fully armed ¹*g.* his own court

Guardians.—*A.V.* ¹*tutors.*
Gal. 4. 2. but is under ¹*g.* and stewards until the term

GUARDS

Guards.—*A. V.* ¹*keepers.*
Acts 12. 6. and ¹*guards* before the door kept the prison
19. he examined the ¹*guards*, and commanded that

Guest-chamber.
Mk. 14. 14. Where is my *guest-chamber. Lu.* 22. 11

Guest *A.V.—see lodge.*

Guests.
Mat. 22. 10. and the wedding was filled with *guests*
11. when the king came in to behold the *guests*

Guide—s—*A. V.* ¹*lead,* ²*leaders.*
Mat. 15. 14. Let them alone: they are blind ²*guides.* And
if the blind ¹*guide* the blind, both shall fall
'23. 16. Woe unto you, ye blind *guides.* 24
Lu. 1. 79. To *guide* our feet into the way of peace
Jno. 16. 13. Spirit of truth, is come, he shall *guide* you
Acts 1. 16. Judas, who was *guide* to them that took Jesus
8. 31. How can I, except some one shall *guide* me?
Rom. 2. 19. that thou thyself art a *guide* of the blind
Rev. 7. 17. shall ¹*g.* them unto fountains of waters of life
see rule.

Guile.—*A.V.* ¹*subtilty.*
Jno. 1. 47. an Israelite indeed, in whom is no *guile!*
Acts 13. 10. O full of all ¹*guile* and all villany [Elymas]
2 *Cor.* 12. 16. being crafty, I caught you with *guile*
1 *Th.* 2. 3. nor of uncleanness, nor in *guile*
1 *Pet.* 2. 1. away therefore all wickedness, and all *guile*
2. long for the spiritual milk which is without *guile*
22. neither was *guile* found in his mouth
3. 10. And his lips that they speak no *guile*
see lie.

Guileless.—*A. V.* ¹*harmless.*
Heb. 7. 26. high priest became us, holy, ¹*guileless*, undefiled

Guiltless.—*A. V.* ¹*blameless.*
Mat. 12. 5. in the temple profane the sabbath, and are ¹*g.?*
7. ye would not have condemned the *guiltless*

Guiltiness *A. V.—see blood guiltiness.*

Guilty.—*A. V.* ¹*danger.*
Mk. 3. 29. never forgiveness, but is ¹*guilty* of an eternal sin
1 *Cor.* 11. 27. unworthily, shall be *guilty* of the body
Jas. 2. 10. yet stumble in one point, he is become *g.* of all
see debtor, judgment, (worthy of) death.

Gulf.
Lu. 16. 26. between us and you there is a great *gulf*

Gushed.
Acts 1. 18. in the midst, and all his bowels *gushed* out

H.

Habitation.—*A.V.* ¹*house,* ²*tabernacle.*
Acts 1. 20. Let his 'Judas' *habitation* be made desolate
7. 46. asked to find a ²*habitation* for the God of Jacob
17. 26. appointed seasons, and the bounds of their *h.*
2 *Cor.* 5. 2. clothed upon with our ¹*h.* which is from heaven
Eph. 2. 22. builded—for a *habitation* of God in the spirit
Jude 6. but left their proper *habitation*, he hath kept
Rev. 18. 2. and is become a *habitation* of devils

Habitations.—*A. V. see tabernacles.*

HALE

Had.—*A.V.* ¹*having,* ²*obtained.*
Mat. 13. 46. and sold all that he *had,* and bought it
18. 25. as he *h.* not wherewith—that he *h.*, and payment
19. 22. he was one that *had* great possessions. *Mk.* 10. 22
22. 28. seven? for they all *h.* her. *Mk.* 12. 23: *Lu.* 20. 33
Mk. 5. 26. and *had* spent all that she *had,* and was nothing
12. 6. He ¹*had* yet one, a beloved son: he sent him last
44. of her want did cast in all that she *had. Lu.* 21. 4
Lu. 7. 42. *had* not wherewith to pay, he forgave them
Jno. 17. 5. glory which I *had* with thee before the world was
Acts 2. 44. were together, and *had* all things common
24. 19. make accusation, if they *had* aught against me
25. 26. after examination *had,* I may have somewhat
28. 19. not that I *had* aught to accuse my nation of
Rom. 4. 11. which he *h.* while he was in uncircumcision. 12
6. 21. What fruit then *had* ye at that time in the things
1 *Cor.* 7. 29. have wives may be as though they *had* none
2 *Cor.* 8. 15. He that gathered much *had* nothing over;
and he that gathered little *had* no lack
Heb. 11. 2. For therein the elders ²*h.* witness borne to them
4. through which he ²*h.* witness borne to him that. 3. 9
1 *Jno.* 2. 7. but an old commandment which ye *had* from
2 *Jno.* 5. but that which we *had* from the beginning
we hath, raise.

Hades.—*A. V.* ¹*hell.*
Mat. 11. 23. thou shalt go down unto ¹*Hades. Lu.* 10. ¹15
16. 18. the gates of ¹*Hades* shall not prevail against it
Lu. 16. 23. in ¹*H.* he lifted up his eyes, being in torments
Acts 2. 27. thou wilt not leave my soul in ¹*Hades*
31. neither was he left in ¹*Hades,* nor did his flesh
Rev. 1. 18. I have the keys of death and of ¹*Hades*
6. 8. his name was Death; and ¹*Hades* followed with him
20. 13. death and ¹*Hades* gave up the dead
14. death and ¹*Hades* were cast into the lake of fire

Hadst.
Heb. 10. 8. sin thou wouldest not, neither *hadst* pleasure

Hail.
Mat. 26. 49. and said, *Hail,* Rabbi; and kissed him
27. 29. *Hail,* King of the Jews! *Mk.* 15. 18: *Jno.* 19. 3
28. 9. behold, Jesus met them, saying, All *hail*
Lu. 1. 28. *Hail,* thou that art highly favoured
Rev. 8. 7. followed *hail* and fire, mingled with blood
11. 19. thunders, and an earthquake, and great *hail*
16. 21. And great *hail*—the plague of the *hail*

Hair.—*A.V.* ¹*hairs.*
Mat. 3. 4. John—had his raiment of camel's *hair. Mk.* 1. 6
5. 36. thou canst not make one *hair* white or black
Lu. 7. 38. wiped them with the ¹*hair* of her head. 44: *Jno.*
11. 2: 12. 3 [*Acts* 27. 34
21. 18. And not a *hair* of your head shall perish.
1 *Cor.* 11. 14. if a man have long *hair,* it is a dishonour
15. woman have long *hair,* it is a glory—for her *hair*
1 *Tim.* 2. 9. not with braided *hair,* and gold or pearls
1 *Pet.* 3. 3. plaiting the *hair,* and of wearing jewels
Rev. 1. 14. And his head and his ¹*hair* were white
6. 12. the sun became black as sackcloth of *hair*
9. 8. And they had *hair* as the *hair* of women

Hairs.
Mat. 10. 30. very *h.* of your head are all numbered. *Lu.* 12. 7
see hair.

Hale—ing.
Lu. 12. 58. lest haply he *hale* thee unto the judge
Acts 8. 3. and *haling* men and women committed them

HALF

Half.
Mk. 6 23. I will give it thee, unto the *half* of my kingdom
Lu. 10. 30. and departed, leaving him *half* dead
    19. 8. the *half* of my goods I give to the poor
Rev. 8. 1. silence in heaven about the space of *half* an hour
    11. 9. look upon their dead bodies three days and a *h.* 11
    12. 14. for a time, and times, and *half* a time
    see shekel.

Hall.—*A.V. see palace, court.*

Hallelujah.—*A.V. ¹alleluia.*
Rev. 19. 1. multitude in heaven, saying, ¹*H.* ¹³, ¹⁴, ¹⁶

Hallowed.
Mat. 6. 9. *Hallowed* be thy name. *Lu.* 11. 2

Halt.
Mat. 18. 8. enter into life maimed or *halt. Mk.* 9. 45
Jno. 5. 3. multitude of them that were sick, blind, *halt*
    see lame.

Hand.—*A.V. ¹hands.*
Mat. 8. 15. he touched her *hand*, and the fever left her
    12. 10. and behold, a man having a withered *hand*
    13. Stretch forth thy *hand. Mk.* 3. 5 : *Lu.* 6. 10
    18. 8. *h.* or thy foot causeth thee to stumble. *Mk.* 9. 43
    22. 13. said to the servants, Bind him *hand* and foot
Lu. 1. 1. as many have taken in *hand* to draw up a narrative
    66. For the *hand* of the Lord was with him
    71. our enemies, and from the *hand* of all that hate us
    22. 21. the *hand* of him that betrayeth me is with me
Jno. 10. 28. no one shall snatch them out of my *hand*
    29. able to snatch them out of the Father's *hand*
    39. to take him : and he went forth out of their *hand*
    11. 44. was dead came forth, bound *hand* and foot
    20. 25. and put my *hand* into his side, I will not believe
    27. reach hither thy *hand*, and put it into my side
Acts 2. 23. the salutation of me Paul with mine own *hand.*
    Col. 4. 18 : 2 *Th.* 3. 17
2 *Cor.* 10. 16. in regard of things ready to our *hand*
Gal. 6. 11. written unto you with mine own *h. Philem.* 19
1 *Pet.* 5. 6. Humble yourselves under the mighty *h.* of God
Rev. 8. 4. before God out of the angel's *hand.* 10. 10
    10. 8. book which is open in the *hand* of the angel
    17. 4. in her *hand* a golden cup full of abominations
    19. 2. avenged the blood of his servants at her *hand*
    20. 4. mark upon their forehead and upon their ¹*hand*
    see hands, his hands, lay (hand), laid.

At Hand.—*A.V. ¹draweth near or nigh, ²nigh.*
Mat. 3. 2. kingdom of heaven is *at hand.* 4. 17 : 10. 7
    26. 18. The Master saith, My time is *at hand*
    45. the hour is *at hand*, and the Son of man is betrayed
    46. he is *at hand* that betrayeth me. *Mk.* 14. 42
Mk. 1. 15. the kingdom of God is *at hand* : repent ye
Lu. 21. 8. The time is ¹*at hand* : go ye not after them
    20. then know that her desolation is ²*at hand*
Jno. 2. 13. the passover of the Jews was *at h.* 6. ²⁴: 11. 55
    7.2. feast of the Jews, the feast of tabernacles, was *at hand*
    19. 42. (for the tomb was nigh *at hand*) they laid Jesus

HAND

Rom. 13. 12. The night is far spent, and the day is *at h.*
Phil. 4. 5. The Lord is *at hand*
Jas. 5. 8. for the coming of the Lord is ¹*at hand*
1 *Pet.* 4. 7. But the end of all things is *at hand*
Rev. 1. 3. written therein : for the time is *at hand.* 22. 10
    see come, present.

by the **Hand.**—*A.V. ¹hands.*
Mat. 9. 25. took her *by the hand. Mk.* 1. 31 : *Lu.* 8. 54
Mk. 5. 41. And taking the child *by the hand*, he saith
    8. 23. he took hold of the blind man *by the hand*
    9. 27. Jesus took him *by the hand*, and raised him up
Acts 2. 23. ye *by the* ¹*hand* of lawless men did crucify
    9. 8. *by the h.*, and brought him into Damascus. 22. 11
    11. 30. to the elders *by the* ¹*hand* of Barnabas and Saul
    13. 11. went about seeking some to lead him *by the hand*
    23. 19. And the chief captain took him *by the hand*
Gal. 3. 19. ordained through angels *by the h.* of a mediator

His **Hand.**
Mat. 3. 12. whose fan is in *his hand. Lu.* 3. 17   [5. 13
    8. 3. stretched forth *his h.* 12. 49 : 14. 31 : *Mk.* 1. 41 : *Lu.*
    26. 23. He that dipped *his hand* with me in the dish
Mk. 3. 1. man—which had *his hand* withered. 3 : *Lu.* 6. 8
    5. stretched it forth : and *his h.* was restored. *Lu.* 6. 10
    7. 32. they beseech him to lay *his hand* upon him
Lu. 9. 62. No man, having put *his hand* to the plough
    15. 22. put a ring on *his hand*, and shoes on his feet
Jno. 3. 35. and hath given all things into *his hand*
    18. 22. officers standing by struck Jesus with *his hand*
Acts 7. 25. God by *his hand* was giving them deliverance
    9. 41. he gave her *his hand*, and raised her up
    26. 1. Then Paul stretched forth *his hand*
    28. 3. a viper came out—and fastened on *his hand.* 4
Rev. 6. 5. he that sat thereon had a balance in *his hand*
    10. 2. and he had in *his hand* a little book open
    14. 9. a mark on his forehead, or upon *his hand*
    14. a golden crown, and in *his hand* a sharp sickle
    20. 1. key of the abyss and a great chain in *his hand*

Hand, *with right and left.*
Mat. 5. 30. if thy *right hand* causeth thee to stumble
    6. 3. let not the *left hand* know what thy *right h.* doeth
    20. 23. to sit on my *right hand*, and on my *left hand.*
    21 : *Mk.* 10. 37, 40   [42 : *Acts* 2. 34 : *Heb.* 1. 13
    22. 44. Sit thou on my *right hand. Mk.* 12. 36 : *Lu.* 20.
    25. 33. sheep on his *right hand*, but the goats on the *left*
    34. say unto them on his *right hand*, Come, ye blessed
    41. Then shall he say also unto them on the *left hand*
    26. 64. ye shall see the Son of man sitting at the *right*
        hand of power. *Mk.* 14. 62 : *Lu.* 22. 69 : *Acts* 7. 56
    27. 29. upon his head, and a reed in his *right hand*
    38. two robbers, one on the *right hand*, and one on the
        left. Mk. 15. 27 : *Lu.* 23. 33
Mk. 16. 19. and sat down at the *right hand* of God
Lu. 6. 6. a man there, and his *right hand* was withered
Acts 2. 25. he is on my *r. hand*, that I should not be moved
    33. Being therefore by the *right hand* of God exalted
    3. 7. he took him by the *right hand*, and raised him up
    5. 31. Him did God exalt with his *r. hand* to be a Prince
    7. 55. saw—Jesus standing on the *right hand* of God. 56
    21. 3. Cyprus, leaving it on the *left hand*, we sailed
Rom. 8. 34. *r. hand* of God, who also maketh intercession
2 *Cor.* 6. 7. righteousness on the *r. hand* and on the *left*
Eph. 1. 20. *sit* at *right hand* in the heavenly places
Col. 3. 1. where Christ is, seated on the *r. hand* of God
Heb. 1. 3. on the *right hand* of the Majesty on high. 8. 1

HAND

Heb. 10. 12. sins for ever, sat down on the *r. hand* of God
12. 2. sat down at the *right hand* of the throne of God
1 *Pet.* 3. 22. who is on the *right hand* of God, having gone
Rev. 1. 16. he had in his *right hand* seven stars. 2O : 2. 1
17. he laid his *right hand* upon me, saying, Fear not
5. 1. the *right hand* of him that sat on the throne. 7
13. 16. be given them a mark on their *right hand*

Handed.—*A. V.* ¹*received by tradition.*
1 *Pet.* 1. 18. vain manner of life ¹*h.* down from your fathers

Handkerchiefs.
Acts 19. 12. unto the sick were carried away from his body *h.*

Handle.
Lu. 24. 39. that it is I myself : *handle* me, and see
Col. 2. 21. *Handle* not, nor taste, nor touch

Handled.—*A. V.* ¹*entreated.*
Mk. 12. 4. wounded in the head, and *handled* shamefully
Lu. 20. 11. him also they beat, and ¹*handled* him shamefully
1 *Jno.* 1. 1. which we beheld, and our hands *handled*

Handling.—*A. V.* ¹*dividing.*
2 *Cor.* 4. 2. nor *handling* the word of God deceitfully
2 *Tim.* 2. 15. ashamed, ¹*handling* aright the word of truth

Handmaid.—*A. V.* ¹*bondmaid,* ²*bondwoman.*
Lu. 1. 38. Behold, the *handmaid* of the Lord
Gal. 4. 22. Abraham had two sons, one by the ¹*handmaid*
23. the son by the ²*handmaid* is born after the flesh
30. Cast out the ²*handmaid* and her son : for the son of the ²*handmaid* shall not inherit with the son
31. we are not children of a ²*h.*, but of the freewoman

Handmaiden—s.
Lu. 1. 48. he hath looked upon the low estate of his *h.*
Acts 2. 18. on my *handmaidens* in those days Will I pour

Handwriting *A. V.*—*see bond.*

Hands.—*A. V.* ¹*hand.*
Mat. 15. 20. to eat with unwashen *hands. Mk.* 7. 2, 5
17. 22. The Son of man shall be delivered up into the *hands* of men. *Mk.* 9. 31; *Lu.* 9. 44; 24. 7 [43
18. 8. having two *hands* or two feet to be cast. *Mk.* 9.
19. 15. he laid his *h.* on them, and departed [*Mk.* 14. 41
26. 45. Son of man is betrayed into the *hands* of sinners.
Mk. 14. 58. temple that is made with *hands*—without *hands*
Lu. 22. 53. ye stretched not forth your *hands* against me
23. 46. Father, into thy *hands* I commend my spirit
24. 39. See my *hands* and my feet. *Lu.* 20. 27
Jno. 13. 9. not my feet only, but also my *h.* and my head
21. 18. stretch forth thy *h.*, and another shall gird thee
Acts 5. 12. by the *hands* of the apostles were many signs
7. 48. dwelleth not in houses made with *hands.* 17. 24
8. 18. laying on of the apostles' *hands* the Holy Ghost
19. whomsoever I lay my *h.*, he may receive the Holy
17. 25. neither is he served by men's *hands* [Ghost
19. 11. God wrought special miracles by the *h.* of Paul
26. that they be no gods, which are made with *hands*
20. 34. know that these *h.* ministered unto my necessities
21. 11. and shall deliver him into the *h.* of the Gentiles
24. 7. took him [Paul] away out of our *hands* [margin]
28. 17. from Jerusalem into the *hands* of the Romans
Rom. 10. 21. spread out my *hands* unto a disobedient and
1 *Cor.* 4. 12. and we toil, working with our own *hands*

HAPLY

2 *Cor.* 5. 1. a house not made with *hands*, eternal
Gal. 2. 9. and Barnabas the right *hands* of fellowship
Eph. 2. 11. called Circumcision, in the flesh, made by *h.*
Col. 2. 11. with a circumcision not made with *hands*
1 *Th.* 4. 11. work with your *h.*, even as we charged you
1 *Tim.* 2. 8. men pray in every place, lifting up holy *h.*
4. 14. with the laying on of the *hands* of the presbytery
2 *Tim.* 1. 6. in thee through the laying on of my *hands*
Heb. 2. 7. And didst set him over the works of thy *hands*
6. 2. teaching of baptisms, and of laying on of *hands*
9. 11. more perfect tabernacle, not made with *hands*
24. entered not into a holy place made with *hands*
10. 31. fearful thing to fall into the *h.* of the living God
12. 12. Wherefore lift up the *hands* that hang down
Jas. 4. 8. Cleanse your *hands*, ye sinners
1 *Jno.* 1. 1. which we beheld, and our *hands* handled
see hand, by the hand, hold, lay, lifted,

His Hands.—*A V.* ¹*hand.*
Mat. 19. 13. [Jesus] lay *his hands* on them. *Mk.* 10. 16
27. 24. Pilate—washed *his hands* before the multitude
Mk. 6. 2. such mighty works wrought by *his hands* ?
8. 23. spit on his eyes, and laid *his hands* upon him. 25
Lu. 24. 40. he shewed them *his hands* and. *Jno.* 20. 20
Jno. 13. 3. the Father had given all things into *his hands*
20. 25. Except I shall see in *his h.* the print of the nails
Acts 9. 12. Ananias coming in, and laying *his* ¹*h.* on him. 17
12. 1. Herod the king put forth *his hands* to afflict
7. And his [Peter] chains fell off from *his hands* [hands
21. 11. taking Paul's girdle, he bound *his* own feet and
2 *Cor.* 11. 33. in a basket by the wall, and escaped *his h.*
Eph. 4. 28. working with *his hands* the thing that is good

Their Hands.
Mat. 4. 6. on *their hands* they shall bear thee up. *Lu.* 4. 11
15. 2. they wash not *their hands* when they eat bread
26. 67. some smote him [Jesus] with the palms of *their hands. Mk.* 14. 65; *Jno.* 19. 3
Mk. 7. 3. except they wash *their hands* diligently, eat not
4. of corn, and did eat, rubbing them in *their hands*
Acts 7. 41. and rejoiced in the works of *their hands*
14. 3. granting signs and wonders to be done by *their h.*
Rev. 7. 9. arrayed in white robes, and palms in *their hands*
9. 20. repented not of the works of *their hands*

Hang—ed.
Mat. 18. 6. millstone should be *h.* about his neck. *Mk.* 9. 42 :
27. 5. he went away and *hanged* himself [*Lu.* 17. 2
Lu. 23. 39. one of the malefactors which were *hanged* railed
Heb. 12. 12. Wherefore lift up the hands that *hang* down
see hangeth, hanging.

Hangeth—ing.—*A. V.* ¹*hang,* ²*hanged.*
Mat. 22. 40. these two commandments ¹*h.* the whole law
Acts 5. 30. whom ye slew, ²*hanging* him on a tree. 10. 39
28. 4. barbarians saw the beast ¹*hanging* from his hand
Gal. 3. 13. Cursed is every one that *hangeth* on a tree

Haply.—*A. V* ¹*anytime.*
Mat. 4. 6. Lest ¹*h.* thou dash thy foot against a stone. *Lu.* 4. 11
5. 25. lest ¹*haply* the adversary deliver thee to the judge
13. 15. Lest ¹*h.* they should perceive with their eyes. *Mk.*
Mk. 11. 13. if *haply* he might find anything thereon ! 4. ¹12
Lu. 14. 29. Lest *haply*, when he hath laid a foundation
21. 34. lest ¹*haply* your hearts be overcharged [God
Acts 5. 39. lest *haply* ye be found even to be fighting against
17. 27. if *haply* they might feel after him, and find him
Heb. 2. 1. lest ¹*haply* we drift away from them
see means.

154

HAPPEN

Happen.
Mk. 10. 32. to tell them the things that were to *h.* unto him

Happened.—*A.V.* ¹*done.*
Lu. 24. 14. communed—of all these things which had *h.*
35. they rehearsed the things that ¹*happened* in the way
Acts 3. 10. amazement at that which had *happened* unto him
1 *Cor.* 10. 11. these things *h.* unto them by way of example
Phil. 1. 12. things which *happened* unto me have fallen out
1 *Pet.* 4. 12. as though a strange thing *happened* unto you
2 *Pet.* 2. 22. *h.* unto them according to the true proverb
see befallen

Happier.
1 *Cor.* 7. 40. she is *h.* if she abide as she is, after my judgement

Happy.
Acts 26. 2. I [Paul] think myself *happy*, king Agrippa
Rom. 14 22. *Happy* is he that judgeth not himself in that
see blessed.

Hard.—*A.V.* ¹*hardly*
Mat. 19. 23. It is ¹*h.* for a rich man to enter into the kingdom
25. 24. I knew thee that thou art a *hard* man
Mk. 10. 24. how *hard* is it for them that trust in riches
Jno. 6. 60. This is a *hard* saying; who can hear it?
Acts 18. 7. whose house joined *hard* to the synagogue
26. 14. it is *hard* for thee to kick against the goad
Heb. 5. 11. many things to say, and *hard* of interpretation
2 *Pet.* 3. 16. are some things *hard* to be understood
Jude 15 *hard* things which ungodly sinners have spoken

Harden.
Heb 3. 8. *Harden* not your hearts. 15 : 4. 7

Hardened.—*A.V.* ¹*blinded.*
Mk. 6. 52. concerning the loaves, but their heart was *h.*
8. 17. neither understand? have ye your heart *hardened*?
Jno. 12. 40. hath blinded their eyes, and he *h.* their heart
Acts 19. 9. some were *h.* and disobedient, speaking evil
Rom. 11 7. the election obtained it, and the rest were ¹*h.*
2 *Cor* 3. 14 but their minds were ¹*hardened*
Heb. 3. 13 To-day; lest any one of you be *hardened*

Hardeneth -ing.—*A.V.* ¹*blindness,* ²*hardness.*
Mk. 3. 5. being grieved at the ²*hardening* of their heart
Rom. 9. 18. mercy on whom he will, and whom he will he *h*
11. 25. a ¹*hardening* in part hath befallen Israel
Eph. 4. 18. because of the ¹*hardening* of their heart

Hardly
Mk. 10. 23. *h.* shall they that have riches enter. *Lu.* 18. 24
Lu 9. 39. it *h.* departeth from him, bruising him sorely
see difficulty, hard.

Hardness.
Mat. 19. 8. for your *h.* of heart suffered you. *Mk.* 10. 5
Mk. 16. 14. upbraided them with their unbelief and *h.*
Rom. 2. 5. but after thy *hardness* and impenitent heart
see hardening, hardship.

Hardship.—*A.V.* ¹*afflictions,* ²*hardness,* ³*trouble.*
2 *Tim.* 1. 8. but suffer ¹*hardship* with the gospel
2. 3. Suffer ²*hardship* with me, as a good soldier
9. wherein I suffer ³*hardship* unto bonds
4. 5. be thou sober in all things, suffer ¹*hardship*

HAST

Harlot.—*A.V.* ¹*whore.*
1 *Cor.* 6. 15. make them members of a *h.* ? God forbid
16. that he that is joined to a *harlot* is one body ?
Heb. 11. 31. By faith Rahab the *harlot* perished not
Jas. 2. 25. was not also Rahab the *h.* justified by works
Rev. 17. 1. I will shew thee the judgement of the great ¹*h.*
15. waters which thou sawest, where the ¹*h.* sitteth [19.¹²
16. these shall hate the ¹*h.*, and shall make her desolate

Harlots.
Mat. 21. 31. *h.* go into the kingdom of God before you
32. but the publicans and the *harlots* believed him
Lu. 15. 30. which hath devoured thy living with *harlots*
Rev. 17. 5. BABYLON THE GREAT, THE MOTHER OF THE H

Harm.—*A.V.* ¹*hurt.*
Acts 16. 28. Do thyself no *harm.* for we are all here
18. 10. no man shall set on thee to ¹*harm* thee [Paul]
28. 5. he shook off the beast—and took no *harm*
21. nor did any of the brethren—speak any *h.* of thee
1 *Pet.* 3. 13. who is he that will *h.* you, if ye be zealous
see amiss, injury.

Harmless.
Mat. 10. 16. wise as serpents, and *harmless* as doves
Phil. 2. 15. ye may be blameless and *h.* children of God
see guileless.

Harp.—*A.V* ¹*harps.*
1 *Cor.* 14. 7. things without life—whether pipe or *harp*
Rev. 5 8. having each one a ¹*harp*, and golden bowls

Harped—ing.
1 *Cor.* 14. 7. how shall it be known what is piped or *h.* ?
Rev. 14. 2. as the voice of harpers *harping* with their harps

Harpers.
Rev. 14. 2. voice which I heard was the voice of *harpers*
18. 22. the voice of *h.* and minstrels and flute-players

Harps
Rev. 14. 2. voice of harpers harping with their *harps*
15. 2. standing by the glassy sea, having *harps* of God
see harp

Harvest.
Mat. 9. 37. The *harvest* truly is plenteous. *Lu.* 10. 2
38. Pray ye therefore the Lord of the *harvest*, that he
send forth labourers into his *harvest*. *Lu.* 10. 2
13 30. Let both grow together until the *harvest* : and in
the time of the *harvest* I will say to the reapers
39. the *harvest* is the end of the world
Mk. 4. 29. putteth forth the sickle, because the *h.* is come
Jno. 4. 35. then cometh the *h.* ?—white already unto *h.*
Rev. 14. 15. for the *harvest* of the earth is over-ripe

Hast.—*A.V.* ¹*saidst.*
Mat 19. 21. sell that thou *hast.* *Mk.* 10. 21 : *Lu.* 18. 22
25. 25. talent in the earth : lo, thou *hast* thine own
Jno. 4. 11. Sir, thou *hast* nothing to draw with—whence
then *hast* thou that living water ?
18. for thou *h.* had five husbands : and he whom thou
now *hast* is not thy husband—this ¹*hast* thou said
Acts 8. 21. Thou *hast* neither part nor lot in this matter
Rom. 14. 22. The faith which thou *h.*, have thou to thyself
1 *Cor.* 4. 7. what *hast* thou that thou didst not receive ?
Philem. 5. faith which thou *hast* toward the Lord Jesus

HAST

Jas. 2. 18. Thou *hast* faith, and I have works
Rev. 2. 6. But this thou *hast*, that thou hatest the works
14. thou *hast* there some that hold the teaching. 15
3. 11. hold fast that which thou *hast*, that no one take

Haste.

Mk. 6. 25. she came in straightway with *h.* unto the king
Lu. 1. 39. and went into the hill country with *haste*
2. 16. came with *haste*, and found both Mary and Joseph
see made, make.

Hasted A.V.—*see hastening.*

Hastening.—A.V. ¹*hasted.*

Acts 20. 16. for he was ¹*hastening*—to be at Jerusalem

Hastily.—A.V. ¹*suddenly.*

1 Tim. 5. 22. Lay hands ¹*hastily* on no man
see quickly.

Hasting A.V.—*see desiring.*

Hate.

Mat. 5. 43. love thy neighbour, and *hate* thine enemy
6. 24. either he will *hate* the one. Lu. 16. 13
24. 10. deliver up one another, and shall *h.* one another
Lu. 1. 71. and from the hand of all that *hate* us
6. 22. Blessed are ye, when men shall *hate* you
27. Love your enemies, do good to them that *hate* you
Jno. 7. 7. The world cannot *hate* you; but me it hateth
Rom. 7. 15. but what I *hate*, that I do
Rev. 2. 6. works of the Nicolaitans, which I also *hate*
17. 16. shall *hate* the harlot, and shall make her desolate
see hateth.

Hated.

Mat. 10. 22. ye shall be *hated.* 24. 9: Mk. 13. 13: Lu. 21. 17
Lu. 19. 14. citizens *hated* him, and sent an ambassage
Jno. 15. 18. ye know that it hath *hated* me before it *h.* you
24. both seen and *hated* both me and my Father
25. written in their law, They *hated* me without a cause
17. 14. world *h.* them, because they are not of the world
Rom. 9. 13. Jacob I loved, but Esau I *hated*
Eph. 5. 29. for no man ever *hated* his own flesh
Heb. 1. 9. Thou hast loved righteousness, and *h.* iniquity

Hateful.—A.V. ¹*haters.*

Rom. 1. 30. backbiters, ¹*hateful* to God, insolent
Tit. 3. 3. living in malice and envy, *hateful*, hating
Rev. 18. 2. a hold of every unclean and *hateful* bird

Haters A.V.—*see hateful.*

Hatest.

Rev. 2. 6. thou *hatest* the works of the Nicolaitans

Hateth.—A.V. ¹*hate.*

Lu. 14. 26. cometh unto me, and ¹*hateth* not his own father
Jno. 3. 20. every one that doeth ill *hateth* the light
7. 7. but me it *hateth*, because I testify of it
12. 25. he that *hateth* his life in this world shall keep it
15. 18. If the world ¹*hateth* you. 1 Jno. 3. ¹13
19. out of the world, therefore the world *hateth* you
23. He hat *hateth* me *hateth* my Father also
1 Jno. 2. 9. and *hateth* his brother, is in the darkness. 11
3. 15. Whosoever *hateth* his brother is a murderer
4. 20. say, I love God, and *hateth* his brother, he is a liar

Hath.—A.V. ¹*had*, ²*have.*

Mat. 5. 23. that thy brother *hath* aught against thee
8. 20. *hath* not where to lay his head. Lu. 9. 58
13. 12. *hath*, to him shall be given—*h.* not, from him
which he *h.* 25. 29: Mk. 4. 25: Lu. 8. ²18: 19. 26

HAVE

Mat. 13. 44. selleth all that he *hath*, and buyeth that field
56. Whence then *hath* this man all these. Mk. 6. 2
Mk. 4. 23. If any man ²*hath* ears to hear. Mat. 11. 15: 13.
9, 43: Lu. 8. 8: 14. 35: Rev. 13. ²9
Lu. 12. 44. that he will set him over all that he *hath*
14. 33. renounceth not all that he *hath*, he cannot be
19. 24. give it unto him that *hath* the ten pounds
25. they said unto him, Lord, he *hath* ten pounds
20. 24. Whose image and superscription *hath* it?
Jno. 12. 48. He that rejecteth me—*h.* one that judgeth him
14. 30. of the world cometh: and he *h.* nothing in me
16. 15. All things whatsoever the Father *hath* are mine
Acts 15. 21. Moses from generations of old *h.* in every city
Rom. 3. 1. What advantage then *hath* the Jew?
4. 1. forefather according to the flesh, *hath* found?
2. was justified by works, he *hath* whereof to glory
8. 9. ²*hath* not the Spirit of Christ, he is none of his
9. 21. Or *hath* not the potter a right over the clay
1 Cor. 14. 26. each one *h.* a psalm, *hath* a teaching, *hath* a
revelation, *hath* a tongue, *hath* an interpretation
2 Cor. 6. 14. what communion *hath* light with darkness?
15. what concord *h.* Christ—what portion *h.* a believer
16. what agreement *hath* a temple of God with idols?
8. 12. according as a man *h.*, not according as he *h.* not
Heb. 7. 6. *hath* taken tithes of Abraham, and *hath* blessed
him that ¹*hath* the promises
Jas. 2. 14. a man say he *hath* faith, but have not works?
1 Jno. 2. 23. *hath* not the Father—*hath* the Father also
3. 17. whoso *hath* the world's goods, and beholdeth
4. 16. and have believed the love which God *hath* in us
5. 12. He that *hath* the Son *hath* the life; he that *hath*
not the Son of God *hath* not the life
2 Jno. 9. *hath* not God—*h.* both the Father and the Son
Rev. 3. 7. he that *hath* the key of David, he that openeth
13. 8. every one whose name *hath* not been written in
the book of life of the Lamb that *hath* been slain
see have.

Hating.

Tit. 3. 3. malice and envy, hateful, *hating* one another
Jude 23. *hating* even the garment spotted by the flesh

Hatred A.V.—*see enmities.*

Haughty.—A.V. ¹*proud.*

Rom. 1. 30. hateful to God, insolent, ¹*haughty*, boastful
2 Tim. 3. 2. ¹*haughty*, railers, disobedient to parents

Have.—A.V. ¹*hath*, ²*receive*, ³*retain.*

Mat. 3. 9. We *have* Abraham to our father. Lu. 3. 8
8. 29. What *have* we to do with thee. Mk. 1. 24: Lu. 4.
13. 12. and he shall *have* abundance. 25. 29 [34
14. 4. It is not lawful for thee to *have* her. Mk. 6. 18
15. 33. Whence should we *have* so many loaves in a desert
34. How many loaves *have* ye? Mk. 6. 38: 8. 5
19. 27. and followed thee; what then shall we *have*?
28. Jesus said—that ye which *have* followed me
26. 11. ye *have* the poor always with you; but me ye
have not always. Mk. 14. 7: Jno. 12. 8
65. what further need *have* we of witnesses?
27. 19. *Have* thou nothing to do with that righteous man
Mk. 2. 17. that are whole *have* no need of a physician
4. 40. Why are ye fearful? *have* ye not yet faith?
7. 24. into a house, and would *have* no man know it
9. 50. the salt *h.* lost its saltness—*Have* salt in yourselves
10. 21. thou shalt *have* treasure in heaven. Lu. 18. 22
11. 22. Jesus answering saith unto them, *H.* faith in God
23. but shall believe—he shall *have* it [them
24. believe that ye *h.* received them, and ye shall *have*
25. forgive, if ye *have* aught against any one

156

HAVE

Lu. 1. 62. signs to his father, what he would *h.* him called
6. 32. what thank *have* ye? 33, 34
11. 6. journey, and I *have* nothing to set before him
12. 4. and after that *have* no more that they can do
24. which *have* no store-chamber nor barn
33. Sell that ye *have*, and give alms [19
14. 18. I *have* bought a field—I pray thee *h.* me excused.
22. 31. Simon, Simon, behold, Satan asked to *have* you
24. 17. What communications are these that ye *have*
41. *Have* ye here anything to eat? *Jno.* 21. 5
Jno. 2. 4. Woman, what *have* I to do with thee?
5. 7. I *have* no man, when the water is troubled, to put
8. 6. that they might *have* whereof to accuse him
Acts 3. 6. gold *have* I none; but what I *h.*, that give I thee
16. 3. Him would Paul *have* to go forth with him
Rom. 1. 28. they refused to ²*have* God in their knowledge
9. 9. season will I come, and Sarah shall *have* a son
14. 22. faith which thou hast, *have* thou to thyself
15. 17. I *have* therefore my glorying in Christ Jesus
1 *Cor.* 6. 19. Holy Ghost which is in you, which ye *have*
7. 2. each man *h.* his own wife—each woman *h.* her own
28. Yet such shall *have* tribulation in the flesh
32. But I would *have* you to be free from cares
40. I think that I also *have* the Spirit of God
8. 1. We know that we all *have* knowledge
9. 4. *Have* we no right to eat and to drink? 5, 6
16. if I preach the gospel, I *have* nothing to glory of
11. 22. *have* ye not—put them to shame that *have* not?
12. 21. hand, I *have* no need of thee—feet, I *h.* no need
25. members should *have* the same care one for another
30. *h.* all gifts of healings? do all speak with tongues?
15. 31. but that glorying in you—which I *have* in Christ
2 *Cor.* 3. 4. such confidence *have* we through Christ
5. 12. may *have* wherewith to answer them that glory
6. 14. what fellowship ¹*have* righteousness and iniquity?
Eph. 4. 28. may *have* whereof to give to him that hath need
Phil. 1. 7. because I *have* you in my heart [flesh
3. 3. glory in Christ Jesus, and *have* no confidence in the
4. might *have* confidence—thinketh to ¹*h.* confidence
17. which do walk even as ye *have* us for an ensample
Col. 1. 4. of the love which ye *have* toward all the saints
Philem. 15. that thou shouldest ²*have* him for ever
Heb. 4. 13. the eyes of him with whom we *have* to do
5. 12. ye *have* need again that some one teach you
8. 3. this high priest also *have* somewhat to offer
13. 5. content with such things as ye *have*
Jas. 4. 2. Ye lust, and *h.* not—ye *h.* not, because ye ask not
1 *Jno.* 4. 21. And this commandment *have* we from him
5. 14. this is the boldness which we *have* toward him
Rev. 2. 4. But I *have* this against thee. 14, 20
10. ye may be tried; and ye shall *h.* tribulation ten days
25. Howbeit that which ye *have*, hold fast till I come
22. 14. may *have* the right to come to the tree of life
see ability, desireth, hath, willeth.

Haven.
Acts 27. 12. *haven* was not commodious—a *haven* of Crete

Having.—*A.V.* ¹*possessed.*
Lu. 8. 43. a woman *having* an issue of blood twelve years
Acts 16. 16. a certain maid ¹*having* a spirit of divination
Rom. 15. 23. *having* no more any place in these regions—
having those many years a longing to come
2 *Cor.* 6. 10. as *h.* nothing, and yet possessing all things
Phil. 1. 23. *having* the desire to depart and be with Christ
Tit. 2. 8. ashamed, *having* no evil thing to say of us
2 *Jno.* 12. *Having* many things to write unto you
Jude 19. make separations, sensual, *having* not the Spirit
see being, had.

HEAL

Havock.—*A.V.* ¹*destroyed,* ²*wasted.*
Acts 9. 21. he that in Jerusalem made ¹*havock* of them
Gal. 1. 13. persecuted the church of God, and made ²*h.* of it
23. preacheth the faith of which he once made ¹*havock*
see waste.

Hay.
1 *Cor.* 3. 12. gold, silver, costly stones, wood, *hay*, stubble

Hazarded—ing.—*A.V.* ¹*regarding.*
Acts 15. 26. *h.* their lives for the name of our Lord Jesus
Phil. 2. 30. ¹*h.* his life to supply that which was lacking

Head.
Mat. 5. 36. Neither shalt thou swear by thy *head*
8. 20. Son of man hath not where to lay his *h. Lu.* 9. 58
10. 30. hairs of your *head* are all numbered. *Lu.* 12. 7
14. 11. his *head* was brought in a charger, and given to
21. 42. was made the *head* of the corner. *Mk.* 12. 10:
Lu. 20. 17: *Acts* 4. 11: 1 *Pet.* 2. 7 [15. 19
27. 30. took the reed and smote him on the *head. Mk.*
Mk. 6. 24. she said, The *h.* of John the Baptist. *Mat.* 14. 8
Lu. 7. 38. and wiped them with the hair of her *head*
46. My *head* with oil thou didst not anoint [34
21. 18. And not a hair of your *head* shall perish. *Acts* 27.
Jno. 13. 9. not my feet only, but also my hands and my *h.*
Rom. 12. 20. thou shalt heap coals of fire upon his *head*
1 *Cor.* 11. 3. the *head* of every man is Christ—the *head* of
the woman is the man—the *head* of Christ is God
4. having his *head* covered, dishonoureth his *head*
5. with her *head* unveiled dishonoureth her *head*
10. sign of authority on her *head*, because of the angels
12. 21. again the *head* to the feet, I have no need of you
Eph. 1. 22. *head* over all. 4. 15: *Col.* 1. 18
5. 23. the husband is the *head* of the wife, as Christ also
is the *head* of the church
Col. 2. 10. who is the *head* of all principality and power
19. not holding fast the *Head*, from whom all the body
Rev. 19. 12. and upon his *head* are many diadems
see bowed, covered, crown.

Headlong.
Lu. 4. 29. led him—that they might throw him down *h.*
Acts 1. 18. falling *headlong*, he burst asunder in the midst

Heady *A.V.—see headstrong.*

Heads.
Mat. 27. 39. railed on him, wagging their *h. Mk.* 15. 29
Lu. 21. 28. lift up your *heads*; because your redemption
Acts 18. 6. Your blood be upon your own *heads*
21. 24. charges for them, that they may shave their *h.*
Rev. 4. 4. and on their *heads* crowns of gold
9. 7. and upon their *heads* as it were crowns like unto gold
19. their tails like unto serpents, had heads
12. 3. red dragon, having seven *h.*—upon his *h.* seven
13. 1. I saw one of his *h.* as though it had been smitten
17. 3. names of blasphemy, having seven *heads.* 7: 13. 1
9. The seven *heads* are seven mountains
18. 19. And they cast dust on their *heads*, and cried

Headstrong.—*A.V.* ¹*heady.*
2 *Tim.* 3. 4. traitors, ¹*headstrong*, puffed up

Heal.
Mat. 8. 7. And he saith unto him, I will come and *h.* him
10. 1. gave them authority—to *h.* all manner of disease
8. *Heal* the sick. *Lu.* 9. 2: 10. 9
12. 10. Is it lawful to *h.* on the sabbath day? *Lu.* 14. 3
13. 15. And I should *heal* them. *Jno.* 12. 40: *Acts* 28. 27
Mk. 3. 2. whether he would *h.* him on the sabbath. *Lu.* 6. 7

157

HEAL

Lu. 4. 23. say unto me this parable, Physician, *h.* thyself
5. 17. the power of the Lord was with him to *heal*
Jno. 4. 47. that he would come down, and *heal* his son
Acts 4. 30. while thou stretchest forth thy hand to *heal*
      see sure.

Healed.—*A.V.* ¹*made whole.*

Mat. 4. 24. he *healed* them. 12. 15 : 15. 30 : 19. 2 : 21. 14:
    Mk. 6. 5, 13 : *Lu.* 4. 40 : 9. 11
8. 8. and my servant shall be *healed.* 13 : *Lu.* 7. 7
10. with a word, and *healed* all that were sick. 14. 14
12. 22. he *healed* him. *Lu.* 14. 4 : 22. 51
15. 28. And her daughter was ¹*healed* from that hour
Mk. 1. 34. he *healed* many that were sick. 3. 10
5. 29. felt in her body that she was *healed* of her plague
Lu. 5. 15. came together to hear, and to be *healed.* 6. 17, 18
6. 19. power came forth from him, and *healed* them all
8. 2. certain women which had been *healed* of evil spirits
43. had spent all—and could not be *healed* of any
47. touched him, and how she was *healed* immediately
9. 42. rebuked the unclean spirit, and *healed* the boy
13. 14. come and be *healed,* and not on—the sabbath
17. 15. when he saw that he was *healed,* turned back
Jno. 5. 13. he that was *healed* wist not who it was
Acts 4. 14. seeing the man which was *healed* standing
5. 16. unclean spirits: and they were *healed* every one
8. 7. that were palsied, and that were lame, were *healed*
28. 8. prayed, and laying his hands on him *healed* him
Heb. 12. 13. not turned out of the way, but rather be *healed*
Jas. 5. 16. pray one for another, that ye may be *healed*
1 *Pet.* 2. 24. by whose stripes ye were *healed*
Rev. 13. 3. and his death-stroke was *healed.* 12
      see cured, whole.

Healeth.—*A.V.* ¹*maketh whole.*

Acts 9. 34. Æneas, Jesus Christ ¹*healeth* thee

Healing.

Mat. 4. 23. and *healing* all manner of disease. 9. 35
Lu. 9. 6. preaching the gospel, and *healing* everywhere
11. and them that had need of *healing* he healed
Acts 4. 22. on whom this miracle of *healing* was wrought
10. 38. who went about doing good, and *healing* all
Rev. 22. 2. leaves of the tree were for the *h.* of the nations
      see healings.

Healings.—*A.V.* ¹*healing.*

1 *Cor.* 12. 9. and to another gifts of ¹*healings.* 28
30. have all gifts of ¹*healings?* do all speak with tongues?

Health.

3 *Jno.* 2. and be in *health,* even as thy soul prospereth
      see safety.

Heap.

2 *Tim.* 4. 3. itching ears, will *heap* to themselves teachers

Heaped *A.V.*—*see laid up.*

Hear.—*A.V.* ¹*heard,* ²*hearers,* ³*hearken.*

Mat. 10. 14. not receive you, nor *h.* your words. *Mk.* 6. 11
11. 4. tell John the things which ye do *hear* and see
5. and the deaf *hear.* *Mk.* 7. 37 : *Lu.* 7. 22
12. 42. to *hear* the wisdom of Solomon. *Lu.* 11. 31
13. 13 hearing they *hear* not, neither do they understand
14. By hearing ye shall *hear.* *Acts* 28. 26
15. *hear* with their ears, And understand. *Acts* 28. 27
16. But blessed are your eyes—and your ears, for they *h.*
17. and to *hear* the things which ye *hear.* *Lu.* 10. 24

HEAR

Mat. 13. 18. *Hear* then ye the parable of the sower
15. 10. and said unto them, *Hear,* and understand
18. 15. if he *hear* thee, thou hast gained thy brother
16. if he *hear* thee not, take with thee one or two more
17. refuse to *hear* them—refuse to *hear* the church also
21. 6. ye shall *hear* of wars. *Mk.* 13. 7 : *Lu.* 21. 9
Mk. 4. 12. and hearing they may *hear,* and not understand
20. such as *hear* the word, and accept it, and bear fruit
23. If any man hath ears to *hear,* let him *hear*
24. Take heed what ye *h.* : with what measure. *Lu.* 8. 18
33. spake he the word unto them, as they were able to *h.*
7. 14. ³*Hear* me all of you, and understand [it
9. 7. my beloved Son : *hear* ye him. *Mat.* 17. 5: *Lu.* 9. 35
12. 29. *Hear,* O Israel ; The Lord our God, the Lord is one
Lu. 5. 15. great multitudes came together to *hear*
6. 27. I say unto you which *hear,* Love your enemies
8. 21. these which *hear* the word of God, and do it. 11. 28
9. 9. but who is this, about whom I *hear* such things ?
15. 1. sinners were drawing near unto him for to *h.* him
16. 2. What is this that I *h.* of thee ? render the account
29. have Moses and the prophets ; let them *hear* them
31. If they *hear* not Moses and the prophets, neither
18. 6. *Hear* what the unrighteous judge saith
Jno. 5. 25. the dead shall *hear*—they that *hear* shall live
30. I can of myself do nothing : as I *hear,* I judge
6. 60. This is a hard saying ; who can *hear* it ?
7. 51. Doth our law judge a man, except it first *hear*
8. 43. Even because ye cannot *hear* my word
47. ye *hear* them not, because ye are not of God
9. 27. ye did not *hear* : wherefore would ye *h.* it again ?
10. 8. robbers : but the sheep did not *hear* them
20. hath a devil, and is mad ; why *hear* ye him ?
12. 47. if any man *hear* my sayings, and keep them not
14. 24. and the word which ye *hear* is not mine
16. 13. what things soever he shall *h.,* these shall he speak
Acts 2. 8. how *hear* we, every man in our own language
22. Ye men of Israel, *hear* these words
33. he hath poured forth this, which ye see and *hear*
10. 22. to send for thee into his house, and to *hear* words
33. to *hear* all things that have been commanded thee
13. 7. and sought to *hear* the word of God
44. city was gathered together to *hear* the word of God
15. 7. by my mouth the Gentiles should *hear* the word
17. 21. either to tell or to *hear* some new thing
32. We will *hear* thee concerning this yet again
19. 2. did not so much as ¹*hear* whether the Holy Ghost
26. And ye see and *hear,* that not alone at Ephesus
21. 22. they will certainly *hear* that thou art come
22. 1. *hear* ye the defence which I now make unto you
23. 35. I will *hear* thy cause—when thine accusers
24. 4. I intreat thee to *h.* us of thy clemency a few words
25. 22. could wish to *hear* the man myself—shalt *h.* him
26. 3. wherefore I beseech thee to *hear* me patiently
29. all that *hear* me this day, might become such as I am
28. 22. But we desire to *hear* of thee what thou thinkest
28. is sent unto the Gentiles : they will also *hear*
Rom. 10. 14. and how shall they *hear* without a preacher ?
18. But I say, Did they not ¹*hear ?* Yea, verily
1 *Cor.* 11. 18. I *hear* that divisions exist among you
14. 21. and not even thus will they *hear* me
Gal. 4. 21. desire to be under the law, do ye not *h.* the law ?
Eph. 4. 29. that it may give grace to them that ²*hear*
Phil. 1. 27. see you or be absent, I may *hear* of your state
30. conflict which ye saw in me, and now *hear* to be
2 *Th.* 3. 11. we *h.* of some that walk among you disorderly
1 *Tim.* 4. 16. save both thyself and them that *hear* thee
2 *Tim.* 2. 14. to the subverting of them that ²*hear*
4. 17. proclaimed, and that all the Gentiles might *hear*

HEAR

Jas. 1. 19. let every man be swift to *hear*, slow to speak
3 *Jno.* 4. to *hear* of my children walking in the truth
Rev. 1. 3. and they that *hear* the words of the prophecy
3. 3. Remember—how thou hast received and didst ¹*hear*
9. 20. idols—neither see, nor *hear*, nor walk
see heard, heareth, hearken, listening.

Heard.—*A.V.* ¹*hear,* ²*hearing,* ³*noised,* ⁴*seen.*

Mat. 5. 21. Ye have *heard* that it was said. 27, 33, 38, 43
6. 7. that they shall be *heard* for their much speaking
11. 2. John *heard* in the prison the works of the Christ
13. 17. things which ye hear, and *h.* them not. *Lu.* 10. 24
14. 1. tetrarch *h.* the report concerning Jesus. *Mk.* 6. 14
15. 12. Pharisees were offended, when they *h.* this saying?
22. 22. when they *h.* it, they marvelled, and left him
26. 65. ye have *heard* the blasphemy. *Mk.* 14. 64
Mk. 4. 15. when they have *h.*, straightway cometh Satan
18. these are they that have ¹*h.* the word. *Lu.* 8. ¹¹², ¹¹³
14. 11. when they *heard* it, were glad, and promised
58. We *heard* him say, I will destroy this temple
Lu. 1. 13. Fear not, Zacharias—thy supplication is *heard*
66. all that *heard* them laid them up in their heart
2. 47. all that *heard* him were amazed at his—answers
4. 23. whatsoever we have *heard* done at Capernaum
5. 1. pressed upon him and ¹*heard* the word of God
10. 39. sat at the Lord's feet, and *heard* his word
12. 3. have said in the darkness shall be *h.* in the light
20. 16. when they *heard* it, they said, God forbid
Jno. 3. 32. What he hath seen and *heard*, of that he beareth
4. 42. we have *heard* for ourselves. *Lu.* 22. 71
6. 45. Every one that hath *heard* from the Father
8. 26. things which I *heard* from him, these speak I
38. ye also do the things which ye ⁴*h.* from your father
40. told you the truth, which I *heard* from God
9. 32. it was never *heard* that any one opened the eyes
40. Pharisees which were with him *heard* these things
12. 29. stood by, and *heard* it, said that it had thundered
34. We have *h.* out of the law that the Christ abideth
15. 15. all things that I *heard* from my Father I have
18. 21. ask them that *heard* me, what I spake unto them
21. 7. Peter *heard* that it was the Lord, he girt his coat
Acts 1. 4. promise of the Father, which—ye *h.* from me
2. 6. sound was ³*heard*, the multitude came together—
every man *h.* them speaking in his own language
37. when they *h.* this, they were pricked in their heart
4. 4. many of them that *heard* the word believed
5. 5. and great fear came upon all that *heard* it
6. 11. We have *heard* him speak blasphemous words
14. we have *heard* him say, that this Jesus of Nazareth
7. 34. have *heard* their groaning, and I am come down
8. 6. spoken by Philip, when they ²*h.*, and saw the signs
30. ran to him, and *h.* him reading Isaiah the prophet
9. 13. I have *h.* from many of this man, how much evil
21. And all that *heard* him [Saul] were amazed
10. 31. Cornelius, thy prayer is *heard*, and thine alms
44. Holy Ghost fell on all them which *heard* the word
46. *heard* them speak with tongues, and magnify God
13. 48. And as the Gentiles *heard* this, they were glad
14. 9. The same *heard* Paul speaking
15. 24. we have *heard* that certain which went out
16. 14. Lydia—one that worshipped God, *heard* us
17. 32. when they *heard* of the resurrection of the dead
19. 5. when they *heard* this, they were baptized
22. 2. when they *heard* that he spake—in the Hebrew
15. witness—unto all men of what thou hast seen and *h.*
24. 24. sent for Paul, and *heard* him concerning the faith
Rom. 10. 14. believe in him whom they have not *heard* ?
15. 21. And they who have not *heard* shall understand

HEARETH

1 *Cor.* 2. 9. Things which eye saw not, and ear *heard* not
2 *Cor.* 12. 4. into Paradise, and *heard* unspeakable words
Gal. 1. 13. ye have *h.* of my manner of life in time past
Eph. 1. 13. ye also, having *heard* the word of the truth
15. having *h.* of the faith in the Lord Jesus. *Col.* 1. 4
4. 21. if so be that ye *heard* him, and were taught in him
Phil. 2. 26. because ye had *heard* that he was sick
4. 9. received and *heard* and saw in me, these things do
Col. 1. 5. for you in the heavens, whereof ye *heard* before
6. since the day ye *heard* and knew the grace of God
9. we also, since the day we *heard* it, do not cease to pray
2 *Tim.* 1. 13. sound words which thou hast *heard* from me
2. 2. the things which thou hast *heard* from me
Heb. 2. 1. more earnest heed to the things that were *heard*
3. was confirmed unto us by them that *heard*
3. 16. For who, when they *heard*, did provoke?
4. 2. they were not united by faith with them that *heard*
5. 7. and having been *heard* for his godly fear
12. 19. which voice they that *h.* intreated that no word
Jas. 5. 11. ye have *heard* of the patience of Job
1 *Jno.* 1. 1. which we have *h.*, that which we have seen. 3
5. this is the message which we have *heard* from him
2. 7. the old commandment is the word which ye *heard*
18. and as ye *heard* that antichrist cometh. 4. 3
24. which ye *heard* from the beginning. 3. 11 : 2 *Jno.* 6
Rev. 5. 13. *h.* I saying, Unto him that sitteth on the throne
7. 4. I *heard* the number of them. 9. 16
8. 13. and I *heard* an eagle, flying in mid heaven
16. 5. And I *heard* the angel of the waters saying
18. 22. trumpeters shall be *heard* no more at all in thee
—the voice of a millstone shall be *heard* no more
23. and of the bride shall be *heard* no more at all
22. 8. I John am he that *heard* and saw these things.
And when I *heard* and saw, I fell down
see heard, heardest, hearkened, listening, received, voice.

Heardest.—*A.V.* ¹*heard.*

Jno. 11. 41. Father, I thank thee that thou ¹*heardest* me

Hearer—s.

Rom. 2. 13. not the *hearers* of a law are just before God
Jas. 1. 22. be ye doers of the word, and not *hearers* only
23. For if any one is a *h.* of the word, and not a doer
25. being not a *hearer* that forgetteth, but a doer
see hear.

Hearest.

Mat. 21. 16. *Hearest* thou what these are saying?
27. 13. *Hearest* thou not how many things they witness
Jno. 3. 8. where it listeth, and thou *hearest* the voice
11. 42. And I knew that thou *hearest* me always

Heareth.—*A.V.* ¹*hear.*

Mat. 7. 24. Every one—which *h.* these words. 26 : *Lu.* 6. 47,
13. 19. When any one *h.* the word of the kingdom [49
20. this is he that *heareth* the word. 22, 23
Lu. 10. 16. He that *heareth* you *heareth* me
Jno. 3. 29. which standeth and *heareth* him, rejoiceth
5. 24. He that *heareth* my word, and believeth him
8. 47. He that is of God *heareth* the words of God
9. 31. God *h.* not sinners—do his will, him he *heareth*
18. 37. Every one that is of the truth *heareth* my voice
2 *Cor.* 12. 6. which he seeth me to be, or *heareth* from me
1 *Jno.* 4. 5. of the world, and the world *heareth* them
6. he that knoweth God *heareth* us—*heareth* us not
5. 14. if we ask anything according to his will, he *h.* us
15. and if we know that he ¹*h.* us whatsoever we ask
Rev. 22. 17. And he that *heareth*, let him say, Come
18. I testify unto every man that *heareth* the words

HEARING

Hearing.—*A.V.* ¹*audience.*

Mat. 13. 13. seeing they see not, and *h.* they hear not
14. By *hearing* ye shall hear, and shall in no wise understand. Mk. 4. 12 : Lu. 8. 10 : Acts 28. 26
15. And their ears are dull of *hearing.* Acts 28. 27
Mk. 6. 2. and many *hearing* him were astonished
Lu. 2. 46. both *hearing* them, and asking them questions
18. 36. *hearing* a multitude going by, he inquired
20. 45. in the ¹*hearing* of all the people he said unto his
Acts 5. 5. Ananias *hearing* these words fell down
9. 7. stood speechless, *h.* the voice, but beholding no man
18. 8. many of the Corinthians *hearing* believed
25. 23. and they were entered into the place of *hearing*
Rom. 10. 17. belief cometh of *h.,* and *h.* by the word of
1 Cor. 12. 17. where were the *h. ?* If the whole were *h.*
Gal. 3. 2. works of the law, or by the *hearing* of faith? 5
Philem. 5. *hearing* of thy love, and of the faith
Heb. 5. 11. seeing ye are become dull of *hearing*
2 Pet. 2. 8. in seeing and *hearing,* vexed his righteous
see decision, heard.

Hearken.—*A.V.* ¹*audience,* ²*hear,* ³*obeyed.*

Acts 3. 22. to him shall ye ²*hearken* in all things
23. every soul, which shall not ²*hearken* to that prophet
4. 19. to *h.* unto you rather than unto God, judge ye
13. 16. Men of Israel, and ye that fear God, ¹*hearken*
15. 13. Brethren, *hearken* unto me. 7. 2
Rom. 10. 16. they did not all ²*hearken* to the glad tidings
Jas. 2. 5. *Hearken,* my beloved brethren ; did not God
see answer, ear, hear.

Hearkened.—*A.V.* ¹*audience,* ²*heard.*

Acts 15. 12. and they ²*hearkened* unto Barnabas and Paul
27. 21. Sirs, ye should have *hearkened* unto me
2 Cor. 6. 2. At an acceptable time I ²*hearkened* unto thee
see voice.

Heart.—*A.V.* ¹*bowels,* ²*hearts,* ³*understanding.*

Mat. 5. 8. Blessed are the pure in *h. :* for they shall see God
28. committed adultery with her already in his *heart*
6. 21. where thy treasure is, there will thy *h.* Lu. 12. 34
11. 29. learn of me ; for I am meek and lowly in *heart*
12. 34. out of the abundance of the *heart.* Lu. 6. 45
40. days and three nights in the *heart* of the earth
13. 15. For this people's *heart* is waxed gross— And understand with their *heart.* Acts 28. 27
19. that which hath been sown in his *heart.* Lu. 8. ²12
15. 8. But their *heart* is far from me. Mk. 7. 6
18. forth out of the *heart :* and they defile the man
19. out of the *heart* come forth evil thoughts. Mk. 7. 21
19. 8. Moses for your hardness of ²*heart* suffered you
22. 37. Thou shalt love the Lord thy God with all thy *heart,* Mk. 12. 30, 33 : Lu. 10. 27
24. 48. say in his *heart,* My lord tarrieth. Lu. 12. 45
Mk. 3. 5. grieved at the hardening of their ²*heart,* he saith
7. 19. goeth not into his *heart,* but into his belly
10. 5. For your hardness of *heart* he wrote you this
11. 23. not doubt in his *heart,* but shall believe
16. 14. with their unbelief and hardness of *heart*
Lu. 1. 51. proud in the imagination of his ²*heart*
66. all that heard them laid them up in their ²*heart*
2. 19. these sayings, pondering them in her *heart*
51. his mother kept all these sayings in her *heart*
6. 45. out of the good treasure of his *heart* bringeth forth
8. 15. honest and good *heart,* having heard the word
9. 47. when Jesus saw the reasoning of their *heart*
21. 25. O foolish men, and slow of *heart* to believe
32. Was not our *heart* burning within us, while he spake
38. wherefore do reasonings arise in your ²*heart ?*

HEART

Jno. 12. 40. hardened their *heart*—perceive with their *h.*
13. 2. devil having already put into the *heart* of Judas
14. 1. Let not your *heart* be troubled. 27
16. 6. these things unto you, sorrow hath filled your *h.*
22. I will see you again, and your *heart* shall rejoice
Acts 2. 26. Therefore my *h.* was glad, and my tongue rejoiced
37. when they heard this, they were pricked in their *h.*
46. food with gladness and singleness of *heart*
4. 32. multitude of them that believed were of one *heart*
5. 3. why hath Satan filled thy *heart* to lie [and soul
4. How is it that thou hast conceived this thing in thy *h.?*
33. when they heard this, were cut to the *heart.* 7. 54
7. 23. it came into his *heart* to visit his brethren
51. Ye stiffnecked and uncircumcised in *heart* and ears
8. 21. for thy [Simon Magus] *h.* is not right before God
22. perhaps the thought of thy *heart* shall be forgiven
11. 23. purpose of *heart* they would cleave unto the Lord
13. 22. David the son of Jesse, a man after my *heart*
15. 8. God, which knoweth the ²*heart,* bare them witness
16. 14. whose *heart* the Lord opened, to give heed
21. 13. What do ye, weeping and breaking my *heart ?*
Rom. 1. 21. and their senseless *heart* was darkened
2. 5. hardness and impenitent *heart* treasurest up
29. circumcision is that of the *heart,* in the spirit
6. 17. became obedient from the *h.* to that form of teaching
9. 2. great sorrow and unceasing pain in my *heart*
10. 1. my *heart's* desire and my supplication to God
6. Say not in thy *heart,* Who shall ascend into heaven?
8. The word is nigh thee, in thy mouth, and in thy *h.*
9. shalt believe in thy *heart* that God raised him
10. with the *heart* man believeth unto righteousness
1 Cor. 2. 9. And which entered not into the *heart* of man
7. 37. stedfast in his *heart,* having no necessity—determined this in his own *heart*
14. 25. the secrets of his *heart* are made manifest
2 Cor. 2. 4. and anguish of *heart* I wrote unto you
3. 15. Moses is read, a veil lieth upon their *heart*
5. 12. them that glory in appearance, and not in *heart*
6. 11. O Corinthians, our *heart* is enlarged
8. 16. earnest care for you into the *heart* of Titus
9. 7. do according as he hath purposed in his *heart*
Eph. 1. 18. having the eyes of your ²*heart* enlightened
4. 18. because of the hardening of their *heart*
5. 19. making melody with your *heart* to the Lord
6. 5. in singleness of your *heart,* as unto Christ
6. doing the will of God from the *heart*
Phil. 1. 7. behalf of you all, because I have you in my *h.*
Col. 3. 12. as God's elect, holy and beloved, a ²*heart* of compassion
22. but in singleness of *heart,* fearing the Lord [passion
1 Th. 2. 17. a short season, in presence, not in *heart*
1 Tim. 1. 5. end of the charge is love out of a pure *heart*
2 Tim. 2. 22. with them that call on the Lord out of a pure *h.*
Philem. 12. sent back to thee—that is, my very ¹*heart*
20. joy of thee in the Lord: refresh my ¹*heart* in Christ
Heb. 3. 10. And said, They do alway err in their ²*heart*
4. 12. quick to discern the thoughts and intents of the *h.*
8. 10. And on their ²*heart* also will I write them
10. 16. I will put my laws on their ²*heart*
22. let us draw near with a true *h.* in fulness of faith
13. 9. it is good that the *heart* be stablished by grace
Jas. 1. 26. deceiveth his *heart,* this man's religion is vain
3. 14. if ye have bitter jealousy and faction in your ²*h.*
1 Pet. 1. 22. love one another from the *heart* fervently
3. 4. but let it be the hidden man of the *heart*
2 Pet. 2. 14. having a *heart* exercised in covetousness
1 Jno. 3. 19. and shall assure our ²*heart* before him
20. our *h.* condemn us —God is greater than our *heart*
21. if our *heart* condemn us not, we have boldness
Rev. 18. 7. she saith in her *heart,* I sit a queen
see evil, harden, hardened, hearts.

160

HEARTILY

Heartily.
Col. 3. 23. whatsoever ye do, work *h.*, as unto the Lord

Hearts.—*A.V.* ¹*bowels,* ²*heart.*
Mat. 9. 4. Wherefore think ye evil in your *hearts* ?
18. 35. if ye forgive not every one his brother from your *h.*
Mk 2. 6. scribes sitting there, and reasoning in their *h.*
8. Why reason ye these things in your *hearts* ? Lu. 5. 22
Lu. 1. 17 to turn the *hearts* of the fathers to the children
2 35. that thoughts out of many *hearts* may be revealed
3. 15. all men reasoned in their *hearts* concerning John
16. 15. in the sight of men; but God knoweth your *hearts*
21. 14. Settle it therefore in your *hearts*, not to meditate
34. lest haply your *hearts* be overcharged with surfeiting
Acts 1. 24. Thou, Lord, which knowest the *hearts* of all men
7 39. and turned back in their *hearts* unto Egypt
14 17. filling your *hearts* with food and gladness
15. 9. between us and them, cleansing their *h.* by faith
Rom. 1. 24. in the lusts of their *hearts* unto uncleanness
2. 15. shew the work of the law written in their *hearts*
5. 5. love of God hath been shed abroad in our *hearts*
8. 27 he that searcheth the *hearts* knoweth what is the
16. 18. fair speech they beguile the *h.* of the innocent
1 Cor. 4. 5. make manifest the counsels of the *hearts*
2 Cor. 1. 22. gave us the earnest of the Spirit in our *hearts*
3. 2 Ye are our epistle, written in our *hearts*
3. not in tables of stone, but in tables that are ²*h.* of flesh
4. 6. who shined in our *hearts*, to give the light
7. 3 ye are in our *h.* to die together and live together
Gal. 4. 6. Spirit of his Son into our *hearts*, crying, Abba
Eph. 3. 17 that Christ may dwell in your *h.* through faith
6. 22. know our state—he may comfort your *h.* Col. 4 8.
Phil. 4. 7. guard your *h.* and your thoughts in Christ Jesus
Col. 2 2. that their *h.* may be comforted, they being knit
3. 15. let the peace of Christ rule in your *hearts*
16. singing with grace in your *hearts* unto God
1 Th. 2. 4. pleasing men, but God which proveth our *hearts*
3. 13. to the end he may stablish your *hearts* unblameable
2 Th. 2. 17. comfort your *hearts* and stablish them
3. 5. the Lord direct your *hearts* unto the love of God
Philem. 7. because the ¹*h.* of the saints have been refreshed
Heb. 10. 22. our *hearts* sprinkled from an evil conscience
Jas. 4. 8. and purify your *hearts*, ye doubleminded
5. 5. ye have nourished your *hearts* in a day of slaughter
8. Be ye also patient; stablish your *hearts*
1 Pet. 3. 15. but sanctify in your *hearts* Christ as Lord
2 Pet. 1. 19. day dawn, and the day-star arise in your *h.*
Rev. 2. 23. I am he which searcheth the reins and *hearts*
17. 17. God did put in their *hearts* to do his mind
see harden, heart.

Heat.
Mat. 20. 12. burden of the day and the scorching *heat*
Lu. 12. 55. blowing, ye say, There will be a scorching *heat*
Acts 28. 3. a viper came out by reason of the *heat*
2 Pet. 3. 10. elements shall be dissolved with fervent *h.* 12
Rev. 7. 16. shall the sun strike upon them, nor any *heat*
16. 9. And men were scorched with great *heat*
see wind.

Heathen *A.V.*—*see Gentiles, proper names.*

Heaven.—*A.V.* ¹*air,* ²*sky.*
Mat. 5. 18. Till *heaven* and earth pass away, one jot
34. the *heaven*, for it is the throne of God. Jas. 5. 12
6. 26. birds of the ¹*heaven.* 8. ¹20: 13. ³32: Mk. 4. ¹32:
Lu. 8. ¹5: 9. ¹58: 13. ¹19: Acts 10. ¹12: 11. ¹6
11. 25. thank thee, O Father, Lord of *heaven*, Lu. 10. 21

HEAVEN

Mat. 16. 2. It will be fair weather: for the ²*h.* is red. ²3
18. 14. it is not the will of your Father which is in *heaven*
23. 22. he that sweareth by the *heaven*, sweareth by the
24. 30. coming on the clouds of *h.* 26. 64: Mk. 14. 62
31. from one end of *heaven* to the other. Mk. 13. 27
85. *H.* and earth shall pass. Mk. 13. 31: Lu. 21. 33
36. not even the angels of *heaven*, neither the Son
Lu. 3. 21. baptized, and praying, the *heaven* was opened
22. voice came out of *h.* Jno. 12. 28: Acts 11. 9: 2 Pet.
4. 25. when the *heaven* was shut up three years [1. 18
12. 56. interpret the face of the earth and the ²*heaven*
15. 18. Father, I have sinned against *heaven.* 21
16. 17. easier for *heaven* and earth to pass away, than
17. 24. lighteneth out of the one part under the *heaven*, shineth unto the other part under *heaven*
Jno. 1. 32. the Spirit descending as a dove out of *heaven*
51. Ye shall see the *heaven* opened, and the angels
3. 13. ascended into *heaven*, but he that descended out of *heaven*, even the Son of man, which is in *heaven*
6. 31. He gave them bread out of *heaven* to eat
32. not Moses that gave you the bread out of *heaven* ; but my Father giveth you the true bread out of *h.*
33. cometh down out of *heaven*, and giveth life [58
41. I am the bread which came down out of *h.* 50, 51,
42. how doth he now say, I am come down out of *h.* ?
Acts 1. 10. looking stedfastly into *heaven* as he went
2. 5. devout men, from every nation under *heaven*
3. 21. whom the *heaven* must receive until the times
4. 12. neither is there any other name under *heaven*
24. thou that didst make the *heaven.* 14. 15: Rev. 14. 7
7. 42. and gave them up to serve the host of *heaven*
49. The *h.* is my throne, And the earth the footstool
9. 3. shone round about him a light out of *heaven*
10. 11. *heaven* opened, and a certain vessel descending
17. 24. being Lord of *heaven* and earth, dwelleth not
1 Cor. 15. 47. the second man is of *heaven*
Col. 1. 23. which was preached in all creation under *h.*
Heb. 11. 12. so many as the stars of ²*heaven* in multitude
Jas. 5. 18. he prayed again ; and the *heaven* gave rain
Rev. 3. 12. Jerusalem, which cometh down out of *heaven*
6. 13. and the stars of the *heaven* fell unto the earth
14. And the *heaven* was removed as a scroll—rolled up
8. 13. I saw, and I heard an eagle, flying in mid *heaven*
10 1. angel coming down out of *heaven.* 18. 1: 20. 1
6. who created the *h.* and the things that are therein
11. 6. power to shut the *heaven*, that it rain not
12. 4. his tail draweth the third part of the stars of *h.*
13. 13. make fire to come down out of *h.* upon the earth
14. 6. And I saw another angel flying in mid *heaven*
16. 21. great hail—cometh down out of *heaven* upon men
18. 20. Rejoice over her, thou *heaven*, and ye saints
19. 11. I saw the *h.* opened; and behold, a white horse
20. 9. fire came down out of *heaven*, and devoured them
11. from whose face the earth and the *heaven* fled
21. 1. I saw a new *heaven* and a new earth : for the first *h.*
10. holy city Jerusalem, coming down out of *heaven*
see birds, fowls, God, heavens, kingdom of heaven.

From **Heaven.**
Mat. 16. 1. sign *from heaven.* Mk. 8. 11 : Lu. 11. 16
21. 25. The baptism of John, whence was it? *from heaven* or *from* men? Mk. 11. 30, 31 : Lu. 20. 4, 5
24. 29. and the stars shall fall *from heaven.* Mk. 13. 25
28. 2. for an angel of the Lord descended *from heaven*
Lu. 9. 54. wilt thou that we bid fire to come down *from h.*
10. 18. I beheld Satan fallen as lightning *from heaven*
29. it rained fire and brimstone *from heaven*
21. 11. and there shall be terrors and great signs *from h.*
22. 43. an angel *from heaven*, strengthening him

HEAVEN

Jno. 3. 27. nothing, except it have been given him *from h.*
31. he that cometh *from heaven* is above all
6. 38. I am come down *from h.*, not to do mine own will
Acts 2. 2. And suddenly there came *from heaven* a sound
11. 5. as it were a great sheet let down *from heaven*
14. 17. in that he did good, and gave you *from h.* rains
22. 6. suddenly there shone *from h.* a great light. 26. 13
Rom. 1. 18. For the wrath of God is revealed *from heaven*
2 *Cor.* 5. 2. clothed upon with our habitation which is *f. h.*
Gal. 1. 8. an angel *from heaven*, should preach unto you
1 *Th.* 1. 10. and to wait for his Son *from heaven*
4. 16. For the Lord himself shall descend *from heaven*
2 *Th.* 1. 7. at the revelation of the Lord Jesus *from heaven*
Heb. 12. 25. who turn away from him that warneth *f. h.*
1 *Pet.* 1. 12. by the Holy Ghost sent forth *from heaven*
Rev. 9. 1. I saw a star *from heaven* fallen unto the earth
10. 4. voice *from heaven.* 8 ; 11. 12 ; 14. 2, 13 ; 18. 4

In **Heaven**, *in the* **Heaven.**

Mat. 5. 12. glad : for great is your reward *in heaven*
16. and glorify your Father which is *in heaven*
45. that ye may be sons of your Father which is *in h.*
6. 1. no reward with your Father which is *in heaven*
9. pray ye : Our Father which art *in heaven*
10. Thy will be done, as *in heaven*, so on earth
20. but lay up for yourselves treasures *in heaven*
7. 11. your Father which is *in heaven* give good things
21. the will of my Father which is *in heaven.* 12. 50
10. 32. also confess before my Father which is *in heaven*
33. also deny before my Father which is *in heaven*
16. 17. unto thee, but my Father which is *in heaven*
19. shall be bound *in heaven*—be loosed *in heaven.* 18. 18
18. 10. *in heaven* their angels do always behold the face
of my Father which is *in heaven*
19. be done for them of my Father which is *in heaven*
19. 21. thou shalt have treasure *in h. Mk.* 10. 21 ; *Lu.* 18. 22
22. 30. in marriage, but are as angels *in h. Mk.* 12. 25
23. 9. for one is your Father, which is *in heaven*
24. 30. shall appear the sign of the Son of man *in heaven*
28. 18. All authority hath been given unto me *in heaven*
Mk. 11. 25. Father also which is *in h.* may forgive you
13. 32. not even the angels *in heaven*, neither the Son
Lu. 6. 23. for behold, your reward is great *in heaven*
10. 20. but rejoice that your names are written *in heaven*
15. 7. shall be joy *in h.* over one sinner that repenteth
19. 38. peace *in heaven*, and glory in the highest
Jno. 3. 13. even the Son of man, which is *in heaven*
Acts 2. 19. And I will shew wonders *in the heaven* above
1 *Cor.* 8. 5. called gods, whether *in heaven* or on earth
Eph. 3. 15. every family *in heaven* and on earth is named
6. 9. both their Master and yours is *in heaven. Col.* 4. 1
Phil. 2. 10. every knee should bow, of things *in heaven*
3. 20. For our citizenship is *in h.* ; from whence also
Heb. 12. 23. the firstborn who are enrolled *in heaven*
1 *Pet.* 1. 4. fadeth not away, reserved *in heaven* for you
Rev. 4. 1. and behold, a door opened *in heaven*
2. there was a throne set *in heaven*, and one sitting
5. 3. no one *in the heaven*, or on the earth, or under
13. And every created thing which is *in the heaven*
8. 1. there followed a silence *in heaven* about the space
11. 15. followed great voices *in heaven*, and they said
19. was opened the temple of God that is *in heaven*
12. 1. And a great sign was seen *in heaven.* 3
7. there was war *in heaven :* Michael and his angels
8. neither was their place found any more *in heaven*
10. I heard a great voice *in heaven*, saying, 19. 1
13. 6. his tabernacle, even them that dwell *in the heaven*
14. 17. angel came out from the temple which is *in h.*
15. 1. I saw another sign *in heaven*, great and marvellous

HEAVENS

Rev. 15. 5. the tabernacle of the testimony *in h.* was opened
19. 14. the armies which are *in heaven* followed him
see heavenly, heavens.

Into **Heaven.**

Mk. 16. 19. was received up *into heaven*, and sat down
Lu. 2. 15. when the angels went away from them *into h.*
24. 51. he parted from them, and was carried up *into h.*
Jno. 3. 13. no man hath ascended *into heaven*, but he that
Acts 1. 11. ye looking *into heaven ?*—up from you *into h.*
—in like manner as ye beheld him going *into h.*
7. 55. looked up stedfastly *into heaven*, and saw the glory
10. 16. straightway the vessel was received up *into h.* 11.
Rom. 10. 6. in thy heart, Who shall ascend *into h. ?* [10
Heb. 9. 24. but *into heaven* itself, now to appear before
1 *Pet.* 3. 22. on the right hand of God, having gone *into h.*
Rev. 11. 12. And they went up *into heaven* in the cloud

To **Heaven** *or unto* **Heaven.**

Mat. 11. 23. shalt thou be exalted *unto heaven ? Lu.* 10. 15
14. 19. looking up *to heaven. Mk.* 6. 41 ; 7. 34 ; *Lu.* 9. 16
Lu. 18. 13. would not lift up so much as his eyes *unto h.*
Jno. 17. 1. lifting up his eyes *to heaven*, he said, Father
2 *Cor.* 12. 2. such a one caught up even to the third *heaven*
Rev. 10. 5. lifted up his right hand *to heaven*, and sware
18. 5. for her sins have reached even *unto heaven*

Heavenly.—*A. V.* [1]*in heaven.*

Mat. 5. 48. perfect, as your [1]*heavenly* Father is perfect
6. 14. your *heavenly* Father will also forgive you
26. into barns ; and your *heavenly* Father feedeth them
32. your *heavenly* Father knoweth that ye have need
15. 13. Every plant which my *heavenly* Father planted not
18. 35. So shall also my *heavenly* Father do unto you
Lu. 2. 13. a multitude of the *heavenly* host praising God
11. 13. more shall your *h.* Father give the Holy Spirit
Jno. 3. 12. how shall ye believe, if I tell you *heavenly* things ?
Acts 26. 19. I was not disobedient unto the *heavenly* vision
1 *Cor.* 15. 48. as is the *h.*, such are they also that are *h.*
49. we shall also bear the image of the *heavenly*
Eph. 1. 3. spiritual blessing in the *heavenly* places in Christ
20. sit at his right hand in the *heavenly* places. 2. 6
3. 10. powers in the *heavenly* places might be made known
6. 12. spiritual hosts of wickedness in the *h.* places
2 *Tim.* 4. 18. and will save me unto his *heavenly* kingdom
Heb. 3. 1. holy brethren, partakers of a *heavenly* calling
6. 4. once enlightened and tasted of the *heavenly* gift
8. 5. serve that which is a copy and shadow of the *h.* things
9. 23. but the *h.* things themselves with better sacrifices
11. 16. they desire a better country, that is, a *heavenly*
12. 22 the city of the living God, the *heavenly* Jerusalem

Heavens.—*A. V.* [1]*heaven.*

Mat. 3. 17. a voice out of the [1]*heavens.* 16 ; *Mk.* 1. [1]11
24. 29. and the powers of the *heavens* shall be shaken.
Mk. 13. [1]26 ; *Lu.* 21. [1]26
Lu. 12. 33. a treasure in the *heavens* that faileth not
Acts 2. 34. For David ascended not into the *heavens*
7. 56. I see the *heavens* opened, and the Son of man
2 *Cor.* 5. 1. house not made with hands, eternal, in the *h.*
Eph. 1. 10. to sum up all things in Christ, the things in the[1]*h.*
4. 10. same also that ascended far above all the *heavens*
Col. 1. 5. the hope which is laid up for you in the [1]*heavens*
16. all things created, in the [1]*heavens*, and upon the earth
20. whether things upon the earth, or things in the [1]*h.*
Heb. 1. 10. And the *heavens* are the works of thy hands
4. 14. great high priest, who hath passed through the *h.*
7. 26. from sinners, and made higher than the *heavens*
8 1. the throne of the Majesty in the *heavens*
9. 23. copies of the things in the *h.* should be cleansed

HEAVENS

2 *Pet.* 3. 5. wilfully forget, that there were *h*. from of old
7. but the *heavens* that now are, and the earth
10. the *heavens* shall pass away with a great noise
12. the *heavens* being on fire shall be dissolved
13. according to his promise, we look for new *heavens*

Heavier.—*A.V.* ¹*greater*.

Jas. 3. 1. knowing that we shall receive ¹*heavier* judgement

Heaviness.

Jas. 4. 9. turned to mourning, and your joy to *heaviness*
see grief, sorrow, troubled.

Heavy.

Mat. 11. 28. all ye that labour and are *heavy* laden
23. 4. they bind *heavy* burdens and grievous to be borne
26. 43. for their eyes were *heavy*. *Mk.* 14. 40
Lu. 9. 32. that were with him were *heavy* with sleep
see troubled.

Hedge—s.—*A.V.* ¹*hedged*.

Mat. 21. 33. planted a vineyard, and set a ¹*h*. about it. *Mk.*
Lu. 14. 23. Go out into the highways and *hedges* [12. 1

Heed.—*A.V.* ¹*attended*, ²*attendance*, ³*believed*, ⁴*regard*.

Acts 3. 5. he gave *heed* unto them, expecting to receive
8. 6. the multitudes gave *heed* with one accord
10. they all gave *heed*, from the least to the greatest
11. they gave ⁴*h*. to him, because that of long time he had
16. 14. to give ¹*heed* unto the things—spoken by Paul
27. 11. centurion gave more ³*h*. to the master and to the
1 *Tim.* 1. 4. neither to give *heed* to fables. *Tit.* 1. 14
4. 1. giving *h*. to seducing spirits and doctrines of devils
13. Till I come, give ²*heed* to reading, to exhortation
Heb. 2. 1. we ought to give the more earnest *heed*
see take heed.

Heel.

Jno. 13. 18. He that eateth my bread lifted up his *heel*

Heifer.

Heb. 9. 13. ashes of a *h*. sprinkling them that have been

Height.

Rom. 8. 39. nor *height*, nor depth, nor any other creature
Eph. 3. 18. the breadth and length and *height* and depth
Rev. 21. 16. and the breadth and the *h*. thereof are equal

Heir—s.

Mat. 21. 38. This is the *heir*. *Mk.* 12. 7: *Lu.* 20. 14
Rom. 4. 13. that he should be *heir* of the world
14. For if they which are of the law be *heirs*, faith is
8. 17. children, then *h.*; *h*. of God, and joint-heirs with
Gal. 3. 29. Abraham's seed, *h*. according to promise [Christ
4. 1. so long as the *heir* is a child, he differeth nothing
7. and if a son, then an *heir* through God
Tit. 3. 7. made *heirs* according to the hope of eternal life
Heb. 1. 2. his Son, whom he appointed *heir* of all things
6. 17. shew more abundantly unto the *h*. of the promise
11. 7. became *heir* of the righteousness which is
9. and Jacob, the *heirs* with him of the same promise
Jas. 2. 5. rich in faith, and *heirs* of the kingdom
see fellow-heirs, inherit, joint-heirs.

Held.—*A.V.* ¹*kept*.

Mat. 26. 63. But Jesus *held* his peace. *Mk.* 14. 61
*Mk.*3. 4. But they *h*. their peace. 9. 34: *Lu.*14. 4: 20. 26: *Acts*
15. 1. council, *h*. a consultation, and bound Jesus [11.18

HERB

Lu. 9. 36. they ¹*held* their peace, and told no man
22. 63. the men that *held* Jesus mocked him [together
Acts 3. 11. as he *held* Peter and John, all the people ran
14. 4. part *h*. with the Jews, and part with the apostles
15. 13. they had *held* their peace, James answered
Rev. 6. 9. slain—for the testimony which they *held*
see holden, took.

Hell.

Mat. 5. 22. Thou fool, shall be in danger of the *hell* of fire
29. and not thy whole body be cast into *hell*. 30
10. 28. destroy both soul and body in *hell*. *Lu.* 12. 5
18. 9 two eyes to be cast into the *hell* of fire. *Mk.* 9. 47
23. 15. twofold more a son of *hell* than yourselves
33. vipers, how shall ye escape the judgement of *h.*?
Mk. 9. 43. having thy two hands to go into *hell*. 45
Jas. 3. 6. wheel of nature, and is set on fire by *hell* [to *h*.
2 *Pet.* 2. 4. angels when they sinned, but cast them down
see Hades.

Helm *A.V.*—*see rudder*.

Helmet.

Eph. 6. 17. the *h*. of salvation, and the sword of the Spirit
1 *Th.* 5. 8. and for a *helmet*, the hope of salvation

Help.—*A.V.* ¹*support*.

Mat. 15. 25. worshipped him, saying, Lord, *help* me
Mk. 9. 22. have compassion on us, and *help* us
24. and said, I believe; *help* thou mine unbelief
Lu. 5. 7. the other boat, that they should come and *help*
10. 40. serve alone? bid her therefore that she *help* me
Acts 16. 9. Come over into Macedonia, and *help* us
20. 35. how that so labouring ye ought to ¹*help* the weak
21. 28. [Jews] crying out, Men of Israel, *help* [day
26. 22. obtained the *h*. that is from God, I stand unto this
Phil. 4. 3. *help* these women, for they laboured with me
Heb. 4. 16. and may find grace to *help* us in time of need

Helped.

Acts 18. 27. and when he was come, he *helped* them much
Rev. 12. 16. And the earth *helped* the woman

Helper—s.

2 *Cor.* 1. 24. are *helpers* of your joy: for by faith ye stand
Heb. 13. 6. The Lord is my *helper*; I will not fear
see fellow-workers.

Helpeth—ing.

Rom. 8. 26. the Spirit also *helpeth* our infirmity
1 *Cor.* 16. 16. to everyone that *h*. in the work and laboureth
2 *Cor.* 1. 11. ye also *helping* together on our behalf

Helps.

Acts 27. 17. they used *helps*, under-girding the ship
1 *Cor.* 12. 28. gifts of healings, *helps*, governments

Hem *A.V.*—*see border*.

Hen.

Mat. 23. 37. as a *hen* gathereth her chickens. *Lu.* 13. 34

Henceforth.—*A.V.* ¹*remaineth*.

1 *Cor.* 7. 29. ¹*henceforth* both those that have wives may be

Herb—s.

Mat. 13. 32. it is greater than the *herbs*. *Mk.* 4. 32
Lu. 11. 42. for ye tithe mint and rue and every *herb*
Rom. 14. 2. but he that is weak eateth *herbs*
Heb. 6. 7. bringeth forth *h*. meet for them for whose sake

HERD

Herd.
Mat. 8. 30. *herd* of many swine. 31: *Mk.* 5. 11 : *Lu.* 8. 32
32. the whole *herd* rushed down. *Mk.* 5. 13 : *Lu.* 8. 33

Here.—*A.V.* ¹*come.*
Mat. 28. 6. He is not *here*; for he is risen. *Mk.* 16. 6 : *Lu.*
Lu. 17. 21. shall they say, Lo, *here* ! or, There ! 23 [24. 6
Jno. 11. 28. The Master is ¹*here*, and calleth thee
Acts 9. 10. Ananias. And he said, Behold, I am *here*, Lord

Heresies.
1 Cor. 11. 19. there must be also *heresies* among you
Gal. 5. 20. wraths, factions, divisions, *heresies*
2 Pet. 2. 1. who shall privily bring in destructive *heresies*

Heresy *A.V.*—*see* sect.

Heretical.—*A.V.* ¹*heretick.*
Tit. 3. 10. that is ¹*h.* after a first and second admonition

Heritage.—*A.V.* ¹*inheritance.*
Eph. 1. 11. in whom also we were made a ¹*heritage*
see charge.

Hewn.
Mat. 3. 10. *hewn* down, and cast into the fire. 7. 19 : *Lu.*
27. 60. *h.* out in the rock. *Mk.* 15. 46 : *Lu.* 23. 53 [3. 9

Hid.—*A.V.* ¹*hide,* ²*hideth.*
Mat. 5. 14. A city set on a hill cannot be *hid*
10. 26. that shall not be revealed ; and *hid*, that shall not be known. *Mk.* 4. 22 : *Lu.* 8. 17 : 12. 2
13. 33. *hid* in three measures of meal. *Lu.* 13. 21
44. treasure—which a man found, and ²*hid*
25. 18. digged in the earth, and *hid* his lord's money
25. I was afraid, and went away and *hid* thy talent
Mk. 7. 24. no man know it : and he could not be *hid*
Lu. 1. 24. conceived, and she *hid* herself five months
8. 47. saw that she was not *hid*, she came trembling
18. 34. and this saying was *hid* from them
19. 42. but now they are *hid* from thine eyes
Jno. 8. 59. but Jesus *hid* himself, and went out. 12. ¹36
Eph. 3. 9. mystery which—hath been *hid* in God. *Col.* 1. 26
Col. 3. 3. For ye died, and your life is *hid* with Christ
1 Tim. 5. 25. and such as are otherwise cannot be *hid*
Heb. 11. 23. By faith Moses, when he was born, was *hid*
Rev. 6. 15. and every bondman and freeman, *h.* themselves
see concealed, face, hidden, hide, veiled.

Hidden.—*A.V.* ¹*hid,* ²*kept secret.*
Mat. 13. 35. I will utter things ²*h.* from the foundation of
44. heaven is like unto a treasure ¹*hidden* in the field
Acts 26. 26. none of these things is *hidden* from him
1 Cor. 2. 7. wisdom that hath been *hidden*, which God
4. 5. bring to light the *hidden* things of darkness
2 Cor. 4. 2. we have renounced the *hidden* things of shame
Col. 2. 3. treasures of wisdom and knowledge ¹*hidden*
1 Pet. 3. 4. but let it be the *hidden* man of the heart
Rev. 2. 17. to him will I give of the *hidden* manna

Hide.—*A.V.* ¹*hid.*
Mat. 11. 25. didst ¹*h.* these things from the wise. *Lu.* 10. ¹21
see cover.

Hideth.—*A.V.* *see hid.*

High, Most High.—*A.V.* ¹*authority,* ²*Highest.*
Lu. 1. 32. and shall be called the Son of the ²*Most High*
35. the power of the ²*Most High* shall overshadow thee

HINDER

Lu. 1. 76. child, shalt be called the prophet of the *Most* ²*H.*
78. Whereby the dayspring from on *high* shall visit us
6. 35. and ye shall be sons of the *Most* ²*High*
24. 49. until ye be clothed with power from on *high*
Jno. 19. 31. (for the day of that sabbath was a *high* day)
Acts 7. 48. the *Most High* dwelleth not in houses made
13. 17. and with a *high* arm led he them forth out of it
Rom. 12. 16. Set not your mind on *high* things
13. 11. it is *high* time for you to awake out of sleep
2 Cor. 10. 5. and every *high* thing that is exalted against
Eph. 4. 8. When he ascended on *h.*, he led captivity captive
Phil. 3. 14. prize of the *high* calling of God in Christ Jesus
1 Tim. 2. 2. for kings and all that are in ¹*high* place
Heb. 1. 3. on the right hand of the Majesty on *high*
Rev. 21. 12. having a wall great and *high*
see God, mountain, (high) priest.

Higher.
Lu. 14. 10. he may say to thee, Friend, go up *higher*
Rom. 13. 1. Let every soul be in subjection to the *h.* powers
Heb. 7. 26. from sinners, and made *h.* than the heavens

Highest.
Mat. 21. 9. Hosanna in the *highest. Mk.* 11. 10 [19. 38
Lu. 2. 14. Glory to God in the *highest*, And on earth peace.
see chief, Most High.

Highly.
Lu. 1. 28. and said, Hail, thou that art *highly* favoured
Acts 12. 20. he was *highly* displeased with them of Tyre
Rom. 12. 3. not to think of himself more *highly* than
Phil. 2. 9. Wherefore also God *highly* exalted him
1 Th. 5. 13. esteem them exceeding *highly* in love

Highminded.
Rom. 11. 20. Be not *highminded*, but fear. 1 Tim. 6. 17
see puffed.

Highways.
Mat. 22. 9. Go ye therefore unto— the *h.* 10 : *Lu.* 14. 23
see way.

Hill—s.
Mat. 5. 14. A city set on a *hill* cannot be hid
Lu. 3. 5. every mountain and *hill* shall be brought low
4. 29. and led him unto the brow of the *hill*
23. 30. Fall on us ; and to the *hills,* Cover us
see Areopagus (proper names), mountain.

Hill *country.*
Lu. 1. 39. and went into the *hill country* with haste
65. noised abroad throughout all the *hill country*

Hinder.
Acts 8. 36. what doth *hinder* me to be baptized ?
Gal. 5. 7. who did *h.* you that ye should not obey the truth?
see hindrance.

Hindered.—*A.V.* ¹*forbade,* ²*let,* ³*suffered.*
Mat. 3. 14. But John would have ¹*hindered* him, saying
Lu. 11. 52. and them that were entering in ye *hindered*
Rom. 1. 13. come unto you (and was ²*hindered* hitherto)
15. 22. I was *h.* these many times from coming to you
1 Th. 2. 18. I Paul once and again ; and Satan *hindered* us
Heb. 7. 23. by death they are ³*h.* from continuing
1 Pet. 3. 7. to the end that your prayers be not *hindered*

Hinder *part, parts A.V.—see stern.*

HINDRANCE

Hindrance.—*A.V.* ¹*hinder.*
1 *Cor.* 9. 12. may cause no ¹*h.* to the gospel of Christ

Hire.—*A.V.* ¹*reward,* ²*wages.*
Mat. 20. 1. to *hire* labourers into his vineyard
    8. pay them their *hire,* beginning from the last
Lu. 10. 7. for the labourer is worthy of his *h.* 1 *Tim.* 5. ¹18
Jas. 5. 4. Behold, the *hire* of the labourers who mowed
2 *Pet.* 2. 13. suffering wrong as the ¹*hire* of wrong-doing
    15. Balaam—who loved the ²*hire* of wrong-doing
Jude 11. ran riotously in the error of Balaam for ¹*hire*

Hired.
Mat. 20. 7. Because no man hath *hired* us
    9. they came that were *hired* about the eleventh hour
Mk. 1. 20. Zebedee in the boat with the *hired* servants
Lu. 15. 17. *hired* servants of my father's have bread enough
    19. make me as one of thy *hired* servants
Acts 28. 30. abode two whole years in his own *h.* dwelling

Hireling.
Jno. 10. 12. He that is a *hireling,* and not a shepherd
    13. he fleeth because he is a *hireling,* and careth not

Hoisted.—*A.V.* ¹*taken up.*
Acts 27. 17. when they had ¹*hoisted* it up, they used helps
    see hoisting.

Hoisting.—*A.V.* ¹*hoisted.*
Acts 27. 40. and ¹*hoisting* up the foresail to the wind

Hold.—*A.V.* ¹*cage.*
Rev. 18. 2. a *h.* of every unclean spirit, and a ¹*h.* of every
    see stronghold, ward.

Hold.—*A.V.* ¹*hands,* ²*keep in memory,* ³*make,* ⁴*took.*
Mat. 6. 24. or else he will *hold* to one. *Lu.* 16. 13
    12. 11. will he not lay *hold* on it, and lift it out?
    14. 3. For Herod had laid *hold* on John. *Mk.* 6. 17
    18. 28. he laid ¹*hold* on him, and took him by the throat
    20. 31. rebuked them, that they should *hold* their peace.
    21. 26. for all *h.* John as a prophet [*Mk.*10. 48: *Lu.*18.39
Mk. 1. 25. *Hold* thy peace, and come out. *Lu.* 4. 35
    3. 21. to lay *hold* on him : for they said, He is beside
    7. 4. things there be, which they have received to *hold*
    8. of God, and *hold* fast the tradition of men
    12. 12. And they sought to lay *hold* on him
    14. 51. over his naked body: and they lay *hold* on him
Lu. 8. 15. having heard the word, ²*hold* it fast
    19. 40. if these shall *hold* their peace, the stones
    20. 20. that they might take *hold* of his speech. 26
    23. 26. they laid *hold* upon one Simon of Cyrene
Jno. 10. 24. How long dost thou ³*hold* us in suspense?
Acts 13. 7. *hold* their peace, declared unto them
    18. 9. Be not afraid, but speak, and *hold* not thy peace
    21. 33. chief captain came near, and laid ¹*hold* on him
Rom. 1. 18. who *hold* down the truth in unrighteousness
1 *Cor.*11. 2. ²*h.* fast the traditions, even as I delivered them
    15. 2. what words I preached unto you, if ye ²*hold* it fast
Phil. 2. 29. in the Lord with all joy; and *h.* such in honour
1 *Th.* 5. 21. *hold* fast that which is good
2 *Th.* 2. 15. brethren, stand fast, and *hold* the traditions
1 *Tim.* 6. 12. *hold* on the life eternal. 19
2. *Tim.* 1. 13. *Hold* the pattern of sound words
Heb. 3. 6. if we *hold* fast our boldness and the glorying
    14. if we *hold* fast the beginning of our confidence
    4. 14. let us *hold* fast our confession. 10. 23
    6. 18. for refuge to lay *hold* of the hope set before us
Rev. 2. 14. some that *hold* the teaching of Balaam
    15. some that *hold* the teaching of the Nicolaitans

HOLY

Rev. 2. 25. that which ye have, *hold* fast till I come. 3. 1
    20. 2. And he laid *hold* on the dragon, the old serpent
    see keep, taken, took, he took.

Holden.—*A.V.* ¹*held,* ²*taken.*
Mat. 4. 24. that were sick, ²*holden* with divers diseases
Lu. 8. 37. him to depart—for they were²*h.* with great fear
    24. 16. eyes were *h.* that they should not know him
Acts 2. 24. it was not possible that he should be *h.* of it
Rom. 7. 6. having died to that wherein we were ¹*holden*
    see stand.

Holdest.
Rev. 2. 13. thou *holdest* fast my name, and didst not deny

Holdeth.
Rev. 2. 1. he that *holdeth* the seven stars in his right hand

Holding.
Mk. 7. 3. eat not, *holding* the tradition of the elders
Phil. 2. 16. *holding* forth the word of life
Col. 2. 19. and not *h.* fast the Head, from whom all the body
1 *Tim.* 1. 19. *holding* faith and a good conscience
    3. 9. *holding* the mystery of the faith in a pure conscience
Tit. 1. 9. *holding* to the faithful word which is according to
Rev. 7. 1. *holding* the four winds of the earth

Holes.—*A.V.* ¹*caves.*
Mat. 8. 20. foxes have *holes,* and the birds. *Lu.* 9. 58
Heb. 12. 38. wandering in deserts—and the ¹*h.* of the earth

Holpen.
Lu. 1. 54. He hath *holpen* Israel his servant

Holiest.—*see holy, holy of holies.*

Holily.
1 *Th.* 2. 10. Ye are witnesses, and God also, how *holily*

Holiness.—*A.V.* ¹*simplicity.*
Lu. 1. 75. In *holiness* and righteousness before him
Rom. 1. 4. with power, according to the spirit of *holiness*
2 *Cor.* 1. 12. that in ¹*h.* and sincerity of God—we behaved
    7. 1. perfecting *holiness* in the fear of God
Eph. 4. 24. created in righteousness and *holiness* of truth
1 *Th.* 3. 13. stablish your hearts unblameable in *holiness*
Heb. 12. 10. that we may be partakers of his *holiness*
    see godliness, reverent, sanctification.

Holy.—*A.V.* ¹*holiest,* ²*sanctuary.*
Mat. 7. 6. Give not that which is *holy* unto the dogs
    24. 15. spoken of by Daniel—standing in the *holy* place
Mk. 1. 24. who thou art, the *Holy* One of God. *Lu.* 4. 34
    6. 20. knowing that he was a righteous man and a *holy*
    8. 38. glory of his Father with the *holy* angels. *Lu.* 9. 26
Lu. 1. 35. that which is to be born shall be called *holy*
    49. done to me great things ; And *holy* is his name
    70. As he spake by the mouth of his *holy* prophets
    72. And to remember his *holy* covenant   [*holy*
    2. 23. Every male that openeth the womb shall be called
Jno. 17. 11. *Holy* Father, keep them in thy name
Acts 2. 27. give thy *Holy* One to see corruption. 13. 35
    3. 14. ye denied the *Holy* and Righteous one   [*anoint*
    4. 27. against thy *holy* Servant Jesus, whom thou didst
    30. may be done through the name of thy *holy* Servant
    6. 13. speak words against this *holy* place, and the law
    7. 33. the place whereon thou standest is *holy* ground
    10. 22. warned of God by a *holy* angel to send for thee
    21. 28. and hath defiled this *holy* place   [*scriptures*
Rom. 1. 2. promised afore by his prophets in the *holy*

HOLY

Rom. 7. 12. the law is *holy*, and the commandment *holy*
11. 16. firstfruit is *h*., so is the lump: and if the root is *h*.
12. 1. to present your bodies a living sacrifice, *holy*
16. 16. Salute one another with a *holy* kiss. 1 *Cor.* 16. 20 :
   2 *Cor.* 13. 12; 1 *Th.* 5. 26   [ye are
1 *Cor.* 3. 17. for the temple of God is *holy*, which temple
7. 14. were your children unclean ; but now they are *holy*
34. that she may be *holy* both in body and in spirit
Eph. 1. 4. that we should be *holy* and without blemish
2. 21. groweth into a *holy* temple in the Lord
5. 27. but that it should be *holy* and without blemish
Col. 1. 22. to present you *holy* and without blemish
3. 12. God's elect, *holy* and beloved, a heart of compassion
1 *Tim.* 2. 8. lifting up *holy* hands, without wrath
2 *Tim.* 1. 9. who saved us, and called us with a *holy* calling
Tit. 1. 8. a lover of good, soberminded, just, *h*., temperate
Heb. 3. 1. *holy* brethren, partakers of a heavenly calling
7. 26. such a high priest became us, *holy*, guileless
9. 2. which is called the ²*Holy* place   [manifest
8. way into the ¹*holy* place hath not yet been made
12. entered in once for all into the *holy* place
24. Christ entered not into a *h*. place made with hands
25. high priest entereth into the *h*. place year by year
10. 19. boldness to enter into the ¹*holy* place by the blood
13. 11. whose blood is brought into the ²*h ly* place
1 *Pet.* 1. 15. called you is *holy*, be ye yourselves also *holy*
16. because it is written, Ye shall be *holy* ; for I am *holy*
2. 5. a *holy* priesthood, to offer up spiritual sacrifices
9. ye are an elect race, a royal priesthood, a *holy* nation
3. 5. the *holy* women also, who hoped in God
2 *Pet.* 1. 18. when we were with him in the *holy* mount
2. 21. knowing it, to turn back from the *h*. commandment
3. 2. words which were spoken before by the *h*. prophets
11. manner of persons ought ye to be in all *holy* living
1 *Jno.* 2. 20. ye have an anointing from the Holy One
Jude 20. building up yourselves on your most *holy* faith
Rev. 3. 7. These things saith he that is *holy*   [Almighty
4. 8. saying Holy, holy, holy, is the Lord God, the
6. 10. How long, O Master, the *holy* and true
14. 10. brimstone in the presence of the *holy* angels
15. 4. and glorify thy name ? for thou only art *holy*
20. 6. *holy* is he that hath part in the first resurrection
21. 10. and shewed me the *holy* city Jerusalem
22. 11. he that is *holy*, let him be made *holy* still
   see city, sacred, saints, spirit.

Holy of holies.—*A. V.* ¹*holiest.*

Heb. 9. 3. tabernacle which is called the ¹*Holy of holies*

Holy One.—*see proper names.*

Holy ones.—*A. V.* ¹*saints.*

Jude 14. the Lord came with ten thousands of his ¹*h. ones*

Home.—*A. V.* ¹*house*—*s,* ²*present.*

Mk. 8. 3. if I send them away fasting to their ¹*home*
26. he sent him away to his ¹*home* [blind man]
Lu. 15. 6. he cometh *home*, he calleth together his friends
Jno. 19. 27. the disciple took her unto his own *home*
20. 10. disciples went away again unto their own *home*
Acts 2. 46. breaking bread at ¹*h*., they did take their food
5. 42. in the temple and at ¹*h*., they ceased not to teach
21. 6. board the ship, but they returned *home* again
1 *Cor.* 11. 34. If any man is hungry, let him eat at *home*
14. 35. let them ask their own husbands at *home*

HONOURABLE

2 *Cor.* 5. 6. whilst we are at *home* in the body, we are
8. absent from the body, and to be at ²*home* with the
9. whether at ²*home* or absent, to be well-pleasing
Tit. 2. 5. soberminded, chaste, workers at *home*, kind
   see family, house.

Honest.

Lu. 8. 15. in an *honest* and good heart, having heard
   see good, honourable, seemly

Honestly.

Rom. 13. 13. Let us walk *h*., as in the day ; not in revelling
1 *Th.* 4. 12. walk *honestly* toward them that are without
Heb. 13. 18. desiring to live *honestly* in all things

Honesty *A. V.*—*see gravity.*

Honey.

Mat. 3. 4. his food was locusts and wild *honey. Mk.* 1. 6
Rev. 10. 9. but in thy mouth it shall be sweet as *honey.* 10

Honour.—*A. V.* ¹*honourable,* ²*reputation.*

Mat. 13. 57. A prophet is not without *h. Mk.* 6. 4: *Jno.* 4. 44
15. 4. *Honour* thy father and thy mother. 19. 19: *Mk.*
   7. 10: 10. 19: *Lu.* 18. 20: *Eph.* 6. 2
6. he shall not *h*. his father. And ye have made void
Jno. 5. 23. may *honour* the Son, even as they *h*. the Father
8. 49. but I *honour* my Father, and ye dishonour me
12. 26. if any man serve me, him will the Father *honour*
Acts 5. 34. Gamaliel, a doctor of the law, had in ²*honour*
Rom. 2. 7. in well-doing seek for glory and *honour*
10. *honour* and peace to every man that worketh good
9. 21. same lump to make one part a vessel unto *honour*
12. 10. in *honour* preferring one another
13. 7. fear to whom fear ; *honour* to whom *honour*
1 *Cor.* 12. 23. we bestow more abundant *honour.* 24
Phil. 2. 29. with all joy ; and hold such in ²*honour*
1 *Th.* 4. 4. his own vessel in sanctification and *honour*
1 *Tim.* 1. 17. the only God, be *h*. and glory for ever and ever
5. 3. *Honour* widows that are widows indeed
17. that rule well be counted worthy of double *honour*
6. 1. count their own masters worthy of all *honour*
16. to whom be *honour* and power eternal
2 *Tim.* 2. 20. some unto *h*., and some unto dishonour. 21
Heb. 2. 7. Thou crownedst him with glory and *honour.* 9
3. 3. he that built the house hath more *h*. than the house
5. 4. And no man taketh the *honour* unto himself
13. 4. Let marriage be had in ¹*honour* among all
1 *Pet.* 1. 7. might be found unto praise and glory and *h*.
2. 17. *Honour* all men—Fear God. *Honour* the king
3. 7. giving *honour* unto the woman, as unto the weaker
2 *Pet.* 1. 17. he received from God the Father *honour*
Rev. 4. 9. living creatures shall give glory and *honour*
11. Worthy—to receive the glory and the *honour.* 5. 12
5. 13. unto the Lamb, be the blessing, and the *h.* 7. 12
Rev. 21. 26. bring the glory and the *honour* of the nations
   see glory, glorify, value.

Honourable.—*A. V.* ¹*honest,* ²*worthy.*

Mk. 15. 43. Joseph of Arimathæa, a councillor of *h*. estate
Lu. 14. 8. lest haply a more *h*. man than thou be bidden
Acts 13. 50. the Jews urged on the devout women of *h*. estate
17. 12. believed ; also of the Greek women of *h*. estate
Rom. 12. 17. for things ¹*h*. in the sight of all men. 2 *Cor.* 8. 12¹
1 *Cor.* 12. 23. of the body, which we think to be less *h*.
2 *Cor.* 13. 7. do that which is ¹*h*., though we be as reprobate
Phil. 4. 8. whatsoever things are ¹*h*., whatsoever things
Jas. 2. 7. Do not they blaspheme the ²*h*. name by the which
   see glory, honour.

HONOURED

Honoured.
Acts 28. 10. who also *honoured* us with many honours
1 *Cor.* 12. 26. one member is *h.*, all the members rejoice

Honoureth.—*A.V.* ¹*draweth nigh.*
Mat. 15. 8. This people ¹*h.* me with their lips. *Mk.* 7. 6
Jno. 5. 23. He that *h.* not the Son *h.* not the Father
see *glorifieth.*

Honours.
Acts 28. 10. who also honoured us with many *honours*

Hook.
Mat. 17. 27. and cast a *hook*, and take up the fish

Hope.—*A.V.* ¹*faith,* ²*trust,* ³*trusteth.*
Mat. 12. 21. And in his name shall the Gentiles ²*hope*
Lu. 6. 34. if ye lend to them of whom ye *hope* to receive
Jno. 5. 45. Moses, on whom ye have set your ²*hope*
Acts 2. 26. Moreover my flesh also shall dwell in *hope*
16. 19. saw that the *hope* of their gain was gone
23. 6. touching the *hope* and resurrection of the dead
24. 15. *hope* toward God, which these also—look for
26. 6. to be judged for the *hope* of the promise
7. serving God—*hope* to attain—concerning this *hope*
27. 20. all *hope* that we should be saved was now taken
28. 20. for because of the *hope* of Israel I am bound
Rom. 4. 18. Who in *hope* believed against *hope*
5. 2. let us rejoice in *hope* of the glory of God
4. and patience, probation ; and probation, *hope*
5. and *h.* putteth not to shame ; because the love of God
8. 20. but by reason of him who subjected it, in *hope*
24. by *h.* were we saved : but *h.* that is seen is not *hope*
25. But if we *hope* for that which we see not
12. 12. rejoicing in *hope* ; patient in tribulation
15. 4. through comfort of the scriptures we might have *h.*
13. God of *hope* fill you with all joy—ye may abound in *h.*
24. (for I ²*h.* to see you in my journey, and to be brought
1 *Cor.* 9. 10. ought to plow in *h.*—thresh in *h.* of partaking
13. 13. But now abideth faith, *hope*, love, these three
16. 7. I ²*hope* to tarry awhile with you, if the Lord permit
2 *Cor.* 1. 7. and our *hope* for you is stedfast
10. on whom we have set our ²*hope* that he will—deliver
13. and I ²*hope* ye will acknowledge unto the end [us
8. 12. Having therefore such a *h.*, we use great boldness
5. 11. I ²*hope* that we are made manifest also in your
10. 15. but having *hope* that, as your faith.groweth
13. 6. I ²*h.* that ye shall know that we are not reprobate
Gal. 5. 5. by faith wait for the *hope* of righteousness
Eph. 1. 18. that ye may know what is the *h.* of his calling
2. 12 having no *hope* and without God in the world
4. 4. one Spirit, even as also ye were called in one *hope*
Phil. 1. 20. and *h.*, that in nothing shall I be put to shame
2. 23. Him therefore I *hope* to send forthwith
Col. 1. 5. because of the *hope* which is laid up for you
23. and not moved away from the *hope* of the gospel
27. which is Christ in you, the *hope* of glory
1 *Th.* 1. 3. labour of love and patience of *hope* in our Lord
2. 19. For what is our *hope*, or joy, or crown of glorying?
4. 13. sorrow not, even as the rest, which have no *hope*
5. 8. and for a helmet, the *hope* of salvation
2 *Th.* 2. 16. eternal comfort and good *hope* through grace
1 *Tim.* 1. 1. God our Saviour, and Christ Jesus our *hope*
4. 10. because we have our ²*hope* set on the living God
5. 5. widow indeed, and desolate, hath her ²*h.* set on God
6. 17. nor have their ²*hope* set on the uncertainty of riches
Tit. 1. 2. in *hope* of eternal life, which God, who cannot lie
2. 13. looking for the blessed *hope* and appearing
3. 7. made heirs according to the *hope* of eternal life

HORSES

Philem. 22. I ²*h.* that through your prayers I shall be granted
Heb. 3. 6. and the glorying of our *hope* firm unto the end
6. 11. diligence unto the fulness of *hope* even to the end
18. fled for refuge to lay hold of the *hope* set before us
19. an anchor of the soul, a *hope* both sure and stedfast
7. 19. better *hope*, through which we draw nigh unto God
10. 23. let us hold fast the confession of our ¹*hope*
1 *Pet.* 1. 3. great mercy begat us again unto a living *hope*
13. be sober and set your *hope* perfectly on the grace
21. so that your faith and *hope* might be in God
3. 15. asketh you a reason concerning the *hope* that is in
1 *Jno.* 3. 3. that hath this *hope* set on him purifieth himself
2 *Jno.* 12. I ²*h.* to come unto you, and to speak face to face
3 *Jno.* 14. I ²*hope* shortly to see thee, and we shall speak
see *hoped, hopeth.*

Hoped.—*A.V.* ¹*hope,* ²*trusted.*
Lu. 23. 8. he *hoped* to see some miracle done by him
24. 21. we ²*h.* that it was he which should redeem Israel
Acts 24. 26. He *h.* withal that money would be given him
1 *Cor.* 16. 19. If in this life only we have ¹*hoped* in Christ
2 *Cor.* 8. 5. and this not as we had *h.*, but first they gave
Eph. 1. 12. we who had before ²*hoped* in Christ
Heb. 11. 1. Now faith is the assurance of things *hoped* for
1 *Pet.* 3. 5. holy women also, who ²*hoped* in God, adorned

Hopeth.—*A.V.* ¹*hope.*
Rom. 8. 24. for who ¹*hopeth* for that which he seeth?
1 *Cor.* 13. 7. *hopeth* all things, endureth all things

Hoping.
1 *Tim.* 3. 14. write I unto thee, *h.* to come unto thee shortly
see *despairing.*

Horn.
Lu. 1. 69. And hath raised up a *horn* of salvation for us

Horns.
Rev. 5. 6. as though it had been slain, having seven *horns*
9. 13. a voice from the *horns* of the golden altar
12. 3. red dragon, having seven heads and ten *horns*
13. 1. having ten *horns*—and on his *horns* ten diadems
11. and he had two *horns* like unto a lamb
17. 3. of blasphemy, having seven heads and ten *h.* 7
12. the ten *horns* that thou sawest are ten kings. 16

Horse.
Rev. 6. 2. And I saw, and behold, a white *horse*. 19. 11
4. And another *horse* came forth, a red *horse*
5. And I saw, and behold, a black *horse*
8. And I saw, and behold, a pale *horse*
19. 19. to make war against him that sat upon the *horse*
21. killed with the sword of him that sat upon the *h.*
see *horses.*

Horsemen.
Acts 23. 23. and *horsemen* threescore and ten. 32
Rev. 9. 16. the number of the armies of the *horsemen* was

Horses.—*A.V.* ¹*horse.*
Jas. 3. 3. if we put the *horses'* bridles into their mouths
Rev. 9. 7. locusts were like unto *horses* prepared for war
17. I saw the *horses*—of the *h.* are as the heads of lions
14. 20. blood—even unto the bridles of the ¹*horses*
19. 14. are in heaven followed him upon white *horses*
18. the flesh of *horses* and of them that sit thereon
see *chariots.*

167

HOSANNA

Hosanna.
Mat. 21. 9. *Hosanna* to the son of David—*Hosanna* in the highest. 15: *Mk*. 11. 9, 10: *Jno*. 12. 13

Hospitality.—*A.V.* ¹*lodged.*
Rom. 12. 13. given to *hospitality*. 1 *Tim*. 3. 2: *Tit*. 1. 8
1 *Tim*. 5. 10. if she hath used ¹*hospitality* to strangers
1 *Pet*. 4. 9. using *h*. one to another without murmuring

Host—s.—*A.V.* ¹*company.*
Lu. 2. 13. a multitude of the heavenly *host* praising God
10. 35. took out two pence, and gave them to the *host*
Rom. 16. 23. my *host*, and of the whole church, saluteth
Heb. 12. 22. and to innumerable ¹*hosts* of angels

Hot.
1 *Tim*. 4. 2. branded in their own conscience as with a *hot*
Rev. 3. 15. nor *hot*: I would thou wert cold or *hot*. 16 [iron

Hour.—*A.V.* ¹*instant*, ²*same day*, ³*time.*
Mat. 8. 13. And the servant was healed in that *hour*
9. 22. the woman was made whole from that *hour*
10. 19. it shall be given you in that *hour*. *Lu*. 12. 12
15. 28. And her daughter was healed from that *hour*
17. 18. and the boy was cured from that *hour*
20. 3. he went out about the third *hour*, and saw others
5. Again he went out about the sixth and the ninth *hour*
6. And about the eleventh *hour* he went out
12. These last have spent but one *hour*
24. 36. of that day and *hour* knoweth no one. *Mk*. 13. 32
44. for in an *hour* that ye think not. *Lu*. 12. 40
50. and in an *hour* when he knoweth not. *Lu*. 12. 46
25. 13. Watch therefore, for ye know not the day nor the *h*.
26. 40. could ye not watch with me one *hour*? *Mk*. 14. 37
45. the *hour* is at hand, and the Son of man is betrayed
55. In that *hour*, said Jesus to the multitudes
27. 45. from the sixth *hour* there was darkness—until the ninth *hour*. *Mk*. 15. 33: *Lu*. 23. 44
46. about the ninth *hour* Jesus cried. *Mk*. 15. 34
Mk. 13. 11. shall be given you in that *hour*, that speak ye
14. 35. if it were possible, the *hour* might pass away
41. it is enough; the *hour* is come. *Jno*. 12. 23: 17. 1
15. 25. it was the third *hour*, and they crucified him
Lu. 1. 10. people were praying without at the ³*h*. of incense
2. 38. Anna—coming up at that very ¹*hour*, she gave
7. 21. In that *hour* he cured many of diseases
10. 21. In that same *hour* he rejoiced in the Holy Spirit
12. 39. had known in what *hour* the thief was coming
13. 31. that very ²*hour* there came certain Pharisees
20. 19. sought to lay hands on him in that very *hour*
22. 14. And when the *hour* was come, he sat down
53. but this is your *hour*, and the power of darkness
59. space of about one *hour* another confidently affirmed
24. 33. rose up that very *hour*, and returned to Jerusalem
Jno. 1. 39. with him that day: it was about the tenth *hour*
2. 4. have I to do with thee? mine *hour* is not yet come
4. 6. sat thus by the well. It was about the sixth *hour*
21. Woman, believe me, the *hour* cometh. 23
52. *hour* when he began to amend—at the seventh *hour*
53. the father knew that it was at that *hour*
5. 25. The *hour* cometh, and now is. 28: 16. 32
7. 30. because his *hour* was not yet come. 8. 20
12. 27. Father, save me from this *hour*. But for this cause came I unto this *hour*
13. 1. Jesus knowing that his *hour* was come
16. 2. the ³*hour* cometh, that whosoever killeth you
21. in travail hath sorrow, because her *hour* is come
25. the ³*hour* cometh, when I shall no more speak
19. 14. of the passover: it was about the sixth *hour*
27. from that *h*. the disciple took her unto his own

HOUSE

Acts 2. 15. seeing it is but the third *hour* of the day
3. 1. temple at the *hour* of prayer, being the ninth *hour*
10. 3. ninth *hour* of the day, an angel of God coming
9. upon the housetop to pray, about the sixth *hour*
30. until this *hour*, I was keeping the ninth *hour*
16. 18. come out of her. And it came out that very *hour*
33. took them the same *hour* of the night, and washed
22. 13. And in that very *hour* I looked up on him
23. 23. spearmen two hundred, at the third *h*. of the night
1 *Cor*. 4. 11. Even unto this present *hour* we both hunger
15. 30. why do we also stand in jeopardy every *hour*?
Gal. 2. 5. in the way of subjection, no, not for an *hour*
1 *Jno*. 2. 18. the last ³*hour*—know that it is the last ³*hour*
Rev. 3. 3. not know what *hour* I will come upon thee
10. I also will keep thee from the *hour* of trial, that *hour* which is to come upon the whole world
8. 1. silence in heaven about the space of half an *hour*
9. 15. been prepared for the *hour* and day and month
11. 13. And in that *hour* there was a great earthquake
14. 7. for the *hour* of his judgement is come
17. 12. authority as kings, with the beast, for one *hour*
18. 10. for in one *hour* is thy judgement come
17. for in one *hour* so great riches is made desolate. 19
see day.

Hours.
Jno. 11. 9. Are there not twelve *hours* in the day?
Acts 5. 7. three *hours* after, when his wife, not knowing
19. 34. space of two *hours* cried out, Great is Diana

House.—*A.V.* ¹*business*, ²*home*, ³*houshould.*
Mat. 2. 11. [wise men] came into the *h*. and saw the young
5. 15. it shineth unto all that are in the *house* [child
7. 24. which built his *house* upon. 26: *Lu*. 6. 48, 49
25. and beat upon that *house*. 27: *Lu*. 6. 48
8. 6. Lord, my servant lieth in the ²*house* sick of the palsy
9. 6. take up thy bed, and go unto thy *house*. 7: *Mk*. 2.
10. as he sat at meat in the *house* [11: *Lu*. 5. 24
28. when he was come into the *house*. *Mk*. 3. 19: 9. 28
10. 6. go rather to the lost sheep of the *h*. of Israel. 15. 4
12. enter into the *house*, salute it. *Mk*. 6. 10: *Lu*. 9. 4
13. If the *house* be worthy, let your peace come. *Lu*. 10.5
14. out of that *house* or that city, shake off the dust
25. have called the master of the *house* Beelzebub
12. 4. into the *h*. of God, and did eat. *Mk*. 2. 26: *Lu*. 6. 4
25. or *house* divided against itself. *Mk*. 3. 25: *Lu*. 11. 17
29. enter into the *house* of the strong man—then he will spoil his *house*. *Mk*. 3. 27 [*Lu*. 11. 24
44. I will return into my *house* whence I came out.
13. 1. went Jesus out of the *house*, and sat by the sea side
57. not without honour, save—in his own *h*. *Mk*. 6. 4
21. 13. My *house* shall be called a *house* of prayer. *Mk*. 11. 17: *Lu*. 19. 46
23. 38. Behold, your *h*. is left unto you desolate. *Lu*. 13. 35
24. 17. the things that are in the *house*. *Mk*. 13. 15
43. master of the *house* had known—and would not have suffered his *house* to be broken through. *Lu*. 12. 39
26. 18. I keep the passover at thy *h*. with my disciples
Mk. 2. 1. it was noised that he was in the *house*
15. he was sitting at meat in his *h*., and many publicans
5. 19. Go to thy ²*h*. unto thy friends, and tell. *Lu*. 8. 39
9. 33. when he was in the *house* he asked them
10. 10. And in the *house* the disciples asked him again
29. no man that hath left *house*, or brethren. *Lu*. 18. 29
13. 34. in another country, having left his *house*
35. when the lord of the *house* cometh
14. 3. in Bethany in the *house* of Simon the leper
14. say to the goodman of the *house*. *Lu*. 22. 11
Lu. 1. 23. he departed unto his *house*. 5. 25
27. whose name was Joseph, of the *house* of David. 2. 4

HOUSE

Lu. 1. 33. he shall reign over the *house* of Jacob for ever
56. about three months, and returned unto her *house*
69. In the *house* of his servant David
2. 49. wist ye not that I must be in my Father's ¹*house*?
5. 29. Levi made him a great feast in his *house*
6. 49. it fell in; and the ruin of that *house* was great
7. 6. not far from the *house*, the centurion sent friends
36. And he entered into the Pharisee's *house*. 37
44. I entered into thine *house*, thou gavest me no water
8. 27. abode not in any *house*, but in the tombs
41. Jairus—and besought him to come into his *h*. 49, 51
9. 61. to bid farewell to them that are at my ²*house*
10. 5. into whatsoever *h*. ye shall enter—Peace be to this *h*.
7. in that same *house* remain—Go not from *house* to *h*.
38. Martha received him into her *house*
12. 52. five in one *house* divided, three against two
14. 1. he went into the *house* of one of the rulers
23. constrain them to come in, that my *h*. may be filled
15. 8. doth not light a lamp, and sweep the *h*., and seek
25. nigh to the *house*, he heard music and dancing
16. 27. that thou wouldest send him to my father's *house*
18. 14. This man went down to his *house* justified
19. 5. come down; for to-day I must abide at thy *house*
9 To-day is salvation come to this *house*
22. 10. follow him into the *house* whereinto he goeth
Jno. 2. 16. make not my Father's *h*. a *h*. of merchandise
4. 53. and himself believed, and his whole *house*
7. 53. And they went every man unto his own *house*
8. 35. the bondservant abideth not in the *h*. for ever
11. 20. but Mary still sat in the *house*
12. 3. *house* was filled with the odour of the ointment
14. 2. In my Father's *house* are many mansions
Acts 2. 2. rushing of a mighty wind, and it filled all the *h*.
36. Let all the *house* of Israel therefore know assuredly
7. 10. made him governor over Egypt and all his *house*
20. Moses—nourished three months in his father's *h*.
42. Forty years in the wilderness, O *house* of Israel?
49. What manner of *house* will ye build me?
9. 11. inquire in the *house* of Judas for one named Saul
10. 2. one that feared God with all his *house*, who gave
6. Simon a tanner, whose *house* is by the sea side. 32
22. by a holy angel to send for thee into his *house*
30. I was keeping the ninth hour of prayer in my *house*
11. 12. and we entered into the man's *house*. 11
13. seen the angel standing in his *house*, and saying
14. shall be saved, thou and all thy *house*. 16. 31
12. 12. he came to the *h*. of Mary the mother of John
16. 15. come unto my [Lydia] *house*, and abide there
32. unto him, and all that were in his [jailor] *house*
34. brought them up into his *house*—rejoiced greatly, with all his *house*
17. 5. an uproar; and assaulting the *house* of Jason
18. 7. *house* of a certain man named Titus Justus—whose *house* joined hard to the synagogue
8. Crispus—believed in the Lord with all his *house*
19. 16. they fled out of that *house* naked and wounded
20. 20. teaching you publicly, and from *house* to *house*
21. 8. entering into the *house* of Philip the evangelist
Rom. 16. 5. church that is in their *house*. 1 *Cor.* 16. 19:
Col. 4. 15: Philem. 2
1 *Cor.* 16. 15. the *h*. of Stephanas, that it is the firstfruits
2 *Cor.* 5. 1. earthly *house* of our tabernacle be dissolved, we have—a *house* not made with hands
1 *Tim.* 3. 4 one that ruleth well his own *house*. 5
15. men ought to behave themselves in the *house* of God
5. 13. idle, going about from *house* to *house*
2 *Tim.* 1. 16. Lord grant mercy unto the *h*. of Onesiphorus
2. 20. in a great *house* there are not only vessels of gold
4. 19. Salute Prisca—and the ²*house* of Onesiphorus

23

HUMBLE

Heb. 3. 2. faithful—as also was Moses in all his *house*
6. Christ as a son, over his *house*; whose *house* are we
8. 8. I will make a new covenant with the *house* of Israel, and with the *house* of Judah. 10
10. 21. having a great priest over the *house* of God
11. 7. Noah—prepared an ark to the saving of his *house*
1 *Pet.* 4. 17. come for judgement to begin at the *h*. of God
2 *Jno.* 10. receive him not into your *h*., and give him no
see build, builded, building, built, dwelling, habitation, home, household, householder.

Household.—*A.V.* ¹*house*.

Mat. 10. 25. how much more shall they call them of his *h*.!
36. a man's foes shall be they of his own *household*
24. 45. whom his lord hath set over his *h*. *Lu*. 12. 42
Acts 16. 15. when she was baptized, and her *household*
Rom. 16. 10. Salute them which are of the *household* of. 11
1 *Cor.* 1. 11. by them which are of the ¹*household* of Chloe
16. I baptized also the *household* of Stephanas
Gal. 6. 10. toward them that are of the *household* of faith
Eph. 2. 19. with the saints, and of the *household* of God
Phil. 4. 22. especially they that are of Cæsar's *household*
1 *Tim.* 5. 8. specially his own ¹*household*, he hath denied
14. widows marry, bear children, rule the ¹*household*

Householder.—*A.V.* ¹*good man of the house*. *see house.*

Mat. 13. 27. the servants of the *householder* came and said
52. kingdom of heaven is like unto a man that is a *h*. 20. 1
20. 11. received it, they murmured against the ¹*h*.
21. 33. man that was a *h*., which planted a vineyard

Household-servants.

Acts 10. 7. he called two of his *household-servants*

Houses.—*A.V.* ¹*temples*.

Mat. 11. 8. they that wear soft raiment are in kings' *houses*
19. 29. every one that hath left *houses*, or. *Mk*. 10. 30
Mk. 12. 40. they which devour widows' *houses*. *Lu*. 20. 47
Lu. 16. 4. they may receive me into their *houses*
Acts 4. 34. as were possessors of lands or *houses* sold them
7. 48. Most High dwelleth not in ¹*h*. made with hands
1 *Cor.* 11. 22. have ye not *houses* to eat and to drink in?
1 *Tim.* 3. 12. ruling their children and their own *houses*
2 *Tim.* 3. 6. For of these are they that creep into *houses*
Tit. 1. 11 men who overthrow whole *houses*

Housetop—s.—*A.V.* ¹*houses*. *see house, housetops.*

Mat. 10. 27. hear ye the ear, proclaim upon the *housetops*
24. 17. that is on the *h*. not go down. *Mk*. 13. ¹16: *Lu*. 17.
Lu. 5. 19. went up to the *housetop*, and let him down [³31
12. 3. chambers shall be proclaimed upon the *housetops*
Acts 10. 9. Peter went up upon the ¹*housetop* to pray

Howbeit.—*A.V.* ¹*notwithstanding*, ²*rather*.

Lu. 10. 20. ¹*Howbeit* in this rejoice not, that the spirits are
11. 41. ²*H*. give for alms those things which are within
12. 31. ²*H*. seek ye his kingdom, and these things shall *In the R.V. the Howbeit is substituted in many cases for and, now, yet, &c. of the A.V.*

Howl.

Jas. 5. 1. Go to now, ye rich, weep and *h*. for your miseries

How long.

Mat. 17. 17. *how long* shall I be with you? *how long* shall I bear with you? *Mk*. 9. 19: *Lu*. 9. 41

Humble.

Mat. 18. 4. Whosoever therefore shall *h*. himself. 23. 12
2 *Cor.* 12. 21. my God should *humble* me before you

169

HUMBLE

Jas. 4. 6. but giveth grace to the *humble*. 1 *Pet*. 5. 5.
10. *Humble* yourselves in the sight of the Lord
1 *Pet*. 5. 6. *Humble* yourselves therefore under the mighty

Humbled.—*A.V.* ¹*abased*.
Mat. 23. 12. shall exalt himself shall be ¹*h*. *Lu*. 14.¹11:18.¹14
Phil. 2. 8. he *h*. himself, becoming obedient even unto death

Humbleminded.—*A.V.* ¹*courteous*.
1 *Pet*. 3. 8. loving as brethren, tenderhearted, ¹*h*.

Humbleness *A. V.*—*see humility*.

Humbleth.
Lu. 14. 11. he that *humbleth* himself shall be exalted. 18. 14

Humiliation.—*A.V.* ¹*vile*.
Acts 8. 33. In his *h*. his judgement was taken away
Phil. 3. 21. fashion anew the body of our ¹*humiliation*

Humility.—*A.V.* ¹*humbleness of mind*.
Col. 2. 18. rob you of your prize by a voluntary *humility*
23. a show of wisdom in will-worship, and *humility*
3. 12. a heart of compassion, kindness, ¹*h*., meekness
1 *Pet*. 5. 5. gird yourselves with *h*., to serve one another
see lowliness.

Hundred.
Mat. 18. 12. if any man have a *hundred* sheep. *Lu*. 15. 4
28. of his fellow-servants, which owed him a *h*.
Mk. 6. 37. go and buy two *h*. pennyworth of bread. *Jno*. 6. 7
Lu. 7. 41. two debtors: the one owed five *hundred* pence
16. 6. And he said, A *hundred* measures of oil
7. owest thou? And he said, A *h*. measures of wheat
Jno. 12. 5. this ointment sold for three *h*. pence. *Mk*. 14. 5
19. 39. myrrh and aloes, about a *hundred* pound weight
21. 8. not far from the land, but about two *h*. cubits off
11. full of great fishes, a *hundred* and fifty and three
Acts 1. 15. persons gathered together, about a *h*. and twenty
5. 36. number of men, about four *h*., joined themselves
7. 6. and entreat them evil, four *hundred* years
13. 19. inheritance, for about four *hundred* and fifty years
23. 23. two *hundred* soldiers—and spearmen two *hundred*
27. 37. in the ship two *h*. threescore and sixteen souls
1 *Cor*. 15. 6. appeared to above five *h*. brethren at once
Gal. 3. 17. the law, which came four *h*. and thirty years
Rev. 13. 18. his number is Six *h*. and sixty and six [after
21. 17. wall thereof, a *hundred* and forty and four cubits
see hundredfold.

Hundredfold.—*A.V.* ¹*hundred*.
Mat. 13. 8. yielded fruit, some a *h*. 23: *Mk*. 4. ¹8,¹20: *Lu*. 8.8
19. 29. for my name's sake, shall receive a *h*. *Mk*. 10. 30

Hundreds.
Mk. 6. 40. they sat down in ranks, by *h*., and by fifties

Hunger.
Mat. 5. 6. Blessed are they that *hunger*. *Lu*. 6. 21
Lu. 6. 25. Woe unto you, ye that are full now! for ye shall *h*.
15. 17. and to spare, and I perish here with *hunger*!
Jno. 6. 35. he that cometh to me shall not *hunger*
Rom. 12. 20. But if thine enemy *hunger*, feed him
1 *Cor*. 4. 11. we both *hunger*, and thirst, and are naked
2 *Cor*. 11. 27. watchings often, in *h*. and thirst, in fastings
Rev. 7. 16. They shall *hunger* no more, neither thirst
see famine, hungry.

Hungered or Hungred.—*A.V.* ¹*hungry*.
Mat. 4. 2. he afterward *hungered*. *Lu*. 4. 2
12. 1. disciples were an *hungred*, and began to pluck ears
3. David did, when he was an *h*. *Mk*. 2. 25: *Lu*. 6. 3

HUSBANDMEN

Mat. 21. 18. as he returned to the city, he *hungered*
25. 35. for I was an *hungred*, and ye gave me meat
37. Lord, when saw we thee an *h*., and fed thee? 44
42. for I was an *hungred*, and ye gave me no meat
Mk. 11. 12. when they were come out from Bethany, he ¹*h*.

Hungry.—*A.V.* ¹*hunger*.
Lu. 1. 53. The *hungry* he hath filled with good things
Acts 10. 10. and he became *hungry*, and desired to eat
1 *Cor*. 11. 21. and one is *hungry*, and another is drunken
34. If any man is ¹*hungry*, let him eat at home
Phil. 4. 12. learned the secret both to be filled and to be *h*.
see hungered.

Hurt.
Mk. 16. 18. any deadly thing, it shall in no wise *hurt* them
Lu. 4. 35. he came out of him, having done him no *hurt*
10. 19. and nothing shall in any wise *hurt* you
Rev. 2. 11. overcometh shall not be *hurt* of the second death
6. 6. and the oil and the wine *hurt* thou not
7. 2. whom it was given to *hurt* the earth and the sea. 3
9. 4. that they should not *hurt* the grass of the earth
10. in their tails is their power to *hurt* men. 19
11. 5. if any man desireth to *hurt* them—desire to *h*. them
see harm, injury.

Hurtful.
1 *Tim*. 6. 9. a snare and many foolish and *hurtful* lusts

Husband.
Mat. 1. 16. and Jacob begat Joseph the *husband* of Mary
19. And Joseph her *husband*, being a righteous man
Mk. 10. 12. if she herself shall put away her *husband*
Lu. 2. 36. Anna—having lived with a *husband* seven years
16. 18. marrieth one that is put away from a *husband*
Jno. 4. 16. Go, call thy *husband*, and come hither
17. I have no *husband*—saidst well, I have no *husband*
18. he whom thou now hast is not thy *husband*
Acts 5. 9. feet of them which have buried thy *husband* are
10. carried her out and buried her by her *husband*
Rom. 7. 2. hath a *husband* is bound by law to the *h*.—If
the *h*. die she is discharged from the law of the *h*.
3. while the *h*. liveth—if the *h*. die, she is free. 1 *Cor*. 7. 39
1 *Cor*. 7. 2. let each woman have her own *husband* [*h*.
3. Let the *h*. render unto the wife—also the wife unto the
4. but the *h*.—also the *husband* hath not power over
10. That the wife depart not from her *husband*
11. or else be reconciled to her *husband*); and that the *husband* leave not his wife
13. unbelieving *husband*—let her not leave her *husband*
14. the unbelieving *husband* is sanctified in the wife
16. O wife, whether thou shalt save thy *h*?—O *husband*
34. things of the world, how she may please her *h*.
2 *Cor*. 11. 2. for I espoused you to one *husband* [the *h*.
Gal. 4. 27. children of the desolate than of her which hath
Eph. 5. 23. the *h*. is the head of the wife, as Christ also
33. and let the wife see that she fear her *husband*
1 *Tim*. 3. 2. without reproach, the *h*. of one wife. *Tit*. 1. 6
Rev. 21. 2. made ready as a bride adorned for her *husband*
see brother.

Husbandman.
Jno. 15. 1. I am the true vine, and my Father is the *h*.
2 *Tim*. 2. 6. It is that laboureth must be the first to partake
Jas. 5. 7. the *husbandman* waiteth for the precious fruit

Husbandmen.
Mat. 21. 33. let it out to *husbandmen*. *Mk*. 12. 1: *Lu*. 20. 9
34. sent his servants to the *h*. 35: *Mk*. 12. 2; *Lu*. 20. 10
38. the *h*., when they saw the son. *Mk*. 12. 7: *Lu*. 20. 14

HUSBANDMEN

Mat. 21. 40. shall come, what will he do unto those *h.* ?
41. will let out the vineyard unto other *husbandmen*
Mk. 12. 2. receive from the *husbandmen* of the fruits
9. he will come and destroy the *husbandmen. Lu.* 20. 16
Lu. 20. 10. but the *husbandmen* beat him

Husbandry.
1 *Cor.* 3. 9. ye are God's *husbandry*, God's building

Husbands.—*A.V.* ¹*men.*
Jno. 4. 18. for thou hast had five *husbands*
1 *Cor.* 14. 35. let them ask their own *husbands* at home
Eph. 5. 22. Wives, be in subjection unto your own *husbands.*
24 : *Col.* 3. 18 : 1 *Pet.* 3. 1
25. *Husbands*, love your wives, even as Christ. *Col.* 3. 19
28. even so ought ¹*husbands* also to love their own wives.
1 *Tim.* 3. 12. Let deacons be *husbands* of one wife
Tit. 2. 4. train the young women to love their *husbands*
5. being in subjection to their own *husbands.* 1 *Pet.* 3. 5
1 *Pet.* 3. 7. Ye *h.*, in like manner, dwell with your wives

Husks.
Lu. 15. 16. would fain have been filled with the *husks*

Hyacinth.—*A.V.* ¹*jacinth.*
Rev. 9. 17. having breastplates as of fire and of ¹*hyacinth*
see *jacinth.*

Hymn—s.—*A.V.* ¹*praises.*
Mat. 26. 30. when they had sung a *hymn. Mk.* 14. 26
Acts 16. 25. Paul and Silas were praying and singing ¹*h.*
Eph. 5. 19. speaking one to another in psalms and *hymns*
Col. 3. 16. admonishing one another with psalms and *h.*

Hypocrisies.
1 *Pet.* 2. 1. Putting away—all guile, and *hypocrisies*

Hypocrisy.—*A.V.* ¹*dissimulation.*
Mat. 23. 28. but inwardly ye are full of *hypocrisy*
Mk. 12. 15. he, knowing their *hypocrisy,* said unto them
Lu. 12. 1. leaven of the Pharisees, which is *hypocrisy*
Rom. 12. 9. Let love be without ¹*hypocrisy*
1 *Tim.* 4. 2. through the *hypocrisy* of men that speak lies
Jas. 3. 17. good fruits, without variance, without *hypocrisy*

Hypocrite.
Mat. 7. 5. Thou *hypocrite*, cast out first the beam. *Lu.* 6. 42
see *hypocrites.*

Hypocrites.—*A.V.* ¹*hypocrite.*
Mat. 6. 2. sound not a trumpet before thee, as the *h.* do
5. when ye pray, ye shall not be as the *hypocrites*
16. Moreover when ye fast, be not, as the *hypocrites*
15. 7. Ye *hypocrites*, well did Isaiah prophesy. *Mk.* 7. 6
22. 18. Why tempt ye me, ye *hypocrites* ?
23. 13. woe unto you, scribes and Pharisees, *h.!* 15, 23, 25,
24. 51. and appoint his portion with the *hypocrites* [27, 29
Lu. 12. 56. Ye *h.*, ye know how to interpret the face of
13. 15. Ye ¹*h.*, doth not each one of you on the sabbath

Hyssop.
Jno. 19. 29. put a sponge full of the vinegar upon *hyssop*
Heb. 9. 19. and *hyssop*, and sprinkled both the book itself

IGNORANT

I.

Idle.—*A.V.* ¹*barren,* ²*slow.*
Mat. 12. 36. that every *idle* word that men shall speak
20. 3. saw others standing in the marketplace *idle.* 6
Lu. 24. 11. And these words appeared—as *idle* talk
1 *Tim.* 5. 13. they learn also to be *idle*—and not only *idle*
Tit. 1. 12. Cretans are alway liars, evil beasts, ²*i.* gluttons
2 *Pet.* 1. 8. they make you to be not ¹*idle* nor unfruitful

Idol.—*A.V.* ¹*idols.*
Acts 7. 41. brought a sacrifice unto the *idol*, and rejoiced
1 *Cor.* 8. 4. that no *idol* is anything in the world. 10. ¹19
7. used until now to the *idol*—sacrificed to an *idol*
10. hast knowledge sitting at meat in an *idol's* temple

Idolater—s.
1 *Cor.* 5. 10. or with *i.* ; for then must ye needs go out of
11. covetous, or an *idolater*, or a reviler   [the world
6. 9. Be not deceived: neither fornicators, nor *idolaters*
10. 7. Neither be ye *idolaters*, as were some of them
Eph. 5. 5. nor covetous man, which is an *idolater*, hath any
Rev. 21. 8. and *idolaters*, and all liars, their part shall be
22. 15. the *i.*, and every one that loveth and maketh a lie

Idolatries.
1 *Pet.* 4. 3. carousings, and abominable *idolatries*

Idolatry.
1 *Cor.* 10. 14. Wherefore, my beloved, flee from *idolatry*
Gal. 5. 20. *idolatry*, sorcery, enmities, strife, jealousies
Col. 3. 5. and covetousness, the which is *idolatry*
see *idols.*

Idols.—*A.V.* ¹*idolatry.*
Acts 15. 20. that they abstain from the pollutions of *idols*
29. abstain from things sacrificed to *idols.* 21. 25
17. 16. was provoked—as he beheld the city full of ¹*idols*
Rom. 2. 22. that abhorrest *idols*, dost thou rob temples ?
1 *Cor.* 8. 1. things sacrificed to *i.* 4, 10: 10. 19: *Rev.* 2. 14, 20
12. 2. ye were led away unto those dumb *idols*
2 *Cor.* 6. 16. what agreement hath a temple of God with *i.* ?
1 *Th.* 1. 9. and how ye turned unto God from *idols*
1 *Jno.* 5. 21. little children, guard yourselves from *idols*
Rev. 9. 20. should not worship devils, and the *idols* of gold

Ignorance.—*A.V.* ¹*ignorantly.*
Acts 3. 17. in *ignorance* ye did it, as did also your rulers
17. 23. What—ye worship in ¹*ignorance*, this set I forth
30. The times of *ignorance* therefore God overlooked
Eph. 4. 18. alienated from the life of God because of the *i.*
1 *Pet.* 1. 14. according to your former lusts in the time of
2. 15. put to silence the *ignorance* of foolish men [your *i.*

Ignorant.—*A.V.* ¹*know not,* ²*understand,* ³*unlearned.*
Acts 4. 13. perceived that they were unlearned and *i.* men
Rom. 1. 13. I would not have you *ignorant*, brethren. 11.
*. 1 *Cor.* 10. 1 ; 12. 1 : 2 *Cor.* 1. 8 : 1 *Th.* 4. 13
6. 3. Or are ye ¹*ignorant* that all we who were baptized
7. 1. Or are ye ¹*ignorant*, brethren (for I speak to men
10. 3. For being *ignorant* of God's righteousness ;
1 *Cor.* 14. 38. if any man is *ignorant*, let him be *ignorant*
2 *Cor.* 2. 11. Satan : for we are not *ignorant* of his devices
2 *Tim.* 2. 23. foolish and ³*ignorant* questionings refuse

171

IGNORANT

Heb. 5. 2. who can bear gently with the *ignorant* and erring
2 *Pet.* 2. 12. railing in matters whereof they are ²*ignorant*
3. 16. which the ⁵*ignorant* and unstedfast wrest
see forget.

Ignorantly.

1 *Tim.* 1. 13. because I did it *ignorantly* in unbelief
see ignorance.

Ill.—A.V. ¹evil.

Jno. 3. 20. every one that doeth ¹*ill* hateth the light
5. 29. they that have done ¹*ill*, unto—judgement
Rom. 13. 10. Love worketh no *ill* to his neighbour

Illuminated A.V.—see enlightened.

Image.

Mat. 22. 20. Whose is this *image*. *Mk.* 12. 16 ; *Lu.* 20. 24
Acts 19. 35. and of the *i.* which fell down from Jupiter?
Rom. 1. 23. incorruptible God for the likeness of an *image*
8. 29. foreordained to be conformed to the *i.* of his Son
1 *Cor.* 11. 7. forasmuch as he is the *image* and glory of God
15. 49. *image* of the earthy—bear the *i.* of the heavenly
2 *Cor.* 3, 18. transformed into the same *i.* from glory to
4. 4. of Christ, who is the *image* of God. *Col.* 1. 15
Col. 3. 10. after the *image* of him that created him
Heb. 1. 3. very *image* of his substance, and upholding all
10. 1. good things to come, not the very *i.* of the things
Rev. 13. 14. that they should make an *image* to the beast
15. to the *image* of the beast, that the *i.* of the beast
should both speak—*i.* of the beast should be killed
14. 9. worshippeth the beast and his *i.* 11: 16. 2: 19. 20
15. 2. victorious from the beast, and from his *image*
20. 4. such as worshipped not the beast, neither his *i.*

Imagination—s.

Lu. 1. 51. scattered the proud in the *i.* of their heart
2 *Cor.* 10. 5. casting down *imaginations*, and every high
see reasonings.

Imagine.

Acts 4. 25. And the peoples *imagine* vain things?

Imitate.—A.V. ¹follow.

2 *Th.* 3. 7. yourselves know how ye ought to ¹*imitate* us
9. ensample unto you, that ye should ¹*imitate* us
Heb. 13. 7. issue of their life, ¹*imitate* their faith
3 *Jno.* 11. Beloved, ¹*imitate* not that which is evil

Imitators.—A.V. ¹followers.

1 *Cor.* 4. 16. be ye ¹*imitators* of me. 11. ¹¹ ; *Phil.* 3. ¹¹⁷
Eph. 5. 1. Be ye therefore ¹*imitators* of God
1 *Th.* 1. 6. And ye became ¹*imitators* of us, and of the Lord
2. 14. became ¹*imitators* of the churches of God
Heb. 6. 12. but ¹*i.* of them who through faith and patience

Immanuel, Emmanuel, see proper names.

Immediately.—A.V. ¹by and by, ²presently, ³soon.

Mat. 21. 19. ²*immediately* the fig tree withered away
20. How did the fig tree ²*immediately* wither away?
Lu. 1. 64. his mouth was opened *i.*, and his tongue loosed
8. 44. and *immediately* the issue of her blood stanched
13. 13. *i.* she was made straight, and glorified God. 47
18. 43. And *immediately* he received his sight   [pear
19. 11. supposed that the kingdom of God was *i.* to ap-
21. 9. but the end is not ¹*immediately*
22. 60. *immediately*, while he yet spake, the cock crew

IMPRISONMENT

Acts 12. 23. And *i.* an angel of the Lord smote him
16. 26. and *immediately* all the doors were opened
Gal. 1. 16. *immediately* I conferred not with flesh and blood

Immortal A.V.—see incorruptible.

Immortality.

1 *Cor.* 15. 53. this mortal must put on *immortality*. 54
1 *Tim.* 6. 16. who only hath *immortality*, dwelling in light
see incorruption.

Immutability.

Heb. 6. 17. the *i.* of his counsel, interposed with an oath

Immutable.

Heb. 6. 18. that by two *immutable* things, in which it is

Impart.—A.V. ¹imparted.

Lu. 3. 11. two coats, let him *impart* to him that hath none
Rom. 1. 11. that I may *impart* unto you some spiritual gift
1 *Th.* 2. 8. pleased to ¹*i.* unto you, not the gospel of God only

Impediment.

Mk. 7. 32. one that was deaf, and had an *i.* in his speech

Impenitent.

Rom. 2. 5. after thy hardness and *i.* heart treasurest up

Implacable.—A.V. ¹truce breakers.

2 *Tim.* 3. 3. without natural affection, ¹*implacable*, slanderers

Implanted.—A.V. ¹engrafted.

Jas. 1. 21. receive with meekness the ¹*implanted* word

Implead A.V.—see accuse.

Importunity.

Lu. 11. 8. because of his *importunity* he will arise and give

Imposed.

Heb. 9. 10. ordinances, *imposed* until a time of reformation

Impossible.—A.V. ¹not possible.

Mat. 17. 20. and nothing shall be *impossible* unto you [27
19. 26. With men this is *impossible*. *Mk.* 10. 27 : *Lu.* 18.
Lu. 17. 1. It is *impossible* but that occasions of stumbling
Heb. 6. 6. it is *i.* to renew them again unto repentance
18. in which it is *impossible* for God to lie
10. 4. it is ¹*impossible* that the blood of bulls and goats
11. 6. without faith it is *i.* to be well-pleasing unto him
see void of power.

Imposters.—A.V. ¹seducers.

2 *Tim.* 3. 13. evil men and ¹*i.* shall wax worse and worse

Impotent.

Acts 4. 9. concerning a good deed done to an *impotent* man
14. 8. at Lystra there sat a certain man, *i.* in his feet
see sick.

Imprisoned.

Acts 22. 19. I *imprisoned* and beat in every synagogue

Imprisonment—s.

2 *Cor.* 6. 5. in stripes, in *imprisonments*, in tumults
Heb. 11. 36. yea, moreover of bonds and *imprisonment*

IMPULSE

Impulse.
Jas 3. 4. rudder, whither the *i.* of the steersman willeth

Impute—ing *A.V.—see reckon, reckoning.*

Imputed.
Rom. 5. 13. but sin is not *imputed* when there is no law
see reckoned, reckoneth.

Incense.—*A.V.* ¹*odours.*
Lu. 1. 10. praying without at the hour of *incense*
Rev. 5. 8. golden bowls full of ¹*i.*, which are the prayers
8. 3. and there was given unto him much *incense*
 4. the smoke of the *i.*, with the prayers of the saints
18. 13. spice, and ¹*i.*, and ointment, and frankincense
see altar, burn.

Inclosed.
Lu. 5. 6. they *inclosed* a great multitude of fishes

Incontinency.
1 *Cor.* 7. 5. that Satan tempt you not because of your *i.*

Incontinent *A.V.—see self-control.*

Incorruptible.—*A.V.* ¹*not corruptible,* ²*immortal,*
³*uncorruptible.*
Rom. 1. 23. and changed the glory of the ³*incorruptible* God
1 *Cor.* 9. 25. a corruptible crown ; but we an *incorruptible*
15. 52. trumpet shall sound, and the dead shall be raised *i.*
1 *Tim.* 1. 17. the King eternal, ²*incorruptible,* invisible
1 *Pet.* 1. 4. an inheritance *incorruptible,* and undefiled
23. not of corruptible seed, but of *incorruptible*
3. 4. ¹*incorruptible* apparel of a meek and quiet spirit

Incorruption.—*A.V.* ¹*immortality.*
Rom. 2. 7. seek for glory and honour and ¹*incorruption*
1 *Cor.* 15. 42. It is sown in corruption ; it is raised in *i.*
 50. neither doth corruption inherit *incorruption* [53
 54. when this corruptible shall have put on *incorruption.*
2 *Tim.* 1. 10. abolished death, and brought life and ¹*i.* to light

Increase.
Lu. 17. 5. apostles said unto the Lord, *Increase* our faith
Jno. 3. 30. He must *increase,* but I must decrease
1 *Cor.* 3. 6. Apollos watered ; but God gave the *increase.* 7
2 *Cor.* 9. 10. and *increase* the fruits of your righteousness
Eph. 4. 16. maketh the *increase* of the body unto the building
Col. 2. 19. and bands, increaseth with the *increase* of God
1 *Th.* 3. 12. Lord make you to *increase* and abound in love
see abound, proceed.

Increased.
Acts 9. 22. But Saul *increased* the more in strength
16. 5. the churches—*increased* in number daily
see advanced, gotten, growth, increasing, multiplied.

Increaseth.—*A.V.* ¹*abound.*
Phil. 4. 17. seek for the fruit that ¹*increaseth* to your account
Col. 2. 19. the body—*increaseth* with the increase of God

Increasing.—*A.V.* ¹*increased.*
Mk. 4. 8. yielded fruit, growing up and ¹*increasing*
Col. 1. 6. bearing fruit, and *i.*, as it doth in you also
10. and *increasing* in the knowledge of God

Incredible.
Acts 26. 8. Why is it judged *incredible* with you, if God
 doth raise the dead?

INHERIT

Indebted.
Lu. 11. 4. we ourselves also forgive every one that is *i.* to us

Indeed.—*A.V.* ¹*of a truth,* ²*verily.*
Mk. 9. 12. Elijah ²*indeed* cometh first, and restoreth
Rom. 2. 25. For circumcision ²*indeed* profiteth
1 *Cor.* 14. 25. declaring that God is among you ¹*indeed*
1 *Pet.* 1. 20. who was foreknown ²*indeed* before

Indignation.—*A.V.* ¹*displeased.*
Mat. 20. 24. moved with *i.* concerning the two. *Mk.* 10. ¹⁴¹
21. 15. saying, Hosanna—they were moved with ¹*i.*
26. 8. *i.*, saying, To what purpose is this waste? *Mk.* 14. 4
Mk. 10. 14. when Jesus saw it, he was moved with ¹*i.*
Lu. 13. 14. ruler of the synagogue, being moved with *i.*
Rom. 2. 8. unto them—shall be wrath and *indignation*
2 *Cor.* 7. 11. clearing of yourselves, yea, what *indignation*
see anger, fierceness, jealousy.

Indulgence.—*A.V.* ¹*liberty,* ²*satisfying.*
Acts 24. 23. [Paul] should have ¹*i.* ; and not to forbid
Col. 2. 23. are not of any value against the ²*i.* of the flesh

Inexcusable *A.V.—see excuse.*

Infants *A.V.—see babes.*

Inferior.
2 *Cor.* 12. 13. ye were made *i.* to the rest of the churches

Infidel *A.V.—see unbeliever.*

Infirmities.
Mat. 8. 17. Himself took our *i.*, and bare our diseases
Lu. 5. 15. to hear, and to be healed of their *infirmities*
 8. 2. healed of evil spirits and *infirmities,* Mary
Rom. 15. 1. strong ought to bear the *infirmities* of the weak
1 *Tim.* 5. 23. stomach's sake and thine often *infirmities*
Heb. 4. 15. be touched with the feeling of our *infirmities*
see diseases, infirmity, weakness—es.

Infirmity. *A.V.* ¹*infirmities.*
Lu. 13. 12. Woman, thou art loosed from thine *infirmity.* 11
Jno. 5. 5. had been thirty and eight years in his *infirmity*
Rom. 6. 19. because of the *infirmity* of your flesh
 8. 26. like manner the Spirit also helpeth our ¹*infirmity*
Gal. 4. 13. an *infirmity* of the flesh I preached
Heb. 5. 2. that he himself also is compassed with *infirmity*
 7. 28. law appointed men high priests, having *infirmity*

Inflicted.
2 *Cor.* 2. 6. punishment which was *inflicted* by the many

Informed.
Acts 21. 21. *informed* concerning thee, that thou teachest. 24
24. 1. they *informed* the governor against Paul. 25. 2, 15

Inhabiters *A.V.—see dwell, earth.*

Inherit-ed.—*A.V.* ¹*heir—s,* ²*obtained.*
Mat. 5. 5. Blessed are the meek ; for they shall *i.* the earth
19. 29. a hundredfold, and shall *inherit* eternal life
25. 34. *inherit* the kingdom prepared for you [18. 18
Mk. 10. 17. may *inherit* eternal life? *Lu.* 10. 25 ;
1 *Cor.* 6. 9. unrighteous shall not *inherit.* 10 ; *Gal.* 5. 21
15. 50. flesh and blood cannot *inherit* the kingdom of
 God ; neither doth corruption *inherit* incorruption
Gal. 4. 30. shall not ¹*inherit* with the son of the freewoman
Heb. 1. 4. hath ²*inherited* a more excellent name than they

INHERIT

Heb. 1. 14. for the sake of them that shall ¹*i.* salvation ?
6. 12. through faith and patience *inherit* the promises
12. 17. afterward desired to *i.* the blessing, he was re-
1 *Pet.* 3. 9. called, that ye should *inherit* a blessing [jected
Rev. 21. 7. He that overcometh shall *inherit* those things

Inheritance.—*A. V.* ¹*lot.*
Mat. 21. 38. let us kill him, and take his *inheritance*
Mk. 12. 7. and the *inheritance* shall be ours. *Lu.* 20. 14
Lu. 12. 13. bid my brother divide the *inheritance* with me
Acts 7. 5. he gave him none *i.* in it, no, not so much
13. 19. he gave them their land for an ¹*inheritance*
20. 32. the *i.* among all them that are sanctified. 26. 18
Gal. 3. 18. if the *i.* is of the law, it is no more of promise
Eph. 1. 14. an earnest of our *i.*, unto the redemption
18. the riches of the glory of his *i.* in the saints
5. 5. idolater, hath any *i.* in the kingdom of Christ
Col. 1. 12. meet to be partakers of the *i.* of the saints
3. 24. ye shall receive the recompense of the *inheritance*
Heb. 9. 15. called may receive the promise of the eternal *i.*
11. 8. place which he was to receive for an *inheritance*
1 *Pet.* 1. 4. unto an *inheritance* incorruptible, and undefiled
see heritage, possession.

Iniquity—ies.—*A. V.* ¹*unrighteousness.*
Mat. 7. 23. depart from me, ye that work *iniquity*
13. 41. things that cause stumbling, and them that do *i.*
23. 28. inwardly ye are full of hypocrisy and *iniquity*
24. 12. because *iniquity* shall be multiplied, the love
Lu. 13. 27. depart from me, all ye workers of *iniquity*
Acts 1. 18. obtained a field with the reward of his *i.*
3. 26. turning away every one of you from your *iniquities*
8. 23. gall of bitterness and in the bond of *iniquity*
Rom. 4. 7. Blessed are they whose *iniquities* are forgiven
6. 19. servants to uncleanness and to *iniquity* unto *i.*
2 *Cor.* 6. 14. what fellowship have righteousness and ¹*i.* ?
Tit. 2. 14. that he might redeem us from all *iniquity*
Heb. 1. 9. Thou hast loved righteousness, and hated *i.*
8. 12. For I will be merciful to their ¹*iniquities*
10. 17. sins and their *iniquities* will I remember no more
Jas. 3. 6. the world of *i.* among our members is the tongue
Rev. 18. 5. and God hath remembered her *iniquities*
see lawlessness, transgression, unrighteousness.

Injurious.
1 *Tim.* 1. 13. and *injurious* : howbeit I obtained mercy
Injured *A. V.*—*see wrong.*

Injury—ies.—*A. V.* ¹*hurt,* ²*harm,* ³*reproaches.*
Acts 27. 10. the voyage will be with ¹*injury* and much loss
21. and have gotten this ²*injury* and loss
2 *Cor.* 12. 10. I take pleasure in weaknesses, in ³*injuries*

Ink.
2 *Cor.* 3. 3. written not with *ink*, but with the Spirit
2 *Jno.* 12. I would not write them with paper and *i.* 3 *Jno.*13

Inn.
Lu. 2. 7. because there was no room for them in the *inn*
10. 34. brought him to an *inn*, and took care of him
Inner.—*A. V.* ¹*secret.*
Mat. 24. 26. Behold, he is in the ¹*inner* chambers [prison
Acts 16. 24. jailor cast them [Paul and Silas] into the *inner*
see chamber—s, inward.

Innocent.—*A. V.* ¹*simple.*
Mat. 27. 24. I am *i.* of the blood of this righteous man
Rom. 16. 18. fair speech they beguile the hearts of the *i.*
see blood.

Innumerable.
Heb. 11. 12. as the sand, which is by the sea shore, *i.*
12. 22. Jerusalem, and to *innumerable* hosts of angels
see thousands.

INSURRECTION

Inordinate *A. V.*—*see passion.*

Inquire—d.—*A. V.* ¹*ask—ed,* ²*demanded,* ³*enquire—d,*
⁴*manner of questions.*
Mat. 2. 4. he ²*i.* of them where the Christ should be born
Lu. 15. 26. called to him one of the servants, and ¹*i.*
18. 36. [blind man] ¹*inquired* what this meant
Jno. 4. 52. So he ²*i.* of them the hour when he began to
16. 19. Do ye ³*i.* among yourselves concerning this¦ amend
21. 12. none of the disciples durst ¹*i.* of him, Who art thou?
Acts 4. 7. they ¹*inquired,* By what power, or in what name
9. 11. ²*i.* in the house of Judas for one named Saul
21. 33. chief captain—²*i.* who he [Paul] was. 23. ³20
24. 20. I, being perplexed how to ⁴*i.* concerning these
2 *Cor.* 8. 23. Whether any ³*inquire* about Titus [things
see judge.

Inquiry.—*A. V.* ¹*enquiry.*
Acts 10. 17. having made ¹*inquiry* for Simon's house
Inside.—*A. V.* ¹*within.*
*Lu.*11.40. did not he that made the outside make the ¹*i.* also

Inscription.
Acts 17. 23. with this *inscription*, TO AN UNKNOWN GOD

Insolent.—*A. V.* ¹*despiteful.*
Rom. 1. 30. hateful to God, ¹*insolent*, haughty, boastful
Inspiration *A. V.*—*see inspired.*

Inspired.—*A. V.* ¹*inspiration.*
2 *Tim.* 3. 16. Every scripture ¹*i.* of God is also profitable

Instant.
Lu. 23. 23. they were *i.* with loud voices, asking—crucified
2 *Tim.* 4. 2. be *instant* in season, out of season ; reprove
see hour, stedfastly.

Instantly *A. V.*—*see earnestly.*
Instruct—ing.—*A. V.* ¹*teach,* ²*teaching.*
1 *Cor.*2.16. mind of the Lord, that he should *instruct* him ?
14. 19. with my understanding—I might ¹*instruct* others
Tit. 2. 12. ²*i.* us, to the intent that, denying ungodliness
see correcting.

Instructed.—*A. V.* ¹*learned,* ²*taught.*
Lu. 1. 4. the things wherein thou wast *instructed*
Acts 7. 22. Moses was ¹*i.* in all the wisdom of the Egyptians
18. 25. [Apollos] *instructed* in the way of the Lord [law
22. 3. ¹*instructed* according to the strict manner of the
Rom. 2. 18. are excellent, being *instructed* out of the law
see disciple, learned, put (forward).

Instruction.
2 *Tim.* 3. 16. for *instruction* which is in righteousness
Instructor—s *A. V.*—*see corrector, tutors.*

Instruments.
Rom. 6. 13. your members unto sin as *i.* of unrighteousness ; but—as *i.* of righteousness unto God

Insurrection—s.—*A. V.* ¹*sedition.*
Mk. 15. 7. Barabbas—that had made *insurrection*, men
who in the *i.* had committed murder. *Lu.* 23. ¹19
Lu. 23. 25. released him that for ¹*insurrection* and murder
Acts 24. 5. a mover of ¹*insurrections* among all the Jews
see rose (up).

174

INTEND

Intend—ing.—*A.V.* ¹*minding.*
Acts 5. 28. and *intend* to bring this man's blood upon us
12. 4. *i.* after the Passover to bring him [Peter] forth
20. 13. set sail for Assos, there *intending* to take in Paul
—¹*intending* himself to go by land
see about, desiring.

Intent—s.
Jno. 11. 15. I was not there, to the *intent* ye may believe
13. 28. knew for what *intent* he spake this unto him
Acts 9. 21. for this *intent*, that he might bring them bound
10. 29. with what *intent* ye sent for me [Peter]
1 *Cor.* 10. 6. the *intent* we should not lust after evil things
Eph. 3. 10. to the *intent* that now unto the principalities
Tit. 2. 12. the *i.* that, denying ungodliness and worldly lusts
Heb. 4. 12. to discern the thoughts and *intents* of the heart

Intercession—s.
Rom. 8. 26. but the Spirit himself maketh *intercession.* 27
34. Christ Jesus—who also maketh *intercession* for us
1 *Tim.* 2. 1. prayers, *i.*, thanksgivings, be made for all
Heb. 7. 25. he ever liveth to make *intercession* for them
see pleadeth.

Interest.—*A.V.* ¹*usury.*
Mat. 25. 27. received back mine own with ¹*i. Lu.* 19. ¹23

Interposed.—*A.V.* ¹*confirmed.*
Heb. 6. 17. immutability of his counsel, ¹*i.* with an oath

Interpret.—*A.V.* ¹*discern.*
Lu. 12. 56. ye know how to ¹*interpret* the face of the earth
—know not how to ¹*interpret* this time
1 *Cor.* 12. 30. do all speak with tongues ? do all *interpret* ?
14. 5. he that speaketh with tongues, except he *interpret*
13. speaketh in a tongue pray that he may *interpret*
27. and that in turn ; and let one *interpret*

Interpretation.—*A.V.* ¹*uttered.*
Jno. 1. 42 Cephas (which is by *interpretation*, Peter)
9. 7. Siloam (which is by *interpretation*, Sent)
Acts. 9. 36. Tabitha, which by *i.* is called Dorcas
13. 8. Elymas the sorcerer (for so—by *interpretation*)
1 *Cor.* 12. 10. to another the *interpretation* of tongues
14. 26. hath a tongue, hath an *interpretation*
Heb. 5. 11. hard of ¹*interpretation*, seeing ye are become
7. 2. being first, by *i.*, King of righteousness   [dull
2 *Pet.* 1. 20. no prophecy of scripture is of private *i.*

Interpreted.—*A.V.* ¹*expounded.*
Mat. 1. 23. Immanuel ; which is, being *i.*, God with us
Mk. 5. 41. being *interpreted*, Damsel, I say unto thee, Arise
15. 22. Golgotha, which is, being *i.*, The place of a skull
34. *i.*, My God, my God, why hast thou forsaken me ?
Lu. 24. 27. he ¹*interpreted* to them in all the scriptures
Jno. 1. 38. Rabbi (which is to say, being *i.*, Master)
41. Messiah (which is, being *interpreted*, Christ)
Acts 4. 36. Barnabas (—being *i.*, Son of exhortation)

Interpreter.
1 *Cor.* 14. 28. if there be no *i.*, let him keep silence

Interrogation.—*A.V.* ¹*answer.*
1 *Pet.* 3. 21. but the ¹*i.* of a good conscience toward God

ISLAND

Intreat—ed, Entreat—ed.—*A.V.* ¹*beseech,* ²*besought,*
³*called,* ⁴*desired,* ⁵*exhort,* ⁶*pray.*
Mat. 22. 6. his servants, and *entreated* them shamefully
Lu. 8. 31. they ²*intreated* him that he would not command them. ²32
15. 28. and his father came out, and *intreated* him
18. 32. and shall be mocked, and shamefully *entreated*
Acts 7. 6. bring them into bondage, and *entreat* them evil
24. 4. I ⁶*i.* thee to hear us of thy clemency a few words
28. 14. and were ⁴*i.* to tarry with them seven days
20. For this cause therefore did I ⁶*intreat* you to see
1 *Cor.* 4. 13. being defamed, we *intreat* : we are made as
2 *Cor.* 6. 1. we ¹*i.* also that ye receive not the grace of God
9. 5. I thought it necessary therefore to ⁵*i.* the brethren
10. 1. I Paul myself *intreat* you by the meekness and
1 *Th.* 2. 2. having suffered before, and been shamefully *e.*
Heb. 12. 19. which voice they that heard *i.* that no word
Jas. 3. 17. then peaceable, gentle, easy to be *i.*   [more
see beseech, entreated, exhort, handled, treated.

Intreating—s.—*A.V.* ¹*did beseech,* ²*desiring.*
Acts 9. 38. ²*intreating* him, Delay not to come on unto us
2 *Cor.* 5. 20. behalf of Christ, as though God were ¹*i.* by us

Intreaty.
2 *Cor.* 8. 4. us with much *intreaty* in regard of this grace

Intruding *A.V.—see dwelling in.*

Intrusted.—*A.V.* ¹*committed,* ¹*put in trust.*
Rom. 3. 2. that they were ¹*i.* with the oracles of God
1 *Cor.* 9. 17. I have a stewardship ¹*intrusted* to me
Gal. 2. 7. when they saw that I had been ¹*i.* with the gospel
1 *Th.* 2. 4. approved of God to be ²*i.* with the gospel
Tit. 1. 3. word in the message, wherewith I was ¹*intrusted*

Inventors.
Rom. 1. 30. insolent, haughty, boastful, *i.* of evil things

Invisible.
Rom. 1. 20. the *invisible* things of him since the creation
Col. 1. 15. who is the image of the *invisible* God
16. things visible and things *invisible*, whether thrones
1 *Tim.* 1. 17. unto the King eternal, incorruptible, *invisible*
Heb. 11. 27. he endured, as seeing him who is *invisible*

Inward.—*A.V.* ¹*inner.*
Lu. 11. 39. *inward* part is full of extortion and wickedness
Rom. 7. 22. I delight in the law of God after the *i.* man
2 *Cor.* 4. 16. yet our *inward* man is renewed day by day
7. 15. his *inward* affection is more abundantly toward you
Eph. 3. 16. with power through his Spirit in the ¹*i.* man

Inwardly.
Mat. 7. 15. sheep's clothing, but *i.* are ravening wolves
Rom. 2. 29. but he is a Jew, which is one *inwardly*

Irksome.—*A.V.* ¹*grievous.*
Phil. 3. 1. to me indeed is not ¹*i.*, but for you it is safe

Iron.
Acts 12. 10. they came unto the *iron* gate that leadeth
1 *Tim.* 4. 2. in their own conscience as with a hot *iron*
Rev. 2. 27. rule them with a rod of *iron.* 12. 5 ; 19. 15
9. 9. had breastplates, as it were breastplates of *iron*
18. 12. most precious wood, and of brass, and *iron*

Island.—*A.V.* ¹*isle.*
Acts 13. 6. gone through the whole ¹*island* unto Paphos
27. 16. under the lee of a small *island* called Clauda

175

ISLAND

Acts 27. 26. Howbeit we must be cast upon a certain *i.*
28. 1. then we knew that the *island* was called Melita
7. to the chief man of the *island*, named Publius
9. had diseases in the *island* came, and were cured
11. ship of Alexandria, which had wintered in the ¹*i.*
Rev. 6. 14. every mountain and *island* were moved
16. 20. every *i.* fled away, and the mountains were not

Isle.
Rev. 1. 9. I John—was in the *isle* that is called Patmos
see island.

Issue.—*A.V.* ¹*end.*
Mat. 9. 20. an *i.* of blood twelve years. *Mk.* 5. 25 : *Lu.* 8.43
Lu. 8. 44. immediately the *issue* of her blood stanched
Heb. 13. 7. considering the ¹*issue* of their life, imitate
see seed.

Issued *A.V.*—*see proceeded, proceedeth.*

Itching.
2 *Tim.* 4. 3. having *i.* ears, will heap to themselves teachers

Ivory.
Rev. 18. 12. and all thyine wood, and every vessel of *ivory*

J.

Jacinth.
Rev. 21. 20 the eleventh, *jacinth* ; the twelfth, amethyst
see hyacinth.

Jailor.—*A.V.* ¹*keeper.*
Acts 16. 23. charging the *jailor* to keep them safely
27. And the ¹*jailor* being roused out of sleep
36. And the ¹*jailor* reported the words to Paul

Jangling *A.V.*—*see talking.*

Jasper.
Rev. 4. 3. he that sat was to look upon like a *jasper* stone
21. 11. as it were a *jasper* stone, clear as crystal
18. And the building of the wall thereof was *jasper*
19. The first foundation was *jasper*

Jealous.
2 *Cor.* 11. 2. For I am *j.* over you with a godly jealousy

Jealousy—ies.—*A.V.* ¹*emulation—s,* ²*envy—ies,* ³*envying—s,* ⁴*indignation,* ⁵*seditions.*
Acts 5. 17. Sadducees), and they were filled with ⁴*jealousy*
7. 9. patriarchs, moved with ²*j.* against Joseph, sold him
13. 45. Jews saw the multitudes, they were filled with ²*j.*
17. 5. Jews, being moved with ²*jealousy*, took unto them
Rom. 10. 19. Moses saith, I will provoke you to *jealousy*
11. 11. unto the Gentiles, for to provoke them to *jealousy*
14. if by any means I may provoke to ¹*jealousy* them
13. 13. chambering and wantonness, not in strife and ³*j.*
1 *Cor.* 3. 3. is among you ³*j.* and strife, are ye not carnal
10. 22. Or do we provoke the Lord to *jealousy* ?
2 *Cor.* 11. 2. For I am jealous over you with a godly *j.*
12. 20. strife, ³*jealousy,* wraths, factions, backbitings
Gal. 5. 20. enmities, strife, ¹*jealousies,* wraths
Jas. 3. 14. if ye have bitter ³*jealousy* and faction. ⁸16

Jeopardy.
Lu. 8. 23. filling with water, and were in *jeopardy*
1 *Cor.* 15. 30. why do we also stand in *jeopardy* every hour ?

JOY

Jesting.
Eph. 5. 4. foolish talking, or *jesting*, which are not befitting

Join.—*A.V.* ¹*keep company.*
Acts 5. 13. of the rest durst no man *join* himself to them
8. 29. Philip, Go near, and *join* thyself to this chariot
9. 26. he [Saul] assayed to *join* himself to the disciples
10. 28. unlawful thing for a—Jew to ¹*join* himself

Joined.—*A.V.* ¹*assented,* ²*married.*
Mat. 19. 6. What therefore God hath *j.* together. *Mk.* 10. 9
Lu. 15. 15. and *joined* himself to one of the citizens
Acts 5. 36. about four hundred, *joined* themselves
18. 7. whose house *joined* hard to the synagogue
24. 9. the Jews also ¹*joined* in the charge, affirming
Rom. 7. 3. she be ²*joined* to another man—²*j.* to another
4. ye should be ²*joined* to another, even to him
1 *Cor.* 6. 16. he that is *joined* to a harlot is one body ?
17. he that is *joined* unto the Lord is one spirit
see cleave, framed, perfected.

Joint—s.
Eph. 4. 16. knit together through that which every *j.* supplieth
Col. 2. 19. knit together through the *j.* and bands
Heb. 4. 12. of both *joints* and marrow, and quick to discern

Joint-heirs.—*A.V.* ¹*heirs.*
Rom. 8. 17. heirs of God, and *joint-heirs* with Christ
1 *Pet.* 3. 7. as being also ¹*joint-heirs* of the grace of life

Jot.
Mat. 5. 18. one *jot* or one tittle shall in no wise pass away

Journey.—*A.V.* ¹*way.*
Mat. 10. 10. no wallet for your *journey*, neither two coats
25. 15. several ability ; and he went on his *journey*
Mk. 6. 8. should take nothing for their *journey*. *Lu.* 9. 3.
Lu. 2. 44. to be in the company, they went a day's *journey*
11. 6. a friend of mine is come to me from a *journey*
15. 13. took his [prodigal] *journey* into a far country
Jno. 4. 6. Jesus—wearied with his *journey*, sat thus
Acts 1. 12. nigh unto Jerusalem, a sabbath day's *j.* off
10. 9. as they were on their *journey*, and drew nigh
21. 5. we departed and went on our ¹*journey*
22. 6. as I made my *journey*, and drew nigh unto Damascus
Rom. 15. 24. I hope to see you in my [Paul] *journey*
1 *Cor.* 16. 6. ye may set me [Paul] forward on my *journey*
11. set him [Timothy] forward on his *journey* in peace
2 *Cor.* 1. 16. to be set forward on my [Paul] ¹*j.* unto Judæa
Tit. 3. 13. Zenas the lawyer and Apollos on their *journey*
3 *Jno.* 6. set forward on their *journey* worthily of God
see go, prospered, sojourning.

Journeyed.—*A.V.* ¹*went.*
Lu. 10. 33. Samaritan, as he *journeyed*, came where he was
Acts 9. 3. as he *j.*—he drew nigh unto Damascus. 22. ¹5
7. men that *journeyed* with him stood speechless. 26. 13
26. 12. as I ¹*journeyed* to Damascus with the authority

Journeying—s.
Lu. 13. 22. teaching, and *journeying* on unto Jerusalem
2 *Cor.* 11. 26. in *journeyings* often, in perils of rivers

Joy.—*A.V.* ¹*gladness,* ²*joyful,* ³*joyfulness.*
Mat. 2. 10. the star, they rejoiced with exceeding great *joy*
13. 20. straightway with *j.* receiveth it. *Mk.* 4. ¹16 : *Lu.* 8. 13
44. in his *joy* he goeth and selleth all that he hath
25. 21. enter thou into the *joy* of thy Lord. 23
28. 8. quickly from the tomb with fear and great *joy*
Lu. 1. 14. And thou shalt have *joy* and gladness
44. the babe leaped in my womb for *joy*
2. 10. I bring you good tidings of great *joy*

176

JOY

Lu. 6. 23. Rejoice in that day, and leap for *joy*
10. 17. And the seventy returned with *joy*, saying
15. 7. so there shall be *joy* in heaven over one sinner
10. there is *joy* in the presence of the angels of God
24. 41. while they still disbelieved for *joy*, and wondered
52. and returned to Jerusalem with great *joy*
Jno. 3. 29. this my *joy* therefore is fulfilled
15. 11. my *joy* may be in you, and that your *joy* may be
16. 20. but your sorrow shall be turned into *joy*
21. for the *joy* that a man is born into the world
22. and your *joy* no one taketh away from you
24. ask, and ye shall receive, that your *j.* may be fulfilled
17. 13. may have my *joy* fulfilled in themselves
Acts 8. 8. And there was much *joy* in that city
12. 14. Rhoda—opened not the gate for ¹*joy*
13. 52. disciples were filled with *j.* and with the Holy Ghost
15. 3. and they caused great *joy* unto all the brethren
Rom 14. 17. and peace and *joy* in the Holy Ghost
15. 13. fill you with all *joy* and peace in believing
32. may come unto you in *joy* through the will of God
2 *Cor.* 1. 24. over your faith, but are helpers of your *joy*
2. 3. confidence in you all, that my *joy* is the *joy* of you all
7. 4. I overflow with ²*joy* in all our affliction
13. joyed the more exceedingly for the *joy* of Titus
8. 2. the abundance of their *joy* and their deep poverty
Gal. 5. 22. But the fruit of the Spirit is love, *joy*, peace
Phil. 1. 4. making my supplication with *joy*, for your
25. with you all, for your progress and *joy* in the faith
2. 2. fulfil ye my *joy*, that ye be of the same mind
17. service of your faith, I *joy*, and rejoice with you all
18. in the same manner do ye also *joy*, and rejoice
29. Receive him therefore in the Lord with all ¹*joy*
4. 1. my *joy* and crown, so stand fast in the Lord
Col. 1. 11. unto all patience and longsuffering with ²*joy*
1 *Th.* 1. 6. in much affliction, with *joy* of the Holy Ghost
19. what is our hope, or *joy*, or crown of glorying?
20. For ye are our glory and our *joy*
3. 9. for all the *joy* wherewith we *joy* for your sakes
2 *Tim.* 1. 4. thy tears, that I may be filled with *joy*
Philem. 7. I had much *joy* and comfort in thy love
20. Yea, brother, let me have *joy* of thee in the Lord
Heb. 12. 2. who for the *joy* that was set before him
13. 17. they may do this with *joy*, and not with grief
Jas. 1. 2. Count it all *joy*—when ye fall into manifold
4. 9. be turned to mourning, and your *joy* to heaviness
1 *Pet.* 1. 8. ye rejoice greatly with *joy* unspeakable
4. 13. ye may rejoice with exceeding *joy*
1 *Jno.* 1. 4. we write, that our *joy* may be fulfilled
2 *Jno.* 12. face to face, that your *joy* may be fulfilled
3 *Jno.* 4. Greater *joy* have I none than this, to hear
Jude 24. without blemish in exceeding *joy*
see gladness, rejoice.

Joyed—ing.
2 *Cor.* 7. 13. we *joyed* the more—for the joy of Titus
Col. 2. 5. in the spirit, *joying* and beholding your order
see rejoice.

Joyful *A.V.*—see joy.

Joyfully.
Lu. 19. 6. came down, and received him *joyfully*
Heb. 10. 34. took *joyfully* the spoiling of your possessions

Joyfulness.—*A.V.* see joy.

Joyous.
Heb. 12. 11. chastening seemeth for the present to be not *j.*

JUDGED

Judge—s.
Mat. 5. 25. the adversary deliver thee to the *judge*, and the *judge* deliver thee to the officer. *Lu.* 12. 58
12. 27. therefore shall they be your *judges*. *Lu.* 11. 19
Lu. 12. 14. who made me a *judge* or a divider over you?
18. 2. There was in a city a *judge*, which feared not
6. Hear what the unrighteous *judge* saith
Acts 7. 27 Who made thee a ruler and a *j.* over us? 35
10. 42. of God to be the *Judge* of quick and dead
13. 20. he gave them *judges* until Samuel the prophet
18. 15. I am not minded to be a *judge* of these matters
24. 10. hast been of many years a *j.* unto this nation
2 *Tim.* 4. 8. of the Lord, the righteous *judge*, shall give to me
Heb. 12. 23. to God the *Judge* of all, and to the spirits
Jas. 2. 4. and become *judges* with evil thoughts?
4. 11. thou art not a doer of the law, but a *judge*
12. One only is the lawgiver and *judge*, even he
5. 9. behold, the *judge* standeth before the doors

Judge (verb).—*A.V.* ¹condemn, ²enquire, ³judged, ⁴judgeth, ⁵judgements.

Mat. 7. 1. *Judge* not, that ye be not *judged*. *Lu.* 6. 37
2. For with what judgement ye *j.*, ye shall be judged
Lu. 12. 57. of yourselves *judge* ye not what is right?
19. 22. Out of thine own mouth will I *judge* thee
Jno. 3. 17. not the Son into the world to ¹*judge* the world
5. 22. neither doth the Father ⁴*judge* any man
30. as I hear, I *judge* : and my judgement is righteous
7. 24. *Judge* not according to appearance, but *judge*
51. Doth our law *judge* a man, except it first hear
8. 15. Ye *judge* after the flesh; I *judge* no man
16. Yea and if I *judge*, my judgement is true [you
26. I have many things to speak and to *j.* concerning
12. 47. I *judge* him not; for I came not to *j.* the world
48. the same shall *judge* him in the last day [law
18 31 Take him yourselves, and *j.* him according to your
Acts 4. 19. hearken unto you rather than unto God, *j.* ye
7. 7. nation to which they shall be in bondage will I *j.*
13. 46. and *judge* yourselves unworthy of eternal life
17. 31. appointed a day, in the which he will *j.* the world
23. 3. sittest thou to *judge* me according to the law
15. though ye would ²*judge* of his case more exactly
Rom. 2. 16. day when God shall *judge* the secrets of men
27. if it fulfil the law, *judge* thee, who with the letter
3. 6. for then how shall God *judge* the world?
11. 3. let not him that eateth not *judge* him that eateth
10 But thou, why dost thou *judge* thy brother?
13. Let us not therefore *judge*—but *judge* ye this rather
1 *Cor.* 4. 3. yea, I *judge* not mine own self
5. Wherefore *judge* nothing before the time
5. 12. Do not ye *judge* them that are within
6. 2. saints shall *j.* the world?—are ye unworthy to *j.*
3. Know ye not that we shall *judge* angels?
4. If then ye have to ⁵*judge*—do ye set them to *judge*
10. 15. I speak as to wise men; *judge* ye what I say
11. 13. *Judge* ye in yourselves: is it seemly that a woman
2 *Cor.* 5. 14. we thus *judge*, that one died for all, therefore
Col. 2. 16. Let no man therefore *judge* you in meat
2 *Tim.* 4. 1. who shall *j.* the quick and the dead. 1 *Pet.* 4. 5
Heb. 10. 30. The Lord shall *judge* his people
13. 4. fornicators and adulterers God will *judge*
Rev. 6. 10. dost thou not *judge* and avenge our blood
16. 5. thou Holy One, because thou didst thus ³*judge*
19. 11. in righteousness he doth *judge* and make war
see decide, discern—ed, judgment—ing.

Judged.—*A.V.* ¹avenged, ²condemned, ³damned, ⁴discerned, ⁵judgeth, ⁶thought.

Mat. 7. 1. Judge not, that ye be not *judged*. *Lu.* 6. 37
2. For with what judgement ye judge, ye shall be *j.*

JUDGED

Lu. 7. 43. he said unto him, Thou hast rightly *judged*
Jno. 3. 18. He that believeth on him is not *ᵃjudged*: he
　　 that believeth not hath been *ᵃjudged* already
16. 11. because the prince of this world hath been *judged*
Acts 16. 15. If ye have *judged* me to be faithful to the Lord
25. 9. there he *judged* of these things before me ? 20
10. Cæsar's judgement-seat, where I ought to be *judged*
26. 6. stand here to be *judged* for the hope of the promise
8. Why is it *ᵃjudged* incredible with you, if God
Rom. 2. 12 sinned under law shall be *judged* by law
3 7 why am I also still *judged* as a sinner ?
1 *Cor.* 2. 14. know them, because they are spiritually *ᵗj.*
15. and he himself is *judged* of no man
4. 3. a very small thing that I should be *judged* of you
5. 3 have already, as though I were present, *j.* him
6. 2. and if the world is *judged* by you, are ye unworthy
10. 29. there why is my liberty *j.* by another conscience ?
11. 31. if we discerned ourselves, we should not be *j.*
32. when we are *judged*, we are chastened of the Lord
14. 24. he is reproved by all, he is *judged* by all
2 *Th.* 2. 12. all might be *ᵃjudged* who believed not the truth
Heb. 10. 29. shall he be *ᵃjudged* worthy, who hath trodden
Jas. 2. 12. as men that are to be *judged* by a law of liberty
5. 9. Murmur not, brethren—that ye be not *ᵃjudged*
1 *Pet.* 4. 6. that they might be *judged* according to men
Rev. 11. 18. and the time of the dead to be *judged*
18. 8. for strong is the Lord God which *ᵃjudged* her
20. for God hath *ᵈjudged* your judgement on her
19. 2. for he hath *judged* the great harlot
20. 12. dead were *j.* out of the things which were written
13. were *judged* every man according to their works
　　 see counted, judge.

Judgement—s.—*A V.* ¹*accusation,* ²*advice,* ⁸*concluded,*
⁴*condemnation,* ⁵*damnation,* ⁶*guilty,* ⁷*judged,* ⁸*sentence.*

Mat. 5. 21. shall be in danger of the *judgement.* 22
7. 2. For with what *j.*, yo judge, ye shall be judged
12. 18. And he shall declare *judgement* to the Gentiles
20. Till he send forth *judgement* unto victory
41. men of Nineveh shall stand up in the *j. Lu.* 11. 32
42 queen of the south shall rise up in the *j. Lu.* 11. 31
23. 23. weightier matters of the law, *judgement,* and mercy
33. how shall ye escape the *ᵟjudgement* of hell?
Mk. 13. 11. when they lead you to *j.*, and deliver you
Lu. 10. 14. more tolerable for Tyre and Sidon in the *j.*
11. 42. and pass over *judgement* and the love of God
Jno. 3. 19. is the *ᵍj.*, that the light is come into the world
5. 22. but he hath given all *judgement* unto the Son
24. hath eternal life, and cometh not into *⁴judgement*
27. and he gave him authority to execute *judgement*
29. have done ill, unto the resurrection of *⁵judgement*
30. and my *judgement* is righteous
7. 24. to appearance, but judge righteous *judgement*
8. 16. Yea and if I judge, my *judgement* is true
9. 39. For *judgement* came I into this world
12. 31. Now is the *judgement* of this world
16. 8. of sin, and of righteousness, and of *judgement*
11. of *j.*, because the prince of this world hath been
Acts 8. 33. In his humiliation his *judgement* was taken away
15. 19. Wherefore my *ᵍj.* is, that we trouble not them
21. 25. giving *ᵍj.* that they should keep themselves from
24. 25. and the *judgement* to come, Felix was terrified
Rom. 2. 2. we know that the *j.* of God is according to truth
3. that thou shalt escape the *judgement* of God?
5. and revelation of the righteous *judgement* of God
3. 4. And mightest prevail when thou comest into *ᵍj.*
10. all the world may be brought under the *ᵍj.* of God
5. 16. for the *judgement* came of one unto condemnation
18. So then as through one trespass the *judgement* came

JUDGING

Rom. 11. 33. how unsearchable are his *judgements*
13. 2. they that withstand shall receive to themselves *⁵j.*
1 *Cor.* 1. 10. in the same mind and in the same *judgement*
4. 3. that I should be judged of you, or of man's *judgement*
7. 25. give my *judgement,* as one that hath obtained mercy
40. happier if she abide as she is, after my *judgement*
11. 29. eateth and drinketh *⁵judgement* unto himself
34. that your coming together be not unto *⁴judgement*
2 *Cor.* 8. 10. herein I give my *²j.* ; for this is expedient
Gal. 5. 10. he that troubleth you shall bear his *judgement*
2 *Th.* 1. 5. is a manifest token of the righteous *j.* of God
1 *Tim.* 5. 24. sins are evident, going before unto *judgement*
Heb. 6. 2. resurrection of the dead, and of eternal *judgement*
9. 27. once to die, and after this cometh *judgement*
10. 27. but a certain fearful expectation of *judgement*
Jas. 2. 13. *j.* is without mercy—mercy glorieth against *j.*
3. 1. knowing that we shall receive heavier *⁴judgement*
5. 12. your nay, nay; that ye fall not under *⁴judgement*
1 *Pet.* 4. 17. For the time is come for *judgement* to begin
2 *Pet.* 2. 4. to pits of darkness, to be reserved unto *judgement*
11. bring not a railing *¹judgement* against them. *Jude* 9
Jude 6. under darkness unto the *judgement* of the great day
15. to execute *judgement* upon all, and to convict all
Rev. 14. 7. for the hour of his *judgement* is come
16. 7. true and righteous are thy *judgements.* 19. 2
17. 1. I will shew thee the *judgement* of the great harlot
18. 10. for in one hour is thy *judgement* come
20. for God *judged* your *judgement* on her
20. 4 they sat upon them, and *j.* was given unto them
　　 see acts, day, discernment, judged, ordinance, righteous, sentence.

Judgement-hall *A.V.—see palace.*

Judgement-seat—s.

Mat. 27. 19. was sitting on the *judgement-seat. Jno.* 19. 13
Acts 18. 12. against Paul, and brought him before the *j.-s.*
16. And he drave them from the *judgement seat*
17. and beat him [Sosthenes] before the *judgement-seat*
25. 6. on the *j.-s.*, and commanded Pau! to be brought
10. I am standing before Cæsar's *judgement-seat*
17 but on the next day sat down on the *j.-s.* [Festus]
Rom. 14. 10. all stand before the *judgement-seat* of God
2 *Cor.* 5. 10. manifest before the *judgement-seat* of Christ
Jas. 2. 6. and themselves drag you before the *j.-seats* ?

Judgest.—*A.V.* ¹*judge.*

Rom. 2. 1. thou art that *judgest*: for wherein thou *judgest*
　　 —thou that *judgest* dost practise the same things
3. O man, who *judgest* them that practise such things
14. 4. Who art thou that *judgest* the servant of another ?
Jas. 4. 11. if thou *¹judgest* the law, thou art not a doer
12. who art thou that *judgest* thy neighbour ?

Judgeth.—*A.V.* ¹*condemneth.*

Jno. 8. 50. there is one that seeketh and *judgeth*
12. 48. receiveth not my sayings, hath one that *j.* him
Rom. 14. 22. Happy is he that *¹judgeth* not himself
1 *Cor.* 2. 15. But he that is spiritual *judgeth* all things
4. 4. but he that *judgeth* me is the Lord
5. 13. whereas them that are without God *judgeth* ?
Jas. 4. 11. *judgeth* his brother—and *judgeth* the law
1 *Pet.* 1. 17. who without respect of persons *judgeth*
2. 23. committed himself to him that *judgeth* righteously
　　 see judge, judged.

Judging.—*A.V.* ¹*judge.*

Mat. 19. 28. *judging* the twelve tribes of Israel. *Lu.* 22. 30
1 *Cor.* 5. 12. have I to do with *¹j.* them that are without?

JURISDICTION

Jurisdiction.
Lu. 23. 7. knew that he was of Herod's *jurisdiction*

Just.
Mat. 5. 45. and sendeth rain on the *just* and the unjust
Lu. 1. 17. disobedient to walk in the wisdom of the *just*
14. 14. be recompensed in the resurrection of the *just*
Acts 24. 15. shall be a resurrection both of the *j.* and unjust
Rom. 2. 13. for not the hearers of a law are *j.* before God
3. 8. whose condemnation is *just*
26. that he might himself be *just*, and the justifier
Phil. 4. 8. whatsoever things are *just*, whatsoever things
Col. 4. 1. render unto your servants that which is *just*
Tit. 1. 8. a lover of good, soberminded, *j.*, holy, temperate
Heb. 2. 2. received a *just* recompense of reward
12. 23. and to the spirits of *just* men made perfect
see righteous.

Just One *A.V.—see Righteous One (proper names).*

Justice.—*A.V.* ¹*vengeance.*
Acts 28. 4. yet ¹*Justice* hath not suffered to live

Justification.
Rom. 4. 25. and was raised for our *justification*
5. 16. free gift came of many trespasses unto *justification*
18. free gift came unto all men to *justification* of life

Justified.—*A.V.* ¹*freed.*
Mat. 11. 19. And wisdom is *j.* by her works. Lu. 7. 35
12. 37. For by thy words thou shalt be *justified*
Lu. 7. 29. and the publicans, *justified* God, being baptized
18. 14. This man went down to his house *justified*
Acts 13. 39. that believeth is *j.*—could not be *j.* by the law
Rom. 2. 13. but the doers of a law shall be *justified*
3. 4. That thou mightest be *justified* in thy words
20. by the works of the law shall no flesh be *j. Gal.* 2. 16
24. being *justified* freely by his grace. *Tit.* 3. 7
28. We reckon therefore that a man is *justified* by faith
4. 2. For if Abraham was *justified* by works, he hath
5. 1. Being therefore *justified* by faith, let us have peace
9. being now *justified* by his blood, shall we be saved
6. 7. for he that hath died is ¹*justified* from sin
8. 30. he also *j.*: and whom he *j.*, them he also glorified
1 Cor. 4. 4. nothing against myself; yet am I not hereby *j.*
6. 11. but ye were *j.* in the name of the Lord Jesus Christ
Gal. 2. 16. a man is not *justified* by the works—*j.* by faith
17. if, while we sought to be *justified* in Christ
3. 11. no man is *justified* by the law in the sight of God
24. bring us unto Christ, that we might be *j.* by faith
5. 4. ye who would be *justified* by the law; ye are fallen
1 Tim. 3. 16. He who was—*justified* in the spirit
Jas. 2. 21. Was not Abraham our father *justified* by works
25. was not also Rahab the harlot *justified* by works

Justifier.
Rom. 3. 26. and the *justifier* of him that hath faith in Jesus

Justifieth.
Rom. 4. 5. but believeth on him that *justifieth* the ungodly
8. 33. to the charge of God's elect? It is God that *j.*

Justify.
Lu. 10. 29. he, desiring to *justify* himself, said unto Jesus
16. 15. Ye are they that *j.* yourselves in the sight of men
Rom. 3. 30. and he shall *justify* the circumcision by faith
Gal. 3. 8. foreseeing that God would *justify* the Gentiles

KEEPETH

Justly.
Lu. 23. 41. we indeed *justly*; for we receive the due reward
see righteously.

K.

Keep.—*A.V.* ¹*believe,* ²*beware,* ³*hold,* ⁴*kept,* ⁵*reserve.*
Mat. 19. 17. enter into life, *keep* the commandments
26. 18. My time is at hand; I *keep* the passover
Mk. 7. 9 that ye may *keep* your tradition
Lu. 11. 28. are they that hear the word of God, and *k.* it
12. 15. Take heed, and ²*k.* yourselves from—covetousness
19. 43. compass thee round, and *keep* thee in on every side
Jno. 8. 51. a man *k.* my word, he shall never see death. 52
55. but I know him, and *keep* his word
12. 7. Suffer her to ⁴*k.* it against the day of my burying
47. if a man hear my sayings, and ¹*keep* them not
14. 15. If ye love me, ye will *keep* my commandments
23. If a man love me, he will *keep* my word
15. 10. If ye *k.* my commandments, ye shall abide in my
20. if they kept my word, they will *keep* yours also
17. 11. *k.* them in thy name which thou hast given me
15. but that thou shouldest *k.* them from the evil one
Acts 5. 3. and to *keep* back part of the price of the land?
15. 5. and to charge them to *keep* the law of Moses
20. from which if ye *keep* yourselves, it shall be well
16. 4. they delivered them the decrees for to *keep*
23. charging the jailor to *k.* them [Paul and Silas] safely
21. 25. *keep* themselves from things sacrificed to idols
Rom. 2. 26. uncircumcision *k.* the ordinances of the law
1 Cor. 5. 8. let us *keep* the feast, not with old leaven
11. I write unto you not to *keep* company, if any man
7. 37. determined—to *keep* his own virgin daughter
14. 28. let him *keep* silence in the church
30. revelation be made to another—let the first ³*k.* silence
34. Let the women *keep* silence in the churches
2 Cor. 11. 9. burdensome unto you, and so will I *k.* myself
Gal. 6. 13. receive circumcision do themselves *keep* the law
Eph. 4. 3. giving diligence to *keep* the unity of the Spirit
1 Tim. 5. 22. of other men's sins: *keep* thyself pure
6. 14. thou *keep* the commandment, without spot
Jas. 1. 27. and to *keep* himself unspotted from the world
2. 10. For whosoever shall *keep* the whole law, and yet
2 Pet. 2. 9. to ⁵*keep* the unrighteous under punishment
1 Jno. 2. 3. we know him, if we *keep* his commandments
3. 22. we receive of him, because we *k.* his commandments
5. 3. is the love of God, that we *keep* his commandments
Jude 21. *keep* yourselves in the love of God
Rev. 1. 3. prophecy, and *keep* the things which are written
3. 3. received and didst hear; and ³*keep* it, and repent
8. didst ⁴*keep* my word, and didst not deny my name
10. thou didst ⁴*keep* the word of my patience, I also
will *keep* thee from the hour of trial
12. 17. rest of her seed which *keep* the commandments
14. 12. saints, they that *k.* the commandments of God
22. 9. with them which *keep* the words of this book
see buffet, door, guard, hold, join, kept.

Keepers.
Acts 5. 23. safety, and the *keepers* standing at the doors
see door watchers, guards, jailors, workers.

Keepest *A.V.—see keeping.*

Keepeth.
Jno. 9. 16. not from God, because he *k.* not the sabbath
14. 21. He that hath my commandments, and *k.* them
24. He that loveth me not *keepeth* not my words

KEEPETH

1 Jno. 2. 4. He that saith, I know him, and k. not his
 5. whoso keepeth his word, in him verily hath the love
 3. 24. he that keepeth his commandments abideth in him
 5. 18. but he that was begotten of God keepeth him
Rev. 2. 26. he that overcometh, and he that k. my works
 16. 15. Blessed is he that watcheth, and k. his garments
 22. 7. that k. the words of the prophecy of this book
   see doeth, guardeth.

Keeping.—A.V. ¹keepest, ²kept.

Lu. 2. 8. and keeping watch by night over their flock
Acts 21. 24. thou thyself also walkest orderly, ¹k the law
 22. 20. I also was—²k. the garments of them that slew
1 Cor. 7. 19. but the keeping of the commandments of God

Kept.—A.V. ¹keep, ²observed, ³preserved, ⁴retained,
 ⁵reserved.

Mk. 6. 20. righteous man and a holy, and ²kept him safe
 9. 10. they k. the saying, questioning among themselves
Lu. 2. 19. But Mary kept all these sayings, pondering. 51
 8. 29. and he was k. under guard, and bound with chains
 19. 20. thy pound, which I kept laid up in a napkin
Jno. 2. 10. thou hast kept the good wine until now
 15. 10. even as I have kept my Father's commandments
 20. if they kept my word, they will keep yours also
 17. 6. thou gavest them to me; and they have k. thy word
 12. I k. them in thy name which thou hast given me
 18. 16. went out and spake unto her that kept the door
 17. The maid therefore that kept the door saith
Acts 5. 2. and kept back part of the price, his wife also
 7. 53. law as it was ordained by angels, and kept it not
 9. 33. Æneas, which had kept his bed eight years
 12. 5. Peter therefore was kept in the prison
 6. and guards before the door kept the prison
 15. 12. And all the multitude kept silence
 23. 35. and he commanded him to be kept. 25. 21
 24. 23. order to the centurion that he should be ¹kept in
 25. 4. Paul was kept in charge at Cæsarea [charge
 21. But when Paul had appealed to be ²kept
Rom. 16. 25. mystery which hath been kept in silence
2 Cor. 11. 9. I k. myself from being burdensome unto you
Gal. 3. 23. before faith came, we were kept in ward
2 Tim. 4. 7. I have finished the course, I have k. the faith
Philem 13. [Onesimus] whom I would fain have ⁴k. with me
Heb. 11. 28. By faith he kept the passover
Jas. 5. 4. which is of you kept back by fraud
Jude 1. beloved in God the Father, and ²k. for Jesus Christ
And angels which kept not their own principality
 see came, fed, guarded, held, keeping, made, observe, shrunk, stayed, stored.

Key—s.

Mat. 16. 19. unto thee the keys of the kingdom of heaven
Lu. 11. 52. for ye took away the key of knowledge
Rev. 1. 18. I have the keys of death and of Hades
 3. 7. he that hath the key of David, he that openeth
 9. 1. the key of the pit of the abyss. 20. 1

Kick.

Acts 26. 14. it is hard for thee to kick against the goad

Kid.

Lu. 15. 29. and yet thou never gavest me a kid

Kill.—A.V. ¹put to death, ²killed, ³killeth, ⁴murder, ⁵slay.

Mat. 5. 21. shalt not k.—whosoever shall k. 19. ⁴18: Rom. 13. 9
 10. 28. k. the body, but are not able to k. the soul. Lu. 12. 4
 17. 23. and they shall kill him. Mk. 9. 31: 10. 34

KILLED

Mat. 21. 38. come, let us kill him. Mk. 12. 7: Lu. 20. 14
 23. 34. some of them shall ye kill and crucify
 24. 9. deliver you up unto tribulation, and shall kill you
 26. 4. they might take Jesus by subtilty, and kill him
Mk. 3. 4. to save a life, or to kill? But they held their peace
 6. 19. Herodias set herself against him, and desired to ²k.
 10. 19. Do not kill. Lu. 18. 20: Jas. 2. 11
Lu. 11. 49. some of them they shall ⁵kill and persecute
 13. 31. go hence: for Herod would fain kill thee
 15. 23. and bring the fatted calf, and k. it, and let us eat
 18. 33. and they shall scourge and ¹kill him
Jno. 5. 18. the Jews sought the more to kill him. 7. 1
 7. 19. none of you doeth the law? Why seek ye to kill me?
 20. Thou hast a devil: who seeketh to kill thee?
 25. Is not this he whom they seek to kill?
 8. 22. Will he kill himself, that he saith, Whither I go
 37. yet ye seek to kill me. 40
 10. 10. The thief cometh not, but that he may steal, and k.
Acts 7. 28. Wouldest thou kill me—killedst the Egyptian
 9. 23. the Jews took counsel together to kill him
 24. watched the gates also day and night—might k. him
 29. Jews; but they went about to ⁵kill him [Saul]
 10. 13. came a voice to him, Rise, Peter; k. and eat. 11. ⁵7
 16. 27. drew his sword, and was about to ⁵kill himself
 21. 31. And as they were seeking to k. him, tidings came
 25. 3. laying wait to kill him on the way
 26. 21. seized me in the temple, and assayed to kill me
 27. 42. the soldiers' counsel was to kill the prisoners
Jas. 4. 2. ye kill, and covet, and cannot obtain
Rev. 2. 23. And I will kill her children with death
 6. 8. to kill with sword, and with famine, and with death
 9. 5. it was given them that they should not kill them
 15. that they should ⁵kill the third part of men
 11. 7. and overcome them, and kill them [killed
 13. 10. ⁵kill with the sword, with the sword must he be
   see killest, put to death, slay.

Killed.—A.V. ¹slain, ²slew.

Mat. 16. 21. be killed, and the third day be raised up. Mk.
   8. 31: 9. 31: Lu. 9. ¹22
 21. 35. beat one, and killed another. Mk. 12. 5
 39. cast him forth out of the vineyard, and ²killed him
 22. 4. my oxen and my fatlings are killed
Lu. 6. laid hold on his servants—and ²k. them. [Lu. 20. 15
Mk. 12. 8. k. him, and cast him forth out of the vineyard.
Lu. 11. 47. prophets, and your fathers killed them. 48
 12. 5. after he hath killed hath power to cast into hell
 13. 4. upon whom the tower in Siloam fell, and ²k. them
 15. 27. and thy father hath killed the fatted calf
Acts 3. 15. and killed the Prince of life; whom God raised
 7. 52. and they ¹k. them which shewed before of the coming
 12. 2. And he k. James the brother of John with the sword
 23. 12. neither eat nor drink till they had killed Paul. ¹14
Rom. 8. 36. For thy sake we are killed all the day long
 11. 3. Lord, they have killed thy prophets, they have
2 Cor. 6. 9. behold, we live; as chastened, and not killed
1 Th. 2. 15. who both k. the Lord Jesus and the prophets
Jas. 5. 6. Ye have condemned, ye have k. the righteous one
Rev. 2. 13. Antipas my witness—who was ¹killed among you
 6. 11. brethren, which should be k. even as they were
 9. 18. By these three plagues was the third part of men k.
 20. And the rest of mankind, which were not killed
 11. 5. desire to hurt them, in this manner must he be k.
 13. ¹killed in the earthquake seven thousand persons
 13. 10. with the sword must he be killed
 15. not worship the image of the beast should be killed
 19. 21. the rest were ¹killed with the sword of him that sat
   see kill, killedst, sacrificed, slain, slew.

KILLEDST

Killedst—est.—*A.V.* ¹*kill,* ²*killed.*
Lu. 15. 30. thou ²*killedst* for him the fatted calf
Jas. 2. 11. if thou dost not commit adultery, but ¹*killest*
　　　　　　see killeth.

Killeth.—*A.V.* ¹*killest.*
Mat. 23. 37. Jerusalem, which ¹*k.* the prophets. *Lu.* 13.¹34
Jno. 16. 2. *k.* you shall think that he offereth service unto
2 *Cor.* 3. 6. for the letter *k.*, but the spirit giveth life [God
　　　　　　see kill.

Killing.
Mk. 12. 5. beating some, and *killing* some

Kin.
Mk. 6. 4. in his own country, and among his own *kin*

Kind—s.—*A.V.* ¹*good,* ²*grain,* ³*none of them.*
Mat. 13. 47. into the sea, and gathered of every *kind*
Mk. 9. 29. This *k.* can come out by nothing, save by prayer
Lu. 6. 35. for he is *kind* toward the unthankful and evil
1 *Cor.* 12. 10. to another divers *kinds* of tongues
13. 4. Love suffereth long, and is *kind*
14. 10. There are, it may be, so many *kinds* of voices in
　　the world, and no ³*kind* is without signification
15. 37. it may chance of wheat, or of some other ²*kind*
Eph. 4. 32. and be ye *kind* one to another, tenderhearted
Tit. 2. 5. ¹*kind,* being in subjection to their own husbands
Jas. 1. 18. that we should be a *k.* of firstfruits of his creatures
3. 7. For every *kind* of beasts and birds
　　　　　see flesh.

Kindled.—*A.V.* ¹*kindleth.*
Lu. 12. 49. and what will I, if it is already *kindled?*
22. 55. when they had *k.* a fire in the midst of the court
Jas. 3. 5. how much wood is ¹*kindled* by how small a fire!
　　　　　see anger.

Kindleth *A.V*—*see kindled*

Kindly.—*A.V.* ¹*courteously.*
Acts 27. 3. Julius treated Paul ¹*kindly,* and gave him leave
　　　　　see tenderly.

Kindness.—*A.V.* ¹*gentleness.*
Acts 28. 2. the barbarians shewed us no common *kindness*
2 *Cor.* 6. 6. in knowledge, in longsuffering, in *kindness*
Gal. 5. 22. longsuffering, ¹*kindness,* goodness
Eph. 2. 7. of his grace in *kindness* toward us in Christ Jesus
Col. 3. 12. a heart of compassion, *kindness,* humility
Tit. 3 4. when the *kindness* of God our Saviour—appeared

Kindred.
Lu. 1. 61. none of thy *kindred* that is called by this name
Acts 4. 6. as many as were of the *kindred* of the high priest
7. 3. Get thee out of thy land, and from thy *kindred*
14. called to him Jacob his father, and all his *kindred*
　　　　　see race, tribe.

Kindreds *A.V.*—*see families, tribes.*

King.
Mat. 1. 6. and Jesse begat David the *king*
2. 9. they, having heard the *king,* went their way
14. 9. the *king* was grieved; but for the sake. *Mk.* 6. 26
18. 23. kingdom of heaven likened unto a certain *k.* 22. 2
21. 5. Behold, thy *King* cometh unto thee. *Jno.* 12. 15
22. 7. But the *king* was wroth; and he sent his armies
11. But when the *king* came in to behold the guests
13. the *king* said to the servants, Bind him hand

KINGDOM

Mat. 25. 34. Then shall the *K.* say unto them on his right
27. 42. He is the *King* of Israel; let him now come. *Mk.*
Mk. 6. 22. the *king* said unto the damsel, Ask of me [15. 32
25. she came in straightway with haste unto the *king*
Lu. 14. 31. what *k.,* as he goeth to encounter another *king*
19. 38. Blessed is the *King* that cometh in the name of
23. 2. and saying that he himself is Christ a *king*
Jno. 1. 49. thou art the Son of God; thou art *K.* of Israel
6. 15. about to come and take him by force, to make him *k.*
12. 13. in the name of the Lord, even the *King* of Israel
18. 37. Art thou a *k.* then?—Thou sayest that I am a *k.*
19. 12. maketh himself a *king* speaketh against Cæsar
14. he saith unto the Jews, Behold, your *King!*
15. Shall I crucify your *K.?*—We have no *k.* but Cæsar
Acts 7. 18. arose another *k.* over Egypt, which knew not
13. 21. And afterward they asked for a *k.*: and God gave
17. 7. saying that there is another *king,* one Jesus [22
25. 14. Festus laid Paul's case before the *king.* 24
26. and specially before thee, *king* Agrippa　　[*king!*
26. 7. concerning this hope I am accused by the Jews, O
13. at midday, O *king,* I saw on the way a light
19. Wherefore, O *king* Agrippa, I was not disobedient
26. For the *king* knoweth of these things
27. *King* Agrippa, believest thou the prophets?
30. And the *king* rose up, and the governor
1 *Tim.* 1. 17. Now unto the *King* eternal, incorruptible
6. 15. *King* of kings, and Lord of lords. *Rev.* 17. 14; 19.
Heb. 7. 1. Melchizedek, *king* of Salem, priest of God [16
2. *King* of righteousness—*King* of Salem—*K.* of peace
11. 23. were not afraid of the *king's* commandment
27. forsook Egypt, not fearing the wrath of the *king*
1 *Pet.* 2. 13. whether it be to the *king,* as supreme
17. Fear God. Honour the *king*
Rev. 9. 11. over them as *king* the angel of the abyss
15. 3. true are thy ways, thou *King* of the ages
　　see great, Israel, Jews (proper names).

Kingdom.—*A.V.* ¹*kings,* ²*kingdom of God,* ³*kingdoms.*
Mat. 4. 23. the gospel of the *kingdom.* 9. 35; 24. 14
6. 10. Thy *kingdom* come. *Lu.* 11. 2
33. seek ye first his ²*kingdom. Lu.* 12. 31
8. 12. the sons of the *kingdom* shall be cast forth
12. 25. Every *kingdom* divided against itself is brought
　　to desolation. *Mk.* 3. 24; *Lu.* 11. 17
26. how then shall his *kingdom* stand? *Lu.* 11. 18
13. 19. When any one heareth the word of the *kingdom*
38. good seed, these are the sons of the *kingdom*
41. gather out of his *k.* all things that cause stumbling
43. shine forth as the sun in the *kingdom* of their Father
16. 28. till they see the Son of man coming in his *kingdom*
20. 21. right hand, and one on thy left hand, in thy *k.*
24. 7. *kingdom* against *kingdom. Mk.* 13. 8; *Lu.* 21. 10
25. 34. inherit the *kingdom* prepared for you
26. 29. when I drink it new with you in my Father's *k.*
Mk. 6. 23. I will give it thee, unto the half of my *kingdom*
11. 10. Blessed is the *k.* that cometh, the *k.* of our father
Lu. 1. 33. and of his *kingdom* there shall be no end
12. 32. Father's good pleasure to give you the *kingdom*
19. 12. went into a far country, to receive for himself a *k.*
15. come back again, having received the *kingdom*
22. 29. and I appoint unto you a *kingdom*
30. that ye may eat and drink at my table in my *k.*
23. 42. remember me when thou comest in thy *kingdom*
Jno. 18. 36. My *kingdom* is not of this world: if my
　　kingdom—now is my *kingdom* not from hence
Acts. 1. 6. dost thou at this time restore the *k.* to Israel?
20. 25. among whom I went about preaching the *k.*
1 *Cor.* 15. 24. when he shall deliver up the *kingdom* to God
Col. 1. 13. translated us into the *k.* of the Son of his love

KINGDOM

1 *Th.* 2. 12. worthily of God, who calleth you into his own *k.*
2 *Tim.* 4. 1. and by his appearing and his *kingdom*
    18. and will save me unto his heavenly *kingdom*
Heb. 1. 8. sceptre of uprightness is the sceptre of thy *k.*
    12. 28. receiving a *kingdom* that cannot be shaken
Jas. 2. 5. and heirs of the *kingdom* which he promised
2 *Pet.* 1. 11. entrance into the eternal *kingdom* of our Lord
Rev. 1. 6. made us to be a ¹*k.*, to be priests unto his God. 5. 10
    9. the tribulation and *k.* and patience which are in Jesus
    11. 15. The ²*k.* of the world is become the ²*k.* of our Lord
    16. 10. throne of the beast; and his *k.* was darkened
    17. 12. ten kings, which have received no *kingdom* as yet
    17. and to give their *kingdom* unto the beast

Kingdom of God.

Mat. 12. 28. then is the *k. of God* come. *Lu.* 10. 9, 11: 11. 20
    19. 24. for a rich man to enter into the *kingdom of God*.
    Mk. 10. 23, 24, 25: *Lu.* 18. 24, 25
    21. 31. harlots go into the *kingdom of God* before you
    43. The *kingdom of God* shall be taken away from you
Mk. 1. 15. the *k. of God* is at hand: repent ye, and believe
    4. 11. is given the mystery of the *k. of God*. *Lu.* 8. 10
    26. So is the *k. of God*, as if a man should cast seed
    30. How shall we liken the *k. of God ? Lu.* 13. 18, 20
    9. 1. till they see the *kingdom of God* come with power
    47. to enter into the *kingdom of God* with one eye
    10. 14. for of such is the *kingdom of God. Lu.* 18. 16
    15. receive the *k. of God* as a little child. *Lu.* 18. 17
    12. 34. Thou art not far from the *kingdom of God*
    14. 25. until that day when I drink it new in the *k. of God*
    15. 43. was looking for the *kingdom of God. Lu.* 23. 51
Lu. 4. 43. I must preach the good tidings of the *k. of God*
    6. 20. Blessed are ye poor: for yours is the *k. of God*
    7. 28. is but little in the *k. of God* is greater than he
    8. 1. bringing the good tidings of the *kingdom of God*
    9. 2. And he sent them forth to preach the *k. of God*
    11. welcomed them, and spake to them of the *k. of God*
    27. taste of death, till they see the *kingdom of God*
    60. go thou and publish abroad the *kingdom of God*
    62. and looking back, is fit for the *kingdom of God*
    13. 28. in the *kingdom of God*, and yourselves cast forth
    29. and shall sit down in the *kingdom of God*
    14. 15. Blessed is he that shall eat bread in the *k. of God*
    16. 16. that time the gospel of the *k. of God* is preached
    17. 20. the *k. of God* cometh—The *k. of God* cometh not
    21. for lo, the *kingdom of God* is within you
    18. 29. or children, for the *kingdom of God's* sake
    19. 11. that the *k. of God* was immediately to appear
    21. 31. know ye that the *kingdom of God* is nigh
    22. 16. not eat it, until it be fulfilled in the *k. of God*
    18. fruit of the vine, until the *k. of God* shall come
Jno. 3. 3. Except a man be born anew, he cannot see the
    5. he cannot enter into the *kingdom of God* [*k. of God*
Acts 1. 3. things concerning the *k. of God.* 8. 12: 19. 8
    14. 22. tribulations we must enter into the *k. of God*
    28. 23. expounded the matter, testifying the *k. of God*
    31. preaching the *kingdom of God*, and teaching
Rom. 14. 17. for the *k. of God* is not eating and drinking
1 *Cor.* 4. 20. the *k. of God* is not in word, but in power
    6. 9. shall not inherit the *k. of God?* 10: *Gal.*5. 21: *Eph.*5. 5
    15. 50. flesh and blood cannot inherit the *k. of God*
Col. 4. 11. my fellow-workers unto the *kingdom of God*
2 *Th.* 1. 5. may be counted worthy of the *kingdom of God*
Rev. 12. 10. salvation, and the power, and the *k. of* our God
    see kingdom.

Kingdom of Heaven.

Mat. 3. 2. for the *k. of heaven* is at hand. 4. 17: 10. 7
    5. 3. for theirs is the *kingdom of heaven.* 10
    19. least in the *kingdom of heaven*—great in the *k. of h.*

KISS

Mat. 5. 20. shall in no wise enter into the *k. of heaven*. 18. 3
    7. 21. Lord, Lord, shall enter into the *kingdom of heaven*
    8. 11. with Abraham, and Isaac, and Jacob, in the *k. of h.*
    11. 11. is but little in the *k. of heaven* is greater than he
    12. until now the *kingdom of heaven* suffereth violence
    13. 11. to know the mysteries of the *kingdom of heaven*
    24. The *kingdom of heaven* is likened unto. 31, 33, 44, 45, 47, 52: 18. 23: 20. 1: 22. 2: 25. 1
    16. 19. I will give unto thee the keys of the *k. of heaven*
    18. 1. Who then is greatest in the *kingdom of heaven ?* 4
    19. 12. eunuchs for the *kingdom of heaven's* sake
    14. forbid them not—for of such is the *kingdom of h.*
    23. hard for a rich man to enter into the *k. of heaven*
    23. 13. because ye shut the *k. of heaven* against men

Kingdoms.

Mat. 4. 8. sheweth him all the *k. of the world. Lu.* 4. 5
Heb. 11. 33. who through faith subdued *kingdoms*
    see kingdom.

Kings.

Mat. 10. 18. before governors and *kings* shall ye be brought for my sake. *Mk.* 13. 9: *Lu.* 21. 12
    11. 8. they that wear soft raiment are in *kings'* houses
    17. 25. the *k.* of the earth, from whom do they receive
Lu. 7. 25. they which—live delicately, are in *kings'* courts
    10. 24. and *k.* desired to see the things which ye see
    22. 25. The *k.* of the Gentiles have lordship over them
Acts 4. 26. The *kings* of the earth set themselves in array
    9. 15. to bear my name before the Gentiles and *kings*
1 *Tim.* 2. 2. for *kings* and all that are in high place
    6. 15. King of *kings* and Lord of lords. *Rev.* 17. 14: 19. 16
Heb. 7. 1. Abraham returning from the slaughter of the *k.*
Rev. 1. 5. and the ruler of the *kings* of the earth
    6. 15. And the *kings* of the earth—hid themselves
    10. 11. Thou must prophesy again over many—*kings*
    16. 12. that the way might be made ready for the *kings*
    14. which go forth unto the *kings* of the whole world
    17. 2. *kings* of the earth committed fornication. 18. 3, 9
    10. and they are seven *kings*; the five are fallen
    12. ten *kings*—receive authority as *kings*, with the beast
    18. great city, which reigneth over the *k.* of the earth
    19. 18. that ye may eat the flesh of *kings*
    19. *kings* of the earth, and their armies, gathered
    21. 24. the *k.* of the earth do bring their glory into it
    see kingdom.

Kinsfolk.—*A.V.* ¹*cousins,* ²*kinsfolks.*

Lu. 1. 58. neighbours and her ¹*kinsfolk* heard that the Lord
    2. 44. sought for him among their *k.* and acquaintance
    21. 16. delivered up even by parents, and brethren, and ²*k.*

Kinsman.

Jno. 18. 26. being a *kinsman* of him whose ear Peter cut off
Rom. 16. 11. Salute Herodion my *kinsman*

Kinsmen.

Lu. 14. 12. call not thy friends, nor thy brethren, nor thy *k.*
Acts 10. 24. called together his *k.* and his near friends
Rom. 9. 3. my brethren's sake, my *k.* according to the flesh
    16. 7. Salute Andronicus and Junias, my *kinsmen*
    21. and Lucius and Jason and Sosipater, my *kinsmen*

Kinswoman.—*A.V.* ¹*cousin.*

Lu. 1. 36. Elisabeth thy ¹*k.*, she also hath conceived

Kiss.

Mat. 26. 48. Whomsoever I shall *kiss*, that is he. *Mk.* 14. 44
Lu. 7. 45. Thou gavest me no *kiss*: but she—hath not ceased to *kiss* my feet

182

KISS

Lu. 22. 47. and he drew near unto Jesus to *kiss* him
48. betrayest thou the Son of man with a *kiss?*
Rom. 16. 16. Salute one another with a holy *kiss*. 1 *Cor.*
16. 20: 2 *Cor.* 13. 12
1 *Th.* 5. 26. Salute all the brethren with a holy *kiss*
1 *Pet.* 5. 14. Salute one another with a *kiss* of love

Kissed.

Mat. 26. 49. Hail, Rabbi; and *kissed* him. *Mk.* 14. 45
Lu. 7. 38. and *kissed* his feet, and anointed them
15. 20. saw him—ran, and fell on his neck, and k. him
Acts 20. 37. and fell on Paul's neck, and *kissed* him

Knee—s.

Mk. 15. 19. and bowing their *knees* worshipped him
Lu. 5. 8. Peter, when he saw it, fell down at Jesus' *knees*
Rom. 11. 4. who have not bowed the *knee* to Baal
14. 11. saith the Lord, to me every k. shall bow. *Phil.* 2. 11
Eph. 3. 14. For this cause I bow my *knees* unto the Father
Heb. 12. 12. hands that hang down, and the palsied *knees*
see *kneeled*.

Kneeled.—A.V. ¹bowed the knee.

Mat. 27. 29. ¹kneeled down before him, and mocked him
Mk. 10. 17. kneeled to him, and asked him, Good Master
Lu. 22. 41. kneeled down and prayed. *Acts* 9. 40: 20. 36
Acts 7. 60. kneeled down, and cried with a loud voice
see *kneeling*.

Kneeling.—A.V. ¹kneeled

Mat. 17. 14. man, k. to him, and saying, Lord, have mercy
Mk. 1. 40. leper, beseeching him, and k. down to him
Acts 21. 5. and, ¹kneeling down on the beach, we prayed

Knew.—A.V. ¹knowledge, ²known.

Mat. 1. 25. and *knew* her not till she had brought forth
7. 23. I never *knew* you : depart from me
14. 35. when the men of that place ¹*knew* him, they sent
25. 24. Lord, I *knew* thee that thou art a hard man
27. 18. he *knew* that for envy they had delivered him
Mk. 1. 34. devils to speak, because they k. him. *Lu.* 4. 41
6. 33. many *knew* them, and they ran there together
38. when they *knew*, they say, Five, and two fishes
54. out of the boat, straightway the people *knew* him
Lu. 6. 8. But he *knew* their thoughts
7. 37. when she *knew* that he was sitting at meat
12. 47. And that servant, which *knew* his lord's will
23. 7. when he *knew* that he was of Herod's jurisdiction
24. 31. And their eyes were opened, and they *knew* him
Jno. 2. 9. servants which had drawn the water *knew*
24. not trust himself unto them, for that he k. all men
25. for he himself *knew* what was in man
4. 1. When therefore the Lord k. how that the Pharisees
53. So the father *knew* that it was at that hour
5. 6 and *knew* that he had been now a long time
6. 6. to prove him : for he himself k. what he would do
64. Jesus *knew* from the beginning who they were
8. 19. if ye ²*knew* me, ye would know my Father also
11. 42. And I *knew* that thou hearest me always
57. if any man *knew* where he was, he should shew it
13. 11. For he *knew* him that should betray him
28. no man at the table *knew* for what intent he spake
17. 8. and ²*knew* of a truth that I came forth from thee
25. but I ¹*knew* thee; and these ¹*knew* that thou didst
18. 2. Judas also, which betrayed him, *knew* the place
Acts 9. 30. when the brethren *knew* it, they brought him
12. 14. when she *knew* Peter's voice, she opened not

KNOW

Acts 16. 3. for they all *knew* that his father was a Greek
22. 29. was afraid, when he *knew* that he was a Roman
28. 1. then we *knew* that the island was called Melita
2 *Cor.* 5. 21. Him who *knew* no sin he made to be sin
Col. 1. 6. ye heard and *knew* the grace of God in truth
see ye *knew*, know, knoweth, knowing, learned, perceived—*ing*.

Knew not.—A.V. ¹known, ²not tell.

Mat. 17. 12. Elijah is come already, and they k. him *not*
24. 39. and they *knew not* until the flood came
Lu. 2. 43. behind in Jerusalem; and his parents k. it *not*
12. 48. he that *knew not*, and did things worthy of stripes
20. 7. answered, that they ²*knew not* whence it was
Jno. 1. 10. He was in the world—and the world k. him n.
31. And I *knew* him *not*. 33
2. 9. now become wine, and *knew not* whence it was
17. 25. O righteous Father, the world ¹*knew* thee *not*
20. 9 For as yet they *knew not* the scripture
14. beholdeth Jesus standing, and k. n. that it was. 21. 4
Acts 7. 18. another king over Egypt, which k. *not* Joseph
13. 27. because they *knew* him *not*, nor the voices of the
19. 32. *knew not* wherefore they were come together
27. 39. And when it was day, they *knew not* the land
1 *Cor.* 1. 21. the world through its wisdom *knew not* God
1 Jno. 3. 1. world knoweth us not, because it k. him *not*

Knewest.

Mat. 25. 26. thou *knewest* that I reap where I sowed not
Lu. 19. 22. Thou *knewest* that I am an austere man
44. because thou *knewest* not the time of thy visitation
Jno. 4. 10. If thou *knewest* the gift of God, and who it is

Knit.

Col. 2. 2. be comforted, they being *knit* together in love
19. the body, being supplied and *knit* together. *Eph.* 4. 16

Knock—ed.

Mat. 7. 7. k., and it shall be opened unto you. *Lu.* 11. 9
Lu. 13. 25. ye begin to stand without, and to k. at the door
Acts 12. 13. And when he *knocked* at the door of the gate
Rev. 3. 20. Behold, I stand at the door and *knock*

Knocketh—ing.

Mat. 7. 8. to him that k. it shall be opened. *Lu.* 11. 10
Lu. 12. 36. when he cometh and *knocketh*, they may—open
Acts 12. 16. But Peter continued *knocking*

Know.— A V. ¹acknowledgement, ²knew, ³known, ⁴knoweth, ⁵perceive, ⁶sure, ⁷understand.

Mat. 6. 3. let not thy left hand k. what thy right hand doeth
9. 30. that no man *know* it. *Mk.* 5. 43: 7. 24: 9. 30
11. 27. neither doth any ⁴*know* the Father, save the Son
13. 11. Unto you it is given to k. the mysteries. *Lu.* 8. 10
24. 30. k. ye that he is nigh, even at the doors. *Mk.* 13. 29
43. But *know* this, that if the master. *Lu.* 12. 39
Lu. 10. 11. howbeit ⁶k. this, that the kingdom of God is come
21. 20. then *know* that her desolation is at hand [God
Jno. 6. 69. believed and ⁶k. that thou art the Holy One of
7. 17. he shall k. of the teaching, whether it be of God
26. the rulers indeed *know* that this is the Christ?
51. first hear from himself and *know* what he doeth?
10. 4. the sheep follow him; for they *know* his voice
14. I *know* mine own, and mine own ³*know* me
13. 35. By this shall all men k. that ye are my disciples
17. 3. that they should *know* thee the only true God
7. Now they ³*know* that all things whatsoever thou
18. 21. behold, these *know* the things which I said

KNOW

Acts 1. 7. It is not for you to *know* times or seasons
2. 36. Let all the house of Israel therefore *k*. assuredly
21. 24. and all shall *know* that there is no truth in
22. 14. hath appointed thee to *know* his will
19. Lord, they themselves *know* that I imprisoned
30. desiring to ³*know* the certainty, wherefore. 23. ⁵28
26. 4. My manner of life—*know* all the Jews
Rom. 2. 2. we ⁰*k*. that the judgement of God is according to
7. 1. (for I speak to men that *know* the law) ⌈truth
15. 29. I ⁶*know* that, when I come unto you, I shall come
1 *Cor.* 2. 14. foolishness unto him ; and he cannot *k*. them
4. 19. I will *k*., not the word of them which are puffed up
8. 2. he knoweth not yet as he ought to *know*
11. 3. have you *k*., that the head of every man is Christ
13. 2. gift of prophecy, and ⁷*know* all mysteries
Gal. 3. 7. *Know* therefore that they which be of faith
Eph. 3. 19. and to *know* the love of Christ which passeth
Phil. 1. 12. Now I would have you ¹*know*, brethren
Col. 2. 1. I would have you ²*k*. how greatly I strive for you
2. that they may ¹*know* the mystery of God
1 *Th.* 2. 1. brethren, *know* our entering in unto you
3. 3. yourselves *know* that hereunto we are appointed
5. I might *k*. your faith, lest by any means the tempter
4. 4. *know* how to possess himself of his own vessel
5. 2. yourselves *k*. perfectly that the day of the Lord
12. brethren, to *know* them that labour among you
2 *Th.* 3. 7. For yourselves *k*. how ye ought to ᶠimitate us
1 *Tim.* 4. 3. by them that believe and *know* the truth
2 *Tim.* 3. 1. But *know* this, that in the last days grievous
Tit. 1. 16. They profess that they *know* God ; but by
Heb. 8. 11. *Know* the Lord : For all shall *know* me
Jas. 2. 20. But wilt thou *know*, O vain man, that faith
5. 20. let him *know*, that he which converteth a sinner
1 *Jno.* 3. 16. Hereby ⁵*k*. we love, because he laid down his life
2 *Jno.* 1. not I only, but also all they that ³*know* the truth
Rev. 2. 23. and all the churches shall *know* that I am he
3. 9. and to *know* that I have loved thee

see certainty, determine, ignorant, knoweth not, understand.

I Know. —*A.V.* ¹*allow*, ²*knew*.

Mat. 28. 5. Fear not ye : for *I know* that ye seek Jesus
Mk. 1. 24. *I know* thee who thou art. *Lu.* 4. 34
Lu. 1. 18. Whereby shall *I know* this ? for I am an old man
Jno. 4. 25. *I k*. that Messiah cometh (which is called Christ)
5. 32. *I know* that the witness which he witnesseth
42. But *I know* you, that ye have not the love of God
7. 29. *I k*. him ; because I am from him, and he sent me
8. 14. *I know* whence I came, and whither I go
37. *I know* that ye are Abraham's seed
55. ye have not known him : but *I k*. him—but *I k*. him
9. 25. one thing *I know*, that, whereas I was blind
10. 14. *I know* mine own, and mine own know me
15. as the Father knoweth me, and *I know* the Father
27. My sheep hear my voice, and I *know* them
11. 22. *I know* that, whatsoever thou shalt ask of God
24. Martha saith unto him, *I k*. that he shall rise again
12. 50. *I know* that his commandment is life eternal
13. 18. I speak not of you all : *I k*. whom I have chosen
Acts 12. 11. Now *I know* of a truth, that the Lord hath sent
19. 15. Jesus *I know*, and Paul *I know* ; but who are ye?
20. 25. And now, behold, *I know* that ye all
29. *I know* that after my departing grievous wolves
24. 10. as *I k*. that thou hast been of many years a judge
26. 27. the prophets ? *I know* that thou believest
Rom. 7. 15. For that which I do ¹*I know* not [good thing
18. *I know* that in me, that is, in my flesh, dwelleth no
14. 14. *I know*, and am persuaded in the Lord Jesus
1 *Cor.* 4. 4. For *I k*. nothing against myself ; yet am I not
13. 12. now *I know* in part ; but then shall *I know* even as

2 *Cor.* 9. 2. for *I know* your readiness, of which I glory
2. 2. *I* ¹*know* a man in Christ, fourteen years ago. ²3
Phil. 1. 19. *I know* that this shall turn to my salvation
25. having this confidence, *I know* that I shall abide
2. 19. may be of good comfort, when *I know* your state
4. 12. *I k*. how to be abased, and *I k*. also how to abound
2 *Tim.* 1. 12. for *I know* him whom I have believed
1 *Jno.* 2. 4. He that saith, *I know* him, and keepeth not
Rev. 2. 2. *I know* thy works. 19: 3. 1, 8, 15
9. *I know* thy tribulation, and thy poverty ⌈is
13. *I k*. where thou dwellest, even where Satan's throne

Know *with negatives.* —*A.V.* ¹*aware*, ²*discern*, ³*known*, ⁴*tell*.

Mat. 21. 27. we ⁴*know not. Mk.* 11. ⁴33
25. 12. Verily I say unto you, I *know* you not
13. ye *know not* the day nor the hour
26. 70. I *know not* what thou sayest. *Mk.* 14. 68 : *Lu.* 22.60
72. I *know not* the man. 74 : *Mk.* 14. 71
Lu. 1. 34. How shall this be, seeing I *know not* a man ?
11. 44. and the men that walk over them ¹*know* it *not*
12. 56. how is it that ye ²*k. not* how to interpret this time ?
13. 25. say to you, I *know* you *not* whence ye are. 27
22. 57. he denied, saying, Woman, I *know* him *not*
23. 34. forgive them ; for they *know not* what they do
24. 16. eyes were holden that they should *not know* him
18. sojourn in Jerusalem and *not know* the things
Jno. 4. 22. Ye worship that which ye *know not*
8. 14. ye ⁴*know not* whence I come, or whither I go
55. if I should say, I *k*. him *not*, I shall be like unto you
9. 12. Where is he ? He saith, I *know not*
21. we *k. not* ; or who opened his eyes, we *know not*
25. answered, Whether he be a sinner, I *know not*
29. but as for this man, we *know not* whence he is
10. 5. for they *know not* the voice of strangers
14. 5. Lord, we *know not* whither thou goest
9. and dost thou *not* ³*know* me, Philip ?
15. 21. because they *know not* him that sent me
16. 18. We *know not* what he saith
20. 2. we *know not* where they have laid him. 13
Rom. 8. 26. we *know not* how to pray as we ought
10. 19. But I say, Did Israel *not know* ?
1 *Cor.* 1. 16. I *know not* whether I baptized any other
2. 2. *not* to *know* anything among you, save Jesus Christ
14. 11. If then I *know not* the meaning of the voice
2 *Cor.* 12. 2. I ⁴*know not* ; or whether out of the body, I *k*.
1 *Th.* 4. 5. even as the Gentiles which *k. not* God [*not*. ⁴3
2 *Th.* 1. 8. rendering vengeance to them that *know not* God
Heb. 3. 10. But they did *not* ³*know* my ways
Jude 10. these rail at whatsoever things they *know not*
Rev. 2. 24. which ³*know not* the deep things of Satan
3. 3. thou shalt *not know* what hour I will come

***May—est*, or *might Know*.**

Mat. 9. 6. But that ye *may know* that the Son of man
hath power. *Mk.* 2. 10 : *Lu.* 5. 24
Lu. 19. 15. that he *might know* what they had gained
Jno. 10. 38. ye *may know* and understand that the Father
14. 31. that the world *may know* that. 17. 23 ⌈is in me
19. 4. that ye *may know* that I find no crime in him
Acts 17. 19. *May* we *know* what this new teaching is
22. 24. he *might know* for what cause they so shouted
1 *Cor.* 2. 16. we *might know* the things that are freely given
2 *Cor.* 2. 4. that ye *might know* the love which I have
9. did I write, that I *might know* the proof of you
Eph. 1. 18. that ye *may know* what is the hope of his calling
6. 22. that ye *may know* our state, and that he may
comfort your hearts. *Col.* 4. 8
Phil. 3. 10. that I *may know* him, and the power of his

KNOW

Col. 4. 6. that ye *may know* how ye ought to answer
1 *Tim.* 3. 15. that thou *mayest k.* how men ought to behave
1 *Jno.* 5. 13. that ye *may know* that ye have eternal life

We Know, Know *we, or shall we* Know.—*A. V.* ¹*sure.*

Mat. 22. 16. *we k.* that thou art true. *Mk.* 12. 14: *Lu.* 20. 21
Jno. 3. 2. *we know* that thou art a teacher come from God
11. We speak that *we do know,* and bear witness
4. 22. we worship that which *we know*
42. *we have heard* for ourselves, and *know* that this is
6. 42. son of Joseph, whose father and mother *we know?*
7. 27. Howbeit *we know* this man whence he is
8. 52. Now *we know* that thou hast a devil
9. 20. *We k.* that this is our son, and that he was born
24. *we know* that this man is a sinner   [blind
29. *We know* that God hath spoken unto Moses
31. *We know* that God heareth not sinners
14. 5. whither thou goest; how *know we* the way?
16. 30. Now ¹*know we* that thou knowest all things
21. 24. and *we know* that his witness is true   [mean
Acts 17. 20. *we* would *know* therefore what these things
Rom. 3. 19. Now *we know* that what things soever the law saith
7. 14. For *we know* that the law is spiritual
8. 22. For *we know* that the whole creation groaneth
28. *we know* that to them that love God all things work
1 *Cor.* 8. 1. *We know* that we all have knowledge
4. *we know* that no idol is anything in the world
13. 9. For *we know* in part, and we prophesy in part
2 *Cor.* 5. 1. For *we know* that if the earthly house
16. *we* henceforth *know* no man after the flesh—yet
now *we know* him so from
1 *Tim.* 1. 8. But *we know* that the law is good
Heb. 10. 30. *we know* him that said, Vengeance belongeth
1 *Jno.* 2. 3. hereby *know we* that *we know* him, if we keep
5. Hereby *know we* that we are in him. 4. 13
18. antichrists; whereby *we know* that it is the last
3. 2. *We know* that, if he shall be manifested
14. *We know* that we have passed out of death into life
19. Hereby *shall we know* that we are of the truth
24. And hereby *we know* that he abideth in us
4. 6. By this *we know* the spirit of truth, and the spirit
5. 2. Hereby *we know* that we love the children of God
15. if *we know* that he heareth us—*we know* that we
18. *We know* that whosoever is begotten of God sinneth
19. *We know* that we are of God, and the whole world
20. *we know* that the Son of God is come—an understanding, that *we know* him that is true

Ye Know, Know *ye, ye, shall or shall ye* Know.—
A. V. ¹*discern,* ²*knew,* ³*known.*

Mat. 7. 11. If *ye* then, being evil, *k.* how to give. *Lu.* 11. 13
16. By their fruits *ye shall know* them. 20
20. 25. *Ye know* that the rulers of the Gentiles lord it
over them. *Mk.* 10. 42   [*Lu.* 21. 30
24. 32. *ye know* that the summer is nigh. *Mk.* 13. 28 :
25. 13. Watch therefore, for *ye know* not the day nor the
26. 2. *Ye know* that after two days the passover cometh
Mk. 4. 13. and how *shall ye know* all the parables?
Lu. 12. 56. Ye hypocrites, *ye* ¹*know* how to interpret the face
21. 31. *know ye* that the kingdom of God is nigh
Jno. 7. 28. Ye both *know* me, and *know* whence I am
8. 19. answered, Ye *know* neither me, nor my Father :
if ye knew me, *ye* would ³*know* my Father also
28. then *shall ye know* that I am he, and that I do
32. *ye shall know* the truth, and the truth shall make
11. 49. *Ye know* nothing at all, nor do ye take account
13. 12. *Know ye* what I have done to you?
17. If *ye know* these things, blessed are ye if ye do them
14. 4. And whither I go, *ye know* the way

KNOW

Jno. 14. 7. from henceforth *ye know* him, and have seen him
17. *ye know* him; for he abideth with you
20. *ye shall know* that I am in my Father, and ye in me
15. 18. *ye know* that it hath hated me before it hated you
Acts 2. 22. in the midst of you, even as *ye* yourselves *know*
3. 16. this man strong, whom *ye* behold and *know*
10. 28. *Ye* yourselves *k.* how that it is an unlawful thing
37. that saying *ye* yourselves *k.*, which was published
15. 7. Brethren, *ye k.* how that a good while ago God
19. 25. *ye know* that by this business we have our wealth
20. 18. *Ye* yourselves *k.*, from the first day that I set foot
34. *Ye* yourselves *know* that these hands ministered
1 *Cor.* 12. 2. *Ye k.* that when ye were Gentiles ye were led
15. 58. *ye know* that your labour is not vain in the Lord
16. 15. *ye know* the house of Stephanas, that it is
2 *Cor.* 8. 9. For *ye know* the grace of our Lord Jesus Christ
13. 6. I hope that *ye shall k.* that we are not reprobate
Gal. 4. 9. but now that *ye* have come to ³*know* God
13. *ye know* that because of an infirmity of the flesh
Eph. 5. 5. *ye know* of a surety, that no fornicator
Phil. 2. 22. But *ye k.* the proof of him, that, as a child
4. 15. *ye* yourselves also *k.*, ye Philippians, that in
1 *Th.* 1. 5. *ye k.* what manner of men we shewed ourselves
2. 2. been shamefully entreated, as *ye know*, at Philippi
5. were we found using words of flattery, as *ye know*
11. as *ye know* how we dealt with each one of you
3. 4. even as it came to pass, and *ye know*
4. 2. For *ye know* what charge we gave you
2 *Th.* 2. 6. And now *ye know* that which restraineth
Heb. 12. 17. For *ye know* that even when he [Esau] afterward desired to inherit the blessing   [at liberty
13. 23. *Know ye* that our brother Timothy hath been set
2 *Pet.* 1. 12. of these things, though *ye know* them   [³14
1 *Jno.* 2. 13. because *ye* ³*k.* him—because *ye* ³*k.* the Father.
20. from the Holy One, and *ye know* all things
21. *ye know* it, and because no lie is of the truth
29. If *ye k.* that he is righteous, *ye k.* that every one
3. 5. *ye k.* that he was manifested to take away sins
15. *ye know* that no murderer hath eternal life
4. 2. Hereby *know ye* the Spirit of God
Jude 5. though *ye* ²*know* all things once for all
see knowing.

Ye Know *not, or* Know *ye not.*

Mat. 20. 22. *Ye know not* what ye ask. *Mk.* 10. 38
24. 42. *ye know not* on what day your Lord cometh
Mk. 4. 13. saith unto them, *Know ye not* this parable?
12. 24. ye err, that *ye now know* not the scriptures
13. 33. watch and pray : for *ye know not* when the time is
35. *ye know not* when the lord of the house cometh
Lu. 1. 26. in the midst of you standeth one whom *ye k. not*
4. 22. Ye worship that which *ye know not*
32. I have meat to eat that *ye know not*
7. 28. he that sent me is true, whom *ye know not*
9. 30. herein is the marvel, that *ye know not* whence he is
Rom. 6. 16. *K. ye not*, that to whom ye present yourselves
1 *Cor.* 3. 16. *K. ye not* that ye are a temple of God. 6. 19
5. 6. *K. ye not* that a little leaven leaveneth the whole
6. 2. Or *k. ye not* that the saints shall judge the world
3. *know ye not* that we shall judge angels?
9. *k. ye not* that the unrighteous shall not inherit
15. *K. ye not* that your bodies are members of Christ?
16. *k. ye not* that he that is joined to a harlot is one body?
9. 13. *Know ye not* that they which minister about
24. *K. ye not* that they which run in a race run all
2 *Cor.* 13. 5. *K. ye n.* as to your own selves, that Jesus Christ
Jas. 4. 4. *know ye not* what shall be on the morrow
14. whereas *ye know not* what shall be on the morrow
1 *Jno.* 2. 21. not written unto you because *ye k. n.* the truth
see ignorant.

KNOWEST

Knowest.—A.V. ¹*tell*.

Mat. 15. 12. *k*. thou that the Pharisees were offended
Mk. 10. 19. Thou *knowest* the commandments. *Lu.* 18. 20
Lu. 22. 34. thou shalt thrice deny that thou *knowest* me
Jno. 1. 48. Nathanael saith unto him, Whence *k*. thou me?
3. 8. the voice thereof, but ¹*k*. not whence it cometh
13. 7. What I do thou *knowest* not now; but thou shalt
16. 30. thou *knowest* all things. 21. 17
19. 10. *k*. thou not that I have power to release thee
21. 15. thou *knowest* that I love thee. 16, 17
Acts 1. 24. Thou, Lord, which *k*. the hearts of all men
25. 10. have I done no wrong, as thou also very well *k*.
Rom. 2. 18. and *knowest* his will, and approvest the things
1 *Cor.* 7. 16 how *k*. thou, O wife—or how *k*. thou, O husband
2 *Tim.* 1. 15. This thou *k*., that all that are in Asia turned
18. ministered at Ephesus, thou *knowest* very well
Rev. 3. 17. and *knowest* not that thou art the wretched one
7. 14. And I say unto him, My lord, thou *knowest*
see understandest.

Knoweth.—A.V. ¹*knew*, ²*known*, ³*understandeth*.

Mat. 6. 8. your Father *k*. what things ye have need of
32. *k*. that ye have need of all these things. *Lu.* 12. 30
11. 27. no one *k*. the Son, save the Father. *Lu.* 10. 22
24. 36. But of that day and hour *k*. no one. *Mk.* 13. 32
Lu. 16. 15. but God *knoweth* your hearts
Jno. 7. 15. How *k*. this man letters, having never learned?
27. but when Christ cometh, no one *k*. whence he is
10. 15. as the Father *knoweth* me, and I know the Father
14. 17. it beholdeth him not, neither *knoweth* him
19. 35. he *k*. that he saith true, that ye also may believe
Acts 15. 8. God, which *k*. the heart, bare them witness
26. 26. For the king *knoweth* of these things
Rom. 8. 27. *knoweth* what is the mind of the Spirit
1 *Cor.* 2. 8. which none of the rulers of this world ¹*knoweth*
11. men *k*. the things of a man—things of God none *k*.
8. 2. If any man thinketh that he *k*. anything, he *k*. not
14. 16. seeing he ³*knoweth* not what thou sayest
2 *Cor.* 11. 11. Wherefore? because I love you not? God *k*.
31. God and Father of the Lord Jesus—*k*. that I lie not
12. 2. I know not; God *knoweth*. 3
2 *Tim.* 2. 19. The Lord *knoweth* them that are his
Jas. 4. 17. To him therefore that *k*. to do good, and doeth
2 *Pet.* 2. 9. The Lord *k*. how to deliver the godly
1 *Jno.* 3. 6. hath not seen him, neither ²*knoweth* him
20. God is greater than our heart, and *knoweth* all things
4. 6. We are of God: he that *knoweth* God heareth us
7. one that loveth is begotten of God, and *knoweth* God
Rev. 2. 17. which no one *knoweth* but he that receiveth it
19. 12. name written, which no one ¹*k*. but he himself
see knowing.

Knoweth not.—A.V. ¹*know*, ²*aware*.

Mat. 24. 50. in an hour when he ²*knoweth* not. *Lu.* 12. ²46
Mk. 4. 27. spring up and grow, he *knoweth* not how
Jno. 7. 49. this multitude which *knoweth* not the law
12. 35. *knoweth* not whither he goeth. 1 *Jno.* 2. 11
15. 15. for the servant *knoweth* not what his lord doeth
Acts 19. 35. men of Ephesus, what man is there who *k*. not
1 *Tim.* 3. 5. if a man ¹*k*. not how to rule his own house
1 *Jno.* 3. 1. the world *k*. us *not*, because it knew him not
4. 8. He that loveth not *knoweth* not God

Knowing.—A.V. ¹*knew*, ²*ye know*, ³*knoweth*, ⁴*known*, ⁵*perceiving*.

Mat. 9. 4. And Jesus *k*. their thoughts. 12. ¹25; *Lu.* 11. 17
22. 29. Ye do err, not *knowing* the scriptures
Mk. 5. 33. trembling, *knowing* what had been done to her
6. 20. Herod feared John, *k*. that he was a righteous man

KNOWLEDGE

Mk. 12. 15. But he, *k*. their hypocrisy, said unto them
28. and ⁵*knowing* that he had answered them well
Lu. 8. 53. laughed him to scorn, *knowing* that she was dead
9. 33. and one for Elijah: not *knowing* what he said
Jno. 6. 61. ¹*knowing* in himself that his disciples murmured
13. 1. Jesus ²*knowing* that his hour was come
3. *knowing* that the Father had given all things
18. 4. *knowing* all the things that were coming upon him
19. 28. Jesus, *knowing* that all things are now finished
21. 12. Who art thou? *knowing* that it was the Lord
Acts 2. 30. *knowing* that God had sworn with an oath to him
5. 7. when his wife, not *k*. what was done, came in
16. 25. *knowing* only the baptism of John
20. 22. not *knowing* the things that shall befall me there
Rom. 1. 21. ¹*knowing* God, they glorified him not as God
32. who, *knowing* the ordinance of God, that they which
2. 4. not *knowing* that the goodness of God leadeth thee to
5. 3. *k*. that tribulation worketh patience [repentance?
6. 6. *k*. this, that our old man was crucified with him
9. *k*. that Christ being raised from the dead dieth no more
13. 11. *knowing* the season, that now it is high time
2 *Cor.* 1. 7. *k*. that, as ye are partakers of the sufferings
4. 14. *knowing* that he which raised up the Lord Jesus
5. 6. *knowing* that, whilst we are at home in the body
11. *Knowing* therefore the fear of the Lord, we persuade
Gal. 2. 16. yet *k*. that a man is not justified by the works
4. 8. at that time, not ¹*knowing* God, ye were in bondage
Eph. 6. 8. *k*. that whatsoever good thing each one doeth
9. *k*. that both their Master and yours is in heaven. *Col.* 4. 1
Phil. 1. 16. *k*. that I am set for the defence of the gospel
Col. 3. 24. *knowing* that from the Lord ye shall receive
1 *Th.* 1. 4. *knowing*, brethren beloved of God, your election
1 *Tim.* 1. 9. *k*. this, that law is not made for a righteous man
6. 4. he is puffed up, *knowing* nothing, but doting
2 *Tim.* 2. 23. *knowing* that they gender strifes
3. 14. *knowing* of whom thou hast learned them
Tit. 3. 11. *knowing* that such a one is perverted
Philem. 21. *k*. that thou wilt do even beyond what I say
Heb. 10. 34. *k*. that ye yourselves have a better possession
11. 8. and he went out, not *knowing* whither he went
Jas. 1. 3. *k*. that the proof of your faith worketh patience
3. 1. *knowing* that we shall receive heavier judgement
1 *Pet.* 1. 18. ³*k*. that ye were redeemed, not with corruptible
5. 9. *knowing* that the same sufferings are accomplished
2 *Pet.* 1. 14. *k*. that the putting off of my tabernacle cometh
20. *knowing* this first, that no prophecy of scripture is
2. 21. than, after ⁴*knowing* it, to turn back from the holy
3. 3. *k*. this first, that in the last days mockers shall come
17. ²*knowing* these things beforehand, beware lest [time
Rev. 12. 12. having great wrath, ³*k*. that he hath but a short
see perceiving.

Knowledge.—A.V. ¹*acknowledge*, ²*acknowledging*, ³*knew*, ⁴*science*, ⁵*understand*.

Lu. 1. 77. To give *knowledge* of salvation unto his people
11. 52. for ye took away the key of *knowledge*
Acts 3. 10. took ³*k*. of him, that it was he which sat for alms
4. 13 took *k*. of them, that they had been with Jesus
17. 13. had *k*. that the word of God was proclaimed
24. 8. thyself, to take *knowledge* of all these things. ⁵11
22. having more exact *knowledge* concerning the Way
26. 5. having ³*k*. of me from the first, if they be willing
Rom. 1. 28. as they refused to have God in their *knowledge*
2. 20. having in the law the form of *k*. and of the truth
3. 20. for through the law cometh the *knowledge* of sin
10. 2. they have a zeal for God, but not according to *k*.
11. 33. the riches both of the wisdom and the *k*. of God
15. 14. are full of goodness, filled with all *knowledge*
1 *Cor.* 1. 5. enriched in him, in all utterance and all *k*.

183

KNOWLEDGE

1 *Cor.* 8. 1. We know that we all have *k*. *K* puffeth up
7. Howbeit in all men there is not that *knowledge*
10. if a man see thee which hast *k*. sitting at meat
11. For through thy *knowledge* he that is weak perisheth
12. 8. and to another the word of *knowledge*
13. 2. and know all mysteries and all *knowledge*
8. whether there be *knowledge*, it shall be done away
14. 6. speak to you either by way of revelation, or of *k*.
37. let him take ¹*knowledge* of the things which I write
15. 34. for some have no *knowledge* of God
2 *Cor.* 2. 14. manifest through us the savour of his *k*.
4. 6. to give the light of the *k*. of the glory of God
6. 6. in pureness, in *k*., in longsuffering, in kindness
8. 7. abound in everything, in faith, and utterance, and *k*.
10. 5. that is exalted against the *knowledge* of God
11. 6. though I be rude in speech, yet am I not in *k*.
Eph. 1. 17. wisdom and revelation in the *knowledge* of him
3. 19. to know the love of Christ which passeth *k*.
4. 13. unity of the faith, and of the *k*. of the Son of God
Phil. 1. 9. your love may abound yet more and more in *k*.
3. 8. to be loss for the excellency of the *k*. of Christ
Col. 1. 9. that ye may be filled with the *k*. of his will
10. and increasing in the *knowledge* of God
2. 3. in whom are all the treasures of wisdom and *k*.
3. 10. put on the new man, which is being renewed unto *k*.
1 *Tim.* 2. 4. and come to the *knowledge* of the truth
6. 20. profane babblings and oppositions of the ⁴*k*.
2 *Tim.* 3. 25. give them repentance unto the ²*k*. of the truth
3. 7. never able to come to the *knowledge* of the truth
Tit. 1. 1. of the truth which is according to godliness
Philem. 6. effectual, in the ²*knowledge* of every good thing
Heb. 10. 26. after that we have received the *k*. of the truth
1 *Pet.* 3. 7. dwell with your wives according to *knowledge*
Pet. 1. 2. peace be multiplied in the *knowledge* of God
3. through the *knowledge* of him that called us
5. in your faith supply virtue; and in your virtue *k*.
6. and in your *knowledge* temperance
8. nor unfruitful unto the *k*. of our Lord Jesus Christ
2. 20. through the *knowledge* of the Lord and Saviour
3. 18. But grow in the grace and *knowledge* of our Lord
see knew, understanding.

Known.—*A.V.* ¹*know*, ²*spread abroad*.

Mat. 12. 7. But if ye had *known* what this meaneth
33. for the tree is *known* by its fruit. *Lu.* 6. 44
24. 43. if the master of the house had *known*. *Lu.* 12. 39
Mk. 6. 14. Herod heard thereof; for his name had become ²*k*.
Lu. 19. 42. If thou hadst *known* in this day, even thou
24. 35. he was *known* of them in the breaking of bread
Jno. 7. 4. and himself seeketh to be *known* openly
14. 7. If ye had *k*. me, ye would have *k*. my Father also
18. 15. that disciple was *k*. unto the high priest. 16
Acts 1. 19. became *known* to all the dwellers at Jerusalem
2. 14. be this *known* unto you, and give ear unto my
4. 10. be it *known* unto you. 13. 38; 28. 28 [words
9. 24. but their plot became *known* to Saul
42. And it became *known* throughout all Joppa
19. 17. this became *known* to all, both Jews and Greeks
28. 22. it is ¹*k*. to us that everywhere it is spoken against
Rom. 1. 19. that which may be *known* of God is manifest
11. 34. For who hath *k*. the mind of the Lord? 1 *Cor*.2.16
1 *Cor.* 2. 8. had they *k*. it, they would not have crucified
8. 3. if any man loveth God, the same is *known* of him
13. 12. then shall I know even as also I have been *known*
14. 7. how shall it be *known* what is piped or harped?
9. how shall it be *known* what is spoken?
2 *Cor.* 3. 2. written in our hearts, *k*. and read of all men
5. 16. though we have *known* Christ after the flesh
6. 9. as unknown, and yet well *known*; as dying

Gal. 4. 9. come to know God, or rather to be *known* of God
Phil. 4. 5. Let your forbearance be *known* unto all men
2 *Tim.* 3. 15. from a babe thou hast *k*. the sacred writings
see follow, knew, know with negatives, ye know, knowing, perceived, proclaimed.

Made, or madest **Known.**—*A.V.* ¹*declared*.

Lu. 2. 15. which the Lord hath *made known* unto us
17. they *m. k.* concerning the saying which was spoken
Jno. 15. 15. heard from my Father I have *made k*. unto you
17. 26. and I ¹*made known* unto them thy name
Acts 2. 28. Thou *madest known* unto me the ways of life
7. 13. second time Joseph was *made k*. to his brethren
Rom. 16. 26. *made k*. unto all the nations unto obedience
Eph. 1. 9. having *made k*. unto us the mystery of his will
3. 3. by revelation was *made k*. unto me the mystery
5. which in other generations was not *made known*
10. might be *made known* through the church
Phil. 4. 6. let your requests be *made known* unto God
2 *Pet.* 1. 16. when we *m. k.* unto you the power and coming
see manifest.

Make—th—ing **Known.**—*A.V.* ¹*certify*, ²*declare*, ³*to wit*.

Mat. 12. 16. that they should not *make* him *k*. *Mk.* 3. 12
Jno. 17. 26. will *make* it ²*known*; that the love wherewith
Acts 15. 18. Saith the Lord, who *maketh* these things *k*.
Rom. 9. 22. and to *make* his power *known*, endured
23. that he might *make known* the riches of his glory
1 *Cor.* 15. 1. Now ¹*make k*. unto you, brethren, the gospel
2 *Cor.* 8. 1. we *made* ³*known* to you the grace of God
Gal. 1. 11. I *made*¹*k*. to you, brethren, as touching the gospel
Eph. 6. 19. to *m. k.* with boldness the mystery of the gospel
21. minister in the Lord, shall *make k*. to you all things
Col. 1. 27. God was pleased to *make k*. what is the riches
4. 7. my affairs shall Tychicus *make* ²*k*. unto you [here
9. They shall *make k*. unto you all things that are done

Not **Known.**

Mat. 10. 26. and hid, that shall *not* be *known*. *Lu.* 8. 17 : 12. 2
Jno. 8. 55. and ye have *not known* him : but I know him
16. 3. because they have *not known* the Father, nor me
Rom. 3. 17. And the way of peace have they *not known*
7. 7. I had *not known* sin—I had *not known* coveting
2 *Pet.* 2. 21. better for them *not* to have *known* the way

L.

LABOUR

Gal. 4. 9. come to know God, or rather to be *known* of God

Labour.—*A.V.* ¹*labours*, ²*weariness*, ³*zeal*.

Mat. 11. 28. All ye that *labour* and are heavy laden
Jno. 4. 38. laboured, and ye are entered into their ¹*labour*
Rom. 16. 6. Salute Mary, who bestowed much *labour* on you
12. Tryphæna and Tryphosa, who *labour* in the Lord
1 *Cor.* 3. 8. receive his own reward according to his own *l*.
15. 58. ye know that your *labour* is not vain in the Lord
2 *Cor.* 11. 27. in ²*labour* and travail, in watchings often
Gal. 4. 11. lest—I have bestowed *labour* upon you in vain
Eph. 4. 28. steal no more: but rather let him *labour*
Phil. 2. 16. I did not run in vain neither *labour* in vain
Col. 1. 29. whereunto I *labour* also, striving according to
4. 13. I have borne witness, that he hath much ³*l*. for you
1 *Th.* 1. 3. your work of faith and *labour* of love
2. 9. For ye remember, brethren, our *labour* and travail
3. 5. tempted you, and our *labour* should be in vain
5. 12. to know them that *labour* among you

LABOUR

2 *Th.* 3. 8. in *labour* and travail, working night and day
1 *Tim.* 4. 10. For to this end we *labour* and strive
5 17. especially those who *labour* in the word
see aim, diligence, laboured, toil, work.

Laboured.—*A.V.* ¹*labour,* ²*tossed.*

Jno. 4. 38. whereon ye have not ¹*l.*: others have *laboured*
Acts 27. 18. as we ²*laboured* exceedingly with the storm
Rom. 16. 12. Salute Persis the beloved, which *l.* much
1 *Cor.* 15. 10. but I *laboured* more abundantly than they all
Phil. 4. 3. help these women, for they *laboured* with me

Labourer,—s.—*A.V.* ¹*workman.*

Mat. 9. 37. but the *labourers* are few. *Lu.* 10. 2
38. send forth *labourers* into his harvest. *Lu.* 10. 2
10. 10. for the ¹*labourer* is worthy of his food
20. 1. in the morning to hire *labourers* into his vineyard
2. when he had agreed with the *labourers* for a penny
8. Call the *labourers,* and pay them their hire
Lu. 10. 7. for the *labourer* is worthy of his hire. 1 *Tim.* 5. 18
Jas. 5. 4. Behold, the hire of the *l.* who mowed your fields
see fellow-workers.

Laboureth—ing.

Acts 20.35. how that so *labouring* ye ought to help the weak
1 *Cor.* 16. 16. every one that helpeth in the work and *l.*
2 *Tim.* 2. 6. The husbandman that *l.* must be the first to
see striving, working.

Labours.

2 *Cor.* 6. 5. in *labours,* in watchings, in fastings
10. 15. that is, in other men's *labours*; but having hope
11. 23. in *labours* more abundantly, in prisons more
Rev 14. 13. that they may rest from their *labours*
see labour.

Lack.—*A.V.* ¹*destitute*

Mat. 19. 20. All these things have I observed: what *l.* I yet?
2 *Cor.* 8. 15. and he that gathered little had no *lack*
Jas. 2. 15. brother or sister be naked, and in ¹*l.* of daily food
see lacking, lacketh, need.

Lacked.

Lu. 22. 35. *lacked* ye anything? And they said, Nothing
Acts 4. 34. neither was there among them any that *lacked*
1 *Cor.* 12. 24. more abundant honour to that part which *l.*
Phil. 4. 10. ye did indeed take thought, but ye *l.* opportunity

Lackest—eth.—*A.V.* ¹*lack.*

Mk. 10. 21. One thing thou *lackest. Lu.* 18. 22
Jas. 1. 5. if any of you ¹*lacketh* wisdom, let him ask of God
2 *Pet.* 1. 9. For he that *lacketh* these things is blind

Lacking.—*A.V.* ¹*behind,* ²*lack,* ³*wanting.*

1 *Cor.* 16. 17. which was *lacking* on your part they supplied
Phil. 2. 30. supply that which was ³*lacking* in your service
*Col.*1.24. fill up—that which is ¹*l.* of the afflictions of Christ
1 *Th.* 3. 10. may perfect that which is *l.* in your faith?
Jas. 1. 4. ye may be perfect and entire, ³*lacking* in nothing

Lad.—*A.V.* ¹*young man.*

Jno. 6.9. There is a *lad* here, which hath five barley loaves
Acts 20. 12. they brought the ¹*lad* alive [Eutychus]

Lade.

Lu. 11. 46. for ye *lade* men with burdens grievous
see put on.

LAID

Laden.—*A.V.* ¹*full.*

Mat. 11. 28. all ye that labour and are heavy *laden*
2 *Tim.* 3. 6. take captive silly women *laden* with sins
Rev. 21. 9. seven bowls, who were ¹*laden* with the seven

Lading.

Acts 27. 10. much loss, not only of the *lading* and the ship

Lady.

2 *Jno.* 1. The elder unto the elect *lady* and her children
5. now I beseech thee, *lady,* not as though I wrote

Laid.—*A V.* ¹*caught,* ²*communicate—d,* ³*declared,* ⁴*put,* ⁵*proved,* ⁶*took.*

Mat. 3. 10. the axe *laid* unto the root of the trees. *Lu.* 3. 9
19. 15. And he *laid* his hands on them. *Lu.* 4. 40
26. 50. *laid* hands on Jesus, and took him. *Mk.* 14. 46
27. 60. *l.* it in his own new tomb. *Mk.* 15. 46: *Lu.* 23. 53: *Acts* 13. 29
Mk. 6. 5. save that he *laid* his hands upon a few sick folk
7. 30. and found the child *laid* upon the bed
15. 47. Mary the mother of Joses beheld where he was *l.*
16. 6. not here: behold, the place where they *laid* him
Lu. 1. 66. all that heard them *laid* them up in their heart
2. 7. swaddling clothes, and *laid* him in a manger
12. 19. Soul, thou hast much goods *l.* up for many years
13. 13. he *laid* his hands upon her: and immediately
16. 20. Lazarus was *laid* at his gate, full of sores
19. 20. here is thy pound, which I kept *laid* up in a napkin
22. austere man, taking up that *l* *laid* not down
23. 55. beheld the tomb, and how his body was *laid*
Jno. 7. 30. and no man *laid* his hand on him. 44
11. 34. Where have ye *laid* him? [Lazarus]
19. 41. a new tomb wherein was never man yet *laid*
42. because of the Jews' Preparation—they *laid* Jesus
20. 2. we know not where they have *laid* him. 13
15. borne him hence, tell me where thou hast *laid* him
Acts 3. 2. whom they *laid* daily at the door of the temple
4. 3. And they *l.* hands on them, and put them in ward
35. and *laid* them at the apostles' feet. 37: 5. 2
5. 15. into the streets, and *l.* them on beds and couches
18. and *laid* hands on the apostles, and put them
6. 6. when they had prayed, they *l.* their hands on them
7. 58. *l.* down their garments at the feet of a young man
8. 17. Then *laid* they their hands on them
9. 37. they *laid* her [Dorcas] in an upper chamber
13. 3. *laid* their hands on them, they sent them away
36. David—was *l.* unto his fathers, and saw corruption
16. 19. gain was gone, they ⁴*laid* hold on Paul and Silas
19. 6. And when Paul had *laid* his hands upon them
20. 3. and a plot was *laid* against him [Paul] by the Jews
21. 27. stirred up all the multitude, and *l.* hands on him
23. 29. nothing *laid* to his charge worthy of death
24. 6. on whom [Paul] also we ⁶*laid* hold
25. 14. Festus ³*laid* Paul's case before the king
16. his defence concerning the matter *laid* against him
Rom. 3. 9. for we before ⁵*laid* to the charge both of Jews
16. 4. who for my life *laid* down their own necks
1 *Cor.* 3. 11. than that which is laid, which is Jesus Christ
9. 16. for necessity is *laid* upon me; for woe is unto me
Gal. 2. 2. I ²*laid* before them the gospel which I preach
Col. 1. 5. the hope which is *laid* up for you in the heavens
2 *Tim.* 4. 8. is *laid* up for me the crown of righteousness
16. may it not be *laid* to their account
1 *Jno.* 3. 16. because he *laid* down his life for us
Rev. 1. 17. And he *laid* his right hand upon me, saying
11. 9. suffer not their dead bodies to be ⁴*laid* in a tomb
see bringing, foundation, (*laid*) *hold, lain, layeth, laying, lying,* [*took.*

LAID

Laid up.—*A.V.* ¹*heaped.*
Jas. 5. 3. Ye have ¹*laid up* your treasure in the last days

Lain.—*A.V.* ¹*laid.*
Lu. 23. 53. hewn in stone, where never man had yet ¹*lain*
Jno. 20. 12. where the body of Jesus had *lain*

Lake.
Lu. 5. 1. he was standing by the *lake* of Gennesaret
  2. and he saw two boats standing by the *lake*
  8. 22. Let us go over unto the other side of the *lake*
  23. there came down a storm of wind on the *lake*
  33. and the herd rushed down the steep into the *lake*
Rev. 20. 10. cast into the *lake* of fire. 19. 20 : 20. 14. 15
  14. This is the second death, even the *lake* of fire
  21. 8. their part shall be in the *lake* that burneth

Lama.—*see Eli, Eloi.*

Lamb.
Acts 8. 32. And as a *lamb* before his shearer is dumb
1 Pet. 1. 19. as of a *l.* without blemish and without spot
Rev. 13. 11. had two horns like unto a *l.*, and he spake as a
    see Lamb, *proper names.*

Lambs.
Lu. 10. 3. I send you forth as *lambs* in the midst of wolves
Jno. 21. 15. He saith unto him, Feed my *lambs*

Lame.—*A.V.* ¹*halt.*
Mat. 11. 5. the *lame* walk. 15. 31: *Lu.* 7. 22
  15. 30. having with them the *lame*, blind, dumb
  21. 14. blind and the *lame* came to him in the temple
Lu. 14. 13. bid the poor, the maimed, the *lame*, the blind
  21. bring in hither the—maimed and blind and ¹*lame*
Acts 3. 2. certain man that was *l.* from his mother's womb
  8. 7. that were palsied, and that were *lame*, were healed
Heb. 12. 13. that which is *l.* be not turned out of the way

Lament.
Jno. 16. 20. ye shall weep and *l.*, but the world shall rejoice
    see weep.

Lamentation.
Acts 8. 2. and made great *lamentation* over him [Stephen]

Lamented.
Lu. 23. 27. and of women who bewailed and *lamented* him

Lamp.—*A.V.* ¹*candle,* ²*light.*
Mat. 5. 15. Neither do men light a ¹*lamp*, and put it under
  the bushel. *Mk.* 4. ¹21: *Lu.* 8. ¹16 : 11. ¹33
  6. 22. The ²*lamp* of the body is the eye. *Lu.* 11. ²34
Lu. 11. 36. as when the ¹*l.* with its bright shining doth
  15. 8. doth not light a ¹*lamp*, and sweep the house
Jno. 5. 35. He was the ²*lamp* that burneth and shineth
2 Pet. 1. 19. take heed, as unto a ²*l.* shining in a dark place
Rev. 18. 23. light of a ¹*l.* shall shine no more at all in thee
  21. 23. and the ²*lamp* thereof is the Lamb
  22. 5. and they need no light of ¹*lamp*, neither light of sun

Lamps.—*A.V.* ¹*lights.*
Mat. 25. 1. ten virgins, which took their *lamps*
  3. when they took their *lamps*, took no oil with them
  4. the wise took oil in their vessels with their *lamps*
  7. those virgins arose, and trimmed their *lamps*
  8. Give us of your oil ; for our *lamps* are going out
Lu. 12. 35. loins be girded about, and your ¹*lamps* burning
Rev. 4. 5. seven *lamps* of fire burning before the throne
    see torch.

LASCIVIOUSNESS

Land.—*A.V.* ¹*afoot,* ²*country,* ³*earth.*
Mat. 4. 15. *land* of Zebulun and the *land* of Naphtali
  9. 26. fame hereof went forth into all that *land*
  31. forth, and spread abroad his fame in all that ²*land*
  10. 15. more tolerable for the *land* of Sodom. 11. 24
  23. 15. for ye compass sea and *land* to make one proselyte
  27. 45. was darkness over all the *l. Mk.* 15. 33 : *Lu.* 23. ²44
Mk. 4. 1. and all the multitude were by the sea on the *land*
  6. 47. in the midst of the sea, and he alone on the *land*
Lu. 5. 3. asked him to put out a little from the *land*
  11. And when they had brought their boats to *land*
  8. 27. when he was come forth upon the *land*
  14. 35. It is fit neither for the *land* nor for the dunghill
  21. 23. for there shall be great distress upon the *land*
Jno. 6. 21. and straightway the boat was at the *land*
  21. 8. for they were not far from the *land*
  9. when they got out upon the *l.*, they see a fire of coals
  11. and drew the net to *land*, full of great fishes
Acts 5. 3. to keep back part of the price of the *land* ?
  8. Tell me whether ye sold the *land* for so much
  7. 3. Get thee out of thy ²*land*—and come into the *land*
  4. Then he came out of the *land* of the Chaldæans—
    father was dead, God removed him into this *land*
  20. 13. intending himself to go by ¹*land*
  27. 39. when it was day, they knew not the *land*
  43. cast themselves overboard, and get first to the *land*
  44. came to pass, that they all escaped safe to the *land*
Heb. 6. 7. For the ²*land* which hath drunk the rain
  11. 9. sojourner in the *l.* of promise, as in a ²*l.* not his own
  29. passed through the Red sea as by dry *land*
    see Benjamin, country, Canaan, darkness, field, Israel, Judah.

Landed.
Acts 18. 22. And when he [Paul] had *landed* at Cæsarea
  21. 3. we sailed unto Syria, and *landed* at Tyro

Landing *A.V.*—*see touching.*

Lands.
Mat. 19. 29. mother, or children, or *lands. Mk.* 10. 29, 30
Acts 4. 34. possessors of *lands* or houses sold them
    see (lands) *belonging.*

Lanes.
Lu. 14. 21. Go out quickly into the streets and *lanes*

Language.—*A.V.* ¹*proper tongue.*
Acts 1. 19. in their ¹*l.* that field was called Akeldama
  2. 6. every man heard them speaking in his own *l.*
  8. how hear we, every man in our own ¹*language*
  21. 40. he spake unto them in the Hebrew ¹*l.* 22. ¹2
  26. 14. saying unto me in the Hebrew ¹*l.*, Saul, Saul

Lanterns.
Jno. 18. 3. cometh thither with *lanterns* and torches

Large.
Mat. 28. 12. gave *l.* money unto the soldiers [chief priests]
Mk. 14. 15. will himself show you a *l.* upper room. *Lu.* 22. 12
Gal. 6. 11. See with how *l.* letters I have written unto you

Lascivious.—*A.V.* ¹*filthy,* ²*pernicious.*
2 Pet. 2. 2. many shall follow their ²*lascivious* doings
  7. Lot, sore distressed by the ¹*lascivious* life of the wicked

Lasciviousness.—*A.V.* ¹*wantonness.*
Mk. 7. 22. wickednesses, deceit, *l.*, an evil eye, railing
2 Cor. 12. 21. fornication and *l.* which they committed

LASCIVIOUSNESS

Gal. 5. 19. which are these, fornication, uncleanness, *l.*
Eph. 4. 19. being past feeling gave themselves up to *l.*
1 *Pet.* 4. 3. and to have walked in *l.*, lusts, winebibbings
2 *Pet.* 2. 18. entice in the lusts of the flesh, by ¹*lasciviousness*
Jude 4. turning the grace of our God into *lasciviousness*

Last.—*A. V.* ¹*uttermost.*

Mat. 5. 26. out thence, till thou have paid the ¹*l.* farthing
12. 45. *last* state of that man becometh worse. *Lu.* 11 26
19. 30. many shall be *last* that are first; and first that are *last*. 20. 16 : *Mk.* 10. 31 : *Lu.* 13. 30
20. 8. their hire, beginning from the *last* unto the first
12. saying, These *last* have spent but one hour
14. it is my will to give unto this *last*, even as unto thee
27. 64. and the *last* error will be worse than the first
Mk. 9. 35. If any man would be first, he shall be *l.* of all
Lu. 12. 59. thence, till thou have paid the very *last* mite
Jno. 8. 9. beginning from the eldest, even unto the *last*
1 *Cor.* 4. 9. God hath set forth us the apostles *last* of all
15. 8. and *last* of all—he appeared to me [Paul] also
26. The *last* enemy that shall be abolished is death
45. The *last* Adam became a life-giving spirit [trump
52. in a moment, in the twinkling of an eye, at the *last*
1 *Pet.* 1. 5. ready to be revealed in the *last* time
1 *Jno.* 2. 18. whereby we know that it is the *last* hour
Jude 18. In the *last* time there shall be mockers
Rev. 1. 17. I am the first and the *last*. 22. 13
2. 8. These things saith the first and the *last*
19. and that thy *last* works are more than the first
15. 1. angels having seven plagues, which are the *l.* 21. 9
see end.

Last day.

Jno. 6. 39. but should raise it up at the *last day*
40. and I will raise him up at the *last day*. 44, 54
7. 37. on the *last day*, the great day of the feast
11. 24. rise again in the resurrection at the *last day*
12. 48. the same shall judge him in the *last day*

Latchet.

Mk. 1. 7. the *latchet* of whose shoes. *Lu* 3. 16 : *Jno.* 1. 27

Late.—*A. V.* ¹*end*

Mat. 28. 1. Now ¹*l.* on the sabbath day, as it began to dawn

Later.—*A. V.* ¹*latter.*

1 *Tim.* 4. 1. in ¹*l.* times some shall fall away from the faith

Latter *A. V.—see later.*

Laud *A. V.—see praise.*

Laugh.

Lu. 6. 21. Blessed are ye that weep now : for ye shall *l.*
25. Woe unto you, ye that *l.* now! for ye shall mourn

Laughed.

Mat. 9. 24. And they *l.* him to scorn. *Mk.* 5. 40 : *Lu.* 8. 53

Laughter.

Jas. 4. 9. let your *laughter* be turned to mourning

Launched.

Lu. 8. 22. other side of the lake : and they *launched* forth
see putting to sea.

Law.

Mat 5. 17. Think not that I came to destroy the *law*
18. one tittle shall in no wise pass away from the *law*
40. And if any man would go to *law* with thee
7. 12. for this is the *law* and the prophets

LAW

Mat. 12. 5. Or have ye not read in the *law*, how that on
22. 36. which is the great commandment in the *law* ?
40. On these two commandments hangeth the whole
23. 23. have left undone the weightier matters of the *l.*
Lu. 2. 22. purification according to the *law* of Moses
23. as it is written in the *law* of the Lord. 24
27. do concerning him after the custom of the *law*
39. things that were according to the *law* of the Lord
5. 17. were Pharisees and doctors of the *law* sitting by
10. 26 What is written in the *law* ? how readest thou ?
16. 16. The *l* and the prophets were until. *Mat* 11. 13
17. earth to pass away, than for one tittle of the *l.* to fail
24. 44. be fulfilled, which are written in the *law* of Moses
Jno. 1. 17. For the *law* was given by Moses ; grace and
45. him, of whom Moses in the *law*, and the prophets
7. 19. Did not Moses give you the *law*, and yet none of
you doeth the *law* ?
23. that the *law* of Moses may not be broken
49. multitude which knoweth not the *law* are accursed
51. Doth our *law* judge a man, except it first hear
8. 5. in the *law* Moses commanded us to stone such
17. in your *law* it is written, that the witness of two men
10. 34. Is it not written in your *l.*, I said, Ye are gods ?
12. 34. heard out of the *law* that the Christ abideth
15. 25. may be fulfilled that is written in their *law*
18. 31. Take him yourselves, and judge him according to
19. 7. We have a *l.*, and by that *l.* he ought to die [your *l.*
Acts 5. 34. Gamaliel, a doctor of the *law*, had in honour
6. 13. speak words against this holy place, and the *law*
7. 53. received the *law* as it was ordained by angels
13. 15. after the reading of the *law* and the prophets
39. ye could not be justified by the *law* of Moses
15. 5. and to charge them to keep the *law* of Moses
18. 13. persuadeth men to worship God contrary to the *l.*
15. questions about words and names and your own *l.*
21. 20. and they are all zealous for the *law*
24. thou thyself also walkest orderly keeping the *law*
28. against the people, and the *law*, and this place
22. 3. instructed according to the strict manner of the *l.*
12. Ananias, a devout man according to the *law*
23. 3. sittest thou to judge me according to the *law*, and
commandest me to be smitten contrary to the *l.* ?
29. I found to be accused about questions of their *law*
24. 14. believing all things which are according to the *law*
25. 8. Neither against the *law* of the Jews, nor against
28. 23. concerning Jesus, both from the *law* of Moses
Rom. 2. 12. sinned without *law*, shall also perish without
law—sinned under *law* shall be judged by *law*
13. not the hearers of a *law*—but the doers of a *law*
14. which have no *l.* do by nature the things of the *l.*,
these, having no *law*, are a *law* unto themselves
15. shew the work of the *law* written in their hearts
17. bearest the name of a Jew, and restest upon the *law*
18. that are excellent, being instructed out of the *law*
20. having in the *law* the form of knowledge
23. thou who gloriest in the *law*, through thy transgression of the *law* dishonourest thou God ?
25. doer of the *l.* : but if thou be a transgressor of the *l.*
26. uncircumcision keep the ordinances of the *law*
27. if it fulfil the *law*—art a transgressor of the *law* ?
3. 19. what things soever the *law* saith, it speaketh to
them that are under the *law* [knowledge of sin
20. works of the *law*—for through the *law* cometh the
21. now apart from the *law*—being witnessed by the *l.*
27. what manner of *l.* ? of works ? Nay : but by a *l.* of faith
28. is justified by faith apart from the works of the *law*
31. make the *law* of none effect—we establish the *law*
4. 13. not through the *law* was the promise to Abraham
14. For if they which are of the *law* be heirs

LAW

Rom. 4. 15. for the *l.* worketh wrath; but where there is no *l.*
16. not to that only which is of the *law*, but to that
5. 13. for until the *law* sin was in the world: but sin is not imputed when there is no *law*
20. the *l.* came in beside, that the trespass might abound
6. 14. for ye are not under *law*, but under grace
7. 1. I speak to men that know the *law*), how that the *l.*
2 the woman--is bound by *law* to the husband--die, she is discharged from the *law* of the husband
3. if the husband die, she is free from the *law* [Christ
4. ye also were made dead to the *l.* through the body of
5. sinful passions, which were through the *law*
6. But now we have been discharged from the *law*
7. Is the *l.* sin?—I had not known sin, except through the *l.*—not known coveting, except the *l.* had said
8. for apart from the *law* sin is dead
9. I was alive apart from the *law* once
12. So that the *law* is holy, and the commandment holy
14. For we know that the *law* is spiritual
16 I consent unto the *law* that it is good
21. 1 find then. the *law*, that, to me who would do good
22. For I delight in the *law* of God after the inward man
23. I see a different *law* in my members, warring against the *law* of my mind, and bringing me into captivity under the *law* of sin which is in my members
25. serve the *l.* of God ; but with the flesh the *l.* of sin
8. 2. the *l.* of the Spirit of life—free from the *law* of sin
3. For what the *law* could not do, in that it was weak
4. the ordinance of the *law* might be fulfilled in us
7. not subject to the *l.* of God, neither indeed can it be
9. 4. the giving of the *law*, and the service of God
31. after a law of righteousness, did not arrive at that *l.*
10. 4. Christ is the end of the *law* unto righteousness
5. doeth the righteousness which is of the *law* shall live
13. 8. he that loveth his neighbour hath fulfilled the *law*
10. love therefore is the fulfilment of the *law*
1 *Cor.* 6. 1. Dare any of you—go to *l.* before the unrighteous
6. but brother goeth to *law* with brother
9. 8 manner of men ? or saith not the *law* also the same ?
9. written in the *law* of Moses, Thou shalt not muzzle
20. to them that are under the *law*, as under the *law*, not being myself under the *law*, that I might gain them that are under the *law*
21. without *l.*, as without *l.*, not being without *l.* to God, but under *l.* to Christ—them that are without *law*
14. 21 In the *l.* it is written, By men of strange tongues
34. women—be in subjection, as also saith the *law*
15. 56. of death is sin ; and the power of sin is the *law*
Gal. 2. 16. not justified by the works of the *law*—Christ, and not by the works of the *law* ; because by the works of the *law* shall no flesh. 3. 11 : *Rom.* 3. 20
19. I through the *law* died unto the *law*, that I might
21. if righteousness is through the *law*, then Christ
3. 2. Received ye the Spirit by the works of the *law*
5. miracles among you, doeth he it by the works of the *l.*
10. For as many as are of the works of the *law* are under
12. and the *law* is not of faith ; but, He that doeth
13. Christ redeemed us from the curse of the *law*
17. the *law*, which came four hundred and thirty years
18. For if the inheritance is of the *law*, it is no more
19. What then is the *law* ? It was added because of
21. Is the *law* then against the promises—a *law* given —righteousness would have been of the *law*
23. we were kept in ward under the *law*, shut up
24. the *law* hath been our tutor to bring us unto Christ
4. 4. his Son, born of a woman, born under the *law*
5. that he might redeem them which were under the *l*
21. that desire to be under the *law*, do ye not hear the *l*. ?
5. 3. that he is a debtor to do the whole *law*

Gal. 5. 4. ye who would be justified by the *law* ; ye are fallen
14. For the whole *law* is fulfilled in one word
18. if ye are led by the Spirit, ye are not under the *law*
23. meekness, temperance: against such there is no *law*
6. 2. Bear ye one another's burdens, and so fulfil the *law*
13. who receive circumcision do themselves keep the *l.*
Eph. 2. 15. the *l.* of commandments contained in ordinances
Phil. 3. 5. as touching the *law*, a Pharisee
6. touching the righteousness which is in the *law*
9. righteousness—of the *law*, but that which is through
1 *Tim.* 1. 7. desiring to be teachers of the *law*
8. we know that the *law* is good, if a man use it lawfully
9. *law* is not made for a righteous man, but for the lawless
Tit. 3. 9. shun—strifes, and fightings about the *law*
Heb. 7. 5. to take tithes of the people according to the *l.*
11. priesthood (under it hath the people received the *l.*)
12. there is made of necessity a change also of the *l.*
16. not after the *law* of a carnal commandment
19. (for the *law* made nothing perfect)
28. For the *law* appointeth men high priests, having
8. 4. there are those who offer the gifts according to the *l.*
9. 19. according to the *law*, he took the blood of the calves
22. And according to the *law*, I may almost say
10. 1. the *law* having a shadow of the good things to come
8. (the which are offered according to the *law*)
Jas. 1. 25. he that looketh into the perfect *l.*, the *l.* of liberty
2. 8. Howbeit if ye fulfil the royal *law*—Thou shalt love
9. being convicted by the *law* as transgressors
10. For whosoever shall keep the whole *law*, and yet
11. but killest, thou art become a transgressor of the *l.*
12. so do, as men that are to be judged by a *law* of liberty
4. 11. speaketh against the *law*, and judgeth the *l.* : but if thou judgest the *l.*, thou art not a doer of the *l*
see book; courts, lawsuits.

Lawful.
Mat. 12. 2. not *l.* to do upon the sabbath *Mk.* 2. 24 . *Lu.* 6. 2
4. it was not *lawful* for him to eat. *Mk.* 2. 26 . *Lu* 6. 4
10. Is it *lawful* to heal on the sabbath day ? *Lu.* 14. 3
12. Wherefore it is *lawful* to do good on the sabbath
14. 4. It is not *lawful* for thee to have her. *Mk.* 6. 18
19. 3. Is it *l.* for a man to put away his wife. *Mk.* 10. 2
20. 15 . Is it not *l.* for me to do what I will with mine own ?
22. 17. Is it *lawful* to give tribute unto Cæsar, or not ? *Mk.* 12. 14 : *Lu.* 20. 22
27. 6. It is not *lawful* to put them into the treasury
Mk. 3. 4. Is it *l.* on the sabbath day to do good. *Lu.* 6. 9
Jno. 5. 10. sabbath, and it is not *l.* for thee to take up thy bed
18. 31. It is not *lawful* for us to put any man to death
Acts. 16. 21. customs which it is not *lawful* for us to receive
22. 25. Is it *l.* for you to scourge a man that is a Roman
1 *Cor.* 6, 12. All things are *l.* for me ; but not all things are expedient. All things are *lawful* for me. 10. 23
2 *Cor.* 12. 4. words, which it is not *l.* for a man to utter
see regular.

Lawfully.
1 *Tim.* 1. 8. the law is good, if a man use it *lawfully*
2 *Tim.* 2. 5 is not crowned, except he have contended *l.*

Lawgiver.
Jas. 4. 12. One only is the *lawgiver* and judge

LAWLESS

Lawless.—A. V ¹unlawful, ²wicked.
Acts 2. 23. by the hand of ²*l.* men did crucify and slay
2 *Th* 2. 8. And then shall be revealed the ²*lawless* one
1 *Tim.* 1. 9. but for the *lawless* and unruly [deeds
2 *Pet.* 2. 8. righteous soul from day to day with their ²*l.*

LAWLESSNESS

Lawlessness.—*A.V.* ¹*iniquity*, ²*transgresseth*, ³*transgression*.
2 *Th*. 2. 7. the mystery of ¹*lawlessness* doth already work
1 *Jno*. 3. 4. doeth sin doeth also ²*l.:* and sin is ³*lawlessness*

Laws
Heb. 8. 10. I will put my *laws* into their mind
10. 16. I will put my *laws* on their heart

Lawsuits.—*A.V.* ¹*law*.
1 *Cor*. 6. 7. a defect in you, that ye have ¹*l.* one with another

Lawyer—s.
Mat. 22. 35. one of them, a *lawyer*, asked him a question
Lu. 7. 30. the Pharisees and the *l.* rejected for themselves
10 25. a certain *lawyer* stood up and tempted him
11. 45. one of the *lawyers* answering saith unto him
46. woe unto you *lawyers* also ! 52
14. 3. spake unto the *lawyers* and Pharisees, saying
Tit. 3. 13. Set forward Zenas the *lawyer* and Apollos

Lay.
Mat. 8. 20. hath not where to *lay* his head. *Lu*. 9. 58
21. 46. when they sought to *lay* hold on him
23. 4. grievous to be borne, and *lay* them on men's
26. 6. Come, see the place where the Lord *lay*
Mk. 1. 30. Simon's wife's mother *lay* sick of a fever
2. 4. let down the bed whereon the sick of the palsy *lay*
Lu. 5. 18 sought to bring him in, and to *lay* him before
25. took up that whereon he *lay*, and departed
8. 42. an only daughter—and she *lay* a dying
Jno. 5. 3. In these *lay* a multitude of them that were sick
11. 38. Now it was a cave, and a stone *lay* against it
Acts 7. 60. Lord, *lay* not this sin to their charge
15. 28. to *lay* upon you no greater burden than these
27. 20. for many days, and no small tempest *lay* on us
28. 8. that the father of Publius *lay* sick of fever
Rom. 8. 33. *lay* anything to the charge of God's elect ?
9. 33. Behold, 1 *lay* in Zion a stone of stumbling
1 *Cor*. 16. 2. let each one of you *lay* by him in store
Heb. 12. 1. *lay* aside every weight, and the sin
1 *Pet*. 2. 6. Behold, I *lay* in Zion a chief corner stone
see putting.

Lay down.
Jno. 10. 15. and I *lay down* my life for the sheep
17. because I *lay down* my life, that I may take it again
18. I *lay* it *down* of myself. I have power to *lay* it *d.*
13 37. I will *lay down* my life for thee. 38
15. 13. that a man *lay down* his life for his friends
1 *Jno*. 3. 16. we ought to *lay down* our lives for the brethren
see dash

Lay hand—s.
Mat. 9. 18. *lay* thy *hand* upon her, and she shall live
Mk. 5. 23. I pray thee, that thou come and *lay* thy *hands*
16. 18. *lay hands* on the sick, and they shall recover
Lu 20. 19. chief priests sought to *lay hands* on him
21. 12. *lay* their *hands* on you, and shall persecute you
Acts 8. 19. on whomsoever I *lay* my *hands*, he may receive
1 *Tim*. 5. 22. *Lay hands* hastily on no man

Lay hold.—*see hold*

Lay up.
Mat. 6. 19. *Lay* not *up* for yourselves treasures upon the
20. but *lay up* for yourselves treasures in heaven
2 *Cor*. 12. 14 children ought not to *lay up* for the parents

LEARN

Layeth.—*A.V.* ¹*giveth*, ²*laid*.
Lu. 12. 21. So is he that *layeth* up treasure for himself
15. 5. found it, he *layeth* it on his shoulders, rejoicing
Jno. 10. 11. good shepherd ¹*l.* down his life for the sheep
13. 4. from supper, and ²*layeth* aside his garments

Laying.—*A.V.* ¹*laid*, ²*put—ting*.
Mk. 10. 16. blessed them, ¹*laying* his hands upon them
Lu. 11. 54. *laying* wait for him, to catch something
Acts 8. 18. through the *laying* on of the apostles' hands
9. 12 Ananias coming in, and ²*laying* his hands on him
25. 3. to Jerusalem ; *laying* wait to kill him on the way
28. 8. Paul entered in, and prayed, and ¹*l.* his hands on him
1 *Tim*. 4. 14. with the *l.* on of the hands of the presbytery
6. 19. *laying* up in store for themselves a good foundation
2 *Tim*. 1. 6 gift of God—through the ²*l.* on of my hands
Heb. 6. 1. not *laying* again a foundation of repentance
2. of the teaching of baptisms, and of *laying* on of hands
see plot, putting (away).

Lead.—*A.V.* ¹*led*, ²*seduce*.
Mk. 13 11. And when they *lead* you to judgement
22. shew signs and wonders, that they may ²*l.* astray
14. 44. take him, and *lead* him away safely
15. 20. And they ¹*lead* him out to crucify him
Jno 13. 15. ass f.om the stall, and *l.* him away to watering ?
Jno 18. 28. They ¹*lead* Jesus therefore from Caiaphas
1 *Cor*. 9. 5. Have we no right to *lead* about a wife that is
1 *Tim*. 2. 2. that we may *lead* a tranquil and quiet life
Heb 8. 9. to *lead* them forth out of the land of Egypt
1 *Jno*. 2. 26. concerning them that would ²*lead* you astray
see astray, bring, guide, take.

Leaders *A.V.—see guides.*

Leadeth.—*A.V* ¹*causeth*.
Mat. 7. 13. broad is the way, that *leadeth* to destruction
14. and straitened the way, that *leadeth* unto life
Jno. 10. 3. his own sheep by name, and *leadeth* them out
Acts 12. 10. unto the iron gate that *leadeth* into the city
Rom. 2. 4. the goodness of God *leadeth* thee to repentance ?
2 *Cor*. 2. 14. God, which always ¹*l.* us in triumph in Christ
see bringeth.

Leaned.
Jno. 21. 20. which also *l.* back on his breast at the supper

Leaning.—*A.V.* ¹*lying*.
Jno. 13. 25. He ¹*leaning* back, as he was, on Jesus' breast
Heb. 11. 21. worshipped, *leaning* upon the top of his staff
see reclining.

Leap—ed.—*A.V.* ¹*leapt*.
Lu. 1. 41. the babe *leaped* in her womb, 44
6. 23. Rejoice in that day, and *leap* for joy
Acts 14. 10. And he *leaped* up and walked
19. 16. man in whom the evil spirit was ¹*leaped* on them

Leaping.
Acts 3. 8. And *leaping* up, he stood, and began to walk
see walking (and leaping).

Learn.—*A.V.* ¹*learned*
Mat. 9. 13. But go ye and *learn* what this meaneth
11. 29. *learn* of me ; for I am meek and lowly in heart
24. 32. from the fig tree *learn* her parable. *Mk*. 13. 28
1 *Cor*. 4. 6. not to go beyond the things which are written
14. 31. prophesy one by one, that all may *learn*
35. if they would *learn* anything, let them ask their own

LEARN

Gal. 3. 2. This only would I *learn* from you. Received ye
Eph. 4. 20. But ye did not so ¹*learn* Christ [tion
1 *Tim.* 2. 11. Let a woman *l.* in quietness with all subjec-
5. 4. let them *learn* first to show piety towards their own
13. withal they *learn* also to be idle [family
Tit. 3. 14. let our people also *learn* to maintain good works
Rev. 14. 3. no man could *learn* the song save the hundred
see taught.

Learned.—*A.V.* ¹*eloquent,* ²*enquired,* ³*instructed,*
⁴*knew,* ⁵*understood.*

Mat. 2. 16. according to the time which he had carefully
²*learned* of the wise men
Mk. 15. 45. when he ⁴*learned* it of the centurion
Jno. 6. 45. the Father, and hath *learned,* cometh unto me
7. 15. How knoweth this man letters, having never *l.* ?
12. 9. common people—of the Jews ⁴*l.* that he was there
Acts 18. 24. Apollos, an Alexandrian by race, a ⁴*learned* man
23 27. rescued him, having ⁵*l.* that he was a Roman
Rom. 16. 17. contrary to the doctrine which ye *learned*
Phil. 4. 9. The things which ye both *learned* and received
11 I have *l.,* in whatsoever state I am, therein to be
12. in all things have I ³*l.* the secret both to be filled
Col. 1. 7. even as ye *learned* of Epaphras
2 *Tim.* 3. 14. abide thou in the things which thou hast
learned—knowing of whom thou hast *learned* them
Heb. 5. 8. yet *l.* obedience by the things which he suffered
see instructed, learn.

Learning.

Acts 26. 24. thy much *learning* doth turn thee to madness
Rom. 15. 4. aforetime were written for our *learning*
2 *Tim.* 3. 7. ever *learning,* and never able to come

Least.—*A.V.* ¹*doubtless.*

Mat. 2. 6. Art in no wise *least* among the princes of Judah
5. 19. break one of these *least* commandments—shall be
called *least* in the kingdom of heaven
25. 40. these my brethren, even these *least.* 45
Lu. 9. 48. he that is *least* among you all, the same is great
12. 26. not able to do even that which is *least,* why are ye
1 *Cor.* 9. 2. I am not an apostle, yet at ¹*least* I am to you
15. 9. I am the *l.* of the apostles, that am not meet to be
Eph. 3. 8. Unto me, who am less than the *least* of all saints
see less, little, account.

Leathern.—*A.V.* ¹*skin.*

Mat. 3. 4. and a *leathern* girdle about his loins. *Mk* 1. ¹⁶

Leave.—*A.V.* ¹*farewell,* ²*laying aside,* ³*left,* ⁴*let,*
⁵*liberty,* ⁶*license,* ⁷*put away,* ⁸*suffer—ed.*

Mat. 5. 24. *leave* there thy gift before the altar
18. 12. doth he not *leave* the ninety and nine. *Lu.* 15. 4
19. 5. For this cause shall a man *leave* his father and
mother. *Mk.* 10. 7: *Eph.* 5. 31
Mk. 7. 8. Ye ²*leave* the commandment of God, and hold fast
12. 19. die, and *l.* a wife behind him, and *leave* no child
Lu. 8. 32. that he would give them ⁶*leave* to enter into
them. And he gave them ⁶*leave. Mk.* 5 13
9. 60. ⁴*Leave* the dead to bury their own dead
10. 40. dost thou not care that my sister did ³*leave* me
11. 42. to have done, and not to *leave* the other undone
19. 44. shall not *leave* in thee one stone upon another
Jno. 14. 18. I will not *leave* you desolate: I come unto you
27. Peace I *leave* with you; my peace I give unto you
16. 28. I *leave* the world, and go unto the Father
32. and shall *leave* me alone: and yet I am not alone
19. 38 the body of Jesus: and Pilate gave him *leave*

LED

Acts 2. 27. Because thou wilt not *leave* my soul in Hades
18. 18. took his *leave* of the brethren, and sailed. ¹21
21. 39. give me ⁸*leave* to speak unto the people
40. when he had given him ⁶*leave,* Paul, standing
27. 3. gave him ⁶*leave* to go unto his friends and refresh
1 *Cor.* 7. 11. that the husband ⁷*leave* not his wife [himself
13. dwell with her, let her not *leave* her husband
2 *Cor.* 2. 13. but taking my *leave* of them, I went forth
Rev. 2. 4. that thou didst ⁵*leave* thy first love
11. 2. the court which is without the temple *l.* without
see fail, farewell, forsake, left.

Leaven.

Mat. 13. 33. The kingdom of heaven is like unto *l. Lu.* 13. 21
16. 6. beware of the *l.* of the Pharisees. 11: *Mk.* 8. 15:
12. he bade them not beware of the *l.* of bread [*Lu.* 12. 1
1 *Cor.* 5. 6. a little *l.* leaveneth the whole lump. *Gal.* 5. 9
7. Purge out the old *leaven,* that ye may be a new lump
8. let us keep the feast, not with old *leaven,* neither
with the *leaven* of malice and wickedness

Leavened.

Mat. 13. 33. measures of meal, till it was all *l. Lu.* 13. 21

Leaveneth.

1 *Cor* 5. 6. a little leaven *l.* the whole lump. *Gal.* 5 9

Leaves.

Mat. 21. 19. nothing thereon, but *leaves. Mk.* 11. 13
24. 32. tender, and putteth forth its *leaves. Mk.* 13. 28
Mk. 11. 13. seeing a fig tree afar off having *leaves* [nations
Rev. 22. 2 the *l.* of the tree were for the healing of the

Leaveth.

Mat. 4 11. the devil *leaveth* him; and behold, angels came
Jno. 10. 12. wolf coming, and *leaveth* the sheep, and fleeth

Leaving.—*A.V.* ¹*left,* ²*sent away.*

Mat. 4. 13. *l.* Nazareth, he came and dwelt in Capernaum
Mk. 4. 36. ²*l.* the multitude, they take him with them
12 21. and the second took her, and died, ¹*l.* no seed
Lu. 10. 30. robbers—beat him, and departed, *l.* him half
Acts 21. 3. in sight of Cyprus, ¹*leaving* it on the left [dead
Rom. 1. 27. the men, *leaving* the natural use of the woman
1 *Pet.* 2. 21. Christ also suffered for you, *l.* you an example
see cease.

Led.—*A.V.* ¹*brought,* ²*carried,* ³*leddest,* ⁴*taking.*

Mat. 4. 1. Then was Jesus *led* up of the Spirit. *Lu.* 4. 1
27. 2. and had bound him away, and delivered him up [him
31. on him his garments, and *led* him away to crucify
Mk. 14. 53. they *led* Jesus away to the high priest. *Mat.*
15. 16. *led* him away within the court [26. 57: *Lu.* 22. 54
Lu. 4. 5. [devil] ⁴*l.* him up, and showed him all the kingdoms.
29. out of the city, and *l.* him unto the brow of the hill. [¹⁹
21. 24. and shall be *led* captive into all the nations
22. 66. they *led* him away into their council [Simon
23. 26. when they *l.* him away, they laid hold upon one
32. others, malefactors, *led* with him to be put to death
24. 50. *l.* them out until they were over against Bethany
Jno. 18. 13. and *led* him to Annas first; for he was father
to Caiaphas [land of Egypt
Acts 7. 40. as for this Moses, which ³*led* us forth out of the
8. 32. He was *led* as a sheep to the slaughter
9. 8. they *led* him by the hand—into Damascus. 22. 11
13. 17. with a high arm ⁴*led* he them forth out of it
21. 38. stirred up to sedition and ⁸*l.* out into the wilderness

LED

Rom. 8. 14. For as many as are *led* by the Spirit of God
1 Cor. 12. 2. when ye were Gentiles ye were ²*led* away unto
    those dumb idols, howsoever ye might be *led*
Gal. 5. 18. if ye are *l*. by the Spirit, ye are not under the law
Eph. 4. 8. he *led* captivity captive, And gave gifts unto men
2 Tim. 3. 6. women laden with sins, *led* away by divers lusts
    see brought, carried, lead.

Leddest A.V.—*see* led.

Left.—A.V. ¹*forsaken*, ²*forsook*, ³*leave*, ⁴*remain*, ⁵*reserved*,
    ⁶*sent away*.

Mat. 4. 20. they straightway *l*. the nets, and followed him.
  8. 15. and the fever *left* her. Mk. 1. 31: Lu. 4. 39 | 22
13. 36. Thou he⁴*l*. the multitudes, and went into the house
16. 4. he *l*. them, and departed. 21. 17: 26. 44: Mk. 8. 13
19. 27. Lo, we have ³*left* all, and followed thee
    29. every one that hath ³*left* houses, or brethren
22. 22. they marvelled, and *l*. him, and went. Mk. 12. 12
25. having no seed *left* his wife unto his brother
23. 23. to have done, and not to have ³*l*. the other undone
33. your house is *l*. unto you desolate. Lu. 13. 35 [21. 6
24. 2. shall not be *l*. here one stone upon. Mk. 13. 2: Lu.
40. taken, and one is *left*. 41: Lu. 17. 34, 35, 36 [margin]
26. 56. all the disciples ³*left* him, and fled. Mk. 14. ²50
Mk. 1. 18. straightway they ²*left* the nets, and followed him
20. and they *left* their father Zebedee in the boat [18. 28
10. 28. we have *l*. all, and have followed thee. Lu. 5. ²11:
29. There is no man that hath *left* house. Lu. 18. 29
12. 20. and the first took a wife, and dying *left* no seed
13. 34. having *left* his house, and given authority
14. 52. but he *left* the linen cloth, and fled naked
Lu. 5. 4. And when he had *l*. speaking, he said unto Simon
20. 31. the seven also *left* no children, and died
Jno. 4. 3. he *left* Judæa, and departed again into Galilee
28. the woman *left* her waterpot, and went away
52. Yesterday at the seventh hour the fever *left* him
Acts 2. 31. Christ, that neither was he *left* in Hades
14. 17. yet he *left* not himself without witness
18. 19. they came to Ephesus, and he *left* them there
21. 32. when they saw—the soldiers, *left* off beating Paul
23. 32. the morrow they *l*. the horsemen to go with him
24. 27. desiring to gain favour—Felix *left* Paul in bonds
25. 14. There is a certain man *left* a prisoner by Felix
Rom. 9. 29. Except the Lord of Sabaoth had *left* us a seed
11. 4. I have ⁵*left* for myself seven thousand men
1 Th. 3. 1. we thought it good to be *left* behind at Athens
   4. 15. we that are alive, that are ⁴*left* unto the coming of
2 Tim. 4. 13. The cloke that I *left* at Troas [the Lord
20. but Trophimus I *left* at Miletus sick
Tit. 1. 5. For this cause *left* I thee in Crete
Heb. 2. 8. he *left* nothing that is not subject to him
   4. 1. a promise being *left* of entering into his rest
Jude 6. own principality, but *left* their proper habitation
    see alone, forsook, leave, leaving, remained.

Legion—s.

Mat. 26. 53. send me more than twelve *legions* of angels?
Mk. 5. 9. My name is *Legion*; for we are many. Lu. 8. 30
15. even him that had the *legion*: and they were afraid

Legs.

Jno. 19. 31. asked of Pilate that their *legs* might be broken
32. soldiers therefore came, and brake the *legs* of the first
33. saw that he was dead already, they brake not his *legs*

Leisure.

Mk 6. 31. they had no *leisure* so much as to eat

LETTERS

Lend.

Lu. 6. 34. if ye *lend*—even sinners *lend* to sinners
  35. do them good, and *lend*, never despairing
11. 5. say to him, Friend, *lend* me three loaves

Lender.—A.V. ¹*creditor*.

Lu. 7. 41. A certain ¹*lender* had two debtors

Length.

Eph. 3. 18. what is the breadth and *l*. and height and depth
Rev. 21. 16. the *length* thereof is as great as the breadth
    —the *l* and the breadth and the height—are equal

Leopard.

Rev. 13. 2. the beast which I saw was like unto a *leopard*

Leper—s.

Mat. 8. 2. there came to him a *leper*. Mk. 1. 40
10. 8. raise the dead, cleanse the *lepers*, cast out devils
11. 5. the lame walk, the *lepers* are cleansed. Lu. 7. 22
26. 6. in the house of Simon the *leper*. Mk. 14. 3
Lu. 4. 27. there were many *l*. in Israel in the time of Elisha
17. 12. there met him ten men that were *lepers*

Leprosy.

Mat. 8. 3. straightway his *leprosy* was cleansed
Mk. 1. 42. the *leprosy* departed from him. Lu 5. 13
Lu. 5. 12. behold, a man full of *leprosy*

Less.—A.V. ¹*least*.

Mat. 13. 32. which indeed is ¹*less* than all seeds. Mk. 4. 31
Mk. 15. 40. Mary the mother of James the *less* and of Joses
2 Cor. 12. 15. love you more abundantly, am I loved the *l*. ?
Eph. 3. 8. who am *less* than the least of all saints
Phil. 2. 28. ye may rejoice, and that I may be the *l*. sorrowful
Heb. 7. 7. without any dispute the *l*. is blessed of the better

Let A. V.—*see* hindered, leave, restraineth.

Let alone, **Let** loose.—*see* alone, loose.

Let down.

Mk. 2. 4. *let down* the bed whereon the sick of the palsy
Lu. 5. 4. and *let down* your nets for a draught
  5. but at thy word I will *let down* the nets
19. *let him down* through the tiles [basket. 2 Cor. 11. 33
Acts 9. 25. for him *d*. through the wall, lowering him in a
11. 5. a great sheet *let down* from heaven. 10. 11
    see lowered.

Let out.—A.V. ¹*let forth*.

Mat. 21. 33. *let it out* to husbandmen. Mk. 12. 1: Lu. 20. ¹9
41. will *let out* the vineyard unto other husbandmen

Letter.—A.V. ¹*epistle*.

Acts 23. 25. he wrote a *letter* after this form
33. and delivered the ¹*letter* to the governor
Rom. 2. 27. who with the *letter* and circumcision art a
29. in the spirit, not in the *letter* [transgressor
7. 6. of the spirit, and not in oldness of the *letter* [killeth
2 Cor. 3. 6. not of the *letter*, but of the spirit: for the *letter*
    see letters, epistle

Letters.—A.V. ¹*letter*.

Jno. 7. 15. How knoweth this man *l*., having never learned?
Acts 9. 2. asked of him *letters* to Damascus
22. 5. from whom also I received *l*. unto the brethren
28. 21. We neither received *letters* from Judæa

LETTERS

1 Cor. 16. 3. whomsoever ye shall approve by *letters*
2 Cor. 10. 9. I may not seem as if I would terrify you by my *l.*
10. For, His *letters*, they say, are weighty and strong
11. what we are in word by *letters* when we are absent
Gal. 6. 11. with how large ¹*letters* I have written unto you
  see epistles.

Lettest.
Lu. 2. 29. Now *lettest* thou thy servant depart, O Lord

Letteth *A.V.—see restraineth*

Levite.—*see Levites, proper names.*

Levitical.—*see proper names.*

Lewd *A.V.—see vile.*

Lewdness *A.V.—see villany.*

Liar.
Jno. 8. 44. for he is a *liar*, and the father thereof
55. say, I know him not, I shall be like unto you, a *liar*
Rom. 3. 4. let God be found true, but every man a *liar*
1 Jno. 1. 10. we have not sinned, we make him a *liar*
2. 4. and keepeth not his commandments, is a *l.* [Christ?
22. Who is the *liar* but he that denieth that Jesus is the
4. 20. I love God, and hateth his brother, he is a *liar*
5. 10. he that believeth not God hath made him a *liar*

Liars.
1 Tim. 1. 10. for men-stealers, for *liars*, for false swearers
Tit. 1. 12. Cretans are alway *liars*, evil beasts, idle gluttons
Rev. 21. 8. all *l.*, their part shall be in the lake that burneth
  see false.

Liberal *A.V.—see liberality.*

Liberality.—*A.V.* ¹bountifulness, ²liberal, ³simplicity.
Rom. 12. 8. he that giveth, let him do it with ³*liberality*
2 Cor. 8. 2. abounded unto the riches of their *liberality*
9. 11. being enriched in everything unto all ¹*liberality*
13. and for the ²*liberality* of your contribution unto them
  see bounty.

Liberally.
Jas. 1. 5. ask of God, who giveth to all *liberally*

Liberty.—*A.V.* ¹go.
Lu. 4. 18. To set at *liberty* them that are bruised
Acts 26. 32. This man [Paul] might have been set at *liberty*
28. 18. examined me, desired to set me at ¹*liberty*
Rom. 8. 21. the *liberty* of the glory of the children of God
1 Cor. 8. 9. this *liberty* of yours become a stumblingblock
10. 29. why is my *liberty* judged by another conscience?
2 Cor. 3. 17. where the Spirit of the Lord is, there is *liberty*
Gal. 2. 4. to spy out our *liberty* which we have in Christ
Heb. 13. 23. our brother Timothy hath been set at *liberty*
Jas. 1. 25. looketh into the perfect law, the law of *liberty*
2. 12. as men that are to be judged by a law of *liberty*
2 Pet. 2. 19. promising them *l.*, while they themselves
  see free, freedom, indulgence, leave.

Licence *A.V.—see leave, opportunity.*

Licked.
Lu. 16. 21. even the dogs came and *licked* his sores

Lie.—*A.V.* ¹guile.
Jno. 8. 44. When he speaketh a *lie*, he speaketh of his own
Acts 5. 3. Satan filled thy heart to *lie* to the Holy Ghost

LIFE

Rom. 1. 25. they exchanged the truth of God for a *lie*
3. 7. But if the truth of God through my *lie* abounded
9. 1. I say the truth in Christ, I *lie* not. 1 Tim. 2. 7
2 Cor. 11. 31. is blessed for evermore, knoweth that I *l.* not
Gal. 1. 20. I write unto you, behold, before God, I *lie* not
Col. 3. 9. *lie* not one to another—ye have put off the old man
2 Th. 2. 11. a working of error, that they should believe a *l.*
Tit. 1. 2. which God, who cannot *lie*, promised before
Heb. 6. 18. things, in which it is impossible for God to *lie*
Jas. 3. 14. glory not and *lie* not against the truth
1 Jno. 1. 6. walk in the darkness, we *l.*, and do not the truth
2. 21. ye know it, and because no *lie* is of the truth
27. is true, and is no *lie*, and even as it taught you
Rev. 3. 9. say they are Jews, and they are not, but do *lie*
14. 5. And in their mouth was found no ¹*lie*
21. 27. or he that maketh an abomination and a *lie*
22. 15. every one that loveth and maketh a *lie*

Lied.
Acts 5. 4. thou hast not *lied* unto men, but unto God

Lies.
1 Tim. 4. 2. through the hypocrisy of men that speak *lies*

Lieth.
Mat. 8. 6. my servant *lieth* in the house sick of the palsy
Rom. 12. 18. as much as in you *l.*, be at peace with all men
1 Jno. 5. 19. the whole world *lieth* in the evil one

Life.—*A.V.* ¹conversation, ²lives, ³living, ⁴soul.
Mat. 2. 20. they are dead that sought the young child's *l.*
6. 25. Be not anxious for your *life*. Lu. 12. 22
7. 14. straitened the way, that leadeth unto *life*
16. 26. and forfeit his ⁴*life*?—in exchange for his ⁴*life*?
  Mk. 8. ⁴36, ⁴37
18. 8. for thee to enter into *life* maimed. 9: Mk. 9. 43, 45
19. 16. good thing shall I do, that I may have eternal *l.*?
17. if thou wouldest enter into *life*, keep the command-
Mk. 3. 4. to save a *life*, or to kill? Lu. 6. 9 [ments
Lu. 12. 15. a man's *life* consisteth not in the abundance
23. For the *life* is more than the food. Mat. 6. 25
Jno. 1. 4. In him was *l.*; and the *l.* was the light of men
3. 36. on the Son hath eternal *life*—shall not see *life*
5. 24. but hath passed out of death into *life*. 1 Jno. 3. 14
26. as the Father hath *life* in himself, even so gave
he to the Son also to have *life* in himself
29. that have done good, unto the resurrection of *life*
40. ye will not come to me, that ye may have *life*
6. 33. out of heaven, and giveth *life* unto the world
35. I am the bread of *life*. 48 [world
51. bread which I will give is my flesh, for the *l.* of the
53. and drink his blood, ye have not *life* in yourselves
63. the words—spoken unto you are spirit, and are *life*
8. 12. in the darkness, but shall have the light of *life*
10. 10. I came that they may have *life*
11. 25. I am the resurrection, and the *life*
13. 38. Wilt thou lay down thy *life* for me?
14. 6. I am the way, and the truth, and the *life*
20. 31. and that believing ye may have *life* in his name.
Acts 2. 28. Thou madest known unto me the ways of *life*
3. 15. and killed the Prince of *life* [*life*
11. 18. Gentiles also hath God granted repentance unto.
17. 25. seeing he himself giveth to all *life*, and breath
26. 4. My manner of *life* then from my youth up
27. 22. there shall be no loss of *life* among you
Rom. 5. 17. reign in *life* through the one, even Jesus
18. free gift came unto all men to justification of *life*

195

LIFE

Rom. 6. 4. so we also might walk in newness of *life*
10. the *life* that he liveth, he liveth unto God
7. 10. the commandment, which was unto *life*
8. 2. the law of the Spirit of *life* in Christ Jesus made
6. but the mind of the spirit is *life* and peace
10. but the spirit is *life* because of righteousness
38. For I am persuaded, that neither death, nor *life*
11. 15. receiving of them be, but *life* from the dead ?
1 *Cor.* 3. 22. the world, or *life*, or death, or things present
14. 7. Even things without *life*, giving a voice
2 *Cor.* 1. 8. insomuch that we despaired even of *life*
2. 16. to the other a savour from *life* unto *life*
3. 6. for the letter killeth, but the spirit giveth *life*
4. 10. that the *life* also of Jesus may be manifested
12. So then death worketh in us, but *life* in you
5. 4. that what is mortal may be swallowed up of *life*
Gal. 2. 20. that *life* which I now live in the flesh I live
Eph. 4. 18. alienated from the *life* of God because of the
Phil. 1. 20. in my body, whether by *life*, or by death
2. 16. holding forth the word of *life*
Col. 3. 3. and your *life* is hid with Christ in God
4. When Christ, who is our *life*, shall be manifested
1 *Tim.* 2. 2. that we may lead a tranquil and quiet *life*
4. 8. having promise of the *life* which now is
2 *Tim.* 1. 1. promise of the *life* which is in Christ Jesus
10. and brought *life* and incorruption to light
Heb. 7. 3. neither beginning of days nor end of *life*
16. but after the power of an endless *life*
13. 7. considering the issue of their ¹*l.*, imitate their faith
Jas. 1. 12. approved, he shall receive the crown of *life*
3. 13. let him show by his good ¹*life* his works
4. 14. What is your *life* ? For ye are a vapour, that
1 *Pet.* 3. 7. as being also joint-heirs of the grace of *life*
10. He that would love *life*, And see good days
2 *Pet.* 1, 3. all things that pertain unto *life* and godliness
2. 7. Lot, sore distressed by the lascivious ¹*life* of the
1 *Jno.* 1. 1. our hands handled, concerning the Word of *l.*
2. the *life* was manifested, and we have seen—and
declare unto you the *life*, the eternal *life*
2. 16. and the vainglory of *life*, is not of the Father
5. 11 God gave unto us eternal *l.*, and this *l.* is in his Son
12. He that hath the Son hath the *life*—hath not the *l.*
16. God will give him *l.* for them that sin not unto death
Rev. 2. 7. to him will I give to eat of the tree of *life*
10. unto death, and I will give thee the crown of *life*
7. 17. shall guide them unto fountains of waters of ³*life*
8. 9. creatures which were in the sea, even they that had *l.*
11. 11. the breath of *life* from God entered into them
12. 11. they loved not their ²*life* even unto death
21. 6. athirst of the fountain of the water of *life* freely
22. 1. he shewed me a river of water of *life*
2. the tree of *life*, bearing twelve manner of fruits
14. that they may have the right to come to the tree of *l*
17. he that will, let him take the water of *life* freely
see *alive*, *book (of life)*, *breath*, *conduct*, *eternal (life)*.

His Life.

Mat. 10. 39. He that findeth *his life* shall lose it; and he that loseth *his life* for my sake shall find it. 16. 25 ; *Mk.* 8. 35 *Lu.* 9. 24 ; 17. 33 ; *Jno.* 12. 25
20. 28. to give *his life* a ransom for many. *Mk.* 10. 45
Lu. 14. 26. *his* own *life* also, he cannot be my disciple
Jno. 10. 11. good shepherd layeth down *his l.* for the sheep
15. 13. that a man lay down *his life* for his friends
Acts 8. 33. For *his life* is taken from the earth
20. 10. Make ye no ado ; for *his life* is in him
Rom. 5. 10. being reconciled, shall we be saved by *his life*
Phil. 2. 30. he came nigh unto death, hazarding *his life*
1 *Jno.* 3. 16. because he laid down *his life* for us

LIGHT

My Life.

Jno. 10. 15. and I lay down *my life* for the sheep
17. I lay down *my life*, that I may take it again
13. 37. I will lay down *my life* for thee
Acts 20. 24. I hold not *my life* of any account
Rom. 11. 3. I [Elijah] am left alone, and they seek *my life*

This Life.

Lu. 8. 14. cares and riches and pleasures of *this life*. 21. 34
Acts 5. 20. speak—to the people all the words of *this Life*
1 *Cor.* 6. 3. things that pertain to *this life* ?
15. 19. If in *this life* only we have hoped in Christ
2 *Tim.* 2. 4. entangleth himself in the affairs of *this life*
1 *Jno.* 5. 11. unto us eternal life, and *this life* is in his Son

Life-giving.—*A.V.* ¹*quickening*.

1 *Cor.* 15. 45. The last Adam became a ¹*life-giving* spirit

Lifetime.

Lu. 16. 25. thou in thy *lifetime* receivedst thy good things
Heb. 2. 15. were all their *lifetime* subject to bondage

Lift.

Mat. 12. 11. will he not lay hold on it, and *lift* it out ?
Lu. 13. 11. bowed—and could in no wise *lift* herself up
21. 28. *lift* up your heads ; because your redemption
Heb. 12. 12. Wherefore *lift* up the hands that hang down
see *exalt*, *eyes*.

Lifted.

Lu. 1. 42. [Elisabeth] *lifted* up her voice with a loud cry
11. 27. woman out of the multitude *lifted* up her voice
17. 13. and they *lifted* up their voices, saying, Jesus
24. 50. and he *lifted* up his hands, and blessed them
Jno. 3. 14. And as Moses *lifted* up the serpent in the wilderness, even so must the Son of man be *lifted*
8. 7. continued asking him, he *l.* up himself, and said. 10
28. When ye have *l.* up the Son of man, then shall ye
12. 32. And I, if I be *lifted* up from the earth
34. sayest thou, The Son of man must be *lifted* up ?
13. 18. oateth my bread *l.* up his heel against me [voice
Acts 2. 14. Peter, standing up with the eleven, *l.* up his
4. 24. they, when they heard it, *l.* up their voice to God
14. 11. saw what Paul had done, they *lifted* up their voice
22. 22. they *lifted* up their voice, and said, Away with such
Rev. 10. 5. And the angel—*l.* up his right hand to heaven
see *eyes*, *puffed*, *raised*.

Lifting.

1 *Tim.* 2. 8. pray in every place, *lifting* up holy hands
see *eyes*.

Light.—*A.V.* ¹*abroad*, ²*darkened*, ³*spirit*.

Mat. 4. 16. Saw a great *light*—did *light* spring up
5. 14. Ye are the *light* of the world
15. Neither do men *light* a lamp, and put it under
16 Even so let your *light* shine before men
6. 22. thy whole body shall be full of *light*. *Lu.* 11. 34, 36
11. 30 For my yoke is easy, and my burden is *light*
17. 2. his garments became white as the *light*
22. 5. But they made *light* of it, and went their ways
24. 29. the moon shall not give her *light*. *Mk.* 13. 24
Mk. 4. 22. secret, but that it should come to ¹*l.* *Lu.* 8. ¹17
Lu. 2. 32. A *l.* for revelation to the Gentiles. *Acts* 13. 47
8. 16. they which enter in may see the *light*. 11. 33
11. 36. lamp with its bright shining doth give thee *light*
15. 8. doth not *light* a lamp, and sweep the house
16. 8. sons of this world—wiser than the sons of the *light*
23. 45. the sun's ²*l.* failing : and the veil of the temple
Jno. 1. 4. the life was the *light* of men [was rent

LIGHT

Jno. 1. 8. He was not the *light*, but—bear witness of the *l.* 7
9. There was the true *l.*, even the *l* which lighteth every
3. 19. the *l.* is come into the world—rather than the *light*
20. that doeth ill hateth the *l.*, and cometh not to the *l*
21. But he that doeth the truth cometh to the *light*
5. 35. willing to rejoice for a season in his *light*
6. 12. not walk in the darkness, but shall have the *l.* of
9. 5. I am the *light* of the world. 8. 12 : 12. 46   [life
11. 9. stumbleth not, because he seeth the *l.* of this world
10. he stumbleth, because the *light* is not in him
12. 35. Yet a little while is the *light* among you. Walk while ye have the *light*
36. While ye have the *light*, believe on the *l.*—sons of *l.*
Acts. 9. 3. shone round about him a *l.* out of heaven. 22. 6
12. 7. stood by him, and a *light* shined in the cell
22. 9. And they that were with me beheld indeed the *l.*
11. when I could not see for the glory of that *light*
26. 13. O king, I saw on the way a *light* from heaven
23. by the resurrection of the dead should proclaim *l.*
Rom. 2. 19. guide of the blind, a *light* of them that are in
13. 12. and let us put on the armour of *light* [darkness
1 *Cor.* 4. 5. who will both bring to *light* the hidden things
2 *Cor.* 4. 4. the *light* of the gospel of the glory of Christ
6. to give the *l.* of the knowledge of the glory of God
17. For our *light* affliction, which is for the moment
11. 14. Satan fashioneth himself into an angel of *light*
Eph. 5. 8. but are now *l.* in the Lord; walk as children of *l.*
9. for the fruit of the *Slight* is in all goodness
13. by the *l.* : for everything that is made manifest is *light*
Col. 1. 12. partakers of the inheritance of the saints in *l.*
1 *Th.* 5. 5. for ye are all sons of *light*, and sons of the day
1 *Tim.* 6. 16. dwelling in *light* unapproachable
2 *Tim.* 1. 10. and brought life and incorruption to *light*
1 *Jno.* 1. 7. but if we walk in the *light*, as he is in the *l.*
2. 9. He that saith he is in the *l.*, and hateth his brother
10. He that loveth his brother abideth in the *light*
Rev. 18. 23. and the *light* of a lamp shall shine no more
21. 11. her *light* was like unto a stone most precious
24. And the nations shall walk amidst the *light* thereof
22. 5. need no *light* of lamp—*l.* of sun—shall give them *l.*
see darkness with light, lamp, lights, shine, shineth, strike.

Lighted.
Lu. 8. 16. no man, when he hath *l.* a lamp, covereth. 11. 33

Lighten.
Rev. 21. 23. for the glory of God did *lighten* it
see revelation.

Lightened—eth.
Lu. 17. 24. for as the lightning, when it *lighteneth*
Acts 27. 38. they *lightened* the ship, throwing out the wheat
Rev. 18. 1. and the earth was *lightened* with his glory

Lighteth.   *see freight.*
Jno. 1. 9. true *light*, even the light which L every man

Lighting.—*A. V.* ¹*falling.*
Acts 27. 41. But ¹*lighting* upon a place where two seas met
see coming.

Lightly—*A. V.* ¹*despise.*
Heb. 12. 5. My son, regard not ¹*lightly* the chastening
see quickly.

Lightness *A. V.*—*see fickleness.*

Lightning—s.
Mat. 24. 27. For as the *lightning* cometh. *Lu.* 17. 24
28. 3. His appearance was as *lightning*, and his raiment
Lu. 10. 18. I beheld Satan fallen as *lightning* from heaven
Rev. 4. 5. *l.* and voices and thunders. 8. 5 : 11. 19 : 16. 18

LINE

Lights.—*A. V.* ¹*light.*
Acts 16. 29. And he called for ¹*lights*, and sprang in
20. 8. there were many *lights* in the upper chamber
Phil. 2. 15. among whom ye are seen as *lights* in the world
Jas. 1. 17. coming down from the Father of *lights*
see lamps.

Like.
Mat. 6. 8. Be not therefore *like* unto them
29. was not arrayed *like* one of these. *Lu.* 12. 27
22. 39. And a second *like* unto it is this, Thou shalt love
Mk. 7. 13. and many such *like* things ye do
Lu. 6. 47. I will shew you to whom he is *like*
48. is *like* a man building a house. 49
7. 31. men of this generation, and to what are they *like* ?
13. 18. Unto what is the kingdom of God *like* ?
21. It is *like* unto leaven, which a woman took
Jno. 8. 55. I know him not, I shall be *like* unto you, a liar
9 9. said, It is he : others said, No, but he is *like* him
Acts 3. 22. from among your brethren, *like* unto me. 7. 37
11. 17. If then God gave unto them the *like* gift as he did
14. 15. We also are men of *like* passions with you
19. 25. together, with the workmen of *like* occupation
Gal. 5. 21. drunkenness, revellings, and such *like*
Heb. 7. 3. but made *like* unto the Son of God
Jas. 5. 17. Elijah was a man of *like* passions with us
2 *Pet.* 1. 1. that have obtained a *like* precious faith with us
1 *Jno.* 3. 2. if he shall be manifested, we shall be *like* him
Rev. 1. 13. one *like* unto a son of man. 14. 14
13. 4. Who is *like* unto the beast ?
see refused, same.

Likeminded.—*A. V.* ¹*one mind.*
Phil. 2 20. For I have no man *l.*, who will care truly
1 *Pet.* 3. 8. Finally, be ye all ¹*likeminded*, compassionate
see (same) mind.

Liken—ed.—*A. V.* ¹*liken,* ²*resemble.*
Mat. 7. 24. shall be ¹*likened* unto a wise man
26. shall be *likened* unto a foolish man
11. 16. whereunto shall I *liken* this generation? *Lu.* 7 31
13. 24. kingdom of heaven is *likened* unto. 18. 23 : 25. 1
Mk. 4. 30. How shall we *l.* the kingdom of God. *Lu.* 13. 20
Lu. 13. 18. kingdom of God like ? and whereunto shall I ²*l.*

Likeness.—*A. V.* ¹*figure,* ²*similitude.*
Acts 14. 11. gods are come down to us in the *likeness* of men
Rom. 5. 14. not sinned after the ²*l.* of Adam's transgression
6. 5. *likeness* of his death—*likeness* of his resurrection
8. 3. sending his own Son in the *likeness* of sinful flesh
Phil. 2. 7. being made in the *l.* of men   [another priest
Heb. 7. 15. if after the ²*l.* of Melchizedek there ariseth
Jas. 3. 9. curse we men, which are made after the ²*l.* of God
1 *Pet.* 3. 21. which also after a true ¹*l.* doth now save you

Likewise.—*A. V.* ¹*in like wise.*
Mat. 20. 5. the sixth and the ninth hour, and did *likewise*
21. 24. I ¹*likewise* will tell you by what authority I do
30. he came to the second, and said *likewise*
Lu. 3. 11. he that hath food, let him do *likewise*
6. 31. men should do to you, do ye also to them *likewise*
10. 37. Jesus said unto him, Go, and do thou *likewise*

Lilies.
Mat. 6. 28. Consider the *lilies* of the field. *Lu.* 12. 27

Limiteth *A. V.*—*see defineth.*

Line *A. V.*—*see province.*

LINEAGE

Lineage *A.V.—see family.*

Linen.
Mat. 27. 59. the body, and wrapped it in a clean *l.* cloth. *Lu.*
Mk. 14. 51. having a *linen* cloth cast about him. 52 [23, 53
15. 46 And he bought a *linen* cloth, and taking him
  down, wound him in the *linen* cloth
Lu. 24. 12. he seeth the *linen* cloths. *Jno.* 20 5, 6, 7
Jno 19. 40. bound it in *linen* cloths with the spices
  see fine (linen), precious (stone).

Lingereth.
2 *Pet* 2. 3. whose sentence now from of old *lingereth* not

Lion.
2 *Tim.* 4. 17. I was delivered out of the mouth of the *lion*
1 *Pet.* 5. 8. your adversary the devil, as a roaring *lion*
Rev. 4. 7. And the first creature was like a *lion*
5 5. the *Lion* that is of the tribe of Judah
10 3. he cried with a great voice, as a *lion* roareth
13. 2 and his mouth as the mouth of a *lion*

Lion of *Judah. —see proper names.*

Lions.
Heb. 11. 33. obtained promises, stopped the mouths of *l.*
Rev. 9. 8. their teeth were as the teeth of *lions*
17. the heads of the horses are as the heads of *lions*

Lips
Mat. 15. 8. This people honoureth me with their *lips. Mk.*
Rom. 3. 13. The poison of asps is under their *lips* [7. 6
1 *Cor.* 14. 21. by the *lips* of strangers will I speak [name
Heb. 13. 15. the fruit of *lips* which make confession to his
1 *Pet.* 3. 10. And his *lips* that they speak no guile

Listed—eth
Mat. 17. 12. did unto him whatsoever they *listed. Mk.* 9. 13
Jno. 3. 8. The wind bloweth where it *listeth*
  see willeth.

Listening.—*A.V.* ¹*attentive to hear,* ²*heard.*
Lu. 19. 48. for the people all hung upon him, ¹*listening*
Acts 16. 25. and the prisoners were ²*listening* to them

Little.—*A.V.* ¹*almost,* ²*least,* ³*long,* ⁴*small,* ⁵*young.*
Mat. 6. 30. O ye of *little* faith? 8. 26 ; 16. 8 ; *Lu.* 12. 28 [²26
11. 11. he that is but ²*l.* in the kingdom of heaven. *Lu.* 7.
14. 31. O thou of *little* faith, wherefore didst thou doubt?
Mk. 3. 9. that a ⁴*little* boat should wait on him
5. 23. My *little* daughter is at the point of death
7. 25. a woman, whose ⁵*l.* daughter had an unclean spirit
Lu. 7. 47. to whom *little* is forgiven, the same loveth *little*
12. 32. Fear not, *little* flock ; for it is your Father's good
16. 10. faithful in a very ²*little*—unrighteous in a very ²*l.*
19. 3. could not for the crowd, because he was *l.* of stature
17. because thou wast found faithful in a very *little*
Jno. 6. 7. not sufficient—that every one may take a *little*
21. 8. the other disciples came in the *little* boat
Acts 14. 28. they tarried no ³*little* time with the disciples
19. 24. brought no ⁴*little* business unto the craftsmen [20
26. 28. With but ⁴*l.* persuasion thou wouldest fain make.
1 *Cor.* 5. 6. a *l.* leaven leaveneth the whole lump? *Gal.* 5. 9
2 *Cor.* 8. 15. he that gathered *little* had no lack
1 *Tim.* 4. 8. bodily exercise is profitable for a *little*
5. 23. but use a *little* wine for thy stomach's sake
Heb. 2. 7. Thou madest him a *l.* lower than the angels, 9
Jas. 3. 5. the tongue also is a *little* member, and boasteth
4. 11. ye are a vapour, that appeareth for a *little* time

LIVE

Rev. 3 8. that thou hast a *little* power, and didst keep
6. 11 they should rest yet for a *little* time
20. 3. after this he must be loosed for a *little* time
  see book, child, (little) children, small.

Little ones.
Mat. 10. 42. give to drink unto one of these *little ones*
18. 6. cause one of these *l. ones*—to stumble. *Mk.* 9. 42:
10. despise not one of these *little ones* [*Lu.* 17. 2
14. that one of these *little ones* should perish

Little *while.*—*A.V.* ¹*season,* ²*short space.*
Lu. 22. 58. And after a *little while* another saw him. *Mk.*
Jno. 7. 33. Yet a *little while* am I with you. 13. 33 [14. 70
12. 35. Yet a *little while* is the light among you
14. 19. Yet a *l. w.,* and the world beholdeth me no more
16. 16. A *little while,* and ye behold me no more ; and
  again a *little while,* and ye shall see me. 17, 19
18. A *little while* ? We know not what he saith
Acts 5. 34. commanded to put the men forth a *little while*
Heb. 10. 37. a very *little while,* He that cometh shall come
1 *Pet.* 1. 6. ye greatly rejoice, though now for a ¹*little w.*
Rev. 17. 10. he must continue a ²*little while*

Live.
Mat. 4. 4. Man shall not *live* by bread alone. *Lu.* 4. 4.
9. 18. lay thy hand upon her, and she shall *live. Mk.* 5. 23
Lu. 7. 25. they which—*live* delicately, are in kings' courts
10. 28. answered right : this do, and thou shalt *live*
20. 38. dead, but of the living : for all *live* unto him
Jno. 5. 25. Son of God ; and they that hear shall *live*
6. 57. and I *live* because of the Father ; so he that eateth
  me, he also shall *live* because of me
58. he that eateth this bread shall *live* for ever
11. 25. believeth on me, though he die, yet shall he *live*
14. 19. because I *live,* ye shall *live* also
Acts 7. 19. cast out their babes to the end they might not *l.*
17. 28. for in him we *live,* and move, and have our being
22. 22. Away with—for it is not fit that he should *live*
25. 24. crying that he ought not to *live* any longer
28. 4. the sea, yet Justice hath not suffered to *live*
Rom. 6. 2. sin, how shall we any longer *live* therein ?
8. we believe that we shall also *live* with him
8. 12. we are debtors, not to the flesh, to *l.* after the flesh
13. for if ye *live* after the flesh, ye must die ; but if—
  ye mortify the deeds of the body, ye shall *live*
14. 8. whether we *live,* we *live* unto the Lord ;—whether
  we *live* therefore, or die, we are the Lord's
11. As I *live,* saith the Lord, to me every knee shall bow
1 *Cor.* 9. 14. proclaim the gospel should *live* of the gospel
2 *Cor.* 4. 11. we which *live* are alway delivered unto death
5. 15. which *live* should no longer *live* unto themselves
6. 9. as dying, and behold, we *live*
7. 3. ye are in our hearts to die together and *live* together
13. 4. are weak in him, but we shall *live* with him
11. *live* in peace : and the God of love and peace
Gal. 2. 14. how compellest thou the Gentiles to *l.* as do the
19. died unto the law, that I might *live* unto God [Jews?
20. yet I *live*—that life which I now *live* in the flesh
  I *live* in faith, the faith which is in the Son
5. 25. If we *l.* by the Spirit, by the Spirit let us also walk
Eph. 6, 3. and thou mayest *live* long on the earth
Phil. 1. 21. For to me to *live* is Christ, and to die is gain
22. to *live* in the flesh,—if this is the fruit of my work
1 *Th.* 3. 6. for now we *live,* if ye stand fast in the Lord
5. 10. wake or sleep, we should *live* together with him
2 *Tim.* 2. 11. if we died with him, we shall also *l.* with him
3. 12. all that would *l.* godly in Christ Jesus shall suffer
Tit. 2. 12. we should *l.* soberly and righteously and godly

LIVE

Heb. 12. 9. in subjection unto the Father of spirits, and *l.* ?
13. 18. desiring to *live* honestly in all things
Jas. 4. 15. If the Lord will, we shall both *live*, and do
1 *Pet.* 2. 24. died unto sins, might *live* unto righteousness
4. 2. that ye no longer should *live* the rest of your time
6. in the flesh, but *live* according to God in the spirit
2 *Pet.* 2. 6. an example unto those that should *live* ungodly
18. just escaping from them that *live* in error [him
1 *Jno.* 4. 9. Son into the world, that we might *l.* through
see be, eat, lived.

Lived.—*A.V.* ¹*alive*, ²*live*, ³*revived.*

Lu. 2. 36. Anna—having *lived* with a husband seven years
Acts 23. 1. Paul—said, Brethren, I have *l.* before God in all
26. 5. straitest sect of our religion I *lived* a Pharisee
Rom. 14. 9. For to this end Christ died, and ³*lived* again
Col. 3. 7. walked aforetime, when ye *lived* in these things
Jas. 5. 5. Ye have *lived* delicately on the earth
Rev. 2. 8. first and the last, which was dead, and ¹*l.* again
13. 14. who hath the stroke of the sword, and ²*lived*
18. 9. and *lived* wantonly with her, shall weep and wail
20. 4. they *l.*, and reigned with Christ a thousand years
5. The rest of the dead *lived* not until the thousand
see waxed.

Lively *A.V.*—*see living.*

Lives.

Acts 15. 26. men that have hazarded their *l.* for the name
27. 10. loss—of the lading and the ship, but also of our *l.*
1 *Jno.* 3. 16. we ought to lay down our *l.* for the brethren
see life.

Livest.

Gal. 2. 14. If thou, being a Jew, *livest* as do the Gentiles
Rev. 3. 1. thou hast a name that thou *l.*, and thou art dead

Liveth.

Jno. 4. 50. Go thy way; thy son *liveth.* 53
11. 26. whosoever *l.* and believeth on me shall never die
Rom. 6. 10. but the life that he *liveth*, he *liveth* unto God
7. 1. dominion over a man for so long time as he *liveth* ?
2. by law to the husband while he *liveth.* 1 *Cor.* 7. 39
3 while the husband *liveth*, she be joined to another
14. 7. For none of us *liveth* to himself, and none dieth to
2 *Cor.* 13. 4. weakness, yet he *l.* through the power of God
Gal. 2. 20. yet no longer I, but Christ *liveth* in me
1 *Tim.* 5. 6. giveth herself to pleasure is dead while she *l.*
Heb. 7. 8. one, of whom it is witnessed that he *liveth*
25. seeing he ever *liveth* to make intercession for them
9¹7. 17. doth it ever avail while he that made it *liveth* ?
1 *Pet.* 1. 23. word of God, which *liveth* and abideth
Rev. 4. 9. that *liveth* for ever and ever. 10 : 10. 6 : 15. 7
see giveth, Living One (proper names).

Living.—*A.V.* ¹*conversation*, ²*lively.*

Mat. 22. 32. God is not the God of the dead, but of the *living.* *Mk.* 12. 27 : *Lu.* 20. 38
Mk. 12. 44. cast in all that she had, even all her *l.* *Lu.* 21. 4
Lu. 8. 43. had spent all her *living* upon physicians
15. 12. And he divided unto them his *living*
13. there he wasted his substance with riotous *living*
30. which hath devoured thy *living* with harlots
24. 5. Why seek ye the *living* among the dead ?
Jno. 4. 10. he would have given thee *living* water
11. from whence then hast thou that *living* water ?
6. 51. I am the *living* bread which came down
57. As the *living* Father sent me, and I live because
7. 38. out of his belly shall flow rivers of *living* water

LOFT

Acts 7. 38. who received ²*living* oracles to give unto us
Rom. 12. 1. present your bodies a *living* sacrifice
14. 9. that he might be Lord of both the dead and the *l.*
1 *Cor.* 15. 45. The first man Adam became a *living* soul
Col. 2. 20. why, as though *l.* in the world, do ye subject
Tit. 3. 3. *l.* in malice and envy, hateful, hating one another
Heb. 10. 20. a new and *living* way, through the veil
1 *Pet.* 1. 3. his great mercy begat us again unto a ²*l.* hope
15. be ye yourselves also holy in all manner of ¹*living*
2. 4. a *living* stone, rejected indeed of men
5. as ²*living* stones, are built up a spiritual house
2 *Pet* 3. 11. ought ye to be in all holy ¹*living* and godliness
Rev. 16. 3. and every *living* soul died—in the sea
see life.

Living *creature*—*see creature.*

Living *God*—*see God.*

Loaf.—*A.V.* ¹*bread.*

Mat. 7. 9. if his son shall ask him for a ¹*l. of.* *Lu.* 11. ¹11
Mk. 8. 14. not in the boat with them more than one *loaf*

Loaves.—*A.V.* ¹*bread.*

Mat. 14. 17. We have here but five *loaves*, and two fishes·
Mk. 6. 41 : *Lu.* 9. 13: *Jno.* 6. 9
19. he took the five *loaves*—and brake and gave the *loaves.* *Mk.* 6. 41 : *Lu.* 9. 16: *Jno.* 6. 11
15. 33. should we have so many ¹*loaves* in a desert
34. How many *loaves* have ye ? *Mk.* 6. 38 : 8. 5
36. and he took the seven *loaves.* *Mk.* 8. 6
16. 9. the five *loaves* of the five thousand. *Mk.* 8. 19
10. Neither the seven *loaves* of the four thousand
Mk. 6. 44. they that ate the *l.* were five thousand men
52. they understood not concerning the *loaves*
Lu. 11. 5. Friend, lend me three *loaves*
Jno. 6. 13. with broken pieces from the five barley *loaves*
26. but because ye ate of the *loaves*, and were filled

Locusts.

Mat. 3. 4. his food was *locusts* and wild honey. *Mk.* 1. 6
Rev. 9. 3. And out of the smoke came forth *locusts*
7. the shapes of the *l.* were like unto horses prepared

Lodge.—*A.V.* ¹*guest.*

Mat. 13. 32. birds—come and *l.* in the branches. *Mk.* 4. 32
Lu. 9. 12. country round about, and *lodge*, and get victuals
19. 7. He is gone in to ¹*l.* with a man that is a sinner
Acts 21. 16. Mnason of Cyprus—with whom we should *l.*

Lodged.—*A.V.* ¹*abode.*

Mat. 21. 17. out of the city to Bethany, and *lodged* there
Lu. 13. 19. birds of the heaven *lodged* in the branches
21. 37. every night he went out, and ¹*l.* in the mount
Acts 10. 23. So he called them in and *lodged* them
see entertained, hospitality, lodging, lodgeth.

Lodgeth.—*A.V.* ¹*lodged.*

Acts 10. 6. he [Peter] *lodgeth* with one Simon a tanner. ¹32

Lodging.—*A.V.* ¹*lodged.*

Acts 10. 18. Simon, which was surnamed Peter, were ¹*l.*
28. 23. came to him [Paul] into his *l.* in great number
Philem. 22. But withal prepare me also a *lodging*

Loft *A.V.*—*see story.*

LOINS

Loins.
Mat. 3. 4. a leathern girdle about his *loins. Mk.* 1. 6
Lu. 12. 35. Let your *loins* be girded about, and your lamps
Acts 2. 30. an oath to him, that of the fruit of his *loins*
Eph. 6. 14. having girded your *loins* with truth
Heb. 7. 5. these have come out of the *loins* of Abraham
10. for he was yet in the *loins* of his father, when
1 *Pet.* 1. 13. Wherefore girding up the *loins* of your mind

Long.—*A.V.* ¹*desire,* ²*great while,* ³*lusteth.*
Mk. 12. 38. which desire to walk in *long* robes. *Lu.* 20. 46
40. for a pretence make *long* prayers. *Lu.* 20. 47
Lu. 23. 8. Herod—was of a *long* time desirous to see him
Acts 27. 21. when they had been *l.* without food, then Paul
28. 6. were ²*long* in expectation, and beheld nothing
Rom. 1. 11. For I *long* to see you, that I may impart
1 *Cor.* 11. 14. if a man have *long* hair, it is a dishonour
15. if a woman have *long* hair, it is a glory to her
13. 4. Love suffereth *long,* and is kind
2 *Cor.* 9. 14. with supplication on your behalf, *long* after
Phil. 1. 8. For God is my witness, how I *long* after you all
Jas. 4. 5. spirit which he made to dwell in us ³*long* unto
1 *Pet.* 2. 2. newborn babes, ¹*long* for the spiritual milk
see longsuffering.

Long ago.—*A V.* ¹*great while.*
Lu. 10. 13. repented ¹*l. ago,* sitting in sackcloth and ashes

Long time.
Mat. 25. 19. after a *long time* the lord of those servants
Lu. 8. 27. for a *long time* he had worn no clothes
20. 9. went into another country for a *long time*
Jno. 5. 6. Jesus—knew that he had been now a *long time*
14. 9. Have I been so *long time* with you—Philip?
Acts 8. 11. of *long time* he had amazed them with his
14. 3. *Long time* therefore they tarried there speaking
see (no) little, (of) old.

Long while.
Acts 20. 11. [Paul] talked with them a *long while,* even till

Longed.
Phil. 2. 26. since he *l.* after you all, and was sore troubled
4. 1. Wherefore, my brethren beloved and *l.* for, my joy

Longing.—*A.V.* ¹*desire,* ²*desiring.*
Rom. 15. 23. having these many years a ¹*l.* to come unto you
2 *Cor.* 5. 2. ²*l.* to be clothed upon with our habitation
7. 7. while he [Titus] told us your ¹*longing*
11. what fear, yea, what *longing,* yea, what zeal
1 *Th.* 3. 6. ²*longing* to see us, even as we also to see you
2 *Tim.* 1. 4. ²*longing* to see thee, remembering thy tears

Longsuffering.—*A.V.* ¹*bear long,* ²*patient.*
Lu. 18. 7. cry to him day and night, and he is ²*l.* over them?
Rom. 2. 4. riches of his goodness and forbearance and *l.*
9. 22. endured with much *longsuffering* vessels of wrath
2 *Cor.* 6. 6. in pureness, in knowledge, in *l.,* in kindness
Gal. 5. 22. fruit of the Spirit is love, joy, peace, *longsuffering*
Eph. 4. 2. with all lowliness and meekness, with *l.*
Col. 1. 11. unto all patience and *longsuffering* with joy
3. 12. kindness, humility, meekness, *longsuffering*
1 *Th.* 5. 14. support the weak, be ²*longsuffering* toward
1 *Tim.* 1. 16. might Jesus Christ show forth all his *l.*
2 *Tim.* 3. 10. my teaching, conduct, purpose, faith, *l.*
4. 2. rebuke, exhort, with all *longsuffering* and teaching
1 *Pet.* 3. 20. the *l.* of God waited in the days of Noah
2 *Pet.* 3. 9. but is *l.* to you-ward, not wishing that any
15. account that the *l.* of our Lord is salvation

LOOKING

Look—*A.V.* ¹*allow,* ²*behold,* ³*see,* ⁴*take heed.*
Mat. 11. 3. cometh, or *look* we for another? *Lu.* 7. 19, 20
Lu. 9. 38. Master, I beseech thee to *look* upon my son
11 35. ⁴*L.* therefore whether the light—be not darkness
21. 28. these things begin to come to pass, *look* up
Jno. 4. 35. *look* on the fields, that they are white already
19. 37. They shall *look* on him whom they pierced
Acts 3. 4. Peter, fastening his eyes upon him—said, *Look*
6. 3. *Look* ye out therefore, brethren, from among you
18. 15. names and your own law, *look* to it yourselves
24. 15. these also themselves ¹*l.* for, that there shall be
2 *Cor.* 3. 7. children of Israel could not ²*l.* stedfastly upon. 13
4. 18. while we *look* not at the things which are seen
10. 7. Ye *look* at the things that are before your face
Eph. 5. 15. ³*Look* therefore carefully how ye walk
1 *Pet.* 1. 12. which things angels desire to *look* into
2 *Pet.* 3. 13. according to his promise, we *l.* for new heavens
14. seeing that ye *l.* for these things, give diligence
2 *Jno.* 8. *Look* to yourselves, that ye lose not the things
Rev. 4. 3. he that sat was to *look* upon like a jasper
5. 3. able to open the book, or to *look* thereon
11. 9. men ³*l.* upon their dead bodies three days and a half
18. 9. when they ²*look* upon the smoke of her burning
see expect, fasten, looked, looking, see, wait.

Looked. — *A.V.* ¹*beheld,* ²*look,* ³*looking,* ⁴*regarded,* ⁵*respect,* ⁶*saw.*
Mk. 3. 5. had *looked* round about on them with anger
5. 32. he *looked* round about to see her that had done
8. 24. And he *looked* up, and said, I see men
25 he ²*looked* stedfastly, and was restored, and saw
10. 23. Jesus *l.* round about, and saith unto his disciples
11. 11. temple; and when he had *looked* round about
Lu. 1. 25. *looked* upon me, to take away my reproach
48. For he hath ⁴*l.* upon the low estate of his handmaiden
6. 10. And he ⁵*looked* round about on them all, and said
22. 61. And the Lord turned, and *looked* upon Peter
Jno. 1. 36. he [John Baptist] ²*l.* upon Jesus as he walked
42. Jesus ¹*looked* upon him, and said, Thou art Simon
13. 22. The disciples *looked* one on another, doubting
20. 11. Mary—stooped and *looked* into the tomb
Acts 7 55 [Stephen] full of the Holy Ghost, *l.* up stedfastly
22. 13. in that very hour I *looked* up on him
Heb. 11. 10. he *l.* for the city which hath the foundations
26. for he *looked* unto the recompense of reward
Rev. 18. 18. as they ⁶*looked* upon the smoke of her burning
see beheld, expected, expectation, fastening, looking, saw, seeing.

Looketh.
Mat. 5. 28. every one that *l.* on a woman to lust after her
Jas. 1. 25. he that *l.* into the perfect law, the law of liberty
see expecteth.

Looking.—*A. V.* ¹*beheld,* ²*beholding,* ³*considering,* ⁴*gazing,* ⁵*look—ed,* ⁶*wait—ed—ing.*
Mat. 14. 19. and *l.* up to heaven, he. *Mk.* 6. ⁵ 41; *Lu.* 9. 16
Mk. 3. 34. And ⁵*l.* round on them which sat round about him
7. 34. and *looking* up to heaven, he sighed, and saith
10. 21. And Jesus ²*looking* upon him loved him
27. Jesus *l.* upon them saith, With men it is impossible
15. 43. who—was ⁶*l.* for the kingdom of God. *Lu.* 23. ⁶51
16. 4. and ⁵*l.* up, they see that the stone is rolled back
Lu. 2. 25. Simeon—⁵*looking* for the consolation of Israel
38. were ⁶*looking* for the redemption of Jerusalem
9 62. put his hand to the plough, and *looking* back, is fit
12. 36. *looking* like unto men ⁶*looking* for their lord
Jno. 20. 5. [Peter] *l.* in, he seeth the linen clothes. *Lu.* 24.
Acts 1. 9. as they were ⁵*looking,* he was taken up [12
10. they were ⁵*looking* stedfastly into heaven as he went
11. why stand ye ⁴*looking* into heaven?

LOOKING

Acts 23. 1. Paul, ²*looking* stedfastly on the council
21. now are they ready, *l*. for the promise from thee
Rom. 4. 20. *looking* unto the promise of God, he wavered not
Gal. 6. 1. ³*looking* to thyself, lest thou also be tempted
Phil. 2. 4. not ⁵*looking* each of you to his own things
Tit. 2. 13. *looking* for the blessed hope and appearing
Heb. 12. 2. *looking* unto Jesus the author and perfecter
15. *looking* carefully lest there be any man that falleth
2 Pet. 3. 12. *looking* for and earnestly desiring the coming
Jude 21. *looking* for the mercy of our Lord Jesus Christ
see beholding, expectation, fastening (his eyes), looked.

Loose.—A.V. ¹*put off.*

Mat. 16. 19. whatsoever thou shalt *loose* on earth. 18. 18
21. 2. with her: *l.* them, and bring. Mk. 11. 2: Lu. 19. 30
Mk. 11. 4. in the open street; and they *loose* him
Lu. 13. 15. each one of you on the sabbath *loose* his ox
19. 31. And if any one ask you, Why do ye *l.* him? 33
Jno. 11. 44. Jesus saith unto them, *L.* him, and let him go
Acts 7. 33. ¹*Loose* the shoes from thy feet
Rev. 5. 2. worthy to open the book, and to *loose* the seals
9. 14. *Loose* the four angels which are bound [thereof?
see unloose.

Loosed.—A.V. ¹*washed.*

Mat. 16. 19. loose on earth shall be *loosed* in heaven. 18. 18
Mk. 7. 35. the bond of his tongue was *loosed*. Lu. 1. 64
Lu. 13. 12. Woman, thou art *loosed* from thine infirmity
16. been *l.* from this bond on the day of the sabbath?
Acts 2. 24. whom God raised up, having *loosed* the pangs
16. 26. and every one's bands were *loosed* [of death
22. 30. [chief captain] *l.* him—and brought Paul down
1 Cor. 7. 27. Art thou bound unto a wife? seek not to be
loosed. Art thou *l.* from a wife? seek not a wife
Rev. 1. 5. him that loveth us, and ¹*loosed* us from our sins
9. 15. And the four angels were *loosed*
20. 3. after this he [Satan] must be *loosed* for a little time
7. Satan shall be *loosed* out of his prison
see discharged, loosing, released, set sail.

Loosing.—A.V. ¹*loosed.*

Mk. 11. 5. What do ye, *loosing* the colt?
Lu. 19. 33. as they were *l.* the colt, the owners thereof said
Acts 27. 40. the same time ¹*loosing* the bands of the rudders
see sail, setting (sail), weighed (anchor).

Lord, *with attributes.—see proper names.*

Lord (*applied to man*).—A.V. ¹*dominion,* ²*exercise lordship,* ³*master,* ⁴*sir.*

Mat. 10. 24. above his master, nor a servant above his *lord*
25. as his master, and the servant as his *lord*
18. 25. his *lord* commanded him to be sold
26. *Lord,* have patience with me, and I will pay
27. *lord* of that servant—released him, and forgave
31. came and told unto their *l.* all that was done. Lu. 14. 21
32. his *lord* called him unto him, and saith to him
34. his *l.* was wroth, and delivered him to the tormentors
20. 25. rulers of the Gentiles ¹*lord* it over them. Mk. 10. 24²
24. 46. whom his *l.* when he cometh shall find. Lu. 12. 37,
48. say in his heart, My *lord* tarrieth. Lu. 12. 45 | 43
50. the *l.* of that servant shall come. 25. 19: Lu. 12. 46
25. 18. digged in the earth, and hid his *lord's* money
20. *Lord,* thou deliveredst unto me. 22
21. His *lord* said—enter thou into the joy of thy *lord.* 23
24. *Lord,* I knew thee that thou art a hard man
Mk. 13 35. know not when the ³*lord* of the house cometh

LOST

Lu. 12. 36. like unto men looking for their *lord* [24. 45
42. faithful and wise steward, whom his *l.* shall set. Mat.
14. 22. Lord, what thou didst command is done. 23
16. 3. my *lord* taketh away the stewardship from me?
5. each one of his *lord's* debtors, he said to the first,
How much owest thou unto my *lord?*
8. And his *lord* commended the unrighteous steward
Lu. 19. 16. *Lord,* thy pound hath made ten pounds
18. Thy pound, *Lord,* hath made five pounds
20. *Lord,* behold, here is thy pound
25. they said unto him, *Lord,* he hath ten pounds
Jno. 15. 15. the servant knoweth not what his *lord* doeth
20. A servant is not greater than his *lord*
Acts 25. 26. I have no certain thing to write unto my *lord*
Rom. 14. 4. to his own ³*lord* he standeth or falleth
Gal. 4. 1. a bondservant, though he is *lord* of all
1 Pet. 3. 6. as Sarah obeyed Abraham, calling him *lord*
Rev. 7. 14. I say unto him, My ⁴*lord,* thou knowest

Lording.—A.V. ¹*lords.*

1 Pet. 5. 3. neither as ¹*l.* it over the charge allotted to you

Lords.

Mk. 6. 21. Herod on his birthday made a supper to his *l.*
1 Cor. 8. 5. as there are gods many, and *lords* many
see lording.

Lordship.—A.V. ¹*dominion.*

Lu. 22. 25. The kings of the Gentiles have *l.* over them
2 Cor. 1. 24. Not that we have ¹*lordship* over your faith
see lord.

Lose.

Mat. 10. 39. his life shall *lose* it. 16. 25: Mk. 8. 35: Lu. 9. 24:
42. he shall in no wise *lose* his reward. Mk. 9. 41 [17. 33
Lu. 9. 25. and *lose* or forfeit his own self?
15. 8. ten pieces of silver, if she *lose* one piece
Jno. 6. 39. which he hath given me I should *lose* nothing
2 Jno. 8. that ye *l.* not the things which we have wrought
see forfeit, loseth, lost.

Loseth.—A.V. ¹*lose.*

Mat. 10. 39. he that *loseth* his life for my sake
Jno. 12. 25. He that loveth his life ¹*loseth* it

Loss.—A.V. ¹*damage,* ²*diminishing.*

Acts 27. 21. and have gotten this injury and *loss.* ¹10
22. for there shall be no *loss* of life among you
Rom. 11. 12. and their ²*loss* the riches of the Gentiles
1 Cor. 3. 15. man's work shall be burned, he shall suffer *loss*
2 Cor. 7. 9. that ye might suffer ¹*loss* by us in nothing
Phil. 3. 7. gain to me, these have I counted *loss* for Christ
8. I count all things to be *loss*—for whom I suffered
the *loss* of all things

Lost.—A.V. ¹*lose.*

Mat. 5. 13. if the salt have *l.* its savour. Mk. 9. 50: Lu. 14. 34
10. 6. to the *lost* sheep of the house of Israel. 15. 24
Lu. 15. 4. having ¹*l.* one of them—go after that which is *l.*
6. with me, for I have found my sheep which was *lost*
9. for I have found the piece which I had *lost*
24. is alive again; he was *l.,* and is found. 32 [margin
19. 10. to seek and to save that which was *lost. Mat.* 18. 11
Jno. 6. 12. pieces which remain over, that nothing be *lost*
18. 9. Of those whom thou hast given me I *lost* not one
see perished—ing.

LOT

Lot—s.

Mat. 27. 35. parted his garments—casting *lots*. *Mk.* 15. 24
Lu. 1. 9. his [Zacharias] *lot* was to enter into the temple
Acts 1. 26. gave *lots* for them; and the *l.* fell upon Matthias
8. 21. Thou hast neither part nor *lot* in this matter
  see inheritance.

Cast Lots *A.V.—see cast.*

Loud.

Lu. 1. 42. she [Elisabeth] lifted up her voice with a *l.* cry
8. 28. with a *loud* voice said, What have I to do with thee
17. 15. turned back, with a *loud* voice glorifying God
19. 37. began to rejoice and praise God with a *loud* voice
23. 23. But they were instant with *loud* voices, asking
  that he might be crucified
Acts 8. 7. spirits, they came out, crying with a *loud* voice
14. 10. said with a *loud* voice, Stand upright on thy feet
26. 24. Festus saith with a *l.* voice, Paul, thou art mad
  see great.

Love.—*A.V.* ¹*charity*, ²*dear*, ³*entertain*, ⁴*kindness*.

Mat. 24. 12. the *love* of the many shall wax cold
Jno. 13. 35. my disciples, if ye have *love* one to another
15. 9. I also have loved you; abide ye in my *love*
10. ye shall abide in my *love*—and abide in his *love*
13. Greater *love* hath no man than this, that a man lay
17. 26. *love* wherewith thou lovedst me may be in them
Rom. 5. 8. But God commendeth his own *love* toward us
8. 35. Who shall separate us from the *love* of Christ?
12. 9. Let *love* be without hypocrisy
10. In *love* of the brethren be tenderly affectioned
13. 10. *L.* worketh no ill—*l.* therefore is the fulfilment of
15. 30. and by the *l.* of the Spirit, that ye strive [the law
1 Cor. 8. 1. Knowledge puffeth up, but ¹*love* edifieth
13. 2. but have not ¹*love*, I am nothing. ¹1, ¹3
4. ¹*l.* suffereth long—*l.* envieth not; ¹*l.* vaunteth not
8. ¹*L.* never faileth: but whether there be prophecies
13. abideth faith, hope, ¹*love*—greatest of these is ¹*love*
14. 1. Follow after ¹*love;* yet desire earnestly spiritual
16. 14. Let all that ye do be done in ¹*love*
24. My *love* be with you all in Christ Jesus
2 Cor. 2. 4. that ye might know the *love* which I have
8. I beseech you to confirm your *love* toward him
5. 14. For the *love* of Christ constraineth us; because
6. 6. kindness, in the Holy Ghost, in *love* unfeigned
8. 7. in all earnestness, and in your *love* to us. 8
24. Shew—in the face of the churches the proof of your *l.*
13. 11. The God of *love* and peace shall be with you
Gal. 5. 6. nor uncircumcision; but faith working through *l.*
13. through *love* be servants one to another
22. But the fruit of the Spirit is *love*, joy, peace
Eph. 2. 4. God, being rich in mercy, for his great *love*
3. 19. know the *love* of Christ which passeth knowledge
6. 23. Peace to the brethren, and *love* with faith
Phil. 1. 9. I pray, that your *love* may abound yet more
16. the one do it of *l.*, knowing that I am set for the defence
2. 1. any comfort in Christ, if any consolation of *love*
2. that ye be of the same mind, having the same *love*
Col. 1. 4. the *love* which ye have toward all the saints
8. who also declared unto us your *love* in the Spirit
13. translated us into the kingdom of the Son of his ²*l.*
3. 14. above all these things put on ¹*love*
1 Th. 1. 3. your work of faith and labour of *love*
3. 6. brought us glad tidings of your faith and ¹*love*
4. 9. concerning *love* of the brethren ye have no need
5. 8. putting on the breastplate of faith and *love*
2 Th. 1. 3. the ¹*l.* of each one of you all toward one another
2. 10. because they received not the *love* of the truth

LOVE

1. *Tim.* 1. 5. the end of the charge is ¹*l.* out of a pure heart
14. abounded exceedingly with faith and *love*
2. 15. if they continue in faith and ¹*l.* and sanctification
4. 12. in manner of life, in ¹*l.*, in faith, in purity [2. ¹22
6. 11. follow after righteousness, godliness, faith, *l.* 2 *Tim.*
2 Tim. 1. 7. spirit of fearfulness; but of power and *love*
3. 10. didst follow my—faith, longsuffering, ¹*l.*, patience
Tit 2. 2. aged men—sound in faith, in ¹*love*, in patience
3. 4. our Saviour, and his *love* toward man, appeared
Philem. 5. hearing of thy *love*, and of the faith which
7. For I had much joy and comfort in thy *love*
9. yet for *love's* sake I rather beseech, being such
Heb. 6. 10. not unrighteous to forget your work and the *l.*
10. 24. to provoke unto *love* and good works
13. 1. Let *love* of the brethren continue
2. Forget not to shew ³*love* unto strangers
1 Pet. 1. 22. unto unfeigned *love* of the brethren
4. 8. above all things being fervent in your ¹*love*—for
  ¹*love* covereth a multitude of sins
5. 14. Salute one another with a kiss of ¹*love*
2 Pet. 1. 7. in your godliness ⁴*love* of the brethren; and in
  your ⁴*love* of the brethren ¹*love*
1 Jno. 2. 15. the world, the *love* of the Father is not in him
3. 1. what manner of *love* the Father hath bestowed
16. Hereby know we *love*, because he laid down his life
4. 7. let us *love* one another: for *love* is of God
8. loveth not knoweth not God; for God is *love*. 16
10. Herein is *love*, not that we loved God
12. God abideth in us, and his *love* is perfected in us
16. believed the *l.* which God hath in us—abideth in *l.*
17. Herein is *love* made perfect with us
18. There is no fear in *l.*: but perfect *l.* casteth out fear
2 Jno. 6. this is *love*, that we should walk after his
3 Jno. 6. who bare witness to thy ¹*love* before the church
Jude 2. Mercy unto you and peace and *love* be multiplied
Rev. 2. 4. against thee, that thou didst leave thy first *love*
19. I know thy works, and thy ¹*love* and faith

Love (*verb*).

Mat. 5. 43. said, Thou shalt *love* thy neighbour, and hate
44. I say unto you, *Love* your enemies. *Lu.* 6. 27, 35
46. if ye *love* them that *l.* you, what reward. *Lu.* 6. 32
6. 5. they *love* to stand and pray in the synagogues
24. will hate the one, and *love* the other. *Lu.* 16. 13
19. 19. Thou shalt *love* thy neighbour as thyself. 22. 39;
  Mk. 12. 31, 33; *Rom.* 13. 9: *Gal.* 5. 14: *Jas.* 2. 8
22. 37. Thou shalt *l.* ve the Lord thy God with all thy
  heart. *Mk.* 12. 30, 33: *Lu.* 10. 27
Lu. 6. 32. even sinners *love* those that *love* them
7. 42. Which of them therefore will *love* him most?
20. 46. long robes, and *l.* salutations. 11. 43: *Mat.* 23. 6
Jno. 8. 42. If God were your Father, he would *love* me
10. 17. the Father *love* me, because I lay down my life
13. 34. *love* one another—ye also *love* one another
14. 15. If ye *love* me, ye will keep my commandments
21. and I will *love* him, and will manifest myself
23. If a man *love* me, he will keep my word: and my
  Father will *love* him
31. the world may know that I *love* the Father [3. 23
15. 12. commandment, that ye *l.* one another. 17: 1 *Jno.*
19. were of the world, the world would *love* its own
21. 15. Lord; thou knowest that I *love* thee. 16, 17
Rom. 8. 28. that *l.* God all things work together for good
13. 8. Owe no man anything, save to *love* one another
1 Cor. 2. 9. things God prepared for them that *love* him
2 *Cor.* 11. 11. because I *love* you not? God knoweth
12. 15. If I *l.* you more abundantly, am I loved the less?
Eph. 5. 25. Husbands, *love* your wives. 28, 33: *Col.* 3. 19
6. 24. Grace be with all them that *love* our Lord Jesus

LOVE

1 *Th.* 4. 9. are taught of God to *love* one another
Tit. 2. 4. to *love* their husbands, to *love* their children
3. 15. Salute them that *love* us in faith
Jas. 1. 12. promised to them that *love* him. 2, 5
1 *Pet.* 1. 8. whom not having seen ye *love*; on whom
22. *love* one another from the heart fervently
2. 17. Honour all men. *Love* the brotherhood
3. 10. He that would *love* life, And see good days
1 *Jno.* 2. 15. *Love* not the world—If any man *l.* the world
3. 11. should *love* one another. 4. 7, 11: 2 *Jno.* 5
14. death into life, because we *love* the brethren
18. My little children, let us not *love* in word
4. 12. if we *love* one another, God abideth in us
19. We *love*, because he first loved us
20. say, I *l.* God—cannot *l.* God whom he hath not seen
21. that he who loveth God *love* his brother also
5. 2. we *love* the children of God, when we *love* God
2 *Jno.* 1. whom I *love* in truth. 3 *Jno.* 1
Rev. 3. 19. As many as I *love*, I reprove and chasten
see loved, loveth loving

Love of God.

Lu. 11. 42. and pass over judgement and the *love of God*
Jno. 5. 42. that ye have not the *love of God* in yourselves
Rom. 5. 5. because the *love of God* hath been shed abroad
8. 39. shall be able to separate us from the *love of God*
2 *Cor.* 13. 14. the *love of God*, and the communion of
2 *Th.* 3. 5. the Lord direct your hearts into the *love of God*
1 *Jno.* 2. 5. verily hath the *love of God* been perfected
3. 17. how doth the *love of God* abide in him?
4. 9. Herein was the *love of God* manifested in us
5. 3. the *love of God*, that we keep his commandments
Jude 21. keep yourselves in the *love of God*, looking for

In Love.—A. V. ¹charitably.

Rom. 14. 15. is grieved, thou walkest no longer *in love*
1 *Cor.* 4. 21. shall I come unto you with a rod, or *in love*
Eph. 1. 4. holy and without blemish before him *in love*
3. 17. that ye, being rooted and grounded *in love*
4. 2. longsuffering, forbearing one another *in love*
15. but speaking truth *in love*, may grow up in all things
16. of the body unto the building up of itself *in love*
5. 2. walk *in love*, even as Christ also loved us
Col. 2. 2. be comforted, they being knit together *in love*
1 *Th.* 3. 12. make you to increase and abound *in love*
5. 13. esteem them exceeding highly *in love* for their
2 *Tim.* 1. 13. hast heard from me, *in faith* and *love*
1 *Jno.* 4. 16. he that abideth *in love* abideth in God
18. no fear *in love*—that feareth is not made perfect *in l.*
2 *Jno.* 3. Christ, the Son of the Father, *in truth and love*

Love of money.—A. V. ¹covetousness.

1 *Tim.* 6. 10. the *love of money* is a root of all kinds of evil
Heb. 13. 5. Be ye free from the ¹*love of money*

Loved.—A. V. ¹love.

Mk. 10. 21. And Jesus looking upon him *loved* him
Lu. 7. 47. which are many, are forgiven; for she *l.* much
Jno. 3. 16. God so *loved* the world, that he gave his only
19. men *loved* the darkness rather than the light
11. 5. Jesus *loved* Martha, and her sister, and Lazarus
36. The Jews therefore said, Behold how he *loved* him!
12. 43. for they *l.* the glory of men more than the glory
13. 1. having *loved* his own—he *loved* them unto the end
34. love one another; even as I have *loved* you. 15. 12
14. 21. he that loveth me shall be *loved* of my Father
28. If ye *loved* me, ye would have rejoiced, because I go
15. 9. as the Father hath *loved* me, I also have *loved* you
16. 27. Father himself loveth you, because ye have *l.* me

LOVETH

Jno. 20. 2. disciple, whom Jesus *loved.* 13. 23: 19. 26: 21. 7, 20
Rom. 8. 37. more than conquerors through him that *l.* us
9. 13. Even as it is written, Jacob I *l.*, but Esau I hated
2 *Cor.* 12. 15. If I love you more abundantly, am I *l.* the less?
Gal. 2. 20. who *loved* me, and gave himself up for me
Eph. 2. 4. for his great love wherewith he *loved* us
5. 2. even as Christ also *loved* you, and gave himself
25. even as Christ also *loved* the church
2 *Th.* 2. 16. which *loved* us and gave us eternal comfort
2 *Tim.* 4. 8. also to all them that have ¹*l.* his appearing
10. Demas forsook me, having *loved* this present world
Heb. 1. 9. Thou hast *l.* righteousness, and hated iniquity
2 *Pet.* 2. 15. son of Beor, who *l.* the hire of wrong-doing
1 *Jno.* 4 10. not that we *loved* God, but that he *loved* us
11. if God so *loved* us, we also ought to love one another
19. We love, because he first *loved* us
Rev. 3. 9 before thy feet, and to know that I have *l.* thee
12. 11. and they *loved* not their life even unto death
see lovedst, loveth.

Lovedst.—A. V. ¹loved.

Jno. 17. 23. and ¹*lovedst* them, even as thou ¹*lovedst* me
24. for thou *l.* me before the foundation of the world
26. love wherewith thou ¹*lovedst* me may be in them

Love-feasts.—A. V. ¹deceivings, ²feasts of charity.

2 *Pet.* 2. 13. revelling in their ¹*love-feasts* while they feast
Jude 12. they who are hidden rocks in your ²*love-feasts*

Lovely.

Phil. 4 8 things are pure, whatsoever things are *lovely*

Lover—s.—A V. ¹covetous, ²despisers.

Lu. 16. 14. the Pharisees, who were ¹*lovers of money*
1 *Tim.* 3. 3. not contentious, no ¹*lover of money*
2 *Tim.* 3. 2. For men shall be *l.* of self, ¹*lovers of money*
3. without self-control, fierce, no ²*lovers of good*
4. *lovers* of pleasure rather than *lovers of God*
Tit. 1. 8. given to hospitality, a *lover of good*, soberminded

Lovest.

Jno. 11. 3 Lord, behold, he whom thou *lovest* is sick
21. 15. Simon, son of John, *lovest* thou me. 16, 17

Loveth.—A. V. ¹love, ²loved

Mat. 10. 37. *l.* father or mother more than me—*l.* son or
Lu. 7. 5. for he *loveth* our nation, and himself built
47. to whom little is forgiven, the same *loveth* little
Jno. 3. 35. The Father *l.* the Son, and hath given. 5. 20
12. 25. He that *loveth* his life loseth it
14. 21. he is that *loveth* me: and he that *loveth* me
shall be loved of my Father
24. He that *loveth* me not keepeth not my words
16. 27. Father himself *l.* you, because ye have loved me
Rom. 13. 8. he that *l.* his neighbour hath fulfilled the law
1 *Cor.* 8. 3. if any man ¹*l.* God, the same is known of him
16. 22. If any man ¹*l.* not the Lord, let him be anathema
2 *Cor.* 9. 7. of necessity: for God *loveth* a cheerful giver
Eph. 5. 28. He that *loveth* his own wife *loveth* himself
Heb. 12. 6. For whom the Lord *loveth* he chasteneth
1 *Jno.* 2. 10. He that *loveth* his brother abideth in the light
3. 10. not of God, neither he that *loveth* not his brother
14. He that *loveth* not abideth in death
4. 7. every one that *loveth* is begotten of God
8. He that *loveth* not knoweth not God; for God is love
20. he that *loveth* not his brother whom he hath seen
21. that be who *loveth* God love his brother also

LOVETH

1 Jno. 5. 1. l. him that begat *loveth* him also that is begotten
3 Jno. 9. Diotrephes, who *loveth* to have the preeminence
Rev. 1. 5. Unto him that ²l. us, and loosed us from our sins
22. 15. and every one that *loveth* and maketh a lie

Loving.—A.V. ¹love.

1 Pet. 3. 8. compassionate, ¹l. as brethren, tenderhearted

Low.

Lu. 1. 48. looked upon the *low* estate of his handmaiden
52. their thrones, And hath exalted them of *low* degree
Jas. 1. 9. But let the brother of *low* degree glory
10. and the rich, in that he is made *low*
see lowly.

Lowered—ing.—A.V. ¹let down, ²strake sail.

Acts 9. 25. let him down through the wall,¹l. him in a basket
27. 17. they ²lowered the gear, and so were driven
30. sailors—had ¹lowered the boat into the sea

Lower—est.

Lu. 14. 9. shalt begin with shame to take the *lowest* place
10. thou art bidden, go and sit down in the *lowest* place
Eph. 4. 9. he also descended into the l. parts of the earth?
Heb. 2. 7. Thou madest him a little *lower* than the angels. 9

Lowliness.—A.V. ¹humility

Acts 20. 19. serving the Lord with all ¹lowliness of mind
Eph. 4. 2. with all l. and meekness, with longsuffering
Phil. 2. 3. in *lowliness* of mind each counting other better

Lowly.—A.V. ¹base, ²cast down, ³low.

Mat. 11. 29. learn of me ; for I am meek and *lowly*
Rom. 12. 16. condescend to things that are ³lowly
2 Cor. 7. 6. he that comforteth the ²lowly, even God
10. 1. I who in your presence am ¹lowly among you

Lowring.

Mat. 16. 3. foul weather to-day : for the heaven is red and l.

Lucre.

1 Tim. 3. 8. not greedy of filthy *lucre*. Tit. 1. 7
Tit. 1. 11. things which they ought not, for filthy l.'s sake
1 Pet. 5. 2. nor yet for filthy *lucre*, but of a ready mind

Lukewarm.

Rev. 3. 16. because thou art l., and neither hot nor cold

Lump.

Rom. 9. 21. same l. to make one part a vessel unto honour
11. 16. And if the firstfruit is holy, so is the *lump*
1 Cor. 5. 6. a little leaven leaveneth the whole l ? Gal. 5. 9
7. Purge out the old leaven, that ye may be a new *lump*

Lunatick A.V.—see *epileptic.*

Lust.

Mat. 5. 28. looketh on a woman to *lust* after her hath
Rom. 1. 27. burned in their *lust* one toward another
1 Cor. 10. 6. we should not l. after evil things, as they also
Gal. 5. 16. Spirit, and ye shall not fulfil the *lust* of the flesh
1 Th. 4. 5. not in the passion of *lust*, even as the Gentiles
Jas. 1. 14. when he is drawn away by his own *lust*

MADNESS

Jas. 1. 15. Then the l., when it hath conceived, beareth sin
4. 2. Ye *lust*, and have not: ye kill, and covet, and cannot
2 Pet. 1. 4. corruption that is in the world by *lust* [obtain
2. 10. that walk after the flesh in the *lust* of defilement
1 Jno. 2. 16. the *lust* of the flesh, and the *lust* of the eyes
17. the world passeth away, and the *lust* thereof
see sin.

Lusted—eth.

1 Cor. 10. 6. not lust after evil things, as they also *lusted*
Gal. 5. 17. flesh l. against the Spirit—Spirit against the flesh
Rev. 18. 14 fruits which thy soul *lusted* after are gone
see long

Lusts.

Mk. 4. 19. *lusts* of other things entering in, choke the word
Jno. 8. 44. and the *lusts* of your father it is your will to do
6. 12. mortal body, that ye should obey the *lusts* thereof
13. 14. make not provision for the flesh, to fulfil the *lusts*
Gal. 5. 24. crucified the flesh with the passions and the l.
Eph. 2. 3. we also all once lived in the *lusts* of our flesh
4. 22. which waxeth corrupt after the *lusts* of deceit
1 Tim. 6. 9. many foolish and hurtful *lusts*, such as drown
2 Tim. 2. 22. flee youthful l., and follow after righteousness
3. 6. women laden with sins, led away by divers *lusts*
4. 3. heap to themselves teachers after their own *lusts*
Tit. 2. 12. that, denying ungodliness and worldly *lusts*, we
3. 3. deceived, serving divers *lusts* and pleasures
1 Pet. 1. 14. to your former l. in the time of your ignorance
2. 11. to abstain from fleshly l., which war against the
4. 2. rest of your time in the flesh to the l. of men [soul
3. have walked in lasciviousness, *lusts*, winebibbings
2 Pet. 2. 18. entice in the l. of the flesh, by lasciviousness
3. 3. come with mockery, walking after their own *lusts*
Jude 16. murmurers, complainers, walking after their l
18. be mockers, walking after their own ungodly *lusts*
see pleasures.

Lying.—A.V. ¹laid, ²lie.

Mat. 8. 14. saw his wife's mother ¹lying sick of a fever
9. 2. a man sick of the palsy, *lying* on a bed
Lu. 2. 12 in swaddling clothes, and *lying* in a manger. 16
Jno. 5. 6. When Jesus saw him [lame man] ¹lying
20. 5. looking in, he seeth the linen clothes *lying*. ²6
7. upon his head, not *lying* with the linen cloths
Acts 23. 16. Paul's sister's son heard of their *lying* in wait
2 Th. 2. 9. with all power and signs and *lying* wonders
see falsehood, leaning, plots.

M.

Mad.—A.V. ¹beside thyself.

Jno. 10. 20. He hath a devil, and is *mad*; why hear ye him?
Acts 12. 15. And they said unto her, Thou art *mad*
26. 11. exceedingly m. against them, I [Saul] persecuted
24. Festus saith with a loud voice, Paul, thou art ¹mad
25. Paul saith, I am not *mad*, most excellent Festus
1 Cor. 14. 23. will they not say that ye are *mad* ?
see madness.

Madness.—A.V. ¹mad.

Lu. 6. 11. they were filled with *madness*; and communed
Acts 26. 24. thy much learning doth turn thee to ¹madness
2 Pet. 2. 16. man's voice and stayed the m. of the prophet

MADE

Made.—*A.V.* ¹become, ²gained, ³kept, ⁴making, ⁵obtained, ⁶put, ⁷taught.

Mat. 9. 16. and a worse rent is *made*. *Mk.* 2. 21
22. thy faith hath *made* thee whole. *Mk* 5 34: 10. 52: *Lu.* 8 48: 17. 19
14. 36. were *made* whole. *Mk.* 6. 56: *Jno.* 5. 9
15. 6. And ye have *made* void the word of God
18. 25. all that he had, and payment to be *made*
19. 4. *made* them—m. them male and female. *Mk.* 10. 6
20. 12. but one hour, and thou hast *m.* them equal unto us
21. 42. The same was ¹*made* the head of the corner. *Mk.* 12. ¹10; *Lu.* 20. ¹17; *Acts* 4. ¹11: 1 *Pet.* 2. 7
22. 5. But they *made* light of it, and went their ways
25. 16. traded with them, and *made* other five talents
27. 64. the sepulchre be *made* sure until the third day
Mk. 2. 27. The sabbath was *m.* for man, and not man for
4. 22. manifested; neither was anything ³*made* secret
11. 17. but ye have *made* it a den of robbers. *Lu.* 19. 46
Lu. 2. 2. This was the first enrolment *made*
6. 50. only believe, and she shall be *made* whole
11. 40. did not he that *made* the outside make the inside
12. 14. Man, who *made* me a judge or a divider over you?
13. 13. and immediately she was *made* straight
14. 12. bid thee again, and a recompense be *made* thee
19. 6. he *made* haste, and came down, and received him
16 Lord, thy pound hath ³*made* ten pounds more. ¹18
Jno. 1. 3. All things were *made* by him; and without him was not anything *made* that hath been *made*
10. was in the world, and the world was *made* by him
4. 46. Cana of Galilee, where he *made* the water wine
5. 6. Wouldest thou be *made* whole?
11. He that *made* me whole, the same said unto me
14. Behold, thou art *made* whole: sin no more
7. 23. wroth—because I *made* a man every whit whole
8. 33. how sayest thou, Ye shall be *made* free?
9. 6. he spat on the ground, and *made* clay. 11, 14
19. 7. to die, because he *made* himself the Son of God
Acts 1. 1. The former treatise I *made*, O Theophilus
20. Let his habitation be *made* desolate
2. 36. God hath *made* him both Lord and Christ
3. 16. hath his name *made* this man strong
4. 9. examined—by what means this man is *made* whole
35 and distribution was *made* unto each
7. 27. Who *made* thee a ruler and a judge over us? [24
48. Most High dwelleth not in houses *m.* with hands. 17.
12. 5. but prayer was *made* earnestly of the church
13. 32. the promise *made* unto the fathers. 26. 6
14. 15. the living God, who *m.* the heaven and the earth.
21. to that city, and had ⁷*made* many disciples [17. 24
15. 7. a good while ago God *made* choice among you
9. he ⁶*made* no distinction between us and them
17. 26. and he *made* of one every nation of men
19. 26. they be no gods, which are *made* with hands
20. 29. the Holy Ghost hath *made* you bishops
23. 13. more than forty which *made* this conspiracy
27. 40. hoisting up the foresail—they *made* for the beach
Rom. 1. 20. being perceived through the things that are *m.*
4. 17. father of many nations have I *made* thee) [Abraham]
5. 19. many were *made* sinners—many be *m.* righteous
6. 18. being *made* free from sin, ye became servants. 22
8. 2. *made* me free from the law of sin and of death
9. 29. as Sodom, and had been *m.* like unto Gomorrah
10. 10. with the mouth confession is *m.* unto salvation
11. 9. Let their table be *made* a snare, and a trap
14. 4. he shall be *m.* to stand : for the Lord hath power
1 *Cor.* 1. 17. lest the cross of Christ should be *made* void
20. hath not God *made* foolish the wisdom of the world?
30. Christ Jesus, who was *m.* unto us wisdom from God
4. 9. we are *m.* a spectacle unto the world, and to angels

1 *Cor.* 4. 13. we are *made* as the filth of the world
12. 13. and were all *made* to drink of one Spirit
15. 22. so also in Christ shall all be *made* alive
2 *Cor.* 2. 2. but he that is *made* sorry by me? 7. 9
3. 6. *made* us sufficient as ministers of a new covenant
10. *m.* glorious hath not been *m.* glorious in this respect
5. 1. house not *made* with hands, eternal, in the heavens
21. who knew no sin he *made* to be sin on our behalf
12. 9. for my power is *made* perfect in weakness [*made*
Gal. 3. 19. seed should come to whom the promise hath been
Eph. 1. 11. in whom also we were ⁵*made* a heritage
2. 6. and *m.* us to sit with him in the heavenly places
11. called Circumcision, in the flesh, *made* by hands
13. were far off are *made* nigh in the blood of Christ
14. For he is our peace, who *made* both one
Eph. 3. 7. whereof I was *made* a minister. *Col.* 1. 23, 25
Phil. 2. 7. servant, being *made* in the likeness of men
Col. 1. 12. who *m.* us meet to be partakers of the inheritance
20. having *made* peace through the blood of his cross
2. 11. with a circumcision not *made* with hands
15. powers, he *m.* a show of them openly, triumphing
1 *Tim.* 1. 9. that law is not *made* for a righteous man
19. thrust from them *m.* shipwreck concerning the faith
2. 1. intercessions, thanksgivings, be *made* for all men
Tit. 3. 7. justified by his grace, we might be *made* heirs
Heb. 1. 2. through whom also he *made* the worlds
2. 17. it behoved him—to be *m.* like unto his brethren
5. 5. Christ also glorified not himself to be *made* a high
9. *m.* perfect, he became—the author of eternal salvation
6. 13. For when God *made* promise to Abraham
7. 3. but *m.* like unto the Son of God, abideth a priest
12. there is *made* of necessity a change also of the law
16. *made*, not after the law of a carnal commandment
19. (for the law *made* nothing perfect)
21. have been *made* priests without an oath
9. 11. and more perfect tabernacle, not *made* with hands
24. Christ entered not into a holy place *m.* with hands
10. 3. there is a remembrance *m.* of sins year by year
13. expecting till his enemies be *made* the footstool
33. being *made* a gazingstock both by reproaches and
11. 3. not been *made* out of things which do appear
34. from weakness were *made* strong, waxed mighty
40. apart from us they should not be *made* perfect
12. 23. and to the spirits of just men *made* perfect
Jas. 1. 10. and the rich, in that he is *made* low
2. 22. his works, and by works was faith *made* perfect
3. 9 men, which are *made* after the likeness of God
2 *Pet.* 2. 6. an overthrow, having ⁴*made* them an example
1 *Jno.* 5. 10. he that believeth not God hath *m.* him a liar
Rev. 1 6. and he *made* us to be a kingdom, to be priests
7. 14. washed their robes, and *made* them white
8. 11. died of the waters, because they were *made* bitter
14. 7. worship him that *made* the heaven and the earth
8. hath *made* all the nations to drink of the wine
17. 2. were *m.* drunken with the wine of her fornication
18. 15. merchants of these things, who were *m.* rich by her
19. *made* rich—for in one hour is she *made* desolate

see arising, *become*, *become*, *born*, *brought*, *given*, *known*, *madest*, *make*, *making*, *place*, *prepared*, *ready*, *set*, *spoken*, *whole*.

Made *manifest.*—*A V.* ¹*make manifest*, ²*manifestly declared.*

Lu. 8. 17. nothing is hid, that shall not be *made manifest*
Jno. 1. 31. but that he should be *made manifest* to Israel
3. 21. to the light, that his works may be *m. manifest*
9. 3. the works of God should be *made manifest* in him
1 *Cor.* 3. 13. each man's work shall be *made manifest*
11. 19. that they which are approved may be *made m.*

MADE

1 *Cor.* 14. 25. the secrets of his heart are *made manifest*
2 *Cor.* 3. 3. being ²*made m.* that ye are an epistle of Christ
5. 11. but we are *made manifest* unto God; and I hope that we are *m. manifest* also in your consciences
11. 6. in everything we have *made it m.* among all men
Eph. 5. 13. all things when they are reproved are *m. m.* by the light: for everything that is ¹*m. m* is light
Heb. 9. 8. way into the holy place hath not yet been *m. m.*
1 *Jno.* 2. 19. *made manifest* how that they all are not of us
Rev. 15. 4. for thy righteous acts have been *m. manifest*
see became, manifested

Made suit.—*A.V.* ¹*dealt.*
Acts 25. 24. all the multitude of the Jews ¹*made suit* to me

Made void.—*see void.*

Madest.—*A.V.* ¹*made.*
Heb. 2. 7. Thou *madest* him a little lower than the angels
Rev. 5 10. and ¹*m.* them to be unto our God a kingdom
see stirred.

Magistrate—s.
Lu. 12. 58. going with thine adversary before the *m.*
Acts 16. 20. when they had brought them unto the *m.*
22. the *magistrates* rent their garments off them
35. *m.* sent the serjeants, saying, Let those men go. 36
38. serjeants reported these words unto the *magistrates*
see rulers.

Magnificence.
Acts 19. 27. Diana—be deposed from her *magnificence*

Magnified.—*A V.* ¹*enlarged,* ²*shewed*
Lu. 1. 58 kinsfolk heard that the Lord had ²*m.* his mercy
Acts 5. 13. howbeit the people *magnified* them
19. 17. and the name of the Lord Jesus was *magnified*
2 *Cor.* 10. 15. we shall be ¹*m.* in you according to our
Phil. 1. 20. so now also Christ shall be *m.* in my body

Magnify.
Lu. 1. 46. Mary said, My soul doth *magnify* the Lord
Acts 10. 46. heard them speak with tongues, and *m.* God
see glorify.

Maid—s.—*A.V.* ¹*damsel.*
Mat. 26. 69. in the court: and a ¹*maid* came. *Jno* 18. ¹17
71. another *maid* saw him. *Mk.* 14. 69: *Lu.* 22 56
Mk. 14. 66. cometh one of the *maids* of the high priest
Acts 12. 13. a ¹*maid* came to answer, named Rhoda
16. 16. a certain ¹*maid* having a spirit of divination
see damsel, maiden.

Maiden.—*A.V.* ¹*maid.*
Lu. 8. 51. and the father of the *maiden* and her mother
54. taking her by the hand, called, saying, ¹*M.,* arise
see maidservants.

Maidservants.—*A.V.* ¹*maidens.*
Lu. 12. 45. shall begin to beat the menservants and the ¹*m.*

Maimed.
Mat. 15. 30. with them the lame, blind, dumb, *maimed*
31. saw the dumb speaking, the *maimed* whole
18. 8. to enter into life *maimed* or halt. *Mk.* 9. 43
Lu. 14. 13. when thou makest a feast, bid the poor, the *m.*
21. bring in hither the poor and *maimed* and blind

Mainsail *A.V.*—*see foresail.*

MAKE

Maintain.
Tit. 3. 8. may be careful to *maintain* good works
14. let our people also learn to *maintain* good works

Majesty.—*A.V.* ¹*mighty power.*
Lu. 9. 43. they were all astonished at the ¹*majesty* of God
Heb. 1. 3. sat down on the right hand of the *Majesty.* 8. 1
2 *Pet.* 1. 16. but we were eyewitnesses of his *majesty*
Jude 25. to the only God our Saviour—be glory, *majesty*
see proper names.

Make.—*A.V.* ¹*call,* ²*made,* ³*maketh,* ⁴*provide,* ⁵*teach.*
Mat. 1. 19. not willing to *make* her a public example
3. 3. *Make* his paths straight. *Mk.* 1. 3: *Lu.* 3. 4: *Jno.*
4. 19. I will *make* you fishers of men. *Mk.* 1. 17 [1. 23
5. 36. thou canst not *make* one hair white or black
8. 2. thou canst *make* me clean. *Mk.* 1. 40; *Lu.* 5. 12
12. 33. *make* the tree good—*make* the tree corrupt
17. 4. I will *m.* here three tabernacles. *Mk* 9. 5 : *Lu.* 9. 33
21. 13. house of prayer: but ye ²*m.* it a den of robbers
23. 15. compass sea and land to *m.* one proselyte—*m.* him
27. 65. guard : go your way, *make* it as sure as ye can
28. 19. Go ye therefore, and ⁵*m.* disciples of all the nations
Mk. 5. 39. Why *make* ye a tumult, and weep? the child
12. 36. Till I *make* thine enemies the footstool of thy feet. *Lu.* 20. 43 : *Acts* 2. 35: *Heb.* 1. 13
40. and for a pretence *make* long prayers. *Lu.* 20. 47
Lu. 5. 33. disciples of John fast often, and *m.* supplications
34. Can ye *make* the sons of the bridechamber fast
11. 40. did not he that made the outside *m.* the inside
12. 33. ⁴*make* for yourselves purses which wax not old
14. 18. they all with one consent began to *make* excuse
15. 19. *make* me as one of thy hired servants
16. 9. *M.* to yourselves friends by means of the mammon
19. 5. Zacchæus, *make* haste, and come down
Jno. 2. 16. *m.* not my Father's house of merchandise
6. 15. to come and take him by force, to *make* him king
8 32. know the truth, and the truth shall *m.* you free
36. If therefore the Son shall *m.* you free, ye shall be
14. 23. will come unto him, and *m.* our abode with him
Acts 2. 28. *make* me full of gladness with thy countenance
4. 24. O Lord, thou that didst ²*m.* the heaven and the earth
7. 40. saying unto Aaron, *M.* us gods which shall go before
44. spake unto Moses, that he should *m.* it according to
50. Did not my hand ²*make* all these things? *Heb.* 8. 5
9. 34. Jesus Christ healeth thee: arise, and *m.* thy bed
10. 15. What God hath cleansed, ¹*make* not thou common
22. 18. *M.* haste, and get thee quickly out of Jerusalem
Rom. 3. 3. want of faith *m.* of none effect the faithfulness
9. 20. to him that formed it, Why didst thou ²*m.* me thus ?
21. to *make* one part a vessel unto honour, and another
13. 14. and *make* not provision for the flesh, to fulfil
14. 4. for the Lord hath power to *make* him stand
19. let us follow after things which *make* for peace
15. 26. to *make* a certain contribution for the poor
1 *Cor.* 6. 15. and *make* them members of a harlot ?
8. 13. I will eat no flesh—that I *m.* not my brother to
9. 18. I may *make* the gospel without charge [stumble
10. 13. with the temptation *make* also the way of escape
2 *Cor.* 2. 2. For if I *make* you sorry, who then is he that
9. 5. *make* up beforehand your aforepromised bounty
8. God is able to *make* all grace abound unto you
Gal. 3. 17. disannul, so as to *m.* the promise of none effect
6. 12. As many as desire to *m.* a fair show in the flesh
1 *Th.* 3. 12. the Lord *m.* you to increase and abound in love
2 *Th.* 3. 9. but to *make* ourselves an ensample unto you
2 *Tim.* 3. 15. sacred writings which are able to *m.* thee wise
Heb. 2. 10. to *make* the author of their salvation perfect

206

MAKE

Heb. 2. 17. to *make* propitiation for the sins of the people
7. 25. he ever liveth to *make* intercession for them
8. 5. warned of God when he is about to *m.* the tabernacle
9. 9. sacrifices that cannot —*m.* the worshipper perfect
10. 1. continually, *make* perfect them that draw nigh
12. 13. and *make* straight paths for your feet [do his will
13. 21. [Lord Jesus] *m.* you perfect in every good thing to
Jas. 3. 18. is sown in peace for them that *make* peace
2 *Pet.* 1. 8. *make* you to be not idle nor unfruitful
10. diligence to *make* your calling and election sure
1 *Jno.* 1. 10. say that we have not sinned, we *m.* him a liar
Rev 3. 9. will *m.* them to come and worship before thy feet
12. I will *m.* him a pillar in the temple of my God
10. 9. eat it up; and it shall *make* thy belly bitter
13. 13. should even ³*m.* fire to come down out of heaven
14. that they should *make* an image to the beast
21. 5. Behold, I *make* all things new
see appoint, cleanse, covenant, create, execute, fire, fulfil, good, hold, known, maketh, mention, prove, ready, set, take, turn, void, war.

Make *manifest.—A.V.* ¹*declare plainly.*
1 *Cor.* 4. 5. and *make manifest* the counsels of the hearts
Col. 4. 4. that I may *make* it *manifest,* as I ought to speak
Heb. 11. 14. say such things ¹*m.* it *m.* that they are seeking
see made manifest.

Maker.
Heb. 11. 10. foundations, whose builder and *maker* is God

Makest.
Lu. 14. 12. thou *makest* a dinner or a supper, call not
13. But when thou *makest* a feast, bid the poor
Jno. 8. 53. prophets are dead: whom *m.* thou thyself?
10. 33. because that thou, being a man, *m.* thyself God
see gloriest.

Maketh.—*A.V.* ¹*causeth,* ²*doeth,* ³*make,* ⁴*worketh.*
Mat. 5. 32. for the cause of fornication, ¹*m.* her an adulteress
45. he *maketh* his sun to rise on the evil and the good
Mk. 7. 87. he *m.* even the deaf to hear, and the dumb to speak
Jno. 19. 12. *maketh* himself a king speaketh against Cæsar
Acts 15. 18 Saith the Lord, who ²*maketh* these things
Rom. 8. 26. *maketh* intercession for us. 27, 34
1 *Cor.* 4. 7. Who *maketh* thee to differ? and what
8. 13. if meat ³*m.* my brother to stumble, I will eat no
2 *Cor.* 2. 2. who then is he that *maketh* me glad [flesh
14. *m.* manifest through us the savour of his knowledge
Gal. 2. 6. (whatsoever they were, it *maketh* no matter to me
Eph. 4. 16. *m.* the increase of the body unto the building
Heb. 1. 7. Who *maketh* his angels winds
Rev. 13. 12. he ¹*m.* the earth and them that dwell therein
21. 27. or he that ⁴*m.* an abomination and a lie. 22. 15
see appointeth, healeth, make, pleadeth, putteth.

Making.—*A V.* ¹*made.*
Mk. 7. 13. *making* void the word of God by your tradition
Jno. 4. 1. heard that Jesus was ¹*making* and baptizing
5. 18. his own Father, *making* himself equal with God
Rom. 1. 10. *making* request, if by any means now
2 *Cor.* 6. 10. as poor, yet *making* many rich
Eph. 2. 15. of the twain one new man, so *making* peace
5. 19. singing and *m.* melody with your heart to the Lord
Phil. 1. 4. on behalf of all *m.* my supplication with joy
see mention, made.

MAN

Male.
Mat. 2. 16. Herod—sent forth, and slew all the *m.* children
19. 4. beginning made them *male* and female. *Mk.* 10. 6
Lu. 2. 23. Every *m.* that openeth the womb shall be called
Gal. 3. 28. there can be no *male* and female

Malefactor—s.—*A.V.* ¹*evil doer.*
Lu 23. 32. there were also two others, *m.,* led with him
33. there they crucified him, and the *malefactors*
39. one of the *m.* which were hanged railed on him
2 *Tim.* 2. 9. suffer hardship unto bonds, as a ¹*malefactor*
see evil doers.

Malice.
1 *Cor.* 5. 8. neither with the leaven of *m.* and wickedness
14. 20. in *malice* be ye babes, but in mind be men
Eph. 4. 31. be put away from you, with all *m. Col.* 3 8
Tit. 3. 3 living in *malice* and envy, hateful, hating
see wickedness

Malicious *A.V.*- *see wicked.*

Maliciousness.
Rom. 1. 29. *maliciousness;* full of envy, murder, strife
see wickedness.

Malignity.
Rom. 1. 29. full of envy, murder, strife, deceit, *malignity*

Mammon.
Mat. 6. 24. Ye cannot serve God and *mammon. Lu.* 16. 13
Lu. 16. 9. friends by means of the *m.* of unrighteousness
11. not been faithful in the unrighteous *mammon*

Man.—*A.V.* ¹*born,* ²*person.*
Mat. 4. 4. *Man* shall not live by bread alone *Lu* 4 4
7. 9. what *man* is there of you. 12. 11: *Lu.* 15. 4
12. 43. spirit, when he is gone out of the *man. Lu* 11. 24
15. 18. those which defile the *man.* 11, 20: *Mk.* 7. 15, 20, 23
19. 6. let not *man* put asunder. *Mk* 10 9
26. 72. I know not the *man* 74
27. 24. I am innocent of the blood of this righteous ²*m.*
Mk. 2. 27. The sabbath was made for *man*—not *man* for
5. 8. Come forth—out of the *man. Lu.* 8. 29
11. 2. a colt—whereon no *man* ever yet sat. *Lu.* 19. 30
Lu. 5. 20. their faith, he said, *M.,* thy sins are forgiven thee
12. 14. *M.,* who made me a judge or a divider over you?
18. 4. Though I fear not God, nor regard *man*
22. 58. art one of them. But Peter said, *Man,* I am not
60. *Man,* I know not what thou sayest
23. 6. Pilate—asked whether the *man* were a Galilean
53. where never *man* had yet lain. *Jno.* 19. 41
Jno. 2. 25. witness concerning *man*—what was in *man*
5. 12. Who is the *m.* that said unto thee, Take up thy bed
34. But the witness which I receive is not from *man*
9. 11. The *man* that is called Jesus made clay
19. 5. Pilate saith unto them, Behold, the *man !*
Acts 17. 31. in righteousness by the *m.* whom he hath ordained
18. 2. Aquila, a ¹*man* of Pontus by race, lately come from
19. 16. the *man* in whom the evil spirit was leaped
35. men of Ephesus, what *m.* is there who knoweth not
21. 11. bind the *man* that oweth this girdle
23. 30. be a plot against the *man,* I sent him to thee
25. 5. anything amiss in the *man,* let them accuse him
22. I also could wish to hear the *man* myself
Rom. 1. Wherefore thou art without excuse, O *man*
3. O *man,* who judgest them that practise such things
4. 6. David also pronounceth blessing upon the *man*

MAN

Rom. 7. 22. I delight in the law of God after the inward *m.*
24. O wretched *man* that I am! who shall deliver me
9. 20. O *man*, who art thou that repliest against God?
10. 5. Moses writeth that the *man* that doeth the
10. with the heart *man* believeth unto righteousness
1 *Cor.* 2. 11. who among men knoweth the things of a *man*, save the spirit of the *man*, which is in him?
5. 13. Put away the wicked *man* from among yourselves
10. 13. no temptation taken you but such as *man* can bear
15. 21. by *man* came death, by *man* came also the
45. The first *man* Adam became a living soul
47. The first *man* is of the earth, earthy: the second *man* is of heaven   [is renewed
2 *Cor.* 4. 16. our outward *m.* is decaying—our inward *man*
Gal. 1. 1. Paul, an apostle—neither through man
11. the gospel—preached by me—not after man
12. neither did I receive it from *m.*, nor was I taught it
Eph. 2. 15. create in himself of the twain one new *man*
3. 16. strengthened--through his Spirit in the inward *m.*
4. 24. put on the new *man*, which after God hath been
Col. 3. 9. put off the old *man* with his doings
10. have put on the new *man*, which is being renewed
1 *Th.* 4. 8. he that rejecteth, rejecteth not *man*, but God
2 *Th.* 2. 3. let no *man* beguile you—*man* of sin be revealed
1 *Tim.* 2. 5. one mediator—himself *man*, Christ Jesus
Tit. 3. 4. God our Saviour, and his love toward *man*
Heb. 2. 6. What is *man*, that thou art mindful of him?
8. 2. tabernacle, which the Lord pitched, not *man*
13. 6. I will not fear; What shall *man* do unto me?
Jas. 1. 8. a doubleminded *man*, unstable in all his ways
2. 20. know, O vain *man*, that faith apart from works is
1 *Pet.* 3. 4. but let it be the hidden *m.* of the heart [barren?
see blessed, evil, foolish, good, men, old, one, poor, rich, righteous.

A Man.—A.V. ¹any man.

Mat. 8. 9. I also am a *man* under authority. *Lu.* 7. 8
10. 35. For I came to set a *man* at variance against his
36. a *man's* foes shall be they of his own household
12. 12. How much then is a *m.* of more value than a sheep?
19. 3. Is it lawful for a *m.* to put away his wife. *Mk.* 10. 2
5. For this cause shall a *man* leave his father and mother. *Mk.* 10. 7; *Eph.* 5. 31
21. 28. *A man* had two sons; and he came to the first
22. 24. If a *man* die, having no children, his brother. *Lu.*
26. 18. Go into the city to such a *man*, and say | 20. ¹28
Mk. 13. 34. when a *man*, sojourning in another country
14. 13. shall meet you a *man* bearing a pitcher. *Lu.* 22. 10
Lu. 1. 34. How shall this be, seeing I know not a *man*?
19. 7. He is gone in to lodge with a *man* that is a sinner
20. 9. *A man* planted a vineyard, and let it out
Jno. 1. 6. came a *m.*, sent from God, whose name was John
30. After me cometh a *man* which is become before me
3. 3. Except a *man* be born anew, he cannot see. 5
4. How can a *man* be born when he is old?
27. *A man* can receive nothing, except it have been
4. 29. Come, see a *man*, which told me all things
7. 23. If a *man* receiveth circumcision on the sabbath—because I made a *man* every whit whole on the
51. Doth our law judge ¹a *man*, except it first hear
8. 40. to kill me, a *man* that hath told you the truth
9. 16. How can a *man* that is a sinner do such signs?
32. never heard that any one opened the eyes of a *m.* born
10. 33. that thou, being a *man*, makest thyself God [blind
11. 9. If ¹a *man* walk in the day, he stumbleth not
10. But if a *man* walk in the night, he stumbleth
14. 23. If a *man* love me, he will keep my word
15. 6. If a *man* abide not in me, he is cast forth
13. that a *man* lay down his life for his friends
16. 21. for the joy that a *man* is born into the world

MAN

Acts 2. 22. Jesus of Nazareth, a *man* approved of God
10. 26. saying, Stand up; I myself also am a *man*
13. 22. David the son of Jesse, a *man* after my heart
16. 9. There was a *m.* of Macedonia standing, beseeching
Rom. 2. 21. preachest a *m.* should not steal, dost thou steal?
22. sayest a *m.* should not commit adultery, dost thou
7. 1. how that the law hath dominion over a *man*
1 *Cor.* 4. 1. Let a *man* so account of us, as of ministers
2. required in stewards, that a *man* be found faithful
6. 18. Every sin that a *man* doeth is without the body
7. 26. namely, that it is good for a *man* to be as he is
8. 10. if ¹a *m.* see thee—sitting at meat in an idol's temple
11. 7. a *man* indeed ought not to have his head veiled
14. if a *man* have long hair, it is a dishonour to him?
28. But let a *man* prove himself, and so let him eat
13. 11. am become a *m.*, I have put away childish things
2 *Cor.* 8. 12. it is acceptable according as a *man* hath
11. 20. ye bear with a *m.*, if he bringeth you into bondage
12. 2. I know a *man* in Christ, fourteen years ago
3. I know such a *man* (whether in the body, or apart
4. words, which it is not lawful for a *man* to utter
Gal. 2. 16. a *man* is not justified by the works of the law
6. 1. Brethren, even if a *m.* be overtaken in any trespass
3. if a *m.* thinketh himself to be something, when he is
Phil. 2. 8. found in fashion as a *man*, he humbled himself
1 *Tim.* 1. 8. the law is good, if a *man* use it lawfully
3. 1. If a *man* seeketh the office of a bishop, he desireth
5. if a *man* knoweth not how to rule his own house
2 *Tim.* 2. 5. if also a. *m.* contend in the games, he is not
21. If a *man* therefore purge himself from these
Tit. 3. 10. *A man* that is heretical after a first and second
Jas 1. 23. a *man* beholding his natural face in a mirror
2. 2. come into your synagogue a *man* with a gold ring
14. if a *man* say he hath faith, but have not works?
18. a *man* will say, Thou hast faith, and I have works
24. Ye see that by works a *man* is justified
5. 17. Elijah was a *man* of like passions with us
1 *Pet.* 2. 19. conscience toward God a *m.* endureth griefs
4. 16. if ¹a *m.* suffer as Christian, let him not be ashamed
2 *Pet.* 2. 19. for of whom a *man* is overcome, of the same
1 *Jno.* 4. 20. If a *man* say, I love God, and hateth his
Rev. 4. 7. the third creature had a face as of a *man*
9. 5. as the torment of a scorpion, when it striketh a *man*

A certain Man.

Lu. 10. 30. *A certain man* was going down from Jerusalem
12. 16. The ground of a *certain* rich *man* brought forth
13. 6. *A certain m.* had a fig tree planted in his vineyard
14. 16. *A c. m.* made a great supper; and he bade many
15. 11. And he said, *A certain man* had two sons
16. 1. There was a *certain* rich *m.*, which had a steward
18. 35. a *certain* blind *man* sat by the way side begging
Acts 3. 2. a *c. m.* that was lame from his mother's womb
14. 8. at Lystra there sat a *c. m.*, impotent in his feet
25. 14. There is a *certain man* left a prisoner by Felix

Any Man.—A.V. ¹every man, ²no man.

Mat. 5. 40. if any *m.* would go to law with thee, and take
16. 24. If *any man* would come after me. *Lu.* 9. 23
22. 46. neither durst *any m.* from that day forth ask him
24. 23. if *any m.* shall say unto you, Lo, here. *Mk.* 13. 21
Mk. 1. 44. See thou say nothing to *any m.* : but go thy way
4. 29. If *any man* hath ears to hear. *Rev.* 13. 9
9. 30. and he would not that *any man* should know it
35. If *any man* would be first, he shall be last of all
Lu. 14. 8. When thou art bidden of *any man* to a marriage
26. If *any man* cometh unto me, and hateth not
19. 8. if I have wrongfully exacted aught of *any man*
Jno. 4. 33. Hath *any man* brought him aught to eat?

MAN

Jno. 5. 22. For neither doth the Father judge ²*any man*
6. 46. Not that *any man* hath seen the Father, save he
51. if *any man* eat of this bread, he shall live for ever
7. 17. If *any man* willeth to do his will, he shall know
37. If *any man* thirst, let him come unto me, and drink
8. 33. and have never yet been in bondage to *any man*
9. 22. that if *any man* should confess him to be Christ
31. heareth not sinners: but if *any m.* be a worshipper
10. 9. by me if *any man* enter in, he shall be saved
11. 57. if *any m.* knew where he was, he should shew it
12. 26. If *any man* serve me, let him follow me—if *any man* serve me, him will the Father honour
47. If *any man* hear my sayings, and keep them not
16. 30. and needest not that *any man* should ask thee
18. 31. It is not lawful for us to put *any man* to death
Acts 2. 45. parted them to all—as ²*any man* had need
10. 28. not call *any man* common or unclean [baptized
47. Can *a. m.* forbid the water, that these should not be
19. 38. have a matter against *any m.*, the courts are open
24. 12. neither—disputing with *any m.* or stirring up a
25.16. not the custom of the Romans to give up *a. m.*, before
Rom. 8. 9. if *any man* hath not the Spirit of Christ, he
1 *Cor.* 3. 12. if *any man* buildeth on the foundation gold
14. If *any man's* work shall abide which he built
15. If *a. man's* work shall be burned, he shall suffer loss
17. If *any man* destroyeth the temple of God, him
18. If *any man* thinketh that he is wise among you
5. 11. if *any m.* that is named a brother be a fornicator
7. 18. Was *any m.* called being circumcised? let him not
8. 2. If *any man* thinketh that he knoweth any thing
3. if *any man* loveth God, the same is known of him
9. 15. than that *any man* should make my glorying void
10. 28. if *any man* say unto you, This hath been offered
11. 16 if *any m.* seemeth to be contentious, we have no
34. If *any man* is hungry, let him eat at home
14. 27. If *any man* speaketh in a tongue, let it be by two
37. If *any man* thinketh himself to be a prophet
38. But if *any man* is ignorant, let him be ignorant
16. 22. If *a. m.* loveth not the Lord, let him be anathema
2 *Cor.* 5. 17. if *any man* is in Christ, he is a new creature
10. 7. If *any man* trusteth in himself that he is Christ's
12. 6. lest *any man* should account of me above that
Gal. 1. 9. If *any man* preacheth unto you any gospel other
Col. 3. 13. forgiving—if *a. m.* have a complaint against any
2 *Th.* 3. 8. neither did we eat bread for nought at *any man's*
14. if *any m.* obeyeth not our word by this epistle [hand
1 *Tim.* 6. 3. If *any man* teacheth a different doctrine
*Heb.*10. 15. lest there be *a. m.* that falleth short of the grace
Jas. 1. 26. If *any man* thinketh himself to be religious
1 *Pet.* 4. 11. if *any man* speaketh—if *any man* ministereth
1 *Jno.* 2. 1. And if *any man* sin, we have an Advocate
15. If *any man* love the world, the love of the Father
5. 16. *any m.* see his brother sinning a sin not unto death
Rev. 3. 20. if *any man* hear my voice and open the door
11. 5. if *any man* desireth to hurt them, fire proceedeth
14. 9. if *any man* worshippeth the beast and his image
22. 18. If *any man* shall add unto them, God shall add
19. if *any m.* shall take away from the words of the book
see any (one), a man, no man.

Each or every Man.

Mat. 16. 27. render unto *every man* according to his deeds.
Rom. 2. 6: *Rev.* 20. 13: 22. 12
20. 9. they received *every man* a penny. 10
Lu. 16. 16. preached, and *every m.* entereth violently into it
Jno. 1. 9. the light which lighteth *every man*
2. 10. *Every man* setteth on first the good wine
16. 32. ye shall be scattered, *every man* to his own
Acts 2. 8. how hear we, *every man* in our own language

MAN

Acts 11. 29. *every man* according to his ability, determined
Rom. 2. 10. and peace to *every man* that worketh good
3. 4. yea, let God be found true, but *every man* a liar
12. 3. For I say—to *every m.*—as God hath dealt to each *m.*
14. 5. Let *each man* be fully assured in his own mind
1 *Cor.* 3. 13. *each man's* work shall be made manifest—
and the fire itself shall prove *each man's* work
4. 5. then shall *each man* have his praise from God
7. 2. let *each man* have his own wife, and let each
7. Howbeit *each man* hath his own gift from God
17. Only, as the Lord hath distributed to *each man*
20. Let *each man* abide in that calling. 24
11. 3. know, that the head of *every man* is Christ
2 *Cor.* 4. 2. commending ourselves to *every m.'s* conscience
Gal. 5. 3. I testify again to *every m.* that receiveth circum-
6. 4. But let *each man* prove his own work [cision
5. For *each man* shall bear his own burden
Col. 1. 28. admonishing *every man* and teaching *every m.*
—that we may present *every m.* perfect in Christ
Heb. 2. 9. he should taste death for *every man* [brother
8. 11. not teach *e. m.* his fellow-citizen, And *e. m.* his
Jas. 1. 14. but *each m.* is tempted, when he is drawn away
19. But let *every man* be swift to hear, slow to speak
1 *Pet.* 3. 15. to give answer to *every man* that asketh you
Rev. 22. 18. I testify unto *every m.* that heareth the words
see any man.

Man of God.

1 *Tim.* 6. 11. But thou, O *man of God*, flee these things
2 *Tim.* 3. 17. that the *man of God* may be complete

No Man.—A.V. ¹*any man.*

Mat. 6. 24. *No man* can serve two masters [8. 56: 9. 21
8. 4. tell *no man.* 16. 20: *Mk.* 7. 36: 8. 30: 9. 9: *Lu.* 5. 14:
9. 16. *no man* putteth a piece of undressed cloth upon an old garment. *Mt.* 2. 21: *Lu.* 5. 36
30. See that *no man* know it. *Mk.* 5. 43: 7. 24
17. 9. the vision to *no m.*, until the Son of man be risen
23. 9. And call *no man* your father on the earth
24. 4. Take heed that *no man.* *Mk.* 13. 15: 1 *Jno.* 3. 7
Mk. 2. 22. *no man* putteth new wine into. *Lu.* 5. 37
5. 4. and ¹*no man* had strength to tame him. 3
9. 39. *no m.* which shall do a mighty work in my name
10. 29. *no man* that hath left house, or. *Lu.* 18. 29
11. 14. *No man* eat fruit from thee heneceforward for ever
Lu. 3. 14. Do violence to *no man*, neither exact anything
5. 39. *no m.* having drunk old wine desireth new
8. 16. *no man*, when he hath lighted a lamp, covereth it.
9. 62. *No man*, having put his hand to the plough [11. 33
10. 4. and salute *no man* on the way
15. 16. swine did eat: and *no man* gave unto him
Jno. 1. 18. *No man* hath seen God at any time. 1 *Jno.* 4. 12
3. 2. for *no m.* can do these signs that thou doest, except
13. And *no man* hath ascended into heaven, but he
32. beareth witness; and *no man* receiveth his witness
5. 7. Sir, I have *no man*, when the water is troubled
6. 44. *No man* can come to me, except the Father. 65
7. 4. For *no man* doeth anything in secret, and himself
30. *no man* laid his hand on him. 44
8. 10. where are they? did *no man* condemn thee?
11. And she said, *No man*, Lord
15. Ye judge after the flesh; I judge *no man*
20. *no m.* took him; because his hour was not yet come
9. 4. the night cometh, when *no man* can work
13. 28. *no m.* at the table knew for what intent he spake
15. 13. Greater love hath *no man* than this
Acts 17. 26. be made desolate, And let *no man* dwell therein
4. 17. that they speak henceforth to *no man* in this name
5. 13. of the rest durst *no man* join himself to them
23. when we had opened, we found *no man* within

209

MAN

Acts 9. 7, hearing the voice, but beholding *no man*
18. 10. and *no man* shall set on thee to harm thee
Rom. 12. 17. Render to *no man* evil for evil
13. 8. Owe *no man* anything, save to love one another
14. 13. this rather, that *no man* put a stumblingblock
1 *Cor.* 2. 15. all things, and he himself is judged of *no man*
3. 11. other foundation can *no man* lay than that which is laid
16. Let *no man* deceive himself
10. 24. Let *no m.* seek his own, but – his neighbour's good
12. 3. *no man* speaking in the Spirit – *no man* can say
14. 2. unto men, but unto God; for *no man* understandeth
2 *Cor.* 5. 16. we henceforth know *no man* after the flesh
7. 2. we wronged *no man*, we corrupted *no man*, we took advantage of *no man*
Gal. 3. 11. Now that *no man* is justified by the law
Eph. 2. 9. not of works, that ¹*no man* should glory
5. 6. Let *no man* deceive you with empty words
29. for *no man* ever hated his own flesh
Phil. 2. 20. I have *no man* likeminded, who will care
Col. 2. 16. Let *no man* therefore judge you in meat, or in
18. Let *no man* rob you of your prize by a voluntary
1 *Th.* 4. 6. that *no man* transgress, and wrong his brother
2 *Th.* 2. 3. let *no man* beguile you in any wise [*Tit.* 2. 15
1 *Tim.* 4. 12. Let *no man* despise thy youth. 1 *Cor.* 16. 10:
5. 22. Lay hands hastily on *no man*, neither be
Tit. 3. 2. to speak evil of *no man*, not to be contentious
Heb. 4. 11. that ¹*no man* fall after the same example
5. 4. And *no man* taketh the honour unto himself
7. 13. *no man* hath given attendance at the altar [Lord
12. 14. sanctification without which *no m.* shall see the
Jas. 1. 13. Let *no man* say when he is tempted – tempteth
3. 8. but the tongue can *no man* tame   ¹*no man*
Rev. 7. 9. multitude, which *no man* could number, out of
13. 17. that *no m.* should be able to buy or to sell, save he
14. 3. and *no man* could learn the song save the hundred
18. 11. for *no man* buyeth their merchandise any more
                                                             see none.

Of Man.

Mat. 8. 27. What manner *of m.* is this, that even the winds
19. 10. If the case *of the man* is so with his wife
Jno. 1. 13. nor of the will *of man*, but of God
Acts 12. 22. saying, The voice of a god, and not *of a man*
Rom. 2. 9. upon every soul *of man* that worketh evil
1 *Cor.* 2. 9. And which entered not into the heart *of man*
11. knoweth the things *of a m.*; save the spirit *of the m.*
4. 3. should be judged *of* you, or *of man's* judgement
Jas. 1. 20. wrath *of m.* worketh not the righteousness of God
24. straightway forgetteth what manner *of man* he was
1 *Pet.* 2. 13. to every ordinance *of man* for the Lord's sake
2 *Pet.* 1. 21. no prophecy ever came by the will *of man*
Rev. 13. 18. of the beast: for it is the number *of a man*
21. 17. the measure *of a man*, that is, of an angel
                                                             see men.

One Man.

Jno. 11. 50. it is expedient for you that *one man* should die for the people. 18. 14
Rom. 5. 12. as through *one man* sin entered into the world
15. gift by the grace of the *one man*, Jesus Christ
19. through the *one man's* disobedience the many were
14. 5. *One man* esteemeth one day above another
1 *Tim.* 5. 9. having been the wife of *one man*

Son of Man (*Christ*).—*see proper names.*

Son of Man (*mankind*).

Heb. 2. 6. Or the *son of man*, that thou visitest him?
Rev. 1. 13. of the candlesticks one like unto a *s. of m.* 14. 14

That Man.

Mat. 12. 45. last state of *t. m.* becometh worse. *Lu.* 11. 26
18. 7. woe to *that man* through whom the occasion
26. 24. but woe unto *that man* through whom the Son of man is betrayed I good were it for *that man* if he had not been born. *Mk.* 14. 21; *Lu.* 22. 22
Rom. 14. 20. it is evil for *that m.* who eateth with offence
2 *Th.* 3. 14. note *that man*, that ye have no company with
Jas. 1. 7. let not *that man* think that he shall receive

This Man.—*A.V.* ¹*fellow.*

Mat. 9. 3. *This* man blasphemeth. *Mk.* 2. 7
12. 24. *This* ¹*man* doth not cast out devils, but by
13. 54. Whence hath *t. m.* this wisdom. 56: *Mk.* 6. 2
26. 61. *This* ¹*man* said, I am able to destroy the temple
71. *This* ¹*man* also was with Jesus. *Lu.* 22. ¹59
27. 47. heard it, said, *This man* calleth Elijah
Mk. 14. 71. I know not *this man* of whom ye speak
15. 39. he said, Truly *this man* was the Son of God
Lu. 7. 39. *This man*, if he were a prophet, would have
14. 9. come and say to thee, Give *this man* place
30. *This man* began to build, and was not able to
15. 2. *This m.* receiveth sinners, and eateth with them
18. 14. *This m.* went down to his house justified rather
19. 14. We will not that *this man* reign over us
22. 56. maid seeing him – said, *This m.* also was with him
23. 2. We found *this* ¹*man* perverting our nation
4. And Pilate said – I find no fault in *this man*. 14
18. Away with *this man*, and release unto us Barabbas
41. our deeds: but *this man* hath done nothing amiss
52. *this man* went to Pilate, and asked for the body of
Jno. 6. 52. How can *this man* give us his flesh to eat?
7. 15. knoweth *this man* letters, having never learned?
27. Howbeit we know *this man* whence he is
31. more signs than those which *this man* hath done?
9. 2. Rabbi, who did sin, *this man*, or his parents. 3
16. *This man* is not from God, because he keepeth
24. Give glory to God: we know that *this man* is
29. but as for *this* ¹*man*, we know not whence he is
33. If *this man* were not from God, he could do nothing
10. 41. all things whatsoever John spake of *this man*
11. 37. Could not *this man*, which opened the eyes – have caused that *this man* also should not die?
47. What do we? for *this man* doeth many signs
18. 17. Art thou also one of *this man's* disciples?
29. What accusation bring ye against *this man*?
40. cried – again, saying, Not *this man*, but Barabbas
19. 12. If thou release *this man*, thou art not Cæsar's
21. to Jesus, Lord, and what shall *this man* do?
Acts 1. 18. *this man* obtained a field with the reward
3. 12. Ye men of Israel, why marvel ye at *this man*?
16. faith in his name hath – made *this man* strong
4. 10. in the name of Jesus Christ – doth *this man* stand
5. 28. and intend to bring *this man's* blood upon us
37. After *this man* rose up Judas of Galilee in the days
6. 13. *This man* ceaseth not to speak words against this
7. 36. *This man* led them forth, having wrought wonders
8. 10. *This man* is that power of God which is called
9. 13. heard from many of *this m.*, how much evil he did
13. 23. Of *this man's* seed hath God according to promise
38. through *this m.* is proclaimed unto you remission
18. 13. ¹*m.* persuadeth men to worship God contrary
25. *This man* had been instructed in the way of the
21. 28. Men of Israel, help: *This* is the *m.*, that teacheth
22. 26. What art thou about to do? for *t. m.* is a Roman
23. 9. strove, saying, We find no evil in *this man*
27. *This man* was seized by the Jews, and was about
24. 5. For we have found *this man* a pestilent fellow

MAN

Acts 25. 24. behold *this m.*, about whom all the multitude
26. 31. *This m.* doeth nothing worthy of death or of bonds
32. *This man* might have been set at liberty, if he had
28. 4. No doubt *this man* is a murderer
Heb. 7. 4. consider how great *this man* was, unto whom
Jas. 1. 25. *this man* shall be blessed in his doing
26. but deceiveth his heart, *this man's* religion is vain

Wise Man.

Mat. 7. 24. shall be likened unto a *wise man*, which built
1 *Cor.* 6. 5. there cannot be found among you one *wise* m.

Man, with woman.

1 *Cor.* 7. 1. It is good for a *man* not to touch a *woman*
11. 3. and the head of the *woman* is the *man*
7. but the *woman* is the glory of the *man*
8. *man* is not of the *woman*; but the *woman* of the *man*
9. was the *m.* created for the *w.*; but the *w.* for the *m.*
11. is the *w.* without the *m.*, nor the *m.* without the *w.*
12. *woman* is of the *man*—the *man* also by the *woman*
1 *Tim.* 2. 12. a *w.* to teach, nor to have dominion over a *m.*

Young Man.

Mat. 19. 20. The *young m.* saith unto him, All these. 22
Mk. 14. 51. And a certain *young man* followed with him
16. 5. into the tomb, they saw a *young man* sitting
Lu. 7. 14. he said, *Young man*, I say unto thee, Arise
Acts 7. 58. laid down their garments at the feet of a *y. m.*
20. 9. *y. m.* named Eutychus, borne down with deep sleep
23. 17. Bring this *young man* unto the chief captain. 18
22. So the chief captain let the *young man* go
see lad.

Man child.

Rev. 12. 5. she was delivered of a son, a *man child*. 13

Manger.

Lu. 2. 7. in swaddling clothes, and laid him in a *manger*

Manifest.—*A.V.* ¹*appear,* ²*declare plainly,* ³*known,* ⁴*manifestly declared,* ⁵*shewed openly,* ⁶*shew.*

Jno. 7. 4. If thou doest these things, ⁶*m.* thyself to the world
14. 21. will love him, and will *manifest* myself unto him
22. *manifest* thyself unto us, and not unto the world?
Acts 4. 16. notable miracle hath been wrought—is *manifest*
7. 13. Joseph's race became ⁵*manifest* unto Pharaoh
10. 40. up the third day, and gave him to be made ⁶*m.*
Rom. 1. 19. which may be known of God is m. in them
10. 20. I became *manifest* unto them that asked not of me
2 *Cor.* 2. 14. maketh *manifest*—the savour of his knowledge
3. 3. being made ⁴*m.* that ye are an epistle of Christ
5. 10. must all be made ¹*m.* before the judgement seat
7. 12. your earnest care for us might be made ¹*m.* unto
Gal. 5. 19. Now the works of the flesh are *manifest*
Phil. 1. 13. my bonds became *m.* in Christ throughout
2 *Th.* 1. 5. a *m.* token of the righteous judgement of God
1 *Tim* 4. 15. that thy progress may be ¹*manifest* unto all
Heb. 4. 13. there is no creature that is not *m.* in his sight
11. 14. they that say such things make it ²*manifest*
1 *Jno.* 3. 2. it is not yet made ¹*manifest* what we shall be
3. 10. In this the children of God are *manifest*
Rev. 3. 18. shame of thy nakedness be not made ⁶*manifest*
see evident, (made) known, (made) manifest, make, manifested.

Manifestation.—*A.V.* ¹*brightness.*

1 *Cor.* 12. 7. to each one is given the *m.* of the Spirit
2 *Cor.* 4. 2. by the *m.* of the truth commending ourselves
2 *Th.* 2. 8. bring to nought by the ¹*m.* of his coming
see revealing.

MANNER

Manifested.—*A.V.* ¹*appear,* ²*appeared,* ³*made manifest,* ⁴*manifest,* ⁵*shewed.*

Mk. 4. 22. nothing hid, save that it should be *manifested*
16. 12. after these things he was ²*m.* in another form
14. afterward he was ²*manifested* unto the eleven
Jno. 2. 11. did Jesus in Cana of Galilee, and *m.* his glory
17 6. I *m.* thy name unto the men whom thou gavest
21. 1. Jesus ⁵*m.* himself again—⁵*m.* himself on this wise.
Rom. 1. 19. for God ⁵*manifested* unto them [614
3. 21. from the law a righteousness of God hath been *m.*
16. 26. now is ³*m.*, and by the scriptures of the prophets
2 *Cor.* 4. 10. the life also of Jesus may be ³*m.* in our body. ³11
Col. 1. 26. but now hath it been ⁵*manifested* to his saints
3. 4. When Christ—shall be ¹*m.*—with him ¹*m.* in glory
1 *Tim.* 3. 16. was ⁴*m.* in the flesh, justified in the spirit
2 *Tim.* 1. 10. been ⁵*m.* by the appearing of our Saviour
Tit. 1. 3. in his own seasons *m.* his word in the message
Heb. 9. 26. ²*m.* to put away sin by the sacrifice of himself
1 *Pet.* 1. 20. was ⁴*m.* at the end of the times for your sake
5. 4. when the chief Shepherd shall be ¹*manifested*
1 *Jno.* 1. 2. (and the life was *manifested*—was *m.* unto us
2. 28. if he shall be ¹*manifested,* we may have boldness
3. 2. if he shall be ¹*manifested*, we shall be like him
5. ye know that he was *manifested* to take away sins
8. the Son of God *m.*, that he might destroy the works
4. 9. Herein was the love of God *manifested* in us

Manifestly *A V.—see manifest.*

Manifold.—*A.V.* ¹*divers.*

Lu. 18. 30. receive *m.* more in this time, and in the world
Eph. 3. 10. known through the church the *m.* wisdom of
Heb. 2. 4. by signs and wonders, and by ¹*m.* powers [God
Jas. 1. 2. when ye fall into ¹*manifold* temptations
1 *Pet.* 1. 6. ye have been put to grief in *m.* temptations
4. 10. as good stewards of the *manifold* grace of God

Mankind.—*A.V.* ¹*men.*

Jas. 3. 7. is tamed, and hath been tamed by *mankind*
Rev. 9. 20. the rest of ¹*m.*, which were not killed with these
see man.

Manna.

Jno. 6. 31. Our fathers ate the *m.* in the wilderness. 49
Heb. 9. 4. wherein was a golden pot holding the *manna*
Rev. 2. 17. overcometh, to him will I give of the hidden *m.*

Manner.—*A.V.* ¹*cause.*

Mat. 4. 23. all *m.* of disease and all *m.* of sickness. 9. 35: 10. 1
5. 11. and say all *manner* of evil against you falsely
6. 9. After this *manner* therefore pray ye: Our Father
8. 27. What *m.* of man is this, that even the winds and
Lu. 7. 39. perceived who and what *m.* of woman this is
Jno. 2. 6. set there after the Jews' *manner* of purifying
Acts 20. 18. after what *m.* I was with you all the time
22. 3. instructed according to the strict *m.* of the law
Rom. 3. 5. (I speak after the *manner* of men). 6. 19: 1 *Cor.* 9. 8: *Gal.* 3. 15
7. 8. sin—wrought in me—all *manner* of coveting
1 *Cor.* 7. 7. one after this *manner*, and another after that
11. 25. In like *manner* also the cup, after supper, saying
15. 32. If after the *manner* of men I fought with beasts
Phil. 2. 18. in the same ¹*manner* do ye also joy
1 *Th.* 1. 5. ye know what *m.* of men we shewed ourselves
9. what *manner* of entering in we had unto you
Jas. 1. 24. forgetteth what *manner* of man he was
1 *Pet.* 1. 11. or what *manner* of time the Spirit of Christ
15. be ye yourselves also holy in all *manner* of living

MANNER

1 Pet. 3. 5. after this *m.* aforetime the holy women also
2 Pet. 3. 11. what *manner* of persons ought ye to be
1 Jno. 3. 1. what *m.* of love the Father hath bestowed
Rev. 11. 5. hurt them, in this *manner* must he be killed
22. 2. tree of life, bearing twelve *manner* of fruits
see conduct, custom, do, every, sort.

In like Manner.

Acts 1. 11. 1 Tim. 2. 9: Heb. 9. 21: Jude 7: Rev. 2. 15.
A.V. even so.—1 Tim. 3. 11
A.V. likewise.—Mat. 21. 36: 22. 26: 27. 41: Mk. 14. 31:
Lu. 10. 32: 13. 3: 16. 25: 22. 20: Jno. 5. 19:
Rom. 8. 26: 1 Tim. 3. 8: 5. 25: Heb. 2. 14: 1 Pet.
3. 7: Jude 8

Manner of life.—A.V. ¹conversation.

Acts 26. 4. My *manner of life* then from my youth up
Gal. 1. 13. ye have heard of my ¹*m. of life* in time past
Eph. 4. 22. put away, as concerning your former ¹*m. of life*
Phil. 1. 27. let your ¹*m. of life* be worthy of the gospel
1 Tim. 4. 12. ensample to them that believe—in ¹*m. of life*
1 Pet. 1. 18. ye were redeemed—from your vain ¹*m. of life*
3. 16. who revile your good ¹*manner of life* in Christ

Manners.

Acts 13. 18. forty years suffered he their *manners*
1 Cor. 15. 33. Evil company doth corrupt good *manners*
Heb. 1. 1. spoken—by divers portions and in divers *m.*

Mansions.

Jno. 14. 2. In my Father's house are many *mansions*

Manslayers.

1 Tim. 1. 9. murderers of mothers, for *manslayers*

Mantle.—A.V. ¹vesture.

Heb. 1. 12. And as a ¹*mantle* shalt thou roll them up

Many.—A.V. ¹great, ²often.

Mat. 7. 13. destruction, and *many* be they that enter in
22. *Many* will say to me in that day, Lord, Lord—by
thy name do *many* mighty works?
8. 11. that *many* shall come from the east and the west
13. 58. he did not *many* mighty works there because
19. 30. But *many* shall be last that are first. Mk. 10. 31
20. 28. and to give his life a ransom for *many*. Mk. 10. 45
22. 14. For *many* are called, but few chosen
24. 5. For *m.* shall come in my name, saying, I am the
Christ; and shall lead *m.* astray. Mk. 13. 6: Lu. 21. 8
12. iniquity shall be multiplied, the love of the *many*
26. 28. blood of the covenant, which is shed for *m.* Mk. 14. 24
27. 53. entered into the holy city, and appeared unto *m.*
Mk. 5. 9. My name is Legion; for we are *many*. Lu. 8. 30
Lu. 1. 1. *many* have taken in hand to draw up a narrative
14. joy and gladness; and *m.* shall rejoice at his birth
16. And *many* of the children of Israel shall he turn
2. 34. set for the falling and rising up of *many* in Israel
4. 25. There were *m.* widows in Israel in the days of Elijah
27. there were *m.* lepers in Israel in the time of Elisha
41. And devils also came out from *many*, crying out
7. 47. Her sins, which are *many*, are forgiven
12. 19. thou hast much goods laid up for *many* years
13. 24. for *many*, I say unto you, shall seek to enter in
14. 16. certain man made a great supper; and he bade *m.*
15. 29. his father, Lo, these *many* years do I serve thee
23. 9. he [Herod] questioned him in *many* words; but he
Jno. 6. 9. two fishes; but what are these among so *many*?

MANY

Jno. 6. 60. *M.* therefore of his disciples—This is a hard saying
66. Upon this *many* of his disciples went back
10. 41. And *many* came unto him; and they said, John
21. 11. for all there were so *many*, the net was not rent
Acts 9. 13. Lord, I have heard from *many* of this man
16. I will shew him how ¹*many* things he must suffer
10. 27. he [Peter] went in, and findeth *m.* come together
12. 12. *many* were gathered together and were praying
24. 10. hast been of *many* years a judge unto this nation
17. Now after *many* years I came to bring alms
26. 10. I both shut up *many* of the saints in prisons
Rom. 4. 17. A Father of *m.* nations have I made thee). 18
5. 15. if by the trespass of the one the *many* died—the
one man, Jesus Christ, abound unto the *many*
19. the *m.* were made sinners—the *m.* be made righteous
12. 5. so we, who are *many*, are one body in Christ
15. 23. having these *many* years a longing to come
16. 2. hath been a succourer of *m.*, and of mine own self
1 Cor. 1. 26. not *m.* wise—not *m.* mighty, not *m.* noble, are
4. 15. yet have ye not *many* fathers   [called
8. 5. as there are gods *many*, and lords *many*
10. 17. seeing that we, who are *m.*, are one bread, one body
33. not seeking mine own profit, but the profit of the *m.*
11. 30. For this cause *m.* among you are weak and sickly
12. 14. For the body is not one member, but *many*
16. 9. for a great door—and there are *many* adversaries
2 Cor. 1. 11. means of *many*, thanks may be given by *m.*
2. 6. this punishment which was inflicted by the *many*
17. For we are not as the *many*, corrupting the word
4. 15. that the grace, being multiplied through the *many*
6. 10. as poor, yet making *many* rich; as having nothing
8. 22. we have ²*many* times proved earnest in *m.* things
9. 2. your zeal hath stirred up very *many* of them
11. 18. Seeing that *many* glory after the flesh, I will
Gal. 1. 14. and I advanced in the Jews' religion beyond *m.*
3. 16. He saith not, And to seeds, as of *m.*; but as of one
Phil. 3. 18. For *many* walk, of whom I told you often
Heb. 2. 10. in bringing *many* sons unto glory, to make
7. 23. they indeed have been made priests *m.* in number
9. 28. having been once offered to bear the sins of *many*
11. 12. sprang of one—so *many* as the stars of heaven
12. 15. trouble you, and thereby the *many* be defiled
Jas. 3. 1. Be not *many* teachers, my brethren
2 Pet. 2. 2. And *many* shall follow their lascivious doings
1 Jno. 2. 18. even now have there arisen *m.* antichrists
4. 1. *m.* false prophets are gone out into the world
2 Jno. 7. For *m.* deceivers are gone forth into the world
Rev. 10. 11. Thou must prophecy again over *m.* peoples
see most.

As Many as.

Mat. 22. 9. as *many as* ye shall find, bid to the marriage
10. gathered together all *as many as* they found
Mk. 6. 56. *as many as* touched him were made whole
Lu. 11. 8. arise and give him *as many as* he needeth
Jno. 1. 12. But *as many as* received him, to them gave he
Acts 2. 39. even *as many as* the Lord our God shall call
3. 24. *as many as* have spoken, they also told of these
5. 36. *as many as* obeyed him, were dispersed. 37
10. 45. were amazed, *as many as* came with Peter
13. 48. as many as were ordained to eternal life believed
Rom. 2. 12. *as many as* have sinned without law—as
many as have sinned under law shall be judged
8. 14. *as many as* are led by the Spirit of God, these are
Gal. 3. 10. *as many as* are of the works of the law
6. 12. *As many as* desire to make a fair show in the flesh
16. And *as many as* shall walk by this rule, peace be
Phil. 3. 15. Let us therefore, *as many as* be perfect
Col. 2. 1. for *as many as* have not seen my face in the flesh

212

MANY

1 *Tim.* 6. 1. Let *as many as* are servants under the yoke
Rev. 2. 24. in Thyatira, *as many as* have not this teaching
3. 19. *As many as* I love, I reprove and chasten
13. 15. cause that *as m. as* should not worship the image

Many *things.*

Mat. 13. 3. he spake to them *many t.* in parables. *Mk.* 4. 2
16. 21. and suffer *many things* of the elders and chief priests. *Mk.* 8. 31; 9. 12; *Lu.* 9. 22; 17. 25
Mat. 25. 21. will set thee over *m. things:* enter thou. 23
27. 13. how *many things* they witness against. *Mk.* 15. 4
19. I have suffered *many things* this day in a dream
Mk. 5. 26. had suffered *many things* of many physicians
6. 34. he began to teach them *many things*
7. 4. and *many* other *things*—washing of cups. 13
15. 3. And the chief priests accused him of *many things*
Lu. 10. 41. art anxious and troubled about *many things*
11. 53. and to provoke him to speak of *many things*
Jno. 8. 26. I have *many things* to speak and to judge
16. 12. I have yet *many things* to say unto you
21. 25. there are also *many* other *things* which Jesus did
Acts 26. 9. that I ought to do *many things* contrary to the
2 *Cor.* 8. 22. we have many times proved earnest in *m. t.*
Gal. 3. 4. Did ye suffer so *many things* in vain?
2 *Tim.* 1. 18. in how *m. things* he ministered at Ephesus
Heb. 5. 11. Of whom we have *many things* to say, and hard
Jas. 3. 2. For in *many things* we all stumble
2 *Jno.* 12. Having *m. things* to write unto you. 3 *Jno.* 13

Maran atha.

1 *Cor.* 16. 22. let him be anathema. *Maran atha*

Marble

Rev. 18. 12. and of brass, and iron, and *marble*

Mariners—*A.V.* ¹*sailors.*

Rev. 18. 17. and ¹*m.*, and as many as gain their living by sea

Mark—s.

Rom. 16. 17. *mark* them which are causing the divisions
Gal. 6. 17. I bear branded on my body the *marks* of Jesus
Phil. 3. 17. *mark* them which so walk even as ye have us
Rev. 13. 16. there be given them a *mark* on their right hand
17. able to buy or to sell, save he that hath the *mark*
14. 9. his image, and receiveth a *mark* on his forehead
11. his image, and whoso receiveth the *m.* of his name
16. 2. sore upon the men which had the *m.* of the beast
19. 20. he deceived them that had received the *mark*
20. 4. received not the *mark* upon their forehead
see goal.

Marked.

Lu. 14. 7. he *marked* how they chose out the chief seats

Market—s *A.V.—see gate, marketplace—s.*

Marketplace—s.—*A.V.* ¹*market—s,* ²*streets.*

Mat. 11. 16. children sitting in the ¹*m.*, which call unto. *Lu.* 20. 3. saw others standing in the *marketplace* idle [7. 32
23. 7. the salutations in the ¹*m. Mk.* 12. 38; *Lu.* 11. 43;
Mk. 6. 56. they laid the sick in the ²*marketplaces* [20. 146
7. 4. when they come from the ¹*m.*, except they wash
Acts 16. 19. dragged them into the *m.* before the rulers
17. 17. [Paul] reasoned—in the ¹*marketplace* every day

Marred *A.V.—see perisheth.*

Marriage.—*A.V.* ¹*wedding.*

Mat. 22. 2. king, which made a *marriage* feast for his son
3. call them that were bidden to the ¹*marriage* feast
4. all things are ready: come to the *marriage* feast

MARVEL

Mat. 22. 9. as many as ye shall find, bid to the *m.* feast
30. nor are given in *marriage. Mk.* 12. 25; *Lu.* 20. 35
24. 38. giving in *m.*, until the day that Noah. *Lu.* 17. 27
25. 10. that were ready went in with him to the *m.* feast
Lu. 12. 36. when he shall return from the ¹*marriage* feast
14. 8. art bidden of any man to a ¹*marriage* feast
20. 34. The sons of this world marry, and are given in *m.*
Jno. 2. 1. the third day there was a *marriage* in Cana
2. Jesus also was bidden, and his disciples, to the *m.*
1 *Cor.* 7. 38. he that giveth—virgin daughter in *m.* doeth well; and he that giveth her not in *m.* shall do better
Heb. 13. 4. Let *marriage* be had in honour among all
Rev. 19. 7. the *marriage* of the Lamb is come, and his wife
9. Blessed are they which are bidden to the *m.* supper

Married.

Mat. 22. 25. seven brethren: and the first *m.* and deceased
Mk. 6. 17. his brother Philip's wife: for he had *m.* her
Lu. 14. 20. another said, I have *m.* a wife, and therefore
17. 27. They ate, they drank, they *married*
1 *Cor.* 7. 10. But unto the *m.* I give charge, yea not I
33. that is *m.* is careful for the things of the world. 34
39. she is free to be *married* to whom she will
see joined, marry.

Marrieth.

Lu. 16. 18. putteth away his wife, and *marrieth* another
— he that *marrieth* one. *Mat.* 19. 9

Marrow.

Heb. 4. 12. dividing of soul and spirit, of both joints and *m.*

Marry.—*A.V.* ¹*married.*

Mat. 5. 32. whosoever shall *marry* her when she is put away committeth adultery [10. 11
19. 9. and shall *m.* another, committeth adultery. *Mk.* 10. is so with his wife, it is not expedient to *marry*
22. 24. his brother shall *m.* his wife, and raise up seed
30. resurrection they neither *m. Mk.* 12. 25; *Lu.* 20. 35
Mk. 10. 12. shall put away her husband, and ¹*m.* another
Lu. 20. 34. The sons of this world *marry*, and are given
1 *Cor.* 7. 9. let them *m.:* for it is better to *m.* than to burn
28. But and if thou *marry*, thou hast not sinned; and if a virgin *marry*, she hath not sinned
36. he sinneth not; let them *marry* [abstain
1 *Tim.* 4. 3. forbidding to *marry*, and commanding to
5. 11. waxed wanton against Christ, they desire to *marry*
14. I desire therefore that the younger widows *marry*

Marrying.

Mat. 24. 38. *marrying* and giving in marriage, until the day

Martyrs.

Rev. 17. 6. and with the blood of the *martyrs* of Jesus
see witness.

Marvel.—*A.V.* ¹*marvellous thing.*

Mk. 5. 20. Jesus had done for him: and all men did *m.*
Jno. 3. 7. *M.* not that I said unto thee, Ye must be born
5. 20. and greater works than these—that ye may *marvel*
28. *Marvel* not at this: for the hour cometh, in which
7. 21. I did one work, and ye all *marvel* [all
9. 30. Why, herein is the ¹*marvel*, that ye know not
Acts 3. 12. Ye men of Israel, why *marvel* ye at this man?
2 *Cor.* 11. 14. And no *marvel;* for even Satan fashioneth
Gal. 1. 6. I *marvel* that ye are so quickly removing
1 *Jno.* 3. 13. *Marvel* not, brethren, if the world hateth you
see wonder.

213

MARVELLED — MEAN

Marvelled.—*A.V.* ¹*admired*, ²*wondered*.

Mat. 8. 10. when Jesus heard it, he *m*., and said. *Lu.* 7. 9
27. *marvelled*, saying, What manner of man is this
9. 33. dumb man spake : and the multitudes *m. Lu.* 11.
21. 20. they *marvelled*, saying, How did the fig tree |²1d
27. 14. insomuch that the governor *m*. greatly. *Mk.* 15. 5
Mk 6. 6. [Jesus] *marvelled* because of their unbelief
12. 17. And they *m*. greatly at him. *Mat.* 22. 22 ; *Lu.* 20. 26
15. 44. Pilate *marvelled* if he were already dead
Lu. 1. 21. for Zacharias, and they *m*. while he tarried
63. wrote, saying, His name is John. And they *m*. all
8. 25. being afraid they ²*m*., saying one to another
11. 38. he *marvelled* that he had not first washed
Jno. 4. 27. they *m*. that he was speaking with a woman
7. 15. Jews therefore *m*., saying, How knoweth this man
Acts 2. 7. And they were all amazed and *marvelled*, saying
4. 13. were unlearned and ignorant men, they *marvelled*
2 *Th.* 1. 10. to be ¹*marvelled* at in all them that believed
see afraid, marvelling.

Marvelling.—*A.V.* ¹*marvelled*, ²*wondered*.

Lu. 2. 33. And his father and his mother were ¹*marvelling*
9. 43. while all were ²*m*. at the things which he did

Marvellous.

Mat. 21. 42. the Lord, And it is *m*. in our eyes ? *Mk.* 12. 11
1 *Pet.* 2. 9. called you out of darkness into his *m*. light
Rev. 15. 1. another sign in heaven, great and *marvellous*
3. Great and *marvellous* are thy works, O Lord God
see marvel.

Master.—*A.V.* ¹*goodman*, ²*lord*.

Mat. 8. 19. *Master*, I will follow thee whithersoever thou
9. 11. eateth your *M*. with the publicans and sinners ?
10. 24. A disciple is not above his *master. Lu.* 6. 40
25. for the disciple that he be as his *master*—If they
have called the *master* of the house Beelzebub
12. 38. scribes—*Master*, we would see a sign from thee
17. 24. Doth not your *master* pay the half-shekel ?
19. 16. *M*., what good thing shall I. *Mk.* 10. 17 : *Lu.* 18. 16
22. 16. *M*., we know that thou art. *Mk.* 12. 14 : *Lu.* 20. 21
23. 10. called masters : for one is your *m*., even the Christ
24. 43. if the ¹*master* of the house had known
26. 18. The *Master* saith, My time is at hand
Mk. 4. 38. *M*., carest thou not that we perish ? *Lu.* 8. 24
5. 35. why troublest thou the *M*. any further ? *Lu.* 8. 49
12. 32. *M*., thou hast well said that he is one. *Lu.* 20. 39
14. 14. The *Master* saith, Where is my guest-chamber
Lu. 3. 12. came also publicans—*M*., what must we do ?
6. 40. every one when he is perfected shall be as his *m*.
7. 40. Simon, I have somewhat—he saith, *Master*, say on
9. 33. Peter said—*Master*, it is good for us to be here
10. 25. lawyer—tempted him, saying, *M*., what shall I do
18. 25. When once the *master* of the house is risen up
14. 21. Then the *master* of the house being angry said
17. 13. their voices, saying, Jesus, *M*., have mercy on us
21. 7. when therefore shall these things be ? [thou ?
Jno. 1. 38. Rabbi—being interpreted, *M*.), where abidest
11. 28. The *Master* is here, and calleth thee [Mary]
13. 13. Ye call me, *Master*, and, Lord : and ye say well
14. If I then, the Lord and the *Master*, have washed
20. 16. in Hebrew, Rabboni ; which is to say, *Master*
Acts 27. 11. the centurion gave more heed to the *master*
Eph. 6. 9. their *Master* and yours is in heaven. *Col.* 4. 1
2 *Tim.* 2. 21. sanctified, meet for the *master's* use
2 *Pet.* 2. 1. denying even the ²*Master* that bought them
see lord, Rabbi (proper names), teacher.

Masterbuilder.

1 *Cor.* 3. 10. as a wise *masterbuilder* I laid a foundation

Mastered.—*A.V.* ¹*overcame*.

Acts 19. 16. evil spirit was leaped on them, and ¹*m*. both

Masteries *A.V.*—*see games.*

Masters.

Mat. 6. 24. No man can serve two *masters. Lu.* 16. 13
15. 27. crumbs which fall from their *masters'* table
23. 10. Neither be ye called *m*. : for one is your master
Acts 16. 16. which brought her *m*. much gain by soothsaying
19. when her *m*. saw that the hope of their gain was gone
Eph. 6. 5. are your *m. Col.* 3. 22 : *Tit.* 2. 9 : 1 *Pet.* 2. 18
9. And, ye *m*., do the same things unto them. *Col.* 4. 1
1 *Tim.* 6. 1. count their own *masters* worthy of all honour
2. that have believing *m*., let them not despise them
see teachers.

Mastery *A.V.*—*see games.*

Matter.—*A.V.* ¹*business*, ²*concerning*, ³*crime*, ⁴*thing*.

Mk. 1. 45. publish it much, and to spread abroad the *m*.
10. 10. the disciples asked him again of this *matter*
Acts 8. 21. Thou hast neither part nor lot in this *matter*
11. 4. But Peter began, and expounded the *matter*
15. 6. apostles and the elders—to consider of this *matter*
18. 14. Gallio said—If indeed it were a *matter* of wrong
19. 38. If therefore Demetrius—have a *m*. against any
24. 22. But Felix—come down, I will determine your *m*.
25. 16. make his defence concerning the ³*m*. laid against
Rom. 16. 2. assist her [Phœbe] in whatsoever ¹*m*. she may
2 *Cor.* 7. 11. ye approved yourselves to be pure in the *m*.[bour
8. 19. to travel with us in the *matter* of this grace
9. 5. as a *matter* of bounty, and not of extortion. 8. 20
Gal. 2. 6. (whatsoever they were, it maketh no *m*. to me
5. 18. good to be zealously sought in a good ⁴*matter*
Phil. 4. 15. no church had fellowship with me in the ²*m*.
1 *Th.* 4. 6. transgress, and wrong his brother in the *matter*
see word.

Matters.—*A.V.* ¹*things*.

Mat. 23. 23. have left undone the weightier *m*. of the law
Lu. 1. 1. concerning those ¹*m*. which have been fulfilled
Acts 18. 15. (Gallio) not minded to be a judge of these *m*.
19. 39. if ye seek anything about other *matters*
25. 20. go to Jerusalem, and there be judged of these *m*.
1 *Cor.* 6. 2. are ye unworthy to judge the smallest *matters* ?
1 *Pet.* 4. 15. or as a meddler in other men's *matters*
2 *Pet.* 2. 12. railing in ¹*matters* whereof they are ignorant

May be.

Jno. 14. 3. that where I am, there ye *may be* also
17. 11. that they *may be* one, even as we are. 21, 22
26. wherewith thou lovedst me *may be* in them, and I
1 *Cor.* 15. 28. that God *may be* all in all [in them

Meal.

Mat. 13. 33. leaven, which a woman took, and hid in three
measures of *meal. Lu.* 13. 21

Mean.—*A.V.* ¹*say*.

Mk. 9. 10. what the rising again from the dead should *m*.
Acts 10. 17. Peter—the vision which he had seen might *m*.
17. 20. we would know therefore what these things *m*.
21. 39. of Tarsus in Cilicia, a citizen of no *mean* city
1 *Cor.* 1. 12. Now this I ¹*mean*, that each one of you
see do, I say.

MEANETH

Meaneth.
Mat. 9. 13. learn what this *meaneth*, I desire mercy. 12. 7
Acts 2. 12. saying one to another, What *meaneth* this?

Meaning.
1 Cor. 14. 11. If then I know not the *meaning* of the voice
  see about.

Means.—A.V. ¹*haply*, ²*perhaps.*
Mat. 5. 26. Thou shalt by no *m*. come out thence. Lu. 12. 59
Acts 4. 9. impotent man, by what *m*. this man is made whole
  27. 12. if by any *means* they could reach Phœnix
Rom. 1. 10. if by any *m*. now at length I may be prospered
  11. 14. if by any *means* I may provoke to jealousy
1 Cor. 8. 9. take heed lest by any *means* this liberty of yours
  9. 22. to all men, that I may by all *means* save some
  27. lest by any *means*, after that I have preached
2 Cor. 1. 11. for the gift bestowed upon us by *m*. of many
  2. 7. lest by any ²*m*. such a one should be swallowed up
  9. 4. lest by any ¹*means*, if there come with me any of
  11. 3. I fear, lest by any *m*., as the serpent beguiled Eve
Gal. 2. 2. lest by any *means* I should be running—in vain
Phil. 3. 11. if by any *m*. I may attain unto the resurrection
1 Th. 3. 5. lest by any *means* the tempter had tempted you
  see reason, ways, wise.

Meant.
Lu 18. 36. a multitude going by, he enquired what this *m*.

Measure.—A.V. ¹*sort.*
Mat. 7. 2. with what *measure* ye mete. Mk. 4. 24: Lu. 6. 38
  23. 32. Fill ye up then the *measure* of your fathers
Mk. 7. 37. And they were beyond *measure* astonished
Lu. 6. 38. and it shall be given unto you; good *m*., pressed
Jno. 3. 34. for he giveth not the Spirit by *measure* [down
Rom. 12. 3. as God hath dealt to each man a *m*. of faith
  15. 15. I write the more boldly unto you in some ¹*measure*
2 Cor. 9. 12. not only filleth up the *m*. of the wants. 11. 9
  10. 13. we will not glory beyond our *measure*, but
  according to the *measure* of the province which
  God apportioned to us as a *measure*. 15
  11. 23. in stripes above *measure*, in deaths oft
Gal. 1. 13. beyond *measure* I persecuted the church of God
Eph. 4. 7. grace given according to the *m*. of the gift of Christ
  13. unto the *m*. of the stature of the fulness of Christ
  16. the working in due *measure* of each several part
Rev. 6. 6. A *measure* of wheat for a penny
  11. 1. Rise, and *measure* the temple of God, and the altar
  2. without the temple leave without, and *m*. it not
  21. 15. for a *measure* a golden reed to *measure* the city
  17. according to the *m*. of a man, that is, of an angel
    see exceedingly, overmuch.

Measured.
Mat. 7. 2. and with what measure ye mete, it shall be
  measured unto you. Mk. 4. 24: Lu. 6. 38
Rev. 21. 16 he *measured* the city with the reed
  17. And he *measured* the wall thereof

Measures.
Mat. 13. 33. and hid in three *measures* of meal. Lu. 13. 21
Lu. 16. 6. And he said, A hundred *measures* of oil. 7
Rev. 6. 6. three *measures* of barley for a penny

Measuring.
2 Cor. 10. 12. *m*. themselves by themselves, and comparing

Meat.—A.V. ¹*table.*
Mat. 9. 10. sat (or sitting) at *meat*. 26. 7: Mk. 2. 15: 6. 22:
  14. 3: 16. 14: Lu. 5. 29: 7. 36, 37, 49: 11. 37:
  14. 15: 24. 30

MEEKNESS

Mat. 14. 9. his oaths, and of them which sat at *m*. with him
  25. 35. I was an hungred, and ye gave me *meat*
  42. I was an hungred, and ye gave me no *meat*
Lu. 12. 37. gird himself, and make them sit down to *meat*
  14. 10. glory in the presence of all that sit at *meat*
  17. 7. Come straightway and sit down to *meat*
  22. 27. greater, he that sitteth at *m*., or—sitteth at *m*.?
Jno. 4. 32. I have *meat* to eat that ye know not
  34. My *meat* is to do the will of him that sent me
  6. 27. Work not for the *meat* which perisheth, but for
    the *meat* which abideth unto eternal life
  55. For my flesh is *m*. indeed, and my blood is drink
  12. 2. Lazarus was one of them that sat at ¹*m* with him
Acts 16. 34. set *meat* before them, and rejoiced greatly
Rom. 14. 15. if because of *meat* thy brother is grieved—
  Destroy not with thy *m*. him for whom Christ did
  20. Overthrow not for *meat's* sake the work of God
1 Cor. 3. 2. I fed you with milk, not with *meat*
  8. 8. But *meat* will not commend us to God
  10. hast knowledge sitting at *meat* in an idol's temple
  13. if *meat* maketh my brother to stumble, I will eat no
  10. 3. and did all eat the same spiritual *meat* [flesh
Col. 2. 16. Let no man therefore judge you in *meat*
Heb. 12. 16. for one mess of *meat* sold his own birthright
  see broken (pieces), to eat, eating, food, something.

Meats.
Mk. 7. 19. This he said, making all *meats* clean
1 Cor. 6. 13. *Meats* for the belly, and the belly for *meats*
1 Tim. 4. 3. forbidding to marry, and—to abstain from *m*.
Heb. 9. 10. (with *m*. and drinks and divers washings) carnal
  13. 9. that the heart be stablished by grace; not by *meats*
    see food, things.

Mediator.
Gal. 3. 19. ordained through angels by the hand of a *m*.
  20. Now a *m*. is not a *mediator* of one; but God is one
1 Tim. 2. 5. one *m*. also between God and men, himself man
Heb. 8. 6. he is the *mediator* of a better covenant
  9. 15. And for this cause he is the *m*. of a new covenant
  12. 24. and to Jesus the *mediator* of a new covenant

Meddler.—A.V. ¹*busybody.*
1 Pet. 4. 15. suffer—or as a ¹*meddler* in other men's matters

Meditate.
Lu. 21. 14. your hearts, not to *m*. beforehand how to answer
  see diligent.

Meek.
Mat. 5. 5. Blessed are the *m*.: for they shall inherit the earth
  11. 29. learn of me; for I am *meek* and lowly in heart
  21. 5. Behold, thy King cometh unto thee, M., and riding
1 Pet. 3. 4. the incorruptible apparel of a *m*. and quiet spirit

Meekness.
1 Cor. 4. 21. with a rod, or in love and a spirit of *meekness*?
2 Cor. 10. 1. intreat you by the *m*. and gentleness of Christ
Gal. 5. 23. *m*., temperance: against such there is no law
  6. 1. restore such a one in a spirit of *meekness*
Eph. 4. 2. with all lowliness and *m*., with longsuffering
Col. 3. 12. a heart of compassion, kindness, humility, *m*.
1 Tim. 6. 11. follow after—faith, love, patience, *meekness*
2 Tim. 2. 25. in *m*. correcting them that oppose themselves
Tit. 3. 2. to be gentle, shewing all *meekness* toward all men
Jas. 1. 21. receive with *meekness* the implanted word
  3. 13. by his good life his works in *meekness* of wisdom
1 Pet. 3. 15. concerning the hope that is in you, yet with *m*.

MEET

Meet.
Mat. 8. 34 And behold, all the city came out to m. Jesus
15. 26. not meet to take the children's bread. Mk. 7. 27
25. 1. their lamps, and went forth to m. the bridegroom
 6. Behold, the bridegroom! Come ye forth to m. him
Mk. 14. 13. shall meet you a man bearing. Lu. 22. 10
Lu. 14. 31. he is able with ten thousand to meet him
15. 32. But it was meet to make merry and be glad
Jno. 12. 13. went forth to m. him, and cried out, Hosanna
Acts 28. 15. came to m. us as far as The Market of Appius
1 Cor. 15. 9. that am not meet to be called an apostle
16. 4. and if it be meet for me to go also, they shall go
Col. 1. 12. the Father, who made us meet to be partakers
1 Th. 4. 17. in the clouds, to meet the Lord in the air
2 Th. 1. 3. to God always for you, brethren, even as it is m.
2 Tim. 2. 21. sanctified, meet for the master's use
Heb. 6. 7. forth herbs meet for them for whose sake it is
see due, right, worthy.

Melody.
Eph. 5. 19. singing and making melody with your heart

Melt.
2 Pet. 3. 12. the elements shall melt with fervent heat?
see dissolved.

Member.
1 Cor. 12. 14. For the body is not one member, but many
19. if they were all one member, where were the body?
26. whether one m. suffereth—or one m. is honoured
Jas. 3. 5. So the tongue also is a little m., and boasteth

Members.
Mat. 5. 29. that one of thy members should perish. 30
Rom. 6. 13. neither present your members unto sin – and
 your members as instruments of righteousness
19. as ye presented your m.—so now present your m.
7. 5. wrought in our members to bring forth fruit unto
23. I see a different law in my m.—bringing me into
 captivity under the law of sin which is in my m.
12. 4. as we have many members—all the members have
5. in Christ, and severally members one of another
1 Cor. 6. 15. your bodies are members of Christ—away the
 members of Christ, and make them m. of a harlot?
12. 12. as the body is one, and hath many members, and
 all the members of the body, being many
18. now hath God set the members each one of them
20. But now are they many members, but one body
22. those m. of the body which seem to be more feeble
25. that the members should have the same care
26. all the m. suffer—all the members rejoice with it
27. ye are the body of Christ, and members severally
Eph. 4. 25. for we are members one of another
5. 30. because we are members of his body
Col. 3. 5. Mortify therefore your m. which are upon the
Jas. 3. 6. world of iniquity among our m. is the tongue
4. 1. of your pleasures that war in your members?
see parts.

Memorial.
Mat. 26. 13. shall be spoken of for a m. of her. Mk. 14. 9
Acts 10. 4. and thine alms are gone up for a m. before God

Memory A.V.—*see hold (fast).*

Men.—A.V. ¹age, ²apostles, ³estates, ⁴man, ⁵mankind.
Mat. 5. 16. Even so let your light shine before men
19. least commandments, and shall teach men so
6. 1. heed that ye do not your righteousness before men
7. 12. ye would that men should do unto you. Lu. 6. 31

MEN

Mat. 9. 8. God, which had given such power unto men
10. 32. confess me before men, him will I also. Lu. 12. 8
33. whosoever shall deny me before men. Lu. 12, 9
13. 25. while men slept, his enemy came and sowed tares
19. 12. eunuchs, which were made eunuchs by men
26. With men this is impossible. Mk. 10. 27; Lu. 18. 27
21. 25. The baptism of John, whence was it? from heaven
 or from men? 26; Mt. 11. 30, 32; Lu. 20. 4, 6
41. He will miserably destroy those miserable men
23. 28. ye also outwardly appear righteous unto men
Mk. 3. 28. their sins shall be forgiven unto the sons of men
6. 21. high captains, and the chief ⁴men of Galilee
8. 24. I see men; for I behold them as trees, walking
27. Who do men say that I am? Mat. 16. 13
Lu. 2. 14. on earth peace among men in whom he is well
52. wisdom and stature, and in favour with God and ⁴m.
5. 10. Fear not; from henceforth thou shalt catch men
11. 31 in the judgement with the men of this generation
32. The men of Nineveh shall stand up in the judgement
12. 36. yourselves like unto men looking for their Lord
18. 11. I thank thee, that I am not as the rest of men
Jno. 5. 41. I receive not glory from men
17. 6. I manifested thy name unto the men whom thou
Acts 1. 11. Ye men of Galilee, why stand ye looking into
21. the men therefore which have companied with us
2. 14. Ye men of Judæa, and all ye that dwell at Jeru-
4. 16. What shall we do to these men? [salem
5. 4. thou hast not lied unto men, but unto God
6. And the young men arose and wrapped him round
10. and the young men came in and found her dead
14. multitudes both of men and women
25. the m. whom ye put in the prison are in the temple
29. We must obey God rather than men
34. commanded to put the ⁴men forth a little while
35. Ye men of Israel, take heed—touching these men
38. Refrain from these men—or this work be of men
8. 3. haling men and women committed them to prison
12. they were baptized, both men and women
9. 2. any that were of the Way, whether men or women
13. 16. Men of Israel, and ye that fear God, hearken
14. 15. We also are men of like passions with you
15. 26. men that have hazarded their lives for the name
16. 17 These men are servants of the Most High God
35. sent the serjeants, saying, Let those men go
17. 22. Paul—said, Ye men of Athens, in all things
19. 35. the townclerk—saith, Ye men of Ephesus
37. these men, which are neither robbers of temples
20. 30. among your own selves shall men arise, speaking
21. 23. We have four men which have a vow on them
26. Then Paul took the men, and the next day
28. crying out, Men of Israel, help
22. 4. delivering into prisons both men and women
24. 16. void of offence toward God and men alway
Rom 1. 27. likewise also the men, leaving the natural use
 of the woman—m. with m. working unseemliness
1 Cor. 1. 25. foolishness of God is wiser than m.—stronger
3. 21. Wherefore let no one glory in men [than men
4. 9. apostles last of all, as men doomed to death—a
 spectacle unto the world, and to angels, and to m.
6. 9. nor abusers of themselves with ⁵men. 1 Tim. 1. ⁵10
14. 2. speaketh in a tongue speaketh not unto men
20. howbeit in malice be ye babes, but in mind be men
21. in the law it is written, By men of strange tongues
16. 13. stand fast in the faith, quit you like men, be strong
2 Cor. 5. 11. Knowing—fear of the Lord, we persuade men
Gal. 1. 1. Paul, an apostle (not from men, neither through
10. am I now persuading men, or God?—seeking to
 please men? if I were still pleasing men
Eph. 3. 5. not made known unto the sons of men, as it

MEN

Eph. 4. 8. led captivity captive, And gave gifts unto *men*
6. 7. as unto the Lord, and not unto *men*. *Col.* 3. 23
1 *Th.* 2. 4. so we speak; not as pleasing *men*, but God
6. nor seeking glory of *men*, neither from you
2 *Th.* 3. 2. delivered from unreasonable and evil *men*
1 *Tim.* 2. 8. I desire therefore that the *men* pray in every
2 *Tim.* 3. 2. For *men* shall be lovers of self, lovers of money
Tit. 2. 6. younger *men* likewise exhort to be soberminded
Heb. 5. 1. high priest—from among *m.*, is appointed for *m.*
14. But solid food is for fullgrown ¹*men*
6. 16. For *men* swear by the greater: and in every dispute
7. 8. And here *men* that die receive tithes
9. 27. it is appointed unto *m.* once to die, and after this
12. 23. and to the spirits of just *men* made perfect
Jas. 3. 9. therewith curse we *men*, which are made after
1 *Pet.* 4. 6. that they—be judged according to *m.* in the flesh
2 *Pet.* 1. 21. but *men* spake from God, being moved by the
1 *Jno.* 2. 13. I write unto you, young *men.* 14
Jude 4. there are certain *men* crept in privily—ungodly *men*, turning the grace of our God
Rev. 9. 4. only such *men* as have not the seal of God
7. their faces were as *men's* faces
10. their power to hurt *men* five months
14. 4. These were purchased from among *men*
16. 18. earthquake, such as was not since there were *m.*
19. 18. flesh of captains, and the flesh of mighty *men*
21. 3. Behold, the tabernacle of God is with *men*
see brethren, chief, evil, husbands, Israel, Judah (proper names), old, rich, righteous, things, two.

All Men.

Mat. 10. 22. And ye shall be hated of *all men* for my name's sake. *Mk.* 13. 13: *Lu.* 21. 17
19. 11. *All men* cannot receive this saying
Mk. 5. 20. Jesus had done for him: and *all m.* did marvel
Lu. 3. 15. *all men* reasoned in their hearts concerning John
6. 26. Woe unto you, when *all m.* shall speak well of you
13. 4. think ye that they were offenders above *all the m.*
Jno. 2. 24. Jesus did not trust—for that he knew *all men*
3. 26. the same baptizeth, and *all men* come to him
11. 48. If we let him thus alone, *all m.* will believe on him
12. 32. I, if I be lifted up from the earth, will draw *all m.*
13. 35. By this shall *all m.* know that ye are my disciples
Acts 1. 24. Thou, Lord, which knowest the hearts of *all m.*
4. 21. for *all men* glorified God for that which was done
17. 30. commandeth *men* that they should *all*—repent
31. whereof he hath given assurance unto *all men*
19. 7. And they were in *all* about twelve *men*
20. 26. that I am pure from the blood of *all men*
21. 28. the man, that teacheth *all m.* everywhere against
22. 15. thou shalt be a witness for him unto *all men*
Rom. 5. 12. death passed unto *all men*, for that all sinned
18. the judgement came unto *all m.* to condemnation—the free gift came unto *all m.* to justification of life
12. 17. for things honourable in the sight of *all men*
18. as much as in you lieth, be at peace with *all men*
16. 19. your obedience is come abroad unto *all men*
1 *Cor.* 7. 7. I would that *all men* were even as I myself
9. 19. though I was free from *all men*, I brought myself
22. I am become all things to *all men*, that I may
10. 33. I also please *all m.* in all things, not seeking mine
15. 19. this life only— e are of *all men* most pitiable
2 *Cor.* 3. 2. written in our hearts, known and read of *all m.*
Gal. 6. 10. let us work that which is good toward *all men*
Eph. 3. 9. to make *all men* see what is the dispensation
Phil. 4. 5. Let your forbearance be known unto *all men*
1 *Th.* 2. 15. please not God, and are contrary to *all men*
3. 12. in love one toward another, and toward *all men*
1 *Tim.* 2. 1. thanksgivings, be made for *all men*

MEN

1 *Tim.* 2. 4. who willeth that *all men* should be saved
4. 10. God, who is the Saviour of *all men*, specially of
2 *Tim.* 3. 9. for their folly shall be evident unto *all men*
Tit. 2. 11. hath appeared, bringing salvation to *all men*
3. 2. be gentle, shewing all meekness toward *all men*
Heb. 12. 14. Follow after peace with *all men*
1 *Pet.* 2. 17. Honour *all men.* Love the brotherhood
3 *Jno.* 12. Demetrius hath the witness of *all men*
Rev. 19. 18. and the flesh of *all men*, both free and bond

Of Men.—A.V. ¹man.

Mat. 4. 19. I will make you fishers *of men. Mk.* 1. 17
5. 13. to be cast out and trodden under foot *of men*
6. 2. and in the streets, that they may have glory *of men*
5. that they may be seen *of men.* 23. 5
16. that they may be seen *of men* to fast. 18
10. 17. But beware *of men:* for they will deliver you
15. 9. as their doctrines the precepts *of men. Mk.* 7. 7
16. 23. things of God, but the things *of men. Mk.* 8. 33
17. 22. The Son of man shall be delivered up into the hands *of men. Mk.* 9. 31: *Lu.* 9. 44: 24. 7
22. 16. thou regardest not the person *of men. Mk.* 12. 14
23. 7. the marketplaces, and to be called *of men*, Rabbi
Mk. 7. 8. and hold fast the tradition *of men*
21. out of the heart *of men*, evil thoughts proceed
Jno. 1. 4. In him was life; and the life was the light *of men*
12. 43. they loved the glory *of men* more than the glory
Acts 5. 36. Theudas—to whom a number *of men*, about
38. for if this counsel or this work be *of men*
14. 11. gods are come down to us in the likeness *of men*
15. 17. That the residue *of men* may seek after the Lord
17. 12. women of honourable estate, and *of men*, not a few
Rom. 1. 18. all ungodliness and unrighteousness *of men*
2. 16. the day when God shall judge the secrets *of men*
29. whose praise is not *of men*, but of God
6. 19. I speak after the manner *of men. Gal.* 3. 15
14. 18. well-pleasing to God, and approved *of men*
1 *Cor.* 2. 5. faith should not stand in the wisdom *of men*
7. 23. with a price; become not bondservants *of men*
9. 8. Do I speak these things after the manner *of* ¹*men?*
13. 1. If I speak with the tongues *of men* and of angels
15. 32. If after the manner *of men* I fought with beasts
2 *Cor.* 8. 21. sight of the Lord, but also in the sight *of men*
Eph. 3. 5. was not made known unto the sons *of men*
4. 14. with every wind of doctrine, by the sleight *of men*
Phil. 2. 7. a servant, being made in the likeness *of men*
Col. 2. 8. and vain deceit, after the tradition *of men*
22. after the precepts and doctrines *of men?*
1 *Th.* 1. 5. ye know what manner *of men* we shewed
2. 6. nor seeking glory *of men*, neither from you
13. ye accepted it not as the word *of men*, but, as it is
1 *Tim.* 6. 5. wranglings *of men* corrupted in mind
Tit. 1. 14. commandments *of men* who turn away from
1 *Pet.* 2. 4. rejected indeed *of men*, but with God elect
15. should put to silence the ignorance of foolish *men*
4. 2. rest of your time in the flesh to the lusts *of men*
1 *Jno.* 5. 9. If we receive the witness *of men*, the witness
Rev. 9. 15. that they should kill the third part *of men.* 18
13. 13 make fire—upon the earth in the sight *of men*
18. 13. horses and chariots and slaves; and souls *of men*
see persons, soldiers, things.

Men *of war A.V.—see* soldiers.

Wise Men.

Mat. 2. 1. *wise men* from the east came to Jerusalem
7. Herod privily called the *wise m.*, and learned of them
16. Herod—mocked of the *w. m.*—learned of the *w. m.*
23. 34. I send unto you prophets, and *wise m.*, and scribes
1 *Cor.* 10. 15. I speak as to *wise men*; judge ye what I say

MENDING

Mending.
Mat. 4. 21. John his brother—*mending* their nets. *Mk.* 1. 19

Men-pleasers.
Eph. 6. 6. notin the way of eyeservice, as *m.-p. Col.* 3. 22

Menservants.
Lu. 12. 45. his coming; and shall begin to beat the *m.*

Men-stealers.
1 *Tim.* 1. 10. for *men-stealers*, for liars, for false swearers

Mention.
Rom. 1. 9. I make *mention* of you, always in my prayers.
Eph. 1. 16 : 1 *Th.* 1. 2 : *Philem.* 4
Heb. 11. 22. faith Joseph, when his end was nigh, made *m.*

Merchandise.
Mat. 22. 5. one to his own farm, another to his *merchandise*
Jno. 2. 16. make not my Father's house a house of *m.*
2 *Pet.* 2. 3. shall they with feigned words make *m.* of you
Rev. 18. 11. for no man buyeth their *merchandise* any more
 12. *merchandise* of gold, and silver, and precious stone
 13. and *merchandise* of horses and chariots and slaves

Merchant—s.
Mat. 13. 45. a man that is a *merchant* seeking goodly pearls
Rev. 18. 3. the *m.* of the earth waxed rich by the power
 11. the *merchants* of the earth weep and mourn over her
 15. The *merchants* of these things, who were made rich
 23. for thy *merchants* were the princes of the earth

Mercies.—*A.V.* ¹*bowels.*
Rom. 12. 1. by the *mercies* of God, to present your bodies
2 *Cor.* 1. 3. the Father of *mercies* and God of all comfort
Phil. 1. 8. I long after you all in the tender ¹*m.* of Christ Jesus
2. 1. if any fellowship of the Spirit, if any tender *m.*
 see compassion—s, blessings.

Merciful.—*A.V.* ¹*mercy.*
Mat. 5. 7. Blessed are the *m.* : for they shall obtain mercy
Lu. 6. 36. Be ye *merciful*, even as your Father is *merciful*
18. 13. God, be *merciful* to me a sinner
Heb. 2. 17. that he might be a *m.* and faithful high priest
8. 12. For I will be *merciful* to their iniquities
Jas. 5. 11. how that the Lord is full of pity, and ¹*merciful*

Mercy.—*A.V.* ¹*compassion,* ²*pity.*
Mat. 5. 7. the merciful: for they shall obtain *mercy*
9. 13. meaneth, I desire *mercy*, and not sacrifice. 12. 7
27. Have *mercy* on us, thou son of David. 20. 30, 31
15. 22. Have *mercy* on me, O Lord, thou son of David.
 Mk. 10. 47, 48 : *Lu.* 18. 38, 39
17. 15. Lord, have *mercy* on my son: for he is epileptic
18. 33. shouldst not thou also have had ¹*mercy* on thy fellow-servant, even as I had ²*mercy* on thee?
23. 23. weightier matters of the law, judgement, and *m.*
Mk. 5. 19. hath done for thee, and how he had ¹*mercy* on thee
Lu. 1. 50. his *mercy* is unto generations and generations
54. Israel his servant, That he might remember *mercy*
58. Lord had magnified his *m.* towards her [Elisabeth]
72. To shew *mercy* towards our fathers
78. Because of the tender *mercy* of our God
10. 37. And he said, He that shewed *mercy* on him
16. 24. Father Abraham, have *mercy* on me
17. 13. Jesus, Master, have *mercy* on us [ten lepers]

MET

Rom. 9. 15. I will have *mercy* on whom I have *mercy*
16. nor of him that runneth, but of God that hath *mercy*
18. So then he hath *mercy* on whom he will
23. vessels of *mercy*, which he afore prepared unto glory
11. 30. ye—have obtained *mercy* by their disobedience
31. by the *m.* shewn to you they also may now obtain *m.*
32. all unto disobedience, that he might have *m.* upon all
12. 8. he that sheweth *mercy*, with cheerfulness
15. 9. that the Gentiles might glorify God for his *mercy*
1 *Cor.* 7. 25. my judgement, as one that hath obtained *m.*
2 *Cor.* 4. 1. even as we obtained *mercy*, we faint not
Gal. 6. 16. walk by this rule, peace be upon them, and *m.*
Eph. 2. 4. God, being rich in *mercy*, for his great love
Phil. 2. 27. sick nigh unto death : but God had *m.* on him
1 *Tim.* 1. 2. Grace, *mercy*, peace, from God the Father
 and Christ Jesus our Lord. 2 *Tim.* 1. 2 : 2 *Jno.* 3
13. howbeit I obtained *m.*, because I did it ignorantly
16. I obtained *mercy*, that in me as chief might Jesus
2 *Tim.* 1. 16. Lord grant *m.* unto the house of Onesiphorus
18. (the Lord grant unto him to find *mercy* of the Lord
Tit. 3. 5. according to his *mercy* he saved us, through the
Heb. 4. 16. throne of grace, that we may receive *m.* [washing
Jas. 2. 13. judgement is without *mercy* to him that hath shewed no *mercy* : *m.* glorieth against judgement
3. 17. easy to be intreated, full of *mercy* and good fruits
1 *Pet.* 1. 3. according to his great *mercy* begat us again
2. 10. had not obtained *m.*, but now have obtained *mercy*
Jude 2. *Mercy* unto you and peace and love be multiplied
21. looking for the *mercy* of our Lord Jesus Christ
22. And on some have ¹*mercy*, who are in doubt
23. and on some have *mercy* with fear
 see compassion, merciful.

Mercy-seat.
Heb. 9. 5. cherubim of glory overshadowing the *mercy-seat*

Merry.
Lu. 12. 19. Soul—take thine ease, eat, drink, be *merry*
15. 23. fatted calf, and kill it, and let us eat, and make *m.*
24. was lost, and is found. And they began to be *merry*
29. never gavest me a kid, that I might make *merry*
32. But it was meet to make *merry* and be glad
Rev. 11. 10. on the earth rejoice over them, and make *merry*
 see cheerful.

Mess.—*A.V.* ¹*morsel.*
Heb. 12. 16. Esau—one ¹*m.* of meat sold his own birthright

Message.—*A.V.* ¹*preaching.*
1 *Th.* 2. 13. the word of the *message*, even the word of God
2 *Tim.* 4. 17. that through me the ¹*m.* might be—proclaimed
Tit. 1. 3. in his own seasons manifested his word in the ¹*m.*
1 *Jno.* 1. 5. this is the *m.* which we have heard from him
3. 11. this is the *m.* which ye heard from the beginning
 see ambassage.

Messenger—s.
Mat. 11. 10. my *m.* before thy face. *Mk.* 1. 2 ; *Lu.* 7. 27
Lu. 7. 24. when the *messengers* of John were departed
9. 52. and sent *messengers* before his face : and they went
2 *Cor.* 8. 23. they are the *messengers* of the churches
12. 7. a thorn in the flesh, a *m.* of Satan to buffet me
Phil. 2. 25. Epaphroditus—your *m.* and minister to my
Jas. 2. 25. justified by works, in that she received the *m.*

Met.
Mat. 8. 28. there *met* him two possessed with devils
28. 9. And behold, Jesus *met* them, saying, All hail
Mk. 5. 2. there *met* him out of the tombs a man. *Lu.* 8. 27

MET

Lu. 9. 37. a great multitude met him. *Jno.* 12. 16
17. 12. there *met* him ten men that were lepers
Jno. 4. 51. And as he was now going down, his servants *met*
11. 20. Martha—went and *met* him. 30   [him
Acts 10. 25. And when—Peter entered, Cornelius *met* him
16. 16. a certain maid having a spirit of divination *met* us
17. 17. marketplace every day with them that *met* with
27. 41. lighting upon a place where two seas *met* [him
Heb. 7. 1. priest of God Most High, who *met* Abraham
10. in the loins of his father, when Melchizedek *m.* him

Mete.

Mat. 7. 2. with what measure ye *mete*. *Mk.* 4. 24 : *Lu.* 6. 38

Midday.

Acts 26. 13. at *m.*, O king, I [Saul] saw on the way a light

Middle.

Eph. 2. 14. and brake down the *middle* wall of partition

Mid heaven.—*A.V.* ¹*midst of heaven.*

Rev. 8. 13. heard an eagle, flying in ¹*mid heaven.* 14. ¹⁶
19. 17. saying to all the birds that fly ¹in *mid heaven*, Come

Midnight.

Mat. 25. 6. at *m.* there is a cry, Behold, the bridegroom !
Mk. 13. 35. cometh, whether at even, or at *midnight*, or
Lu. 11. 5. at *m.*, and say to him, Friend, lend me three
Acts 16. 25. about *m.* Paul and Silas were praying and singing
20. 7. Paul—prolonged his speech until *midnight* [ing
27. 27. about *m.* the sailors surmised that they were draw-

Midst.—*A.V.* ¹*among.*

Mat. 10. 16. I send you forth as sheep in the *m.* of wolves
14. 24. boat was now in the *midst* of the sea. *Mk.* 6. 47
18. 2. child, and set him in the *midst* of them. *Mk.* 9. 36
20. together in my name, there am I in the *m.* of them
Lu. 2. 46. in the temple, sitting in the *m.* of the doctors
4. 30. [Jesus] passing through the *m.* of them went his
6. 8. withered, Rise up, and stand forth in the *midst*
21. 21. let them that are in the *midst* of her depart out
22. 27. I am in the ¹*midst* of you as he that serveth
23. 45. the veil of the temple was rent in the *midst*
24. 36. himself stood in the *m.* of them. *Jno.* 20. 19, 26
Jno. 7. 14. the *m.* of the feast Jesus went up into the temple
8. 3. in adultery ; and having set her in the *midst*. 9
19. 18. on either side one, and Jesus in the *midst*
Acts 1. 15. Peter stood up in the *midst* of the brethren
18. falling headlong, he burst asunder in the *midst*
2. 22. signs, which God did by him in the *midst* of you
17. 22. Paul stood in the *midst* of the Areopagus
Phil. 2. 15. in the *m.* of a crooked and perverse generation
Heb. 2. 12. In the *midst* of the congregation will I sing
Rev. 1. 13. in the *midst* of the candlesticks one like unto
2. 1. in the *midst* of the seven golden candlesticks
4. 6. in the *midst* of the throne. 5. 6 : 7. 17
5. 6. and in the *midst* of the elders, a Lamb standing
    see mid heaven.

Might.—*A.V.* ¹*power.*

Eph. 1. 19. that working of the strength of his ¹*might*
6. 10. in the Lord, and in the strength of his ¹*might*
Col. 1. 11. according to the ¹*might* of his glory
2 *Th.* 1. 9. face of the Lord and from the glory of his ¹*m.*
2 *Pet.* 2. 11. angels, though greater in *might* and power
Rev. 7. 12. honour, and power, and *might*, be unto our God
    see dominion, power.

MIND

Mightier.

Mat. 3. 11. cometh after me is *m.* than I. *Mk.* 1. 7 : *Lu.* 3. 16

Mightily.

Acts 19. 20. So *m.* grew the word of the Lord and prevailed
Col. 1. 29. his working, which worketh in me ¹*mightily*
    see cried out, powerfully.

Mighty.—*A.V.* ¹*strong,* ²*valiant,* ³*violence,* ⁴*wonderful.*

Mat. 7. 22. and by thy name do many ⁴*mighty* works ?
11. 20. wherein most of his *mighty* works were done
21. *m.* works had been done in Tyre. 23 : *Lu.* 10. 13
13. 54. this man this wisdom, and these *mighty* works ?
58. he did not many *mighty* works there. *Mk.* 6. 5
Mk. 6. 2. what mean such *m.* works wrought by his hands ?
Lu. 1. 49. he that is *mighty* hath done to me great things
15. 14. there arose a *mighty* famine in that country
19. 37. praise God with a loud voice for all the *m.* works
24. 19. Jesus—a prophet *mighty* in deed and word
Acts 2. 2. a sound as of the rushing of a *mighty* wind
11. speaking in our tongues the ⁴*mighty* works of God
7. 22. Moses—was *mighty* in his words and works
18. 24. Apollos—and he was *mighty* in the scriptures
1 *Cor.* 1. 26. not many *mighty*, not many noble, are called
2 *Cor.* 10. 4. *m.* before God to the casting down of strong
12. 12. by signs and wonders and *mighty* works [holds]
Heb. 11. 34. were made strong, waxed ⁴*mighty* in war
1 *Pet.* 5. 6. Humble yourselves—under the *m.* hand of God
Rev. 16. 18. so great an earthquake, so *mighty*
18. 2. he cried with a ¹*mighty* voice, saying, Fallen
21. Thus with a ²*mighty* fall shall Babylon
19. 6. voice of *mighty* thunders, saying, Hallelujah
    see great, majesty, might, power, powerful, powers, princes, strong, wrought.

Mile.

Mat. 5. 41. compel thee to go one *mile*, go with him twain

Milk.

1 *Cor.* 3. 2. I fed you with *milk*, not with meat
9. 7. who feedeth a flock, and eateth not of the *milk*
Heb. 5. 12. such as have need of *milk*, and not of solid food
13. For every one that partaketh of *milk* is without
1 *Pet.* 2. 2. as newborn babes, long for the spiritual *milk*

Mill.

Mat. 24. 41. two women shall be grinding at the *mill*

Millstone.

Mat. 18. 6. profitable for him that a great *millstone* should
    be hanged about his neck. *Mk.* 9. 42 : *Lu.* 17. 2
Rev. 18. 21. took up a stone as it were a great *millstone*
22. and the voice of a *millstone* shall be heard no more

Mind.—*A.V.* ¹*affection,* ²*agree,* ³*minded,* ⁴*minds,* ⁵*remembrance,* ⁶*understanding,* ⁷*will.*

Mat. 22. 37. with all thy *mind*. *Mk.* 12. 30 : *Lu.* 10. 27
Mk. 5. 15. clothed and in his right *mind*. *Lu.* 8. 35
14. 72. And Peter called to *mind* the word, how that Jesus
Lu. 1. 29. cast in her *mind* what manner of salutation
12. 29. ye shall drink, neither be ye of doubtful *mind*
24. 45. opened he their ⁶*m.*, that they might understand
Acts 17. 11. received the word with all readiness of *mind*
20. 19. serving the Lord with all lowliness of *mind*
Rom. 1. 28. God gave them up unto a reprobate *mind*
7. 23. members, warring against the law of my *mind*
25. So then I myself with the *m.* serve the law of God
8. 5. are after the flesh do *mind* the things of the flesh

MIND

Rom. 8. 6. For the *²mind* of the flesh is death; but the *³mind* of the spirit is life and peace
7. because the *m.* of the flesh is enmity [of the Spirit
27. that searcheth the hearts knoweth what is the *mind*
11. 34. For who hath known the *mind* of the Lord?
12. 2. be ye transformed by the renewing of your *mind*
16. Be of the same *mind* one toward another. Set not your *mind* on high things, but condescend
14. 5. Let each man be fully assured in his own *mind*
15. 5. grant you to be of the same *³m.* one with another
1 *Cor.* 1. 10. that ye be perfected together in the same *m.*
2. 16. For who hath known the *mind* of the Lord, that he should instruct him? But we have the *m.* of Christ
14. 20. be not children in *⁵mind*—but in *⁶mind* be men
2 *Cor.* 13. 11. be of the same *mind, Phil.* 2. 2
Eph. 2. 3. doing the desires of the flesh and of the *mind*
4. 17. Gentiles also walk, in the vanity of their *mind*
23. that ye be renewed in the spirit of your *mind*
Phil. 2. 2. being of one accord, of one *mind*
3. in lowliness of *mind* each counting other better than
5. this *mind* in you, which was also in Christ Jesus
3. 19. glory is in their shame, who *mind* earthly things
4. 2. I exhort Syntyche, to be of the same *m.* in the Lord
Col. 1. 21. time past alienated and enemies in your *mind*
2. 18. he hath seen, vainly puffed up by his fleshly *mind*
3. 2. Set your *¹mind* on the things that are above
2 *Th.* 2. 2. that ye be not quickly shaken from your *mind*
1 *Tim.* 4. 6. If thou put the brethren in *⁵m.* of these things
6. 5. men corrupted in *⁴mind.* 2 *Tim.* 3. *¹*8
Tit. 1. 15. both their *mind* and their conscience are defiled
3. 1. Put them in *mind* to be in subjection to rulers
Philem. 14. but without thy *mind* I would do nothing
Heb. 8. 10. I will put my laws into their *mind*
10. 16. And upon their *⁴mind* also will I write them
1 *Pet.* 1. 13. girding up the loins of your *mind,* be sober
4. 1. arm ye yourselves also with the same *mind*
5. 2. nor yet for filthy lucre, but of a ready *mind*
2 *Pet.* 3. 1. I stir up your sincere *⁴mind* by putting you in
Rev. 17. 9. Here is the *mind* which hath wisdom
13. Those have one *mind,* and they give their power
17. For God did put in their hearts to do his *⁷mind,* and to come to one *⁸mind*
see accord, discipline, humility, likeminded, readiness, remembrance, zeal.

Minded.—*A.V.* *¹counsel,* *²determined,* *³disposed,* *⁴think,* *⁵willing.*
Mat. 1. 19. Joseph—was *minded* to put her away privily
Acts 5. 33. cut to the heart, and were *¹minded* to slay them
15. 37. Barnabas was *²minded* to take with them John
18. 27. when he was *³minded* to pass over into Achaia
2 *Cor.* 1. 15. in this confidence I was *minded* to come
17. When I therefore was thus *m.,* did I shew fickleness?
Gal. 5. 10. that ye will be none otherwise *minded* [all
Phil. 1. 7. it is right for me to be thus *⁴m.* on behalf of you
3. 15. Let us therefore, as many as be perfect, be thus *m.*; and if in any thing ye are otherwise *minded*
Heb. 6. 17. Wherein God, being *⁵m.* to shew more abundantly
see counsel, highminded, likeminded, mind, soberminded.

Mindest.—*A.V.* *¹savourest.*
Mat. 16. 23. for thou *¹m.* not the things of God. *Mk.* 8. *¹*33

Mindful.
Heb. 2. 6. What is man, that thou art *mindful* of him?
11. 15. if indeed they had been *mindful* of that country
see remember, remembering.

Minding *A.V.—see intending.*

MINISTERETH

Minds.
Acts 28. 6. changed their *m.,* and said that he was a god
2 *Cor.* 3. 14. their *m.* were hardened: for until this very day
4. 4. in whom the god of this world hath blinded the *m.*
11. 3. your *m.* should be corrupted from the simplicity
see mind, souls, thoughts.

Mingle—d.—*A.V.* *¹fill—ed.*
Mat. 27. 34. gave him wine to drink *mingled* with gall
Mk. 15. 23. offered him wine *mingled* with myrrh
Lu. 13. 1. whose blood Pilate had *m.* with their sacrifices
Rev. 8. 7. there followed hail and fire, *mingled* with blood
15. 2. I saw it as it were a glassy sea *mingled* with fire -
18. 6. the cup which she *¹mingled,* *¹m.* unto her double

Minister.—*A.V.* *¹ministered,* *²servant.*
Mat. 20. 26. shall be your *minister. Mk.* 10. 43
Mk. 9. 35. first, he shall be last of all, and *²minister* of all
Acts 26. 16. to appoint thee a *minister* and a witness
Rom. 13. 4. for he is a *minister* of God to thee for good—he is a *minister* of God, an avenger for wrath
15. 8. Christ hath been made a *m.* of the circumcision
16. that I should be a *m.* of Christ Jesus unto the Gentiles
Gal. 2. 17. is Christ a *minister* of sin? God forbid
Eph. 3. 7. whereof I was made a *minister. Col.* 1, 23, 25 [7
6. 21. Tychicus, the beloved brother and faithful *m. Col.* 4.
Phil. 2. 25. Epaphroditus—your messenger and *¹minister*
Col. 1. 7. Epaphras—who is a faithful *minister* of Christ
1 *Th.* 3. 2. Timothy, our brother and God's *minister*
1 *Tim.* 4. 6. thou shalt be a good *minister* of Christ Jesus
Heb. 8. 2. a *m.* of the sanctuary, and of the true tabernacle
see attendant.

Minister (verb).—*A.V.* *¹ministered,* *²ministry,* *³service.*
Mat. 20. 28. not to be ministered unto, but to *m. Mk.* 10. 45
25. 44. sick, or in prison, and did not *minister* unto thee?
Acts 24. 23. not to forbid any of his friends to *m.* unto him
Rom. 15. 27. they owe it—to *m.* unto them in carnal things
1 *Cor.* 9. 13. they which *minister* about sacred things eat of
16. 15. have set themselves to *²minister* unto (the saints)
2 *Cor.* 11. 8. taking wages of them that I might *³minister*
1 *Tim.* 1. 4. endless genealogies, the which *m.* questionings
Philem. 13. that in thy behalf he might *¹minister* unto me
Heb. 6. 10. ye ministered unto the saints, and still do *m.*
1 *Pet.* 1. 12. but unto you, did they *minister* these things
see give, ministereth, ministering, service.

Ministered.—*A.V.* *¹administered.*
Mat. 4. 11. angels came and *m.* unto him. *Mk.* 1. 13
8. 15. she arose, and *m.* unto him. *Mk.* 1, 31; *Lu.* 4. 39
20. 28. Son of man came not to be *m.* unto. *Mk.* 10. 45
Mk. 15. 41. and *m.* unto him; and many other women
Lu. 8. 3. Susanna, and many others, which *m.* unto them
Acts 13. 2. *m.* to the Lord, and fasted, the Holy Ghost
19. 22. into Macedonia two of them that *m.* unto him
20. 34. these hands *ministered* unto my necessities
2 *Cor.* 3. 3. ye are an epistle of Christ, *m.* by us [¹20
8. 19. this grace, which is *¹m.* by us to the glory of the Lord.
2 *Tim.* 1. 18. and in how many things he *m.* at Ephesus
Heb. 6. 10. ye *m.* unto the saints, and still do minister
see minister, supplied.

Ministereth.—*A.V.* *¹minister.*
1 *Pet.* 4. 11. if any man *¹m.,* ministering as of the strength
see supplieth.

MINISTERING

Ministering.—*A.V.* ¹*minister,* ²*ministry.*

Mat. 27. 55. had followed Jesus from Galilee, *m.* unto him
Rom. 15. 16. *ministering* the gospel of God
 25. I go unto Jerusalem, ¹*ministering* unto the saints
2 Cor. 8. 4. the fellowship in the *ministering* to the saints
 9. 1. as touching the *m.* to the saints, it is superfluous
Eph. 4. 12. perfecting of the saints, unto the work of ²*m.*
2 Tim. 4. 11. Mark—for he is useful to me for ²*ministering*
Heb. 1. 14. Are they not all *ministering* spirits, sent forth
 10. 11. day by day *m.* and offering oftentimes the same
1 Pet. 4. 10. as each hath received a gift, ¹*ministering* it
 11. if any man *ministereth, m.* as of the strength
  see ministry.

Ministers.

Lu. 1. 2. were eyewitnesses and *ministers* of the word
Rom. 13. 6. for they are *ministers* of God's service
1 Cor. 3. 5. is Paul? *Ministers* through whom ye believed
 4. 1. so account of us, as of *ministers* of Christ
2 Cor. 3. 6. made us sufficient as *m.* of a new covenant
 6. 4. everything commending ourselves, as *m.* of God
 11. 15. *m.* also fashion themselves as *m.* of righteousness
 23. Are they *ministers* of Christ?—I more; in labours
Heb. 1 7. his angels winds, And his *ministers* a flame of fire

Ministration—s.—*A V.* ¹*administration—s,* ²*ministry,*
³*service.*

Lu. 1. 23. when the days of his *ministration* were fulfilled
Acts 6. 1. their widows were neglected in the daily *m.* [²*m.*
 12. 25. Barnabas and Saul—when they had fulfilled their
Rom. 15. 31. that my ³*m.* which I have for Jerusalem may
1 Cor. 12. 5. diversities of ¹*ministrations,* and the same Lord
2 Cor. 8. 7. But if the *m.* of death, written, and engraven
 8. shall not rather the *m.* of the spirit be with glory?
 9. *m.* of condemnation is glory—*m.* of righteousness
 6. 3. that our ²*ministration* be not blamed [exceed
 9. 12. For the ¹*ministration* of this service—aboundeth
 13. through—proving of you by this *m.* they glorify God

Minstrels.—*A.V.* ¹*musicians.*

Rev. 18. 22. the voice of harpers and ¹*m.* and flute-players
  see flute-players.

Ministry.—*A.V.* ¹*ministering,* ²*office,* ³*service.*

Acts 1. 17. received his [Judas] portion in this *ministry*
 25. to take the place in this *ministry* and apostleship
 6. 4. stedfastly in prayer, and in the *ministry* of the word
 20. 24. I may accomplish my course, and the *ministry*
 21. 19. God had wrought among the Gentiles by his *m.*
Rom. 11. 13. I am an apostle of the Gentiles, I glorify my ²*m.*
 12. 7. or ¹*ministry,* let us give ourselves to our ¹*ministry*
2 Cor. 4. 1. Therefore seeing we have this *m.,* even as we
 5. 18. and gave unto us the *ministry* of reconciliation
Col. 4. 17. say to Archippus, Take heed to the *ministry*
2 Tim. 4. 5. do the work of an evangelist, fulfil thy *ministry*
Heb. 8. 6. hath he obtained a *ministry* the more excellent
 9. 21. and all the vessels of the *ministry* he sprinkled
Rev. 2. 19. thy love and faith and ³*ministry* and patience
  see minister, ministered, ministering, ministration, service.

Mint.

Mat. 23. 23. ye tithe *m.* and anise and cummin. *Lu.* 11. 42

Miracle—s.

Lu. 23. 8. Herod—hoped to see some *miracle* done by him
Acts 4. 16. a notable *m.* hath been wrought through them
 22. more than forty years old, on whom this *miracle*
 8. 13. beholding signs and great *m.* wrought, he was
 19. 11. God wrought special *m.* by the hands of Paul

MOCKING

1 Cor. 12. 10. and to another workings of *miracles*
 28. teachers, then *miracles,* then gifts of healings
 29. are all teachers? are all workers of *miracles?*
Gal. 3. 5. supplieth to you the Spirit, and worketh *m.*
  see mighty work, sign, signs.

Mire.

2 Pet. 2. 22. sow that had washed to wallowing in the *mire*

Mirror.—*A.V.* ¹*glass.*

1 Cor. 13. 12. For now we see in a ¹*mirror,* darkly
2 Cor. 3. 18. face reflecting as a ¹*m.* the glory of the Lord
Jas. 1. 23. a man beholding his natural face in a ¹*mirror*

Mischief *A.V.*—*see villany.*

Miserable.—*A.V.* ¹*wicked.*

Mat. 21. 41. He will miserably destroy those ¹*miserable* men
Rev. 3. 17. thou art the wretched one and *m.* and poor
  see pitiable.

Miserably.

Mat. 21. 41. He will *miserably* destroy those miserable men

Misery—ies.

Rom. 3. 16. Destruction and *misery* are in their ways
Jas. 5. 1. weep and howl for your *m.* that are coming

Mist—s.—*A.V.* ¹*clouds.*

Acts 13. 11. there fell on him [Elymas] a *m.* and a darkness
2 Pet. 2. 17. without water, and ¹*mists* driven by a storm
  see blackness.

Mite—s.

Mk. 12. 42. poor widow, and she cast in two *m. Lu.* 21. 2
Lu. 12. 59. till thou have paid the very last *mite*

Mixed *A.V.*—*see united.*

Mixture.

Jno. 19. 39. Nicodemus—bringing a *m.* of myrrh and aloes
  see unmixed.

Mock.

Mat. 20. 19. shall deliver him unto the Gentiles to *mock*
Mk. 10. 34. and they shall *mock* him, and shall spit
Lu. 14. 29. to finish, all that behold begin to *mock* him

Mocked.

Mat. 2. 16. Herod, when he saw that he was *mocked*
 27. 29. and *mocked* him, saying, Hail, King of the Jews!
  31: *Mk.* 15. 20: *Lu.* 22. 63: 23. 11, 36
Lu. 18. 32. and shall be *mocked,* and shamefully entreated
Acts 17. 32. the resurrection of the dead, some *mocked*
Gal. 6. 7. Be not deceived; God is not *mocked*

Mockers.—*A.V.* ¹*scoffers.*

2 Pet. 3. 3 the last days ¹*mockers* shall come with mockery
Jude 18. In the last time there shall be *mockers*

Mockery.

2 Pet. 3. 3. last days the mockers shall come with *mockery*

Mocking—s.

Mat. 27. 41. the chief priests *mocking* him. *Mk.* 15. 31
Acts 2. 13. others *m.* said, They are filled with new wine
Heb. 11. 36. others had trial of *mockings* and scourgings

MODERATION

Moderation *A.V.—see forbearance.*

Modest.
1 Tim. 2, 9. that women adorn themselves in m. apparel

Moisture.
Lu. 8. 6. it withered away, because it had no moisture

Moment.
Lu. 4. 5. shewed him all the kingdoms of the world in a m.
1 Cor. 15. 52. but we shall all be changed, in a moment
2 Cor. 4. 17. our light affliction, which is for the moment

Money.—*A.V.* ¹covetous.
Mat. 22. 19. Shew me the tribute m. And they brought
25. 18. digged in the earth, and hid his lord's money
27. put my money to the bankers. Lu. 19. 23
28. 12. they gave large money unto the soldiers, saying
15. So they took the m., and did as they were taught
Mk. 6. 8. bread, no wallet, no m. in their purse. Lu. 9. 3
12. 41. how the multitude cast money into the treasury
14. 11. and promised to give him [Judas] m. Lu. 22. 5
Lu. 19. 15. servants, unto whom he had given the money
Jno. 2. 14. and doves, and the changers of money sitting
15. and he poured out the changers' money
Acts 4. 37. having a field, sold it, and brought the money
8. 18. Holy Ghost was given, he offered them money
20. thought to obtain the gift of God with money
24. 26. hoped withal that m. would be given him of Paul
1 Tim. 3. 3. not contentious, no lover of ¹money
6. 10. For the love of money is a root of all kinds of evil
see lovers, shekel, silver.

Money-changers.
Mat. 21. 12. overthrew the tables of the m.-c. Mk. 11. 15

Month.
Lu. 1. 26. in the sixth month the angel Gabriel was sent
36. this is the sixth m. with her that was called barren
Rev. 9. 15. prepared for the hour and day and month and
22. 2. twelve manner of fruits, yielding its fruit every m.

Months.
Lu. 1. 24. Elisabeth—conceived ; and she hid herself five m.
56. Mary abode with her about three months
4. 25. was shut up three years and six months. Jas. 5. 17
Jno. 4. 35. yet four months, and then cometh the harvest?
Acts 7. 20. Moses—was nourished three months in his father's house. Heb. 11. 23
18. 11. a year and six months, teaching the word
19. 8. and spake boldly for the space of three months
20. 3. when he had spent three months there [Greece]
28. 11. after three m. we set sail in a ship of Alexandria
Gal. 4. 10. Ye observe days, and months, and seasons
Rev. 9. 5. that they should be tormented five months
11. 2. city shall they tread under foot forty and two m.
13. 5. authority to continue forty and two months

Moon.
Mat. 24. 29. the moon shall not give her light. Mk. 13. 24
Acts 2. 20. the moon into blood, Before the day of the Lord
1 Cor. 15. 41. of the sun, and another glory of the moon
Col. 2. 16. in respect of a feast day or a new moon
Rev. 6. 12. and the whole moon became as blood
8. 12. sun was smitten, and the third part of the moon
12. 1. arrayed with the sun, and the moon under her feet
21. 23. city hath no need of the sun, neither of the moon

MORTAL

Sun and Moon.—*see sun.*

Moored.—*A.V.* ¹drew.
Mk. 6. 53. land unto Gennesaret, and ¹m. to the shore

More.—*A.V.* ¹far more.
Mat. 5. 37. Nay, nay : and whatsoever is more than these
47. brethren only, what do ye more than others?
6. 25. Is not the life more than the food. Lu. 12. 23 [13
7. 11. children, how much m. shall your Father. Lu. 11.
11. 9. unto you, and much m. than a prophet. Lu. 7. 26
20. 10. they supposed that they would receive more
Mk. 4. 24. and more shall be given unto you
7. 36. the more he charged them, so much the more
12. 43. This poor widow cast in more than all. Lu. 21. 3
Lu. 10. 35. whatsoever thou spendest m., I, when I come
12. 48. commit much, of him will they ask the more
18. 30. manifold more in this time, and in the world to
Jno. 15. 2. he cleanseth it, that it may bear more fruit
Acts 5. 14. believers were the more added to the Lord
23. 13. m. than forty which made this conspiracy. 21
Rom. 8. 37. in all these things we are m. than conquerors
1 Cor. 9. 19. bondage to all, that I might gain the more
2 Cor. 4. 17. worketh for us ¹more and more exceedingly
Phil. 1. 9. that your love may abound yet more and more
1 Th. 4. 1. that ye abound more and more. 10
Heb. 7. 15. what we say is yet more abundantly evident
12. 25. much more shall not we escape, who turn away
26. Yet once m. will I make to tremble not the earth. 27
Rev. 2. 19. and that thy last works are more than the first
see abundantly, beyond, exceedingly.

Morning.
Mat. 16. 3. And in the morning, It will be foul weather
20. 1. went out early in the morning to hire labourers
21. 18. in the m. as he returned to the city, he hungered
27. 1. when m. was come, all the chief priests. Mk. 15. 1
Mk. 1. 35. in the morning, a great while before day
11. 20. passed by in the morning, they saw the fig tree
13. 35. at midnight, or at cockcrowing, or in the morning
Lu. 21. 38. the people came early in the morning to hear
Jno. 8. 2. early in the m. he came again into the temple
Rev. 2. 28. I will give him the morning star
22. 16. the offspring of David, the bright, the m. star
see dawn, day, daybreak.

Morrow, to-morrow.—*A.V.* ¹day following, ²next day.
Mat. 6. 30. and to-morrow is cast into the oven. Lu. 12. 28
34. Be not therefore anxious for the m. : for the m.
Lu. 10. 35. And on the morrow he took out two pence
13. 32. and perform cures to-day and to-morrow
33. Howbeit I must go on my way to-day and to-morrow
Jno. 1. 43. On the ¹m. he was minded to go forth into Galilee
6. 22. On the ¹morrow the multitude which stood on the
12. 12. On the ²m. a—multitude that had come to the feast
Acts 20. 7. discoursed with them, intending to depart on
25. 22. To-morrow, saith he, thou shalt hear him [the m.
1 Cor. 15. 32. let us eat and drink, for to-morrow we die
Jas. 4. 13. To-day or to-morrow we will go into this city
14. whereas ye know not what shall be on the morrow

Morsel *A.V.—see mess.*

Mortal.—*A.V.* ¹mortality.
Rom. 6. 12. Let not sin therefore reign in your m. body
8. 11. shall quicken also your m. bodies through his Spirit
1 Cor. 15. 53. this mortal must put on immortality. 54
2 Cor. 4. 11. of Jesus may be manifested in our m. flesh
5. 4. that what is ¹mortal may be swallowed up of life

222

MORTALITY

Mortality *A.V.—see mortal.*

Mortify.
Rom. 8. 13. if by the spirit ye *mortify* the deeds of the body
Col. 3. 5. *Mortify* therefore your members which are

Most.—*A.V.* ¹*many.*
1 *Cor.* 10. 5. with ¹*most* of them God was not well pleased
Phil. 1. 14. and that ¹*most* of the brethren in the Lord

Mote.
Mat. 7. 3. And why beholdest thou the *mote. Lu.* 6. 41
4. Let me cast out the *mote* out of thine eye. *Lu.* 6. 42
5. then shalt thou see clearly to cast out the *m. Lu.* 6. 42

Moth.
Mat. 6. 19. the earth, where *moth* and rust doth consume
20. heaven, where neither *moth* nor rust. *Lu.* 12. 33

Moth-eaten.
Jas. 5. 2. and your garments are *moth-eaten*

Mother.
Mat. 1. 18. When his *mother* Mary had been betrothed
2. 13. Arise and take the young child and his *m.* 14, 20, 21
8. 14. Peter's house, he saw his wife's *mother* lying sick of a fever. *Mk.* 1. 30; *Lu.* 4. 38
10. 35. and the daughter against her *mother. Lu.* 12. 53
37. He that loveth father or *m.* more than me is not worthy
12. 46. his *m.* and his brethren stood. *Mk.* 3. 31; *Lu.* 8. 19
47. thy *mother* and thy brethren. *Mk.* 3. 32; *Lu.* 8. 20
48. Who is my *m.?* and who are my brethren? *Mk.* 3. 33
49. Behold, my *mother* and my brethren! *Mk.* 3. 34
50. he is my brother, and sister, and *mother. Mk.* 3. 35
13. 55. carpenter's son? is not his *mother. Mk.* 6. 28
14. 8. being put forward by her *mother* [Herodias]
11. and she brought it to her *mother. Mk.* 6. 28
19. 12. eunuchs, which were so born from their *m.'s* womb
20. 20. Then came to him the *m.* of the sons of Zebedee
Lu. 1. 15. with the Holy Ghost, even from his *m.'s* womb
43. that the *mother* of my Lord should come unto me?
60. his *mother* answered and said, Not so; but he shall
2. 33. And his father and his *mother* were marvelling
48. his *mother* said unto him, Son, why hast thou
51. his *mother* kept all these sayings in her heart
7. 12. the only son of his *mother,* and she was a widow
15. began to speak. And he gave him to his *mother*
8. 21. My *mother* and brethren are these which hear
Jno. 2. 1. and the *mother* of Jesus was there. 3
5. His *mother* saith unto the servants, Whatsoever
12. to Capernaum, he, and his *mother,* and his brethren
3. 4. can he enter a second time into his *mother's* womb
19. 25. by the cross of Jesus his *m.,* and his *m.'s* sister
26. saw his *m.*—saith unto him, Woman, behold, thy
27. Then saith he to the disciple, Behold, thy *m.!* [son!
Acts 3. 2. certain man that was lame from his *m.'s* womb. 14. 8
12. 12. [Peter] to the house of Mary the *mother* of John
Rom. 16. 13. Salute Rufus the chosen in the Lord, and his *m.*
Gal. 1. 15. God, who separated me, even from my *m.'s* womb
4. 26. Jerusalem that is above is free, which is our *mother*
2 *Tim.* 1. 5. thy grandmother Lois, and thy *mother* Eunice
Rev. 17. 5. BABYLON THE GREAT, THE *MOTHER* OF THE HARLOTS AND OF THE ABOMINATIONS
see parents, father.

Mother in law.
Mat. 10. 35. the daughter in law against her *mother in law. Lu.* 12. 53.

MOURNING

Mothers.
Mk. 10. 30. *m.,* and children, and lands, with persecutions
1 *Tim.* 1, 9. of fathers and murderers of *mothers* [ters
5. 2. the elder women as *mothers;* the younger as sis-

Motions *A.V.—see passions.*

Mount.
Acts 7. 30. in the wilderness of *m.* Sinai, in a flame of fire
38. the angel which spake to him in the *mount* Sinai
Gal. 4. 24. two covenants; one from *mount* Sinai
25. Now this Hagar is *mount* Sinai in Arabia
Heb. 8. 5. to the pattern that was shewed thee in the *m.*
12. 18. not come unto a *mount* that might be touched
2 *Pet.* 1. 18. when we were with him in the holy *mount*

Mount of *Olives.—see proper names.*

Mountain.—*A.V.* ¹*hill,* ²*mountains.*
Mat. 4. 8. [Jesus] went up into the *mountain.* 14. 23; 15. 29. *Mk.* 3. 13; 6. 46. *Lu.* 6. 12; 9. 28; *Jno.* 6. 3, 15
8. 1. And when he was come down from the *mountain*
17. 1. and John—into a high *mountain* apart. *Mk.* 9. 2
9. down from the *m*, Jesus commanded them. *Mk.* 9. 9
20. ye shall say unto this *m.,* Remove. 21. 21; *Mk.* 11. 23
28. 16. unto the *m.* where Jesus had appointed them
Mk. 5. 11. on the ²*m.* side a great herd of swine feeding
Lu. 3. 5. every *mountain* and hill shall be brought low
8. 32. a herd of many swine feeding on the *mountain*
9. 37. come down from the ¹*m.,* a great multitude met him
Jno. 4. 20. Our fathers worshipped in this *mountain*
21. neither in this *m.,* nor in Jerusalem, shall ye worship
Heb. 12. 20. If even a beast touch the *m*, it shall be stoned
Rev. 6. 14. every *mountain* and island were moved
8. 8. a great *mountain* burning with fire was cast into
21. 10. he carried me away in the Spirit to a *mountain*

Mountains.
Mat. 18. 12. leave the ninety and nine, and go unto the *m.*
24. 16. let them that are in Judea flee unto the *mountains. Mk.* 13. 14; *Lu.* 21. 21
Mk. 5. 5. night and day, in the tombs and in the *mountains*
Lu. 23. 30. shall they begin to say to the *m.,* Fall on us
1 *Cor.* 13. 2. if I have all faith, so as to remove *mountains*
Heb. 11. 38. wandering in deserts and *m.* and caves
Rev. 6. 15. hid—in the caves and in the rocks of the *m.*
16. and they say to the *mountains* and to the rocks
16. 20. island fled away, and the *m.* were not found
17. 9. The seven heads are seven *mountains*
see mount.

Mourn—ed.—*A.V.* ¹*bewail,* ²*mourned,* ³*wail.*
Mat. 5. 4. Blessed are they that *m.:* for they shall be com-
9. 15. Can the sons of the bride-chamber *mourn* [forted
11. 17. we wailed, and ye did not *mourn*
24. 30. then shall all the tribes of the earth *mourn*
Mk. 16. 10. had been with him, as they *mourned* and wept
Lu. 6. 25. Woe unto you, ye that laugh now! for ye shall *m.*
1 *Cor.* 5. 2. ye are puffed up, and did not rather ²*mourn*
2 *Cor.* 12. 21. I should ¹*m.* for many of them that have
Jas. 4. 9. Be afflicted, and *mourn,* and weep [sinned
Rev. 1. 7. all the tribes of the earth shall ³*mourn* over him
18. 11. merchants of the earth weep and *mourn* over her
see wailed.

Mourning.—*A.V.* ¹*sorrow,* ²*wailing.*
Mat. 2. 18. great *m.,* Rachel weeping for her children
2 *Cor.* 7. 7. he told us your longing, your *m.,* your zeal

MOURNING

Jas. 4. 9. let your laughter be turned to *mourning*
Rev. 18. 7. of torment and ¹*mourning*—in no wise see ¹m.
    8. her plagues come, death, and *mourning*, and famine
    15. afar off for the fear of her torment, weeping and ²m.
    21. 4. neither shall there be ¹*mourning*, nor crying [²19

Mouth.

Mat. 4. 4. word that proceedeth out of the *mouth* of God
    5. 2. and he opened his m. and taught them   [Lu. 6. 45
    12. 34. out of the abundance of the heart the m. speaketh.
    13. 35. I will open my m. in parables; I will utter things
    15. 11. Not that which entereth into the m. defileth the
        man; but that which proceedeth out of the *mouth*
      17. whatsoever goeth into the *mouth* passeth into the
      18. proceed out of the *mouth* come forth out of the heart
    17. 27. when thou hast opened his *mouth*, thou shalt find
    18. 16. the *mouth* of two witnesses or three. 2 Cor. 13. 1
    21. 16. Out of the *mouth* of babes and sucklings
Lu. 1. 64. his [Zacharias] *mouth* was opened immediately
    70. (As he spake by the *mouth* of his holy prophets
    4. 22. words of grace which proceeded out of his *mouth*
    11. 54. wait for him, to catch something out of his *mouth*
    19. 22. Out of thine own *mouth* will I judge thee
    21. 15. for I will give you a m. and wisdom, which all your
    22. 71. for we ourselves have heard from his own *mouth*
Jno. 19. 29. upon hyssop, and brought it to his *mouth*
Acts 1. 16. by the *mouth* of David concerning Judas
    3. 18. by the m. of all the prophets, that his Christ. 21
    4. 25. by the *mouth* of our father David thy servant
    8. 32. as a lamb—is dumb, So he openeth not his *mouth*
    35. Philip opened his m., and beginning from this scrip-
    10. 34. Peter opened his m., and said, Of a truth [ture
    11. 8. or unclean hath ever entered into my *mouth*
    15. 7. by my *mouth* the Gentiles should hear the word
    27. shall tell you the same things by word of *mouth*
    18. 14. Paul was about to open his *mouth*, Gallio said
    22. 14. Righteous One, and to hear a voice from his m.
    23. 2. them that stood by him to smite him on the *mouth*
Rom. 3. 14. Whose *mouth* is full of cursing and bitterness
    19. that every *mouth* may be stopped
    10. 8. The word is nigh thee, in thy m. and in thy heart
    9. if thou shalt confess with thy *mouth* Jesus as Lord
    10. with the *mouth* confession is made unto salvation
    15. 6. with one accord ye may with one *mouth* glorify
2 Cor. 6. 11. Our *mouth* is open unto you, O Corinthians
Eph. 4. 29. speech proceed out of your *mouth*. Col. 3. 8
    6. 19. utterance may be given unto me in opening my m.
2 Th. 2. 8. Lord Jesus shall slay with the breath of his m.
2 Tim. 4. 17. I was delivered out of the *mouth* of the lion
Jas. 3. 10. same m. cometh forth blessing and cursing
1 Pet. 2. 22. no sin, neither was guile found in his *mouth*
Jude 16. (and their *mouth* speaketh great swelling words)
Rev. 1. 16. proceeded a sharp two-edged sword
    2. 16. war against them with the sword of my *mouth*
    3. 16. I will spew thee out of my *mouth*
    9. 19. the power of the horses is in their *mouth*
    10. 9. in thy *mouth* it shall be sweet as honey. 10
    11. 5. fire proceedeth out of their *mouth*, and devoureth
    12. 15. serpent cast out of his *mouth* after the woman
    16. the earth opened her m., and swallowed up the river
    13. 2. and his *mouth* as the *mouth* of a lion
    5. a *mouth* speaking great things and blasphemies. 6
    14. 5. And in their *mouth* was found no lie
    16. 13. out of the *mouth* of the dragon—*mouth* of the
        beast—*mouth* of the false prophet, three unclean
    19. 15. out of his *mouth* proceedeth a sharp sword

Mouths.

Tit. 1. 11. whose *mouths* must be stopped; men who

MULTITUDE

Heb. 11. 33. obtained promises, stopped the m. of lions
Jas. 3. 3. if we put the horses' bridles into their *mouths*
Rev. 9. 17. their *mouths* proceedeth fire and smoke. 18

Move.—A.V. ¹remove.

Mat. 23. 4. themselves will not m. them with their finger
Acts 17. 28. for in him we live, and m., and have our being
Rev. 2. 5. and will ¹*move* thy candlestick out of its place

Moved.—A.V. ¹sore displeased.

Mat. 9. 36. [Jesus] was *moved* with compassion. Mk. 1. 41
    18. 27. lord of that servant, being m. with compassion
    20. 24. the ten heard it, they were m. with indignation
    21. 15. they [chief priests] were ¹m. with indignation
Acts 2. 25. on my right hand, that I should not be *moved*
    7. 9. the patriarchs, *moved* with jealousy against Joseph
    17. 5. But the Jews, being *moved* with jealousy
    21. 30. all the city was m., and the people ran together
Col. 1. 23. not *moved* away from the hope of the gospel
1 Th. 3. 3. that no man be *moved* by these afflictions
Heb. 11. 7. Noah—m. with godly fear, prepared an ark
2 Pet. 1. 21. men spake from God, being m. by the Holy
Rev. 6. 14. and every mountain and island were *moved*
                      see shaken, stirred

Mover.

Acts 24. 5. a *mover* of insurrections among all the Jews

Much.—A.V ¹great, ²greatly.

Mat. 26. 9. this ointment might have been sold for *much*
    15. 23. and beseecheth with him ²m., saying, My little daughter
Lu. 6. 34. lend to sinners, to receive again as *much*
    7. 47. sins, which are many, are forgiven; for she loved m.
    12. 48. to whomsoever *much* is given, of him shall *much*
        be required: and to whom they commit *much*
    16. 10. is faithful also in m.—unrighteous also in *much*
Jno. 6. 11. also of the fishes as *much* as they would
    12. 24. if it die, it beareth *much* fruit. 15. 5
    14. 30. I will no more speak *much* with you
Acts 18. 27. he helped them *much* which had believed
    26. 29. whether with little or with m., not thou only, but
Rom. 1. 15. So, as *much* as in me is, I am ready to preach
    3. 2. M. every way: first of all, that they were intrusted
    12. 18. as *much* as in you lieth, be at peace with all men
    16. 12. Persis—which laboured *much* in the Lord
1 Cor. 16. 12. touching Apollos—I besought him ²m. to come
2 Cor. 8. 15. He that gathered *much* had nothing over
Col. 4. 13. him witness, that he [Epaphras] hath ¹m. labour
Jas. 5. 16. supplication of a righteous man availeth *much*
              see abundantly, exceedingly, people, times

Multiplied.—A.V. ¹abound, ²abundant.

Mat. 24. 12. because iniquity shall be ¹*multiplied*
Acts 6. 7. and the number of the disciples ¹m. in Jerusalem
    7. 17. the people grew and *multiplied* in Egypt
    9. 31. in the comfort of the Holy Ghost, was *multiplied*
    12. 24. But the word of God grew and *multiplied*
2 Cor. 4. 15. that the grace, being ²m. through the many
1 Pet. 1. 2. Grace to you and peace be m. 2 Pet. 1. 2; Jude 2
                      see multiplying.

Multiply—ing.—A.V. ¹multiplied.

Acts 6. 1. days, when the number of the disciples was m.
2 Cor. 9. 10. shall supply and *multiply* your seed for sowing
Heb. 6. 14. and ¹*multiplying* I will *multiply* thee

Multitude.—A.V. ¹company, ²people.

Mat. 13. 2. all the *multitude* stood on the beach. Mk. 4. 1
    14. 5. [Herod] put him to death, he feared the *multitude*

MULTITUDE

Mat. 14. 14. And he came forth, and saw a—*m.* *Mk.* 6. ²34
15. 10. he called to him the *m.*, and said unto them
32. I have compassion on the *multitude. Mk.* 8. 2
33. loaves in a desert place, as to fill so great a *multitude?*
35. he commanded the *multitude* to sit down. *Mk.* 8. ²6
17. 14. when they were come to the *multitude*
21. 8. the *multitude* spread their garments in the way
26. we fear the ²*multitude*; for all hold John as a prophet
27. 15. the governor was wont to release unto the ²*m.*
24. Pilate—washed his hands before the *multitude*
Mk. 5. 21. a great ²*multitude* was gathered unto him
24. a great ²*multitude* followed him. *Mat.* 20. 29
31. Thou seest the *multitude* thronging thee
Lu. 2. 13. suddenly there was with the angel a *multitude*
5. 29. there was a great ¹*m.* of publicans and of others
6. 17. a great ¹*m.* of his disciples, and a great number
8. 40. as Jesus returned, the ²*multitude* welcomed him
9. 37. from the mountain, a great ²*multitude* met him
38. a man from the ¹*multitude* cried, saying, Master
11. 27. a certain woman out of the ¹*m.* lifted up her voice
12. 1. many thousands of the *m.* were gathered together
13. one out of the ¹*multitude* said unto him, Master
13. 17. all the ²*m.* rejoiced for all the glorious things
22. 6. deliver him unto them in the absence of the *m.*
47. behold, a *multitude*, and he that was called Judas
Jno. 5. 13. himself away, a *multitude* being in the place
6. 5. lifting up his eyes, and seeing that a great¹*m.* cometh
24. when the ²*m.* therefore saw that Jesus was not there
7. 12. Not so, but he leadeth the ¹*multitude* astray
43. there arose a division in the ²*m.* because of him
49. this ²*m.* which knoweth not the law are accursed
12. 12. morrow a great ²*m.* that had come to the feast
21. 6. were not able to draw it for the *multitude* of fishes
Acts 4. 32. the *m.* of them that believed were of one heart
6. 5. saying pleased the whole *m.*: and they chose Stephen
14. 14. Barnabas and Paul—sprang forth among the ²*m.*
16. 22. And the *multitude* rose up together against them
21. 27. stirred up all the ²*multitude*, and laid hands
Heb. 11. 12. so many as the stars of heaven in *multitude*
Jas. 5. 20. soul from death, and shall cover a *m.* of sins
1 *Pet.* 4. 8. for love covereth a *multitude* of sins
Rev. 19. 1. I heard as it were—voice of a great ²*multitude*
see company, crowd, multitudes.

Multitudes.—*A.V.* ¹*multitude*, ²*people.*

Mat. 4. 25. great *multitudes* from Galilee and Decapolis
5. 1. seeing the *multitudes*, he went up into the mountain
7. 28. the ²*multitudes* were astonished at his teaching
8. 1. great *multitudes* followed him. 19. 2
18. when Jesus saw great *multitudes* about him
9. 8. when the *multitudes* saw it, they were afraid
33. the dumb man spake: and the *multitudes* marvelled
36. when he saw the *m.*, he was moved with compassion
11. 7. Jesus began to say unto the *multitudes* concerning
12. 23. all the ²*multitudes* were amazed, and said, Is this
46. While he was yet speaking to the ²*multitudes*
13. 2. there were gathered unto him great *multitudes*
34. All these things spake Jesus in parables unto the ¹*m.*
36. he left the ¹*multitudes*, and went into the house
14. 13. when the ²*multitudes* heard. 15. send the ¹*multitudes* away. 22. 19. ¹*multitudes* to sit down—to the ¹*multitudes.* 15. ¹36. 23. sent the *multitudes* away. 15. ¹39
15. 30. there came unto him great *multitudes*
21. 9. the *m.* that went before him, and that followed
Lu. 3. 10. the ²*m.* asked him, saying, What then must we do?
4. 42. the ²*m.* sought after him, and came unto him
8. 45. the ¹*multitudes* press thee and crush thee
9. 18. Who do the ²*multitudes* say that I am?

MUST

Jno. 7. 12. much murmuring among the ²*m.* concerning him
Acts 5. 14. added to the Lord, *m.* both of men and women
8. 6. the ²*multitudes* gave heed with one accord
13. 45. Jews saw the *m.*, they were filled with jealousy
14. 11. when the ²*multitudes* saw what Paul had done
18. with these sayings scarce restrained they the ²*m.*
19. having persuaded the ²*multitudes*, they stoned Paul
Rev. 17. 15. where the harlot sitteth, are peoples, and *m.*
see great.

Murder—s.

Mat. 15. 19. heart come forth evil thoughts, *m. Mk.* 7. 21
Mk. 15. 7. who in the insurrection had committed *murder*
Lu. 23. 19. and for *murder*, was cast into prison. 25
Rom. 1. 29. full of envy, *murder*, strife, deceit, malignity
Rev. 9. 21. and they repented not of their *murders*
see kill.

Murderer.

Jno. 8. 44. He was a *murderer* from the beginning
Acts 3. 14. and asked for a *m.* to be granted unto you
28. 4. said one to another, No doubt this man is a *m.*
1 *Pet.* 4. 15. For let none of you suffer as a *murderer*
1 *Jno.* 3. 15. Whosoever hateth his brother is a *m.*: and ye
know that no *m.* hath eternal life abiding in him

Murderers.

Mat. 22. 7. king—sent his armies, and destroyed those *m.*
Acts 7. 52. ye have now become betrayers and *murderers*
1 *Tim.* 1. 9. for *murderers* of fathers and *m.* of mothers
Rev. 21. 8. unbelieving, and abominable, and *m.* 22. 15
see assassins (proper names)

Murmur.—*A.V.* ¹*grudge.*

Jno. 6. 43. said unto them, *M.* not among yourselves
1 *Cor.* 10. 10. Neither *murmur* ye, as some of them
Jas. 5. 9. ¹*Murmur* not, brethren, one against another

Murmured.

Mat. 20. 11. And when they received it, they *murmured*
Mk. 14. 5. to the poor. And they *murmured* against her
Lu. 5. 30. And the Pharisees and their scribes *m.* 15. 2
19. 7. all *murmured*, saying, He is gone in to lodge with
Jno. 6. 41. *m.* concerning him, because he said, I am the
61. Jesus knowing in himself that his disciples *m.* breed
1 *Cor.* 10. 10. Neither *murmur* ye, as some of them *m.*
see murmuring.

Murmurers.

Jude 16. These are *m.*, complainers, walking after their

Murmuring—s.—*A.V.* ¹*grudging*, ²*murmured.*

Jno. 7. 12. there was much *m.* among the multitudes
32. The Pharisees heard the multitude ²*murmuring*
Acts 6. 1. arose a *murmuring* of the Grecian Jews against
Phil. 2. 14. Do all things without *m.* and disputings
1 *Pet.* 4. 9. using hospitality one to another without ¹*m.*

Mused *A.V.*—*see reasoned.*

Music.

Lu. 15. 25. nigh to the house, he heard *music* and dancing

Musicians *A.V.*—*see minstrels.*

Must.—*A.V.* ¹*ought.*

Mat. 18. 7. it *must* needs be that the occasions come
26. 54. scriptures be fulfilled, that thus it *must* be?
Mk. 9. 11. The scribes say that Elijah *must* first come
13. 7. be not troubled: these things *m.* needs. *Lu.* 21. 9

MUST

Lu. 2. 49. wist ye not that I *m.* be in my Father's house?
14. 18. bought a field, and I *m.* needs go out and see it
Jno. 3. 7. I said unto thee, Ye *must* be born anew
4. 4. And he *must* needs pass through Samaria
Acts 5. 29. We ¹*must* obey God rather than men
9. 6. city, and it shall be told thee what thou *must* do
16. 30. said, Sirs, what *must* I do to be saved?
Rom. 13. 5. Wherefore ye *must* needs be in subjection
1 *Cor.* 5. 10. for then *must* ye needs go out of the world
11. 19. For there *must* be also heresies among you
2 *Cor.* 11. 30. If I *must* needs glory, I will glory of
1 *Tim.* 3. 7. *m.* have good testimony from them that are
8. Deacons in like manner *must* be grave, not [without
2 *Tim.*2. 6. laboureth *m.* be the first to partake of the fruits
Tit. 1. 7. For the bishop *must* be blameless. 1 *Tim.* 3. 2
Heb. 9. 16. testament is, there *m.* of necessity be the death
Rev. 4. 1. I will shew thee the things which *must* come
22. 6. things which *must* shortly come to pass
we behoved, needful.

Mustard *seed.*
*Mat.*13.31. like unto a grain of *m. seed. Mk.*4.31, *Lu.*13.19
17. 20. If ye have faith as a grain of *m. seed. Lu.* 17. 6

Mutual *A.V.—see others.*

Muzzle.
1 *Cor.* 9. 9. Thou shalt not *muzzle* the ox when he treadeth out the corn. 1 *Tim.* 5. 18.

Myrrh.
Mat. 2. 11. gifts, gold and frankincense and *myrrh*
Mk. 15. 23. they offered him wine mingled with *myrrh*
Jno. 19. 39. bringing a mixture of *myrrh* and aloes

Mysteries.
Mat. 13. 11. Unto you it is given to know the *m. Lu.* 8. 10
1 *Cor.* 4. 1. and stewards of the *mysteries* of God
13. 2. and know all *mysteries* and all knowledge
14. 2. but in the spirit he speaketh *mysteries*

Mystery.—*A.V.* ¹*testimony.*
Mk. 4. 11. Unto you is given the *mystery* of the kingdom
Rom. 11. 25. would not—have you ignorant of this *mystery*
16. 25. according to the revelation of the *mystery*
1 *Cor.* 2. 1. proclaiming to you the ¹*mystery* of God
7. but we speak God's wisdom in a *mystery*
15. 51. I tell you a *mystery :* We shall not all sleep
Eph. 1. 9. made known unto us the *mystery* of his will
3. 3. by revelation was made known unto me the *m.*
4. perceive my understanding in the *mystery* of Christ
9. make all men see what is the dispensation of the *m.*
5. 32. This *m.* is great: but I speak in regard of Christ
6. 19. known with boldness the *mystery* of the gospel
Col. 1. 26. the *mystery* which hath been hid from all ages
27. riches of the glory of this *m.* among the Gentiles
2. 2. that they may know the *m.* of God, even Christ
4. 3. door for the word, to speak the *mystery* of Christ
2 *Th.* 2. 7. the *mystery* of lawlessness doth already work
1 *Tim.* 3. 9. the *mystery* of the faith in a pure conscience
16. without controversy great is the *m.* of godliness
Rev. 1. 20. the *m.* of the seven stars which thou sawest
10. 7. about to sound, then is finished the *m.* of God
17. 5. *MYSTERY,* BABYLON THE GREAT, THE MOTHER OF
7. I will tell thee the *mystery* of the woman

NAME

N.

Nails.
Jno. 20. 25. the *nails,* and put my finger—print of the *nails*

Nailing.
Col. 2. 14. taken it out of the way, *nailing* it to the cross

Naked.
Mat. 25. 36. *naked,* and ye clothed me. 43
38. and took thee in ? or *naked,* and clothed thee ? 44
Mk. 14. 51. linen cloth cast about him, over his *naked* body
52. he left the linen cloth, and fled *naked*
Jno. 21. 7. (for he was *naked*), and cast himself into the sea
Acts 19. 16. so that they fled out of that house *naked*
1 *Cor.* 4. 11. we both hunger, and thirst, and are *naked*
2 *Cor.* 5. 3. being clothed we shall not be found *naked*
Heb. 4. 13. all things are *n.* and laid open before the eyes
Jas. 2. 15. If a brother or sister be *naked,* and in lack
Rev. 3. 17. miserable and poor and blind and *naked*
16. 15. and keepeth his garments, lest he walk *naked*
17. 16. and shall make her desolate and *naked*

Nakedness.
Rom. 8. 35. or famine, or *nakedness,* or peril, or sword?
2 *Cor.* 11. 27. in fastings often. in cold and *nakedness*
Rev. 3. 18. shame of thy *nakedness* be not made manifest

Name.—*A.V.* ¹*behalf,* ²*call,* ³*called,* ⁴*names.*
Mat. 10. 41. receiveth a prophet in the *name* of a prophet
—a righteous man in the *name* of a righteous man
42. a cup of cold water only, in the *name* of a disciple
28. 19. baptizing them into the *name* of the Father and
Lu. 1. 59. called him Zacharias after the *name* of his father
6. 22. reproach you, and cast out your *name* as evil
Jno. 3. 18. not believed on the *name* of the only begotten
5. 43. come in my Father's *name,* and ye receive me not
—shall come in his own *name,* him ye will receive
10. 3. and he calleth his own sheep by *name*
25. that I do in my Father's *name,* these bear witness
Acts 2. 38. baptized every one of you in the *name* of Jesus
3. 6. In the *name* of Jesus Christ of Nazareth, walk
4. 7. what power, or in what *name,* have ye done this?
10. that in the *name* of Jesus Christ of Nazareth
12. neither is there any other *name* under heaven
17. speak henceforth to no man in this *n.* 18: 5. 28, 40
30. wonders may be done through the *name* of thy holy
5. 41. counted worthy to suffer dishonour for the *Name*
8. 12. and the *n.* of Jesus Christ, they were baptized. 16
9. 21. made havock of them which called on this *name?*
27. Damascus he had preached boldly in the *n.* of Jesus
15. 26. hazarded their lives for the *n.* of our Lord Jesus
16. 18. in the *name* of Jesus Christ to come out of her
19. 13. to ³*n.* over them which had the evil spirits the *n.*
26. 9. to do many things contrary to the *name* of Jesus
Rom. 2. 17. if thou bearest the ³*n.* of a Jew, and restest upon
24. *name* of God is blasphemed among the Gentiles
1 *Cor.* 1. 10. beseech you, brethren, through the *n.* of our
13. or were ye baptized into the *name* of Paul?
5. 4. in the *name* of our Lord Jesus. *Eph.* 5. 20
Phil. 2. 9. gave unto him the *n.* which is above every *n.*
10. that in the *name* of Jesus every knee should bow
1 *Tim.* 6. 1. *n.* of God and the doctrine be not blasphemed

NAME

2 *Tim.* 2. 19. the *n.* of the Lord depart from unrighteousness
Heb. 1. 4. hath inherited a more excellent name than they
Jas. 2. 7. Do not they blaspheme the honourable *name*
1 *Pet.* 4. 14. reproached for the *name* of Christ, blessed
   16. be ashamed ; but let him glorify God in this ¹*name*
1 *Jno.* 3. 23. should believe in the *name* of his Son. 5. 13
3 *Jno.* 7. for the sake of the *Name* they went forth, taking
   14. Salute the friends by *name*   [nothing
Rev. 2. 17. a new *name* written, which no one knoweth
 3. 1. hast a *name* that thou livest, and thou art dead
   12. write upon him the *name* of my God—*name* of the
       city of my God—mine own new *name*
 8. 11. and the *name* of the star is called Wormwood
 9. 11. in the Greek tongue he hath the *name* Apollyon
13. 8. whose *n.* hath not been written in the book. 17. ⁴8
   17. he that hath the mark, even the *name* of the beast
       or the number of his *name*   ;their foreheads
   14. 1. having his *n.*, and the *n.* of his Father, written on
   16. 9. they blasphemed the *name* of the God which hath
   17. 5. upon her forehead a *name* written, MYSTERY
   19. 12. a *n.* written, which no one knoweth but he himself
   16. on his thigh a *name* written, KING OF KINGS
       see my name, thy name, names.

His Name.

Mat. 1. 21. thou shalt call *his name* Jesus. *Lu.* 1. 31 : 2. 21
   23. And they shall call *his name* Immanuel
12. 21. And in *his name* shall the Gentiles hope
Mk. 6. 14. Herod heard thereof; for *his name* had become
Lu. 1. 13. and thou shalt call *his name* John. 63 [known
   24. 47. remission of sins should be preached in *his name*
Jno. 1. 12. even to them that believe on *his name*
  2. 23. many believed on *his name*, beholding his signs
  5. 43. shall come in *his* own *name*, him ye will receive
 20. 31. that believing ye may have life in *his name*
Acts 3. 16. faith in *his name* hath *his name* made this man
 10. 43. all the prophets witness, that through *his name*
 13. 8. But Elymas the sorcerer (for so is *his name*
 15. 14. to take out of them a people for *his name*
Rom. 1. 5. of faith among all the nations, for *his n.*'s sake
Heb. 6. 10. and the love which ye shewed toward *his name*
 13. 15. the fruit of lips which make confession to *his n.*
1 *Jno.* 2. 12. sins are forgiven you for *his name's* sake
Rev. 3. 5. in no wise blot *his n.* out—I will confess *his n.*
  6. 8. he that sat upon him, *his name* was Death
  9. 11. *his name* in Hebrew is Abaddon
 13. 6. blasphemies against God, to blaspheme *his name*
   17. the beast or the number of *his name.* 15. 2
 14. 11. and whoso receiveth the mark of *his name*
 22. 4. and *his name* shall be on their foreheads

My Name.—A.V. ¹*mine own name.*

Mat. 10. 22. ye shall be hated of all men for *my name's*
       sake. 24. 9: *Mk.* 13. 13 : *Lu.* 21. 17
 18. 5. child in *my n.* receiveth me. *Mk.* 9. 37: *Lu.* 9. 48
   20. are gathered together in *my name*, there am I
 19. 29. for *my name's* sake, shall receive a hundredfold
 24. 5. many shall come in *my name. Mk.* 13. 6 : *Lu.* 21. 8
Mk. 5. 9. he saith unto him, *My name* is Legion
  9. 39. mighty work in *my name*, and be able quickly to
 16. 17. in *my name* shall they cast out devils   [speak
Lu. 21. 12. before kings and governors for *my n.'s* sake
Jno. 14. 13. whatsoever ye shall ask in *my name*, that will
       I do. 14 : 15. 16: 16. 23, 24, 26
   26. Holy Spirit, whom the Father will send in *my n.*
 15. 21. things will they do unto you for *my name's* sake
Acts 9. 15. he is a chosen vessel unto me, to bear *my name*
   16. many things he must suffer for *my name's* sake
 15. 17. the Gentiles, upon whom *my name* is called

NATION

Rom. 9. 17. and that *my name* might be published abroad
1 *Cor.* 1. 15. say that ye were baptized into ¹*my name*
Rev. 2. 3. and didst bear for *my name's* sake
   13. holdest fast *my name*, and didst not deny my faith
 3. 8. didst keep my word, and didst not deny *my name*

Thy Name.—A.V. ¹*thine own name.*

Mat. 6. 9. Hallowed be *thy name. Lu.* 11. 2
 7. 22. prophesy by *thy name*, and by *thy name* cast out
       devils, and by *thy name* do many mighty works ?
Mk. 9. 38. one casting out devils in *thy name. Lu.* 9. 49
Lu. 8. 30. is *thy name?* And he said, Legion. *Mk.* 5. 9
 10. 17. the devils are subject unto us in *thy name*
Jno. 12. 28. Father, glorify *thy n.* There came therefore
 17. 6. I manifested *thy name* unto the men. 26
   11. Holy Father, keep them in ¹*thy n.* which thou. 12
Acts 9. 14. chief priests to bind all that call upon *thy name*
Rom. 15. 9. among the Gentiles, And sing unto *thy name*
Heb. 2. 12. I will declare *thy name* unto my brethren
Rev. 11. 18. the saints, and to them that fear *thy name*
 15. 4. Who shall not fear, O Lord, and glorify *thy name?*

Name *of the Lord.—see Lord, proper names.*

Named—eth.—A.V. ¹*called.*

Lu. 6. 13. chose—twelve, whom also he *n.* apostles. 14
Rom. 15. 20. the gospel, not where Christ was already *n.*
1 *Cor.* 5. 11. if any man that is ¹*n.* a brother be a fornicator
Eph. 1. 21. name that is *named*, not only in this world
 3. 15. every family in heaven and on earth is *named*
 5. 3. or covetousness, let it not even be *n.* among you
2 *Tim.* 2. 19. Let every one that *n.* the name of the Lord
Heb. 5. 10. ¹*n.*—a high priest after the order of Melchizedek
       see called.

Names.—A.V. ¹*name.*

Mat. 10. 2. Now the *n.* of the twelve apostles are these
Lu. 10. 20. rejoice that your *names* are written in heaven
Acts 18. 15. but if they are questions about words and *n.*
Phil. 4. 3. whose *names* are in the book of life
Rev. 3. 4. a few *n.* in Sardis which did not defile their
 13. 1. upon his heads ¹*names* of blasphemy   [garments
 17. 3. full of *names* of blasphemy, having seven heads
 21. 12. *names* written thereon—*n.* of the twelve tribes
   14. on them twelve *names* of the twelve apostles
       see name.

Napkin.

Lu. 19. 20. thy pound, which I kept laid up in a *napkin*
Jno. 11. 44. his face was bound about with a *napkin*
 20. 7. the *napkin*, that was upon his head, not lying with

Narrative.—A.V. ¹*declaration.*

Lu. 1. 1. many have taken in hand to draw up a ¹*narrative*

Narrow.—A.V. ¹*strait.*

Mat. 7. 13. Enter ye in by the ¹*narrow* gate. *Lu.* 13. 24
   14. For ¹*narrow* is the gate, and straitened the way
       see straitened.

Nation.—A.V. ¹*nations*, ²*people.*

Mat. 21. 43. given to a *nation* bringing forth the fruits
 24. 7. *nation* shall rise against *n. Mk.* 13. 8: *Lu.* 21. 10
Lu. 7. 5. for he loveth our *nation*, and himself built us
 23. 2. We found this man perverting our *nation*
Jno. 11. 48. come and take away both our place and our *n.*
   50. for the people, and that the whole *nation* perish not
   51. prophesied that Jesus should die for the *nation*
   52. not for the *nation* only, but that he might also
 18. 35. Thine own *nation* and the chief priests delivered

NATION

Acts 2. 5. Jews, devout men, from every *n*. under heaven
7. 7. the *n*. to which they shall be in bondage will I judge
10. 22. well reported of by all the *nation* of the Jews
28. of another *n*. ; and yet unto me hath God shewed
35. but in every *nation* he that feareth him
17. 26. he made of one every ¹*nation* of men for to dwell
24. 2. by thy providence evils are corrected for this *n*.
10. hast been of many years a judge unto this *nation*
17. I came to bring alms to my *nation*, and offerings
26. 4. was from the beginning among mine own *nation*
28. 19. not that I had aught to accuse my *nation* of
Rom. 10. 19. jealousy with that which is no ²*n*., With a *n*.
1 *Pet*. 2. 9. an elect race, a royal priesthood, a holy *nation*
Rev. 5. 9. tribe, and tongue, and people, and *nation*. 13. ¹⁷
7. 9. no man could number, out of every ¹*nation*, and of
14. 6. that dwell on the earth, and unto every *nation*
see countrymen, generation, race.

Nations.—*A.V.* ¹*Gentiles*.
Mat. 24. 9. shall be hated of all the *n*. for my name's sake
14. testimony unto all the *n*. *Mk*. 13. 10: *Lu*. 24. 47
25. 32. and before him shall be gathered all the *nations*
28. 19. make disciples of all the *nations*, baptizing them
Mk. 11. 17. called a house of prayer for all the *nations* ?
Lu. 12. 30. these things do the *nations* of the world seek
21. 24. and shall be led captive into all the *nations*
25. and upon the earth distress of the *nations*, in perplexity
Acts 7. 45. when they entered on the possession of the ¹*n*.
13. 19. when he had destroyed seven *nations* in the land
14. 16. suffered all the *nations* to walk in their own ways
Rom. 1. 5. unto obedience of faith among all the *nations*
4. 17. A father of many *nations* have I made thee). 18
16. 26. made known unto all the *nations* unto obedience
Gal. 3. 8. saying, In thee shall all the *nations* be blessed
1 *Tim*. 3. 16. seen of angels, preached among the ¹*nations*
Rev. 2. 26. to him will I give authority over the *nations*
10. 11. prophesy again over many peoples and *nations*
11. 2. for it hath been given unto the ¹*nations*
9. and *nations* do men look upon their dead bodies
13. And the *nations* were wroth, and thy wrath came
12. 5. a man child, who is to rule all the *n*. with a rod
14. 8. made all the *nations* to drink of the wine. 18. 3
15. 4. for all the *n*. shall come and worship before thee
16. 19. three parts, and the cities of the *nations* fell
17. 15. are peoples, and multitudes, and *nations*
18. 23. for with thy sorcery were all the *nations* deceived
19. 15. that with it he should smite the *nations*
20. 3. that he should deceive the *nations* no more. 8
21. 24. the *nations* shall walk amidst the light thereof
26. shall bring the glory and the honour of the *nations*
22. 2. leaves of the tree were for the healing of the *n*.
s.e Gentiles (proper names); nation.

Natural.
Rom. 1. 26. for their women changed the *natural* use into
27. also the men, leaving the *natural* use of the woman
31. without *natural* affection. 2 *Tim*. 3. 3
11. 21. for if God spared not the *natural* branches. 24
1 *Cor*. 2. 14. *n*. man receiveth not the things of the Spirit
15. 44. it is sown a *n*. body—there is a *natural* body
46. which is *natural* ; then that which is spiritual
Jas. 1. 23. a man beholding his *natural* face in a mirror
see animals.

Naturally.
Jude 10. understand *n*., like the creatures without reason
see truly.

NECKS

Nature.
Rom. 1. 26. natural use into that which is against *nature*
2. 14. have no law do by *nature* the things of the law
27. uncircumcision which is by *nature*, if it fulfil
11. 24. by *nature* a wild olive tree—grafted contrary to *n*.
1 *Cor*. 11. 14. Doth not even *nature* itself teach you
Gal. 2. 15. Jews by *nature*, and not sinners of the Gentiles
4. 8. in bondage to them which by *nature* are no gods
Eph. 2. 3. were by *nature* children of wrath, even as the rest
Jas. 3. 6. body, and setteth on fire the wheel of *nature*
2 *Pet*. 1. 4. ye may become partakers of the divine *nature*

Naughtiness *A.V.*—*see wickedness*.

Nay.
Mat. 5. 37. your speech be, Yea, yea; *Nay*, nay. *Jas*. 5. 12
13. 29. he saith, *Nay* ; lest haply while ye gather up
Lu. 12. 51. come to give peace in the earth? I tell you, *Nay*
13. 3. *Nay* : but, except ye repent, ye shall all. 5
16. 30. *Nay*, father Abraham ; but if one go to them
Acts 16. 37. do they now cast us out privily? *nay* verily
Rom. 3. 27. law? of works? *Nay* : but by a law of faith
9. 20. *Nay* but, O man, who art thou that repliest
2 *Cor*. 1. 17. there should be the yea yea and the *nay nay* ?
16. our word toward you is not yea and *nay*
19. was not yea and *nay*, but in him is yea

Near.
Acts 10. 24. called together his kinsmen and his *n*. friends
see nigh.

Nearer.
Rom. 13. 11. salvation *n*. to us than when we first believed

Necessary.—*A.V.* ¹*necessity*.
Acts 13. 46. It was *n*. that the word of God should first
28. upon you no greater burden than these *n*. things
1 *Cor*. 12. 22. body which seem to be more feeble are *n*.
2 *Cor*. 9. 5. I thought it *n*. therefore to intreat the brethren
Phil. 2. 25. I counted it *n*. to send to you Epaphroditus
Tit. 3. 14. learn to maintain good works for *necessary* uses
Heb. 8. 3. ¹*n*. that this high priest also have somewhat to offer
9. 23. *necessary* therefore that the copies of the things
see needed.

Necessities.—*A.V.* ¹*necessity*.
Acts 20. 34. these hands ministered unto my *necessities*
Rom. 12. 13. communicating to the ¹*necessities* of the saints
2 *Cor*. 6. 4. In afflictions, in *necessities*, in distresses
12. 10. pleasure in weaknesses, in injuries, in *necessities*

Necessity.
1 *Cor*. 7. 37. no *n*., but hath power as touching his own
9. 16. *n*. is laid upon me ; for woe is unto me, if I preach
2 *Cor*. 9. 7. or of *necessity* : for God loveth a cheerful giver
Philem. 14. that thy goodness should not be as of *necessity*
Heb. 7. 12. is made of *necessity* a change also of the law
9. 16. there must of *necessity* be the death of him that
see necessary, necessities, need.

Neck.
Mat. 18. 6. profitable for him that a great millstone should
be hanged about his *neck*. *Mk*. 9. 42 : *Lu*. 17. 2
Lu. 15. 20. with compassion, and ran, and fell on his *neck*
Acts 15. 10. put a yoke upon the *neck* of the disciples
20. 37. they all wept sore, and fell on Paul's *neck*

Necks.
Rom. 16. 4. who for my life laid down their own *necks*

NEED

Need.—*A.V.* ¹*lack,* ²*necessity,* ³*needeth,* ⁴*wants.*

Mat. 3, 14. I have *need* to be baptized of thee
  6. 8. for your Father knoweth what things ye have *need* of, before ye ask him. 32: *Lu.* 12. 30
  9. 12. have no *n.* of a physician. *Mk.* 2. 17: *Lu.* 5. 31
  14. 16. They have no *n.* to go away; give ye them to eat
  21. 3. The Lord hath *n.* of them. *Mk.* 11. 3: *Lu.* 19. 31, 34
  26. 65. spoken blasphemy; what further *need* have we of witnesses? *Mk.* 14. 63: *Lu.* 22. 71
Mk. 2, 25. never read what David did, when he had *need*
Lu. 9. 11. and them that had *need* of healing he healed
  15. 7. righteous persons, which *need* no repentance
Jno. 13. 29. Buy what things we have *need* of for the feast
Acts 2. 45. to all, according as any man had *need.* 4. 35
Rom. 16. 2. in whatsoever matter she may have *n.* of you
1 *Cor.* 7. 36. if *need* so requireth, let him do what he will
  12. 21. eye cannot say to the hand, I have no *need* of thee: or—head to the feet, I have no *need* of you
  24. whereas our comely parts have no *need*   [tion
2 *Cor.* 3. 1. or *need* we, as do some, epistles of commenda-
Eph. 4. 28. have whereof to give to him that hath ³*need*
Phil. 2. 25. and your messenger and minister to my ⁴*need*
  4. 16. ye sent once and again unto my ²*need*
  19. my God shall fulfil every *need* of yours
1 *Th.* 1. 8. so that we *need* not to speak anything
  4. 9. concerning love—ye have no *need* that one write
  12. may walk honestly—and may have ¹*need* of nothing
  5. 1. seasons, brethren, ye have no *need* that aught be
Heb. 4. 16. and may find grace to help us in time of *need*
  5. 12. *need* again that some one teach—*need* of milk
  7. 11. *need* was there that another priest should arise
  10. 36. *need* of patience, that, having done the will
1 *Pet.* 1. 6. while, if *need* be, ye have been put to grief
1 *Jno.* 2. 27. and ye *need* not that any one teach you
  3. 17. the world's goods, and beholdeth his brother in *n.*
Rev. 3. 17. have gotten riches, and have *need* of nothing
  22. 5. they *n.* no light of lamp, neither light of sun. 21. 23
    see want.

Needed.—*A.V.* ¹*necessary.*

Jno. 2. 25. *needed* not that any one should bear witness
Acts 17. 25. *n.* anything, seeing he himself giveth to all life
  28. 10. they put on board such things as we ¹*needed*

Needest.—eth.

Lu. 11. 8. he will arise and give him as many as he *n.*
Jno. 13. 10. is bathed *needeth* not save to wash his feet
  16. 30. and *needest* not that any man should ask thee
2 *Tim.* 2. 15. a workman that *needeth* not to be ashamed
Heb. 7. 27. *n.* not daily, like those high priests, to offer
    see need.

Needful.—*A.V.* ¹*must needs.*

Lu. 10. 42. one thing is *needful*: for Mary hath chosen
Acts 13. 5. It is ¹*n.* that the scripture should be fulfilled
Phil. 1. 24. to abide in the flesh is more *n.* for your sake
Jas. 2. 16. ye give them not the things *needful* to the body
    see constrained.

Needle.

Mat. 19. 24. It is easier for a camel to go through a *needle's* eye. *Mk.* 10. 25: *Lu.* 18. 25

Needs.—*A.V.* ¹*doubtless.*

2 *Cor.* 12. 1. I must ¹*n.* glory, though it is not expedient
    see behoved, needful.

NEW

Neglect.

1 *Tim.* 4. 14. *Neglect* not the gift that is in thee
Heb. 2. 3. how shall we escape, if we *n.* so great salvation?
    see refuse.

Neglected.

Acts 6. 1. their widows were *n.* in the daily ministration

Neglecting *A.V.*—*see severity.*

Negligent *A.V.*—*see ready.*

Neighbour.—*A.V.* ¹*another.*

Mat. 5. 43. love thy *neighbour,* and hate thine enemy
  19. 19. Thou shalt love thy *n.* as thyself. 22. 39: *Mk.* 12. 31: *Lu.* 10. 27: *Rom.* 13. 9: *Gal.* 5. 14: *Jas.* 2. 8
Mk. 12. 33. to love his *n.* as himself, is much more than
Lu. 10. 29. said unto Jesus, And who is my *neighbour?*
  36. proved *n.* unto him that fell among the robbers?
Acts 7. 27. he that did his *n.* wrong thrust him away
Rom. 13. 8. he that loveth his ¹*n.* hath fulfilled the law
  10. Love worketh no ill to his *neighbour*
  15. 2. please his *n.* for that which is good. 1 *Cor.* 10. ¹24
Gal. 6. 4. glorying in—himself alone, and not of his ¹*n.*
Eph. 4. 25. speak ye truth each one with his *neighbour*
    see fellow-citizen.

Neighbourhood.—*A.V.* ¹*quarters.*

Acts 28. 7. in the ¹*n.* of that place were lands belonging

Neighbours.

Lu. 1. 58. her *n.* and her kinsfolk heard that the Lord
  14. 12. nor rich *neighbours*; lest haply they also bid thee
  15. 9. friends and *neighbours,* saying, Rejoice. 6
Jno. 9. 8. *n.* therefore, and they which saw him aforetime

Nephews *A.V.*—*see grandchildren.*

Nests.

Mat. 8. 20. birds of the heaven have *n.*; but the. *Lu.* 9. 58

Net.

Mat. 4. 18. casting a *net* into the sea. *Mk.* 1. 16
  13. 47. the kingdom of heaven is like unto a *net*
Jno. 21. 6. Cast the *net* on the right side of the boat
  8. dragging the *net* full of fishes
  11. drew the *net* to land, full—the *net* was not rent
    see nets.

Nets.—*A.V.* ¹*net.*

Mat. 4. 20. left the *nets,* and followed him. *Mk.* 1. 18
  21. mending their *nets*; and he called. *Mk.* 1. 19
Lu. 5. 2. gone out of them, and were washing their *nets*
  4. into the deep, and let down your *nets* for a draught
  5. but at thy word I will let down the ¹*nets*
  6. multitude of fishes; and their ¹*nets* were breaking

New.

Mat. 9. 17. do men put *new* wine into old wine-skins—*new* wine into fresh wine-skins. *Mk.* 2. 22: *Lu.* 5. 37, 38
  13. 52. forth out of his treasure things *new* and old
  26. 29. when I drink it *new* with you. *Mk.* 14. 25
  27. 60. laid it in his own *new* tomb, which he had hewn
Mk. 1. 27. What is this? a *new* teaching!
  2. 21. the *new* from the old, and a worse rent is made
  16. 17. they shall speak with *new* tongues
Lu. 5. 36. piece from a *new* garment—else he will rend the *new*—piece from the *n.* will not agree with the old
  39. no man having drunk old wine desireth *new*
  22. 20. the *new* covenant in my blood. 1 *Cor.* 11. 25
Jno. 13. 34. A *new* commandment I give unto you
  19. 41. a *new* tomb wherein was never man yet laid

NEW

Acts 2. 13. mocking said, They are filled with *new* wine
17. 19. May we know what this *new* teaching is
21. but either to tell or to hear some *new* thing)
1 *Cor.* 5. 7. out the old leaven, that ye may be a *new* lump
2 *Cor.* 3. 6. sufficient as ministers of a *new* covenant
5. 17. if any man is in Christ, he is a *new* creature—
passed away ; behold, they are become *new*
Gal. 6. 15. nor uncircumcision, but a *new* creature
Eph. 2. 15. of the twain one *new* man, so making peace
4. 24. and put on the *new* man. *Col.* 3. 10
Heb. 9. 15. he is the mediator of a *new* covenant
10. 20. dedicated for us, a *new* and living way
2 *Pet.* 3. 13. we look for *new* heavens and a *new* earth
1 *Jno.* 2. 7. no *new* commandment write I unto you
8. Again, a *new* commandment write I unto you
2 *Jno.* 5. not as though I wrote to thee a *n.* commandment
Rev. 2. 17. a *new* name written, which no one knoweth
3. 12. *new* Jerusalem—and mine own *new* name. 21. 2
5. 9. And they sing a *new* song, saying. 14. 3
21. 1. And I saw a *new* heaven and a *new* earth
5. on the throne said, Behold, I make all things *new*
see undressed.

Newborn.

1 *Pet.* 2. 2. as *newborn* babes, long for the spiritual milk

Newness.

Rom. 6. 4. so we also might walk in *newness* of life
7. 6. so that we serve in *newness* of the spirit

Next.—*A.V.* ¹another.

Mat. 10. 23. they persecute you in this city, flee into the ¹*n.*
Mk. 1. 38. Let us go elsewhere into the *next* towns
Lu. 9. 37. the *next* day. *Acts* 20. 15 : 21. 26 : 27. 3, 18
Acts 13. 42. be spoken to them the *next* sabbath. 44

Nigh.—*A.V.* ¹near, ²ready.

Mat. 24. 32. ye know—summer is *n. Mk.* 13. ¹28: *Lu.* 21. 30
33. know ye that he is ¹*n.*, even at the doors. *Mk.* 13. 29
Lu. 19. 11. a parable, because he was *nigh* to Jerusalem
21. 28. your heads ; because your redemption draweth *n.*
31. know ye that the kingdom of God is *nigh*
Jno. 19. 20. where Jesus was crucified was *nigh* to the city
42. (for the tomb was *nigh* at hand)
Eph. 2. 13. far off are made *nigh* in the blood of Christ
17. were far off, and peace to them that were *nigh*
Phil. 2. 27. for indeed he was sick *nigh* unto death
Heb. 6. 8. thistles, it is rejected and *nigh* unto a curse
8. 13. waxeth aged is ²*nigh* unto vanishing away
see came, come, draw, drawing, drew, (at) hand, honoureth.

Night.

Mat. 2. 14. and took the young child and his mother by *n.*
14. 25. fourth watch of the *night* he came. *Mk.* 6. 48
26. 31. All ye shall be offended in me this *night*
34. this *night*, before the cock crow, thou shalt deny me
28. 13. His disciples came by *night*, and stole him away
Lu. 2. 8. and keeping watch by *night* over their flock
5. 5. Master, we toiled all *night*, and took nothing
6. 12. and he continued all *night* in prayer to God
12. 20. this *night* is thy soul required of thee
17. 34. In that *night* there shall be two men on one bed
21. 37. every *night* he went out, and lodged in the mount
Jno. 3. 2. the same came unto him by *night*. 19. 39
9. 4. the *night* cometh, when no man can work
11. 10. But if a man walk in the *night*, he stumbleth
13. 30. the sop went out straightway : and it was *night*
21. 3. and that *night* they took nothing

NONE

Acts 5. 19. angel of the Lord by *night* opened the prison
9. 25. took him by *night*, and let him down through the
12. 6. the same *night* Peter was sleeping between two
16. 9. a vision appeared to Paul in the *night*. 18. 9
33. same hour of the *night*, and washed their stripes
23. 11. the *night* following the Lord stood by him
23. two hundred, at the third hour of the *night*
31. Paul, and brought him by *n.* to Antipatris. 17. 10
27. 23. there stood by me this *night* an angel of the God
27. But when the fourteenth *night* was come
Rom. 13. 12. The *night* is far spent, and the day is at hand
1 *Cor.* 11. 23. Jesus in the *night* in which he was betrayed
1 *Th.* 5. 2. day of the Lord so cometh as a thief in the *night*
5. we are not of the *night*, nor of darkness
7. they that sleep sleep in the *n.*—are drunken in the *n.*
Rev. 21. 25. (for there shall be no *night* there). 22. 5
see day and night.

Nights.

Mat. 4. 2. when he had fasted forty days and forty *nights*
12. 40. as Jonah was three days and three *nights* in the
belly—Son of man be three days and three *nights*

Nine.

Lu. 17. 17. Were not the ten cleansed ? but where are the *n.?*
see ninety and nine.

Ninety and nine.

Mat. 18. 12. doth he not leave the *n.* and *n.* 13. *Lu.* 15. 4, 7

Ninth.

Mat. 20. 5. went out about the sixth and the *ninth* hour
27. 45. land until the *ninth* hour. *Mk.* 15. 33 : *Lu.* 23. 44
46. *ninth* hour Jesus cried with a loud voice. *Mk.* 15. 34
Acts 3. 1. at the hour of prayer, being the *ninth* hour
10. 3. vision openly, as it were about the *ninth* hour. 30
Rev. 21. 20. the *ninth*, topaz ; the tenth, chrysoprase

Noble.

Acts 17. 11. were more *noble* than those in Thessalonica
1 *Cor.* 1. 26. not many mighty, not many *noble*, are called
see excellent.

Nobleman.

Lu. 19. 12. A certain *nobleman* went into a far country
Jno. 4. 46. there was a certain *nobleman*, whose son was sick
49. *n.* saith unto him, Sir, come down ere my child die

Noise.

2 *Pet.* 3. 10. the heavens shall pass away with a great *n.*
see tumult, voice.

Noised.

Mk. 2. 1. it was *noised* that he was in the house
Lu. 1. 65. all these sayings were *noised* abroad
see heard, sound.

Noisome.

Rev. 16. 2. it became a *n.* and grievous sore upon the men

None.—*A.V.* ¹no man.

Mk. 10. 18. ¹*none* is good save one, even God. *Lu.* 18. 19
12. 31. There is *none* other commandment greater
32. said that he is one ; and there is *none* other but he
Lu. 1. 61. *none* of thy kindred that is called by this name
3. 11. coats, let him impart to him that hath *none*
4. 26. unto *none* of them was Elijah sent, but only to
27. and *none* of them was cleansed, but only Naaman

230

NONE

Lu. 11. 24. seeking rest; and finding *none*, he saith, I will
13. 6. he came seeking fruit thereon, and found *none*
14. 24. *none* of those men which were bidden shall taste
Jno. 7. 19. give you the law, and yet *none* of you doeth
15. 24. the works which *n.* other did, they had not had
16. 5. *none* of you asketh me, Whither goest thou? [sin
Acts 3. 6. Peter said, Silver and gold have I *none* [tized
8. 16. fallen upon *n.* of them: only they had been bap-
24. *n.* of the things which ye have spoken come upon me
11. 19. speaking the word to *none* save only to Jews
19. 17. And Gallio cared for *none* of these things
25. 11. if *n.* of those things is true, whereof these accuse
Rom. 3. 10. There is *none* righteous, no, not one [*me*
11. There is *n.* that understandeth, There is *n.* that
9. 9 hath not the Spirit of Christ, he is *n.* of his [seeketh
14. 7. *n.* of us liveth to himself, and ¹*none* dieth to himself
1 *Cor.* 1. 14. I thank God that I baptized *none* of you, save
2. 8. which *none* of the rulers of this world knoweth
7. 29. that have wives may be as though they had *none*
9. 15. But I have used *none* of these things
Gal. 1. 19. other of the apostles saw I *none*, save James
1 *Th.* 5. 15. See that *n.* render unto any one evil for evil
1 *Tim.* 5. 14. give *none* occasion to the adversary
1 *Pet.* 4. 15 let *n.* of you suffer as a murderer, or a thief
see nothing, one.

Noon.

Acts 22 6. about *noon*, suddenly there shone from heaven

North.

Lu. 13. 29. from the east and west, and from the *north*
Rev. 21. 13. and on the *north* three gates [and south

North-east.—*A.V.* ¹*north-west*.

Acts 27. 12. haven of Crete, looking ¹*n.-east* and south-east.

Notable.

Mat. 27. 16. had then a *notable* prisoner, called Barabbas
Acts 2. 20. day of the Lord come, That great and *n.* day
4. 16. a *n.* miracle hath been wrought through them

Note.

Rom. 16. 7. who are of *note* among the apostles
2 *Th* 3. 14. *n.* that man, that ye have no company with him

Nothing.—*A.V.* ¹*none*, ²*anything.*

Mat. 5. 13. thenceforth good for *nothing*, but to be cast out
10. 26. for there is *nothing* covered, that shall not be revealed. *Mk.* 4. 22: *Lu.* 12. 2
15. 32. and have *nothing* to eat. *Mk.* 8. 1, 2
17. 20. and *nothing* shall be impossible unto you
21. 19. found *nothing* thereon, but leaves. *Mk.* 11. 13
23. 16. Whosoever shall swear by the temple, it is *n.*
18 Whosoever shall swear by the altar, it is *nothing*
26. 62. Answerest thou *nothing*? *Mk.* 14. 60: 15. 4
27. 12. he answered *nothing. Mk.* 14. 61: *Lu.* 23. 9
19. Have thou *nothing* to do with that righteous man
24. when Pilate saw that he prevailed *nothing*
Mk. 1. 44. say *nothing* to any man: but go thy way, shew
5. 26. had spent all that she had, and was *n.* bettered
6. 8. take *nothing* for their journey, save a staff. *Lu.* 9. 3
7. 15. there is *nothing* from without the man, that
9. 29. This kind can come out by *nothing*, save by prayer
16. 8. they said ²*nothing* to any one; for they were afraid
Lu 4. 2. And he did eat *nothing* in those days
5. 5. Master, we toiled all night, and took *n. Jno.* 21. 3

NOTHING

Lu. 9. 17 *nothing* is hid, that shall not be made manifest
10. 19. the enemy: and *n.* shall in any wise hurt you
11. 6. from a journey, and I have *n.* to set before him
22. 35. lacked ye any thing? And they said, *Nothing*
23. 15. *n.* worthy of death. *Acts* 23. 29; 25. 25; 26. 31
41. reward of our deeds: but this man hath done *n.*
Jno. 3. 27. can receive *n.*, except it have been given him
4. 11 Sir, thou hast *nothing* to draw with, and the well
5. 19. The Son can do *nothing* of himself. 30
6. 12. pieces which remain over, that *nothing* be lost
39 I should lose *nothing*, but should raise it up
63. the spirit that quickeneth, the flesh profiteth *n.*
7. 26. he speaketh openly, and they say *n.* unto him
8. 28. I am he, and that I do *nothing* of myself, but
54. If I glorify myself, my glory is *nothing*
9. 33. If this man were not from God, he could do *nothing*
11. 49. Caiaphas—said unto them, Ye know *n.* at all
12. 19. Behold how ye prevail *nothing*: lo, the world
14. 30. prince of the world cometh: and he hath *n.* in me
15. 5. much fruit: for apart from me ye can do *nothing*
16. 23. And in that day ye shall ask me *nothing*
24. Hitherto have ye asked *nothing* in my name: ask
18. 20. Jews come together; and in secret spake I *nothing*
Acts 4. 14. they could say *nothing* against it
21. finding *nothing* how they might punish them
10. 20. and go with them, *nothing* doubting [my mouth
11. 8. *nothing* common or unclean hath ever entered into
17. 21. spent their time in *nothing* else, but either to tell
19. 36. ye ought to be quiet, and to do *nothing* rash
23 14 curse, to taste *nothing* until we have killed Paul
26. 22. saying ¹*n.* but what the prophets and Moses did
27. 33. wait and continue fasting, having taken *nothing*
28. 17. though I had done *nothing* against the people
Rom. 14. 14. that *nothing* is unclean of itself
1 *Cor.* 4. 4. For I know *nothing* against myself; yet am I
5. Wherefore judge *nothing* before the time, until
7 19. Circumcision is *n.*, and uncircumcision is *nothing*
9. 16. If I preach the gospel, I have *nothing* to glory of
13. 2. remove mountains, but have not love, I am *nothing*
3. be burned, but have not love, it profiteth me *nothing*
2 *Cor.* 6 10. as having *nothing*, and yet possessing all things
7. 9. that ye might suffer loss by us in *nothing*
8. 15. He that gathered much had *nothing* over
12. 11. in *n.* was I behind the very chiefest apostles, though
13. 8. For we can do *nothing* against the truth [I am *n.*
Gal. 2. 6. who were of repute imparted *nothing* to me
4 1. so long as the heir is a child, he differeth *nothing*
5. 2. circumcision, Christ will profit you *nothing*
6. 3. something, when he is *nothing*, he deceiveth himself
Phil. 1. 20. and hope, that in *nothing* shall I be put to shame
28. and in *nothing* affrighted by the adversaries
2 3 doing *nothing* through faction or through vainglory
4. 6. In *nothing* be anxious; but in everything by prayer
1 *Th.* 4. 12. and may have need of *nothing*
1 *Tim.* 4. 4. creature of God is good, and *n.* is to be rejected
5. 21. without prejudice, doing *nothing* by partiality
6. 4. he is puffed up, knowing *nothing*, but doting
7. for we brought *nothing* into the world
Tit. 1. 15. that are defiled and unbelieving *nothing* is pure
3. 13. diligently, that *nothing* be wanting unto them
Philem. 14. but without thy mind I would do *nothing*
Heb. 2. 8. he left *nothing* that is not subject to him
19. (for the law made *nothing* perfect), and a bringing in
Jas. 1. 6. ye may be perfect and entire, lacking in *nothing*
6. But let him ask in faith, *nothing* doubting
3 *Jno.* 7. they went forth, taking *nothing* of the Gentiles
Rev. 3. 17. have gotten riches, and have need of *nothing*
see anything, reject, truth, word.

231

NOTICE

Notice *A.V.*—*see promised.*

Nought.—*A.V.* ¹*destroy,* ²*freely,* ³*none effect.*
Acts 5. 36. obeyed him, were dispersed, and came to *nought*
Rom. 9. 6. as though the word of God hath come to ³*n.*
1 *Cor.* 1. 28. might bring to *nought* the things that are
  2. 6. rulers of this world, which are coming to *nought*
  6. 13. God shall bring to ¹*nought* both it and them
2 *Cor.* 11. 7. I preached to you the gospel of God for ²*n.* ?
2 *Th.* 2. 8. bring to ¹*n.* by the manifestation of his coming
  3. 8. neither did we eat bread for *n.* at any man's hand
Heb. 2. 14. bring to ¹*nought* him that had the power of death
  see disrepute, (made) desolate, overthrown.

Set at Nought.—*A.V.* ¹*despise*—*d.*
Mk. 9. 12. and be *set at nought* ? *Lu.* 23. 11
Lu. 18. 9. they were righteous, and ¹*set* all others *at nought*
Acts 4. 11. stone which was *set at n.* of you the builders
Rom. 14. 3. him that eateth ¹*set at n.* him that eateth not
  10. why dost thou *set at nought* thy brother?
Heb. 10. 28. A man that hath ¹*set at nought* Moses' law
Jude 8. ¹*set at nought* dominion, and rail at dignities

Nourish—ed.—*A.V.* ¹*feed.*
Acts 7. 20. he was *n.* three months in his father's house
  21. Pharaoh's daughter took him up, and *nourished* him
1 *Tim.* 4. 6. *n.* in the words of the faith, and of the good
Jas. 5. 5. ye have *n.* your hearts in a day of slaughter
Rev. 12. 6. there they may ¹*n.* her a thousand two hundred
  14. *nourished* for a time, and times, and half a time
  see fed.

Nourisheth.
Eph. 5. 29. his own flesh; but *nourisheth* and cherisheth it

Nourishment *A.V.*—*see supplied*

Novice.
1 *Tim.* 3. 6. not a *novice*, lest being puffed up he fall

Number
Lu. 22. 3. Judas—Iscariot, being of the *n.* of the twelve
Jno. 6. 10. sat down, in *n.* about five thousand. *Acts* 4. 4
Acts 5. 36. to be somebody; to whom a *number* of men
  6. 1. when the *number* of the disciples was multiplying. 7
  11, 21. a great *n.* that believed turned unto the Lord
  16. 5. in the faith, and increased in *number* daily
Rom. 9. 27. If the *n.* of the children of Israel be as the
2 *Cor.* 10. 12. For we are not bold to *number* or compare
Rev. 5. 11. the *n.* of them was ten thousand times ten
  7. 4. I heard the *number* of them which were sealed
  9. a great multitude, which no man could *number*
  9. 16. the *number* of the armies—I heard the *n.* of them
  13. 17. name of the beast or the *number* of his name
  18. count the *number* of the beast; for it is the *number*
    of a man; and his *number* is Six hundred and
  15. 2. from his image, and from the *number* of his name
  20. 8. to the war; the *number* of whom is as the sand
  see enrolled.

Numbered.
Mat. 10. 30. hairs of your head are all *numbered.* *Lu.* 12. 7
Acts 1. 17. he was *numbered* among us, and received his
  26. Matthias; and he was *n.* with the eleven apostles

Nurse.
1 *Th.* 2. 7. as when a *nurse* cherisheth her own children

Nurture.—*A.V.* ¹*bring up.*
Eph. 6. 4. ¹*n.* them in the chastening and admonition of
  see chastening.

OBEY

O.

Oath.
Mat. 14. 7. he promised with an *oath* to give her
  26. 72. he denied with an *oath*, I know not the man
Lu. 1. 73. *o.* which he sware unto Abraham our father
Acts 2. 30. that God had sworn with an *oath* to him
Heb. 6. 16. in every dispute of theirs the *oath* is final
  17. immutability of his counsel, interposed with an *o.*
  7. 20. as it is not without the taking of an *oath* [saith
  21. priests without an *o.*; but he with an *o.* by him that
  28. the *oath.* which was after the law, appointeth a Son
Jas. 5. 12. nor by any other *oath*: but let your yea be yea
  see curse, oaths.

Oaths.—*A.V* ¹*oath.*
Mat. 5. 33. shalt perform unto the Lord thine *oaths*
  14. 9. but for the sake of his ¹*oaths*, and of them. *Mk.* 6.¹26

Obedience.—*A.V.* ¹*obedient,* ²*obey—ing,* ³*professed subjection.*
Rom. 1. 5. unto *obedience* of faith among all the nations
  5. 19. so through the *obedience* of the one shall the many
  6. 16. as servants unto ³*o.*—or of *o.* unto righteousness?
  15. 18. wrought through me, for the ¹*o.* of the Gentiles
  16. 19. your *obedience* is come abroad unto all men
  26. known unto all the nations unto *obedience* of faith
2 *Cor.* 7. 15. whilst he remembereth the *obedience* of you all
  9. 13. they glorify God for the ³*o.* of your confession
  10. 5. every thought into captivity to the *o.* of Christ
  6. avenge all disobedience, when your *o.* shall be fulfilled
Philem. 21. Having confidence in thine *obedience* I write
Heb. 5. 8. yet learned *o.* by the things which he suffered
1 *Pet.* 1. 2. in sanctification of the Spirit, unto *obedience*
  14. as children of ¹*obedience*, not fashioning yourselves
  22. Seeing ye have purified your souls in your ²*obedience*
  see subjection.

Obedient.—*A V.* ¹*obey—ed.*
Acts 6. 7. company of the priests were *obedient* to the faith
  7. 39. to whom our fathers would not be ¹*obedient*
Rom. 6. 17. servants of sin, ye became ¹*o.* from the heart
2 *Cor.* 2. 9. proof of you, whether ye are *o.* in all things
Eph. 6. 5. Servants, be *o.* unto them that according to
Phil. 2. 8. humbled himself, becoming *o.* even unto death
Tit. 3. 1. subjection to rulers, to authorities, to be ¹*obedient*
  see obedience, subjection.

Obey.
Mat. 8. 27. What manner of man is this, that even the
  winds and the sea *obey* him? *Mk.* 4. 41: *Lu.* 8. 25
Mk. 1. 27. even the unclean spirits, and they *obey* him
Acts 5. 29. We must *obey* God rather than men   [him
  32. Holy Ghost, whom God hath given to them that *o.*
Rom. 2. 8. *obey* not the truth, but *obey* unrighteousness
  6. 12. mortal body, that ye should *obey* the lusts thereof
  16. unto obedience, his servants ye are whom ye *obey*
Gal. 5. 7. who did hinder you that ye should not *obey*
Eph. 6. 1. Children, *obey* your parents. *Col.* 3. 20
Col. 3. 22. Servants, *obey* in all things them that are
2 *Th.* 1. 8. that *obey* not the gospel of our Lord Jesus
Heb. 5. 9. unto all them that *obey* him the author of
  13. 17. *Obey* them that have the rule over you [obey us
Jas. 3. 3. horses' bridles into their mouths, that they may
1 *Pet.* 3. 1. that, even if any *obey* not the word, they may
  4. 17 what shall be the end of them that *obey* not
  see obedient, obeyed, obeyeth.

232

OBEYED

Obeyed.—*A.V.* ¹*obey.*
Lu. 17. 6. planted in the sea; and it would have ¹o. you
Acts 5. 36. as many as *obeyed* him, were dispersed. 37
Phil. 2. 12. have always *obeyed*, not in my presence only
Heb. 11. 8. Abraham, when he was called, *obeyed* to go out
1 *Pet.* 3. 6. as Sarah *obeyed* Abraham, calling him lord
  see hearken, obedient.

Obeyeth.—*A.V.* ¹*believeth,* ²*obey.*
Jno. 3. 36 he that ¹*obeyeth* not the Son shall not see life
2 *Th.* 3. 14. if any man ²*obeyeth* not our word

Obeying *A.V.*—*see obedience.*

Object *A.V.*—*see accusation.*

Observation.
Lu. 17. 20. The kingdom of God cometh not with *o.*

Observe—d.—*A.V.* ¹*beheld,* ²*kept.*
Mat. 19. 20. All these things have I ²o. *Mk.* 10. 20; *Lu.* 18.
  23. 3. all things—they bid you, these do and *observe* [²21
  28. 20. teaching them to *observe* all things whatsoever I
Acts 16. 21. to receive, or to *observe*, being Romans
  17. 23. I passed along, and ¹o. the objects of your worship
Gal. 4. 10. Ye o. days, and months, and seasons, and years
1 *Tim.* 5. 21. that thou o. these things without prejudice
  see kept.

Obtain.—*A.V.* ¹*purchased.*
Mat. 5. 7. Blessed are the merciful: for they shall *o.* mercy
Acts 8. 20. because thou hast thought to ¹o. the gift of God
Rom. 11. 31. shewn to you they also may now *obtain* mercy
2 *Tim.* 2. 10. that they also may *obtain* the salvation
Heb. 11. 35. that they might *obtain* a better resurrection
Jas. 4. 2. ye kill, and covet, and cannot *obtain*
  see attain, obtaining, receive.

Obtained.—*A.V.* ¹*attained,* ²*purchased,* ³*received.*
Acts 1. 18. this man ²o. a field with the reward of his
  22. 28. With a great sum o. I this citizenship ¦iniquity
  26. 22. Having therefore o. the help that is from God
  27. 13. supposing that they had *obtained* their purpose
Rom. 11. 7. Israel seeketh for, that he o. not—election o. it
  30. now have *obtained* mercy by their disobedience
1 *Cor.* 7. 25. as one that hath *obtained* mercy of the Lord
2 *Cor.* 4. 1. even as we ³*obtained* mercy, we faint not
Phil. 3. 12. I have already ¹o., or am already made perfect
1 *Tim.* 1. 13. I o. mercy, because I did it ignorantly. 16
Heb. 6. 15. having patiently endured, he o. the promise
  8. 6. now hath he *obtained* a ministry the more excellent
  9. 12. into the holy place, having o. eternal redemption
  11. 33. *obtained* promises, stopped the mouths of lions
1 *Pet.* 2. 10. which had not *obtained* mercy, but now have o.
2 *Pet.* 1. 1. have *obtained* a like precious faith with us
  see had, inherited, made, received.

Obtaining.—*A.V.* ¹*obtain.*
1 *Th.* 5. 9. not unto wrath, but unto the ¹o. of salvation
2 *Th.* 2. 14. to the *obtaining* of the glory of our Lord Jesus

Occasion.—*A.V.* ¹*offence,* ²*offended.*
Mat. 11. 6. whosoever shall find none ²*occasion* of. *Lu.* 7.²23
  18. 7. woe to that man through whom the ¹o. cometh
Rom. 7. 8. but sin, finding *occasion*, wrought in me. 11
  14. 13. in his brother's way, or an *occasion* of falling
2 *Cor.* 5. 12. giving you *occasion* of glorying on our behalf
  11. 12. I may cut off o. from them which desire an o

OFFERED

Gal. 5. 13. use not your freedom for an *o.* to the flesh
1 *Tim.* 5. 14. give none *o.* to the adversary for reviling
1 *Jno.* 2. 10. there is none *occasion* of stumbling in him

Occasions.—*A.V.* ¹*offences.*
Mat. 18. 7. because of ¹*occasions* of stumbling! for it must
  needs be that the ¹*occasions* come. *Lu.* 17. ¹1
Rom. 16. 17. causing the divisions and *o.* of stumbling

Occupation.
Acts 19. 25. together, with the workmen of like *occupation*
  see trade.

Occupied.
Heb. 13. 9. wherein they that *o.* themselves were not profited

Occupieth *A.V.*—*see filleth.*

Occupy *A.V.*—*see trade.*

Odour.—*A.V.* ¹*savour.*
Jno. 12. 3. house was filled with the *odour* of the ointment
Eph. 5. 2. and a sacrifice to God for an ¹o. of a sweet smell
Phil. 4. 18. from you, an *odour* of a sweet smell, a sacrifice

Odours *A.V.*—*see incense.*

Offence.
Acts 24. 16. to have a conscience void of *o.* toward God
Rom. 9. 33. of stumbling and a rock of *offence*. 1 *Pet.* 2. 8
  14. 20. it is evil for that man who eateth with *offence*
Phil. 1. 10. sincere and void of *o.* unto the day of Christ
  see occasion, sin, stumbling, stumblingblock, trespass.

Offences *A.V.*—*see occasions of stumbling, trespasses.*

Offend *A.V.*—*see stumble, stumbling.*

Offended.
Mat. 13. 57. And they were *offended* in him. *Mk.* 6. 3
  15. 12. The Pharisees were o., when they heard this
  26. 31. ye shall be *offended* because of me this night. *Mk.* 14. 27
  33. said unto him, If all shall be *offended* in thee, I
    will never be *offended*. *Mk.* 14. 29
  see occasion, sinned, stumbled, stumbleth, stumbling.

Offenders.—*A.V.* ¹*sinners.*
Lu. 13. 4. think ye that they were ¹o. above all the men
  see wrong-doers.

Offer.—*A.V.* ¹*offered.*
Mat. 5. 24. thy brother, and then come and *offer* thy gift
  8. 4. *offer* the gift that Moses. *Mk.* 1. 44: *Lu.* 5. 14
Lu. 2. 24. to *offer*—A pair of turtledoves, or two young
  6. 29. smiteth thee on the one cheek *offer* also the other
Acts 7. 42. Did ye ¹o. unto me slain beasts and sacrifices
Heb. 5. 1. that he may o. both gifts and sacrifices for sins
  3. people, so also for himself, to *offer* for sins. 7. 27
  8. 3. every high priest is appointed to *offer*—necessary
    that this high priest also have somewhat to *offer*
  9. 25. nor yet that he should *offer* himself often
  13. 15. Through him then let us *offer* up a sacrifice
1 *Pet.* 2. 5. holy priesthood, to *offer* up spiritual sacrifices
  see add, give.

Offered.—*A.V.* ¹*gave him to drink,* ²*presented.*
Mat. 2. 11. opening their treasures they ²o. unto him gifts
Mk. 15. 23. *offered* him wine mingled with myrrh
Acts 8. 18. Holy Ghost was given, he *offered* them money
  21. 26. until the offering was *offered* for every one

OFFERED

Phil. 2. 17. o. upon the sacrifice and service of your faith
2 *Tim.* 4. 6. For I am already being *offered*
Heb. 5. 7. in the days of his flesh, having o. up prayers
7. 27. this he did once for all, when he *offered* up himself
9. 9. to which are *offered* both gifts and sacrifices
14. *offered* himself without blemish unto God, cleanse
28. Christ also, having been once o. to bear the sins
10. 2. Else would they not have ceased to be *offered*
12. when he had *offered* one sacrifice for sins for ever
11. 4. faith Abel o. unto God a more excellent sacrifice
17. By faith Abraham, being tried, *offered* up Isaac
Jas. 2. 21. justified by works, in that he *offered* up Isaac
see offer, offereth, offering, sacrificed.

Offereth.—*A.V.* ¹*doeth,* ²*offered.*
Jno. 16. 2. shall think that he ¹*offereth* service unto God
Heb. 9. 7. blood, which he ²o. for himself, and for the errors

Offering—s.—*A.V.* ¹*bring,* ²*gifts,* ³*offered.*
Mat. 5. 23. If therefore thou art ¹o. thy gift at the altar
Lu. 21. 5. temple—adorned with goodly stones and ²o.
23. 36. coming to him, *offering* him vinegar
Acts 21. 26. until the o. was offered for every one of them
24. 17. I came to bring alms to my nation, and *offerings*
Rom. 15. 16. o. up of the Gentiles might be made acceptable
Eph. 5. 2. an *offering* and a sacrifice to God for an odour
Heb. 10. 5. Sacrifice and *offering* thou wouldest not. 8
10. sanctified through the o. of the body of Jesus Christ
11. and *offering* oftentimes the same sacrifices
14. by one *offering* he hath perfected for ever them
18. where remission of these is, there is no more *offering*
11. 17. Abraham—was ³*offering* up his only begotten son
see gifts, sacrifices.

Office.—*A.V.* ¹*bishoprick.*
Lu. 1. 8. while he executed the priest's *office* before God
Acts 1. 20. His [Judas Iscariot] ¹*office* let another take
Rom. 12. 4. and all the members have not the same *office*
1 *Tim.* 3. 1. the *office* of a bishop, he desireth a good work
Heb. 7. 5. the priest's o. have commandment to take tithes
see ministry, serve, served.

Officer.
Lu. 12. 58. judge shall deliver thee to the *officer,* and the *officer* shall cast thee into prison. *Mat.* 5. 25

Officers.—*A.V.* ¹*servants.*
Mat. 26. 58. Peter—sat with the ¹o., to see the end. *Mk.* 14. 154
Mk. 14. 65. the ¹o. received him with blows of their hands
Jno. 7. 32. and the Pharisees sent *officers* to take him
46. The *officers* answered, Never man so spake
18. 3. Judas—having received the band of soldiers, and o.
12. captain, and the *officers* of the Jews, seized Jesus
18. the servants and the *officers* were standing there
22. one of the *officers* standing by struck Jesus
19. 6. the *officers* saw him, they cried out, saying, Crucify
Acts 5. 22. o. that came found them not in the prison. 26

Offscouring.
1 *Cor.* 4. 13. the *offscouring* of all things, even unto now

Offspring.—*A.V.* ¹*generation.*
Mat. 3. 7. Ye ¹*offspring* of vipers. 12. ¹34: 23. ¹33: *Lu.* 3. ¹7
Acts 17. 28. For we are also his *offspring.* 29
Rev. 22. 16. I am the root and the *offspring* of David

Oft.
Mat. 9. 14. Why do we and the Pharisees fast *oft*
18. 21. how *oft* shall my brother sin against me, and I
1 *Cor.* 11. 25. as *oft* as ye drink it, in remembrance of me

OLD

2 *Cor.* 11. 23. in stripes above measure, in deaths *oft*
2 *Tim.* 1. 16. Onesiphorus: for he *oft* refreshed me [upon it
Heb. 6. 7. land which hath drunk the rain that cometh *oft*
see diligently, oft-times.

Often.
Mat. 23. 37. how *often* would I have gathered. *Lu.* 13. 34
Mk. 5. 4. he had been *often* bound with fetters and chains
Lu. 5. 33. The disciples of John fast *often*
2 *Cor.* 11. 26. For as *often* as ye eat this bread, and drink
Cor. 11. 26. in journeyings *often,* in perils of rivers
27. in watchings *often*—in fastings *often*
Phil. 3. 18. many walk, of whom I told you o., and now tell
1 *Tim.* 5. 23. thy stomach's sake and thine *often* infirmities
Heb. 9. 25. nor yet that he should offer himself *often*
26. else must he *often* have suffered since the foundation
Rev. 11. 6. every plague, as *often* as they shall desire

Oftener.
Acts 24. 26. he sent for him the *oftener,* and communed

Oft-times *or* **Oftentimes.**—*A.V.* ¹*oft.*
Mat. 17. 15. for *oft-times* he falleth into the fire, and ¹*oft-times* into the water. *Mk.* 9. 22
Lu. 8. 29. o. it had seized him: and he was kept under guard
Jno. 18. 2. Jesus *oft-times* resorted thither with his disciples
Acts 26. 11. And punishing them ¹o. in all the synagogues
Rom. 1. 13. o. I purposed to come unto you (and was hindered
Heb. 10. 11. offering o. the same sacrifices, the which can
see many (times).

Oil.
Mat. 25. 3. foolish, when they took their lamps, took no *oil*
4. the wise took *oil* in their vessels with their lamps
8. Give us of your *oil;* for our lamps are going out
Mk. 6. 13. and anointed with *oil* many that were sick
Lu. 7. 46. My head with *oil* thou didst not anoint
10. 34. his wounds, pouring on them *oil* and wine
16. 6. And he said, A hundred measures of *oil*
Rev. 6. 6. and the *oil* and the wine hurt thou not
18. 13. frankincense, and wine, and *oil,* and fine flour

Ointment—s.
Mat. 26. 7. exceeding precious o. *Mk.* 14. 3: *Lu.* 7. 37
9. this o. might have been sold for. *Mk.* 14. 5: *Jno.* 12. 5
12. in that she poured this o. upon my body, she did it
Mk. 14. 4. purpose hath this waste of the *ointment* been
Lu. 7. 38. his feet, and anointed them with the o. 46
23. 56. they returned, and prepared spices and *ointments*
Jno. 11. 2. that Mary which anointed the Lord with o.
12. 3. Mary therefore took a pound of o.—odour of the o
Rev. 18. 13. and spice, and incense, and *ointment*

Old.—*A.V.* ¹*age,* ²*decayeth,* ³*long time,* ⁴*past.*
Mat. 2. 16. borders thereof, from two years *old* and under
5. 21. have heard that it was said to them of *old* time. 33
9. 16. cloth upon an *old* garment. *Mk.* 2. 21 : *Lu.* 5. 36
17. new wine into *old* wine-skins. *Mk.* 2. 22 : *Lu.* 5. 37
13. 52. forth out of his treasure things new and *old*
Mk. 5. 42. she [Jairus' daughter] was twelve years ¹*old*
Lu. 1. 18. I am an *old* man, and my wife well stricken in
36. she also hath conceived a son in her *old* age
2. 42. he was twelve years *old,* they went up after the
5. 36. the new will not agree with the *old.* *Mk.* 2. 21
39. *old* wine desireth new; for he saith, The *old* is good
9. 8. that one of the *old* prophets was risen again
Jno. 3. 4. How can a man be born when he is *old?*
8. 57. not yet fifty years *old,* and hast thou seen Abraham?
21. 18. when thou shalt be *old,* thou shalt stretch forth

234

OLD

Acts 2. 17. And your *old* men shall dream dreams
4. 22. more than forty years *old*, on whom this miracle
7. 23. well-nigh forty years *old*, it came into his heart
15. 21. Moses from generations of *old* hath in every city
Rom. 4. 19. (he being about a hundred years *old*)
6. 6. that our *old* man was crucified with him
1 *Cor.* 5. 7. Purge out the *old* leaven, that ye may be
8. let us keep the feast, not with *old* leaven
2 *Cor.* 3. 14. reading of the *old* covenant the same veil
5. 17. a new creature: the *old* things are passed away
Eph. 4. 22. the *old* man, which waxeth corrupt
Col. 3. 9. ye have put off the *old* man with his doings
1 *Tim.* 4. 7. refuse profane and *old* wives' fables
5. 9. enrolled as a widow under threescore years *old*
Heb. 1. 1. having of ¹*old* time spoken unto the fathers
8. 13. made the first *old*—becoming ²*old* and waxeth aged
2 *Pet.* 1. 9. having forgotten the cleansing from his *old* sins
2. 3. whose sentence now from of ³*old* lingereth not
3. 5. forget, that there were heavens from of *old*
1 *Jno.* 2. 7. an *old* commandment—the o. commandment is
Jude 4. who were of *old* set forth unto this condemnation
Rev. 12. 9. the *old* serpent, he that is called the Devil
20 2. he laid hold on the dragon, the *old* serpent
see aforetime, ancient, early, ever, wax.

Oldness.

Rom. 7. 6. newness of the spirit, and not in *oldness* of the

Olive, olive tree—s.

Rom. 11. 17. being a wild *olive*—fatness of the *olive* tree
24. by nature a wild *olive tree*—into a good *olive tree*—
be grafted into their own *olive tree*?
Rev. 11. 4. These are the two *olive* trees and the two
see Mount of Olives (proper names), olives.

Olives.—A.V. ¹olive berries.

Jas. 3. 12. can a fig tree, my brethren, yield ¹*olives*

Omega, *see proper names.*

Omitted A.V.—*see left undone.*

Omnipotent A.V.—*see Almighty.*

Once.—A.V. ¹sometimes, ²times past.

Rom. 6. 10. the death that he died, he died unto sin *once*
Gal. 1. 23. He that ²*once* persecuted us now preacheth the faith of which he *once* made havock
Eph. 2. 3. among whom we also all ²*once* lived in the lusts
13. ye that ¹*once* were far off are made nigh in the blood
5. 8. for ye were ¹*once* darkness, but are now light
Heb. 7. 27. this he did *once* for all, when he offered up him-
9. 7. the high priest alone, *once* in the year [self
12. entered in *once* for all into the holy place
26. now *once* at the end of the ages hath he been mani-
27. appointed unto men *once* to die [fested
28. having been o. offered to bear the sins. 10. 10: 1 *Pet.*
10. 2. the worshippers, having been *once* cleansed [3. 18
1 *Pet.* 26. Yet *once* more will I make to tremble. 27

One.—A.V. ¹angel, ²any, ³certain, ⁴man, ⁵none, ⁶only, ⁷other, ⁸particularly, ⁹same.

Mat. 5. 18. *one* jot or *one* tittle shall in no wise pass away
19. break *one* of these least commandments
29. that *one* of thy members should perish. 30
6. 24. he will hate the *one*, and love the other; or else
he will hold to o., and despise the other. *Lu.* 16. 13
10. 29. not *one* of them shall fall on the ground without

ONE

Mat. 17. 4. three tabernacles; *one* for thee, and *one* for Moses, and *one* for Elijah. *Mk.* 9. 5: *Lu.* 9. 33
18. 9. enter into life with *one* eye, rather than
10. See that ye despise not *one* of these little ones
12. hundred sheep, and *one* of them be gone astray. *Lu.*
14. that *one* of these little ones should perish [15. 4
19. 5. shall cleave to his wife; and the twain shall become *one* flesh? 6: *Mk.* 10. 8: 1 *Cor.* 6. 16
17. *One* there is who is good. *Mk.* 10. 18: *Lu.* 18. 19
20. 12. saying, These last have spent but *one* hour
23. 8. *one* is your teacher, and all ye are brethren
9. for *one* is your Father, which is in heaven
10. for *one* is your master, even the Christ
24. 40. *one* is taken, and ⁷*one* is left. 7. 11: *Lu.* 17. 34, 35
25 15. unto *one* he gave five talents—to another o. 16, 21
40. Inasmuch as ye did it unto *one* of these my brethren
45. did it not unto o. of these least, ye did it not unto me
26. 21. Verily I say unto you, that *one* of you shall betray me. *Mk.* 14. 18: *Jno.* 13. 21
73. thou also art *one* of them. *Mk.* 14. 69, 70: *Lu.* 22. 58
Mk. 2 7. who can forgive sins but ⁶*one*, even God?
9. 37. Whosoever shall receive *one* of such little children
12. 6. He had yet *one*, a beloved son; he sent him last
29. The Lord our God, the Lord is *one*. 32
14. 19. and to say unto him *one* by *one*, Is it I?
15. 6. at the feast he used to release unto them o. prisoner
Lu. 5. 12. while he was in ³*one* of the cities, behold, a man
17. came to pass on ⁸o. of those days, that he was teaching
6. 29. smiteth thee on the *one* cheek offer also the other
7. 8. I say to this *one*, Go, and he goeth; and to another
12. there was carried out *one* that was dead
41. the *one* owed five hundred pence, and the other fifty
12. 6. not *one* of them is forgotten in the sight of God
52. be from henceforth five in *one* house divided
15. 7. joy in heaven over *one* sinner that repenteth. 10
16. 17 to pass away, than for *one* tittle of the law to fall
Jno. 5. 45. there is *one* that accuseth you, even Moses
6. 70. choose you the twelve, and *one* of you is a devil?
7. 21. I did *one* work, and ye all marvel
8. 41. of fornication; we have *one* Father, even God
50. own glory: there is *one* that seeketh and judgeth
10. 16. and they shall become *one* flock, *one* shepherd
30. I and the Father are *one*
11. 52. gather together into *one* the children of God
17. 11. that they may be *one*, even as we are. 21, 22
23. that they may be perfected into *one*
18. 9. Of those whom thou hast given me I lost not ⁶*one*
Acts 1. 22. of these must *one* become a witness with us
4. 32. that believed were of *one* heart and soul; and not
²*one* of them said that aught of the things
7. 26. strove, and would have set them at *one* again
13. 41. no wise believe, if ⁴*one* declare it unto you
17. 26. and he made of *one* every nation of men
21. 19. he rehearsed ⁴*one* by *one* the things which God
24. 21. except it be for this *one* voice, that I cried
28. 25. departed, after that Paul had spoken *one* word
Rom. 3. 10. written, There is none righteous, no, not *one*
12. none that doeth good, no, not so much as *one*
30. if so be that God is *one*, and he shall justify
5. 15. For if by the trespass of the *one* the many died—
the gift by the grace of the *one* man
16. not as through *one* that sinned, so is the gift: for
the judgement came of *one* unto condemnation
17. death reigned through the o.—in life through the o.
18. through o. trespass—through o. act of righteousness
19. *one* man's disobedience—obedience of the *one*
1 *Cor.* 3. 4. For when *one* saith, I am of Paul; and another
8. Now he that planteth and he that watereth are *one*
4. 6. no *one* of you be puffed up for the *one* against

ONE

1 Cor. 6. 5. there cannot be found among you *one* wise man
17. But he that is joined unto the Lord is *one* spirit
7. 7. *one* after this manner, and another after that
8. 4. and that there is no God but *one*
6. yet to us there is *one* God—and *one* Lord, Jesus Christ
9. 24. run all, but *one* receiveth the prize? [bread
10. 17. *one* bread, *one* body : for we all partake of the *one*
11. 21. each *one* taketh before other his own supper ;
and *one* is hungry, and another is drunken
12. 8. to o. is given through the Spirit the word of wisdom
9. to another gifts of healings, in the ⁹*one* Spirit
11. all these worketh the *one* and the same Spirit
12. For as the body is *one*, and hath many members
13. in *one* Spirit were we all baptized into *one* body—
and were all made to drink of *one* Spirit
14. For the body is not *one* member, but many
14. 27. most three, and that in turn ; and let *one* interpret
31. ye all can prophesy *one* by *one*, that all may learn
41. *one* glory of the sun—*one* star differeth
15. 39. *one* flesh of men, and another flesh of beasts
40. the glory of the celestial is *one*, and the glory
2 Cor. 2. 6. Sufficient to such a ⁴*one* is this punishment
7. lest by any means such a *one* should be swallowed up
16. to the *one* a savour from death unto death
5. 14. we thus judge, that *one* died for all, therefore all died
Gal. 3. 16. not, And to seeds, as of many ; but as of *one*
20. a mediator is not a mediator of *one* ; but God is *one*
29. for ye are all *one* man in Christ Jesus
4. 22. *one* by the handmaid, and *one* by the freewoman
5. 14. the whole law is fulfilled in *one* word, even in this
17. flesh ; for these are contrary the *one* to the other
Eph. 2. 14. For he is our peace, who made both *one*
18. through whom we both have our access in *one* Spirit
4. 4. *one* body, and *one* Spirit—*one* hope of your calling
5. *one* Lord, *one* faith, *one* baptism
6. *one* God and Father of all, who is over all
7. But unto each *one* of us was the grace given
Phil. 1. 27. stand fast in *one* spirit, with *one* soul
2. 2. being of *one* accord, of *one* mind. Rev. 17. 13
1 Tim. 2. 5. there is *one* God, *one* mediator also between
3. 2. the husband of *one* wife. 12: Tit. 1. 6
Heb. 2. 11. and they that are sanctified are all of *one*
3. 4. For every house is builded by some ⁴*one*
10. 12. he, when he had offered *one* sacrifice for sins
14. For by o. offering he hath perfected for ever them
11. 12. there sprang of *one*—so many as the stars
Jas. 2. 10. yet stumble in *one* point, he is become guilty
19. Thou believest that God is *one* ; thou doest well
4. 12. *One* only is the lawgiver and judge
1 Jno. 5. 8. the water, and the blood : and the three agree in o.
Rev. 11. 1. and ⁴*one* said, Rise, and measure the temple
17. 10. the *one* is, the other is not yet come
see first, man, same, thing.

Only.—*A.V.* ¹*alone.*

Mat. 4. 10. thy God, and him *only* shalt thou serve. Lu. 4. 8
Lu. 7. 12. was carried out one that was dead, the *only* son
8. 42. had an *only* daughter, about twelve years of age
9. 38. look upon my son ; for he is mine *only* child
Jno. 17. 3. that they should know thee the *only* true God
20. Neither for these ¹*only* do I pray, but for them also
Rom. 16. 27. to the *only* wise God. 1 Tim. 1. 17: Jude 25
1 Tim. 6. 15. who is the blessed and *only* Potentate
16. who *only* hath immortality, dwelling in light
Jude 4. denying our *only* Master and Lord, Jesus Christ
Rev. 15. 4. glorify thy name ? for thou *only* art holy
see alone, begotten, one.

Onset.—*A.V.* ¹*assault.*

Acts 14. 5. made an ¹o. both of the Gentiles and of the Jews

OPENLY

Onward.—*A.V.* ¹*transgresseth.*

2 Jno. 9. Whosoever goeth ¹o. and abideth not in the teaching

Open.—*A.V.* ¹*opened,* ²*receive.*

Mat. 25. 11. saying, Lord, Lord, *open* to us. Lu. 13. 25
Lu. 12. 36. cometh and knocketh, they may straightway o.
Acts 16. 27. seeing the prison doors *open*, drew his sword
19. 38. the courts are *open*, and there are proconsuls
Rom. 3. 13. Their throat is an *open* sepulchre
2 Cor. 6. 11. Our mouth is *open* unto you, O Corinthians
7. 2. ²*Open* your hearts to us : we wronged no man
Col. 4. 3. that God may *open* unto us a door for the word
Heb. 4. 13. are naked and laid ¹*open* before the eyes of him
6. 6. Son of God afresh, and put him to an *open* shame
Rev. 5. 2. Who is worthy to *open* the book, and. 3, 4
5. the Root of David, hath overcome, to *open* the book
9. Worthy art thou to take the book, and to *open* the
10. 2. he had in his hand a little book *open*. 8 [seals
see evident, eyes, mouth, opened, unveiled.

Opened.—*A.V.* ¹*open.*

Mat. 3. 16. lo, the heavens were o. Lu. 3. 21 : Acts 7. 56
7. 7. knock, and it shall be o. unto you. 8 : Lu. 11. 9, 10
27. 52. tombs were o. ; and many bodies of the saints
Mk. 7. 34. saith unto him, Ephphatha, that is, Be *opened*
35. And his ears were *opened*, and the bond of his tongue
Lu. 4. 17. he *opened* the book, and found the place where
24. 32. in the way, while he *opened* to us the scriptures ?
45. Then o. he their mind, that they might understand
Jno. 1. 51. Ye shall see the heaven ¹*opened*, and the angels
Acts 5. 19. angel of the Lord by night o. the prison doors
23. but when we had *opened*, we found no man within
10. 11. the heaven o., and a certain vessel descending
12. 10. iron gate—which *opened* to them of its own accord
14. she *opened* not the gate for joy, but ran in
16. when they had o., they saw him, and were amazed
14. 27. he had *opened* a door of faith unto the Gentiles
16. 14. whose heart the Lord *opened*, to give heed
26. were o. ; and every one's hands were loosed
1 Cor. 16. 9. great door and effectual is *opened*. 2 Cor. 2. 12
Rev. 3. 8. (behold, I have set before thee a door ¹*opened*
4. 1. I saw, and behold, a door *opened* in heaven
6. 1. I saw when the Lamb *opened* one of the seven seals
3. he o. the second. 5. o. the third. 7. o. the fourth
9. o. the fifth seal. 12. o. the sixth. 8. 1. o. the seventh
9. 2. he o. the pit of the abyss ; and there went up a smoke
11. 19. And there was *opened* the temple of God
15. 5. tabernacle of the testimony in heaven was *opened*
19. 11. I saw the heaven o. ; and behold, a white horse
20. 12. books were *opened*—o.. which is the book of life
see open, opening, rent.

Openeth—ing.—*A.V.* ¹*opened,* ²*place.*

Mat. 2. 11. ¹o. their treasures they offered unto him gifts
Lu. 2. 23. Every male that o. the womb shall be called holy
Jno. 10. 3. To him the porter *openeth* ; and the sheep hear
Acts 8. 32. shearer is dumb, So he ¹*openeth* not his mouth
17. 3. *opening* and alleging, that it behoved the Christ to
Jas. 3. 11. the fountain send forth from the same ²o. sweet
Rev. 3. 7. hath the key of David, he that o., and none shall
shut, and that shutteth, and none *openeth*

Openly.—*A.V.* ¹*boldly,* ²*evidently.*

Mk. 8. 32. And he spake the saying *openly*
Jno. 7. 4. and himself seeketh to be known *openly*
13. no man spake *openly* of him for fear of the Jews
26. he speaketh ¹*openly*, and they say nothing unto him
11. 54. Jesus therefore walked no more o. Mk. 1. 45
18. 20. I have spoken o. to the world ; I ever taught

OPENLY

Acts 10. 3. He [Cornelius] saw in a vision ²*openly*
Gal. 3. 1. before whose eyes Jesus Christ was ²*o.* set forth
Col. 2. 15. he made a show of them *openly*, triumphing
    see manifest, publicly.

Operation—s *A.V.—see working—s.*

Opportunity.—*A.V.* ¹*convenient time,* ²*licence.*

Mat. 26. 16. he sought *opportunity* to deliver him. *Lu.* 22. 6
Acts 25. 16. and have had ²*opportunity* to make his defence
1 *Cor.* 16. 12. he [Apollos] will come when he shall have ¹*o.*
Gal. 6. 10. as we have o., let us work that which is good
Phil. 4. 10. ye did indeed take thought, but ye lacked o.
Heb. 11. 15. they would have had *opportunity* to return

Oppose—ed—eth.

Acts 18. 6. when they *opposed* themselves, and blasphemed
2 *Th.* 2. 4. he that o. and exalteth himself against all
2 *Tim.* 2. 25. in meekness correcting them that *oppose*

Oppositions.

1 *Tim.* 6. 20. o. of the knowledge which is falsely so called

Oppress—ed.

Acts 7. 24. and avenged him that was *oppressed*, smiting
10. 38. and healing all that were *oppressed* of the devil
Jas. 2. 6. Do not the rich *oppress* you, and themselves drag

Oracles.

Acts 7. 38. who received living *oracles* to give unto us
Rom. 3. 2. that they were intrusted with the *oracles* of God
Heb. 5. 12. the first principles of the *oracles* of God [God
1 *Pet.* 4. 11. if any man speaketh, speaking as it were o. of

Oration.

Acts 12. 21. Herod—sat on the throne, and made an o.

Orator.

Acts 24. 1. Ananias came—with an *orator*, one Tertullus

Ordain.—*A.V.* ¹*ordained.*

1 *Cor.* 7. 17. so let him walk. And so o. I in all the churches
9. 14. the Lord ¹*o.* that they which proclaim the gospel
    see appoint.

Ordained.—*A.V.* ¹*disposition.*

Acts 7. 53. received the law as it was ¹*ordained* by angels
10. 42. *ordained* of God to be the Judge of quick and dead
13. 48. as many as were *ordained* to eternal life believed
16. 4. decrees for to keep, which had been o. of the apostles
17. 31. in righteousness by that man whom he hath o.
Rom. 13. 1. the powers that be are *ordained* of God
Gal. 3. 19. o. through angels by the hand of a mediator
    see appointed, become, foreordained, ordain, prepared, set (forth).

Order.

Lu. 1. 3. to write unto thee in o., most excellent Theophilus
8. priest's office before God in the *order* of his course
Acts 11. 4. expounded the matter unto them in *order*
16. 23. through the region of Galatia and Phrygia in *order*
1 *Cor.* 11. 34. the rest will I set in *order* whensoever I come
14. 40. But let all things be done decently and in *order*
15. 23. each in his own *order* : Christ the firstfruits
16. 1. as I gave *order* to the churches of Galatia
Col. 2. 5. in the spirit, joying and beholding your *order*
Tit. 1. 5. set in *order* the things that were wanting
Heb. 7. 11. after the *order* of Melchizedek, and not be reckoned after the *order* of Aaron ? 5. 6, 10.

OUGHT

Orderly.

Acts 21. 24. thyself also walkest *orderly*, keeping the law

Ordinance.—*A.V.* ¹*judgment,* ²*righteousness.*

Rom. 1. 32. who, knowing the ¹*ordinance* of God, that they
8. 4. the ²*ordinance* of the law might be fulfilled
13. 2. resisteth the power, withstandeth the o. of God
1 *Pet.* 2. 13. Be subject to every *ordinance* of man

Ordinances.—*A.V.* ¹*righteousness.*

Lu. 1. 6. commandments and o. of the Lord blameless
Rom. 2. 26. uncircumcision keep the ¹*o.* of the law
Eph. 2. 15. the law of commandments contained in o.
Col. 2. 14. having blotted out the bond written in *ordinances*
20. in the world, do ye subject yourselves to *ordinances*
Heb. 9. 1. the first covenant had *ordinances* of divine service
10. carnal o., imposed until a time of reformation
    see traditions.

Ornament *A.V.—see apparel.*

Other—s.—*A.V.* ¹*another,* ²*mutual,* ³*other men.*

Rom. 1. 12. comforted in you, each of us by the ²*other's* faith
1 *Cor.* 4. 6. be puffed up for the one against the ¹*other*
2 *Cor.* 8. 13. I say not this, that ³*o.* may be eased, and ye
    see one, strangers.

Ought *A.V. (anything)—see aught.*

Ought.—*A.V.* ¹*oughtest.*

Mat. 23. 23. these ye *ought* to have done. *Lu.* 11. 42
Mk. 13. 14. of desolation standing where he *ought* not
Lu. 12. 12. teach you in that very hour what ye o. to say
13. 14. There are six days in which men *ought* to work
16. o. not this woman, being a daughter of Abraham
18. 1. that they *ought* always to pray, and not to faint
Jno. 4. 20. the place where men *ought* to worship
13. 14. ye also *ought* to wash one another's feet
19. 7. We have a law, and by that law he *ought* to die
Acts 17. 29. we *ought* not to think that the Godhead is like
19. 36. ye *ought* to be quiet, and to do nothing rash
20. 35. how that so labouring ye *ought* to help the weak
24. 19. who *ought* to have been here before thee
25. 10. Cæsar's judgement-seat, where I o. to be judged
24. crying that he *ought* not to live any longer
26. 9. that I o. to do many things contrary to the name
Rom. 8. 26. for we know not how to pray as we *ought*
12. 3. not to think of himself more highly than he *ought*
15. 1. strong *ought* to bear the infirmities of the weak
1 *Cor.* 8. 2. he knoweth not yet as he *ought* to know
11. 7. man indeed *ought* not to have his head veiled
10. this cause o. the woman to have a sign of authority
2 *Cor.* 2. 3. sorrow from them of whom I *ought* to rejoice
12. 11. for I *ought* to have been commended of you
14. children *ought* not to lay up for the parents, but
Eph. 5. 28. so o. husbands also to love their own wives
6. 20. I may speak boldly, as I *ought* to speak. *Col.* 4. 4
Col. 4. 6. ye may know how ye *ought* to answer each one
1 *Th.* 4. 1. that, as ye received of us how ye *ought* to walk
2 *Th.* 3. 7. yourselves know how ye *ought* to imitate us
1 *Tim.* 3. 15. ¹*o.* to behave thomselves in the house of God
5. 13. busybodies, speaking things which they *ought* not
Tit. 1. 11. teaching things which they *ought* not
Heb. 2. 1. we *ought* to give the more earnest heed
5. 12. time ye *ought* to be teachers, ye have need again
Jas. 3. 10. My brethren, these things *ought* not so to be
4. 15. ye o. to say, If the Lord will, we shall both live
2 *Pet.* 3. 11. what manner of persons *ought* ye to be
1 *Jno.* 2. 6. *ought* himself also to walk even as he walked

237

OUGHT

1 *Jno.* 3. 16. wo o. to lay down our lives for the brethren
4. 11. if God so loved us, we also o. to love one another
3 *Jno.* 8. We therefore *ought* to welcome such
see beloved, bound, must, should.

Oughtest.
Mat. 25. 27. thou *oughtest* therefore to have put my money
see ought.

Outer.
Mat. 8. 12. be cast forth into the o. darkness. 22. 13 : 25. 30

Outran.—*A.V.* ¹*outrun.*
Jno. 20. 4. and the other disciple ¹*outran* Peter

Outrun *A.V.*—*see outran.*

Outside.—*A.V.* ¹*without.*
Mat. 23. 25. ye cleanse the *outside* of the cup. *Lu.* 11. 39
26. that the *outside* thereof may become clean also
Lu. 11. 40. he that made the ¹*outside* make the inside also ?

Outward.
Rom. 2. 28. neither is that circumcision, which is *outward*
2 *Cor.* 4. 16. though our o. man is decaying, yet our inward
1 *Pet.* 3. 3. let it not be the o. adorning of plaiting the hair
see face, outwardly.

Outwardly.—*A.V.* ¹*outward.*
Mat. 23. 27. whited sepulchres, which ¹o. appear beautiful
28. ye also *outwardly* appear righteous unto men
Rom. 2. 28. he is not a Jew, which is one *outwardly*

Outwent.
Mk. 6. 33. on foot from all the cities, and *outwent* them

Oven.
Mat. 6. 30. to-morrow is cast into the *oven*. *Lu.* 12. 28

Over.—*A.V.* ¹*had the charge.*
Acts 8. 27. eunuch—who was ¹*over* all her treasure

Over against.—*A.V.* ¹*far.*
Mat. 21. 2. Go into the village that is *over against* you
Lu. 24. 50. led them out until they were ¹o. against Bethany

Over you.—*A.V.* ¹*your behalf.*
Rom. 16. 19. I rejoice therefore ¹*over you*

Overboard.—*A.V.* ¹*into the sea,* ²*ship.*
Acts 27. 18. next day they began to throw the freight ²o.
43. which could swim should cast themselves ¹*overboard*

Overcame.
Rev. 3. 21. with me in my throne, as I also *overcame,* and sat
12. 11. they o. him because of the blood of the Lamb
see mastered.

Overcharge *A.V.*—*see press.*

Overcharged.
Lu. 21. 34. your hearts be *overcharged* with surfeiting

Overcome.—*A.V.* ¹*overcometh,* ²*prevailed.*
Lu. 11. 22. o. him, he taketh from him his whole armour
Jno. 16. 33. be of good cheer; I have *overcome* the world
Rom. 12. 21. Be not *overcome* of evil, but o. evil with good
2 *Pet.* 2. 19. of whom a man is o., of the same is he also

OVERTHROW

2 *Pet.* 2. 20. again entangled therein and o., the last state is
1 *Jno.* 2. 13. because ye have *overcome* the evil one. 14
4. 4. Ye are of God, my little children, and have o. them
5. 4. this is the victory that hath ¹*overcome* the world
Rev. 5. 5. the Root of David, hath ²o., to open the book
11. 7. shall make war with them, and *overcome* them
13. 7. to make war with the saints, and to *overcome* them
17. 14. and the Lamb shall *overcome*—they also shall o.
see prevail.

Overcometh.
1 *Jno.* 5. 4. whatsoever is begotten of God o. the world
5. who is he that o. the world, but he that believeth
Rev. 2. 7. that o., to him will I give to eat of the tree of life
11. He that o. shall not be hurt of the second death
17. that o , to him will I give of the hidden manna
26. he that *overcometh,* and he that keepeth my works
3. 5. He that *overcometh* shall thus be arrayed in white
12. He that *overcometh,* I will make him a pillar
21. He that o., I will give to him to sit down with me
21. 7. He that *overcometh* shall inherit these things
see overcome.

Overflow—**ed.**—*A.V.* ¹*exceeding.*
2 *Cor.* 7. 4. I ¹*overflow* with joy in all our affliction
2 *Pet.* 3. 6. world—that then was, being o. with water

Overflowing.—*A.V.* ¹*superfluity.*
Jas. 1. 21. putting away all filthiness and ¹*overflowing* of

Overlooked.—*A.V.* ¹*winked at.*
Acts 17. 30. times of ignorance therefore God ¹*overlooked*

Overmuch.—*A.V.* ¹*above measure,* ²*beyond measure.*
2 *Cor.* 2. 7. one should be swallowed up with his o. sorrow
10. 14. we stretch not ourselves ²o., as though we reached
12. 7. should not be exalted ¹*overmuch,* there was given
to me a thorn—that I should not be exalted ¹o.

Over-ripe.—*A.V.* ¹*ripe.*
Rev. 14. 15. for the harvest of the earth is ¹*over-ripe*

Overseers *A.V.*—*see bishops.*

Overshadow—**ed**—**ing.**—*A.V.* ¹*shadowing.*
Mat. 17. 5. cloud *overshadowed* them. *Mk.* 9. 6 : *Lu.* 9. 34
Lu. 1. 35. power of the Most High shall *overshadow* thee
Acts 5. 15. Peter—at the least his shadow might o. some
Heb. 9. 5. cherubim of glory ¹*overshadowing* the mercy-seat

Oversight.
1 *Pet.* 5. 2. exercising the *oversight,* not of constraint

Overtake—**en.**—*A.V.* ¹*come upon.*
Jno. 12. 35. ye have the light, that darkness ¹o. you not
Gal. 6. 1. Brethren, even if a man he o. in any trespass
1 *Th.* 5. 4. that that day should *overtake* you as a thief

Overthrew.
Mat. 21. 12. in the temple, and *overthrew* the tables of the
money-changers. *Mk.* 11 15 : *Jno.* 2. 15

Overthrow—*A.V.* ¹*destroy,* ²*subvert.*
Acts 5. 39. if it is of God, ye will not be able to o. them
Rom. 14. 20. ¹*Overthrow* not for meat's sake the work of God
2 *Tim.* 2. 18. past already, and *overthrow* the faith of some
Tit. 1. 11. men who ²*overthrow* whole houses
2 *Pet.* 2. 6. into ashes condemned them with an *overthrow*

Overthrown.—*A.V.* ¹*come to nought.*
Acts 5. 38. or this work be of men, it will be ¹*overthrown*
1 *Cor.* 10. 5. for they were *overthrown* in the wilderness

Owe—d.—*A.V.* ¹*duty.*
Mat. 18. 24. which *owed* him ten thousand talents
28. fellow-servants, which *owed* him a hundred pence
Lu. 7. 41. the one o. five hundred pence, and the other fifty
Rom. 13. 8. *Owe* no man anything, save to love one another
15. 27. they ¹*owe* it to them also to minister unto them

Owest—eth.
Mat. 18. 28. by the throat, saying, Pay what thou *owest*
Lu. 16. 5. How much *owest* thou unto my lord ? 7
Philem. 18. wronged thee at all, or *oweth* thee aught
19. thou *owest* to me even thine own self besides

Own.—*A.V.* ¹*due,* ²*proper,* ³*purchased.*
Mat. 20. 15. for me to do what I will with mine *own* ?
Lu. 16. 12. who will give you that which is your *own* ?
Jno. 1. 11. He came unto his *o.*—his *own* received him not
8. 44. When he speaketh a lie, he speaketh of his *own*
13. 1. having loved his *own* which were in the world
15. 19. of the world, the world would love its *own*
16. 32. ye shall be scattered, every man to his *own*
Acts 5. 4. Whiles it remained, did it not remain thine *own* ?
Rom. 8. 32. He that spared not his *own* Son
1 *Cor.* 6. 19. ye have from God ? and ye are not your *own*
7. 2. have his *own* wife—have her *own* husband
7. Howbeit each man hath his ²*own* gift from God
10. 24. no man seek his *own,* but each his neighbour's good
13. 5. seeketh not its *own,* is not provoked
Eph. 1. 14. unto the redemption of God's ³*own* possession
Phil. 2. 21. all seek their *own,* not the things of Jesus
1 *Tim.* 2. 6. the testimony to be borne in its ¹*own* times
5. 8. if any provideth not for his *o.,* and—his *o.* household
Tit. 1. 3. but in his ¹*own* seasons manifested his word

Own *age.*—*A.V.* ¹*equals.*
Gal. 1. 14. advanced in the Jews' religion beyond many of mine ¹*own age*

Owner—s.
Lu. 19. 33. loosing the colt, the *owners* thereof said [the *o.*
Acts 27. 11. centurion gave more heed to the master and to

Owneth.
Acts 21. 11. bind the man that *owneth* this girdle

Ox.
Lu. 13. 15. each one of you on the sabbath loose his *ox*
14. 5. shall have an ass or an *ox* fallen into a well
1 *Cor.* 9. 9. Thou shalt not muzzle the *ox* when he treadeth out the corn. 1 *Tim.* 5. 18

Oxen.
Mat. 22. 4. my *oxen* and my fatlings are killed
Lu. 14. 19. bought five yoke of *oxen,* and I go to prove
Jno. 2. 14. found in the temple those that sold *oxen.* 15
Acts 14. 13. brought *oxen* and garlands unto the gates
1 *Cor.* 9. 10. Is it for the *oxen* that God careth

P.

Paid.
Mat. 5. 26. out thence, till thou have *paid. Lu.* 12. 59
Heb. 7. 9. Abraham—who receiveth tithes, hath *p.* tithes

Pain—s.—*A.V.* ¹*pained,* ²*sorrow.*
Rom. 8 22. the whole creation groaneth and travaileth in *p.*
9. 2. I have great sorrow and unceasing ²*p.* in my heart
Rev. 12. 2. travailing in birth, and in ¹*pain* to be delivered
16. 10. they gnawed their tongues for *pain*
11. blasphemed—because of their *pains* and their sores
21. 4. mourning, nor crying, nor *pain,* any more
see pangs.

Pained *A.V.*—*see pain.*

Painfulness *A.V.*—*see travail.*

Pair.
Lu. 2. 24. A *pair* of turtledoves, or two young pigeons

Palace.—*A.V.* ¹*common hall,* ²*judgment hall.*
Mat. 27. 27. soldiers of the governor took Jesus into the ¹*p.*
Jno. 18. 28. lead Jesus—into the ²*palace*—not into the ²*p.*
33. Pilate therefore entered again into the ²*palace.* 19. 29
Acts 23. 35. he commanded him to be kept in Herod's ²*p.*
see court, prætorian guard.

Pale.
Rev. 6. 8. I saw, and behold, a *pale* horse

Palms.
Mat. 26. 67. and some smote him with the *p.* of their hands
see blows.

Palm trees, Palms.
Jno. 12. 13. took the branches of the *p. trees,* and went forth
Rev. 7. 9. white robes, and *palms* in their hands

Palsied.—*A V.* ¹*feeble,* ²*palsies,* ³*palsy.*
Mat. 4. 24. brought unto him all that were—²*palsied*
Lu. 5. 18. men bring on a bed a man that was ³*palsied*
24. (he said unto him that was ³*palsied*)—Arise
Acts 8. 7. many that were ²*palsied*—were healed
9. 33. kept his bed eight years ; for he was ³*palsied*
Heb. 12. 12. the hands that hang down, and the ¹*p.* knees

Palsies *A V.*—*see palsied.*

Palsy.
Mat. 8. 6. Lord, my servant lieth in the house sick of the *p.*
9. 2. brought to him a man sick of the *palsy*—said unto the sick of the *palsy,* Son. 6: *Mk.* 2. 3, 4, 5, 9, 10
see palsied.

Pangs.—*A.V.* ¹*pains.*
Acts 2. 24. God raised up, having loosed the ¹*pangs* of death

Paper.
2 *Jno.* 12. I would not write them with *paper* and ink

Paps *A.V.*—*see breasts.*

Parable.—*A.V.* ¹*comparison,* ²*figure,* ³*proverb.*
Mat. 13. 18. Hear then ye the *parable. Lu.* 8. 11 : 21. 29
24. Another *parable* set he before them. 31, 33 : 21. 33 : *Lu.* 5. 36 : 6. 39 : 8. 4 : 12. 16 : 13. 6 : 14. 7 : 15. 3 : 18. 1, 9 : 19. 11 : 20. 9 : *Jno.* 10. 6

PARABLE

Mat. 13. 34. without a *parable* spake he nothing unto them. *Mk.* 4. 34
36. Explain unto us the *p.* 15. 15 ; *Mk.* 7. 17 : *Lu.* 8. 9
24. 32. now from the fig tree learn her *p. Mk.* 13. 28
Mk. 4. 13 saith unto them, Know ye not this *parable ?*
30. kingdom of God? or in what ¹*p.* shall we set it forth?
12. 12. perceived that he spake the *p.* against them. *Lu.*20.
Lu. 4. 23. Doubtless ye will say unto me this ²*parable.* [19
12. 41. speakest thou this *p.* unto us, or even unto all ?
Heb. 9. 9. which is a ²*parable* for the time now present
11. 19. from whence he did also in a ²*p.* receive him back
see parables.

Parables.—*A.V.* ¹*parable.*

Mat. 13. 3. he spake to them many things in *parables.* 13, 34, 53 : 22. 1 ; *Mk.* 3. 23 : 4. 2, 33 ; 12. 1
10. Why speakest thou unto them in *parables ?*
35. prophet, saying, I will open my mouth in *parables*
21. 45. his *parables,* they perceived that he spake of them
Mk. 4. 10. the twelve asked of him the ¹*parables*
11. that are without, all things are done in *parables*
13. and how shall ye know all the *parables ?*
Lu. 8. 10. to the rest in *p.* ; that seeing they may not see

Paradise.—*see proper names.*

Parcel.

Jno. 4. 5. near to the *parcel* of ground that Jacob gave

Parchments.

2 *Tim.* 4. 13. and the books, especially the *parchments*

Parents.—*A V.* ¹*Joseph and his mother.*

Mat. 10. 21. children shall rise up against *p. Mk.* 13. 12
Lu. 2. 27. when the *parents* brought in the child Jesus
41. his *p.* went every year to Jerusalem at the feast
43. behind in Jerusalem ; and his ¹*parents* knew it not
8. 56. her *parents* were amazed : but he charged them
18. 29. left house, or wife, or brethren, or *parents*
21. 16. But ye shall be delivered up even by *parents*
Jno. 9. 2. Rabbi, who did sin, this man, or his *parents.* 3
22. These things said his *p.,* because they feared. 18,
Rom. 1. 30. disobedient to *parents.* 2 *Tim.* 3. 2 [20, 23
2 *Cor.* 12. 14. children ought not to lay up for the *parents,* but the *parents* for the children
Eph. 6. 1. Children, obey your *parents. Col.* 3. 20
1 *Tim.* 5. 4. to requite their *parents :* for this is acceptable
Heb. 11. 23. Moses—was hid three months by his *parents*

Part.—*A.V.* ¹*parted,* ²*stood with me.*

Mk. 13. 27. *part* of the earth to the uttermost *p. of heaven*
15. 24. they crucify him, and ¹*p.* his garments among them
Lu. 10. 42. for Mary hath chosen the good *part*
11. 36. whole body be full of light, having no *part* dark
39. your inward *p.* is full of extortion and wickedness
17. 24. out of the one *part*—shineth unto the other *part*
Jno. 13. 8. If I wash thee not, thou hast no *p.* with me
19. 23. garments, and—four parts, to every soldier a *p.*
Acts 5. 2. back *part* of the price—brought a certain *p.* 3
8. 21. Thou hast neither *part* nor lot in this matter
14. 4. *part* held with the Jews, and *p.* with the apostles
19. 32. more *part* knew not wherefore they were come
23. 6. Paul perceived that the one *part* were Sadducees
27. 12. the more *part* advised to put to sea from thence
Rom. 11. 25. a hardening in *part* hath befallen Israel
1 *Cor.* 13. 9. we know in *part,* and we prophesy in *part.* 12
10. that which is in *part* shall be done away

PARTED

1 *Cor.* 15. 6. of whom the greater *part* remain until now
16. 17. that which was lacking on your *part* they supplied
2 *Cor.* 1. 14. as also ye did acknowledge us in *part*
2. 5. he hath caused sorrow, not to me, but in *part*
Eph. 4. 16. working in due measure of each several *part*
2 *Tim.* 4. 16. At my first defence no one took my ²*part*
Tit. 2. 8. he that is of the contrary *part* may be ashamed
Heb. 7. 2. to whom also Abraham divided a tenth *p.* of all
Rev. 6. 8. given unto them authority over the fourth *p.* of
8. 7. third *p.* of the earth—third *p.* of the trees was burnt
8. the third *part* of the sea became blood [up
9. third *part* of the creatures—third *part* of the ships
10. and it fell upon the third *part* of the rivers
11. the third *part* of the waters became wormwood
12. the third *part* of the sun was smitten—third *part* of the moon—third *part* of the stars—third *part* of them should be darkened, and the day should not shine for the third *part* of it
9. 15. that they should kill the third *part* of men. 18
11. 13. earthquake, and the tenth *part* of the city fell
12. 4. his tail draweth the third *p.* of the stars of heaven
20. 6. holy is he that hath *part* in the first resurrection
21. 8. and all liars, their *part* shall be in the lake
22. 19. God shall take away his *part* from the tree of life
see partook, place, portion.

Partake.—*A.V.* ¹*partaker—s.*

1 *Cor.* 9. 12. If others ¹*p.* of this right over you, do not we
10. 17. one body ; for we all ¹*partake* of the one bread
21. ye cannot ¹*p.* of the table of the Lord, and of the
30. If I by grace ¹*partake,* why am I evil spoken of
1 *Tim.* 5. 2. because they that ¹*p.* of the benefit are believing
2 *Tim.* 2. 6. that laboureth must be the first to ¹*p.* of the fruits

Partaker.—*A.V.* ¹*companion,* ²*partakest.*

Rom. 11. 17. ²*partaker* with them of the root of the fatness
1 *Cor.* 9. 23. gospel's sake, that I may be a joint *p.* thereof
1 *Tim.* 5. 22. neither be *partaker* of other men's sins
1 *Pet.* 5. 1. a *partaker* of the glory that shall be revealed
Rev. 1. 9. I John, your brother and ¹*partaker* with you
see partake, partaketh, partaking.

Partakers, fellow-partakers.—*A.V.* ¹*companions.*

Mat. 23. 30. not have been *partakers* with them in the blood
Rom. 15. 27. Gentiles have been made *p.* of their spiritual
2 *Cor.* 1. 7. as ye are *p.* of the sufferings, so also are ye
Eph. 5. 7. Be not ye therefore *partakers* with them
Phil. 1. 7. ye all are *partakers* with me of grace
Col. 1 12. made us meet to be *partakers* of the inheritance
Heb. 3. 1. holy brethren, *p.* of a heavenly calling, consider
14. for we are become *partakers* of Christ, if we hold
6. 4. and were made *partakers* of the Holy Ghost
10. 33. becoming ¹*partakers* with them that were so used
12. 8. without chastening, whereof all have been made *p.*
10. our profit, that we may be *partakers* of his holiness
1 *Pet.* 4. 13. insomuch as ye are *p.* of Christ's sufferings
2 *Pet.* 1. 4. ye may become *partakers* of the divine nature
see communion, fellowship, partake, portion, sharers.

Partaketh—ing.—*A.V.* ¹*partaker,* ²*useth.*

Heb. 5. 13. every one that ²*p.* of milk is without experience
1 *Cor.* 9. 10. he that thresheth, to thresh in hope of ¹*p.*
2 *Jno.* 11. he that giveth him greeting ¹*p* in his evil works

Partakest *A.V.*—*see partaker.*

Parted—ing.—*A.V.* ¹*departed,* ²*gotten,* ³*withdrawn.*

Mat. 27. 35. had crucified him, they *parted* his garments.
Lu. 23. 34 : *Jno.* 19. 24

PARTED

Lu. 9. 33. as they were ¹*p.* from him, Peter said unto Jesus
22. 41. he was ²*parted* from them about a stone's cast
24. 51. while he blessed them, he *parted* from them
Acts 2. 45. *p.* them to all, according as any man had need
15. 39. so that they ¹*parted* asunder one from the other
21. 1. we were ²*parted* from them, and had set sail
Philem. 15. perhaps he was—¹*p.* from thee for a season
see part.

Partial *A.V.—see divided.*

Partiality.
1 *Tim.* 5. 21. without prejudice, doing nothing by *partiality*
see variance.

Particular *A.V.—see severally.*

Particularly *A.V.—see one by one, severally.*

Parting *asunder.—A.V.* ¹*cloven.*
Acts 2. 3. there appeared unto them tongues ¹*p. asunder*

Partition.
Eph. 2. 14. and brake down the middle wall of *partition*

Partly.
1 *Cor.* 11. 18. divisions exist among you ; and I *p.* believe
Heb. 10. 33. *partly,* being made a gazingstock both by reproaches—*partly,* becoming partakers with them

Partner—s.
Lu. 5. 7. they beckoned unto their *partners*
10. sons of Zebedee, which were *partners* with Simon
2 *Cor.* 8. 23. Titus, he is my *partner* and my fellow-worker
Philem. 17. countest me a *partner,* receive him as myself

Partook.—*A.V.* ¹*took part.*
Heb. 2. 14. also himself in like manner ¹*p.* of the same

Parts.—*A.V.* ¹*coasts,* ²*members,* ³*quarters,* ⁴*regions.*
Mat. 2. 22. he withdrew into the *parts* of Galilee
15. 21. withdrew into the ¹*parts* of Tyre and Sidon
16. 13. when Jesus came into the ¹*p.* of Cæsarea Philippi
Mk. 8. 10. and came into the *parts* of Dalmanutha
Jno. 19. 23. took his garments, and made four *parts*
Acts 2. 10. in Egypt and the *parts* of Libya about Cyrene
9. 32. as Peter went throughout all ⁸*parts,* he came
16. 3. because of the Jews that were in those ²*parts*
20. 2. when he [Paul] had gone through those *p.*—he came
1 *Cor.* 12. 23. those ²*p.* of the body, which we think to be less honourable—uncomely *parts* have more abun-
24. whereas our comely *parts* have no need [dant
2 *Cor.* 10. 16. to preach the gospel even unto the ⁴*p.* beyond
Eph. 4. 9. descended into the lower *parts* of the earth?] you
Rev. 16. 19. the great city was divided into three *parts*
see ends, regions.

Pass.—*A.V.* ¹*go.*
Mat. 5. 18. Till heaven and earth *pass* away, one jot—in no wise *pass* away from the law. *Lu.* 16. 17
8. 28. fierce, so that no man could pass by that way
24. 34. This generation shall not *pass* away, till all these things be accomplished. *Mk.* 13. 30, 31 : *Lu.* 21. 33
35. Heaven and earth shall *pass* away, but my words shall not *pass* away. *Mk.* 13. 31 : *Lu.* 21. 33
26. 39. if it be possible, let this cup *pass* away from me
42. Father, if this cannot *pass* away, except I drink it

PASSIONS

Mk. 14. 35. possible, the hour might *pass* away from him
Lu. 11. 42. and *pass* over judgement and the love of God
16. 26. they which would *pass* from hence to you may not
19. 4. tree to see him : for he was to *pass* that way
Jno. 4. 4. he must needs ¹*pass* through Samaria
1 *Cor.* 16. 5. for I do *pass* through Macedonia. 2 *Cor.* 1. 16
Jas. 1. 10. as the flower of the grass he shall *pass* away
1 *Pet.* 1. 17. *pass* the time of your sojourning in fear
2 *Pet.* 3. 10. the heavens shall *pass* away with a great noise
see cross, go, going, passed, past.

Passed—*A.V.* ¹*departed,* ²*pass,* ³*past.*
Mat. 9. 27. as Jesus ¹*passed* by—two blind men followed him
27. 39. they that *passed* by railed on him. *Mk.* 15. 29
Mk. 2. 14. as he *passed* by, he saw Levi the son of Alphæus
6. 48. on the sea ; and he would have *passed* by them
11. 20. *passed* by in the morning, they saw the fig tree
Lu. 10. 31. saw him, he *passed* by on the other side. 32
Jno. 5. 24. hath *passed* out of death into life. 1 *Jno.* 3. 14
9. 1. as he *passed* by, he saw a man blind from his birth
Acts 12. 10. they went out, and *passed* on through one street
17. 23. as I *passed* along, and observed the objects of your
Rom. 5. 12. so death *p.* unto all men, for that all sinned
1 *Cor.* 16. 5. you, when I shall have ²*p.* through Macedonia
2 *Cor.* 5. 17. the old things are ³*passed* away
Heb. 4. 14. high priest, who hath *p.* through the heavens
11. 29. By faith they *passed* through the Red sea
Rev. 21. 1. first heaven and the first earth are *passed* away
4. nor pain, any more : the first things are *passed* away
see crossed, passing, spent, went.

Passeth.—*A.V.* ¹*done,* ²*walketh.*
Mat. 12. 43. ²*passeth* through waterless places. *Lu.* 11. ²24
Lu. 18. 37. told him, that Jesus of Nazareth *passeth* by
1 *Cor.* 7. 31. the fashion of this world *p.* away. 1 *Jno.* 2. 17
2 *Cor.* 3. 11. if that which ¹*passeth* away was with glory
Eph. 3. 19. to know the love of Christ which *p.* knowledge
Phil. 4. 7. the peace of God, which *p.* all understanding

Passing.—*A.V.* ¹*abolished,* ²*departed,* ³*done,* ⁴*passed,* ⁵*past,* ⁶*remission.*
Mat. 20. 30. when they heard that Jesus was ⁴*p.* by, cried
Mk. 15. 21. they compel one ⁴*p.* by, Simon of Cyrene [ont·
Lu. 4. 30. he *p.* through the midst of them went his way
17. 11. was ⁴*p.* through the midst of Samaria and Galilee
Acts 8. 40. [Philip] *passing* through he preached the gospel
13. 14. But they, Paul's company] ²*p.* through from Perga
16. 8. and *passing* by Mysia, they came down to Troas
Rom. 3. 25. because of the ⁶*p.* over of the sins done afore-
2 *Cor.* 3. 7. which glory was ⁵*passing* away [time
13. on the end of that which was ¹*passing* away
1 *Jno.* 2. 8. the darkness is ⁵*p.* away, and the true light
see coasting.

Passion.—*A.V.* ¹*inordinate affection,* ²*concupiscence.*
Acts 1. 3. he also shewed himself alive after his *passion*
Col. 3. 5. fornication, uncleanness, ¹*passion,* evil desire
1 *Th.* 4. 5. not in the ²*passion* of lust, even as the Gentiles

Passions.—*A.V.* ¹*affections,* ²*motions.*
Acts 14. 15. We also are men of like *passions* with you
Rom. 1. 26. For this cause God gave them up unto vile ¹*p.*
7. 5. the sinful ²*passions,* which were through the law
Gal. 5. 24. have crucified the flesh with the ¹*p.* and the lusts
Jas. 5. 17. Elijah was a man of like *passions* with us

PASSOVER

Passover.—*A.V.* ¹*Easter.*
Mat. 26. 2. after two days the *passover* cometh
17. Where wilt thou that we make ready for thee to eat the *passover*? 18: *Mk.* 14. 12, 14: *Lu.* 22. 8, 11
19. they made ready the *passover. Mk.* 14. 16: *Lu.* 22. 13
Mk. 14. 12. they sacrificed the *passover. Lu.* 22. 7
Lu. 22. 15. desired to eat this *p.* with you before I suffer
Jno. 2. 13. And the *p.* of the Jews was at hand. 11. 55
23. Now when he was in Jerusalem at the *passover*
11. 55. to Jerusalem—before the *p.*, to purify themselves
12. 1. Jesus—six days before the *p.* came to Bethany
18. 28. not be defiled, but might eat the *passover*
39. that I should release unto you one at the *passover*
19. 14. Now it was the Preparation of the *passover*
Acts 12. 4. [Herod] intending after the ¹*P.* to bring him
1 *Cor.* 5. 7. our *p.* also hath been sacrificed, even Christ
Heb. 11. 28. By faith he [Moses] kept the *passover*
see feast, keep.

Past.—*A.V.* ¹*pass.*
Mat. 14. 15. time is already *p.*; send the multitudes away
Mk. 16. 1. when the sabbath was *past*, Mary Magdalene
Acts 12. 10. when they were *p.* the first and the second ward
Rom. 11. 30. as ye in time *past* were disobedient to God
33. his judgements, and his ways *past* tracing out!
1 *Cor.* 7. 36. daughter, if she be ¹*past* the flower of her age
Gal. 1. 13. heard of my manner of life in time *past*
Eph. 4. 19. who being *past* feeling gave themselves up to
2 *Tim.* 2. 18. erred, saying that the resurrection is *past*
Heb. 11. 11. power to conceive seed when she was *p.* age
1 *Pet.* 2. 10. which in time *past* were no people, but now
4. 3. For the time *past* may suffice to have wrought
Rev. 9. 12. The first Woe is *p.*: behold, there come yet two
11. 14. The second Woe is *past*: behold, the third Woe
see aforetime, came, forewarn, gone, old(time), once, passed, passing.

Pastors.
Eph. 4. 11. evangelists; and some, *pastors* and teachers

Pasture.
Jno. 10. 9 shall go in and go out, and shall find *pasture*

Paths.
Mat. 3. 3. Make his *paths* straight. *Mk.* 1 3: *Lu.* 3. 4
Heb. 12. 13. and make straight *paths* for your feet

Patience.—*A.V.* ¹*patient continuance,* ²*patient waiting.*
Mat. 18. 26. have *p.* with me, and I will pay thee all. 29
Lu. 8. 15. hold it fast, and bring forth fruit with *patience*
21. 19. In your *patience* ye shall win your souls
Rom. 2. 7. to them that by ¹*patience* in well-doing seek
5. 3. knowing that tribulation worketh *patience*
4. and *patience*, probation; and probation, hope
8. 25. which we see not, then do we with *p.* wait for it
15. 4. through *p.* and through comfort of the scriptures
5. the God of *patience* and of comfort grant you to be
2 *Cor.* 6. 4. ourselves, as ministers of God, in much *p.*
12. 12. were wrought among you in all *patience*, by signs
Col. 1. 11. unto all *patience* and longsuffering with joy
1 *Th.* 1. 3. and *patience* of hope in our Lord Jesus Christ
2 *Th.* 1. 4. glory in you in the churches of God for your *p.*
3. 5. love of God, and into the ²*patience* of Christ
1 *Tim.* 6. 11. godliness, faith, love, *patience*, meekness
2 *Tim.* 3. 10. faith, longsuffering, love, *patience*
Tit. 2. 2. aged men be—sound in faith, in love, in *patience*
Heb. 6. 12. who through faith and *p.* inherit the promises
10. 36. need of *p.*, that, having done the will of God
12 1. let us run with *p.* the race that is set before us

PEACE

Jas. 1. 3. that the proof of your faith worketh *patience*
4. let *patience* have its perfect work, that ye may be
5. 10. example of suffering and of *patience*, the prophets
11. ye have heard of the *patience* of Job, and have seen
2 *Pet.* 1. 6. in your temperance *p.*; and in your *patience*
Rev. 1. 9. and kingdom and *patience* which are in Jesus
2 2. I know thy works, and thy toil and *patience.* 3, 19
3. 10. Because thou didst keep the word of my *patience*
13. 10. Here is the *p.* and the faith of the saints. 14. 12
see patient.

Patient.—*A.V.* ¹*patience.*
Rom. 12. 12. rejoicing in hope; *patient* in tribulation
2 *Cor.* 1. 6. your comfort, which worketh in the *p.* enduring
Jas. 5. 7. for the precious fruit of the earth, being ¹*patient*
8. Be ye also *patient*; stablish your hearts. 7
see forbearing, longsuffering, patience.

Patiently.
Acts 26. 3. wherefore I beseech thee to hear me *patiently*
Heb. 6. 15. having *p.* endured, he obtained the promise
1 *Pet.* 2. 20. buffeted for it, ye shall take it *p.*? but if, when ye do well, and suffer—ye shall take it *patiently*

Patriarch—s.
Acts 2. 29. I may say unto you freely of the *p.* David
7. 8. begat Jacob, and Jacob the twelve *patriarchs*
9. the *patriarchs*, moved with jealousy against Joseph
Heb. 7. 4 unto whom Abraham, the *patriarch*, gave a

Pattern.—*A.V.* ¹*figures,* ²*form.*
2 *Tim.* 1. 13. Hold the ²*pattern* of sound words
Heb. 8. 5. make all things according to the *pattern* (that
9. 24. place made with hands, like in ¹*pattern* to the true
see copies, ensample.

Pavement—*see proper names.*

Pay.
Mat. 17 24. Doth not your master *pay* the half-shekel?
18. 25. as he had not wherewith to *pay. Lu.* 7. 42
26. have patience with me, and I will *pay* thee all. 29
28. by the throat, saying, *Pay* what thou owest
30 into prison, till he should *pay* that which was due
34. tormentors, till he should *pay* all that was due
Rom 13. 6. For this cause ye *pay* ¹tribute also

Payment.
Mat. 18 25 all that he had, and *payment* to be made

Peace.—*A.V.* ¹*close,* ²*peaceably,* ³*quietness,* ⁴*rest.*
Mat. 10 13. house be worthy, let your *peace* come upon it: but if it be not worthy, let your *peace* return
31. Think not that I came to send *peace*—I came not to send *peace*, but a sword *Lu.* 12. 51
20, 31. rebuked them, that they should hold their *peace*
Mk. 4. 39. the wind, and said unto the sea, Peace, be still
9. 50. salt in yourselves, and be at *p.* one with another
Lu. 1. 79. To guide our feet into the way of *peace*
2. 14. And on earth *p.* among men in whom he is well
29. depart, O Lord, According to thy word, in *peace*
9. 36. they held their ¹*peace*, and told no man
10. 6. son of *p.* be there, your *peace* shall rest upon him
11. 21. guardeth his own court, his goods are in *peace*
14. 32. an ambassage, and asketh conditions of *peace*
19. 38. *peace* in heaven, and glory in the highest
42. the things which belong unto *peace*! but now
Jno. 14. 27. *Peace* I leave with you; my *p.* I give unto you

PEACE

Jno. 16. 33. spoken unto you, that in me ye may have *p.*
Acts. 9. 31. church throughout all Judæa—had *¹peace*
  10. 36. preaching good tidings of *peace* by Jesus Christ
  12. 20. they asked for *p* , because their country was fed
  24. 2. Seeing that by thee we enjoy much *²peace*
Rom. 1. 7. *peace* from God our Father. 1 *Cor.* 1. 3 : 2 *Cor.*
    1. 2 : *Gal.* 1. 3 : *Eph.* 1. 2 : *Phil.* 1. 2 : *Col.* 1. 2 :
    1 *Th.* 1. 1 : 2 *Th.* 1. 2 : 1 *Tim.* 1. 2 : 2 *Tim.* 1. 2 :
    Tit. 1. 4 : *Philem.* 3 : 2 *Jno.* 3
  2. 10. honour and *peace* to every man that worketh good
  3 17. And the way of *peace* have they not known
  5. 1. justified by faith, let us have *peace* with God
  8. 6. but the mind of the spirit is life and *peace*
  12. 18. as much as in you lieth, be at *²p.* with all men
Rom. 14. 17. not eating and drinking, but righteousness and
  19 let us follow after things which make for *peace* ¦*p.*
  15. 13. fill you with all joy and *peace* in believing
1 *Cor.* 7. 15. but God hath called us in *peace*
  14. 33. for God is not a God of confusion, but of *peace*
  16. 11. But set him forward on his journey in *peace*
2 *Cor.* 13. 11. be of the same mind ; live in *peace*
Gal. 5. 22. the fruit of the Spirit is love, joy, *peace*
Eph. 2. 14. For he is our *peace*, who made both one
  15. create in himself—one new man, so making *peace*
  17. preached *p.* to you that were far off, and *p.* to them
  4. 3 to keep the unity of the Spirit in the bond of *peace*
  6. 15. shod—with the preparation of the gospel of *peace*
Phil. 4. 7. *peace* of God, which passeth all understanding
Col. 3. 15. And let the *peace* of Christ rule in your hearts
1 *Th.* 5. 3. When they are saying, Peace and safety, then
  13. Be at *peace* among yourselves |sudden
2 *Th.* 3. 16. Lord of *p.* himself give you *peace* at all times
2 *Tim.* 2. 22. follow after righteousness, faith, love, *peace*
Heb. 7. 2. also King of Salem, which is, King of *peace*
  11. 31. Rahab the harlot—received the spies with *peace*
  12. 14. Follow after *peace* with all men
Jas. 2. 16. Go in *peace*, be ye warmed and filled
  3. 18. is sown in *peace* for them that make *peace*
1 *Pet.* 3. 11. Let him seek *peace*, and pursue it
2 *Pet.* 3. 14 give diligence that ye may be found in *peace*
Jude 2. Mercy unto you and *peace* and love be multiplied
Rev. 1. 4. Grace to you and *peace*, from him which is
  6. 4. it was given to take *peace* from the earth
    see (good) things, held, hold, made.

Peace *be.*

Lu. 10. 5. first say, Peace *be* to this house
  24. 36. Peace *be* unto you. *Jno.* 20. 19, 21, 26   [of God
Gal. 6. 16. *p. be* upon them, and mercy, and upon the Israel
Eph. 6. 23. Peace *be* to the brethren, and love with faith
1 *Pet.* 1. 2. Grace to you and *peace be.* 2 *Pet.* 1. 2
  5. 14. Peace *be* unto you all that are in Christ
3 *Jno.* 14. Peace *be* unto thee. The friends salute thee

God *of* Peace.

Rom. 15. 33. Now the *God of peace* be with you all. Amen
  16. 20. *God of peace* shall bruise Satan under your feet
Phil. 4. 9. *God of peace* shall be with you. 2 *Cor.* 13. 11
1 *Th.* 5. 23. the *God of peace* himself sanctify you wholly
Heb. 13. 20. Now the *God of peace*, who brought again

Peaceable.

Heb. 12. 11. afterward it yieldeth *peaceable* fruit unto them
Jas. 3. 17. wisdom that is from above is first pure, then *p.*
    see tranquil.

Peaceably *A.V.—see peace.*

PEOPLE

Peacemakers.

Mat. 5. 9. Blessed are the *peacemakers :* for they shall be

Pearl—s.

Mat. 7. 6. neither cast your *pearls* before the swine
  13. 45. a man that is a merchant seeking goodly *pearls*
  46. having found one *pearl* of great price
1 *Tim.* 2. 9. not with braided hair, and gold or *pearls*
Rev. 17. 4. with gold and precious stone and *p.* 18. 12, 16
  21. 21. the twelve gates were twelve *pearls ;* each one of
    the several gates was of one *pearl*

Peculiar *A.V.—see possession.*

Pen.

3 *Jno.* 13. unwilling to write them to thee with ink and *pen*

Pence.

Mat. 18. 28. fellow-servants, which owed him a hundred *p.*
Mk. 14. 5. sold for above three hundred *pence. Jno.* 12. 5
Lu. 7. 41. the one owed five hundred *p.*, and the other fifty
  10. 35. on the morrow he took out two *pence*, and gave

Penny.

Mat. 20. 2. agreed with the labourers for a *penny* a day
  9. eleventh hour, they received every man a *penny.* 10
  13. no wrong : didst not thou agree with me for a *p ?*
  22. 19. tribute money. And they brought unto him a *p.*
Mk. 12. 15. tempt ye me ? bring me a *penny. Lu.* 20. 24
Rev. 6. 6. saying, A measure of wheat for a *penny*, and
    three measures of barley for a *penny*

Pennyworth.

Mk. 6. 37. and buy two hundred *pennyworth* of bread
Jno. 6. 7. Two hundred *pennyworth* of bread is not sufficient

Pentecost—*see proper names.*

Penury *A.V.—see want.*

People.

Mat. 1. 21. is he that shall save his *people* from their sins
  4. 16. The *people* which sat in darkness saw a great light
  23. healing all manner of disease—among the *people*
  13. 15. For this *p.'s* heart is waxed gross. *Acts* 28. 26, 27
  15. 8 This *people* honoureth me with their lips. *Mk.* 7. 6
  26. 5. Not during the feast, lest a tumult arise among the *p.*
Mk. 11. 32. feared the *p. :* for all—held John to be a prophet
Lu. 1. 17. to make ready for the Lord a *p.* prepared for him
  21 And the *people* were waiting for Zacharias
  68. visited and wrought redemption for his *people.* 7 16
  77. To give knowledge of salvation unto his *people*
  2. 10. great joy which shall be to all the *people*
  3. 15. as the *p.* were in expectation, and all men reasoned
  7. 12. a widow : and much *p.* of the city was with her
  8. 47. declared in the presence of all the *p.* for what cause
  9. 13. except we should go and buy food for all this *people*
  18. 43. all the *p.*, when they saw it, gave praise unto God
  19. 47. principal men of the *p.* sought to destroy him
  48. for the *people* all hung upon him, listening
  20. 6. say, From men ; all the *people* will stone us
  19. and they feared the *people.* 22. 2 : *Acts* 5. 26
  45. And in the hearing of all the *people* he said
  21. 23. distress upon the land, and wrath unto this *people*
  23. 5. stirreth up the *p.*, teaching throughout all Judæa
  14. unto me this man, as one that perverteth the *people*
  24. 19. mighty in deed and word before God and all the *p.*
Jno. 11. 50. that one man should die for the *people.* 18. 14
  12. 9. The common *p.* therefore of the Jews learned that
Acts 2. 47. and having favour with all the *people*

243

PEOPLE

Acts 3. 23. shall be utterly destroyed from among the *p.*
  4. 2. being sore troubled because they taught the *people*
  17. But that it spread no further among the *people*
  21. how they might punish them, because of the *people*
  5. 12. signs and wonders wrought among the *people*
  13. join himself to them: howbeit the *people* magnified
  20. stand and speak in the temple to the *people*
  34. doctor of the law, had in honour of all the *people*
  37. Judas—drew away some of the *people* after him
  7. 34. I have surely seen the affliction of my *people*
  10. 2. gave much alms to the *people*, and prayed to God
  41. not to all the *people*, but unto witnesses that were
  42. And he charged us to preach unto the *people*
  11. 24. and much *people* was added unto the Lord
  12. 4 after the Passover to bring him forth to the *people*
  22. the *people* shouted, saying, The voice of a god
  13. 17. The God of this *people* Israel chose our fathers
      and exalted the *people* when they sojourned
  24. the baptism of repentance to all the *people* of Israel
  31. who are now his witnesses unto the *people*
  15. 14. God did visit the Gentiles, to take out of them a *p.*
  17. 5. they sought to bring them forth to the *people*
  18. 10 to harm thee: for I have much *people* in this city
  19. 26 hath persuaded and turned away much *people*
  30. when Paul was minded to enter in unto the *people*
  33. Alexander—would have made a defence unto the *p.*
  21. 39. thee, give me leave to speak unto the *people*
  40. Paul—beckoned with the hand unto the *people*
  23. 5. Thou shalt not speak evil of a ruler of thy *people*
  26. 17. delivering thee from the *people*, and from the
  23. proclaim light both to the *p.* and to the Gentiles
  28. 17. though I had done nothing against the *people*
Rom. 9. 25. I will call that my *p.*, which was not my *p.*
  26. where it was said unto them, Ye are not my *people*
  10. 21. hands unto a disobedient and gainsaying *people*
  11. 1. Did God cast off his *people?* God forbid
  15. 10. saith, Rejoice, ye Gentiles, with his *people*
1 *Cor.* 10. 7. written, The *people* sat down to eat and drink
  14. 21. lips of strangers will I speak unto this *people*
2 *Cor.* 6. 16. their God, and they shall be my *p. Heb.* 8. 10
Heb. 4. 9. therefore a sabbath rest for the *people* of God
  5. 3. for the *people*, so also for himself, to offer. 7. 27
  7. 11. priesthood (for under it hath the *p.* received the law)
  9. 7. for himself, and for the errors of the *people*. 2. 17
  19. been spoken by Moses unto all the *p.*—all the *p.*
  10. 30. And again, The Lord shall judge his *people*
  11. 25. rather to be evil entreated with the *p.* of God
  13. 12. that he might sanctify the *p.* through his own
1 *Pet.* 2. 9. a holy nation, a *p.* for God's own possession
  10. in time past were no *people*, but now are the *p.* of
2 *Pet.* 2. 1. arose false prophets also among the *people*
Jude 5. how that the Lord, having saved a *people*
Rev. 5. 9. men of every tribe, and tongue, and *people*
  see crowd, multitude—s, nation, peoples.

Peoples.—*A.V.* ¹*people.*

Lu. 2. 31. hast prepared before the face of all ¹*peoples*
Acts 4. 25. Gentiles rage, And the ¹*p.* imagine vain things?
Rom. 15. 11. And let all the ¹*peoples* praise him
Rev. 10. 11 Thou must prophesy again over many *peoples*
  11. 9. from among the ¹*peoples* and tribes and tongues
  17. 15. where the harlot sitteth, are *p.*, and multitudes
  21. 3. dwell with them, and they shall be his ¹*peoples*

Perceive.—*A.V.* ¹*perceived,* ²*see,* ³*understand.*

Mat. 13. 14. shall in no wise *p. Mk.* 4. 12: *Acts* 28. 26
  15. Lest haply they should ²*p.* with their. *Acts* 28. 27
  15. 17. ³*Perceive* ye not, that. 16. ³9, ³11: *Mk.* 8. 17
Mk. 7. 18. *P.* ye not, that whatsoever from without goeth

PERFECT

Lu. 9. 45. from them, that they should not ¹*perceive* it
Jno. 4. 19. Sir, I *perceive* that thou art a prophet
  12. 40. Lest they should—⁵*perceive* with their heart
Acts 10. 34. a truth I *p.* that God is no respecter of persons
  17. 22. I *perceive* that ye are somewhat superstitious
  27. 10. Sirs, I *p.* that the voyage will be with injury
  see behold, know, perceived, see.

Perceived.—*A.V.* ¹*discovered,* ²*knew,* ³*known,* ⁴*perceive,*
  ⁵*understood.*

Mat. 21. 45. *perceived* that he spake of them. *Lu.* 20. 19
  22. 18. Jesus *p.* their wickedness, and said. *Lu.* 20. 23
Mk. 12. 12. they ²*p.* that he spake the parable against them
  15. 10. he ²*p.* that for envy the chief priests had delivered
Lu. 1. 22. they *perceived* that he had seen a vision [him
  7. 39. would have ²*p.* who and what manner of woman
  8. 46. I ⁴*perceived* that power had gone forth from me
  18. 34. they ³*perceived* not the things that were said
Jno. 6. 27. They ²*p.* not that he spake to them of the Father
  16. 19. Jesus ²*p.* that they were desirous to ask him
Acts 4. 13. and had *perceived* that they were unlearned
  19. 34. But when they ²*p.* that he [Paul] was a Jew
  23. 6. Paul *perceived* that the one part were Sadducees
  27. 39. they ¹*perceived* a certain bay with a beach
Rom. 1. 20. being ⁵*p.* through the things that are made
Gal. 2. 9. when they *p.* the grace that was given unto me
  see found, perceive, perceiving.

Perceivest *A.V.*—*see considerest.*

Perceiving.—*A.V.* ¹*knew,* ²*knowing,* ³*perceived,* ⁴*understood.*

Mat. 12. 15. And Jesus ¹*perceiving* it withdrew from thence
  26. 10. Jesus ¹*perceiving* it said unto them. 16. ³8
Mk. 5. 30. Jesus ²*perceiving* in himself that the power
  8. 17. Jesus ¹*perceiving* it saith unto them, Why reason
Lu. 5. 22. Jesus ³*perceiving* their reasonings. *Mk.* 2. ³8
  9. 11 the multitudes ¹*perceiving* it followed him
Jno. 6. 15. ³*p.* that they were about to come and take him
  see knowing, saw, seeing.

Perdition.—*A.V.* ¹*destruction.*

Jno. 17. 12. not one of them perished, but the son of *p.*
Phil. 1. 28. which is for them an evident token of *perdition*
  3. 19. whose end is ¹*perdition,* whose god is the belly
2 *Th.* 2. 3. the man of sin be revealed, the son of *perdition*
1 *Tim.* 6. 9. such as drown men in destruction and *p.*
Heb. 10. 39. we are not of them that shrink back unto *p.*
Rev. 17. 8. out of the abyss, and to go into *perdition.* It
  see destruction.

Perfect.—*A.V.* ¹*perform.*

Mat. 5. 48. Ye—shall be *p.*, as your heavenly Father is *p.*
  19. 21. If thou wouldest be *p.*, go, sell that thou hast
Acts 3. 16. faith—hath given him this *perfect* soundness
Rom. 12. 2. good and acceptable and *perfect* will of God
1 *Cor.* 2. 6. Howbeit we speak wisdom among the *perfect*
  13. 10. when that which is *perfect* is come, that which
2 *Cor.* 12. 9. for my power is made *perfect* in weakness
Phil. 1. 6. he which began a good work in you will ¹*p.* it
  3. 12. already obtained, or am already made *perfect*
  15. therefore, as many as be *perfect*, be thus minded
Col. 1. 28. that we may present every man *p.* in Christ
  4. 12. stand *p.* and fully assured in all the will of God
1 *Th.* 3. 10. may *p.* that which is lacking in your faith?
Heb. 2. 10. to make the author of their salvation *perfect*
  5. 9. made *p.*, he became unto all them that obey him
  7. 19. (for the law made nothing *p.*), and a bringing in
  9. 9. touching the conscience, make the worshipper *p.*
  11. greater and more *perfect* tabernacle, not made with

PERFECT

Heb. 10. 1. continually, make *perfect* them that draw nigh
11. 40. that apart from us they should not be made *p.*
12. 23. and to the spirits of just men made *perfect*
13. 21. make you *p.* in every good thing to do his will
Jas. 1. 4. let patience have its *p.* work, that ye may be *p.*
17. Every good gift and every *p.* boon is from above
25. he that looketh into the *p.* law, the law of liberty
2. 22. and by works was faith made *perfect*
3. 2. stumbleth not in word, the same is a *perfect* man
1 *Pet.* 5. 10. suffered a little while, shall himself *perfect*
1 *Jno.* 4. 17. Herein is love made *perfect* with us
18. but *p.* love casteth out fear—is not made *p.* in love
see complete, exact, fulfilled, fullgrown, perfected, strict.

Perfected.—*A.V.* ¹consecrated,²perfectly joined,³perfect.

Mat. 21. 16. of babes and sucklings thou hast *p.* praise?
Lu. 6. 40. every one when he is ³*p.* shall be as his master
13. 32. and the third day I am *perfected*
Jno. 7. 23. that they may be ³*perfected* into one
1 *Cor* 1. 10. that ye be ²*perfected* together in the same mind
2 *Cor.* 13. 11. Be ³*p.*; be comforted; be of the same mind
Gal. 3. 3. begun in the Spirit, are ye now ³*p.* in the flesh?
Heb. 7. 28. appointeth a Son, ¹*perfected* for evermore
10. 14. he hath *perfected* for ever them that are sanctified
1 *Jno.* 2. 5. in him verily hath the love of God been *perfected*
4. 12. God abideth in us, and his love is *perfected* in us

Perfecter.—*A.V.* ¹*finisher.*

Heb. 12. 2. looking unto Jesus the author and ¹*p.* of our

Perfecting.—*A.V.* ¹*perfection.*

2 *Cor.* 7. 1. *perfecting* holiness in the fear of God
13. 9. this we also pray for, even your ¹*perfecting*
Eph. 4. 12. for the *perfecting* of the saints, unto the work

Perfection.

Lu. 8. 14. of this life, and bring no fruit to *perfection*
Heb. 6. 1. and press on unto *perfection*; not laying again
7. 11. if there was *p.* through the Levitical priesthood
see perfecting.

Perfectly.—*A.V.* ¹*to the end.*

1 *Th.* 5. 2. know *p.* that the day of the Lord so cometh
1 *Pet.* 1. 13. be sober and set your hope ¹*p.* on the grace
see carefully, exactly, perfected.

Perfectness.

Col. 3. 14. put on love, which is the bond of *perfectness*

Perform.—*A.V.* ¹*do.*

Mat. 5. 33. but shalt *perform* unto the Lord thine oaths
Lu. 13 32. I cast out devils and ¹*p.* cures to-day and to-morrow
Rom. 4. 21. what he had promised, he was able also to *p.*
see complete, perfect.

Performance *A.V.—see fulfilment, completion.*

Performed *A.V.—see come to pass, accomplished.*

Peril.

Rom. 8. 35. famine, or nakedness, or *peril*, or sword?

Perilous *A.V.—see grievous.*

Perils.

2 *Cor.* 11. 26. in *perils* of rivers, in *perils* of robbers, in *perils*
from my countrymen, in *perils* from the Gentiles,
in *perils* in the city, in *perils* in the wilderness,
in *perils* in the sea, in *perils* among false brethren

PERPLEXED

Perish.—*A.V.* ¹*fall.*

Mat. 5. 29. that one of thy members should *perish.* 30
8. 25. saying, Save, Lord; we *perish. Lu.* 8. 24
9. 17. the wine is spilled, and the skins *perish. Lu.* 5. 37
18. 14. that one of these little ones should *perish*
26. 52. that take the sword shall *perish* with the sword
Mk. 4. 38. Master, carest thou not that we *perish?*
Lu. 13. 3. except ye repent, ye shall all in like manner *p.* 5
33. it cannot be that a prophet *perish* out of Jerusalem
15. 17. have bread enough and to spare, and I *perish*
21. 18. And not a hair of your head shall *p. Acts* 27. ¹34
Jno. 3. 16. whosoever believeth on him should not *perish*
10. 28. unto them eternal life; and they shall never *perish*
11. 50. and that the whole nation *perish* not
Acts 8. 20. Thy silver *perish* with thee, because thou hast
13. 41. Behold, ye despisers, and wonder, and *perish*
Rom. 2. 12. sinned without law shall also *perish* without law
Col. 2. 22. (all which things are to *perish* with the using)
Heb. 1. 11. They shall *perish*; but thou continuest
2 *Pet.* 3. 9. not wishing that any should *p.*, but that all
see decaying, destroyed, perisheth, perishing.

Perish'd.—*A.V.* ¹*departed,* ²*destroyed,* ³*lost.*

Mat. 8. 32. into the sea, and *perished* in the waters
Lu. 11.51. who *perished* between the altar and the sanctuary
Jno. 17. 12. I guarded them, and not one of them ¹*perished*
Acts 5. 37. he also *perished*; and all, as many as obeyed him
1 *Cor.* 10. 9. some of them tempted, and ²*p.* by the serpents
15. 18. which are fallen asleep in Christ have *perished*
Heb. 11. 31. By faith Rahab the harlot *perished* not
2 *Pet.* 3. 6. being overflowed with water, *perished*
Jude 11. and *perished* in the gainsaying of Korah
Rev. 18.14. all things that were dainty and sumptuous are ¹*p.*

Perisheth.—*A.V.* ¹*perish,* ²*spilled.*

Mk. 2. 2¹. wine will burst the skins, and the wine ²*perisheth*
Jno. 6. 27. Work not for the meat which *perisheth*
1 *Cor.* 8. 11. through thy knowledge he that is weak ¹*p.*
Jas. 1. 11. and the grace of the fashion of it *perisheth*
1 *Pet.* 1. 7. being more precious than gold that *perisheth*

Perishing.—*A.V.* ¹*lost,* ²*perish.*

1 *Cor.* 1. 18. word of the cross is to them that are ²*p.* foolish-
2 *Cor.* 2. 15. being saved, and in them that are ²*p.* [ness
4. 3. it is veiled in them that are ¹*perishing*
2 *Th.* 2. 10. of unrighteousness for them that are ²*perishing*

Perjured *A.V.—see swearers.*

Permission.

1 *Cor.* 7. 6. I say by way of *p.*, not of commandment

Permit.—*A.V.* ¹*suffer.*

1 *Cor.* 16. 7. to tarry a while with you, if the Lord *permit*
1 *Tim.* 2. 12. I ¹*permit* not a woman to teach
Heb. 6. 3. And this will we do, if God *permit*

Permitted.

Acts 26. 1. said unto Paul, Thou art *p.* to speak for thyself
1 *Cor.* 14. 34. for it is not *permitted* unto them to speak

Pernicious *A.V.—see lascivious.*

Perplexed.—*A.V.* ¹*did many things,* ²*doubted,* ³*in doubt.*

Mk. 6. 20. Herod—heard him, he was much ¹*p. Lu.* 9. 7
Lu. 24. 4. while they were *p.* thereabout, behold, two men
Acts 2. 12. were all amazed, and were ³*perplexed*

245

PERPLEXED

Acts 5. 24. they were much *²perplexed* concerning them
10. 17. while Peter was much *²perplexed* in himself
25. 20. I, being *²p.* how to inquire concerning these things
2 *Cor.* 4. 8. pressed—yet not straitened ; *p.*, yet not unto
Gal. 4. 20. for I am *²perplexed* about you [despair

Perplexity.

Lu. 21. 25. upon the earth distress of nations, in *perplexity*

Persecute.—A.V. ¹*persecuted.*

Mat. 5. 11. when men shall reproach you, and *persecute*
44. pray for them that *persecute* you [you
10. 23. when they *p.* you in this city, flee into the next
23. 34. and *persecute* from city to city
Lu. 11. 49. and some of them they shall kill and *p.* 21. 12
Jno 5. 16. for this cause did the Jews *persecute* Jesus
15. 20. If they persecuted me, they will also *persecute* you
Acts 7. 52. Which of the prophets did not your fathers ¹*p. ?*
Rom. 12. 14. Bless them that *p.* you ; bless, and curse not

Persecuted.—A.V. ¹*persecution.*

Mat. 5. 10. Blessed are they that have been *p.* for righteous-
12. so *p.* they the prophets which were before you [ness'
Jno. 15. 20. If they *p.* me, they will also persecute you
Acts 22. 4. and I *p.* this Way unto the death, binding
26. 11. I *persecuted* them even unto foreign cities
1 *Cor.* 4. 12. being reviled, we bless ; being *p.*, we endure
15. 9. because I *persecuted* the church of God. *Gal.* 1. 13
Gal. 1. 23. He that once *p* us now preacheth the faith
4. 29. he that was born after the flesh *persecuted* him
5.11. still preach circumcision, why am I still ¹*persecuted ?*
6. 12. circumcised ; only that they may not be ¹*persecuted*
Rev. 12. 13. he *persecuted* the woman which brought forth
see persecute, pursued, drave.

Persecutest.

Acts 9. 4. Saul, Saul, why *p.* thou me? 22. 7 ; 26. 14
5. I am Jesus whom thou *persecutest.* 22. 8 ; 26. 15

Persecuting.

Phil. 3. 6. as touching zeal, *persecuting* the church

Persecution.

Mat. 13. 21. or *p* ariseth because of the word. *Mk.* 4. 17
Acts 8. 1. that day a great *persecution* against the church
13. 50. stirred up a *persecution* against Paul and Barnabas
Rom. 8. 35. love of Christ? shall tribulation—or *persecution*
2 *Tim.* 3. 12. live godly in Christ Jesus shall suffer *p.*
see persecuted, tribulation.

Persecutions.

Mk. 10. 30. lands, with *p.* ; and in the world to come
2 *Cor.* 12. 10. in *persecutions,* in distresses, for Christ's sake
2 *Th.* 1. 4. for your patience and faith in all your *persecutions*
2 *Tim.* 3. 10. *p.,* sufferings ; what things befell me at Antioch
11. what *p.* I endured ; and out of them all the Lord

Persecutor.

1 *Tim.* 1. 13. though I was before a blasphemer, and a *p.*

Perseverance.

Eph. 6. 18. and watching thereunto in all *perseverance*

Person.

Mat. 22. 16. regardest not the *p.* of men. *Mk.* 12. 14 : *Lu.* 20. 21
2 *Cor.* 2. 10. for your sakes have I forgiven it in the *p.* of

PERTAINING

Eph. 5. 5. nor unclean *person,* nor covetous man
Heb. 12. 16. or profane *person,* as Esau, who for one mess
Philem. 12. whom I have sent back to thee in his own *p.*
see man, substance.

Persons.—A.V. ¹*men,* ²*names.*

Lu. 15. 7. more than over ninety and nine righteous *p.*
Acts 1. 15. there was a multitude of ²*p.* gathered together
10. 34. I perceive that God is no respecter of *persons*
17. 17. synagogue with the Jews and the devout *persons*
2 *Cor.* 1. 11. thanks may be given by many *p.* on our behalf
2 *Pet.* 3. 11. what manner of *persons* ought ye to be
Jude 16. shewing respect of *p.* for the sake of advantage
Rev. 11. 13. killed in the earthquake seven thousand ¹*p.*
see swearers.

Persuade.

Mat. 28. 14. we will *persuade* him, and rid you of care
2 *Cor.* 5. 11. Knowing—the fear of the Lord, we *p.* men
see persuading.

Persuaded.—A.V. ¹*believed,* ²*trust.*

Mat. 27. 20. chief priests and the elders *p.* the multitudes
Lu. 16. 31. neither will they be *p.,* if one rise from the dead
20. 6. for they be *persuaded* that John was a prophet
Acts 14. 19. having *p.* the multitudes, they stoned Paul
17. 4. some of them were ¹*p.*, and consorted with Paul
18. 4. every sabbath, and *persuaded* Jews and Greeks
19. 26. this Paul hath *p.* and turned away much people
21. 14. when he would not be *persuaded,* we ceased
26. 26. I am *p.* that none of those things is hidden
Rom. 8. 38. I am *persuaded,* that neither death, nor life
14. 14. am *p.* in the Lord Jesus, that nothing is unclean
15. 14. *p.* of you, my brethren, that ye yourselves are full
2 *Tim.* 1. 5. mother Eunice ; and, I am *p.,* in thee also
12. I am *persuaded* that he is able to guard that which
Heb. 6. 9. But, beloved, we are *p.* better things of you
13. 18. we are ²*persuaded* that we have a good conscience
see assured, urged.

Persuadeth.

Acts 18. 13. *p.* men to worship God contrary to the law

Persuaded *A.V.—see persuasion*

Persuading.—A.V. ¹*persuade.*

Acts 19. 8. and *p.* as to the things concerning the kingdom
28. 23. *p.* them concerning Jesus, both from the law
Gal. 1. 10. For am I now ¹*persuading* men, or God ?

Persuasive-ness.—A.V. ¹*enticing.*

1 *Cor.* 2. 4. speech and my preaching were not in ¹*p.* words
Col. 2. 4. no one may delude you with ¹*p.* of speech

Persuasion.—A.V. ¹*persuadest*

Acts 26. 28. With but little ¹*p.* thou wouldest fain make me
Gal. 5. 8. This *persuasion* came not of him that calleth you

Pertain.

1 *Cor.* 6. 3. how much more, things that *p.* to this life
2 *Pet.* 1. 3. granted unto us all things that *pertain* unto life
see pertaining.

Pertaineth *A.V.—see belongeth.*

Pertaining.—A.V. ¹*pertain.*

Rom. 15. 17. glorying in Christ Jesus in things ¹*p.* to God
1 *Cor.* 6. 4. If then ye have to judge things *p.* to this life
Heb. 2. 17. faithful high priest in things *p.* to God 5. 1
see according, concerning, touching.

PERVERSE

Perverse.
Mat. 17. 17. O faithless and *perverse* generation. *Lu.* 9. 41
Acts 20. 30. speaking *p.* things, to draw away the disciples
Phil. 2. 15. crooked and *p.* generation, among whom ye
see wranglings.

Pervert.
Acts 13. 10. not cease to *p.* the right ways of the Lord?
Gal. 1. 7. trouble you, and would *p.* the gospel of Christ

Perverted.—*A.V.* ¹*subverted.*
Tit. 3. 11. knowing that such a one is ¹*perverted*

Perverteth—ing.
Lu. 23. 2. We found this man *perverting* our nation
14. brought unto me this man, as one that *p.* the people

Pestilences.
Lu. 21. 11. and in divers places famines and *pestilences*

Pestilent.
Acts 24. 5. For we have found this man a *pestilent* fellow

Petitions.
1 *Jno.* 5. 15. we have the *p.* which we have asked of him

Pharisee—s.—*see proper names.*

Philosophers.
Acts 17. 18. the Epicurean and Stoic *p.* encountered him

Philosophy.
Col. 2. 8. that maketh spoil of you through his *philosophy*

Phylacteries.
Mat. 23. 5. for they make broad their *p.*, and enlarge

Physician—s.
Mat. 9. 12. a *p.*, but they that are sick. *Mk.* 2. 17 : *Lu.* 5. 31
Mk. 5. 26. suffered many things of many *p. Lu.* 8. 43
Lu. 4. 23. say unto me this parable, *Physician*, heal thyself
Col. 4. 14. Luke, the beloved *physician*, and Demas salute

Piece.
Mat. 9. 16. a *p.* of undressed cloth upon an old garment.
Lu. 5. 36. the *piece* from the new [*Mk.* 2. 21 : *Lu.* 5. 36
15. 8. if she lose one *piece*, doth not light a lamp
9. Rejoice with me, for I have found the *piece* which
24. 42 And they gave him a *piece* of a broiled fish
see field, shekel.

Pieces.—*A.V.* ¹*meat*
Mat. 15. 37. which remained over of the broken ¹*pieces*
21. 44. falleth on this stone shall be broken to *p. Lu.* 20. 18
26. 15. they weighed unto him thirty *pieces* of silver
27. 3. brought back the thirty *pieces* of silver. 5, 6, 9
Lu. 15. 8 what woman having ten *pieces* of silver, if she
Acts 19. 19. and found in fifty thousand *pieces* of silver
23. 10. fearing lest Paul should be torn in *pieces* by them

Pierce—d.
Lu. 2. 35. yea and a sword shall *p.* through thine own soul
Jno. 19. 34. one of the soldiers with a spear *pierced* his side
37. They shall look on him whom they *pierced* [sorrows
1 *Tim.* 6. 10. have *pierced* themselves through with many
Rev. 1. 7. every eye shall see him, and they which *p.* him

PLACE

Piercing.
Heb. 4. 12. *piercing* even to the dividing of soul and spirit

Piety.
1 *Tim.* 5. 4. first to shew *piety* towards their own family

Pigeons.
Lu. 2. 24. A pair of turtledoves, or two young *pigeons*

Pilgrims.
Heb. 11. 13. confessed that they were strangers and *p.*
1 *Pet.* 2. 11. and *pilgrims*, to abstain from fleshly lusts

Pillar.
1 *Tim.* 3. 15. church—the *pillar* and ground of the truth
Rev. 3. 12. He that overcometh, I will make him a *pillar*

Pillars.
Gal. 2. 9. James and Cephas and John—reputed to be *p.*
Rev. 10. 1. face was as the sun, and his feet as *pillars* of fire

Pillow *A.V.*—*see cushion*

Pineth.
Mk. 9. 18 and grindeth his teeth, and *pineth* away

Pinnacle.
Mat. 4. 5 he set him on the *p.* of the temple. *Lu.* 4 9

Pipe.
1 *Cor* 14. 7 without life, giving a voice, whether *p.* or harp

Piped.
Mat. 11. 17. We *p.* unto you, and ye did not dance. *Lu.* 7. 32
1 *Cor.* 14. 7. how shall it be known what is *p.* or harped?

Pipers *A.V.*—*see flute-players.*

Pit—s.—*A.V.* ¹*chains,* ²*ditch.*
Mat. 12. 11. sheep, and if this fall into a *pit* on the sabbath
15. 14. blind guide the blind, both shall fall into a ²*pit*
2 *Pet.* 2. 4. and committed them to ¹*pits* of darkness
see abyss.

Pitched.
Heb 8. 2. of the true tabernacle, which the Lord *pitched*

Pitcher
Mk 14 13. a man bearing a *pitcher* of water. *Lu.* 22. 10

Pitiable.—*A.V.* ¹*miserable.*
1 *Cor* 15 19. we are of all men most ¹*pitiable*

Pitiful *A.V.*—*see pity, tenderhearted.*

Pity.—*A.V* ¹*pitiful.*
Jas. 5. 11. seen—that the Lord is full of ¹*pity*, and merciful
see mercy.

Place.—*A.V.* ¹*authority,* ²*part,* ³*plain,* ⁴*rooms,* ⁵*wont to be made.*
Mat. 14. 35. when the men of that *p.* knew him, they sent
23. 6. love the chief ⁴*place* at feasts
26. 52. Put up again thy sword into its *place*
27. 33. a *place* called Golgotha, that is to say, The *place* of a skull. *Mk.* 15. 22 : *Lu.* 23. 33 : *Jno.* 19. 17
28. 6. Come, see the *place* where the Lord lay. *Mk.* 16. 6

PLACE

Mk 6. 11. And whatsoever *place* shall not receive you
Lu. 4. 17. book, and found the *place* where it was written
  6. 17. came down with them, and stood on a level ²*place*
  10. 1. two and two before his face into every city and *p.*
  32. Levite also, when he came to the *p.*, and saw him
  14. 9. Give this man *p.*—shame to take the lowest ⁴*place*
  10. thou art bidden, go and sit down in the lowest ⁴*p.*
  16. 28. lest they also come into this *place* of torment
  23. 5. And beginning from Galilee even unto this *place*
Jno. 4. 20. in Jerusalem is the *p.* where men ought to worship
  5. 13. conveyed himself away, a multitude being in the *p.*
  11. 6. he abode—two days in the *place* where he was
  30. was still in the *place* where Martha met him)
  48. Romans will come and take away both our *place*
  14. 2. I go to prepare a *place* for you. 3
  18. 2. Judas also, which betrayed him, knew the *place*
  19. 41. in the *p.* where he was crucified there was a garden
Acts 1. 25. ³*p.* in this ministry and apostleship, from which
  Judas fell away, that he might go to his own *place*
  2. 1. they were all together in one *place*
  4. 31. when they had prayed, the *place* was shaken
  6. 14. Jesus of Nazareth shall destroy this *place*
  7. 7. shall they come forth, and serve me in this *place*
  33. *p.* whereon thou [Moses] standest is holy ground
  49. Or what is the *place* of my rest?
  8. 32. *p.* of the scripture which he was reading was this
  16. 13. where we supposed there was a ⁵*place* of prayer
  21. 12. both we and they of that *place* besought him
  28. teacheth—against the people, and the law, and this *p.*
  25. 23. and they were entered into the *place* of hearing
Rom. 9. 26. in the *p.* where it was said—Ye are not my
  12. 19. Avenge not—but give *place* unto wrath [people
  15. 23. now, having no more any *place* in these regions
1 *Cor.* 1. 2 with all that call upon the name of our Lord
  Jesus Christ in every *place* [say the Amen
  14. 16. how shall he that filleth the ⁴*place* of the unlearned
2 *Cor.* 2. 14. the savour of his knowledge in every *place*
Gal. 2. 5. we gave *place* in the way of subjection, no, not
Eph. 4. 27. neither give *place* to the devil
1 *Th.* 1. 8. in every *p.* your faith to God-ward is gone forth
1 *Tim.* 2. 2. for kings and all that are in high ¹*place*
Heb. 4. 5. in this *p.* again, They shall not enter into my rest
  5. 6. he saith also in another *place*, Thou art a priest
  8. 7. faultless, then would no *place* have been sought
  11. 8. Abraham, when he was called, obeyed to go out
    unto a *place* which he was to receive [sought it
  12. 17. he found no *place* of repentance), though he
Rev. 2. 5. and will move thy candlestick out of its *place*
  12. 6. where she hath a *place* prepared of God
  8. neither was their *place* found any more in heaven
  14. that she might fly into the wilderness unto her *place*
  16. 16. the *place* which is called in Hebrew Har-Magedon
  20. 11. fled away; and there was found no *place* for them
  see course, desert, holy, opening, somewhere, steep, street.

Places.—*A.V.* ¹*ground.*

Mat. 13. 20. he that was sown upon the rocky *p. Mk.* 4. ¹16
  24. 7. there shall be famines and earthquakes in divers
  places. Mk. 13. 8: *Lu.* 21. 11
Acts 24. 3. we accept it in all ways and in all *places*
  27. 2. about to sail unto the *places* on the coast of Asia
Eph. 6. 12. spiritual hosts of wickedness in the heavenly *p.*
Rev. 6. 14. mountain and island were moved out of their *p.*
  see heavenly, rest.

Plague.—*A.V.* ¹*plagues.*

Mk. 5. 29. felt in her body that she was healed of her *plague*
  34. go in peace, and be whole of thy *plague*
Rev. 11. 6. power—to smite the earth with every ¹*p.*, as often
  16. 21. *p.* of the hail; for the *p.* thereof is exceeding great

PLEASE

Plagues.

Mk. 3. 10. as many as had *plagues* pressed upon him
Lu. 7. 21. he cured many of diseases and *plagues*
Rev. 9. 20. mankind, which were not killed with these *p.*
  15. 1. seven angels having seven *plagues.* 6, 8: 21. 9
  16. 9. name of the God which hath the power over these *p.*
  18. 4. and that ye receive not of her *plagues*
  8. Therefore in one day shall her *plagues* come, death
  22. 18. God shall add unto him the *p.* which are written
  see plague.

Plain.

Mk. 7. 35. his tongue was loosed, and he spake *plain*
  see (level) place.

Plainly.

Jno. 10. 24. If thou art the Christ, tell us *plainly*
  11. 14. Jesus—said unto them *plainly*, Lazarus is dead
  16. 25. but shall tell you *plainly* of the Father
  29. now speakest thou *plainly*, and speakest no proverb
  see manifest.

Plainness *A.V.—see boldness.*

Plaited—ing.—*A.V.* ¹*platted.*

Mat. 27. 29. *plaited* a crown of thorns. *Mk.* 15. 17: *Jno.* 19. 2
1 *Pet.* 3. 3. not be the outward adorning of *p.* the hair

Planks.—*A.V.* ¹*boards.*

Acts 27. 44. some on ¹*planks*, and some on other things

Plant.

Mat. 15. 13. Every *p.* which my heavenly Father planted not

Planted.

Mat. 15. 13. Every plant which my heavenly Father *p.* not
  21. 33. which *planted* a vineyard. *Mk.* 12. 1: *Lu.* 20. 9
Lu. 13. 6. man had a fig tree *planted* in his vineyard
  17 6. Be thou rooted up, and be thou *planted* in the sea
  28. they bought, they sold, they *planted*, they builded
1 *Cor.* 3. 6. I *p.*, Apollos watered; but God gave the increase
  see united.

Planteth.

1 *Cor.* 3. 7. So then neither is he that *planteth* anything
  8. Now he that *planteth* and he that watereth are one
  9. 7 who *p.* a vineyard. and eateth not the fruit thereof?

Platted *A V.—see plaited*

Platter.

Mat 23. 25. outside of the cup and of the *platter. Lu.* 11. 39
  26. cleanse first the inside of the cup and of the *platter*

Play.

1 *Cor.* 10. 7. sat down to eat and drink, and rose up to *play*

Pleadeth.—*A.V.* ¹*maketh intercession.*

Rom. 11. 2. Elijah? how he ¹*p.* with God against Israel

Please.

Rom. 8. 8. they that are in the flesh cannot *please* God
  15. 1. infirmities of the weak, and not to *p.* ourselves
  2. each—*please* his neighbour for that which is good
1 *Cor.* 7. 32. is careful—how he may *please* the Lord
  33. for the things of the world, how he may *p.* his wife
  34. how she may *please* her husband
  10. 33. *p.* all men in all things, not seeking mine own
Gal. 1. 10. men, or God? or am I seeking to *please* men?

248

PLEASE

1 *Th.* 2. 15. and *p.* not God, and are contrary to all men
4. 1. received of us how ye ought to walk and to *p.* God
2 *Tim.* 2. 4. may *please* him who enrolled him as a soldier
see pleasing, well-pleasing.

Pleased.

Mat. 14. 6. danced in the midst, and *p.* Herod. *Mk.* 6. 22
Acts 6. 5. saying *p.* the whole multitude : and they chose
12. 3. when he saw that it *pleased* the Jews, he proceeded
Rom. 15. 3. For Christ also *pleased* not himself
1 *Cor.* 12. 18. God set the members—even as it *pleased* him
15. 38. God giveth it a body even as it *pleased* him
Col. 1. 27. God was *p.* to make known what is the riches
see content, pleasing, pleasure, well-pleased, well-pleasing.

Pleasing.—*A.V.* ¹*please*—*d.*

Jno. 8. 29. I do always the things that are ¹*pleasing* to him
Gal. 1. 10. if I were still ¹*p.* men, I should not be a servant
Col. 1. 10. to walk worthily of the Lord unto all *pleasing*
1 *Th.* 2. 4. so we speak ; not as *pleasing* men, but God
1 *Jno.* 3. 22. and do the things that are *pleasing* in his sight
see well-pleasing.

Pleasure.—*A.V.* ¹*pleased*, ²*pleasures.*

Lu. 12. 32. Father's good *pleasure* to give you the kingdom
Rom. 15. 26. it hath been the good ¹*p.* of Macedonia. ¹²⁷
1 *Cor.* 1. 21. God's good ¹*p.* through the foolishness of the
2 *Cor.* 12. 10. Wherefore I take *pleasure* in weaknesses
Gal. 1. 15. it was the good ¹*p.* of God, who separated me
Eph. 1. according to the good *pleasure* of his will. 9
Phil. 2. 13. both to will and to work, for his good *pleasure*
Col. 1. 19. good ¹*pleasure* of the Father that in him should
2 *Th.* 2. 12. not the truth, but had *p.* in unrighteousness
1 *Tim.* 5. 6. she that giveth herself to *p.* is dead while she
2 *Tim.* 3. 4. lovers of ²*pleasure* rather than lovers of God
Heb. 10. 6. sacrifices for sin thou hadst no *pleasure.* 8
38. if he shrink back, my soul hath no *pleasure* in him
Jas. 5. 5. lived delicately on the earth, and taken your *p.*
2 *Pet.* 2. 13. men that count it *p.* to revel in the day-time
see consent, delicately, desire, favour, good, will.

Pleasures—*A.V.* ¹*lusts.*

Lu. 8. 14. riches and *pleasures* of this life, and bring no fruit
Tit. 3. 3. deceived, serving divers lusts and *pleasures*
Heb. 11. 25. than to enjoy the *pleasures* of sin for a season
Jas. 4. 1. even of your ¹*pleasures* that war in your members?
3. ye ask amiss, that ye may spend it in your ¹*pleasures*
see pleasure.

Plenteous.—*A.V.* ¹*great.*

Mat. 9. 37. harvest truly is *p.*, but the labourers. *Lu.* 10. ¹²

Plentifully.

Lu. 12. 16. ground of a certain rich man brought forth *p.*

Plot—s.—*A.V.* ¹*laid wait*, ²*laying await*, ³*lying in wait.*

Acts 9. 24. but their ²*plot* became known to Saul
20. 19. which befell me by the ³*plots* of the Jews. ¹³
23. 30. when it was shewn to me that there would be a ¹*p.*

Plough.

Lu. 9. 62. put his hand to the *plough*, and looking back, is fit

Plow—eth.

1 *Cor.* 9. 10. because he that *ploweth* ought to *plow* in hope

Plowing.

Lu. 17. 7. of you, having a servant *plowing* or keeping sheep

POOR

Pluck.

Mat. 5. 29. eye causeth thee to stumble, *pluck* it out. 18. 9
12. 1. began to *pluck* ears of corn, and to eat. *Mk.* 2. 23
see snatch.

Plucked.

Lu. 6. 1. his disciples *plucked* the ears of corn, and did eat
Gal. 4. 15. if possible, ye would have *plucked* out your eyes
Jude 12. without fruit, twice dead, *plucked* up by the roots
see rent, rooted.

Poets.

Acts 17. 28. as certain even of your own *poets* have said

Point—s.—*A.V.* ¹*ready*, ²*signify*, ³*sum.*

Mk. 5. 23. My little daughter is at the *point* of death
Lu. 7. 2. centurion's servant—was sick and at the ¹*p.* of death
Jno. 4. 47. heal his son ; for he was at the *point* of death
Heb. 4. 15. hath been in all *points* tempted like as we are
8. 1. things which we are saying the chief ³*point* is this
Jas. 2. 10. stumble in one *point*, he is become guilty of all
1 *Pet.* 1 11. Spirit of Christ which was in them did ²*p.* unto

Poison.

Rom. 3. 13. The *poison* of asps is under their lips
Jas. 3. 8. it is a restless evil, it is full of deadly *poison*

Polluted *A.V.*—*see defiled.*

Pollutions.

Acts 15. 20. that they abstain from the *pollutions* of idols
see defilements.

Pomp.

Acts 25. 23. Agrippa was come, and Bernice, with great *p.*

Pondered *A.V.*—*see pondering.*

Pondering.—*A.V.* ¹*pondered.*

Lu. 2. 19. Mary kept all these sayings, ¹*p.* them in her heart

Pool.

Jno. 5. 2. there is in Jerusalem by the sheep gate a *pool*
4. went down at certain seasons into the *pool* [margin]
7. I have no man—to put me into the *pool*
9. 7. said unto him, Go, wash in the *pool* of Siloam

Poor.

Mat. 5. 3. Blessed are the *poor* in spirit. *Lu.* 6. 20
11. 5. the *poor* have good tidings preached. *Lu.* 7. 22
19. 21. thou hast, and give to the *poor. Mk.* 10. 21 : *Lu.* 18. 22
26. 9. sold for much, and given to the *p. Mk.* 14.5: *Jno.*12.5
11. ye have the *p.* always with you. *Mk.* 14. 7 : *Jno.* 12. 8
Mk. 12. 42. *p.* widow, and she cast in two mites. *Lu.* 21. 2
43. *p.* widow cast in more than all they. *Lu.* 21. 3
Lu. 4. 18. anointed me to preach good tidings to the *poor*
14. 13. when thou makest a feast, bid the *poor*
21. bring in hither the *poor* and maimed and blind
19. 8. Lord, the half of my goods I give to the *poor*
Jno. 12. 6. this he said, not because he cared for the *poor*
13. 29. that he should give something to the *poor*
Rom. 15. 26. contribution for the *poor* among the saints
1 *Cor.* 13. 3. if I bestow all my goods to feed the *poor*
2 *Cor.* 6. 10. as *poor*, yet making many rich
8. 9. he was rich, yet for your sakes he became *poor*
9. 9. scattered abroad, he hath given to the *poor*
Gal. 2. 10. they would that we should remember the *poor*
Jas. 2. 2. there come in also a *poor* man in vile clothing
3. ye say to the *p.* man, Stand thou there, or sit under
5. God choose them that are *p.* as to the world to be rich

POOR

Jas. 2. 6. But ye have dishonoured the *poor* man
Rev. 3. 17. art the wretched one and miserable and *poor*
13. 16. rich and the *p.*—that there be given them a mark

Porch

Mat. 26. 71. out into the *porch*, another maid saw him
Mk. 14. 68. he went out into the *porch*; and the cock crew
Jno. 10. 23. Jesus was walking in the temple in Solomon's *p.*
Acts 3. 11. people ran together unto them in the *porch*
5. 12. they were all with one accord in Solomon's *porch*

Porches

Jno. 5. 2. called in Hebrew Bethesda, having five *porches*

Porter

Mk. 13. 34. his work, commanded also the *porter* to watch
Jno. 10. 3. To him the *porter* openeth; and the sheep hear

Portion—s.—*A V.* ¹*part,* ²*partakers,* ⁸*times.*

Mat. 24. 51. and appoint his *portion* with the hypocrites
Lu. 12. 42. give them their *portion* of food in due season?
46. and appoint his *portion* with the unfaithful
15. 12. give me the *p.* of thy substance that falleth to me
Acts 1. 17. and received his ¹*portion* in this ministry [altar?
1 *Cor.* 9. 13. wait upon the altar have their ²*p.* with the
2 *Cor.* 6. 15 or what ¹*p.* hath a believer with an unbeliever?
Heb. 1. 1. God, having of old time spoken—by divers ⁸*p.*

Possess—ed.

Acts 4. 32. aught of the things which he *p.* was his own
1 *Cor.* 7. 30. and those that buy, as though they *possessed* not
1 *Th.* 4. 4. to *p.* himself of his own vessel in sanctification
see devil, get, having, win.

Possesseth—ing.

Lu. 12. 15 not in the abundance of the things which be *p.*
2 *Cor.* 6. 10. as having nothing, and yet *possessing* all things

Possession—s.—*A. V.* ¹*goods,* ²*peculiar,* ³*substance.*

Mat. 19. 22. he was one that had great *p.* *Mk.* 10. 22
Acts 2. 45 sold their *possessions* and goods, and parted them
5. 1. Ananias, with Sapphira his wife, sold a *possession*
7. 5. promised that he would give it to him in *possession*
45. Joshua when they entered on the *p* of the nations
Eph. 1. 14 unto the redemption of God's own *possession*
Tit. 2. 14. unto himself a people for his own ²*p.* 1 *Pet.* 2. ²⁹
Heb. 10. 34. took joyfully the spoiling of your ¹*possessions,*
knowing that ye yourselves have a better ²*p.*
see belonging.

Possessors.

Acts 4. 34. as many as were *p* of lands or houses sold them

Possible

Mat. 19. 26. with God all things are *p* *Mk.* 10. 27; *Lu.* 18. 27
24. 24. lead astray, if *possible,* even the elect *Mk.* 13. 22
26. 39. if it be *possible,* let this cup pass away from me
Mk. 9. 23. All things are *possible* to him that believeth
14. 35. if it were *p.,* the hour might pass away from him
36. Abba, Father, all things are *possible* unto thee
Acts 2. 24. not *possible* that he should be holden of it
20. 16. *p.* for him, to be at Jerusalem the day of Pentecost
Rom. 12. 18. *possible,* as much as in you lieth, be at peace
1 *Cor.* 11. 20 it is not *possible* to eat the Lord's supper
Gal. 4. 15. if *possible,* ye would have plucked out your eyes
see impossible.

Pot—s.

Mk. 7. 4. received to hold, washings of cups, and *pots*
Heb. 9. 4 wherein was a golden *pot* holding the manna

POWER

Potentate—*see proper names.*

Potter.

Mat. 27. 7. and bought with them the *potter's* field. 10
Rom. 9. 21. hath not the *potter* a right over the clay
Rev. 2. 27. as the vessels of the *potter* are broken to shivers

Pound—s.

Lu. 19. 13. ten servants of his, and gave them ten *pounds*
16. Lord, thy *pound* hath made ten *pounds* more
18. Thy *pound,* Lord, hath made five *pounds*
20. here is thy *pound,* which I kept laid up in a napkin
24. Take away from him the *pound,* and give it unto
him that hath the ten *pounds.* 25
Jno. 12. 3. Mary therefore took a *p.* of ointment of spikenard
19. 39. myrrh and aloes, about a hundred *pound* weight

Pour—ed.—*A V.* ¹*shed*

Mat. 26 7. ointment—*p.* it upon his head. 12: *Mk.* 14. 3
Lu. 22. 20. blood, even that which is ¹*poured* out for you
Jno. 2. 15. and he *poured* out the changers' money
Acts 2. 17. I will *pour* forth of my Spirit upon all flesh 18
2 33. he hath ¹*poured* forth this, which ye see and hear
10, 45. Gentiles also was *p.* out the gift of the Holy Ghost
Tit. 3. 6. Holy Ghost which he ¹*poured* out upon us richly
Rev 16. 1 *pour* out the seven bowls of the wrath of God
2. went, and *poured* out his bowl. 3, 4, 8, 10, 12, 17
6. for they ¹*poured* out the blood of saints and prophets
see prepared.

Poureth—ing.

Lu. 10. 34. bound up his wounds, *p.* on them oil and wine
Jno. 13. 5. Then he *poureth* water into the bason, and began

Poverty.

2 *Cor.* 8. 2. *p.* abounded unto the riches of their liberality
9. poor, that ye through his *poverty* might become rich
Rev. 2. 9. I know thy tribulation, and thy *poverty*

Powder *A.V.—see dust.*

Power.—*A.V.* ¹*able,* ²*abundance,* ³*might,* ⁴*mighty,* ⁵*strength,* ⁶*violence,* ⁷*virtue.*

Mat. 9. 6. may know that the Son of man hath *power* on
earth to forgive sins. *Mk.* 2. 10: *Lu.* 5. 24
8. glorified God, which had given such *power* unto men
24. 30. clouds of heaven with *power.* *Mk.* 13. 26: *Lu* 21 27
26. 64. sitting at the right hand of *power.* *Mk.* 14 .62
Mk. 5. 30. Jesus, perceiving—that the ⁷*p.* proceeding from
9 1. till they see the kingdom of God come with *power*
Lu. 1. 17. before his face in the spirit and *power* of Elijah
4. 14. Jesus returned in the *power* of the Spirit
36. and *power* he commandeth the unclean spirits
5. 17. and the *power* of the Lord was with him to heal
6. 19. for ⁷*power* came forth from him, and healed them all
9. 1. the twelve—and gave them *p.* and authority over
10. 19. I have given you—over all the *p.* of the enemy
12. 5. after he hath killed hath *power* to cast into hell
22. 53. but this is your hour, and the *power* of darkness
24. 49. until ye be clothed with *power* from on high
Jno. 10. 18. I have *p.* to lay it down—*p.* to take it again
19. 10. I have *p.* to release thee, and have *p.* to crucify
11. no *power* against me, except it were given thee
Acts 1. 8. ye shall receive *p.,* when the Holy Ghost is come
3. 12. as though by our own *p.* or godliness we had made
4. 7. By what *p.,* or in what name, have ye done this?
5. 4. and after it was sold, was it not in thy *power ?*
6. 8. Stephen, full of grace and *p.,* wrought great wonders

POWER

Acts 8. 19. saying, Give me also this *p.*, that on whomsoever
10. 38. God anointed him with the Holy Ghost and with *p.*
25. 5. Let them—which are of ¹*p.* among you, go down
26. 18. and from the *power* of Satan unto God
Rom. 1. 4. who was declared to be the Son of God with *p.*
20. that are made, even his everlasting *p.* and divinity
9 17. raise thee up, that I might shew in thee my *power*
22. his wrath, and to make his *power* known, endured
13. 1. for there is no *power* but of God
2. resisteth the *p.*, withstandeth the ordinance of God
3. thou have no fear of the *p* ? do that which is good
14. 4. the Lord hath ¹*power* to make him stand [Ghost
15 13. ye may abound in hope, in the *power* of the Holy
19. the ⁴*p.* of signs and wonders, in the *p.* of the Holy
1 *Cor.* 2. 4. in demonstration of the Spirit and of *p* [Ghost
4. 19. word of them which are puffed up, but the *power*
20. For the kingdom of God is not in word, but in *power*
5. 4. and my spirit, with the *power* of our Lord Jesus
6. 12. but I will not be brought under the *power* of any
14. and will raise up us through his *power*
7 4. wife hath not *p.*—husband hath not *p.* over his own
37. hath *p.* as touching his own will, and hath deter
15. 24. abolished all rule and all authority and *p.* [uined
43. it is sown in weakness; it is raised in *power*
56. sting of death is sin; and the ⁵*power* of sin is the law
2 *Cor.* 4. 7. the exceeding greatness of the *power* may be of God
8. 3. according to their *p.*—beyond their *power*, they gave
12. 9 for my ⁵*power* is made perfect in weakness
Eph. 1. 19. greatness of his *power* to us-ward who believe
21. far above all rule, and authority, and *power*
2. 2. according to the prince of the *power* of the air
3. 7. given me according to the working of his *power*
16. strengthened with ⁵*power* through his Spirit
20. according to the *power* that worketh in us
Phil. 3. 10. may know him, and the *p.* of his resurrection
Col. 1. 11. strengthened with all ⁵*p.*, according to the might
13. who delivered us out of the *power* of darkness
2. 10. who is the head of all principality and *power*
1 *Th.* 1. 5. not unto you in word only, but also in *power*
2 *Th.* 1. 7. Lord Jesus from heaven with the angels of his ⁴*p.*
11. and fulfil every—work of faith, with *power*
2. 9. to the working of Satan with all *power* and signs
1 *Tim.* 6. 16. to whom be honour and *p.* eternal. Amen
2 *Tim.* 1. 7. gave us not a spirit of fearfulness, but of *p.*
3. 5. holding a form of godliness, but having denied the *p.*
Heb. 1. 3. upholding all things by the word of his *power*
2. 14. bring to nought him that had the *power* of death
7. 16. but after the *power* of an endless life
11 34. quenched the ⁶*power* of fire, escaped the edge
2 *Pet.* 1. 3. his divine *p.* hath granted unto us all things
16. when we made known unto you the *p.* and coming
2. 11. whereas angels, though greater in might and *p.*
Jude 25. our Lord, be glory, majesty, dominion and *power*
Rev. 3. 8. that thou hast a little ⁵*p.*, and didst keep my word
4. 11. receive the glory and the honour and the *power*
5. 12. Lamb—slain to receive the *power*, and riches
7. 12. honour, and *power*, and might, be unto our God
9. 3. *power* was given them, as the scorpions—have *power*
10. in their tails is their *power* to hurt men five months
19. For the *power* of the horses is in their mouth
11. 6 have the *p.* to shut the heaven—*p.* over the waters
12. 10 salvation, and the ⁵*p.*, and the *kingdom* of our God
13. 2. the dragon gave him his *power*, and his throne
14. 18 from the altar, he that hath *power* over fire
15. 8. smoke from the glory of God, and from his *power*
16. 9. the God which hath the *power* over these plagues
17. 13. they give their ⁵*p.* and authority unto the beast
18. 3. merchants—waxed rich by the ²*p* of her wantonness

PRAISE

Rev. 19. 1. Salvation, and glory, and *p.* belong to our God
20. 6. over these the second death hath no *power*
see able, authority, dominion, might, right, rule, strength.

Power of God.

Mat. 22. 29. said unto them, Ye do err, not knowing the
scriptures, nor the *power of God*. *Mk.* 12. 24
Lu. 22. 69. be seated at the right hand of the *p. of God*
Rom. 1. 16. the gospel : for it is the *p. of G.* unto salvation
1 *Cor.* 1. 18. us which are being saved it is the *p. of God*
24. Christ the *power of God*, and the wisdom of God
2. 5. not stand in the wisdom of men, but in the *p.of God*
2 *Cor.* 6. 7 in the word of truth, in the *power of God*
13 4. crucified through weakness, yet he liveth through
the *p. of God*—live with him through the *p. of God*
2 *Tim.* 1. 8. hardship with the gospel—to the *power of God*
1 *Pet.* 1. 5. by the *power of God* are guarded through faith
see majesty.

Powerful.—*A.V.* ¹*mighty.*

2 *Cor.* 13. 3. who—is not weak, but is ¹*powerful* in you
see active, strong.

Powerfully.—*A.V.* ¹*mightily.*

Acts 18. 28. he [Apollos] ¹*powerfully* confuted the Jews

Powers.—*A.V.* ¹*mighty works*, ²*miracles.*

Mat 14. 2. therefore do these ¹*p.* work in him. *Mk.* 6. ¹14
24. 29. *p.* of the heavens shall be shaken. *Mk.*13. 25: *Lu.*21.
Rom. 8. 38. things present, nor things to come, nor *p.* [26
13. 1 every soul be in subjection to the higher *powers*—
the *powers* that be are ordained of God [known
Eph. 3, 10. the *p.* in the heavenly places might be made
6 12. but against the principalities, against the *powers*
Col. 1. 16. or *p.* ; all things have been created through him
2. 15 and the *powers*, he made a shew of them openly
Heb. 2. 4. by signs and wonders, and by manifold ¹*powers*
6. 5. and the *powers* of the age to come
1 *Pet* 3. 22. and *powers* being made subject unto him
see authorities, right.

Practices *A. V.—see covetousness.*

Practise—d.—*A.V.* ¹*commit*, ²*do*, ³*doest*, ⁴*used.*

Acts 19. 19. not a few of them that ⁴*practised* curious arts
Rom. 1. 32. they which ¹*practise* such things are worthy of
death—but also consent with them that ²*p.* them
2. 1. thou that judgest doest ³*practise* the same things
2. judgement of God—against them that ²*p.* such things
3. who judgest them that ²*practise* such things
Gal. 5. 21. they which ²*p.* such things shall not inherit

Prætorian *guard.*—*A.V.* ¹*palace.*

Phil. 1.13. manifest in Christ throughout the whole ¹*p.guard*

Prætorium.—*see proper names.*

Praise.—*A.V.* ¹*confess*, ²*laud*, ³*psalms.*

Mat. 21. 16. and sucklings thou hast perfected *praise* ?
Lu. 18. 43. people, when they saw it, gave *praise* unto God
19. 37. disciples began to rejoice and *praise* God
Rom. 2. 29. whose *praise* is not of men, but of God
13. 3. do that which is good, and thou shalt have *praise*
15.9. Therefore will I give ¹*p.* unto thee among the Gentiles
11. *Praise* the Lord, all ye Gentiles ; And let all the
peoples ²*praise* him
1 *Cor.* 4. 5. then shall each man have his *praise* from God
11. 2. I *praise* you that ye remember me in all things

251

PRAISE

1 Cor. 11. 17. in giving you this charge, I *praise* you not. 22
2 Cor. 8. 18. the brother whose *p.* in the gospel is spread
Eph. 1. 6. to the *praise* of the glory of his grace
  12. that we should be unto the *praise* of his glory. 14
Phil. 1. 11. Jesus Christ, unto the glory and *praise* of God
  4. 8. and if there be any *praise*, think on these things
Heb. 2. 12. midst of the congregation will I sing thy *praise*
  13. 15. Through him then let us offer up a sacrifice of *p.*
Jas. 5. 13. Is any cheerful? let him sing ²*praise*
1 Pet. 1. 7. proved by fire, might be found unto *praise*
  2. 14. and for *praise* to them that do well
Rev. 19. 5. Give *praise* to our God, all ye his servants
    see excellencies, glory, gave glory, hymns.

Praised *A.V.—see blessing.*

Praising.

Lu. 2. 13. a multitude of the heavenly host *praising* God
  20. the shepherds returned, glorifying and *praising* God
Acts. 2. 47. *praising* God, and having favour with all
  3. 8. walking, and leaping, and *praising* God. 9

Prating.

3 John. 10. *prating* against us with wicked words

Pray.—*A.V.* ¹*prayest,* ²*wish.*

Mat. 5. 44. *pray* for them that persecute you. Lu. 6. 28
  6. 5. when ye ¹*pray,* ye shall not be as the hypocrites:
    for they love to stand and *pray* in the synagogues
  6. shut thy door, *pray* to thy Father which is in secret
  9. this manner therefore *pray* ye: Our Father. Lu. 11. 2
  9. 38. *P.* ye therefore the Lord of the harvest. Lu. 10. 2
  14. 23. mountain apart to *p.* Mk. 6. 46: Lu. 6. 12: 9. 28
  19. 13. that he should lay his hands on them, and *pray*
  21. 30. And *pray* us that your flight be not. Mk. 13. 18
  26. 36. Sit ye here, while I go yonder and *pray.* Mk. 14. 32
  41. Watch and *pray,* that ye enter not into temptation.
    Mk. 13. 33: 14. 38: Lu. 22. 40, 46
Mk. 11. 24. whatsoever ye *pray* and ask for, believe that
Lu. 11. 1 Lord, teach us to *pray,* even as John also taught
  14. 19. I go to prove them: I *p.* thee have me excused
  18. 1. that they ought always to *pray,* and not to faint
  10. Two men went up into the temple to *pray;* the one
Jno. 14. 16. I will *pray* the Father, and he shall give. 16. 26
  17. 9. I *pray* for them: I *pray* not for the world
  15. I *pray* not that thou shouldest take them from the
  20. Neither for these only do I *pray,* but for them also
Acts 8. 22. *pray* the Lord, if perhaps the thought of thy
  24. Simon—said, *Pray* ye for me to the Lord
  10. 9. Peter went up upon the housetop to *pray*
Rom. 8. 26. for we know not how to *pray* as we ought
1 Cor. 11. 13. is it seemly that a woman *pray* unto God
  14. 13. speaketh in a tongue *pray* that he may interpret
  14. For if I *pray* in a tongue, my spirit prayeth
  15. I will *p.* with the spirit—*p.* with the understanding
2 Cor. 13. 7. Now we *pray* to God that ye do no evil
  9. this we also ²*pray* for, even your perfecting
Phil. 1. 9. I *pray,* that your love may abound yet more
1 Th. 5. 17. *pray* without ceasing
  25. Brethren, *pray* for us. 2 Th. 3. 1; Heb. 13. 18
2 Th. 1. 11. we also *pray* always for you. Col. 1. 9
1 Tim. 2. 8. I desire therefore that the men *pray* in every
Jas. 5. 13. Is any among you suffering? let him *pray*
  14. elders of the church; and let them *pray* over him
  16. your sins one to another, and *pray* one for another
3 Jno. 2. I ²*pray* that in all things thou mayest prosper
    see beseech, intreat, praying, request.

PRAYEST

Prayed.—*A.V.* ¹*besought.*

Mat. 26. 39. *prayed,* saying, O my Father—let this cup
  pass away. 42, 44: Mk. 14. 35, 39; Lu. 22. 41
Mk. 1. 35. desert place, and there *prayed.* Lu. 5. 16
Lu. 8. 38. the man from whom the devils were gone out ¹*p.*
  18. 11. The Pharisee stood and *prayed* thus with himself
  22. 44. And being in an agony he *prayed* more earnestly
Jno. 4. 31. the disciples *prayed* him, saying, Rabbi, eat
Acts 1. 24. they *prayed,* and said, Thou, Lord, which
  4. 31. when they had *prayed,* the place was shaken
  6. 6. when they had *prayed,* they laid their hands on
  8. 15. who, when they were come down, *prayed* for them
  9. 40. Peter—*prayed;* and turning to the body, he said
  10. 2. much alms to the people, and *prayed* to God alway
  48. Then *prayed* they him to tarry certain days
  13. 3. Then, when they had fasted and *prayed.* 14. 23
  20. 36. he kneeled down, and *prayed* with them all
  21. 5. and kneeling down on the beach, we *prayed*
  22. 17. while I *prayed* in the temple, I fell into a trance
  28. 8. *prayed,* and laying his hands on him healed him
Jas. 5. 17. he *prayed* fervently that it might not rain
  18. And he *prayed* again; and the heaven gave rain
    see asked, beseeching, besought, prayer, praying, supplication.

Prayer.—*A.V.* ¹*prayed.*

Mat. 17. 21. goeth not out save by *p.* [margin]. Mk. 9. 29
  21. 13. shall be called a house of *p.* Mk. 11. 17: Lu. 19. 46
  22. shall ask in *prayer,* believing, ye shall receive
Lu. 6. 12. and be continued all night in *prayer* to God
  22. 45. rose up from his *p.,* he came unto the disciples
Acts 1. 14. all with one accord continued stedfastly in *p.*
  3. 1. Peter and John—into the temple at the hour of *p.*
  6. 4. But we will continue stedfastly in *prayer*
  10. 30. I was keeping the ninth hour of ¹*p.* in my house
  31. Cornelius, thy *prayer* is heard, and thine alms
  12. 5. but *prayer* was made earnestly of the church
  16. 13. where we supposed there was a place of *prayer*
  16. were going to the place of *prayer,* that a certain
Rom. 12. 12. continuing stedfastly in *prayer* [maid
1 Cor. 7. 5. that ye may give yourselves unto *prayer*
Eph. 6. 18. all *prayer* and supplication praying at all seasons
Phil. 4. 6. In nothing be anxious; but in everything by *p.*
Col. 4. 2. Continue stedfastly in *prayer,* watching therein
1 Tim. 4. 5. it is sanctified through the word of God and *p.*
Jas. 5. 15. the *prayer* of faith shall save him that is sick
1 Pet. 4. 7. be ye—of sound mind, and be sober unto *prayer*
    see supplication.

Prayers.

Mk. 12. 40. for a pretence make long *prayers.* Lu. 20. 47
Acts 2. 42. fellowship, in the breaking of bread and the *p.*
  10. 4. Thy *prayers* and thine alms are gone up
Rom. 1. 9. make mention of you, always in my *prayers.*
    Eph. 1. 16; 1 Th. 1. 2: Philem. 4
  15. 30. strive together with me in your *prayers* to God
Col. 4. 12. always striving for you in his *prayers*
1 Tim. 2. 1. first of all, that supplications, *prayers*
  5. 5. in supplications and *prayers* night and day
Philem. 22. through your *p.* I shall be granted unto you
1 Pet. 3. 7. to the end that your *prayers* be not hindered
Rev. 5. 8. full of incense, which are the *prayers* of the saints
  8. 3. much incense, that he should add it unto the *p.*
  4. with the *prayers* of the saints, went up before God
    see supplications.

Prayest—eth.

Mat. 6. 6. when thou *p.,* enter into thine inner chamber
Acts 9. 11. Saul, a man of Tarsus: for behold, he *prayeth*
1 Cor. 14. 14. my spirit *p.,* but my understanding is unfruitful
    see pray, praying.

PRAYING

Praying.—*A.V.* ¹*pray,* ²*prayed,* ³*prayeth.*

Mat. 6. 6. And in ¹*praying* use not vain repetitions
Mk. 11. 25. stand p., forgive, if ye have aught against any
Lu. 1. 10. multitude of the people were *praying* without
   3. 21. been baptized, and *praying*, the heaven was opened
   9. 18. he was *praying* alone, the disciples were with him
   29. was ²p., the fashion of his countenance was altered
  11. 1. as he was p. in a certain place, that when he ceased
Acts 11. 5. I was in the city of Joppa *praying*
  12. 12. many were gathered together and were *praying*
  16. 25. about midnight Paul and Silas were ²p. and singing
1 *Cor.*11 4. man p. or prophesying, having his head covered
  5. woman ³p. or prophesying with her head unveiled
Eph. 6. 18. p. at all seasons in the Spirit, and watching
Col. 1. 3. *praying* always for you
  4. 3. withal *praying* for us also, that God may open
1 *Th.* 3. 10. night and day *praying* exceedingly
Jude 20. on your most holy faith, *praying* in the Holy Spirit
    see beseeching.

Preach.—*A.V.* ¹*preached.*

Mat. 4. 17. began Jesus to *preach*, and to say, Repent ye
  10. 7. *preach*, saying, The kingdom of heaven is at hand
  11. 1. departed thence to teach and *preach* in their cities
Mk. 1. 38. next towns, that I may p. there also. *Lu.* 4. 43
  3. 14. that he might send them forth to *preach*. *Lu.* 9. 2
Lu. 4. 18. anointed me to *preach* good tidings to the poor
Acts 5. 42. they ceased not to teach and to *preach* Jesus
  10. 42. And he charged us to *preach* unto the people
  15. 21. hath in every city them that *preach* him
Rom. 10. 8. that is, the word of faith, which we *preach*
  15. and how shall they *preach*, except they be sent?
1 *Cor.* 1. 23. but we *preach* Christ crucified
  15. 11. I or they, so we *preach*, and so ye believed
2 *Cor.* 4. 5. we p. not ourselves, but Christ Jesus as Lord
  11. 4. preacheth another Jesus whom we did not ¹*preach*
Gal. 1. 16. that I might *preach* him among the Gentiles
  5. 11. if I still p. circumcision, why am I still persecuted?
Eph. 3. 8. to p. unto the Gentiles the unsearchable riches
Phil. 1. 15. Some indeed p. Christ even of envy and strife
2 *Tim.* 4. 2. *preach* the word ; be instant in season, out of
    see bring, preached, proclaim, publish, speak.

Preached.—*A.V.* ¹*preach,* ²*published.*

Mat. 11. 5. the poor have good tidings p. to them. *Lu.* 7. 22
Mk. 1. 4. ¹p. the baptism of repentance unto remission
  7. p., saying, There cometh after me he that is mightier
  6. 12. they went out, and p. that men should repent
  13. 10. the gospel must first be ²p. unto all the nations
  16. 20. and p. everywhere, the Lord working with them
Lu. 9. 18. With many other exhortations therefore p. he
  16. 16. from that time the gospel of the kingdom of God is
  24. 47. remission of sins should be p. in his name [p.
Acts 8. 25. p. the gospel to many villages of the Samaritans
  35. from this scripture, *preached* unto him Jesus
  9. 27. and how at Damascus he had *preached* boldly
  10. 37. from Galilee, after the baptism which John p.
  13. 24. when John had first *preached* before his coming
  17. 18. because he *preached* Jesus and the resurrection
1 *Cor.* 9. 27. have p. to others, I myself should be rejected
  15. 2. in what words I p. it unto you, if ye hold it fast
  12. if Christ is p. that he hath been raised from the dead
2 *Cor.* 1. 19. Jesus Christ, who was p. among you by us
Eph. 2. 17. came and p. peace to you that were far off
Col. 1. 23. which was *preached* in all creation under heaven
1 *Tim.* 3. 16. p. among the nations, believed on in the world
Heb. 4. 2. had good tidings p. unto us, even as also they

PREFERRED

Heb. 4. 6. before p. failed to enter in because of disobedience
1 *Pet.* 3. 19. he went and p. unto the spirits in prison
    see appointed, discoursed, preach, preaching, proclaimed, spake, spoken.

Preacher.

Rom. 10. 14. and how shall they hear without a *preacher*?
1 *Tim.* 2. 7. whereunto I was appointed a p. 2 *Tim.* 1, 11
2 *Pet.* 2. 5. but preserved Noah with seven others, a p. of

Preachest—eth.

Acts 19. 13. I adjure you by Jesus whom Paul *preacheth*
Rom. 2. 21. that *preachest* a man should not steal, dost thou
2 *Cor.* 11. 4. if he that cometh *preacheth* another Jesus
Gal. 1. 23. now p. the faith of which he once made havock

Preaching.—*A.V.* ¹*preached.*

Mat. 3. 1. cometh John the Baptist, *preaching*. *Lu.* 3. 3
  12. 41. they repented at the p. of Jonah. *Lu.* 11. 32
Mk. 1. 39. synagogues throughout all Galilee, ¹p. *Lu.* 4. ¹44
Lu. 8. 1. *preaching* and bringing the good tidings
Acts 8. 4. scattered abroad went about *preaching* the word
  12. Philip p. good tidings concerning the kingdom
  10. 36. *preaching* good tidings of peace by Jesus Christ
  11. 20. spake unto the Greeks also, p. the Lord Jesus
  15. 35. and Barnabas tarried in Antioch, teaching and p.
  20. 25. ye all, among whom I went about p. the kingdom
  28. 31. *preaching* the kingdom of God, and teaching
Rom. 16. 25. to my gospel and the p. of Jesus Christ
1 *Cor.* 1. 21. through the foolishness of the p. to save them
  2. 4. my p. were not in persuasive words of wisdom
  15. 14. if Christ hath not been raised, then is our p. vain
    see discoursed, message, proclaimed, speaking, word.

Precede.—*A.V.* ¹*prevent.*

1 *Th.* 4. 15. in no wise ¹*precede* them that are fallen asleep

Precept *A.V.—see commandment.*

Precepts.—*A.V.* ¹*commandments.*

Mat. 15. 9. Teaching as their doctrines the ¹p. of men. *Mk.*
Col. 2. 22. after the ¹*precepts* and doctrines of men? [7. 17

Precious.—*A.V.* ¹*costly,* ²*white linen.*

Mat. 26. 7. exceeding p. ointment, and she poured it
Jno. 12. 3. pound of ointment of spikenard, very ¹*precious*
Jas. 5. 7. the husbandman waiteth for the *precious* fruit
1 *Pet.* 1. 7. proof of your faith, being more p. than gold
  19. but with p. blood, as of a lamb without blemish
  2. 4. rejected indeed of men, but with God elect, p.
  6. I lay in Zion a chief corner stone, elect, *precious*
2 *Pet.* 1. 1. that have obtained a like *precious* faith with us
  4. granted unto us his p. and exceeding great promises
Rev. 15. 6. seven angels—arrayed with ²*precious* stone
  18. 12. vessel made of most *precious* wood, and of brass
    see preciousness.

Preciousness.—*A.V.* ¹*precious.*

1 *Pet.* 2. 7. For you therefore which believe is the ¹p.

Predestinate—d *A.V.—see foreordained.*

Preeminence.

Col. 1. 18. in all things he might have the *preeminence*
3 *Jno.* 9. Diotrephes, who loveth to have the *preeminence*

Preferred *A.V.—see become.*

PREFERRING

Preferring.
Rom. 12. 10. in honour *preferring* one another
see partiality, prejudice.

Prejudice.—*A.V.* ¹*preferring*.
1 *Tim.* 5. 21. without ¹*prejudice*, doing nothing by partiality

Premeditate *A.V.*—*see beforehand.*

Preparation.
Jno. 19. 14. the *Preparation* of the passover. 31, 42 :
  Mat. 27. 62 ; *Mk.* 15. 42 ; *Lu.* 23. 54
Eph. 6. 15. shod your feet with the *p.* of the gospel of peace
  see proper names.

Prepare.—*A.V.* ¹*prepared.*
Mat. 11. 10. Who shall *p.* thy way. *Mk.* 1. 2 ; *Lu.* 7. 27
26. 12. she did it to *prepare* me for burial
Jno. 14. 2. I go to *prepare* a place for you. 3
1 *Cor.* 14. 8. uncertain voice, who shall *p.* himself for war ?
Philem. 22. But withal *prepare* me also a lodging
Heb. 10. 5. But a body didst thou ¹*prepare* for me
  see make ready.

Prepared.—*A.V.* ¹*made,* ²*ordained,* ³*poured,* ⁴*provided,*
  ⁵*ready.*
Mat. 20. 23. for them for whom it hath been *p. Mk.* 10. 40
25. 34. inherit the kingdom *p.* for you from the foundation
Lu. 1. 17. to make ready for the Lord a people *p.* for him
2. 31. thou hast *prepared* before the face of all peoples
12. 20. things which thou hast ⁴*p.*, whose shall they be ?
23. 56. returned, and *prepared* spices and ointments. 24. 1
Rom. 9. 23. vessels of mercy, which he afore *prepared*
1 *Cor.* 2. 9. things God *prepared* for them that love him
2 *Cor.* 9. 2. that Achaia hath been ⁵*p.* for a year past. ⁵3
Eph. 2. 10. God afore ²*p.* that we should walk in them
2 *Tim.* 2. 21. meet for the master's use, *p.* unto every good
Heb. 9. 2. For there was a tabernacle ¹*prepared*, the first
6. these things having been thus ²*prepared*, the priests
11. 7. moved with godly fear, *p.* an ark to the saving of
16. their God : for he hath *prepared* for them a city
Rev. 8. 6. seven trumpets *prepared* themselves to sound
9. 7. the locusts were like unto horses *prepared* for war
15. which had been *prepared* for the hour and day and
12. 6. wilderness, where she hath a place *p.* of God
14. 10. wrath of God, which is ³*p.* unmixed in the cup
  see (made) ready, (make) ready, prepare.

Preparing.
1 *Pet.* 3. 20. days of Noah, while the ark was a *preparing*

Presbytery.
1 *Tim.* 4. 14. with the laying on of the hands of the *p.*

Presence.—*A.V.* ¹*before,* ²*coming.*
Lu. 1. 19. I am Gabriel, that stand in the *presence* of God
8. 47. declared in the ¹*p.* of all the people for what cause
12. 9. in the ¹*p.* of men shall be denied in the ¹*p.* of the angels
13. 26. We did eat and drink in thy *presence*
14. 10. have glory in the *presence* of all that sit at meat
15. 10. there is joy in the *presence* of the angels of God
Jno. 20. 30. signs—did Jesus in the *p.* of the disciples
Acts 3. 16. given him this perfect soundness in the *p.* of
19. come seasons of refreshing from the *p.* of the Lord
5. 41. departed from the *presence* of the council, rejoicing
27. 35. bread, he gave thanks to God in the *p.* of all
2 *Cor.* 10. 1. I who in your *presence* am lowly among you
10. weighty and strong ; but his bodily *p.* is weak

PRESS

Phil. 1. 26. glorying may abound in—me through my ²*p.*
2. 12. ye have always obeyed, not as in my *presence* only
1 *Th.* 2. 17. of you for a short season, in *p.*, not in heart
Jude 24. set you before the *p.* of his glory without blemish
Rev. 14. 10. with fire and brimstone in the *presence* of
  the holy angels, and in the *presence* of the Lamb
  see before, face.

Present.—*A.V.* ¹*at hand.*
Lu. 13. 1. some *present* at that very season which told him
Acts 10. 33. we are all here *p.* in the sight of God, to hear
21. 18. with us unto James ; and all the elders were *p.*
25. 24. King Agrippa, and all men which are here *present*
28. 2. received us all, because of the *present* rain
Rom. 7. 18. to will is *present* with me, but to do that which
21. law, that, to me who would do good, evil is *present*
8. 18. sufferings of this *present* time are not worthy to be
38. nor things *present*, nor things to come [compared
11. 5. at this *present* time also there is a remnant
1 *Cor.* 3. 22. things *p.*, or things to come ; all are yours
4. 11. Even unto this *present* hour we both hunger, and
5. 3. *p.* in spirit, have already, as though I were *p.*, judged
7. 26. this is good by reason of the *present* distress
2 *Cor.* 10. 2. beseech you, that I may not when *p.* shew
11. such are we also in deed who we are *present* [courage
11. 9. when I was *present* with you and was in want
13. 2. I do say beforehand, as when I was *p.* the second
10. absent, that I may not when *p.* deal sharply [time
Gal. 1. 4. he might deliver us out of this *present* evil world
4. 18. at all times, and not only when I am *p.* with you
20. wish to be *p.* with you now, and to change my voice
2 *Th.* 2. 2. as that the day of the Lord is now ¹*present*
2 *Tim.* 4. 10. Demas forsook me, having loved this *p.* world
Tit. 2. 12. live soberly and righteously and godly in this *p.*
Heb. 9. 9. which is a parable for the time now *p.* [world
12. 11. All chastening seemeth for the *p.* to be not joyous
  see abiding, at home.

Present—ed.—*A.V.* ¹*shew,* ²*yield—ed.*
Lu. 2. 22. up to Jerusalem, to *present* him to the Lord
Acts 9. 41. calling the saints and widows, he *p.* her alive
23. 33. the letter to the governor, *presented* Paul also
Rom. 6. 13. neither ²*present* your members unto sin—but
  ²*present* yourselves unto God
16. Know ye not, that to whom ye ²*present* yourselves
19. for as ye ²*presented* your members as servants—
  even so now ²*present* your members as servants
12. 1. to *present* your bodies a living sacrifice, holy
2 *Cor.* 4. 14. raise *p.* us also with Jesus, and shall *p.* us
11. 2. that I might *present* you as a pure virgin to Christ
Eph. 5. 27. that he might *present* the church to himself
Col. 1. 22. to *present* you holy and without blemish
28. that we may *present* every man perfect in Christ
2 *Tim.* 2. 15. Give diligence to ¹*p.* thyself approved unto
  see offered, set.

Presently *A.V.*—*see immediately, forthwith.*

Preserve—d.—*A.V.* ¹*saved.*
Mat. 9. 17. into fresh wine-skins, and both are *preserved*
Lu. 17. 33. whosoever shall lose his life shall *preserve* it
1 *Th.* 5. 23. may your spirit and soul and body be *p.* entire
2 *Pet.* 2. 5. but ¹*preserved* Noah with seven others
  see kept, save.

Press *A.V.*—*see crowd.*

Press—ed.—*A.V.* ¹*follow,* ²*go,* ³*overcharge,* ⁴*troubled,*
  ⁵*urge.*
Mk. 3. 10. *p.* upon him that they might touch him [word
Lu. 5. 1. while the multitude *p.* upon him and heard the

254

PRESS

Lu. 6. 38. good measure, *pressed* down, shaken together
8. 45. Master, the multitudes *press* thee and crush thee
11. 53. scribes and the Pharisees began to ⁵*p.* upon him
2 *Cor.* 2. 5. (that I ³*press* not too heavily) to you all
4. 8. we are ⁴*pressed* on every side, yet not straitened
Phil. 3. 12. but I ¹*press* on, if so be that I may apprehend
14. I *p.* on toward the goal unto the prize of the high
Heb. 6. 1. cease to speak—³*p.* on unto perfection [calling
see constrained, weighed.

Presseth.—*A.V.* ¹*cometh.*
2 *Cor.* 11. 28. that which ¹*p.* upon me daily, anxiety for all
see entereth.

Presumptuous *A.V.*—*see daring.*

Pretence.—*A.V.* ¹*shew.*
Mk. 12. 40. and for a *p.* make long prayers. *Lu.* 20. 147
Phil. 1. 18. whether in *p.* or in truth, Christ is proclaimed

Prevail—ed.—*A.V.* ¹*accounted worthy,* ²*overcome.*
Mat. 16. 18. the gates of Hades shall not *prevail* against it
27. 24. So when Pilate saw that he *prevailed* nothing
Lu. 21. 36. that ye may ¹*prevail* to escape all these things
23. 23. he might be crucified. And their voices *prevailed*
Jno. 12. 19. Behold how ye *prevail* nothing
Acts 19. 16. and *prevailed* against them, so that they fled
20. So mightily grew the word of the Lord and *p.*
Rom. 3. 4. mightest ²*p.* when thou comest into judgement
Rev. 12. 8. and they *p.* not, neither was their place found
see overcome.

Prevent—ed *A.V.*—*see precede, spake first.*

Price—d.—*A.V.* ¹*sum,* ²*value—d.*
Mat. 13. 46. found one pearl of great *p.,* he went and sold
27. 6. into the treasury, since it is the *price* of blood
9. thirty pieces of silver, the *price* of him that was
²*p.,* whom certain of the children of Israel did ²*p.*
Acts 5. 2. and kept back part of the *price,* his wife also being
7. 16. laid in the tomb that Abraham bought for a ¹*p.*
19. 19. counted the *p.* of them, and found it fifty thousand
1 *Cor.* 6. 20. for ye were bought with a *price.* 7. 23
1 *Pet.* 3. 4. which is in the sight of God of great *price*
see silver.

Prices.
Acts 4. 34. brought the *prices* of the things that were sold

Pricked.
Acts 2. 37. when they heard this, they were *p.* in their heart

Pricks *A.V.*—*see goad.*

Pride.
Mk. 7. 22. an evil eye, railing, *pride,* foolishness
see vainglory.

Priest.—*A.V.* ¹*priesthood,* ²*priests.*
Mat. 8. 4. shew thyself to the *priest.* *Mk.* 1. 44 : *Lu.* 5. 14
Lu. 1. 5. *priest* named Zacharias, of the course of Abijah
8. while he executed the *priest's* office before God
10. 31. by chance a certain *p.* was going down that way
Acts. 14. 13. *p.* of Jupiter whose temple was before the city
19. 14. seven sons of one Sceva, a Jew, a chief ²*priest*
Heb. 7. 3. like unto the Son of God), abideth a *p.* continually
5. that receive the ¹*priest's* office have commandment
11. what—need was there that another *p.* should arise
15. likeness of Melchizedek there ariseth another *p.*

PRIESTS

Heb. 7. 17. Thou art a *priest* for ever. 21
8. 4. if he were on earth, he would not be a *priest* at all
10. 11. every *p.* indeed standeth day by day ministering
21. having a great *priest* over the house of God

High Priest.
Mat. 26. 3. unto the court of the *high priest.* 58 : *Mk.* 14.
54 : *Lu.* 22. 54
51. servant of the *high priest,* and struck off his ear.
Mk. 14. 47 : *Lu.* 22. 50 : *Jno.* 18. 10, 26 [*Jno.* 18. 24
57. led him away to—Caiaphas the *high p.* *Mk.* 14. 53 :
62. the *high priest* stood up, and said, 63 : *Mk.* 14. 60, 61
65. the *high priest* rent his garments. *Mk.* 14. 63
Mk. 2. 26. when Abiathar was *high priest,* and did eat
Jno. 11. 51. being *high priest* that year. 49 : 18. 13
18. 15. that disciple was known unto the *high priest.* 16
22. Answerest thou the *high priest* so ?
Acts 4. 6. Annas the *high priest* was there, and—as many
as were of the kindred of the *high priest.* 5. 17, 27
7. 1. And the *high priest* said, Are these things so ?
22. 5. As also the *high priest* doth bear me witness. 9. 1
23. 4. stood by said, Revilest thou God's *high priest* ?
5. I wist not, brethren, that he was *high priest*
Heb. 2. 17. might be a merciful and faithful *high priest*
3. 1. consider the Apostle and *High P.* of our confession
4. 14. a great *high priest,* who hath passed through
15. we have not a *high priest* that cannot be touched
5. 5. Christ—glorified not himself to be made a *high p.*
10. *high priest* after the order of Melchizedek. 6. 20
7. 26. such a *high priest* became us, holy, guileless
8. 1. We have such a *high priest,* who sat down
3. every *high priest* is appointed to offer both gifts. 5. 1
9. 11. Christ having come a *high p.* of the good things
25. as the *high p.* entereth into the holy place year. 7
13. 11. blood is brought into the holy place by the *high p.*
see chief priests.

Priesthood, High-Priesthood.—*A.V.* ¹*high priests.*
Lu. 3. 2. in the ¹*high-priesthood* of Annas and Caiaphas
Heb. 7. 11. if there was perfection through the Levitical *p.*
12. For the *priesthood* being changed, there is made
24. abideth for ever, hath his *priesthood* unchangeable
1 *Pet.* 2. 5. a holy *priesthood,* to offer up spiritual sacrifices
9. But ye are an elect race, a royal *p.,* a holy nation
see priest—s.

Priests.—*A.V.* ¹*priesthood.*
Mat. 12. 4. that were with him, but only for the *priests* ?
5. the *priests* in the temple profane the sabbath
Mk. 2. 26. not lawful to eat save for the *priests.* *Lu.* 6. 4
Lu. 17. 14. Go and shew yourselves unto the *priests*
Acts 4. 1. the *priests* and the captain of the temple—came
6. 7. company of the *priests* were obedient to the faith
Heb. 7. 14. as to which tribe Moses spake—concerning ¹*p.*
21. have been made *priests* without an oath
23. been made *priests* many in number, because
9. 6. the *priests* go in continually into the first tabernacle
Rev. 1. 6. us to be a kingdom, to be *p.* unto his God. 5. 10
20. 6. be *priests* of God and of Christ, and shall reign
see Levites, priest.

Chief Priests.—*see chief.*

High Priests.
Heb. 7. 27. needeth not daily, like those *high priests,* to offer
28. the law appointeth men *high priests,* having infirmity
see priesthood.

PRINCE

Prince.—*A.V.* ¹*chief.*
Mat. 9. 34. By the *prince* of the devils casteth he out devils. 12. 24 : *Mk.* 3. 22 : *Lu.* 11. ¹15
Jno. 12. 31. now shall the *prince* of this world be cast out
14. 30. *prince* of the world cometh : and he hath nothing
16. 11. because the *prince* of this world hath been judged
Acts 3. 15. and killed the *Prince* of life ; whom God raised
5. 31. to be a *P.* and a Saviour, for to give repentance
Eph. 2. 2. according to the *prince* of the power of the air
see ruler.

Princes.—*A.V.* ¹*great men,* ²*mighty.*
Mat. 2. 6. Art in no wise least among the *princes* of Judah
Lu. 1. 52. He hath put down ²*princes* from their thrones
Rev. 6. 15. And the kings of the earth, and the ¹*princes*
18. 23. thy merchants were the ¹*princes* of the earth
see rulers.

Principal.—*A.V.* ¹*chief.*
Lu. 19. 47. the scribes and the ¹*p.* men of the people sought
Acts 25. 23. *p.* men of the city, at the command of Festus

Principality—ies.—*A.V.* ¹*estate.*
Rom. 8. 38. nor angels, nor *principalities,* nor things present
Eph. 3. 10. the intent that now unto the *p.* and the powers
6. 12. not against flesh and blood, but against the *p.*
Col. 1. 16. whether thrones or dominions or *p.* or powers
2. 10. in him—is the head of all *principality* and power
15. put off—the *p.* and the powers, he made a show
Jude 6. angels which kept not their own ¹*principality*
see rule, rulers.

Principles.
Heb. 5. 12. rudiments of the first *p.* of the oracles of God
6. 1. cease to speak of the first *p.* of Christ, and press on

Print.
Jno. 20. 25. Except I shall see in his hands the *print* of the nails, and put my finger into the *p.* of the nails

Prison.
Mat. 5. 25. and thou be cast into *prison. Lu.* 12. 58
11. 2. John heard in the *prison* the works of the Christ
14. 3. him in *prison* for the sake of Herodias. *Mk.* 6. 17
10. sent, and beheaded John in the *prison. Mk.* 6. 27
18. 30. into *p.,* till he should pay that which was due
25. 39. thee sick, or in *prison,* and came unto thee ? 36
43. sick, and in *prison,* and ye visited me not. 44
Lu. 3. 20. this above all, that he shut up John in *prison*
22. 33. with thee I am ready to go both to *prison* and to
23. 19. and for murder, was cast into *prison.* 25
Jno. 3. 24. For John was not yet cast into *prison*
Acts 5. 19. angel of the Lord by night opened the *p.* doors
22. found them not in the *prison.* 25
8. 3. haling men and women committed them to *prison*
12. 4. put him in *prison,* and delivered him to four
5. Peter therefore was kept in the *prison*
6. and guards before the door kept the *prison*
17. the Lord had brought him forth out of the *prison*
16. 23. stripes upon them, they cast them into *prison*
27. and seeing the *prison* doors open, drew his sword
37. that are Romans, and have cast us into *prison*
40. they went out of the *p.,* and entered into the house
1 *Pet.* 3. 19. he went and preached unto the spirits in *p.*
Rev. 2. 10. devil is about to cast some of you into *prison*
20. 7. are finished, Satan shall be loosed out of his *p.*
see cell, delivered, prison-house, prisons, ward.

PROCEED

Prisoner.—*A.V.* ¹*in bonds.*
Mat. 27. 15. wont to release unto the multitude one *p.*
16. And they had then a notable *prisoner* [*Mk.* 15. 6
Acts 23. 18. Paul the *prisoner* called me unto him
25. 14. There is a certain man left a ¹*prisoner* by Felix
27. unreasonable, in sending a *p.,* not withal to signify
28. 17. nothing against the people—yet was delivered *p.*
Eph. 3. 1. Paul, the *p.* of Christ. 4. 1 : 2 *Tim.* 1. 8 : *Philem.* 9
see fellow-prisoner.

Prisoners.
Acts 16. 25. singing hymns unto God, and the *prisoners* were
27. 1. delivered Paul and certain other *p.* to a centurion
42. the soldiers' counsel was to kill the *prisoners*
see fellow-prisoners.

Prison-house.—*A.V.* ¹*prison.*
Acts 5. 21. sent to the ¹*prison-house* to have them brought
23. The ¹*prison-house* we found shut in all safety
16. 26. the foundations of the ¹*prison-house* were shaken

Prisons.—*A.V.* ¹*prison.*
Lu. 21. 12. delivering you up to the synagogues and *p.*
Acts 22. 4. and delivering into *p.* both men and women
26. 10. shut up many of the saints in ¹*prisons*
2 *Cor.* 11. 23. in *prisons* more abundantly, in stripes above

Private.
2 *Pet.* 1. 20. no prophecy of scripture is of *p.* interpretation

Privately.—*A.V.* ¹*alone.*
Mk. 4. 34. but ¹*privately* to his own disciples he expounded
7. 33. he took him aside from the multitude *privately*
9. 28. his disciples asked him *privately* 13. 3 : *Mat* 24. 3
Lu. 10. 23. And turning to the disciples, he said *privately*
Acts 23. 19. chief captain—going aside asked him *privately*
Gal. 2. 2. but *privately* before them who were of no repute
see apart.

Privily.—*A.V.* ¹*unawares.*
Mat. 1. 19. was minded to put her away *privily*
2. 7. Then Herod *p.* called the wise men, and learned
Acts 16. 37. and do they now cast us out *p.* ? nay verily
Gal. 2. 4. because of the false brethren ¹*privily* brought in, who came in *privily* to spy out our liberty
2 *Pet.* 2. 1. who shall *privily* bring in destructive heresies
Jude 4. For there are certain men crept in ¹*privily*

Privy.
Acts 5. 2. part of the price, his wife also being *privy* to it

Prize.—*A.V.* ¹*reward,* ²*robbery.*
1 *Cor.* 9. 24. in a race run all, but one receiveth the *prize* ?
Phil. 2. 6. counted it not a ²*p.* to be on an equality with God
3. 14. I press on toward the goal unto the *prize*
Col. 2. 18. Let no man rob you of your ¹*prize* by a voluntary

Probation.—*A.V.* ¹*experience.*
Rom. 5. 4. patience, ¹*probation ;* and ¹*probation,* hope

Proceed.—*A.V.* ¹*come,* ²*increase,* ³*proceeded.*
Mat. 15. 18. the things which *proceed* out of the mouth
Mk. 7. 15. the things which ¹*p.* out of the man are those
21. out of the heart of men, evil thoughts *proceed*
23. all these evil things ¹*proceed* from within
Eph. 4. 29. Let no corrupt speech *p.* out of your mouth

PROCEED

2 *Tim.* 2. 16. they will ²*proceed* further in ungodliness
3. 9. they shall *proceed* no further : for their folly
Rev. 4. 5. out of the throne ²*proceed* lightnings and voices
    see come.

Proceeded.—*A.V.* ¹*issued.*

Lu. 4. 22. wondered at the words of grace which *proceeded*
Acts 12. 3. he [Herod] *proceeded* to seize Peter also
Rev. 9. 18. and the brimstone, which ¹*p.* out of their mouths
    see came, came forth, proceed.

Proceedeth.—*A.V.* ¹*cometh,* ²*goeth,* ³*issued.*

Mat. 4. 4. not live by bread alone, but by every word that *p.*
15. 11. that which ¹*p.* out of the mouth, this defileth
Mk. 7. 20. That which ¹*p.* out of the man, that defileth
Jno. 15. 26. the Spirit of truth, which *p.* from the Father
Rev. 9. 17. out of their mouths ³*proceedeth* fire and smoke
11. 5. fire *proceedeth* out of their mouth, and devoureth
19. 15. out of his mouth ²*proceedeth* a sharp sword
    see cometh.

Proceeding.

Mk. 5. 30. Jesus, perceiving—that the power *p.* from him had
Rev. 22. 1. water of life, bright as crystal, *p.* out of the throne

Proclaim.—*A.V.* ¹*preach,* ²*shew.*

Mat. 10. 27. what ye hear in the ear, ¹*p.* upon the housetops
Lu. 4. 18. sent me to ¹*proclaim* release to the captives
19. To ¹*proclaim* the acceptable year of the Lord
Acts 16. 17. servants of—God, which ²*p.* unto you the way
17. 3. Jesus, whom—I ¹*proclaim* unto you, is the Christ
26. 23. by the resurrection of the dead should ²*p.* light
1 *Cor.* 9. 14. they which ¹*p.* the gospel should live of the gospel
11. 26. drink the cup, ye ²*p.* the Lord's death till he come
Phil. 1. 17. but the other ¹*p.* Christ of faction, not sincerely
Col. 1. 28. whom we ¹*proclaim,* admonishing every man
Rev. 14. 6. having an eternal gospel to ¹*p.* to them that dwell

Proclaimed.—*A.V.* ¹*known,* ²*preached—ing,* ³*spoken of.*

Lu. 12. 3. shall be *proclaimed* upon the housetops
Acts 4. 2. and ²*p.* in Jesus the resurrection from the dead
8. 5. Philip went down—and ²*p.* unto them the Christ
9. 20. in the synagogues he ²*p.* Jesus, that he is the Son
13. 5. they ²*p.* the word of God in the synagogues
38. through this man is ²*p.* unto you remission of sins
15. 36. visit the brethren in every city wherein we ²*p.*
17. 13. the word of God was ²*p.* of Paul at Berœa also
Rom. 1. 8. your faith is ³*p.* throughout the whole world
Phil. 1. 18. Christ is ²*proclaimed ;* and therein I rejoice
2 *Tim.* 4. 17. that through me the message might be fully ¹*p.*

Proclaiming.—*A.V.* ¹*declaring.*

1 *Cor.* 2. 1. ¹*proclaiming* to you the mystery of God
Rev. 5. 2. I saw a strong angel *p.* with a great voice

Proconsul—s.—*A.V.* ¹*deputy—ies.*

Acts 13. 7. which was with the ¹*proconsul,* Sergius Paulus
8. seeking to turn aside the ¹*proconsul* from the faith
12. the ¹*proconsul,* when he saw what was done
18. 12. when Gallio was ¹*proconsul* of Achaia
19. 38. the courts are open, and there are ¹*proconsuls*

Profane.

Mat. 12. 5. the priests in the temple *profane* the sabbath
Acts 24. 6. who moreover assayed to *profane* the temple
1 *Tim.* 1. 9. for the unholy and *profane,* for murderers
4. 7. but refuse *profane* and old wives' fables   [2. 16
6. 20. turning away from the *profane* babblings. 2 *Tim.*
Heb. 12. 16. be any fornicator, or *profane* person, as Esau

PROMISE

Profess.

Mat. 7. 23. then will I *profess* unto them, I never knew you
Tit. 1. 16. They *p.* that they know God ; but by their works

Professed *A.V.*—*see confess.*

Professing.

Rom. 1. 22. *P.* themselves to be wise, they became fools
1 *Tim.* 2. 10. (which becometh women *professing* godliness)
6. 21. which some *p.* have erred concerning the faith

Profession—s *A.V.*—*see confession, obedience.*

Profit.—*A.V.* ¹*advantageth.*

Mk. 8. 36. doth it *profit* a man, to gain the whole world
Rom. 3. 1. or what is the *profit* of circumcision ?
1 *Cor.* 7. 35. And this I say for your own *profit*
10. 33. not seeking mine own *p.,* but the *p.* of the many
12. 7. given the manifestation of the Spirit to *p.* withal
14. 6. with tongues, what shall I *profit* you, unless I
15. 32. what doth it ¹*profit* me ? If the dead are not raised
Gal. 5. 2. circumcision, Christ will *profit* you nothing
2 *Tim.* 2. 14. that they strive not about words, to no *profit*
Heb. 4. 2. word of hearing did not *profit* them, because
12. 10. he for our *p.,* that we may be partakers of his holi-
Jas. 2. 14. What doth it *p.,* my brethren, if a man say [ness
16. things needful to the body ; what doth it *profit* ?

Profitable.—*A.V.* ¹*better,* ²*profiteth.*

Mat. 5. 29. it is *p.* for thee that one of thy members. 30
18. 6. it is ¹*profitable* for him that a great millstone
Acts 20. 20. shrank not from declaring unto you anything
that was *profitable*   [is *p.* for all things
1 *Tim.* 4. 8. bodily exercise is ²*p.* for a little ; but godliness
2 *Tim.* 3. 16. is also *profitable* for teaching, for reproof
Tit. 3. 8. These things are good and *profitable* unto men
Philem. 11. [Onesimus] now is *profitable* to thee and to me
    see useful.

Profited—eth.—*A.V.* ¹*advantaged.*

Mat. 15. 5. That wherewith thou mightest have been
profited by me is given to God. *Mk.* 7. 11
16. 26. what shall a man be *p.,* if he shall gain. *Lu.* 9. ¹25
Jno. 6. 63. spirit that quickeneth ; the flesh *p.* nothing
Rom. 2. 25. circumcision indeed *p.,* if thou be a doer of the
1 *Cor.* 13. 3. but have not love, it *p.* me nothing   [law
Heb. 13. 9. not by meats, wherein they—were not *profited*
    see advanced, profitable.

Profiting *A.V.*—*see progress.*

Progress.—*A.V.* ¹*furtherance,* ²*profiting.*

Phil. 1. 12. fallen out rather unto the ¹*progress* of the gospel
25. abide with you all, for your ¹*p.* and joy in the faith
1 *Tim.* 4. 15. that thy ²*progress* may be manifest unto all

Prolonged.—*A.V.* ¹*continued.*

Acts 20. 7. Paul—¹*prolonged* his speech until midnight

Promise.

Lu. 24. 49. I send forth the *promise* of my Father upon you
Acts 1. 4. but to wait for the *promise* of the Father
2. 33. received of the Father the *p.* of the Holy Ghost
39. For to you is the *promise,* and to your children
7. 17. time of the *p.* drew nigh, which God vouchsafed
13. 23. according to *promise* brought unto Israel a Saviour
32. good tidings of the *promise* made unto the fathers
23. 21. now are they ready, looking for the *p.* from thee
26. 6. to be judged for the hope of the *p.* made of God

PROMISE

Acts 26. 7. unto which *p.* our twelve tribes, earnestly serving
Rom. 4. 13. not through the law was the *p.* to Abraham
14. faith is made void, and the *promise*—of none effect
16 to the end that the *p.* may be sure to all the seed
20. looking unto the *promise* of God, he wavered not
9. 8. the children of the *promise* are reckoned for a seed
9. this is a word of *promise*, According to this season
Gal. 3. 14. that we might receive the *promise* of the Spirit
17. disannul, so as to make the *promise* of none effect
18. For if the inheritance is of the law, it is no more of *p.*; but God hath granted it to Abraham by *p.*
19. seed should come to whom the *p.* hath been made
22. the *promise* by faith in Jesus Christ might be given
29. Abraham's seed, heirs according to *promise*
4. 23. the son by the freewoman is born through *promise*
28. we, brethren, as Isaac was, are children of *promise*
Eph. 1. 13. ye were sealed with the Holy Spirit of *promise*
2. 12. and strangers from the covenants of the *promise*
3. 6. and fellow-partakers of the *promise* in Christ Jesus
6. 2. (which is the first commandment with *promise*)
1 *Tim.* 4. 8. having *p.* of the life which now is, and of that
2 *Tim.* 1. 1. according to the *p.* of the life which is in Christ
Heb. 4. 1. lest haply, a *p.* being left of entering into his rest
6. 13. *p.* to Abraham, since he could swear by none greater
15. having patiently endured, he obtained the *promise*
17. unto the heirs of the *promise* the immutability
9. 15. may receive the *promise* of the eternal inheritance
10. 36. done the will of God, ye may receive the *promise*
11. 9. became a sojourner in the land of *promise*—and Jacob, the heirs with him of the same *promise*
39. witness borne to them—received not the *promise*
2 *Pet.* 3. 4. saying, Where is the *promise* of his coming?
9. The Lord is not slack concerning his *promise*
13. according to his *promise*, we look for new heavens
1 *Jno.* 2. 25. And this is the *promise* which he promised us
  see promising.

Promised, aforepromised.—*A.V.* ¹*notice.*

Mat. 14. 7. he *promised* with an oath to give her whatsoever
Mk. 14. 11. were glad, and *promised* to give him money
Acts 7. 5. he *p.* that he would give it to him in possession
Rom. 1. 2. which he *promised* afore by his prophets
4. 21. that, what he had *p.*, he was able also to perform
2 *Cor.* 9. 5. make up beforehand your ¹*aforepromised* bounty
Tit. 1. 2. eternal life, which God, who cannot lie, *promised*
Heb. 10. 23. that it waver not; for he is faithful that *p.*
11. 11. since she counted him faithful who had *promised*
12. 26. now he hath *p.*, saying, Yet once more will I
Jas. 1. 12. the Lord *promised* to them that love him. 2. 5
1 *Jno.* 2. 25. promise which he *p.* us, even the life eternal
  see consented.

Promises.

Rom. 9. 4. and the service of God, and the *promises*
15. 8. might confirm the *promises* given unto the fathers
2 *Cor.* 1. 20. many soever be the *p.* of God, in him is the yea
7. 1. Having therefore these *p.*, beloved, let us cleanse
Gal. 3. 16. to Abraham were the *p.* spoken, and to his seed
21. Is the law then against the *promises* of God?
Heb. 6. 12. who through faith and patience inherit the *p.*
7. 6. and hath blessed him that hath the *promises*
8. 6. covenant, which hath been enacted upon better *p.*
11. 13. These all died in faith, not having received the *p.*
17. he that had gladly received the *p.* was offering up
33. obtained *promises*, stopped the mouths of lions
2 *Pet.* 1. 4. unto us his precious and exceeding great *p.*

Promising.—*A.V.* ¹*promise.*

2 *Pet.* 2. 19. ¹*promising* them liberty, while they themselves are bondservants of corruption

PROPHESYING

Pronounced—eth.—*A.V.* ¹*describeth.*

Rom. 4. 6. as David also ¹*p.* blessing upon the man. 9

Proof—s.—*A.V.* ¹*trial*, ²*trying.*

Acts 1. 3. shewed himself alive after his passion by many *p.*
2 *Cor.* 2. 9. I write, that I might know the *proof* of you
8. 2. how that in much ¹*proof* of affliction the abundance
24. in the face of the churches the *proof* of your love
13. 3. ye seek a *proof* of Christ that speaketh in me
Phil. 2. 22. ye know the *proof* of him, that, as a child
Jas. 1. 3. the ²*proof* of your faith worketh patience
1 *Pet.* 1. 7. the ¹*proof* of your faith, being more precious
  see fulfil.

Proper *A.V.*—*see language, own, goodly.*

Prophecies.

1 *Cor.* 13. 8. whether there be *p.*, they shall be done away
1 *Tim.* 1. 18. according to the *prophecies* which went before

Prophecy.

Mat. 13. 14. unto them is fulfilled the *prophecy* of Isaiah
Rom. 12. 6. whether *p.*, let us prophesy according to the
1 *Cor.* 12. 10. to another *p.*; and to another discernings
13. 2. if I have the gift of *p.*, and know all mysteries
1 *Tim.* 4. 14. gift that is in thee, which was given thee by *p.*
2 *Pet.* 1. 19. we have the word of *prophecy* made more sure
20. no *prophecy* of scripture is of private interpretation
21. For no *prophecy* ever came by the will of man
Rev. 1. 3. that hear the words of the *prophecy*. 22. 18
11. 6. that it rain not during the days of their *prophecy*
19. 10. for the testimony of Jesus is the spirit of *prophecy*
22. 7. keepeth the words of the *prophecy* of this book. 10
19. of this *prophecy*, God shall take away his part

Prophesied.

Mat. 11. 13. all the prophets and the law *p.* until John
Lu. 1. 67. Zacharias was filled with the Holy Ghost, and *p.*
Jno. 11. 51. he *p.* that Jesus should die for the nation
Acts 19. 6. they spake with tongues, and *prophesied*
1 *Pet.* 1. 10. who *p.* of the grace that should come unto you
Jude 14. Enoch, the seventh from Adam, *p.*, saying
  see prophesy.

Prophesieth.

1 *Cor.* 14. 3. he that *p.* speaketh unto men edification
4. but he that *prophesieth* edifieth the church
5. greater is he that *prophesieth* than he that speaketh
  see prophesying.

Prophesy.—*A.V.* ¹*prophesied.*

Mat. 7. 22. Lord, Lord, did we not ¹*prophesy* by thy name
15. 7. Ye hypocrites, well did Isaiah *p.* of you. *Mk.* 7. 16
26. 68. *P.* unto us, thou Christ. *Mk.* 14. 65: *Lu.* 22. 64
Acts 2. 17. And your sons and your daughters shall *p.* 18
21. 9. four daughters, virgins, which did *prophesy*
Rom. 12. 6. let us *p.* according to the proportion of our faith
1 *Cor.* 13. 9. we know in part, and we *prophesy* in part
14. 1. spiritual gifts, but rather that ye may *prophesy*. 15
24. But if all *p.*, and there come in one unbelieving
31. For ye all can *p.* one by one, that all may learn
39. desire earnestly to *prophesy*, and forbid not to speak
Rev. 10. 11. Thou must *prophesy* again over many peoples
11. 3. they shall *p.* a thousand two hundred and three-score days, clothed in sackcloth

Prophesying—s.—*A.V.* ¹*prophesieth.*

1 *Cor.* 11. 4. praying or *prophesying*, having his head covered
5. praying or ¹*prophesying* with her head unveiled

PROPHESYING

1 *Cor.* 14. 6. of knowledge, or of *p*., or of teaching?
22. *prophesying* is for a sign, not to the unbelieving, but
1 *Th.* 5. 20. despise not *prophesyings*

Prophet.—*A.V.* ¹*prophets.*

Mat. 1. 22. was spoken by the Lord through the *prophet*
  2. 15, 17: 3. 3: 4. 14: 8. 17: 12. 17: 13. 35: 21.
  4: 24. 15: 27. 9: *Lu.* 3. 4: *Jno.* 1. 23: 12. 38:
  Acts 2. 16: 28. 25
2. 5. of Judæa: for thus it is written by the *prophet*
10. 41. He that receiveth a *prophet* in the name of a
  prophet shall receive a *prophet's* reward
11. 9. But wherefore went ye out? to see a *prophet*?
  —much more than a *prophet*. *Lu.* 7. 26
12. 89. no sign be given to it but the sign of Jonah the *p*.
13. 57. A *prophet* is not without honour, save in his own
  country. *Mk.* 6. 4: *Jno.* 4. 44
14. 5. because they counted him as a *prophet*
21. 11. This is the *p*., Jesus, from Nazareth of Galilee
26. for all hold John as a *prophet*. *Mk.* 11. 32: *Lu.* 20. 6
46. feared the multitudes, because they took him for a *p*.
Mk. 1. 2. Even as it is written in Isaiah the ¹*prophet*
6. 15. It is a *prophet*, even as one of the prophets
Lu. 1. 76. child, shalt be called the *p*. of the Most High
4. 17. delivered unto him the book of the *prophet* Isaiah
24. No *prophet* is acceptable in his own country
27. many lepers in Israel in the time of Elisha the *p*.
7. 16. saying, A great *prophet* is arisen among us
39. This man. if he were a *prophet*, would have perceived
13. 33. it cannot be that a *prophet* perish out of Jerusalem
24. 19. Jesus of Nazareth, which was a *p*. mighty in deed
Jno. 1. 21. Art thou the *prophet*? And he answered, No
25. not the Christ, neither Elijah, neither the *prophet*?
4. 19. Sir, I perceive that thou art a *prophet*   ¦7. 40
6. 14. This is of a truth the *p*. that cometh into the world.
7. 52. Search, and see that out of Galilee ariseth no *p*.
9. 17. opened thine eyes? And he said, He is a *prophet*
Acts 2. 30. Being—a *p*., and knowing that God had sworn
3. 22. A *prophet* shall the Lord God raise up. 7. 37
23. every soul, which shall not hearken to that *prophet*
7. 48. not in houses made with hands; as saith the *p*.
8. 28. in his chariot, and was reading the *prophet* Isaiah
34. I pray thee, of whom speaketh the *prophet* this?
13. 20. he gave them judges until Samuel the *prophet*
21. 10. from Judæa a certain *prophet*, named Agabus
1 *Cor.* 14. 37. If any man thinketh himself to be a *prophet*
Tit. 1. 12. a *p*. of their own, said, Cretans are alway liars
2 *Pet.* 2. 16. man's voice and stayed the madness of the *p*.

Prophets.

Mat. 2. 23. spoken by the *prophets*. *Lu.* 18. 31: *Jno.* 6. 45
5. 12. so persecuted they the *prophets*. *Lu.* 6. 23
17. Think not that I came to destroy the law or the *p*.
7. 12. also unto them: for this is the law and the *prophets*
11. 13. all the *prophets* and the law prophesied until John
13. 17. many *prophets* and righteous men desired to see
  the things which ye see. *Lu.* 10. 24
16. 14. or one of the *prophets*. *Mk.* 6. 15: 8. 28
22. 40. commandments hangeth the whole law, and the *p*.
23. 29. ye build the sepulchres of the *prophets*. *Lu.* 11. 47
30. partakers with them in the blood of the *prophets*
31. that ye are sons of them that slew the *prophets*
34. behold, I send unto you *prophets*
37. Jerusalem, which killeth the *prophets*. *Lu.* 13. 34
26. 56. scriptures of the *prophets* might be fulfilled
Lu. 1. 70. by the mouth of his holy *p*. *Acts* 3. 21: 2 *Pet.* 3. 2
9. 8. that one of the old *prophets* was risen again. 19
11. 49. I will send unto them *prophets* and apostles

PROSELYTE

Lu. 11. 50. that the blood of all the *p*., which was shed
13. 28. all the *p*., in the kingdom of God, and yourselves
16. 16. The law and the *prophets* were until John
29. They have Moses and the *p*.; let them hear them. 31
24. 25. to believe in all that the *prophets* have spoken!
27. Moses and from all the *prophets*, he interpreted
Jno. 1. 45. Moses in the law, and the *p*., did write. *Lu.* 24. 44
8. 52. Abraham is dead, and the *prophets*. 53
Acts 3. 18. by the mouth of all the *p*., that his Christ
24. all the *p*. from Samuel and them that followed
25. Ye are the sons of the *p*., and of the covenant
7. 42. written in the book of the *prophets*, Did ye offer
52. Which of the *p*. did not your fathers persecute?
10. 43. To him bear all the *p*. witness, that through his
11. 27. came down *p*. from Jerusalem unto Antioch
13. 1. at Antioch, in the church that was there, *prophets*
15. after the reading of the law and the *prophets*
27. knew him not, nor the voices of the *prophets*
40. that come upon you, which is spoken in the *p*.
15. 15. And to this agree the words of the *prophets*
32. Judas and Silas, being themselves also *prophets*
24. 14. to the law, and which are written in the *prophets*
26. 22. what the *p*. and Moses did say should come
27. King Agrippa, believest thou the *prophets*?
28. 23. and from the *prophets*, from morning till evening
Rom. 1. 2. which he promised afore by his *prophets*
3. 21. being witnessed by the law and the *prophets*
11. 3. Lord, they have killed thy *p*., they have digged
16. 26. now is manifested, and by the scriptures of the *p*.
1 *Cor.* 12. 28. first apostles, secondly *p*., thirdly teachers
29. are all *prophets*? are all teachers?
14. 29. And let the *prophets* speak by two or three
32. the spirits of the *prophets* are subject to the *p*.
Eph. 2. 20. built upon the foundation of the apostles and *p*.
3. 5. now been revealed unto his holy apostles and *p*.
4. 11. he gave some to be apostles; and some, *prophets*
1 *Th.* 2. 15. who both killed the Lord Jesus and the *p*.
Heb. 1. 1. of old time spoken unto the fathers in the *p*.
11. 32. of David and Samuel and the *prophets*
Jas. 5. 10. Take, brethren, for an example—the *prophets*
1 *Pet.* 1. 10. Concerning which salvation the *p*. sought
Rev. 10. 7. tidings which he declared to his servants the *p*.
11. 10. because these two *prophets* tormented them
18. to give their reward to thy servants the *prophets*
16. 6. for they poured out the blood of saints and *p*.
18. 20. apostles, and ye *prophets*; for God hath judged
22. 6. the God of the spirits of the *p*., sent his angel
9. fellow-servant with thee and with thy brethren the *p*.
  see prophet.

Prophetess.

Lu. 2. 36. And there was one Anna, a *prophetess*
Rev. 2. 20. the woman Jezebel, which calleth herself a *p*.

Propitiation.—*A.V.* ¹*reconciliation.*

Rom. 3. 25. whom God set forth to be a *propitiation*
Heb. 2. 17. to make ¹*propitiation* for the sins of the people
1 *Jno.* 2. 2. and he is the *propitiation* for our sins. 4. 10

Proportion.

Rom. 12. 6. let us prophesy according to the *p*. of our faith

Proposed *A.V.*—*see determined.*

Proselyte—s.

Mat. 23. 15. ye compass sea and land to make one *p*.
Acts 2. 10. sojourners from Rome, both Jews and *p*.
6. 5. and Nicolas a *proselyte* of Antioch
13. 43. of the Jews and of the devout *p*. followed Paul

PROSPER — PUBLIC

Prosper.—*A.V.* ¹*prospered.*
1 *Cor.* 16. 2. lay by him in store, as he may ¹*prosper*
3 *Jno.* 2. I pray that in all things thou mayest *prosper*

Prospered—eth.—*A.V.* ¹*prosperous journey*
Rom. 1. 10. be ¹*p.* by the will of God to come unto you
3 *Jno.* 2. and be in health, even as thy soul *prospereth*
see prosper.

Prosperous *A.V.*—*see prospered.*

Protest.
1 *Cor.* 15. 31. I *protest* by that glorying in you, brethren

Proud.
Lu. 1. 51. He hath scattered the *proud* in the imagination
Jas. 4. 6. God resisteth the *proud.* 1 *Pet.* 5. 5
see haughty, puffed.

Prove.—*A.V.* ¹*examine,* ²*make,* ³*try.*
Lu. 14. 19. bought five yoke of oxen, and I go to *p.* them
Jno. 6. 6. this he said to *prove* him : for he himself knew
Acts 24. 13. Neither can they *p.* to thee the things. 25. 7
Rom. 12. 2. that ye may *p.* what is the good and acceptable
1 *Cor.* 3. 13. the fire itself shall ³*prove* each man's work
11. 28. let a man ¹*prove* himself, and so let him eat
2 *Cor.* 13. 5. whether ye be in the faith ; *p.* your own selves
Gal. 2. 18. which I destroyed, I ²*prove* myself a transgressor
6. 4. But let each man *prove* his own work
1 *Th.* 5. 21. *prove* all things ; hold fast that which is good
1 *Pet.* 4. 12. trial—which cometh upon you to ²*prove* you
1 *Jno.* 4. 1. ³*prove* the spirits, whether they are of God
see proving.

Proved.—*A.V.* ¹*tried.*
2 *Cor.* 8. 22. whom we have many times *proved* earnest
1 *Tim.* 3. 10. let these also first be *p.;* thou let them serve
1 *Pet.* 1. 7. more precious than gold—¹*proved* by fire
see proving.

Proverb—s.
Jno. 16. 25. in *proverbs*—no more speak unto you in *p.*
29. now speakest thou plainly, and speakest no *p.*
2 *Pet.* 2. 22. happened unto them according to the true *p.*
see parable.

Proveth.—*A.V.* ¹*trieth.*
1 *Th.* 2. 4. pleasing men, but God which ¹*proveth* our hearts

Provide—d—eth.—*A.V.* ¹*provide*
Acts 23. 24. *p.* beasts, that they might set Paul thereon
1 *Tim.* 5. 8. if any ¹*provideth* not for his own, and specially
Heb. 11. 40. God having *p.* some better thing concerning
see get, make, prepared, take thought.

Providence
Acts 24. 2. by thy *p.* evils are corrected for this nation

Province.—*A.V.* ¹*line,* ²*rule.*
Acts 23. 34. when he had read it, he asked of what *p.* he was
25. 1. Festus therefore, having come into the *province*
2 *Cor.* 10.13. according to the measure of the ²*p.* which God
15. according to our ²*province* unto further abundance
16. and not to glory in another's ¹*province* in regard of

Proving.—*A.V.* ¹*evidence,* ²*experiment,* ³*prove,* ⁴*proved.*
Acts 9. 22. confounded the Jews—*p.* that this is the Christ

2 *Cor.* 8. 8. but as ³*p.* through the earnestness of others
9. 13. through the ²*proving* of you by this ministration
Eph. 5. 10. *proving* what is well-pleasing unto the Lord
Heb. 3. 9. Wherewith your fathers tempted me by ⁴*p.* me
11. 1. faith is—the ¹*proving* of things not seen

Provision.
Rom. 13. 14. and make not *provision* for the flesh

Provocation.
Heb 3. 8. Harden not your hearts, as in the *provocation.* 15

Provoke.
Lu. 11. 53. and to *provoke* him to speak of many things
Rom. 10.19. *p.* you to jealousy with that which is no nation.
1 *Cor.* 10. 22. Or do we *p.* the Lord to jealousy? [11. 11, 14
Eph. 6. 4. And, ye fathers, *p.* not your children to wrath. *Col.*
Heb. 3. 16. For who, when they heard, did *provoke* ? [3. 21
10. 24. one another to *provoke* unto love and good works

Provoked—ing.—*A.V.* ¹*stirred.*
Acts 17. 16. his spirit was ¹*provoked* within him
1 *Cor* 13. 5. is not *provoked,* taketh not account of evil
Gal. 5. 26. Let us not be vainglorious, *p.* one another
see stirred.

Prudence.—*A V.* ¹*understanding.*
1 *Cor.* 1. 19. And the ¹*prudence* of the prudent will I reject
Eph. 1. 8. abound toward us in all wisdom and *prudence*

Prudent.
1 *Cor.* 1. 19. And the prudence of the *prudent* will I reject
Psalm. *see understanding.*
Acts 13. 33. written in the second *psalm,* Thou art my Son
35. he saith also in another *psalm,* Thou wilt not give
1 *Cor.* 14. 26. When ye come together, each one hath a *p.*

Psalms.
Lu. 20. 42. David himself saith in the book of *Psalms*
24. 44. the prophets, and the *psalms,* concerning me
Acts 1. 20. For it is written in the book of *Psalms*
Eph. 5. 19. speaking one to another in *psalms* and hymns
Col. 3. 16. admonishing one another with *p.* and hymns
see praise.

Publican—s.
Mat. 5. 46. do not even the *publicans* the same ?
9. 10. many *p.* and sinners came. *Mk.* 2. 15 : *Lu.* 5. 29
11. Why eateth your Master with the *p. Mk.* 2. 16 : *Lu*
10. 3. Thomas, and Matthew the *publican* [5. 30
11 19. a friend of *publicans* and sinners ! *Lu.* 7. 34
18. 17. let him be unto thee as the Gentile and the *p.*
21. 31. *p.* and the harlots go into the kingdom of God before
32. but the *publicans* and the harlots believed him [you
Lu. 3. 12. And there came also *publicans* to be baptized
5. 27. beheld a *p.,* named Levi, sitting at the place of toll
7. 29. and the *publicans,* justified God, being baptized
15. 1. all the *p.* and sinners were drawing near unto him
18. 10. to pray ; the one a Pharisee, and the other a *p.*
11. adulterers, or even as this *publican* [as his eyes
13. the *p.,* standing afar off, would not lift up so much
19. 2. Zacchæus ; and he was a chief *publican*

Public.—*A.V.* ¹*common.*
Mat. 1. 19. not willing to make her a *public* example
Acts 5. 18. hands on the apostles, and put them in ¹*p.* ward

PUBLICLY

Publicly.—*A.V.* ¹*openly*

Jno. 7. 10. then went he also up, not ¹*p.*, but—in secret
Acts 16. 37. They have beaten us ¹*publicly*, uncondemned
18. 28. confuted the Jews, and that *publicly*, shewing
20. 20. shrank not from—teaching you *publicly*

Publish.—*A.V.* ¹*preach.*

Mk. 1. 45. he went out, and began to *publish* it much
5. 20. he went his way, and began to *publish* in Decapolis
Lu. 9. 60. go thou and ¹*p.* abroad the kingdom of God

Published—ing.—*A.V.* ¹*declared.*

Mk. 7. 36. so much the more a great deal they *published* it
Lu. 8. 39. *p.* throughout the whole city how great things
Acts 10. 37. that saying ye yourselves know, which was *p.*
Rom. 9. 17. my name might he ¹*p.* abroad in all the earth
see preached, spread.

Puffed—eth.—*A.V.* ¹*highminded*, ²*lifted*, ³*proud.*

1 *Cor.* 4. 6. no one of you be *p.* up for the one against the
18. some are *p.* up, as though I were not coming [other
19. not the word of them which are *p.* up, but the power
5. 2. And ye are *puffed* up, and did not rather mourn
8. 1. Knowledge *puffeth* up, but love edifieth
13. 4. love vaunteth not itself, is not *puffed* up
Col. 2. 18. vainly *puffed* up by his fleshly mind
1 *Tim.* 3. 6. not a novice, lest being ²*puffed* up he fall
6. 4. he is ³*puffed* up, knowing nothing
2 *Tim.* 3. 4. headstrong, ¹*puffed* up, lovers of pleasure

Pull.

Lu. 12. 18. I will *pull* down my barns, and build greater
see cast out, draw, torn.

Pulling *A.V.*—*see casting, snatching.*

Punish—ed.

Acts 4. 21. finding nothing how they might *punish* them
22. 5. unto Jerusalem in bonds, for to be *punished*
see punishment.

Punishing.—*A.V.* ¹*punished.*

Acts 26. 11. And ¹*p.* them oftentimes in all the synagogues

Punishment.—*A.V.* ¹*punished*, ²*torment*, ³*vengeance.*

Mat. 25. 46. And these shall go away into eternal *p.*
2 *Cor.* 2. 6. Sufficient to such a one is this *punishment*
2 *Th.* 1. 9. who shall suffer ¹*p.*, even eternal destruction
Heb. 10. 29. of how much sorer *p.*, think ye, shall he be
2 *Pet.* 2. 9. and to keep the unrighteous under ¹*p.* unto
1 *Jno.* 4. 18. casteth out fear, because fear hath ²*punishment*
Jude 7. suffering the ³*punishment* of eternal fire
see vengeance.

Purchase—d.—*A.V.* ¹*redeemed.*

Acts 20. 28. which he *purchased* with his own blood
Rev. 5. 9. didst ¹*p.* unto God with thy blood men of every
14. 3. even they that had been ¹*p.* out of the earth. 14
see gain, obtain, obtained, own.

Pure.—*A.V.* ¹*chaste*, ²*clean*, ³*clear.*

Acts 15. that I am *pure* from the blood of all men
2 *Cor.* 7. 11. ye approved yourselves to be ²*p.* in the matter
11. 2. that I might present you as a ¹*pure* virgin to Christ
Phil. 4. 8. are just, whatsoever things are *p.* [conscience
1 *Tim.* 3. 9. holding the mystery of the faith in a *pure*
5. 22. partaker of other men's sins: keep thyself *pure*
2 *Tim.* 1. 3. serve from my forefathers in a *p.* conscience

PURPOSE

Tit. 1. 15. To the *pure* all things are *pure*: but to them
that are defiled and unbelieving nothing is *pure*
Heb. 10. 22. and our body washed with *pure* water
Jas. 1. 27. *Pure* religion and undefiled before our God
3. 17. But the wisdom that is from above is first *pure*
1 *Jno.* 3. 3. this hope set on him purifieth himself—he is *p.*
Rev. 15. 6. arrayed with precious stone, *pure* and bright
19. 8. array herself in fine linen, bright and ²*pure*. ²14
21. 18. and the city was *pure* gold, like unto ²*pure* glass
see clean, sincere.

Pureness.

2 *Cor.* 6. 6. in *pureness*, in knowledge, in longsuffering

Purge.

1 *Cor.* 5. 7. *P.* out the old leaven, that ye may be a new lump
2 *Tim.* 2. 21. If a man therefore *purge* himself from these
see cleanse—ed—ing, purification.

Purgeth *A.V.*—*see cleanseth.*

Purging *A.V.*—*see clean, cleansing.*

Purification.—*A.V.* ¹*purged.*

Lu. 2. 22. when the days of their *p.* according to the law
Acts 21. 26. declaring the fulfilment of the days of *p.*
Heb. 1. 3. when he had made ¹*purification* of sins, sat down

Purified—eth.

Acts 24. 18. amidst which they found me *p.* in the temple
1 *Pet.* 1. 22. Seeing ye have *p.* your souls in your obedience
1 *Jno.* 3. 3. that hath this hope set on him *purifieth* himself
see cleansed.

Purify.

Jno. 11. 55. to Jerusalem—before the passover, to *p.* them-
Acts 21. 24. these take, and *p.* thyself with them [selves
Tit. 2. 14. and *p.* unto himself a people for his own posses-
Jas. 4. 8. and *purify* your hearts, ye doubleminded [sion

Purifying.

Jno. 2. 6. set there after the Jews' manner of *purifying*
3. 25. There arose therefore a questioning—about *p.*
Acts 21. 26. and the next day *purifying* himself with them
see cleanness, cleansing.

Purity.

2 *Cor.* 11. 3. your minds should be corrupted from—the *p.*
1 *Tim.* 4. 12. be thou an ensample—in love, in faith, in *p.*
5. 2. the younger as sisters, in all *purity*

Purloining.

Tit. 2. 10. not *purloining*, but shewing all good fidelity

Purple.

Mk. 15. 17. And they clothe him with *purple*. *Jno.* 19. 2, 5
20. had mocked him, they took off from him the *purple*
Lu. 16. 19. rich man, and he was clothed in *purple*
Acts 16. 14. woman named Lydia, a seller of *purple*
Rev. 17. 4. the woman was arrayed in *purple* and scarlet
18. 12. fine linen, and *purple*, and silk
16. city, she that was arrayed in fine linen and *purple*

Purpose.

Mat. 26. 8. saying, To what *p.* is this waste? *Mk.* 14. 4
Acts 11. 23. with *p.* of heart they would cleave unto the Lord
27. 13. supposing that they had obtained their *purpose*
43. desiring to save Paul, stayed them from their *p.*
Rom. 8. 28. to them that are called according to his *p.*
9. 11. the *p.* of God according to election might stand
17. For this very *purpose* did I raise thee [Pharaoh] up

PURPOSE

2 Cor. 1. 17. the things that I p., do I purpose according
Eph. 1. 11. according to the p. of him who worketh all
3. 11. to the eternal p. which he purposed in Christ
6. 22. I have sent unto you for this very purpose. Col. 4. 8
2 Tim. 1. 9. but according to his own purpose and grace
3. 10. thou didst follow my teaching, conduct, purpose
see end.

Purposed.—*A.V.* ¹purposeth.

Acts 19. 21. Paul purposed in the spirit, when he had passed
Rom. 1. 13. that oftentimes I purposed to come unto you
2 Cor. 9. 7. each man do—as he hath ¹purposed in his heart
Eph. 1. 9. according to his good pleasure which he p.
3. 11. eternal purpose which he purposed in Christ Jesus

Purposeth *A.V.*—see purposed.

Purse—s.—*A.V.* ¹bags.

Mat. 10. 9. no gold, nor silver, nor brass in your purses
Mk. 6. 8. no bread, no wallet, no money in their purse
Lu. 10. 4. Carry no purse, no wallet, no shoes. 22. 35
12. 33. make for yourselves ¹purses which wax not old
22. 36. But now, he that hath a purse, let him take it

Pursue—ed.—*A.V.* ¹ensue, ²persecuted.

2 Cor. 4. 9. ²pursued, yet not forsaken ; smitten down
1 Pet. 3. 11. Let him seek peace, and ¹pursue it

Put.—*A.V.* ¹appointed, ²bring, ³depart, ⁴divorced,
⁵instructed, ⁶launch—ed, ⁷putteth, ⁸stretched, ⁹thrust.

Mat. 1. 19. was minded to put her away privily
5. 15. a lamp, and put it under the bushel. Mk. 4. 21
31. Whosoever shall p. away his wife. 19. 9 ; Mk. 10. 11
32. shall marry her when she is ⁴put away. Lu. 16. 18
6. 25. nor yet for your body, what ye shall p. on. Lu.12.22
9. 17. Neither do men put new wine into old wine-skins
—they p. new wine into fresh. Mk. 2. 22 ; Lu. 5. 38
25. But when the crowd was put forth, he entered in
12. 18. I will p. my Spirit upon him, And he shall declare
14. 3. John, and bound him, and put him in prison
8. she, being ⁶put forward by her mother, saith
19. 6. let not man put asunder. Mk. 10. 9.
21. 7. and the colt, and put on them their garments
22. 34. heard that he had put the Sadducees to silence
25. 27. therefore to have put my money to the bankers
26. 52. Put up again thy sword. Jno. 18. 11
27. 6. It is not lawful to put them into the treasury
28. and put on him a scarlet robe. 31   [Jno. 19. 2
29. crown of thorns and p. it upon his head. Mk. 15. 17:
48. with vinegar, and put it on a reed. Mk. 15. 36
Mk. 5. 40. he, having put them all forth, taketh the father
6. 9. and, said he, put not on two coats
7. 33. and put his fingers into his ears, and he spat
10. 2. lawful for a man to p. away his wife ? 4 ; Mat. 19. 3,
12. put away her husband, and marry another   [7, 8
Lu. 1. 52. He hath put down princes from their thrones
5. 3. asked him to ⁶put out a little from the land
4. he said unto Simon, ⁶Put out into the deep
9. 62. put his hand to the plough, and looking back
15. 22. best robe, and p. it on him—p. a ring on his hand
16. 4. that, when I am put out of the stewardship
Jno. 5. 7. when the water is troubled, to p. me into the pool
9. 15. He p. clay upon mine eyes, and I washed, and do see
10. 4. When he hath ⁷put forth all his own, he goeth
12. 6. having the bag took away what was put therein
42. confess it, lest they should be p. out of the synagogue
13. 2. devil having already put into the heart of Judas
16. 2. put you out of the synagogues. 9. 22 ; 12. 42
19. 19. Pilate wrote a title also, and put it on the cross

PUTTING

Jno. 19. 29. they p. a sponge full of the vinegar upon hyssop
20. 25. and put my finger into the print of the nails,
and ⁶put my hand into his side, I will not believe
Acts 1. 23. they ¹put forward two, Joseph called Barsabbas
4. 3. and put them in ward unto the morrow. 5. 18
5. 25. men whom ye put in the prison are in the temple
34. and commanded to put the men forth a little while
9. 40. But Peter put them all forth, and kneeled down
12. 1. Herod the king ⁸put forth his hands to afflict
4. when he had taken him, he put him [Peter] in prison
15. 10. why tempt ye God, that ye should put a yoke
27. 2. embarking in a ship of Adramyttium—we ⁶p. to sea
12. the more part advised to ⁶put to sea from thence
Rom. 13. 12. and let us put on the armour of light
14. But put ye on the Lord Jesus Christ
14. 13. no man put a stumblingblock in his brother's way
1 Cor. 4. 17. who shall ²put you in remembrance of my ways
5. 13. Put away the wicked man from among yourselves
13. 11. become a man, I have put away childish things
15. 25. he must reign, till he hath put all his enemies
under his feet. 27 ; Eph. 1. 22 ; Heb. 2. 8
53. this corruptible must put on incorruption, and this
mortal must put on immortality. 54
Gal. 3. 27. as were baptized into Christ did put on Christ
Eph. 4. 24. p. on the new man, which after God hath been
31. and railing, be put away from you   [created
6. 11. Put on the whole armour of God, that ye may
Col. 3. 8. put ye also away all these ; anger, wrath, malice
9. seeing that ye have put off the old man. Eph. 4. 22
10. and have put on the new man, which is being
12. Put on therefore, as God's elect, holy and beloved
14. and above all these things put on love   [things
1 Tim. 4. 6. If thou put the brethren in mind of these
2 Tim. 1. 6. For the which cause I p. thee in remembrance
2. 14. Of these things put them in remembrance
Tit. 3. 1. Put them in mind to be in subjection to rulers
Philem. 18. or oweth thee aught, put that to mine account
Heb. 2. 13. And again, I will put my trust in him
6. 6. Son of God afresh, and put him to an open shame
8. 10. I will put my laws into their mind. 10. 16
9. 26. to put away sin by the sacrifice of himself
Jas. 3. 3. we put the horses' bridles into their mouths
1 Pet. 2. 15. put to silence the ignorance of foolish men
2 Pet. 1. 12. always to put you in remembrance. Jude 5
Rev. 17. 17. God did put in their hearts to do his mind
see abolished, arrayed, cast, delivered, entrusted, laid, laying, leave,
loose, made, putteth, putting, set, stretched, subject—ed—ion, thrust.

Putteth.—*A.V.* ¹maketh, ²put, ³setteth, ⁴shooteth.

Mat. 5. 32. every one that ²putteth away his wife. 19. 18
9. 16. no man p. a piece of undressed cloth. Lu. 5. 36
24. 32. and putteth forth its leaves, ye know. Mk. 13. 28
Mk. 2. 22. putteth new wine into old wine-skins. Lu. 5. 37
4. 29. he p. forth the sickle, because the harvest is come
32. greater than all the herbs, and ⁴p. out great branches
Lu. 8. 16. or putteth it under a bed ; but ³p. it on a stand
11. 33. when he hath lighted a lamp, putteth it in a cellar
Rom. 5. 5. and hope ¹putteth not to shame   [Titus
2 Cor. 8. 16. ²p. the same earnest care—into the heart of
see put.

Putting.—*A.V.* ¹launched, ²lay apart, ³laying, ⁴put.

Acts 19. 33. the Jews p. him forward. And Alexander
27. 4. but ¹putting to sea from thence, we sailed under
Rom. 15. 15. as p. you again in remembrance, because of
Eph. 4. 25. putting away falsehood, speak ye truth each one
Col. 2. 11. in the putting off of the body of the flesh
1 Th. 5. 8. putting on the breastplate of faith and love
Jas. 1. 21. Wherefore ²putting away all filthiness

262

PUTTING

1 *Pet.* 2. 1. ⁸*Putting* away therefore all wickedness
3. 3. wearing jewels of gold, or of *putting* on apparel
21. not the *putting* away of the filth of the flesh
2 *Pet.* 1. 13. to stir you up by *putting* you in remembrance
14. the ⁴*putting* off of my tabernacle cometh swiftly
see appointing, laying.

Q.

Quake.—*A.V.* ¹*shake.*
Mat. 27. 51. the earth did *quake;* and the rocks were rent
28. 4. for fear of him the watchers did ¹*quake*
Heb. 12. 21. that Moses said, I exceedingly fear and *quake*

Quarrel *A V* —*see complaint, set.*

Quarter.
Mk. 1. 45 and they came to him from every *quarter*

Quarters *A.V.*—*see corners, neighbourhood, parts.*

Quaternions
Acts 12. 4. and delivered him to four *q.* of soldiers

Queen.
Mat. 12. 42. *q.* of the south shall rise up in the judgement.
Acts 8. 27. Candace, *queen* of the Ethiopians [*Lu.* 11. 31
Rev. 18. 7. in her heart, I sit a *queen*, and am no widow

Quench—**ed.**
Mat. 12. 20. And smoking flax shall he not *quench*
Mk. 9. 48. worm dieth not, and the fire is not *quenched*
Eph. 6 16. able to *quench* all the fiery darts of the evil one
1 *Th.* 5. 19. *Quench* not the Spirit
Heb. 11. 34. *quenched* the power of fire, escaped the edge
see unquenchable.

Question—**s.**—*A.V.* ¹*enquire,* ²*question,* ³*thing.*
Mat. 21. 24. Jesus answered—I also will ask you one
⁸*question. Mk.* 11. 29 ; *Lu.* 20. ³3
22. 35. a lawyer, asked him a *question*, tempting him
41 Pharisees—gathered together, Jesus asked them a *q*
46 from that day forth ask him any more *q. Mk.* 12. 34 :
Mk. 8. 11. Pharisees came forth, and began to *q.* [*Lu.* 20. 40
9. 16 And he asked them, What *question* ye with them?
Lu. 2. 46. doctors, both hearing them, and asking them *q.*
22. 23. they began to ¹*q.* among themselves, which of them
Acts 15. 2. unto the apostles and elders about this *question*
18. 15. if they are ²*questions* about words and names
23. 6 resurrection of the dead I am called in *q.* 24. 21
29. I found to be accused about *questions* of their law
25. 19. certain *questions* against him of their own religion
26. 3. because thou art expert in all customs and *questions*
1 *Cor.* 10. 25. eat, asking no *question* for conscience sake. 27
see accused, inquire, questioned, questionings, these things.

Questioned—**ing**—**s.**—*A.V.* ¹*disputation,* ²*disputing,*
³*question*—*s,* ⁴*reasoned,* ⁵*reasoning.*
Mk. 1. 27. *q.* among themselves, saying, What is this?
9. 10. *q.* among themselves what the rising again
14. multitude about them, and scribes *q.* with them
12. 28. one of the scribes came, and heard them ⁵*q.*
Lu. 23. 9. And he [Herod] *q.* him [Jesus] in many words

QUIT

Lu. 24. 15. while they communed and ⁴*questioned* together
Jno. 3. 25. a ³*q.* on the part of John's disciples with a Jew
Acts 15. 2. Paul and Barnabas had—dissension and ¹*q.*
7. when there had been much ²*questioning,* Peter rose
1 *Tim.* 1. 4. minister ³*q.,* rather than a dispensation of God
6. 4. but doting about ²*questionings* and disputes
2. *Tim.* 2. 23. foolish and ignorant ³*q.* refuse. *Tit.* 3. ⁸9

Quick.
Acts 10. 42. to be the Judge of *quick* and dead
2 *Tim.* 4. 1. Jesus, who shall judge the *quick* and the dead
Heb. 4. 12. and *quick* to discern the thoughts and intents
1 *Pet.* 4. 5. account to him that is ready to judge the *quick*

Quicken—**ed.**—*A.V.* ¹*quickened.*
Rom. 8. 11. shall *q.* also your—bodies through his Spirit
1 *Cor.* 15. 36. thyself sowest is not *quickened,* except it die
Eph. 2. 1. And you did he ¹*quicken,* when ye were dead
5. *quickened* us together with Christ. *Col.* 2. ¹13
1 *Pet.* 3 18. put to death in the flesh, but *q.* in the spirit

Quickeneth.
Jno. 5. 21. *q.* them, even so the Son also *q.* whom he will
6. 63. the spirit that *q.*; the flesh profiteth nothing
Rom. 4. 17. believed, even God, who *quickeneth* the dead
1 *Tim.* 6. 13. in the sight of God, who *quickeneth* all things

Quickening *A.V.*—*see lifegiving.*

Quickly.—*A.V.* ¹*hastily,* ²*lightly,* ³*soon*
Mat. 5 25. Agree with thine adversary *quickly*
28. 7. go *quickly*, and tell his disciples, He is risen
8. they departed *quickly* from the tomb with fear
Mk. 9. 39. my name, and be able ²*q.* to speak evil of me
Lu. 14. 21. Go out *quickly* into the streets and lanes
16. 6. Take thy bond, and sit down *q.* and write fifty
Jno. 11. 29. when she heard it, arose *q.,* and went unto. ¹31
13. 27. Jesus—saith unto him, That thou doest, do *q.*
Acts 12. 7. saying, Rise up *quickly.* And his chains fell off
22. 18. Make haste, and get thee *q.* out of Jerusalem
Gal. 1. 6. I marvel that ye are so ³*quickly* removing
2 *Th.* 2. 2. to the end that ye be not ³*quickly* shaken
Rev. 2. 16. Repent therefore ; or else I come to thee *q.*
22. 20. Yea : I come *q.*—come, Lord Jesus. 3. 11 : 22. 7, 12

Quicksands.—*see Syrtis, proper names.*

Quiet—**ed.**—*A.V.* ¹*appeased,* ²*silence.*
Acts 19. 36. when the townclerk had ¹*q.* the multitude
36. we ought to be *quiet*, and to do nothing rash
22. 2. in the Hebrew language, they were the more ²*q.*
1 *Th.* 4. 11. study to be *quiet*, and to do your own business
1 *Tim.* 2. 2. that we may lead a tranquil and *quiet* life
1 *Pet.* 3. 4. incorruptible apparel of a meek and *q.* spirit

Quietness.—*A.V.* ¹*silence.*
2 *Th.* 3. 12. that with *quietness* they work, and eat
1 *Tim.* 2. 11. Let a woman learn in ¹*q.* with all subjection
12. nor to have dominion over a man, but to be in ¹*q.*
see peace.

Quit.—*A.V.* ¹*delivered.*
Lu. 12. 58. on the way give diligence to be ¹*quit* of him
1 *Cor.* 16. 13. Watch ye—*quit* you like men, be strong

RABBI

R.

Rabbi—Rabboni.—*see proper names.*

Rabble.—*A.V.* ^{1}*baser sort.*
Acts 17. 5. took unto them certain vile fellows of the ^{1}r.

Raca.
Mat. 5. 22. whosoever shall say to his brother, *Raca*

Race.—*A.V.* ^{1}*born,* ^{2}*generation,* ^{3}*kindred,* ^{4}*nation.*
Mk. 7. 26. woman was a Greek, a Syrophœnician by ^{4}*race*
Acts 7. 13. Joseph's ^{3}*race* became manifest unto Pharaoh
19. The same dealt subtilly with our ^{3}*race*
18. 24. certain Jew named Apollos, an Alexandrian by ^{1}r.
1 *Cor.* 9. 24. which run in a *race* run all, but one receiveth
Heb. 12. 1. run with patience the *race* that is set before us
1 *Pet.* 2. 9. But ye are an elect ^{3}*race,* a royal priesthood

Rage.
Acts 4. 25. Why did the Gentiles *rage,* And the peoples

Raging.
Lu. 8. 24. rebuked the wind and the *raging* of the water
see wild.

Rail.—*A.V.* ^{1}*speak evil.*
2 *Pet.* 2. 10. they tremble not to ^{1}*rail* at dignities
Jude 8. set at nought dominion, and ^{1}*rail* at dignities
10. these ^{1}*rail* at whatsoever things they know not

Railed.—*A.V.* ^{1}*reviled.*
Mat. 27. 39. they that passed by ^{1}*railed* on him. *Mk.* 15. 29
Lu. 23. 39. malefactors which were hanged *railed* on him

Railer *A.V.*—*see reviler.*

Railers.—*A.V.* ^{1}*blasphemers.*
2 *Tim.* 3. 2. shall be lovers of self—boastful, haughty, ^{1}r.

Railing—s.—*A.V.* ^{1}*blasphemy—ies,* ^{2}*evil speaking,* ^{3}*speak evil.*
Mat. 15. 19. out of the heart come—thefts, false witness, ^{1}r.
Mk. 7. 22. an evil eye, ^{1}*railing,* pride, foolishness
Eph. 4. 31. wrath, and anger, and clamour, and ^{2}r., be put
Col. 3. 8. ^{1}*railing,* shameful speaking out of your mouth
1 *Tim.* 6. 4. whereof cometh envy, strife, *railings,* evil
2 *Pet.* 2. 11. angels—bring not a r. judgement against them
12. ^{3}*railing* in matters whereof they are ignorant
Jude 9. durst not bring against him a *railing* judgement
see reviling.

Raiment.—*A.V.* ^{1}*array,* ^{2}*clothing.*
Mat. 3. 4. John himself had his *raiment* of camel's hair
6. 25. than the food, and the body than the r. ? *Lu.* 12. 23
28. why are ye anxious concerning *raiment* ? Consider
11. 8. clothed in soft r. ?—they that wear soft ^{2}r. *Lu.* 7. 25
28. 3. as lightning, and his *raiment* white as snow
Lu. 9. 29. and his *raiment* became white and dazzling
Acts 18. 6. he shook out his *raiment,* and said unto them
1 *Tim.* 2. 9. braided hair, and gold or pearls or costly ^{1}r.
see clothing, covering, garments.

RAISED

Rain—s.—*A.V.* ^{1}*rain.*
Mat. 5. 45. sendeth *rain* on the just and the unjust
7. 25. the *rain* descended, and the floods came. 27
Acts 14. 17. gave you from heaven ^{1}r. and fruitful seasons
28. 2. and received us all, because of the present *rain*
Heb. 6. 7. the land which hath drunk the *rain* that cometh
Jas. 5. 17. Elijah—prayed fervently that it might not *rain*
18. [Elijah] prayed again ; and the heaven gave *rain*
Rev. 11. 6. that it r. not during the days of their prophecy

Rainbow.
Rev. 4. 3. there was a *rainbow* round about the throne
10. 1. and the *rainbow* was upon his head

Rained.
Lu. 17. 29. Sodom it r. fire and brimstone from heaven
Jas. 5. 17. and it *rained* not on the earth for three years

Raise.—*A.V.* ^{1}*add,* ^{2}*raised,* ^{3}*rear.*
Mat. 3. 9. to *raise* up children unto Abraham. *Lu.* 3. 8
10. 8. Heal the sick, *raise* the dead, cleanse the lepers
22. 24. his brother shall marry his wife, and *raise* up
seed unto his brother, *Mk.* 12. 19 : *Lu.* 20. 28
Jno. 2. 19. this temple, and in three days I will r. it up. ^{3}20
6. 40. I will *raise* him up at the last day. 39, 44, 54
Acts 2. 32. This Jesus did God ^{2}*raise* up, whereof we all
3. 22. A prophet shall the Lord God *raise* up. 7. 37
26 8. incredible with you, if God doth *raise* the dead ?
Rom. 9. 17. For this very purpose did I ^{2}*raise* thee up
1 *Cor.* 6. 14. and will *raise* up us through his power
2 *Cor.* 4. 14. the Lord Jesus shall *raise* up us also with Jesus
Phil. 1. 17. thinking to ^{1}r. up affliction for me in my bonds
Heb. 11. 19. accounting that God is able to *raise* up
Jas. 5. 15. him that is sick, and the Lord shall *raise* him up
see rose.

Raised.—*A.V.* ^{1}*arose,* ^{2}*lift—ed,* ^{3}*rise—n,* ^{4}*rose,* ^{5}*took.*
Mat. 11. 5. deaf hear, and the dead are r. up. *Lu.* 7. 22
16. 21. the third day be *raised* up, 17. 23 : 20. ^{3}19 : *Lu.* 9. 22
26. 32. But after I am ^{3}*raised* up, I will go before you
27. 52. bodies of the saints that had fallen asleep were ^{1}r.
Mk. 1. 31. took her by the hand, and ^{2}*raised* her up
9. 27. Jesus took him by the hand and ^{2}*raised* him up
12. 26. But as touching the dead, that they are ^{3}*raised*
Lu. 1. 69. And hath *raised* up a horn of salvation for us
20. 37. But that the dead are *raised,* even Moses shewed
Jno. 2. 22. When therefore he was ^{3}*raised* from the dead
12. 1. whom Jesus *raised* from the dead. 9, 17
Acts 2. 24. whom God *raised* up. 3. 15, 26 : 4. 10 : 5. 30 :
10. 40 : 13. 30, 33, 34, 37 : 17. 31 : *Rom.* 10. 9 : 1
Cor. 6. 14 : 2 *Cor.* 4. 14 : *Gal.* 1. 1 : *Eph.* 1. 20 : 1
Th. 1. 10 : 1 *Pet.* 1. 21
3. 7. [Peter] took him by the right hand, and ^{2}r. him up
10. 26. But Peter ^{5}*raised* him up, saying, Stand up
13. 22. he *raised* up David to be their king
Rom. 4. 24. who believe on him that *raised* Jesus our Lord
25. and was *raised* for our justification
6. 4. that like as Christ was *raised* from the dead
9. Christ being *raised* from the dead dieth no more
4. joined to another, even to him who was *raised*
8. 11. Spirit of him that *raised* up Jesus—r. up Christ
34. yea rather, that was ^{3}*raised* from the dead
1 *Cor.* 15. 4. that he hath been ^{4}*raised* on the third day
12. if Christ is preached that he hath been ^{4}*raised*
13. no resurrection—neither hath Christ been ^{3}*raised*
14. if Christ hath not been ^{3}*raised,* then is our preaching

RAISED

1 *Cor.* 15. 15. of God that he *raised* up Christ; whom he raised not up, if so be that the dead are not ⁸*raised*
16. if the dead are not ³*r* , neither hath Christ been *r.*
17. if Christ hath not been *raised*, your faith is vain
20. Christ been ⁸*raised* from the dead, the firstfruits
35. some one will say, How are the dead *raised ?*
42. sown in corruption; it is *raised* in incorruption
43. it is *raised* in glory—it is *raised* in power
44. sown a natural body; it is *raised* a spiritual body
52. the dead shall be *raised* incorruptible
Eph. 2. 6. *raised* us up with him, and made us to sit
Col. 2. 12. wherein ye were also ⁸*raised*—God, who *r.* him
8. 1. If then ye were ⁸*raised* together with Christ
see arose, awoke, brought, raise, resurrection, risen, stirred.

Raiseth.

Jno. 5. 21. For as the Father *raiseth* the dead [dead
2 *Cor.* 1. 9. not trust in ourselves, but in God which *r.* the

Raising *A.V* —*see stirring.*

Ran.—*A. V.* ¹*run*, ²*running.*

Mat. 27. 48. one of them *ran*, and took a sponge. *Mk.* 15. 36
28. 8. [women] ¹*ran* to bring his disciples word
Mk. 6. 33. many knew them, and they *ran* there together
55. and *ran* round about that whole region
10. 17. there ²*ran* one to him, and kneeled to him
Lu. 15. 20. with compassion, and *ran*, and fell on his neck
19. 4. he *r.* on before, and climbed up into a sycamore tree
24. 12. But Peter arose, and *ran* unto the tomb [ciple
Jno. 20. 4. And they *ran* both together: and the other dis-
Acts 3. 11. all the people *r.* together unto them in the porch
8. 30. And Philip *ran* to him, and heard him reading
12. 14. but *r.* in, and told that Peter stood before the gate
21. 30. the people *ran* together; and they laid hold on
32. and centurions, and *ran* down upon them [Paul
27. 41. where two seas met, they *ran* the vessel aground
Jude 11. and *ran* riotously in the error of Balaam for hire
see rushed, sprang.

Ranks.

Mk. 6. 40. And they sat down in *ranks*, by hundreds

Ransom.

Mat. 20. 28. and to give his life a *r.* for many. *Mk.* 10. 45
1 *Tim.* 2. 6. who gave himself a *ransom* for all

Rash.—*A.V.* ¹*rashly.*

Acts 19. 36. ye ought to be quiet, and to do nothing ¹*rash*

. **Rashly** *A.V.*—*see rash.*

Rather.

Mat. 10. 6. but go *r.* to the lost sheep of the house of Israel
28. *rather* fear him which is able to destroy both soul
18. 8. *rather* than having two hands or two feet to be
9. *r.* than having two eyes to be cast into the hell of fire
25. 9. go ye *rather* to them that sell, and buy for yourselves
27. 24. but *rather* that a tumult was arising, he took water
Mk. 5. 26. nothing bettered, but *rather* grew worse
15. 11. that he should *rather* release Barabbas unto them
Lu. 11. 28. Yea *rather*, blessed are they that hear the word
12. 51. I tell you, Nay; but *rather* division [of God
17. 8. and will not *rather* say unto him, Make ready
18. 14. down to his house justified *rather* than the other
Jno. 3. 19. and men loved the darkness *r.* than the light

35

READEST

Acts 5. 29. We must obey God *rather* than men
Rom. 8. 34. Christ Jesus that died, yea *r.*, that was raised
14. 13. but judge ye this *r.*, that no man put a stumbling-
1 *Cor.* 5. 2. ye are puffed up, and did not *r.* mourn [block
6. 7. Why not *r.* take wrong ? why not *r.* be defrauded ?
7. 21. but if thou canst become free, use it *rather*
14. 1. spiritual gifts, but *rather* that ye may prophesy
19. I had *r.* speak five words with my understanding
2 *Cor.* 2. 7. ye should *rather* forgive him and comfort him
3. 8. how shall not *r.* the ministration of the spirit be
5. 8. and are willing *rather* to be absent from the body
12. 9. therefore will I *rather* glory in my weaknesses
Gal. 4. 9. come to know God, or *rather* to be known of God
Eph. 4. 28. steal no more: but *rather* let him labour
5. 4. which are not befitting: but *rather* giving of thanks
11. works of darkness, but *rather* even reprove them
Phil. 1. 12. have fallen out *r.* unto the progress of the gospel
1 *Tim.* 1. 4. *r.* than a dispensation of God which is in faith
6. 2. but let them serve them the *rather*, because they
Philem. 9. yet for love's sake I *rather* beseech [of God
Heb. 11. 25. choosing *r.* to be evil entreated with the people
12. 9. shall we not much *rather* be in subjection unto the
13. turned out of the way, but *rather* be healed [Father
see exceedingly, howbeit.

Ravening.

Mat. 7. 15. sheep's clothing, but inwardly are *r.* wolves
see extortion.

Ravens.

Lu. 12. 24. Consider the *ravens*, that they sow not

Reach.—*A.V.* ¹*attain.*

Jno. 20. 27. *R.* hither thy finger—and *r.* hither thy hand
Acts 27. 12. if by any means they could ¹*reach* Phœnix
2 *Cor.* 10. 13. to us as a measure, to *reach* even unto you

Reached.

2 *Cor.* 10. 14. as though we *reached* not unto you
Rev. 18. 5. for her sins have *reached* even unto heaven
see stretch.

Reaching.—*A.V.* ¹*coveted.*

1 *Tim.* 6. 10. which some ¹*r.* after have been led astray
see stretching.

Read.

Mat. 12. 3. Have ye not *read.* 5. 19. 4 : 21. 16, 42 : 22. 31 :
Mk. 2. 25 : 12. 10, 26 : *Lu.* 6. 3
Lu. 4. 16. on the sabbath day, and stood up to *read*
Jno. 19. 20. This title therefore *read* many of the Jews
Acts 13. 27. prophets which are *read* every sabbath. 15. 21
15. 31. And when they had *read* it, they rejoiced [was
23. 34. when he had *r.* it, he asked of what province he
2 *Cor.* 1. 13. none other things unto you, than what ye *r.*
3. 2. written in our hearts, known and *read* of all men
15. whensoever Moses is *r.*, a veil lieth upon their heart
Eph. 3. 4. whereby, when ye *read*, ye can perceive
Col. 4. 16. when this epistle hath been *read*—cause that
it be *read* also—and that ye also *read* the epistle
1 *Th.* 5. 27. this epistle be *read* unto all the brethren
see reading.

Readest-**eth.**

Mat. 24. 15. (let him that *readeth* understand). *Mk.* 13. 14
Lu. 10. 26. What is written in the law? how *readest* thou?
Acts 8. 30. Understandest thou what thou *readest ?*
Rev. 1. 3. Blessed is he that *readeth*, and they that hear

265

READINESS

Readiness.—*A.V.* ¹*forwardness,* ²*ready mind,* ³*willing mind.*

Acts 17. 11. they received the word with all *r.* of mind
2 *Cor.* 8. 11. that as there was the *r.* to will, so there may
    12. if the ³*readiness* is there, it is acceptable according
    19. to the glory of the Lord, and to shew our ²*readiness*
  9. 2. I know your ¹*readiness,* of which I glory
  10. 6. and being in *readiness* to avenge all disobedience

Reading.—*A.V.* ¹*read.*

Acts 8. 28. and was ¹*reading* the prophet Isaiah. ¹30, ¹32
  13. 15. And after the *reading* of the law and the prophets
2 *Cor.* 3. 14. this very day at the *reading* of the old covenant
1 *Tim.* 4. 13. Till I come, give heed to *reading*

Ready.—*A.V.* ¹*negligent,* ²*prepare—d.*

Mat. 3. 3. Make ye ²*ready* the way of the Lord. *Mk.* 1. ²3 : *Lu.* 1. ²76 : 3. ²4
  22. 4. Behold, I have made ²*ready* my dinner—all things are *ready* : come to the marriage feast. *Lu.* 14. 17
  8. The wedding is *ready,* but they that were bidden
  24. 44. Therefore be ye also *ready. Lu.* 12. 40
  25. 10. they that were *r.* went in with him to the marriage
  26. 17. Where wilt thou that we make ²*r. Mk.* 14. ²12 : *Lu.* 19. made *r.* the passover. *Mk.*14. 16: *Lu.*22. 13 [22. ²8, ²9
Mk. 14. 15. he will—shew you a large upper room furnished and ²*ready* : and there make *r.* for us. *Lu.* 22. 12
Lu. 1. 17. to make *ready* for the Lord a people prepared
  9. 52. village of the Samaritans, to make *ready* for him
  12. 47. which knew his lord's will, and made not ²*ready*
  17. 8. say unto him, Make *ready* wherewith I may sup
  22. 33. Lord, with thee I am *r.* to go both to prison and
Jno. 7. 6. not yet come; but your time is alway *ready*
Acts 10. 10. while they made *ready,* he fell into a trance
  21. 13. for I am *r.* not to be bound only, but also to die
  23. 15. or ever he come near, are *ready* to slay him
  21. now are they *r.,* looking for the promise from thee
  23. Make *r.* two hundred soldiers to go as far as Cæsarea
Rom. 1. 15. I am *ready* to preach the gospel to you also
2 *Cor.* 9. 5. that the same might be *r.,* as a matter of bounty
  12. 14. this is the third time I am *ready* to come to you
1 *Tim.* 6. 18. in good works, that they be *r.* to distribute
Tit. 3. 1. to be *ready* unto every good work
1 *Pet.* 1. 5. a salvation *r.* to be revealed in the last time
  3. 15. being *ready* always to give answer to every man
  4. 5. to him that is *ready* to judge the quick and the dead
  5. 2. nor yet for filthy lucre, but of a *ready* mind
2 *Pet.* 1. 12. I shall be ¹*r.* always to put you in remembrance
Rev. 3. 2. the things that remain, which were *ready* to die
  16. 12. that the way might be made ²*ready* for the kings
  19. 7. and his wife hath made herself *ready*
  21. 2. made ²*ready* as a bride adorned for her husband
see about, already, nigh, point, prepared, readiness, willing.

Reap.

Mat. 6. 26. they sow not, neither do they *reap. Lu.* 12. 24
  25. 26. thou knewest that I *reap* where I sowed not
Jno. 4. 38. to *reap* that whereon ye have not laboured
1 *Cor.* 9. 11. is it a great matter if we shall *r.* your carnal
2 *Cor.*9. 6. He that soweth sparingly shall *r.* also sparingly;
    —soweth bountifully shall *reap* also bountifully
Gal. 6. 7. whatsoever a man soweth, that shall he also *r.*
  8. his own flesh shall of the flesh *reap* corruption;
    —soweth unto the Spirit shall of the Spirit *reap*
  9. for in due season we shall *reap,* if we faint not
Rev. 14. 15. sickle, and *reap* : for the hour to *reap* is come

REASONING

Reaped.

Jas. 5. 4. cries of them that *r.* have entered into the ears
*Rev.*14. 16. his sickle upon the earth; and the earth was *r.*

Reapers.

Mat. 13. 30. I will say to the *r.,* Gather up first the tares
  39. harvest is the end of the world; and the *r.* are angels

Reapest—eth.

Lu. 19. 21. and *reapest* that thou didst not sow
Jno. 4. 36. He that *reapeth* receiveth wages—he that soweth and he that *reapeth* may rejoice together
  37. One soweth, and another *reapeth*

Reaping.

Mat. 25. 24. *reaping* where thou didst not sow. *Lu.* 19. 22

Rear *A.V.*—*see raise.*

Reason.—*A.V.* ¹*brute,* ²*means.*

Mat. 16. 8. why *reason* ye among yourselves. *Mk.* 8. 17
Lu. 5. 21. And the scribes and the Pharisees began to *r.*
  22. What *reason* ye in your hearts? *Mk.* 2. 8
Jno. 6. 18. And the sea was rising by *r.* of a great wind
  12. 11. because that by *r.* of him many of the Jews went
*Acts*18. 14. O ye Jews, *r.* would that I should bear with you
  26. 3. a viper came out by *reason* of the heat
Rom. 8. 20. but by *reason* of him who subjected it
2 *Cor.* 3. 10. by *reason* of the glory that surpasseth
Heb. 5. 3. and by *reason* thereof is bound, as for the people
  12. when by *reason* of the time ye ought to be teachers
  14. who by *reason* of use have their senses exercised
1 *Pet.* 3. 15. asketh you a *reason* concerning the hope
2 *Pet.* 2. 2. by *r.* of whom the way of the truth shall be evil
  12. as creatures without ¹*reason,* born mere animals
*Jude*10. understand naturally, like the creatures without¹*r.*
Rev. 8. 13. by *reason* of the other voices of the trumpet
  9. 2. sun and the air were darkened by *r.* of the smoke
  13. 14. dwell on the earth by ²*reason* of the signs
  18. 19. had their ships in the sea by *r.* of her costliness 1
    see fit.

Reasonable.

Rom. 12. 1. which is your *reasonable* service

Reasoned.—*A.V.* ¹*disputed,* ²*mused,* ³*thought.*

Mat. 16. 7. And they *reasoned* among themselves. 21. 25: *Mk.* 11. 31: *Lu.* 20. 5
Mk. 2. 8. perceiving in his spirit that they so *reasoned*
  8. 16. they *reasoned* one with another. *Lu.* 20. 14
Lu. 3. 15. all men ²*r.* in their hearts concerning John
  12. 17. he ³*r.* within himself, saying, What shall I do
Acts 17. 2. sabbath days *r.* with them from the scriptures
  17. So he ¹*r.* in the synagogue with the Jews. 18. 4, 19
  24. 25. And as he *reasoned* of righteousness
    see questioned—ing.

Reasoneth.—*A.V.* ¹*speaketh.*

Heb. 12. 5. which ¹*reasoneth* with you as with sons

Reasoning—s.—*A.V.* ¹*disputed—ing,* ²*imaginations,* ³*thought—s.*

Mk. 2. 6. scribes sitting there, and *reasoning* in their hearts
  9. 33. What were ye ¹*reasoning* in the way?
Lu. 5. 22. But Jesus perceiving their ³*reasonings,* answered
  9. 46. And there arose a *reasoning* among them

REASONING

Lu. 9. 47. when Jesus saw the ²*reasoning* of their heart
24. 38. wherefore do ²*reasonings* arise in your heart?
Acts 19. 8. three months, ¹*reasoning* and persuading
9. separated the disciples, ¹*reasoning* daily in the school
Rom. 1. 21. but became vain in their ²*reasonings*
1 *Cor.* 3. 20. The Lord knoweth the ²*reasonings* of the wise
see questioning.

Rebuke.

Mat. 16. 22. and began to *rebuke* him, saying. *Mk.* 8. 32
Lu. 17. 3. if thy brother sin, *rebuke* him ; and if he repent
19. 39. Pharisees—said unto him, Master, *r.* thy disciples
1 *Tim.* 5. 1. Rebuke not an elder, but exhort him
2 *Tim.* 4. 2. reprove, *rebuke*, exhort, with all longsuffering

Rebuked.—*A.V.* ¹*charged*.

Mat. 8. 26. and *r.* the winds and the sea. *Mk.* 4. 39: *Lu.* 8. 24
17. 18. And Jesus *r.* him. *Mk.* 1. 25: 9. 25: *Lu.* 4. 35: 9. 42
19. 13. and the disciples *r.* them. *Mk.* 10. 13: *Lu.* 18. 15
20. 31. And the multitude *rebuked* them
Mk. 8. 33. *rebuked* Peter, and saith, Get thee behind me
10. 48. many ¹*r.* him, that he should hold his peace. *Lu.*
Lu. 4. 39. And he stood over her, and *r.* the fever [18. 39
9. 55. But he turned, and *rebuked* them
2 *Pet.* 2. 16. but he was *rebuked* for his own transgression
see rebuking, reproved.

Rebuking.—*A.V.* ¹*rebuked*.

Lu. 4. 41. And *r.* them, he suffered them not to speak
23. 40. and ¹*r.* him said, Dost thou not even fear God

Receipt *A.V.*—*see toll.*

Receive.—*A.V.* ¹*obtain*, ²*received*, ³*take*.

Mat. 10. 14. whosoever—not *r.* you. *Mk.* 6. 11: *Lu.* 9. 5: 10. 10
41. prophet shall *receive* a prophet's reward—righteous man shall *receive* a righteous man's reward
11. 5. the blind *receive* their sight, and the lame walk
14. if ye are willing to *receive* it, this is Elijah
17. 25. from whom do they ²*receive* toll or tribute ? [9. 48
18. 5. whoso shall *r.* one such little child. *Mk.* 9. 37: *Lu.*
19. 11. All men cannot *r.* this saying, but they to whom
12. He that is able to *receive* it, let him *receive* it
29. my name's sake, shall *r.* a hundredfold. *Mk.* 10. 30
20. 10. they supposed that they would ²*receive* more
21. 22. whatsoever ye shall ask in prayer—ye shall *r.*
34. sent his servants—to *receive* his fruits. *Mk.* 12. 2
Mk. 10. 15. Whosoever shall not *receive* the kingdom of God as a little child. *Lu.* 18. 17
51. Rabboni, that I may *receive* my sight. *Lu.* 18. 41
12. 40. those shall *r.* greater condemnation. *Lu.* 20. 47
Lu. 6. 34. lend to them of whom ye hope to *r.*—to *r.* again
8. 13. they have heard, *r.* the word with joy. *Mk.* 4. 16
9. 48. whosoever shall *r.* me receiveth him that sent me
53. they did not *receive* him, because his face was as
10. 8. into whatsoever city ye enter, and they *receive* you
16. 4. of the stewardship, they may *r.* me into their houses
9. they may *receive* you into the eternal tabernacles
18. 30. who shall not *receive* manifold more in this time
42. *Receive* thy sight. *Acts* 22. 13
19. 12. into a far country, to *r.* for himself a kingdom
23. 41. we *r.* the due reward of our deeds : but this man
Jno. 3. 11. we have seen ; and ye *receive* not our witness
27. A man can *r.* nothing, except it have been given him
5. 34. But the witness which I *receive* is not from man
41. I *receive* not glory from men

RECEIVE

Jno. 5. 43. Father's name, and ye *r.* me not—him ye will *r.*
44. How can ye believe, which *r.* glory one of another
6. 21. They were willing therefore to ²*r.* him into the boat
7. 39. Spirit, which they that believed on him were to *r.*
14. 3. I come again, and will *receive* you unto myself
17. even the Spirit of truth : whom the world cannot *r.*
16. 24. ask, and ye shall *r.*, that your joy may be fulfilled
20. 22. saith unto them, *Receive* ye the Holy Ghost
Acts 1. 8. ye shall *r.* power, when the Holy Ghost is come
2. 38. and ye shall *receive* the gift of the Holy Ghost
3. 5. gave heed unto them, expecting to *r.* something
21. whom the heaven must *receive* until the times of
7. 59. and saying, Lord Jesus, *receive* my spirit
8. 15. prayed for them, that they might *r.* the Holy Ghost
19. I lay my hands, he may *receive* the Holy Ghost
9. 12. laying his hands on him, that he might *r.* his sight. 17
10. 43. believeth on him shall *r.* remission of sins. 26. 18
16. 21. set forth customs which it is not lawful for us to *r.*
19. 27. encouraged him, and wrote to the disciples to *r.* him
19. 2. Did ye ²*receive* the Holy Ghost when ye believed ?
20. 35. It is more blessed to give than to *receive*
22. 18. they will not *r.* of thee testimony concerning me
Rom. 5. 17. much more shall they that *r.* the abundance
13. 2. they that withstand shall *r.* to themselves judgement
14. 1. But him that is weak in faith *receive* ye
15. 7. *r.* ye one another, even as Christ also received you
16. 2. that ye *r.* her in the Lord, worthily of the saints
1 *Cor.* 3. 8. but each shall *r.* his own reward according to
14. abide which he built thereon, he shall *r.* a reward
4. 7. that thou didst not *r. ?* but if thou didst *receive* it
9. 25. they do it to ¹*receive* a corruptible crown
14. 5. except he interpret, that the church may *r.* edifying
2 *Cor.* 5. 10. that each one may *r.* the things done in the body
6. 1. intreat also that ye *r.* not the grace of God in vain
17. touch no unclean thing ; And I will *receive* you
11. 4. or if ye *r.* a different spirit, which ye did not ²*r.*
16. yet as foolish *r.* me, that I also may glory a little
Gal. 1. 12. neither did I ²*r.* it from man, nor was I taught it
3. 14. that we might *r.* the promise of the Spirit through
4. 5. that we might *r.* the adoption of sons [the Lord
Eph. 6. 8. each one doeth, the same shall he *r.* again from
Phil. 2. 29. *Receive* him therefore in the Lord with all joy
Col. 3. 24. from the Lord ye shall *receive* the recompense
25. shall *receive* again for the wrong that he hath done
4. 10. and Mark—if he come unto you, *receive* him)
1 *Tim.* 5. 19. Against an elder *receive* not an accusation
Philem. 17. If then thou countest me a partner, *r.* him as
Heb. 4. 16. that we may ¹*receive* mercy, and may find grace
7. 5. sons of Levi that *r.* the priest's office have commandment
8. and here men that die *receive* tithes
9. 15. *r.* the promise of the eternal inheritance. 10. 36
11. 8. a place which he was to *receive* for an inheritance
19. from whence he did also in a parable ²*r.* him back
Jas. 1. 7. think that he shall *receive* anything of the Lord
12. been approved, he shall *receive* the crown of life
21. *receive* with meekness the implanted word
3. 1. knowing that we shall *receive* heavier judgement
4. 3. Ye ask, and *receive* not, because ye ask amiss
5. 7. patient over it, until it *r.* the early and latter rain
1 *Pet.* 5. 4. ye shall *receive* the crown of glory
1 *Jno.* 3. 22. and whatsoever we ask, we *receive* of him
2 *Jno.* 10. and bringeth not this teaching, *receive* him not
3 *Jno.* 10. neither doth he himself *receive* the brethren
Rev. 4. 11. Worthy art thou, our Lord and our God, to *receive* the glory and the honour [the power
5. 12. Worthy is the Lamb that hath been slain to *receive*
17. 12. but they *r.* authority as kings, with the beast
18. 4. her sins, and that ye *receive* not of her plagues
see accept, given, have, open, receiveth, suffer, welcome

RECEIVED

Received.—*A.V.* ¹*heard,* ²*obtained,* ³*strike,* ⁴*taken,* ⁵*took.*
Mat. 6. 2. They have *received* their reward. 5, 16
10. 8. freely ye *received,* freely give
17. 24. they that *received* the half-shekel came to Peter
20. 9. they *received* every man a penny. 10
11. And when they *received* it, they murmured against
34. and straightway they *received* their sight
25. 16. *received* the five talents went and traded with
17. that *received* the two gained other two. 22 ' them. 20
18. he that *received* the one went away and digged. 24
27. I should have *received* back mine own with interest
Mk. 7. 4. things there be, which they have *received* to hold
10. 52. And straightway he *received* his sight. *Lu.* 18. 43
14. 65. the officers ⁵*r.* him with blows of their hands
15. 23. wine mingled with myrrh : but he *received* it not
16. 19. was *r.* up into heaven, and sat down at the right
Lu. 2. 28. then he ⁵*received* him into his arms [hand
6. 24. rich ! for ye have *received* your consolation
9. 51. *r.* up, he stedfastly set his face to go to Jerusalem
10. 38. Martha *received* him into her house
15. 27. because he hath *received* him safe and sound
19. 6. and came down, and *received* him joyfully
15. he was come back again, having *r.* the kingdom
22. 17. he ⁵*received* a cup, and when he had given thanks
Jno. 1. 11. and they that were his own *received* him not
12. But as many as *r.* him, to them gave he the right
16. For of his fulness we all *received,* and grace for grace
3. 33. He that hath *r.* his witness hath set his seal to this
4. 45. Galilæans *received* him, having seen all the things
9. 11. so I went away and washed, and I *received* sight
15. Pharisees also asked him how he *received* his sight
18. been blind, and had *received* his sight—called the
parents of him that had *received* his sight
10. 18. This commandment *received* I from my Father
13. 30. He then having *r.* the sop went out straightway
17. 8. I have given unto them ; and they *received* them
18. 3. Judas then, having *received* the band of soldiers
19. 30. When Jesus therefore had *received* the vinegar
Acts 1. 2. until the day in which he was ⁴*received* up. 22
9. and a cloud *received* him out of their sight
11. this Jesus, which was ⁴*r.* up from you into heaven
17. numbered among us, and ⁴*received* his portion
2. 33. and having *received* of the Father the promise
41. They then that *received* his word were baptized
3. 7. his feet and his ankle-bones *received* strength
7. 38. who *received* living oracles to give unto us
53. ye who *r.* the law as it was ordained by angels
8. 14. heard that Samaria had *received* the word of God
17. and they *received* the Holy Ghost
9. 18. *received* his sight ; and he arose and was baptized
10. 16. the vessel was *received* up into heaven
47. which have *received* the Holy Ghost as well as we ?
11. 1. the Gentiles also had *received* the word of God
15. 4. to Jerusalem, they were *received* of the church
16. 24. having *r* such a charge, cast them into—prison
17. 7. whom Jason hath *r. :* and these all act contrary
11. they *received* the word with all readiness of mind
20. 24. and the ministry which I *r.* from the Lord Jesus
21. 17. the brethren *received* us gladly
22. 5. from whom also I *r.* letters unto the brethren
26. 10. having *received* authority from the chief priests
28. 2. for they kindled a fire, and *received* us all
7. Publius ; who *r.* us, and entertained us three days
21. We neither *r.* letters from Judæa concerning thee
30. hired dwelling, and *r.* all that went in unto him
Rom. 1 5. through whom we *r.* grace and apostleship
4. 11. and he *received* the sign of circumcision
5. 11. through whom we have now *r.* the reconciliation

RECEIVETH

Rom. 8. 15. For ye *received* not the spirit of bondage again
unto fear ; but ye *received* the spirit of adoption
14. 3. him that eateth ; for God hath *received* him
15 7. even as Christ also *received* you, to the glory of God
1 *Cor.* 2. 12. But we *received,* not the spirit of the world
4. 7. why dost thou glory, as if thou hadst not *r.* it ?
11. 23. For I *r.* of the Lord that which also I delivered
15. 1. gospel which I preached unto you, which also ye *r.*
3. I delivered unto you first of all that which also I *r.*
2 *Cor.* 7. 15. how with fear and trembling ye *received* him
11. 24. Of the Jews five times *r.* I forty stripes save one
Gal. 1. 9. any gospel other than that which ye *received*
3. 2. *Received* ye the Spirit by the works of the law
4. 14. but ye *received* me as an angel of God
Phil. 4. 9. The things which ye both learned and *received*
18. I am filled, having *received* from Epaphroditus
Col. 2. 6. As therefore ye *received* Christ Jesus the Lord
4. 10. (touching whom ye *received* commandments
17. Take heed to the ministry which thou hast *r.* in
1 *Th.* 1. 6. having *received* the word in much affliction
2. 13. when ye ¹*received* from us the word of the message
4. 1. as ye *received* of us how ye ought to walk
2 *Th.* 2. 10. because they *received* not the love of the truth
3. 6. and not after the tradition which they *received* of us
1 *Tim.* 3. 16. believed on in the world, *received* up in glory
4. 3. abstain from meats, which God created to be *r.*
4. nothing is to be rejected, if it be *r.* with thanksgiving
Heb. 2. 2. disobedience *r.* a just recompense of reward
7. 11. (for under it hath the people *received* the law)
10. 26. sin wilfully after that we have *r.* the knowledge
11. 11. Sarah herself *received* power to conceive seed
13. These all died in faith, not having *r.* the promises
17. he that had gladly *r.* the promises was offering up
31. By faith Rahab—having *r.* the spies with peace
35. Women *received* their dead by a resurrection
39. borne to them through their faith, *r.* not the promise
Jas. 2. 25. Rahab the harlot—*received* the messengers
1 *Pet.* 4. 10. according as each hath *received* a gift [glory
2 *Pet.* 1. 17. For he *r.* from God the Father honour and
1 *Jno.* 2. 27. the anointing which ye *r.* of him abideth in you
2 *Jno.* 4. even as we *r.* commandment from the Father
Rev. 2. 27. as I also have *received* of my Father
3. 3. Remember—how thou hast *received* and didst hear
17. 12. which have *received* no kingdom as yet
19. 20. he deceived them that had *r.* the mark of the beast
20. 4. and *received* not the mark upon their forehead
see accepted, handed, obtained, receive, sown, taken, took, welcome.

Receivedst.
Lu. 16. 25. that thou in thy lifetime *r.* thy good things

Receiveth.—*A.V.* ¹*receive.*
Mat. 7. 8. for every one that asketh *receiveth.* *Lu.* 11. 10
10. 40. He that *r.* you *r.* me, and he that *r.* me *r.* him
that sent me. *Mk.* 9. ¹37 : *Lu.* 9. 48 : *Jno.* 13. 20
41. He that *r.* a prophet—that *r.* a righteous man
13. 20. and straightway with joy *receiveth* it
18. 5. one such little child in my name *receiveth* me
Lu. 15. 2. This man *r.* sinners, and eateth with them
Jno. 3. 32. he beareth witness ; and no man *r.* his witness
4. 36. He that respeth *r.* wages, and gathereth fruit
7. 23. If a man ¹*receiveth* circumcision on the sabbath
12. 48. and *r.* not my sayings, hath one that judgeth him
1 *Cor.* 2. 14. natural man *r.* not the things of the Spirit of
9. 24. in a race run all, but one *r.* the prize ? [God
Heb. 6. 7. sake it is also tilled, *receiveth* blessing from God
7. 9. even Levi, who *receiveth* tithes, hath paid tithes
12. 6. And scourgeth every son whom he *receiveth*

RECEIVETH

3 Jno. 9. to have the preeminence among them, r. us not
Rev. 2. 17. which no one knoweth but he that receiveth it
14. 9. any man—¹receiveth a mark on his forehead
11. and whoso receiveth the mark of his name

Receiving.
Acts 17. 15. and r. a commandment unto Silas and Timothy
Rom. 1. 27. r. in themselves that recompense of—error
11. 15. what shall the receiving of them be, but life
Phil. 4. 15. in the matter of giving and r., but ye only
Heb. 12. 28. receiving a kingdom that cannot be shaken
1 Pet. 1. 9. r. the end of your faith, even the salvation

Reckon.—A.V. ¹conclude, ²impute, ³suppose, ⁴think.
Mat. 18. 24. And when he had begun to reckon
Rom. 3. 28. We ¹r. therefore that a man is justified by faith
4. 8. the man to whom the Lord will not ²reckon sin
6. 11. Even so r. ye also yourselves to be dead unto sin
8. 18. For I r. that the sufferings of this present time
2 Cor. 10. 11. Let such a one ⁴reckon this, that, what we are
11. 5. I ³reckon that I am not a whit behind

Reckoned.—A.V.¹accounted,²called,³counted,⁴imputed.
Lu. 22. 37. And he was reckoned with transgressors
Rom. 2. 26. uncircumcision be ⁴reckoned for circumcision?
4. 3. and it was ³reckoned unto him for righteousness.
⁸5, 9, ⁴22; Gal. 3. ¹⁰; Jas. 2. ⁴23
4. the reward is not reckoned as of grace [cumcision
10. How then was it reckoned? when he was in cir-
11. that righteousness might be ⁴reckoned unto them
23. for his sake alone, that it was ⁴reckoned unto him
24. but for our sake also, unto whom it shall be ⁴r.
9. 8. the children of the promise are ³reckoned for a seed
Heb. 7. 11. not be ²reckoned after the order of Aaron?

Reckonest.—A.V. ¹thinkest.
Rom. 2. 3. And ¹r. thou this, O man, who judgest them

Reckoneth.—A.V. ¹imputeth.
Rom. 4. 6. blessing upon the man, unto whom God ¹r.
see reckoning.

Reckoning.—A.V. ¹account, ²imputing, ³reckoneth.
Mat. 18. 23. which would make a ¹r. with his servants
25. 19. cometh, and maketh a ³reckoning with them
2 Cor. 5. 19. not ²reckoning unto them their trespasses

Reclining.—A.V. ¹leaning.
Jno. 13. 23. There was at the table ¹r. in Jesus' bosom

Recommended A.V.—see commended, committed.

Recompense.—A.V. ¹repay, ²reward.
Mat. 6. 4. thy Father which seeth in secret shall ²r. thee
Lu. 14. 12. bid thee again, and a recompense be made thee
14. because they have not wherewith to recompense thee
Rom. 1. 27. receiving—that r. of their error which was due
11. 9. a stumblingblock, and a recompense unto them
12. 19. I will ¹recompense, saith the Lord. Heb. 10. 30
2 Cor. 6. 13. Now for a recompense in like kind
Col. 3. 24. from the Lord ye shall receive the ²recompense
2 Th. 1. 6. to recompense affliction to them that afflict you
Heb. 2. 2. disobedience received a just recompense of reward
10. 35. boldness, which hath great recompense of reward
11. 26. for he looked unto the recompense of reward
see render.

REDEMPTION

Recompensed.
Lu. 14. 14. thou shalt be r. in the resurrection of the just
Rom. 11. 35. and it shall be recompensed unto him again?

Reconcile.
Eph. 2. 16. and might r. them both in one body unto God
Col. 1. 20. through him to reconcile all things unto himself

Reconciled.
Mat. 5. 24. first be reconciled to thy brother—then come
Rom. 5. 10. while we were enemies, we were reconciled to
God—much more, being r., shall we be saved
1 Cor. 7. 11. remain unmarried, or else be r. to her husband)
2 Cor. 5. 18. who reconciled us to himself through Christ
20. we beseech you—be ye reconciled to God
Col.1. 21. in time past alienated—yet now hath he reconciled

Reconciliation.—A.V. ¹atonement.
Rom. 5. 11. through whom we have now received the ¹r.
2 Cor. 5. 18. and gave unto us the ministry of reconciliation
19. having committed unto us the word of reconciliation
see propitiation.

Reconciling.
Rom. 11. 15. casting away of them is the r. of the world
2 Cor. 5. 19. God was in Christ r. the world unto himself

Record A.V.—see witness, testify.

Recover.—A.V. ¹do well.
Mk. 16. 18. lay hands on the sick, and they shall recover
Jno. 11. 12. Lord, if he is fallen asleep, he will ¹recover
2 Tim. 2. 26. they may recover themselves out of the snare

Recovering.
Lu. 4. 18. And recovering of sight to the blind

Red.
Mat. 16. 2. It will be fair weather; for the heaven is red. 3
Rev. 6. 4. And another horse came forth, a red horse
12. 3. behold, a great red dragon, having seven heads

Redeem.—A.V. ¹redeemed.
Lu. 24. 21. it was he which should ¹redeem Israel
Gal. 4. 5. that he might r. them which were under the law
Tit. 2. 14. that he might redeem us from all iniquity

Redeemed.
Gal. 3. 13. Christ redeemed us from the curse of the law
1 Pet. 1. 18. knowing that ye were redeemed
see purchase, purchased, redeem, redemption.

Redeeming.
Eph. 5. 16. redeeming the time. Col. 4. 5

Redemption.—A.V. ¹redeemed.
Lu. 1. 68. he hath visited and wrought ¹r. for his people
2. 38. all them that were looking for the r. of Jerusalem
21. 28. because your redemption draweth nigh
Rom. 3. 24. justified freely by his grace through the r.
8. 23. our adoption, to wit, the redemption of our body
1 Cor. 1. 30. and righteousness and sanctification, and r.
Eph. 1. 7. in whom we have our r. through his blood. Col.
14. unto the redemption of God's own possession [1. 14
4. 30. ye were sealed unto the day of redemption
Heb. 9. 12. having obtained eternal redemption
15. having taken place for the r. of the transgressions

REDOUND

Redound *A.V.—see abound.*

Reed.
Mat. 11. 7. a *reed* shaken with the wind? *Lu.* 7. 24
12. 20. A bruised *reed* shall he not break
27. 29. and a *reed* in his right hand
30. took the *r.* and smote him on the head. *Mk.* 15. 19
48. vinegar, and put it on a *reed*, and gave him to drink. *Mk.* 15. 36
Rev. 11. 1. And there was given me a *reed* like unto a rod
21. 15. had for a measure a golden *r.* to measure the city
16. he measured the city with the *r.*, twelve thousand

Refined.—*A.V.* ¹*burned*, ²*tried.*
Rev. 1. 15. unto burnished brass, as if it had been ¹*refined*
3. 18. I counsel thee to buy of me gold ²*refined* by fire

Reflecting.—*A.V.* ¹*beholding.*
2 *Cor.* 3. 18. with unveiled face ¹*r.*—the glory of the Lord

Reformation.
Heb. 9. 10. ordinances, imposed until a time of *reformation*

Refrain.
Acts 5. 38. *Refrain* from these men, and let them alone
1 *Pet.* 3. 10. Let him *refrain* his tongue from evil

Refresh.
Acts 27. 3. to go unto his friends and *refresh* himself
Philem. 20. *refresh* my heart in Christ

Refreshed.
1 *Cor.* 16. 18. For they *refreshed* my spirit and yours
2 *Cor.* 7. 13. Titus, because his spirit hath been *r.* by you
2 *Tim.* 1. 16. house of Onesiphorus: for he oft *r.* me
Philem. 7. hearts of the saints have been *r.* through thee
see rest.

Refreshing.
Acts 3.19. come seasons of *r.* from the presence of the Lord

Refuge.
Heb. 6. 18. who have fled for *refuge* to lay hold of the hope

Refuse.—*A.V.* ¹*avoid*, ²*neglect*, ³*reject.*
Mat. 18. 17. if he ²*refuse* to hear them, tell it unto the church: and if he ²*refuse* to hear the church
Acts 25. 11. any thing worthy of death, I *refuse* not to die
1 *Tim.* 4. 7. but *refuse* profane and old wives' fables
5. 11. But younger widows *refuse*
2 *Tim.* 2. 23. foolish and ignorant questionings ¹*refuse*
Tit. 3. 10. after a first and second admonition ³*refuse*
Heb. 12. 25. See that ye *refuse* not him that speaketh

Refused.—*A.V.* ¹*like.*
Acts 7. 35. This Moses whom they *refused*, saying
Rom. 1. 28. even as they ¹*r.* to have God in their knowledge
Heb. 11. 24. *r.* to be called the son of Pharaoh's daughter
12. 25. when they *r.* him that warned them on earth
see rejected.

Regard.—*A.V.* ¹*concerning*, ²*despise*, ³*respect.*
Lu. 18. 4. Though I fear not God, nor *regard* man
Eph. 5. 32. I speak ¹*regard* of Christ and of the church
Heb. 12. 5. ²*regard* not lightly the chastening of the Lord
Jas. 2. 3. ye have ³*r.* to him that weareth the fine clothing
see heed.

REIGN

Regarded.
Lu. 18. 2. judge, which feared not God, and *r.* not man
Heb. 8. 9. And I *regarded* them not, saith the Lord
see looked.

Regardest.
Mat. 22. 16. for thou *r.* not the person of men. *Mk.* 12. 14

Regardeth.
Rom. 14. 6. He that *regardeth* the day, *r.* it unto the Lord

Regarding *A.V.—see hazarding.*

Regeneration.
Mat. 19. 28. that ye which have followed me, in the *r.*
Tit. 3. 5. he saved us, through the washing of *regeneration*

Region.—*A.V.* ¹*country.*
Mat. 3. 5. and all the *region* round about Jordan
4. 16. which sat in the *region* and shadow of death
14. 35. sent into all that ¹*region* round about. *Lu.* 3. 3
Mk. 1. 28. all the *region* of Galilee round about. *Lu.* 4. 14
6. 55. and ran round about that whole *region*
Lu. 3. 1. tetrarch of the *region* of Ituræa and Trachonitis
4. 37. rumour concerning him into every place of the ¹*r.* 7.
Acts 13. 49. was spread abroad throughout all the *r.* [17
14. 6. Lystra and Derbe, and the *region* round about
16. 6. went through the *r.* of Phrygia and Galatia. 18. ¹20

Regions.—*A.V.* ¹*parts.*
Acts 8. 1. scattered abroad throughout the *r.* of Judæa
Rom. 15. 23. having no more any place in these ¹*regions*
2 *Cor.* 11. 10. shall stop me of this glorying in the *r.* of
Gal. 1. 21. I came into the *r.* of Syria and Cilicia [Achaia
see parts.

Regret.—*A.V.* ¹*repent*, ²*repented.*
2 *Cor.* 7. 8. I do not ¹*regret* it, though I did ¹*regret*
10. a repentance which bringeth no ²*regret*

Regular.—*A.V.* ¹*lawful.*
Acts 19. 39. matters, it shall be settled in the ¹*r.* assembly

Rehearsed.—*A.V.* ¹*declared*, ²*told.*
Lu. 24. 35. they ²*r.* the things that happened in the way
Acts 10. 8. [Cornelius] having ¹*r.* all things unto them
14. 27. *r.* all things that God had done with them. 15. ¹4
15. 14. Symeon hath ¹*r.* how first God did visit the Gentiles
21. 19. he [Paul] *r.* one by one the things which God

Rehearsing.—*A.V.* ¹*declaring.*
Acts 15. 12. hearkened unto Barnabas and Paul ¹*r.* what signs

Reign.—*A.V.* ¹*reigned.*
Lu. 1. 33. and he shall *r.* over the house of Jacob for ever
19. 14. We will not that this man *reign* over us [them
27. mine enemies, which would not that I should *r.* over
Rom. 5. 17. the gift of righteousness *r.* in life through the
21. even so might grace *r.* through righteousness [one
6. 12. Let not sin therefore *reign* in your mortal body
1 *Cor.* 4. 8. that ye did *r.*, that we also might *r.* with you
15. 25. For he must *r.*, till he hath put all his enemies
2 *Tim.* 2. 12. if we endure, we shall also *reign* with him
Rev. 5. 10. kingdom and priests; and they *r.* upon the earth

270

REIGN

Rev. 11. 15. and he shall *reign* for ever and ever
  17. thou hast taken thy great power, and didst ¹*reign*
  20. 6. and shall *reign* with him a thousand years
  22. 5. and they shall *reign* for ever and ever
    see reigning, rule.

Reigned.

Rom. 5. 14. Nevertheless death *r.* from Adam until Moses
  17. trespass of the one, death *reigned* through the one
  21. that, as sin *r.* in death, even so might grace reign
1 *Cor.* 4. 8. already ye are become rich, ye have *r.* without us
Rev. 20. 4. they lived, and *r.* with Christ a thousand years
    see reign.

Reigneth.

Rev. 17. 18. great city, which *r.* over the kings of the earth
  19. 6. for the Lord our God, the Almighty, *reigneth*

Reigning.—*A.V.* ¹*reign.*

Mat. 2. 22. Archelaus was ¹*r.* over Judæa in the room of

Reins.

Rev. 2. 23. know that I am he which searcheth the *reins*

Reject.—*A.V.* ¹*bring to nothing.*

Mk. 6. 26. and of them that sat at meat, he would not *r.* her
  7. 9. Full well do ye *reject* the commandment of God
1 *Cor.* 1. 19. the prudence of the prudent will I ¹*reject*
    see refuse.

Rejected.—*A.V.* ¹*castaway,* ²*cast off,* ³*disallow—ed,* ⁴*refused.*

Mat. 21. 42. The stone which the builders *rejected. Mk.* 12. 10: *Lu.* 20. 17: 1 *Pet.* 2. ³⁷
Mk. 8. 31. and be *rejected* by the elders. *Lu.* 9. 22
Lu. 7. 30. Pharisees and the lawyers *r.* for themselves
  17. 25. suffer many things and be *r.* of this generation
1 *Cor.* 9. 27. I have preached to others, I myself should be¹*r.*
Gal. 4. 14. in my flesh ye despised not, nor *rejected*
1 *Tim.* 4. 4. nothing is to be ⁴*rejected,* if it be received with
  5. 12. because they have ²*rejected* their first faith
Heb. 6. 8. it is *rejected* and nigh unto a curse
  12. 17. desired to inherit the blessing, he was *rejected*
1 *Pet.* 2. 4. a living stone, ³*rejected* indeed of men

Rejecteth.—*A.V.* ¹*despiseth.*

Lu. 10. 16. he that ¹*rejecteth* you, ¹*rejecteth* me; and he that ¹*rejecteth* me ¹*rejecteth* him that sent me
Jno. 12. 48. He that *r.* me, and receiveth not my sayings
1 *Th.* 4. 8. Therefore he that ¹*rejecteth,* ¹*r.* not man, but God

Rejoice.—*A.V.* ¹*glad,* ²*glory,* ³*joy,* ⁴*rejoiced.*

Mat. 5. 12. *Rejoice,* and be exceeding glad: for great is
Lu. 1. 14. and many shall *rejoice* at his birth
  6. 23. *Rejoice* in that day, and leap for joy
  10. 20. in this *r.* not—but *r.* that your names are written
  15. 6. *Rejoice* with me, for I have found. 9
  19. 37. whole multitude of the disciples began to *rejoice*
Jno. 4. 36. he that soweth and he that reapeth may *rejoice*
  5. 35. ye were willing to *rejoice* for a season in his light
  16. 20. ye shall weep and lament, but the world shall *r.*
  22. I will see you again, and your heart shall *rejoice*
Rom. 5. 2. let us *rejoice* in hope of the glory of God
  3. we also *r.* in our tribulations
  11. we also ⁵*r.* in God through our Lord Jesus Christ
  12. 15. *R.* with them that *r.*; weep with them that weep
  15. 10. *Rejoice,* ye Gentiles, with his people [you wise
  16. 19. I ¹*rejoice* therefore over you: but I would have

RELEASE

1 *Cor.* 7. 30. those that *rejoice,* as though they rejoiced not
  12. 26. member is honoured, all the members *r.* with it
  16. 17. I ¹*rejoice* at the coming of Stephanas
2 *Cor.* 2. 3. sorrow from them of whom I ought to *rejoice*
  7. 9. I *rejoice,* not that ye were made sorry, but that
  16. I *rejoice* that in everything I am of good courage
  13. 9. we ¹*rejoice,* when we are weak, and ye are strong
Gal. 4. 27. *Rejoice,* thou barren that bearest not
Phil. 1. 18. is proclaimed; and therein I *r.,* yea, and will *r.*
  2. 17. service of your faith, I joy, and *rejoice* with you all
  18. in the same manner do ye also joy, and *r.* with me
  28. when ye see him [Epaphroditus] again, ye may *r.*
  3. 1. Finally, my brethren, *rejoice* in the Lord
  4. 4. *Rejoice* in the Lord alway: again I will say, *Rejoice*
  10. But I ⁴*rejoice* in the Lord greatly, that now
Col. 1. 24. Now I *rejoice* in my sufferings for your sake
1 *Th.* 5. 16. *Rejoice* alway
1 *Pet.* 1. 6. Wherein ye greatly *r.,* though now for a little
  8. believing, ye *rejoice* greatly with joy unspeakable
  4. 13. as ye are partakers of Christ's sufferings, *rejoice;* that at the revelation of his glory also ye may ¹*r.*
2 *Jno.* 4. I ⁴*rejoice* greatly that I have found certain of thy
Rev. 11. 10. they that dwell on the earth *rejoice* over them
  12. 12. *rejoice,* O heavens, and ye that dwell in them
  18. 20. *Rejoice* over her, thou heaven, and ye saints
  19. 7. Let us ¹*rejoice* and be exceeding glad
    see glory, rejoiced.

Rejoiced.—*A.V.* ¹*rejoice.*

Mat. 2. 10. when they saw the star, they *rejoiced*
Lu. 1. 47. my spirit hath *rejoiced* in God my Saviour
  58. mercy towards her; and they *rejoiced* with her
  10. 21. same hour he *rejoiced* in the Holy Spirit, and said
  13. 17. the multitude *rejoiced* for all the glorious things
Jno. 8. 56. Your father Abraham *rejoiced* to see my day
  14. 28. If ye loved me, ye would have ¹*rejoiced*
Acts 7. 41. and *rejoiced* in the works of their hands
  15. 31. when they had read it, they *r.* for the consolation
  16. 34. *r.* greatly, with all his house, having believed
1 *Cor.* 7. 30. those that rejoice, as though they *rejoiced* not
2 *Cor.* 7. 7. your zeal for me; so that I *rejoiced* yet more
3 *Jno.* 3. For I *rejoiced* greatly, when brethren came
    see rejoice.

Rejoiceth.

Mat. 18. 13. he *r.* over it more than over the ninety and nine
Jno. 3. 29. *r.* greatly because of the bridegroom's voice
1 *Cor.* 13. 6. *r.* not in unrighteousness, but *r.* with the truth
    see glorieth.

Rejoicing.

Lu. 15. 5. he layeth it on his shoulders, *rejoicing*
Acts 5. 41. *rejoicing* that they were counted worthy to suffer
  8. 39. he went on his way *rejoicing*
Rom. 12. 12. *rejoicing* in hope; patient in tribulation
2 *Cor.* 6. 10. as sorrowful, yet alway *r.*; as poor, yet making
    see glorying.

Release—d.—*A.V.* ¹*deliverance,* ²*forgive—n,* ³*let go,* ⁴*loosed,* ⁵*released.*

Mat. 18. 27. ⁴*released* him, and forgave him the debt
  27. 15. feast the governor was wont to *r.* unto the multitude one prisoner. *Mk.* 15. ⁵⁶: *Jno.* 18. 39
  17. Pilato said unto them, Whom will ye that I *release* unto you? 21: *Mk.* 15. 9: *Jno.* 18. 39
  26. *r.* he unto them Barabbas. *Mk.* 15. 15: *Lu.* 23. 25
Mk. 15. 11. should rather *release* Barabbas. *Lu.* 23. 18
Lu. 4. 18. He hath sent me to proclaim ¹*r.* to the captives
  6. 37. ²*release,* and ye shall be ²*released*

RELEASE

Lu. 23. 16. I will therefore chastise him, and *r* him. ³22
Jno. 19. 10. power to *r.* thee, and have power to crucify
12. Pilate sought to *release* him—³*release* this man.
Lu. 23. 20: *Acts* 3.⁵13

Relief—*A.V.* ¹*rest.*
Acts 11. 29. determined to send *relief* unto the brethren
2 *Cor.* 2. 13. I had no ¹*r.* for my spirit because I found not
7. 5. our flesh had no ¹*relief*, but we were afflicted

Relieve—d.
1 *Tim.* 5. 10 if she hath *relieved* the afflicted
16. believeth hath widows, let her *relieve* them—that it may *relieve* them that are widows indeed

Religion.—*A.V.* ¹*superstition.*
Acts. 25. 19. questions against him of their own ¹*religion*
26. 5. after the straitest sect of our *religion* I lived
Gal. 1. 13. of life in time past in the Jews' *religion.* 14
Jas. 1. 26. but deceiveth his heart, this man's *r.* is vain
27. Pure *r.* and undefiled before our God and Father

Religious.
Jas. 1. 26. to be *religious*, while he bridleth not his tongue
see devout

Remain.
Lu. 10. 7. in that same house *remain*, eating and drinking
Jno. 6. 12. Gather up the broken pieces which *remain*
19. 31. that the bodies should not *remain* on the cross
Acts 5. 4. Whiles it remained, did it not *r.* thine own?
1 *Cor.* 7. 11. if she depart, let her *remain* unmarried
15. 6. of whom the greater part *remain* until now
Heb. 12. 27. that those things which are not shaken may *r.*
Rev. 3. 2. stablish the things that *remain*, which were ready
see abide, left.

Remained.—*A.V.* ¹*left.*
Mat. 11. 23. which were done in thee, it would have *r.*
14. 20. *remained* over of the broken pieces. 15. ¹37: *Mk.* 8. ¹8: *Lu.* 9. 17: *Jno.* 6 13
Lu. 1. 22. making signs unto them, and *remained* dumb
Acts 5. 4. Whiles it *r.*, did it not remain thine own?
27. 41. the foreship struck and *remained* unmoveable

Remainest *A.V.*—*see continuest.*

Remaineth.
Jno. 9. 41. but now ye say, We see: your sin *remaineth*
2 *Cor.* 3. 11. much more that which *remaineth* is in glory
14. until this very day—the same veil *r.* unlifted
Heb. 4. 6. it *remaineth* that some should enter thereinto
9. There *r.* therefore a sabbath rest for the people
10. 26. there *remaineth* no more a sacrifice for sins
see abideth, henceforth.

Remaining *A.V*—*see abiding.*

Remember.—*A.V.* ¹*mindful,* ²*remembrance.*
Mat. 16. 9. neither *remember* the five loaves. *Mk.* 8. 18
27. 63. Sir, we *remember* that that deceiver said
Lu. 1. 54. holpen Israel his servant, That he might ²*r.* mercy
72. And to *remember* his holy covenant [good things
16. 25. Son, *r.* that thou in thy lifetime receivedst thy
17. 32. *Remember* Lot's wife
23. 42. *remember* me when thou comest in thy kingdom
24. 6. He is not here, but is risen: *r.* how he spake

REMISSION

Jno. 15. 20. *R.* the word that I said unto you, A servant
16. 4. that when their hour is come, ye may *remember*
Acts 20. 35. help the weak, and to *r.* the words of the Lord
1 *Cor.* 11. 2. that ye *remember* me in all things, and hold
Gal. 2. 10. only they would that we should *r.* the poor
Eph. 2. 11. *r.*, that aforetime ye, the Gentiles in the flesh
Col. 4. 18. *Remember* my bonds. Grace be with you
1 *Th.* 2. 9. For ye *r.*, brethren, our labour and travail
2 *Th.* 2. 5. *R.* ye not, that, when I was yet with you
2 *Tim.* 2. 8. *Remember* Jesus Christ, risen from the dead
Heb. 8. 12. And their sins will I *remember* no more. 10. 17
13. 3. *Remember* them that are in bonds, as bound with
7. *Remember* them that had the rule over you
2 *Pet.* 3. 2. ¹*remember* the words which were spoken
Jude. 17. *remember* ye the words which have been spoken
Rev. 2. 5. *Remember* therefore from whence thou art fallen
3. 3. *R.* therefore how thou hast received and didst hear
see remembering, remembrance.

Remembered.—*A.V.* ¹*remembrance.*
Mat. 26. 75. And Peter *remembered* the word. *Lu.* 22. 61
Lu. 24. 8. And they *remembered* his words
Jno. 2. 17. His disciples *r.* that it was written, The zeal
22. When—he was raised from the dead, his disciples *r.*
12. 16. when Jesus was glorified, then *remembered* they
Acts 11. 16. And I *remembered* the word of the Lord
Rev. 16. 19. Babylon the great was ¹*r.* in the sight of God
18. 5. and God hath *remembered* her iniquities

Rememberest—eth.
Mat. 5. 23. there *r.* that thy brother hath aught against thee
Jno. 16. 21. of the child, she *r.* no more the anguish
2 *Cor.* 7. 15. whilst he *remembereth* the obedience of you all

Remembering.—*A.V.* ¹*mindful,* ²*remember.*
Acts 20. 31. ²*remembering* that by the space of three years
1 *Th.* 1. 3. *remembering* without ceasing your work of faith
2 *Tim* 1. 4. ¹*r.* thy tears, that I may be filled with joy

Remembrance.—*A V* ¹*mind,* ²*remember.*
Mk. 11. 21. Peter calling to *remembrance* saith unto him
Lu. 22. 19. this do in *remembrance* of me. 1 *Cor.* 11. 24, 25
Jno. 14. 26. and bring to your *r.* all that I said unto you
Acts 10. 31. prayer is heard, and thine alms are had in *r.*
Rom. 15. 15. putting you again in ¹*r.*, because of the grace
1 *Cor.* 4. 17. Timothy—who shall put you in *r.* of my ways
Phil. 1. 3. I thank my God upon all my *remembrance* of you
1 *Th.* 3. 6. and that ye have good *remembrance* of us always
2 *Tim.* 1. 3. *remembrance* is my *r.* of thee in my supplications
6. I put thee in *r.* that thou stir up the gift of God
2. 14. Of those things put them in *r.*, charging them
Heb. 10. 3. in those sacrifices there is a *r.* made of sins
32. But call to *r.* the former days, in which, after
2 *Pet.* 1. 12. to put you in *remembrance.* *Jude* 5
13. to stir you up by putting you in *remembrance*
15. may be able after my decease to call these things to *r.*
3. 1. I stir up your sincere mind by putting you in *r.*
3 *Jno.* 10. I will bring to ²*r.* his [Diotrephes] works
see mind, remember, remembered, reminded.

Reminded.—*A.V.* ¹*call to remembrance.*
2 *Tim.* 1. 5. having been ¹*r.* of the unfeigned faith that is in

Remission.—*A.V.* ¹*forgiveness.*
Mat. 26. 28. which is shed for many unto *remission* of sins
Mk. 1. 4. baptism of repentance unto *r.* of sins. *Lu.* 3. 3
Lu. 1. 77. salvation unto his people In the *r.* of their sins
24. 47. and *r.* of sins should be preached in his name

REMISSION

Acts 2. 38. in the name of Jesus Christ unto the *r.* of your sins
5. 31. to give repentance to Israel, and ¹*remission* of sins
10. 43. believeth on him shall receive *remission* of sins
13. 38. through this man is proclaimed unto you ¹*r.* of sins
26. 18. that they may receive ¹*r.* of sins and an inheritance
Heb. 9. 22. apart from shedding of blood there is no *r.*
10. 18. where *r.* of these is, there is no more offering
see passing.

Remit—ted *A.V.*—*see forgive*—n.

Remnant.

Rom. 9. 27. it is the *remnant* that shall be saved
11. 5. there is a *r.* according to the election of grace
see rest.

Remove—d.—*A.V.* ¹*departed,* ²*take away.*

Mat. 17. 20. mountain, *Remove* hence—and it shall *remove*
Mk. 14. 36. ²*remove* this cup from me. *Lu.* 22. 42
Acts 7. 4. when his father was dead, God *removed* him
13. 22. when he had *removed* him, he raised up David
1 *Cor.* 13. 2. if I have all faith, so as to *remove* mountains
Rev. 6. 14. And the heaven was ¹*removed* as a scroll
see move, removing, taken.

Removing.—*A.V.* ¹*removed.*

Gal. 1. 6. I marvel that ye are so quickly ¹*r.* from him
Heb. 12. 27. once more, signifieth the *r.* of those things

Rend—*A.V.* ¹*rent.*

Mat. 7. 6. under their feet, and turn and *rend* you
Lu. 5. 36. else he will ¹*rend* the new, and also the piece
Jno. 19. 24. Let us not *rend* it, but cast lots for it

Render—ed.—*A.V.* ¹*give,* ²*recompense,* ³*reward*—ed.

Mat. 16. 27. he ⁸*r.* unto every man according to his deeds.
21. 41. shall *r.* him the fruits in their seasons [*Rom.* 2. 6
22. 21. *Render* therefore unto Cæsar the things that are Cæsar's. *Mk.* 12. 17: *Lu.* 20. 25
Rom. 12. 17. ²*Render* to no man evil for evil
13. 7. *Render* to all their dues: tribute to whom tribute
1 *Cor.* 7. 3. Let the husband *render* unto the wife her due
Col. 4. 1. Masters, ¹*r.* unto your servants that which is just
1 *Th.* 3. 9. what thanksgiving can we *r.* again unto God
5. 15. See that none *render* unto any one evil for evil
2 *Tim.* 4. 14. the Lord will ⁸*r.* to him according to his works
Rev. 18. 6. ³*Render* unto her even as she ⁴*rendered*
22. 12. to ¹*render* to each man according as his work is

Rendering—*A.V.* ¹*taking.*

2 *Th.* 1. 8. ¹*rendering* vengeance to them that know not God
1 *Pet.* 3. 9. not *r.* evil for evil, or reviling for reviling

Renew—ed.

2 *Cor.* 4. 16. yet our inward man is *renewed* day by day
Eph. 4. 23. and that ye be *renewed* in the spirit of your mind
Col. 3. 10. new man, which is being *r.* unto knowledge
Heb. 6. 6. impossible to *renew* them again unto repentance

Renewing.

Rom. 12. 2. be ye transformed by the *r.* of your mind
Tit. 3. 5. regeneration and *renewing* of the Holy Ghost

Renounced

2 *Cor.* 4. 2. but we have *r.* the hidden things of shame

Renounceth.—*A.V.* ¹*forsaketh.*

Lu. 14. 33. whosoever he be of you that ¹*renounceth* not all

REPENTED

Rent.—*A.V.* ¹*broken,* ²*opened,* ³*plucked.*

Mat. 9. 16. and a worse *rent* is made. *Mk.* 2. 21
27. 51. veil of the temple was *rent* in twain—and the rocks were *rent. Mk.* 15. 38: *Lu.* 23. 45
Mk. 1. 10. [John] saw the heavens ²*rent* asunder
5. 4. the chains had been ³*rent* asunder by him
14. 63. And the high priest *rent* his clothes
Jno. 21. 11. for all there were so many, the net was not ¹*r.*
see rend, torn.

Repay.

Lu. 10. 35. I, when I come back again, will *repay* thee
Philem. 19. write it with mine own hand, I will *repay* it
see recompense.

Repent.—*A.V.* ¹*repented.*

Mat. 3. 2. *Repent* ye; for the kingdom of heaven is at hand. 4. 17: *Mk.* 1. 15
21. 32. when ye saw it, did not even ¹*repent* yourselves
Mk. 6. 12. and preached that men should *repent*
Lu. 13. 5. except ye *repent,* ye shall all likewise perish. 3
16. 30. if one go to them from the dead, they will *repent*
17. 3. rebuke him; and if he *repent,* forgive him. 4
Acts 2. 38. *Repent* ye, and be baptized every one of you
8. 19. *R.* ye therefore, and turn again, that your sins
8. 22. *Repent* therefore of this thy wickedness, and pray
17. 30. men that they should all everywhere *repent*
26. 20. Gentiles, that they should *r.* and turn to God
Heb. 7. 21. The Lord sware and will not *repent* himself
Rev. 2. 5. and *r.,* and do the first works—except thou *r.*
16. *Repent* therefore; or else I come to thee quickly
21. time that she should *r.*; and she willeth not to ¹*r.*
22. great tribulation, except they *repent* of her works
3. 3. received and didst hear; and keep it, and *repent*
19. I reprove and chasten : be zealous therefore, and *r.*
see regret.

Repentance.—*A.V.* ¹*repented*

Mat. 3. 8. Bring forth therefore fruit worthy of *r. Lu.* 3. 8
11. I indeed baptize you with water unto *repentance*
Mk. 1. 4. preached the baptism of *repentance* unto remission of sins. *Lu.* 3. 3: *Acts* 13. 24: 19. 4
Lu. 5. 32. not come to call the righteous but sinners to *r.*
15. 7. righteous persons, which need no *repentance*
24. 47. *r.* and remission of sins should be preached in his
Acts 5. 31. a Saviour, for to give *r.* to Israel [name
11. 18. Gentiles also hath God granted *r.* unto life
20. 21. both to Jews and to Greeks *r.* toward God
26. 20. turn to God, doing works worthy of *repentance*
Rom. 2. 4. that the goodness of God leadeth thee to *r.* ?
11. 29. the gifts and the calling of God are without *r.*
2 *Cor.* 7. 9. but that ye were made sorry unto *repentance*
10. godly sorrow worketh *repentance* unto salvation, a ¹*repentance* which bringeth no regret
2 *Tim.* 2. 25. if peradventure God may give them *repentance*
Heb. 6. 1. not laying again a foundation of *repentance*
6. it is impossible to renew them again unto *repentance*
12. 17. (for he found no place of *repentance*)
2 *Pet.* 3. 9. should perish, but that all should come to *r.*

Repented.

Mat. 11. 20. works were done, because they *repented* not
21. done in you, they would have *r.* long ago. *Lu.* 10. 13
12. 41. they *r.* at the preaching of Jonah. *Lu.* 11. 32
21. 29. I will not: but afterward he *r.* himself, and went
27. 3. *repented* himself, and brought back the thirty pieces
2 *Cor.* 12. 21. and *r.* not of the uncleanness and fornication
see regret.

REPENTED

Rev. 9. 20. which were not killed with these plagues, *r.* not
21. and they *r.* not of their murders, nor of their
16. 9. power over these plagues; and they *r.* not. 11
    see repent, repentance.

Repenteth.
Lu. 15. 7. joy in heaven over one sinner that *repenteth.* 10

Repetitions.
Mat. 6. 7. in praying use not vain *r.*, as the Gentiles do

Repliest.
Rom. 9. 20. O man, who art thou that *r.* against God?

Report.—*A.V.* ¹*fame,* ²*rumour,* ³*shew—ed,* ⁴*tidings.*
Mat. 4. 24. the ¹*report* of him went forth into all Syria
14. 1. Herod the tetrarch heard the ¹*r.* concerning Jesus
Mk. 1. 28. the ¹*r.* of him went out straightway everywhere
Lu. 5. 15. so much the more went abroad the ¹*r.* concerning
7. 17. And this ²*report* went forth concerning him
Jno. 12. 38. Lord, who hath believed our *r.? Rom.* 10. 16
Acts 6. 3. seven men of good *r.,* full of the Spirit [church
11. 22. the ⁴*r.* concerning them came to the ears of the
28. 21. brethren come hither and ³*r.* or speak any harm
2 *Cor.* 6. 8. by evil *r.* and good *r.;* as deceivers, and yet true
Phil. 4. 8. are lovely, whatsoever things are of good *report*
1 *Th.* 1. 9. For they themselves ²*report* concerning us
    see declaring, reported, testimony, witness.

Reported.—*A.V.* ¹*report,* ²*told.*
Acts 4. 23. own company, and *r.* all that the chief priests
10. 22. feareth God, and well ¹*r.* of by all the nation
16. 2. The same was well *reported* of by the brethren
38. the serjeants ²*r.* these words unto the magistrates
23. 12. devout man according to the law, well ¹*r.* of
Rom. 3. 8. and why not (as we be slanderously *reported*
1 *Cor.* 5. 1. It is actually *reported* that there is fornication
1 *Tim.* 5. 10. well *reported* of for good works; if she hath
    see announce, spread.

Reproach.—*A.V.* ¹*blameless,* ²*in his teeth,* ³*revile,*
    ⁴*unrebukable.*
Mat. 5. 11. Blessed are ye when men shall ³*r.* you. *Lu.* 6. 22
27. 41. crucified with him cast upon him the same ²*r.*
Lu. 1. 25. he looked upon me, to take away my *reproach*
1 *Tim.* 3. 2. The bishop therefore must be without ¹*reproach*
7. lest he fall into *reproach* and the snare of the devil
5. 7. These things also command, that they may be with-
6. 14. without spot, without ⁴*reproach* [out ³*reproach*
Heb. 11. 26. accounting the *reproach* of Christ greater riches
13. 13. unto him without the camp, bearing his *reproach*
    see disparagement, strive.

Reproached—est.—*A.V.* ¹*reviled.*
Mk. 15. 32. they that were crucified with him, ¹*r.* him
Lu. 11. 45. in saying this thou *reproachest* us also [me
Rom. 15. 3. The reproaches of them that *r.* thee fell upon
1 *Pet.* 4. 14. are *r.* for the name of Christ, blessed are ye

Reproaches.
Rom. 15. 3. The *reproaches* of them that reproached thee
Heb. 10. 33. made a gazingstock both by *r.* and afflictions
    see injuries.

Reproachfully *A.V.*—*see reviling.*

RESERVED

Reprobate.—*A.V.* ¹*reprobates.*
Rom. 1. 28. God gave them up unto a *reprobate* mind
2 *Cor.* 13. 5. Jesus Christ is in you? unless indeed ye be ¹*r.*
6. I hope that ye shall know that we are not ¹*reprobate*
7. may do that which is honourable, though we be as ¹*r.*
2 *Tim.* 3. 8. men corrupted in mind, *r.* concerning the faith
Tit. 1. 16. and unto every good work *reprobate*

Reproof.
2 *Tim.* 3. 16. is also profitable for teaching, for *reproof*

Reprove—d.—*A.V.* ¹*convinced,* ²*rebuke,* ³*rebuked.*
Lu. 3. 19. Herod the tetrarch, being *reproved* by him
Jno. 3. 20. to the light, lest his works should be *reproved*
1 *Cor.* 14. 24. he is ¹*reproved* by all, he is judged by all
Eph. 5. 11. works of darkness, but rather even *r.* them
13. all things when they are *r.* are made manifest
1 *Tim.* 5. 20. Them that sin ²*reprove* in the sight of all
2 *Tim.* 4. 2. *reprove,* rebuke, exhort, with all longsuffering
Tit. 1. 13. For which cause ²*reprove* them sharply. 2. ²15
Heb. 12. 5. Nor faint when thou art ³*reproved* of him
Rev. 3. 19. As many as I love, I ²*reprove* and chasten
    see convict, respect.

Reputation *A.V.*—*see emptied, repute, honour.*

Repute—d.—*A.V.* ¹*reputation,* ²*seemed.*
Gal. 2. 2. but privately before them who were of ¹*repute*
6. who were ²*reputed*—who were of ²*repute*
9. and Cephas and John, they who were ²*r.* to be pillars

Request—s.—*A.V.* ¹*desire,* ²*pray,* ³*request.*
Rom. 1. 10. making *request,* if by any means now
Phil. 4. 6. let your ³*requests* be made known unto God
19. 23. I at my coming should have *r.* it with interest?
1 *Jno.* 5. 16. do I say that he should make ²*request*
    see supplication.

Required.
Lu. 11. 50. may be *required* of this generation. 51
12. 20. this night is thy soul *required* of thee
48. much is given, of him shall much be *required*
1 *Cor.* 4. 2. it is *r.* in stewards, that a man be found faithful
    see ask, asked, requireth.

Requireth.—*A.V.* ¹*require.*
1 *Cor.* 7. 36. if need so ¹*requireth,* let him do what he will

Requiring *A.V.*—*see asking.*

Requite.
1 *Tim.* 5. 4. to shew piety—and to *requite* their parents

Rescued.
Acts 23. 27. I came upon them with the soldiers, and *r.* him

Resemble *A.V.*—*see liken—ed.*

Reserve *A.V.*—*see keep.*

Reserved.
1 *Pet.* 1. 4. that fadeth not away, *r.* in heaven for you
2 *Pet.* 2. 4. pits of darkness, to be *reserved* unto judgement
17. for whom the blackness of darkness hath been *r. Jude*
3. 7. being *reserved* against the day of judgement [13
    see kept, left.

RESIDUE

Residue.
Acts 15. 17. That the *r.* of men may seek after the Lord
see rest.

Resist.
Mat. 5. 39. but I say unto you, *Resist* not him that is evil
Acts 7. 51. ye do always *r.* the Holy Ghost: as your fathers
Jas. 4. 7. but *resist* the devil, and he will flee from you
5. 6. killed the righteous one ; he doth not *resist* you
see withstand.

Resisted—eth.—*A.V.* ¹withstood.
Rom. 13. 2. he that *r.* the power, withstandeth the ordinance
Gal. 2. 11. Cephas came to Antioch, I ¹*r.* him to the face
Heb. 12. 4. Ye have not yet *r.* unto blood, striving against
Jas. 4. 6. God *resisteth* the proud. 1 *Pet.* 5. 5 [sin
see withstandeth.

Resolved.
Lu. 16. 4. I am *r.* what to do, that, when I am put out

Resort *A.V.—see come.*

Resorted.—*A.V.* ¹come.
Mk. 2. 13. multitude *r.* unto him, and he taught them
Lu. 8. 4. and they of every city ¹*resorted* unto him
Jno. 18. 2. Jesus oft-times *r.* thither with his disciples
see came, come.

Respect.—*A.V.* ¹admiration.
Jno. 16. 8. he is come, will convict the world in *r.* of sin
Rom. 2. 11. there is no *r.* of persons. *Eph.* 6. 9 : *Col.* 3. 25
2 *Cor.* 3. 10. hath not been made glorious in this *respect*
Phil. 4. 11. Not that I speak in *respect* of want ; for I have
Col. 2. 16. or in drink, or in *respect* of a feast day [learned
Jas. 2. 1. the Lord of glory, with *respect* of persons
9. but if ye have *respect* of persons, ye commit sin
1 *Pet.* 1. 17. as Father, who without *r.* of persons judgeth
Jude 16. shewing ¹*r.* of persons for the sake of advantage
see looked, regard.

Respecter.
Acts 10. 34. I perceive that God is no *respecter* of persons

Rest.—*A.V.* ¹refreshed.
Mat. 11. 29. and are heavy laden, and I will give you *rest*
29. and ye shall find *rest* unto your souls
12. 43. seeking *rest*, and findeth it not. *Lu.* 11. 24
26. 45. Sleep on now, and take your *rest*. *Mk.* 14. 41
Mk. 6. 31. apart into a desert place, and *rest* a while
Lu. 10. 6. peace be there, your peace shall *rest* upon him
Jno. 11. 13. thought that he spake of taking *rest* in sleep
Acts 7. 49. Or what is the place of my *rest* ?
Rom. 15. 32. will of God, and together with you find ¹*rest*
2 *Cor.* 12. 9. that the strength of Christ may *rest* upon me
Heb. 3. 11. They shall not enter into my *rest.* 18
4. 1. a promise being left of entering into his *rest*
3. For we which have believed do enter into that *rest*
—They shall not enter into my *rest.* 5 [spoken
8. if Joshua had given them *rest*, he would not have
9. There remaineth therefore a sabbath *r.* for the people
10. he that is entered into his *r.* hath himself also rested
11. Let us therefore give diligence to enter into that *r.*
Rev. 4. 8. and they have no *rest* day and night. 14. 11
6. 11. that they should *rest* yet for a little time
14. 13. that they may *rest* from their labours
see dwell, peace, relief, rested.

RESURRECTION

Rest *(remainder).* — *A.V.* ¹*other*, ²*places*, ³*remnant*, ⁴*residue.*
Mat. 22. 6. and the ³*rest* laid hold on his servants
27. 49. the *rest* said, Let be ; let us see whether Elijah
Mk. 16. 13. they went away and told it unto the ⁴*rest*
Lu. 12. 26. why are ye anxious concerning the *rest* ?
18. 11. I thank thee, that I am not as the ¹*rest* of men
24. 9. these things to the eleven, and to all the *rest*
Acts 2. 37. and said unto Peter and the *r.* of the apostles
5. 13. of the *rest* durst no man join himself to them
27. 44. and the *rest*, some on planks, and some on
Rom. 11. 7. obtained it, and the *rest* were hardened
1 *Cor.* 7. 12. But to the *rest* say I, not the Lord
11. 34. And the *r.* will I set in order whensoever I come
2 *Cor.* 13. 2. that have sinned heretofore, and to all the ¹*rest*
Phil. 1. 13. the whole prætorian guard, and to all the ²*rest*
1 *Pet.* 4. 2. should live the *rest* of your time in the flesh
Rev. 2. 24. But to you I say, to the *r.* that are in Thyatira
9. 20. And the *rest* of mankind, which were not killed
11. 13. the ³*r.* were affrighted, and gave glory to the God
12. 17. went away to make war with the ³*r.* of her seed
19. 21. the ³*r.* were killed with the sword of him that sat
20. 5. The *rest* of the dead lived not until the thousand

Rested.—*A.V.* ¹ceased, ²rest.
Lu. 23. 56. And on the sabbath they *rested* according
Heb. 4. 4. And God ²*r.* on the seventh day from all his works
10. hath himself also ¹*rested* from his works

Restest—eth.
Rom. 2. 17. bearest the name of a Jew, and *r.* upon the law
1 *Pet.* 4. 14. Spirit of glory and the Spirit of God *r.* upon you

Restitution *A.V.—see restoration.*

Restless—*A.V.* ¹unruly.
Jas. 3. 8. tongue can no man tame; it is a ¹*restless* evil

Restoration.—*A.V.* ¹restitution.
Acts 3. 21. until the times of ¹*restoration* of all things

Restore.
Mat. 17. 11. Elijah indeed cometh, and shall *r.* all things
Lu. 19. 8. exacted aught of any man, I *restore* fourfold
Acts 1. 6. dost thou at this time *r.* the kingdom to Israel ?
Gal. 6. 1. *restore* such a one in a spirit of meekness

Restored.
Mk. 3. 5. and his hand was *restored*. *Mat.* 12. 13: *Lu.* 6. 10
8. 25. and was *restored*, and saw all things clearly
Heb. 13. 19. do this, that I may be *r.* to you the sooner

Restoreth.
Mk. 9. 12. Elijah indeed cometh first, and *r.* all things

Restrained—eth.—*A.V.* ¹let—teth, ²withholdeth.
Acts 14. 18. with these sayings scarce *restrained* they the
2 *Th.* 2. 6. And now ye know that which ²*r.* [multitudes
7. only there is one that ¹*restraineth* now

Resurrection.—*A.V.* ¹raised, ²rise.
Mat. 22. 23. which say that there is no *resurrection*. *Mk.*
12. 18 : *Lu.* 20. 27 : *Acts* 23. 8 : 1 *Cor.* 15. 12
28. In the *resurrection* therefore whose wife shall she
be of the seven ? *Mk.* 12. 23 : *Lu.* 20. 33
30. For in the *r.* they neither marry, nor. *Lu.* 20. 35
31. touching the *r.* of the dead, have ye not read
27. 53. forth out of the tombs after his *r.* they entered

RESURRECTION

Lu. 14. 14. thou shalt be recompensed in the r. of the just
20. 36. sons of God, being sons of the *resurrection*
Jno. 5. 29. unto the r. of life—unto the r. of judgement
11. 24. I know that he shall rise again in the *resurrection*
25. Jesus said—I am the *resurrection*, and the life
Acts 1. 22. must one become a witness with us of his r.
2. 31. he foreseeing this spake of the r. of the Christ
4. 2. and proclaimed in Jesus the r. from the dead
33. gave the apostles their witness of the *resurrection*
17. 18. because he preached Jesus and the *resurrection*
32. when they heard of the *resurrection* of the dead
23. 6. r. of the dead I am called in question. 24. 21
24. 15. that there shall be a r. both of the just and unjust
26. 23. first by the ²r. of the dead should proclaim light
Rom. 1. 4. spirit of holiness, by the *resurrection* of the dead
6. 5. we shall be also by the likeness of his *resurrection*
1 Cor. 15. 13. if there is no r. of the dead, neither hath
21. by man came death, by man came also the r.
42. So also is the *resurrection* of the dead. It is sown in
Phil. 3. 10. that I may know him, and the power of his r.
11. if by any means I may attain unto the *resurrection*
2 Tim. 2. 18. erred, saying that the r. is past already
Heb. 6. 2. of r. of the dead, and of eternal judgement
11. 35. Women received their dead by a *resurrection*—
that they might obtain a better *resurrection*
1 Pet. 1. 3. a living hope by the r. of Jesus Christ. 3. 21
Rev. 20. 5. years should be finished. This is the first r.
6. holy is he that hath part in the first *resurrection*

Retain—ed.
Jno. 20. 23. whose soever sins ye *retain*, they are *retained*
see have, kept.

Return.—A.V. ¹go again, ²returned, ³turn.
Mat. 2. 12. in a dream that they should not *return* to Herod
10. 13. if it be not worthy, let your peace *return* to you
12. 44. he saith, I will *return* into my house [Lu. 17. 31
24. 18. let him that is in the field not r. back. Mk. 13. ⁸16:
Lu. 8. 39. *Return* to thy house, and declare how great
12. 36. their lord, when he shall r. from the marriage
19. 12. to receive for himself a kingdom, and to *return*
Acts 13. 34. now no more to *return* to corruption
15. 16. After these things I will *return*, And I will build
36. Let us ¹*return* now and visit the brethren in every
18. 21. and saying, I will r. again unto you, if God will
20. 3. he determined to *return* through Macedonia
Heb. 11. 15. they would have had opportunity to ²*return*
see turn.

Returned.—A.V. ¹came again, ²turned back.
Mat. 21. 18. in the morning as he r. to the city, he hungered
Lu. 1. 56. three months, and *returned* unto her house
2. 20. the shepherds r., glorifying and praising God
39. they r. into Galilee, to their own city Nazareth
45. they ²*returned* to Jerusalem, seeking for him
4. 1. Jesus, full of the Holy Spirit, r. from the Jordan
14. Jesus r. in the power of the Spirit into Galilee
8. 37. and he entered into a boat, and *returned*
40. as Jesus *returned*, the multitude welcomed him
55. her [Jairus' daughter] spirit ¹r., and she rose up
9. 10. apostles, when they were r., declared unto him
10. 17. And the seventy *returned* with joy [God
17. 18. Were there none found that r. to give glory to
23. 48. things that were done, r. smiting their breasts
56. they *returned*, and prepared spices and ointments
24. 9. *returned* from the tomb, and told all these things
33. they rose up that very hour, and r. to Jerusalem. 52
Acts 1. 12. Then r. they unto Jerusalem from the mount
5. 22. found them not in the prison; and they *returned*

REVELATION

Acts 8. 25. *returned* to Jerusalem, and preached the gospel
12. 25. Barnabas and Saul *returned* from Jerusalem
13. 13. John departed from them and r. to Jerusalem
14. 21. [Paul and Barnabas] r. to Lystra, and to Iconium
21. 6. we went on board the ship, but they r. home again
23. 32. horsemen to go with him, and r. to the castle
Gal. 1. 17. and again I *returned* unto Damascus
1 Pet. 2. 25. are now r. unto the Shepherd and Bishop of
see came, come (back), return.

Returning.
Lu. 7. 10. *returning* to the house, found the servant whole
Acts 8. 28. and he [eunuch] was r. and sitting in his chariot
Heb. 7. 1. met Abraham r. from the slaughter of the kings

Reveal.—A.V. ¹revealed.
Mat. 11. 25. and didst ¹*reveal* them unto babes. Lu. 10. ¹21
27. to whomsoever the Son willeth to r. him. Lu. 10. 22
Gal. 1. 16. to r. his Son in me, that I might preach him
Phil. 3. 15. otherwise minded, even this shall God *reveal*

Revealed.
Mat. 10. 26. nothing covered, that shall not be r. Lu. 12. 2
16. 17. flesh and blood hath not *revealed* it unto thee
Lu. 2. 26. it had been r. unto him by the Holy Spirit
35. that thoughts out of many hearts may be *revealed*
17. 30. be in the day that the Son of man is *revealed*
Jno. 12. 38. to whom hath the arm of the Lord been r. ?
Rom. 1. 17. For therein is *revealed* a righteousness of God
18. For the wrath of God is *revealed* from heaven
8. 18. compared with the glory which shall be r. to us-
1 Cor. 2. 10 unto us God r. them through the Spirit [ward
3. 13. day shall declare it, because it is *revealed* in fire
Gal. 3. 23. unto the faith which should afterwards be r.
Eph. 3. 5. as it hath now been r. unto his holy apostles
2 Th. 2. 3. and the man of sin be r., the son of perdition
6. to the end that he may be *revealed* in his own season
8. And then shall be *revealed* the lawless one
1 Pet. 1. 5. a salvation ready to be r. in the last time
12. To whom it was *revealed*, that not unto themselves
5. 1. am also a partaker of the glory that shall be *revealed*
see reveal, revelation.

Revealing.—A.V. ¹manifestation.
Rom. 8. 19. creation waiteth for the ¹r. of the sons of God

Revel.—A.V. ¹riot.
2 Pet. 2. 13. that count it pleasure to ¹r. in the day-time

Revelation. — A.V. ¹appearing, ²coming, ³lighten, ⁴revealed.
Lu. 2. 32. A light for ³*revelation* to the Gentiles
Rom. 2. 5. wrath and r. of the righteous judgement of God
16. 25. r. of the mystery which hath been kept in silence
1 Cor. 1. 7. waiting for the ²r. of our Lord Jesus Christ
14. 6. unless I speak to you either by way of *revelation*
26. hath a teaching, hath a *revelation*, hath a tongue
30. if a ⁴*revelation* be made to another sitting by
Gal. 1. 12. but it came to me through r. of Jesus Christ
2. 2. And I went up by r.; and I laid before them
Eph. 1. 17. may give unto you a spirit of wisdom and r.
3. 3. by *revelation* was made known unto me the mystery
2 Th. 1. 7. ¹r. of the Lord Jesus from heaven
1 Pet. 1. 7. and honour at the ⁴*revelation* of Jesus Christ
13. brought unto you at the *revelation* of Jesus Christ
4. 13. that at the ⁴r. of his glory also ye may rejoice
Rev. 1. 1. The *Revelation* of Jesus Christ, which God gave

REVELATIONS

Revelations.
2 *Cor.* 12. 1. I will come to visions and r. of the Lord
7. by reason of the exceeding greatness of the *revelations*

Revelling—s.—*A.V.* ¹*rioting,* ²*sporting.*
Rom. 13. 13. as in the day ; not in ¹r. and drunkenness
Gal. 5. 21. r., and such like : of the which I forewarn you
1 *Pet.* 4. 3. lusts, winebibbings, *revellings,* carousings
2 *Pet.* 2. 13. ²*revelling* in their love-feasts while they feast

Revenge *A. V.*—*see avenge, avenging.*

Revenger *A.V.*—*see avenger.*

Reverence.
Mat. 21. 37. They will r. my son. *Mk.* 12. 6 : *Lu.* 20. 13
Heb. 12. 9. chasten us, and we gave them *reverence*
28. service well-pleasing to God with *reverence* and awe
see *fear.*

Reverent.—*A.V.* ¹*becometh holiness.*
Tit. 2. 3. that aged women likewise be ¹r. in demeanour

Revile—d.—*A.V.* ¹*accuse.*
Jno. 9. 28. they r. him, and said, Thou art his disciple
1 *Cor.* 4. 12. being *reviled,* we bless ; being persecuted
1 *Pet.* 2. 23. who, when he was *reviled, reviled* not again
3. 16. put to shame who ¹*revile* your good manner of life
see *railed, reproach, reproached.*

Reviler—s.—*A V.* ¹*railer.*
1 *Cor.* 5. 11. a brother be a fornicator—or a ¹r., or a drunkard
6. 10. nor r., nor extortioners, shall inherit the kingdom

Revilest.
Acts 23. 4. that stood by said, *R.* thou God's high priest?

Reviling.—*A.V* ¹*blasphemously,* ²*railing,* ³*speak reproachfully.*
Lu. 22. 65. other things spake they against him, ¹r. him
1 *Tim.* 5. 14. give none occasion to the adversary for ³r.
1 *Pet.* 3. 9. not rendering evil for evil, or ²*reviling* for ²r.

Revived.—*A.V.* ¹*flourished.*
Rom. 7. 9. when the commandment came, sin *revived*
Phil. 4. 10. at length ye have ¹*revived* your thought for me
see *lived.*

Reward.
Mat. 5. 12. great is your *reward* in heaven. *Lu.* 6. 23
46. If ye love them that love you, what *reward* have ye?
6. 1. else ye have no *reward* with your Father [5, 16
2. Verily I say unto you, They have received their r.
10. 41. receive a prophet's *reward*—a righteous man's r.
42. he shall in no wise lose the due *reward. Mk.* 9. 41
Lu. 6. 35. never despairing ; and your *reward* shall be great
23. 41. justly ; for we receive the due *reward* of our deeds
Acts 1. 18. obtained a field with the *reward* of his iniquity
Rom. 4. 4. the r. is not reckoned as of grace, but as of debt
1 *Cor.* 3. 8. but each shall receive his own *reward*
14. abide which he built thereon, he shall receive a r.
9. 17. if I do this of mine own will, I have a *reward*
18. What then is my r. ? That, when I preach the gospel
Heb. 2. 2. disobedience received a just recompense of r.
10. 35. boldness, which hath great recompense of *reward*
11. 26. for he looked unto the recompense of *reward*

RICHES

2 *Jno.* 8. have wrought, but that ye receive a full *reward*
Rev. 11. 18. the time to give their *reward* to thy servants
22. 12. I come quickly ; and my *reward* is with me
see *hire, prize, recompense, render, wrong.*

Rewarded *A.V.*—*see rendered.*

Rewarder.
Heb. 11. 6. God—is a *rewarder* of them that seek after him

Rich.
Mat. 19. 23. It is hard for a *rich* man to enter into the
kingdom. 24 : *Mk.* 10. 25 : *Lu.* 18. 25
27. 57. came a *rich* man from Arimathea, named Joseph
Mk. 12. 41. and many that were *rich* cast in much
Lu. 1. 53. And the *rich* he hath sent empty away
6. 24. woe unto you that are *rich* ! for ye have received
12. 16. The ground of a certain *rich* man brought forth
21. treasure for himself, and is not *rich* toward God
14. 12. call not thy friends—nor *rich* neighbours
16. 1. There was a certain *rich* man, which had a steward
19. a certain *rich* man, and he was clothed in purple
21. fed with the crumbs that fell from the r. man's table
22. and the *rich* man also died, and was buried
18. 23. he became exceeding sorrowful ; for he was very r.
19. 2. and he was a chief publican, and he was *rich*
21. 1. the *rich* men—casting their gifts into the treasury
Rom. 10. 12. Lord of all, and is r. unto all that call upon him
1 *Cor.* 4. 8. Already are ye filled, already ye are become r.
2 *Cor.* 6. 10. rejoicing ; as poor, yet making many *rich*
8. 9. though he was r., yet for your sakes he became poor,
that ye through his poverty might become *rich*
Eph. 2. 4. God, being *rich* in mercy, for his great love
1 *Tim.* 6. 9. they that desire to be r. fall into a temptation
17. Charge them that are *rich* in this present world
18. that they do good, that they be *rich* in good works
Jas. 1. 10. and the *rich,* in that he is made low
11. so also shall the *rich* man fade away in his goings
2. 5. God choose—poor as to the world to be r. in faith
6. Do not the r. oppress you, and themselves drag you
5. 1. Go to now, ye r., weep and howl for your miseries
Rev. 2. 9. thy poverty (but thou art r.), and the blasphemy
3. 17. Because thou sayest, I am r., and have gotten riches
18. gold refined by fire, that thou mayest become *rich*
6. 15. and the chief captains, and the r., and the strong
13. 16. the *rich* and the poor, and the free and the bond
18. 3. and the merchants of the earth waxed *rich.* 15
19. wherein were made r. all that had—ships in the sea

Riches.—*A.V.* ¹*goods.*
Mat. 13. 22. the deceitfulness of r., choke the word. *Mk.* 4.19
Mk. 10. 23. How hardly shall they that have *riches* enter
into the kingdom of God ! 24 : *Lu.* 18. 24
Lu. 8. 14. choked with cares and r. and pleasures of this life
16. 11. who will commit to your trust the true *riches* ?
Rom. 2. 4. Or despisest thou the *riches* of his goodness
9. 23. that he might make known the *riches* of his glory
11. 12. is the r. of the world, and their loss the r. of the
33. O the depth of the r. both of the wisdom [Gentiles
2 *Cor.* 8. 2. abounded unto the *riches* of their liberality
Eph. 1. 7. trespasses, according to the *riches* of his grace
18. what the *riches* of the glory of his inheritance
2. 7. he might shew the exceeding *riches* of his grace
3. 8. the Gentiles the unsearchable *riches* of Christ
16. he would grant you, according to the r. of his glory
Phil. 4. 19. every need of yours according to his r. in glory
Col. 1. 27. to make known—the *riches* of the glory of this mystery
2. 2. in love, and unto all r. of the full assurance [of r.
1 *Tim.* 6. 17. nor have their hope set on the uncertainty

RICHES

Heb. 11. 26. [Moses] accounting the reproach of Christ greater *riches* than the treasures of Egypt
Jas. 5. 2. Your *riches* are corrupted, and your garments
Rev. 3. 17. have gotten ¹*riches*, and have need of nothing
5. 12. Lamb that hath been slain to receive the—*riches*
18. 17. for in one hour so great *riches* is made desolate

Richly.—*A.V.* ¹*abundantly.*
Col. 3. 16. Let the word of Christ dwell in you *richly*
1 *Tim.* 6. 17. God, who giveth us *richly* all things to enjoy
Tit. 3. 6. which he poured out upon us ¹*richly*
2 *Pet.* 1. 11. shall be ¹*richly* supplied unto you the entrance

Rid.—*A.V.* ¹*secure.*
Mat. 28. 14. we will persuade him, and ¹*rid* you of care

Riding.—*A.V.* ¹*sitting.*
Mat. 21. 5. thy king cometh unto thee—¹*r.* upon an ass

Right.—*A.V.* ¹*meet,* ²*power*—*s.*
Mat. 20. 4. whatsoever is *right* I will give you
Mk. 5. 15. sitting, clothed and in his *r.* mind. *Lu.* 8. 35
Lu. 10. 28. Thou hast answered *r.*: this do, and thou shalt
12. 57. even of yourselves judge ye not what is *r.?* [live
Jno. 1. 12. to them gave he the ²*r.* to become children of
Acts 4. 19. Whether it be *r.* in the sight of God to [God
8. 21. for thy heart [Simon Magus] is not *r.* before God
13. 10. wilt thou not cease to pervert the *r.* ways of the
Rom. 9. 21. hath not the potter a ²*r.* over the clay [Lord?
1 *Cor.* 9. 4. Have we no ²*right* to eat and to drink?
5. Have we no ²*right* to lead about a wife
6. have we not a ²*right* to forbear working?
12. If others partake of this ²*r.*—we did not use this ²*r.*
18. so as not to use to the full my ²*right* in the gospel
Eph. 6. 1. obey your parents in the Lord: for this is *right*
Phil. 1. 7. even as it is ¹*right* for me to be thus minded
2 *Th.* 3. 9. because we have not the ²*right,* but to make
Heb. 13. 10. an altar, whereof they have no *right* to eat
2 *Pet.* 1. 13. I think it ¹*r.,* as long as I am in this tabernacle
2. 15. forsaking the *right* way, they went astray [life
Rev. 22. 14. they may have the *right* to come to the tree of
see side.

Righteous.—*A.V.* ¹*judgements,* ²*just,* ³*righteousness.*
Mat. 1. 19. Joseph her husband, being a ²*righteous* man
9. 13. I came not to call the *r.,* but. *Mk.* 2. 17 : *Lu.* 5. 32
10. 41. he that receiveth a *righteous* man in the name of a *righteous* man shall receive a *r.* man's reward
13. 17. and *r.* men desired to see the things which ye see
43. Then shall the *righteous* shine forth as the sun
49. sever the wicked from among the ²*righteous*
23. 28. Even so ye also outwardly appear *righteous* unto
29. and garnish the tombs of the *righteous* [men
35. all the *r.* blood shed—from the blood of Abel the *r.*
25. 37. Then shall the *r.* answer him, saying, Lord
46. eternal punishment: but the *r.* into eternal life
27. 19. Have thou nothing to do with that ²*righteous* man
24. I am innocent of the blood of this ²*righteous* man
Mk. 6. 20. knowing that he [John] was a ²*righteous* man
Lu. 1. 6. And they were both *righteous* before God
2. 25. Simeon; and this man was ²*righteous* and devout
15. 7. over ninety and nine ²*righteous* persons
18. 9. which trusted in themselves that they were *r.*
20. 20. which feigned themselves to be ²*righteous*
23. 47. saying, Certainly this was a *righteous* man
50. Joseph—a councillor, a good man and a ²*righteous*

RIGHTEOUSNESS

Jno. 5. 30. I judge: and my judgement is ²*righteous*
7. 24. to appearance, but judge *righteous* judgement
17. 25. O *righteous* Father, the world knew thee not
Acts 10. 22. Cornelius a centurion, a ²*righteous* man
Rom. 1. 17. the ²*r.* shall live by faith. *Gal.* 3. ²11 : *Heb.* 10. ²38
2. 5. and revelation of the *righteous* judgement of God
3. 10. as it is written, There is none *righteous,* no, not one
5. 7. For scarcely for a *righteous* man will one die
19. obedience of the one shall the many be made *r.*
7. 12. the commandment holy, and ²*righteous,* and good
2 *Th.* 1. 5. a manifest token of the *r.* judgement of God
6. if so be that it is a *r.* thing with God to recompense
1 *Tim.* 1. 9. knowing this, that law is not made for a *r.* man
2 *Tim.* 4. 8. which the Lord, the *r.* judge, shall give to me
Heb. 11. 4. he had witness borne to him that he was *r.*
Jas. 5. 6. ye have killed the ²*r.* one; he doth not resist you
16. The supplication of a *righteous* man availeth much
1 *Pet.* 3. 12. the eyes of the Lord are upon the *righteous*
18. suffered for sins once, the ²*r.* for the unrighteous
4. 18. if the *r.* is scarcely saved, where shall the ungodly
2 *Pet.* 2. 7. delivered ²*righteous* Lot, sore distressed
8. for that *r.* man—vexed his *r.* soul from day to day
1 *Jno.* 1. 9. he is faithful and ²*r.* to forgive us our sins
2. 1. Advocate with the Father, Jesus Christ the *r.*
29. If ye know that he is *r.,* ye know that every one
3. 7. he that doeth righteousness is *r.,* even as he is *r.*
12. Because his works were evil, and his brother's *r.*
Rev. 15. 3. ²*r.* and true are thy ways, thou King of the ages
4. for thy ¹*righteous* acts have been made manifest
16. 5. *Righteous* art thou, which art and which wast
7. the Almighty, true and *r.* are thy judgements. 19. 2
19. 8. for the fine linen is the ³*righteous* acts of the saints
22. 11. he that is *righteous,* let him do righteousness still
see righteousness.

Righteous One.—*see proper names.*

Righteously.—*A.V.* ¹*justly,* ²*righteousness.*
1 *Cor.* 15. 34. Awake up ²*righteously,* and sin not
1 *Th.* 2. 10. how holily and ¹*righteously* and unblameably
Tit. 2. 12. we should live soberly and *righteously* and godly
1 *Pet.* 2. 23. committed himself to him that judgeth *r.*

Righteousness.—*A.V.* ¹*alms,* ²*righteous.*
Mat. 3. 15. thus it becometh us to fulfil all *righteousness*
5. 6. Blessed are they that hunger and thirst after *r.*
10. Blessed are they that have been persecuted for *r.*
20. except your *r.* shall exceed the *r.* of the scribes
6. 1. Take heed that ye do not your ¹*r.* before men
33. But seek ye first his kingdom, and his *righteousness*
21. 32. For John came unto you in the way of *righteousness*
Lu. 1. 75. In holiness and *r.* before him all our days
Jno. 16. 8. convict the world in respect of sin, and of *r.*
10. of *righteousness,* because I go to the Father
Acts 10. 35. that feareth him, and worketh *r.,* is acceptable
13. 10. thou enemy of all *r.,* wilt thou not cease to pervert
17. 31. he will judge the world in *r.* by the man whom
24. 25. as he reasoned of *righteousness,* and temperance
Rom. 1. 17. For therein is revealed a *r.* of God by faith
3. 5. if our unrighteousness commendeth the *r.* of God
21. apart from the law a *r.* of God hath been manifested
22. even the *r.* of God through faith in Jesus Christ
25. to shew his *r.,* because of the passing over. 26
4. 3. and it was reckoned unto him for *righteousness.* 5, 9, 22: *Gal.* 3. 6: *Jas.* 2. 23
4. 6. unto whom God reckoneth *r.* apart from works
11. a seal of the *r.* of the faith—that *r.* might be reckoned
13. heir of the world, but through the *r.* of faith
5. 17. receive the abundance of grace and of the gift of *r.*

RIGHTEOUSNESS

Rom. 5. 18. through one act of *r.* the free gift came unto all
21. so might grace reign through *r.* unto eternal life
6. 13. your members as instruments of *r.* unto God. 19
16. whether of sin unto death, or of obedience unto *r.* ?
18. being made free from sin, ye became servants of *r.*
20. servants of sin, ye were free in regard of *r.*
8. 10. but the spirit is life because of *righteousness*
9. 30. Gentiles, which followed not after *r.*, attained to *righteousness*, even the *r.* which is of faith
31. Israel, following after a law of *r.*, did not arrive
10. 3. being ignorant of God's *righteousness*—did not subject themselves to the *righteousness* of God
4. For Christ is the end of the law unto *righteousness*
5. doeth the *r.* which is of the law shall live thereby
6. But the *righteousness* which is of faith saith thus
10. for with the heart man believeth unto *righteousness*
14. 17. kingdom of God is not eating and drinking, but *r.*
1 *Cor.* 1. 30. was made unto us wisdom from God, and *r.*
2 *Cor.* 3. 9. doth the ministration of *r.* exceed in glory
5. 21. that we might become the *r.* of God in him
6. 7. by the armour of *r.* on the right hand and on the left
14. fellowship have *righteousness* and iniquity?
9. 9. His *righteousness* abideth for ever
10. seed for sowing, and increase the fruits of your *r.*
11. 15. ministers also fashion themselves as ministers of *r.*
Gal. 2. 21. if *r.* is through the law—Christ died for nought
3. 21. make alive, verily *r.* would have been of the law
5. 5. we through the Spirit by faith wait for the hope of *r.*
Eph. 4. 24. new man, which after God hath been created in
5. 9. the fruit of the light is in all goodness and *r.*   [*r.*
6. 14. and having put on the breastplate of *righteousness*
Phil. 1. 11. being filled with the fruits of *righteousness*
3. 6. touching the *r.* which is in the law, found blameless
9. not having a *r.* of mine own—the *r.* which is of God
1 *Tim.* 6. 11. and follow after *righteousness*. 2 *Tim.* 2. 22
2. *Tim.* 3. 16. for correction, for instruction which is in *r.*
4. 8. henceforth there is laid up for me the crown of *r.*
Tit. 3. 5. not by works done in *righteousness*, which we did
Heb. 1. 9. Thou hast loved *righteousness*, and hated iniquity
5. 13. of milk is without experience of the word of *r.*
7. 2. (being first, by interpretation, King of *righteousness*
11. 7. heir of the *r.* which is according to faith
33. who through faith subdued kingdoms, wrought *r.*
12. 11. exercised thereby, even the fruit of *righteousness*
Jas. 1. 20. the wrath of man worketh not the *r.* of God
3. 18. And the fruit of *r.* is sown in peace for them
1 *Pet.* 2. 24. we, having died unto sins, might live unto *r.*
3. 14. if ye should suffer for *r.* sake, blessed are ye
2 *Pet.* 1. 1. precious faith with us in the *r.* of our God
2. 5. preserved Noah with seven others, a preacher of *r.*
21. better for them not to have known the way of *r.*
3. 13. new heavens and a new earth, wherein dwelleth *r.*
1 *Jno.* 2. 29. every one also that doeth *r.* is begotten of him
3. 7. he that doeth *righteousness* is righteous
10. whosoever doeth not *righteousness* is not of God
Rev. 19. 11. and in *r.* he doth judge and make war
22. 11. he that is righteous, let him do *²righteousness* still
see ordinance—s, righteous, righteously, uprightness.

Rightly.

Lu. 7. 43. he said unto him, Thou hast *rightly* judged
20. 21. Master, we know that thou—teachest *rightly*
see aright.

Ring.

Lu. 15. 22. put a *ring* on his hand, and shoes on his feet
Jas. 2. 2. into your synagogue a man with a gold *ring*

Ringleader.

Acts 24. 5. and a *ringleader* of the sect of the Nazarenes

RISETH

Riot.—*A.V.* ¹*excess,* ²*uproar.*

Acts 19. 40. danger to be accused concerning this day's ²*riot*
Eph. 5. 18. be not drunken with wine, wherein is ¹*riot*
Tit. 1. 6. children that believe, who are not accused of *r.*
1 *Pet.* 4. 4. that ye run not—into the same excess of *riot*
see revel.

Rioting *A.V.—see revelling.*

Riotous.

Lu. 15. 13. there he wasted his substance with *r.* living

Riotously.—*A.V.* ¹*greedily.*

Jude 11. and ran ¹*riotously* in the error of Balaam for hire

Ripe, over-ripe.—*A.V.* ¹*brought forth,* ²*ripe.*

Mk. 4. 29. when the fruit is ¹*ripe*, straightway he putteth
Rev. 14. 15. for the harvest of the earth is ²*over-ripe*
18. vine of the earth; for her grapes are fully *ripe*

Rise.—*A.V.* ¹*arise,* ²*risen,* ³*rose.*

Mat. 5. 45. maketh his sun to *rise* on the evil and the good
10. 21. children shall *rise* up against parents. *Mk.* 13. 12
12. 42. The queen of the south shall *rise* up. *Lu.* 11. 31
24. 7. For nation shall *r.* against nation. *Mk.* 13. 8: *Lu.*
27. 63. After three days I *rise* again. *Mk.* 8. 31 [21. 10
Mk. 4. 27. and should sleep and *rise* night and day
9. 31. after three days he shall *r.* again. 10. 34: *Lu.* 18.
10. 49. Be of good cheer: *rise*, he calleth thee [33: 24. 7
12. 25. when they shall have *risen* from the dead, they neither
Lu. 6. 8. *Rise* up, and stand forth in the midst   [marry
11. 7. with me in bed; I cannot *rise* and give thee?
8. I say unto you, Though he will not *r.* and give him
16. 31. will they be persuaded, if one ³*rise* from the dead
22. 46. *rise* and pray, that ye enter not into temptation
24. 46. it is written—Christ should suffer, and *rise* again
Jno. 11. 23. Jesus saith unto her, Thy brother shall *r.* again
24. I know that he shall *rise* again in the resurrection
20. 9. the scripture, that he must *r.* again from the dead
Acts 10. 13. voice to him, *Rise*, Peter; kill and eat. 11. ¹7
12. 7. angel—smote Peter—saying, ¹*Rise* up quickly
17. 3. it behoved the Christ to suffer, and to ²*rise* again
1 *Th.* 4. 16. and the dead in Christ shall *rise* first
Rev. 11. 1. one said, *Rise*, and measure the temple of God
see arise, ariseth, coming, resurrection, risen, rising, stand.

Risen.—*A.V.* ¹*raised,* ²*rise,* ³*up.*

Mat. 6. when the sun was ²*risen*, they were scorched
14. 2. This is John the Baptist; he is *risen* from the dead. *Mk.* 6. 14, 16: *Lu.* 9. 7
17. 9. until the Son of man be *r.* from the dead. *Mk.* 9. 9
27. 64. and say unto the people, He is *r.* from the dead
28. 6. He is not here; for he is *r. Mk.* 16. 6: *Lu.* 24. 6
7. tell his disciples, He is *risen* from the dead
Mk. 3. 26. if Satan hath ²*risen* up against himself
16. 9. Now when he was *risen* early on the first day
14. which had seen him after he was *risen. Jno.* 21. 14
Lu. 9. 8. that one of the old prophets was *risen* again. 19
13. 25. When once the master of the house is *risen* up
24. 34. The Lord is *risen* indeed, and hath appeared
2 *Tim.* 2. 8. Remember Jesus Christ, ¹*risen* from the dead
see arisen, ariseth, raised, rise.

Riseth—ing.—*A.V.* ¹*arose,* ²*rise.*

Mk. 9. 10. what the *rising* again from the dead should mean
Lu. 2. 34. child is set for the falling and *rising* up of many
12. 54. When ye see a cloud ²*rising* in the west

RISETH

Jno. 6. 18. the sea was ¹r. by reason of a great wind [ments
13. 4. [Jesus] r. from supper, and layeth aside his gar.
see rose.

River—s.—*A.V.* ¹*flood*, ²*waters.*

Mat. 3. 6. they were baptized of him in the r. Jordan. *Mk.* 1. 5
Jno. 7. 38. out of his belly shall flow *rivers* of living water
Acts 16. 13. went forth without the gate by a *river* side
2 *Cor.* 11. 26. in journeyings often, in perils of ²*rivers*
Rev. 8. 10. and it fell upon the third part of the *rivers*
12. 15. out of his mouth after the woman water as a ¹*river*
16. swallowed up the ¹*river* which the dragon cast out
16. 4. the third poured out his bowl into the *rivers*
12. his bowl upon the great *river*, the *river* Euphrates
22. 1. And he shewed me a *river* of water of life [life
2. on this side of the *river* and on that was the tree of

Roareth—ing.

Lu. 21. 25. in perplexity for the *roaring* of the sea
1 *Pet.* 5. 8. the devil, as a *roaring* lion, walketh about
Rev. 10. 3. cried with a great voice, as a lion *roareth*

Rob—bed.—*A.V.* ¹*beguile*, ²*sacrilege.*

Rom. 2. 22. thou that abhorrest idols, dost thou ²r. temples?
2 *Cor.* 11. 8. I *robbed* other churches, taking wages of them
Col. 2. 18. Let no man ¹*rob* you of your prize

Robber—s.—*A.V.* ¹*thief*, ²*thieves.*

Mat. 21. 13. ye make it a den of ²r. *Mk.* 11. ²17: *Lu.* 19. ²46
26. 55. Are ye come out as against a ¹r. *Mk.* 14. ¹48: *Lu.* 22.
27. 38. crucified with him two ²r. ²44: *Mk.* 15. ²27 [¹52
Lu. 10. 36. neighbour unto him that fell among the ²r.? ²30
Jno. 10. 1. other way, the same is a thief and a *robber*
8. All that came before me are thieves and *robbers*
18. 40. Now Barrabas was a *robber*
Acts 19. 37. these men, which are neither r. of temples
2 *Cor.* 11. 26. in perils of rivers, in perils of *robbers*

Robbery *A.V.*—*see prize.*

Robe—s.—*A.V.* ¹*clothing*, ²*do his commandments*,
³*garment*, ⁴*robes.*

Mat. 27. 28. they stripped him, and put on him a scarlet r.
31. mocked him, they took off from him the *robe*
Mk. 12. 38. scribes, which desire to walk in long ¹r. *Lu.* 20.
16. 5. arrayed in a white ³r.; and they were amazed [46
Lu. 15. 22. Bring forth quickly the best r., and put it on him
Rev. 6. 11. And there was given them to each one a white ⁴r.
7. 9. and before the Lamb, arrayed in white *robes*
13. These which are arrayed in the white *robes*
14. they washed their *robes*, and made them white
22. 14. Blessed are they that wash their ²r., that they may
see apparel, garment.

Rock—s.—*A.V.* ¹*spots.*

Mat. 7. 24. wise man, which built his house upon the r. *Lu.*
25. fell not; for it was founded upon the *rock* [6. 48
16. 18. and upon this *rock* I will build my church
27. 51. the earth did quake; and the *rocks* were rent
60. new tomb, which he had hewn out in the r. *Mk.* 15. 46
Lu. 8. 6. And other fell on the *rock*; and as soon as it grew
13. those on the *rock* are they which, when they have
Rom. 9. 33. stone of stumbling and a r. of offence. 1 *Pet.* 2. 8
1 *Cor.* 10. 4. a spiritual r. that followed them: and the r. was
Jude 12. who are hidden ¹*rocks* in your love-feasts [Christ
Rev. 6. 15. hid themselves in the caves and in the *rocks*
16. say to the mountains and to the *rocks*, Fall on us
see rocky.

ROSE

Rocky.—*A.V.* ¹*rocks*, ²*stony.*

Mat. 13. 5. others fell upon the ²r. places. ²20: *Mk.* 4. ²5, ²16
Acts 27. 29. lest haply we should be cast ashore on ¹r. ground

Rod—s.

Acts 16. 22. and commanded to beat them with *rods*
1 *Cor.* 4. 21. shall I come unto you with a *rod*, or in love
2 *Cor.* 11. 25. Thrice was I beaten with *rods*
Heb. 9. 4. the manna, and Aaron's *rod* that budded
Rev. 2. 27. he shall rule them with a r. of iron. 12. 5: 19. 15
11. 1. And there was given me a reed like unto a *rod*

Roll.—*A.V.* ¹*volume.*

Heb. 10. 7. (In the ¹*roll* of the book it is written of me)

Roll—ed.—*A.V.* ¹*fold*, ²*wrapped.*

Mat. 27. 60. he *rolled* a great stone to the door. *Mk.* 15. 46
28. 2. came and *rolled* away the stone, and sat upon it
Mk. 16. 3. Who shall *roll* us away the stone from the door
4. they see that the stone is *rolled* back. *Lu.* 24. 2
Jno. 20. 7. with the linen cloths, but ²r. up in a place by
Heb. 1. 12. And as a mantle shalt thou ¹*roll* them up [itself
Rev. 6. 14. heaven was removed as a scroll when it is r. up

Roman.—*A.V.* ¹*free.*

Acts 22. 28. Paul said, But I am a ¹*Roman* born
see proper names.

Roof.

Mat. 8. 8. that thou shouldest come under my r. *Lu.* 7. 6
Mk. 2. 4. they uncovered the *roof* where he [Jesus] was

Room.

Mat. 2. 22. over Judæa in the *room* of his father Herod
Mk. 2. 2. so that there was no longer *room* for them
14. 15. himself shew you a large upper *room*. *Lu.* 22. 12
Lu. 2. 7. because there was no *room* for them in the inn
14. 22. thou didst command is done, and yet there is r.
see chamber, place, seat, seats, succeded.

Root—s.

Mat. 3. 10. now is the axe laid unto the *root*. *Lu.* 3. 9
13. 6. because they had no *root*, they withered. *Mk.* 4. 6
21. not r. in himself, but endureth. *Mk.* 4. 17: *Lu.* 8. 13
29 up the tares, ye *root* up the wheat with them
Mk. 11. 20. the fig tree withered away from the *roots*
Rom. 11. 16. and if the *root* is holy, so are the branches
17. didst become partaker with them of the *root*
18. it is not thou that bearest the r., but the *root* thee
15. 12. There shall be the *root* of Jesse
1 *Tim.* 6. 10. the love of money is a r. of all kinds of evil
Heb. 12. 15. lest any r. of bitterness springing up trouble you
Jude 12. without fruit, twice dead, plucked up by the *roots*
Rev. 5. 5. the R. of David, hath overcome, to open the book
22. 16. I am the *root* and the offspring of David

Rooted.—*A.V.* ¹*plucked.*

Mat. 15. 13. my heavenly Father planted not, shall be r. up
Lu. 17. 6. Be thou ¹r. up, and be thou planted in the sea
Eph. 3. 17. that ye, being *rooted* and grounded in love
Col. 2. 7. *rooted* and builded up in him, and stablished

Ropes.

Acts 27. 32. Then the soldiers cut away the r. of the boat

Rose.—*A.V.* ¹*arose*, ²*insurrection*, ³*rising.*

Mk. 1. 35. a great while before day, he ³r. up and went out
5. 42. And straightway the damsel ¹*rose* up. *Lu.* 8. ¹55

ROSE

Lu. 4. 29. they *rose* up, and cast him forth out of the city
38. he ¹*rose* up—and entered into the house
39. immediately she ¹*rose* up and ministered unto them
5. 25. he r. up before them, and took up that whereon he
28. And he forsook all, and r. up and followed him [lay
22 45. when he r. up from his prayer, he came unto the
24. 33. they r. up that—hour, and returned to Jerusalem
Jno. 11. 31. when they saw Mary, that she *rose* up quickly
Acts 5. 17. the high priest *rose* up, and all they that were
36. For before these days *rose* up Theudas [with him
37. *rose* up Judas of Galilee in the days of the enrolment
10. 41. who did eat and drink with him after he *rose*
14. 20. he [Paul] *rose* up, and entered into the city
15. 5. there *rose* up certain of the sect of the Pharisees
16. 22. And the multitude *rose* up together against them
18. 12. the Jews with one accord ²*rose* up against Paul
26. 30. the king *rose* up, and the governor, and Bernice
1 *Cor.* 10. 7. sat down to eat and drink, and *rose* up to play
2 *Cor.* 5. 15. him who for their sakes died and *rose* again
1 *Th.* 4. 14. if we believe that Jesus died and *rose* again
see awoke, goeth, raise, raised, rise, sprang.

Rough.—*A.V.* ¹*fierce.*

Lu. 3. 5. crooked shall become straight, And the r. ways
Jas. 3. 4. ships—are driven by ¹*rough* winds [smooth

Roused—*A.V.* ¹*awaking.*

Acts 16. 27. the jailor being ¹*roused* out of sleep

Rowed—ing.

Mk. 6. 48. And seeing them distressed in r., for the wind
Jno. 6. 19. When therefore they had r. about five and twenty

Royal.

Acts 12. 21. Herod arrayed himself in r. apparel, and sat
Jas. 2. 8. if ye fulfil the r. law, according to the scripture
1 *Pet.* 2. 9. But ye are an elect race, a *royal* priesthood

Rubbing.

Lu. 6. 1. ears of corn, and did eat, r. them in their hands

Rudder—s.—*A.V.* ¹*helm,* ²*rudder.*

Acts 27. 40. at the same time loosing the bands of the ²r.
Jas. 3. 4. ships—are yet turned about by a very small ¹r.

Rude.

2 *Cor.* 11. 6. though I be *rude* in speech—not in knowledge

Rudiments.—*A.V.* ¹*elements.*

Gal. 4. 3. were held in bondage under the ¹r. of the world
9. turn ye back again to the weak and beggarly ¹r.
Col. 2. 8. after the r. of the world, and not after *Christ*
20. If ye died with Christ from the r. of the world

Rue.

Lu. 11. 42. for ye tithe mint and *rue* and every herb

Ruin—s.

Lu. 6. 49. it fell in; and the *ruin* of that house was great
Acts 15. 16. And I will build again the *ruins* thereof

Rule.—*A.V.* ¹*guide,* ²*power,* ³*principality,* ⁴*reign.*

Mk. 10. 42. which are accounted to *rule* over the Gentiles
Lu. 20. 20. so as to deliver him up to the ²r. and—authority
Rom. 15. 12. he that ariseth to ⁴*rule* over the Gentiles
1 *Cor.* 15. 24. when he shall have abolished all *rule*

RUN

Gal. 6. 16. as many as shall walk by this r., peace be upon
Eph. 1. 21. far above all ³r., and authority, and power [them
Phil. 3. 16. attained, by that same *rule* let us walk
Col. 3. 15. And let the peace of Christ *rule* in your hearts
1 *Tim.* 3. 5. if a man knoweth not how to *rule* his own house
5. 14. younger widows marry—¹*rule* the household
17. Let the elders that *rule* well be counted worthy
Heb. 13. 7. Remember them that had the r. over you. 17, 24
Rev. 2. 27. *rule* them with a rod of iron. 12. 5 : 19. 15
see province, shepherd.

Ruler.—*A.V.* ¹*governor,* ²*prince.*

Mat. 9. 18. there came a *ruler*, and worshipped him
23. And when Jesus came into the *ruler's* house
Mk. 5. 36. *ruler* of the synagogue. 35, 38: *Lu.* 8. 41, 49: 13. 14
Lu. 18. 18. a certain *ruler* asked him, saying, Good Master
Jno. 2. 8. Draw out now, and bear unto the ¹r. of the feast
9. And when the *ruler* of the feast tasted the water
3. 1. named Nicodemus, a *ruler* of the Jews
Acts 7. 27. Who made thee a r. and a judge over us? 35
35. him hath God sent to be both a r. and a deliverer
18. 8. Crispus, the *ruler* of the synagogue, believed
17. all laid hold on Sosthenes, the r. of the synagogue
23. 5. Thou shalt not speak evil of a *ruler* of thy people
Rev. 1. 5. firstborn of the dead, and the ²*ruler* of the kings
see set (over).

Rulers. — *A.V.* ¹*chief,* ²*magistrates,* ³*princes,*
⁴*principalities.*

Mat. 20. 25. the ³*rulers* of the Gentiles lord it over them
Mk. 5. 22. cometh one of the r. of the synagogue, Jaïrus
Lu. 12. 11. the ²*rulers*, and the authorities, be not anxious
14. 1. when he went into the house of one of the ¹*rulers*
23. 13. called together the chief priests and the *rulers*
35. And the *rulers* also scoffed at him, saying
24. 20. our *rulers* delivered him up to be condemned
Jno. 7. 26. that the r. indeed know that this is the Christ?
48. Hath any of the *rulers* believed on him
12. 42. even of the *rulers* many believed on him
Acts 3. 17. in ignorance ye did it, as did also your *rulers*
4. 26. kings—in array, And the r. were gathered together
13. 15. the *rulers* of the synagogue sent unto them
27. and their *rulers*, because they knew him not
14. 5. Jews with their r., to entreat them shamefully
16. 19. Paul and Silas, and dragged them—before the r.
17. 8. they troubled the multitude and the r. of the city
Rom. 13. 3. For *rulers* are not a terror to the good work
1 *Cor.* 2. 6. the ³r. of this world, which are coming to nought
8. which none of the ³*rulers* of this world knoweth
Eph. 6. 12. against the world-*rulers* of this darkness
Tit. 3. 1. Put them in mind to be in subjection to ⁴*rulers*
see governors.

Ruleth—ing.

Rom. 12. 8. he that *ruleth*, with diligence; he that sheweth
1 *Tim.* 3. 4. one that *ruleth* well his own house
12. *ruling* their children and their own houses well

Rumour—s.—*A.V.* ¹*fame.*

Mat. 24. 6. ye shall hear of wars and r. of wars. *Mk.* 18. 7
Lu. 4. 37. And there went forth a ¹*rumour* concerning him
see report.

Run.—*A.V.* ¹*have free course.*

1 *Cor.* 9. 24. they which *run* in a race *run* all, but one
receiveth the prize? Even so r., that ye may attain
26. I therefore so *run*, as not uncertainly
Gal. 2. 2. I should be running, or had *run*, in vain
Phil. 2. 16. I did not *run* in vain neither labour in vain

RUN

2 *Th.* 3. 1. word of the Lord may ¹*run* and be glorified
Heb. 12. 1. let us *r.* with patience the race that is set before us
1 *Pet.* 4. 4. that ye *r.* not with them into the same excess
see ran, running.

Runneth.

Jno. 20. 2. She [Mary Magdalene] *r.* therefore, and cometh
Rom. 9. 16. not of him that willeth, nor of him that *runneth*
see spilled.

Running.—*A.V.* ¹*run.*

Mk. 9. 15. greatly amazed, and *running* to him saluted him
25. when Jesus saw that a multitude came *r.* together
Lu. 6. 38. measure, pressed down, shaken together, *r.* over
Acts 27. 16. And *r.* under the lee of a small island called Cauda
Gal. 2. 2. lest by any means I should be ¹*r.*, or had run
5. 7. Ye were ¹*running* well; who did hinder you
see ran, rushing.

Rushed.—*A.V.* ¹*ran.*

Mat. 8. 32. whole herd ¹*rushed* down the steep into the
sea. *Mk.* 5. ¹13; *Lu.* 8. ¹33   [with one accord
Acts 7. 57. stopped their ears, and ¹*r.* upon him [Stephen]
19. 29. and they *rushed* with one accord into the theatre

Rushing.—*A.V.* ¹*running.*

Acts 2. 2. from heaven a sound as of the *r.* of a mighty wind
Rev. 9. 9. sound of chariots, of many horses ¹*r.* to war

Rust—ed.—*A.V.* ¹*cankered.*

Mat. 6. 19. where moth and *rust* doth consume. 20
Jas. 5. 3. Your gold and your silver are ¹*rusted;* and their
rust shall be for a testimony against you

S.

Sabachthani.—*see Eli.*

Sabaoth.—*see proper names.*

Sabbath.—*A.V.* ¹*sabbath day—s.*

Mat. 12. 2. it is not lawful to do upon the ¹*sabbath. Lu.* 6. ¹9
5. the priests in the temple profane the *sabbath*
8. the Son of man is lord of the ¹*s. Mk.* 2. 28; *Lu.* 6. 5
24. 20. flight be not in the winter, neither on a ¹*sabbath*
Mk. 2. 27. The *s.* was made for man, and not man for the *s.*
6. 2. when the ¹*sabbath* was come, he began to teach
15. 42. the Preparation, that is, the day before the *s.*
16. 1. And when the *sabbath* was past, Mary Magdalene
Lu. 6. 1. it came to pass on a *sabbath*, that he was going
6. on another *s.*, that he entered into the synagogue
7. whether he would heal on the ¹*sabbath*   [of the ¹*s.*
13. 14. Jesus had healed on the ¹*s.*—and not on the day
15. doth not each one of you on the *s.* loose his ox
14. 1. rulers of the Pharisees on a ¹*sabbath* to eat bread
3. Is it lawful to heal on the ¹*sabbath*, or not?
23. 54. day of the Preparation, and the *sabbath* drew on
56. on the ¹*s.* they rested according to the commandment
Jno. 5. 16. because he did these things on the ¹*sabbath*
18. he not only brake the *sabbath*, but also called God
7. 22. and on the ¹*sabbath* ye circumcise a man. ¹23
23. because I made a man every whit whole on the ¹*s.?*
9. 16. not from God, because he keepeth not the ¹*sabbath*

SADDUCEES

Acts 13. 27. which are read every ¹*sabbath.* 15. ¹21
42. might be spoken to them the next *sabbath*
44. the next ¹*s.* almost the whole city was gathered
18. 4. And he reasoned in the synagogue every *sabbath*
see sabbath day.

Sabbath *day.—see p.* 77.

Sackcloth.

Mat. 11. 21. repented long ago in *s.* and ashes. *Lu.* 10. 13
Rev. 6. 12. and the sun became black as *sackcloth* of hair
11. 3. and they shall prophesy—clothed in *sackcloth*

Sacred.—*A.V.* ¹*holy.*

1 *Cor.* 9. 13. they which minister about ¹*sacred* things
2 *Tim.* 3. 15. from a babe thou hast known the ¹*s.* writings

Sacrifice.

Mat. 9. 13. I desire mercy, and not *sacrifice.* 12. 7
Lu. 2. 24. to offer a *sacrifice* according to that which is
Acts 7. 41. in those days, and brought a *s.* unto the idol
14. 13. and would have done *s.* with the multitudes
18. scarce restrained they the multitudes from doing *s.*
Rom. 12. 1. to present your bodies a living *sacrifice*, holy
1 *Cor.* 10. 20. things which the Gentiles *s.*, they *s.* to devils
28. This hath been offered in *sacrifice*, eat not
Eph. 5. 2. and a *s.* to God for an odour of a sweet smell
Phil. 2. 17. upon the *sacrifice* and service of your faith
4. 18. a *sacrifice* acceptable, well-pleasing to God
Heb. 9. 26. to put away sin by the *sacrifice* of himself
10. 5. *Sacrifice* and offering thou wouldest not
12. when he had offered one *sacrifice* for sins for ever
26. there remaineth no more a *sacrifice* for sins
11. 4. Abel offered unto God a more excellent *sacrifice*
13. 15. Through him then let us offer up a *s.* of praise
see sacrifices.

Sacrificed.—*A.V.* ¹*killed*, ²*offered.*

Mk. 14. 12. when they ¹*sacrificed* the passover. *Lu.* 22. ¹7
Acts 15. 29. that ye abstain from things ²*s.* to idols. 21. ²25
1 *Cor.* 5. 7. For our passover also hath been *sacrificed*
8. 1. things ²*s.* to idols. ²4, ²7, ²10: 10. ²19: *Rev.* 2. 14, 20

Sacrifices.—*A.V.* ¹*offering*, ²*sacrifice.*

Mk. 12. 33. more than all whole burnt offerings and *s.*
Lu. 13. 1. whose blood Pilate had mingled with their *s.*
Acts 7. 42. Did ye offer unto me slain beasts and *sacrifices*
1 *Cor.* 10. 18. they which eat the *s.* communion with the
Heb. 5. 1. that he may offer both gifts and *s.* for sins
7. 27. not daily, like those high priests, to offer up ²*s.*
8. 3. high priest is appointed to offer both gifts and *s.*
9. 9. according to which are offered both gifts and *s.*
23. but the heavenly things themselves with better *s.*
10. 1. they can never with the same *s.* year by year
3. But in those *sacrifices* there is a remembrance
6. In whole burnt offerings and *sacrifices* for sin
8. ²*S.* and offerings and whole burnt offerings and ¹*s.*
11. and offering oftentimes the same *sacrifices*
13. 16. for with such *sacrifices* God is well pleased
1 *Pet.* 2. 5. a holy priesthood, to offer up spiritual ²*s.*

Sacrilege *A.V.—see rob.*

Sad.

Mat. 6. 16. be not, as the hypocrites, of a *sad* countenance
Lu. 24. 17. And they stood still, looking *sad*

Sadducees.—*see proper names.*

SAFE

Safe.
Lu. 15. 27. because he hath received him *safe* and sound
Acts 23. 24. set Paul thereon, and bring him *s.* unto Felix
27. 44. came to pass, that they all escaped *s.* to the land
Phil. 3. 1. indeed is not irksome, but for you it is *safe*

Safely.
Mk. 14. 44. take him, and lead him away *safely*
Acts 16. 23. charging the jailor to keep them *safely*

Safety.—*A.V.* ¹*health.*
Acts 5. 23. The prison-house we found shut in all *safety*
27. 34. you to take some food : for this is for your ¹*safety*
1 *Th.* 5. 3. When they are saying, Peace and *safety*

Said.—*A.V.* ¹*commanded,* ²*saidst,* ³*spoken,* ⁴*told.*
Mat. 5. 21. Ye heard that it was *said.* 27, 31, 33, 38, 43
15. 4. For God ¹*said,* Honour thy father and thy mother
27. But she *said,* Yea, Lord : for even the dogs eat
20. 13. he answered and *said* to one of them, Friend
26. 35. Likewise also *said* all the disciples. *Mk.* 14, 31
64. Jesus saith unto him, Thou hast *said.* 25
27. 63. Sir, we remember that that deceiver *said*
Mk. 3. 21. for they *said,* He is beside himself
30. because they *said,* He hath an unclean spirit
11. 6. they *said* unto them even as Jesus had ¹*said*
16. 8. they *said* nothing to any one; for they were afraid
Lu. 1. 13. But the angel *said* unto him, Fear not. 30 : 2. 10
2. 24. according to that which is *said* in the law
4. 12. It is *said,* Thou shalt not tempt the Lord thy God
9. 7. it was *said* by some, that John was risen
49. And John answered and *said,* Master, we saw one
12. 3. whatsoever ye have ³*s.* in the darkness shall be heard
18. 34. they perceived not the things that were ³*said*
19. 34. And they *said,* The Lord hath need of him
20. 39. answering *said,* Master, thou hast well *s. Mk.* 12. 32
23. 46. and having *said* this, he gave up the ghost
24. 23. a vision of angels, which *said* that he was alive
24. and found it even so as the women had *said*
Jno. 1. 23. Make straight the way of the Lord, as *s.* Isaiah
4. 18. is not thy husband : this hast thou ¹*said*
7. 38. He that believeth on me, as the scripture hath *said*
8. 11. And she *said,* No man, Lord
11. 28. And when she had *said* this, she went away
12. 41. These things *said* Isaiah, because he saw his
50. even as the Father hath *said* unto me, so I speak
20. 14. When she had thus *said,* she turned herself back
Acts 2. 38. And Peter *said* unto them, Repent ye
4. 23. the chief priests and the elders had *s.* unto them
5. 8. land for so much. And she *said,* Yea, for so much
7. 37. This is that Moses, which *said* unto the children
12. 15. they *said* unto her—And they *s.,* It is his angel
17. 28. as certain even of your own poets have *said*
Rom. 7. 7. except the law had *said,* Thou shalt not covet
9. 12. it was *said* unto her, The elder shall serve
2 *Cor.* 4. 6. Seeing it is God, that ¹*said,* Light shall shine
6. 16. even as God *said,* I will dwell in them
13. 2. I have ⁴*said* beforehand, and I do say beforehand
Gal. 1. 9. As we have ⁴*said* before, so say I now again
Heb. 3. 15. while it is *said,* To-day if ye shall hear. 4. 7
7. 13. he of whom these things are ³*said* belongeth to
10. 30. For we know him that *said,* Vengeance belongeth
11. 18. to whom it was *said,* In Isaac shall thy seed be
13. 5. for himself hath *said,* I will in no wise fail thee
Rev. 5. 14. And the four living creatures *said,* Amen

SAILED

Rev. 6. 11. it was *said* unto them, that they should rest yet
9. 4. it was ¹*s.* unto them that they should not hurt the
see answered, called, saith, say, saying, spake.

He Said, Said he.—*A.V.* ¹*saith,* ²*spake,* ³*spoken.*
Mat. 27. 43. for *he said,* I am the Son of God
28. 6. He is not here ; for he is risen, even as *he said*
Mk. 14. 16. and found as *he* had *said. Lu.* 19. 32 : 22. 13
16. 7. there shall ye see him, as *he said* unto you
Lu. 9. 33. and one for Elijah : not knowing what *he said*
18. 17. as *he said* these things, all his adversaries
Jno. 6. 6. And this *he said* to prove him : for he himself
59. These things *said he* in the synagogue
9. 17. opened thine eyes ? And *he said,* He is a prophet
11. 51. Now this *he ²said* not of himself
12. 6. this *he said,* not because he cared for the poor
33. this *he said,* signifying by what manner of death
18. 6. When therefore *he said* unto them, I am he
19. 30. *he said,* It is finished : and he bowed his head
20. 18. when *he* had ²*said* these things unto her
20. And when *he* had *said* this. 22 : *Acts* 7. 60
Acts 1. 4. the promise of the Father, which, ¹*said he,* ye
9. 5. And *he said,* Who art thou, Lord ? And *he said,* I am
20. 35. how *he* himself *said,* It is more blessed to give
23. 7. And when *he* had so *said,* there arose a dissension
27. 35. when *he* had ²*said* this, and had taken bread
2 *Cor.* 12. 9. *he* hath *said* unto me, My grace is sufficient
Heb. 1. 5. For unto which of the angels *said he.* 13
4. 4. For *he* hath ²*said* somewhere of the seventh day
10. 9. then hath *he said,* Lo, I am come to do thy will
15. beareth witness to us : for after *he* hath *said*
Jas. 2. 11. For *he* that *said,* Do not commit adultery
Rev. 22. 6. *he said* unto me, These words are faithful and
see he saith.

I Said, Said I.—*A.V.* ¹*spake.*
Jno. 1. 30. is he of whom I *said,* After me cometh. ¹15
3. 7. Marvel not that *I said* unto thee, Ye must be born
10. 34. Is it not written in your law, *I said,* Ye are gods ?
36. because *I said,* I am the Son of God ?
11. 40. Said *I* not unto thee, that, if thou believedst
42. of the multitude which standeth around *I said* it
14. 26. bring to your remembrance all that *I said* unto
28. Ye heard how *I said* to you, I go away
16. 4. these things *I s.* not unto you from the beginning
18. 21. behold, these know the things which *I said*
Acts 11. 8. But *I said,* Not so, Lord : for nothing common
2 *Cor.* 7. 3. for *I* have *said* before, that ye are in our hearts
9. 3. that, even as *I said,* ye may be prepared
Gal. 2. 14. *I said* unto Cephas before them all, If thou
Heb. 10. 7. Then *said I,* Lo, I am come
see I say, spake, spoken.

Saidst *A.V.*—*see hast, said.*

Sail.—*A.V.* ¹*forth,* ²*loosing,* ³*sailed.*
Acts 16. 11. Setting ²*sail* therefore from Troas, we made
18. 21. unto you, if God will, he set ³*sail* from Ephesus
20. 3. as he was about to set *sail* for Syria
13. But he, going before to the ship, set ³*sail* for Assos
16. For Paul had determined to *sail* past Ephesus
21. 2. unto Phœnicia, we went aboard, and set ¹*sail*
27. 1. it was determined that we should *sail* for Italy
2. which was about to *sail* unto the—coast of Asia
24. God hath granted thee all them that *sail* with thee
see gear, sailing.

Sailed.—*A.V.* ¹*departed.*
Lu. 8. 23. But as they *sailed* he fell asleep
Acts 13. 4. from thence they *sailed* to Cyprus. 15. 39

SAILED

Acts 14. 26. and thence they *s*. to Antioch, from whence
18. 18. and *sailed* thence for Syria. 21. 3
20. 6. And we *sailed* away from Philippi after the days
27. 4. to sea from thence, we *s*. under the lee of Cyprus
5. when we had *sailed* across the sea which is off Cilicia
7. we had *s*. slowly many days—*s*. under the lee of Crete
13. they weighed anchor and *sailed* along Crete
28. 10. when we ¹*sailed*, they put on board such things
see sail.

Saileth.- *A.V.* ¹*company in ships.*

Rev. 18. 17. shipmaster, and every one that ¹*s*. any whither

Sailing.—*A.V.* ¹*sailed.*

Acts 20. 15. And ¹*s*. from thence, we came—against Chios
27. 6. found a ship of Alexandria *sailing* for Italy
see crossing, voyage.

Sailors.—*A.V.* ¹*shipmen.*

Acts 27. 27. about midnight the ¹*s*. surmised that they were
30. as the ¹*sailors* were seeking to flee out of the ship
see mariners.

Saint.

Phil. 4. 21. Salute every *saint* in Christ Jesus

Saints.—*A.V.* ¹*all,* ²*holy.*

Mat. 27. 52. the *saints* that had fallen asleep were raised
Acts 9. 13. how much evil he did to thy *saints* at Jerusalem
32. came down also to the *saints* which dwelt at Lydda
41. calling the *s*. and widows, he presented her alive
26. 10. and I [Saul] both shut up many of the *s*. in prisons
Rom. 1. 7. in Rome, beloved of God, called to be *saints*
8. 27. because he maketh intercession for the *saints*
12. 13. communicating to the necessities of the *saints*
15. 25. I go unto Jerusalem, ministering unto the *saints*
26. certain contribution for the poor among the *saints*
31. my ministration—may be acceptable to the *saints*
16. 2. that ye receive her in the Lord, worthily of the *s*.
15. and all the *saints* that are with them. Heb. 13. 24
1 Cor. 1. 2. sanctified in Christ Jesus, called to be *saints*
6. 1. before the unrighteous, and not before the *saints* ?
2. Or know ye not that the *s*. shall judge the world ?
14. 33. but of peace ; as in all the churches of the *saints*
16. 1. Now concerning the collection for the *saints*
15. have set themselves to minister unto the *saints*)
2 Cor. 1. 1. with all the *s*. which are in the whole of Achaia
8. 4. and the fellowship in the ministering to the *saints*
9. 1. For as touching the ministering to the *saints*
12. not only filleth up the measure of the wants of the *s*.
13. 13. All the *saints* salute you. Phil. 4. 22
Eph. 1. 1. to the *saints* which are at Ephesus [Col. 1. 4
15. among you, and which ye shew toward all the *s*.
18. the riches of the glory of his inheritance in the *s*.
2. 19. but ye are fellow-citizens with the *saints*
3. 8. Unto me, who am less than the least of all *saints*
18. be strong to apprehend with all the *s*.—the breadth
4. 12. for the perfecting of the *saints*, unto the work of
5. 3. not be named among you, as becometh *saints*
6. 18. in all perseverance and supplication for all the *s*.
Phil. 1. 1. to all the *s*. in Christ Jesus which are at Philippi
Col. 1. 2. to the *saints* and faithful brethren in Christ
12. partakers of the inheritance of the *saints* in light
26. but now hath it been manifested to his *saints*
1 Th. 3. 13. coming of our Lord Jesus with all his *saints*
2 Th. 1. 10. he shall come to be glorified in his *saints*
1 Tim. 5. 10. if she hath washed the *saints'* feet
Philem. 5. toward the Lord Jesus, and toward all the *saints*
7. the hearts of the *s*. have been refreshed through thee
Heb. 6. 10. in that ye ministered unto the *saints*

SAITH

Jude 3. faith which was once for all delivered unto the *s*.
Rev. 5. 8. which are the prayers of the *saints*. 8. 3, 4
11. 18. to thy servants the prophets, and to the *saints*
13. 7. to make war with the *s*., and to overcome them
10. Here is the patience and the faith of the *s*. 14. 12
16. 6. for they poured out the blood of *saints* and prophets
17. 6. the woman drunken with the blood of the *saints*
18. 20. Rejoice over her, thou heaven, and ye ²*saints*
24. in her was found the blood of prophets and of *saints*
19. 8. for the fine linen is the righteous acts of the *s*.
20. 9. and compassed the camp of the *saints* about
22. 21. The grace of the Lord Jesus be with the ¹*saints*
see ages, holy (ones).

Saith.—*A.V.* ¹*calleth,* ²*said,* ³*speaketh.*

Mat. 7. 21. Not every one that *saith* unto me, Lord, Lord
26. 18. The Master *saith*, My time is at hand
35. Peter ²*s*. unto him, Even if I must die with thee
Mk. 2. 14. and he ²*saith* unto him, [Levi] Follow me
8. 29. Peter—*saith* unto him, Thou art the Christ
Lu. 18. 6. Hear what the unrighteous judge *saith*
Jno. 4. 10. who it is that *saith* to thee, Give me to drink
19. 28. scripture might be accomplished, *saith*, I thirst
Acts 2. 17. in the last days, *saith* God, I will pour forth
25. David ³*saith* concerning him, I beheld the Lord
7. 48. not in houses made with hands ; as *s*. the prophet
21. 11. Thus *saith* the Holy Ghost, So shall the Jews
Rom. 3. 19. we know that what things soever the law *s*.
4. 3. what *saith* the scripture ? 10. 6 : Gal. 4. 30
9. 17. For the scripture *saith* unto Pharaoh, For this very
10. 6. the righteousness which is of faith ²*saith* thus
11. For the scripture *s*., Whosoever believeth on him
16. For Isaiah *saith*. 20 ; 15. 12
19. First Moses *saith*, I will provoke you to jealousy
11. 2. Or wot ye not what the scripture *saith* of Elijah ?
4. But what *saith* the answer of God unto him ?
1 Cor. 3. 4. For when one *saith*, I am of Paul. 1. 12
9. 8. or *saith* not the law also the same ? [anathema
12. 3. no man speaking in the Spirit of God ¹*s*., Jesus is
14. 34. let them be in subjection, as also *saith* the law
1 Tim. 4. 1. the Spirit ³*saith* expressly, that in later times
5. 18. For the scripture *saith*, Thou shalt not muzzle
Heb. 3. 7. as the Holy Ghost *saith*, To-day if ye shall hear
7. 21. but be with an oath by him that ²*saith* of him
Jas. 2. 23. and the scripture was fulfilled which *saith*
Rev. 2. 7. the Spirit *s*. to the churches. 11, 17, 29 : 3. 6, 13, 22
8. write ; These things *s*. the first and the last ¹*sword
12. These things *s*. he that hath the sharp two-edged
18. These things *s*. the Son of God, who hath his eyes
3. 1. These things *s*. he that hath the seven Spirits of God
7. These things *saith* he that is holy, he that is true
14. These things *saith* the Amen, the faithful and true
14. 13. yea, *s*. the Spirit, that they may rest from their
18. 7. for she *saith* in her heart, I sit a queen
22. 20. *s*., Yea : I come quickly. Amen : come, Lord Jesus
see speaketh.

He Saith, Saith he.—*A.V.* ¹*said.*

Mk. 11. 23. believe that what *he saith* cometh to pass
Jno. 5. 7. Whatsoever *he saith* unto you, do it
16. 18. What is this that *he s*. ?—We know not what *he s*.
19. 35. and he knoweth that *he saith* true
21. 15. *He saith* unto him, Yea, Lord—*He saith* unto
him, Feed my lambs. 16, ¹17
Acts 22. 2. Hebrew—they were the more quiet : and *he saith*
Rom. 9. 15. For *he saith* to Moses, I will have mercy
25. As *he saith* also in Hosea, I will call that my people
10. 21. to Israel *he saith*, All the day long did I spread
15. 10. again *he s*., Rejoice, ye Gentiles, with his people

SAITH

1 Cor. 6. 16. The twain, *saith he*, shall become one flesh
9. 10. or *saith he* it altogether for our sake?
2 Cor. 6. 2. (for *he saith*, At an acceptable time I hearkened
Gal. 3. 16. He *saith* not, And to seeds, as of many
Heb. 8. 5. for, See, *saith he*, that thou make all things
13. In that *he saith*, A new covenant, he hath made
see he said.

Saith *the Lord.—see Lord.*

Sake.—*A.V.* ¹*because of me,* ²*sakes,* ³*us,* ⁴*you.*

Mat. 5. 10. have been persecuted for righteousness' *sake*
11. all manner of evil against you falsely, for my *sake*
10. 18. shall ye be brought for my *s.* Mk. 13. 9 : Lu. 21. 12
22. all men for my name's *s.* 24. 9 : Mk. 13. 13 : Lu. 21. 17
39. life for my *s.* shall find it. 16. 25 : Mk. 8. 35 : Lu. 9. 24
14. 3. put him in prison for the *s.* of Herodias. Mk. 6. 17
9. but for the *sake* of his oaths, and of them. Mk. 6. 26
19. 12. eunuchs for the kingdom of heaven's *sake*
29. children, or lands, for my name's *sake*. Mk. 10. 29
24. 22. for the elect's *s.* those days shall be shortened. Mk.
Lu. 6. 22. your name as evil, for the Son of man's *s.* [13. 20
18. 29. parents, or children, for the kingdom of God's *s.*
Jno. 12. 9. and they came, not for Jesus' *sake* only
30. This voice hath not come for my ¹*sake*
14. 11. or else believe me for the very works' *sake*
15. 21. these things will they do unto you for my name's *s.*
Acts 9. 16. many things he must suffer for my name's *sake*
Rom. 4. 23. Now it was not written for his *sake* alone
24. but for our ³*s.* also, unto whom it shall be reckoned
8. 36. For thy *sake* we are killed all the day long
11. 28. enemies for your *s.*—beloved for the fathers' ²*sake*
13. 5. because of the wrath, but also for conscience *sake*
1 Cor. 4. 10. We are fools for Christ's *sake*, but ye are wise
9. 10. or saith he it altogether for our ²*s.*? Yea, for our ²*s.*
23. And I do all things for the gospel's *sake*
10. 25. eat, asking no question for conscience *sake*. 27
28. eat not, for his *s.* that shewed it, and for conscience *s.*
2 Cor. 4. 10. and ourselves as your servants for Jesus' *sake*
11. are alway delivered unto death for Jesus' *sake*
12. 10. in persecutions, in distresses, for Christ's *sake*
Col. 1. 24. I rejoice in my sufferings for your ⁴*sake*—for
his body's *sake*, which is the church
3. 6. for which things' *sake* cometh the wrath of God
1 Th. 1. 5. men we shewed ourselves toward you for your *s.*
5. 13. exceeding highly in love for their work's *sake*
1 Tim. 5. 23. but use a little wine for thy stomach's *sake*
2 Tim. 2. 10. Therefore I endure all things for the elect's ²*s.*
Tit. 1. 11. which they ought not, for filthy lucre's *sake*
Philem. 9. yet for love's *sake* I rather beseech
Heb. 1. 14. for the *sake* of them that shall inherit salvation?
1 Pet. 2. 13. every ordinance of man for the Lord's *sake*
3. 14. But and if ye should suffer for righteousness' *sake*
1 Jno. 2. 12. your sins are forgiven you for his name's *sake*
2 Jno. 2. for the truth's *sake* which abideth in us
3 Jno. 7. for the *sake* of the Name they went forth
Rev. 2. 3. hast patience and didst bear for my name's *sake*
see because (of), behalf, concerning, sakes.

Sakes.

Jno. 11. 15. I am glad for your *sakes* that I was not there
12. 30. voice hath not come for my sake, but for your *sakes*
17. 19. And for their *sakes* I sanctify myself
1 Cor. 4. 6. transferred to myself and Apollos for your *sakes*
2 Cor. 2. 10. for your *s.* have I forgiven it in the person of
4. 15. For all things are for your *sakes* [Christ
5. 15. who for their *sakes* died and rose again
8. 9. though he was rich, yet for your *s.* he became poor
1 Th. 3. 9. for all the joy wherewith we joy for your *sakes*
see of them, sake.

SALUTED

Salt.

Mat. 5. 13. Ye are the *salt* of the earth : but if the *salt*
Mk. 9. 50. *Salt* is good : but if the *salt* have lost its saltness—Have *salt* in yourselves. Lu. 14. 34
Col. 4. 6. speech be alway with grace, seasoned with *salt*
Jas. 3. 12. neither can *salt* water yield sweet

Salted.

Mat. 5. 13. lost its savour, wherewith shall it be *salted?*
Mk. 9. 49. For every one shall be *salted* with fire

Saltness.

Mk. 9. 50. but if the salt have lost its *saltness*

Salutation.

Lu. 1. 29. what manner of *salutation* this might be
41. when Elisabeth heard the *salutation* of Mary
44. when the voice of thy *s.* came into mine ears
1 Cor. 16. 21. The *salutation* of me Paul with mine own
hand. Col. 4. 18 : 2 Th. 3. 17

Salutations.—*A.V.* ¹*greetings.*

Mat. 23. 7. and the ¹*salutations* in the marketplaces. Mk.
12. 38 : Lu. 11. ¹43 : 20. ¹46

Salute'.—*A. V.* ¹*greet.*

Mat. 5. 47. And if ye *salute* your brethren only
10. 12. And as ye enter into the house, *salute* it
Mk. 15. 18. began to *salute* him, Hail, King of the Jews!
Lu. 10. 4. no shoes : and *salute* no man on the way
Rom. 16. 3. ¹*Salute* Prisca and Aquila my fellow-workers
5. ¹*salute* the church—*Salute* Epænetus my beloved
6. ¹*Salute* Mary, who bestowed much labour on you
7. *Salute* Andronicus and Junias, my kinsmen
8. ¹*Salute* Ampliatus. 9. *Salute* Urbanus
10. *Salute* Apelles—*S.* them which are of the household
11. *Salute* Herodion—¹*Salute* them of the household
12. *Salute* Tryphena and Tryphosa—*Salute* Persis
13. *S.* Rufus. 14. *S.* Asyncritus. 15. *S.* Philologus
16. *S.* one another with a holy kiss. All the churches
of Christ *salute* you. 1 Cor. 16. ¹20 : 2 Cor. 13. ¹12
22. I Tertius, who write the epistle, *salute* you
1 Cor. 16. 19. The churches of Asia *salute* you. Aquila
and Prisca *salute* you much in the Lord
2 Cor. 13. 13. All the saints *salute* you. Phil. 4. 22
Phil. 4. 21. *Salute* every saint in Christ Jesus. The
brethren which are with me ¹*salute* you
Col. 4. 14. Luke, the beloved physician, and Demas ¹*s.* you
15. *Salute* the brethren that are in Laodicea
1 Th. 5. 26 ¹*Salute* all the brethren with a holy kiss
2 Tim. 4. 19 *Salute* Prisca and Aquila, and the house of
Tit. 3. 15. All that are with me *s.* thee. ¹*S.* them that love
Heb. 13. 24. *S.* all them that have the rule—Italy *s.* you
1 Pet. 5. 14. ¹*Salute* one another with a kiss of love
2 Jno. 13. The children of thine elect sister ¹*salute* thee
3 Jno. 14. The friends *s.* thee. ¹*S.* the friends by name
see saluted, saluteth.

Saluted.—*A.V.* ¹*salute.*

Mk. 9. 15. greatly amazed, and running to him *s.* him
Lu. 1. 40. into the house of Zacharias and *s.* Elizabeth
Acts 18. 22. the church, and went down to Antioch
21. 7. we arrived at Ptolemais ; and we *s.* the brethren
19. when he had *saluted* them, he rehearsed one by one
25. 13. and Bernice arrived at Cæsarea, and ¹*s.* Festus

SALUTETH

Saluteth.—*A.V.* ¹*greeteth*, ²*salute.*
Rom. 16. 21. Timothy my fellow-worker ²*saluteth* you
23. Gaius my host—*saluteth* you. Erastus—*saluteth* you
Col. 4. 10. Aristarchus my fellow-prisoner *saluteth* you
12. Epaphras—a servant of Christ Jesus, *saluteth* you.
2 *Tim.* 4. 21. Eubulus ¹*s.* thee, and Pudens [*Philem.* ²23
1 *Pet.* 5. 13. Babylon, elect together with you, *saluteth* you

Salvation.—*A.V.* ¹*saved.*
Lu. 1. 69. And hath raised up a horn of *salvation* for
71. ¹*S.* from our enemies, and from the hand of all
77. To give knowledge of *salvation* unto his people
2. 30. For mine eyes have seen thy *salvation*
3. 6. And all flesh shall see the *salvation* of God
19. 9. To-day is *salvation* come to this house
Jno. 4. 22. we worship that which we know : for *salvation*
Acts 4. 12. And in none other is there *salvation*
13. 26. to us is the word of this *salvation* sent forth
47. shouldest be for *s.* unto the uttermost part of the
16. 17. which proclaim unto you the way of *salvation*
28. 28. this *salvation* of God is sent unto the Gentiles
Rom. 1. 16. it is the power of God unto *s.* to every one that
10. 10. and with the mouth confession is made unto *s.*
11. 11. but by their fall *s.* is come unto the Gentiles
13. 11. now is *s.* nearer to us than when we first believed
2 *Cor.* 1. 6. afflicted, it is for your comfort and *salvation*
6. 2. And in a day of *salvation* did I succour thee—behold,
now is the day of *salvation*)
7. 10. For godly sorrow worketh repentance unto *s.*
Eph. 1. 13. the word of the truth, the gospel of your *s.*
6. 17. take the helmet of *s.*, and the sword of the Spirit
Phil. 1. 19. For I know that this shall turn to my *salvation*
28. evident token of perdition, but of your *salvation*
2. 12. work out your own *s.* with fear and trembling
1 *Th.* 5. 8. and for a helmet, the hope of *salvation*
9. but unto the obtaining of *salvation* through our Lord
2 *Th.* 2. 13. God chose you from the beginning unto *s.*
2 *Tim.* 2. 10. that they also may obtain the *s.* which is in
3. 15. which are able to make thee wise unto *salvation*
Tit. 2.11. the grace of God hath appeared, bringing *s.* to all
Heb. 1. 14. for the sake of them that shall inherit *s.* ?
2. 3. how shall we escape, if we neglect so great *salvation* ?
10. to make the author of their *salvation* perfect
5. 9. he became unto all—the author of eternal *salvation*
6. 9. better things of you, and things that accompany *s.*
9. 28. sin, to them that wait for him, unto *salvation*
1 *Pet.* 1. 5. of God are guarded through faith unto a *s.*
9. the end of your faith, even the *salvation* of your souls
10. Concerning which *salvation* the prophets sought
2. 2. that ye may grow thereby unto *salvation*
2 *Pet.* 3. 15. the longsuffering of our Lord is *salvation*
Jude 3. to write unto you of our common *salvation*
Rev. 7. 10. *Salvation* unto our God which sitteth on the
12. 10. voice in heaven, saying, Now is come the *s.*
19. 1. *S.*, and glory, and power, belong to our God

Same.—*A.V.* ¹*like*, ²*likeminded*, ³*one*, ⁴*selfsame.*
Mat. 5. 46. do not even the publicans the *same* ?
21. 42. The *s.* was made the head. *Lu.* 20. 17: 1 *Pet.* 2. 7
24. 13. to the end, the *same* shall be saved. *Mk.* 13. 13
26. 23. with me in the dish, the *same* shall betray me
44. a third time, saying again the *s.* words. *Mk.* 14. 39
27. 44. crucified with him cast upon him the *s.* reproach
Mk. 3. 35. the *same* is my brother, and sister, and mother
Lu. 6. 33. what thank have ye ? for even sinners do the *s.*
7. 47. to whom little is forgiven, the *same* loveth little
9. 24. lose his life for my sake, the *same* shall save it

SANCTIFICATION

Lu. 9. 48. he that is least among you all, the *s.* is great
16. 1. a steward ; and the *same* was accused unto him
Jno. 1. 2. The *same* was in the beginning with God
7. The *s.* came for witness, that he might bear witness
33. the *same* is he that baptizeth with the Holy Spirit
7. 18. the *same* is true, and no unrighteousness is in him
10. 1. but climbeth up some other way, the *s.* is a thief
12. 48. the *same* shall judge him in the last day
15. 5. and I in him, the *same* beareth much fruit
Acts 7. 19. The *same* dealt subtilly with our race
13. 33. God hath fulfilled the *same* unto our children
14. 9. The *same* heard Paul speaking: who, fastening
15. 27. Judas and Silas—shall tell you the *s.* things by
16. 17. The *same* following after Paul and us cried out
18. 3. because he was of the *s.* trade, he abode with them
Rom. 1. 32. not only do the *s.*, but also consent with them
2. 1. thou that judgest dost practise the *same* things. 3
10. 12. for the *same* Lord is Lord of all, and is rich
12. 4. and all the members have not the *same* office
16. Be of the *same* mind. 15. ³⁵: 1 *Cor.* 1. 10: 2 *Cor.*
13. ¹¹¹ : *Phil.* 2. ²² : 4. 2
13. 3. good, and thou shalt have praise from the *same*
1 *Cor.* 1 10. that ye all speak the *same* thing—*s.* judgement
9. 8. manner of men ? or saith not the law also the *same* ?
10. 3 and did all eat the *same* spiritual meat
4. and did all drink the *same* spiritual drink
11. 5. it is one and the *same* thing as if she were shaven
12. 4. there are diversities of gifts, but the *same* Spirit
5. diversities of ministrations, and the *same* Lord
6. but the *same* God, who worketh all things in all
8. word of knowledge, according to the *s.* Spirit. 9, ¹¹11
15. 39. All flesh is not the *same* flesh : but there is one
2 *Cor.* 4. 13. But having the *same* spirit of faith
9. 5. that the *s.* might be ready, as a matter of bounty
12. 18. walked we not by the *same* Spirit ?—*s.* steps ?
Gal. 3. 7. which be of faith, the *s.* are sons of Abraham
Eph. 4. 10. He that descended is the *s.* also that ascended
6. 8. the *same* shall he receive again from the Lord
9. And, ye masters, do the *same* things unto them
Phil. 1. 30. having the *same* conflict which ye saw in me
2. 2. that ye be of the ²*same* mind, having the *same* love
18. in the *same* manner do ye also joy, and rejoice
3. 1. To write the *s.* things to you, to me indeed is not
16. already attained, by that *same* rule let us walk
1 *Th.* 2. 14. suffered the ¹*s.* things of your own countrymen
2 *Tim.* 2. 2. the *same* commit thou to faithful men
Heb. 1. 12. thou art the *same*, And thy years shall not fail
2. 14. he also himself in like manner partook of the *s.*
11. 9. the heirs with him of the *same* promise
13. 8. Jesus Christ is the *same* yesterday and to-day
Jas. 3. 2. If any stumbleth not in word, the *s.* is a perfect man
1 *Pet.* 4. 1. arm ye yourselves also with the *same* mind
10. ministering the *same* sufferings are accomplished
2 *Pet.* 2. 19. of the *same* is he also brought into bondage
3. 7. by the *same* word have been stored up for fire
1 *Jno.* 2. 23. denieth the Son, the *s.* hath not the Father
see one.

Sanctification.—*A.V.* ¹*holiness.*
Rom. 6. 19. now present your members as servants—unto ¹*s.*
4. know how to possess himself of his own vessel in *s.*
7. God called us not for uncleanness, but in ¹*s.*
2 *Th.* 2. 13. in *sanctification* of the Spirit. 1 *Pet.* 1. 2
1 *Tim.* 2. 15. faith and love and ¹*sanctification* with sobriety
Heb. 12. 14. ¹*s.* without which no man shall see the Lord

SANCTIFIED

Sanctified.—*A.V.* ¹*sanctifieth.*

Mat. 23. 17. or the temple that hath ¹*sanctified* the gold?
Jno. 10. 36. whom the Father *s.* and sent into the world
17. 19. that they themselves also may be *s.* in truth
Acts 20. 32. among all them that are *sanctified.* 26. 18
Rom. 15. 16. made acceptable, being *s.* by the Holy Ghost
1 *Cor.* 1. 2. even them that are *sanctified* in Christ Jesus
6. 11. but ye were washed, but ye were *sanctified*
7. 14. the unbelieving husband is *s.*—wife is *sanctified*
1 *Tim.* 4. 5. for it is *s.* through the word of God and prayer
2 *Tim.* 2. 21. *sanctified,* meet for the master's use
Heb. 2. 11. and they that are *sanctified* are all of one
10. 10. By which will we have been *sanctified*
14. he hath perfected for ever them that are *sanctified*
29. the blood of the covenant, wherewith he was *s.*
    see beloved.

Sanctifieth.

Mat. 23. 19. the gift, or the altar that *sanctifieth* the gift?
Heb. 2. 11. both he that *s.* and they that are sanctified
    see sanctify, sanctified.

Sanctify.—*A.V.* ¹*sanctifieth.*

Jno. 17. 17. *Sanctify* them in the truth: thy word is truth
19. And for their sakes I *sanctify* myself
Eph. 5. 26. that he might *sanctify* it, having cleansed it
1 *Th.* 5. 23. And the God of peace himself *s.* you wholly
Heb. 9. 13. ¹*sanctify* unto the cleanness of the flesh
13. 12. that he might *s.* the people through his own blood
1 *Pet.* 3. 15. but *sanctify* in your hearts Christ as Lord

Sanctuary.—*A.V.* ¹*temple.*

Mat. 23. 35. ye slew between the ¹*s.* and the altar. *Lu.* 11.¹51
27. 5. cast down the pieces of silver into the ¹*sanctuary*
Heb. 8. 2. a minister of the *s.,* and of the true tabernacle
9. 1. divine service, and its *s.,* a *sanctuary* of this world
    see holy.

Sand.

Mat. 7. 26. foolish man, which built his house upon the *s.*
Rom. 9. 27. number—children of Israel be as the *s.* of the sea
Heb. 11. 12. as the *s.,* which is by the sea shore, innumerable
Rev. 13. 1. and he stood upon the *sand* of the sea
20. 8. the number of whom is as the *sand* of the sea.

Sandals.

Mk. 6. 9. go shod with *s.:* and, said he, put not on two coats
Acts 12. 8. Gird thyself, and bind on thy *sandals*

Sang *A.V.*—*see sing, singing.*

Sapphire.

Rev. 21. 19. the second, *sapphire;* the third, chalcedony

Sardine *A.V.*—*see sardius.*

Sardius.—*A.V.* ¹*sardine.*

Rev. 4. 3. to look upon like a jasper stone and a ¹*sardius*
21. 20. the sixth, *sardius;* the seventh, chrysolite

Sardonyx.

Rev. 21. 20. the fifth, *sardonyx;* the sixth, sardius

Sat.—*A.V.* ¹*set,* ²*sitting.*

Mat. 4. 16. The people which *sat* in darkness saw a great light, And to them which *sat* in the region
9. 10. as he *sat* at meat in the house
14. 9. of them which *sat* at meat with him. *Mk.* 6. 26
26. 55. I *sat* daily in the temple teaching

SAVE

Mat. 26. 58. Peter—entered in, and *sat* with the officers
27. 36. and they ²*sat* and watched him there
28. 2. came and rolled away the stone, and *sat* upon it
Mk. 3. 34. looking round on them which *sat* round about
11. 2. colt tied, whereon no man ever yet *s. Lu.* 19. 30
16. 19. into heaven, and *s.* down at the right hand of God
Lu. 7. 15. the dead *sat* up, and began to speak
10. 39. called Mary, which also *sat* at the Lord's feet
22. 55. ¹*sat* down together, Peter *sat* in the midst of them
Jno. 4. 6. Jesus—wearied with his journey, *s.*—by the well
9. 8. said, Is not this he that *sat* and begged?
11. 20. and met him; but Mary still *sat* in the house
12. 14. found a young ass, *s.* thereon. *Mat.* 21.¹7: *Mk.* 11.7
Acts 2. 3. like as of fire; and it *sat* upon each one of them
3. 10. he which *sat* for alms at the Beautiful Gate
9. 40. and when she [Dorcas] saw Peter, she *sat* up
25. 6. on the morrow he ²*sat* on the judgement seat
26. 30. governor, and Bernice, and they that *s.* with them
Rev. 4. 3. he that *sat* was to look upon like a jasper stone
6. 2. white horse, and he that *sat* thereon had a bow
4. and to him that *sat* thereon it was given to take
5. black horse; and he that *sat* thereon had a balance
8. and he that *sat* upon him, his name was Death
9. 17. horses in the vision, and them that *sat* on them
19. 11. and he that *sat* thereon, called Faithful and True
19. to make war against him that *sat* upon the horse
    see set, sitting, sit.

Sat down.—*A.V.* ¹*set.*

Mat. 5. 1. when he had ¹*sat down,* his disciples came
9. 10. many publicans and sinners came and *sat down*
13. 48. they *sat down,* and gathered the good into vessels
Mk. 12. 41. And he *sat down* over against the treasury
Lu. 4. 20. gave it back to the attendant, and *sat down*
5. 3. *sat down,* and taught the multitudes out of the boat
22. 14. And when the hour was come, he *sat down*
55. had *sat down* together, Peter sat in the midst
Jno. 6. 10. the men *sat down,* in number about five thousand
8. 2. came unto him; and he *sat down,* and taught
13. 12. taken his garments, and ¹*sat down* again
Acts 13. 14. and they went into the synagogue—and *sat d.*
16. 13. and we *sat down,* and spake unto the women
1 *Cor.* 10. 7. The people *sat down* to eat and drink
Heb. 8. 1. high priest, who ¹*sat down* on the right hand. 12.¹2
10. 12. *sat down* on the right hand of God. 1. 3
Rev. 3. 21. ¹*sat down* with my Father in his throne
    see sitting.

Satan.—*see proper names.*

Satisfied.—*A.V.* ¹*filled.*

Rom. 15. 24. I shall have been ¹*satisfied* with your company)

Satisfy *A.V.*—*see fill.*

Satisfying *A.V.*—*see indulgence.*

Save.—*A.V.* ¹*but,* ²*heal,* ³*preserve.*

Mat. 1. 21. he that shall *save* his people from their sins
8. 25. awoke him, saying, *Save,* Lord; we perish
14. 30. to sink, he cried out, saying, Lord, *save* me
16. 25. would *s.* his life shall lose it. *Mk.* 8. 35: *Lu.* 9. 24
27. 40. Thou that destroyest the temple, and buildest it in three days, *save* thyself. *Mk.* 15. 30
42. He saved others; himself he cannot *save. Mk.* 15. 31
49. let us see whether Elijah cometh to *save* him
Mk. 3. 4. or to do harm? to *save* a life, or to kill? *Lu.* 6. 9
Lu. 7. 3. asking him that he would come and ²*s.* his servant
19. 10. For the Son of man came—to *s.* that which was
23. 35. let him *save* himself, if this is the Christ [lost
37. If thou art the King of the Jews, *save* thyself

SAVE

Lu. 23. 39. Art not thou the Christ? *save* thyself and us
Jno. 12. 27. Father, *save* me from this hour
    47. I came not to judge the world, but to *save* the world
Acts 2. 40. *Save* yourselves from this crooked generation
    27. 43. But the centurion, desiring to *save* Paul
Rom. 11. 14. if by any means I may—*save* some of them
1 *Cor.* 1. 21. through the foolishness of the preaching to *s.*
    7. 16. shalt *save* thy husband?—shalt *save* thy wife?
    9. 22. to all men, that I may by all means *save* some
Gal. 2. 16. of the law, ¹*save* through faith in Jesus Christ
1 *Tim.* 1. 15. Christ Jesus came into the world to *s.* sinners
    4. 16. in doing this thou shalt *s.* both thyself and them
2 *Tim.* 4. 18. Lord will deliver me—and will ³*save* me
Heb. 5. 7. unto him that was able to *save* him from death
    7. 25. he is able to *save* to the uttermost them that
Jas. 1. 21. implanted word, which is able to *s.* your souls
    2. 14. but have not works? can that faith *save* him?
    4. 12. and judge, even he who is able to *s.* and to destroy
    5. 15. the prayer of faith shall *save* him that is sick
    20. from the error of his way shall *s.* a soul from death
1 *Pet.* 3. 21. which also after a true likeness doth now *save*
Jude 23. and some *save*, snatching them out of the fire

Saved.

Mat. 19. 25. Who then can be *saved?* *Mk.* 10. 26 : *Lu.* 18. 26
    24. 22. no flesh would have been *saved*. *Mk.* 13. 20
    27. 42. He *saved* others. *Mk.* 15. 31 : *Lu.* 23. 35
Lu. 7. 50. Thy faith hath *saved* thee ; go in peace
    8. 12. that they may not believe and be *saved*
    13. 23. said unto him, Lord, are they few that be *saved?*
Jno. 3. 17. but that the world should be *saved* through him
    5. 34. howbeit I say these things, that ye may be *saved*
Acts 2. 47. added to them day by day those that were being *s.*
    4. 12. given among men, wherein we must be *saved*
    15. 1. circumcised—the custom of Moses, ye cannot be *s.*
    16. 30. Sirs, what must I do to be *saved?*
    27. 20. all hope that we should be *s.* was now taken away
    31. Except these abide in the ship, ye cannot be *saved*
Rom. 8. 24. by hope were we *saved :* but hope that is seen
    10. 1. supplication to God is for them, that they may be *s.*
1 *Cor.* 1. 18. unto us which are being *s.* it is the power of God
    5. 5. that the spirit may be *saved* in the day of the Lord
    10. 33. but the profit of the many, that they may be *s.*
    15. 2. [the gospel] by which also ye are *saved*
2 *Cor.* 2. 15. savour of Christ unto God, in them that are being *s.*
Eph. 2. 8. for by grace have ye been *s.* through faith [*saved*
1 *Th.* 2. 16. speak to the Gentiles that they may be *saved*
2 *Th.* 2. 10. love of the truth, that they might be *saved*
1 *Tim.* 2. 4. who willeth that all men should be *saved*
2 *Tim.* 1. 9. who *saved* us, and called us with a holy calling
Tit. 3. 5. but according to his mercy he *saved* us
1 *Pet.* 3. 20. few, that is, eight souls, were *s.* through water
    4. 18. if the righteous is scarcely *s.*—shall the ungodly
Jude 5. the Lord, having *s.* a people out of the land of Egypt
see salvation, preserved, whole.

Shall be Saved, or shalt be Saved.

Mat. 10. 22. he that endureth to the end, the same *shall be saved.* 24. 13 : *Mk.* 13. 13
Mk. 16. 16. He that believeth and is baptized *shall be s.*
Jno. 10. 9. by me if any man enter in, he *shall be saved*
Acts 2. 21. whosoever shall call on the name of the Lord *shall be saved.* *Rom.* 10. 13
    11. 14. speak unto thee words, whereby thou *shalt be s.*
    15. 11. we *shall be s.* through the grace of the Lord Jesus
    16. 31. Believe on the Lord Jesus, and thou *shalt be saved*. *Rom.* 10. 9

SAW

Rom. 5. 9. *shall* we *be saved* from the wrath of God
    10. being reconciled, *shall* we *be saved* by his life
    9. 27. sand of the sea, it is the remnant that *shall be saved*
    11. 26. and so all Israel *shall be s.* : even as it is written
1 *Cor.* 3. 15. but he himself *shall be s.* ; yet so as through fire
1 *Tim.* 2. 15. but she *shall be s.* through the childbearing

Saving.

Mat. 5. 32. his wife, *saving* for the cause of fornication
Heb. 10. 39. them that have faith unto the *saving* of the soul
    11. 7. Noah—prepared an ark to the *saving* of his house

Saviour.

Eph. 5. 23. Christ—being himself the *saviour* of the body
see proper names.

Savour.

Mat. 5. 13. if the salt have lost its *savour.* *Lu.* 14. 34 [ledge
2 *Cor.* 2. 14. maketh manifest through us the *s.* of his know-
    15. For we are a sweet *savour* of Christ unto God
    16. a *s.* from death unto death—a *s.* from life unto life
see odour.

Savourest *A.V.—see mindest.*

Saw.—*A.V.* ¹*beheld*, ²*looked*, ³*perceiving*, ⁴*seeing*, ⁵*seen.*

Mat. 2. 2. we ⁵*s.* his star in the east, and are come to worship
    9. the star, which they *saw* in the east. 10
    11. and *saw* the young child with Mary his mother
    16. Herod, when he *s.* that he was mocked of the wise men
    3. 16. he *saw* the Spirit of God descending. *Mk.* 1. 10
    4. 16. The people which sat in darkness *S.* a great light
    8. 34. when they *s.* him, they besought—he would depart
    12. 2. the Pharisees, when they *saw* it, said unto him
    22. insomuch that the dumb man spake and *saw*
    13. 17. to see the things which ye see, and ⁵*saw* them not
    17. 8. they *saw* no one, save Jesus only. *Mk.* 9. 8
    18. 31. when his fellow-servants *saw* what was done
    21. 15. priests and scribes *saw* the wonderful things
    32. ye, when ye ⁵*saw* it, did not even repent yourselves
    38. But the husbandmen, when they *saw* the son
    22. 11. *s.* there a man which had not on a wedding-garment
    25. 37. Lord, when *saw* we thee an hungred. 44
    38. when *saw* we thee a stranger, and took thee in?
    39. And when *saw* we thee sick, or in prison
    26. 71. another maid *s.* him [Peter]. *Mk.* 14. 69 : *Lu.* 22. 58
    27. 3. when he *saw* that he was condemned, repented
    28. 17. And when they *saw* him, they worshipped him
Mk. 8. 25. and was restored, and *saw* all things clearly
    9. 15. multitude, when they ¹*s.* him, were greatly amazed
    38. Master, we *saw* one casting out devils. *Lu.* 9. 49
Lu. 2. 17. And when they ⁴*saw* it, they made known
    5. 12. man full of leprosy : and when he ⁴*saw* Jesus
    7. 13. the Lord *saw* her, he had compassion on her
    8. 28. when he *saw* Jesus, he cried out, and fell down
    34. when they that fed them *saw* what had come to pass
    47. when the woman *saw* that she was not hid
    9. 32. when they were fully awake, they *saw* his glory
    47. when Jesus ³*saw* the reasoning of their heart
    10. 32. Levite also, when he came to the place, and ²*s.* him
    15. 20. while he was yet afar off, his father *saw* him
    17. 15. one of them, when he *saw* that he was healed
    19. 41. he drew nigh, he ¹*saw* the city and wept over it
    24. 24. as the women had said : but him they *saw* not
Jno. 1. 48. when thou wast under the fig tree, I *s.* thee. 50
    6. 14. When therefore the people ⁵*s.* the sign which he did
    26. Ye seek me, not because ye *saw* signs

SAW

Jno. 8. 56. Abraham rejoiced to see my day; and he *saw* it
9. 8. they which ⁵*saw* him aforetime, that he was a beggar
12. 41. These things said Isaiah, because he s. his glory
20. 8. came first to the tomb, and he *saw*, and believed
20. disciples therefore were glad, when they s. the Lord
Acts. 4. 20. but speak the things which we ⁵*saw* and heard
6. 15. *saw* his face as it had been the face of an angel
7. 55. and saw the glory of God, and Jesus standing
8. 6. when they heard, and ⁴*saw* the signs which he did
18. Now when Simon s. that through the laying on of
39. caught away Philip; and the eunuch s. him no more
9. 8. and when his eyes were opened, he *saw* nothing
35. And all that dwelt at Lydda and at Sharon s. him
40. and when she [Dorcas] *saw* Peter, she sat up
10. 3. He *saw* in a vision openly, as it were about
12. 3. when he *saw* that it pleased the Jews, he proceeded
13. 12. the proconsul, when he s. what was done, believed
36. David—was laid unto his fathers, and s. corruption
37. but he whom God raised up *saw* no corruption
16. 19. her masters s. that the hope of their gain was gone
21. 27. when they *saw* him in the temple, stirred up all
26. 13. I *saw* on the way a light from heaven
28. 15. whom when Paul *saw*, he thanked God
1 Cor. 2. 9. Things which eye ⁵*saw* not, and ear heard not
Gal. 1. 19. But other of the apostles s. I none, save James
2. 7. when they *saw* that I had been intrusted with the
14. But when I *saw* that they walked not uprightly
Phil. 1. 30. having the same conflict which ye *saw* in me
4. 9. received and heard and ⁵*saw* in me, these things do
Heb. 3. 9. your fathers—*saw* my works forty years
11. 23. because they *saw* he [Moses] was a goodly child
Rev. 1. 2. of Jesus Christ, even of all things that he *saw*
17. And when I *saw* him, I fell at his feet as one dead
4. 1. After these things I ²*saw*, and. 6. ²8: 14. ²14: 15. ²5
5. 6. I ¹*saw* in the midst of the throne—a Lamb standing
12. 13. the dragon s. that he was cast down to the earth
14. 1. I ²s., and behold, the Lamb standing on the mount
14. and on the cloud I *saw* one sitting like unto
22. 8. I John am he that heard and ⁵*saw* these things.
And when I heard and ⁵*saw*, I fell down
see beheld, beholdeth, beholding, looked, seeing, seen, seest.

Sawest.—A.V. ¹*seen.*

Rev. 1. 19. Write therefore the things which thou ¹*sawest*
20. the mystery of the seven stars which thou *sawest*
17. 12. the ten horns that thou *sawest* are ten kings. 16
15. The waters which thou *sawest*, where the harlot
18. the woman whom thou *sawest* is the great city

Sawn.

Heb. 11. 37. they were stoned, they were *sawn* asunder

Say.—A. V. ¹*deny,* ²*said,* ³*speak,* ⁴*tell.*

Mat. 3. 9. think not to *say* within yourselves. Lu. 3. 8
5. 11. and *say* all manner of evil against you falsely
7. 22. Many will *say* to me in that day, Lord, Lord
8. 8. only ³*say* the word, and my servant shall. Lu. 7. 7
9. 28. to do this? They ²*say* unto him, Yea, Lord
13. 51. understood all these things? They *say* unto him
16. 13. Who do men *say* that the Son of man is? Mk.
8. 27: Lu. 9. 18
14. Some *say* John the Baptist; some, Elijah
15. But who *say* ye that I am? Mk. 8. 29: Lu. 9. 20
21. 3. if any one *say* aught unto you, ye shall *say*, The
Lord hath need. Mk. 11. 3   [11. 31: Lu. 20. 5
25. If we shall s., From heaven; he will s. unto us. Mk.
26. if we shall *say*, From men. Mk. 11. 32: Lu. 20. 6
23. 3. do not ye after their works; for they *say*, and do not
26. 22. exceeding sorrowful, and began to *say* unto him

SAY

Mk. 1. 44. See thou *say* nothing to any man
11. 33. they answered Jesus and ²*say*, We know not
Lu. 4. 23. Doubtless ye will *say* unto me this parable
7. 40. Simon, I have somewhat to *say* unto thee.   And
he saith, Master, *say* on
10. 10. go out into the streets thereof and *say*
12. 11. or what ye shall answer, or what ye shall *say*
12. teach you in that very hour what ye ought to *say*
13. 32. Go and ⁴*say* to that fox, Behold, I cast out devils
20. 27. they which ¹*say* that there is no resurrection
22. 70. And he said unto them, Ye *say* that I am
Jno. 4. 20. ye *say*, that in Jerusalem is the place where
35. Say not ye, There are yet four months, and then
7. 26. he speaketh openly, and they *say* nothing unto him
8. 48. *Say* we not well that thou art a Samaritan
54. of whom ye *say*, that he is your God   [you
55. if I should *say*, I know him not, I shall be like unto
10. 36. *say* ye of him, whom the Father sanctified
12. 49. hath given me a commandment, what I should s.
13. 13. Ye call me, Master, and, Lord: and ye *say* well
16. 12. I have yet many things to *say* unto you
Acts 2. 29. Brethren, I may ³*say* unto you freely of the
4. 14. seeing the man—they could *say* nothing against it
6. 14. for we have heard him *say*, that this Jesus
13. 15. any word of exhortation for the people, *say* on
17. 18. And some said, What would this babbler *say* ?
21. 23. Do therefore this that we *say* to thee
23. 18. unto thee, who hath something to *say* to thee
24. 20. men themselves *say* what wrong-doing they found
26. 22. what the prophets and Moses did *say* should come
Rom. 3. 5. what shall we *say* ? Is God unrighteous
8. and as some affirm that we *say*), Let us do evil
4. 1. What then shall we *say*. 6. 1: 7. 7: 8. 31: 9. 14, 30
9. 20. Shall the thing formed *say* to him that formed it
10. 6. *Say* not in thy heart, Who shall ascend   [Spirit
1 Cor. 12. 3: no man can *say*, Jesus is Lord, but in the Holy
14. 16. unlearned say the Amen at thy giving of thanks
23. will they not *say* that ye are mad?   [rection
15. 12. how *say* some among you that there is no resur-
2 Cor. 9. 4. we (that we *say* not, ye) should be put to shame
10. 10. For, His letters, they *say*, are weighty and strong
Col. 4. 17. *say* to Archippus, Take heed to the ministry
1 Th. 4. 15. this we *say* unto you by the word of the Lord
1 Tim. 1. 7. though they understand neither what they s.
Tit. 2. 8. be ashamed, having no evil thing to *say* of us
Philem. 19. I *say* not unto thee how that thou owest to me
Heb. 5. 11. Of whom we have many things to *say*
7. 9. And, so to *say*, through Abraham even Levi
9. 11. with hands, that is to *say*, not of this creation
10. 20. way, through the veil, that is to *say*, his flesh
11. 14. For they that *say* such things make it manifest
13. 6. without fear of what men *say*, The Lord is my helper
Jas. 1. 13. Let no man *say* when he is tempted
4. 13. Go to now, ye that *say*, To-day or to-morrow
15. For that ye ought to *say*, If the Lord will, we shall
1 Jno. 1. 6. If we *say* that we have fellowship with him
8. If we *say* that we have no sin, we deceive. 10
4. 20. If a man *say*, I love God, and hateth his brother
5. 16. not concerning this do I *say* that he should make
Rev. 2. 9. which *say* they are Jews, and they are not. 3. 9
24. to you I *say*, to the rest that are in Thyatira
22. 17. Spirit and the bride *say*—let him *say*, Come
see answer, call, saying, speak.

I Say, Say I.—A.V. ¹*mean,* ²*said,* ³*speak,* ⁴*tell.*

Mat. 8. 9. I *say* to this one, Go, and he goeth. Lu. 7. 8
18. 22. I *say* not unto thee, Until seven times; but
Mk. 2. 11. I *say* unto thee, Arise. 5. 41: Lu. 5. 24: 7. 14
13. 37. what I *say* unto you I *say* unto all, Watch

SAY

Lu. 4. 25. of a truth I ⁴say unto you, There were many
6. 46. Lord, Lord, and do not the things which I say?
7. 47. Wherefore I say unto thee, Her sins, which are
12. 59. I ⁴say unto thee, Thou shalt by no means come out
23. 43. Verily I say unto thee, To-day shalt thou be
Jno. 4. 35. behold, I say unto you, Lift up your eyes
5. 34. howbeit I say these things, that ye may be saved
8. 45. because I ⁴say the truth, ye believe me not
46. If I say truth, why do ye not believe me?
12. 27. what shall I say? Father, save me from this
16. 26. I say not unto you, that I will pray the Father
Acts 21. 37. saith unto the chiefcaptain, May I ³s. something
Rom. 3. 26. for the shewing, I say, of his righteousness
9. 1. I say the truth in Christ, I lie not, my conscience
1 Cor. 6. 5. I ³say this to move you to shame
7. 6. But this I ³say by way of permission
12. to the rest ³say I, not the Lord
7. 29. But this I say, brethren, the time is shortened
35. And this I ²say for your own profit
10. 15. I speak as to wise men; judge ye what I say
19. What say I then? that a thing sacrificed to idols
20. But I say, that the things which the Gentiles
29. conscience, I say, not thine own, but the other's
11. 22. What shall I say to you? shall I praise you
15. 50. Now this I say. 2 Cor. 9. 6: Gal. 3. 17: 5. 16:
Eph. 4. 17: Col. 2. 4
2 Cor. 7. 3. I ³say it not to condemn you: for I have said
8. 13. I ¹say not this, that others may be eased
Gal. 1. 9. As we have said before, so say I now again
5. 2. I Paul say unto you, that, if ye receive circumcision
2 Tim. 2. 7. Consider what I say; for the Lord shall give
Philem. 21. that thou wilt do even beyond what I say
Heb. 11. 32. And what shall I more say? for the time
Rev. 7. 14. And I ²say unto him, My lord, thou knowest
see mean, I speak.

Sayest.

Mat. 26. 70. saying, I know not what thou sayest
27. 11. Art thou the King of the Jews? And Jesus said
unto him, Thou sayest. Mk. 15. 2: Lu. 23. 3
Mk. 5. 31. thronging thee, and s. thou, Who touched me?
14. 68. I neither know, nor understand what thou sayest
Lu. 20. 21. Master, we know that thou sayest and teachest
Jno. 1. 22. What sayest thou [John] of thyself? [rightly
8. 5. to stone such: what then sayest thou of her?
33. how sayest thou, Ye shall be made free?
52. Abraham is dead—and thou sayest, If a man keep
9. 17. the blind man again, What sayest thou of him
12. 34. sayest thou, The Son of man must be lifted up?
14. 9. how sayest thou, Shew us the Father?
18. 34. Jesus answered, Sayest thou this of thyself
37. Jesus answered, Thou sayest that I am a king
Rom. 2. 22. that sayest a man should not commit adultery
1 Cor. 14. 16. seeing that he knoweth not what thou s. ?
Rev. 3. 17. Because thou sayest, I am rich, and have gotten

Saying.—A.V. ¹said, ²say, ³spoken, ⁴words.

Mat. 15. 12. Pharisees were offended—they heard this s.?
17. 5. behold, a voice out of the cloud, ¹saying, This is
19. 11. All men cannot receive this saying, but they to
22. when the young man heard the s., he went away
21. 16. said unto him, Hearest thou what these are ²s. ?
26. 44. prayed a third time, saying again the same words
28. 15. this saying was spread abroad among the Jews
Mk. 7. 29. said unto her, For this saying go thy way
8. 32. And he spake the saying openly. And Peter took
9. 10. they kept the s., questioning among themselves.
32. [disciples] understood not the saying [Lu. 2. 50
10. 22. But his countenance fell at the saying

SCATTER

Mk. 13. 6. Many shall come in my name, saying, I am he
14. 68. But he denied, s., I neither know, nor understand
Lu. 1. 29. [Mary] was greatly troubled at the saying
2. 17. the saying which was spoken to them [shepherds]
9. 45. were afraid to ask him about this saying
11. 45. Master, in saying this thou reproachest us also
18. 34. this saying was hid from them [disciples]
20. 26. they were not able to take hold of the ⁴saying
Jno. 4. 37. For herein is the saying true, One soweth
6. 60. This is a hard saying; who can hear it?
19. 8. When Pilate therefore heard this saying
12. the Jews cried out, saying, If thou release this man
21. 23. This s. therefore went forth among the brethren
Acts 6. 5. And the saying pleased the whole multitude
7. 29. Moses fled at this saying, and became a sojourner
40. s. unto Aaron, Make us gods which shall go before us
11. 7. a voice saying unto me, Rise, Peter; kill and eat
16. 35. the magistrates sent the serjeants, saying, Let
36. reported the words to Paul, saying, The magistrates
19. 28. cried out, s., Great is Diana of the Ephesians
26. 22. saying nothing but what the prophets and Moses
1 Cor. 15. 54. s. that is written, Death is swallowed up
1 Tim. 1. 15. Faithful is the s. 3. 1 : 4. 9 : 2 Tim. 2. 11 : Tit. 3. 8
Heb. 8. 1. in the things which we are ³s. the chief point
Rev. 13. 14. saying to them that dwell on the earth
14. 13. voice from heaven s., Write, Blessed are the dead
see affirming, speaking, supposing, word, words.

Sayings.—A.V. ¹things, ²words.

Lu. 1. 65. and all these sayings were noised abroad
2. 19. Mary kept all these ¹sayings, pondering them
51. his mother kept all these sayings in her heart
7. 1. After he had ended all his sayings in the ears of
9. 28. about eight days after these sayings, he took
Jno. 10. 21. These are not the ²s. of one possessed with a
12. 47. if any man hear my ²sayings, and keep them not
48. rejecteth me, and receiveth not my ²sayings
Acts 14. 18. with these sayings scarce restrained they
see word, words.

Scales.

Acts 9. 18. there fell from his eyes as it were scales

Scarce—ly.

Acts 14. 18. with these sayings scarce restrained they
Rom. 5. 7. scarcely for a righteous man will one die
1 Pet. 4. 18. if the righteous is scarcely saved, where
see difficulty.

Scarlet.

Mat. 27. 28. stripped him, and put on him a scarlet robe
Heb. 9. 19. and scarlet wool and hyssop, and sprinkled
Rev. 17. 3. a woman sitting upon a scarlet-coloured beast
4. the woman was arrayed in purple and scarlet
18. 12. merchandise of—purple, and silk, and scarlet
16. arrayed in fine linen and purple and scarlet

Scatter—ed.—A.V. ¹dispersed, ²grind, ³strawed.

Mat. 9. 36. scattered, as sheep not having a shepherd
21. 44. it shall fall, it will ²scatter him as dust. Lu. 20. ²18
25. 24. gathering where thou didst not ³scatter. ²26
26. 31. the flock shall be scattered abroad. Mk. 14. 27
Lu. 1. 51. hath scattered the proud in the imagination
Jno. 11. 52. the children of God that are scattered abroad
16. 32. ye shall be scattered, every man to his own
Acts 5. 37. as many as obeyed him, were ¹scattered abroad
8. 1. all scattered abroad throughout the regions of Judæa

SCATTERED

Acts 8. 4. that were *scattered* abroad went about preaching
11. 19. that were *scattered* abroad upon the tribulation
2 *Cor.* 9. 9. He hath ¹*scattered* abroad, he hath given
see dispersed, dispersion.

Scattereth.
Mat. 12. 30. that gathereth not with me *s*. *Lu.* 11. 23
Jno. 10. 12. and the wolf snatcheth them, and *scattereth*

Sceptre.
Heb. 1. 8. the *s*. of uprightness is the *s*. of thy kingdom

Schism.
1 *Cor.* 12. 25. that there should be no *schism* in the body

School.
Acts 19. 9. [Paul] reasoning daily in the *school* of Tyrannus

Schoolmaster *A.V.—see tutor.*

Science *A.V.—see knowledge.*

Scoffed.—*A.V.* ¹*derided.*
Lu. 16. 14. Pharisees, who were lovers of money—¹*s*. at him
23. 35. the rulers also ¹*scoffed* at him, saying, He saved

Scoffers *A.V.—see mockers.*

Scorch—ed—ing.—*A.V.* ¹*burning.*
Mat. 13. 6. the sun was risen, they were *scorched. Mk.* 4. 6
20. 12. borne the burden of the day and the *scorching* heat
Jas. 1. 11. For the sun ariseth with a ¹*scorching* wind
Rev. 16. 8. and it was given unto it to *scorch* men with fire
9. And men were *scorched* with great heat

Scorn.
Mat. 9. 24. they laughed him to *scorn. Mk.* 5. 40: *Lu.* 8. 53

Scorpion—s.
Lu. 10. 19. authority to tread upon serpents and *scorpions*
11. 12. if he shall ask an egg, will he give him a *scorpion?*
Rev. 9. 3. as the *scorpions* of the earth have power
5. as the torment of a *scorpion*, when it striketh a man
10. And they have tails like unto *scorpions*, and stings

Scourge.
Mat. 10. 17. in their synagogues they will *scourge* you
20. 19. the Gentiles to mock, and to *s. Mk.* 10. 34: *Lu.* 18.
23. 34. some of them shall ye *s.* in your synagogues [33
Jno. 2. 15. he made a *scourge* of cords, and cast all out
Acts 22. 25. lawful for you to *s.* a man that is a Roman

Scourged—eth.
Mat. 27. 26. but Jesus he *scourged. Mk.* 15. 15: *Jno.* 19. 1
Heb. 12. 6. And *scourgeth* every son whom he receiveth

Scourging—s.
Acts 22. 24. that he should be examined by *scourging*
Heb. 11. 36. others had trial of mockings and *scourgings*

Scribe—s.
Mat. 2. 4. [Herod] gathering—the chief priests and *scribes*
5. 20. exceed the righteousness of the *s.* and Pharisees
7. 29. having authority, and not as their *s. Mk.* 1. 22
8. 19. there came a *s.*, and said unto him, Master, I will
9. 3. the *s.* said within themselves, This man blasphemeth
12. 38. certain of the *scribes* and Pharisees answered him

SCRIPTURE

Mat. 13. 52. every *scribe* who hath been made a disciple
15. 1. from Jerusalem Pharisees and *s.*, saying. *Mk.* 7. 1
16. 21. suffer many things of—chief priests and *scribes*
17. 10. say the *s.* that Elijah must first come? *Mk.* 9. 11
20. 18. the Son of man shall be delivered unto the chief
priests and *scribes. Mk.* 10. 33
21. 15. the *scribes* saw the wonderful things that he did
23. 2. The *scribes* and the Pharisees sit on Moses' seat
13. woe unto you, *s.* and Pharisees. 15, 23, 25, 27, 29
34. I send unto you prophets, and wise men, and *s.*
26. 57. where the *scribes* and the elders were gathered
27. 41. mocking him, with the *s.* and elders. *Mk.* 15. 31
Mk. 2. 6. the *scribes* sitting there, and reasoning in their
16. the *scribes* of the Pharisees—eating with the sinners
3. 22. the *scribes* which came down from Jerusalem said
7. 5. and the *scribes* ask him, Why walk not thy disciples
8. 31. be rejected by the elders, and the chief priests,
and the *scribes. Lu.* 9. 22
9. 14. multitude—and *scribes* questioning with them
11. 18. the chief priests and the *scribes* heard it, and
sought how they might destroy him. *Lu.* 19. 47
27. the chief priests, and the *scribes*, and the elders
12. 28. one of the *s.* came, and heard them questioning
32. the *s.* said unto him, Of a truth, Master. *Lu.* 20. 39
35. How say the *s.* that the Christ is the son of David?
38. Beware of the *s.*, which desire to walk. *Lu.* 20. 46
14. 1. the *scribes* sought how they might take him
43. swords and staves, from—the *scribes* and the elders
53. led Jesus away to the high priest—the *s. Lu.* 22. 66
15. 1. and *s.*, and the whole council, held a consultation
Lu. 5. 21. the *scribes* and the Pharisees began to reason
30. Pharisees and their *scribes* murmured. 15. 2
6. 7. the *scribes* and the Pharisees watched him
11. 53. the *scribes* and the Pharisees began to press
20. 1. there came upon him the chief priests and the *s.*
19. *s.* and the chief priests sought to lay hands on him
22. 2. the *s.* sought how they might put him to death
23. 10. the *scribes* stood, vehemently accusing him
Jno. 8. 3. the *scribes* and the Pharisees bring a woman
Acts 4. 5. and *scribes* were gathered together in Jerusalem
6. 12. stirred up the people, and the elders, and the *s.*
23. 9. the *scribes* of the Pharisees' part stood up
1 *Cor.* 1. 20. Where is the wise? where is the *scribe?*

Scrip *A.V.—see wallet.*

Scripture.—*A.V.* ¹*he.*
Mk. 12. 10. Have ye not read even this *scripture*; The stone
15. 28. And the *s.* was fulfilled, which saith [margin]
Lu. 4. 21. To-day hath this *scripture* been fulfilled
Jno. 2. 22. believed the *scripture*, and the word which Jesus
7. 38. the *scripture* hath said, out of his belly shall flow
42. the *scripture* said that the Christ cometh of the seed
10. 35. (and the *scripture* cannot be broken)
13. 18. that the *s.* may be fulfilled. 17. 12: 19. 24, 28, 36
19. 37. another *scripture* saith, They shall look on him
20. knew not the *scripture*, that he must rise again
Acts 1. 16. it was needful that the *s.* should be fulfilled
8. 32. the *s.* which he [eunuch] was reading was this
35. Philip—from this *scripture*, preached unto him
Rom. 4. 3. what saith the *s.?* And Abraham believed God
9. 17. For the *scripture* saith unto Pharaoh
10. 11. the *scripture* saith, Whosoever believeth on him
11. 2. Or wot ye not what the *scripture* saith of Elijah?
Gal. 3. 8. the *scripture*, foreseeing that God would justify
22. the *scripture* hath shut up all things under sin
4. 30. what saith the *scripture?* Cast out the handmaid
1 *Tim.* 5. 18. the *scripture* saith, Thou shalt not muzzle
2 *Tim.* 3. 16. Every *s.* inspired of God is also profitable

SCRIPTURE

Jas. 2. 8. if ye fulfil the royal law, according to the *s.*
23, the *s.* was fulfilled which saith, And Abraham
4. 5. Or think ye that the *scripture* speaketh in vain ?
6. Wherefore the *¹s.* saith, God resisteth the proud
1 *Pet.* 2. 6. is contained in *s.*, Behold, I lay in Zion a chief
2 *Pet.* 1. 20. no prophecy of *s.* is of private interpretation

Scriptures.

Mat. 21. 42. Did ye never read in the *s.*, The stone
22. 29. Ye do err, not knowing the *scriptures*. *Mk.* 12. 24
26. 54. How then should the *scriptures* be fulfilled
56. that the *scriptures* of the prophets might be fulfilled
Mk. 14. 49. that the *scriptures* might be fulfilled
Lu. 24. 27. he interpreted to them in all the *scriptures*
32. in the way, while he opened to us the *scriptures?*
45. opened he their mind—understand the *scriptures*
Jno. 5. 39. Ye search the *scriptures*, because ye think that
Acts 17. 2. Paul—reasoned with them from the *scriptures*
11. examining the *scriptures* daily, whether these things
18. 24. he [Apollos] was mighty in the *scriptures*
28. shewing by the *scriptures* that Jesus was the Christ
Rom. 1. 2. promised afore by his prophets in the holy *s.*
15. 4. through comfort of the *s.* we might have hope
16. 26. but now is manifested, and by the *scriptures*
1 *Cor.* 15. 3. Christ died—according to the *scriptures*
4. he hath been raised—according to the *scriptures*
2 *Pet.* 3. 16. wrest, as they do also the other *scriptures*
see (*sacred*) *writings.*

Scroll.

Rev. 6. 14. And the heaven was removed as a *scroll*

Sea—s.

Mat. 4. 13. dwelt in Capernaum, which is by the *sea*
15. the land of Naphtali, Toward the *sea*
18. [Jesus] and walking by the *sea* of. *Mk.* 1. 16
8. 26. he arose, and rebuked the winds and the *sea*
27. even the winds and the *sea* obey him? *Mk.* 4. 41
15. 29. Jesus—came nigh unto the *sea* of Galilee
17. 27. go thou to the *sea*, and cast a hook
23. 15. ye compass *sea* and land to make one proselyte
Mk. 3. 7. Jesus with his disciples withdrew to the *sea*
4. 1. all the multitude were by the *sea* on the land
39. and said unto the *sea*, Peace, be still
5. 21. gathered unto him; and he was by the *sea*
Jno. 6. 1. went away to the other side of the *s.* of Galilee. 25
16. his disciples went down unto the *sea*
17. and were going over the *sea* unto Capernaum
18. And the *sea* was rising by reason of a great wind
21. 1. Jesus manifested himself—at the *sea* of Tiberias
Acts 14. 15. God, who made the heaven—and the *s. Rev.* 10. 6
17. 14. brethren sent forth Paul to go as far as to the *sea*
27. 5. when we had sailed across the *s.* which is off Cilicia
27. 41. lighting upon a place where two *seas* met
28. 4. though he hath escaped from the *sea*, yet Justice
1 *Cor.* 10. 1. under the cloud, and all passed through the *sea*
Rev. 4. 6. as it were a glassy *sea* like unto crystal
7. 2. to whom it was given to hurt the earth and the *sea*
8. saying, Hurt not the earth, neither the *sea*
12. 12. Woe for the earth and for the *sea*
14. 7. worship him that made the heaven—and *sea*
15. 2. I saw as it were a glassy *sea*—by the glassy *sea*
18. 17. as many as gain their living by *sea*, stood afar off
20. 13. And the *sea* gave up the dead which were in it
21. 1. first earth are passed away; and the *sea* is no more
see in the sea.

In, or into the **Sea.**—*A.V.* ¹*unto the sea,* ²*upon the sea.*

Mat. 4. 18. casting a net *into the sea*. *Mk.* 1. 16
8. 24. there arose a great tempest *in the sea*

SEAL

Mat. 8. 32. herd rushed down the steep *into the s. Mk.* 5. 13
13. 47. like unto a net, that was cast *into the sea*
21. 21. Be thou taken up and cast *into the sea*. *Mk.* 11. 23
Mk. 4. 1. so that he entered into a boat, and sat *in the sea*
5. 13. two thousand; and they were choked *in the sea*
9. 42. neck, and he were cast *into the sea. Lu.* 17. 2
Lu. 17. 6. Be thou rooted up, and be thou planted *in the sea*
Jno. 21. 7. Simon Peter—cast himself *into the sea*
Acts 27. 30. and had lowered the boat *into the sea*
38. throwing out the wheat *into the sea*
40. casting off the anchors, they left them ¹*in the sea*
1 *Cor.* 10. 2. unto Moses in the cloud and *in the sea*
2 *Cor.* 11. 26. in the wilderness, in perils *in the sea*
Jas. 3. 7. creeping things and things *in the sea*, is tamed
Rev. 8. 8. mountain burning with fire was cast *into the sea*
9. the third part of the creatures which were *in the sea*
16. 3. second [angel] poured out his bowl ²*into the sea*—
every living soul died—*in the sea*
18. 19. made rich all that had their ships *in the sea*
21. as it were a great millstone, and cast it *into the sea*
see overboard.

Of, or out of the **Sea.**

Mat. 18. 6. that he should be sunk in the depth *of the sea*
Mk. 5. 1. they came to the other side *of the sea*
Lu. 21. 25. in perplexity for the roaring *of the sea*
Jno. 6. 22. the multitude—on the other side *of the sea*
25. when they found him on the other side *of the sea*
Rom. 9. 27. children of Israel be as the sand *of the sea*
Jas. 1. 6. for he that doubteth is like the surge *of the sea*
Jude 13. wild waves *of the s.*, foaming out their own shame
Rev. 8. 8. the third part *of the sea* became blood
13. 1. he stood upon the sand *of the sea.* And I saw a
beast coming up *out of the sea*
20. 8. the number of whom is as the sand *of the sea*

On, or upon the **Sea.**

Mat. 14. 25. he came unto them, walking *upon the sea.*
26: *Mk.* 6. 48, 49: *Jno.* 6. 19   [*the sea*
Rev. 5. 13. every created thing—under the earth, and *on*
7. 1. no wind should blow on the earth, and *on the sea*
10. 2. and he set his right foot *upon the sea*
5. the angel which I saw standing *upon the sea.* 8
see into the sea.

Sea *coast.—see coast.*

Sea *shore.*

Heb. 11. 12. as the sand, which is by the *s. s.*, innumerable

Sea *side.*

Mat. 13. 1. Jesus out of the house, and sat by the *sea side*
Mk. 2. 13. [Jesus] went forth again by the *sea side*
4. 1. he [Jesus] began to teach by the *sea side*
Acts 10. 6. tanner, whose house is by the *sea side.* 32

Seal—s.

Jno. 3. 33. hath set his *seal* to this, that God is true
Rom. 4. 11. circumcision, a *seal* of the righteousness
1 *Cor.* 9. 2. the *seal* of mine apostleship are ye in the Lord
2 *Tim.* 2. 19. having this *seal*, The Lord knoweth them
Rev. 5. 1. a book—close sealed with seven *seals*
2. Worthy art thou—and to open the *seals* thereof? 5
9. Worthy art thou—and to open the *seals* thereof
6. 1. I saw when the Lamb opened one of the seven *seals*
3. the second *seal.* 5. the third *seal.* 7. the fourth
seal. 9. the fifth *seal.* 12. the sixth *seal.* 8. 1.
the seventh *seal*
7. 2. another angel—having the *seal* of the living God

SEAL

Rev. 9. 4. hurt—only such men as have not the *s.* of God
10. 4. *Seal* up the things which the seven thunders
22. 10. *Seal* not up the words of the prophecy of this book
    see sealed.

Sealed.—*A. V.* ¹*seal.*

Jno. 6. 27. him the Father, even God, hath *sealed*
Rom. 15. 28. and have *sealed* to them this fruit
2 *Cor.* 1. 22. who also *sealed* us, and gave us the earnest
Eph. 1. 13. also believed, ye were *s.* with the Holy Spirit
4. 30. the Holy Spirit of God, in whom ye were *sealed*
Rev. 5. 1. a book—close *sealed* with seven seals
7. 3. till we shall have *sealed* the servants of our God
4. the number of them which were *s.*—*sealed* out of
5. Of the tribe of Judah were *sealed.* 6 [every tribe
20. 3. into the abyss, and shut it, and ¹*sealed* it over him

Sealing.

Mat. 27. 66. made the sepulchre sure, *sealing* the stone

Seam.

Jno. 19. 23. the coat was without *seam*, woven from the top

Search—ed.—*A. V.* ¹*enquire.*

Mat. 2. 8. Go and *search* out carefully—the young child
10. 11. city or village ye shall enter, ¹*s.* out who in it
Jno. 5. 39. Ye *search* the scriptures, because ye think
7. 52. *S.*, and see that out of Galilee ariseth no prophet
1 *Pet.* 1. 10. the prophets sought and *searched* diligently

Searcheth—ing.

Rom. 8. 27. he that *searcheth* the hearts knoweth what is
1 *Cor.* 2. 10. for the Spirit *searcheth* all things
1 *Pet.* 1. 11. *searching* what time or what manner of time
Rev. 2. 23. I am he which *searcheth* the reins and hearts
    see examining.

Seared *A.V.*—*see branded.*

Season—ed.—*A. V.* ¹*always*, ²*time.*

Mat. 11. 25. At that ²*season* Jesus answered. 12. 2]
14. 1. At that ²*season* Herod the tetrarch heard the report
21. 34. when the ²*season* of the fruits drew near
Mk. 9. 50. lost its saltness, wherewith will ye *season* it?
11. 13. for it was not the ²*season* of figs.
12. 2. at the *s.* he sent to the husbandmen. *Lu.* 20. 10
Lu. 1. 20. my words, which shall be fulfilled in their *season*
4. 13. temptation, he departed from him for a *season*
12. 42. give them their portion of food in due *season?*
13. 1. were some present at that very *season* which told
14. 34. lost its savour, wherewith shall it be *seasoned?*
21. 36. watch ye at every ¹*season*, making supplication
Jno. 5. 35. ye were willing to rejoice for a *season* in his light
Acts 7. 20. At which ²*season* Moses was born
13. 11. thou shalt be blind, not seeing the sun for a *season*
24. 25. when I have a convenient *season*, I will call thee
Rom. 3. 26. of his righteousness at this present ²*season*
9. 9. According to this ²*season* will I come, and Sarah
1 *Cor.* 7. 5. except it be by consent for a ²*season*
2 *Cor.* 7. 8. epistle made you sorry, though but for a *season*
Col. 4. 6. speech be always with grace, *seasoned* with salt
1 *Th.* 2. 17. being bereaved of you for a short ²*season*
2 *Th.* 2. 6. that he may be revealed in his own ²*season*
2 *Tim.* 4. 2. be instant in *season*, out of *season*; reprove
Philem. 15. he was therefore parted from thee for a *s.*
Heb. 11. 25. than to enjoy the pleasures of sin for a *season*
    see seasons, time, while, little while.

SECRET

Seasons.—*A. V.* ¹*season*, ²*times.*

Mat. 21. 41. shall render him the fruits in their *seasons*
*Jno.*5. 4. angel of the Lord went down at certain ¹*s.* [margin]
Acts 1. 7. It is not for you to know times or *seasons*
3. 19. so there may come ²*seasons* of refreshing
14. 17. gave you from heaven rains and fruitful *seasons*
Gal. 4. 10. Ye observe days, and months, and ²*s.*, and years
1 *Th.* 5. 1. But concerning the times and the *seasons*
Tit. 1. 3. in his own ²*seasons* manifested his word

Seat—s.—*A.V.* ¹*room—s.*

Mat. 21. 12. *seats* of them that sold the doves. *Mk.* 11. 15
23. 2. The scribes and the Pharisees sit on Moses' *seat*
6. the chief *seats* in the synagogues. *Mk.* 12. 39: *Lu.*
    11. 43 : 20. 46
Lu. 14. 7. he marked how they chose out the chief ¹*seats*
8. to a marriage feast, sit not down in the chief ¹*seat*
    see judgement-seat, mercy-seat, throne, thrones.

Seated.—*A.V.* ¹*sit*, ²*sitteth.*

Lu. 22. 69. henceforth shall the Son of man be ¹*s.* at the
Col. 3. 1. where Christ is, ²*s.* on the right hand of God

Second.—*A.V.* ¹*again*, ²*another.*

Mat. 21. 30. he came to the *second*, and said likewise
22. 26. the *s.* also, and the third. *Mk.* 12. 21 : *Lu.* 20. 30
39. And a *second* like unto it is this. *Mk.* 12. 31
26. 42. Again a *second* time he went away, and prayed
Mk. 14. 72. straightway the *second* time the cock crew
Lu. 12. 38. if he shall come in the *second* watch
19. 18. the *second* came, saying, Thy pound, Lord
Jno. 3. 4. can he enter a *s.* time into his mother's womb
4. 54. This is again the *second* sign that Jesus did
9. 24. they called a ¹*second* time the man that was blind
21. 16. He saith to him again a *s.* time, Simon, son of John
Acts 7. 13. the *second* time Joseph was made known
10. 15. the *second* time, What God hath cleansed. 11. 19
12. 10. they were past the first and the *second* ward
13. 33. it is written in the *second* psalm, Thou art my Son
1 *Cor.* 15. 47. the *second* man is of heaven
2 *Cor.* 1. 15. that ye might have a *second* benefit
13. 2. as when I was present the *second* time
Tit. 3. 10. after a first and *second* admonition refuse
Heb. 8. 7. would no place have been sought for a *second*
9. 3. And after the *second* veil, the tabernacle which is
7. but into the *second* the high priest alone, once
28. shall appear a *second* time, apart from sin
10. 9. taketh away the first, that he may establish the *s.*
2 *Pet.* 3. 1. This is now, beloved, the *second* epistle
Rev. 2. 11. shall not be hurt of the *second* death. 20. 6
4. 7. and the *second* creature like a calf
6. 8. opened the *s.* seal, I heard the *s.* living creature
8. 8. And the *second* angel sounded, and as it were a great
11. 14. The *s.* Woe is past : behold, the third Woe cometh
14. 8. a ²*second* angel, followed, saying, Fallen, fallen
16. 3. And the *second* poured out his bowl into the sea
19. 3. a ¹*second* time they say, Hallelujah
20. 14. This is the *s.* death, even the lake of fire. 21. 8
21. 19. The first foundation was jasper ; the *s.*, sapphire
    see day.

Secondarily *A.V.*—*see secondly.*

Secondly.—*A.V.* ¹*secondarily.*

1 *Cor.* 12. 28. first apostles, ¹*s.* prophets, thirdly teachers

Secret—s—ly.

Mat. 6. 4. in *secret :* and thy Father which seeth in *s.* 6
18. thy Father which is in *s.*—Father, which seeth in *s.*

293

SECRET

Mk. 4. 22. neither was anything made *secret*. Lu. 8. 17
Jno. 7. 4. For no man doeth anything in *secret*
    10. went he also up, not publicly, but as it were in *secret*
    11. 26. she went away, and called Mary her sister *secretly*
    18. 20. I have spoken openly—and in *s.* spake I nothing
    19. 38. Joseph—but *secretly* for fear of the Jews
Rom. 2. 16. the day when God shall judge the *secrets* of men
1 Cor. 14. 25. the *secrets* of his heart are made manifest
Eph. 5. 12. things which are done by them in *secret*
Phil. 4. 12. have I learned the *secret* both to be filled
    see cellar, hidden, inner, silence.

Sect.—*A.V.* ¹*heresy.*

Acts 5. 17. (which is the *sect* of the Sadducees)
    15. 5. certain of the *sect* of the Pharisees who believed
    24. 5. and a ringleader of the *sect* of the Nazarenes
    14. after the Way which they call a ¹*sect*, so serve I
    26. 5. the straitest *sect* of our religion I lived a Pharisee
    28. 22. as concerning this *sect*, it is known to us that

Secure *A.V.*—*see rid.*

Security.

Acts 17. 9. when they had taken *security* from Jason

Sedition—s.—*A.V.* ¹*uproar.*

Acts 21. 38. which before these days stirred up to ¹*sedition*
    see divisions, insurrection, jealousies.

Seduce *A.V.*—*see lead, seduceth.*

Seducers *A.V.*—*see impostors.*

Seduceth—ing.—*A.V.* ¹*seduce.*

1 Tim. 4. 1. giving heed to *seducing* spirits and doctrines
Rev. 2. 20. she teacheth and ¹*seduceth* my servants

See.—*A V.* ¹*behold,* ²*look,* ³*perceive,* ⁴*seen,* ⁵*take heed.*

Mat. 5. 8. the pure in heart: for they shall *see* God
    16. that they may *see* your good works   [6. 42
    7. 5. then shalt thou *see* clearly to cast out the mote. Lu.
    8. 4. *See* thou tell no man. 9. 30: Mk. 1. 44.
    11. 8. But what went ye out for to *see* ? 9: Lu. 7. 25, 26
    13. 16. But blessed are your eyes, for they *see*. Lu. 10. 23
    17. righteous men desired to *see* the things. Lu. 10. 24
    16. 28. taste of death, till they *see* the Son of man
    18. 10. ⁵*See* that ye despise not one of these little ones
    24. 6. wars: *see* that ye be not troubled   [Lu. 21. 27
    30. they shall *see* the Son of man coming on the clouds.
    26. 58. and sat with the officers, to *see* the end
    27. 4. What is that to us? *See* thou to it
    49. let us *see* whether Elijah cometh. Mk. 15. 36
    28. 1. and the other Mary to *see* the sepulchre
    6. Come, *see* the place where the Lord lay
    10. they depart into Galilee, and there shall they *see* me
Mk. 4. 12. seeing they may *see*, and not perceive. Acts 28. 26
    5. 14. to *see* what it was that had come to pass. Lu. 8. 35
    32. looked round about to *s.* her that had done this thing
    6. 38. How many loaves have ye? go and *see*
    8. 24. I *see* men; for I behold them as trees, walking
    9. 1. taste of death, till they ⁴*see* the kingdom. Lu. 9. 27
    12. 15. bring me a penny, that I may *see* it
Lu. 2. 15. Let us now go even unto Bethlehem, and *see*
    3. 6. And all flesh shall *see* the salvation of God
    8. 16. they which enter in may *see* the light. 11. 33
    20. Thy mother and thy brethren—desiring to *see* thee
    9. 9. And he [Herod] sought to *see* him. 23. 8
    14. 18. bought a field, and I must needs go out and *see* it
    17. 22. ye shall desire to *see* one of the days of the Son

SEE

Lu. 19. 3. he [Zacchæus] sought to *see* Jesus. 4
    23. 8. he hoped to ⁴*see* some miracle done by him
    24. 39. ¹*See* my hands—it is I myself: handle me, and *see*
Jno. 1. 33. Upon whomsoever thou shalt *see* the Spirit
    39. Come, and ye shall *see*. 46: 11. 34
    50. thou shalt *see* greater things than these
    4. 29. Come, *see* a man, which told me all things that ever
    7. 52. Search, and ²*see* that out of Galilee ariseth no
    8. 51. If a man keep my word, he shall never *see* death
    56. Your father Abraham rejoiced to *see* my day
    9. 15. clay upon mine eyes, and I washed, and do *see*
    19. ye say was born blind? how then doth he now *see* ?
    25. I know, that, whereas I was blind, now I *see*
    39. that they which *see* not may *see*—which *see* may
    11. 40. believedst, thou shouldest *see* the glory of God?
    12. 9. but that they might *see* Lazarus also
    16. 22. I will *see* you again, and your heart shall rejoice
    20. 25. Except I shall *s.* in his hands the print of the nails
    27. Reach hither thy finger, and ¹*see* my hands
Acts 2. 17. And your young men shall *see* visions
    27. Neither wilt thou give thy Holy One to *see*. 13. 35
    31. was he left in Hades, nor did his flesh *see* corruption
    7. 56. I [Stephen] *see* the heavens opened, and the Son
    8. 23. For I ³*see* that thou art in the gall of bitterness
    15. 36. visit the brethren—and *see* how they fare
    19. 21. After I have been there, I [Paul] must also *s.* Rome
    22. 14. thee to know his will, and to *see* the Righteous One
    28. 20. therefore did I intreat you to *see* and to speak
Rom. 1. 11. For I long to *see* you, that I may impart unto you
    7. 23. but I *see* a different law in my members
    15. 21. They shall *see*, to whom no tidings of him came
    24. (for I hope to *see* you in my journey
1 Cor. 8. 10. if a man *see* thee which hast knowledge
    16. 10. if Timothy come, *see* that he be with you
2 Cor. 7. 8. for I ³*see* that that epistle made you sorry
    8. 7. *see* that ye abound in this grace also
Gal. 6. 11. *See* with how large letters I have written
Eph. 3. 9. to make all men *see* what is the dispensation
    33. and let the wife *see* that she fear her husband
Phil. 1. 27. whether I come and *see* you or be absent
    2. 23. so soon as I shall *see* how it will go with me
1 Th. 3. 6. longing to *see* us, even as we also to *see* you
    5. 15. *See* that none render unto any one evil for evil
1 Tim. 6. 16. whom no man hath seen, nor can *see*
2 Tim. 1. 4. night and day longing to *see* thee
Heb. 8. 5. *See*, saith he, that thou make all things according
    12. 14. the sanctification without which no man shall *s.*
    25. *See* that ye refuse not him that speaketh
    13. 23. with whom, if he come shortly, I will *see* you
1 Pet. 3. 10. He that would love life, And *see* good days
1 Jno. 5. 16. If any man *see* his brother sinning a sin
3 Jno. 14. but I hope shortly to *see* thee, and we shall speak
Rev. 1. 7. with the clouds; and every eye shall *see* him
    12. And I turned to *see* the voice which spake with me
    3. 18. eyesalve to anoint thine eyes, that thou mayest *see*
    9. 20. which can neither *see*, nor hear, nor walk
    16. 15. lest he walk naked, and they *see* his shame)
    18. 7. am no widow, and shall in no wise *see* mourning
    19. 10. he saith unto me, *See* thou do it not. 22. 9
    see behold, look, perceive, seeing, sight, visit.

We with See.

Mat. 12. 38. Master, *we* would *see* a sign from thee
Mk. 15. 32. that *we* may *see* and believe. Jno. 6. 30
Jno. 9. 41. now ye say, *We see*: your sin remaineth
    12. 21. came to Philip—saying, Sir, *we* would *see* Jesus
1 Cor. 13. 12. For now *we see* in a mirror, darkly
Heb. 3. 19. And *we see* that they were not able to enter in
1 Jno. 3. 2. be like him; for *we* shall *see* him even as he is

SEE

Ye with See.
Mat. 11. 4. the things which *ye* do hear and *s.* [*Acts* 28. 26
13. 14. seeing *ye* shall *see*, and shall in no wise perceive.
17. things which *ye s.*, and saw them not. *Lu.* 10. 23, 24
24. 15. When therefore *ye see* the abomination. *Mk.* 13. 14
33. when *ye see* all these things, know ye that he is nigh.
Mk. 13. 29 : *Lu.* 21. 31
26. 64. Henceforth *ye* shall *see* the Son of man sitting at the right hand of power. *Mk.* 14. 62
27. 24. of the blood of this righteous man : *see ye* to it
28. 7. into Galilee ; there shall *ye see* him. *Mk.* 16. 7
Lu. 12. 54. When *ye see* a cloud rising in the west
55. when *ye see* a south wind blowing, ye say
13. 28. when *ye* shall *see* Abraham, and Isaac, and Jacob
21. 20. But when *ye see* Jerusalem compassed with armies
30. when they now shoot forth, *ye see* it and know
Jno. 1. 51. *Ye* shall *see* the heaven opened, and the angels
4. 48. Except *ye see* signs and wonders, ye will in no wise
16. 16. again a little while, and *ye* shall *see* me. 17, 19
Acts 2. 33. he hath poured forth this, which *ye see* and hear
19. 26. And *ye see* and hear, that not alone at Ephesus
Phil. 2. 28. when *ye see* him again, ye may rejoice
Heb. 10. 25. so much the more, as *ye see* the day drawing nigh
Jas. 2. 24. *Ye see* that by works a man is justified
1 *Pet.* 1. 8. on whom, though now *ye see* him not, yet

See, *with not or cannot.*
Mat. 13. 13. parables ; because seeing they *see* not. *Lu.* 8. 10
23. 39. Ye shall *not see* me henceforth. *Lu.* 13. 35
24. 2. *See* ye *not* all these things ? verily I say unto you
Mk. 8. 18. Having eyes, *see* ye *not* ? and having ears
Lu. 2. 26. that he should *not see* death, before he had seen
17. 22. days of the Son of man, and ye shall *not see* it
Jno. 3. 3. born anew, he *cannot see* the kingdom of God
36. but he that obeyeth not the Son shall *not see* life
9. 39. came I into this world, that they which *see not* may
18. 26. Did *not* I *see* thee in the garden with him ?
Acts 22. 11. I [Paul] could *not see* for the glory of that light
Rom. 8. 25. if we hope for that which we *see not*
11. 8. a spirit of stupor, eyes that they should *not see*
10. Let their eyes be darkened, that they may *not see*
Heb. 2. 8. now we *see not* yet all things subjected to him
11. 5. Enoch was translated that he should *not see* death

Seed.—*A.V.* ¹*issue.*
Mat. 13. 24. a man that sowed good *seed* in his field
27. Sir, didst thou not sow good *seed* in thy field ?
37. He that soweth the good *seed* is the Son of man
38. the good *seed*, these are the sons of the kingdom
22. 24. raise up *s.* unto his brother. *Mk.* 12. 19 : *Lu.* 20. 28
25. no ¹*s.* left his wife unto his brother. *Mk.* 12. 20, 21, 22
Mk. 4. 4. as he sowed, some *seed* fell by the way side
26. as if a man should cast *seed* upon the earth. 27
31. It is like a grain of mustard *s.*, which, when it is sown
Lu. 8. 5. The sower went forth to sow his *seed*
11. Now the parable is this : The *seed* is the word of God
Jno. 7. 42. Christ cometh of the *s.* of David. *Rom.* 1. 3 : 2 *Tim.*
Acts 2. 30. in thy *s.* shall all the families—be blessed [2. 8
7. 5. give it to him in possession, and to his *s.* after him
6. that his *seed* should sojourn in a strange land
13. 23. Of this man's *s.* hath God according to promise
Rom. 4. 16. that the promise may be sure to all the *seed*
18. to that which had been spoken, So shall thy *seed* be
9. 7. because they are Abraham's *s.*—In Isaac shall
thy *seed* be called. *Heb.* 11. 18
8. the children of the promise are reckoned for a *seed*
29. Except the Lord of Sabaoth had left us a *seed*
1 *Cor.* 15. 38. and to each *seed* a body of its own

SEEK

2 *Cor.* 9. 10. he that supplieth *seed* to the sower—shall supply and multiply your *seed* for sowing
Gal. 3. 16. to his *seed*. He saith not, And to seeds, as of many ; but—to thy *seed*, which is Christ
19. till the *seed* should come to whom the promise
Heb. 11. 11. Sarah herself received power to conceive *seed*
1 *Pet.* 1. 23. begotten again, not of corruptible *seed*
1 *Jno.* 3. 9. doeth no sin, because his *seed* abideth in him
Rev. 12. 17. to make war with the rest of her *seed*
see Abraham, sown.

Seeds.
Mat. 13. 4. as he sowed, some *seeds* fell by the way side
32. which indeed is less than all *s.* ; but when. *Mk.* 4. 31
Gal. 3. 16. He saith not, And to *seeds*, as of many

Seeing.—*A.V.* ¹*beheld,* ²*beholding,* ³*looked,* ⁴*perceiving,* ⁵*saw,* ⁶*see.*
Mat. 5. 1. And *seeing* the multitudes, he [Jesus] went up
9. 2. Jesus *seeing* their faith said unto the sick. *Mk.* 2. ⁵5
13. 13. because *seeing* they see not. *Lu.* 8. 10. [26. 26
14. *s.* ye shall see, and shall in no wise. *Mk.* 4. 12 : *Acts*
15. 31. and the lame walking, and the blind ⁶*seeing*
Mk. 8. 33. he turning about, and ³*s.* his disciples, rebuked
11. 13. And *seeing* a fig tree afar off having leaves
Lu. 22. 56. certain maid ¹*s.* him—said, This man also was
23. 49. women—from Galilee, stood afar off, ²*seeing* those
Jno. 9. 7. He went—and washed, and came *seeing* [things
21. 21. Peter therefore *seeing* him saith to Jesus
Acts 3. 3. *s.* Peter and John about to go into the temple
4. 14. And ²*seeing* the man which was healed standing
7. 24. *seeing* one of them suffer wrong, he defended him
13. 11. thou shalt be blind, not *seeing* the sun for a season
14. 9. and ⁴*seeing* that he had faith to be made whole
16. 27. jailor—*s.* the prison doors open, drew his sword
Heb. 11. 27. he endured, as *seeing* him who is invisible
1 *Pet.* 1. 22. *Seeing* ye have purified your souls in your
2 *Pet.* 1. 9. is blind, ⁶*s.* only what is near, having forgotten
2. 8. in *seeing* and hearing, vexed his righteous soul
see beholding, foreseeing, saw.

Seek.—*A.V.* ¹*affect,* ²*desire,* ³*enquire,* ⁴*go,* ⁵*seeketh.*
Mat. 2. 13. Herod will *seek* the young child to destroy him
6. 32. For after all these things do the Gentiles *seek*
33. But *seek* ye first his kingdom. *Lu.* 12. 31
7. 7. *seek*, and ye shall find ; knock, and it shall. *Lu.* 11. 9
18. 12. the mountains, and ⁵*seek* that which goeth astray ?
28. 5. I know that ye *seek* Jesus. *Mk.* 16. 6
Mk. 3. 32. mother and thy brethren without *seek* for thee
8. 12. Why doth this generation *seek* a sign ?
Lu. 12. 30. all these things do the nations of the world *s.*
13. 24. many, I say unto you, shall *seek* to enter in
15. 8. sweep the house, and *s.* diligently until she find it ?
17. 33. Whosoever shall *seek* to gain his life shall lose it
19. 10. the Son of man came to *s.* and to save that which
24. 5. Why *seek* ye the living among the dead ?
Jno. 1. 38. Jesus—saith unto them, What *seek* ye ?
4. 23. for such doth the Father ¹*s.* to be his worshippers
6. 26. Ye *s.* me, not because ye saw signs, but because ye
7. 19. Why ⁴*seek* ye to kill me ? [Jesus]
25. Is not this he whom they *seek* to kill ?
34. Ye shall *seek* me, and shall not find me. 36 : 13. 33
8. 21. ye shall *seek* me, and shall die in your sin
37. ye are Abraham's *seed* ; yet ye *seek* to kill me. 40
18. 4. Jesus—saith unto them, Whom *seek* ye ?
8. if therefore ye *seek* me, let these go their way
Acts 10. 19. Spirit said unto him, Behold, three men *s.* thee
21. Peter—said, Behold, I am he whom ye *seek*
11. 25. [Barnabas] went forth to Tarsus to *seek* for Saul

SEEK

Acts 17. 27. that they should *s*. God, if haply they might
19. 39. But if ye *⁸seek* any thing about other matters
Rom. 2. 7. them that by patience in well-doing *s*. for glory
1 *Cor.* 1. 22. Jews ask for signs, and Greeks *s*. after wisdom
10. 24. Let no man *s*. his own, but each his neighbour's
14. 12. *seek* that ye may abound unto the edifying
2 *Cor.* 13. 3. seeing that ye *seek* a proof of Christ [¹*s*. them
Gal. 4. 17. They zealously ¹*s*. you in no good way—ye may
Phil. 2. 21. For they all *s*. their own, not the things of Jesus
4. 17. Not that I ²*s*. for the gift ; but I ²*seek* for the fruit
Col. 3. 1. *seek* the things that are above, where Christ is
Heb. 11. 6. he is a rewarder of them that *seek* after him
13. 14. but we *seek* after the city which is to come
Rev. 9. 6. in those days men shall *seek* death
see *Lord, seeketh, seeking, seen, sought.*

Seek not.

Lu. 12. 29. *s. not* ye what ye shall eat, and what ye shall
Jno. 5. 30. I *seek not* mine own will, but the will of him
44. the glory that cometh from the only God ye *s. not?*
8. 50 I *seek not* mine own glory : there is one that seeketh
1 *Cor.* 7. 27. *seek not* to be loosed—*seek not* a wife
2 *Cor.* 12. 14. not be a burden to you : for I *s. not* yours, but

Seeketh—est.—*A.V.* ¹*goeth about,* ²*seek.*

Mat. 7. 8. and he that *seeketh* findeth. *Lu.* 11. 10
12. 39. adulterous generation *seeketh* after a sign. 16. 4
Lu. 11. 29. an evil generation : it ²*seeketh* after a sign
Jno. 4. 27. yet no man said, What *seekest* thou ?
7. 4. in secret, and himself *seeketh* to be known openly
18. *seeketh* his own glory : but he that *seeketh* the glory
20. Thou hast a devil : who ¹*seeketh* to kill thee?
8. 50. there is one that *seeketh* and judgeth
20. 15. Woman, why weepest thou ? whom *seekest* thou ?
Rom. 3. 11. There is none that *seeketh* after God
11. 7. What then ? That which Israel *seeketh* for
1 *Cor.* 13. 5. [love] *seeketh* not its own, is not provoked
see *seek.*

Seeking.—*A.V.* ¹*desiring,* ²*going about,* ³*seek,* ⁴*sought.*

Mat. 12. 43. *seeking* rest, and findeth it not. *Lu.* 11. 24
46. his brethren stood without, ¹*s*. to speak to him. ¹47
13. 45. a man that is a merchant *seeking* goodly pearls
Mk. 1. 37. and say unto him, All are ³*seeking* thee
8. 11. the Pharisees—*seeking* of him a sign from heaven
Lu. 2. 45. they returned to Jerusalem, *seeking* for him
13. 6. he came ⁴*seeking* fruit thereon, and found none
7. these three years I come *seeking* fruit on this fig tree
Jno. 6. 24. came to Capernaum, *seeking* Jesus
11. 8. the Jews were but now ⁴*seeking* to stone thee
Acts 13. 8. Elymas—*seeking* to turn aside the proconsul
11. *seeking* some to lead him by the hand [own
Rom. 10. 3. God's righteousness, and ²*s*. to establish their
1 *Cor.* 10. 33. not *s*. mine own profit, but the profit of
Gal. 1. 10. or am I ³*seeking* to please men ? if I were still
1 *Th.* 2. 6. nor ⁴*seeking* glory of men, neither from you
Heb. 11. 14. they are ³*seeking* after a country of their own
1 *Pet.* 5. 8. walketh about, *seeking* whom he may devour

Seem.

1 *Cor.* 12. 22. those members—which *s*. to be more feeble
2 *Cor.* 10. 9. I may not *seem* as if I would terrify you
Heb. 4. 1. any one of you should *seem* to have come short
see *seemeth.*

Seemed *A.V.—see appeared, reputed.*

SEEN

Seemeth.—*A.V.* ¹*seem.*

Acts 17. 18. He *seemeth* to be a setter forth of strange gods
25. 27. it *s*. to me unreasonable, in sending a prisoner
1 *Cor.* 11. 16. if any man ¹*seemeth* to be contentious
Heb. 12. 11. All chastening *s*. for the present to be not
see *thinketh.*

Seemly.—*A.V.* ¹*comely,* ²*honest.*

1 *Cor.* 7. 35. for that which is ¹*s*., and that ye may attend
11. 13. is it ¹*s*. that a woman pray unto God unveiled ?
1 *Pet.* 2. 12. having your behaviour ²*s*. among the Gentiles

Seen.—*A.V.* ¹*appear,* ²*appeared,* ³*saw,* ⁴*shine*—*eth.*

Mat. 6. 1. do not your righteousness before men, to be *seen*
5. corners of the streets, that they may be *seen* of men
16. that they may be ¹*seen* of men to fast. ¹18
9. 33. marvelled, saying, It was never so *seen* in Israel
23. 5. all their works they do for to be *seen* of men
24. 27. from the east, and is ⁴*seen* even unto the west
Mk. 9. 9. they should tell no man what things they had *seen*
16. 11. heard that he was alive, and had been *seen* of her
14. believed not them which had *s*. him after he was
Lu. 1. 22. perceived that he had *seen* a vision
2. 20. for all the things that they had heard and *s*. 19. 37
26. before he [Simeon] had *seen* the Lord's Christ
30. For mine eyes have *seen* thy salvation
5. 26. We have *seen* strange things to-day
7. 22. tell John what things ye have *seen* and heard
9. 36. told no man—of the things which they had *seen*
24. 23. saying, that they had also *seen* a vision of angels
Jno. 1. 18. No man hath *seen* God at any time
34 And I have ³*seen*, and have borne witness
3. 11. we do know, and bear witness of that we have *s*.
32. What he hath *seen* and heard—beareth witness
4. 45. the Galilæans—having *seen* all the things
5. 37. Ye have neither heard his voice—nor *s*. his form
6. 36. ye have *seen* me, and yet believe not
46. Not that any man hath *seen* the Father—he hath *s*.
8. 38. I speak the things which I have *s*. with my Father
57. not yet fifty years old, and hast thou *s*. Abraham ?
9. 37. Thou hast both *seen* him, and he it is that speaketh
14. 7. from henceforth ye know him, and have *seen* him
9. he that hath *seen* me hath *seen* the Father [Father
15. 24. have they both *seen* and hated both me and my
19. 35. he that hath ³*seen* hath borne witness [the Lord
20. 18. Mary Magdalene cometh and telleth—I have *seen*
25. disciples therefore said unto him, We have *s*. the Lord
29. Because thou hast *seen* me, thou hast believed :
blessed are they that have not *seen*
Acts 7. 34. I have surely *seen* the affliction of my people
44. make it according to the figure that he had *seen*
9. 12. he hath *seen* a man named Ananias coming in
27. declared unto them how he [Paul] had *s*. the Lord
10. 17. the vision which he had *seen* might mean
11. 13. told us how he [Cornelius] had *seen* the angel
23. [Barnabas] had *seen* the grace of God, was glad
13. 31. he [Jesus] was *seen* for many days of them
16. 10. And when he [Paul] had *seen* the vision
40. had *seen* the brethren, they comforted them
21. 29. had before *seen* with him in the city Trophimus
22. 15. for him unto all men of what thou hast *seen*. 26. 16
Rom. 1. 20. are clearly *seen*, being perceived through the
8. 24. but hope that is *seen* is not hope [things
1 *Cor.* 9. 1. have I not *seen* Jesus our Lord ?
2 *Cor.* 4. 18. things which are *seen*—things which are not
seen—are *seen* are temporal—not *seen* are eternal
Phil. 2. 15. among whom ye are ⁴*s*. as lights in the world
Col. 2. 1. as many as have not *seen* my face in the flesh
18. dwelling in the things which he hath *seen*

296

SEEN

1 *Tim.* 3. 16. *seen* of angels, preached among the nations
6. 16. whom no man hath *seen*, nor can see
Heb. 11. 1. things hoped for, the proving of things not *s.*
3. so that what is *seen* hath not been made out of things
7. Noah, being warned—concerning things not *seen*
13. promises, but having *seen* them and greeted them
Jas. 5. 11. ye have heard of the patience of Job, and have *s.*
1 *Pet.* 1. 8. whom not having *seen* ye love ; on whom
1 *Jno.* 1. 1. that which we have *seen* with our eyes
2. was manifested, and we have *seen*, and bear witness
3. that which we have *seen* and heard declare we
3. 6. whosoever sinneth hath not *seen* him. 3 *Jno.* 11
4. 20. he that loveth not his brother whom he hath *seen*,
cannot love God whom he hath not *seen*
Rev. 11. 19. there was *seen* in his temple the ark
12. 1. a great sign was ²*seen* in heaven ; a woman arrayed
see appearing, beheld, heard, saw, sawest, see.

Seest.—*A. V.* ¹*saw.*

Mk. 5 31. Thou *seest* the multitude thronging thee
8. 23. he asked him, ¹*Seest* thou aught ?
13. 2. Jesus said—*Seest* thou these great buildings ?
Lu. 7. 44. said unto Simon, *Seest* thou this woman ?
Acts 21. 20. Thou *seest*, brother, how many thousands
Jas. 2. 22. Thou *seest* that faith wrought with his works
Rev. 1. 11. What thou *seest*, write in a book, and send it to

Seeth.—*A. V.* ¹*beheld.*

Mat. 6. 4. thy Father which *seeth* in secret. 6, 18
Lu. 16. 23. and *seeth* Abraham afar off. and Lazarus
24. 12. Peter—looking in, he ¹*seeth* the linen cloths
Jno. 1. 29. On the morrow he *seeth* Jesus coming unto him
5. 19. nothing of himself, but what he *s.* the Father doing
9. 21. but how he now *seeth*, we know not; or who opened
11. 9. he stumbleth not, because he *seeth* the light
20. 1. and *seeth* the stone taken away from the tomb
21. 20. Peter—*s.* the disciple whom Jesus loved following
Rom. 8. 24. for who hopeth for that which he *seeth* ?
2 *Cor.* 12. 6. account of me above that which he *seeth* me
see beholdeth.

Seize.—*A. V.* ¹*take.*

Mat. 26. 55. against a robber with swords and staves to ¹*seize*
Acts 12. 3. he [Herod] proceeded to ¹*seize* Peter also [me ?

Seized.—*A. V.* ¹*caught,* ²*taken,* ³*took.*

Lu. 8. 29. For oftentimes it [unclean spirit] had ¹*s.* him
22. 54. they ³*s.* him, [Jesus] and led him away. *Jno.* 18.³12
Acts 6. 12. the scribes, and came upon him, and ¹*s.* him
19. 29. the theatre, having ¹*seized* Gaius and Aristarchus
23. 27. This man was ²*seized* by the Jews
26. 21. this cause the Jews ¹*seized* me [Paul] in the temple

Self.—*A. V.* ¹*own selves.*

Lu 9. 25. whole world, and lose or forfeit his own *self* ?
Jno. 17. 5. O Father, glorify thou me with thine own *self*
1 *Cor.* 4. 3. man's judgement: yea, I judge not mine own *self*
2 *Tim.* 3. 2. For men shall be lovers of ¹*self*
Philem. 19. thou owest to me even thine own *self* besides
1 *Pet.* 2. 24. who his own *self* bare our sins in his body

Self-control.—*A. V.* ¹*incontinent.*

2 *Tim.* 3. 3. without ¹*self-control,* fierce, no lovers of good

Selfsame.

2 *Cor.* 7. 11. this *selfsame* thing, that ye were made sorry
see hour, same, very.

SEND

Selfwilled.

Tit. 1. 7. the bishop—not *s.*, not soon angry, no brawler
2 *Pet.* 2. 10. Daring, *s.*, they tremble not to rail at dignities

Sell—er.

Mat. 19. 21. If thou wouldest be perfect, go, *sell* that thou
hast. *Mk.* 10. 21: *Lu.* 18. 22   ʳselves
25. 9. go ye rather to them that *sell*, and buy for your-
Lu. 12. 33. *Sell* that ye have, and give alms
22. 36. let him *sell* his cloke, and buy a sword
Acts 16. 14. Lydia, a *seller* of purple, of the city of Thyatira
Rev. 13. 17. no man should be able to buy or to *sell*
see trade.

Selleth.

Mat. 13. 44. *selleth* all that he hath, and buyeth that field

Selves.

Acts 20. 30. from among your own *selves* shall men arise
2 *Cor.* 8. 5. first they gave their own *selves* to the Lord
13. 5. Try your own *selves*, whether—prove your own
selves—know ye not as to your own *selves*
Jas. 1. 22. not hearers only, deluding your own *selves*

Senate.

Acts 5. 21. called the council together, and all the *senate*

Send.—*A. V.* ¹*sent,* ²*suffer,* ³*thrust.*

Mat. 8. 31. ²*send* us away into the herd of swine. *Mk.* 5. 12
9. 38. he *send* forth labourers into his harvest. *Lu.* 10. 2
10. 34. Think not that I came to *send* peace on the earth :
I came not to *send* peace, but a sword
12. 20. Till he *send* forth judgement unto victory
13. 41. shall *send* forth his angels. 24. 31 : *Mk.* 13. 27
14. 15. *s.* the multitudes away. ¹22 : *Mk.* 6. 36 : *Lu.* 9. 12
15. 23. *Send* her away ; for she crieth after us
21. 3. and straightway he will *send* them. *Mk.* 11. 3
26. 53. even now *s.* me more than twelve legions of angels ?
Mk. 3. 14. that he might *send* them forth to preach
5. 10. that he would not *s.* them away out of the country
6. 7. the twelve, and began to *s.* them forth by two and two
12. 13. they *send* unto him certain of the Pharisees
Lu. 16. 24. Father Abraham—*send* Lazarus. 27
Jno. 11. 42. that they may believe that thou didst ¹*send* me
14. 26. even the Holy Spirit, whom the Father will *send*
17. 3. him whom thou didst ¹*send*, even Jesus Christ
8. from thee, and they believed that thou didst *s.* me. 125
18. As thou didst ¹*send* me into the world, even so sent I
23. the world may know that thou didst ¹*send* me. ¹21
Acts 3. 20. may *send* the Christ who hath been appointed
10. 5. now *send* men to Joppa, and fetch. 32 : 11. 13
22. warned of God by a holy angel to *send* for thee
11. 29. determined to *send* relief unto the brethren
15. 22. their company, and *send* them to Antioch. 25
25. 3. that he would *send* for him to Jerusalem
25. to the emperor I determined to *send* him
Phil. 2. 19. I hope in the Lord Jesus to *send* Timothy. 23
25. I counted it necessary to *send* to you Epaphroditus
Jas. 3. 11. Doth the fountain *send* forth from the same
Rev. 1. 11. write in a book, and *s.* it to the seven churches
11. 10. and they shall *send* gifts one to another [is come
14. 15. ³*S.* forth thy sickle, and reap : for the hour to reap
18. ⁵*Send* forth thy sharp sickle, and gather the clusters
see cast, sendeth, sending, sent.

I with Send.

Mat. 10. 16. Behold, *I send* you forth as sheep. *Lu.* 10. 3
11. 10. Behold, *I s.* my messenger before thy face. *Mk.* 1. 2 :
15. 32. *I* would not *send* them away fasting   [*Lu.* 7. 27

SEND

Mat. 23. 34. behold, I s. unto you prophets, and wise men
Mk. 8. 3. if I send them away fasting to their home
Lu. 11. 49. I will send unto them prophets and apostles
20. 13. I will send my beloved son: it may be they will
24. 49. behold, I send forth the promise of my Father
Jno. 13. 20. receiveth whomsoever I send receiveth me
15. 26. the Comforter—whom I will send unto you. 16. 7
20. 21. as the Father hath sent me, even so send I you
Acts 7. 34. now come, I will send thee into Egypt
22. 21. I will send thee forth far hence unto the Gentiles
25. 21. to be kept till I should send him to Cæsar
25. 27. from the Gentiles, unto whom I send thee
1 Cor. 16. 3. them will I send to carry your bounty
Tit. 3. 12. When I shall send Artemas unto thee

Sendeth.—A.V. ¹send, ²sent.

Mat. 5. 45. and sendeth rain on the just and the unjust
Mk. 6. 45. while he himself ²sendeth the multitude away
11. 1. mount of Olives, he s. two of his disciples. 14. 13
Lu. 14. 32. he s. an ambassage, and asketh conditions of
2 Th. 2. 11. God ¹sendeth them a working of error [peace

Sending.—A.V. ¹send, ²sent.

Acts 11. 30. ²s. it to the elders by the hand of Barnabas
25. 27. seemeth to me unreasonable, in ¹s. a prisoner
Rom. 8. 3. God, sending his own Son in the likeness

Senseless.—A.V. ¹foolish.

Rom. 1. 21. and their ¹senseless heart was darkened

Senses.

Heb. 5. 14. by reason of use have their senses exercised

Sensual.

Jas. 3. 15. This wisdom—but is earthly, sensual, devilish
Jude 19. who make separations, s., having not the Spirit

Sent.—A.V. ¹send.

Mat. 10. 40. he that receiveth me receiveth him that sent
me. Mk. 9. 37; Lu. 9. 48; Jno. 13. 20
15. 24. I was not sent but unto the lost sheep of the house
21. 1. mount of Olives, then Jesus sent two disciples
22. 7. sent his armies, and destroyed those murderers
23. 37. and stoneth them that are sent unto her! Lu. 13. 34
27. 19. sitting on the judgement-seat, his wife s. unto him
Mk. 3. 31. standing without, they s. unto him, calling him
6. 27. straightway the king sent forth a soldier
Lu. 1. 19. I am Gabriel—sent to speak unto thee. 26
4. 26. and unto none of them was Elijah sent
7. 6. the centurion sent friends to him [Jesus]
20. John the Baptist hath sent us unto thee
10. 1. and sent them two and two before his face
16. he that rejecteth me, rejecteth him that sent me
19. 14. But his citizens hated him, and s. an ambassage
20. 11. s. yet another servant—and s. him away empty. 10
23. 11. in gorgeous apparel sent him back to Pilate
Jno. 1. 6. a man, sent from God, whose name was John
22. that we may give an answer to them that sent us
24. And they had been sent from the Pharisees
3. 17. God sent not the Son into the world to judge
28. I am not the Christ, but, that I am sent before him
34. he whom God hath sent speaketh the words of God
4. 34. My meat is to do the will of him that sent me
5. 23. honoureth not the Father which sent him
24. believeth him that sent me, hath eternal life. 12. 44
30. own will, but the will of him that sent me. 6. 38, 39
33. Ye have sent unto John, and he hath borne witness
6. 44. except the Father which sent me draw him

SENT

Jno. 6. 57. As the living Father sent me, and I live because
7. 16. My teaching is not mine, but his that sent me
18. he that seeketh the glory of him that sent him
32. priests and the Pharisees sent officers to take him
33. a little while am I with you—I go unto him that s. me
8. 16. I am not alone, but I and the Father that sent me
18. the Father that sent me beareth witness of me
9. 4. We must work the works of him that sent me
7. the pool of Siloam (which is by interpretation, Sent)
10. 36. whom the Father sanctified, and s. into the world
11. 3. The sisters therefore sent unto him, saying, Lord
12. 45. that beholdeth me beholdeth him that sent me
49. which sent me, he hath given me a commandment
13. 16. neither one that is s. greater than he that s. him
14. 24. ye hear is not mine, but the Father's who sent me
15. 21. because they know not him that sent me
16. 5. But now I go unto him that sent me
18. 24. Annas therefore sent him bound unto Caiaphas
20. 21. as the Father hath sent me, even so send I you
Acts 3. 26. God—raised up his Servant, sent him to bless
5. 21. sent to the prison-house to have them brought
7. 35. him hath God ¹s. to be both a ruler and a deliverer
8. 14. they sent unto them Peter and John [10. 17
9. 38. hearing that Peter was there, s. two men unto him.
10. 29. gainsaying, when I was sent for—ye sent for me
36. The word which he [God] sent unto the children of
11. 11. three men—having been s. from Cæsarea unto me
13. 15. rulers of the synagogue sent unto them
15. 27. We have sent therefore Judas and Silas
16. 36. Paul—The magistrates have sent to let you go
19. 31. his friends, sent unto him, and besought him
28. 28. this salvation of God is sent unto the Gentiles
Rom. 15. how shall they preach, except they be sent ?
1 Cor. 1. 17. Christ sent me not to baptize, but to preach
2 Cor. 8. 18. we have s. together with him the brother. 22
Phil. 4. 16. in Thessalonica ye sent once and again unto
1 Th. 3. 2. and s. Timothy, our brother and God's minister
1 Pet. 2. 14. or unto governors, as s. by him for vengeance
1 Jno. 4. 9 God hath sent his only begotten Son
10. loved God, but that he loved us, and sent his Son
14. the Father hath sent the Son to be the Saviour
Rev. 22. 6. God—sent his angel to shew unto his servants
see came, send, sending.

Sent away.

Mat. 14. 23. And after he had s. the multitudes a. 15. 39
Mk. 8. 9. about four thousand: and he sent them away
26. And he sent him away to his house
12. 3. beat him, and sent him away empty. Lu. 20. 10, 11
Lu. 1. 53. And the rich he hath sent empty away
8. 38. be with him: but he sent him away, saying,
Acts 13. 3. laid their hands on them, they sent them away
17. 10. the brethren—s. away Paul and Silas by night
see leaving, left, sendeth, sent forth, taken.

He Sent.

Mat. 11. 2. John heard in the prison—he sent by his [12
21. 36. Again, he s. other servants. Mk. 12. 4, 5: Lu. 20. 11
37. But afterward he sent unto them his son. Mk. 12. 6
Lu. 19. 20. [Jesus] he sent two of the disciples
23. 7. of Herod's jurisdiction, he sent him unto Herod
Jno. 1. 33. but he that sent me to baptize with water
5. 38. for whom he sent, him ye believe not
6. 29. that ye believe on him whom he hath sent
7. 28. but he that sent me is true, whom ye know not. 8. 26
29. I know him; because I am from him, and he sent me
8. 29. And he that s. me is with me; he hath not left me
42. for neither have I come of myself, but he sent me
Acts 24. 26. [Felix] wherefore also he s. for him the oftener
Rev. 1. 1. and he sent and signified it by his angel

SENT

1 Sent, Sent 1.
Lu. 4. 43. to the other cities also: for therefore was *I sent*
22. 35. When *I sent* you forth without purse
Jno. 4. 38. *I sent* you to reap that whereon ye have not
17. 18. even so *sent I* them into the world
Acts 10. 20. nothing doubting: for *I* have *sent* them
33. Forthwith therefore *I s.* to thee; and thou hast well
1 *Cor.* 4. 17. For this cause have *I sent* unto you Timothy
2 *Cor.* 9. 3. But *I* have *sent* the brethren, that our glorying
12. 17. by any one of them whom *I* have *sent* unto you?
18. I exhorted Titus, and *I sent* the brother with him
Eph. 6. 22. [Tychicus] whom *I* have *s.* unto you. *Col.* 4. 8
Phil. 2. 28. *I* have *sent* him therefore the more diligently
1 *Th.* 3. 5. *I—sent* that I might know your faith
Philem. 12. whom *I* have *s.* back to thee in his own person
Rev. 22. 16. *I* Jesus have *sent* mine angel to testify

Sent forth, Sent out.—*A.V.* ¹*sent away*, ²*sent down*, ³*sent out.*

Mat. 2. 16. Herod—*s. forth*, and slew all the male children
10. 5. These twelve Jesus *sent forth*, and charged them
22. 3. and *s. forth* his servants to call them. 4: *Lu.* 14. 17
Mk. 1, 43. strictly charged him, and straightway ¹*s.* him *out*
6. 17. Herod—had *sent forth* and laid hold upon John
Lu. 20. 20. And they watched him, and *sent forth* spies
Acts 7. 12. Jacob—²*sent forth* our fathers the first time
9. 30. to Cæsarea, and *sent* him *forth* to Tarsus
11. 22. they *sent forth* Barnabas as far as Antioch
13. 4. they, being *sent forth* by the Holy Ghost
26. to us is the word of this salvation *sent forth*
17. 14. brethren ¹*sent forth* Paul to go as far as to the sea
Gal. 4. 4. God *sent forth* his Son, born of a woman
6. God *sent forth* the Spirit of his Son into our hearts
Heb. 1, 14. ministering spirits, *sent forth* to do service
Jas. 2. 25. messengers, and *s.* them *o.* another way? [Rahab]
1 *Pet.* 1. 12. by the Holy Ghost ²*sent forth* from heaven
Rev. 5. 6. the seven Spirits of God, *sent f.* into all the earth

Sent with Lord.—*see Lord (proper names).*

Sentence.—*A.V.* ¹*judgment.*
Lu. 23. 24. Pilate gave *sentence* that what they asked
Acts 25. 15. asking for ¹*sentence* against him [Paul]
2 *Pet.* 2. 3. whose ¹*sentence* now from of old lingereth not
see answer, judgement.

Separate.
Mat. 25. 32. he shall *separate* them one from another
Lu. 6. 22. Blessed are ye—when they shall *separate* you
Acts 13. 2. *Separate* me Barnabas and Saul for the work
Rom. 8. 35. Who shall *separate* us from the love of Christ?
39. shall be able to *separate* us from the love of God
2 *Cor.* 6. 17. among them, and be ye *separate*, saith the Lord
see separated, separations.

Separated—eth.—*A.V.* ¹*divideth*, ²*separate.*
Mat. 25. 32. as the shepherd ¹*s.* the sheep from the goats
Acts 19. 9. *s.* the disciples, reasoning daily in the school
Rom. 1. 1. Paul—an apostle, *s.* unto the gospel of God
Gal. 1. 15. the good pleasure of God, who *separated* me
2. 12. [Peter] drew back and *separated* himself, fearing
Heb. 7. 26. a high priest—undefiled, ²*separated* from sinners

Separations.—*A.V.* ¹*separate.*
Jude 19. who make ¹*s.*, sensual, having not the Spirit

Sepulchre—s.—*A.V.* ¹*tombs.*
Mat. 23. 27. for ye are like unto whited *sepulchres*
29. ye build the ¹*sepulchres* of the prophets
27. 61. other Mary, sitting over against the *sepulchre*

SERVANT

Mat. 27. 64. Command therefore that the *s.* be made sure. 66
28. 1. and the other Mary to see the *sepulchre*
Rom. 3. 13. Their throat is an open *sepulchre*
see tomb, tombs.

Serjeants.
Acts 16. 35. sent the *serjeants*, saying, Let those men go
38. And the *s.* reported these words unto the magistrates

Serpent—s.
Mat. 7. 10. ask for a fish, will give him a *serpent*? *Lu.* 11. 11
10. 16. be ye therefore wise as *s.*, and harmless as doves
23. 33. Ye *serpents*, ye offspring of vipers, how shall ye
Mk. 16. 18. they shall take up *serpents*, and if they drink
Lu. 10. 19. I have given you authority to tread upon *s.*
Jno. 3. 14. as Moses lifted up the *serpent* in the wilderness
1 *Cor.* 10. 9. some of them tempted, and perished by the *s.*
2 *Cor.* 11. 3. as the *serpent* beguiled Eve in his craftiness
Rev. 9. 19. in their tails: for their tails are like unto *s.*
12. 9. the old *s.*, he that is called the Devil and Satan. 20.
14. and times, and half a time, from the face of the *s.* [2
15. the serpent cast out of his mouth—water as a river
see creeping things.

Servant.—*A.V.* ¹*child*, ²*son.*
Mat. 8. 6. my *servant* lieth in the house sick of the palsy
8. only say the word, and my *s.* shall be healed. *Lu.* 7. 7
9. and to my *servant*, Do this, and he doeth it. *Lu.* 7. 8
13. And the *servant* was healed in that hour
10. 24. nor a *servant* above his lord. *Jno.* 13. 16: 15. 20
25. that he be as his master, and the *servant* as his lord
12. 18. Behold, my *servant* whom I have chosen
18. 26. The *s.* therefore fell down and worshipped him
27. the lord of that *s.*, being moved with compassion
28. that *s.* went out, and found one of his fellow-servants
32. Thou wicked *servant*, I forgave thee all that debt
20. 27. you shall be your *servant*. 23. 11: *Mk.* 10. 44
24. 45. Who then is the faithful and wise *s.*, whom his
46. Blessed is that *servant*, whom his lord. *Lu.* 12. 43
48. that evil *servant* shall say in his heart. *Lu.* 12. 45
50. lord of that *servant* shall come in a day. *Lu.* 12. 46
25. 21. Well done, good and faithful *servant*. 23: *Lu.* 19. 17
26. Thou wicked and faithful *servant*. *Lu.* 19. 22
30. cast ye out the unprofitable *servant* into the outer
26. 51. smote the *s.* of the high priest, and struck off
his ear. *Mk.* 14. 47: *Lu.* 22. 50: *Jno.* 18. 10
Mk. 12. 2. he sent to the husbandmen a *s.* 4: *Lu.* 20. 10, 11
Lu. 1. 54. He hath holpen Israel his *servant*
2. 29. Now lettest thou thy *servant* depart, O Lord
7. 2. centurion's *s.*, who was dear unto him, was sick
3. asking him that he would come and save his *s.*
10. returning to the house, found the *servant* whole
12. 47. And that *servant*, which knew his lord's will
14. 17. sent forth his *servant* at supper time to say
21. the *servant* came, and told his lord. 22
23. And the lord said unto the *servant*, Go out into the
16. 13. No *servant* can serve two masters
17. 7. who is there of you, having a *servant* plowing
9. Doth he thank the *s.* because he did the things
Jno. 12. 26. where I am, there shall also my *servant* be
15. 15. the *servant* knoweth not what his lord doeth
18. 10. Now the *servant's* name was Malchus
Acts 3. 13. God of our fathers, hath glorified his ²*S.* Jesus
26. God, having raised up his ²*S.*, sent him to bless you
4. 27. in this city against thy holy ¹*Servant* Jesus
30. done through the name of thy holy ¹*Servant* Jesus
Rom. 1. 1. Paul, a *servant* of Jesus Christ, called to be an
14. 4. Who art thou that judgest the *s.* of another?
16. 1. Phœbe our sister, who is a *servant* of the church
Gal. 1. 10. pleasing men, I should not be a *s.* of Christ
Phil. 2. 7. emptied himself, taking the form of a *servant*

SERVANT

Col. 4. 12. Epaphras, who is one of you, a *servant* of Christ
2 *Tim.* 2. 24. And the Lord's *servant* must not strive
Tit. 1. 1. Paul, a *servant* of God, and an apostle of Jesus
Philem. 16. no longer as a *s.*, but more than a *servant*
Heb. 3. 5. Moses indeed was faithful in all his house as a *s.*
Jas. 1. 1. James, a *servant* of God and of the Lord Jesus
2 *Pet.* 1. 1. Simon Peter, a *servant* and apostle of Jesus
Jude 1. Judas, a *s.* of Jesus Christ, and brother of James
Rev. 1 1. signified it by his angel unto his *servant* John
15. 3. And they sing the song of Moses the *s.* of God
   see bondage, bondservant, minister.

Servant *David.—see David (proper names).*

Servants.—A.V. ¹*serve.*

Mat. 13. 27. And the *s.* of the householder came and said. 28
18. 23. king, which would make a reckoning with his *s.*
21. 34. he sent his *servants* to the husbandmen. 35
36. Again, he sent other *s.* more than the first. 22. 4
22. 3. sent forth his *s.* to call them that were bidden
6. laid hold on his *s.*, and entreated them shamefully
8. Then saith he to his *servants,* The wedding. 10
13. Then the king said to the *servants,* Bind him
25. 14. called his own *servants,* and delivered unto them
19. the lord of those *s.* cometh, and maketh a reckoning
Mk. 13. 34. left his house, and given authority to his *s.*
Lu. 12. 37. Blessed are those *servants,* whom the lord. 38
15. 26. he called to him one of the *servants,* and enquired
17. 10. We are unprofitable *servants* ; we have done
19. 13. he called ten *s.* of his, and gave them ten pounds
15. he commanded these *servants—*to be called to him
Jno. 2. 5. His mother saith unto the *s.,* Whatsoever he
9. (but the *servants* which had drawn the water knew)
15. 15. No longer do I call you *servants ;* for the servant
18. 26. One of the *s.* of the high priest, being a kinsman
36. were of this world, then would my *servants* fight
Acts 2. 18. on my *s.* and on my handmaidens in those days
4. 29. grant unto thy *servants* to speak thy word
10. 7. he called two of his household-*servants*
16. 17. These men are *servants* of the Most High God
Rom. 6. 16. as *s.* unto obedience, his *s.* ye are whom ye
17. whereas ye were *servants* of sin, ye became obedient
18. free from sin, ye became *servants* of righteousness
19. as ye presented your members as *s.* to uncleanness
—now present your members as *s.* to righteousness
20. when ye were *servants* of sin, ye were free in regard
22. being made free from sin, and become *s.* to God
2 *Cor.* 4. 5. and ourselves as your *servants* for Jesus' sake
Gal. 5. 13. through love be ¹*servants* one to another
Eph. 6. 5. *Servants,* be obedient unto them that—are your
masters. *Col.* 3. 22 ; *Tit.* 2. 9 : 1 *Pet.* 2. 18
6. as *servants* of Christ, doing the will of God
Phil. 1. 1. Paul and Timothy, *servants* of Christ Jesus
Col. 4. 1. Masters, render unto your *s.* that which is just
1 *Tim.* 6. 1. Let as many as are *servants* under the yoke
Rev. 1. to shew unto his *s.,* even the things which. 22. 6
2. 20. teacheth and seduceth my *servants* to commit
7. 3. till we shall have sealed the *servants* of our God
11. 18. to give their reward to thy *servants* the prophets
19. 2. hath avenged the blood of his *servants* at her hand
5. Give praise to our God, all ye his *servants*
22. 3. be therein : and his *servants* shall do him service
   see bondservants, officers.

Hired **Servants.—***see hired.*

Servants *the prophets.—see prophets.*

Serve.—A.V. ¹*be subject to,* ²*service,* ³*use the office,*
⁴*worship.*

Mat. 4. 10. thy God, and him only shalt thou *s. Lu.* 4. 8

SERVING

Mat. 6. 24. No man can *serve* two masters—Ye cannot *serve*
God and mammon. *Lu.* 16. 13
Lu. 1. 74. of our enemies, Should *serve* him without fear
10. 40. care that my sister did leave me to *serve* alone ?
12. 37. sit down to meat, and shall come and *serve* them
15. 29. Lo, these many years do I *serve* thee, and I never
17. 8. and gird thyself, and *serve* me, till I have eaten
22. 26. and he that is chief, as he that doth *serve*
Jno 12. 26. If any man *serve* me, let him follow me—if
any man *serve* me, him will the Father
Acts 6. 2. we should forsake the word of God, and *serve* tables
7. 7. shall they come forth, and *serve* me in this place
42. and gave them up to ⁴*serve* the host of heaven
24. 14. after the Way—so ⁴*serve* I the God of our fathers
27. 23. angel of the God whose I am, whom also I *serve*
Rom. 1. 9. God is my witness, whom I *serve* in my spirit
7. 6. so that we *serve* in newness of the spirit
25. I myself with the mind *serve* the law of God
16. 18. For they that are such *serve* not our Lord Christ
1 *Th.* 1. 9. from idols, to *serve* a living and true God
1 *Tim.* 3. 10. then let them ²*serve* as deacons [partake
6. 2. let them ²*serve* them the rather, because they that
2 *Tim.* 1. 3. I thank God, whom I *s.* from my forefathers
Heb. 8. 5. who *serve* that which is a copy and shadow of
9. 14. from dead works to *serve* the living God ?
13. 10. they have no right to eat which *s.* the tabernacle
1 *Pet.* 5. 5. gird yourselves with humility, to ¹*s.* one another
Rev. 7. 15. and they *serve* him day and night in his temple
   see bondage, servants, service.

Serve *the Lord.—see Lord.*

Served.—A.V. ¹*used the office,* ²*worshipped.*

Jno. 12. 2. made him a supper there : and Martha *served*
Acts 13. 36. For David, after he had—*s.* the counsel of God
17. 25. neither is he ²*served* by men's hands
Rom. 1. 25. and *s.* the creature rather than the Creator
Phil. 2. 22. he *served* with me in furtherance of the gospel
1 *Tim.* 3. 13. they that have ¹*served* well as deacons
   see worshipping.

Serveth.—A.V. ¹*goeth a warfare.*

Lu. 22. 27. greater, he that sitteth at meat, or he that *s. ?*
—but I am in the midst of you as he that *serveth*
Rom. 14. 18. he that herein *s.* Christ is well-pleasing to God
1 *Cor.* 9. 7. What soldier ever ¹*serveth* at his own charges ?
   see sign.

Service—s.—A.V. ¹*minister,* ²*ministry,* ³*serve,* ⁴*service.*

Jno. 16. 2. killeth you shall think that he offereth *service*
Rom. 9. 4. of the law, and the *s.* of God, and the promises
12. 1. acceptable to God, which is your reasonable *s.*
2 *Cor.* 9. 12. the ministration of this *s.* not only filleth up
Eph. 6. 7. with good will doing *service,* as unto the Lord
Phil. 2. 17. if I am offered upon the sacrifice and *s.* of your
30. to supply that which was lacking in your *service*
1 *Tim.* 1. 12. counted me faithful, appointing me to his ³*s.*
Heb. 1. 14. not all ministering spirits, sent forth to do ¹*s.*
9. 1. first covenant had ordinances of divine *service*
6. into the first tabernacle, accomplishing the ⁴*services*
12. 28. whereby we may offer ⁸*s.* well-pleasing to God
Rev. 22. 3. and his servants shall do him ³*service*
   see bondage, ministration, ministry, serve, worshipper.

Serving.

Lu. 10. 40. Martha was cumbered about much *serving*
Acts 20. 19. *serving* the Lord with all lowliness of mind
26. 7. twelve tribes, earnestly *serving* God night and day
Rom. 12. 11. fervent in spirit; *serving* the Lord
Tit. 3. 3. disobedient, deceived, *s.* divers lusts and pleasures

SET

Set.—*A.V.* ¹*addicted,* ²*bring,* ³*brought,* ⁴*conduct,* ⁵*declare,* ⁶*go,* ⁷*made,* ⁸*made or make ruler,* ⁹*ordained,* ¹⁰*present,* ¹¹*put,* ¹²*quarrel,* ¹³*setteth,* ¹⁴*sit,* ¹⁵*teach.*

Mat. 4. 5. and he ¹³*set* him on the pinnacle of the temple
5. 14. A city *set* on a hill cannot be hid
10. 35. For I came to *set* a man at variance against his
13. 24. Another parable ¹¹*set* he before them
18. 2. called to him a little child, and *set* him in the midst. *Mk.* 9. 36: *Lu.* 9. 47
24. 45. whom his lord hath ⁸*set* over his household
47. that he will ⁸*set* him over all that he hath
25. 21. I will ⁸*set* thee over many things. ⁸23
33. and he shall *set* the sheep on his right hand
27. 37. they *set* up over his head his accusation written
Mk. 1. 32. And at even, when the sun did *set*, they brought
6. 19. Herodias ¹²*set* herself against him [John] [9. 16
41. gave to the disciples to *set* before them. 8. 6, 7: *Lu.*
12. 1. planted a vineyard, and *set* a hedge about it
Lu. 2. 34. this child is *set* for the falling and rising up
7. 8. For I also am a man *set* under authority
10. 8. eat such things as are *set* before you. 1 *Cor.* 10. 27
34. he *set* him on his own beast, and brought him
11. 6. from a journey, and I have nothing to *s.* before him
19. 35. their garments upon the colt, and *s.* Jesus thereon
Jno. 2. 6. there were six waterpots of stone *set* there
3. 33. He that hath received his witness hath *s.* his seal
6. 11. he distributed to them that were *set* down
8. 3. taken in adultery; and having *set* her in the midst
Acts 1. 7. seasons, which the Father hath ¹¹*s.* within his own
2. 30. fruit of his loins he would ¹⁴*set* one upon his throne
4. 7. And when they had *set* them in the midst
6. 13. and *set* up false witnesses, which said, This man
7. 5 not so much as to *set* his foot on: and he promised
26. would have *set* them at one again, saying, Sirs
12 21. And upon a *set* day Herod arrayed himself
13. 47. I have *set* thee for a light of the Gentiles
15. 16. build again the ruins thereof, And I will *s.* it up
16. 21. ¹⁵*set* forth customs which it is not lawful for us
17. 23. What therefore ye worship in ignorance, this ⁸*s.*
18. 10. and no man shall *set* on thee to harm thee
21. 4. said to Paul—that he should not ⁵*set* foot in
22. 30. brought Paul down, and *set* him before them
23. 24. provide beasts, that they might *set* Paul thereon
Rom. 3. 25. whom God *set* forth to be a propitiation
1 *Cor.* 4. 9. God hath *set* forth us the apostles last of all
6. 4. do ye *set* them to judge who are of no account
12. 18. But now hath God *set* the members each one
28. God hath *set* some in the church, first apostles
16. 6. that ye may ²*set* me forward on my journey
11. But ¹*set* him forward on his journey in peace
15. house of Stephanas—have ¹*s.* themselves to minister
2 *Cor.* 1. 16. to be ⁵*set* forward on my journey unto Judea
Gal. 3. 1. Jesus Christ was openly *set* forth crucified?
5. 1. With freedom did Christ ⁷*set* us free
Phil. 1. 16. knowing that I am *set* for the defence of the
Col. 3. 2. Set your mind on the things that are above
Heb. 2. 7. And didst *set* him over the works of thy hands
6. 18. fled for refuge to lay hold of the hope *set* before us
12. 1. run with patience the race that is *set* before us
2. who for the joy that was *set* before him endured
3 *Jno.* 6. whom thou wilt do well to ²*set* forward on their
Jude 1. 7. are *set* forth as an example, suffering the punishment
24. and to ¹⁰*set* you before the presence of his glory
Rev. 3. 8. (behold, I have *set* before thee a door opened
4. 2. there was a throne *set* in heaven, and one sitting
10. 2. and he *set* his right foot upon the sea
see day, face, fastened, liberty, nought, order, sat, sit, sitting, setteth, sealed.

SEVEN

Set—ting *sail.*—*A.V.* ¹*loosed,* ²*loosing.*

Acts 13. 13 Paul and his company ¹*set sail* from Paphos
16. 11. ²*S. sail* therefore from Troas, we made a straight
27. 21. not have ¹*set sail* from Crete, and have gotten this

Setter.

Acts 17. 18. He seemeth to be a *setter* forth of strange gods

Setteth.—*A.V.* ¹*set.*

Jno. 2. 10 Every man ¹*setteth* on first the good wine
Jas. 3. 6. and *setteth* on fire the wheel of nature
see putteth, set.

Setting.—*A.V.* ¹*shewing.*

Lu. 4. 40. And when the sun was *setting,* all they that
2 *Th.* 2. 4. temple of God, ¹*setting* himself forth as God

Settle.

Lu. 21. 14. S. it therefore in your hearts, not to meditate

Settled.—*A.V.* ¹*determined.*

Acts 19. 39. matters, it shall be ¹*s.* in the regular assembly
see stedfast.

Seven.

Mat. 12. 45. taketh with himself *s.* other spirits. *Lu.* 11. 26
15. 34. How many loaves have ye?—they said, S. *Mk.* 8. 5
36. and he took the *s.* loaves and the fishes. *Mk.* 8. 6
37. remained over the broken pieces, *s.* baskets. *Mk.* 8. 8
16. 10. the *seven* loaves of the four thousand. *Mk.* 8. 20
18. 21. and I forgive him? until *seven* times?
22. Until *seven* times; but, Until seventy times *seven*
22. 25. there were with us *s.* brethren. *Mk.* 12. 20: *Lu.* 20. 29
28. whose wife shall she be of the *s.*? for they all had
Mk. 12. 22. and the *seven* left no seed. *Lu.* 20. 31
23. for the *seven* had her to wife. *Lu.* 20. 33
16. 9. from whom he had cast out *seven* devils. *Lu.* 8. 2
Lu. 2. 36. a husband *seven* years from her virginity
17. 4. sin against thee *s.* times in the day, and *s.* times
Acts 6. 3. Look ye out—*seven* men of good report
13. 19. And when he had destroyed *seven* nations
19. 14. And there were *seven* sons of one Sceva, a Jew
21. 4. found the disciples, we tarried there *seven* days
8. Philip the evangelist, who was one of the *seven*
27. when the *seven* days were almost completed
Rev. 1. 4. John to the *seven* churches which are in Asia— from the *s.* Spirits which are before his throne. 11
12. having turned I saw *seven* golden candlesticks. 20
16. in his right hand *seven* stars. 20: 2. 1: 3. 1
20. The *seven* stars are the angels of the *seven* churches: and the *seven* candlesticks are *seven* churches
2. 1. walketh in the midst of the *s.* golden candlesticks
3. 1. *seven* Spirits of God, and the *seven* stars. 4. 5; 5. 6
4. 5. there were *seven* lamps of fire burning
5. 1. a book written—close sealed with *seven* seals
5. to open the book and the *seven* seals thereof
6. a Lamb standing—having *seven* horns, and *seven* eyes
8. 2. I saw the *s.* angels—given unto them *s.* trumpets. 6
10. 3. the *seven* thunders uttered their voices. 4
4. Seal up the things which the *s.* thunders uttered
12. 3. *s.* heads and ten horns—*s.* diadems. 13. 1: 17. 3. 7
15. 1. *seven* angels having *seven* plagues. 6, 8: 21. 9
16. 1. saying to the *s.* angels, Go ye, and pour out the *s.*
17. 1. one of the *s.* angels that had the *s.* bowls. 15. 7: 21. 9
9. The *seven* heads are *seven* mountains, on which
10. they are *s.* kings; the five are fallen, the one is
11. an eighth, and is of the *seven*; and he goeth into

301

SEVENTH SHARPNESS

Seventh.
Mat. 22. 26. second also, and the third, unto the *seventh*
Jno. 4. 52. Yesterday at the *seventh* hour the fever left him
Jude 14. to these also Enoch, the *s.* from Adam, prophesied
Rev. 8. 1. And when he opened the *seventh* seal
10. 7. in the days of the voice of the *seventh* angel
11. 15. the *seventh* angel sounded; and there followed
16. 17. And the *seventh* poured out his bowl upon the
21. 20. the sixth, sardius; the *seventh*, chrysolite

Seventy.
Mat. 18. 22. Until seven times; but, Until *s.* times seven
Lu. 10. 1. the Lord appointed *s.* others, and sent them
17. And the *seventy* returned with joy, saying, Lord

Sever—ed.—A.V. ¹become of no effect.
Mat. 13. 49. and *s.* the wicked from among the righteous
Gal. 5. 4. Ye are ¹*severed* from Christ, ye who would be

Several.
Mat. 25. 15. to each according to his *several* ability
Rev. 21. 21. each one of the *several* gates was of one pearl

Severally.—A.V. ¹every one, ²particular, ³particularly.
Rom. 12. 5. one body in Christ, and ¹*s.* members. 1 Cor. 12. ²27
1 Cor. 12. 11. dividing to each one *severally* even as he will
Eph. 5. 33. do ye also ²*severally* love each one his own wife
Heb. 9. 5. of which things we cannot now speak ³*severally*

Severity.—A.V. ¹neglecting of.
Rom. 11. 22. Behold then the goodness and *severity* of God: toward them that fell, *severity*
Col. 2. 23. will-worship, and humility, and ¹*s.* to the body

Seweth.
Mk. 2. 21. No man *s.* a piece of undressed cloth on an old

Shadow.
Mk. 4. 32. birds of the heaven can lodge under the *s.* thereof
Acts 5. 15. as l'eter came by, at the least his *shadow* might
Col. 2. 17. which are a *shadow* of the things to come
Heb. 8. 5. a copy and *shadow* of the heavenly things
10. 1. law having a *shadow* of the good things to come
Jas. 1. 17. no variation, neither *s.* that is cast by turning
see *death.*

Shadowing A.V.—see overshadowing.

Shake.
Mat. 10. 14. *s.* off the dust of your feet. Mk. 6. 11: Lu. 9. 5
Lu. 6. 48. brake against that house, and could not *shake* it
see *quake, tremble.*

Shaken.—A.V. ¹moved.
Mat. 11. 7. a reed *shaken* with the wind? Lu. 7. 24
24. 29. powers of the heavens shall be *s.* Mk. 13. 25: Lu. 21. 26
Lu. 6. 38. good measure, pressed down, *shaken* together
Acts 4. 31. when they had prayed, the place was *shaken*
16. 26. foundations of the prison-house were *shaken*
2 Thes. 2. 2. be not quickly *shaken* from your mind, nor yet
Heb. 12. 27. the removing of those things that are *shaken*
—that those things which are not *s.* may remain
28. receiving a kingdom that cannot be ¹*shaken*
Rev. 6. 13. unripe figs, when she is *shaken* of a great wind

Shambles.
1 Cor. 10. 25. Whatsoever is sold in the *shambles,* eat

Shame.—A.V. ¹ashamed, ²confound, ³confounded, ⁴dishonesty.
Lu. 13. 17. all his adversaries were put to ¹*shame*
14. 9. shalt begin with *shame* to take the lowest place
Rom. 5. 5. hope putteth not to ¹*shame;* because the love
9. 33. believeth—shall not be put to ¹*s.* 10. ¹11: 1 Pet. 2. ²6
1 Cor. 1. 27. that he might put to ²*s.* them that are wise—
that he might put to ²*s.* the things that are strong
4. ¹4. I write not these things to *shame* you
6. 5. I say this to move you to *shame.* 15. 34
11. 6. if it is a *shame* to a woman to be shorn or shaven
22. despise ye the church of God, and put them to *s.*
2 Cor. 4. 2. renounced the hidden things of ⁴*shame*
7. 14. I was not put to ¹*shame.* 10. ¹8
9. 4. find you unprepared, we—should be put to ¹*shame*
Eph. 5. 12. by them in secret it is a *shame* even to speak of
Phil. 1. 20. that in nothing shall I be put to ¹*shame*
3. 19. the belly, and whose glory is in their *shame*
Heb. 6. 6. Son of God afresh, and put him to an open *shame*
12. 2. Jesus—endured the cross, despising *shame*
1 Pet. 3. 16. may be put to ¹*s.* who revile your good manner
Jude 13. wild waves of the sea, foaming out their own *s.*
Rev. 3. 18. the *shame* of thy nakedness he not made manifest
16. 15. lest he walk naked, and they see his *shame*)
see *dishonour, shameful.*

Shamefacedness A.V.—see shamefastness.

Shamefastness.—A.V. ¹shamefacedness.
1 Tim. 2. 9. in modest apparel, with ¹*shamefastness*

Shameful.—A.V. ¹filthy, ²shame.
1 Cor. 14. 35. it is ²*s.* for a woman to speak in the church
Col. 3. 8. railing, ¹*shameful* speaking out of your mouth

Shamefully.—A.V. ¹despitefully, ²spitefully.
Mat. 22. 6. laid hold on his servants, and entreated them ²*s.*
Mk. 12. 4. wounded in the head, and handled *s.* Lu. 20. 11
Lu. 18. 32. shall be mocked, and ²*shamefully* entreated
Acts 14. 5. to entreat them ¹*shamefully,* and to stone them
1 Thes. 2. 2. and been *shamefully* entreated, as ye know

Shapes.
Rev. 9. 7. And the *s.* of the locusts were like unto horses
see *form.*

Sharers.—A.V. ¹partakers.
Heb. 2. 14. Since then the children are ¹*s.* in flesh and blood

Sharp.
Acts 15. 39. And there arose a *s.* contention, so that they
Rev. 2. 12. saith he that hath the *sharp* two-edged sword
14. 14. and in his hand a *sharp* sickle. 17, 18
19. 15. out of his mouth proceedeth a *sharp* sword. 1. 16

Sharper.
Heb. 4. 12. word of God is living, and active, and *s.* than

Sharply.—A.V. ¹sharpness.
2 Cor. 13. 10. that I may not when present deal ¹*sharply*
Tit. 1. 13. reprove them *sharply,* that they may be sound

Sharpness A.V.—see sharply.

SHAVE

Shave—n.
Acts 21. 24. charges for them, that they may *s.* their heads
1 *Cor.* 11, 5. it is one and the same thing as if she were *s.*
    6. if it is a shame to a woman to be shorn or *shaven*

Shearer.
Acts 8. 32. And as a lamb before his *shearer* is dumb

Sheath.
Jno. 18. 11. unto Peter, Put up the sword into the *sheath*

Shed.
Mat. 26. 28. is shed for many unto remission of sins
Rom. 5. 5. the love of God hath been *s.* abroad in our hearts
    see poured.

Shed *blood.—see blood.*

Shedding.
Heb. 9. 22. apart from *s.* of blood there is no remission

Sheep.—*A.V.* ¹*cattle.*
Mat. 7. 15. prophets, which come to you in *s.'s* clothing
    9. 36. as *sheep* not having a shepherd. *Mk.* 6. 34
    10. 6. go rather to the lost *s.* of the house of Israel. 15. 24
    16. I send you forth as *sheep* in the midst of wolves
    12. 11. one *s.*, and if this fall into a pit on the sabbath
    12. How much then is a man of more value than a *s.!*
    18. 12. if any man have a hundred *s.*, and one. *Lu.* 15. 4
    25. 32. as the shepherd separateth the *s.* from the goats
    33. he shall set the *s.* on his right hand, but the goats
    26. 31. the shepherd, and the *s.*—shall be scattered. *Mk.*
Lu. 15 6. for I have found my *s.* which was lost [14. 27
Jno. 2. 14. in the temple those that sold oxen and *s.* 15
    5. 2. Now there is in Jerusalem by the *sheep* gate a pool
    10. 1. entereth not by the door into the fold of the *sheep*
    2. entereth in by the door is the shepherd of the *sheep*
    3. the *s.* hear his voice : and he calleth his own *s.* 27
    4. he goeth before them, and the *sheep* follow him
    7. I say unto you, I am the door of the *sheep*
    8. thieves and robbers : but the *s.* did not hear them
    11. the good shepherd layeth down his life for the *s.* 15
    12. whose own the *sheep* are not—leaveth the *sheep*
    13. because he is a hireling, and careth not for the *sheep*
    16. And other *sheep* I have, which are not of this fold
    26. But ye believe not, because ye are not of my *sheep*
    21. 16. He saith unto him, Feed my *sheep.* 17
Acts 8. 32. He was led as a *sheep* to the slaughter
Rom. 8. 36. We were accounted as *sheep* for the slaughter
Heb. 13. 20. again from the dead the great shepherd of the
1 *Pet.* 2. 25. For ye were going astray like sheep [*sheep*
Rev. 18. 13. fine flour, and wheat, and cattle, and *sheep*
    see ox, oxen.

Sheepfold *A.V.—see fold.*

Sheepskins.
Heb. 11. 37. they went about in *sheepskins*, in goatskins

Sheet.
Acts 10. 11. a great *sheet*, let down by four corners. 11. 5

Shekel, *half-shekel.*—*A.V.* ¹*tribute,* ²*tribute money,* ³*piece of money.*
Mat. 17. 24. they that received the ²*half-s.* came to Peter,
    and said, Doth not your master pay the ¹*h.-shekel ?*
    27. thou shalt find a ³*s.* : that take, and give unto them

SHEWBREAD

Shepherd—s.—*A.V.* ¹*rule.*
Mat. 2. 6. Which shall be ¹*shepherd* of my people Israel
    9. 36. scattered, as sheep not having a *s. Mk.* 6. 34
    25. 32. as the *s.* separateth the sheep from the goats
    26. 31. I will smite the *shepherd. Mk.* 14. 27
Lu. 2. 8. there were *shepherds*—abiding in the field
    15. *shepherds* said one to another, Let us now go
    18. things which were spoken unto them by the *s.*
    20. And the *s.* returned, glorifying and praising God
Jno. 10. 2. he that entereth in by the door is the *shepherd*
    11. I am the good *shepherd* : the good *shepherd* layeth
    down his life for the sheep. 14
    12. He that is a hireling, and not a *shepherd*
    16. and they shall become one flock, one *s.* [sheep
Heb. 13. 20. brought again from the dead the great *s.* of the
1 *Pet.* 2. 25. unto the *Shepherd* and Bishop of your souls
    5. 4. when the chief *Shepherd* shall be manifested
Jude 12. *shepherds* that without fear feed themselves
Rev. 7. 17. Lamb—shall be their *s.*, and shall guide them

Shew, Show.—*A.V.* ¹*declaration,* ²*declare,* ³*tell,* ⁴*use.*
Mat. 8. 4. go thy way, *shew* thyself to the priest, and
    offer the gift. *Mk.* 1. 44: *Lu.* 5. 14
    16. 1. asked him to *shew* them a sign from heaven
    21. began Jesus to *shew* unto his disciples, how that
    18. 15. ³*shew* him his fault between thee and him alone
    22. 19. *Shew* me the tribute money. *Lu.* 20. 24
    24. 1. came to him to *s.* him the buildings of the temple
    24. and shall *shew* great signs and wonders. *Mk.* 13. 22
Mk. 14. 15. *s.* you a large upper room furnished. *Lu.* 22. 12
Lu. 6. 47. doeth them, I will *shew* you to whom he is like
    17. 14. said unto them, Go and *s.* yourselves unto the priests
Jno. 5. 20. greater works than these will he *shew* him
    11. 57. if any man knew where he was, he should *s.* it
    14. 8. Lord, *show* us the Father, and it sufficeth us. 9
Acts 1. 24. *s.* of these two the one whom thou hast chosen
    7. 3. and come into the land which I shall *shew* thee
    9. 16. I will *shew* him how many things he must suffer
Rom. 2. 15. they *s.* the work of the law written in their hearts
    3. 25. through faith, by his blood, to ²*s.* his righteousness
    9. 17. raise thee up, that I might *shew* in thee my power
    22. What if God, willing to *shew* his wrath [you
1 *Cor.* 12. 31. And a still more excellent way *shew* I unto
2 *Cor.* 1. 17. when I—was thus minded, did I ⁴*s.* fickleness ?
    8. 19. to the glory of the Lord, and to ¹*shew* our readiness
    24. *S.* ye therefore unto them in the face of the churches
Gal. 6. 12. As many as desire to make a fair *s.* in the flesh
Eph. 2. 7. he might *shew* the exceeding riches of his grace
Col. 2. 15. he made a *show* of them openly, triumphing over
    23. Which things have indeed a *show* of wisdom [ing
1 *Tim.* 1. 16. might Jesus Christ *s.* forth all his longsuffer-
    5. 4. learn first to *shew* piety towards their own family
    6. 15. which in its own times he shall *shew*, who is the
Heb. 6. 11. each one of you may *shew* the same diligence
    17. God, being minded to *s.* more abundantly unto the
Jas. 2. 18. *shew* me thy faith apart from thy works, and I
    by my works will *shew* thee my faith
    3. 13. let him *s.* by his good life his works in meekness
1 *Pet.* 2. 9. that ye may *shew* forth the excellencies of him
Rev. 1. 1. to *shew* unto his servants, even the things. 22. 6
    4. 1. I will *shew* thee the things which must come to pass
    17. 1. I will *shew* thee the judgement of the great harlot
    21. 9. I will *shew* thee the bride, the wife of the Lamb
    see bring, declare, go thy way, manifest, present, pretence, proclaim, report, tell.

Shewbread.
Mat. 12. 4. [David] and did eat the *s. Mk.* 2. 26: *Lu.* 6. 4
Heb. 9. 2. a tabernacle—and the table, and the *shewbread*

SHEWED

Shewed.—*A.V.* ¹*were.*

Lu. 1. 51. He hath *shewed* strength with his arm
4. 5. and *shewed* him all the kingdoms of the world
20. 37. that the dead are raised, even Moses *shewed*
24. 40. he *shewed* them his hands and his feet. *Jno.* 20. 20
Jno. 10. 32. Many good works have I *shewed* you
Acts 1. 3. to whom he also *shewed* himself alive
7. 52. *shewed* before of the coming of the Righteous One
10. 28. God *s.* that I should not call any man common
1 *Cor.* 10. 28. in sacrifice, eat not, for his sake that *s.* it
1 *Th.* 1. 5. Ye know what manner of men we *¹s.* ourselves
Heb. 6. 10. and the love which ye *shewed* toward his name
Rev. 21. 10. and *shewed* me the holy city Jerusalem
22. 1. And he *shewed* me a river of water of life
6. before the feet of the angel which *s.* me these things
see appeared, declared, declaring, example, foreshewed, kindness, manifested, mercy, report, signified, told, wrought.

Shewest—eth.

Mat. 4. 8. and *sheweth* him all the kingdoms of the world
Jno. 2. 18. What sign *shewest* thou unto us
5. 20. Father loveth the Son, and *sheweth* him all things
see mercy.

Shewing.

Lu. 1. 80. in the deserts till the day of his *s.* unto Israel
Acts 9. 39. *s.* the coats and garments which Dorcas made
18. 28. *s.* by the scriptures that Jesus was the Christ
Tit. 2. 7. *shewing* thyself an ensample of good works; in thy doctrine *shewing* uncorruptness
10. not purloining, but *shewing* all good fidelity
3. 2. to be gentle, *shewing* all meekness toward all men
see bringing, setting.

Shewn.—*A.V.* ¹*appear.*

Rom. 7. 13. that it might be ¹*s.* to be sin, by working death
see mercy.

Shield.

Eph. 6. 16. withal taking up the *shield* of faith

Shine.—*A.V.* ¹*give light,* ²*shone.*

Mat. 5. 16. Even so let your light *shine* before men
13. 43. Then shall the righteous *shine* forth as the sun
17. 2. his face did *shine* as the sun, and his garments
Lu. 1. 79. To ¹*shine* upon them that sit in darkness
2 *Cor.* 4. 6. God, that said, Light shall *shine* out of darkness
Eph. 5. 14. from the dead, and Christ shall ¹*shine* upon thee
Rev. 8. 12. day should not ²*shine* for the third part of it
18. 23. light of a lamp shall *shine* no more at all in thee
21. 23. no need of the sun, neither of the moon, to *shine*
see dawn, seen.

Shined.

Acts 12. 7. stood by him, and a light *shined* in the cell
2 *Cor.* 4. 6. who *shined* in our hearts, to give the light
see shone.

Shineth.—*A.V.* ¹*giveth light,* ²*shining.*

Mat. 5. 16. it ¹*shineth* unto all that are in the house
Lu. 17. 24. *shineth* unto the other part under heaven
Jno. 1. 5. And the light *shineth* in the darkness
5. 35. He was the lamp that burneth and ²*shineth*
1 *Jno.* 2. 8. darkness is passing away—true light already *s.*
Rev. 1. 16. countenance was as the sun *s.* in his strength
see dazzling, glistering, seen, shining.

Shining.—*A.V.* ¹*shineth.*

Lu. 11. 36. lamp with its bright *s.* doth give thee light
Acts 26. 13. above the brightness of the sun, *s.* round
2 *Pet.* 1. 19. take heed, as unto a lamp ¹*s.* in a dark place
see dazzling, glistering, shineth.

SHORE

Ship—s.

Acts 20. 13. we, going before to the *ship*, set sail for Assos
88. And they brought him on his way unto the *ship*
21. 2. having found a *ship* crossing over unto Phœnicia
3. Tyre: for there the *ship* was to unlade her burden
6. we went on board the *ship*, but they returned home
27. 2. And embarking in a *ship* of Adramyttium
30. as the sailors were seeking to flee out of the *ship*
31. Except these abide in the *ship*, ye cannot be saved
37. in the *s.* two hundred threescore and sixteen souls
38. lightened the *ship*, throwing out the wheat
39. counsel whether they could drive the *ship* upon it
44. planks, and some on other things from the *ship*
28. 11. after three months we set sail in a *ship* of
Jas. 3. 4. Behold, the *ships* also, though they are so great
Rev. 8. 9. and the third part of the *ships* was destroyed
18. 19. wherein were made rich all that had their *ships*
see boat, boats, overboard, saileth.

Shipmaster.

Rev. 18. 17. And every *s.*, and every one that saileth

Shipmen *A.V.*—*see sailors.*

Shipping *A.V.*—*see boats.*

Shipwreck.

2 *Cor.* 11. 25. once was I stoned, thrice I suffered *shipwreck*
1 *Tim.* 1. 19. made *shipwreck* concerning the faith

Shivers.

Rev. 2. 27. as the vessels of the potter are broken to *shivers*

Shod.

Mk. 6. 9. to go *s.* with sandals: and—put not on two coats
Eph. 6. 15. *s.* your feet with the preparation of the gospel

Shoe—s.

Mat. 3. 11. whose *shoes* I am not worthy to bear
10. 10. neither two coats, nor *shoes*, nor staff
Mk. 1. 7. whose *shoes* I am not worthy to stoop down and unloose. *Lu.* 3. 16: *Jno.* 1. 27: *Acts* 13. 25
Lu. 10. 4. Carry no purse, no wallet, no *shoes*. 22. 35
15. 22. put a ring on his hand, and *shoes* on his feet
Acts 7. 33. Loose the *shoes* from thy feet: for the place

Shone.—*A.V.* ¹*appeared,* ²*shined.*

Lu. 2. 9. the glory of the Lord *shone* round about them
Acts 9. 3. suddenly there ²*s.* round about him a light. 22. 6
27. 20 neither sun nor stars ¹*s.* upon us for many days
see shine.

Shook.

Acts 13. 51. But they *shook* off the dust of their feet
18. 6. he *shook* out his raiment, and said unto them
28. 5. Howbeit he *shook* off the beast into the fire
Heb. 12. 26. whose voice then *shook* the earth

Shoot.

Lu. 21. 30. when they now *s.* forth, ye see it and know

Shooteth *A.V.*—*see putteth.*

Shore.

Mk. 6. 53. the land unto Gennesaret, and moored to the *s.*
see beach.

Sea Shore.—*see sea.*

304

SHORN

Shorn.
Acts 18. 18. Paul—having *shorn* his head in Cenchrea
1 *Cor.* 11. 6. let her also be *shorn :* but if it is a shame to a woman to be *shorn* or shaven, let her be veiled

Short.
Rom. 9. 28. word upon the earth, finishing it and cutting
1 *Th.* 2. 17. being bereaved of you for a *short* season [it *s.*
Rev. 12. 12. knowing that he hath but a *short* time
  see little while, shortened.

Shortened.—*A.V.* ¹*short.*
Mat. 24. 22. except those days had been *shortened*—for the elect's sake those days shall be *shortened. Mk.* 13. 20
1 *Cor.* 7. 29. But this I say, brethren, the time is ¹*shortened*

Shortly.
Acts 25. 4. he himself was about to depart thither *shortly*
Rom. 16 20. shall bruise Satan under your feet *shortly*
1 *Cor.* 4. 19. I will come to you *shortly,* if the Lord will
Phil. 2. 19. I hope—to send Timothy *shortly* unto you
  24. I trust in the Lord that I myself also shall come *s.*
1 *Tim.* 3. 14. hoping to come unto thee *shortly*
2 *Tim.* 4. 9. Do thy diligence to come *shortly* unto me
Heb. 13. 23. with whom, if he come *shortly,* I will see you
3 *Jno.* 14. but I hope *shortly* to see thee, and we shall speak
Rev. 1. 1. the things which must *s.* come to pass. 22. 6
  see swiftly.

Should.—*A.V.* ¹*ought.*
2 *Cor.* 2. 7. ye ¹*should* rather forgive him and comfort him

Shoulders.
Mat. 23. 4. and lay them on men's *s. ;* but they themselves
Lu. 15. 5. found it, he layeth it on his *shoulders,* rejoicing

Shout.
1 *Th.* 4. 16. shall descend from heaven, with a *shout*
  see shouted.

Shouted.—*A.V.* ¹*cried,* ²*shout.*
Lu. 23. 21. but they ¹*shouted,* saying, Crucify, crucify him
Acts 12. 22. people ²*shouted,* saying, The voice of a god
  21. 34. And some ¹*shouted* one thing, some another
  22. 24. for what cause they so ¹*shouted* against him

Show.—*see shew.*

Shower.
Lu. 12. 54. ye say, There cometh a *s. ;* and so it cometh

Shrank.—*A.V.* ¹*kept back,* ²*shunned.*
Acts 20. 20. how that I ¹*s.* not from declaring unto you
  27. I ²*s.* not from declaring unto you the whole counsel

Shrines.
Acts 19. 24. Demetrius, a silversmith, which made silver *s.*

Shrink.—*A.V.* ¹*draw.*
Heb. 10. 38. if he ¹*s.* back, my soul hath no pleasure in him
  39. we are not of them that ¹*shrink* back unto perdition

Shudder.—*A.V.* ¹*tremble.*
Jas. 2. 19. the devils also believe, and ¹*shudder*

40

SICKLY

Shun.—*A.V.* ¹*avoid.*
2 *Tim.* 2. 16. But *shun* profane babblings : for they will
Tit. 3. 9. but ¹*shun* foolish questionings, and genealogies

Shunned *A.V.*—*see shrank.*

Shut.—*A.V.* ¹*concluded,* ²*exclude,* ³*shutteth.*
Mat. 23. 13. ye *shut* the kingdom of heaven against men
Lu. 3. 20. above all, that he *shut* up John in prison
  4. 25. when the heaven was *shut* up three years and six
Acts 5. 23. The prison-house we found *shut* in all safety
  26. 10. I both *shut* up many of the saints in prisons
Rom. 11. 32. For God hath ¹*shut* up all unto disobedience
Gal. 3. 22. the scripture hath ¹*s.* up all things under sin
  23. *shut* up unto the faith which should—be revealed
  4. 17. they desire to ²*shut* you out, that ye may seek them
Rev. 3. 7. he that openeth, and none shall ³*shut.* 8
  11. 6. power to *shut* the heaven, that it rain not
  20. 3. into the abyss, and *shut* it, and sealed it over him
  21. 25. And the gates thereof shall in no wise be *s.* by day
  see door, doors.

Shutteth.
1 *Jno.* 3. 17. and *shutteth* up his compassion from him
Rev. 3. 7. and that *shutteth,* and none openeth
  see shut.

Sick.—*A.V.* ¹*diseased,* ²*impotent.*
Mat. 4. 24. brought unto him all that were *s.* 14. ¹35 : *Mk.*
  8. 14. wife's mother lying *s.* of a fever. *Mk.* 1. 30 [1. ¹32
  16. and healed all that were *sick.* 14. 14 : *Mk.* 1. 34
  9. 12. physician, but they that are *s. Mk.* 2. 17 ; *Lu.* 5. 31
  10. 8. Heal the *sick,* raise the dead. *Lu.* 9. 2 : 10. 9
  25. 36. I was *sick,* and ye visited me : I was in prison. 43
  39. And when saw we thee *sick,* or in prison. 44
Mk. 6. 5. save that he laid his hands upon a few *sick* folk
  13. and anointed with oil many that were *sick*
  55. to carry about on their beds those that were *sick*
  56. they laid the *sick* in the marketplaces
  16. 18. lay hands on the *sick,* and they shall recover
Lu. 4. 40. all they that had any *sick*—brought them
  7. 2. centurion's servant, who was dear unto him, was *s.*
Jno. 4. 46. a certain nobleman, whose son was *sick*
  5. 3. lay a multitude of them that were ²*sick*
  7. The ²*sick* man answered him, Sir, I have no man
  6. 2. signs which he did on them that were ¹*sick*
  11. 1. Now a certain man was, *s.,* Lazarus of Bethany. 2
  3. Lord, behold, he whom thou lovest is *sick*
  6. When therefore he heard that he was *sick,* he abode
Acts 5. 15. they even carried out the *sick* into the streets
  16. bringing *sick* folk, and them that were vexed
  9. 37. in those days, that she [Dorcas] fell *sick,* and died
  19. 12. unto the *sick* were carried—handkerchiefs
  28. 8. the father of Publius lay *sick* of fever
Phil. 2. 26. troubled, because ye had heard that he was *s.*
  27. for indeed he was *sick* nigh unto death : but God
2 *Tim.* 4. 20. but Trophimus I left at Miletus *sick*
Jas. 5. 14. Is any among you *sick ?* let him call for the
  15. and the prayer of faith shall save him that is *sick*
  see palsy.

Sickle.
Mk. 4. 29. straightway he putteth forth the *sickle*
Rev. 14. 14. and in his hand a sharp *sickle.* 17, 18
  15. Send forth thy *sickle,* and reap. 16, 18, 19

Sickly.
1 *Cor.* 11. 30. many among you are weak and *sickly*

SICKNESS

Sickness.
Mat. 4. 23. and healing—all manner of *sickness*. 9. 35 : 10. 1
Jno. 11. 4. he said, This *sickness* is not unto death
   see diseases.

Side.
Mat. 8. 18. unto the other *s*. 28 : 14. 22 : 16. 5 : Mk. 4. 35 : Lu.
Mk. 16. 5. they saw a young man sitting on the right *s*. [8. 22
Lu. 1. 11. standing on the right *side* of the altar of incense
   9. 47. he took a little child, and set him by his *side*
   10. 31. saw him, he passed by on the other *side*. 32
   19. 43. compass thee round, and keep thee in on every *s*.
Jno. 6. 25. when they found him on the other *side* of the sea
   19. 18. on either *side* one, and Jesus in the midst
   34. one of the soldiers with a spear pierced his *side*
   20. 20. he shewed unto them his hands and his *side*
   25. and put my hand into his *side*, I will not believe
   27. reach hither thy hand, and put it into my *side*
   21. 6. Cast the net on the right *side* of the boat
Acts 12. 7. smote Peter on the *side*, and awoke him
   16. 13. we went forth without the gate by a river *side*
2 Cor. 4. 8. we are pressed on every *side*. 7. 5
   7. 5. no relief, but we were afflicted on every *s*. [of life
Rev. 22. 2. on this *s*. of the river and on that was the tree
   see beyond, of the sea, sea, sea side, way.

Sift.
Lu. 22. 31. Satan asked to have you, that he might *s*. you as

Sighed.
Mk. 7. 34. looking up to heaven, he *sighed*, and saith
   8. 12. And he *sighed* deeply in his spirit, and saith

Sight.—A.V. ¹*before*, ²*discovered*, ³*see*.
Mat. 11. 5. the blind receive their *sight*. Lu 7. ³22
   26. so it was well-pleasing in thy *sight*. Lu. 10. 21
   20. 34. and straightway they received their *sight*
Mk. 10. 51. Rabboni, that I may receive my *s*. Lu. 18. 41
   52. And straightway he received his *sight*, and followed
      him in the way. Lu. 18. 43
Lu. 4. 18. And recovering of *sight* to the blind
   7. 21. on many that were blind he bestowed *sight*
   12. 6. not one of them is forgotten in the ¹*sight* of God
   15. 18. have sinned against heaven, and in thy ¹*sight*. 21
   16. 15. justify yourselves in the ¹*sight* of men—an
      abomination in the *sight* of God
   18. 42. And Jesus said unto him, Receive thy *sight*
   23. 48. multitudes that came together to this *sight*
   24. 31. knew him; and he vanished out of their *sight*
Jno. 9. 11. I went away and washed, and I received *sight*
   15. asked him how he received his *sight*. 18
   18. parents of him that had received his *sight*
Acts 1. 9. and a cloud received him out of their *sight*
   4. 19. Whether it be right in the *sight* of God to hearken
   7. 31. when Moses saw it, he wondered at the *sight*
   46. [David] who found favour in the ¹*sight* of God
   9. 9. he was three days without *sight*
   12. hands on him, that he might receive his *sight*
   18. received his *sight*; and he arose and was baptized
   10. 31. alms are had in remembrance in the *sight* of God
   33. we are all here present in the ¹*sight* of God
   21. 3. And when we had come in ²*sight* of Cyprus
   22. 13. Brother Saul, receive thy *sight*. 9. 17
Rom. 3. 20. of the law shall no flesh be justified in his *sight*
   12. 17. thought for things honourable in the *s*. of all men
2 Cor. 2. 17. in the *sight* of God, speak we in Christ. 12. ¹19
   4. 2. to every man's conscience in the *sight* of God

SIGNIFYING

2 Cor. 5. 7. (for we walk by faith, not by *sight*)
   7. 12. care for us might be made manifest—in the *s*. of God
Gal. 3. 11. no man is justified by the law in the *s*. of God
1 Tim. 2. 3. acceptable in the *sight* of God our Saviour. 5.¹⁴
   21. I charge thee in the ¹*sight* of God. 2 Tim. 4. ¹1
   6. 12. confess the good confession in the ¹*s*. of—witnesses
   13. I charge thee in the *sight* of God, who quickeneth
Heb. 4. 13. no creature that is not manifest in his *sight*
   13. 21. working in us that which is well-pleasing in his *s*.
1 Pet. 3. 4. which is in the *sight* of God of great price
1 Jno. 3. 22. and do the things that are pleasing in his *s*.
Rev. 13. 13. make fire to come down—in the *sight* of men
   14. was given him to do in the *sight* of the beast
   16. 19. Babylon the great was remembered in the ¹*s*. of God
      see appearance.

Sights A.V.—*see terrors.*

Sign.—A.V. ¹*miracle*, ²*serveth not*, ³*wonder*.
Mat. 12. 38. Master, we would see a *sign* from thee
   39. seeketh after a *sign*; and there shall no *s*. be given
      to it but the *s*. of Jonah. 16. 4 : Mk. 8. 12 : Lu. 11. 29
   16. 1. asked him to shew them a *sign* from heaven. Mk.
      8. 11 : Lu. 11. 16
   24. 3. and what shall be the *sign* of thy coming
   30. and then shall appear the *sign* of the Son of man
   26. 48. Now he that betrayed him gave them a *sign*
Mk. 13. 4. what shall be the *s*. when these things, Lu. 21. 7
Lu. 2. 12. And this is the *sign* unto you; Ye shall find
   34. and for a *sign* which is spoken against
   11. 30. as Jonah became a *sign* unto the Ninevites
Jno. 2. 18. What *sign* shewest thou unto us. 6. 30
   4. 54. This is again the second ¹*sign* that Jesus did
   10. 41. John indeed did no ¹*s*.: but all things whatsoever
   12. 18. for that they heard that he had done this ¹*sign*
Acts 28. 11. island, whose *sign* was The Twin Brothers
Rom. 4. 11. and he received the *sign* of circumcision
1 Cor. 14. 22. tongues are for a *sign*—prophesying is for a ²*s*.
Rev. 12. 1. a great ³*s*. was seen in heaven; a woman arrayed
   15. 1. And I saw another *sign* in heaven
      see signs.

Signification.

1 Cor. 14. 10. and no kind is without *signification*

Signified.—A.V. ¹*declared*, ²*shewed*.
Acts 11. 28. *s*. by the Spirit that there should be a great
   23. 22. Tell no man that thou hast ²*s*. these things to me
1 Cor. 1. 11. it hath been ¹*signified* unto me concerning you
2 Pet. 1. 14. as our Lord Jesus Christ ²*signified* unto me
Rev. 1. 1. *signified* it by his angel unto his servant John

Signifieth.
Heb. 12. 27. *s*. the removing of those things that are shaken

Signify.
Acts 23. 15. *signify* to the chief captain that he bring him
   25. 27. not withal to *signify* the charges against him
      see declaring, point.

Signifying.
Jno. 12. 33. *s*. by what manner of death he should die. 18. 32
   21. 19. *s*. by what manner of death he should glorify God
Heb. 9. 8. the Holy Ghost this *signifying*, that the way into

SIGNS

Signs.—*A.V.* ¹*beckoned,* ²*miracles,* ³*sign,* ⁴*wonders.*
Mat. 16. 3. ye cannot discern the *signs* of the times
24. 24. false prophets, and shall shew great *s. Mk.* 13. 22
Mk. 16. 17. And these *signs* shall follow them that believe
20. and confirming the word by the *signs* that followed
Lu. 1. 22. he [Zacharias] continued making ¹*s.* unto them
62. made *s.* to his father, what he would have him called
21. 11. shall be terrors and great *signs* from heaven
25. there shall be *signs* in sun and moon and stars
Jno. 2. 11. This beginning of his ²*signs* did Jesus in Cana
23. many believed—beholding his ²*signs* which he did
3. 2. for no man can do these ²*signs* that thou doest
4. 48. Except ye see *s.* and wonders, ye will in no wise
6. 2. beheld the ²*s.* which he did on them that were sick
26. Ye seek me, not because ye saw ²*signs*
7. 31. will he do more ²*signs* than those which this man
9. 16. How can a man that is a sinner do such ²*signs* ?
11. 47. What do we ? for this man doeth many ²*signs*
12. 37. though he had done so many ²*signs* before them
20. 30. Many other *signs* therefore did Jesus
Acts 2. 19. And *signs* on the earth beneath ; Blood, and fire
22. and wonders and *signs,* which God did by him
43. wonders and *signs* were done by the apostles. 5. 12
4. 30. *signs* and wonders may be done through the name
6. 8. Stephen—wrought great wonders and ²*signs*
7. 36. having wrought wonders and *signs* in Egypt
8. 6. by Philip, when they heard, and saw the ²*signs*
13. beholding *signs* and great miracles wrought
14. 3. granting *s.* and wonders to be done by their hands
15.12. Barnabas and Paul rehearsing what ²*s.* and wonders
Rom. 15. 19. in the power of *signs* and wonders
1 *Cor.* 1. 22. Seeing that Jews ask for ²*s.,* and Greeks seek
2 *Cor.* 12. 12. Truly the *signs* of an apostle—by *signs* and
2 *Thes.* 2. 9. working of Satan with all power and *signs*
Heb. 2. 4. witness with them, both by *signs* and wonders
Rev. 13. 13. he doeth great ⁴*s.,* that he should even make
14. he deceiveth—by reason of the ²*s.* which it was given
16. 14. for they are spirits of devils, working ²*signs*
19. 20. the false prophet that wrought the ²*s.* in his sight

Silence.—*A.V.* ¹*secret.*
Mat. 22. 34. that he had put the Sadducees to *silence*
Acts 21. 40. when there was made a great *silence,* he spake
Rom. 16. 25. the mystery which hath been kept in ¹*silence*
1 *Pet.* 2. 15. put to *silence* the ignorance of foolish men
Rev. 8. 1. there followed a *s.* in heaven about the space of
see quiet, quietness.

Keep and kept **Silence.**—*see keep, kept.*

Silent.—*A.V.* ¹*dumb.*
Lu. 1. 20. thou [Zacharias] shalt be ¹*s.* and not able to speak

Silk.
Rev. 18. 12. fine linen, and purple, and *silk,* and scarlet

Silly.
2 *Tim.* 3. 6. take captive *silly* women laden with sins

Silver.—*A.V.* ¹*money.*
Mat. 10. 9. Get you no gold, nor *s.,* nor brass in your purses
26. 15. they weighed unto him thirty pieces of *silver*
27. 3. Judas—brought back the thirty pieces of *silver*
6. the chief priests took the pieces of *silver.* 9
Lu. 15. 8. Or what woman having ten pieces of *silver*
Acts 3. 6. Peter said, *Silver* and gold have I none
7. 16. tomb that Abraham bought for a price in ¹*silver*
8. 20. Thy ¹*s.* perish with thee, because thou hast thought

SIN

Acts 19. 24. which made *silver* shrines of Diana
1 *Cor.* 3. 12. any man buildeth on the foundation gold, *s.*
Rev. 18. 12. merchandise of gold, and *silver*
see gold, price.

Silversmith.
Acts 19. 24. Demetrius, a *s.,* which made silver shrines

Similitude *A.V.*—*see likeness.*

Simple.
Rom. 16. 19. wise unto that which is good, and *s.* unto—evil
see innocent.

Simplicity.
2 *Cor.* 11. 3. corrupted from the *s.*—that is toward Christ
see holiness, liberality.

Sin.—*A.V.* ¹*damnation,* ²*offence,* ³*sins,* ⁴*sinned,* ⁵*trespass.*
Mat. 12. 31. Every *sin* and blasphemy shall be forgiven
18. 15. if thy brother ⁵*sin* against thee, go, shew him his
21. how oft shall my brother *sin* against me [fault
Mk. 3. 29. blaspheme against the Holy Spirit—is guilty of
Lu. 17. 3. if thy brother ⁵*sin,* rebuke him [an eternal ¹*sin*
4. if he ⁵*sin* against thee seven times in the day
Jno. 1. 29. which taketh away the *sin* of the world !
5. 14. *sin* no more, lest a worse thing befall thee
8. 7. He that is without *sin* among you, let him first
11. go thy way ; from henceforth sin no more]
21. ye shall seek me, and shall die in your ³*sin*
34. Every one that committeth *sin* is the bondservant
9. 2. Rabbi, who did *sin,* this man, or his parents [of *sin*
3. Neither did this man ⁴*sin,* nor his parents
41. If ye were blind, ye would have no *sin :* but now
ye say, We see : your *sin* remaineth
15. 22. If I had not come—they had not had *sin :* but
now they have no excuse for their *sin.* 24
16. 8. will convict the world in respect of *sin*
9. of *sin,* because they believe not on me
19. 11. he that delivered me unto thee hath greater *sin*
Acts 7. 60. Lord, lay not this *sin* to their charge
Rom. 3. 9. Jews and Greeks, that they are all under *sin*
20. through the law cometh the knowledge of *sin*
5. 12. *sin* entered into the world, and death through *sin*
13. until the law was in the world : but *sin* is not
20. where *sin* abounded, grace did abound more
21. as *sin* reigned in death, even so might grace reign
6. 1. Shall we continue in *sin,* that grace may abound ?
2. We who died to *sin,* how shall we any longer live
6. that the body of *sin* might be done away, that so we
should no longer be in bondage to *sin*
7. for he that hath died is justified from *sin*
10. the death that he died, he died unto *sin* once
11. reckon ye also yourselves to be dead unto *sin*
12. Let not *sin* therefore reign in your mortal body
13. neither present your members unto *sin* as
14. For *sin* shall not have dominion over you
15. shall we *sin,* because we are not under law
16. whom ye obey ; whether of *sin* unto death
17. were servants of *sin,* ye became obedient
18. being made free from *sin,* ye became. 22
20. For when ye were servants of *sin,* ye were free
23. For the wages of *sin* is death ; but the free gift
7. 7. Is the law *sin* ?—I had not known *sin* [dead. 11
8. but *sin,* finding occasion—for apart from the law *s.* is
9. commandment came, *sin* revived, and I died
13. But *sin,* that it might be shown to be *sin*—through
the commandments. might become exceeding sinful

SIN

Rom. 7. 14. law is spiritual: but I am carnal, sold under *sin*
17. no more I that do it, but *s.* which dwelleth in me. 20
23. bringing me into captivity under the law of *sin*
25. but with the flesh the law of *sin*. 6. 2
6. 3. as an offering for *sin*, condemned *sin* in the flesh
10. if Christ is in you, the body is dead because of *sin*
14. 23. not of faith; and whatsoever is not of faith is *sin*
1 *Cor.* 6. 18. Every *s.* that a man doeth is without the body
8. 12. conscience when it is weak, ye *sin* against Christ
15. 34. Awake up righteously, and *sin* not
56. The sting of death is *s.*; and the power of *s.* is the law
2 *Cor.* 5. 21. Him who knew no *s.* he made to be *s.* on our
11. 7. did I commit a ²*sin* in abasing myself [behalf
Gal. 2. 17. is Christ a minister of *sin* ? God forbid
3. 22. the scripture hath shut up all things under *sin*
Eph. 4. 26. Be ye angry, and *sin* not: let not the sun go
2 *Th.* 2. 3. and the man of *s.* be revealed, the son of perdition
1 *Tim.* 5. 20. Them that *sin* reprove in the sight of all
Heb. 3. 13. of you be hardened by the deceitfulness of *sin*
4. 15. in all points tempted like as we are, yet without *sin*
9. 26. end of the ages hath he been manifested to put away
28. shall appear a second time, apart from *sin* [*sin*
10. 6. and sacrifices for *sin* thou hadst no pleasure. 8
18. remission of these is, there is no more offering for *s.*
26. For if we *sin* wilfully after that we have received
11. 25. than to enjoy the pleasures of *sin* for a season
12. 1. every weight, and the *s.* which doth so easily beset us
4. have not yet resisted unto blood, striving against *sin*
13. 11. an offering for *sin*, are burned without the camp
Jas. 1. 15. when it hath conceived, beareth *sin*: and the *s.*
2. 9. if ye have respect of persons, ye commit *sin*
4. 17. knoweth to do good, and doeth it not, to him it is *sin*
1 *Pet.* 2. 22. did no *sin*, neither was guile found in his mouth
4. 1. hath suffered in the flesh hath ceased from *sin*
2 *Pet.* 2. 14. full of adultery, and that cannot cease from *sin*
1 *Jno.* 1. 7. blood of Jesus his Son cleanseth us from all *s.*
8. If we say that we have no *sin*, we deceive ourselves
2. 1. that ye may not *sin*. And if any man *sin*, we have
3. 4. Every one that doeth *sin*—and *sin* is lawlessness
5. manifested to take away sins; and in him is no *sin*
8. he that doeth *sin* is of the devil; for the devil sinneth
9. begotten of God doeth no *sin*—and he cannot *sin*
5. 16. sinning a *sin* not unto death—life for them that
sin not unto death. There is a *sin* unto death
17. unrighteousness is *s.*: and there is a *s.* not unto death
see offering, sinning.

Since.—*A.V.* ¹*because.*

Heb. 6. 13. ¹*since* he could swear by none greater, he swore

Sincere.—*A.V.* ¹*pure.*

Phil. 1. 10. that ye may be *sincere* and void of offence
2 *Pet.* 3. 1. in both of them I stir up your ¹*sincere* mind
see spiritual.

Sincerely.
Phil. 1. 17. proclaim Christ of faction, not *sincerely*

Sincerity.
1 *Cor.* 5. 8. with the unleavened bread of *s.* and truth
2 *Cor.* 1. 12. in holiness and *sincerity* of God, not in
2. 17. but as of *sincerity*, but as of God, in the sight
8. 8. proving—the *sincerity* also of your love
see uncorruptness.

Sinful.—*A.V.* ¹*sins.*
Mk. 8. 38. in this adulterous and *sinful* generation
Lu. 5. 8. Depart from me; for I am a *sinful* man, O Lord
24. 7. must be delivered up into the hands of *sinful* men

SINNERS

Rom. 7. 5. the ¹*s.* passions, which were through the law
13. commandment *sin* might become exceeding *sinful*
8. 3. sending his own Son in the likeness of *sinful* flesh

Sing.—*A.V.* ¹*sung.*

Rom. 15. 9. among the Gentiles, And *sing* unto thy name
1 *Cor.* 14. 15. I will *sing* with the spirit, and I will *sing*
with the understanding also
Jas. 5. 13. Is any cheerful? let him *sing* praise
Rev. 5. 9. they ¹*sing* a new song, saying, Worthy art thou
14. 3. they ¹*sing* as it were a new song before the throne
15. 3. And they *s.* the song of Moses the servant of God
see praise, praises.

Singing.—*A.V.* ¹*sang.*

Acts 16. 25. Paul and Silas were praying and ¹*singing* hymns
Eph. 5. 19. *singing* and making melody with your heart
Col. 3. 16. *singing* with grace in your hearts unto God

Single.

Mat. 6. 22. if therefore thine eye be *single*. *Lu.* 11. 34

Singleness.

Acts 2. 46. their food with gladness and *singleness* of heart
Eph. 6. 5. in *s.* of your heart, as unto Christ. *Col.* 3. 22

Sink.

Mat. 14. 30. beginning to *sink*, he cried out, saying, Lord
Lu. 5. 7. filled both the boats, so that they began to *sink*
9. 44. Let these words *sink* into your ears

Sinned.—*A.V.* ¹*offended.*

Mat. 27. 4. I have *sinned* in that I betrayed innocent blood
Lu. 15. 18. Father, I have *sinned* against heaven. 21
Acts 25. 8. nor against Cæsar, have I ¹*sinned* at all
Rom. 2. 12. have *sinned* without law—have *s.* under law
5. 23. for all have *s.*, and fall short of the glory of God
5. 12. death passed unto all men, for that all *sinned*
14. had not *s.* after the likeness of Adam's transgression
16. And not as through one that *sinned*, so is the gift
1 *Cor.* 7. 28. if thou marry, thou hast not *s.*—she hath not *s.*
2 *Cor.* 12. 21. I should mourn for many of them that have *s.*
13. 2. being absent, to them that have *sinned* heretofore
Heb. 3. 17. forty years? was it not with them that *sinned*
2 *Pet.* 2. 4. For if God spared not angels when they *sinned*
1 *Jno.* 1. 10. If we say that we have not *s.*, we make him a liar
see sin.

Sinner.

Lu. 7. 37. a woman which was in the city, a *sinner*. 39
15. 7. joy in heaven over one *sinner* that repenteth. 10
18. 13. saying, God, be merciful to me a *sinner*
19. 7. He is gone in to lodge with a man that is a *sinner*
Jno. 9. 16. How can a man that is a *sinner* do such signs?
24. Give glory to God: we know that this man is a *sinner*
25. Whether he be a *sinner*, I know not: one thing
Rom. 3. 7. why am I also still judged as a *sinner* ?
Jas. 5. 20. he which converteth a *sinner* from the error
1 *Pet.* 4. 18. where shall the ungodly and *sinner* appear?

Sinners.

Mat. 9. 10. publicans and *s.* came and sat down. *Mk.* 2. 15
11. Why eateth your Master with the publicans and
sinners ? *Mk.* 2. 16: *Lu.* 5. 30 [*Mk.* 2. 17: *Lu.* 5. 32
13. for I came not to call the righteous, but *sinners*.
11. 19. a friend of publicans and *sinners* ! *Lu.* 7. 34
26. 45. the Son of man is betrayed unto the hands of *s.*
Lu. 6. 32. even *s.* love those that love them [*Mk.* 14. 41

308

SINNERS

Lu. 6. 33. what thank have ye? for even *s.* do the same
34. even *sinners* lend to *s.*, to receive again as much
13. 2. Think ye that these Galileans were *sinners*
15. 1. publicans and *s.* were drawing near unto him
2. This man receiveth *sinners*, and eateth with them
Jno. 9. 31. We know that God heareth not *sinners*
Rom. 5. 8. while we were yet *sinners*, Christ died for us
19. one man's disobedience the many were made *s.*
Gal. 2. 15. We being Jews by nature, and not *s.* of the
17. in Christ, we ourselves also were found *sinners*
1 *Tim.* 1. 9. for the ungodly and *s.*, for the unholy and
15. that Christ Jesus came into the world to save *s.*
Heb. 7. 26. guileless, undefiled, separated from *sinners*
12. 3. that hath endured such gainsaying of *sinners*
Jas. 4. 8. Cleanse your hands, ye *sinners ;* and purify
Jude 15. hard things which ungodly *sinners* have spoken
    see offenders.

Sinneth.

1 *Cor.* 6. 18. fornication *sinneth* against his own body
7. 36. do what he will ; he *sinneth* not ; let them marry
Tit. 3. 11. that such a one is perverted, and *sinneth*
1 *Jno.* 3. 6. Whosoever abideth in him *sinneth* not: whosoever *s.* hath not seen him, neither knoweth him
8. for the devil *sinneth* from the beginning
5. 18. We know that whosoever is begotten of God *s.* not

Sinning.—A.V. ¹sin.

1 *Cor.* 8. 12. And thus, ¹*sinning* against the brethren
1 *Jno.* 5. 16. If any man see his brother ¹*sinning* a sin

Sins.—A.V. ¹faults.

Mat. 9. 2. Son, be of good cheer ; thy *sins* are forgiven. 5
26. 28. which is shed for many unto remission of *sins*
Mk. 1. 4. John—preached—unto remission of *s.* *Lu.* 3. 3
Lu. 24. 47. and remission of *sins* should be preached
Jno. 8. 24. ye shall die in your *sins*—die in your *sins*
9. 34. Thou wast altogether born in *sins*
20. 23. whose soever *sins* ye forgive—*sins* ye retain
Acts 2. 38. every one of you—unto the remission of your *s.*
3. 19. turn again, that your *sins* may be blotted out
10. 43. through his name—shall receive remission of *s.*
22. 16. arise, and be baptized, and wash away thy *sins*
Rom. 3. 25. the passing over of the *sins* done aforetime
4. 7. Blessed are they—And whose *sins* are covered
1 *Cor.* 15. 17. your faith is vain ; ye are yet in your *sins*
Eph. 2. 1. ye were dead through your trespasses and *sins*
1 *Tim.* 5. 22. neither be partaker of other men's *sins*
24. Some men's *sins* are evident, going before unto
2 *Tim.* 3. 6. take captive silly women laden with *sins*
Heb. 1. 3. when he had made purification of *sins*, sat down
2. 17. to make propitiation for the *sins* of the people
5. 1. that he may offer both gifts and sacrifices for *sins*
3. as for the people, so also for himself, to offer for *sins*
7. 27. first for his own *s.*, and then for the *s.* of the people
9. 28. Christ—once offered to bear the *sins* of many
10. 2. would have had no more conscience of *sins ?*
3. there is a remembrance made of *sins* year by year
4. blood of bulls and goats should take away *sins*
11. sacrifices, the which can never take away *sins*
12. when he had offered one sacrifice for *sins* for ever
26. there remaineth no more a sacrifice for *sins*
Jas. 5. 16. Confess therefore your ¹*sins* one to another
20. and shall cover a multitude of *sins*
1 *Pet.* 2. 24. we, having died unto *sins*, might live unto
3. 18. Because Christ also suffered for *sins* once
4. 8. for love covereth a multitude of *sins*
2 *Pet.* 1. 9. having forgotten the cleansing from his old *s.*

SISTERS

1 *Jno.* 3. 5. know that he was manifested to take away *sins*
Rev. 18. 4. that ye have no fellowship with her *sins*
5. for her *sins* have reached even unto heaven
    see sin, sinful, trespass, trespasses.

Dear Sins.—*see bear.*

Our Sins.

1 *Cor.* 15. 3. Christ died for *our sins* according to the
Gal. 1. 4. [Lord Jesus Christ] who gave himself for *our s.*
1 *Pet.* 2. 16. who his own self bare *our sins* in his body
1 *Jno.* 1. 9. If we confess *our sins*—to forgive us *our sins*
2. 2. he is the propitiation for *our sins.* 4. 10
Rev. 1. 5. and loosed us from *our sins* by his blood

Their Sins.

Mat. 1. 21. it is he that shall save his people from *their s.*
3. 6. in the river Jordan, confessing *their sins.* *Mk.* 1. 5
Mk. 3. 28. *their sins* shall be forgiven unto the sons of men
Lu. 1. 77. unto his people In the remission of *their sins*
Rom. 11. 27. When I shall take away *their sins*
1 *Th.* 2. 16. to fill up *their sins* alway : but the wrath
Heb. 8. 12. *their sins* will I remember no more. 10. 17

Sir.

Mat. 13. 27. *Sir*, didst thou not sow good seed in thy field ?
21. 30. he answered and said, I go, *sir :* and went not
27. 63. *Sir*, we remember that that deceiver said
Jno. 4. 11. *Sir*, thou hast nothing to draw with
15. *Sir*, give me this water, that I thirst not
19. *Sir*, I perceive that thou art a prophet
49. *Sir*, come down ere my child die
5. 7. *Sir*, I have no man, when the water is troubled
12. 21. asked him, saying, *Sir*, we would see Jesus
20. 15. *Sir*, if thou hast borne him hence, tell me where
    see lord.

Sirs.

Acts 7. 26. *Sirs*, ye are brethren ; why do ye wrong
14. 15. *Sirs*, why do ye these things ? We also are men
16. 30. *Sirs*, what must I do to be saved ?   [wealth
19. 25. *Sirs*, ye know that by this business we have our
27. 10. *Sirs*, I perceive that the voyage will be with injury
21. *Sirs*, ye should have hearkened unto me
25. Wherefore, *sirs*, be of good cheer : for I believe God

Sister.

Mk. 3. 35. same is my brother, and *s.*, and mother. *Mat.* 12. 50
Lu. 10. 39. And she had a *sister* called Mary, which also sat
40. not care that my *sister* did leave me to serve alone ?
Jno. 11. 1. the village of Mary and her *sister* Martha
5. Now Jesus loved Martha, and her *sister*, and Lazarus
19. 25. cross of Jesus his mother, and his mother's *sister*
Acts 23. 16. Paul's *sister's* son heard of their lying in wait
Rom. 16. 1. I commend unto you Phœbe our *sister*
15. Salute Philologus and Julia, Nereus and his *sister*
1 *Cor.* 7. 15. the brother or *sister* is not under bondage
Jas. 2. 15. If a brother or *sister* be naked, and in lack
2 *Jno.* 13. The children of thine elect *sister* salute thee

Sister's son.—*see cousin.*

Sisters.

Mat. 13. 56. And his *s.*, are they not all with us ? *Mk.* 6. 3
19. 29. that hath left houses, or brethren, or *s.* *Mk.* 10. 29
Mk. 10. 30. in this time, houses, and brethren, and *sisters*
Lu. 14. 26. brethren, and *sisters*, yea, and his own life also
Jno. 11. 3. The *sisters* therefore sent unto him, saying
1 *Tim.* 5. 2. the younger as *sisters*, in all purity

SIT

Sit.—*A.V.* ¹*sat,* ²*set,* ³*sitteth,* ⁴*sitting.*
Mat. 8. 11. shall *sit* down with Abraham, and Isaac
14. 19. he commanded the multitudes to *sit* down. 15.
    35 : *Mk.* 6. 39 ; 8. 6
19. 28. Son of man shall *sit* on the throne of his glory, ye
    also shall *sit* upon twelve thrones. 25. 31 : *Lu.* 22.30
20. 21. two sons may *sit,* one on thy right hand. *Mk.* 10. 37
23. but to *sit* on my right hand. *Mk.* 10. 40
23. 44. *Sit* thou on my right hand. *Mk.* 12. 36 ; *Lu.*
    20. 42 ; *Acts* 2. 34 ; *Heb* 1. 13
23. 2. The scribes and the Pharisees *sit* on Moses' seat
Mk. 14. 32. *Sit* ye here, while I pray. *Mat.* 26. 36
Lu. 1. 79. To shine upon them that *sit* in darkness
7. 32. like unto children that ⁴*sit* in the marketplace
9. 14. Make them *sit* down in companies. 15
12. 37. gird himself, and make them *sit* down to meat
13. 29. and shall *sit* down in the kingdom of God
14. 8. to a marriage feast, *sit* not down in the chief seat
10. art bidden, go and *sit* down in the lowest place
28. doth not first ³*sit* down and count the cost. ³31
16. 6. Take thy bond, and *sit* down quickly, and write fifty
17. 7. Come straightway and *sit* down to meat
Jno. 6. 10. Jesus said, Make the people *sit* down
Acts 8. 31. besought Philip to come up and *sit* with him
Eph. 1. 20. and made him to ²*sit* at his right hand
2. 6. made us to *sit* with him in the heavenly places
Jas. 2. 3. *Sit* thou here in a good place—or *sit* under my
Rev. 3. 21. I will give to him to *sit* down with me
11. 16. four and twenty elders, which ¹*sit* before God
18. 7. for she saith in her heart, I *sit* a queen
19. 18. flesh of horses and of them that *sit* thereon
    see seated, set, sitting.

Sittest.
Acts 23. 3. *sittest* thou to judge me according to the law

Sitteth.
Mat. 23. 22. throne of God, and by him that *sitteth* thereon
Lu. 22. 27. For whether is greater, he that *s.* at meat, or
    he that serveth ? is not he that *sitteth* at meat ?
2 *Thes.* 2. 4. so that he *sitteth* in the temple of God
Rev. 5. 13. Unto him that *s.* on the throne—be the blessing
6. 16. hide us from the face of him that *s.* on the throne
7. 10. Salvation unto our God which *sitteth* on the throne
15. he that *sitteth* on the throne shall spread his
17. 1. great harlot that *sitteth* upon many waters. 15
9. seven mountains, on which the woman *sitteth*
    see seated, sit, sitting.

Sitting.—*A.V.* ¹*sat,* ²*eat down,* ³*set down,* ⁴*sit,* ⁵*sitteth.*
Mat. 9. 9. Matthew, *s.* at the place. *Mk.* 2. 14 : *Lu.* 5. 27
11. 16. like unto children *sitting* in the marketplaces
20. 30. behold, two blind men *sitting* by the way side
26. 20. when even was come, he was ³*sitting* at meat
64. Son of man *s.* at the right hand of power. *Mk.* 14. 62
27. 19. while he was ³*sitting* on the judgement-seat
61. and the other Mary, *s.* over against the sepulchre
Mk. 2. 6. there were certain of the scribes *sitting* there
3. 32. And a multitude was ¹*sitting* about him
5. 15. *sitting,* clothed and in his right mind. *Lu.* 8. 35
10. 46. a blind beggar, was ¹*sitting* by the way side
14. 54. Peter—was ¹*sitting* with the officers
16. 5. they saw a young man *sitting* on the right side
Lu. 2. 46. in the temple, *sitting* in the midst of the doctors
5. 17. Pharisees and doctors of the law *sitting* by
10. 13. repented long ago, *sitting* in sackcloth and ashes
Jno. 2. 14. in the temple—the changers of money *sitting*
12. 15. thy King cometh, *sitting* on an ass's colt
20. 12. she beholdeth two angels in white *sitting*

SLAIN

Acts 2. 2. it filled all the house where they were *sitting*
8. 28. [eunuch] *sitting* in his chariot, and was reading
1 *Cor.* 8. 10. knowledge ⁴*sitting* at meat in an idol's temple
14. 30. if a revelation be made to another ⁵*sitting* by
Rev. 4. 4. upon the thrones I saw four and twenty elders *s.*
14. 14. I saw one ¹*sitting* like unto a son of man
17. 3. a woman ⁴*sitting* upon a scarlet-coloured beast
    see riding, sat, sit.

Six.

Lu. 4. 25. was shut up three years and *s.* months. *Jas.* 5. 17
Jno. 2. 6. there were *six* waterpots of stone set there
Acts 11. 12. And these *six* brethren also accompanied me
18. 11. And he dwelt there a year and *six* months
Rev. 4. 8. living creatures, having each one—*six* wings
    see days, hundred.

Sixth.

Mat. 20. 5. went out about the *sixth* and the ninth hour
27. 45. from the *sixth* hour there was darkness over all
    the land. *Mk.* 15. 33 : *Lu.* 23. 44
Jno. 4. 6. by the well. It was about the *sixth* hour
19. 14. of the passover : it was about the *sixth* hour
Acts 10. 9. upon the housetop to pray, about the *sixth* hour
Rev. 6. 12. And I saw when he opened the *sixth* seal
9. 13. the *sixth* angel sounded, and I heard a voice
14. saying to the *sixth* angel, which had the trumpet
16. 12. And the *sixth* poured out his bowl upon the great
21. 20. the *sixth,* sardius ; the seventh, chrysolite

Sixty.
Mat. 13. 8. some a hundredfold, some *sixty.* 23

Sixtyfold.
Mk. 4. 8. brought forth, thirtyfold, and *sixtyfold.* 20

Skin *A.V.—see leathern.*

Skins.—*A.V.* ¹*bottles.*
Mat. 9. 17. else the ¹*skins* burst, and the wine is spilled,
    and the ¹*skins* perish. *Mk.* 2. ¹22 : *Lu.* 5. ¹37
    see wineskins.

Skull.
Mat. 27. 33. called Golgotha, that is to say, The place of
    a *skull. Mk.* 15. 22 ; *Jno.* 19. 17

Sky *A.V.—see heaven.*

Slack—ness.
2 *Pet.* 3. 9. The Lord is not *slack* concerning his promise,
    as some count *slackness*

Slain.—*A.V.* ¹*killed.*
Acts 5. 36. who was *slain ;* and all, as many as obeyed him
7. 42. Did ye offer unto me *slain* beasts and sacrifices
13. 28. yet asked they of Pilate that he should be *slain*
23. 21. neither to eat nor to drink till they have ¹*s.* him
27. seized by the Jews, and was about to be ¹*s.* of them
Eph. 2. 16. the cross, having *slain* the enmity thereby
Heb. 11. 37. tempted, they were *slain* with the sword
Rev. 5. 6. a Lamb standing, as though it had been *slain*
9. for thou wast *slain,* and didst purchase unto God
12. Worthy is the Lamb that hath been *slain.* 13. 8
6. 9. souls of them that had been *s.* for the word of God
18. 24. and of all that have been *slain* upon the earth
    see killed, slay.

310

SLANDERERS

Slanderers.—*A.V.* ¹*false accusers.*

1 *Tim.* 3. 11. Women—must be grave, not *slanderers*
2 *Tim.* 3. 3. implacable, ¹*slanderers*, without self-control
Tit. 2. 3. not ¹*slanderers* nor enslaved to much wine

Slanderously.

Rom. 3. 8. (as we be *s.* reported, and as some affirm

Slaughter.

Acts 8. 32. He was led as a sheep to the *slaughter*
9. 1. Saul, yet breathing threatening and *slaughter*
Rom. 8. 36. We were accounted as sheep for the *slaughter*
Heb. 7. 1. met Abraham returning from the *s.* of the kings
Jas. 5. 5. ye have nourished your hearts in a day of *s.*

Slaves.

Rev. 18. 13. chariots and *slaves*; and souls of men

Slay.—*A.V.* ¹*consume,* ²*kill,* ³*slain.*

Lu. 19. 27. bring hither, and *slay* them before me
Acts 2. 23. by the hand of lawless men did crucify and ³*s.*
5. 33. cut to the heart, and were minded to *slay* them
23. 15. or ever he come near, are ready to ²*slay* him
2 *Th.* 2. 8. whom the Lord Jesus shall ¹*slay* with the breath
Rev. 6. 4. and that they should ²*slay* one another
see kill.

Sleep.

Mat. 1. 24. And Joseph arose from his *sleep*, and did as
26. 45. *Sleep* on now, and take your rest. *Mk.* 14. 41
Mk. 4. 27. and should *sleep* and rise night and day
Lu. 9. 32. they that were with him were heavy with *sleep*
22. 46. Why *s.* ye? rise and pray, that ye enter not into
Jno. 11. 11. but I go, that I may awake him out of *sleep*
13. thought that he spake of taking rest in *sleep*
Acts 13. 36. David—served the counsel of God, fell on *sleep*
16. 27. And the jailor being roused out of *sleep*
20. 9. Eutychus, borne down with deep *sleep*—by his *s.*
Rom. 13. 11. it is high time for you to awake out of *sleep*
1 *Cor.* 11. 30. you are weak and sickly, and not a few *sleep*
15. 51. We shall not all *s.*, but we shall all be changed
1 *Th.* 5. 6. so then let us not *sleep*, as do the rest
7. For they that *sleep sleep* in the night
10. that, whether we wake or *sleep*, we should live
see asleep.

Sleepest.

Mk. 14. 37. Simon, *s.* thou? couldest thou not watch
Eph. 5. 14. Awake, thou that *s.*, and arise from the dead

Sleepeth.

Mat. 9. 24. is not dead, but *sleepeth*. *Mk.* 5. 39: *Lu.* 8. 52
see asleep.

Sleeping.—*A.V.* ¹*asleep.*

Mat. 26 40. disciples, and findeth them ¹*s.* ¹43. *Mk.*14.37,¹40
Mk. 13. 36. lest coming suddenly he find you *sleeping*
Lu. 22. 45. disciples, and found them *sleeping* for sorrow
Acts 12. 6. Peter was *sleeping* between two soldiers

Sleight.

Eph. 4. 14. by the *sleight* of men, in craftiness

Slept.

Mat. 13. 25. while men *s.*, his enemy came and sowed tares
25. 5. the bridegroom tarried, they all slumbered and *s.*
28. 13. came by night, and stole him away while we *slept*
see asleep.

SMITEST

Slew.—*A.V.* ¹*killed.*

Mat. 2. 16. *slew* all the male children—in Bethlehem
23. 31. ye are sons of them that ¹*slew* the prophets
35. whom ye *s* between the sanctuary and the altar
Acts 5. 30. whom ye *slew*, hanging him on a tree. 10. 39
22. 20. keeping the garments of them that *slew* him
Rom. 7. 11. beguiled me, and through it *slew* me
1 *Jno.* 3. 12. *slew* his brother. And wherefore *slew* he him?

Slip *A.V.*—*see drift, killed.*

Slothful.

Mat. 25. 26. Thou wicked and *s.* servant, thou knewest
Rom. 12. 11. in diligence not *slothful*; fervent in spirit
see sluggish.

Slow.

Lu. 24. 25. O foolish men, and *slow* of heart to believe
Jas. 1. 19. swift to hear, *slow* to speak, *slow* to wrath
see idle.

Slowly.

Acts 27. 7. And when we had sailed *slowly* many days

Sluggish.—*A.V.* ¹*slothful.*

Heb. 6. 12. not ¹*s.*, but imitators of them who through faith

Slumber *A.V.*—*see stupor.*

Slumbered—eth.

Mat. 25. 5. while the bridegroom tarried, they all *s.*
2 *Pet.* 2. 3. and their destruction *slumbereth* not

Small.—*A.V.* ¹*little.*

Mat. 15. 34. Seven, and few ¹*small* fishes
Acts 12. 18. there was no *small* stir among the soldiers
15. 2. Paul and Barnabas had no *small* dissension
19. 23. there arose no *small* stir concerning the Way
27. 20. and no *small* tempest lay on us, all hope that
1 *Cor.* 4. 3. a very *s.* thing that I should be judged of you
Jas. 3. 4. are yet turned about by a very *small* rudder
5. how much wood is kindled by how ¹*small* a fire!
see great, little.

Smallest.

1 *Cor.* 6. 2. are ye unworthy to judge the *smallest* matters?

Smell.—*A.V.* ¹*sweetsmelling.*

Eph. 5. 2. sacrifice to God for an odour of a sweet ¹*smell*
Phil. 4. 18. an odour of a sweet *s.*, a sacrifice acceptable

Smelling.

1 *Cor.* 12. 17. If the whole were hearing, where were the *s.*?

Smite.

Mat. 26. 31. I will *smite* the shepherd. *Mk.* 14. 27
Lu. 22. 49. Lord, shall we *smite* with the sword?
Acts 23. 2. commanded them that stood by him to *s.* him on
3. God shall *smite* thee, thou whited wall
Rev. 11. 6. and to *smite* the earth with every plague
19. 15. sword, that with it he should *smite* the nations
see beat, killed.

Smitest—eth—*A.V.* ¹*smite.*

Mat. 5. 39. whosoever ¹*s.* thee on thy right cheek. *Lu.* 6. 29
Jno. 18. 23. but if well, why *smitest* thou me?
2 *Cor.* 11. 20. exalteth himself, if he ¹*s.* you on the face

SMITING

Smiting.—*A.V.* ¹*smote.*
Lu. 23. 48. multitudes—returned ¹*smiting* their breasts
Acts 7. 24. avenged him that was oppressed, ¹*smiting* the

Smitten.—*A.V.* ¹*cast,* ²*wounded.*
Acts 23. 3. commandest me to be s. contrary to the law?
2 *Cor.* 4. 9. ¹*smitten* down, yet not destroyed
Rev. 8. 12. and the third part of the sun was *smitten*
 13. 3. as though it had been ²*smitten* unto death

Smoke.
Acts 2. 19. Blood, and fire, and vapour of *smoke*
Rev. 8. 4. And the *smoke* of the incense, with the prayers
 9. 2. a *smoke* out of the pit, as the *smoke* of a great furnace—darkened by reason of the *smoke* of the pit
 3. And out of the *smoke* came forth locusts
 17. out of their mouths proceedeth fire and *smoke.* 18
 14. 11. the s. of their torment goeth up for ever and ever
 15. 8. temple was filled with s. from the glory of God
 18. 9. when they look upon the *smoke* of her burning. 18
 19. 3. And her *smoke* goeth up for ever and ever

Smoking.
Mat. 12. 20. And *smoking* flax shall he not quench

Smooth.—*A.V.* ¹*good words.*
Lu. 3. 5. shall become straight, And the rough ways *smooth*
Rom. 16. 18. by their ¹*smooth* and fair speech they beguile

Smote.—*A.V.* ¹*beat,* ²*struck.*
Mat. 7. 27. the winds blew, and ¹*smote* upon that house
 26. 51. drew his sword, and ²*smote* the servant of the high priest. *Mk.* 14. 47: *Lu.* 22. 50
 67. some *smote* him with the palms of their hands
 27. 30. took the reed and s. him on the head. *Mk.* 15. 19
Lu. 18. 13. publican—s. his breast, saying, God, be merciful
Acts 12. 7. angel—*smote* Peter on the side, and awoke him
 23. immediately an angel of the Lord s. him [Herod]
see beat, smiting, struck.

Snare.
Lu. 21. 35. as a *snare* : for so shall it come upon all
Rom. 11. 9. Let their table be made a *snare,* and a trap
1 *Cor.* 7. 35. not that I may cast a *snare* upon you
1 *Tim.* 3. 7. fall into reproach and the *snare* of the devil
 6. 9. desire to be rich fall into a temptation and a *snare*
2 *Tim.* 2. 26. recover themselves out of the s. of the devil

Snatch.—*A.V.* ¹*pluck.*
Jno. 10. 28. no one shall ¹*snatch* them out of my hand
 29. no one is able to ¹s. them out of the Father's hand

Snatcheth.—*A.V.* ¹*catcheth.*
Mat. 13. 19. cometh the evil one, and ¹s. away that which
Jno. 10. 12. wolf ¹*snatcheth* them, and scattereth them

Snatching.—*A.V.* ¹*pulling.*
Jude 23. some save, ¹*snatching* them out of the fire

Snow.
Mat. 28. 3. [angel] his raiment white as *snow*
Rev. 1. 14. his head and his hair were—white as *snow*

SOLD

Sober.—*A.V.* ¹*watch.*
2 *Cor.* 5 13. whether we are of *sober* mind, it is unto you
1 *Thes.* 5. 6. let us not sleep—but let us watch and be *sober*
 8. But let us, since we are of the day, be *sober*
2 *Tim.* 4. 5. be thou ¹*sober* in all things, suffer hardship
1 *Pet.* 1. 13. girding up the loins of your mind, be *sober*
 4. 7. of sound mind, and be ¹*sober* unto prayer
 5. 8. Be *sober,* be watchful : your adversary the devil
see soberminded, temperate.

Soberly.
Rom. 12. 3. but so to think as to think s., according as God
Tit. 2. 12. we should live *soberly* and righteously

Soberminded.—*A.V.* ¹*sober.*
1 *Tim.* 3. 2. The bishop therefore must be—¹s. *Tit.* 1. ¹⁸
Tit. 2. 2. aged men be temperate, grave, ¹*soberminded*
 5. to be ¹*soberminded,* chaste, workers at home
 6. younger men likewise exhort to be *soberminded*

Soberness.
Acts 26. 25. but speak forth words of truth and *soberness*

Sobriety.
1 *Tim.* 2. 9. modest apparel, with shamefastness and s.
 15. if they continue in faith and love—with *sobriety*

Soft.
Mat. 11. 8. out for to see? a man clothed in *soft* raiment?
 Behold, they that wear *soft* raiment. *Lu.* 7. 25

Softly.
Acts 27. 13. And when the south wind blew *softly*

Sojourn—ed.—*A.V.* ¹*dwelt,* ²*stranger.*
Lu. 24. 18. Dost thou alone ²*sojourn* in Jerusalem
Acts 7. 6. that his seed should *sojourn* in a strange land
 13. 17. the people when they ¹s. in the land of Egypt
see sojourner.

Sojourner—s.—*A.V.* ¹*foreigners,* ²*sojourned,* ³*stranger—s.*
Acts 2. 10. ³s. from Rome, both Jews and proselytes
 7. 29. Moses fled—and became a ³s. in the land of Midian
Eph. 2. 19. So then ye are no more strangers and ¹*sojourners*
Heb. 11. 9. By faith he became a ²s. in the land of promise
1 *Pet.* 1. 1. elect who are ³*sojourners* of the Dispersion
 2. 11. I beseech you as ³*sojourners* and pilgrims

Sojourning.—*A.V.* ¹*journey.*
Mk. 13. 34. It is when a man, ¹*sojourning* in another country
Acts 17. 21. all the Athenians and the strangers s. there
1 *Pet.* 1. 17. pass the time of your *sojourning* in fear

Sold.
Mat. 10. 29. Are not two sparrows *sold* for a farthing?
 13. 46. went and *sold* all that he had, and bought it
 18. 25. his lord commanded him to be *sold,* and his wife
 21. 12. that *sold* and bought—seats of them that *sold* the doves. *Mk.* 11. 15 ; *Lu.* 19. 45 : *Jno.* 2. 16
 26. 9. have been *sold* for much. *Mk.* 14. 5 : *Jno.* 12. 5
Lu. 12. 6. Are not five sparrows *sold* for two farthings?
 17. 28. they bought, they *sold,* they planted
Jno. 12. 6. found in the temple those that *sold* oxen
Acts 2. 45. they *sold* their possessions and goods
 4. 34. possessors of lands or houses *sold* them, and brought the prices of the things that were *sold*

SOLD

Acts 4. 37. [Barnabas] having a field, *sold* it, and brought
5. 1. Ananias, with Sapphira his wife, *sold* a possession
4. after it was *sold*, was it not in thy power?
8. Tell me whether ye *sold* the land for so much
Rom. 7. 14. the law is spiritual: but I am carnal, *s.* under sin
1 *Cor.* 10. 25. Whatsoever is *sold* in the shambles, eat
Heb. 12. 16. Esau, who for one mess of meat *sold* his own

Soldier.—*A.V.* ¹*executioner.*

Mk. 6. 27. straightway the king sent forth a ¹*soldier*
Jno. 19. 23. made four parts, to every *soldier* a part
Acts 10. 7. a devout *soldier* of them that waited on him
28. 16. Paul was suffered to abide by himself with the *s.*
2 *Tim.* 2. 3. Suffer—as a good *soldier* of Christ Jesus
4. that he may please him who enrolled him as a *soldier*

Soldiers.—*A.V.* ¹*army,* ²*men,* ³*men of war.*

Mat. 8. 9. having under myself *soldiers. Lu.* 7. 8
28. 12. they gave large money unto the *soldiers*
Mk. 15. 16. the *soldiers* led him away. *Mat.* 27. 27
Lu. 3 14. *s.* also asked him, saying, And we, what must
23. 11. Herod with his ³*s.* set him at nought [Jesus]
36. the *soldiers* also mocked him, coming to him
Jno. 18. 3. Judas—having received the band of ²*soldiers*
19. 2. And the *soldiers* plaited a crown of thorns
23. The *s.* therefore, when they had crucified Jesus
24. These things therefore the *soldiers* did
32. The *s.* therefore came, and brake the legs of the first
34. one of the *soldiers* with a spear pierced his side
Acts 12. 4. four quaternions of *soldiers* to guard him
6. Peter was sleeping between two *soldiers*
18. there was no small stir among the *soldiers*
21. 32. took *soldiers*—when they saw—the *soldiers*
35. he was borne of the *s.* for the violence of the crowd
23. 10. commanded the *s.* to go down and take him
23. Make ready two hundred *soldiers* to go as far as
27. [Lysias] I came upon with the ¹*s.*, and rescued
31. So the *s.*, as it was commanded them, took Paul
27. 31. Paul said to the centurion and to the *soldiers*
32. Then the *soldiers* cut away the ropes of the boat
42. And the *soldiers'* counsel was to kill the prisoners

Solid.—*A.V.* ¹*strong.*

Heb. 5. 12. such as have need of milk, and not of ¹*solid* food
14. But ¹*solid* food is for fullgrown men

Solitary *A.V.*—*see desert place.*

Some.—*A.V.* ¹*divers.*

Mk. 8. 3. and ¹*some* of them are come from far
Acts 19. 9. when ¹*some* were hardened and disobedient

Somebody.

Acts 5. 36. rose up Theudas, giving himself out to be *s.*
see someone.

Some one.—*A.V.* ¹*somebody.*

Lu. 8. 46. But Jesus said, ¹*Some one* did touch me

Something.—*A.V.* ¹*certain thing,* ²*meat.*

Mk. 5. 43. and he commanded that *something* should be
given her to eat. *Lu.* 8. ²55
Acts 23. 17. unto the chief captain: for he hath ¹*s.* to tell
Gal. 6. 3. For if a man thinketh himself to be *something*

Sometime—s *A.V.*—*see aforetime, time past, once.*

SON

Somewhat.

Gal. 2. 6. from those who were reputed to be *somewhat*
Heb. 8. 3. that this high priest also have *s.* to offer

Somewhere.—*A.V.* ¹*certain place.*

Heb. 2. 6. one hath ¹*s.* testified, saying, What is man
4. 4. For he hath said ¹*somewhere* of the seventh day

Son.—*A.V.* ¹*child.*

Mat. 1. 1. Jesus Christ, the *son* of David, the *s.* of Abraham
21. And she shall bring forth a *son.* 23: *Lu.* 1, 31
10. 37. he that loveth *son* or daughter more than me
11. 27. no one knoweth the *Son*, save the Father—the
Father, save the *Son*, and he to whomsoever the
Son willeth to reveal him. *Lu.* 10. 22
13. 55. Is not this the carpenter's *son* ?
21. 28. and said, *Son*, go work to-day in the vineyard
38. the husbandmen, when they saw the *son*, said
22. 42. What think ye of the Christ? whose *son* is he?
They say unto him, The *son* of David (yourselves
23. 15. ye make him twofold more a ¹*son* of hell than
Mk. 2. 5. *Son*, thy sins are forgiven. *Mat.* 9. 2
6. 3. Is not this the carpenter, the *son* of Mary
12. 6. Ho had yet one, a beloved *son* : he sent him last
13. 32. knoweth no one—neither the *Son*, but the Father
14. 61. Art thou the Christ, the *Son* of the Blessed?
Lu. 1. 13. thy wife Elisabeth shall bear thee a *son*
32. and shall be called the *Son* of the Most High
36. Elisabeth—also hath conceived a *son* in her old age
57. Elisabeth's time—and she brought forth a *son*
2. 48. *Son*, why hast thou thus dealt with us?
3. 23. being the *son* (as was supposed) of Joseph
4. 22. Is not this Joseph's *son* ? *Jno.* 6. 42
7. 12. the only *son* of his mother, and she was a widow
10. 6. if a son of peace be there, your peace shall rest
11. 11. which of you that is a father shall *son* ask a loaf
12. 53. divided, father against *son*, and *son* against father
15. 13. the younger *son* gathered all together
21. *son* said—no more worthy to be called thy *son*
31. *S.*, thou art ever with me, and all that is mine is thine
16. 25. *Son*, remember that thou in thy lifetime
19. 9. forasmuch as he also is a *son* of Abraham
Jno. 1. 18. the only begotten *Son*, which is in the bosom
45. prophets—write, Jesus of Nazareth, the *s.* of Joseph
3. 17. For God sent not the *Son* into the world to judge
35. The Father loveth the *Son.* 5. 20
36. He that believeth on the *Son* hath eternal life; but
he that obeyeth not the *Son* shall not see life
4. 46. nobleman, whose *son* was sick at Capernaum
5. 19. The *Son* can do nothing of himself—these the *Son*
21. the *Son* also quickeneth whom he will [also doeth
22. but he hath given all judgement unto the *Son*
23. that all may honour the *Son*—He that honoureth
not the *Son* honoureth not the Father
26. so gave he to the *Son* also to have life in himself
6. 40. every one that beholdeth the *Son*, and believeth
8. 35. bondservant abideth not—the *son* abideth for ever
36. If therefore the *Son* shall make you free
9. 19. Is this your *son*, who ye say was born blind? 20
14. 13. that the Father may be glorified in the *Son*
17. 1. glorify thy *Son*, that the *Son* may glorify thee
12. not one of them perished, but the *son* of perdition
21. 15. Simon, *son* of John, lovest thou me. 16, 17
Acts 4. 36. Barnabas—(*Son* of exhortation), is
7. 21. and nourished him [Moses] for her own *son* [ness
13. 10. thou ¹*son* of the devil, thou enemy of all righteous-
22. and said, I have found David the *son* of Jesse

SON

Acts 23. 6. Paul—Brethren, I am a Pharisee, a *s.* of Pharisees
16. Paul's sister's *son* heard of their lying in wait
Rom. 9. 9. this season will I come, and Sarah shall have a *s.*
1 *Cor.* 15. 28. shall the *Son* also himself be subjected to him
Gal. 4. 7. no longer a bondservant, but a *son*; and if a *son*
Col. 1. 13. us into the kingdom of the *Son* of his love
2 *Th.* 2. 3. the man of sin be revealed, the *son* of perdition
Heb. 1. 5. I will be to him a Father—he shall he to me a *S.?*
    8. of the *Son* he saith, Thy throne, O God, is for ever
3. 6. Christ as a *son*, over his house; whose house are we
5. 8. though he was a *Son*, yet learned obedience
7. 28. appointeth a *Son*, perfected for evermore
11. 24. the Father hath sent the *Son* to be called the *son* of Pharoh's
12. 6. scourgeth every *son* whom he receiveth [daughter
    7. what *son* is there whom his father chasteneth not?
2 *Pet.* 2. 15. followed the way of Balaam the *son* of Beor
1 *Jno.* 2. 22. even he that denieth the Father and the *Son*
23. Whosoever denieth the *S.*—he that confesseth the *S.*
24. ye also shall abide in the *Son*, and in the Father
4. 14. the Father hath sent the *Son* to be the Saviour
5. 12. He that hath the *Son* hath the life
2 *Jno.* 3. Jesus Christ, the *S.* of the Father, in truth and love
    9. the same hath both the Father and the *Son*
    see child, cousin.

His Son.

Mat. 7. 9. if *his son* shall ask him for a loaf. *Lu.* 11. 11
21. 37. But afterward he sent unto them *his son*
22. 2. certain king—made a marriage feast for *his son*
45. Lord, how is he *his son?* *Mk.* 12. 37: *Lu.* 20. 44
Lu. 15. 25. Now *his elder son* was in the field
Jno. 3. 16. the world, that he gave *his* only begotten *Son*
4. 5. ground that Jacob gave to *his son* Joseph
47. that he would come down, and heal *his son*
51. his servants met him, saying, that *his son* lived
Rom. 1. 9. I serve in my spirit in the gospel of *his Son*
5. 10. reconciled to God through the death of *his Son*
8. 3. God, sending *his own Son* in the likeness
29. foreordained to be conformed to the image of *his S.*
32. He that spared not *his own Son*, but delivered him
1 *Cor.* 1. 9. ye were called into the fellowship of *his Son*
Gal. 1. 16. to reveal *his Son* in me, that I might preach
4. 4. God sent forth *his Son*, born of a woman
6. God sent forth the Spirit of *his Son* into our hearts
1 *Th.* 1. 10. to wait for *his Son* from heaven
Heb. 1. 2. spoken unto us in *his Son*, whom he appointed
11. 17. Abraham—offering up *his* only begotten *son*
Jas. 2. 21. he offered up Isaac *his son* upon the altar?
1 *Jno.* 1. 3. fellowship—and with *his Son* Jesus Christ
7. the blood of Jesus *his Son* cleanseth us from all sin
3. 23. believe in the name of *his Son* Jesus Christ
4. 9. God hath sent *his* only begotten *Son* into the world
10. sent *his Son* to be the propitiation for our sins
5. 9. that he hath borne witness concerning *his Son* 10
11. God gave—us eternal life, and this life is in *his Son*
20. are in him that is true, even in *his Son* Jesus Christ
    see servant.

My Son.

Mat. 2. 15. Out of Egypt did I call *my son*
3. 17. This is *my* beloved *S.* 17. 5: *Mk.* 1. 11: 9. 7: *Lu.* 3.
17. 15. Lord, have mercy on *my son* [22: 9. 35: 2 *Pet.* 1. 17
21. 37. They will reverence *my son*. *Mk.* 12. 6
Mk. 9. 17. Master, I brought unto thee *my son*
Lu. 9. 38. Master, I beseech thee to look upon *my son*
15. 24. this *my son* was dead, and is alive again
20. 13. What shall I do? I will send *my* beloved *son*
Heb. 12. 5. *My son*, regard not lightly the chastening
Rev. 21. 7. I will be his God, and he shall be *my son*

Thy Son.

Lu. 9. 41. with you, and bear with you? bring hither *thy s.*
15. 19. no more worthy to be called *thy son.* 21
30. but when this *thy son* came, which hath devoured
Jno. 4. 50. Go thy way; *thy son* liveth. 53
17. 1. glorify *thy Son*, that the Son may glorify thee
19. 26. he saith unto his mother, Woman, behold, *thy son!*

Son of God.—*see proper names.*

Son of Man.—*see p.* 210.

Song.

Rev. 5. 9. they sing a new *song*, saying, Worthy art thou
14. 3. they sing as it were a new *song* before the throne
    —and no man could learn the *song*
15. 3. the *song* of Moses—and the *song* of the Lamb

Songs.

Eph. 5. 19. psalms and hymns and spiritual *s. Col.* 3. 16

Sons.—*A.V.* ¹*children.*

Mat. 5. 45. that ye may be ¹*s.* of your Father which is in
8. 12. the ¹*s.* of the kingdom shall be cast forth [heaven
9. 15. Can the ¹*sons* of the bride-chamber mourn [11. 19
12. 27. devils, by whom do your ¹*s.* cast them out? *Lu.*
13. 38. these are the ¹*sons* of the kingdom; and the tares
    are the ¹*sons* of the evil one
17. 25. toll or tribute? from their ¹*s.*, or from strangers?
26. Jesus said unto him, Therefore the ¹*sons* are free
20. 20. the mother of the ¹*sons* of Zebedee with her *sons*
21. Command that these my two *sons* may sit
21. 28. A man had two *sons*. *Lu.* 15. 11
23. 31. ye are the ¹*sons* of them that slew the prophets
26. 37. took with him Peter and the two *sons* of Zebedee
Mk. 3. 17. Boanerges, which is, *Sons* of thunder
Lu. 6. 35. ye shall be ¹*sons* of the Most High
16. 8. ¹*sons* of this world—wiser than the ¹*sons* of the light
20. 34. The ¹*sons* of this world marry, and are given in
36. ¹*sons* of God, being ¹*sons* of the resurrection [*sons*
Jno. 4. 12. our father Jacob—drank thereof himself, and his
12. 36. believe on the light, that ye may become ¹*s.* of light
Acts 3. 25. Ye are the ¹*sons* of the prophets
7. 29. in the land of Midian, where he begat two *sons*
19. 14. there were seven *sons* of one Sceva, a Jew
Gal. 3. 7. which be of faith, the same are ¹*s.* of Abraham
4. 5. that we might receive the adoption of *sons*
6. because ye are *sons*, God sent forth the Spirit
22 Abraham had two *sons*, one by the handmaid
Eph. 1. 5. having foreordained us unto adoption as ¹*sons*
2. 2 the spirit that now worketh in the ¹*s.* of disobedience
5. 6. cometh the wrath of God upon the ¹*s.* of disobedience.
1 *Th.* 5. 5. ye are all ¹*s.* of light, and ¹*s.* of the day [*Col.* 3. 16
Heb. 2. 10. it became him—in bringing many *s.* unto glory
11. 21. Jacob—dying, blessed each of the *sons* of Joseph
12. 5. exhortation, which reasoneth with you as with ¹*s.*
7. God dealeth with you as with *sons*
8. without chastening—then are ye bastards, and not *s.*
    see children, daughters.

Sons of God.—*A.V.* ¹*children of God.*

Mat. 5. 9. peacemakers: for they shall be called ¹*s.* of God
Lu. 20. 36. ¹*sons of God*, being sons of the resurrection
Rom. 8. 14. led by the Spirit of God, these are *sons of God*
19. waiteth for the revealing of the *sons of God*
9. 26. There shall they be called ¹*sons of the living God*
Gal. 3. 26. ye are all ¹*sons of God*, through faith, in Christ
    see children of God.

SOON

Soon.
Phil. 2. 23. I hope to send forthwith, so *soon* as I shall see
Tit. 1. 7. not selfwilled, not *soon* angry, no brawler
 see immediate, immediately, quickly.

Sooner.
Heb. 13. 19. that I may be restored to you the *sooner*

Soothsaying.
Acts 16. 16. brought her masters much gain by *soothsaying*

Sop.
Jno. 13. 26. He it is, for whom I shall dip the *sop*—when he
 had dipped the *s.*, he taketh and giveth it to Judas
 27. after the *sop*, then entered Satan into him
 30. He then having received the *s.* went out straightway

Sorcerer—s.
Acts 13. 6. they found a certain *sorcerer*—Bar-Jesus
 8. But Elymas the *sorcerer*—withstood them
Rev. 21. 8. and *s.*, and idolaters, and all liars, their part
 22. 15. Without are the dogs, and the *sorcerers*

Sorceries.
Acts 8. 11. long time he had amazed them with his *s.*
Rev. 9. 21. repented not of their murders, nor of their *s.*
 see sorcery.

Sorcery.—*A.V.* ¹*sorceries,* ²*witchcraft.*
Acts 8. 9. Simon—which beforetime in the city used *s.*
Gal. 5. 20. idolatry, ²*sorcery,* enmities, strife
Rev. 18. 23. with thy ¹*sorcery* were all the nations deceived

Sore.—*A.V.* ¹*very.*
Mat. 26. 37. began to be sorrowful and ¹*s.* troubled. *Mk.* 14.
Mk. 6. 51. and they were amazed in themselves [133
Acts 20. 37. they all wept *sore*, and fell on Paul's neck
Rev. 16. 2. became a noisome and grievous *s.* upon the men
 see grievously, moved.

Sorely.
Lu. 9. 39. hardly departeth from him, bruising him *sorely*

Sorer.
Heb. 10. 29. of how much *sorer* punishment, think ye

Sores.
Lu. 16. 20. Lazarus was laid at his gate, full of *sores*
 21. yea, even the dogs came and licked his *sores*
Rev. 16. 11. because of their pains and their *sores*

Sorrow.—*A.V.* ¹*grief,* ²*grieved,* ³*heaviness.*
Lu. 22. 45. the disciples, and found them sleeping for *s.*
Jno. 16. 6. because I have spoken—*s.* hath filled your heart
 20. but your *sorrow* shall be turned into joy
 21. A woman when she is in travail hath *sorrow*
 22. ye therefore now have *sorrow* : but I will see you
Rom. 9. 2. I have great *sorrow* and unceasing pain
2 *Cor.* 2. 1. I would not come again to you with ³*sorrow*
 3. I should have *s.* from them of whom I ought to rejoice
 5. if any hath caused ¹*sorrow*, he hath caused ²*sorrow*
 7. swallowed up with his overmuch *sorrow* [death
 7. 10. godly *s.* worketh repentance—the *s.* of the world—
Phil. 2. 27. that I might not have *sorrow* upon *sorrow*
1 *Th.* 4. 13. that ye *sorrow* not, even as the rest
 see mourning, pain.

SOUGHT

Sorrowed *A.V.*—*see sorry.*

Sorrowful.—*A.V.* ¹*grieved.*
Mat. 19. 22. he went away *s. Mk.* 10. ¹22; *Lu.* 18. 23
 26. 22. they were exceeding *sorrowful. Mk.* 14. 19
 37. and began to be *sorrowful* and sore troubled
 38. My soul is exceeding *s.*, even unto death. *Mk.* 14. 34
Jno. 16. 20. ye shall be *sorrowful*, but your sorrow shall be
2 *Cor.* 6. 10. as *sorrowful*, yet alway rejoicing
Phil. 2. 28. ye may rejoice, and that I may be the less *s.*

Sorrowing.
Lu. 2. 48. thy father and I sought thee *sorrowing*
Acts 20. 38. *s.* most of all for the word which he had spoken

Sorrows.
1 *Tim.* 6. 10. pierced themselves through with many *s.*
 see travail.

Sorry.—*A.V.* ¹*grieved,* ²*sorrowed.*
Mat. 17. 23. And they were exceeding *sorry*
 18. 31. saw what was done, they were exceeding *sorry*
Mk. 6. 26. And the king was exceeding *sorry*
2 *Cor.* 2. 2. For if I make you *s.*—he that is made *s.* by me ?
 4. not that ye should be made ¹*sorry*, but that ye might
 7. 8. though I made you *sorry* with my epistle—I see
 that that epistle made you *sorry*
 9. I rejoice, not that ye were made *sorry*—made ²*s.* unto
 repentance—were made *s.* after a godly sort. ²11
 see grieved, sorrowed.

Sort.—*A.V.* ¹*manner.*
1 *Cor.* 3. 13. prove each man's work of what *sort* it is
2 *Cor.* 7. 9. were made sorry after a godly ¹*sort.* 11

Sought.—*A.V.* ¹*affected,* ²*desired,* ³*endeavoured,* ⁴*enquired,* ⁵*seek.*
Mat. 2. 20. they are dead that *s.* the young child's life
 21. 46. they *s.* to lay hold on him. *Mk.* 12. 12; *Lu.* 20. 19
 26. 16. [Judas] *s.* opportunity to. *Mk.* 14. 11: *Lu.* 22. 6
 59. council *s.* false witness against Jesus. *Mk.* 14. 55
Mk. 11. 18. *s.* how they might destroy him. 14. 1 ; *Lu.* 19.
Lu. 2. 44. they *s.* for him among their kinsfolk. [47 ; 22. 2
 48. thy father and I *sought* thee sorrowing
 49. How is it that ye *s.* me ? wist ye not that I must be
 4. 42. into a desert place : and the multitudes *s.* after him
 5. 18. man that was palsied : and they *s.* to bring him in
 6. 19. And all the multitude *sought* to touch him
 9. 9. he [Herod] ²*sought* to see him
 11. 16. tempting him, *sought* of him a sign from heaven
 19. 3. [Zacchæus] *sought* to see Jesus who he was
Jno. 5. 18. the Jews *sought* the more to kill him
 7. 11. The Jews therefore *sought* him at the feast
 30. They *sought* therefore to take him. 10. 39
 11. 56. They *sought* therefore for Jesus, and spake
 19. 12. Upon this Pilate *sought* to release him
Acts 12. 19. when Herod had *s.* for him, and found him not
 13. 7. Barnabas and Saul, and ⁴*s.* to hear the word of God
 16. 10. straightway we ²*s.* to go forth into Macedonia
 17. 5. they *sought* to bring them together to the people
Rom. 9. 32. Because they *sought* it not by faith
 10. 20. I was found of them that *sought* me not
Gal. 2. 17. while we ⁵*sought* to be justified in Christ
 4. 18. it is good to be zealously ¹*sought* in a good matter
2 *Tim.* 1. 17. when he was in Rome, he *s.* me diligently
Heb. 8. 7. then would no place have been *s.* for a second
 12. 17. though he *sought* it diligently with tears
1 *Pet.* 1. 10. which salvation the prophets ⁴*s.*, and searched
 see measure, seeking.

315

SOUL

Soul.
Mat. 10. 28. not able to kill the *soul*—destroy both *soul*
12. 18. My beloved in whom my *soul* is well pleased
22. 37. love the Lord—with all thy *s*. *Mk*. 12. 30: *Lu*. 10
26. 38. My *s*. is exceeding sorrowful. *Mk*. 14. 34 [27
Lu. 1. 46. My *soul* doth magnify the Lord
2. 35. yea and a sword shall pierce through thine own *s*.
12. 19. I will say to my *soul*, Soul, thou hast much goods
20. Thou foolish one, this night is thy *s*. required of thee
Jno. 12. 27. Now is my *s*. troubled; and what shall I say?
Acts 2. 27. Because thou wilt not leave my *soul* in Hades
43. fear came upon every *soul* : and many wonders
3. 23. every *soul*, which shall not hearken to that prophet
4. 32. them that believed were of one heart and *soul*
Rom. 2. 9. anguish, upon every *s*. of man that worketh evil
13. 1. Let every *s*. be in subjection to the higher powers
2 *Cor*. 1. 23. I call God for a witness upon my *soul*
1 *Th*. 5. 23. your spirit and *s*. and body be preserved entire
Heb. 4. 12. and piercing even to the dividing of *s*. and spirit
6. 19. which we have as an anchor of the *soul*, a hope
10. 38. shrink back, my *soul* hath no pleasure in him
39. of them that have faith unto the saving of the *soul*
Jas. 5. 20. shall save a *soul* from death, and shall cover
1 *Pet*. 2. 11. fleshly lusts, which war against the *soul*
2 *Pet*. 2. 8. vexed his righteous *soul* from day to day
3 *Jno*. 2. and be in health, even as thy *soul* prospereth
Rev. 16. 3. every living *soul* died, even the things that were
18. 14. the fruits which thy *soul* lusted after are gone
see life.

Souls.—*A. V.* ¹*minds.*
Mat. 11. 29. and ye shall find rest unto your *souls*
Lu. 21. 19. In your patience ye shall win your *souls*
Acts 2. 41. added unto them—about three thousand *souls*
7. 14. and all his kindred, threescore and fifteen *souls*
14. 2. Jews that were disobedient stirred up the ¹*s*. of the
22. confirming the *souls* of the disciples [Gentiles
15. 24. troubled you with words, subverting your *souls*
27. 37. in the ship two hundred threescore and sixteen *s*
1 *Th*. 2. 8. not the gospel of God only, but also our own *s*.
Heb. 12. 3. that ye wax not weary, fainting in your ¹*souls*
13. 17. for they watch in behalf of your *souls*
Jas. 1. 21. word, which is able to save your *souls*
1 *Pet*. 1. 9. end of your faith, even the salvation of your *s*.
22. Seeing ye have purified your *souls* in your obedience
2. 25. returned unto the Shepherd and Bishop of your *s*.
3. 20. wherein few, that is, eight *souls*, were saved
4. 19. commit their *s* in well-doing unto a faithful Creator
2 *Pet*. 2. 14. cannot cease from sin; enticing unstedfast *s*.
Rev. 6. 9. underneath the altar the *s*.—that had been slain
18. 13. and chariots and slaves; and *souls* of men
20. 4. I saw the *souls* of them that had been beheaded

Sound.—*A. V.* ¹*noised abroad,* ²*wholesome.*
Mat. 6. 2. thou doest alms, *sound* not a trumpet before thee
24. 31. he shall send forth his angels with a great *sound*
Lu. 15. 27. because he hath received him safe and *sound*
Acts 2. 2. came from heaven a *sound* as of the rushing
6. when this ¹*s*. was heard, the multitude came together
Rom. 10. 18. Their *sound* went out into all the earth
1 *Cor*. 15. 52. for the trumpet shall *sound*, and the dead
1 *Tim*. 1. 10. any other thing contrary to the *s*. doctrine
6. 3. a different doctrine, and consenteth not to ²*s*. words
2 *Tim*. 1. 13. Hold the pattern of *sound* words
4. 3. come when they will not endure the *sound* doctrine
Tit. 1. 9. may be able both to exhort in the *sound* doctrine
13. reprove them sharply, that they may be *s*. in the faith
2. 1. speak—the things which befit the *sound* doctrine

SOWEST

Tit. 2. 2. aged men be temperate—*sound* in faith, in love
8. *sound* speech, that cannot be condemned
Heb. 12. 19. *sound* of a trumpet, and the voice of words
1 *Pet*. 4. 7. be ye therefore of *sound* mind, and be sober
Rev. 8. 6. seven angels—prepared themselves to *sound*
13. trumpet of the three angels, who are yet to *sound*
9. 9. the *s*. of their wings was as the *sound* of chariots
10. 7. seventh angel, when he is about to *sound*
see discipline, voice.

Sounded.
Acts 27. 28. they *sounded*, and found twenty fathoms—
they *sounded* again, and found fifteen fathoms
1 *Th*. 1. 8. For from you hath *sounded* forth the word
Rev. 8. 7. the first *sounded*, and there followed hail
8. And the second angel *sounded*. 10. third angel *s*.
12. fourth angel *sounded*. 9. 1. fifth angel *sounded*
13. sixth angel *sounded*. 11. 15. seventh angel *sounded*

Sounding.
1 *Cor*. 13. 1. but have not love, I am become *sounding* brass

Soundness.
Acts 3. 16. given him this perfect *soundness* in the presence

Sounds.
1 *Cor*. 14. 7. if they give not a distinction in the *sounds*

South.
Mat. 12. 42. The queen of the *south* shall rise up. *Lu*. 11. 31
Lu. 12. 55. when ye see a *south* wind blowing, ye say
13. 29. and from the north and *south*, and shall sit down
Acts 8. 26. Arise, and go toward the *south* unto the way
27. 13. And when the *south* wind blew softly
Rev. 21. 13. the north three gates; and on the *s*. three gates

South-east.—*A. V.* ¹*south-west.*
Acts 27. 12. haven of Crete, looking north-east and ¹*s*.

Sow.
2 *Pet*. 2. 22. and the *sow* that had washed to wallowing

Sow.—*A. V.* ¹*sown*
Mat. 6. 26. the birds of the heaven, that they *sow* not
13. 3. the sower went forth to *sow*. *Mk*. 4. 3: *Lu*. 8. 5
27. Sir, didst thou not *sow* good seed in thy field?
25. 24. reaping where thou didst not ¹*sow*. *Lu*. 19. 21, 22
Lu. 12. 24. Consider the ravens, that they *sow* not

Sowed.—*A. V.* ¹*sown.*
Mat. 13. 4. as he *sowed*, some seeds fell by the way side.
Mk. 4. 4: *Lu*. 8. 5
24. unto a man that *sowed* good seed in his field
25. his enemy came and *sowed* tares. 39
31. grain of mustard seed, which a man took, and *sowed*
25. 26. thou knowest that I reap where I *sowed* not
1 *Cor*. 9. 11. If we ¹*sowed* unto you spiritual things

Sower.
Mat. 13. 3. the *sower* went forth to sow. *Mk*. 4. 3: *Lu*. 8. 5
18. Hear then ye the parable of the *sower*
Mk. 4. 14. The *sower* soweth the word
2 *Cor*. 9. 10. that supplieth seed to the *sower* and bread

Sowest.
1 *Cor*. 15. 36. that which thou thyself *s*. is not quickened
37. thou *sowest*, thou *sowest* not the body that shall be

SOWETH

Soweth.
Mat. 13. 37. He that *soweth* the good seed is the Son of man
Mk. 4. 14. The sower *soweth* the word
Jno. 4. 36. he that *soweth* and he that reapeth may rejoice
37. One *soweth*, and another reapeth
2 Cor. 9. 6. He that *soweth* sparingly—he that s. bountifully
Gal. 6. 7. whatsoever a man *soweth*, that shall he also reap
8. *soweth* unto his own flesh—*soweth* unto the Spirit

Sowing.—A.V. ¹*sown*.
2 Cor. 9. 10. shall supply and multiply your seed for ¹*sowing*

Sown.—A.V. ¹*received seed*.
Mat. 13. 19. s. in his heart—¹s. by the way side. Mk. 4. 15
20. he that was ¹s. upon the rocky places. Mk. 4. 16
22. he that was ¹*sown* among the thorns. Mk. 4. 18
23. he that was ¹*sown* upon the good ground. Mk. 4. 20
Mk. 4. 31. when it is s. upon the earth, though it be less. 32
1 Cor. 15. 42. It is *sown* in corruption; it is raised in
43. it is *sown* in dishonour—it is *sown* in weakness
44. it is *sown* a natural body; it is raised a spiritual
Jas. 3. 18. And the fruit of righteousness is *sown* in peace
  see sow, sowed, sowing.

Space.
Lu. 22. 59. after the *space* of about one hour another
Acts 1. 3. appearing unto them by the *space* of forty days
5. 7. the *space* of three hours after, when his wife
13. 21. tribe of Benjamin, for the *space* of forty years
19. 8. spake boldly for the *space* of three months
10. and this continued for the *space* of two years
34. all with one voice about the *space* of two hours cried
20. 31. that by the *space* of three years I ceased not
Rev. 8. 1. silence in heaven about the *space* of half an hour
  see far, little while, time, while.

Spake.—A.V. ¹*preached*, ²*prevented*, ³*said*, ⁴*speaking*, ⁵*spoken*, ⁶*talked*, ⁷*waxed bold*.
Mat. 9. 18. While he *spake*. 26. 47; Mk. 5. 35; 14. 43;
  Lu. 8. 49; 11. 37; 22. 47, 60 [Lu. 11. 14
33. devil was cast out, the dumb man *spake*. 12. 22;
16. 11. I *spake* not to you concerning bread? [Simon?
17. 25. Jesus ²s. first to him, saying, What thinkest thou
21. 45. Pharisees—perceived that he *spake* of them
Mk. 2. 2. about the door: and he ¹s. the word unto them
6. 50. ⁶*spake* with them, and saith—Be of good cheer
7. 35. his tongue was loosed, and he *spake* plain
8. 32. and he *spake* the saying openly
12. 12. perceived that he *spake* the parable against them
26. how God *spake* unto him, saying, I am the God of
Lu. 1. 55. (As he *spake* unto our fathers)
70. (As he *spake* by the mouth of his holy prophets
2. 38. gave thanks unto God, and *spake* of him to all
50. understood not the saying which he *spake*
4. 36. they *spake* together, one with another, saying
7. 39. *spake* within himself, saying, This man, if he were
9. 11. and *spake* to them of the kingdom of God
31. s. of his decease which he was about to accomplish
22. 65. And many other things *spake* they against him
23. 20. Pilate *spake* unto them again, desiring to release
24. 6. remember how he *spake* unto you, when he was yet
32. not our heart burning within us, while he ⁶*spake*
36. as they *spake* these things, he himself stood
44. These are my words which I *spake* unto you
Jno. 2. 22. his disciples remembered that he ³*spake* this
4. 50. The man believed the word that Jesus ⁵*spake*

SPAT

Jno. 7. 13. no man *spake* openly of him for fear of the Jews
39. But this *spake* he of the Spirit, which they that
46. The officers answered, Never man so *spake*
8. 27. perceived not that he *spake* to them of the Father
10. 6. This parable *spake* Jesus unto them—understood
  not what things they were which he *spake*
41. whatsoever John *spake* of this man were true
11. 11. These things ³*spake* he: and after this he saith
13. they thought that he ⁵*spake* of taking rest in sleep
12. 38. might be fulfilled, which he *spake*. 18. 9, 32
41. Isaiah, because he saw his glory; and he s. of him
48. the word that I ⁵*spake*, the same shall judge him
49. For I ²*spake* not from myself; but the Father which
13. 22. looked one on another, doubting of whom he s.
28. no man at the table knew for what intent he *spake*
18. 20. taught in synagogues—and in secret ³s. I nothing
21. 19. this he *spake*, signifying by what manner of death
Acts 3. 21. whereof God ⁵s. by the mouth of his holy prophets
6. 10. the wisdom and the Spirit by which he *spake*
7. 6. God *spake* on this wise, that his seed should sojourn
9. 29. he *spake* and disputed against the Grecian Jews
10. 44. While Peter yet s. these words, the Holy Ghost
13. 46. Paul and Barnabas ⁷*spake* out boldly, and said
14. 1. so *spake*, that a great multitude both of Jews
22. 9. they heard not the voice of him that *spake* to me
26. 31. they ⁶*spake* one to another, saying, This man
28. 25. Well *spake* the Holy Ghost by Isaiah the prophet
1 Cor. 13. 11. When I was a child, I *spake* as a child
2 Cor. 7. 14. but as we *spake* all things to you in truth
Heb. 7. 14. as to which tribe Moses s. nothing concerning
13. 7. rule over you, which ⁵s. unto you the word of God
Jas. 5. 10. the prophets who ⁶*spake* in the name of the Lord
2 Pet. 1. 21. men s. from God, being moved by the Holy
2. 16. a dumb ass ⁴*spake* with man's voice and stayed the
Rev. 1. 12. I turned to see the voice which *spake* with me
13. 11. horns like unto a lamb, and he *spake* as a dragon
17. 1. voice that had the seven bowls, and ⁶s. 21. 60, ⁶15
  see contradicted, defence, Lord or God (proper names), he said, I said, speak, speaketh, speaking, spoken.

Spare.
Lu. 15. 17. bread enough and to *spare*, and I perish
Rom. 11. 21. natural branches, neither will he *spare* thee
1 Cor. 7. 28. have tribulation in the flesh: and I would s. you
2 Cor. 1. 23. that to *spare* you I forbare to come unto Corinth
13. 2. that, if I come again, I will not *spare*

Spared.
Rom. 8. 32. He that *spared* not his own Son
11. 21. if God *spared* not the natural branches
2 Pet. 2. 4. if God *spared* not angels when they sinned
5. and s. not the ancient world, but preserved Noah

Sparing.—ly.
Acts 20. 29. wolves shall enter in among you, not s. the flock
2 Cor. 9. 6. He that soweth *sparingly* shall reap also s.

Sparrows.
Mat. 10. 29. Are not two *sparrows* sold for a farthing?
31. ye are of more value than many *sparrows*. Lu. 12. 7
Lu. 12. 6. Are not five *sparrows* sold for two farthings?

Spat.—A.V. ¹*spit*.
Mat. 27. 30. they ¹*spat* upon him, and took the reed
Mk. 7. 33. and he ¹*spat*, and touched his tongue
Jno. 9. 6. When he had thus spoken, he *spat* on the ground

317

SPEAK

Speak.—¹*preach,* ²*say,* ³*spake,* ⁴*speaketh,* ⁵*speaking,* ⁶*talk.*

Mat. 10. 19. how or what ye shall *speak*—what ye shall *s.*
20. For it is not ye that *speak. Mk.* 13. 11 [*Mk.* 13. 11
27. tell you in the darkness, *speak* ye in the light
12. 32. whosoever shall ⁴*speak* a word against the Son of man—⁴*speak* against the Holy Spirit. *Lu.* 12. 10
34. how can ye, being evil, *speak* good things?
36. every idle word that men shall *speak,* they shall give
46. his brethren stood without, seeking to *s.* to him. 47
Mk. 1. 34. suffered not the devils to *speak. Lu.* 4. 41
2. 7. Why doth this man thus *speak?* he blasphemeth
7. 37. maketh even the deaf to hear, and the dumb to *s.*
9. 39. my name, and be able quickly to *speak* evil of me
13. 11. shall be given you in that hour, that *speak* ye
14. 71. I know not this man of whom ye *speak*
16. 17. they shall *speak* with new tongues
Lu. 1. 19. I am Gabriel—I was sent to *speak* unto thee
20. thou shalt be silent and not able to *speak*
22. when he came out, he could not *speak* unto them
6. 26. Woe unto you, when all men shall *s.* well of you!
11. 53. to provoke him to *speak* of many things
Jno. 3. 11. We *s.* that we do know, and bear witness of that
8. 26. I have many things to ²*s.* and to judge concerning
9. 21. he is of age; he shall *speak* for himself [you
14. 30. I will no more ⁶*speak* much with you
16. 13. for he shall not *s.* from himself—these shall he *s.*
Acts 2. 4. the Holy Spirit, and began to *s.* with other tongues
7. are not all these which *speak* Galileans?
3. 22. in all things whatsoever he shall ²*speak* unto you
4. 17. *speak* henceforth to no man in this name. 5. 40
20. we cannot but *speak* the things which we saw
29. to *s.* thy word with all boldness. 18. 26 : *Phil.* 1. 14
5. 20. Go ye, and stand and *s.* in the temple [1 *Th.* 2. 2
6. 11. We have heard him *speak* blasphemous words
10. 46. they heard them *s.* with tongues, and magnify God
16. 6. forbidden of the Holy Ghost to ¹*s.* the word in Asia
18. 9. Be not afraid, but *speak,* and hold not thy peace
21. 39. give me leave to *speak* unto the people
23. 5. Thou shalt not *speak* evil of a ruler of thy people
30. charging his accusers also to ²*speak* against him
26. 1. Thou art permitted to *speak* for thyself
25. but *speak* forth words of truth and soberness
Rom. 15. 18. I will not dare to *s.* of any things save those
1 *Cor.* 1. 10. that ye all *speak* the same thing [6, 7
2. 13. we *s.,* not in words which man's wisdom teacheth,
3. 1. And I—could not *speak* unto you as unto spiritual
12. 30. do all *speak* with tongues? 14. 23
14. 5. Now I would have you all ⁵*speak* with tongues
28. let him *speak* to himself, and to God
29. let the prophets *speak* by two or three
35. shameful for a woman to *speak* in the church. 34
39. to prophesy, and forbid not to *speak* with tongues
2 *Cor.* 2. 17. in the sight of God, *speak* we in Christ. 12. 19
4. 13. we also believe, and therefore also we *speak*
12. 6. I shall not be foolish; for I shall ²*speak* the truth
Eph. 4. 25. putting away falsehood, *s.* ye truth each one
5. 12. done by them in secret it is a shame even to *s.* of
Col. 4. 3. a door for the word, to *s.* the mystery of Christ
4. that I may make it manifest, as I ought to *speak*
1 *Th.* 1. 8. so that we need not to *speak* anything
2. 2. to *s.* unto you the gospel of God in much conflict
4. so we *s.;* not as pleasing men, but God which proveth
16. forbidding us to *speak* to the Gentiles
1 *Tim.* 4. 2. through the hypocrisy of men that ⁵*speak* lies
Tit. 2. 1. *s.* thou the things which befit the sound doctrine
15. These things *speak* and exhort and reprove
3. 2. to *speak* evil of no man, not to be contentious
Heb. 2. 5. did he subject the world to come, whereof we *s.*

SPEAKETH

Heb. 6. 9. persuaded better things of you—though we thus *s.*
9. 5. of which things we cannot now *speak* severally
Jas. 1. 19. let every man be swift to hear, slow to *speak*
2. 12. So *speak* ye, and so do, as men that are to be
4. 11. *Speak* not one against another, brethren
1 *Pet.* 2. 12. wherein they *speak* against you as evil-doers
3. 10. And his lips that they *speak* no guile
1 *Jno.* 4. 5. therefore *speak* they as of the world
2 *Jno.* 12. I hope to come unto you, and to *s.* face to face. 3
Rev. 13. 15. the image of the beast should both *s.* [*Jno.* 14
see rail—*ing, rid, say, speaketh, speaking, spoken, uttering.*

I Speak.—*A.V.* ¹*have I spoken,* ²*say I.*

Mat. 13. 13. Therefore *speak I* to them in parables
Jno. 4. 26. *I that speak* unto thee am he
7. 17. whether it be of God, or whether *I s.* from myself
8. 28. as the Father taught me, *I speak* these things. 26
38. *I s.* the things which I have seen with my Father
12. 49. what I should say, and what *I should speak*
50. *I speak,* even as the Father hath said—so *I speak*
13. 18. *I s.* not of you all : I know whom I have chosen
14. 10. words that I say unto you *I s.* not from myself
16. 25. when *I* shall no more *speak* unto you in proverbs
17. 13. these things *I s.* in the world, that they may have
Acts 11. 15. as *I* began to *s.,* the Holy Ghost fell on them
26. 26. the king knoweth—unto whom also *I speak* freely
Rom. 3. 5. (*I s.* after the manner of men.) 6. 19 : *Gal.* 3. 15
7. 1. (for *I speak* to men that know the law)
11. 13. But *I speak* to you that are Gentiles
1 *Cor.* 9. 8. Do *I* ¹*s.* these things after the manner of men?
10. 15. *I speak* as to wise men ; judge ye what I say
13. 1. If *I speak* with the tongues of men and of angels
14. 6. profit you, unless *I speak* to you either by way
18. *I speak* with tongues more than you all
19. *I had rather speak* five words with my understanding
21. by the lips of strangers will *I s.* unto this people
15. 34. *I speak* this to move you to shame
2 *Cor.* 4. 13. I believed, and therefore did *I* ¹*speak*
13. 3. (*I speak* as unto my children), be ye also enlarged
11. 17. That which *I speak, I speak* not after the Lord
21. *I s.* by way of disparagement—(*I s.* in foolishness)
23. ministers of Christ ? (*I speak* as one beside himself)
Eph. 5. 32. *I speak* in regard of Christ and of the church
6. 20. that in it *I* may *speak* boldly, as *I* ought to *speak*
Phil. 4. 11. Not that *I speak* in respect of want
1 *Tim.* 2. 7. (*I speak* the truth, I lie not)
see I say.

Speaker.

Acts 14. 12. Paul, Mercury, because he was the chief *speaker*

Speakest.—*A.V.* ¹*talkest.*

Mat. 13. 10. Why *speakest* thou unto them in parables ?
Lu. 12. 41. Lord, *speakest* thou this parable unto us
Jno. 4. 27. no man said—Why ¹*speakest* thou with her?
16. 29. disciples say, Lo, now *s.* thou plainly—*s.* no proverb
19. 10. Pilate therefore saith—S. thou not unto me ?
see spoken.

Speaketh.—*A.V.* ¹*saith,* ²*spake,* ³*speak,* ⁴*speaking,* ⁵*talketh.*

Mat. 10. 20. the Spirit of your Father that *speaketh* in you
12. 34. the abundance of the heart the mouth *s. Lu.* 6. 45
Lu. 5. 21. Who is this that *speaketh* blasphemies ?
Jno. 3. 31. is of the earth, and of the earth he *speaketh*
34. whom God hath sent *speaketh* the words of God
7. 18. He that *s.* from himself seeketh his own glory
26. lo, he *s.* openly, and they say nothing unto him
8. 44. When he *speaketh* a lie, he *speaketh* of his own
9. 37. hast both seen him, and he it is that ¹*s.* with thee
13. 24. Tell us who it is of whom he ²*speaketh*

318

SPEAKETH

Jno. 19. 12. maketh himself a king *speaketh* against Cæsar
Acts 8. 34. I pray thee, of whom *speaketh* the prophet this?
Rom. 3. 19. law saith, it ¹*speaketh* to them that are under
1 *Cor.* 14. 2. he that *speaketh* in a tongue *speaketh* not
    unto men—in the spirit he *speaketh* mysteries
  3. he that prophesieth *speaketh* unto men edification
  4. He that *speaketh* in a tongue edifieth himself
  5. greater is he that prophesieth than he that *speaketh*
 11. be to him that *s.* a barbarian—he that *s.* will be
 13. let him that *speaketh* in a tongue pray that he may
2 *Cor.* 13. 3. ye seek a proof of Christ that ⁴*speaketh* in me
Heb. 11. 4. through it he being dead yet *speaketh*
 12. 24. blood—that *speaketh* better than that of Abel
 25. See that ye refuse not him that *speaketh*
Jas. 4. 5. think ye that the scripture ¹*speaketh* in vain?
 11. He that *s.* against a brother—*s.* against the law
1 *Pet.* 4. 11. if any man ³*speaketh*, speaking as it were
Jude 16. (and their mouth *speaketh* great swelling words)
   see reasoneth, saith, speak, warneth.

Speaking.—*A.V.* ¹*preaching,* ²*saying,* ³*spake,* ⁴*speak,*
   ⁵*talked—ing.*

Mat. 6. 7. that they shall be heard for their much *speaking*
 15. 31. multitude wondered, when they saw the dumb ⁴*s.*
Jno. 4. 27. they marvelled that he was ⁵*s.* with a woman
 42. Now we believe, not because of thy ²*speaking*
Acts 3. 3. and *s.* the things concerning the kingdom of God
 2. 6. every man heard them ⁴*s.* in his own language
 11. we do hear them ⁴*speaking* in our tongues
 11. 19. ¹*speaking* the word to none save only to Jews
 14. 3. they tarried there *speaking* boldly in the Lord
 9. The same [cripple] heard Paul ⁴*speaking*
 19. 9. ²*speaking* evil of the Way before the multitude
 20. 30. *s.* perverse things, to draw away the disciples
1 *Cor.* 12. 3. no man *speaking* in the Spirit of God saith
 14. 6. if I come unto you *speaking* with tongues
 9. what is spoken? for ye will be ⁴*speaking* into the air
Eph. 4. 15. *s.* truth in love, may grow up in all things
 5. 19. *speaking* one to another in psalms and hymns
1 *Tim.* 5. 13. busybodies, *s.* things which they ought not
1 *Pet.* 2. 1. hypocrisies, and envies, and all evil *speakings*
 4. 4. into the same excess of riot, *speaking* evil of you
 11. ⁴*speaking* as it were oracles of God
2 *Pet.* 3. 16. epistles, *speaking* in them of these things
Rev. 4. 1. I heard, a voice as of a trumpet ⁵*speaking*
 10. 8. voice which I heard—again ³*speaking* with me
 13. 5. a mouth *speaking* great things and blasphemies
   see railing, spake, speak, speaketh.

Spear.

Jno. 19. 34. one of the soldiers with a *s.* pierced his side

Spearmen

Acts 23. 23. threescore and ten, and *spearmen* two hundred

Special.

Acts 19. 11. God wrought *s.* miracles by the hands of Paul

Specially.

Acts 25. 26. before you, and *s.* before thee, king Agrippa
1 *Tim.* 4. 10. Saviour of all men, *s.* of them that believe
 5. 8. provideth not for his own, and *s.* his own household
Tit. 1. 10. and deceivers, *s.* they of the circumcision
Philem. 16. a brother beloved, *specially* to me
   see especially.

Spectacle.

1 *Cor.* 4. 9. for we are made a *spectacle* unto the world

SPIKENARD

Speech—es.—*A.V.* ¹*communication,* ²*speeches,* ³*words.*

Mat. 5. 37. let your ¹*speech* be, Yea, yea; Nay, nay
 26. 73. art one of them; for thy *speech* bewrayeth thee
Mk. 7. 32. deaf, and had an impediment in his *speech*
Lu. 20. 20. they might take hold of his ³*speech*
Jno. 8. 43. Why do ye not understand my *speech?*
Acts 14. 11. saying in the *speech* of Lycaonia, The gods
 20. 7. Paul—prolonged his *speech* until midnight
Rom. 16. 18. by their smooth and fair ²*speech* they beguile
1 *Cor.* 2. 1. And I—came not with excellency of *speech*
 4. my *s.* and my preaching were not in persuasive words
 14. 9. unless ye utter by the tongue ³*s.* easy to be understood
2 *Cor.* 3. 12. Having—such a hope, we use great boldness of *s.*
 7. 4. Great is my boldness of *speech* toward you
 10. 10. presence is weak, and his *speech* of no account
 11. 6. I be rude in *speech,* yet am I not in knowledge
Eph. 4. 29. Let no corrupt ¹*s.* proceed out of your mouth
Col. 4. 6. Let your *speech* be always with grace
Tit. 2. 8. sound *speech,* that cannot be condemned
   see things, word.

Speechless.

Mat. 22. 12. not having a wedding garment? And he was *s.*
Acts 9. 7. men that journeyed with him stood *speechless*
   see dumb.

Speed.

Acts 17. 15. Silas and Timothy—come to him with all *s.*
   see greeting.

Speedily.

Lu. 18. 8. I say unto you, that he will avenge them *s.*

Spend.—*A.V.* ¹ *consume,* ²*continue.*

Acts 20. 16. that he [Paul] might not have to *s.* time in Asia
2 *Cor.* 12. 15. And I will most gladly *spend* and be spent
Jas. 4. 3. because ye ask amiss, that ye may ¹*spend* it in
 13. to-morrow we will go into this city, and ²*s.* a year there

Spendest

Lu. 10. 35. care of him; and whatsoever thou *s.* more

Spent.—*A.V.* ¹*abode,* ²*passed,* ³*tarried,* ⁴*wrought.*

Mat. 20. 12. These last have ⁴*spent* but one hour
Mk. 5. 26. and had *spent* all that she had. *Lu.* 8. 43
 6. 35. when the day was now far *spent*—day is now
   far ²*spent. Lu.* 24. 29
Lu. 15. 14. when he had *s.* all, there arose a mighty famine
Acts 15. 33. after they had ³*spent* some time there
 17. 21. spent their time in nothing else, but either to
 20. 3. he had ⁴*spent* three months there, and a plot
 27. 9. much time was *spent,* and the voyage was. 18. 23
Rom. 13. 12. The night is far *spent,* and the day is at hand
2 *Cor.* 12. 15. I will most gladly spend and be *s.* for your souls

Spew.—*A.V.* ¹*spue.*

Rev. 3. 16. hot nor cold, I will *spew* thee out of my mouth

Spice—s.

Lu. 24. 1. tomb, bringing the *spices.* 23. 56: *Mk.* 16. 1
Jno. 19. 40. bound it in linen cloths with the *spices*
Rev. 18. 13. cinnamon, and *s.,* and incense, and ointment

Spies.

Lu. 20. 20. And they watched him, and sent forth *spies*
Heb. 11. 31. Rahab—received the *spies* with peace

Spikenard

Mk. 14. 3. an alabaster cruse of ointment of *s. Jno.* 12. 3

SPILLED

Spilled.—*A.V.* ¹*runneth out.*
Mat. 9. 17. else the skins burst, and the wine is ¹*spilled*
Lu. 5. 37. wine will burst the skins, and itself will be *s.*
          see perisheth.

Spin.
Mat. 6. 28. they toil not, neither do they *spin. Lu.* 12. 27

Spirit.—*A.V.* ¹*ghost,* ²*Holy Ghost,* ³*spiritually.*
Mat. 4. 1. Then was Jesus led up of the *Spirit. Lu.* 4. 1
5. 3. Blessed are the poor in *s.:* for theirs is the kingdom
22. 43. How then doth David in the *S.* call him Lord
26. 41. the *spirit* indeed is willing. *Mk.* 14. 38
27. 50. Jesus—loud voice, and yielded up his ¹*s Jno.* 19.¹30
Mk. 1. 10. the *S.* as a dove descending upon him. *Jno.* 1. 32
12. the *Spirit* driveth him forth into the wilderness
2. 8. Jesus, perceiving in his *s.* that they so reasoned
6. 12. And he sighed deeply in his *spirit*
9. 17. I brought—my son, which hath a dumb *spirit*
25. rebuked the unclean *spirit,* saying unto him, Thou
dumb and deaf *spirit*
Lu. 1. 17. go before his face in the *s.* and power of Elijah
80. the child grew, and waxed strong in *spirit*
2. 27. [Simeon] came in the *Spirit* into the temple
4. 14. Jesus returned in the power of the *S.* into Galilee
8. 55. And her *spirit* returned, and she rose up
9. 39. a *spirit* taketh him, and he suddenly crieth out
13. 11. woman which had a *s.* of infirmity eighteen years
24. 37. affrighted, and supposed that they beheld a *spirit*
39. a *spirit* hath not flesh and bones, as ye behold me
Jno. 1. 33. see the *Spirit* descending, and abiding upon him
3. 5. Except a man be born of water and the *Spirit*
6. that which is born of the *Spirit* is spirit
8. so is every one that is born of the *Spirit*
34. for he giveth not the *Spirit* by measure
4. 23. shall worship the Father in *spirit* and truth
24. God is a *S.:* and they—must worship in *s.* and truth
6. 63. It is the *spirit* that quickeneth—the words that I
have spoken unto you are *spirit,* and are life
7. 39. this spake he of the *S.*—for the ²*S.* was not yet
11. 33. Jesus—groaned in the *s.,* and was troubled. 13. 21
14. 17. the *S.* of truth: whom the world cannot receive
15. 26. from the Father, even the *Spirit* of truth
16. 13. Howbeit when he, the *Spirit* of truth, is come
Acts 2. 4. other tongues, as the *S.* gave them utterance
6. 10. not able to withstand the wisdom and the *Spirit*
8. 29. And the *Spirit* said unto Philip, Go near
10. 19. the *S.* said unto him—three men seek thee. 11. 12
11. 28. Agabus—signified by the *S.* that there should be
16. 7. and the *Spirit* of Jesus suffered them not
16. certain maid having a *spirit* of divination met us
18. Paul—turned and said to the *spirit,* I charge thee
17. 16. at Athens, his *spirit* was provoked within him
18. 25. being fervent in *spirit. Rom.* 12. 11
20. 22. I go bound in the *spirit* unto Jerusalem. 19. 21
21. 4. said to Paul through the *S.,* that he should not set
23. 8. no resurrection, neither angel, nor *spirit*
9. what if a *spirit* hath spoken to him, or an angel?
Rom. 1. 4. Son of God with power, according to the *s.* of
2. 29. circumcision is that of the heart, in the *spirit*
7. 6. so that we serve in newness of the *spirit*
8. 2. law of the *S.* of life in Christ Jesus made me free
4. who walk not after the flesh, but after the *spirit*
5. they that are after the *spirit* the things of the *spirit*
6. but the mind of the ³*spirit* is life and peace
9. but in the *s.*—if any man hath not the *S.* of Christ
10. but the *spirit* is life because of righteousness
11. the *Spirit* of him that raised up Jesus from the
dead dwelleth in you—quicken—through his *S.*

SPIRIT

Rom. 8. 13. if by the *spirit* ye mortify the deeds of the body
15. received not the *spirit* of bondage again unto fear;
but ye received the *spirit* of adoption
16. The *Spirit* himself beareth witness with our *spirit*
23. ourselves also, which have the first-fruits of the *S.*
26. the *Spirit* also helpeth our infirmity—the *Spirit*
himself maketh intercession for us
27. the hearts knoweth what is the mind of the *Spirit*
11. 8. God gave them a *s.* of stupor, eyes that they should
15. 30. by the love of the *Spirit,* that ye strive together
1 *Cor.* 2. 4. in demonstration of the *Spirit* and of power
10. revealed them through the *S.:* for the *S.* searcheth
11. save the *spirit* of the man, which is in him?
12. not the *s.* of the world, but the *s.* which is of God
13. man's wisdom teacheth, but which the ²*S.* teacheth
4. 21. with a rod, or in love and a *spirit* of meekness?
5. 3. I verily, being absent in body but present in *spirit*
5. that the *s.* may be saved in the day of the Lord Jesus
6. 17. he that is joined unto the Lord in one *spirit*
7. 34. that she may be holy both in body and in *spirit*
12. 4. diversities of gifts, but the same *Spirit.* 8, 9, 11
7. the manifestation of the *Spirit* to profit withal
8. to one is given through the *Spirit* the word of wisdom
9. to another gifts of healings, in the one *Spirit*
13. For in one *Spirit* were we all baptized—and were
all made to drink of one *Spirit*
14. 2. but in the *spirit* he speaketh mysteries
15. I will pray with the *spirit*—I will sing with the *s.*
16. Else if thou bless with the *spirit,* how shall he
15. 45. The last Adam became a life-giving *spirit*
2 *Cor.* 1. 22. gave us the earnest of the *S.* in our hearts. 5. 5
3. 6. not of the letter, but of the *spirit:* for the letter
killeth, but the *spirit* giveth life
8. rather the ministration of the *spirit* be with glory?
17. the Lord is the *S.:* and where the *S.* of the Lord is
4. 13. But having the same *spirit* of faith, according to
7. 1. cleanse ourselves from all defilement of flesh and *s.*
13. because his *spirit* hath been refreshed by you all
11. 4. receive a different *spirit,* which ye did not receive
12. 16. walked we not by the same *Spirit?*
Gal. 3. 2. Received ye the *Spirit* by the works of the law
3. having begun in the *Spirit,* are ye now perfected
5. He therefore that supplieth to you the *Spirit*
14. we might receive the promise of the *S.* through faith
4. 6. God sent forth the *S.* of his Son into our hearts
29. persecuted him that was born after the *Spirit*
5. 5. For we through the *Spirit* by faith wait for the hope
16. Walk by the *Spirit,* and ye shall not fulfil the lust
17. flesh lusteth against the *S.,* and the *S.* against the flesh
18. But if ye are led by the *S.,* ye are not under the law
22. the fruit of the *Spirit* is love, joy, peace
25. If we live by the *Spirit,* by the *S.* let us also walk
6. 1. restore such a one in a *spirit* of meekness
8. he that soweth unto the *Spirit* shall of the *S.* reap
18. grace of our Lord Jesus Christ be with yours. *Philem.*
Eph. 1. 13. ye were sealed with the Holy *S.* of promise [25
17. may give unto you a *s.* of wisdom and revelation
2. 2. the *s.* that now worketh in the sons of disobedience
18. we both have our access in one *S.* unto the Father
22. builded—for a habitation of God in the *Spirit*
3. 5. unto his holy apostles and prophets in the *Spirit*
16. may be strengthened with power through his *S.*
4. 3. to keep the unity of the *Spirit* in the bond of peace
4. There is one body, and one *Spirit,* even as also ye
23. that ye be renewed in the *spirit* of your mind
5. 18. not drunken with wine—but be filled with the *S.*
6. 17. the sword of the *Spirit,* which is the word of God
18. praying at all seasons in the *Spirit,* and watching
Phil. 1. 19. and the supply of the *Spirit* of Jesus Christ

SPIRIT

Phil. 1. 27. that ye stand fast in one *spirit*, with one soul
2. 1 if any fellowship of the *Spirit*, if any tender mercies
3. 3. we are the circumcision, who worship by the *Spirit*
Col. 1. 8. who also declared unto us your love in the *S.*
2. 5. absent in the flesh, yet am I with you in the *spirit*
1 *Th.* 5. 19. Quench not the *Spirit*
23. may your *spirit* and soul and body be preserved
2 *Th.* 2. 2. nor yet be troubled, either by *spirit*, or by word
13. in sanctification of the *S.* and belief of the truth
1 *Tim.* 3. 16. manifested in the flesh, justified in the *spirit*
4. 1. But the *Spirit* saith expressly, that in later times
2 *Tim.* 1. 7. God gave us not a *spirit* of fearfulness
4. 22. The Lord be with thy *spirit*. Grace be with you
Heb. 4. 12. even to the dividing of soul and *spirit*
9. 14. Christ, who through the eternal *S.* offered himself
10. 29. and hath done despite unto the *Spirit* of grace ?
Jas. 2. 26. as the body apart from the *spirit* is dead
4. 5. Doth the *spirit* which he made to dwell in us long
1 *Pet.* 1. 2. in sanctification of the *Spirit*, unto obedience
11. the *Spirit* of Christ which was in them did point
3. 4. incorruptible apparel of a meek and quiet *spirit*
18. put to death in the flesh, but quickened in the *spirit*
4. 6. but live according to God in the *spirit*
14. the *S.* of glory and the *S.* of God resteth upon you
1 *Jno.* 3. 24. we know that he abideth in us, by the *Spirit*
4. 1. believe not every *spirit*, but prove the spirits
3. every *s.* which confesseth that Jesus Christ is come
3. and every *spirit* which confesseth not Jesus is not
of God : and this is the *spirit* of the antichrist
6. By this we know the *s.* of truth, and the *s.* of error
13. he in us, because he hath given us of his *Spirit*
5. 7. And it is the *Spirit* that beareth witness, because
the *Spirit* is the truth
8. bear witness, the *S.*, and the water, and the blood
Jude 19. make separations, sensual, having not the *Spirit*
Rev. 1. 10. I was in the *Spirit* on the Lord's day
2. 7. He that hath an ear, let him hear what the *Spirit*
saith to the churches. 11, 17, 29 : 3. 6, 13, 22
4. 2. I was in the *Spirit* : and behold, there was a throne
14. 13. yea, saith the *Spirit*, that they may rest from
17. 3. And he carried me away in the *Spirit*. 21. 10
18. 2. of devils, and a hold of every unclean *spirit*
19. 10. the testimony of Jesus is the *spirit* of prophecy
22. 17. And the *Spirit* and the bride say, Come
see apparition, breath, evil spirit, light, unclean, word.

Spirit of God.

Mat. 3. 16. he saw the *Spirit of God* descending as a dove
12. 28. if I by the *Spirit of God* cast out devils
Rom. 8. 9. that the *S. of God* dwelleth in you. 1 *Cor.* 3. 16
14. as many as are led by the *S. of God*, these are sons
1 *Cor.* 2. 11. things of God none knoweth, save the *S. of God*
14. receiveth not the things of the *Spirit of God*
6. 11. of the Lord Jesus Christ, and in the *S. of* our *God*
7. 40. I think that I also have the *Spirit of God*
12. 3. no man speaking in the *Spirit of God* saith
2 *Cor.* 3. 3. not with ink, but with the *S. of* the living *God*
Eph. 4. 30. grieve not the Holy *Spirit of God*
1 *Pet.* 4. 14. the *Spirit* of glory and the *S. of G.* resteth upon
1 *Jno.* 4. 2. Hereby know ye the *Spirit of God*   [you
see Holy Ghost (proper names).

My Spirit.

Mat. 12. 18. I will put *my Spirit* upon him
Lu. 1. 47. *my spirit* hath rejoiced in God my Saviour
23. 46. Father, into thy hands I commend *my spirit*
Acts 2. 17. I will pour forth of *my Spirit* upon all flesh. 18
7. 59. Lord Jesus, receive *my spirit*
Rom. 1. 9. whom I serve in *my spirit* in the gospel

42

SPOIL

1 *Cor.* 5. 4. ye being gathered together, and *my spirit*
14. 14. if I pray in a tongue, *my spirit* prayeth
16. 18. For they refreshed *my spirit* and yours
2 *Cor.* 2. 13. no relief for *my s.*, because I found not Titus

Spirits.

Mat. 8. 16. he cast out the *spirits* with a word   [11. 26
12. 45. seven other *spirits* more evil than himself. *Lu.*
Lu. 10. 20. rejoice not, that the *spirits* are subject unto you
1 *Cor.* 12. 10. and to another discernings of *spirits*
14. 32. the *s.* of the prophets are subject to the prophets
1 *Tim.* 4. 1. giving heed to seducing *spirits* and doctrines
Heb. 1. 14. Are they not all ministering *spirits*, sent forth
12. 9. in subjection unto the Father of *spirits*, and live ?
23. and to the *spirits* of just men made perfect
1 *Pet.* 3. 19. he went and preached unto the *s.* in prison
1 *Jno.* 4 1. prove the *spirits*, whether they are of God
Rev. 16. 14. they are *spirits* of devils, working signs
22. 6. the Lord, the God of the *spirits* of the prophets
see evil spirit, seven, unclean, winds.

Spiritual.—*A.V.* ¹*sincere.*

Rom. 1. 11. I may impart unto you some *spiritual* gift
7. 14. For we know that the law is *spiritual*
15. 27. been made partakers of their *spiritual* things
1 *Cor.* 2. 13. teacheth ; comparing *spiritual* things with *s.*
15. But he that is *spiritual* judgeth all things
3. 1. And I—could not speak unto you as unto *spiritual*
9. 11. If we sowed unto you *spiritual* things
10. 3. and did all eat the same *spiritual* meat
4. did all drink the same *spiritual* drink—of a *s.* rock
12. 1. concerning *spiritual* gifts, brethren, I would not
14. 1. Follow after love ; yet desire earnestly *s.* gifts
12. since ye are zealous of *spiritual* gifts, seek that
37. thinketh himself to be a prophet, or *spiritual*
15. 44. it is raised a *s.* body—there is also a *s.* body
46. that is not first which is *s.*—then that which is *s.*
Gal. 6. 1. any trespass, ye which are *spiritual*, restore
Eph. 1. 3. hath blessed us with every *spiritual* blessing
5. 19. psalms and hymns and *spiritual* songs. *Col.* 3. 16
6. 12. against the *spiritual* hosts of wickedness
1 *Pet.* 2. 2. for the ¹*spiritual* milk which is without guile
5. are built up a *s.* house—to offer up *s.* sacrifices

Spiritually.

1 *Cor.* 2. 14. know them, because they are *s.* judged
Rev. 11. 8. city, which *s.* is called Sodom and Egypt
see spirit.

Spit.—*A.V.* ¹*spitted.*

Mat. 26. 67. Then did they *s.* in his face. *Mk.* 14. 65 : 15. 19
Mk. 8. 23. when he had *spit* on his eyes, and laid his hands
10. 34. shall mock him, and shall *spit* upon him
Lu. 18. 32. and shamefully entreated, and ¹*spit* upon
see spat.

Spitefully *A.V.—see shamefully.*

Spitted *A.V.—see spit.*

Spittle.

Jno. 9. 6. made clay of the *spittle*, and anointed his eyes

Spoil—s.

Mat. 12. 29. house of the strong man, and *spoil* his goods
—then he will *spoil* his house. *Mk.* 3. 27.
Lu. 11. 22. armour wherein he trusted, and divideth his *s.*
Col. 2. 8. maketh *spoil* of you through his philosophy
Heb. 7. 4. Abraham—gave a tenth out of the chief *spoils*

321

SPOILING

Spoiling.
Heb. 10. 34. took joyfully the *spoiling* of your possessions

Spoken.—*A.V.* ¹*made*, ²*preached*, ³*said*, ⁴*spake*, ⁵*speak*, ⁶*speakest*, ⁷*told*.
Mat. 2. 17. which was *s*. by Jeremiah the prophet. 27. 9
 23. fulfilled which was *s*. by the prophets. 13. 35: 21. 4
 3. 3. this is he that was *spoken* of by Isaiah the prophet
 4. 14. which was *s*. by Isaiah the prophet. 8. 17: 12. 17
 22. 31. have ye not read that which was *spoken* [Daniel
 24. 15. abomination of desolation, which was *spoken* of by
 26. 13. this woman hath done shall be ⁷*s*. of for a memorial.
 65. saying, He hath *spoken* blasphemy   [*Mk*. 14. 9
Mk. 5. 36. Jesus, not heeding the word *spoken*, ⁶aith
Lu. 1. 45. things which have been ⁷*spoken* to her [Mary]
 2. 18. wondered at the things which were ⁷*s*. unto them. ⁷20
 33. marvelling at the things which were *s*. concerning
 34. in Israel; and for a sign which is *spoken* against
 12. 3. what ye have *s*. in the ear in the inner chambers
 19. 28. when he had thus *spoken*. *Jno.* 9. 6: 11. 43:
  18. 1: *Acts* 19. 41: 20. 36   [have *spoken*!
 24. 25. slow of heart to believe in all that the prophets
Jno. 6. 63. the words that I have ⁵*s*. unto you are spirit
 8. 25. Even that which I have also ³*spoken* unto you
 9. 29. We know that God hath ⁴*spoken* unto Moses
 11. 13. Now Jesus had ⁴*spoken* of his death
 12. 29. others said, An angel hath ⁴*spoken* to him [25, 33
 14. 25. These things have I *s*. unto you. 15. 11: 16. 1, ⁴4, ³6,
 15. 3. ye are clean because of the word which I have *s*.
 22. If I had not come and *spoken* unto them
 18. 20. Jesus answered him, I have ⁴*s*. openly to the world
 23. If I have *spoken* evil, bear witness of the evil
 21. 19. when he had *s*. this, he saith unto him, Follow me
Acts 2. 16. that which hath been *s*. by the prophet Joel
 3. 24. as many as have *s*., they also told of these days
 8. 6. heed—unto the things that were ⁴*spoken* by Philip
 24. none of the things which ye have *spoken* come
 25. when they had testified and ²*s*. the word of the Lord
 9. 27. the Lord in the way, and that he had *s*. to him
 13. 40. that come upon you, which is *s*. in the prophets
 42. they besought that these words might be ²*spoken*
 46. the word of God should first be *spoken* to you
 14. 25. when they had ²*s*. the word in Perga, they went
 16. 14. give heed unto the things which were *s*. by Paul
 17. 19. what this new teaching is, which is ⁶*s*. by thee?
 20. 36. sorrowing most of all for the word which he had ⁴*s*.
 23. 9. what if a spirit hath *spoken* to him, or an angel?
 27. 11. than to those things which were *spoken* by Paul
 25. it shall be even so as it hath been ⁷*spoken* unto me
 28. 22. it is known to us that everywhere it is *s*. against
 25. they departed, after that Paul had *spoken* [been *s*.
Rom. 4. 18. of many nations, according to that which had
 14. 16. Let not then your good be evil *spoken* of
 1 *Cor.* 10. 30. evil *s*. of for that for which I give thanks?
 14. 9. how shall it be known what is *spoken*?
Gal. 3. 16. Now to Abraham were the promises ²*spoken*
Heb. 1. 1. God, having of old time ⁴*spoken* unto the fathers
 2. hath at the end of these days *s*. unto us in his Son
 2. 2. if the word *spoken* through angels proved stedfast
 3. 5. those things which were afterward to be *spoken*
 4. 8. he would not have *spoken* afterward of another day
 9. 19. when every commandment had been *s*. by Moses
 12. 19. that no word more should be *spoken* unto them
 1 *Pet.* 3. 16. ye are ⁵*s*. against, they may be put to shame
 2 *Pet.* 2. 2. of whom the way of the truth shall be evil *s*. of
 3. 2. remember the words which were *s*. before. *Jude* 17
Jude 15. which ungodly sinners have *spoken* against him
 see gainsaid, Lord, proclaimed, said, he said, saying, spake, I speak, tidings.

SPRUNG

Sponge.—*A.V.* ¹*spunge*.
Mat. 27. 48. one of them ran, and took a ¹*sponge*, and filled
  it with vinegar. *Mk.* 15. ¹36: *Jno.* 19. ¹29

Sporting *A.V.*—*see* revelling.

Spot—**s.**
Eph. 5. 27. a glorious church, not having *spot* or wrinkle
 1 *Tim.* 6. 14. keep the commandment, without *spot*
 1 *Pet.* 1. 19. a lamb without blemish and without *spot*
 2 *Pet.* 2. 13. revel in the day-time, *spots* and blemishes
 3. 14. ye may be found in peace, without *s*. and blameless
   see blemish, rocks.

Spotted.
Jude 23. hating even the garment *spotted* by the flesh

Sprang.—*A.V.* ¹*blew*, ²*ran*, ³*rose*, ⁴*sprung*.
Mat. 13. 5. and straightway they ⁴*sprang* up. *Mk.* 4. 5
 26. But when the blade ⁴*sprang* up
Mk. 10. 50. he [blind man]—⁴*s*. up, and came to Jesus
Acts 14. 14. Barnabas and Paul—rent their garments, and
   ²*sprang* forth
 16. 29. [Jailor] he called for lights, and *sprang* in
 28. 13. after one day a south wind ¹*sprang* up
Heb. 11. 12. there *sprang* of one, and him as good as dead
   see grew.

Spread.—*A.V.* ¹*blaze*, ²*dwell*, ³*published*, ⁴*reported*, ⁵*stretched*.
Mat. 9. 31. and *spread* abroad his fame in all that land
 21. 8. multitude *spread* their garments in the way.
   Mk. 11. 8: *Lu.* 19. 36
 28. 15. this saying was ⁴*spread* abroad among the Jews
Mk. 1. 45. publish it much, and to ¹*s*. abroad the matter
Acts 4. 17. But that it *spread* no further among the people
 13. 49. And the word of the Lord was ³*spread* abroad
Rom. 10. 21. All the day long did I ⁵*spread* out my hands
Rev. 7. 15. sitteth on the throne shall ²*s*. his tabernacle
   see gone (forth), known.

Spring.—*A.V.* ¹*sprung*.
Mat. 4. 16. To them did light ¹*spring* up
Mk. 4. 27. seed should *s*. up and grow, he knoweth not how

Springing.
Jno. 4. 14. in him a well of water *s*. up unto eternal life
Heb. 12. 15. root of bitterness *springing* up trouble you

Springs.—*A.V.* ¹*wells*.
2 *Pet.* 2. 17. These are ¹*springs* without water, and mists

Sprinkled.—*A.V.* ¹*dipped*.
Heb. 9. 19. *sprinkled* both the book itself, and all the people
 21. and all the vessels of the ministry he *sprinkled*
 10. 22. having our hearts *s*. from an evil conscience
Rev. 19. 13. arrayed in a garment ¹*sprinkled* with blood

Sprinkling.
Heb. 9. 13. ashes of a heifer *s*. them that have been defiled
 11. 28. kept the passover, and the *sprinkling* of the blood
 12. 24. blood of *sprinkling* that speaketh better than
 1 *Pet.* 1. 2. unto obedience and *s*. of the blood of Jesus

Sprung.—*A.V.* ¹*sprang*.
Heb. 7. 14. evident that our Lord hath ¹*sprung* out of Judah
   see grew, sprang, spring.

SPUE

Spue *A.V.—see spew.*

Spunge *A.V.—see sponge.*

Spy.

Gal. 2. 4. who came in privily to *spy* out our liberty

Stablish—*A.V.* ¹*strengthen.*

Lu. 22. 32. thou hast turned again, ¹*stablish* thy brethren
Rom. 16. 25. able to *stablish* you according to my gospel
1 *Th.* 3. 13. he may *s.* your hearts unblameable. 2 *Th.* 2. 17
2 *Th.* 3. 3. who shall *s.* you, and guard you from the evil one
Jas. 5. 8. Be ye also patient; *stablish* your hearts
1 *Pet* 5. 10. shall himself perfect, *stablish,* strengthen you
Rev. 3. 2. watchful, and ¹*stablish* the things that remain
see establish.

Stablished.

Col. 2. 7. *stablished* in your faith, even as ye were taught
Heb. 13. 9. it is good that the heart be *stablished* by grace
see established.

Stablisheth—ing.—*A.V.* ¹*strengthening.*

Acts 18. 23. Phrygia in order, ¹*stablishing* all the disciples
2 *Cor.* 1. 21. he that *s.* us with you in Christ—is God

Staff.—*A.V.* ¹*staves.*

Mat. 10. 10. two coats, nor shoes, nor ¹*staff. Lu.* 9. ¹³
Mk. 6. 8. nothing for their journey, save a *staff* only
Heb. 11. 21. worshipped, leaning upon the top of his *staff*

Staggered *A.V.—see wavered.*

Stairs.

Acts 21. 40. Paul, standing on the *stairs,* beckoned. 35

Stall.

Lu. 13. 15. sabbath loose his ox or his ass from the *stall*

Stanched.

Lu. 8. 44. immediately the issue of her blood *stanched*

Stand.—*A.V.* ¹*brought,* ²*candlestick,* ³*continue,* ⁴*holden up,* ⁵*rise,* ⁶*standing,* ⁷*stood.*

Mat. 5. 15. under the bushel, but on the ²*stand. Lu.* 11. ³³
6. 5. love to ⁶*stand* and pray in the synagogues
12. 25. divided against itself shall not *stand. Mk.* 3. 24, 25
26. how then shall his kingdom *s. ? Mk.* 3. 26 : *Lu.* 11. 18
41. of Nineveh shall ⁵*s.* up in the judgement. *Lu.* 11. ⁵³²
47. thy mother and thy brethren *s.* without. *Lu.* 8. 20
16. 28. ⁶*s.* here, which shall in no wise taste of death. *Mk.*
20. 6. Why *stand* ye here all the day idle ? [9. 1 : *Lu.* 9. 27
Mk. 3. 3. man that had his hand withered, *S.* forth. *Lu.* 6. 8
4. 21. under the bed, and not to be put on the ²*s.? Lu.* 8.²¹⁶
11. 25. And whensoever ye *stand* praying, forgive
13. 9. before governors and kings shall ye ¹*s.* for my sake
Lu. 1. 19. I am Gabriel, that *stand* in the presence of God
13. 25. ye begin to *s.* without, and to knock at the door
21. 36. prevail to escape—and to *s.* before the Son of Man
Acts 1. 11. why *stand* ye looking into heaven ?
4. 10. in him doth this man *stand* here before you whole
5. 20. Go ye, and *stand* and speak in the temple
8. 38. he commanded the chariot to *stand* still
10. 26. saying, *Stand* up ; I myself also am a man
14. 10. *Stand* upright on thy feet. And he leaped

STANDING

Acts 26. 6. I *s.* here to be judged for the hope of the promise
16. But arise, and *stand* upon thy feet
22. obtained the help that is from God, I ³*s.* unto this day
27. 24. Fear not, Paul ; thou must ¹*stand* before Cæsar
Rom. 5. 2. by faith into this grace wherein we *stand*
9. 11. purpose of God according to election might *stand*
14. 4. made to ⁴*s.*; for the Lord hath power to make him *s.*
10. we shall all *stand* before the judgement-seat of God
1 *Cor.* 2. 5. your faith should not *s.* in the wisdom of men
15. 1. which also ye received, wherein also ye *stand*
30. why do we also *stand* in jeopardy every hour ?
2 *Cor.* 1. 24. are helpers of your joy : for by faith ye *stand*
Eph. 6. 11. able to stand against the wiles of the devil
13. in the evil day, and, having done all, to *stand*
14. *Stand* therefore, having girded your loins with truth
Col. 4. 12. *s.* perfect and fully assured in all the will of God
Jas. 2. 3. and ye say to the poor man, *Stand* thou there
Rev. 3. 20. Behold, I *stand* at the door and knock
6. 17. day of their wrath is come ; and who is able to *s.* ?
8. 2. I saw the seven angels which ⁷*stand* before God
18. 15. shall *stand* afar off for the fear of her torment
see standeth, standing.

Stand *fast*.

1 *Cor.* 16. 13. Watch ye, *stand fast* in the faith
Gal. 5. 1. *stand fast* therefore, and be not entangled again
Phil. 1. 27. *stand fast* in one spirit, with one soul striving
4. 1. so *stand fast* in the Lord, my beloved
1 *Th.* 3. 8. now we live, if ye *stand fast* in the Lord
2 *Th.* 2. 15. brethren, *stand fast,* and hold the traditions
1 *Pet.* 5. 12. the true Grace of God : *stand* ye fast therein

Standest.

Acts 7. 33. the place whereon thou *standest* is holy ground
Rom. 11. 20. they were broken off, and thou *s.* by thy faith

Standeth.—*A.V.* ¹*stand.*

Jno. 1. 26. in the midst of you *s.* one whom ye know not
3. 29. friend of the bridegroom, which *s.* and heareth him
11. 42. because of the multitude which ¹*s.* around I said it
Rom. 14. 4. to his own lord he *standeth* or falleth
1 *Cor.* 7. 37. But he that *standeth* stedfast in his heart
10. 12. let him that thinketh he *standeth* take heed
2 *Tim.* 2. 19. the firm foundation of God *s.,* having this seal
Heb. 10. 11. every priest indeed *s.* day by day ministering
Jas. 5. 9. behold, the judge *standeth* before the doors
Rev. 10. 8. angel that *s.* upon the sea and upon the earth

Standing.—*A.V.* ¹*degree,* ²*stand,* ³*stood.*

Mat. 20. 3. saw others *standing* in the marketplace idle.
24. 15. abomination of—³*s.* in the holy place. *Mk.* 13. 14 6
Mk. 3. 31. mother and his brethren ; and, *standing* without
5. 1. he was ³*standing* by the lake of Gennesaret
2. he saw two boats *standing* by the lake
7. 38. and ³*standing* behind at his feet, weeping
18. 13. But the publican, *standing* afar off, would not lift
Jno. 18. 5. which betrayed him, was ³*standing* with them
16. but Peter was ³*standing* at the door without
18. the servants and the officers were ³*standing* there
22. one of the officers ³*standing* by struck Jesus
25. Simon Peter was ³*standing* and warming himself. 18
19. 25. ³*standing* by the cross of Jesus his mother. 26
20. 11. Mary was ³*standing* without at the tomb weeping
14. beholdeth Jesus *s.,* and knew not that it was Jesus
Acts 2. 14. But Peter, *standing* up with the eleven
4. 14. the man which was healed *standing* with them
5. 23. in all safety, and the keepers *standing* at the doors
25. are in the temple *standing* and teaching the people

323

STANDING

Acts 7. 55 the glory of God, and Jesus *s*. on the right hand of
16. 9. man of Macedonia ³*s*., beseeching him [God. 56
21. 40. Paul, ³*standing* on the stairs, beckoned
22. 13. ³*standing* by me said unto me, Brother Saul
   20. I also was *standing* by, and consenting
24. 21. I cried *s*. among them, Touching the resurrection
25. 10. Paul said, I am ²*s*. before Cæsar's judgement-seat
1 *Tim*. 3. 13. deacons gain to themselves a good ¹*standing*
Heb. 9. 8. while as the first tabernacle is yet *standing*
Rev. 5. 6. and in the midst of the elders, a Lamb ⁵*standing*
7. 1. I saw four angels *standing* at the four corners
   9. peoples and tongues, ³*standing* before the throne
   11. all the angels were ³*standing* round about the throne
10. 5. And the angel which I saw ²*standing* upon the sea
11. 4. the two candlesticks, *standing* before the Lord
14. 1. behold, the Lamb ⁵*standing* on the mount Zion
15. 2. ²*standing* by the glassy sea, having harps of God
18. 10. *standing* afar off for the fear of her torment
19. 17. I saw an angel *standing* in the sun
20. 12. dead, the great and the small, ²*s*. before the throne
   see compacted, stand.

Star.

Mat. 2. 2. we saw his *star* in the east. 9
   7. learned of them carefully what time the *s*. appeared
   10. And when they saw the *star*, they rejoiced
Acts 7. 43. Moloch, And the *star* of the god Rephan
1 *Cor*. 15. 41. one *star* differeth from another *star* in glory
Rev. 2. 28. and I will give him the morning *star*
8. 10. there fell from heaven a great *star*. 9. 1
   11. the name of the *star* is called Wormwood
22. 16. the offspring of David, the bright, the morning *s*.
   see day-star.

Stars.

Mat. 24. 29. and the *stars* shall fall from heaven. *Mk*. 13. 25
Lu. 21. 25. there shall be signs in sun and moon and *stars*
Acts 27. 20. neither sun nor *s*. shone upon us for many days
1 *Cor*. 15. 41. another glory of the *s*.; for one *star* differeth
Heb. 11. 12. so many as the *stars* of heaven in multitude
Jude 13. wandering *s*., for whom the blackness of darkness
Rev. 1. 16. he had in his right hand seven *s*. 20: 2. 1: 3. 1
6. 13. and the *stars* of the heaven fell unto the earth
8. 12. part of the moon, and the third part of the *s*. 12. 1
12. 1. and upon her head a crown of twelve *stars*

State.—*A. V*. ¹*affairs*, ²*end*.

Mat. 12. 45. last *s*. of that man becometh worse. *Lu*. 11. 26
Phil. 1. 27. see you or be absent, I may hear of your ¹*s*.
2. 19. of good comfort, when I know your *state*
   20. likeminded, who will care truly for your *state*
4. 11. whatsoever *state* I am, therein to be content [first
2 *Pet*. 2. 20. the last ²*s*. is become worse with them than the
   see affairs.

Stature.

Mat. 6. 27. anxious can add one cubit unto his *s*.? *Lu*. 12.
Lu. 2. 52. Jesus advanced in wisdom and *stature* [25
   19. 3. crowd, because he [Zacchæus] was little of *stature*
Eph. 4. 13. measure of the *stature* of the fulness of Christ

Staves.

Mat. 26. 47. a great multitude with swords and *s*. *Mk*. 14. 43
   55. Are ye come out as against a robber with swords
      and *staves*. *Mk*. 14. 48: *Lu*. 22. 52
   see staff.

STEWARD

Stayed.—*A. V*. ¹*forbade*, ²*kept*.

Lu. 4. 42. came unto him, and would have *stayed* him
Acts 19. 22. [Paul] he himself *stayed* in Asia for a while
27. 43. to save Paul, ²*stayed* them from their purpose
2 *Pet*. 2. 16. ass spake with man's voice and ¹*s*. the madness

Steal.

Mat. 6. 19. where thieves break through and *steal*
   20. where thieves do not break through nor *s*.   [13. 9
19. 18. Thou shalt not *s*. *Mk*. 10. 19 : *Lu*. 18. 20: *Rom*.
27. 64. lest haply his disciples come and *steal* him away
Jno. 10. 10. The thief cometh not, but that he may *steal*
Rom. 2. 21. preachest a man should not *s*., dost thou *s*.?
Eph. 4. 28. Let him that stole *steal* no more

Stedfast.—*A. V*. ¹*settled*.

1 *Cor*. 7. 37. he that standeth *stedfast* in his heart
15 58. Wherefore, my beloved brethren, be ye *stedfast*
2 *Cor*. 1. 7. and our hope for you is *stedfast*
Col. 1. 23. continue in the faith, grounded and ¹*stedfast*
Heb. 2. 2. the word spoken through angels proved *stedfast*
6. 19. a hope both sure and *s*. and entering into that
1 *Pet*. 5. 9. whom withstand *stedfast* in your faith
   see firm.

Stedfastly.—*A. V*. ¹*earnestly*, ²*instant*.

Mk. 8. 25. he looked *stedfastly*, and was restored, and saw
Lu. 9. 51. he *stedfastly* set his face to go to Jerusalem
22. 56. certain maid—looking ¹*s*. upon him, [Peter] said
Acts 1. 10. they were looking *s*. into heaven as he went
   14. with one accord continued *stedfastly* in prayer. 6. 4
   2. 42. they continued *stedfastly* in the apostles' teaching
   7. 55. looked up *s*. into heaven, and saw the glory [Stephen]
   14. Paul, looking ¹*stedfastly* on the council, said
Rom. 12. 12. patient in tribulation; continuing ²*s*. in prayer
2 *Cor*. 3. 7. Israel could not look *s*. upon the face of Moses
   13. children of Israel should not look *s*. on the end
Col. 4. 2. Continue *stedfastly* in prayer, watching therein

Stedfastness.

Col. 2. 5. beholding your order, and the *s*. of your faith
2 *Pet*. 3. 17. beware lest—ye fall from your own *stedfastness*

Steep.—*A. V*. ¹*steep place*.

Mat. 8. 32. down the ¹*s*. into the sea. *Mk*. 5. ¹13: *Lu*. 8. ¹33

Steersman.—*A. V*. ¹*governor*.

Jas. 3. 4. rudder, whither the impulse of the ¹*s*. willeth

Steppeth.

Jno. 5. 7. while I am coming, another *s*. down before me

Steps.

Rom. 4. 12. walk in the *s*. of that faith of our father Abraham
2 *Cor*. 12. 18. walked we not in the same *steps*?
1 *Pet*. 2. 21. an example, that ye should follow his *steps*

Stern.—*A. V*. ¹*hinder part*.

Mk. 4. 38. he himself [Jesus] was in the ¹*stern*, asleep
Acts 27. 29. they let go four anchors from the *stern*
   41. the ¹*stern* began to break up by the violence

Steward.

Mat. 20. 8. lord of the vineyard saith unto his *steward*
Lu. 8. 3. Joanna the wife of Chuza Herod's *steward*
12. 42. Who then is the faithful and wise *steward*

STEWARD

Lu. 16. 1. There was a certain rich man, which had a *s.*
  2. for thou canst be no longer *steward.* 3
  8. his lord commended the unrighteous *steward*
Tit. 1. 7. the bishop must be blameless, as God's *steward*

Stewards.—*A.V.* [1]*governors.*

1 *Cor.* 4. 1. ministers of Christ, and *s.* of the mysteries of God
  2. required in *stewards,* that a man be found faithful
Gal. 4. 2. under guardians and [1]*stewards* until the term
1 *Pet.* 4. 10. good *stewards* of the manifold grace of God

Stewardship.—*A.V.* [1]*dispensation of the gospel.*

Lu. 16. 2. render the account of thy *stewardship*
  3. my lord taketh away the *stewardship* from me? 4
1 *Cor.* 9. 17. I have a [1]*stewardship* intrusted to me

Sticks

Acts 28. 3. when Paul had gathered a bundle of *sticks*

Stiffnecked.

Acts 7. 51. Ye *s.* and uncircumcised in heart and ears

Still.

Mk. 4. 39. and said unto the sea, Peace, be *still*
Jno. 11. 20. met him: but Mary *still* sat in the house

Sting.—*A.V.* [1]*victory.*

1 *Cor.* 15. 55. where is thy victory? O death, where is thy [1]*s.?*
  56. The *sting* of death is sin; and the power of sin is
                see victory.

Stings.

Rev. 9. 10. they have tails like unto scorpions, and *stings*

Stinketh.

Jno. 11. 39. saith unto him, Lord, by this time he *stinketh*

Stir.

Acts 12. 18. there was no small *stir* among the soldiers
  19. 23. there arose no small *stir* concerning the Way
2 *Tim.* 1. 6. *stir* up the gift of God, which is in thee
2 *Pet.* 1. 13. *s.* you up by putting you in remembrance. 3. 1

Stirred.—*A.V.* [1]*madest,* [2]*moved,* [3]*provoked,* [4]*raised.*

Mat. 21. 10. all the city was [2]*stirred,* saying, Who is this?
Mk. 15. 11. the chief priests [3]*stirred* up the multitude
Acts 6. 12. they *stirred* up the people, and the elders. 21. 27
  13. 50. [4]*s.* up a persecution against Paul and Barnabas
  14. 2. Jews that were disobedient *stirred* up the souls
  21. 38. which before these days [1]*stirred* up to sedition
2 *Cor.* 9. 2. your zeal hath [3]*stirred* up very many of them
              see provoked.

Stirreth—ing.—*A.V.* [1]*raising,* [2]*stirred.*

Lu. 23. 5. the more urgent, saying, He *stirreth* up the people
Acts 17. 13. [2]*stirring* up and troubling the multitudes
  24. 12. disputing with any man or [1]*stirring* up a crowd

Stock.

Acts 13. 26. Brethren, children of the *stock* of Abraham
Phil. 3. 5. of the *stock* of Israel, of the tribe of Benjamin

Stocks.

Acts 16. 24. and made their [Paul and Silas] feet fast in the *s.*

Stoic.—*A.V.* [1]*Stoicks.*

Acts 17. 18. the Epicurean and [1]*S.* philosophers encountered

STONES

Stole.

Mat. 28. 13. His disciples came by night, and *s.* him away
Eph. 4. 28. Let him that *stole* steal no more

Stomach.

1 *Tim.* 5. 23. but use a little wine for thy *stomach's* sake

Stone.—*A.V.* [1]*stoned,* [2]*stones.*

Mat. 4. 6. haply thou dash thy foot against a *s. Lu.* 4. 11
  7. 9. ask him for a loaf, will give him a *stone. Lu.* 11. 11
  21. 42. The *stone* which the builders rejected. *Mk.* 12. 10:
        Lu. 20. 17: *Acts* 4. 11: 1 *Pet.* 2. 7
  44. falleth on this *stone* shall be broken. *Lu.* 20. 18
  24. 2. There shall not be left here one *stone* upon
    another. *Mk.* 13. 2: *Lu.* 19. 44: 21. 6
  27. 66. made the sepulchre sure, sealing the *stone*
Mk. 15. 46. he rolled a *stone* against the door of the tomb
  16. 3. Who shall roll us away the *stone* from the door
Lu. 4. 3. command this *stone* that it become bread
  20. 6. if we shall say, From men; all the people will *s.* us
  22. 41. parted from them about a *stone's* cast
  23. 53. laid him in a tomb that was hewn in *stone*
  24. 2. found the *stone* rolled away from the tomb. *Mat.*
    28. 2: *Mk.* 16. 4: *Jno.* 20. 1
Jno. 2. 6. there were six waterpots of *stone* set there
  8. 5. Moses commanded us to [1]*stone* such
  7. without sin among you, let him first cast a *stone*
  10. 31. The Jews took up stones again to *stone* him
  32. for which of those works do ye *stone* me?
  33. For a good work we *s.* thee not, but for blasphemy
  11. 8. the Jews were but now seeking to *stone* thee
  38. Now it was a cave, and a *stone* lay against it
  39. Jesus saith, Take ye away the *stone*   [eyes
  41. So they took away the *s.* And Jesus lifted up his
Acts 14. 5. to entreat them shamefully, and to *stone* them
  17. 29. the Godhead is like unto gold, or silver, or *stone*
2 *Cor.* 3. 3. not in tables of *s.,* but in tables that are hearts
1 *Pet.* 2. 4. unto whom coming, a living *stone* [of flesh
Rev. 2. 17. I will give him a white *s.,* and upon the *s.* a new
  9. 20. idols of gold—of *stone,* and of wood [name
  16. 21. hail, every *stone* about the weight of a talent
  18. 12. silver, and precious [2]*stone,* and pearls
  16. decked with gold and precious [2]*stone* and pearl!
  21. angel took up a *stone* as it were a great millstone
  21. 11. light was like unto a *stone* most precious
    see corner stone, Peter (proper names), stumbling.

Stoned.

Mat. 21. 35. and killed another, and *stoned* another
Acts 5. 26. feared the people, lest they should be *stoned*
  7. 59. And they *s.* Stephen, calling upon the Lord. 58
  14. 19. they *stoned* Paul, and dragged him out of the city
2 *Cor* 11. 25. Thrice was I beaten with rods, once was I *s.*
Heb. 11. 37. they were *stoned,* they were sawn asunder
  12. 20. a beast touch the mountain, it shall be *stoned*
              see stone.

Stones.

Mat. 3. 9. God is able of these *s.* to raise up children. *Lu.*
  4. 3. command that these *stones* become bread [3. 8
Mk. 5. 5. crying out, and cutting himself with *stones*
  13. 1. Master, behold, what manner of *stones*
Lu. 19. 40. if these should hold their peace, the *s.* will cry out
  21. 5. temple, how it was adorned with goodly *stones*
Jno. 8. 59. They took up *s.* therefore to cast at him. 10. 31
1 *Cor.* 3. 12. on the foundation gold, silver, costly *stones*
2 *Cor.* 3. 7. the ministration of death—engraven on *stones*
1 *Pet.* 2. 5. as living *stones,* are built up a spiritual house
Rev. 21. 19. adorned with all manner of precious *stones*
              see stone.

STONEST

Stonest.—*A.V. see stoneth.*
Stoneth.—*A.V.* ¹*stonest.*
Mat. 23. 37. ¹*stoneth* them that are sent unto her! *Lu.*13.¹34
Stony *A.V. -see rocky.*
Stood.—*A.V.* ¹*abode.*
Mat. 2. 9. it came and *s.* over where the young child was
 12. 46. his mother and his brethren *stood* without
 13. 2. and all the multitude *stood* on the beach
 20. 32. Jesus *stood* still, and called them [blind men]
 27. 11. Now Jesus *stood* before the governor
 47. some of them that *stood* there. *Mk.* 11. 5
Lu. 4. 39. he *stood* over her, and rebuked the fever
 6. 8. man that had his hand withered—arose and *s.* forth
 7. 14. touched the bier: and the bearers *stood* still
 9. 32. saw his glory, and the two men that *s.* with him
 17. 12. ten men that were lepers, which *stood* afar off
 18. 11. The Pharisee *stood* and prayed thus with himself
 23. 49. from Galilee, *stood* afar off, seeing these things
 24. 36. he himself *s.* in the midst of them. *Jno.* 20. 19, 26
Jno. 6. 22. multitude which *s.* on the other side of the sea
 8. 44. murderer from the beginning, and ¹*stood* not in the
 21. 4. day was now breaking, Jesus *stood* on the beach
Acts 3. 8. And leaping up, he *stood*, and began to walk
 9. 7. men that journeyed with him *stood* speechless
 10. 17. made inquiry for Simon's house, *s.* before the gate
 30. a man *stood* before me in bright apparel
 12. 14. ran in, and told that Peter *stood* before the gate
 14. 20. as the disciples *stood* round about him, he rose up
 17. 22. Paul *stood* in the midst of the Areopagus
 24. 20. what wrong-doing they found, when I *s.* before the
 25. 7. down from Jerusalem *s.* round about him [council
 27. 21. Paul *stood* forth in the midst of them
2 Tim. 4. 17. But the Lord *s.* by me, and strengthened me
Rev. 8. 3. another angel came and *stood* over the altar
 11. 11. they *stood* upon their feet; and great fear fell
 12. 4. and the dragon *stood* before the woman which was
 13. 1. and he *stood* upon the sand of the sea
 18. 17. as many as gain their living by sea, *s.* afar off
    see part, standing.

Stood by.
Mat. 26.73. that *s. by* came and said to Peter. *Mk.* 14. 69, 70
Mk. 14. 47. certain one of them that *s. by* drew his sword
 15. 35. some of them that *stood by,* when they heard it. 39
Lu. 19. 24. said unto them that *s. by,* Take away from him
 24. 4. two men *stood by* them in dazzling apparel
*Jno.*12.29. that *s. by,* and heard it, said that it had thundered
Acts 1. 10. two men *stood by* them in white apparel
 9. 39. all the widows *stood by* him weeping, and shewing
 22. 25. Paul said unto the centurion that *stood by*
 23. 2. commanded them that *stood by* him to smite him
 4. they that *s. by* said, Revilest thou God's high priest ?
 11. the Lord *stood by* him, and said, Be of good cheer
 27. 23. there *stood by* me this night an angel of the God
    see standing.

Stood up.—*A.V.* ¹*arose.*
Mk. 14. 57. there ¹*stood up* certain, and bare false witness
 60. the high priest *stood up* in the midst. *Mat.* 26. ¹62
Lu. 4. 16. on the sabbath day, and *stood up* to read
 10. 25. a certain lawyer *stood up* and tempted him
Acts 15. in these days Peter *stood up* in the midst
 5. 34. there *stood up* one in the council, a Pharisee
 11. 28. there *stood up* one of them named Agabus
 13. 16. Paul *stood up,* and beckoning with the hand said
 25. 18. Concerning whom, when the accusers *stood up*
    see array.

STRANGE

Stoop.
Mk. 1. 7. shoes I am not worthy to *s.* down and unloose
Stooped—ing.
Lu. 24. 12. *s.* and looking in, he seeth the linen. *Jno.* 20. 5
Jno. 8. 6. Jesus *stooped* down, and with his finger wrote. 8
 20. 11. as she wept, she *stooped* and looked into the tomb
Stop.
2 Cor. 11. 10. no man shall *stop* me of this glorying
Stopped.
Acts 7. 57. *stopped* their ears, and rushed upon him
Rom. 3. 19. under the law; that every mouth may be *s.*
Tit. 1. 11. whose mouths must be *s.;* men who overthrow
Heb. 11. 33. obtained promises, *s.* the mouths of lions

Store—d.—*A.V.* ¹*kept in store.*
1 Cor. 16. 2. lay by him in *store,* as he may prosper
1 Tim. 6. 19. laying up in *s.* for themselves a good foundation
2 Pet. 3. 7. by the same word have been ¹*stored* up for fire

Store-chamber.—*A.V.* ¹*storehouse.*
Lu. 12. 24. which have no ¹*store-chamber* nor barn

Storehouse.—*A.V. see store-chamber.*

Storm.—*A.V.* ¹*tempest.*
Mk. 4. 37. And there ariseth a great *storm* of wind
Lu. 8. 23. there came down a *storm* of wind on the lake
Acts 27. 18. as we laboured exceedingly with the ¹*storm*
2 Pet. 2. 17. springs without water, and mists driven by a ¹*s.*

Story.—*A.V.* ¹*loft.*
Acts 20. 9. Eutychus—fell down from the third ¹*story*

Straight.
Mat. 3. 3. Make his paths *s. Mk.*1. 3 : *Lu.* 3. 4 : *Jno.*1. 23
Lu. 3. 5. And the crooked shall become *straight*
 13. 13. she was made *straight,* and glorified God
Acts 9. 11. go to the street which is called *Straight*
Heb. 12. 13. and make *straight* paths for your feet

Strain.
Mat. 23. 24. Ye blind guides, which *strain* out the gnat

Strait.
Phil. 1. 23. But I am in a *strait* betwixt the two
    see narrow.

Straitened.—*A.V.* ¹*distressed,* ²*narrow.*
Mat. 7. 14. narrow is the gate, and ²*straitened* the way
Lu. 12. 50. how am I *straitened* till it be accomplished !
2 Cor. 4. 8. we are pressed on every side, yet not ¹*straitened*
 6. 12. not *s.* in us, but ye are *s.* in your own affections

Straitest.
Acts 26. 5. after the *straitest* sect of our religion I lived

Strake *A.V.—see lowered.*

Strange.
Lu. 5. 26. saying, We have seen *strange* things to-day
Acts 7. 6. that his seed should sojourn in a *strange* land
 17. 18. He seemeth to be a setter forth of *strange* gods
 20. thou bringest certain *strange* things to our ears
Heb. 13. 9. Be not carried away by divers and *s.* teachings

326

STRANGE

1 Pet. 4. 4. they think it *strange* that ye run not with them
12. think it not *strange* concerning the fiery trial among you—as though a *strange* thing happened
Jude 7. as Sodom and Gomorrah—gone after *strange* flesh
see foreign.

Stranger.

Mat. 25. 35. I was a *stranger*, and ye took me in. 43
38. when saw we thee a *stranger*? 44
Lu. 17. 18. returned to give glory to God, save this *stranger*?
Jno. 10. 5. a s. will they not follow, but will flee from him
see sojourn.

Strangers.—A.V. ¹other.

Mat. 17. 25. tribute? from their sons, or from *strangers*? 26
27. 7. bought—the potter's field, to bury *strangers* in
Jno. 10. 5. for they know not the voice of *strangers*
Acts 17. 21. all the Athenians and the s. sojourning there
1 Cor. 14. 21. by the lips of ¹s. will I speak unto this people
Eph. 2. 12. and s. from the covenants of the promise
19. So then ye are no more *strangers* and sojourners
1 Tim. 5. 10. if she hath used hospitality to *strangers*
Heb. 11. 13. having confessed that they were s. and pilgrims
13. 2. Forget not to shew love unto *strangers*
3 Jno. 5. doest toward them that are brethren and *strangers*
see elect, sojourners.

Strangled.

Acts 15. 20. from what is s., and from blood. 29: 21. 25

Strawed A.V.—see scattered.

Stream.—A.V. ¹flood.

Lu. 6. 48. the *stream* brake against that house. 49
Rom. 12. 15. cause her to be carried away by the ¹*stream*

Street.—A.V. ¹place where two ways met.

Mk. 11. 4. colt tied at the door without in the open ¹*street*
Acts 9. 11. go to the *street* which is called Straight
12. 10. went out, and passed on through one *street*
Rev. 11. 8. their dead bodies lie in the s. of the great city
21. 21. and the *street* of the city was pure gold
22. 2. [river of water] in the midst of the *street* thereof

Streets.

Mat. 6. 5. corners of the *streets*. that they may be seen. 2
12. 19. Neither shall any one hear his voice in the *streets*
Lu. 10. 10. go out into the *streets* thereof and say
13. 26. in thy presence, and thou didst teach in our s.
14. 21. into the *streets* and lanes of the city, and bring in
Acts 5. 15. that they even carried out the sick into the *streets*
see market-places.

Strength.—A.V. ¹ability, ²cannot, ³power.

Mk. 12. 33. to love him with all the heart, and—the *strength*
Lu. 1. 51. He hath shewed *strength* with his arm
10. 27. love the Lord thy God with all thy—s. Mk. 12. 30
16. 3. I have not ²*strength* to dig ; to beg I am ashamed
Acts 9. 22. his feet and his ankle bones received *strength*
9. 22. Saul increased the more in *strength*
2 Cor. 12. 9. that the ³*strength* of Christ may rest upon me
Eph. 1. 19. according to that working of the ³s. of his might
6. 10. be strong in the Lord, and in the ³s. of his might
1 Pet. 4. 11. ministering as of the ¹s. which God supplieth
Rev. 1. 16. countenance was as the sun shineth in his s.
see authority, might, power.

Strengthen.

1 Pet. 5. 10. shall himself perfect, stablish, *strengthen* you
see stablish.

STRIPES

Strengthened.—A.V. ¹established, ²strong.

Acts 9. 19. he [Saul] took food and was *strengthened*
16. 5. So the churches were ¹*strengthened* in the faith
Eph. 3. 16. ye may be s. with power through his Spirit
Col. 1. 11. s. with all power, according to the might
2 Tim. 2. 1. Thou therefore, my child, be ²*strengthened*
4. 17. the Lord stood by me, and *strengthened* me
Phil. 4. 13. I can do all things in him that *strengtheneth* me

Strengthening.

Lu. 22. 43. an angel from heaven, *strengthening* him
see stablishing.

Stretch.—A.V. ¹reached.

Mat. 12. 13. *Stretch* forth thy hand. Mk. 3. 5: Lu. 6. 10
Jno. 21. 18. s. forth thy hands, and another shall gird thee
2 Cor. 10. 14. For we ¹*stretch* not ourselves overmuch

Stretched.—A.V. ¹put.

Mat. 8. 3. he ¹s. forth his hand. 12. 49: 14. 31: Mk. 1. ¹41:
12. 13. And he *stretched* it forth. Mk. 3. 5 [Lu. 5. ¹13
26. 51. s. out his hand, and drew his sword, and smote
Lu. 22. 53. in the temple, ye s. not forth your hands against
Acts 26. 1. Then Paul *stretched* forth his hand [me
see put, spread.

Stretchest—ing.—A.V. ¹reaching, ²stretching.

Acts 4. 30. while thou ²*stretchest* forth thy hand to heal
Phil. 3. 13. ¹s. forward to the things which are before

Stricken.

Lu. 1. 7. they both were now well *stricken* in years. 18

Strict.—A.V. ¹perfect.

Acts 22. 3. instructed according to the ¹s. manner of the law

Strife—s.—A.V. ¹debate, ²strifes, ³strivings.

Rom. 1. 29. full of envy, murder, ¹*strife*, deceit
13. 13. Let us walk honestly—not in *strife* and jealousy
1 Cor. 3. 3. there is among you jealousy and *strife*
2 Cor. 12. 20. lest by any means there should be ²*strife*
Gal. 5. 20. *strife*, jealousies, wraths, factions, divisions
Phil. 1. 15. Some indeed preach Christ even of envy and s.
1 Tim. 6. 4. whereof cometh envy, ¹*strife*, railings
2 Tim. 2. 23. refuse, knowing that they gender *strifes*
Tit. 3. 9. genealogies, and ³s., and fightings about the law
see contention, disputes, faction.

Strike—eth.—A.V. ¹light.

Rev. 7. 16. neither shall the sun ¹*strike* upon them
9. 5. torment of a scorpion, when it *striketh* a man
see received.

Striker.

1 Tim. 3. 3. no brawler, no *striker*; but gentle. Tit. 1. 7

String A.V.—see bond.

Stripes.

Lu. 12. 47. to his will, shall be beaten with many *stripes*
48. worthy of *stripes*, shall be beaten with few *stripes*
Acts 16. 23. *stripes* upon them, they cast them into prison
33. and washed their *stripes*; and was baptized
2 Cor. 11. 23. in *stripes* above measure, in deaths oft. 6. 5
24. Of the Jews five times received I forty s. save one
1 Pet. 2. 24. by whose *stripes* ye were healed

STRIPPED

Stripped.
Mat. 27. 28. they *s.* him, and put on him a scarlet robe
Lu. 10. 30. robbers, which both *stripped* him and beat him

Strive.—*A.V.* ¹*conflict,* ²*suffer reproach.*
Mat. 12. 19. He shall not *strive,* nor cry aloud
Lu. 13. 24. *Strive* to enter in by the narrow door
Rom. 15. 30. ye *strive* together with me in your prayers
Col. 2. 1. I would have you know how greatly I ¹*s.* for you
1 *Tim.* 4. 10. For to this end we labour and ²*strive*
2 *Tim.* 2. 14. that they *strive* not about words, to no profit
24. the Lord's servant must not *strive,* but be gentle
see contend, contended.

Strived *A.V.*—*see aim.*

Striveth.
1 *Cor.* 9. 25. every man that *s.* in the games is temperate

Striving.—*A.V.* ¹*labouring fervently.*
Phil. 1. 27. with one soul *striving* for the faith of the gospel
Col. 1. 29. I labour also, *striving* according to his working
4. 12. always ¹*striving* for you in his prayers
Heb. 12. 4. not yet resisted unto blood, *striving* against sin
see fightings, strifes.

Stroke.—*A.V.* ¹*wound.*
Rev. 13. 14. who hath the ¹*stroke* of the sword, and lived
see death-stroke.

Strolling.—*A.V.* ¹*vagabond.*
Acts 19. 13. certain also of the ¹*strolling* Jews, exorcists

Strong.—*A.V.* ¹*able,* ²*mighty,* ³*powerful.*
Mat. 12. 29. how can one enter into the house of the
s. man—except he first bind the *s.* man? *Mk.*3. 27
Lu. 1. 80. child grew, and waxed *strong* in spirit. 2. 40
11. 21. *strong* man fully armed guardeth his own court
Acts 3. 16. faith in his name hath—made this man *strong*
Rom. 4. 20. waxed *s.* through faith, giving glory to God
15. 1. we that are *strong* ought to bear the infirmities
1 *Cor.* 1. 27. put to shame the things that are ²*strong*
4. 10. we are weak, but ye are *strong;* ye have glory
16. 13. stand fast in the faith, quit you like men, be *strong*
2 *Cor.* 10. 10. His letters, they say, are weighty and ³*strong*
12. 10. for when I am weak, then am I *strong*
13. 9. we rejoice, when we are weak, and ye are *strong*
Eph. 3. 18. may be ¹*strong* to apprehend with all the saints
6. 10. Finally, be *strong* in the Lord, and in the strength
*Heb.*5. 7. offered up prayers and supplications with *s.* crying
6. 18. we may have a *strong* encouragement, who have
11. 34. from weakness were made *strong,* waxed mighty
1 *Jno.* 2. 14. ye are *s.,* and the word of God abideth in you
Rev. 5. 2. I saw a *s.* angel proclaiming with a great voice
10. 1. I saw another ²*strong* angel coming down
18. 8. for *strong* is the Lord God which judged her
10. the great city, Babylon, the ²*strong* city!
see solid, strengthened, working.

Stronger.
Lu. 11. 22. when a *stronger* than he shall come upon him
1 *Cor.* 1. 25. the weakness of God is *stronger* than men
10. 22. provoke the Lord to jealousy? are we *s.* than he?

Strong holds.
2 *Cor.* 10. 4. mighty before God to the casting down of *s. h.*)

STUMBLING

Strove.—*A.V.* ¹*compelled.*
Jno. 6. 52. The Jews therefore *strove* one with another
Acts 7. 26. he [Moses] appeared unto them as they *strove*
23. 9. and *strove,* saying, We find no evil in this man
26. 11. punishing them—I ¹*s.* to make them blaspheme

Struck.—*A.V.* ¹*cut,* ²*smote,* ³*stuck fast.*
Mat. 26. 51. smote the servant of the high priest, and
²*struck* off his ear. *Mk.* 14. ¹47: *Lu.* 22. ¹50
68. thou Christ: who is he that ²*s.* thee? [his right ear
Jno. 18. 10. Peter—²*s.* the high priest's servant, and cut off
22. one of the officers standing by *s.* Jesus. *Lu.* 22. ²64
19. 3. and they ²*struck* him with their hands
Acts 27. 41. and the foreship ³*s.* and remained unmoveable
see smote.

Stubble.
1 *Cor.* 3. 12. silver, costly stones, wood, hay, *stubble*

Stuck fast *A.V.*—*see struck.*

Study.
1 *Th.* 4. 11. *study* to be quiet, and to do your own business
see diligence.

Stuff *A.V.*—*see goods.*

Stumble—d.—*A.V.* ¹*fall,* ²*offend*—*ed,* ³*stumbled.*
Mat. 5. 29. if thy right eye causeth thee to ²*s.* 18 ²9: *Mk.*9. ²47
30. if thy right hand causeth thee to ²*s.* 18. ²8: *Mk.*9. ²43
17. 27. lest we cause them to ²*stumble,* go thou to the sea
18. 6. cause one of these little ones which believe on me
to ²*stumble. Mk.* 9. ²42: *Lu.* 17. ²2
24. 10. then shall many ²*stumble,* and shall deliver up
Mk. 4. 17. because of the word, straightway they ²*stumble*
9. 45. if thy foot cause thee to ²*stumble,* cut it off
Jno. 6. 61. Jesus—said unto them, Doth this cause you to ²*s.?*
16. 1. that ye should not be made to ²*stumble*
Rom. 9. 32. They *stumbled* at the stone of stumbling
11. 11. I say then, Did they ³*stumble* that they might fall?
1 *Cor.* 8. 13. if meat maketh my brother to ²*stumble,* I will
eat no flesh—make not my brother to ²*stumble*
Jas. 2. 10. keep the whole law—yet ²*stumble* in one point
3. 2. For in many things we all ²*stumble*
1 *Pet.* 2. 8. for they *stumble* at the word, being disobedient
2 *Pet.* 1. 10. if ye do these things, ye shall never ¹*stumble*

Stumbleth.—*A.V.* ¹*offend*—*ed.*
Mat. 13. 21. because of the word, straightway he ¹*stumbleth*
Jno. 11. 9. If a man walk in the day, he *stumbleth* not
10. he ¹*stumbleth,* because the light is not in him
Rom. 14. 21. nor to do anything whereby thy brother *s.*
Jas. 3. 2. If any ¹*s.* not in word, the same is a perfect man

Stumbling.—*A.V.* ¹*falling,* ²*offence,* ³*offences,* ⁴*offend,* ⁵*offended.*
Mat. 11. 6. find none occasion of ³*stumbling* in me. *Lu.* 7. ⁵²³
13. 41. out of his kingdom all things that cause ³*stumbling*
18. 7. Woe unto the world because of occasions of
³*stumbling! Lu.* 17. ³1
Rom. 9. 32. They *stumbled* at the stone of *s.* [1 *Pet.* 2. 8
33. Behold, I lay in Zion a stone of *s.* and a rock of offence.
14. 13. causing the divisions and occasions of ³*stumbling*
1 *Cor.* 10. 32. Give no occasion of ²*stumbling.* 2 *Cor.* 6. ²3
1 *Jno.* 2. 10. light, and there is none occasion of *s.* in him
Jude 24. unto him that is able to guard you from ¹*stumbling*

STUMBLINGBLOCK

Stumblingblock.—*A.V.* ¹*offence.*
Mat. 16. 23. thou [Peter] art a ¹*stumblingblock* unto me
Rom. 11. 9. table be made a snare, and a trap, And a *s.*
    14. 13. that no man put a *s.* in his brother's way
1 *Cor.* 1. 23. but we preach Christ crucified, unto Jews a *s.*
    8. 9. lest by any means this liberty of yours become a *s.*
Gal. 5. 11. then hath the ¹*s.* of the cross been done away
Rev. 2. 14. who taught Balak to cast a *stumblingblock*

Stumblingstone *A.V.*—*see stumbling.*

Stupor.—*A.V.* ¹*slumber.*
Rom. 11. 8. is written, God gave them a spirit of ¹*stupor*

Subdue *A.V.*—*see subject.*

Subdued.
Heb. 11. 33. who through faith *subdued* kingdoms
    see subjected.

Subject.—*A.V.* ¹*put in subjection,* ²*put under,* ³*subdue,* ⁴*submit—ed.*
Lu. 2. 51. came to Nazareth; and he was *subject* unto them
    10. 17. even the devils are *subject* unto us in thy name
    20. rejoice not, that the spirits are *subject* unto you
Rom. 8. 7. for it is not *subject* to the law of God
    10. 3. did not ⁴*s.* themselves to the righteousness of God
1 *Cor.* 14. 32. the spirits of the prophets are *s.* to the prophets
    15. 27. he is excepted who did ²*subject* all things, ¹28
Eph. 5. 24. as the church is *s.* to Christ, so let the wives
Phil. 3. 21. able even to ³*subject* all things unto himself
Col. 2. 20. why, as--living in the world, do yes. yourselves
Heb. 2. 5. not unto angels did he ¹*s.* the world to come
    8. he left nothing that is not ²*subject* to him [bondage
    15. through fear of death were all their lifetime *s.* to
Jas. 4. 7. Be ⁴*s.* therefore unto God; but resist the devil
1 *Pet.* 2. 13. Be ⁴*subject* to every ordinance of man
    3. 22. authorities and powers being made *s.* unto him
    5. 5. Likewise, ye younger, be ⁴*subject* unto the elder
    see subjected, subjection.

Subjected.—*A.V.* ¹*put in subjection,* ²*put under,* ³*subdued,* ⁴*subject.*
Rom. 8. 20. For the creation was ⁴*s.* to vanity—who *s.* it
1 *Cor.* 15. 28. when all things have been ²*subjected*—the
    Son also himself be ⁴*subjected* to him
Heb. 2. 8. in that he ¹*subjected* all things—we see not yet
    all things ²*subjected* to him

Subjecting.—*A.V.* ¹*submitting.*
Eph. 5. 21. ¹*subjecting* yourselves one to another

Subjection.—*A.V.* ¹*obedience,* ²*obedient,* ³*under,* ⁴*subject,* ⁵*submit.*
Rom. 13. 1. Let every soul be in ⁴*s.* to the higher powers
    5. Wherefore ye must needs be in ⁴*subjection*
1 *Cor.* 14. 34. let them be in ¹*s.*, as also saith the law
    15. 27. He put all things in ³*s.*—All things are put in ³*s.*
    16. that ye also be in ⁵*subjection* unto such [*Eph.* 1. ⁵22
Gal. 2. 5. gave place in the way of *s.*, no, not for an hour
Eph. 5. 22. Wives, be in ⁵*s.* unto your own husbands. *Col.*
    3. ⁵18: 1 *Pet.* 3. 1
1 *Tim.* 2. 11. Let a woman learn in quietness with all *s.*
    3. 4. having his children in *s.* with all gravity [3. 5
Tit. 2. 5. being in ²*subjection* to their own husbands. 1 *Pet.*
    9. servants to be in ²*s.* to their own masters. 1 *Pet.* 2. ⁴18
    3. 1. Put them in mind to be in ⁴*subjection* to rulers
Heb. 2. 8. Thou didst put all things in *s.* under his feet
    12. 9. rather be in *subjection* unto the Father of spirits
    see bondage, obedience, subject, subjected.

SUDDENLY

Submit.
Heb. 13. 17. *s.* to them: for they watch in behalf of your souls
    see subject, subjection.

Submitted *A.V.*—*see subject.*

Submitting *A.V.*—*see subjecting.*

Suborned.
Acts 6. 11. Then they *suborned* men, which said, We have
    heard him speak

Substance.—*A.V.* ¹*goods,* ²*person.*
Lu. 8. 3. which ministered unto them of their *substance*
    15. 12. give me the portion of thy ¹*s.* that falleth to me
    13. he wasted his *substance* with riotous living
Heb. 1. 3. of his glory, and the very image of his ²*substance*
    see assurance, possession.

Subtilly.
Acts 7. 19. The same dealt *subtilly* with our race

Subtilty.—*A.V.* ¹*craft.*
Mat. 26. 4. they might take Jesus by *subtilty,* and kill him
Mk. 14. 1. might take him with ¹*subtilty,* and kill him
    see craftiness, guile.

Subvert *A.V.*—*see overthrow.*

Subverted *A.V.*—*see perverted.*

Subverting.
Acts 15. 24. troubled you with words, *subverting* your souls
2 *Tim.* 2. 14. words, to no profit, to the *s.* of them that hear

Succeeded.—*A.V.* ¹*room.*
Acts 24. 27. Felix ¹*succeeded* by Porcius Festus

Succour.—*A.V.* ¹*succoured.*
2 *Cor.* 6. 2. in a day of salvation did I *succour* thee
Heb. 2. 18. he is able to *succour* them that are tempted

Succoured *A.V.*—*see succour.*

Succourer.
Rom. 16. 2. she herself also hath been a *succourer* of many

Suck.—*A.V.* ¹*sucked.*
Mat. 24. 19. But woe unto them that are with child and—
    that give *s.* in those days! *Mk.* 13. 17: *Lu.* 21. 23
Lu. 11. 27. and the breasts which thou didst ¹*suck*
    23. 29. Blessed—and the breasts that never gave *suck*

Sucklings.
Mat. 21. 16. Out of the mouth of babes and *sucklings*

Sudden.
1 *Th.* 5. 3. Peace and safety, then *s.* destruction cometh

Suddenly.—*A.V.* ¹*unawares.*
Mk. 9. 8. *suddenly* looking round about, they saw no one
    13. 36. lest coming *suddenly* he find you sleeping
Lu. 2. 13. *suddenly* there was with the angel a multitude
    9. 39. a spirit taketh him, and he *suddenly* crieth out
    21. 34. lest haply—that day come on you ¹*suddenly*
Acts 2. 2. And *suddenly* there came from heaven a sound
    9. 3. and *s.* there shone round about him a light. 22. 6
    16. 26. and *suddenly* there was a great earthquake
    28. 6. that he would have swollen, or fallen down dead *s.*
    see hastily.

SUFFER

Suffer.—A.V. ¹*endure,* ²*receive,* ³*suffered.*
Mat. 3. 15. *Suffer* it now : for thus it becometh us to fulfil
8. 21. Lord, *s.* me first to go and bury my father. *Lu.* 9. 59
16. 21. Jerusalem, and *suffer* many things of the elders.
  17. 12 : *Mk.* 8. 31 : 9. 12 : *Lu.* 9. 22 : 17. 25
19. 14. *Suffer* the little children. *Mk.* 10. 14 : *Lu.* 18. 16
23. 13. neither *s.* ye them that are entering in to enter
Mk. 7. 12. no longer *suffer* him to do aught for his father
11. 16. not *suffer* that any man should carry a vessel
Lu. 22. 15. to eat this passover with you before I *suffer*
51. Jesus answered and said, *Suffer* ye thus far
24. 26. Behoved it not the Christ to ³*suffer* these things
46. written, that the Christ should *s. Acts* 3. 18 : 26. 23
Jno. 12. 7. *s.* her to keep it against the day of my burying
Acts 5. 41. counted worthy to *s.* dishonour for the Name
7. 24. seeing one of them *suffer* wrong, he defended
9. 16. how many things he must *s.* for my name's sake
17. 3. it behoved the Christ to ³*suffer,* and to rise again
Rom. 8. 17. with Christ ; if so be that we *suffer* with him
1 *Cor.* 3. 15. man's work shall be burned, he shall *s.* loss
10. 13. not *s.* you to be tempted above that ye are able
12. 26. one member suffereth, all the members *s.* with it
2 *Cor.* 1. 6. of the same sufferings which we also *suffer*
7. 9. that ye might ²*suffer* loss by us in nothing
Gal. 3. 4. Did ye ³*suffer* so many things in vain ?
Phil. 1. 29. to believe on him, but also to *s.* in his behalf
1 *Th.* 3. 4. we told you beforehand that we are to *s.* affliction
2 *Th.* 1. 5. the kingdom of God, for which ye also *suffer*
2 *Tim.* 1. 12. For the which cause I *suffer* also these things
2. 3. ¹*Suffer* hardship with me, as a good soldier of Christ
9. wherein I *suffer* hardship unto bonds, as a malefactor
3. 12. live godly in Christ Jesus shall *suffer* persecution
4. 5. But be thou sober in all things, ¹*suffer* hardship
1 *Pet.* 2. 20. do well, and *s.* for it, ye shall take it patiently
3. 14. if ye should *s.* for righteousness' sake, blessed are
17. God should so will, that ye *suffer* for well-doing
4. 15. let none of you *suffer* as a murderer
16. if a man *s.* as a Christian, let him not be ashamed
19. let them also that *s.* according to the will of God
Rev. 2. 10. Fear not the things which thou art about to *s.*
11. *s.* and *s.* not their dead bodies to be laid in a tomb
see bear (with), endure, entreat, give leave, permit, send, strive, suffereth.

Suffered.—A.V. ¹*suffereth.*
Mat. 19. 8. Moses—*suffered* you to put away your wives
24. 43. would not have *s.* his house to be broken through
27. 19. I have *suffered* many things this day in a dream
Mk. 1. 34. he *suffered* not the devils to speak. *Lu.* 4. 41
5. 19. And he *suffered* him not, but saith unto him
26. and had *suffered* many things of many physicians
37. And he *s.* no man to follow with him. *Lu.* 8. 51
10. 4. Moses *suffered* to write a bill of divorcement
Lu. 13. 2. Galilæans, because they have *s.* these things ?
Acts 13. 18. forty years *suffered* he their manners
14. 16. *s.* all the nations to walk in their own ways
16. 7. the Spirit of Jesus *suffered* them not
19. 30. unto the people, the disciples *suffered* him not
28. 4. from the sea, yet Justice hath not ¹*suffered* to live
16. Paul was *suffered* to abide by himself
2 *Cor.* 7. 12. nor for his cause that *suffered* the wrong
11. 25. once was I stoned, thrice I *suffered* shipwreck
Phil. 3. 8. for whom I *suffered* the loss of all things ʻtreated
14. ye also *s.* the same things of your own countrymen
Heb. 2. 18. in that he himself hath *suffered* being tempted
5. 8. yet learned obedience by the things which he *s.*
9. 26. else must he often have *s.* since the foundation
13. 12. through his own blood, *suffered* without the gate

1 *Pet.* 2. 21. Christ also *s.* for you, leaving you an example
23. when he *suffered,* threatened not ; but committed
3. 18. Because Christ also *suffered* for sins once
4. 1. as Christ *suffered* in the flesh—for he that hath
suffered in the flesh hath ceased from sin
5. 10. after that ye have *suffered* a little while
see hindered, leave, suffer, suffereth.

Sufferest.
Rev. 2. 20. that thou *sufferest* the woman Jezebel

Suffereth.—A.V. ¹*suffer,* ²*suffered,* ³*vexed.*
Mat. 3. 15. to fulfil all righteousness. Then he ²*s.* him
11. 12. now the kingdom of heaven *suffereth* violence
17. 15. he is epileptic, and ³*suffereth* grievously ʃsuffer
1 *Cor.* 12. 26. whether one member ¹*s.,* all the members
13. 4. Love *s.* long, and is kind ; love envieth not
see suffered.

Suffering.—A.V. ¹*afflicted.*
Acts 27. 7. against Cnidus, the wind not further *suffering* us
Heb. 2. 9. Jesus, because of the *suffering* of death crowned
Jas. 5. 10. for an example of *suffering* and of patience
5. 10. Is any among you ¹*suffering* ? let him pray
1 *Pet.* 2. 19. a man endureth griefs, *suffering* wrongfully
Jude 7. *suffering* the punishment of eternal fire

Sufferings.—A.V. ¹*afflictions.*
Rom. 8. 18. For I reckon that the *s.* of this present time
2 *Cor.* 1. 5. For as the *sufferings* of Christ abound unto us
6. which worketh in the patient enduring of the same *s.*
7. as ye are partakers of the *sufferings,* so also are ye
Phil. 3. 10. the fellowship of his *s.,* becoming conformed
Col. 1. 24. Now I rejoice in my *sufferings* for your sake
2 *Tim.* 3. 11. persecutions, ¹*s. ;* what things befell me
Heb. 2. 10. author of their salvation perfect through *s.*
10. 32. ye endured a great conflict of ¹*sufferings*
1 *Pet.* 1. 11. it testified beforehand the *sufferings* of Christ
4. 13. insomuch as ye are partakers of Christ's *sufferings*
5. 1. fellow-elder, and a witness of the *sufferings* of Christ
9. that the same ¹*s.* are accomplished in your brethren

Suffice.
1 *Pet.* 4. 3. For the time past may *suffice* to have wrought

Sufficeth.
Jno. 14. 8. Lord, shew us the Father, and it *sufficeth* us

Sufficiency.
2 *Cor.* 3. 5. as from ourselves ; but our *s.* is from God
9. 8. that ye, having always all *sufficiency* in everything

Sufficient.—A.V. ¹*able.*
Mat. 6. 34. *Sufficient* unto the day is the evil thereof
Jno. 6. 7. Philip—Two hundred pennyworth of bread is not *s.*
2 *Cor.* 2. 6. *Sufficient* to such a one is this punishment
16. life unto life. And who is *sufficient* for these things ?
3. 5. not that we are *sufficient* of ourselves, to account
6. who also made us ¹*s.* as ministers of a new covenant
12. 9. My grace is *sufficient* for thee : for my power

Sum.—A.V. ¹*gather together in one.*
Acts 22. 28. With a great *sum* obtained I this citizenship
Eph. 1. 10. of the times, to ¹*sum* up all things in Christ
see point, price.

Summed up.—A.V. ¹*briefly comprehended.*
Rom. 13. 9. it is ¹*s.* up in this word, namely, Thou shalt

330

SUMMER

Summer.
Mat. 24. 32. fig tree—tender, and putteth forth its leaves,
  ye know that the *s.* is nigh. *Mk.* 13. 28 : *Lu.* 21. 30

Sumptuous—ly.—*A.V.* ¹*goodly.*
Lu. 16. 19. in purple and fine linen, faring *s.* every day
Rev. 18. 14. things that were dainty and ¹*s.* are perished

Sun
Mat. 5. 45. he maketh his *sun* to rise on the evil and
  13. 6. when the *s.* was risen, they were scorched. *Mk.* 4. 6
  43. Then shall the righteous shine forth as the *sun*
  17. 2. his face did shine as the *sun*, and his garments
  24. 29. the *s.* shall be darkened, and the moon. *Mk.* 13. 24
Mk. 1. 32. And at even, when the *sun* did set. *Lu.* 4. 40
  16. 2. they come to the tomb when the *sun* was risen
Lu. 21. 25. shall be signs in *sun* and moon and stars
  23. 45. the *sun's* light failing: and the veil of the temple
Acts 2. 20. The *sun* shall be turned into darkness
  13. 11. shalt be blind, not seeing the *sun* for a season
  26. 13. light from heaven, above the brightness of the *s.*
  27. 20. And when neither *sun* nor stars shone upon us
1 *Cor.* 15. 41. There is one glory of the *sun*, and another
Eph. 4. 26. let not the *sun* go down upon your wrath
Jas. 1. 11. For the *sun* ariseth with the scorching wind
Rev. 1. 16. his countenance was as the *sun* shineth
  6. 12. the *sun* became black as sackcloth of hair
  7. 16. neither shall the *s.* strike upon them, nor any heat
  8. 12. the third part of the *sun* was smitten
  9. 2. and the *sun* and the air were darkened by reason
  10. 1. his face was as the *sun*, and his feet as pillars
  12. 1. a woman arrayed with the *sun*, and the moon under
  16. 8. the fourth poured out his bowl upon the *sun*
  19. 17. I saw an angel standing in the *sun*
  21. 23. And the city hath no need of the *sun*
  22. 5. they need no light of lamp, neither light of *sun*

Sunder *A.V.*—*see asunder.*

Sundry *A.V.*—*see old.*

Sung.
Mat. 26. 30. And when they had *sung* a hymn. *Mk.* 14. 26
  see sing.

Sunk.—*A.V.* ¹*drowned.*
Mat. 18. 6. he should be ¹*sunk* in the depth of the sea
  see borne.

Sunrising.—*A.V.* ¹*east.*
Rev. 7. 2. I saw another angel ascend from the ¹*sunrising*
  16. 12. ready for the kings that come from the ¹*sunrising*

Sup
Lu. 17. 8. Make ready wherewith I may *sup*
Rev. 3. 20. I will come in to him, and will *sup* with him

Superfluity.—*A.V.* ¹*abundance.*
Mk. 12. 44. all did cast in of their ¹*superfluity.* *Lu.* 21. ¹4
  see overflowing.

Superfluous.
2 *Cor.* 9. 1. it is *superfluous* for me to write to you

Superscription.
Mat. 22.20. Whose is this image and *s.*? *Mk.* 12. 16: *Lu.*
Mk. 15. 26. And the *s.* of his accusation. *Lu.* 23. 38. | 20. 24

SUPPORT

Superstition *A.V.*—*see religion.*

Superstitious.
Acts 17. 22. in all things I perceive that ye are somewhat *s.*

Supped.—*A.V.* ¹*supper.*

Supper.—*A.V.* ¹*supped.*
Mk. 6. 21. Herod on his birthday made a *supper*
Lu. 14. 12. When thou makest a dinner or a *s.*, call not
  16. A certain man made a great *s.*; and he bade many
  17. and he sent forth his servant at *supper* time
  24. none of those men which were bidden shall taste of
  22. 20. And the cup in like manner after *supper* [my *s.*
Jno. 12. 2. So they made him a *s.* there: and Martha
  13. 2. And during *s.*, the devil having already put into the
  4. [Jesus] riseth from *supper*, and layeth aside ₁heart
  21. 20. which also leaned back on his breast at the *supper*
1 *Cor.* 11. 20. it is not possible to eat the Lord's *supper*
  21. each one taketh before other his own *supper*
  25. In like manner also the cup, after ¹*supper*
Rev. 19. 9. Blessed—hidden to the marriage *s.* of the Lamb
  17. Come and be gathered—unto the great *supper* of God

Supplication—s.—*A.V.* ¹*fervent prayer*, ²*prayed*,
  ³*prayer—s*, ⁴*request.*
Lu. 1. 13. because [Zacharias] thy ³*supplication* is heard
  2. 37. worshipping with fastings and ³*supplications*
  5. 33. disciples of John fast often, and make ³*supplications*
  21. 36. watch ye at every season, making ³*supplication*
  22. 32. I made ²*s.* for thee, that thy faith fail not
Rom. 10. 1. my heart's desire and my ³*supplication* to God
2 *Cor.* 1. 11. helping together on our behalf by your ³*s.*
  9. 14. while they themselves also, with ³*s.* on your behalf
Eph. 6. 18. with all prayer and *s.*—*s.* for all the saints
Phil. 1. 4. always in every ³*s.* of mine—making my ⁴*s.*
  19. this shall turn to my salvation, through your ³*s.*
  4. 6. but in everything by prayer and *supplication*
1 *Tim.* 2. 1. I exhort therefore, first of all, that *supplications*
  5. 5. and continueth in *s.* and prayers night and day
2 *Tim.* 1. 3. how unceasing is my remembrance of thee in my
Heb. 5. 7. and *supplications* with strong crying and tears [*s.*
Jas. 5. 16. The ¹*s.* of a righteous man availeth much
1 *Pet.* 3. 12. upon the righteous, And his ears unto their ³*s.*

Supplied—eth.—*A.V.* ¹*giveth*, ²*ministered—eth.*
1 *Cor.* 16. 17. which was lacking on your part they *s.*
2 *Cor.* 9. 10. he that ²*s.* seed to the sower and bread for food
  11. 9. Macedonia, *supplied* the measure of my want
Gal. 3. 5. He therefore that ²*supplieth* to you the Spirit
Eph. 4. 16. through that which every joint *supplieth*
Col. 2. 19. whom all the body, being ²*s.* and knit together
1 *Pet.* 4. 11. ministering as of the strength which God ¹*s.*
2 *Pet.* 1. 11. for thus shall be richly ²*supplied* unto you
  see filleth up.

Supply.—*A.V.* ¹*add.*
2 *Cor.* 8. 14. being a *s.*—abundance also may become a *s.*
Phil. 1. 19. through your supplication and the *s.* of the Spirit
  2. 30. hazarding his life to *supply* that which was lacking
2 *Pet.* 1. 5. in your faith ¹*supply* virtue
  see fulfil.

Support.
1 *Th.* 5. 14. *support* the weak, be longsuffering toward all
  see help.

SUPPOSE

Suppose.—*A.V.* ¹*think.*
Lu. 7. 43. He, I *suppose*, to whom he forgave the most
Jno. 21. 25. I *s.* that even the world itself would not contain
Acts 2. 15. these are not drunken, as ye *suppose* [the books
13. 25. What ¹*suppose* ye that I am? I am not he
see account, reckon, think.

Supposed.—*A.V.* ¹*thought,* ²*wont.*
Mat. 20. 10. they *supposed* that they would receive more
Mk. 6. 49. walking on the sea, *s.* that it was an apparition
Lu. 3. 23. being the son (as was *supposed*) of Joseph
19 11. they ¹*s.* that the kingdom of God was immediately
24. 37. affrighted, and *supposed* that they beheld a spirit
Acts 7. 25. and he *s.* that his brethren understood [Moses]
16. 13. where we ²*supposed* there was a place of prayer
21. 29. Ephesian, whom they *s.* that Paul had brought
25. 18. brought no charge of such evil things as I *s.*
see counted.

Supposing.—*A.V. saying.*
Lu. 2. 44. but *supposing* him to be in the company
Jno 11. 31. ¹*s.* that she was going unto the tomb to weep
20. 15. She, [Mary Magdalene] *s.* him to be the gardener
Acts 14. 19. out of the city, *s.* that he [Paul] was dead
16. 27. *supposing* that the prisoners had escaped
27. 13. *supposing* that they had obtained their purpose
1 *Tim.* 6. 5. *supposing* that godliness is a way of gain
see thinking.

Supreme.
1 *Pet.* 2. 13. Be subject—to the king, as *supreme*

Sure.
Mat. 27. 64. Command therefore that the sepulchre be
made *sure* [ye can
65. Ye have a guard: go your way, make it as *sure* as
66. So they went, and made the sepulchre *sure*
Acts 13. 34. give you the holy and *sure* blessings of David
Rom. 4. 16. that the promise may be *sure* to all the seed
Heb. 6. 19. an anchor of the soul, a hope both *s.* and stedfast
2 *Pet.* 1. 10. diligence to make your calling and election *s.*
19. we have the word of prophecy made more *sure*
see firm, know, we know.

Surely *A.V.*—*see of a truth.*

Surety.
Heb. 7. 22. Jesus become the *surety* of a better covenant
see of a truth.

Surfeiting.
Lu. 21. 34. haply your hearts be overcharged with *surfeiting*

Surge.—*A.V.* ¹*wave.*
Jas. 1. 6. he that doubteth is like the ¹*surge* of the sea

Surmised.—*A.V.* ¹*deemed.*
Acts 27. 27. about midnight the sailors ¹*surmised* that they

Surmisings.
1 *Tim.* 6. 4. whereof cometh envy, strife, railings, evil *s.*

Surname—d.—*A.V.* ¹*surname.*
Mk. 3. 16. and Simon he *surnamed* Peter
17. them he *s.* Boanerges, which is, Sons of thunder
Acts 1. 23. Barsabbas, who was *surnamed* Justus
4. 36. Joseph, who by the apostles was *s.* Barnabas
10. 5. and fetch one Simon, who is ¹*surnamed* Peter. 18
11. 13. and fetch Simon, whose *surname* is Peter
12. 12. the mother of John whose *surname* was Mark
see called.

SWELLING

Surpasseth.—*A.V.* ¹*excelleth.*
2 *Cor.* 3. 10. by reason of the glory that ¹*surpasseth*

Suspense.—*A.V.* ¹*doubt.*
Jno. 10. 24. How long dost thou hold us in ¹*suspense?*

Sustenance.
Acts 7. 11. and our fathers found no *sustenance*

Swaddling.
Lu. 2. 7. she wrapped him in *swaddling* clothes. 12

Swallow—ed.—*A.V.* ¹*drowned.*
Mat. 23. 24. which strain out the gnat, and *s.* the camel
1 *Cor.* 15. 54. Death is *swallowed* up in victory
2 *Cor.* 2. 7. such a one should be *s.* up with his—sorrow
5. 4. that what is mortal may be *swallowed* up of life
Heb. 11. 29. which the Egyptians assaying to do were ¹*s.* up
Rev. 12. 16. the earth opened her mouth, and *s.* up the river

Sware.—*A.V.* ¹*sworn.*
Mk. 6. 23. [Herod] *s.* unto her, Whatsoever thou shalt ask
Lu. 1. 73. The oath which he *sware* unto Abraham [4. ¹³
Heb. 3. 11. As I *sware* in my wrath, They shall not enter.
18. And to whom *sware* he that they should not enter
6. 13. could swear by none greater, he *sware* by himself
7. 21. The Lord *sware* and will not repent himself
Rev. 10. 6. and *sware* by him that liveth for ever and ever

Swear.—*A.V.* ¹*sweareth.*
Mat. 5. 34. but I say unto you, *Swear* not at all
36. Neither shalt thou *swear* by thy head [of the temple
23. 16. Whosoever shall *s.* by the temple—*s.* by the gold
18. *swear* by the altar—¹*swear* by the gift that is upon it
26. 74. Then began he to curse and to *swear.* *Mk.* 14. 71
Heb. 6. 13. since he could *swear* by none greater, he sware
16. For men *swear* by the greater: and in every dispute
Jas. 5. 12. But above all things, my brethren, *swear* not
see sweareth.

Swearers.—*A.V.* ¹*perjured persons.*
1 *Tim.* 1. 10. for men-stealers, for liars, for false ¹*swearers*

Sweareth.—*A.V.* ¹*swear.*
Mat. 23. 20. He therefore that ¹*s.* by the altar, *s.* by it
21. And he that ¹*sweareth* by the temple, *sweareth* by it
22. he that ¹*s.* by the heaven, *s.* by the throne of God
see swear.

Sweat.
Lu. 22. 44. his *s.* became as it were great drops of blood

Sweep.
Lu. 15. 8. doth not light a lamp, and *sweep* the house

Sweet.—*A.V.* ¹*fresh.*
Eph. 5. 2. sacrifice to God for an odour of a *sweet* smell
Jas. 3. 11. from the same opening *sweet* water and bitter?
12. neither can salt water yield ¹*sweet*
Rev. 10. 9. in thy mouth it shall be *sweet* as honey. 10
see savour.

Sweetsmelling *A.V.*—*see smell.*

Swelling.
2 *Pet.* 2. 18. For, uttering great *swelling* words of vanity
Jude 16. (and their mouth speaketh great *swelling* words)

Swellings.
2 Cor. 12. 20. backbitings, whisperings, *swellings*, tumults

Swept.
Mat. 12. 44. he findeth it empty, *swept*. Lu. 11. 25

Swerved.
1 Tim. 1. 6. from which things some having *swerved*

Swift.
Rom. 3. 15. Their feet are *swift* to shed blood
Jas. 1. 19. let every man be *swift* to hear, slow to speak
2 Pet. 2. 1. bringing upon themselves *swift* destruction

Swiftly.—A.V. ¹shortly.
2 Pet. 1. 14. putting off of my tabernacle cometh ¹*swiftly*

Swim.
Acts 27. 42. lest any of them should *swim* out, and escape
43. they which could *swim* should cast themselves

Swine.
Mat. 7. 6. neither cast your pearls before the *swine*
8. 30. a herd of many *swine* feeding. Mk. 5. 11: Lu. 8. 32
31. send us away into the herd of *swine*. Mk. 5. 12
32. went into the *swine*. Mk. 5. 13, 16: Lu. 8. 33
Lu. 15. 15. he sent him into his fields to feed *swine*
16. been filled with the husks that the *swine* did eat

Swollen.
Acts 28. 6. they expected that he would have *swollen*

Sword.
Mat. 10. 34. I came not to send peace, but a *sword* [18. 10
26. 51. drew his *s*., and smote the servant. Mk. 14. 47: Jno.
52. Put up again thy *sword* into its place: for all they
that take the *s*. shall perish with the *s*. Jno. 18. 11
Lu. 2. 35. a *sword* shall pierce through thine own soul
22. 36. let him sell his cloke, and buy a *sword*
49. Lord, shall we smite with the *sword*? [the *sword*
Acts 12. 2. he [Herod] killed James the brother of John with
16. 27. jailor—drew his *s*., and was about to kill himself
Rom. 8. 35. or famine, or nakedness, or peril, or *sword*?
13. 4. be afraid; for he beareth not the *sword* in vain
Eph. 6. 17. the *s*. of the Spirit, which is the word of God
Heb. 4. 12. active, and sharper than any two-edged *sword*
11. 34. escaped the edge of the *sword*, from weakness
37. were tempted, they were slain with the *sword*
Rev. 1. 16. out of his mouth proceeded a sharp two-edged *s*.
2. 12. saith he that hath the sharp two-edged *sword*
16. war against them with the *sword* of my mouth
6. 4. and there was given unto him a great *sword*
8. to kill with *s*., and with famine, and with death
13. 10. kill with the *sword*, with the *s*. must he be killed
14. the beast, who hath the stroke of the *s*., and lived
19. 15. out of his mouth proceedeth a sharp *sword*
21. the rest were killed with the *sword* of him that
sat upon the horse, even the *s*. which came forth

Swords.
Mat. 26. 47. a great multitude with *s*. and staves. Mk. 14. 43
55. Are ye come out as against a robber with *swords*
and staves to seize me? Mk. 14. 48: Lu. 22. 52
Lu. 22. 38. And they said, Lord, behold, here are two *s*.

Sworn.
Acts 2. 30. knowing that God had *s*. with an oath to him
see *sware, vouchsafed*.

Sycamine.
Lu. 17. 6. ye would say unto this *s*. tree, Be thou rooted up

Sycomore.
Lu. 19. 4. [Zacchæus] climbed up into a *sycomore* tree

Synagogue.—A.V. ¹*assembly*, ²*congregation*.
Mat. 12. 9. [Jesus] departed thence, and went into their *s*.
13. 54. he taught them in their *s*. Mk. 1. 21 : 3. 1 : 6. 2.
Mk. 1. 23. in their *s*. a man with an unclean. Lu. 4. 33
29. of the *synagogue*—into the house of Simon. Lu. 4. 38
5. 22. one of the rulers of the *s*. 36, 38: Lu. 8 41, 49: 13. 14
Lu. 4. 16. entered—into the *synagogue* on the sabbath day
20. the eyes of all in the *s*. were fastened on him
28. they were all filled with wrath in the *synagogue*
7. 5. he loveth our nation, and himself built us our *s*.
Jno. 6. 59. in the *synagogue*, as he taught in Capernaum
9. 22. confess him to be Christ, he—be put out of the *s*.
12. 42. lest they should be put out of the *synagogue*
Acts 6. 9. that were of the *s*. called the *s*. of the Libertines
13. 14. to Antioch of Pisidia; and they went into the *s*.
15. the rulers of the *synagogue* sent unto them
43. when the ²*s*. broke up—proselytes followed Paul
14. 1. Iconium—they entered together into the *s*. of the
17. 1. to Thessalonica, where was a *synagogue* of the Jews
10. unto Berœa—went into the *synagogue* of the Jews
17. So he reasoned in the *s*. with the Jews. 18. 4
18. 7. Titus Justus—whose house joined hard to the *s*.
8. And Crispus, the ruler of the *synagogue*, believed
17. laid hold on Sosthenes, the ruler of the *synagogue*
26. he began to speak boldly in the *synagogue*. 19. 8
22. 19. I [Paul] imprisoned and beat in every *synagogue*
Jas. 2. 2. there come into your ¹*s*. a man with a gold ring
Rev. 2. 9. Jews, and they are not, but are a *s*. of Satan
3. 9. Behold, I give of the *synagogue* of Satan
see *synagogues*.

Synagogues.—A.V. ¹*synagogue*.
Mat. 4. 23. Jesus went about in all Galilee, teaching in
their *synagogues*. 9. 35: Mk. 1. 39: Lu. 4. 44 : 13. 10
6. 2. sound not a trumpet—as the hypocrites do in the *s*.
5. they love to stand and pray in the *synagogues*
10. 17. in their *synagogues* they will scourge you. 23. 34
23. 6. chief seats in the *s*. Mk. 12. 39: Lu. 11. 43: 20. 46
Mk. 13. 9. and in the *synagogues* shall ye be beaten
Lu. 4. 15. And he taught in their *s*., being glorified of all
12. 11. And when they bring you before the *synagogues*
21. 12. delivering you up to the *synagogues* and prisons
Jno. 16. 2. They shall put you out of the *synagogues*
18. 20. I ever taught in ¹*synagogues*, and in the temple
Acts 9. 2. asked of him letters to Damascus unto the *s*.
20. straightway in the *synagogues* he proclaimed Jesus
13. 5. they proclaimed the word of God in the *synagogues*
15. 21. Moses—being read in the *synagogues* every sabbath
24. 12. or stirring up a crowd, nor in the *synagogues*
26. 11. [Saul] punishing them oftentimes in all the ¹*s*.

T.

Tabernacle.—A.V. ¹*dwell*.
Acts 7. 43. ye took up the *tabernacle* of Moloch, And the star
44. Our fathers had the *tabernacle* of the testimony
15. 16. I will build again the *tabernacle* of David
2 Cor. 5. 1. if the earthly house of our *tabernacle* be dissolved
4. For indeed we that are in this *tabernacle* do groan

TABERNACLE

Heb. 8. 2. a minister of the sanctuary, and of the true *t.*
5. about to make the *tabernacle :* for, See, saith he
9. 2. there was a *tabernacle* prepared, the first, wherein
3. the *tabernacle* which is called the Holies of holies
6. priests go in continually into the first *tabernacle*
8. while as the first *tabernacle* is yet standing
11. through the greater and more perfect *t.*, not made
21. the *t.* and all the vessels—sprinkled in like manner
13.10. they have no right to eat which serve the *tabernacle*
2 *Pet.* 1. 13. as long as I am in this *tabernacle,* to stir you up
14. the putting off of my *tabernacle* cometh swiftly
Rev. 7. 15. sitteth on the throne shall spread his *1t.* over
13. 6. to blaspheme his name, and his *tabernacle*
15. 5. temple of the *t.* of the testimony in heaven
21. 3. Behold, the *tabernacle* of God is with men
see habitation.

Tabernacles.—*A. V. 1habitations.*

Mat. 17. 4. I will make here three *t. Mk.* 9. 5 ; *Lu.* 9. 33
Lu. 16. 9. they may receive you into the eternal *1t.*
see tents, feast.

Table.

Mat. 15. 27. Yea, Lord : for even the dogs eat of the crumbs which fall from their masters' *table. Mk.* 7. 28
Lu. 16. 21. the crumbs that fell from the rich man's *table*
22. 21. hand of him that betrayeth me is with me on the *t.*
30. ye may eat and drink at my *table* in my kingdom
Jno. 13. 28. no man at the *table* knew for what intent he
Rom. 11. 9. Let their *table* be made a snare, and a trap
1 *Cor.* 10. 21. ye cannot partake of the *table* of the Lord, and of the *table* of devils
Heb. 9. 2. wherein were the candlestick, and the *table*
see meat.

Writing **Table** *A. V—see tablet.*

Tables.

Mat. 21. 12. and overthrew the *t. Mk.* 11. 15 ; *Jno.* 2. 15
Acts 6. 2. forsake the word of God, and serve *tables*
2 *Cor.* 3. 3. not in *t.* of stone, but in *t.* that are hearts of flesh
Heb. 9. 4. Aaron's rod that budded, and the *tables* of the

Tablet.—*A. V. 1table.*

Lu. 1. 63. And he asked for a writing *1tablet,* and wrote

Tackling.

Acts 27. 19. cast out with their own hands the *t.* of the ship

Tail—s.

Rev. 9. 10. And they have *tails* like unto scorpions— and in their *tails* is power to hurt men
19. in their *tails :* for their *tails* are like unto serpents
12. 4. And his *tail* draweth the third part of the stars

Take.—*A. V. 1apprehend, 2carry, 3lead, 4make, 5receive, 6seize, 7taketh, 8took.*

Mat. 1. 20. fear not to *take* unto thee Mary thy wife
2. 13. Arise and *take* the young child and his mother. 20
9. 6. *t.* up thy bed. *Mk.* 2. 9, 11 ; *Lu.* 5. 24 ; *Jno.* 5. 8, 12
10. 38. *7t.* his cross and follow after me, is not worthy
11. 12. and men of violence *take* it by force
29. *Take* my yoke upon you, and learn of me
15. 26. it not meet to *t.* the children's bread. *Mk.* 7. 27
16. 5. to the other side and forgot to *take* bread. *Mk.* 8. 14
24. let him deny himself, and *take* up his cross, and follow me. *Mk.* 8. 84 ; *Lu.* 9. 23
17. 27. *take* up the fish that first cometh up—that *take*
18. 16. *t.* with thee one or two more, that at the mouth

TAKE

Mat. 20. 14. *Take* up that which is thine, and go thy way
21. 38. come, let us kill him, and *6take* his inheritance
24. 17. on the housetop not go down to *t.* out. *Mk.* 13. 15
25. 28. *Take* ye away therefore the talent from him
26. 4. *t.* Jesus by subtilty. *Mk.* 14. 1 ; *Jno.* 7. 30, 32 : 10. 39
26. and said, *Take,* eat ; this is my body. *Mk.* 14. 22
45. Sleep on now, and *t.* your rest. *Mk.* 14. 41
52. for all they that *take* the sword shall perish with
Mk. 4. 36. they *8take* him with them, even as he was
6. 8. should *take* nothing for their journey. *Lu.* 9. 3
12. 19. that his brother should *take* his wife. *Lu.* 20. 28
14. 44. I shall kiss, that is he ; *take* him, and lead him
15. 24. casting lots upon them, what each should *take*
36. let us see whether Elijah cometh to *take* him down
16. 18. speak with new tongues ; they shall *t.* up serpents
Lu. 6. 4. and did *take* and eat the shewbread, and gave also
10. 35. gave them to the host, and said, *Take* care of him
12. 19. goods laid up for many years ; *take* thine ease
14. 9. shalt begin with shame to *take* the lowest place
16. 6. *Take* thy bond, and sit down quickly. 7
19. 24. *Take* away from him the pound, and give it
22. 17. cup—*Take* this, and divide it among yourselves
36. he that hath a purse, let him *take* it   [house
Jno. 2. 16. T. these things hence ; make not my Father's
5. 10. it is not lawful for thee to *2take* up thy bed
6. 7. is not sufficient—that every one may *take* a little
15. about to come and *t.* him by force, to make him king
10. 17. I lay down my life, that I may *take* it again
18. I have power to lay it down, and I have power to *take* it again
11. 57. he should shew it, that they might *take* him
16. 14. he shall *5take* of mine, and shall declare it unto you
17. 15. not that thou shouldest *take* them from the world
18. 31. Pilate—*Take* him yourselves, and judge him
19. 6. Pilate—*Take* him yourselves, and crucify him *7t.*
Acts 1. 20. no man dwell therein: and, His office let another
15. 14. visit the Gentiles, to *take* out of them a people
37. Barnabas was minded to *take* with them John also
38. Paul thought not good to *take* with them him
20. 13. sail for Assos, there intending to *take* in Paul
21. 24. [a vow on them] these *take,* and purify thyself
27. 33. Paul besought them all to *take* some food. 34
1 *Cor.* 6. 7. Why not rather *take* wrong?
15. shall I then *take* away the members of Christ
2 *Cor.* 11. 32. king guarded the city—in order to *1take* me
12. 10. Therefore I *take* pleasure in weaknesses
17. Did I *1take* advantage of you by any one of them
18. Did Titus *4take* any advantage of you?
Eph. 6. 13. Wherefore *take* up the whole armour of God
17. And *take* the helmet of salvation
1 *Tim.* 3. 5. how shall he *take* care of the church of God ?)
2 *Tim.* 3. 6. *3take* captive silly women laden with sins
4. 11. *Take* Mark, and bring him with thee
Heb. 2. 16. For verily not of angels doth he *8take* hold
7. 5. have commandment to *take* tithes of the people
Jas. 5. 10. *Take,* brethren, for an example of suffering
1 *Pet.* 2. 20. ye shall *take* it patiently ? but if, when ye do well, and suffer for it, ye shall *take* it patiently
Rev. 3. 11. that which thou hast, that no one *t.* thy crown
5. 9. Worthy art thou to *t.* the book, and to open the seals
6. 4. to him that sat thereon it was given to *take* peace
10. 8. go, *take* the book which is open [from the earth
9. he saith unto me, *Take* it, and eat it up
22. 17. he that will, let him *take* the water of life freely
see hold, receive, seize, taketh, testify, withhold.

Take away.

Mat. 5. 40. *take away* thy coat, let him have thy cloke also
Lu. 1. 25. *take away* my [Elisabeth] reproach among men

TAKE

Lu. 17. 31. goods in the house, let him not go—to *t.* them
Jno. 11. 39. Jesus saith, Take ye away the stone [away
48. Jesus saith, Take ye away the stone [away
19. 38. Joseph—asked of Pilate that he might *take away*
Rom. 11. 27. When I shall *take away* their sins
Heb. 10. 4. blood of bulls and goats should *take away* sins
11. sacrifices, the which can never *take away* sins
1 Jno. 3. 5. that he was manifested to *take away* sins
Rev.22.19. any man shall *t. away* from the words of the book
—God shall *take away* his part from the tree of life
see remove.

Take heed.—A.V. ¹beware.

Mat. 6. 1. Take heed that ye do not your righteousness
16. 6. Take heed and beware of the leaven. Mk. 8. 15
24. 4. T. h. that no man lead you astray. Mk. 13. 5: Lu.
Mk. 4. 24. Take heed what ye hear [21. 8
13. 9. *take* ye heed to yourselves: for they shall deliver
23. But *take* ye *heed*: behold, I have told you all
33. Take ye *heed*, watch and pray: for ye know not
Lu. 8. 18. Take heed therefore how ye hear
12. 15. Take *h.*, and keep yourselves from all covetousness
17. 3. Take heed to yourselves: if thy brother sin
21. 34. *take* heed to yourselves, lest haply your hearts
Acts 5. 35. *take heed* to yourselves as touching these men
20. 28. Take heed unto yourselves, and to all the flock
1 Cor. 3. 10. let each man *take h.* how he buildeth thereon
8. 9. *take heed* lest by any means this liberty of yours
10. 12. let him that thinketh he standeth *t. h.* lest he fall
Gal. 5. 15. *take h.* that ye be not consumed one of another
Col. 2. 8. ¹*T. h.* lest there shall be any one that maketh spoil
4. 17. Take heed to the ministry which thou [of you
1 Tim. 4. 16. Take heed to thyself, and to thy teaching
Heb.3.12. Take *h.*, brethren, lest—an evil heart of unbelief
2 Pet. 1. 19. *take heed*, as unto a lamp shining in a dark
see look, see.

Take thought.—A.V. ¹provide—ing.

Rom. 12. 17. ¹Take *t.* for things honourable in the sight
2 Cor. 8. 21. for we ¹*take* thought for things honourable

Taken.—A.V. ¹apprehended, ²caught, ³hold, ⁴received, ⁵removed, ⁶sent away, ⁷took.

Mat. 9. 15. the bridegroom shall be *taken* away. Mk. 2. 20: Lu. 5. 35
13. from him shall be *taken* away even that which he hath. 25. 29: Mk. 4. 25: Lu. 8. 18: 19. 26
21.21. Be thou⁵*t.* up and cast into the sea. Mk. 3. ¹²³
43. The kingdom of God shall be taken away from you
24.40. two men be in the field; one is *taken*. Lu. 17. 34
41. two women—one is *taken*. Lu. 17. 35
26. 57. they that had ³*taken* Jesus led him away
28. 12. had *taken* counsel, they gave large money
Mk. 6. 46. after he had ⁶*taken* leave of them, he departed
Lu. 1. 1. Forasmuch as many have *taken* in hand to draw
5. 9. at the draught of the fishes which they had *taken*
9. 17. and there was *taken* up that which remained over
10. 42. chosen the good part, which shall not be *t. away*
Jno. 7. 44. would have *taken* him; but no man laid hands
8. 3. the Pharisees bring a woman *taken* in adultery
19. 31.legs—broken, and that they might be *taken* away
20. 1. and seeth the stone *taken* away from the tomb
2. They have *taken* away the Lord. 13
21. 10. Bring of the fish which ye have now ²*taken*
Acts 1. 9. he was *taken* up; and a cloud received him
8. 33. In his humiliation his judgement was *taken* away
—For his life is *taken* from the earth
12. 4. when he had ¹*taken* him, he put him in prison

TALENT

Acts 20. 9. Eutychus—third story, and was *taken* up dead
27. 20. all hope that we should be saved was now *t.* away
33. ye wait and continue fasting, having *taken* nothing
35. and had ⁷*taken* bread, he gave thanks to God
1 Cor. 5. 2 he that had done this deed might be *t.* away
10. 13. There hath no temptation *taken* you but such as
2 Cor. 3. 16. turn to the Lord, the veil is *taken* away
Col. 2. 14. hath ⁷*t.* it out of the way, nailing it to the cross
2 Th. 2. 7. restraineth now, until he be *t.* out of the way
2 Tim. 2. 26. having been *t.* captive by the Lord's servant
Heb. 5. 1. every high priest, being *taken* from among men
7. 6. counted from them hath ⁴*taken* tithes of Abraham
2 Pet. 2. 12. born mere animals to be *taken* and destroyed
Rev. 5. 8. And when he had *taken* the book
11. 17. because thou hast *taken* thy great power
19. 20. And the beast was *taken*, and with him
see bereaved, enrolled, exacted, he took, hoisted, received, seized, took.

Takest.

Lu. 19. 21. an austere man: thou *takest* up that thou

Taketh.—A.V. ¹take, ²took.

Mat. 4. 5. Then the devil *taketh* him into the holy city
8. *taketh* him unto an exceeding high mountain
9. 16. *t.* from the garment, and a worse rent. Mk. 2. 21
12. 45. *taketh* with himself seven other spirits. Lu. 11. 26
17. 1. Jesus *t.* with him Peter, and James. Mk. 9. 2: 14. 33
Mk. 4. 15. Satan, and *taketh* away the word. Lu. 8. 12
5 40. he, having put them all forth, *taketh* the father
9. 18. it *taketh* him, it dasheth him down. Lu. 9. 39
Lu. 6. 29. from him that *taketh* away thy cloke withhold
30. of him that *t.* away thy goods ask them not again
11. 22. he *taketh* from him his whole armour wherein
16. 3. my lord *taketh* away the stewardship from me?
Jno. 1. 29. Lamb of God, which *taketh* away the sin
10. 18. No one *taketh* it away from me, but I lay it down
15. 2. branch in me that beareth not fruit, he *t.* it away
16. 15. he ¹*taketh* of mine, and shall declare it unto you
22. your joy no one *taketh* away from you
21. 13. Jesus cometh, and *taketh* the bread, and giveth
1 Cor. 11. 21. each one *taketh* before other his own supper
2 Cor. 11. 20. devoureth you, if he ¹*taketh* you captive
Heb. 2. 16. not of angels doth he take hold, but he ²*t.* hold
5. 4. And no man *taketh* the honour unto himself
10. 9. He *taketh* away the first, that he may establish
Rev. 5. 7. he ²*taketh* it out of the right hand of him
8. 5. And the angel ²*taketh* the censer; and he filled it
see take, visiteth.

Taking.—A.V. ¹took.

Mk. 15. 46. ¹*t.* him down, wound him in the linen cloth
Lu. 19. 22. austere man, *taking* up that I laid not down
Jno. 11. 13. they thought that he spake of *t.* rest in sleep
Acts 12. 25. ¹*t.* with them John whose surname was Mark
21. 11. [Agabus] ¹*t.* Paul's girdle, he bound his own feet
2 Cor. 2. 13. but *taking* my leave of them, I went forth
11. 8. I robbed other churches, *taking* wages of them
Gal. 2. 1. again to Jerusalem—*taking* Titus also with me
Eph. 6. 16. withal *taking* up the shield of faith
Phil. 2. 7. emptied himself, ¹*taking* the form of a servant
3 Jno. 7. they went forth, *taking* nothing of the Gentiles
see anxious, exercising, finding, led, rendering.

Talent.

Mat. 25. 24. he also that had received the one *talent* came
25. and went away and hid thy *talent* in the earth
28. Take ye away therefore the *talent* from him
Rev. 16. 21. hail, every stone about the weight of a *talent*

TALENTS

Talents.
Mat. 18. 24. which owed him ten thousand *talents*
25. 15. And unto one he gave five *talents*. 16, 20, 22, 28

Tales A.V.—see *talk*.

Talitha cumi.
Mk. 5. 41. the child by the hand, he saith unto her T. c.

Talk.—A.V. ¹*tales*, ²*words*.
Mat. 22. 15. counsel how they might ensnare him in his *t*.
Mk. 12. 13. that they might catch him in ²*talk*
Lu. 24. 11. words appeared in their sight as idle ¹*talk*
see *speak*.

Talked.
Lu. 9. 30. *t*.with him two men, which were Moses and Elijah
Acts 10. 27. [Peter] as he *talked* with him, he went in
20. 11. eaten, and had *talked* with them a long while
see *spake, speaking, communed*.

Talkers.
Tit. 1. 10. unruly men, vain *talkers* and deceivers

Talkest A.V.—see *speakest*.

Talketh A.V.—see *speaketh*.

Talking.—A.V. ¹*jangling*.
Mat. 17. 3. Moses and Elijah *talking* with him. Mk. 9. 4
Eph. 5. 4. nor filthiness, nor foolish *talking*, or jesting
1 Tim. 1. 6. have turned aside unto vain ¹*talking*
see *speaking*.

Tame.
Mk. 5. 4. no man had strength to *tame* him
Jas. 3. 8. the tongue can no man *tame*; it is a restless evil

Tamed.
Jas. 3. 7. is *tamed*, and hath been *tamed* by mankind

Tanner.
Acts 9. 43. in Joppa with one Simon a *tanner*. 10. 6, 32

Tare.
Mk. 9. 20. the spirit *tare* him grievously. Lu. 9. 42

Tares.
Mat. 13. 25. men slept, his enemy came and sowed *tares*
26. brought forth fruit, then appeared the *tares* also
27. good seed in thy field ? whence then hath it *tares* ?
29. lest haply while ye gather up the *tares*, ye root up
30. I will say to the reapers, Gather up first the *tares*
36. Explain unto us the parable of the *tares* of the field
38. the *tares* are the sons of the evil one
40. As therefore the *tares* are gathered up and burned

Tarried.—A.V. ¹*abode*, ²*continued*, ³*had been*.
Mat.25.5. while the bridegroom *tarried*, they all slumbered
Lu. 1. 21. they marvelled while he *tarried* in the temple
2. 43. the boy Jesus *tarried* behind in Jerusalem
Jno. 3. 22. Jesus—there he *t*. with them, and baptized
11. 54. Ephraim; and there he ²*tarried* with the disciples
Acts 12. 19. Herod—went down—to Cæsarea, and ¹*t*. there
14. 3. Long time therefore they ¹*tarried* there speaking
28. they ¹*tarried* no little time with the disciples

TAUGHT

Acts 18. 18. Paul, having *tarried* after this yet many days
20. 6. to Troas—where we ¹*tarried* seven days
21. 4. having found the disciples, we *t*. there seven days
10. as we *tarried* there many days, there came—Agabus
25. 14. as they ³*t*. there many days, Festus laid Paul's case
28. 12. touching at Syracuse, we *tarried* there three days
Gal. 1. 18. I went up to Jerusalem to visit Cephas, and ¹*t*.
see *abode, spent, waiting*.

Tarriest—eth.—A.V. ¹*delayeth*.
Mat. 24. 48. servant shall say in his heart, My lord ¹*tarrieth*
Acts 22. 16. And now why *t*. thou? arise, and be baptized

Tarry.—A.V. ¹*abide*.
Lu. 24 49. but *tarry* ye in the city, until ye be clothed
Jno. 21. 22. If I will that he *tarry* till I come. 23
Acts 10. 48. Then prayed they him to *tarry* certain days
28. 14. were intreated to *tarry* with them seven days
1 Cor. 16. 7. for I hope to *tarry* a while with you
8. But I will *tarry* at Ephesus until Pentecost
1 Tim. 1. 3. As I exhorted thee to ¹*tarry* at Ephesus
3. 15. but if I *tarry* long, that thou mayest know
Heb. 10. 37. He that cometh shall come, and shall not *t*.
see *abide, wait*.

Tarrying.—A.V. ¹*abiding*.
Acts 16. 12. we were in this city ¹*tarrying* certain days

Taste.—A.V. ¹*eat*.
Mat. 16. 28. shall in no wise *t*. of death. Mk. 9. 1.: Lu. 9. 27
Lu. 14. 24. which were bidden shall *taste* of my supper
Jno. 8. 52. keep my word, he shall never *taste* of death
Acts 23. 14. bound ourselves under a—curse, to ¹*t*. nothing
Col. 2. 21. Handle not, nor *taste*, nor touch [man
Heb. 2. 9. by the grace of God he should *t*. death for every

Tasted.
Mat. 27. 34. mingled with gall: and when he had *tasted* it
Jno. 2. 9. when the ruler of the feast *tasted* the water
Heb. 6. 4. once enlightened and *tasted* of the heavenly gift
5. and *tasted* the good word of God, and the powers
1 Pet. 2. 3. if ye have *tasted* that the Lord is gracious

Tattlers.
1 Tim. 5. 13. not only idle, but *tattlers* also and busybodies

Taught.—A.V. ¹*learn*.
Mat. 5. 2. [Jesus] *taught* them. Mk. 2. 13: 4. 2: 9. 31:
10. 1: 11. 17: Lu. 5. 3
7. 29. he *taught* them as one having authority. Mk. 1. 22
13. 54. [Jesus] *t*. them in their synagogue. Lu. 4. 15: 6. 6
15. So they took the money, and did as they were *t*.
Mk. 6. 30. they had done, and whatsoever they had *taught*
12. 35. as he *taught* in the temple. Jno. 7. 14: 8. 2, 20
Lu. 11. 1. teach us to pray—as John also *t*. his disciples
Jno. 6. 45. And they shall all be *taught* of God
8. 28. but as the Father *taught* me, I speak these things
18. 20. I ever *taught* in synagogues, and in the temple
Acts 4. 2. sore troubled because they *taught* the people
5. 21. into the temple about daybreak, and *taught*
11. 26. with the church, and *taught* much people
15. 1. from Judæa and *t*. the brethren, saying, Except
18. 25. [Apollos] *t*. carefully the things concerning Jesus
Gal. 1. 12. receive it from man, nor was I *taught* it
6. 6. let him that is *taught* in the word communicate
Eph. 4. 21. if so be that ye heard him, and were *t*. in him
Col. 2. 7. stablished in your faith, even as ye were *taught*
1 Th. 4. 9. yourselves are *t*. of God to love one another

TAUGHT

2 *Th.* 2. 15. and hold the traditions which ye were *taught*
1 *Tim.* 1. 20. that they might be ¹*taught* not to blaspheme
1 *Jno.* 2. 27. even as it *taught* you, ye abide in him
Rev. 2. 14. Balaam, who *t.* Balak to cast a stumblingblock
see instructed, made, teach, teaching.

Taverns *A.V.—see proper names.*

Taxed *A.V.—see enrol, enrolled.*

Taxing *A.V.—see enrolment.*

Teach.—*A.V.* ¹*taught.*

Mat. 5, 19. and shall *teach* men so, shall be called least—
  and *teach* them, he shall be called great [cities
11. 1. Jesus—departed thence to *t.* and preach in their
Mk. 6. 34. he began to *teach* them many things. 2
8. 31. to *teach* them, that the Son of man must suffer
Lu. 11. 1. Lord, *teach* us to pray, even as John also
12. 12. Holy Spirit shall *teach* you in that very hour
13. 26. and thou didst ¹*teach* in our streets
Jno. 7. 35. will he go unto—Greeks, and *teach* the Greeks?
9. 34. Thou wast—born in sins, and dost thou *teach* us?
14. 26. send in my name, he shall *teach* you all things
Acts 1. 1. all that Jesus began both to do and to *teach*
4. 18. not to speak at all nor *teach* in the name of Jesus
5. 28. We straitly charged you not to *teach* in this name
42. they ceased not to *teach* and to preach Jesus
1 *Cor.* 4. 17. even as I *teach* everywhere in every church
11. 14. nature itself *teach* you, that, if a man have long
1 *Tim.* 1. 3. charge certain men not to *t.* a different doctrine
2. 12. But I permit not a woman to *teach*
3. 2. The bishop therefore must be—apt to *teach*
4. 11. These things command and *teach*
6. 2. These things *teach* and exhort
2 *Tim.* 2. 2. faithful men, who shall be able to *teach* others
24. must not strive, but be gentle towards all, apt to *t.*
Heb. 5. 12. again that some one *teach* you the rudiments
8. 11. they shall not *teach* every man his fellow-citizen
1 *Jno.* 2. 27. and ye need not that any one *teach* you
see disciples, instruct, make, set, teacheth, train.

Teacher.—*A.V.* ¹*master.*

Mat. 23. 8. one is your ¹*teacher,* and all ye are brethren
Jno. 3. 2. know that thou art a *teacher* come from God
10. Art thou the ¹*teacher* of Israel, and understandest
Rom. 2. 20. a corrector of the foolish, a *teacher* of babes
1 *Tim.* 2. 7. a *teacher* of the Gentiles in faith and truth
2 *Tim.* 1. 11. appointed a preacher, and an apostle, and a *t.*

Teachers.—*A.V.* ¹*masters.*

Acts 13. 1. at Antioch—prophets and *t.,* Barnabas, and
1 *Cor.* 12. 28. first apostles, secondly prophets, thirdly *t.*
20. Are all apostles? are all prophets? are all *teachers*?
Eph. 4. 11. evangelists; and some, pastors and *teachers*
1 *Tim.* 1. 7. desiring to be *teachers* of the law
2 *Tim.* 4. 3. will heap to themselves *t.* after their own lusts
Tit. 2. 3. aged women—*teachers* of that which is good
Heb. 5. 12. when by reason of the time ye ought to be *t.*
Jas. 3. 1. be not many ¹*teachers,* my brethren
2 *Pet.* 2. 1. among you also there shall be false *teachers*

Teachest.

Mat. 22. 16. *t.* the way of God in truth. *Mk.* 12. 14: *Lu.* 20. 21
Acts 21. 21. thou *t.* all the Jews which are among the Gentiles
Rom. 2. 21. thou—that *teachest* another, *t.* thou not thyself?

TEARING

Teacheth.—*A.V.* ¹*teach.*

Acts 21. 28. This is the man, that *t.* all men everywhere
Rom. 12. 7. he that *teacheth,* to his teaching
1 *Cor.* 2. 13. not in words which man's wisdom *teacheth,*
  but which the Spirit *teacheth;* comparing
Gal. 6. 6. communicate unto him that *t.* in all good things
1 *Tim.* 6. 3. If any man ¹*teacheth* a different doctrine
1 *Jno.* 2. 27. his anointing *t.* you concerning all things
Rev. 2. 20. Jezebel—she ¹*t.* and seduceth my servants

Teaching.—*A.V.* ¹*doctrine,* ²*taught.*

Mat. 4. 23. *t.* in their synagogues. 9. 35: *Lu.* 4. ²31: 13. 10
7. 28. multitudes were astonished at his ¹*teaching.* 22.
  ¹33: *Mk.* 1. ¹22: *Lu.* 4. ¹32
15. 9. do they worship me, T. as their doctrines. *Mk.* 7. 7
16. 12. beware—of the ¹*teaching* of the Pharisees
26. 55. I sat daily in the temple *teaching.* *Mk.* 14. 49
28. 20. *teaching* them to observe all things whatsoever
Mk. 1. 27. What is this? a new ¹*teaching!*
4. 2. and said unto them in his ¹*teaching.* 12. ¹38
6. 6. And he went round about the villages *teaching*
Lu. 5. 17. he was *t.;* and there were Pharisees and doctors
21. 37. *teaching* in the temple. 19. ²47: 20. ²1: *Mat.* 21.
  23: *Jno.* 7. ²28
23. 5. He stirreth up the people, *t.* throughout all Judæa
Jno. 7. 16. My ¹*teaching* is not mine, but his that sent me
17. he shall know of the ¹*teaching,* whether it be of God
18. 19. asked Jesus of his disciples, and of his ¹*teaching*
Acts 2. 42. they continued stedfastly in the apostles' ¹*t.*
5. 25. in the temple standing and *teaching* the people
28. ye have filled Jerusalem with your ¹*teaching*
13. 12. proconsul—being astonished at the ¹*t.* of the Lord
15. 35. But Paul and Barnabas tarried in Antioch, *t.*
17. 19. May we know what this new ¹*teaching* is
18. 11. there a year and six months, *t.* the word of God
20. 20. ²*teaching* you publicly, and from house to house
28. 31. *t.* the things concerning the Lord Jesus Christ
Rom. 6. 17. obedient from the heart to that form of ¹*t.*
12. 7. or he that teacheth, to his *teaching*
1 *Cor.* 14. 6. or of knowledge, or of prophesying, or of ¹*t.*?
26. each one hath a psalm, hath a ¹*teaching*
Col. 1. 28. admonishing every man and *teaching* every man
3. 16. *teaching* and admonishing one another with psalms
1 *Tim.* 4. 13. give heed to reading, to exhortation, to ¹*t*
16. Take heed to thyself, and to thy ¹*teaching*
5. 17. those who labour in the word and in ¹*teaching*
2 *Tim.* 3. 10. thou didst follow my ¹*teaching,* conduct
16. scripture inspired of God is also profitable for ¹*t.*
4. 2. exhort, with all longsuffering and ¹*teaching*
Tit. 1. 9. the faithful word which is according to the ²*t.*
11. *teaching* things which they ought not
Heb. 6. 2. of the ¹*teaching* of baptisms, and of laying on
2 *Jno.* 9. abideth not in the ¹*t.* of Christ—abideth in the ¹*t.*
10. cometh unto you, and bringeth not this ¹*teaching*
Rev. 2. 14. there some that hold the ¹*teaching* of Balaam
15. some that hold the ¹*teaching* of the Nicolaitans
24. in Thyatira, as many as have not this ¹*teaching*
see instructing.

Teachings.—*A.V.* ¹*doctrines.*

Heb. 13. 9. carried away by divers and strange ¹*teachings*

Tear.—*A.V.* ¹*tears.*

Rev. 7. 17. God shall wipe away every ¹*t.* from their. 21. 14

Teareth *A.V.—see dasheth.*

Tearing.—*A.V.* ¹*torn.*

Mk. 1. 26. And the unclean spirit, ¹*tearing* him and crying

TEARS

Tears.
Lu. 7. 38. she began to wet his feet with her *tears*. 44
Acts 20. 19. lowliness of mind, and with *t*., and with trials
  31. admonish every one night and day with *tears*
2 Cor. 2. 4. I wrote unto you with many *tears*
2 Tim. 1. 4. longing to see thee, remembering thy *tears*
Heb. 5. 7. supplications with strong crying and *tears*
12. 17. repentance), though he sought it diligently with *t*.
  see tear.

Tedious.
Acts 24. 4. that I be not further *tedious* unto thee [Felix]

Teeth.
Mk. 9. 18. foameth, and grindeth his *teeth* [dumb spirit]
Rev. 9. 8. their *teeth* were as the *teeth* of lions
  see gnashing, reproach.

Tell.—A.V. ¹answer, ²ask, ³bring thee word, ⁴shew, ⁵told.
Mat. 2. 13. flee into Egypt, and be thou there until I ³*t*. thee
  8. 4. See thou *tell* no man. Mk. 7. 36; Lu. 5. 14: 8. 56
11, 4. Go your way and ⁴*tell* John the things
16. 20. should *tell* no man. 17. 9: Mk. 8. 30: 9. 9: Lu. 9. 21
18. 17. if he refuse to hear them, *tell* it unto the church
21. 5. *Tell* ye the daughter of Zion, Behold, thy King
24. if ye *tell* me, I likewise will *tell* you by what
22. 4. servants, saying, *Tell* them that are bidden
17. *Tell* us therefore, What thinkest thou?
21. 3. *Tell* us, when shall these things be? Mk. 13. 4
26. 63. that thou *t*. us whether thou be the Christ. Lu.
28. 7. *tell* his disciples, He is risen. Mk. 16. 7 | 22. 67
Mk. 1. 30. sick of a fever; and straightway they *tell* him
5. 19. unto thy friends, and *tell* them how great things
10. 32. to *tell* them the things that were to happen
Lu. 7. 22. *tell* John what things ye have seen and heard
20. 2. *Tell* us: By what authority doest thou these
3. I also will ask you a question; and ¹*tell* me
22. 34. I *tell* thee, Peter, the cock shall not crow this
Jno. 10. 24. If thou art the Christ, *tell* us plainly
12. 22. Andrew cometh, and Philip, and they ⁵*tell* Jesus
13. 24. ³*Tell* us who it is of whom he speaketh
16. 25. proverbs, but shall ⁴*tell* you plainly of the Father
18. 34. Sayest thou this of thyself, or did others *tell* it thee
20. 15. borne him hence, *tell* me where thou hast laid him
Acts 5. 8. *Tell* me whether ye sold the land for so much
12. 17. he said, ⁴*Tell* these things unto James
15. 27. Judas and Silas, who themselves also shall *t*. you
17. 21. either to *tell* or to hear some new thing)
22. 27. *Tell* me, art thou a Roman? And he said, Yea
23. 17. chief captain: for he hath something to *tell* him
19. What is that thou hast to *tell* me?
22. let the young man go, charging him, *Tell* no man
1 Cor. 15. 51. Behold, I ⁴*tell* you a mystery
Gal. 4. 21. *Tell* me, ye that desire to be under the law
Heb. 11. 32. for the time will fail me if I *tell* of Gideon
Rev. 17. 7. I will *tell* thee the mystery of the woman
  see declare, knew not, know (with negatives), knowest, say, I say, shew.

I Tell you.
Mat. 10. 27. What *I tell you* in the darkness, speak ye
21. 27. Neither *tell I you* by. Mk. 11. 29, 33: Lu. 20 8
Lu. 9. 27. But *I tell you* of a truth, There be some of them
12. 51. come to give peace in the earth? *I tell you*, Nay
13. 3. *I tell you*, Nay: but, except ye repent. 5
27. *I tell you*, I know not whence ye are
19. 40. *I tell you* that, if these shall hold their peace
22. 67. If *I tell you*, ye will not believe

TEMPLE

Jno. 3. 12. shall ye believe, if *I tell you* heavenly things?
13. 19. *I tell you* before it come to pass, that, when it
16. 7. *I tell you* the truth; It is expedient for you that
Gal. 4. 16. your enemy, because *I tell you* the truth?
Phil. 3. 18. I told you often, and now *tell you* even weeping
  see forewarn, I say.

Telleth.—A.V. ¹told.
Jno. 12. 22. Philip cometh and *telleth* Andrew
20. 18. Mary Magdalene cometh and ¹*telleth* the disciples

Tempered.
1 Cor. 12. 24. but God *tempered* the body together

Temperance.
Acts 24. 25. as he reasoned of righteousness, and *temperance*
Gal. 5. 23. meekness, *t*.: against such there is no law
2 Pet. 1. 6. in your knowledge *t*.; and in your *t*. patience

Temperate.—A.V. ¹sober, ²vigilant.
1 Cor. 9. 25. And every man that striveth in the games is *t*.
1 Tim. 3. 2. The bishop—husband of one wife, ²*temperate*
3. 11. not slanderers, ¹*temperate*, faithful in all things
Tit. 1. 8. a lover of good, soberminded, just, holy, *t*.
2. 2. that aged men be *temperate*, grave, soberminded

Tempest.
Mat. 8. 24. there arose a great *tempest* in the sea
Acts 27. 20. and no small *tempest* lay on us
Heb. 12. 18. and unto blackness, and darkness, and *tempest*
  see storm.

Tempestuous.
Acts 27. 14. a *tempestuous* wind, which is called Euraquilo

Temple.
Mat. 4. 5. set him on the pinnacle of the *temple*. Lu. 4. 9
12. 6. that one greater than the *temple* is here
23. 16. shall swear by the *temple*—by the gold of the *t*.
17. the gold, or the *temple* that hath sanctified the gold?
21. he that sweareth by the *temple*, sweareth by it
24. 1. And Jesus went out from the *temple*—shew him
  the buildings of the *temple*. Mk. 13. 1: Lu. 21. 5
26. 61. I am able to destroy the *t*. of God. Mk. 14. 58
27. 40. that destroyest the *t*., and buildest it. Mk. 15. 29
51. the veil of the *t*. was rent. Mk. 15. 38: Lu. 23. 45
Mk. 11. 16. should carry a vessel through the *temple*
Lu. 2. 37. a widow—which departed not from the *temple*
Jno. 2. 15. scourge of cords, and cast all out of the *temple*
19. Destroy this *temple*, and in three days I will raise
20. Forty and six years was this *temple* in building
21. he spake of the *temple* of his body
8. 59. Jesus hid himself, and went out of the *temple*
Acts 3. 2. the door of the *t*. which is called Beautiful. 10
19. 27. the *t*. of the great goddess Diana be made of no
21. 30. on Paul, and dragged him out of the *temple*
24. 6. who moreover assayed to profane the *temple*
25. 8. Jews, nor against the *temple*, nor against Cæsar
1 Cor. 3. 16. Know ye not that ye are a *temple* of God
17. If any man destroyeth the *temple* of God, him shall
  God destroy; for the *t*. of God is holy, which *t*. ye
6. 19. your body is a *temple* of the Holy Ghost [are
8. 10. hast knowledge sitting at meat in an idol's *temple*
9. 13. eat of the things of the *t*., and they which wait
2 Cor. 6. 16. And what agreement hath a *temple* of God
  with idols? for we are a *temple* of the living God
Eph. 2. 21. groweth into a holy *temple* in the Lord
Rev. 7. 15. they serve him day and night in his *temple*

TEMPLE

Rev. 11. 1. Rise, and measure the *temple* of God
    2. the court which is without the *temple* leave without
    19. there was opened the *temple* of God that is in heaven;
        and there was seen in his *temple* the ark
    14. 15. another angel came out from the *temple*. 17
    15. 5. the *temple* of the tabernacle of the testimony in
      6. came out from the *temple* the seven angels
      8. And the *temple* was filled with smoke from the glory
    16. 1. I heard a great voice out of the *temple*. 17
    21. 22. And I saw no *temple* therein : for the Lord God
        the Almighty, and the Lamb, are the *t.* thereof
          see sanctuary.

In or into the Temple.

Mat. 12. 5. the priests *in the temple* profane the sabbath
    21. 12. Jesus entered *into the temple* of God, and cast out
        all them that sold and bought *in the temple*. *Mk.*
        11. 15: *Lu.* 19. 45: *Jno.* 2. 14
    14. And the blind and the lame came to him *in the t.*
    15. children that were crying *in the temple* and saying
    23. when he was come *into the t*. *Mk.* 11. 27 : *Jno.* 10. 23
    26. 55. I sat daily *in the t.* teaching. *Mk.* 12. 35 : 14. 49;
        Lu. 19. 47: 20. 1 : 21. 37 : 22. 53 : *Jno.* 7. 14, 28:
        8. 2, 20 : 18. 20
Mk. 11. 11. he entered into Jerusalem, *into the temple*
Lu. 1. 21. Zacharias—marvelled while he tarried *in the t.*
    22. perceived that he had seen a vision *in the temple*
    2. 27. he [Simeon] came in the Spirit *into the temple*
    46. they found him [Jesus] *in the temple*, sitting in the
    18. 10. Two men went up *into the temple* to pray
    21. 38. people came early in the morning to him *in the t.*
    24. 53. were continually *in the temple*, blessing God
Jno. 5. 14. Afterward Jesus findeth him *in the temple*
    11. 56. as they stood *in the temple*, What think ye ?
Acts 2. 46. with one accord *in the t.*, and breaking bread
    3. 1. Peter and John were going up *into the temple*
    2. to ask alms of them that entered *into the temple*
    3. seeing Peter and John about to go *into the temple*
    8. he entered with them *into the t.*, walking, and leaping
    5. 20. Go ye, and stand and speak *in the temple*. 21
    25. men whom ye put in the prison are in the *temple*
    42. *in the temple* and at home, they ceased not to teach
    21. 26. Paul—himself with them went *into the temple*
    27. Jews from Asia, when they saw him *in the temple*
    28. he brought Greeks also *into the temple*
    29. they supposed that Paul had brought *into the temple*
    22. 17. [Paul] and while I prayed *in the temple*, I fell
    24. 12. neither *in the temple* did they find me disputing
    18. they found me purified *in the temple*, with no crowd
    26. 21. For this cause the Jews seized me *in the temple*
2 Th. 2. 4. so that he sitteth *in the temple* of God
Rev. 3. 12. I will make him a pillar *in the temple* of my God
    15. 8. and none was able to enter *into the temple*

Temple-keeper.—*A.V.* ¹worshipper.

Acts 19. 35. Ephesians is ¹*temple-keeper* of the great Diana

Temples.—*A.V.* ¹*churches*, ²*commit sacrilege*.

Acts 17. 24. dwelleth not in *temples* made with hands
    19. 37. which are neither robbers of ¹*t.* nor blasphemers
Rom. 2. 22. that abhorrest idols, dost thou rob ²*temples ?*
        see houses.

Temporal.

2 Cor. 4. 18. for the things which are seen are *temporal*

TEN

Tempt.

Mat. 4. 7. Thou shalt not *t.* the Lord thy God. *Lu.* 4. 12
    22. 18. Why *tempt* ye me, ye hypocrites ? *Mk.* 12. 15
Acts 5. 9. ye have agreed together to *tempt* the Spirit
    15. 10. why *tempt* ye God, that ye should put a yoke
1 Cor. 7. 5. Satan *t.* you not because of your incontinency
    10. 9. Neither let us *tempt* the Lord, as some of them

Temptation.—*A.V.* ¹*temptations.*

Mat. 6. 13. And bring us not into *temptation*. *Lu.* 11. 4
    26. 41. that ye enter not into *t.* *Mk.* 14. 38 : *Lu.* 22. 40, 46
Lu. 4. 13. when the devil had completed every *t.*, he
    8. 13. for a while believe, and in time of *t.* fall away
1 Cor. 10. 13. There hath no *t.* taken you but such as man
        can bear—will with the *t.* make also the way
Gal. 4. 14. that which was a *temptation* to you in my flesh
1 Tim. 6. 9. they that desire to be rich fall into a *t.*
Heb. 3. 8. Like as in the day of the *t.* in the wilderness
Jas. 1. 12. Blessed is the man that endureth *temptation*
2 Pet. 2. 9. knoweth how to deliver the godly out of ¹*t.*
        see trial.

Temptations.

Lu. 22. 28. which have continued with me in my *t.*
Jas. 1. 2. joy, my brethren, when ye fall into manifold *t.*
1 Pet. 1. 6. ye have been put to grief in manifold *t.*
        see temptation, trials.

Tempted.

Mat. 4. 1. to be *tempted* of the devil. *Mk.* 1. 13 : *Lu.* 4. 2
Lu. 10. 25. a certain lawyer stood up and *tempted* him
1 Cor. 10. 9. Lord, as some of them *tempted*, and perished
    13. not suffer you to be *tempted* above that ye are able
Gal. 6. 1. looking to thyself, lest thou also be *tempted*
1 Th. 3. 5. lest by any means the tempter had *tempted* you
Heb. 2. 18. he himself hath suffered being *tempted*, he is
        able to succour them that are *tempted*
    3. 9. Wherewith your fathers *tempted* me by proving me
    4. 15. hath been in all points *tempted* like as we are
    11. 37. they were sawn asunder, were *tempted*
Jas. 1. 13. Let no man say when he is *tempted*, I am
        tempted of God : for God cannot be *t.* with evil
    14. but each man is *tempted*, when he is drawn away

Tempter.

Mat. 4. 3. And the *t.* came and said unto him, If thou
1 Th. 3. 5. lest by any means the *tempter* had tempted you

Tempteth.

Jas. 1. 13. tempted with evil, and he himself *t.* no man

Tempting.

Mat. 16. 1. *t.* him asked him to shew. *Mk.* 8. 11 : *Lu.* 11. 16
    19. 3. Pharisees, *tempting* him—Is it lawful. *Mk.* 10. 2
    22. 35. a lawyer, asked him a question, *tempting* him
Jno. 8. 6. *t.* him, that they might have whereof to accuse

Ten.

Mat. 20. 24. And when the *ten* heard it, they were moved.
    25. 1. *ten* virgins, which took their lamps [*Mk.* 10. 41
    28. give it unto him that hath the *ten* talents
Lu. 15. 8. Or what woman having *ten* pieces of silver
    17. 12. there met him *ten* men that were lepers
    17. Jesus answering said, Were not the *ten* cleansed ?
    19. 13. *ten* servants of his, and gave them *ten* pounds
    16. Lord, thy pound hath made *ten* pounds more
    17. have thou authority over *ten* cities

TEN

Lu. 19. 24. give it unto him that hath the *ten* pounds
25. they said unto him, Lord, he hath *ten* pounds
Rev. 12. 3. red dragon, having seven heads and *ten* horns
13. 1. a beast coming up out of the sea, having *ten* horns
—on his horns *ten* diadems [7, 12, 16
17. 3. of blasphemy, having seven heads and *ten* horns.
12. the *ten* horns that thou sawest are *ten* kings

Tend.—*A.V.* ¹*feed.*

Jno. 21. 16. He saith unto him, ¹*Tend* my sheep
1 *Pet.* 5. 2. ¹*Tend* the flock of God which is among you

Tender.

Mat. 24. 32. her branch is now become *tender. Mk.* 13. 28
Lu. 1. 78. Because of the *tender* mercy of our God
see mercies, merciful.

Tenderhearted.—*A.V.* ¹*pitiful.*

Eph. 4. 32. *tenderhearted,* forgiving each other. even as God
1 *Pet.* 3. 8. loving as brethren, ¹*tenderhearted*

Tenderly.—*A.V* ¹*kindly.*

Rom. 12. 10. brethren be ¹*t.* affectioned one to another

Tenth.

Jno. 1. 39. abode with him that day: it was about the *t.* hour
Heb. 7. 2. Abraham divided a *tenth* part of all. 4
Rev. 21. 20. the *tenth,* [foundation] chrysoprase

Tentmakers.

Acts 18. 3. for by their trade they were *tentmakers*

Tents.—*A.V.* ¹*tabernacles.*

Heb. 11. 9. dwelling in ¹*tents,* with Isaac and Jacob

Terrestrial.

1 *Cor.* 15. 40. bodies *t.*—and the glory of the *t.* is another

Terrible *A.V.*—*see fearful.*

Terrified.—*A.V.* ¹*trembled.*

Lu. 21. 9. ye shall hear of wars and tumults, be not *terrified*
24. 37. But they were *t.* and affrighted, and supposed that
Acts 24. 25. Felix was ¹*terrified,* and answered, Go thy way
see affrighted.

Terrify.

2 *Cor.* 10. 9. I may not seem as if I would *t.* you by my letters

Terror—s.—*A.V.* ¹*amazement,* ²*fearful sights.*

Lu. 21. 11. there shall be ²*t.* and great signs from heaven
Rom. 13. 3. For rulers are not a *terror* to the good work
1 *Pet.* 3. 6. if ye do well, and are not put in fear by any ¹*t.*
see fear.

Testament.

Heb. 9. 16. For where a *t.* is, there must of necessity be
17. For a *t.* is of force where there hath been death
see covenant.

Testified.—*A.V.* ¹*testify.*

Jno. 4. 39. because of the word of the woman, who *testified*
44. For Jesus himself *t.,* that a prophet hath no honour
13. 21. Jesus—he was troubled in the spirit, and *testified*
Acts 2. 40. And with many other words he ¹*t.,* and exhorted
8. 25. when they had *testified* and spoken the word
23. 11. for as thou hast *t.* concerning me at Jerusalem

TETRARCH

1 *Th.* 4. 6. as also we forewarned you and *testified*
Heb. 2. 6. But one hath somewhere *t.,* saying, What is man
1 *Pet* 1. 11. when it *t.* beforehand the sufferings of Christ
see borne witness, testifying, testimony, witness—ed.

Testifieth.—*A.V.* ¹*witnesseth.*

Acts 20. 23. the Holy Ghost ¹*t.* unto me in every city
Rev. 22. 20. He which *t.* these things saith, Yea: I come
see witness, witnessed.

Testify.—*A.V.* ¹*take to record.*

Lu. 16. 28. five brethren; that he may *testify* unto them
Jno. 7. 7. but me it hateth, because I *testify* of it
Acts 10. 42. to *t.* that this is he which is ordained of God
20. 24. to *testify* the gospel of the grace of God
26. 1 ¹*testify* unto you this day, that I am pure
26. 5. if they be willing to *t.,* how that after the straitest
Gal. 5. 3. I *testify* again to every man that receiveth
Eph. 4. 17. and *testify* in the Lord, that ye no longer walk
Rev. 22. 16. I Jesus have sent mine angel to *t.* unto you
18. I *testify* unto every man that heareth the words
see bear witness, testified.

Testifying.—*A.V.* ¹*charged,* ²*testified,* ³*witnessing.*

Acts 18. 5. ²*t.* to the Jews that Jesus was the Christ
20. 21. *t.* both to Jews and to Greeks repentance
26. 22. I stand unto this day ³*t.* both to small and great
28. 23. ²*t.* the kingdom of God, and persuading them
1 *Th.* 2. 11. exhorting you, and encouraging you, and ¹*t.*
1 *Pet.* 5. 12. exhorting, and *t.* that this is the true grace of
see witness.

Testimony.—*A.V.* ¹*report,* ²*testified,* ³*witness.*

Mat. 8. 4. gift—for a *t.* unto them. *Mk.* 1. 44; *Lu.* 5. 14
10. 18. shall ye be brought for my sake, for a *t. Mk.* 13. 9
24. 14 preached in the whole world for a ³*testimony*
Mk. 6. 11. dust that is under your feet for a *t. Lu.* 9. 5
Lu. 21. 13. It shall turn unto you for a *testimony*
Acts 7. 44. Our fathers had the tabernacle of the ³*testimony*
22. 18. they will not receive of thee *t.* concerning me
1 *Cor.* 1. 6 even as the *t.* of Christ was confirmed in you
2 *Cor.* 1. 12. our glorying is this, the *t.* of our conscience
2 *Th.* 1. 10. (because our *testimony* unto you was believed)
1 *Tim.* 2. 6. the ²*testimony* to be borne in its own times
3. 7. Moreover he must have good ¹*testimony*
2 *Tim.* 1. 8. Be not ashamed therefore of the *t.* of our Lord
Tit. 1. 13. This ²*t.* is true. For which cause reprove them
Heb. 3. 5. Moses—for a *t.* of those things which were
Jas. 5. 3. their rust shall be for a ³*testimony* against you
Rev. 1. 2. and of the *t.* of Jesus Christ, even of all things
9. Patmos, for the word of God and the *t.* of Jesus
6. 9. slain for the word of God, and for the *t.* which they
11. 7. and when they shall have finished their *testimony*
12. 11. the Lamb, and because of the word of their *t.*
17. commandments of God, and hold the *t.* of Jesus
15. 5. temple of the tabernacle of the *t.* in heaven
19. 10. thy brethren that hold the *t.* of Jesus: worship
God: for the *t.* of Jesus is the spirit of prophecy
20. 4. them that had been beheaded for the ³*t.* of Jesus
see mystery, witness.

Tetrarch.

Mat. 14. 1. Herod the *tetrarch* heard the report, *Lu.* 9. 7
Lu. 3. 1. Herod being *t.* of Galilee, and his brother Philip
t. of the region of Ituræa—Lysanias *t.* of Abilene
19. Herod the *tetrarch,* being reproved by him [John]
Acts 13. 1. Manaen the foster-brother of Herod the *t.*

THANK

Thank.
Mat. 11. 25. I *thank* thee, O Father—didst hide. Lu. 10. 21
Lu. 6. 32. If ye love them that love you, what *t*. have ye?
  17. 9. Doth he *thank* the servant because he did [33, 34
  18. 11. God, I *t*. thee, that I am not as the rest of men
Jno. 11. 41. Father, I *thank* thee that thou heardest me
Rom. 1. 8. I *t*. my God through Jesus Christ for you all
  7. 25. I *t*. God through Jesus Christ our Lord. So then I
1 Cor. 1. 4. I *t*. my God always concerning you, for the grace
  14. I *thank* God that I baptized none of you
  14. 18. I *thank* God, I speak with tongues more than
Phil. 1. 3. I *thank* my God upon all my remembrance
1 Th. 2. 13. this cause we also *thank* God without ceasing
1 Tim. 1. 12. I *t*. him that enabled me, even Christ Jesus
2 Tim. 1. 3. I *thank* God, whom I serve from my forefathers
Philem. 4. I *t*. my God always, making mention of thee
see thanks.

Thanked.
Acts 28. 15. when Paul saw, he *t*. God, and took courage
see thanks.

Thankful.
Col. 3. 15. ye were called in one body; and be ye *thankful*
see thanks.

Thankfulness.
Acts 24. 3. in all places, most excellent Felix, with all *t*.

Thanks.—A.V. ¹*thank—ed—ful.*
Mat. 26. 27. he took a cup, and gave *t*. Mk. 14. 23 : Lu. 22. 17
Mk. 8. 6. he took the seven loaves, and having given
  thanks. Mat. 15. 36 : Jno. 6. 11, 23
Lu. 2. 38. she [Anna] gave *t*. unto God, and spake of him
  17. 16. fell upon his face at his feet, giving him *thanks*
  22. 19. took bread, and when he had given *thanks*,
  he brake it. Acts 27. 35 : 1 Cor. 11. 24
Rom. 1. 21. glorified him not as God, neither gave ¹*thanks*
  6. 17. But ¹*t*. be to God, that, whereas ye were servants
  14. 6. he giveth God *t*.—eateth not, and giveth God *t*.
1 Cor. 14. 16. unlearned say the Amen at thy giving of *t*.
  15. 57. but *thanks* be to God, which giveth us the victory
2 Cor. 1. 11. *thanks* may be given by many persons
  2. 14. *thanks* be unto God, which always leadeth us
  8. 16. *thanks* be to God, which putteth the same—care
  9. 15. *Thanks* be to God for his unspeakable gift
Eph. 5. 4. are not befitting: but rather giving of *thanks*
  20. giving *thanks* always for all things in the name
Col. 1. 12. giving *t*. unto the Father, who made us meet
  3. 17. giving *thanks* to God the Father through him
2 Th. 1. 3. We are bound to give ¹*t*. to God alway for you
Rev. 4. 9. and *thanks* to him that sitteth on the throne
see confession, give, thanksgiving—s.

Thanksgiving.—A.V. ¹*thanks.*
2 Cor. 4. 15. cause the *t*. to abound unto the glory of God
  9. 11. which worketh through us *thanksgiving* to God
Phil. 4. 6. everything by prayer and supplication with *t*.
Col. 2. 7. as ye were taught, abounding in *thanksgiving*
  4. 2. prayer, watching therein with *thanksgiving*
1 Th. 3. 9. For what ¹*t*. can we render again unto God
1 Tim. 4. 3. created to be received with *t*. by them
  4. rejected, if it be received with *thanksgiving*
Rev. 7. 12. Blessing, and glory, and wisdom, and *t*.

Thanksgivings.—A.V. ¹*giving of thanks.*
2 Cor. 9. 12. aboundeth also through many *t*. unto God
1 Tim. 2. 1. intercessions, ¹*t*., be made for all men

THING

Thankworthy A.V.—*see acceptable.*

Theatre.
Acts 19. 29. rushed—into the *theatre*, having seized Gaius
  31. besought him not to adventure himself into the *t*.

Thefts.
Mat. 15. 19. fornications, *thefts*, false witness. Mk. 7. 22
Rev. 9. 21. repented not of—fornication, nor of their *t*.

Thief.
Mat. 24. 43. in what watch the *thief* was coming. Lu. 12. 39
Lu. 12. 33. where no *thief* draweth near, neither moth
Jno. 10. 1. but climbeth up some other way, the same is a *t*.
  10. The *thief* cometh not, but that he may steal
  12. 6. but because he was a *thief*, and having the bag
1 Th. 5. 2. the day of the Lord so cometh as a *thief*
  4. that that day should overtake you as a *thief*
1 Pet. 4. 15. For let none of you suffer as a murderer, or a *t*.
2 Pet. 3. 10. But the day of the Lord will come as a *thief*
Rev. 3. 3. thou shalt not watch, I will come as a *thief*
  16. 15. (Behold, I come as a *thief*. Blessed is he that
see robber.

Thieves.
Mat. 6. 19. and where *thieves* break through and steal
  20. and where *thieves* do not break through nor steal
Jno. 10. 8. All that came before me are *thieves* and robbers
1 Cor. 6. 10. nor *thieves*, nor covetous, nor drunkards
see robbers.

Thigh.
Rev. 19. 16. on his *thigh* a name written, KING OF KINGS

Thing.—A.V. ¹*deed.*
Mk. 5. 32. about to see her that had done this *thing*
  10. 21. One *t*. thou lackest: go, sell whatsoever. Lu. 18. 22
  16. 18. serpents, and if they drink any deadly *thing*
Lu. 2. 15. unto Bethlehem, and see this *thing* that is come
  10. 42. but one *thing* is needful: for Mary hath chosen
  22. 23. which of them it was that should do this *thing*
Jno. 5. 14. sin no more, lest a worse *thing* befall thee
  9. 25. one *thing* I know, that, whereas I was blind
Acts 5. 4. that thou hast conceived this *t*. in thine heart?
  10. 28. it is an unlawful *thing* for a man that is a Jew
  12. 12. And when he [Peter] had considered the *thing*
  17. 21. either to tell or to hear some new *thing*)
  19. 32. Some therefore cried one *t*., and some another
  21. 34. And some shouted one *thing*, some another
  25. 26. Of whom I have no certain *thing* to write
Rom. 9. 20. Shall the *t*. formed say to him that formed it
  13. 6. attending continually upon this very *thing*
1 Cor. 1. 10. that ye all speak the same *thing*
  5. 3. judged him that hath so wrought this ¹*thing*
  8. 7. eat as of a *thing* sacrificed to an idol
  11. 5. it is one and the same *thing* as if she were shaven
2 Cor. 5. 5. he that wrought us for this very *thing* is God
  6. 17. And touch no unclean *thing*; And I will receive
  7. 11. this selfsame *thing*, that ye were made sorry
  10. 5. casting down imaginations, and every high *thing*
  12. 8. Concerning this *thing* I besought the Lord thrice
Eph. 5. 27. not having spot or wrinkle or any such *thing*
Phil. 1. 6. being confident of this very *thing*, that he
  3. 18. but one *thing* I do, forgetting the things which
2 Th. 3. is a righteous *thing* with God to recompense
1 Tim. 1. 10. any other *t*. contrary to the sound doctrine
Heb. 10. 29. wherewith he was sanctified, an unholy *thing*
  31. It is a fearful *t*. to fall into the hands of the living

THING

1 Pet. 4. 12. as though a strange *thing* happened unto you
2 Pet. 3. 8. But forget not this one *thing*, beloved, that one
1 Jno. 2. 8. which *thing* is true in him and in you
Rev. 9. 4. hurt the grass of the earth, neither any green *t.*
  see evil, good, great, question, something.

Any Thing, Anything.—A.V. ¹*nothing*.

Mat. 18. 19. two of you shall agree on earth, as touching *a.*
Mk. 4. 22. neither was *a.* made secret, but that. Lu. 8. 17
9. 22. if thou canst do *anything*, have compassion on
11. 13. fig tree—if haply he might find *a.* thereon
13. 15. nor enter in, to take *anything* out of his house
Lu. 22. 35. When I sent you forth—lacked ye *anything?*
Jno. 1. 3. without him was not *anything* made that hath
7. 4. For no man doeth *anything* in secret, and himself
14. 14. If ye shall ask me *a. t.* in my name, that will I do
Acts 10. 14. I have never eaten *any thing* that is common
17. 25. by men's hands, as though he needed *anything*
20. 20. I shrank not from declaring unto you ¹*anything*
25. 11. and have committed *anything* worthy of death
Rom. 8. 33. Who shall lay *a.* to the charge of God's elect?
13. 8. Owe no man *anything*, save to love one another
14. 14. to him who accounteth *anything* to be unclean
21. nor to do *anything* whereby thy brother stumbleth
1 Cor. 2. 2. I determined not to know *anything* among you
3. 7. So then neither is he that planteth *anything*
8. 2. If any man thinketh that he knoweth *anything*
4. we know that no idol is ¹*anything* in the world
10. 19. sacrificed to idols is *anything*, or that an idol is *a.?*
14. 35. would learn *a.*, let them ask their own husbands
2 Cor. 2. 10. But to whom ye forgive *a.*, I forgive also—I
  have forgiven *anything*, for your sakes have I
3. 5. of ourselves, to account *anything* as from ourselves
6. 3. giving no occasion of stumbling in *anything*
7. 14. For if in *anything* I have gloried to him
Gal. 5. 6. circumcision availeth *a.*, nor uncircumcision. 6. 15
Phil. 3. 15. and if in *anything* ye are otherwise minded
1 Th. 1. 8. is gone forth ; so that we need not to speak *a.*
Jas. 1. 7. think that he shall receive *anything* of the Lord
1 Jno. 5. 14. if we ask *anything* according to his will
Rev. 21. 27. in no wise enter into it *anything* unclean
  see aught, nothing, things.

Every Thing, Everything.—A.V. ¹*all things*.

Mat. 8. 33. went away into the city, and told *every thing*
1 Cor. 1. 5. that in *every thing* ye were enriched in him
2 Cor. 6. 4. but in ¹*e.* commending ourselves, as ministers
7. 11. In ¹*every thing* ye approved yourselves to be pure
16. I rejoice that in ¹*every thing* I am of good courage
8. 7. But as ye abound in *every thing*, in faith, and
9. 8. having always all sufficiency in ¹*every thing*
11. ye being enriched in *every thing* unto all liberality
11. 6. in ¹*every thing* we have made it manifest among all
9. in ¹*every thing* I kept myself from being burdensome
Eph. 5. 24. the wives also be to their husbands in *e.*
Phil. 4. 6. but in *every thing* by prayer and supplication
1 Th. 5. 18. in *e.* give thanks: for this is the will of God

Things.—A.V. ¹*anything*, ²*meats*, ³*men*, ⁴*speeches*.

Mat. 7. 11. your Father which is in heaven give good *things*
11. 4. tell John the *things* which ye do hear and see
13. 17. to see the *t.* which ye see—to hear. Lu. 10. 24
52. out of his treasure *things* new and old [8. 33
16. 23. mindest not the *t.* of God, but the *t.* of men. Mk.
22. 21. unto Cæsar the *things* that are Cæsar's; and unto
  God the *things* that are God's. Mk. 12. 17; Lu. 20. 25

THINGS

Mat. 24. 17. housetop not go down to take out the ¹*things*
25. 23. faithful over a few *things*—over many *things*
Mk. 4. 19. the lusts of other *t.* entering in, choke the word
7. 15. but the *things* which proceed out of the man·
10. 32. began to tell them the *t.* that were to happen unto
Lu. 5. 26. We have seen strange *things* to-day   [him
6. 46. why call ye me, Lord, Lord, and do not the *t.* which
9. 43. all were marvelling at all the *things* which he did
10. 23. Blessed are the eyes which see the *t.* that ye see
12. 15. man's life consisteth not in the abundance of the *t.*
20. the *t.* which thou hast prepared, whose shall they be?
48. did *things* worthy of stripes, shall be beaten
18. 27. The *t.* which are impossible with men are possible
19. 42. *t.* which belong unto peace ! but now they are hid
23. 48. when they beheld the *things* that were done
24. 18. and not know the *things* which are come to pass
27. in all the scriptures the *things* concerning himself
Jno. 1. 50. thou shalt see greater *things* than these
3. 12. If I told you earthly *things*, and ye believe not, how
  shall ye believe, if I tell you heavenly *things?*
8. 29. for I do always the *things* that are pleasing to him
16. 13. but what *things* soever he shall hear—and he
  shall declare unto you the *things* that are to come
Acts 1. 3. speaking the *t.* concerning the kingdom of God
4. 20. we cannot but speak the *things* which we saw
25. Gentiles rage, And the peoples imagine vain *things?*
32. not one of them said that aught of the *t.* which he
  possessed was his own ; but they had all *t.* common
15. 27. shall tell you the same *things* by word of mouth
29. ²*things* sacrificed to idols—*things* strangled. 21. 25
16. 14. heed unto the *things* which were spoken by Paul
17. 20. thou bringest certain strange *things* to our ears
18. 25. and taught carefully the *things* concerning Jesus
19. 8. persuading as to the *t.* concerning the kingdom
20. 22. Jerusalem, not knowing the *t.* that shall befall me
30. speaking perverse *t.*, to draw away the disciples
24. 13. Neither can they prove to thee the *t.* whereof
26. 24. And some believed the *things* which were spoken
Rom. 1. 20. For the invisible *t.* of him—are clearly seen,
  being perceived through the *things* that are made
2. 1. thou that judgest dost practise the same *things*
14. have no law do by nature the *things* of the law
18. and approvest the *things* that are excellent
4. 17. and calleth the *t.* that are not, as though they were
6. 21. What fruit then had ye at that time in the *things*
8. 5. do mind the *things* of the flesh—the *t.* of the spirit
38. nor *things* present, nor *things* to come, nor powers
10. 15. feet of them that bring glad tidings of good *t.!*
12. 16. Set not your mind on high *things*, but condescend to ³*things* that are lowly
17. Take thought for *things* honourable in the sight
14. 19. let us follow after *t.* which make for peace, and *t.*
15. 4. For whatsoever *things* were written aforetime
27. if the Gentiles have been made partakers of their
  spiritual *t.*, they owe it—unto them in carnal *t.*
1 Cor. 1. 27. God chose the foolish *things* of the world—the
  weak *things* of the world—the *t.* that are strong
28. the base *things* of the world, and the *things* that are
  despised—and the *things* that are not, that he
  might bring to nought the *things* that are
2. 9. *Things* which eye saw not—Whatsoever *things* God
10. Spirit searcheth all *things*, yea, the deep *t.* of God
11. who among men knoweth the *t.* of a man, save—
  even so the *things* of God none knoweth, save
12. we might know the *things* that are freely given
13. Which *things* also we speak—comparing spiritual *t.*
14. the natural man receiveth not the *t.* of the Spirit
3. 22. or *t.* present, or *things* to come; all are yours
4. 5. both bring to light the hidden *things* of darkness

THINGS

1 Cor. 4. 6. not to go beyond the *things* which are written
6. 3. how much more, *things* that pertain to this life?
4. If then ye have to judge *things* pertaining to this life
7. 32. unmarried is careful for the *t.* of the Lord. 34
33. married is careful for the *things* of the world. 34
8. 1. Now concerning *things* sacrificed to idols
9. 11. If we sowed unto you spiritual *t.*—carnal *things*?
13. they which minister about sacred *t.* eat of the *t.*
10. 20. But I say, that the *things* which the Gentiles
13, 11. become a man, I have put away childish *things*
14. 7. Even *things* without life, giving a voice
37. let him take knowledge of the *things* which I write
2 Cor. 1. 13. For we write none other *things* unto you
17. or the *things* that I purpose, do I purpose
4. 2. we have renounced the hidden *things* of shame
18. while we look not at the *things* which are seen, but at the *things* which are not seen : for the *things* which are seen are temporal ; but the *t.* which are
5. 10. that each one may receive the *t.* done in the body
17. he is a new creature : the old *t.* are passed away
8. 21. we take thought for *things* honourable, not only
10. 7. Ye look at the *things* that are before your face
16. not to glory in another's province in regard of *t.*
11. 30. I will glory of the *t.* that concern my weakness
Gal. 2. 18. if I build up again those *t.* which I destroyed
4. 24. Which *things* contain an allegory
5. 17. that ye may not do the *things* that ye would
Eph. 1. 10. the *t.* in the heavens, and the *t.* upon the earth
6. 9. And, ye masters, do the same *things* unto them
Phil. 1. 10. so that ye may approve the *t.* that are excellent
12. the *things* which happened unto me have fallen out
2. 4. not looking each of you to his own *things*, but each
10. every knee should bow, of *things* in heaven and *things* on earth and *things* under the earth
21. all seek their own, not the *things* of Jesus Christ
3. 1. To write the same *things* to you, to me indeed
19. glory is in their shame, who mind earthly *things*
4. 8. whatsoever *things* are true—*things* are honourable —*things* are just—*things* are pure—*things* are lovely—*t.* are of good report—think on these *t.*
9. The *things* which ye both learned—these *things* do
18. from Epaphroditus the *things* that came from you
Col. 1. 16. *things* visible and *t.* invisible, whether thrones
20. whether *t.* upon the earth, or *things* in the heavens
2. 17. are a shadow of the *things* to come. Heb. 10. 1
18. dwelling in the *things* which he hath seen
23. Which *things* have indeed a show of wisdom
3. 2. your mind on the *t.* that are above, not on the *t.*
6. for which *things*' sake cometh the wrath of God
1 Th. 2. 14. for ye also suffered the same *things* of your
2 Th. 3. 4. that ye both do and will do the *things*
1 Tim. 5. 13. busybodies, speaking *t.* which they ought not
2 Tim. 2. 2. the *things* which thou hast heard from me
3. 14. abide thou in the *things* which thou hast learned
Tit. 1. 5. shouldest set in order the *t.* that were wanting
11. teaching *t.* which they ought not, for filthy lucre's
2. 1. speak thou the *things* which befit the sound doctrine
Heb. 2. 1. more earnest heed to the *things* that were heard
17. and faithful high priest in *things* pertaining to God
5. 1. appointed for men in *things* pertaining to God
8. learned obedience by the *things* which he suffered
6. 9. But, beloved, we are persuaded better *things* of you, and *things* that accompany salvation
18. two immutable *things*, in which it is impossible
8. 1. Now in the *things* which we are saying the chief
5. which is a copy and shadow of the heavenly *things*
9. 23. *things* in the heavens should be cleansed with these ; but the heavenly *things*—with better

THINGS

Heb. 10. 1. the law having a shadow of the good *things* to come, not the very image of the *things*
11. 1. Now faith is the assurance of *things* hoped for, the proving of *things* not seen
3. hath not been made out of *things* which do appear
7. Noah, being warned of God concerning *things*
20. blessed Jacob and Esau, even concerning *t.* to come
Jas. 3. 7. of creeping *things* and *things* in the sea, is tamed
1 Pet. 1. 12. but unto you, did they minister these *things* —which *things* angels desire to look into
18. ye were redeemed, not with corruptible *things*
2 Pet. 3. 16. wherein are some *things* hard to be understood
1 Jno. 2. 15. world, neither the *things* that are in the world
Jude 10. rail at whatsoever *things* they know not
15. of all the hard *t.* which ungodly sinners have spoken
Rev. 1. 1. the *t.* which must shortly come to pass. 22. 6
19. Write therefore the *things* which thou sawest, and the *t.* which are, and the *t.* which shall come to pass
2. 14. But I have a few *things* against thee, because thou hast—to eat *things* sacrificed to idols
3. 2. watchful, and stablish the *things* that remain
4. 1. I will shew thee the *things* which must come to pass
10. 6. created the heaven and the *things* that are therein —earth and the *things*—the sea and the *things*
see creeping, evil, good, great, matters, perplexed, good tidings.

All Things.

Mat. 7. 12. *All things* therefore whatsoever ye would that
11. 27. *All t.* have been delivered unto me of my. Lu. 10.
13. 41. gather out of his kingdom *all things* that |22
17. 11. cometh, and shall restore *all things.* Mk. 9. 12
19. 26. but with God *all things* are possible. Mk. 10. 27
21. 22. *all things,* whatsoever ye shall ask in prayer
22. 4. *all t.* are ready : come to the marriage. Lu. 14. 17
23. 3. *all things*—they bid you, these do and observe
26. altar, sweareth by it, and by *all things* thereon
28. 11. told unto the chief priests *all* the *t.* that were come
20. teaching them to observe *all things* whatsoever
Mk. 4. 11. that are without, *all things* are done in parables
34. to his own disciples he expounded *all things*
6. 30. the apostles—told him *all things,* whatsoever they
7. 37. He hath done *all t.* well : he maketh even the deaf
9. 23. *All things* are possible to him that believeth
11. 24. *All things* whatsoever ye pray and ask for
13. 23. behold, I have told you *all things* beforehand
14 36. Abba, Father, *all things* are possible unto thee
Lu. 1. 3. having traced the course of *all things* accurately
2. 20. praising God for *all* the *things* that they had heard
39. *all things* that were according to the law of the Lord
11. 41 within ; and behold, *all things* are clean unto you
13. 17. multitude rejoiced for *all* the glorious *things*
18. 31. and *all* the *things* that are written by the prophets
21. 22. days of vengeance, that *all t.* which are written
32. not pass away, till *all things* be accomplished
24. 44. how that *all things* must needs be fulfilled
Jno. 1. 3. *All things* were made by him ; and without him
3. 35. the Son, and hath given *all things* into his hand
4. 25. when he is come, he will declare unto us *all things*
29. see a man, which told me *all t.* that ever I did. 39
5. 20. Father loveth the Son, and sheweth him *all things*
10. 41. *all things* whatsoever John spake of this man
13. 3. Jesus, knowing that the Father had given *all t.*
14. 26. teach you *all t.*, and bring to your remembrance
15. 15. for *all things* that I heard from my Father
16. 15. *All things* whatsoever the Father hath are mine
30. Now know we that thou knowest *all things*
17. 7. they know that *all t.* whatsoever thou hast given me
10. *all t.* that are mine are thine, and thine are mine

343

THINGS

Jno. 16. 4. Jesus—knowing *all* the *things* that were coming
19. 28. Jesus, knowing that *all things* are now finished
21. 17. Lord, thou knowest *all things;* thou knowest
Acts 2. 44. were together, and had *all things* common. 4. 32
3. 21. until the times of restoration of *all things*
22. like unto me; to him shall ye hearken in *all things*
10. 33. present—to hear *all t.* that have been commanded
39. we are witnesses of *all things* which he did
13. 39. every one that believeth is justified from *all things*
17. 24. The God that made the world and *all t.* therein
25. giveth to all life, and breath, and *all things*
20. 35. In *all things* I gave you an example
22. 10. and there it shall be told thee of *all things*
24. 14. believing *all things* which are according to the law
26. 2. touching *all* the *things* whereof I am accused
Rom. 8. 28. love God *all things* work together for good
32. shall he not also with him freely give us *all things ?*
11. 36. of him, and through him, and unto him, are *all t.*
14. 2. One man hath faith to eat *all things :* but he
20. *All things* indeed are clean; howbeit it is evil
1 Cor. 2. 10. the Spirit searcheth *all things,* yea, the deep
15. But he that is spiritual judgeth *all things*
3. 21. let no one glory in men. For *all things* are yours
4. 13. filth of the world, the offscouring of *all things*
6. 12. *All things* are lawful for me; but not *all things*
are expedient. *All things* are lawful for me
8. 6. one God, the Father, of whom are *a. t.*—and one
Lord, Jesus Christ, through whom are *all things*
9. 12. we bear *all things*, that we may cause no hindrance
22. I am become *all things* to all men
23. And I do *all things* for the gospel's sake
25. striveth in the games is temperate in *all things*
10. 23. *All things* are lawful; but *all t.* are not expedient.
All things are lawful; but *all things* edify not
33. even as I also please all men in *all things*
11. 2. that ye remember me in *all things,* and hold fast
12. but *all things* are of God. 2 Cor. 5. 18
12. 6. the same God, who worketh *all things* in all
13. 7. beareth *all things,* believeth *all things,* hopeth
all things, endureth *all things*
14. 26. Let *all things* be done unto edifying
40. But let *all things* be done decently and in order
15. 27. For, He put *all t.* in subjection under his feet—
All things are put—who did subject *a. t.* unto him
28. when *all things* have been subjected—himself be
subjected to him that did subject *all things*
2 Cor. 2. 9. whether ye are obedient in *all things*
4. 15. For *all things* are for your sakes, that the grace
6. 10. as having nothing, and yet possessing *all things*
7. 14. we spake *all things* to you in truth, so our glorying
12. 19. But *all things,* beloved, are for your edifying
Gal. 3. 10. continueth not in *all things* that are written
Eph. 1. 10. fulness of the times, to sum up *all t.* in Christ
11. who worketh *all things* after the counsel of his will
22. he put *all things* in subjection under his feet, and
gave him to be head over *all things* to the church
3. 9. ages hath been hid in God who created *all things*
4. 10. above all the heavens, that he might fill *all things)*
15. grow up in *all things* into him, which is the head
5. 13. But *all things* when they are reproved are made
20. giving thanks always for *all things* in the name
6. 10. hath made known to you *all things.* Col. 4. 9
Phil. 2. 14. Do *all things* without murmurings
3. 8. I count *all things* to be loss for—Christ Jesus my
Lord: for whom I suffered the loss of *all things*
21. is able even to subject *all things* unto himself
4. 12. and in *all things* have I learned the secret
13. I can do *all things* in him that strengtheneth me
18. But I have *all things,* and abound

THINGS

Col. 1. 16. in him were *all things* created—*all things* have
17. he is before *all things,* and in him *all things* consist
18. that in *all things* he might have the preeminence
20. and through him to reconcile *all things* unto himself
3. 20. Children, obey your parents in *all things*
22. Servants, obey in *all t.* them that are your masters
1 Th. 5. 21. prove *all things ;* hold fast that which is good
1 Tim. 3. 11. Women—temperate, faithful in *all things*
4. 8. but godliness is profitable for *all things*
6. 13. in the sight of God, who quickeneth *all things*
17. God, who giveth us richly *all things* to enjoy
2 Tim. 2. 7. the Lord shall give thee understanding in *all t.*
10. Therefore I endure *all things* for the elect's sake
4. 5. But be thou sober in *all things,* suffer hardship
Tit. 1. 15. To the pure *all things* are pure
2. 7. in *all t.* shewing thyself an ensample of good works
9. and to be well-pleasing to them in *all things*
10. adorn the doctrine of God our Saviour in *all things*
Heb. 1. 2. his Son, whom he appointed heir of *all things*
3. upholding *all things* by the word of his power
2. 8. Thou didst put *all things* in subjection—be subjected *all things*—we see not yet *all t.* subjected
10. for whom are *all things,* and through whom are *all t.*
17. in *all things* to be made like unto his brethren
3. 4. but he that built *all things* is God
4. 13. *all things* are naked and laid open before the eyes
8. 5. thou make *all things* according to the pattern
9. 22. almost say, *all things* are cleansed with blood
13. 18. desiring to live honestly in *all things*
Jas. 5. 12. But above *all things,* my brethren, swear not
1 Pet. 4. 7. But the end of *all things* is at hand: be ye
8. above *all things* being fervent in your love
11. that in *all t.* God may be glorified through Jesus
2 Pet. 1. 3. *all things* that pertain unto life and godliness
3. 4. *all things* continue as they were from the beginning
1 Jno. 2. 20. anointing from the Holy One, and ye know *a. t.*
27. his anointing teacheth you concerning *all things*
3. 20. God is greater than our heart, and knoweth *all t.*
3 Jno. 2. that in *all things* thou mayest prosper [he saw
Rev. 1. 2. testimony of Jesus Christ, even of *all things* that
4. 11. for thou didst create *all t.*—of thy will they were
21. 5. on the throne said, Behold, I make *all things* new
see every thing, these things.

Such Things.

Mk. 7. 13. tradition—and many such like *things* ye do
Lu. 9. 9. who is this, about whom I hear *such things ?*
10. 7. eating and drinking *such things* as they give. 8
Acts 25. 18. no charge of *such evil things* as I supposed
28. 10. they put on board *such things* as we needed
Rom. 1. 32. practise *such things* are worthy of death. 2. 2
2. 3. judgest them that practise *s. t.,* and doest the same
Gal. 5. 21. practise *such t.* shall not inherit the kingdom
Heb. 11. 14. *such t.* make it manifest that they are seeking
13. 5. content with *such things* as ye have [after
see these things. those things.

These **Things.**—*A.V.* ¹all *things,* ²*questions,* ³*such
things,* ⁴*those things,* ⁵*words.*

Mat. 1. 20. he thought on *these things,* behold, an angel
4. 9. All *these things* will I give thee, if thou wilt fall
6. 32. after all *these things* do the Gentiles seek—Father
knoweth that ye have need of all *these t.* Lu. 12. 30
33. all *these things* shall be added unto you. Lu. 12. 31
11. 25. thou didst hide *these t.* from the wise. Lu. 10. 21
13. 34. All *these things* spake Jesus in parables
51. Have ye understood all *these things ?*
56. Whence then hath this man all *these t. ?* Mk 6. 2
15. 20. *these* are the *things* which defile the man
19. 20. All *these things* have I observed. Mk. 10. 20

THINGS

Mat. 21. 23. By what authority doest thou *these things?* 24, 27: Mk. 11. 28, 29, 33: Lu. 20. 2, 8
23. 36. All *these things* shall come upon this generation
24. 2. See ye not all *these things?* verily I say. Lu. 21. 6
3. when shall *these things* be? Mk. 13. 4: Lu. 21. 7:
6. *these t.* must needs come to. Mk. 13. ⁸7: Lu. 21. 9
8. all *these things* are the beginning of travail
33. *these t.*, know ye that he. Mk. 13. 29: Lu. 21. 28, 31
34. till all *these things* be accomplished. Mk. 13. 30
Mk. 2. 8. Why reason ye *these things* in your hearts?
Lu. 1. 20. not able to speak, until the day that *these things*
13. 2. Galilæans, because they have suffered ³*these t.?*
14. 6. they could not answer again unto *these things*
15. 26. servants, and inquired what *these t.* might be
16. 14. who were lovers of money, heard all *these things*
18. 34. And they understood none of *these things*
21. 12. before all *these things,* they shall lay their hands
36. that ye may prevail to escape all *these things*
23. 31. For if they do *these things* in the green tree
24. 14. they communed with each other of all *these t.*
21. now the third day since *these t.* came to pass
26. Behoved it not the Christ to suffer *these things*
48. Ye are witnesses of *these things*
Jno. 2. 16. that sold the doves be said, Take *these things*
18. shewest thou unto us, seeing that thou doest *t. t.?*
3. 9. Nicodemus answered—How can *these things* be?
10. teacher of Israel, and understandest not *these t.?*
5. 16. because he did *these things* on the sabbath
34. howbeit I say *these things,* that ye may be saved
7. 4. If thou doest *these things,* manifest thyself
32. Pharisees heard the multitudes murmuring ⁴*these t.*
8. 28. as the Father taught me, I speak *these things*
9. 22. *These* ⁵*things* said his parents, because they feared
12. 16. *These things* understood not his disciples—remembered they that *these things* were written of him, and that they had done *these things*
41. *These things* said Isaiah, because he saw his glory
13. 17. If ye know *these things,* blessed are ye if ye do
15. 21. But all *these things* will they do unto you. 16. 3
19. 24. they cast lots. *These t.* therefore the soldiers did
36. *these t.* came to pass, that the scripture might
Acts 5. 32. And we are witnesses of *these t.* Jno. 21. 24
7. 1. the high priest said, Are *these things* so?
50. Did not my hand make all *these things?* [heart
54 Now when they heard *these t.,* they were cut to the
14. 15. Sirs, why do ye *these things?* We also are men
15. 18. who maketh *these t.* known from the beginning
28. no greater burden than *these* necessary *things*
17. 11. examining the scriptures daily, whether ⁴*these t.*
20. would know therefore what *these things* mean
18. 17. And Gallio cared for none of ⁴*these things*
19. 36. Seeing then that *these things* cannot be gainsaid
24. 9. [Jews] affirming that *these things* were so
25. 9. to Jerusalem, and there be judged of *these things*
20. perplexed how to inquire concerning ²*these t.*
26. 26. For the king knoweth of *these things*—none of *these things* is hidden from him
Rom. 8. 31. What then shall we say to *these things?*
37. in all *these things* we are more than conquerors
1 Cor. 9. 8. Do I speak *t. things* after the manner of men?
15. I have used none of *these t.:* and I write not *t. t.*
10. 6. Now *these things* were our examples
2 Cor. 2. 16. And who is sufficient for *these things?*
Eph. 5. 6. because of *these things* cometh the wrath of God
Phil. 4. 8. if there be any praise, think on *these things*
9. *these t.* do: and the God of peace shall be with you
Col. 3. 14. and above all *these things* put on love
1 Tim. 4. 6. put the brethren in mind of *these things*
11. *These things* command and teach. 5. 7: 6. 2

THINK

1 Tim. 4. 15. Be diligent in *t. t.;* give thyself wholly. 16
6. 11. O man of God, flee *these things;* and follow after
2 Tim. 1. 12. I suffer also *these t.:* yet I am not ashamed
2. 14. Of *these things* put them in remembrance
Tit. 2. 15. *These things* speak and exhort and reprove
3. 8. Faithful is the saying, and concerning *these things*
—*These things* are good and profitable unto men
Heb. 7. 13. he of whom *t. t.* are said belongeth to another
Jas. 3. 10. My brethren, *these things* ought not so to be
2 Pet. 1. 8. For if *these things* are yours and abound
9. For he that lacketh *these things* is blind, seeing only
10. if ye do *these things,* ye shall never stumble
12. always to put you in remembrance of *these things*
15. able after my decease to call *t. t.* to remembrance
3. 11. Seeing that *these things* are thus all to be dissolved
14. beloved, seeing that ye look for ⁸*these things*
16. in all his epistles, speaking in them of *these things*
17. beloved, knowing *these things* beforehand
Jude 10. in *these things* are they destroyed
Rev. 21. 7. He that overcometh shall inherit ¹*these things*
22. 8. I John am he that heard and saw *these things*—feet of the angel which shewed me *these things*
16. to testify unto you *t. things* for the churches
20. He which testifieth *t. things* saith—I come quickly *see sayings.*

Those Things.—A.V. ¹*such things.*

Lu. 11. 41. Howbeit give for alms ¹*t. t.* which are within
Acts 27. 11. than to *t. things* which were spoken by Paul
Rom. 1. 28. to do *those things* which are not fitting
6. 21. now ashamed? for the end of *those things* is death
2 Cor. 11. 23. Beside *those things* that are without
Heb. 3. 5. for a testimony of *those t.* which were afterward
12. 27. signifieth the removing of *those things*—that *those things* which are not shaken may remain *see these things.*

What Things.

Mat. 6. 8. your Father knoweth *w. things* ye have need of
18. 18. *W. t.* soever ye shall bind—*w. t.* soever ye shall loose
Mk. 9. 9. should tell no man *what things* they had seen
Lu. 7. 22. tell John *what things* ye have seen and heard
24. 19. And he [Jesus] said unto them, *What things?*
Jno. 5. 19. for *what things* soever he doeth, these the Son
10 6. they understood not *w. things* they were [Christ
Phil. 3. 7. *w. t.* were gain to me, these have I counted loss for

Think.—A.V. ¹*suppose.*

Mat. 3. 9. and *think* not to say within yourselves, We have
5. 17. *Think* not that I came to destroy the law or the
6. 7. they *think* that they shall be heard for their much
9. 4. Wherefore *think* ye evil in your hearts? [speaking
10. 34. *Think* not that I came to send peace. Lu. 12. ¹51
18. 12. How *think* ye? if any man have a hundred sheep
21. 28. But what *think* ye? A man had two sons
22. 42. What *think* ye of the Christ? Whose son is he?
24. 44. in an hour that ye *think* not the Son of man cometh. Lu. 12. 40 [death. Mk. 14. 64
26. 66. what *t.* ye? They answered—He is worthy of
Lu. 13. 2. ¹*T.* ye that these Galilæans were sinners above
4. *think* ye that these were offenders above all the men
Jno. 5. 39. because ye *t.* that in them ye have eternal life
45. *Think* not that I will accuse you to the Father
11. 56. spake—what *think* ye, that he will not come to the feast? [gold
16. 2. killeth you shall *t.* that he offereth service unto God
Acts. 17. 29. we ought not to *t.* that the Godhead is like unto
26. 2. I *think* myself happy, king Agrippa
Rom. 12. 3. not to *think* of himself more highly than he ought to *think;* but so to *think* as to *t.* soberly

THINK

1 Cor. 4. 9. I *think*, God hath set forth us the apostles
7. 26. I *think* therefore that this is good by reason of the
40. I *think* that I also have the Spirit of God
12. 23. parts of the body, which we *think* to be less
2. Cor. 11. 16. Let no man *think* me foolish [honourable
12. 19. Ye *think* all this time that we are excusing
Eph. 3. 20. able to do—above all that we ask or *think*
Phil. 4. 8. if there be any praise, *think* on these things
Heb. 10. 29. of how much sorer punishment, ¹*think* ye
Jas. 1. 7. let not that man *t.* that he shall receive anything
4. 5. Or *think* ye that the scripture speaketh in vain?
1 Pet. 4. 4. wherein they *think* it strange that ye run not
12. *think* it not strange concerning the fiery trial
2 Pet. 1. 13. I *t.* it right, as long as I am in this tabernacle
see account, consider, count, minded, reckon, suppose, thinketh.

Thinkest.

Mat. 17. 25. What *t.* thou, Simon? the kings of the earth
22. 17. What *thinkest* thou? Is it lawful to give tribute
26. 53. *thinkest* thou that I cannot beseech my Father
Lu. 10. 36. Which of these three, *t.* thou, proved neighbour
Acts 28. 22. desire to hear of thee what thou *thinkest*
see reckonest.

Thinketh.—A.V. ¹*seem*, ²*seemeth*, ³*think*.

Lu. 8. 18. taken away even that which he ²*thinketh* he hath
1 Cor. 3. 18. If any man ³*thinketh* that he is wise
7. 36. if any man ³*t.* that he behaveth himself unseemly
8. 2. If any man ³*thinketh* that he knoweth any thing
10. 12. let him that *thinketh* he standeth take heed
14. 37. If any man ³*thinketh* himself to be a prophet
Gal. 6. 3. if a man ³*thinketh* himself to be something
Phil. 3. 4. if any other man *thinketh* to have confidence
Jas. 1. 26. If any man ¹*thinketh* himself to be religious

Thinking.—A.V. ¹*supposing*.

Phil. 1. 17. ¹*t.* to raise up affliction for me in my bonds

Third.

Mat. 22. 26. the *t.*, unto the seventh. Mk. 12. 21; Lu. 20. 31
26. 44. prayed a *third* time, saying again the same words
Mk. 14. 41. he cometh the *third* time, and saith unto them
Lu. 12. 38. if in the *third*, [watch] and find them so
20. 12. And he sent yet a *t.*: and him also they wounded
Jno. 21. 14. *third* time that Jesus was manifested
17. *third* time, Simon, son of John, lovest thou me?—
grieved because he said unto him the *third* time
Acts 20. 9. he [Eutychus] fell down from the *third* story
2 Cor. 12. 2. such a one caught up even to the *third* heaven
14. Behold, this is the *third* time I am ready to come
13. 1. This is the *third* time I am coming to you
Rev. 4. 7. the *third* creature had a face as of a man
6. 5. opened the *t.* seal, I heard the *third* living creature
8. 7. the *third* part of the earth—*third* part of the trees
8. the *third* part of the sea became blood
9. there died the *third* part of the creatures—the *third*
part of the ships was destroyed [the rivers
10. the *t.* angel sounded—and it fell upon the *t.* part of
11. the *third* part of the waters became wormwood
12. the *third* part of the sun—*third* part of the moon—
t. part of the stars—*t.* part of them—*t.* part of it
11. 14. second Woe is past—the *t.* Woe cometh quickly
14. 9. another angel, a *third*, followed them
16. 4. And the *third* poured out his bowl into the rivers
21. 19. the second, sapphire; the *third*, chalcedony
see day, hour, part.

Thirdly.

1 Cor. 12. 28. prophets, *thirdly* teachers, then miracles

THOUGHTS

Thirst.

Mat. 5. 6. that hunger and *thirst* after righteousness
Jno. 4. 13. Every one that drinketh—shall *thirst* again
14. the water that I shall give him shall never *thirst*
15. Sir, give me this water, that I *thirst* not
6. 35. he that believeth on me shall never *thirst*
7. 37. If any man *thirst*, let him come unto me
19. 28. that all things are now finished—saith, I *thirst*
Rom. 12. 20. feed him; if he *thirst*, give him to drink
1 Cor. 4. 11. we both hunger, and *thirst*, and are naked
2 Cor. 11. 27. in hunger and *thirst*, in fastings often
Rev. 7. 16. hunger no more, neither *thirst* any more

Thirsty.

Mat. 25. 35. I was *thirsty*, and ye gave me drink
42. I was *thirsty*, and ye gave me no drink
see athirst.

Thirty.—A.V. ¹*thirtyfold*.

Mat. 13. 8. yielded fruit, some a hundredfold—some ¹*t.* 23
26. 15. they weighed unto him [Judas] *t.* pieces of silver
27. 3. repented himself, and brought back the *t.* pieces
9. And they [chief priests] took the *t.* pieces of silver
Lu. 3. 23. Jesus—when he began to teach, was about *thirty*
Jno. 5. 5. had been *thirty* and eight years in his infirmity
6. 19. rowed about five and twenty or *thirty* furlongs
see thirtyfold.

Thirtyfold.—A.V. ¹*thirty*.

Mk. 4. 8. and brought forth, ¹*thirtyfold*, and sixtyfold. 20
see thirty.

Thistles.—A.V. ¹*briers*.

Mat. 7. 16. Do men gather grapes of thorns, or figs of *t.*?
Heb. 6. 8. beareth thorns and ¹*thistles*, it is rejected

Thongs.

Acts 22. 25. when they had tied him [Paul] up with the *t.*

Thorn—s.

Mat. 7. 16. Do men gather grapes of *thorns*, or figs. Lu. 6.44
13. 7. *thorns*; and the *t.* grew up. Mk. 4. 7; Lu. 8. 7, 14
22. And he that was sown among the *thorns*
27. 29. they plaited a crown of *t.* Mk. 15. 17; Jno. 19. 2
Mk. 4. 18. others are they that are sown among the *thorns*
Jno. 19. 5. Jesus—came out, wearing the crown of *thorns*
2 Cor. 12. 7. there was given to me [Paul] a *t.* in the flesh
Heb. 6. 8. if it beareth *thorns* and thistles, it is rejected

Thought.—A.V. ¹*care*, ²*careful*.

Mat. 1. 20. when he [Joseph] *thought* on these things
Mk. 14. 72. when he [Peter] *thought* thereon, he wept
Lu. 7. 7. neither *thought* I myself worthy to come unto
Jno. 11. 13. they *thought* that he spake of taking rest
Acts 8. 20. because thou hast *thought* to obtain the gift
22. if perhaps the *t.* of thy heart shall be forgiven thee
10. 19. while Peter *thought* on the vision, the Spirit said
12. 9. wist not that it was true—but *t.* he saw a vision
15. 38. Paul *thought* not good to take with them him
26. 9. I verily *thought* with myself, that I ought to do
1 Cor. 13. 11. I felt as a child, I *thought* as a child
2 Cor. 9. 5. I *thought* it necessary therefore to intreat
10. 5. bringing every *thought* into captivity
Phil. 4. 10. your ¹*t.* for me; wherein ye did indeed take ²*t.*
see anxious, counted, judged, reasoned—ing, supposed.

Thoughts.—A.V. ¹*minds*.

Mat. 9. 4. Jesus knowing their *t.* 12. 25; Lu. 6. 8; 11. 17
15. 19. out of the heart come forth evil *thoughts.* Mk. 7. 21

THOUGHTS

Lu. 2. 35. that *thoughts* out of many hearts may be revealed
Rom. 2. 15. their *thoughts* one with another accusing
Phil. 4. 7. guard your hearts and your ¹*t.* in Christ Jesus
Heb. 4. 12. quick to discern the *t.* and intents of the heart
Jas. 2. 4. and become judges with evil *thoughts* ?
    see reasonings.

Thousand.

Mat. 14. 21. they that did eat were about five *thousand.*
  Mk. 6. 44 : *Lu.* 9. 14 : *Jno.* 6. 10
15. 38. did eat were about four *thousand* men. *Mk.* 8. 9
16. 9. remember the five loaves of the five *t. Mk.* 8. 19
10. Neither the seven loaves of the four *t. Mk.* 8. 20
18. 24. one—which owed him ten *thousand* talents
Mk. 5. 13. into the sea, in number about two *thousand*
Lu. 14. 31. whether he is able with ten *t.* to meet him—
  cometh against him with twenty *thousand* ?
Acts 2. 41. added unto them in that day about three *t.* souls
4. 4. the number of the men came to be about five *t.*
19. 19. and found it fifty *thousand* pieces of silver
21. 38. the four *thousand* men of the Assassins?
Rom. 11. 4. seven *t.* men, who have not bowed the knee
1 *Cor.* 4. 15. though ye should have ten *t.* tutors in Christ
10. 8. fell in one day three and twenty *thousand*
14. 19. than ten *thousand* words in a tongue
2 *Pet.* 3. 8. one day—as a *t.* years, and a *t.* years as one day
Rev. 5. 11. ten *thousand* times ten *thousand.* 9. 16
7. 4. sealed, a hundred and forty and four *t.* 14. 1, 3
5. Of the tribe of Judah were sealed twelve *t.* 6, 7, 8
11. 3. shall prophesy a *t.* two hundred and threescore days
13. killed in the earthquake seven *thousand* persons
12. 6. nourish her a *t.* two hundred and threescore days
14. 20. as far as a *thousand* and six hundred furlongs
20. 2. and bound him for a *thousand* years
3. until the *thousand* years should be finished. 5, 7
4. and reigned with Christ a *thousand* years
21. 16. measured the city—twelve *thousand* furlongs

Thousands.—*A.V.* ¹*innumerable.*

Lu. 12. 1. many ¹*thousands* of the multitude were gathered
Acts 21. 20. Thou seest, brother, how many *t.* there are
Rev. 5. 11. times ten thousand, and *thousands of thousands*

Threaten—ed.

Acts 4. 17. let us *threaten* them, that they speak henceforth
21. when they had further *threatened* them, let them go
1 *Pet.* 2. 23. when he suffered, *threatened* not

Threatening—s.—*A.V.* ¹*threatenings.*

Acts 4. 29. And now, Lord, look upon their *threatenings*
9. 1. Saul, yet breathing ¹*threatening* and slaughter
Eph. 6. 9. and forbear *t.* : knowing that both their Master

Three.

Mat. 13. 33. and hid in *three* measures of meal. *Lu.* 13. 21
17. 4. I will make here *t.* tabernacles. *Mk.* 9. 5 : *Lu.* 9. 33
18. 16. at the mouth of two witnesses or *t.* 2 *Cor.* 13. 1
20. where two or *three* are gathered together
Lu. 10. 36. Which of these *three*—proved neighbour
11. 5. and say to him, Friend, lend me *three* loaves
12. 52. one house divided, *t.* against two, and two against *t.*
Acts 5. 7. about the space of *t.* hours after, when his wife
10. 19. Behold, *three* men seek thee [Peter]
11. 11. forthwith *three* men stood before the house
28. 15. The Market of Appius, and The *Three* Taverns
1 *Cor.* 13. 13. But now abideth faith, hope, love, these *t.*
14. 27. speaketh—let it be by two, or at the most *three*
29. let the prophets speak by two or *three*
1 *Tim.* 5. 19. except at the mouth of two or *t.* witnesses

THRONE

Heb. 10. 28. on the word of two or *three* witnesses
1 *Jno.* 5. 8. *three* who bear witness—the *three* agree in one
Rev. 6. 6. and *three* measures of barley for a penny
6. 13. voices of the trumpet of the *three* angels ⁷killed
9. 18. By these *three* plagues was the third part of men
16. 13. *three* unclean spirits, as it were frogs
19. And the great city was divided into *three* parts
21. 13. on the east were *three* gates—north *three* gates
  —south *three* gates—west *three* gates
  see days, hundred, thousand, thrice, years.

Threescore.

Lu. 24. 13. Emmaus, which was *t.* furlongs from Jerusalem
Acts 7. 14. and all his kindred, *threescore* and fifteen souls
23. 23. and horsemen *threescore* and ten   [years old
1 *Tim.* 5. 9. Let none be enrolled as a widow under *t.*

Thresh—eth.

1 *Cor.* 9. 10. and he that *t.*, to *thresh* in hope of partaking

Threshing-floor.—*A.V.* ¹*floor.*

Mat. 3. 12. he will throughly cleanse his ¹*t.-floor. Lu.* 3. ¹17

Threw.—*A.V.* ¹*cast.*

Lu. 19. 35. they ¹*threw* their garments upon the colt
Acts 22. 23. And as they cried out, and ¹*t.* off their garments
  see cast, dashed.

Thrice.—*A.V.* ¹*three times.*

Mat. 26. 34. before the cock crow, thou shalt deny me *thrice.*
  75 : *Mk.* 14. 30, 72 : *Lu.* 22. 34, 61 : *Jno.* 13. 38
Acts 10. 16. And this was done *t.* : and—the vessel. 11. ¹10
2 *Cor.* 11. 25. *T.* was I beaten with rods—*t.* I suffered ship-
12. 8. Concerning this thing I besought the Lord *t.* [wreck

Throat.

Mat. 18. 28. and took him by the *throat*, saying, Pay what
Rom. 3. 13. Their *throat* is an open sepulchre

Throne.—*A.V.* ¹*God,* ²*seat.*

Mat. 5. 34. neither by the heaven, for it is the *t.* of God. 23. ²2
19. 28. when the Son of man shall sit on the *throne.* 25. 31
Lu. 1. 32. the Lord God shall give unto him the *t.* of—David
Acts 2. 30. of his loins he would set one upon his *throne*
7. 49. The heaven is my *t.*, And the earth the footstool
12. 21. Herod arrayed himself—and sat on the *throne*
Heb. 1. 8. Thy *throne*, O God, is for ever and ever
4. 16. draw near with boldness unto the *throne* of grace
8. 1. who sat down on the right hand of the *throne.* 12. 2
Rev. 1. 4. from the seven Spirits which are before his *t.* [is
2 13. I know where thou dwellest, even where Satan's ²*t.*
3. 21. to sit down with me in my *throne*, as I—sat down
  with my Father in his *throne*
4. 2. was a *throne* set in heaven—one sitting upon the *t.*
3. and there was a rainbow round about the *throne*
4. And round about the ²*t.* were four and twenty thrones
5. out of the *throne* proceed lightnings—there were
  seven lamps of fire burning before the *throne*
6. and before the *throne*, as it were a glassy sea—and
  in the midst of the *throne*, and round about the *t.*
9. honour and thanks to him that sitteth on the *throne*
10. fall down before him that sitteth on the *throne*—
  crowns before the *throne.* 7. 11   ¹a book. 7
5. 1. I saw in the right hand of him that sat on the *throne*
6. And I saw in the midst of the *t.*—a Lamb standing
11. I heard a voice of many angels round about the *t.*
13. Unto him that sitteth on the *t.*, and unto the Lamb
6. 16. hide us from the face of him that sitteth on the *t.*

THRONE

Rev. 7. 9. and peoples and tongues, standing before the *t.*
10. Salvation unto our God which sitteth on the *throne*
15. Therefore are they before the *t.* of God—he that sitteth on the *t.* shall spread his tabernacle over
17. Lamb—in the midst of the *t.* shall be their shepherd
8. 3. upon the golden altar which was before the *throne*
12. 5. her child was caught up unto God, and unto his *t.*
13. 2. the dragon gave him his power, and his ²*throne*
14. 3. and they sing as it were a new song before the *t.*
16. 10. the fifth poured out his bowl upon the ²*throne*
17. temple, from the *throne*, saying, It is done. 19. 5
19. 4. and worshipped God that sitteth on the *throne*
20. 11. And I saw a great white *throne*
12. the great and the small, standing before the ¹*throne*
21. 5. he that sitteth on the *t.* said, Behold, I make all
22. 1. bright as crystal, proceeding out of the *t.* of God
3. and the *t.* of God and of the Lamb shall be therein

Thrones.—*A.V.* ¹*seats.*

Mat. 19. 28. ye also shall sit upon the twelve *t. Lu.* 22. 30
Lu. 1. 52. He hath put down princes from their ¹*thrones*
Col. 1. 16. whether *thrones* or dominions or principalities
Rev. 4. 4. throne were four and twenty ¹*t.* : and upon the ¹*t.*
11. 16. elders, which sit before God on their ¹*thrones*
20. 4. And I saw *thrones*, and they sat upon them

Throng—ed.

Mk. 3. 9. because of the crowd, lest they should *t.* him
Lu. 8. 42. But as he went the multitudes *t.* him. *Mk.* 5. 24
see crush.

Thronging.

Mk. 5. 31. Thou seest the multitude *thronging* thee

Throughly *A.V.*—*see completely.*

Throw.—*A.V.* ¹*cast.*

Lu. 4. 29. that they might ¹*t.* him [Jesus] down headlong

Throwing.—*A.V.* ¹*cast.*

Acts 27. 38. lightened the ship, ¹*t.* out the wheat into the sea

Thrown.—*A.V.* ¹*cast.*

Mat. 24. 2. that shall not be *t.* down. *Mk.* 13. 2: *Lu.* 21. 6
Lu. 4. 35. And when the devil had *t.* him down in the midst
17. 2. about his neck, and he were ¹*thrown* into the sea
see cast down.

Thrust.—*A.V.* ¹*drave*, ²*put.*

Acts 7. 27. But he that did his neighbour wrong *t.* him away
39. fathers would not be obedient, but *t.* him from them
45. which God ¹*t.* out before the face of our fathers
13. 46. Seeing ye ²*t.* is from you, and judge yourselves
1 *Tim.* 1. 19. some having ²*t.* from them made shipwreck
see brought, cast forth, drive, put, send.

Thunder—s.—*A.V.* ¹*thunderings.*

Mk. 3. 17. Boanerges, which is, Sons of *thunder*
Rev. 4. 5. proceed lightnings and voices and ¹*t.* 16. 18 : 19. ¹⁶
6. 1. living creatures saying as with a voice of *t.*, Come
8. 5. and there followed ¹*thunders*, and voices. 11. ¹⁹
10. 3. when he cried, the seven *t.* uttered their voices. 4
14. 2. many waters, and as the voice of a great *thunder*

Thundered.

Jno. 12. 29. that stood by, and heard it, said that it had *t.*

Thunderings.—*A.V. see thunders.*

TIME

Thyine.

Rev. 18. 12. and all *thyine* wood, and every vessel of ivory

Tidings.—*A.V.* ¹*gospel*, ²*spoken.*

Acts 21. 31. to kill him, *t.* came up to the chief captain
Rom. 10. 15. them that bring glad *tidings* of good things!
16. they did not all hearken to the glad ¹*tidings*
15. 21. They shall see, to whom no ²*tidings* of him came
see report.

Good Tidings.—*A.V.* ¹*glad tidings*, ²*gospel*, ³*things.*

Mat. 11. 5. poor have ²*good tidings* preached to them
Lu. 1. 19. Gabriel—and to bring thee these ¹*good tidings*
2. 10. I bring you *good tidings* of great joy
4. 18. anointed me to preach ²*good tidings* to the poor
43. I must preach the *good tidings* of the kingdom of God
8. 1. bringing the ¹*good tidings* of the kingdom of God
Acts 8. 12. Philip preaching ²*g. t.* concerning the kingdom
13. 32. And we bring you ¹*good t.* of the promise made
Heb. 4. 2. we have had ²*good tidings* preached unto us
1 *Pet.* 1. 25. this is the word of ²*g. t.* which was preached

Tied.—*A.V.* ¹*bound.*

Mat. 21. 2. ye shall find an ass *t. Mk.* 11. 2, 4 ; *Lu.* 19. 30
Acts 22. 25. when they had ¹*tied* him up with the thong

Tiles.—*A.V.* ¹*tiling.*

Lu. 5. 19. and let him down through the ¹*t.* with his couch

Tiling.—*A.V.* ¹*see tiles.*

Tilled.—*A.V.* ¹*dressed.*

Heb. 6. 7. herbs meet for them for whose sake it is also ¹*t.*

Time.—*A.V.* ¹*ago*, ²*season—s*, ³*sometimes*, ⁴*space*, ⁵*times.*

Mat. 1. 11. at the *time* of the carrying away to Babylon
2. 7. learned of them carefully what *t.* the star appeared
16. according to the *t.* which he had carefully learned
8. 29. art thou come hither to torment us before the *time* ?
13. 30. and in the *t.* of the harvest I will say to the reapers
26. 18. The Master saith, My *time* is at hand [hand
Mk. 1. 15. The *t.* is fulfilled, and the kingdom of God is at
9. 21. How long ¹*time* is it since this hath come unto him ?
13. 33. watch and pray: for ye know not when the *time* is
Lu. 1. 57. Now Elisabeth's *time* was fulfilled
4. 5. all the kingdoms of the world in a moment of *time*
27. there were many lepers in Israel in the *t.* of Elisha
7. 45. Thou gavest me no kiss: but she, since the *time*
8. 13. a while believe, and in *time* of temptation fall away
19. 44. because thou knewest not the *time* of thy visita-
21. 8. saying, I am he ; and, The *time* is at hand [tion
Jno. 1. 18. No man hath seen God at any *time.* 1 *Jno.* 4. 12
5. 37. Ye have neither heard his voice at any *time*
7. 6. My *time* is not yet come ; but your *t.* is alway ready
8. is not yet fulfilled
Acts 1. 21. all the *time* that the Lord Jesus went in and
7. 17. But as the *time* of the promise drew nigh [hear
15. 33. had spent some ²*t.* there, they were dismissed
17. 21. spent their *t.* in nothing else, either to tell or to
20. 16. after what manner I was with you all the ²*time*
Rom. 13. 11. now it is high *t.* for you to awake out of sleep
1 *Cor.* 4. 5. Wherefore judge nothing before the *time*
7. 29. But this I say, brethren, the *time* is shortened
2 *Cor.* 6. 2. At an acceptable *time* I hearkened unto thee
Eph. 5. 16. redeeming the *t.*, because the days are evil. *Col.*
Col. 1. 21. you, being in ⁵*time* past alienated [4. 5

TIME

1 *Th.* 2. 5. at any *t.* were we found using words of flattery
2 *Tim.* 4. 6. and the *time* of my departure is come
Heb. 1. 1. God, having of old ⁵*time* spoken unto the fathers
    5. For unto which of the angels said he at any *time*
    4. 16. and may find grace to help us in *time* of need
    5. 12. For when by reason of the *t.* ye ought to be teachers
    9. 9. which is a parable for the *time* now present
    10. ordinances, imposed until a *time* of reformation
    11. 32. for the *time* will fail me if I tell of Gideon
Jas. 4. 14. For ye are a vapour, that appeareth for a little *t.*
1 *Pet.* 1. 11. searching what *time* or what manner of *time*
    17. pass the *time* of your sojourning in fear
    4. 2. no longer should live the rest of your *t.* in the flesh
Jude 25. dominion and power, before all *time*, and now
Rev. 1. 3. for the *time* is at hand. 22. 10
    2. 21. I gave her ⁴*time* that she should repent
    10. 6. and sware—that there shall be *time* no longer
    11. 18. the *t.* of the dead to be judged, and the *t.* to give
    12. 12. great wrath, knowing that he hath but a short *t.*
    14. where she is nourished for a *time*—and half a *time*
see day, days, haply, generations, hour, season, that time, while.

That Time.—*A.V.* ¹*same time.*

Mat. 4. 17. From *that time* began Jesus to preach
    16. 21. From *t. t.* began Jesus to shew unto his disciples
    26. 16. And from *t. t.* he sought opportunity to deliver him
Lu. 16. 16. from *that t.* the gospel of the kingdom of God
Acts 12. 1. *t. t.* Herod—put forth his hands to afflict certain
    19. 23. about ¹*that t.* there arose no small stir concerning
Eph. 2. 12. that ye were at *that time* separate from Christ

This Time.

Mk. 10. 30. but he shall receive a hundredfold now in *t. t.*
Lu. 12. 56. how is it that ye know not how to interpret *t. t.?*
    18. 30. who shall not receive manifold more in *this time*
Jno. 11. 39. Lord, by *t. t.* he stinketh : for he hath been dead
Acts 1. 6. Lord, dost thou at *this time* restore the kingdom
    24. 25. Felix—answered, Go thy way for *this time*
Rom. 8. 18. that the sufferings of *t.* present *t.* are not worthy
    11. 5. Even so then at *t.* present *t.* also there is a remnant
2 *Cor.* 8. 14. your abundance being a supply at *t.* present *t.*
see season.

Times.—*A.V.* ¹*much,* ²*world began.*

Mat. 16. 3. but ye cannot discern the signs of the *times*
Lu. 21. 24. until the *times* of the Gentiles be fulfilled
Acts 1. 7. It is not for you to know *times* or seasons
    3. 21. the heaven must receive until the *t.* of restoration
    17. 30. The *t.* of ignorance therefore God overlooked
Rom. 15. 22. I was hindered these many ¹*t.* from coming
    16. 25. bone kept in silence through ²*times* eternal
2 *Cor.* 11. 24. Of the Jews five *times* received I forty stripes
Eph. 1. 10. unto a dispensation of the fulness of the *times*
1 *Th.* 5. 1. But concerning the *times* and the seasons
1 *Tim.* 4. 1. in later *t.* some shall fall away from the faith
    6. 15. in its own *times* he shall shew, who is the blessed
2 *Tim.* 1. 9. given us in Christ Jesus before ²*times* eternal
    3. 1. that in the last days grievous *times* shall come
Tit. 1. 2. who cannot lie, promised before ²*times* eternal
1 *Pet.* 1. 20. but was manifested at the end of the *times*
see many, past, portions, seasons, seven, thrice, times.

Tinkling *A.V.*—*see clanging.*

Tip.

Lu. 16. 24. that he may dip the *tip* of his finger in water

TOLD

Tithe.

Mat. 23. 23. for ye *tithe* mint and anise and cummin
Lu. 11. 42. Pharisees! for ye *t.* mint and rue and every herb

Tithes.

Lu. 18. 12. I give *tithes* of all that I get
Heb. 7. 5. have commandment to take *t.* of the people
    6. hath taken *tithes* of Abraham, and hath blessed him
    8. And here men that die receive *tithes*
    9. even Levi, who receiveth *tithes*, hath paid *tithes*

Title.

Jno. 19. 19. And Pilate wrote a *title* also, and put it on the
    20. This *title* therefore read many of the Jews [cross

Tittle.

Mat. 5. 18. one jot or one *tittle* shall in no wise pass away
Lu. 16. 17. than for one *tittle* of the law to fall

Together.—*A.V.* ¹*accord,* ²*appear.*

Acts 2. 1. they were all ¹*together* in one place
    22. 30. commanded—all the council to come ²*together*

Toil—ed.—*A.V.* ¹*labour.*

Mat. 6. 28. lilies—how they grow; they *t.* not. *Lu.* 12. 27
Lu. 5. 5. Master, we *toiled* all night, and took nothing
1 *Cor.* 4. 12. and we ¹*toil*, working with our own hands
Rev. 2. 2. I know thy works, and thy ¹*toil* and patience

Toiling *A.V.*—*see distressed.*

Token.

Mk. 14. 44. he that betrayed him had given them a *token*
Phil. 1. 28. which is for them an evident *t.* of perdition
2 *Th.* 1. 5. a manifest *token* of the righteous judgement
    3. 17. mine own hand, which is the *token* in every epistle

Told.—*A.V.* ¹*answered,* ²*foretold,* ³*shewed.*

Mat. 14. 12. and they went and *told* Jesus
    24. 25. Behold, I have *told* you beforehand
    28. 7. there shall ye see him : lo, I have *told* you
    11. guard came into the city, and ³*told* unto the chief
Mk. 5. 14. and *told* it in the city. *Mat.* 8. 33 : *Lu.* 8. 34
    33. fell down before him, and *told* him all the truth
    8. 28. they ³*told* him, saying, John the Baptist [9, 10
    16. 13. went away and *told* it unto the rest. 10 : *Lu.* 24.
Lu. 7. 18. disciples of John ³*told* him of all these things
    8. 36. they that saw it *told* them how that it was
    9. 36. And they held their peace, and *told* no man
    13. 1. some present—which *told* him of the Galilæans
    14. 21. servant came, and ³*told* his lord these things
Jno. 3. 12. If I *told* you earthly things, and ye believe not
    4. 29. Come, see a man, which *told* me all things
    5. 15. and *told* the Jews that it was Jesus
    8. 40. seek to kill me, a man that hath *told* you the truth
    9. 27. I *told* you even now, and ye did not hear. 10. 25
    14. 2. mansions ; if it were not so, I would have *told* you
    29. I have *told* you before it come to pass, that, when
    16. 4. may remember them, how that I *told* you
    18. 8. I *told* you that I am he : if therefore ye seek me
Acts 3. 24. prophets from Samuel—also ²*told* of these days
    9. 6. and it shall be *told* thee what thou must do
    11. 13. he [Cornelius] ³*told* us how he had seen the angel
    23. 16. entered into the castle, and *told* Paul

TOLD

2 Cor. 7. 7. while he *told* us your longing, your mourning
Phil. 3. 18. many walk, of whom I *told* you often
1 Th. 3. 4. we *t*. you beforehand that we are to suffer affliction
2 Th. 2. 5. Remember ye not—I *told* you these things?
see forewarn, rehearsed, reported, said, spoken, tell, telleth.

Tolerable.
Mat. 10. 15. It shall be more *tolerable* for the land of Sodom. 11. 22, 24 : Lu. 10. 12, 14

Toll.—A.V. ¹custom, ²receipt of custom.
Mat. 9. 9. saw a man, called Matthew, sitting at the place of ²*toll*. Mk. 2. ²14 : Lu. 5. ²27
17. 25. kings—from whom do they receive ¹*t*. or tribute?

Tomb—s.—A.V. ¹grave—s, ²sepulchre—s.
Mat. 8. 28. coming forth out of the *t*. Mk. 5. 2, 3, 5 : Lu. 8. 27
23. 29. and garnish the ²*tombs* of the righteous [saints
27. 52. and the ¹*t*. were opened ; and many bodies of the
53. coming forth out of the ¹*t*. after his resurrection
60. and laid it in his own new *t*.—a great stone to the door of the ²*t*. Mk. 15. ²46 : Lu. 23. ²53 : Acts 13. ²29
28. 8. they departed quickly from the ²*tomb* with fear
Mk. 6. 29. took up his [John] corpse, and laid it in a *tomb*
16. 2. they come to the ²*tomb* when the sun was risen
3. roll us away the stone from the door of the ²*tomb*?
5. And entering into the ²*tomb*, they saw a young man
8. And they went out, and fled from the ²*tomb*
Lu. 11. 44. for ye are as the ¹*tombs* which appear not
47. for ye build the ²*tombs* of the prophets. ²48
23. 55. the women—followed after, and beheld the ²*tomb*
24. 1. at early dawn, they came unto the ²*t*. Jno. 20. ²1
2. found the stone rolled away from the ²*t*. Jno. 20. ²1
9. [women]returned from the²*t*., and told all these things
12. Peter arose, and ran unto the ²*tomb*. Jno. 20. 6
22. women—amazed us, having been early at the ²*tomb*
24. of them that were with us went to the ²*tomb*
Jno. 5. 28. all that are in the ¹*tombs* shall hear his voice
11. 17. that he [Lazarus] had been in the ¹*t*. four days
31. she [Mary] was going unto the ¹*tomb* to weep there
38. Jesus—groaning in himself cometh to the ¹*tomb*
12. 17. when he called Lazarus out of the ¹*tomb*
19. 41. there was a garden ; and in the garden a new ²*t*.
42. Preparation (for the ²*tomb* was nigh at hand)
20. 2. They have taken away the Lord out of the ²*tomb*
3. disciple, and they went toward the ²*tomb*. ²4, ²8
11. Mary was standing without at the ²*tomb*—she stooped and looked into the ²*tomb*
Acts 2. 29. David—and his ²*tomb* is with us unto this day
7. 16. and laid in the ²*tomb* that Abraham bought
Rev. 11. 9. suffer not their dead bodies to be laid in a ¹*t*.
see sepulchres.

Tongue.—A.V. tongues.
Mk. 7. 33. and he spat, and touched his *tongue*
35. and the bond of his *tongue* was loosed. Lu. 1. 64
Lu. 16. 24. tip of his finger in water and cool my *tongue*
Acts 2. 26. my heart was glad, and my *tongue* rejoiced
Rom. 14. 11. And every ¹*tongue* shall confess to God
1 Cor. 14. 2. For he that speaketh in a *tongue* speaketh not unto men. 4, 13, 14, 19, 27
9. unless ye utter by the *t*. speech easy to be understood
26. each one—hath a *tongue*, hath an interpretation
Phil. 2. 11. every *t*. should confess that Jesus Christ is Lord
Jas. 1. 26. while he bridleth not his *tongue*
3. 5. So the *tongue* also is a little member
6. And the *t*. is a fire—among our members is the *t*.
8. but the *tongue* can no man tame ; it is a restless evil
1 Pet. 3. 10. Let him refrain his *tongue* from evil

TOOK

1 Jno. 3. 18. let us not love in word, neither with the *tongue*
Rev. 5. 9. every tribe, and *tongue*, and people. 13. ¹⁷ : 14. 6
9. 11. and in the Greek *tongue* he hath the name Apollyon
see language.

Tongues.
Mk. 16. 17. they shall speak with new *tongues*
Acts 2. 3. appeared unto them *tongues* parting asunder
4. and began to speak with other *tongues*, as the Spirit
11. speaking in our *tongues* the mighty works of God
10. 46. heard them speak with *tongues*, and magnify God
19. 6. and they spake with *tongues*, and prophesied
Rom. 3. 13. With their *tongues* they have used deceit
1 Cor. 12. 10. to another divers kinds of *tongues* ; and to another the interpretation of *tongues*. 28
30. do all speak with *tongues*? do all interpret?
13. 1. If I speak with the *tongues* of men and of angels
8. whether there be *tongues*, they shall cease
14. 5. Now I would have you all speak with *tongues*—prophesieth than he that speaketh with *tongues*
6. if I come unto you speaking with *tongues*
18. I thank God, I speak with *tongues* more than you all
21. By men of strange *t*. and by the lips of strangers
22. Wherefore *t*. are for a sign, not to them that believe
23. all speak with *t*., and there come in men unlearned
39. to prophesy, and forbid not to speak with *tongues*
Rev. 7. 9. of all tribes and peoples and *tongues*
10. 11. prophesy—over many peoples and nations and *t*.
11. 9. from among the peoples and tribes and *tongues*
16. 10. and they gnawed their *tongues* for pain
17. 15. peoples, and multitudes, and nations, and *tongues*
see tongue.

Took.—A.V. ¹bare, ²caught, ³felt, ⁴held, ⁵laid hold, ⁶taken.
Mat. 1. 24. Joseph arose—and *took* unto him his wife
8. 17. Himself *t*. our infirmities, and bare our diseases
12. 14. Pharisees went out, and ⁴*took* counsel against him
13. 31. which a man *t*., and sowed in his field. Lu. 13. 19
33. leaven, which a woman *took*, and hid. Lu. 13. 21
14. 31. Jesus stretched forth his hand, and ²*t*. hold of him
16. 7. among themselves, saying, We ⁶*took* no bread
22. Peter *t*. him, and began to rebuke him. Mk. 8. 32
18. 28. and *t*. him by the throat, saying, Pay what thou
21. 39. ²*took* him, and cast him forth out of the vineyard
24. 39. until the flood came, and *took* them all away
25. 3. *took* their lamps, *took* no oil with them
4. wise *took* oil in their vessels with their lamps
35. I was a stranger, and ye *took* me in. 38
43. I was a stranger, and ye *took* me not in [Mk. 14 49
26. 55. sat daily in the temple teaching, and ye⁵*t*. me not.
28. 9. and ⁴*took* hold of his feet, and worshipped him
Mk. 1. 31. he came and *t*. her by the hand, and raised her
12. 20. the first *t*. a wife, and dying left no seed. Lu. 20. 29
21. the second *took* her, and died. Lu. 20. 31
Lu. 5. 5. Master, we toiled all night, and ⁶*took* nothing
11. 52. lawyers! for ye ⁶*took* away the key of knowledge
Jno. 12. 6. having the bag ¹*took* away what was put therein
19. 27. the disciple *took* her unto his own home
20. 8. then—that; and that night they ²*took* nothing
Acts 1. 16. Judas, who was guide to them that *took* Jesus
9. 27. Barnabas *t*. him, and brought him to the apostles
19. 13. exorcists, *took* upon them to name over them
28. 5. shook off the beast into the fire, and ³*t*. no harm
15. when Paul saw, he thanked God, and *took* courage
1 Cor. 11. 23. night in which he was betrayed *took* bread
Heb. 8. 9. the day that I *t*. them by the hand to lead them
10. 34. and *t*. joyfully the spoiling of your possessions
Rev. 10. 10. And I *t*. the little book out of the angel's hand
see counsel, hold, laid (hold), raised, seized, taketh, taking.

TOOK

He **Took.**—*A.V.* ¹*received*, ²*taken.*

Mat. 15. 36. *h. t.* the seven loaves and the fishes. *Mk.* 8. 6
26. 27. And *he took* a cup, and gave thanks
37. *he took* with him Peter and the two sons. *Lu.* 9. 28
27. 24. *he took* water, and washed his hands
Mk. 6. 41. *he* ²*t.* the five loaves and the two fishes. *Lu.* 9. 16
7. 33. *he took* him aside from the multitude privately
8. 23. And *he took* hold of the blind man by the hand
9. 36. *he took* a little child, and set him in the midst
10. 16. *he took* them in his arms, and blessed them
Lu. 10. 35. *he took* out two pence, and gave them to the host
14. 4. *he took* him, and healed him, and let him go
18. 31. And *he took* unto him the twelve. *Mk.* 10. 32
22. 19. *he t.* bread, and when he had given thanks. 24. 30
23. 53. *he took* it down, and wrapped it in a linen cloth
Acts 9. 19. *he* [Paul] ¹*took* food and was strengthened
16. 33. *he took* them the same hour of the night
Heb. 9. 19. *he took* the blood of the calves and the goats
see partook, received, taken, taketh, taking.

Took leave.—*A.V.* ¹*embraced.*

Acts 20. 1. Paul having sent for the disciples—¹*t. l.* of them

They Took.—*A.V.* ¹*caught.*

Mat. 21. 46. because *they took* him for a prophet
27. 31. had mocked him, *they took* off from him the robe
28. 15. So *t. t.* the money, and did as they were taught
Mk. 12. 3. *they* ¹*took* him, and beat him, and sent him
8. *they took* him, and killed him, and cast him forth
Jno. 11. 41. So *they took* away the stone
19. 17. *They took* Jesus therefore: and he went out
Acts 4. 13. *they took* knowledge of them, that they had
13. 29. *they took* him down from the tree, and laid him
18. 26. *they took* him unto them, and expounded
see raised, take.

Took up.

Mat. 14. 12. and *took up* the corpse, and buried him. *Mk* 6. 29
20. *took up* that which remained. 15. 37: *Mk.* 6. 43: 8. 8
16. 9. how many baskets ye *took up* ? 10: *Mk.* 8. 19, 20
Mk. 2. 12. and straightway *took up* the bed. *Lu.* 5. 25
Jno. 8. 59. *took up* stones therefore to cast at him. 10. 31
Acts 7. 21. he was cast out, Pharaoh's daughter *took* him *up*
43. And ye *took up* the tabernacle of Moloch
21. 15. after these days we *took up* our baggage
Rev. 18. 21. a strong angel *took up* a stone as it were a great
see raised.

Tooth.

Mat. 5. 38. An eye for an eye, and a *tooth* for a *tooth*

Top.

Mat. 27. 51. in twain from the *t.* to the bottom. *Mk.* 15. 38
Jno. 19. 23. coat was without seam, woven from the *top*
Heb. 11. 21. Jacob—leaning upon the *top* of his staff

Topaz.

Rev. 21. 20. the ninth, *topaz* ; the tenth, chrysoprase

Torch—es.—*A.V.* ¹*lamp*

Jno. 18. 3. cometh thither with lanterns and *torches*
Rev. 8. 10. fell from heaven a great star, burning as a ¹*torch*

Torment—s.

Mat. 4. 24. holden with divers diseases and *torments*
8. 29. art thou come hither to *torment* us before the time?
Mk. 5. 7. I adjure thee by God, *torment* me not. *Lu.* 8. 28

TOUCHETH

Lu. 16. 23. in Hades he lifted up his eyes, being in *torments*
28. lest they also come into this place of *torment*
Rev. 9. 5. their *torment* was as the *torment* of a scorpion
14. 11. the smoke of their *t.* goeth up for ever and ever
18. 7. so much give her of *torment* and mourning
10. standing afar off for the fear of her *torment.* 15
see punishment.

Tormented.

Mat. 8. 6. sick of the palsy, grievously *tormented*
Rev. 9. 5. but that they should be *tormented* five months
11. 10. because these two prophets *tormented* them
14. 10. he shall be *tormented* with fire and brimstone
20. 10. they shall be *tormented* day and night for ever
see anguish, (evil) entreated.

Tormentors.

Mat. 18. 34. and delivered him to the *tormentors*

Torn.—*A.V.* ¹*pulled*, ²*rent.*

Mk. 9. 26. having cried out, and ²*torn* him much
Acts 23. 10. lest Paul should be ¹*torn* in pieces by them
see tearing.

Tortured.

Heb. 11. 35. others were *t.*, not accepting their deliverance

Tossed.

Eph. 4. 14. no longer children, *tossed* to and fro
Jas. 1. 6. surge of the sea driven by the wind and *tossed*
see distressed, laboured.

Touch.—*A.V.* ¹*touched.*

Mat. 9. 21. If I do but *touch* his garment. *Mk.* 5. 28
14. 36. only *touch* the border of his garment. *Mk.* 6. 56
Mk. 3. 10. upon him that they might *touch* him. *Lu.* 6. 19
8. 22. a blind man, and beseech him to *touch* him
Lu. 8. 46. Some one did ¹*touch* me: for I perceived that
11. 46. ye yourselves *touch* not the burdens
18. 15. babes, that he should *touch* them. *Mk.* 10. 13
Jno. 20. 17. Jesus saith to her, *Touch* me not
1 *Cor.* 7. 1. It is good for a man not to *touch* a woman
2 *Cor.* 6. 17. And *touch* no unclean thing
Col. 2. 21. Handle not, nor taste, nor *touch*
Heb. 11. 28. destroyer of the firstborn should not *t.* them
12. 20. If even a beast *t.* the mountain, it shall be stoned

Touched.—*A.V.* ¹*arrived.*

Mat. 8. 3. and *touched* him, saying. *Mk.* 1. 41: *Lu.* 5. 13
15. And he *touched* her hand, and the fever left her
9. 20. and *touched* the border of. *Mk.* 5. 27: *Lu.* 8. 44
29. Then *touched* he their eyes, saying. 20. 34
14. 36. as many as *touched* were made whole. *Mk.* 6. 56
17. 7. Jesus came and *touched* them and said, Arise
Mk. 5. 30. Who *touched* my garments? 31: *Lu.* 8. 45
7. 33. and he spat, and *touched* his tongue
Lu. 7. 14. And he came nigh and *touched* the bier
8. 47. of all the people for what cause she *touched* him
22. 51. And he *touched* his ear, and healed him
Acts 20. 15. the next day we ¹*touched* at Samos
27. 3. And the next day we *touched* at Sidon
Heb. 4. 15. not a high priest that cannot be *touched*
12. 18. not come unto a mount that might be *touched*
see touch.

Toucheth.

Lu. 7. 39. what manner of woman this is which *t.* him
1 *Jno.* 5. 18. and the evil one *toucheth* him not

TOUCHING

Touching.—*A.V.* ¹*concerning,* ²*landing,* ³*over,* ⁴*pertaining,* ⁵*whereby.*

Mat. 18. 19. as *touching* anything that they shall ask
22. 31. *t.* the resurrection of the. *Mk.* 12. 26 : *Acts* 24. 21
Lu. 23. 14. *touching* those things whereof ye accuse him
Acts 5. 35. take heed to yourselves as *touching* these men
19. 40. and as ⁵*t.* it we shall not be able to give account
21. 25. But as *touching* the Gentiles which have believed
26. 2. *touching* all the things whereof I am accused
28. 12. And ²*touching* at Syracuse, we tarried there
Rom. 11. 28. As ¹*touching* the gospel, they are enemies—
as *touching* the election, they are beloved
1 *Cor.* 7. 37. no necessity, but hath power as ³*t.* his own will
16. 12. But as *touching* Apollos the brother
2 *Cor.* 9. 1. For as *touching* the ministering to the saints
Gal. 1. 20. Now *touching* the things which I write unto you
Phil. 3. 5. as *touching* the law, a Pharisee
6. as ¹*touching* zeal, persecuting the church ; as *t.* the
Col. 4. 10. Barnabas (*t.* whom ye received commandments
2 *Th.* 3. 4. we have confidence in the Lord *touching* you
Heb. 6. 4. as *touching* those who were once enlightened
9. 9. as ⁴*t.* the conscience, make the worshipper perfect
see concerning.

Toward.—*A.V.* ¹*by the way.*

Mat. 4. 15. Naphthali, ¹*Toward* the sea, beyond Jordan

Towel.

Jno. 13. 4. and he took a *towel,* and girded himself
5. disciples' feet, and to wipe them with the *towel*

Tower.

Mat. 21. 33. built a *t.*, and let it out to husbandmen *Mk.* 12. 1
Lu. 13. 4. Or those eighteen, upon whom the *t.* in Siloam
14. 28. which of you, desiring to build a *tower* [fell

Townclerk.

Acts 19. 35. And when the *t.* had quieted the multitude

Towns.

Mk. 1. 38. Let us go elsewhere into the next *towns*
see village.

Traced.—*A.V.* ¹*understanding.*

Lu. 1. 3. having ¹*traced* the course of all things accurately

Tracing out.—*A.V.* ¹*finding out.*

Rom. 11. 33. judgements, and his ways past ¹*tracing out !*

Trade.—*A.V.* ¹*buy and sell,* ²*craft,* ³*occupation,* ⁴*occupy.*

Lu. 19. 13. ⁴*Trade* ye herewith till I come
Acts 18. 3. because he was of the same ²*trade,* he abode with
them—for by their ³*trade* they were tentmakers
19. 27. not only is there danger that this our ²*t.* come into
Jas. 4. 13. spend a year there, and ¹*t.*, and get gain ;`disrepute
see gain.

Traded—ing.

Mat. 25. 16. he that received the five talents went and *t.*
Lu. 19. 15. might know what they had gained by *trading*

Tradition—s.—*A.V.* ¹*ordinances.*

Mat. 15. 2. disciples transgress the *t.* of the elders ? *Mk.* 7. 5
3. transgress the commandment of God because of
your *tradition ?* 6 : *Mk.* 7. 9, 13
Mk. 7. 8. holding the *tradition* of the elders. 8
1 *Cor.* 11. 2. remember me in all things, and hold fast the ¹*t.*
Gal. 1. 14. exceedingly zealous for the *t.* of my fathers

TRANSGRESSOR

Col. 2. 8. vain deceit, after the *tradition* of men
2 *Th.* 2. 15. and hold the *traditions* which ye were taught
3. 6. not after the *tradition* which they received of us
see handed down.

Train.—*A.V.* ¹*teach.*

Tit. 2. 4. ¹*train* the young women to love their husbands

Traitor—s.

Lu. 6. 16. and Judas Iscariot, which was the *traitor*
2 *Tim.* 3. 4. *t.,* headstrong—rather than lovers of God

Trample.

Mat. 7. 6. pearls before the swine, lest haply they *t.* them

Trance.

Acts 10. 10. while they made ready, he fell into a *trance*
11. 5. and in a *trance* I saw a vision, a certain vessel
22. 17. while I prayed in the temple, I fell into a *trance*

Tranquil.—*A.V.* ¹*peaceable.*

1 *Tim.* 2. 2. that we may lead a ¹*tranquil* and quiet life

Transferred.

1 *Cor.* 4. 6. I have in a figure *transferred* to myself

Transfigured.

Mat. 17. 2. and he was *transfigured* before them. *Mk.* 9. 2

Transformed.—*A.V.* ¹*changed.*

Rom. 12. 2. but be ye *t.* by the renewing of your mind
2 *Cor.* 3. 18. are ¹*t.* into the same image from glory to
see fashioned.

Transforming.—*A.V.* *see fashioning.*

Transgress.—*A.V.* ¹*go beyond.*

Mat. 15. 2. Why do thy disciples *transgress* the tradition
3. Why do ye also *transgress* the commandment of God
1 *Th.* 4. 6. no man ¹*transgress,* and wrong his brother

Transgressed.

Lu. 15. 29. and I never *t.* a commandment of thine
see transgressor.

Transgressest—eth.—*see doeth lawlessness, onward.*

Transgression—s.—*A.V.* ¹*breaking,* ²*iniquity.*

Rom. 2. 23. through thy ¹*t.* of the law dishonourest thou
4. 15. where there is no law, neither is there *t.* [God ?
5. 14. had not sinned after the likeness of Adam's *t.*
Gal. 3. 19. What then is the law ? It was added because of *t.*
1 *Tim.* 2. 14. woman being beguiled hath fallen into *t.*
Heb. 2. 2. every *t.* and disobedience received a just
9. 15. redemption of the *t.* that were under the first
2 *Pet.* 2. 16. he was rebuked for his own ²*transgression*
see lawlessness.

Transgressor—s.—*A.V.* ¹*breaker—s,* ²*transgress—ed.*

Mk. 15. 28. And he was reckoned with *t.* [margin] *Lu.* 22. 37.
Rom. 2. 25. if thou be a ¹*t.* of the law, thy circumcision is
27. circumcision art a ²*transgressor* of the law ?
Gal. 2. 18. I prove myself a *transgressor*
Jas. 2. 9. being convicted by the law as *transgressors*
11. but killest, thou art become a *t.* of the law

TRANSLATED

Translated—tion.
Col. 1. 13. and *t.* us into the kingdom of the Son of his love
Heb. 11. 5. By faith Enoch was *t.*—because God *t.* him: for before his *t.* he hath had witness borne to him

Transparent.
Rev. 21. 21. city was pure gold, as it were *transparent* glass

Trap.
Rom. 11. 9. Let their table be made a snare, and a *trap*

Travail.—*A.V.* ¹*painfulness,* ²*sorrows.*
Mat. 24. 8. these things are the beginning of ²*t. Mk.* 13. 28
Jno. 16. 21. A woman when she is in *travail* hath sorrow
2 *Cor.* 11. 27. in labour and ¹*travail,* in watchings often
Gal. 4. 19. I am again in *t.* until Christ be formed in you
1 *Th* 2. 9. For ye remember, brethren, our labour and *t.*
5. 3. upon them, as *travail* upon a woman with child
2 *Th.* 3. 8. but in labour and *t.*, working night and day

Travailest—eth.
Rom. 8. 22. the whole creation groaneth and *t.* in pain
Gal. 4. 27. Break forth and cry, thou that *travailest* not

Travailing.
Rev. 12. 2. and she crieth out, *travailing* in birth

Travel.
Acts 19. 29. men of Macedonia, Paul's companions in *travel*
2 *Cor.* 8. 19. appointed by the churches to *travel* with us

Travelled.
Acts 11. 19. *travelled* as far as Phœnicia, and Cyprus

Travelling *A.V.—see going.*

Tread.
Lu. 10. 19. authority to *tread* upon serpents and scorpions
Rev. 11. 2. and the holy city shall they *tread* under foot

Treadeth.
1 *Cor.* 9. 9. Thou shalt not muzzle the ox when he *treadeth* out the corn. 1 *Tim.* 5. 18
Rev. 19. 15. he *treadeth* the winepress of the fierceness

Treasure.
Mat. 6. 21. thy *t.* is, there will thy heart be also. *Lu.* 12. 34
12. 35. The good man out of his good *treasure*—the evil man out of his evil *treasure. Lu.* 6. 45
13. 44. The kingdom of heaven is like unto a *treasure*
52. bringeth forth out of his *t.* things new and old
19. 21. give to the poor, and thou shalt have *treasure* in heaven. *Mk.* 10. 21: *Lu.* 18. 22
Lu. 12. 21. So is he that layeth up *treasure* for himself
33. a *treasure* in the heavens that faileth not
Acts 8. 27. a eunuch—who was over all her *treasure*
2 *Cor.* 4. 7. But we have this *treasure* in earthen vessels
Jas. 5. 3. Ye have laid up your *treasure* in the last days

Treasurer.—*A.V.* ¹*chamberlain.*
Rom. 16. 23. Erastus the ¹*treasurer* of the city saluteth you

Treasurest.
Rom. 2. 5. *treasurest* up for thyself wrath in the day of wrath

TRENCH

Treasures.
Mat. 2. 11. and opening their *t.* they offered unto him gifts
6. 19. Lay not up for yourselves *treasures* upon the earth
20. but lay up for yourselves *treasures* in heaven
Col. 2. 3. in whom are all the *treasures* of wisdom
Heb. 11. 26. accounting the reproach of Christ greater riches than the *treasures* of Egypt

Treasury.
Mat. 27. 6. It is not lawful to put them into the *treasury*
Mk. 12. 41. And he sat down over against the *treasury*—multitude cast money into the *treasury*
43. casting into the *treasury. Lu.* 21. 1
Jno. 8. 20. These words spake he in the *treasury*

Treated.—*A.V.* ¹*entreated.*
Acts 27. 3. Julius ¹*t.* Paul kindly, and gave him leave to go

Treatise.
Acts 1. 1. The former *treatise* I made, O Theophilus

Tree.—*A.V.* ¹*book.*
Mat. 3. 10. every *tree* therefore that bringeth not forth good fruit is hewn down. 7. 19: *Lu.* 3. 9
7. 17. Even so overy good *tree* bringeth forth good fruit —corrupt *t.* bringeth forth evil fruit. 18: *Lu.* 6. 43
12. 33. Either make the *tree* good—or make the *tree* corrupt—for the *tree* is known. *Lu.* 6. 44 [13. 19
13. 32. it is greater than the herbs, and becometh a *t. Lu.*
Acts 5. 30. Jesus, whom ye slew, hanging him on a *t.* 10. 39
13. 29. they took him down from the *tree*, and laid him
Gal. 3. 13. Cursed is every one that hangeth on a *tree*
1 *Pet.* 2. 24. bare our sins in his body upon the *tree*
Rev. 2. 7. to him will I give to eat of the *tree* of life
7. 1. no wind should blow—or on the sea, or upon any *t.*
9. 4. neither any green thing, neither any *tree*
22. 2. this side of the river and on that was the *t.* of life
14. that they may have the right to come to the *t.* of life
19. God shall take away his part from the ¹*tree* of life
see fig tree.

Trees.
Mat. 3. 10. now is the axe laid unto the root of the *t. Lu.* 3. 9
21. 8. and others cut branches from the *trees*
Mk. 8. 24. I see men; for I behold them as *trees*, walking
Lu. 21. 29. Behold the fig tree, and all the *trees*
Jude 12. autumn *trees* without fruit, twice dead, plucked up
Rev. 7. 3. Hurt not the earth, neither the sea, nor the *trees*
8. 7. and the third part of the *trees* was burnt up
see fields.

Tremble.—*A.V.* ¹*afraid,* ²*shake.*
Heb. 12. 26. will I make to ²*tremble* not the earth only
2 *Pet.* 2. 10. they ¹*tremble* not to rail at dignities
see shudder.

Trembled.
Acts 7. 32. And Moses *trembled,* and durst not behold *see terrified, trembling.*

Trembling.—*A.V.* ¹*trembled.*
Mk. 5. 33. But the woman fearing and *trembling. Lu.* 8. 47
16. 8. for ¹*t.* and astonishment had come upon them
Acts 16. 29. and, *t.* for fear, fell down before Paul and Silas
1 *Cor.* 2. 3. and in fear, and in much *trembling*
2 *Cor.* 7. 15. how with fear and *trembling* ye received him
Eph. 6. 5. with fear and *t.*, in singleness of your heart
Phil. 2. 12. work out your own salvation with fear and *t.*

Trench *A.V.—see bank.*

TRESPASS

Trespass.—*A.V.* ¹*fault,* ²*offence.*
Rom. 5. 15. not as the ²*trespass,* so also is the free gift.
 For if by the ²*trespass* of the one the many died
 17. For if, by the ²*trespass* of the one, death reigned
 18. So then as through one ²*t.* the judgement came
 20. law came in beside, that the ²*trespass* might abound
Gal. 6. 1. even if a man be overtaken in any ¹*trespass*
 see sin.

Trespasses.—*A.V.* ¹*offences,* ²*sins.*
Mat. 6. 14. For if ye forgive men their *t. Mk.* 11. 25
 15. But if ye forgive not men their *t.,* neither will your
 Father forgive your *trespasses. Mk.* 11. 26 [margin]
Rom. 4. 25. who was delivered up for our ¹*trespasses*
 5. 16. but the free gift came of many ¹*trespasses*
2 Cor. 5. 19. not reckoning unto them their *trespasses*
Eph. 1. 7. through his blood, the forgiveness of our ²*t.*
 2. 1. quicken, when ye were dead through your *t.* ²5
Col. 2. 13. being dead through your ²*trespasses*—having
 forgiven us all our *trespasses*

Trial—s—*A.V.* ¹*temptation—s.*
Acts 20. 19. ¹*trials* which befell me by the plots of the Jews
Heb. 11. 36. others had *trial* of mockings and scourgings
1 Pet. 4. 12. think it not strange concerning the fiery *trial*
Rev. 3. 10. I also will keep thee from the hour of ¹*trial*
 see proof.

Tribe.—*A.V.* ¹*kindred—s,* ²*tribes.*
Heb. 7. 13. For he of whom these things are said belongeth to another *tribe*   [priests
 14. as to which *tribe* Moses spake nothing concerning
Rev. 5. 9. purchase unto God—men of every ¹*t.,* and tongue
 7. 4. sealed out of every ²*tribe* of the children of Israel
 5. Of the *tribe* of—were sealed twelve thousand. 6, 7, 8
 13. 7. authority over every ¹*tribe* and people and tongue

Tribes.—*A.V.* ¹*kindreds.*
Mat. 24. 30. and then shall all the *tribes* of the earth mourn
Acts 26. 7. unto which promise our twelve *tribes*   [sion
Jas. 1. 1. James—to the twelve *t.* which are of the Disper-
Rev. 1. 7. all the ¹*tribes* of the earth shall mourn over him
 7. 9. a great multitude—of all ¹*t.* and peoples and tongues
 11. 9. from among the peoples and ¹*tribes* and tongues
 21. 12. names of the twelve *tribes* of the children of Israel
 see tribe.

Tribulation.—*A.V.* ¹*afflicted,* ²*affliction,* ³*persecution,*
 ⁴*trouble.*
Mat. 13. 21. when *t.* or persecution ariseth. *Mk.* 4. ³17
 24. 9. Then shall they deliver you up unto ¹*tribulation*
 21. for then shall be great *tribulation. Mk.* 13. ²19
 29. after the *tribulation* of those days. *Mk.* 13. 24
Jno. 16. 33. In the world ye have *tribulation*   [Stephen
Acts 11. 19. scattered abroad upon the ²*t.* that arose about
Rom. 2. 9. *tribulation* and anguish, upon every soul
 5. 3. knowing that *tribulation* worketh patience
 8. 35. from the love of Christ ? shall *tribulation*
 12. 12. patient in *t.;* continuing stedfastly in prayer
1 Cor. 7. 28. Yet such shall have ⁴*tribulation* in the flesh
Rev. 1. 9. your brother and partaker with you in the *t.*
 2. 9. I know thy *tribulation,* and thy poverty
 10. and ye shall have *tribulation* ten days
 22. that commit adultery with her into great *tribulation*
 7. 14. These are they which come out of the great *t.*
 see affliction, tribulations.

Tribulations.—*A.V.* ¹*tribulation.*
Acts 14. 22 through many ¹*t.* we must enter into the kingdom

TROUBLED

Rom. 5. 3. but let us also rejoice in our *tribulations*
Eph. 3. 13. that ye faint not at my *tribulations* for you

Tribute.
Mat. 17. 25. from whom do they receive toll or *tribute ?*
 22. 17. Is it lawful to give *tribute* unto Cæsar, or not ?
     Mk. 12. 14 ; *Lu.* 20. 22
 19. Shew me the *tribute* money
Lu. 23. 2. and forbidding to give *tribute* to Cæsar
Rom. 13. 6. For this cause ye pay *tribute* also
 7. Render to all their dues : *tribute* to whom *t.* is due
 see afflictions, shekel.

Tried.
Heb. 11. 17. By faith Abraham, being *tried,* offered up
Rev. 2. 10. that ye may be *t. ;* and ye shall have tribulation
 see approved, proved, try, refined.

Trieth *A.V.—see proveth.*

Trimmed.
Mat. 25. 7. those virgins arose, and *trimmed* their lamps

Triumph—ing.
2 Cor. 2. 14. which always leadeth us in *triumph* in Christ
Col. 2. 15. made a show of them openly, *t.* over them in it

Trodden.
Mat. 5. 13. but to be cast out and *trodden* under. *Lu.* 6. 5
Lu. 21. 24. Jerusalem shall be *t.* down of the Gentiles
Heb. 10. 29. who hath *trodden* under foot the Son of God
Rev. 14. 20. the winepress was *trodden* without the city

Trode.
Lu. 12. 1. insomuch that they *trode* one upon another

Trouble.
Mat. 26. 10. Why *trouble* ye the woman ? *Mk.* 14. 6
Lu. 7. 6. Lord, *trouble* not thyself : for I am not worthy
 8. 49. Thy daughter is dead ; *trouble* not the Master
 11. 7. *Trouble* me not : the door is now shut
Acts 15. 19. which *trouble* not them which from among
 16. 20. These men, being Jews, do exceedingly *t.* our city
Gal. 1. 7. there are some that *t.* you, and would pervert
 6. 17. From henceforth let no man *trouble* me
Heb. 12. 15. lest any root of bitterness springing up *t.* you
 see ado, afflict, affliction, hardship, tribulation, unsettle.

Troubled.—*A.V.* ¹*grieved,* ²*heaviness,* ³*heavy,* ⁴*vexed.*
Mat. 2. 3. when Herod the king heard it, he was *troubled*
 14. 26. walking on the sea, they were *t. Mk.* 6. 50
 24. 6. see that ye be not *troubled. Mk.* 13. 7.
 26. 37. and began to be sorrowful and sore ²*troubled*
Lu. 1. 12. And Zacharias was *troubled* when he saw him
 29. But she was greatly *troubled* at the saying
 6. 18. they that were ⁴*troubled* with unclean spirits
 10. 41. Martha, thou art anxious and *t.* about many things
 24. 38. Why are ye *t. ?* and wherefore do reasonings
Jno. 5. 4. seasons into the pool, and *t.* the water [margin]
 7. Sir, I have no man, when the water is *troubled*
 11. 33. he groaned in the spirit, and was *troubled.* 13. 21
 12. 27. Now is my soul *troubled ;* and what shall I say ?
 14. 1. Let not your heart be *troubled.* 27
Acts 2. being sore ¹*t.* because they taught the people
 15. 24. certain which went out from us have *t.* you with
 16. 18. Paul, being sore ⁴*troubled,* turned and said
 17. 8. And they *troubled* the multitude and the rulers
Phil. 2. 26. sore ³*t.,* because ye had heard that he was sick
2 Th. 2. 2. nor yet be *troubled,* either by spirit, or by word
1 Pet. 3. 14. and fear not their fear, neither be *troubled*
 see afflicted, pressed.

TROUBLEST

Troublest.
Mk. 5. 35. why *troublest* thou the Master any further?

Troubleth.
Lu. 18. 5. yet because this widow *troubleth* me
Gal. 5. 10. but he that *t.* you shall bear his judgement

Troubling.
Jno. 5. 4. first after the *troubling* of the water [margin]

Trucebreakers A.V.—*see implacable.*

True.—A.V. ¹*truth.*
Mat. 22. 16. Master, we know that thou art *t.* Mk. 12. 14
Lu. 16. 11. who will commit to your trust the *t.* riches?
Jno. 1. 9. There was the *true* light, even the light which
3. 33. hath set his seal to this, that God is *true*
4. 23. when the *t.* worshippers shall worship the Father
37. For herein is the saying *true*, One soweth
5. 31. If I bear witness of myself, my witness is not *true*
32. the witness which he witnesseth of me is *true*
6. 32. but my Father giveth you the *true* bread
7. 18. the same is *true*, and no unrighteousness is in him
28. but he that sent me is *true*, whom ye know not
8. 13. bearest witness of thyself; thy witness is not *true*
14. if I bear witness of myself, my witness is *true*
16. Yea and if I judge, my judgement is *true*
17. it is written, that the witness of two men is *true*
10. 41. whatsoever John spake of this man were *true*
15. 1. I am the *t.* vine, and my Father is the husbandman
19. 35. hath borne witness, and his witness is *t.* 21. 24
Acts 12. 9. and he wist not that it was *t.* which was done
Rom. 3. 4. let God be found *true*, but every man a liar
2 Cor. 6. 8. as deceivers, and yet *true*
Phil. 4. 3. I beseech thee also, *true* yokefellow
8. Finally, brethren, whatsoever things are *true*
Heb. 8. 2. the *true* tabernacle, which the Lord pitched
9. 24. place made with hands, like in pattern to the *true*
10. 22. let us draw near with a *true* heart in fulness
1 Pet. 5. 12. testifying that this is the *true* grace of God
2 Pet. 2. 22. according to the *t.* proverb, The dog turning
1 Jno. 2. 8. which thing is *true* in him and in you—the
true light already shineth. ¹27
5. 20. know him that is *t.*, and we are in him that is *t.*
3 Jno. 12. and thou knowest that our witness is *true*
Rev. 3. 7. These things saith he that is holy, he that is *t.*
14. saith the Amen, the faithful and *true* witness
6. 10. How long, O Master, the holy and *true* [ages
15. 3. righteous and *true* are thy ways, thou King of the
16. 7. *true* and righteous are thy judgements. 19. 2
19. 9. And he saith unto me, These are the *true* words of God
11. and he that sat thereon, called Faithful and *True*
21. 5. Write: for those words are faithful and *true*. 22. 6
see faithful, truth.

True God.
Jno. 17. 3. that they should know thee the only *true* God
1 Th. 1. 9. from idols, to serve a living and *true* God
1 Jno. 5. 20. This is the *true* God, and eternal life

Truly.—A.V. ¹*naturally.*
Mk. 15. 39. *Truly* this man was the Son of God
Phil. 2. 20. who will care ¹*truly* for your state
see of a truth.

Trump.
1 Cor. 15. 52. in the twinkling of an eye, at the last *trump*
1 Th. 4. 16. voice of the archangel, and with the *t.* of God

TRUTH

Trumpet—s.
Mat. 6. 2. doest alms, sound not a *trumpet* before thee
24. 31. send forth his angels with a great sound of a *t.*
1 Cor. 14. 8. if the *trumpet* give an uncertain voice
15. 52. the *t.* shall sound, and the dead shall be raised
Heb. 12. 19. and the sound of a *t.*, and the voice of words
Rev. 1. 10. I heard behind me a great voice, as of a *t.* 4.1
8. 2. there were given unto them seven *trumpets*. 6
13. by reason of the other voices of the *t.* of the three
9. 14. saying to the sixth angel, which had the *t.* [Angels

Trumpeters.
Rev. 18. 22. and *trumpeters* shall be heard no more at all

Trust.—A.V. ¹*commit.*
Mk. 10. 24. how hard is it for them that *trust* in riches
Lu. 16. 11. who will commit to your *trust* the true riches?
Jno. 2. 24. But Jesus did not ¹*trust* himself unto them
2 Cor. 1. 9. that we should not *t.* in ourselves, but in God
Phil. 2. 24. but I *t.* in the Lord that I myself also shall come
1 Tim. 1. 11. blessed God, which was committed to my *t.*
Heb. 2. 13. And again, I will put my *trust* in him
see confidence, hope, intrusted, persuaded, trusteth.

Trusted.
Lu. 11. 22. from him his whole armour wherein he *trusted*
18. 9. which *t.* in themselves that they were righteous
see hoped, trusteth.

Trusteth.—A.V. ¹*trust—ed.*
Mat. 27. 43. He ¹*trusteth* on God; let him deliver him now
2 Cor. 10. 7. If any man ¹*t.* in himself that he is Christ's
see hope.

Truth.—A.V. ¹*nothing*, ²*true*, ³*verity.*
Mk. 5. 33. fell down before him, and told him all the *truth*
Jno. 1. 14. begotten from the Father), full of grace and *t.*
17. grace and *truth* came by Jesus Christ
4. 23. the true worshippers shall worship—in spirit and
5. 33. and he hath borne witness unto the *truth* [*t.* 24
8. 32. ye shall know the *t.*, and the *t.* shall make you free
40. to kill me, a man that hath told you the *truth*
44. and stood not in the *t.*, because there is no *t.* in him
45. But because I say the *truth*, ye believe me not
46. If I say *truth*, why do ye not believe me?
14. 6. I am the way, and the *truth*, and the life
16. 7. Nevertheless I tell you the *truth* | the *truth*
13. the Spirit of *t.*, is come, he shall guide you into all
17. 17. Sanctify them in the *truth* : thy word is *truth*
18. 37. that I should bear witness unto the *truth*. Every one that is of the *truth* heareth
38. Pilate saith unto him, What is *truth* ?
Acts 21.24. and all shall know that there is no ¹*t.* in the things
26. 25. but speak forth words of *truth* and soberness
Rom. 1. 18. who hold down the *truth* in unrighteousness
25. they exchanged the *truth* of God for a lie
2. 2. the judgement of God is according to *truth*
8. and obey not the *truth*, but obey unrighteousness
20. having—the form of knowledge and of the *truth*
3. 7. But if the *truth* of God through my lie abounded
9. 1. I say the *truth* in Christ, I lie not. 1 Tim. 2. 7
15. 8. a minister of the circumcision for the *truth* of God
1 Cor. 5. 8. with the unleavened bread of sincerity and *t.*
13. 6. not in unrighteousness, but rejoiceth with the *t.*
2 Cor. 4. 2. but by the manifestation of the *truth*
6. 7. in the word of *truth*, in the power of God
7. 14. we spake all things to you in *t.*—was found to be *t.*
11. 10. As the *truth* of Christ is in me, no man shall stop

TRUTH

2 Cor. 12. 6. for I shall speak the *truth*: but I forbear
13. 8. For we can do nothing against the *t.*, but for the *t.*
Gal. 2. 5. that the *t.* of the gospel might continue with you
14. they walked not uprightly according to the *truth*
4. 16. I become your enemy, because I tell you the *truth?*
5. 7. who did hinder you that ye should not obey the *t.?*
Eph. 1. 13. having heard the word of the *truth*
4. 15. but speaking *truth* in love, may grow up in all
21. and were taught in him, even as *truth* is in Jesus
24. created in righteousness and holiness of ²*truth*
25. putting away lying each one with his neighbour
6. 9. is in all goodness and righteousness and *truth*)
6. 14. having girded your loins with *truth* [of the gospel
Col. 1. 5. whereof ye heard before in the word of the *truth*
2 Th. 2. 10. because they received not the love of the *truth*
12. they all might be judged who believed not the *truth*
13. in sanctification of the Spirit and belief of the *truth*
1 Tim. 2. 4. and come to the knowledge of the *truth*
7. a teacher of the Gentiles in faith and ³*truth*
3. 15. the living God, the pillar and ground of the *truth*
4. 3. by them that believe and know the *truth*
6. 5. of men corrupted in mind and bereft of the *truth*
2 Tim. 2. 15. handling aright the word of *truth*
18. men who concerning the *truth* have erred
25. repentance unto the knowledge of the *truth*
3. 7. never able to come to the knowledge of the *truth*
8. withstood Moses, so do these also withstand the *t.*
4. 4. and will turn away their ears from the *truth*
Tit. 1. 1. faith of God's elect, and the knowledge of the *t.*
14. commandments of men who turn away from the *t.*
Heb. 10. 26. we have received the knowledge of the *truth*
Jas. 1. 18. his own will he brought us forth by the word of *t.*
3. 14. glory not and lie not against the *truth*
5. 19. if any among you do err from the *truth*
1 Pet. 1. 22. purified your souls in your obedience to the *t.*
2 Pet. 2. 2. of whom the way of the *t.* shall be evil spoken of
1 Jno. 1. 6. walk in the darkness, we lie, and do not the *t.*
8. we deceive ourselves, and the *truth* is not in us
2. 4. is a liar, and the *truth* is not in him
21. because ye know not the *truth*—no lie is of the *truth*
3. 18. neither with the tongue; but in deed and *truth*
19. Hereby shall we know that we are of the *truth*
5 7. that beareth witness, because the Spirit is the *truth*
2 Jno. 1. whom I love in *t.*—also all they that know the *t.*
2. for the *truth's* sake which abideth in us
3 Jno. 3. unto thy *truth*, even as thou walkest in *truth*
8. that we may be fellow-workers with the *truth*
12. Demetrius hath the witness of all men, and of the *t.*
see true, in truth.

In Truth.—*A.V.* ¹*through truth.*

Mat. 22. 16. and teachest the way of God *in truth*
Jno. 8. 44. He was a murderer—stood not in the *truth*
17. 17. Sanctify them ¹*in* the *truth*: thy word is truth
19. they themselves also may be sanctified ¹*in truth*
2 Cor. 7. 14. but as we spake all things to you *in truth*
Phil. 1. 18. in pretence or *in truth*, Christ is proclaimed
Col. 1. 6. and knew the grace of God *in truth*
1 Th. 2. 13. but, as it is *in truth*, the word of God
2 Pet. 1. 12. are established *in* the *truth* which is with you
2 Jno. 1. elect lady and her children, whom I love *i. t.* 3 Jno. 1
3. the Son of the Father, *in truth* and love
4. certain of thy children walking *in truth.* 3 Jno. 4
3 Jno. 3. unto thy truth, even as thou walkest *in truth*
see of a truth.

Of a Truth.—*A.V.* ¹*in truth,* ²*surely,* ³*of a surety,*
⁴*the truth,* ⁵*freely.*

Mat. 14. 33. *Of a truth* thou art the Son of God

TURN

Mat. 26. 73. ²*Of a truth* thou also art one of them. *Mk.* 14.
²70: *Lu.* 22. 59
Mk. 12. 14. ¹*of a truth* teachest the way of God. *Lu.* 20.⁵21
32. ⁴*Of a t.*, Master, thou hast well said that he is one
Lu. 4. 25. But *of a truth* I say unto you. 12. 44 : 21.3
9. 27. I tell you *of a truth*, There be some—that stand
Jno. 6. 14. This is *of a truth* the prophet. 7. 40
Acts 4. 27. *of a t.* in this city against thy holy Servant Jesus
10. 34. *Of a truth* I perceive that God is no respecter of
12. 11. Now I know ³*of a truth*, that the Lord hath sent
see indeed.

Try.—*A.V.* ¹*examine,* ²*tried.*

2 Cor. 13. 5. ¹*T.* your own selves, whether ye be in the faith
Rev. 2. 2. and didst ²*t.* them which call themselves apostles
3. 10. to *try* them that dwell upon the earth
see prove.

Trying.—*A.V. see proof.*

Tumult *A.V.*—¹*ado,* ²*noise,* ³*uproar.*

Mat. 9. 23. the crowd making a ²*tumult. Mk.* 5. 38
26. 5. lest a ³*tumult* arise among the people. *Mk.* 14. ³2
27. 24. rather that a *tumult* was arising, he took water
Mk. 5. 39. Why make ye a ¹*tumult*, and weep?
Acts 24. 18. with no crowd, nor yet with *tumult*
see uproar.

Tumults.—*A.V.* ¹*commotions.*

Lu. 21. 9. ye shall hear of wars and ¹*t.*, be not terrified
2 Cor. 6. 5. in *tumults*, in labours, in watchings
12. 20. factions, backbitings, whisperings, swellings, *t.*

Turn.—¹*avoid,* ²*convert—ed,* ³*course,* ⁴*eschew,* ⁵*make,*
⁶*return,* ⁷*turned.*

Mat. 5. 39. on thy right cheek, *turn* to him the other also
42. from him that would borrow of thee *turn* not thou
7. 6. trample them under their feet, and ⁷*t.* and rend you
13.15. ²*t.* again, And I should heal. *Jno.* 12. ²40 : *Acts* 28. ⁹27
18. 3. Except ye ²*turn*, and become as little children
Mk. 4. 12. should ²*turn* again, and it should be forgiven
Lu. 1. 16. children of Israel shall he *turn* unto the Lord
17. to *turn* the hearts of the fathers to the children
10. 6. rest upon him: but if not, it shall *turn* to you again
11. 24. I will ⁶*t.* back unto my house whence I came out
17. 4. seven times *turn* again to thee, saying, I repent
21. 13. It shall *turn* unto you for a testimony
Acts 3. 19. Repent ye therefore, and ²*t* again, that your sins
13. 8. seeking to *turn* aside the proconsul from the faith
46. unworthy of eternal life, lo, we *turn* to the Gentiles
14. 15. that ye should *turn* from these vain things
15. 19. which from among the Gentiles ⁷*turn* to God
26. 18. that they may *turn* from darkness to light
20. that they should repent and *turn* to God
24. thy much learning doth ⁵*turn* thee to madness
Rom. 11. 26. He shall *turn* away ungodliness from Jacob
16. 17. doctrine which ye learned: and ¹*t.* away from them
1 Cor. 14. 27. two, or at the most three, and that in ³*turn*
2 Cor. 3. 16. whensoever it shall *turn* to the Lord, the veil
Gal. 4. 9. how *t.* ye back again to the weak and beggarly
Phil. 1. 19. For I know that this shall *turn* to my salvation
2 Tim. 3. 5. denied the power thereof: from these also *turn*
4. 4. and will *turn* away their ears from the truth, and
⁷*turn* aside unto fables   [the truth
Tit. 1. 14. commandments of men who *turn* away from

TURN

Heb. 12. 25. who *turn* away from him that warneth from
Jas. 3. 3. we *turn* about their whole body also [heaven
1 Pet. 3. 11. let him ¹*turn* away from evil and do good
2 Pet. 2. 21. to *turn* back from the holy commandment
Rev. 11. 6. power over the waters to *turn* them into blood
    see return.

Turned.—*A.V.* ¹*converted,* ²*gone out of the way.*
Mat. 16. 23. But he *turned,* and said unto Peter
Mk. 5. 30. Jesus—*t.* him about in the crowd, and said [25
Lu. 7. 9. Jesus—marvelled at him, and *t.* and said. 9. 55: 14.
17. 15. that he was healed, *t.* back, with a loud voice
22. 32. when once thou hast ¹*turned* again, stablish thy
61. And the Lord *t.,* and looked upon Peter [brethren
Jno. 16. 20. but your sorrow shall be *turned* into joy
20. 14. she *turned* herself back, and beholdeth Jesus
Acts 2. 20. The sun shall be *turned* into darkness
7. 39. and *turned* back in their hearts unto Egypt
42. But God *turned,* and gave them up [the Lord
9. 35. at Lydda and in Sharon saw him, and they *t.* to
11. 21. a great number that believed *turned* unto the Lord
17. 6. These that have *turned* the world upside down
19. 26. this Paul hath persuaded and *t.* away much people
Rom. 3. 12. They have all ²*turned* aside, they are together
1 Th. 1. 9. and how ye *turned* unto God from idols
1 Tim. 1. 6. some having swerved have *turned* aside
5. 15. for already some are *turned* aside after Satan
2 Tim. 1. 15. that all that are in Asia *turned* away from me
Heb. 11. 34. *turned* to flight armies of aliens
12. 13. that that which is lame be not *t.* out of the way
Jas. 3. 4. are yet *turned* about by a very small rudder
4. 9. let your laughter be *turned* to mourning
Rev. 1. 12. I *turned* to see the voice—having *turned* I saw
    see returned, turn, turneth, turning, withdrew.

Turneth.—*A.V.* ¹*turned.*
Jno. 20. 16. She [Mary]¹*turneth* herself, and saith unto him

Turning.—*A.V.* ¹*avoiding,* ²*turned.*
Mk. 8. 33. But he ²*turning* about, and seeing his disciples
Acts 3. 26. in *t.* away every one of you from your iniquities
1 Tim. 6. 20. ¹*turning* away from the profane babblings
Jas. 1. 17. no variation, neither shadow that is cast by *t.*
2 Pet. 2. 22. The dog ²*turning* to his own vomit again
Jude 4. *turning* the grace of our God into lasciviousness

Turtle doves.
Lu. 2. 24. A pair of *turtle doves,* or two young pigeons

Tutor—s.—*A.V.* ¹*instructors,* ²*schoolmaster.*
1 Cor. 4. 15. though ye should have ten thousand ¹*t.* in
Gal. 3. 24. the law hath been our ²*t.* to bring us unto Christ
25. now that faith is come, we are no longer under a ²*t.*
    see guardians.

Twain.—*A.V.* ¹*both,* ²*two.*
Mat. 5. 41. compel thee to go one mile, go with him *twain*
19. 5. and the *twain* shall become one flesh? Mk. 10. 8:
    1 Cor. 6. ²16: Eph. 5. ²31   [10. 8
6. So that they are no more *twain,* but one flesh. Mk.
21. 31. Whether of the *t.* did the will of his father?
27. 21. Whether of the *t.* will ye that I release unto you?
51. the veil of the temple was rent in *t.* [Mk. 15. 38
Eph. 2. 15. that he might create in himself of the *t.* one
Rev. 19. 20. they ¹*t.* were cast alive into the lake of fire

Twelfth.
Rev. 21. 20. the eleventh, jacinth; the *twelfth,* amethyst

TWO

Twelve.
Mat. 9. 20. an issue of blood *t.* years. Mk. 5. 25: Lu. 8. 43
10. 1. called unto him his *t.* disciples. Mk. 3. 14: Lu. 6. 13
2. the names of the *t.* apostles are. 5. [Lu. 9. 17: Jno. 6. 13
14. 20 the broken pieces, *t.* baskets full. Mk. 6. 43: 8. 19
19. 28. ye also shall sit upon *t.* thrones, judging the
    twelve tribes. Lu. 22. 30.   [Mk. 14. 17
26. 20. he was sitting at meat with the *twelve* disciples
47. Judas, one of the *t.* 14. Mk. 14. 10, 43: Lu. 22. 3, 47:
53. send me more than *t.* legions of angels? [Jno. 6. 71
Mk. 4. 10. with the *twelve.* 11. 11: Lu. 8. 1: 9. 12
5. 42. and walked; for she was *t.* years old. Lu. 8. 42
6. 7. called unto him the *twelve.* 10, 32: Lu. 9. 1: 18. 31
14. 20. It is one of the *twelve,* he that dippeth with me
Lu. 2. 42. And when he was *t.* years old, they went up
Jno. 6. 67. Jesus said therefore unto the *twelve*
70. Did not I choose you the *t.,* and one of you is a devil?
11. 9. Are there not *twelve* hours in the day?
20. 24. Thomas, one the *twelve,* called Didymus
Acts 6. 2. And the *twelve* called the multitude—unto them
7. 8. Isaac begat Jacob, and Jacob the *t.* patriarchs
19. 7. And they were in all about *twelve* men
24. 11. not more than *t.* days since I went up to worship
26. 7. unto which promise our *twelve* tribes, earnestly
1 Cor. 15. 5. that he appeared to Cephas; then to the *t.*
Jas. 1. 1. to the *twelve* tribes which are of the Dispersion
Rev. 7. 5. Of the tribe of—were sealed *t.* thousand. 6, 7, 8
12. 1. and upon her head a crown of *twelve* stars
21. 12 having *twelve* gates, and at the gates *twelve*
    angels—names of the *twelve* tribes
14. And the wall of the city had *twelve* foundations, and
    on them *t.* names of the *t.* apostles of the Lamb
21. And the *twelve* gates were *twelve* pearls
22. 2. the tree of life, bearing *twelve* manner of fruits
    see thousand.

Twenty—Four and Twenty.
Acts 27. 28. and they sounded, and found *twenty* fathoms
Rev. 4. 4. about the throne were *four and twenty* thrones
    —upon the thrones I saw *four and twenty* elders
5. 8. and the *four and twenty* elders fell down before
    the Lamb. 4. 10: 11. 16: 19. 4
    see thousand.

Twice.
Mk. 14. 30. even this night, before the cock crow *t.* 72
Lu. 18. 12. I fast *twice* in the week; I give tithes of all
Jude 12. without fruit, *twice* dead, plucked up by the roots

Twinkling.
1 Cor. 15. 52. in the *twinkling* of an eye, at the last trump

Two.
Mat. 2. 16. from *two* years old and under
6. 24. No man can serve *two* masters. Lu. 16. 13
8. 28. there met him *two* possessed with devils
9. 27. *two* blind men followed him, crying out
18. 8. than having *two* hands or *two* feet. Mk 9. 43, 45
9. rather than having *two* eyes to be cast. Mk. 9. 47
16. hear thee not, with take with thee one or *two* more, that
    at the mouth of *t.* witnesses. 2 Cor. 13. 1: Heb. 10. 28
19. that if *two* of you shall agree on earth as touching
20. For where *two* or three are gathered together
22. 40. On these *two* commandments hangeth the whole
24. 40. Then shall *t.* men be in the field. Lu. 17. 36 [marg.]
41. *Two* women shall be grinding at the mill. Lu. 17. 35
25. 15. unto one he gave five talents, to another *two*
17. he also that received the *two* gained other *two*

357

TWO

Mk. 6. 7. and began to send them forth by *two* and *two.*
    Mat. 21. 1 ; *Mk.* 11. 1 ; 14. 13 ; *Lu.* 10. 1 ; 19. 29
12. 42. came a poor widow, and she cast in *two* mites
16. 12. was manifested in another form unto *two* of them
Lu. 3. 11. He that hath *two* coats, let him impart to him
7. 41. A certain lendor had *two* debtors
9. 3. nor bread, nor money ; neither have *two* coats
30. with him *two* men, which were Moses and Elijah. 32
10. 35. And on the morrow he took out *two* pence
12. 52. three against *two*, and *two* against three
17. 34. *two* men on one bed ; the one shall be taken
18. 10. *Two* men went up into the temple to pray
23. 32. there were also *two* others, malefactors. *Jno.* 19. 18
24. 4. *two* men stood by them in dazzling apparel
    13. *two* of them were going that very day to—Emmaus
Jno. 1. 40. One of the *two* that heard John speak. 35, 37
8 17. that the witness of *two* men is true
21. 2. sons of Zebedee, and *two* other of his disciples
Acts 1. 10. *two* men stood by them in white apparel
    24. shew of these *two* the one whom thou hast chosen
9. 38. that Peter was there, sent *two* men unto him
19. 10. And this continued for the space of *two* years
24. 27. But when *two* years were fulfilled, Felix was
28. 30. he abode *two* whole years in his own hired
1 *Cor.* 14. 27. man speaketh in a tongue, let it be by *t.* 29
Gal. 4. 24. for these women are *two* covenants
Phil. 1. 23. But I am in a strait betwixt the *two*
1 *Tim.* 5. 19. except at the mouth of *two* or three witnesses
Heb. 6. 18. that by *two* immutable things, in which it is
Rev. 9. 12. there come yet *two* Woes hereafter
11. 3. And I will give unto my *two* witnesses
    4. These are the *two* olive trees and the *two* candlesticks
12. 14. And there were given to the woman the *two* wings
13. 11. and he had *two* horns like unto a lamb
    see *twain.*

Two-edged.—*A.V.* ¹*two edges.*

Heb. 4. 12. and sharper than any *two-edged* sword
Rev. 1. 16. mouth proceeded a sharp *two-edged* sword. 2. ¹12

Twofold.

Mat. 23. 15. ye make him *twofold* more a son of hell

U.

Unapproachable.—*A.V.* ¹*approach.*

1 *Tim.* 6 16. dwelling in light ¹*unapproachable*

Unawares.

Heb. 13. 2. for thereby some have entertained angels *u.*
    see *privily, suddenly.*

Unbelief.

Mat. 13. 58. not many mighty works there because of their *u.*
Mk. 6. 6. And he marvelled because of their *unbelief*
9. 24. I believe ; help thou mine *unbelief*
16. 14. and he upbraided them with their *unbelief* [strong
Rom. 4. 20. [Abraham] wavered not through *u.*, but waxed
11. 20. Well ; by their *unbelief* they were broken off
    23. if they continue not in their *unbelief*, shall be grafted
1 *Tim.* 1. 13. because I did it ignorantly in *unbelief*
Heb. 3. 12. shall be in any one of you an evil heart of *u.*
    19. they were not able to enter in because of *unbelief*
    see *disobedience, faith.*

UNCLEAN

Unbeliever—s.—*A.V.* ¹*infidel.*

1 *Cor.* 6. 6. to law with brother, and that before *u.* ¹
2 *Cor.* 6. 14. Be not unequally yoked with *unbelievers*
    15. what portion hath a believer with an ¹*unbeliever* ?
1 *Tim.* 5. 8. denied the faith, and is worse than an ¹*u.*
    see *unbelieving, unfaithful.*

Unbelieving.—*A.V.* ¹*believe not,* ²*believeth not,*
    ³*unbelievers.*

1 *Cor.* 7. 12. If any brother hath an ²*unbelieving* wife
    13. the woman which hath an ²*unbelieving* husband
    14. the *unbelieving* husband is sanctified in the wife,
        and the *u.* wife is sanctified in the brother
    15. Yet if the *unbelieving* departeth, let him depart
14. 22. to them that believe, but to the ¹*u.*—not to the ¹*u.*
    23. there come in men unlearned or ³*unbelieving.* ²24
2 *Cor.* 4. 4. this world hath blinded the minds of the ¹*u.*
Tit. 1. 15. to them that are defiled and *u.* nothing is pure
Rev. 21. 8. But for the fearful, and *unbelieving*
    see *disobedient.*

Unblameable—y.

1 *Th.* 2. 10. righteously and *u.* we behaved ourselves
3. 13. the end he may stablish your hearts *u.* in holiness
    see *blemish.*

Unceasing—ly.—*A.V.* ¹*without ceasing,* ²*continual.*

Rom. 1. 9. ¹*u.* I make mention of you, always in my prayers
9. 2. I have great sorrow and ²*u.*, pain in my heart
2 *Tim.* 1. 3. how ¹*unceasing* is my remembrance of thee

Uncertain.

1 *Cor.* 14. 8. For if the trumpet give an *uncertain* voice
    see *uncertainty.*

Uncertainly.

1 *Cor.* 9. 26. I therefore so run, as not *uncertainly*

Uncertainty.—*A.V.* ¹*uncertain.*

1 *Tim.* 6. 17. nor have their hope set on the ¹*u.* of riches

Unchangeable.

Heb. 7. 24. hath his priesthood *unchangeable*

Uncircumcised.

Acts 7. 51. Ye stiffnecked and *u.* in heart and ears
11. 3. Thou wentest in to men *uncircumcised*
1 *Cor.* 7. 18. let him not become *uncircumcised*
    see *uncircumcision.*

Uncircumcision.—*A.V.* ¹*not circumcised,* ²*uncircumcised.*

Rom. 2. 25. thy circumcision is become *uncircumcision*
    26. If therefore the *uncircumcision* keep the ordinances
        —shall not his *u.* be reckoned for circumcision ? 27
3. 30. and the *uncircumcision* through faith
4. 9. blessing then pronounced—or upon the *u.* also ? 10
    11. of the faith which he had while he was in *uncircumcision*—though they be in ¹*uncircumcision.* ²12
1 *Cor.* 7. 18. Hath any been called in *uncircumcision* ?
    19. and *uncircumcision* is nothing ; but the keeping of
Gal. 2. 7. that I had been intrusted with the gospel of the *u.*
5. 6. nor *u.* ; but faith working through love. 6. 15
Eph. 2. 11. Gentiles in the flesh, who are called *U.* [flesh
Col. 2. 13. dead through your trespasses and the *u.* of your
3. 11. cannot be Greek and Jew, circumcision and *u.*

Unclean.—*A.V.* ¹*defileth,* ²*filthiness.*

Lu. 4. 33. a man, which had a spirit of an *unclean* devil
Acts 10. 14. never eaten anything that is common and *u.*
    28. should not call any man common or *unclean.* [11. 8

UNCLEAN

Rom. 14. 14. that nothing is *unclean* of itself—any thing to be *unclean*, to him it is *unclean*
1 *Cor.* 7. 14. else were your children *unclean*
2 *Cor.* 6. 17. And touch no *u.* thing; And I will receive you
Eph. 5. 5. nor *unclean* person, nor covetous man
Rev. 17. 4. even the ²*unclean* things of her fornication
18. 2. a hold of every *unclean* and hateful bird
21. 27. in no wise enter into it anything ¹*unclean*
   see defiled.

Unclean Spirit—s.—*A.V.* ¹*foul spirit.*

Mat. 10. 1. and gave them authority over *u. spirits. Mk.* 6. 7
12. 43. the *unclean spirit*, when he is gone out. *Lu.* 11. 24
Mk. 1. 23. in their synagogue a man with an *unclean s.*
26. the *unclean spirit*, tearing him and crying
27. he commandeth even the *unclean spirits. Lu.* 4. 36
3. 11. And the *unclean spirits*—fell down before him
30. because they said, He hath an *unclean spirit*
5. 2. met him out of the tombs a man with an *u. spirit*
8. Come forth, thou *u. spirit*, out of the man. *Lu.* 8. 29
13. And the *unclean spirits* came out, and entered into
7. 25. whose little daughter had an *unclean spirit*
9. 25. he rebuked the ¹*unclean spirit*, saying unto him
Lu. 6. 18. troubled with *u. spirits* were healed. *Acts* 5. 16
9. 42. Jesus rebuked the *unclean s.*, and healed the boy
Acts 8. 7. *u. spirits*, they came out, crying with a loud voice
Rev. 16. 13. three *unclean spirits*, as it were frogs
18. 2. habitation of devils, and a hold of every ¹*u. spirit*

Uncleanness.

Mat. 23. 27. dead men's bones, and of all *uncleanness*
Rom. 1. 24. Wherefore God gave them up—unto *uncleanness*
6. 19. your members are servants to *uncleanness*
2 *Cor.* 12. 21. and repented not of the *uncleanness*
Gal. 5. 19. are manifest, which are these, fornication, *u.*
Eph. 4. 19. to work all *uncleanness* with greediness
5. 3. and all *uncleanness*, or covetousness, let it not even
Col. 3. 5. fornication, *uncleanness*, passion, evil desire
1 *Th.* 2. 3. For our exhortation is not of error, nor of *u.*
4. 7. God called us not for *u.*, but in sanctification
   see defilement.

Unclothed.

2 *Cor.* 5. 4. not for that we would be *unclothed*

Uncomely.

1 *Cor.* 12. 23. and our *uncomely* parts have more abundant
   see unseemly.

Uncondemned.

Acts 16. 37. They have beaten us publicly, *uncondemned*
22. 25. Is it lawful for—that is a Roman, and *uncondemned*?

Uncorruptible *A.V.*—*see incorruptible.*

Uncorruptness.—*A.V.* ¹*sincerity.*

Eph. 6. 24. love our Lord Jesus Christ in ¹*uncorruptness*
Tit. 2. 7 in thy doctrine shewing *uncorruptness*

Uncovered.

Mk. 2. 4. they *uncovered* the roof where he was
   see unveiled.

Unction *A.V.*—*see anointing.*

Undefiled.

Heb. 7. 26. a high priest—holy, guileless, *undefiled*
13. 4. in honour among all, and let the bed be *undefiled*
Jas. 1. 27. Pure religion and *undefiled* before our God
1 *Pet.* 1. 4. unto an inheritance incorruptible, and *undefiled*

UNDERSTOOD

Undergirding.

Acts 27. 17. they used helps, *under-girding* the ship

Understand.—*A.V.* ¹*believe,* ²*know,* ³*understanding.*

Mat. 13. 14. and shall in no wise *u.* 13: *Acts* 28. 26
15. 10. Hear, and *understand. Mk.* 7. 14
24. 15. (let him that readeth *understand.*) *Mk.* 13. 14
Mk. 4. 12. lest at any time they may hear, and not *understand.*
   Mat. 13. 15: *Lu.* 8. 10: *Acts* 28. 27
8. 21. Do ye not yet *understand*?
14. 68. I neither know, nor *understand* what thou sayest
Lu. 24. 45. that they might *understand* the scriptures
Jno. 8. 43. Why do ye not *understand* my speech?
10. 38. ye may know and ¹*u.* that the Father is in me
13. 7. not now; but thou shalt ²*understand* hereafter
Rom. 15. 21. they who have not heard shall *understand*
1 *Cor.* 12. 3. Wherefore I give you to *understand*
Eph. 5. 17. not foolish, but ³*u.* what the will of the Lord is
1 *Tim.* 1. 7. teachers of the law, though they ³*u.* neither
Heb. 11. 3. By faith we *u.* that the worlds have been framed
Jude 10. what they ²*u.* naturally, like the creatures
   see perceive, know, ignorant, knowledge.

Understandest.—*A.V.* ¹*knowest.*

Jno. 3. 10. teacher of Israel, and ¹*u.* not these things?
Acts 8. 30. *Understandest* thou what thou readest?

Understandeth.

Mat. 13. 19. word of the kingdom, and *understandeth* it not
23. he that heareth the word, and *understandeth* it
Rom. 3. 11. There is none that *understandeth*
1 *Cor.* 14. 2. but unto God; for no man *understandeth*
   see knoweth.

Understanding.—*A.V.* ¹*foolish,* ²*knowledge,* ³*prudent,* ⁴*wise.*

Mat. 11. 25. hide these things from the wise and ⁴*u. Lu.* 10. ⁵21
15. 16. Are ye also even yet without *u.*? *Mk.* 7. 18
Mk. 12. 33. love him with all the heart, and with all the *u.*
Lu. 2. 47. were amazed at his *u.* and his answers
Acts 13. 7. Sergius Paulus, a man of ³*understanding*
Rom. 1. 31. without *understanding*, covenant breakers
10. 19. With a nation void of ¹*u.* will I anger you
1 *Cor.* 14. 14. my spirit prayeth, but my *u.* is unfruitful
15. and I will pray with the *understanding* also—I will sing with the *understanding* also
19. I had rather speak five words with my *u.*
2 *Cor.* 10. 12. comparing themselves—are without ⁴*u.*
Eph. 3. 4. ye can perceive my ²*u.* in the mystery of Christ
4. 18. being darkened in their *understanding*
Phil. 4. 7. And the peace of God, which passeth all *u.*
Col. 1. 9. in all spiritual wisdom and *understanding*
2. 2. unto all riches of the full assurance of *u.*
2 *Tim.* 2. 7. the Lord shall give thee *u.* in all things
Jas. 3. 13. Who is wise and *understanding* among you?
1 *Jno.* 5. 20. Son of God is come, and hath given us an *u.*
Rev. 13. 18. He that hath *understanding*, let him count
   see mind, prudence, heart, traced, understand.

Understood.

Mat. 13. 51. Have ye *understood* all these things?
16. 12. Then *u.* they how that he bade them not beware
17. 13. Then *u.* the disciples that he spake unto them
Mk. 9. 32. But they *u.* not the saying, and were afraid. 6. 52:
   Lu. 2. 50: 9. 45: 18. 34: *Jno.* 10. 6: 12. 16

UNDERSTOOD

Acts 7. 25. supposed that his brethren *understood* how
    that God—but they *understood* not
23. 34. when he *understood* that he was of Cilicia
1 *Cor*.14. 9. unless ye utter by the tongue speech easy to be *u*.
2 *Pet*. 3. 16. wherein are some things hard to be *u*.
    see perceived, perceiving, learned, thought.

Undone.—*A.V.* [1]*omitted.*

Mat. 23. 23. and have left [1]*undone* the weightier matters—
    and not to have left the other *undone. Lu.* 11. 42

Undressed.—*A.V.* [1]*new.*

Mat. 9. 16. no man putteth a piece of [1]*u.* cloth. *Mk.* 2. [1]21

Unequally.

2 *Cor.* 6. 14. Be not *unequally* yoked with unbelievers

Unfaithful.—*A.V.* [1]*unbelievers.*

Lu. 12. 46. and appoint his portion with the [1]*unfaithful*

Unfeigned.

2 *Cor.* 6. 6. in the Holy Ghost, in love *unfeigned*
1 *Tim.* 1. 5. a good conscience and faith *unfeigned*
2 *Tim.* 1. 5. reminded of the *unfeigned* faith that is in thee
1 *Pet.* 1. 22. your obedience to the truth unto *u.* love of the

Unfruitful.

Mat. 13. 22. and he becometh *unfruitful. Mk.* 4. 19
1 *Cor.* 14. 14. but my understanding is *unfruitful*
Eph. 5. 11. no fellowship with the *u.* works of darkness
Tit. 3. 14. for necessary uses, that they be not *unfruitful*
2 *Pet.* 1. 8. they make you to be not idle nor *unfruitful*

Ungodliness.—*A.V.* [1]*ungodly.*

Rom. 1. 18. is revealed from heaven against all *ungodliness*
11. 26. He shall turn away *ungodliness* from Jacob
2 *Tim.* 2. 16. they will proceed further in *ungodliness*
Tit. 2. 12. denying *ungodliness* and worldly lusts
Jude 15. convict all the ungodly of all their works of [1]*u.*

Ungodly.

Rom. 4. 5. but believeth on him that justifieth the *ungodly*
5. 6. yet weak, in due season Christ died for the *ungodly*
1 *Tim.* 1. 9. the lawless and unruly, for the *u.* and sinners
1 *Pet.* 4. 18. where shall the *ungodly* and sinner appear?
2 *Pet.* 2. 5. brought a flood upon the world of the *ungodly*
    6. example unto those that should live *ungodly*
3. 7. the day of judgement and destruction of *u.* men
Jude 4. *ungodly* men, turning the grace of our God
    15. to convict all the *ungodly*—which they have *un-
    godly* wrought—*ungodly* sinners have spoken
    18. mockers, walking after their own *ungodly* lusts
    see ungodliness.

Unholy.

1 *Tim.* 1. 9. and sinners, for the *unholy* and profane
2 *Tim.* 3. 2. disobedient to parents, unthankful, *unholy*
Heb. 10. 29. an *unholy* thing, and hath done despite

United.—*A.V.* [1]*mixed,* [2]*planted together.*

Rom. 6. 5. become [2]*u.* with him by the likeness of his death
Heb. 4. 2. because they were not [1]*united* by faith

Unity.

Eph. 4. 3. the *unity* of the Spirit in the bond of peace
13. till we all attain unto the *unity* of the faith

UNPROFITABLENESS

Unjust.

Mat. 5. 45. and sendeth rain on the just and the *unjust*
Lu. 18. 11. as the rest of men, extortioners, *unjust*
Acts 24. 15. resurrection both of the just and *unjust*
    see unrighteous, unrighteousness.

Unknown.

Acts 17. 23. with this inscription, TO AN *UNKNOWN* GOD
2 *Cor.* 6. 9. as *unknown,* and yet well known
Gal. 1. 22. And I was still *u.* by face unto the churches

Unlade.

Acts 21. 3. for there the ship was to *unlade* her burden

Unlawful.

Acts 10. 28. it is an *unlawful* thing for a man that is a Jew
    see lawless.

Unlearned.

Acts 4. 13. perceived that they were *u.* and ignorant men
1 *Cor.* 14. 16. he that filleth the place of the *unlearned* say
    23. and there come in men *unlearned* or unbelieving. 24
    see ignorant.

Unleavened.

Mat. 26. 17. day of *u.* bread. *Mk.* 14. 1, 12: *Lu.* 22. 1, 7
Acts 12. 3. seize Peter also. And those were the days of *u.*
20. 6. we sailed away from Philippi after the days of *u.*
1 *Cor.* 5. 7. that ye may be a new lump, even as ye are *u.*
    8. but with the *unleavened* bread of sincerity and truth

Unlifted.—*A.V.* [1]*untaken away.*

2 *Cor.* 3. 14. same veil remaineth [1]*unlifted*; which veil is

Unloose.—*A.V.* [1]*loose.*

Mk. 1. 7. of whose shoes I am not worthy to stoop down
    and *unloose. Lu.* 3. 16: *Jno.* 1. 27: *Acts* 13. [1]25

Unmarried.

1 *Cor.* 7. 8. But I say to the *unmarried* and to widows
    11. let her remain *unmarried,* or else be reconciled
    32. *unmarried* is careful for the things of the Lord. 34

Unmerciful.

Rom. 1. 31. without natural affection, *unmerciful*

Unmixed.—*A.V.* [1]*without mixture.*

Rev. 14. 10. wrath of God, which is prepared [1]*unmixed*

Unmoveable.

Acts 27. 41. and the foreship struck and remained *u.*
1 *Cor.* 15. 58. my beloved brethren, be ye stedfast, *u.*

Unprepared.

2 *Cor.* 9. 4. with me any of Macedonia, and find you *u.*

Unprofitable.

Mat. 25. 30. And cast ye out the *unprofitable* servant
Lu. 17. 10. We are *unprofitable* servants; we have done
Rom. 3. 12. they are together become *unprofitable*
Tit. 3. 9. for they are *unprofitable* and vain
Philem. 11. who was aforetime *unprofitable* to thee
Heb. 13. 17. for this were *unprofitable* for you

Unprofitableness.

Heb. 7. 18. of its weakness and *unprofitableness*

UNQUENCHABLE

Unquenchable.—*A.V.* ¹*never shall be quenched.*

Mat. 3. 12. the chaff he will burn up with *u.* fire. *Lu.* 3. 17
Mk. 9. 43. two hands to go into hell, into the ¹*u.* fire

Unreasonable.

Acts 25. 27. For it seemeth to me *unreasonable*
2 *Th.* 3. 2. that we may be delivered from *u.* and evil men

Unrebukeable *A.V.—see reproach.*

Unreproveable.—*A.V.* ¹*blameless.*

1 *Cor.* 1. 8. that ye be ¹*u.* in the day of our Lord Jesus Christ
Col. 1. 22. without blemish and *unreproveable* before him

Unrighteous.—*A.V.* ¹*unjust.*

Lu. 16. 8. And his lord commended the ¹*u.* steward
10. ¹*unrighteous* in a very little is ¹*u.* also in much
11. ye have not been faithful in the *u.* mammon
18. 6. Hear what the ¹*unrighteous* judge saith
Rom. 3. 5. Is God *unrighteous* who visiteth with wrath?
1 *Cor.* 6. 1. go to law before the ¹*u.*, and not before the saints?
9. that the *u.* shall not inherit the kingdom of God?
Heb. 6. 10. for God is not *unrighteous* to forget your work
1 *Pet.* 3. 18. suffered for sins once, the righteous for the ¹*u.*
2 *Pet.* 2. 9. and to keep the ¹*unrighteous* under punishment
Rev. 22. 11. He that is ¹*u.*, let him do unrighteousness still

Unrighteousness.—*A.V.* ¹*iniquity*, ²*unjust.*

Lu. 16. 9. by means of the mammon of *unrighteousness*
Jno. 7. 18. the same is true, and no *unrighteousness* is in him
Rom. 1. 18. all ungodliness and *unrighteousness* of men, who hold down the truth in *unrighteousness*
29. being filled with all *unrighteousness*, wickedness
2. 8. obey not the truth, but obey *unrighteousness*
3. 5. But if our *u.* commendeth the righteousness of God
6. 13. your members unto sin as instruments of *u.*
9. 14. Is there *unrighteousness* with God? God forbid
1 *Cor.* 13. 6. rejoiceth not in ¹*unrighteousness*
2 *Th.* 2. 10. with all deceit of *unrighteousness* for them
12. not the truth, but had pleasure in *unrighteousness*
2 *Tim.* 2. 19. nameth the name of the Lord depart from ¹*u.*
1 *Jno.* 1. 9. forgive us our sins, and to cleanse us from all *u.*
5. 17. All *unrighteousness* is sin: and there is a sin
Rev. 22. 11. He that is unrighteous, let him do ¹*u.* still
see iniquity, wrong-doing.

Unripe.—*A.V.* ¹*untimely.*

Rev. 6. 13. as a fig tree casteth her ¹*unripe* figs

Unruly.—*A.V.* ¹*disobedient.*

1 *Tim.* 1. 9. law is not—but for the lawless and ¹*unruly*
Tit. 1. 6. who are not accused of riot or *unruly*
10. For there are many *unruly* men, vain talkers
see disorderly, restless.

Unsearchable.

Rom. 11. 33. how *unsearchable* are his judgements
Eph. 3. 8. to preach unto the Gentiles the *u.* riches of Christ

Unseemliness.—*A.V.* ¹*that which is unseemly.*

Rom. 1. 27. men with men working ¹*unseemliness*

Unseemly.—*A.V.* ¹*uncomely.*

1 *Cor.* 7. 36. he behaveth himself ¹*u.* toward his virgin
13. 5. doth not behave itself *unseemly* [daughter
see unseemliness.

UPPERMOST

Unsettle.—*A.V.* ¹*trouble.*

Gal. 5. 12. they which ¹*u.* you would even cut themselves off

Unskilful *A.V.—see experience.*

Unspeakable.

2 *Cor.* 9. 15. Thanks be to God for his *unspeakable* gift
12. 4. caught up into Paradise, and heard *u.* words
1 *Pet.* 1. 8. with joy *unspeakable* and full of glory

Unspotted.

Jas. 1. 27. to keep himself *unspotted* from the world

Unstable.

Jas. 1. 8. a doubleminded man, *unstable* in all his ways
see unstedfast.

Unstedfast.—*A.V.* ¹*unstable.*

2 *Pet.* 2. 14. that cannot cease from sin; enticing ¹*u.* souls
3. 16. which the ignorant and ¹*unstedfast* wrest

Untaken *A.V.—see unlifted.*

Unthankful.

Lu. 6. 35. for he is kind toward the *unthankful* and evil
2 *Tim.* 3. 2. disobedient to parents, *unthankful*, unholy

Untimely *A.V.—see unripe.*

Untoward *A.V.—see crooked.*

Unveiled.—*A.V.* ¹*open*, ²*uncovered.*

1 *Cor.* 11. 5. praying or prophesying with her head ²*u.*
13. seemly that a woman pray unto God ²*unveiled*?
2 *Cor.* 3. 18. But we all, with ¹*u.* face reflecting as a mirror

Unwashen.

Mat. 15. 20. but to eat with *unwashen* hands. *Mk.* 7. 2
see defiled.

Unwise.—*A.V.* ¹*fools.*

Eph. 5. 15. Look—carefully how ye walk, not as ¹*unwise*
see foolish.

Unworthy.

Acts 13. 46. and judge yourselves *unworthy* of eternal life
1 *Cor.* 6. 2. are ye *unworthy* to judge the smallest matters?

Unworthily.

1 *Cor.* 11. 27. eat the bread or drink the cup of the Lord *u.*

Upbraid.

Mat. 11. 20. Then began he to *upbraid* the cities wherein

Upbraided—eth.

Mk. 16. 14. and he *upbraided* them with their unbelief
Jas. 1. 5. who giveth to all liberally and *upbraideth* not

Upholding.

Heb. 1. 3. *upholding* all things by the word of his power

Upper.

Mk. 14. 15. he will—shew you a large *u.* room. *Lu.* 22. 12
Acts 1. 13. they [disciples] went up into the *upper* chamber
19. 1. Paul having passed through the *upper* country
see chamber, chambers.

Uppermost *A.V.—see chief.*

UPRIGHT

Upright.
Acts 14. 10. Stand *upright* on thy feet [Paul to cripple]

Uprightly.
Gal. 2. 14. But when I saw that they walked not *uprightly*

Uprightness.—A.V. ¹*righteousness*.
Heb. 1. 8. the sceptre of ¹u. is the sceptre of thy kingdom

Uproar.—A.V. ¹*tumult*.
Acts 17. 5. Jews, being moved—set the city on an *uproar*
20. 1. And after the *uproar* was ceased, Paul—took leave
21. 34. when he could not know the certainty for the ¹u.
    see confusion, riot, sedition, tumult.

Upside *down*.
Acts 17. 6. These that have turned the world *upside down* are come hither also

Urge A.V.—*see press*.

Urged.—A.V. ¹*persuaded*.
Acts 13. 43. ¹*urged* them to continue in the grace of God

Urgent.—A.V. ¹*fierce*.
Lu. 23. 5. they were the more ¹u., saying, He stirreth up

Use—s.—A.V. ¹*abuse*, ²*used*.
1 Cor. 9. 18. not to ¹*use* to the full my right in the gospel. ²12
Tit. 3. 14. to maintain good works for necessary *uses*
    see deal, entreat, serve, shew, using.

Used.—A.V. ¹*with conscience*.
1 Cor. 8. 7. but some, being ¹*used* until now to the idol
9. 15. But I have *used* none of these things
Heb. 10. 33. becoming partakers with them that were so u.
    see practised, served, use, using.

Useful.—A.V. ¹*profitable*.
2 Tim. 4. 11. for he is ¹*useful* to me for ministering

Useth A.V.—*see partaketh*.

Using.—A.V. ¹*use*, ²*used*.
Col. 2. 22. (all which things are to perish with the *using*)
1 Th. 2. 5. at any time were we found ²*u*. words of flattery
1 Pet. 2. 16. not u. your freedom for a cloke of wickedness
4. 9. ¹*using* hospitality one to another without murmuring

Usury A.V.—*see interest*.

Utter.
Mat. 13. 35. I will *utter* things hidden from the foundation
1 Cor. 14. 9. u. by the tongue speech easy to be understood
2 Cor. 12. 4. words, which it is not lawful for a man to u.

Utterance.—A.V. ¹*word*.
Acts 2. 4. with other tongues, as the Spirit gave them u.
1 Cor. 1. 5. ye were enriched in him, in all *utterance*
2 Cor. 8. 7. abound in everything, in faith, and *utterance*
Eph. 6. 19. that *utterance* may be given unto me

VAINGLORY

Uttered.—A.V. ¹*cried*.
Mk. 15. 37. Jesus ¹u. a loud voice, and gave up the ghost
Rom. 8. 26. with groanings which cannot be *uttered*
Rev. 10. 3. the seven thunders *uttered* their voices. 4
4. Seal up the things which the seven thunders *uttered*
    see interpretation.

Uttering.—A.V. ¹*speak*.
2 Pet. 2. 18. ¹*uttering* great swelling words of vanity

Utterly.
Rev. 18. 8. she shall be *utterly* burned with fire
    see altogether.

Uttermost.—A.V. ¹*ends*.
Mk. 13. 27. the *uttermost* part of the earth to the u. part
Acts 1. 8. and unto the *uttermost* part of the earth
13. 47. be for salvation unto the ¹u. part of the earth
1 Th. 2. 16. the wrath is come upon them to the *uttermost*
Heb. 7. 25. he is able to save to the *uttermost* them that
    see ends, last.

V.

Vagabond A.V.—*see strolling*.

Vail A.V.—*see veil*.

Vain.—A.V. ¹*in vain*, ²*vanities*.
Mat. 6. 7. And in praying use not *vain* repetitions
Acts 4. 25. And the peoples imagine *vain* things?
14. 15. turn from these ²v. things unto the living God
Rom. 1. 21. but became *vain* in their reasonings
1 Cor. 3. 20. reasonings of the wise, that they are *vain*
15. 10. grace which was bestowed upon me was not found v.
14. our preaching *vain*, your faith also is *vain*. 17
58. ye know that your labour is not ¹*vain* in the Lord
Col. 2. 8. and *vain* deceit, after the tradition of men
1 Th. 2. 1. in unto you, that it hath not been found ¹*vain*
1 Tim. 1. 6. have turned aside unto *vain* talking
Tit. 1. 10. many unruly men, *vain* talkers and deceivers
3. 9. about the law; for they are unprofitable and *vain*
Jas. 1. 26. deceiveth his heart, this man's religion is *vain*
2. 20. O v. man, that faith apart from works is barren?
1 Pet. 1. 18. from your *vain* manner of life handed down
    see empty.

In Vain.
Mat. 15. 9. But *in vain* do they worship me. Mk. 7. 7
Rom. 13. 4. for he beareth not the sword *in vain*
1 Cor. 15. 2. if ye hold it fast, except ye believed *in vain*
2 Cor. 6. 1. that ye receive not the grace of God *in vain*
Gal. 2. 2. I should be running, or had run, *in vain*
3. 4. so many things *in vain*? if it be indeed *in vain*
4. 11. any means I have bestowed labour upon you *in v*.
Phil. 2. 16. I did not run *in vain* neither labour *in vain*
1 Th. 3. 5. tempted you, and our labour should be *in vain*
Jas. 4. 5. Or think ye that the scripture speaketh *in vain*?
    see rain, void.

Vainglorious.—A.V. ¹*vain glory*.
Gal. 5. 26. Let us not be ¹v., provoking one another

Vainglory.—A.V. ¹*pride*.
Phil. 2. 3. nothing through faction or through *vainglory*
1 Jno. 2. 16. the ¹*vainglory* of life, is not of the Father
    see vainglorious.

VAINLY

Vainly.
Col. 2. 18. *vainly* puffed up by his fleshly mind

Valiant *A.V.—see mighty.*

Valley.
Lu. 3. 5. Every *v.* shall be filled, And every mountain

Value—d.—*A.V.* ¹*better*, ²*honour.*
Mat. 6. 26. Are not ye of much more ¹*v.* than. *Lu.* 12. ¹24
10. 31. ye are of more *v.* than many sparrows. *Lu.* 12. 7
12. 12. How much then is a man of more¹*v.* than a sheep!
Col. 2. 23. not of any ²*v.* against the indulgence of the flesh
see price, priced.

Vanish *A.V.—see done, vanishing.*

Vanished.
Lu. 24. 31. they knew him; and he *v.* out of their sight

Vanisheth.
Jas. 4. 14. appeareth for a little time, and then *v.* away

Vanishing.—*A.V.* ¹*vanish.*
Heb. 8. 13. and waxeth aged is nigh unto ¹*vanishing* away

Vanities *A.V.—see vain (things).*

Vanity.
Rom. 8. 20. For the creation was subjected to *vanity*
Eph. 4. 17. as the Gentiles also walk, in the *v.* of their mind
2 *Pet.* 2. 18. For, uttering great swelling words of *vanity*

Vapour.
Acts 2. 19. Blood, and fire, and *vapour* of smoke   ¹time
Jas. 4. 14. For ye are a *vapour*, that appeareth for a little

Variableness *A.V.—see variation.*

Variance.—*A.V.* ¹*partiality.*
Mat. 10. 35. For I came to set a man at *v.* against his father
Jas. 3. 17. without ¹*variance*, without hypocrisy

Variation.—*A.V.* ¹*variableness.*
Jas. 1. 17. from the Father of lights, with whom can be no ¹*v.*

Vaunteth.
1 *Cor.* 13. 4. love *vaunteth* not itself, is not puffed up

Vauntings.—*A.V.* ¹*boastings.*
Jas. 4. 16. But now ye glory in your ¹*vauntings*

Vehemently.
Mk. 14. 31. But he spake exceeding *vehemently*, If I must die
Lu. 11. 53. the Pharisees began to press upon him *v.*
23. 10. the scribes stood, *vehemently* accusing him

Veil—ed.—*A.V.* ¹*cover*, ²*covered*, ³*hid*, ⁴*vail.*
Mat. 27. 51. *v.* of the temple was rent. *Mk.* 15. 38 : *Lu.* 23. 45
1 *Cor.* 11. 6. For if a woman is not ²*veiled*—let her be *v.*
7. a man indeed ought not to have his head ¹*veiled*
2 *Cor.* 3. 14. same ⁴*v.* remaineth unlifted; which ⁴*v.* is done
15. whensoever Moses is read, a ⁴*v.* lieth upon their heart
16. it shall turn to the Lord, the ⁴*veil* is taken away
4. 3. if our gospel is ³*v.*, it is ³*v.* in them that are perishing

VICTORIOUS

Heb. 6. 19. entering into that which is within the *veil*
9. 3. And after the second *veil*, the tabernacle which
10. 20. a new and living way, through the *veil*

Vengeance.—*A.V.* ¹*punishment.*
Lu. 21. 22. For these are days of *vengeance*   [10. 30
Rom. 12. 19. for it is written, *V.* belongeth unto me. *Heb.*
2 *Th.* 1. 8. rendering *vengeance* to them that know not God
1 *Pet.* 2. 14. as sent by him for ¹*vengeance* on evil-doers
see justice, punishment, wrath.

Verily.—*A.V.* ¹*doubtless.*
Phil. 3. 8. Yea ¹*verily*, and I count all things to be loss
see indeed.

Verity *A.V.—see truth.*

Very.—*A.V.* ¹*express*, ²*selfsame.*
2 *Cor.* 5. 5. he that wrought us for this ²*very* thing is God
Heb. 1. 3. and the ¹*very* image of his substance

Vessel.—*A.V.* ¹*vessels.*
Mk. 11. 16. any man should carry a *v.* through the temple
Lu. 8. 16. hath lighted a lamp, covereth it with a *vessel*
Jno. 19. 29 There was set there a *vessel* full of vinegar
Acts 9. 15. Go thy way: for he is a chosen *vessel* unto me
10. 11. the heaven opened, and a certain *v.* descending.
Rom. 9. 21. to make one part a *vessel* unto honour 16 : 11. 5
1 *Th.* 4. 4. know how to possess himself of his own *vessel*
2 *Tim.* 2. 21. he shall be a *vessel* unto honour, sanctified
1 *Pet.* 3. 7. giving honour unto the woman, as unto the
weaker *vessel*   [of most precious wood
Rev. 18. 12. every ¹*vessel* of ivory, and every ¹*vessel* made

Vessels.
Mat. 13. 48. gathered the good into *vessels*, but the bad
25. 4. but the wise took oil in their *v.* with their lamps
Mk. 7. 4. washings of cups, and pots, and brasen *vessels*
Rom. 9. 22. *vessels* of wrath fitted unto destruction
23. make known the riches of his glory upon *v.* of mercy
2 *Tim.* 2. 20. in a great house there are not only *v.* of gold
Heb. 9. 21. all the *vessels* of the ministry he sprinkled
Rev. 2. 27. as the *v.* of the potter are broken to shivers
see vessel.

Vesture.
Jno. 19. 24. And upon my *vesture* did they cast lots
see garment, mantle.

Vex *A.V.—see afflict.*

Vexed.
Mat. 15. 22. my daughter is grievously *vexed* with a devil
Acts 5. 16. and them that were *v.* with unclean spirits
2 *Pet.* 2. 8. Lot, *vexed* his righteous soul from day to day
see suffereth, troubled.

Vial—s *A.V.—see bowl—s.*

Victory.—*A.V.* ¹*sting.*
Mat. 12. 20. Till he send forth judgement unto *victory*
1 *Cor.* 15. 54. Death is swallowed up in *victory*
55. O death where is thy ¹*victory!*
57. giveth us the *v.* through our Lord Jesus Christ
1 *Jno.* 5. 4. the *victory* that hath overcome the world
see sting, victorious.

Victorious.—*A.V.* ¹*gotten the victory.*
Rev. 15. 2. and them that come ¹*victorious* from the beast

VICTUALS

Victuals.
Lu. 9. 12. and get v. : for we are here in a desert place
    see food.

Vigilant *A.V.—see temperate, watchful.*

Vile.—*A.V. ¹evil, ²lewd.*
Acts 17. 5. Jews—took unto them certain ²vile fellows
Rom. 1. 26. God gave them up unto vile passions
Jas. 2. 2. and there come in also a poor man in v. clothing
3. 16. there is confusion and every ¹vile deed
    see humiliation.

Village—s.—*A.V. ¹town—s.*
Mat. 9. 35. Jesus went about all the cities and the villages
    Mk. 6. 6: Lu. 8. 1; 9. ¹⁶: 13. 22
10. 11. into whatsoever city or ¹v. ye shall enter ⌈9. ¹¹²
14. 15. away, that they may go into the v. Mk. 6. 36: Lu.
21. 2. the v. that is over against you. Mk. 11. 2: Lu. 19. 30
Mk. 6. 56. wheresoever he entered, into v., or into cities
8. 23. blind man by the hand, and brought him out of
26. Do not even enter into the ¹village ⌈the ¹village
27. Jesus went forth—into the ¹v. of Cæsarea Philippi
Lu. 10. 38. he entered into a certain village. 9. 52, 56
24. 13. going that very day to a village named Emmaus
28. And they drew nigh unto the village
Jno. 7. 42. from Bethlehem, the ¹village where David was?
11. 1. Lazarus of Bethany, of the ¹village of Mary
30. Jesus was not yet come into the ¹village
Acts 8. 25. preached the gospel to many v. of the Samaritans

Villany.—*A.V. ¹lewdness, ²mischief.*
Acts 13. 10. O full of all guile and all ²villany
18. 14. If—it were a matter of wrong or of wicked ¹villany

Vine.
Mat. 26. 29. not drink henceforth of this fruit of the vine.
Jno. 15. 1. I am the true vine [Mk. 14. 25: Lu. 22. 18
4. cannot bear fruit of itself, except it abide in the vine
5. I am the vine, ye are the branches
Jas. 3. 12. can a fig tree—yield olives, or a vine figs?
Rev. 14. 18. gather the clusters of the vine of the earth
    see vintage.

Vinedresser.—*A.V. ¹dresser of his vineyard.*
Lu. 13. 7. he said unto the ¹v., Behold, these three years

Vinegar.
Mat. 27. 48. sponge, and filled it with v. Mk. 15. 36: Jno.
Lu. 23. 36. coming to him, offering him vinegar [19. 29
Jno. 19. 29. There was set there a vessel full of vinegar
30. When Jesus therefore had received the vinegar
    see wine.

Vineyard.
Mat. 20. 1. early in the morning to hire labourers into his v.
21. 28. Son, go work to-day in the vineyard [2, 4, 7, 8
33. which planted a v. Mk. 12. 1, 2: Lu. 20. 9, 10
39. cast him forth out of the v. Mk. 12. 8: Lu. 20. 15
40. When therefore the lord of the v. shall come. Mk. 12. 9
41. let out the vineyard unto other husbandmen. Mk.
    12. 9: Lu. 20. 16
Lu. 13. 6. A certain man had a fig tree planted in his v.
20. 13. the lord of the vineyard said, What shall I do. 15
1 Cor. 9. 7. who planteth a vineyard, and eateth not

Vintage.—*A.V. ¹vine.*
Rev. 14. 19. and gathered the ¹vintage of the earth

VISIT

Violence.—*A.V. ¹violent.*
Mat. 11. 12. the kingdom of heaven suffereth violence, and
    men of ¹violence take it by force
Lu. 3. 14. Do violence to no man, neither exact anything
Acts 5. 26. and brought them, but without violence
21. 35. borne of the soldiers for the violence of the crowd
27. 41. the stern began to break up by the v. of the waves
    see mighty fall, power.

Violent *A.V.—see violence.*

Viper—**s.**
Mat. 3. 7. Ye offspring of vipers. 12. 34 : 23. 33 : Lu. 3. 7
Acts 28. 3. a viper came out by reason of the heat

Virgin.—*A.V. ¹her.*
Mat. 1. 23. Behold, the virgin shall be with child
Lu. 1. 27. to a virgin betrothed—virgin's name was Mary
1 Cor. 7. 28. and if a virgin marry, she hath not sinned
34. is a difference also between the wife and the virgin
36. behaveth himself unseemly toward his v. daughter
37. to keep his own virgin daughter, shall do well
38. he that giveth his own ¹virgin daughter in marriage
2 Cor. 11. 2. I might present you as a pure virgin to Christ

Virginity.
Lu. 2. 36. with a husband seven years from her virginity

Virgins.
Mat. 25. 1. kingdom of heaven be likened unto ten virgins
7. Then all those v. arose, and trimmed their lamps
11. Afterward come also the other virgins, saying
Acts 21. 9. four daughters, virgins, which did prophesy
1 Cor. 7. 25. Now concerning v. I have no commandment
Rev. 14. 4. were not defiled with women ; for they are v.

Virtue.
Phil. 4. 8. if there be any virtue, and if there be any praise
2 Pet. 1. 3. him that called us by his own glory and virtue
5. in your faith supply virtue ; and in your v. knowledge
    see power.

Visible.
Col. 1. 16. things visible and things invisible, whether

Vision.
Mat. 17. 9. Tell the vision to no man, until the Son of man
Lu. 1. 22. perceived that he had seen a vision in the temple
24. 23. that they had also seen a vision of angels
Acts 9. 10. and the Lord said unto him in a vision, Ananias
10. 3. He [Cornelius] saw in a vision openly
17. Peter was much perplexed—what the vision. 19
11. 5. and in a trance I saw a vision, a certain vessel
12. 9. done by the angel, but thought he saw a vision
16. 9. And a vision appeared to Paul in the night. 10: 18. 9
26. 19. I was not disobedient unto the heavenly vision
Rev. 9. 17. And thus I saw the horses in the vision

Visions.
Acts 2. 17. And your young men shall see visions
2 Cor. 12. 1. I will come to v. and revelations of the Lord

Visit.—*A.V. ¹see, ²visited.*
Lu. 1. 78. Whereby the dayspring from on high shall ²visit
Acts 7. 23. it came into his heart to visit his brethren
15. 14. rehearsed how first God did visit the Gentiles
36. Let us return now and visit the brethren
Gal. 1. 18. I went up to Jerusalem to ¹visit Cephas
Jas. 1. 27. to v. the fatherless and widows in their affliction

VISITATION — VOYAGE

Visitation.
Lu. 19. 44. because thou knewest not the time of thy *v.*
1 *Pet.* 2. 12. glorify God in the day of *visitation*

Visited.
Mat. 25. 36. I was sick, and ye *visited* me
 43. sick, and in prison, and ye *visited* me not
Lu. 1. 68. For he hath *visited* and wrought redemption
 7. 16. arisen among us: and, God hath *visited* his people
  see visit.

Visitest—eth.—*A.V.* ¹*taketh vengeance.*
Rom. 3. 5. Is God unrighteous who ¹*visiteth* with wrath?
Heb. 2. 6. Or the son of man, that thou *visitest* him?

Vocation *A.V.*—*see calling.*

Voice.—*A.V.* ¹*cry,* ²*noise,* ³*sound.*
Mat. 3. 3. The *v.* of one crying. *Mk.* 1. 3: *Lu.* 3. 4: *Jno.* 1. 23
 3. 17. and lo, a *voice* out of the heavens. *Mk.* 1. 11: *Lu.* 3. 22
 12. 19. Neither shall any one hear his *v.* in the streets
 17. 5. a *voice* out of the cloud, saying. *Mk.* 9. 7: *Lu.* 9. 35
Lu. 1. 44. when the *v.* of thy salutation came into mine ears
 9. 36. when the *voice* came, Jesus was found alone
Jno. 3. 8. The wind bloweth—thou hearest the ³*v.* thereof
 29. rejoiceth greatly because of the bridegroom's *voice*
 5. 25. the dead shall hear the *voice* of the Son of God. 28
 10. 3. and the sheep hear his *voice.* 16, 27
  4. the sheep follow him: for they know his *voice*
  5. for they know not the *voice* of strangers
 12. 28. a *v.* out of heaven, saying, I have both glorified it
 30. This *voice* hath not come for my sake
 18. 37. Every one that is of the truth heareth my *voice*
Acts 9. 7. hearing the *voice,* but beholding no man
 10. 13. there came a *voice* to him, Rise, Peter. 11. 7
 15. And a *v.* came unto him again the second time. 11. 9
 12. 14. And when she [Rhoda] knew Peter's *voice*
 22. [Herod] The *voice* of a god, and not of a man
 19. 34. they perceived that he was a Jew, all with one *v.*
 22. 14. know his will—and to hear a *voice* from his mouth
 24. 21. except it be for this one *voice,* that I cried
1 *Cor.* 14. 7. Even things without life, giving a ³*voice*
 8. if the trumpet give an uncertain ³*v.,* who shall prepare
 11. If then I know not the meaning of the *voice*
1 *Th.* 4. 16. with a shout, with the *voice* of the archangel
Heb. 3. 15. To-day if ye shall hear his *voice.* 4. 7
 12. 19. sound of a trumpet, and the *voice* of words
 26. whose *voice* then shook the earth
2 *Pet.* 1. 17. such a *voice* to him from the excellent glory
 2. 16. a dumb ass spake with man's *voice* and stayed
Rev. 1. 12. I turned to see the *voice* which spake with me
 15. his *voice* as the ³*voice* of many waters. 14. 2
 3. 20. if any man hear my *voice* and open the door
 6. 1. I heard—saying as with a ²*voice* of thunder. 14. 2
 8. 13. an eagle—saying with a great *voice,* Woe, woe, woe
 10. 3. he cried with a great *voice,* as a lion roareth
 7. but in the days of the *voice* of the seventh angel
 14. 2. *voice* which I heard was as the *voice* of harpers
 18. with a great ¹*voice* to him that had the sharp sickle
 16. 17. there came forth a great *voice* out of the temple
 18. 2. And he cried with a mighty *voice,* saying, Fallen
 22. the ³*v.* of harpers and minstrels—³*v.* of a millstone
 19. 5. a *v.* came forth from the throne, saying, Give praise
 6. *v.* of a great multitude—*v.* of many waters—*v.* of mighty
  see cried, crying, lifted, loud, vote.

Voice, *with heard.*
Mat. 2. 18. A *voice* was *heard* in Ramah
Jno. 5. 37. Ye have neither *heard* his *voice* at any time

Acts 9. 4. and h. a *v.* saying unto him, Saul. 22. 7: 26. 14
 11. 7. I *heard* also a *voice* saying unto me, Rise, Peter
 22. 9. but they *heard* not the *voice* of him that spake
Heb. 12. 19. which *v.* they that *h.* intreated that no word
2 *Pet.* 1. 18. this *v.* we ourselves *h.* come out of heaven
Rev. 1. 10. I *heard* behind me a great *voice,* as of a trumpet
 5. 11. I *heard* a *v.* of many angels round about the throne
 6. 6. I *h.*—a *v.* in the midst of the four living creatures
 7. I *h.* the *v.* of the fourth living creature saying, Come
 9. 13. I *heard* a *voice* from the horns of the golden altar
 10. 4. *heard* a *voice* from heaven. 8: 11. 12: 14. 2, 13: 18. 4
 14. 2. I *h.* a *voice* from heaven—*v.* of many waters—*v.* of a
  great thunder—*v.* which I *h.* was as the *v.* of harpers
 16. 1. I *heard* a great *voice* out of the temple, saying
 19. 1. I *h.* as it were a great *voice* of a great multitude. 6
 21. 3. I *heard* a great *voice* out of the throne saying

Voice *of the Lord.*—*see Lord.*

Voices.
Lu. 23. 23. they were instant with loud *v.*—their *v.* prevailed
Acts 13. 27. they knew him not, nor the *v.* of the prophets
1 *Cor.* 14. 10. so many kinds of *voices* in the world
Rev. 4. 5. lightnings and *v.* and thunders. 8. 5: 11. 19: 16. 18
 8. 13. the other *voices* of the trumpet of the three angels
 10. 3. the seven thunders uttered their *voices.* 4
 11. 15. and there followed great *voices* in heaven
  see loud.

Void.—*A.V.* ¹*disannulleth,* ²*foolish,* ³*frustrate,* ⁴*impossible,* ⁵*none effect,* ⁶*vain.*
Mat. 15. 6. ye have made ⁵*void* the word of God. *Mk.* 7. ⁵13
Lu. 1. 37. For no word from God shall be ⁴*void* of power
Acts 24. 16. to have a conscience *void* of offence toward God
Rom. 4. 14. which are of the law be heirs, faith is made *v.*
 10. 19. With a nation ²*void* of understanding will I anger
1 *Cor.* 1. 17. lest the cross of Christ should be made ⁵*void*
 9. 15. than that any man should make my glorying *void*
2 *Cor.* 9. 3. our glorying on your behalf may not be made ⁶*v.*
Gal. 2. 21. I do not make ¹*void* the grace of God
 3. 15. no one maketh it ¹*void,* or addeth thereto
  see effect.

Volume *A.V.*—*see roll.*

Voluntary.
Col. 2. 18. by a *v.* humility and worshipping of the angels

Vomit.
2 *Pet.* 2. 22. The dog turning to his own *vomit* again

Vote.—*A.V.* ¹*voice.*
Acts 26. 10. put to death, I gave my ¹*vote* against them

Vouchsafed.—*A.V.* ¹*sworn.*
Acts 7. 17. promise drew nigh, which God ¹*vouchsafed*

Vow.
Acts 18. 18. for he [Paul] had a *vow*
 21. 23. We have four men which have a *vow* on them

Voyage.—*A.V.* ¹*course,* ²*sailing.*
Acts 21. 7. when we had finished the ¹*voyage* from Tyre
 27. 9. the ²*voyage* was now dangerous, because the Fast
 10. I perceive that the *voyage* will be with injury

WAGES

W.

Wages.
Lu. 3. 14. and be content with your *wages*
Jno. 4. 36. He that reapeth receiveth *wages*
Rom. 6. 23. For the *wages* of sin is death
2 *Cor.* 11. 8. I robbed other churches, taking *w.* of them
see hire.

Wagging.
Mat. 27. 39. railed on him, *wagging* their heads. *Mk.* 15. 29

Wail—ed.—*A.V.* ¹*lament,* ²*mourned.*
Mat. 11. 17. we ²*wailed,* and ye did not mourn
Lu. 7. 32. we ²*wailed,* and ye did not weep ⌐over her
Rev. 18. 9. lived wantonly with her, shall weep and ¹*wail*
see mourn, wailing.

Wailing.—*A.V.* ¹*wailed.*
Mk. 5. 38. and many weeping and ¹*wailing* greatly
see mourning, weeping.

Wait.—*A.V.* ¹*look,* ²*tarried,* ³*tarry.*
Mk. 3. 9. that a little boat should *wait* on him
Acts 1. 4. but to *wait* for the promise of the Father
23. 21. there lie in *wait* for him—more than forty men
27. 33. fourteenth day that ye ²*wait* and continue fasting
Rom. 8. 25. then do we with patience *wait* for it
1 *Cor.* 9. 13. they which *w.* upon the altar have their portion
11. 33. ye come together to eat, ⁶*wait* one for another
Gal. 5. 5. by faith *wait* for the hope of righteousness
Phil. 3. 20. from whence also we ¹*wait* for a Saviour
1 *Th.* 1. 10. and to *wait* for his Son from heaven
Heb. 9. 28. to them that ¹*wait* for him, unto salvation
see laying, looking, plot.

Waited.
Acts 10. 7. devout soldier of them that *w.* on him continually
17. 16. Now while Paul *waited* for them at Athens
1 *Pet.* 3. 20. longsuffering of God *w.* in the days of Noah
see looking, waiting.

Waiteth.
Rom. 8. 19. creation *w.* for the revealing of the sons of God
Jas. 5. 7. *waiteth* for the precious fruit of the earth

Waiting.—*A.V.* ¹*tarried,* ²*waited.*
Lu. 1. 21. And the people were ³*waiting* for Zacharias
8. 40. welcomed him; for they were all *waiting* for him
Acts 10. 24. And Cornelius was ²*waiting* for them
20. 5. and were ¹*waiting* for us at Troas
Rom. 8. 23. groan within ourselves, *w.* for our adoption
1 *Cor.* 1. 7. *w.* for the revelation of our Lord Jesus Christ
see looking.

Wake.
1 *Th.* 5. 10. whether we *wake* or sleep, we should live

Walk.—*A.V.* ¹*walked.*
Mat. 9. 5. Arise, and *walk?* *Mk.* 2. 9; *Lu.* 5. 23; *Jno.* 5.
8, 11, 12; *Acts* 3. 6   [*Lu.* 7. 22
11. 5. the blind receive their sight, and the lame *walk.*
Mk. 7. 5. Why *w.* not thy disciples according to the tradition
Lu. 1. 17. the disobedient to *w.* in the wisdom of the just
11. 44. and the men that *walk* over them know it not
20. 46. scribes, which desire to *walk* in long robes

WALKEDST

Lu. 21. 17. What communications are these that ye have
one with another, as ye *walk?*
Jno. 7. 1. for he would not *w.* in Judæa, because the Jews
8. 12. he that followeth me shall not *w.* in the darkness
11. 9. If a man *walk* in the day, he stumbleth not
10. But if a man *walk* in the night, he stumbleth
12. 35, 17. while ye have the light, that darkness overtake
Acts 3. 8. And leaping up, he stood, and began to ¹*walk*
12. own power or godliness we had made him to *walk?*
14. 16. suffered all the nations to *walk* in their own ways
21. 21. their children, neither to *walk* after the customs
Rom. 4. 12. of the circumcision, but who also *w.* in the steps
6. 4. so we also might *walk* in newness of life
8. 4. who *walk* not after the flesh, but after the spirit
13. 13. Let us *walk* honestly, as in the day
1 *Cor.* 7. 17. as God hath called each, so let him *walk*
2 *Cor.* 5. 7. (for we *walk* by faith, not by sight)
6. 16. as God said, I will dwell in them, and *w.* in them
10. 3. For though we *walk* in the flesh, we do not war
Gal. 5. 16. But I say, *Walk* by the Spirit. 25
6. 16. And as many as shall *walk* by this rule, peace be
Eph. 2. 10. God afore prepared that we should *w.* in them
4. 1. beseech you to *walk* worthily of the calling
17. that ye no longer *walk* as the Gentiles also *walk*
5. 2. *walk* in love, even as Christ also loved you
8. are now light in the Lord: *walk* as children of light
15. Look therefore carefully how ye *w.*, not as unwise
Phil. 3. 16. already attained, by that same rule let us *walk*
17. and mark them which so *walk* even as ye have us
18. For many *walk,* of whom I told you often
Col. 1. 10. to *walk* worthily of the Lord. 1. *Th.* 2. 12
2. 6. received Christ Jesus the Lord, so *walk* in him
4. 5. *Walk* in wisdom toward them that are without
1 *Th.* 4. 1. ought to *w.* and to please God, even as ye do *w.*
12. ye may *walk* honestly toward them that are without
2 *Th.* 3. 11. hear of some that *walk* among you disorderly
2 *Pet.* 2. 10. but chiefly them that *walk* after the flesh
1 *Jno.* 1. 6. fellowship with him, and *walk* in the darkness
7. but if we *walk* in the light, as he is in the light
2. 6. ought himself also to *walk* even as he walked
2 *Jno.* 6. *walk* after his commandments—ye should *w.* in it
Rev. 3. 4. and they shall *walk* with me in white
9. 20. which can neither see, nor hear, nor *walk*
16. 15. and keepeth his garments, lest he *walk* naked
21. 24. And the nations shall *w.* amidst the light thereof
see walking, way.

Walked.
Mat. 14. 29. Peter—*w.* upon the waters, to come to Jesus
Mk. 5. 42. straightway the damsel rose up, and *walked*
16. 12. as they *walked,* on their way into the country
Jno. 1. 36. [John] looked upon Jesus as he *walked*
5. 9. made whole, and took up his bed and *walked*
6. 66. disciples went back, and *walked* no more with him
7. 1. And after these things Jesus *walked* in Galilee
11. 54. Jesus therefore *walked* no more openly
Acts 14. 8. from his mother's womb, who never had *w.*
10. And he leaped up and *walked*
2 *Cor.* 10. 2. as if we *walked* according to the flesh
12. 18. *walked* we not by the same Spirit? *walked* we
not in the same steps?
Gal. 2. 14. But when I saw that they *walked* not uprightly
E ph. 2. 2. ye *walked* according to the course of this world
1 *Pet.* 4. 3. and to have *w.* in lasciviousness. *Col.* 3. 7
1 *Jno.* 2. 6. ought himself also to walk even as he *walked*
see walk.

Walkedst, Walkest.
Jno. 21. 18. and *walkedst* whither thou wouldest

366

WALKEDST

Acts 21. 24. but that thou thyself also *walkest* orderly
Rom. 14. 15. thou *walkest* no longer in love
3 *John* 3. even as thou *walkest* in truth

Walketh.

Jno. 12. 35. that *walketh* in the darkness. 1 *Jno.* 2. 11
2 *Th.* 3. 6. from every brother that *walketh* disorderly
1 *Pet.* 5. 8. the devil, as a roaring lion, *walketh* about
Rev. 2. 1. he that *w.* in the midst of the seven golden
see passeth.

Walking.—A.V. ¹*walk.*

Mat. 4. 18. And *walking* by the sea of Galilee, he saw two
14. 25. [Jesus] *w.* upon the sea. 26. *Mk.* 6. 48, 49:
15. 31. the lame ¹*walking*, and the blind seeing [*Jno.*6. 19
Mk. 8. 24. I see men ; for I behold them as trees, *walking*
11. 27. as he was *w.* in the temple, there come to him
Lu. 1. 6. before God, *walking* in all the commandments
Acts 3. 8. with them into the temple, *w.*, and leaping. 9
9. 31. and, *walking* in the fear of the Lord, and in the
2*Cor.* 4. 2. not *walking* in craftiness, nor handling the word
2 *Pet.* 3. 3. *walking* after their own lusts. *Jude* 16, ¹18
2 *Jno.* 4. thy children *walking* in truth. 3 *Jno.* ¹4

Wall—s.

Acts 9. 25. down through the *w.*, lowering him in a basket
23. 3. God shall smite thee, thou whited *w.* [2 *Cor.* 11. 33
Eph. 2. 14. brake down the middle *wall* of partition
Heb. 11. 30. By faith the *walls* of Jericho fell down
Rev. 21. 14. the *w.* of the city had twelve foundations
17. And he measured the *wall* thereof
18. And the building of the *wall* thereof was jasper

Wallet.—A.V. ¹*scrip.*

*Mat.*10.10. no ¹*w.* for your journey. *Mk.*6. ¹8: *Lu.*9.¹3: 10.¹4
Lu. 22.35. When I sent you forth without purse, and ¹*wallet*
36. now—let him take it, and likewise a ¹*wallet*

Wallowed.

Mk. 9. 20. fell on the ground, and *wallowed* foaming

Wallowing.

2 *Pet.* 2. 22. the sow that had washed to *w.* in the mire

Wandered *A.V.—see wandering, went.*

Wandering.—A.V. ¹*wandered.*

Heb. 11. 38. ¹*wandering* in deserts and mountains
Jude 13. foaming out their own shame ; *wandering* stars
see going.

Want—s.—A.V. ¹*need,* ²*penury,* ³*want,* ⁴*wanted.*

Mk. 12. 44. but she of her *w.* did cast in all that she had.
Lu. 15. 14. famine—and he began to be in *w.* [*Lu.* 21. ²4
2 *Cor.* 8. 14. supply at this present time for their *w.*,that their
abundance also may become a supply for your *w.*
9. 12. filleth up the measure of the ³*wants* of the saints
11. 9. was in ⁴*want*—supplied the measure of my *want*
Phil. 4. 11. Not that I speak in respect of *want*
12. learned the secret,—both to abound and to be in ¹*w.*
see need.

Wanted *A.V.—see failed, wants.*

Wanting.

Tit. 1. 5. shouldest set in order the things that were *w.*
3. 13. that nothing be *wanting* unto them
see lacking.

WARNED

Wanton.—A.V. ¹*deliciously.*

1 *Tim.* 5. 11. when they have waxed *wanton* against Christ
Rev. 18. 7. she glorified herself, and waxed ¹*wanton*

Wantonly.—A.V. ¹*deliciously.*

Rev. 18. 9. kings—lived ¹*w.* with her, shall weep and wail

Wantonness.—A.V. ¹*delicacies.*

Rom. 13. 13. not in chambering and *wantonness*
Rev. 18. 3. waxed rich by the power of her ¹*wantonness*
see lasciviousness.

War.—A.V. ¹*battle,* ²*fight,* ³*fought.*

Lu. 14. 31. king, as he goeth to encounter another king in *w.*
1 *Cor.* 14. 8. an uncertain voice, who shall prepare himself
2 *Cor.* 10. 3. we do not *war* according to the flesh [for ¹*war* ?
1 *Tim.* 1. 18. that by them thou mayest *w.* the good warfare
Heb. 11. 34. waxed mighty in ²*war*, turned to flight armies
Jas. 4. 1. even of your pleasures that *w.* in your members ?
2. ye fight and *war* ; ye have not, because ye ask not
1 *Pet.* 2. 11. from fleshly lusts, which *w.* against the soul
Rev. 2. 16. I will make ²*war* against them with the sword
9. 7. locusts were like unto horses prepared for ¹*war*
9. sound of their wings—of many horses rushing to ¹*w.*
11. 7. the beast—shall make *war* with them [to ³*war*
12. 7. *war* in heaven : Michael and his angels going forth
17. went away to make *war* with the rest of her seed
13. 4. unto the beast? and who is able to *war* with him ?
7. given unto him to make *war* with the saints
16. 14. to gather them together unto the ¹*w.* of the great
17. 14. These shall *war* against the Lamb [day
19. 11. in righteousness he doth judge and make *war*
19. to make *war* against him that sat upon the horse
20. 8. Gog and Magog, to gather them together to the ¹*w.*
see encounter.

Men of War.—*see soldiers.*

Ward.—A.V. ¹*hold,* ²*prison.*

Acts 4. 3. on them, and put them in ¹*w.* unto the morrow
5. 18. the apostles, and put them in public ²*ward*
12. 10. when they were past the first and the second *w.*

Ware.

2 *Tim.* 4. 15. of whom be thou *ware* also
see aware, worn.

Warfare.

2 *Cor.* 10. 4. (for the weapons of our *w.* are not of the flesh
1 *Tim.* 1. 18. by them thou mayest war the good *warfare*
see serveth.

Warmed.

Jas. 2. 16. Go in peace, be ye *warmed* and filled
see earning.

Warming.—A.V. ¹*warmed.*

Mk. 14. 54. and ¹*warming* himself in the light of the fire
67. and seeing Peter *warming* himself. *Jno.* 18. ¹18, ¹25

Warn.—A.V. ¹*forewarn.*

Lu. 12. 5. I will ¹*warn* you whom ye shall fear
see admonish.

Warned.—A.V. ¹*admonished,* ²*spake.*

Mat. 2. 12. And being *warned* of God in a dream. 22
3. 7. who *w.* you to flee from the wrath to come ? *Lu.* 3. 7
Acts 10. 22. was *warned* of God by a holy angel to send

WARNED

Heb. 8. 5. even as Moses is ¹warned of God when he is
11. 7. By faith Noah, being warned of God when he is
12. 25. they refused him that ²warned them on earth

Warneth.—A.V. ¹speaketh.
Heb. 12. 25. turn away from him that ¹w. from heaven

Warning A.V.—see admonishing.

Warred.—A.V. ¹fought.
Rev. 12. 7. and the dragon ¹warred and his angels

Warring.
Rom. 7. 23. warring against the law of my mind

Wars.
Mat. 24. 6. And ye shall hear of wars and rumours of wars. Mk. 13. 7: Lu. 21. 9
Jas. 4. 1. Whence come wars and whence come fightings

Wash.—A.V. ¹do his commandments.
Mat. 6. 17. fastest, anoint thy head, and wash thy face
15. 2. for they w. not their hands when they eat bread
Mk. 7. 3. except they wash their hands diligently. 4
Jno. 9. 7. Go, wash in the pool of Siloam. 11
13. 8. If I wash thee not, thou hast no part with me
Acts 22. 16. arise, and be baptized, and wash away thy sins
Rev. 22. 14. Blessed are they that ¹wash their robes
see feet.

Washed.
Mat. 27. 24. Pilate—washed his hands before the multitude
Lu. 11. 38. marvelled that he had not first w. before dinner
Jno. 9. 7. He went away therefore, and w., and came seeing.
Acts 9. 37. [Dorcas] died: and when they had w. her 11, 15.
16. 33. same hour of the night, and washed their stripes
1 Cor. 6. 11. but ye were washed, but ye were sanctified
Heb. 10. 22. and our body washed with pure water
2 Pet. 2. 22. and the sow that had washed to wallowing
Rev. 7. 14. they washed their robes, and made them white
see bathed, feet, loosed.

Washing—s.—A.V. ¹washing.
Mk. 7. 4. ¹washings of cups, and pots, and brasen vessels
Lu. 5. 2. gone out of them, and were washing their nets
Eph. 5. 26. cleansed it by the w. of water with the word
Tit. 3. 5. he saved us, through the washing of regeneration
Heb. 9. 10. (with meats and drinks and divers washings)

Waste.—A.V. ¹havock.
Mat. 26. 8. To what purpose is this waste? Mk. 14. 4
Acts 8. 3. Saul laid ¹w. the church, entering into every house

Wasted—ing.—A.V. ¹wasted.
Lu. 15. 13. far country; and there he wasted his substance
16. 1. accused unto him that he was ¹wasting his goods
see havock.

Watch.
Mat. 14. 25. And in the fourth watch of the night. Mk. 6. 48
24. 42. W. therefore. 25. 13: Mk. 13. 35: Lu. 21. 36: Acts
43. known in what watch the thief was coming 20. 31
26. 38. abide ye here, and watch with me. Mk. 14. 34
40. could ye not watch with me one hour? Mk. 14. 37
41. Watch and pray. Mk. 13. 33: 14. 38
Mk. 13. 34. commanded also the porter to watch. 35, 37
Lu. 2. 8. and keeping watch by night over their flock
12. 38. And if he shall come in the second watch

WATER

1 Cor. 16. 13. W. ye, stand fast in the faith, quit you like men
1 Th. 5. 6. let us not sleep—but let us watch and be sober
Heb. 13. 17. for they watch in behalf of your souls
Rev. 3. 3. If therefore thou shalt not w., I will come as a thief
see guard, sober, watching.

Watched.
Mat. 24. 43. he would have watched. Lu. 12. 39
27. 36. and they sat and watched him there
Mk. 3. 2. And they watched him. Lu. 6. 7
Lu. 20. 20. And they watched him, and sent forth spies
Acts 9. 24. they watched the gates also day and night
see watching.

Watchers.—A.V. ¹keepers.
Mat. 28. 4. for fear of him the ¹watchers did quake

Watcheth.
Rev. 16. 15. Blessed is he that watcheth

Watchful.—A.V. ¹vigilant.
1 Pet. 5. 8. Be sober, be ¹w.: your adversary the devil
Rev. 3. 2. Be thou w., and establish the things that remain

Watching.—A.V. ¹watch, ²watched.
Mat. 27. 54. watching Jesus, when they saw the earthquake
Lu. 12. 37. the lord when he cometh shall find watching
14. 1. on a sabbath to eat bread, that they were ²w. him
Eph. 6. 18. and watching thereunto in all perseverance
Col. 4. 2. in prayer, ¹watching therein with thanksgiving

Watchings.
2 Cor. 6. 5. in labours, in watchings, in fastings
11. 27. in watchings often, in hunger and thirst

Water.
Mat. 3. 11. I indeed baptize you with water unto repentance. Mk. 1. 8: Lu. 3. 16: Jno. 1. 26, 31, 33
16. went up straightway from the water. Mk. 1. 10 [41
10. 42. one of these little ones a cup of cold w. only. Mk. 9.
17. 15. he falleth into the fire, and oft-times into the w.
27. 24. Pilate—took water, and washed his hands
Mk. 14. 13. a man bearing a pitcher of water. Lu. 22. 10
Lu. 7. 44. thou gavest me no water for my feet
8. 23. and they were filling with w., and were in jeopardy
24. rebuked the wind and the raging of the water
25. even the winds and the water, and they obey him?
16. 24. Lazarus, that he may dip the tip of his finger in w.
Jno. 2. 7. Fill the waterpots with water [knew
9. ruler of the feast tasted the water—drawn the water
3. 5. Except a man be born of water and the Spirit
23. Ænon near to Salim, because there was much w.
4. 10. he would have given thee living water. 11, 15
13. Every one that drinketh of this w. shall thirst
14. drinketh of the water—water that I shall give—a well of water springing up unto eternal life
46. Cana of Galilee, where he made the water wine
5. 4. at certain seasons into the pool, and troubled the water—after the troubling of the water [margin
7. Sir, I have no man, when the water is troubled
7. 38. out of his belly shall flow rivers of living water
13. 5. Then he poureth water into the bason
19. 34. straightway there came out blood and water
Acts 1. 5. for John indeed baptized with water. 11, 16
8. 36. they came unto a certain water—Behold, here is w.
38. and they both went down into the water. 39
10. 47. Can any man forbid the water, that these should
Eph. 5. 26. cleansed it by the washing of w. with the word
Heb. 9. 19. blood of the calves and the goats, with water
10. 22. and our body washed with pure water

WATER

Jas. 3. 11. from the same opening sweet w. and bitter ?
1 Pet. 3. 20. eight souls, were saved through water
2 Pet. 2. 17. These are springs without water, and mists
3. 5. and an earth compacted out of w. and amidst w.
6. the world—being overflowed with water, perished
1 Jno. 5. 6. This is he that came by water and blood—
    water only, but with the water and with the blood
8. who bear witness, the Spirit, and the w., and the blood
Jude 12. clouds without water, carried along by winds
Rev. 12. 15. of his mouth after the woman water as a river
16. 12. Euphrates ; and the water thereof was dried up
22. 1. And he shewed me a river of water of life
17. let him take the water of life freely. 21. 6
    see waters.

Bitter Water—Draw Water—Drink Water.—see
    bitter, draw, drink.

Watered—eth.

1 Cor. 3. 6. I planted, Apollos w.; but God gave the increase
7. neither he that watereth; but God that giveth. 8

Watering.

Lu. 13. 15. from the stall, and lead him away to watering ?

Waterless.—A.V. ¹dry.

Mat. 12. 43. passeth through ¹waterless places. Lu. 11. 24

Waterpot—s.

Jno. 2. 6. Now there were six waterpots of stone set there
7. Jesus saith unto them, Fill the waterpots with water
4. 28. So the woman left her waterpot, and went away

Waters.—A.V. ¹water.

Mat. 8. 32. into the sea, and perished in the waters
14. 28. bid me come unto thee upon the ¹waters
29. Peter—walked upon the ¹waters, to come to Jesus
Mk. 9. 22. into the fire and into the waters, to destroy him
Rev. 1. 15. and his voice as the voice of many waters
7. 17. shall guide them unto fountains of waters of life
8. 10. part of the rivers, and upon the fountains of the w.
11. third part of the waters—men died of the waters
11. 6. power over the waters to turn them into blood
14. 2. as the voice of many waters, and as the voice of a
7. heaven and the earth and sea and fountains of waters
16. 4. howl into the rivers and the fountains of the w.
5. I heard the angel of the waters saying, Righteous
17. 1. the great harlot that sitteth upon many waters
15. The waters which thou sawest, where the harlot
    see rivers.

Wave A.V.—*see surge.*

Waver.—A.V. ¹without wavering.

Heb. 10. 23. the confession of our hope that it ¹waver not

Wavered.—A.V. ¹staggered.

Rom. 4. 20. he [Abraham] ¹wavered not through unbelief

Wavereth A.V.—*see doubteth.*

Wavering A.V.—*see doubting, waver.*

Waves.

Mat. 8. 24. insomuch that the boat was covered with the w.
14. 24. distressed by the waves; for the wind was contrary
Mk. 4. 37. storm of wind, and the waves beat into the boat
Acts 27. 41. the stern began to break up by the violence of
Jude 13. wild waves of the sea, foaming out | the waves
    see billows.

WAY

Wax.—A.V. ¹be wearied.

Mat. 24. 12. the love of the many shall wax cold
Lu. 12. 33. make for yourselves purses which wax not old
2 Tim. 3. 13. But evil men and impostors shall wax worse
Heb. 1. 11. And they all shall wax old as doth a garment
12. 3. that ye ¹wax not weary, fainting in your souls
    see waxed.

Waxed.—A.V. ¹lived, ²was, ³wax, ⁴were.

Mat. 13. 15. For this people's heart is w. gross. Acts 28. 27
Lu. 1. 80. And the child grew, and w. strong in spirit. 2. 40
Rom. 4. 20. ²w. strong through faith, giving glory to God
1 Th. 2. 2. at Philippi, we ⁴waxed bold in our God
1 Tim. 5. 11. for when they have ³w. wanton against Christ
Heb. 11. 34. waxed mighty in war, turned to flight armies
Rev. 18. 3. and the merchants of the earth waxed rich
17. she glorified herself, and ¹waxed wanton

Waxeth.—A.V. ¹is.

Eph. 4. 22. which ¹waxeth corrupt after the lusts of deceit
Heb. 8. 13. and waxeth aged is nigh unto vanishing away

Waxing A.V.—*see being.*

Way.—A.V. ¹concerning, ²forth, ³highway, ⁴walk.

Mat. 2. 12. they departed into their own country another w.
5. 25. whiles thou art with him in the way
7. 13. and broad is the way, that leadeth to destruction
14. and straitened the way, that leadeth unto life
8. 28. so that no man could pass by that way
10. 5. Go not into any way of the Gentiles
11. 10. shall prepare thy w. before thee. Mk. 1. 2: Lu. 7. 27
13. 4. as he sowed some seeds fell by the way side. 19:
    Mk. 4. 4, 15: Lu. 8. 5, 12
20. 30. two blind men sitting by the way side. Mk. 10. 46
21. 8. their garments in the way—spread them in the
    way. Mk. 11. 8 ; Lu. 19. 36
19. seeing a fig tree by the way side, he came to it
32. For John came unto you in the way of righteousness
22. 16. and teachest the way of God in truth. Mk. 12. 14 :
Mk. 8. 3. they will faint in the way   [Lu. 20. 21
27. and in the w. he asked his disciples, saying unto them
9. 33. What were ye reasoning in the way ?   [9. 57
10. 32. they were in the way, going up. Mat. 20. 17 : Lu.
Lu. 1. 79. To guide our feet into the way of peace
5. 14. go thy way, and shew thyself to the priest
19. And not finding by what way they might bring him
8. 14. as they go on their ²way they are choked
10. 4. and salute no man on the way
31. a certain priest was going down that way
13. 33. I must go on my ⁴way to-day and to-morrow
14. 32. is yet a great way off, he sendeth an ambassage
18. 35. a certain blind man sat by the way side begging
19. 4. tree to see him : for he was to pass that way
21. 32. burning within us, while he spake to us in the w. 35
Jno. 10. 1. of the sheep, but climbeth up some other way
14. 4. And whither I go, ye know the way
5. Thomas saith unto him—how know we the way ?
6. I am the way, and the truth, and the life
Acts 9. 2. that if he found any that were of the Way
17. even Jesus, who appeared unto thee in the way
27. unto them how he had seen the Lord in the way
15. 3. therefore, being brought on their way. 16. 4
16. 17. which proclaim unto you the way of salvation
18. 26. expounded unto him the w. of God more carefully
19. 9. speaking evil of the Way before the multitude
23. there arose no small stir concerning the Way
22. 4. I persecuted this Way unto the death
24. 14. that after the Way which they call a sect

WAY

Acts 24. 22. Felix, having more exact knowledge concerning
Rom. 3, 2. Much every *way* : first of all [the *Way*
17. And the *way* of peace have they not known
14. 13. no man put a stumblingblock in his brother's *w.*
15. 24. to be brought on my *way* thitherward by you
1 *Cor.* 10. 13. with the temptation make also the *w.* of escape
12. 31. And a still more excellent *way* shew I unto you
16. 7. For I do not wish to see you now by the *way*
2 *Cor.* 11. 21. I speak by ¹*way* of disparagement
Phil. 1. 18. only that in every *way*, whether in pretence or
Col. 2. 14. hath taken it out of the *w.*, nailing it to the cross
1 *Th.* 3. 11. and our Lord Jesus, direct our *way* unto you
2 *Th.* 2. 7. restraineth now, until he be taken out of the *w.*
Heb. 9. 8. the *w.* into the holy place hath not yet been made
10. 20. *way* which he dedicated for us, a new and living *w.*
12. 13. that which is lame be not turned out of the *way*
Jas. 2. 25. messengers, and sent them out another *way* ?
5. 20. which converteth a sinner from the error of his *w.*
2 *Pet.* 2. 2. the *way* of the truth shall be evil spoken of
15. forsaking the right *way*—followed the *way* of Balaam
21. not to have known the *way* of righteousness
Jude 11. Woe unto them! for they went in the *w.* of Cain
Rev. 16. 12. that the *way* might be made ready for the kings
see afar, away, erring, journey, toward, turned.

Way *of the Lord A.V.—see Lord.*

Ways.—*A.V.* ¹*means.*

Lu. 1. 76. before the face of the Lord to make ready his *w.*
3. 5. shall become straight, And the rough *ways* smooth
Acts 2. 28. Thou madest known unto me the *ways* of life
14. 16. suffered all the nations to walk in their own *ways*
Rom. 3. 16. Destruction and misery are in their *ways*
11. 33. his judgements, and his *ways* past tracing out!
1 *Cor.* 4. 17. who shall put you in remembrance of my *ways*
2 *Th.* 3. 16. give you peace at all times in all ¹*ways*
Heb. 3. 10. But they did not know my *ways*
Jas. 1. 8. a doubleminded man, unstable in all his *ways*
Rev. 15. 3. righteous and true are thy *ways*, thou King
see doings, goings.

Weak.—*A.V.* ¹*without strength.*

Mat. 26. 41. but the flesh is *weak. Mk.* 14. 38
Acts 20. 35. so labouring ye ought to help the *weak*
Rom. 5. 6. we were yet ¹*weak*, in due season Christ died
8. 3. could not do, in that it was *weak* through the flesh
14. 1. But him that is *weak* in faith receive ye
2. faith to eat all things; but he that is *w.* eateth herbs
15. 1. strong ought to bear the infirmities of the *weak*
1 *Cor.* 1. 27. and God chose the *weak* things of the world
4. 10. we are *weak*, but ye are strong
8. 7. and their conscience being *weak* is defiled
10. conscience, if he is *w.*, be emboldened to eat things
11. For through thy knowledge he that is *w.* perisheth
12. and wounding their conscience when it is *weak*
9. 22. To the *weak* I became weak—gain the *weak*
11. 30. For this cause many among you are *w.* and sickly
2 *Cor.* 10. 10. but his bodily presence is *weak*
11. 21. of disparagement, as though we had been *weak*
29. Who is *weak*, and I am not *weak* ?
12. 10. for when I am *weak*, then am I strong
13. 3. who to you-ward is not *weak*, but is powerful in you
4. For we are *w.* in him, but we shall live with him
9. For we rejoice, when we are *weak*, and ye are strong
Gal. 4. 9. how turn ye back again to the *weak*—rudiments
1 *Th.* 5. 14. support the *weak*, be longsuffering toward all
see weakened.

WEEK

Weakened.—*A.V.* ¹*weak.*

Rom. 4. 19. being ¹*w.* in faith he considered his own body

Weaker.

1 *Pet.* 3. 7. honour unto the woman, as unto the *w.* vessel

Weakness.—*A.V.* ¹*infirmities.*

1 *Cor.* 1. 25. and the *weakness* of God is stronger than men
2. 3. And I was with you in *weakness*, and in fear
15. 43. it is sown in *weakness* ; it is raised in power
2 *Cor.* 11. 30. I will glory of the things that concern my ¹*w.*
12. 9. for my power is made perfect in *weakness*
13. 4. for he was crucified through *weakness*
Heb. 7. 18. because of its *weakness* and unprofitableness
11. 34. from *weakness* were made strong

Weaknesses.—*A.V.* ¹*infirmities.*

2 *Cor.* 12. 9. Most gladly—will I rather glory in my ¹*w.* 15
10. Wherefore I take pleasure in *weaknesses*

Wealth.

Acts 19. 25. ye know that by this business we have our *w.*
see good.

Weapons.

Jno. 18. 3. thither with lanterns and torches and *weapons*
2 *Cor.* 10. 4. (for the *w.* of our warfare are not of the flesh

Wear.—*A.V.* ¹*weary.*

Mat. 11. 8. they that *wear* soft raiment are in kings' houses
Lu. 9. 12. And the day began to *wear* away
18. 5. lest she ¹*wear* me out by her continual coming

Weareth.

Jas. 2. 3. ye have regard to him that *w.* the fine clothing

Wearied.

Jno. 4. 6. Jesus therefore, being *wearied* with his journey
see weary.

Wearing.

Jno. 19. 5. Jesus therefore came out, *w.* the crown of thorns
1 *Pet.* 3. 3. plaiting the hair, and of *wearing* jewels of gold

Weariness *A.V.—see labour.*

Weary.—*A.V.* ¹*fainted,* ²*wearied.*

Gal. 6. 9. let us not be *weary* in well-doing. 2 *Th.* 3. 13
Heb. 12. 3. that ye wax not ²*weary*, fainting in your souls
Rev. 2. 3. for my name's sake, and hast not grown ¹*weary*
see wear.

Weather.

Mat. 16. 2. It will be fair *weather* : for the heaven is red
3. in the morning, It will be foul *weather* to-day

Wedding—Wedding-garment.

Mat. 22. 8. The *wedding* is ready, but they that were bidden
10. and the *wedding* was filled with guests
11. he saw there a man which had not on a *w.-garment*
12. how camest thou in hither not having a *w.-garment* ?
see marriage.

Week.

Mat. 28. 1. began to dawn toward the first day of the *w.*
Mk. 16. 2, 9; *Lu.* 24. 1; *Jno.* 20. 1, 19; *Acts* 20. 7;
Lu. 18. 12. I fast twice in the *week* [1 *Cor.* 16. 2

WEEP

Weep.—*A.V.* ¹*bewail,* ²*wept.*
Mk. 5. 39. Why make ye a tumult, and *weep* ?
Lu. 6. 21. Blessed are ye that *weep* now: for ye shall laugh
  25. ye that laugh now ! for ye shall mourn and *weep*
  7. 13. had compassion on her, and said unto her, *W.* not
  32. we wailed, and ye did not ²*weep*
  8. 52. *Weep* not ; for she is not dead, but sleepeth
  23. 28. *weep* not for me, but *weep* for yourselves
Jno. 11. 31. that she was going unto the tomb to *weep* there
  16. 20. I say unto you, that ye shall *weep* and lament
Rom. 12. 15. *weep* with them that *weep*
1 *Cor.* 7. 30. and those that *weep,* as though they wept not
Jas. 4. 9. Be afflicted, and mourn, and *weep*
  5. 1. Go to now, ye rich, *weep* and howl for your miseries
Rev. 5. 5. one of the elders saith unto me, *Weep* not
  18. 9. kings of the earth—shall ¹*weep* and wail over her
  11. merchants of the earth *weep* and mourn over her
            see weeping.

Weepest.
Jno. 20. 13. Woman, why *weepest* thou ? 15

Weeping.—*A.V.* ¹*wailing,* ²*weep,* ³*wept.*
Mat. 2. 18. *Weeping* and great mourning, Rachel *weeping*
  8. 12. there shall be the *weeping* and gnashing of teeth.
  13. ¹42, ¹50: 22. 13 : 24. 51 : 25. 30 : *Lu.* 13. 28
Lu. 7. 38. *weeping,* she began to wet his feet with her tears
  8. 52. all were ³*weeping,* and bewailing her. *Mk.* 5. ³38
Jno. 11. 33. Jesus therefore saw her *weeping*—Jews also *w.*
  20. 11. But Mary was standing without at the tomb *w.*
Acts 9. 39. and all the widows stood by him *weeping*
  21. 13. What do ye, ²*weeping* and breaking my heart ?
Phil. 3. 18. I told you often, and now tell you even *weeping*
Rev. 18. 15. fear of her torment, ¹*weeping* and mourning. 19

Weighed.—*A.V.* ¹*covenanted,* ²*pressed.*
Mat. 26. 15. they ¹*weighed* unto him thirty pieces of silver
2 *Cor.* 1. 8. we were ²*weighed* down exceedingly

Weighed Anchor.—*A.V.* ¹*loosing thence.*
Acts 27. 13. they ¹*weighed anchor* and sailed along Crete

Weight.
2 *Cor.* 4. 17. more exceedingly an eternal *weight* of glory
Heb. 12. 1. lay aside every *weight,* and the sin which doth
Rev. 16. 21. every stone about the *weight* of a talent

Weightier.
Mat. 23. 23. and have left undone the *w.* matters of the law

Weighty.
2 *Cor.* 10. 10. His letters, they say, are *weighty* and strong

Welcome—d.—*A.V.* ¹*receive,* ²*received.*
Lu. 8. 40. Jesus returned, the multitude *welcomed* him
  9. 11. he ²*welcomed* them and spake to them of the
3 *Jno.* 8. We ought therefore to ¹*welcome* such

Well—s.
Jno. 4. 6. and Jacob's *well* was there—sat thus by the *w.*
  11. thou hast nothing to draw with, and the *w.* is deep
  12. greater than our father Jacob, which gave us the *w.*
  14. shall become in him a *well* of water springing up
            see springs.

Well (adverb).
Mat. 15. 7. *w.* did Isaiah prophesy of you, saying. *Mk.* 7. 6
  25. 21. *W.* done, good and faithful servant. 23 : *Lu.* 19. 17

WENT

Mk. 7. 37. He hath done all things *well :* he maketh even
  12. 28. and knowing that he had answered them *well*
Lu. 6. 26. Woe unto you, when all men shall speak *w.* of you !
  13. 9. and if it bear fruit thenceforth, *well ;* but if not
  20. 39. Master, thou hast *well* said
Jno. 4. 17. Thou saidst *well,* I have no husband
  8. 48. Say we not *well* that thou art a Samaritan
  13. 13. Ye call me, Master, and, Lord : and ye say *well*
  18. 23. but if *well,* why smitest thou me ?
Acts 15. 29. if ye keep yourselves it shall be *well* with you !
  28. 25. *Well* spake the Holy Ghost by Isaiah the prophet
1 *Cor.* 7. 37. keep his own virgin daughter, shall do *well*
  38. his own virgin daughter in marriage doeth *well*
Gal. 5. 7. Ye were running *well ;* who did hinder you
Phil. 4. 14. Howbeit ye did *well,* that ye had fellowship
1 *Tim.* 3. 4. one that ruleth *well* his own house
  5. 17. Let the elders that rule *well* be counted worthy
Jas. 2. 19. Thou believest that God is one ; thou doest *well*
          see do well, doing, doeth.

Well *beloved A.V.—see beloved, my beloved.*

Well-doing.
Rom. 2. 7. by patience in *well-doing* seek for glory
Gal. 6. 9. let us not be weary in *well-doing.* 2 *Th.* 3. 13
1 *Pet.* 2. 15. that by *well-doing* ye should put to silence
  3. 17. that ye suffer for *well-doing* than for evil-doing
  4. 19. commit their souls in *w.-d.* unto a faithful Creator

Well pleased.—*A.V.* ¹*willing.*
Mat. 3. 17. my beloved Son, in whom I am *well p.* 12. 18 :
  17. 5 : *Mk.* 1. 11 : *Lu.* 3. 22 : 2 *Pet.* 1. 17
Lu. 2. 14. peace among men in whom he is *well pleased*
1 *Cor.* 10. 5. with most of them God was not *well pleased*
1 *Th.* 2. 8. we were ¹*well pleased* to impart unto you
Heb. 13. 16. for with such sacrifices God is *well pleased*

Well-pleasing.—*A.V.* ¹*acceptable,* ²*acceptably,* ³*accepted,*
         ⁴*please—d,* ⁵*seemed good.*
Mat. 11. 26. for so it was ⁵*well-p.* in thy sight. *Lu.* 10. ²21
Rom. 14. 18. he that herein serveth Christ is ¹*w.-pleasing*
2 *Cor.* 5. 9. at home or absent, to be ³*well-pleasing* unto
Eph. 5. 10. proving what is ¹*well-pleasing* unto the Lord
Phil. 4. 18. a sacrifice acceptable, *well-pleasing* to God
Col. 3. 20. obey your parents in all things, for this is *w.-p.*
Tit. 2. 9. subjection to their own masters, and to be ⁴*w.-p.*
Heb. 11. 5. witness borne to him that he had been ⁴*w.-p.*
  6. without faith it is impossible to be ⁴*well-pleasing*
  12. 28. whereby we may offer service ²*well-p.* to God
  13. 21. working in us that which is *well-p.* in his sight

Went. — *A.V.* ¹*came,* ²*departed,* ³*gone,* ⁴*passed,*
      ⁵*wandered,* ⁶*went up.*
Mat. 2. 9. star, which they saw in the east, *w.* before them
  21. 9. the multitudes that *went* before him. *Mk.* 11. 9
  29. he afterward he repented himself, and *went*
  30. he answered and said, I go, sir : and *went* on ⁶35
  26. 39. he *w.* forward a little, and fell on his face. *Mk.* 14.
Mk. 1. 20. with the hired servants, and *went* after him
  6. 6. And he *went* round about the villages. *Lu.* 8. 1
Lu. 2. 3. And all *went* to enrol themselves, even one to
  17. 14. as they *went,* they were cleansed
  18. 14. This man *went* down to his house justified
  30. And they that *went* before him rebuked him
  22. 47. Judas, one of the twelve, *went* before them
  23. 52. *went* to Pilate, and asked for the body of Jesus
Jno. 4. 45. Galilæans—for they also *went* unto the feast
  6. 66. Upon this many of his disciples *went* back

371

WENT

Jno. 7. 53. And they *went* every man unto his own house
8. 1. but Jesus *went* unto the mount of Olives
18. 6. I am he, they *went* backward, and fell to the ground
Acts 1. 10. they were looking stedfastly into heaven as he ⁶*w.*
7. 15. And Jacob *went* down into Egypt; and he died
8. 4. were scattered abroad *w.* about preaching the word
5. And Philip *went* down to the city of Samaria
38. and they both *went* down into the water [priest
9. 1. Saul, yet breathing threatening—*w.* unto the high
29. the Grecian Jews; but they *went* about to kill him
32. as Peter ⁴*went* throughout all parts, he came down
10. 21. And Peter *went* down to the men, and said—I am he
38. Jesus of Nazareth—who *went* about doing good
12. 17. And he departed, and *went* to another place
19. And he *went* down from Judæa to Cæsarea
13. 11. he *w.* about seeking some to lead him by the hand
42. as they ⁵*went* out, they besought that these words
15. 38. withdrew—and *went* not with them to the work
20. 10. Paul *went* down, and fell on him, and embracing
25. among whom I ³*went* about preaching the kingdom
1 Tim. 1. 18. according to the prophecies which *w.* before
2 Tim. 4. 10. Demas forsook me—and ²*went* to Thessalonica
Heb. 11. 37. they ⁵*went* about in sheepskins [Balaam
2 Pet. 2. 15. they⁵*went* astray, having followed the way of
see assayed, came, entered, go, goeth, going, gone, journeyed, went away, went forth.

Went aside A.V. ¹*see withdrew, going.*

Went away.—A.V. ¹come, ²departed—ing, ³gone,
⁴went, ⁵went her, his, or their way—s.
Mat. 8. 33. fed them fled, and ⁵*went away* into the city
13. 25. tares also among the wheat, and ⁵*went away*
19. 22. he *went away* sorrowful. Mk. 10. 22
25. 10. while they ⁴*w. away* to buy, the bridegroom came
26. 44. and *w. a.*, and prayed a third time. 42: Mk. 14. 39
Mk. 6. 32. they ²*went away* in the boat to a desert place
7. 24. he ⁴*w. away* into the borders of Tyre. Jno. 10. 40
30. she ¹*went away* unto her house, and found the child
11. 4. ⁵*went away*, and found a colt tied. Lu. 19. ⁵32
14. 10. Judas Iscariot—⁴*w. a.* unto the chief priests. Lu.
Lu. 2. 15. when the angels ⁵*went away* from them [22. ⁵¹
Jno. 4. 28. left her waterpot, and ⁵*went away* into the city
5. 15. The man ¹*went away*, and told the Jews
6. 22. into the boat, but that his disciples ²*went a.* alone
9. 7. He ⁵*went away* therefore, and washed. ⁴11
11. 28. she ⁵*went away*, and called Mary her sister
46. But some of them ⁵*went away* to the Pharisees
12. 11. many of the Jews *w. away*, and believed on Jesus
20. 10. disciples *went away* again unto their own home
see went forth.

Went forth.—A.V. ¹came out, ²departed, ³escaped,
⁴went abroad, ⁵went away, ⁶went out.
Mat. 9. 31. they ²*w. forth*, and spread abroad his fame. ⁶32
13. 3. Behold, the sower *went forth* to sow
25. 1. and *went forth* to meet the bridegroom
Mk. 2. 12. took up the bed, and *went forth* before them all
9. 30. they ²*w. f.* from thence, and passed through Galilee
16. 20. they *went forth*, and preached everywhere
Lu. 5. 27. he *went forth*, and beheld a publican
Jno. 10. 39. to take him: and he ⁵*w. forth* out of their hand
21. 23. This saying therefore ¹*w. f.* among the brethren
Acts 10. 23. he arose and ⁵*went forth* with them
11. 25. he ²*went forth* to Tarsus to seek for Saul
1 Cor. 14. 36. was it from you that the word of God ¹*w. f.* ?
3 Jno. 7. for the sake of the Name they *went forth*

WENT

Went his, their way or ways.—A.V. ¹departed.
Mat. 11. 7. as these ¹*went their way*, Jesus began to say
20. 4. into the vineyard—And they *went their way*
22. 5. they made light of it, and *went their ways*
22. marvelled, and left him, and *went their way*
Lu. 4. 30. But he passing through the midst of them *went*
8. 39. And he *w. his way*, publishing throughout [his *w.*
Jno. 4. 50. Jesus spake unto him, and he *went his way*
Acts 8. 36. And as they *went on the way*, they came unto
39. saw him no more, for he *went on his way* rejoicing
see departed, went away.

Went in, or into.—A.V. ¹came in, ²entered, ³gone.
Mat. 8. 32. And they came out, and *went into* the swine
13. 36. and *went into* the house. Lu. 11. 37 [12: 20. 9
21. 33. and *w. into* another country. Mk. 12. 1: Lu. 19.
25. 10. ready *went in* with him to the marriage feast
Mk. 6. 51. he *went up* unto them *into* the boat
15. 43. and he boldly *went in* unto Pilate, and asked for
Lu. 1. 39. Mary arose in these days and *went into* the hill
24. 29. And he *went in* to abide with them [country
Acts 1. 21. the Lord Jesus *went in* and went out among us
10. 27. And as he talked with him, he *went in* [2, 10
13. 14. they *w. i.* the synagogue on the sabbath day. 17.
18. 7. ²*went into* the house of a certain man named Titus
28. 30. [Paul] received all that ¹*went in* unto him
Jude 11. for they ⁵*went in* the way of Cain
see enter, entered.

Went out.—A.V. ¹departed, ²departing, ³went.
Mat. 3. 5. Then *went out* unto him Jerusalem
11. 7. What *went ye out* into the wilderness to behold ?
8, 9: Lu. 7. 24, 25, 26
17. 18. rebuked him; and the devil ¹*went out* from him
20. 1. *went out* early in the morning to hire labourers
3. And he *went out* about the third hour. 5, 6
22. 10. And those servants *went out* into the highways
26. 75. he *w. o.*, and wept bitterly. Mk. 14. 68: Lu. 22. 62
Mk. 3. 21. friends heard it, they *w. out* to lay hold on him
6. 1. And he [Jesus] *went out* from thence
12. And they *w. o.*, and preached that men should repent
7. 31. again he ²*went out* from the borders of Tyre
Lu. 8. 35. And they *went out* to see what had come to pass
Jno. 8. 9. And they, when they heard it, *w. out* one by one
59. Jesus hid himself, and *went out* of the temple
11. 31. Mary, that she rose up quickly and *went out*
13. 30. having received the sop *went out* straightway
18. 16. *went out* and spake unto her that kept the door
Acts 1. 21. the Lord Jesus went in and *went out* among us
15. 24. certain which *w. out* from us have troubled you
17. 33. Thus Paul ¹*went out* from among them
19. 12. and the evil spirits *went out*
Rom. 10. 18. Their sound ³*went out* into all the earth
Heb. 11. 8. and he *went out*, not knowing whither he went
1 Jno. 2. 19. They *w. o.* from us—*w. o.*, that they might be
see came forth, went forth.

Went up.—A.V. ¹arose, ascended, ²gone.
Mat. 3. 16. Jesus, when he was baptized, *w. up* straightway
5. 1. he *w. up* into the mountain. 14. 23: 15. 29: Lu. 9. 28
Lu. 18. 10. Two men *went up* into the temple to pray
Jno. 7. 10. gone up unto the feast, then *went he* also *up*
Acts 10. 9. Peter *went up* upon the housetop to pray
18. 22. he [Paul] ¹*went up* and saluted the church
24. 11. I *went up* to worship at Jerusalem. Gal. 1. 18 : 2. 1
25. 1. Festus—after three days ²*went up* to Jerusalem
Gal. 2. 2. And I *went up* by revelation
Rev. 8. 4. with the prayers of the saints, ²*w. up* before God

WENT

Rev. 9. 2. there ¹*went up* a smoke out of the pit
11. 12. they ²*went up* into heaven in the cloud
20. 9. they *went up* over the breadth of the earth
see going, went.

Wentest.

Acts 11. 3. Thou *wentest* in to men uncircumcised

Wept.

Mat. 26. 75. And he went out, and *wept* bitterly. *Mk.* 14. 72: *Lu.* 22. 62
Mk. 16. 10. been with him, as they mourned and *wept*
Lu. 19. 41. he saw the city and *wept* over it
Jno. 11. 35. Jesus *wept*
20. 11. as she *wept*, she stooped and looked into the tomb
Acts 20. 37. And they all *wept* sore, and fell on Paul's neck
1 *Cor.* 7. 30. those that weep, as though they *wept* not
Rev. 5. 4. And I *w.* much, because no one was found worthy
see weep, weeping.

West.

Mat. 8. 11. many shall come from the east and the *west*
24. 27. and is seen unto the *west* [*Lu.* 13. 29
Lu. 12. 54. When ye see a cloud rising in the *west*
Rev. 21. 13. and on the *west* three gates
for south-west see south-east.

Wet—ted.—*A.V.* ¹*wash,* ²*washed.*

Lu. 7. 38. she began to ¹*wet* his feet with her tears. 244

Whale.

Mat. 12. 40. three days and three nights in the belly of the *w.*

Wheat.

Mat. 3. 12. he will gather his *w.* into the garner. *Lu.* 3. 17
13. 25. enemy came and sowed tares also among the *w.*
29. gather up the tares, ye root up the *wheat* with them
30. but gather the *wheat* into my barn
Lu. 16. 7. he said, A hundred measures of *wheat*
22. 31. Satan asked—that he might sift you as *wheat*
Jno. 12. 24. Except a grain of *wheat* fall into the earth
Acts 27. 38. throwing out the *wheat* into the sea
1 *Cor.* 15. 37. but a bare grain, it may chance of *wheat*
Rev. 6. 6. A measure of *wheat* for a penny
18. 13. fine flour, and *wheat*, and cattle, and sheep

Wheel.—*A.V.* ¹*course.*

Jas. 3. 6. and setteth on fire the ¹*wheel* of nature

Wherewith.—*A.V.* ¹*sufficient.*

Lu. 14. 28. whether he have ¹*wherewith* to complete it?

While.—*A.V.* ¹*season,* ²*space,* ³*time.*

Mk. 4. 17. but endure for a ³*while*; then, when tribulation
Acts 5. 34. commanded to put the men forth a little ²*while*
19. 22. he [Paul] himself stayed in Asia for a ¹*while*
see long, long ago.

Whisperers.

Rom. 1. 29. strife, deceit, malignity; *whisperers*

Whisperings.

2 *Cor.* 12. 20. backbitings, *whisperings*, swellings

Whit.

Jno. 7. 23. I made a man every *whit* whole on the sabbath?
13. 10. save to wash his feet, but is clean every *whit*
2 *Cor.* 11. 5. I am not a *w.* behind the very chiefest apostles

White.

Mat. 5. 36. thou canst not make one hair *white* or black

WHOLLY

Mat. 17. 2. his garments became *w.* as the light. *Mk.* 9. 3:
28. 3. and his raiment *white* as snow. [*Lu.* 9. 29
Mk. 16. 5. arrayed in a *white* robe; and they were amazed
Jno. 4. 35. the fields, that they are *w.* already unto harvest
20. 12. beholdeth two angels in *white* sitting
Acts 1. 10. two men stood by them in *white* apparel
Rev. 1. 14. his hair were *white* as *white* wool, *white* as snow
2. 17. I will give him a *white* stone
3. 4. they shall walk with me in *w.*; for they are worthy
5. shall thus be arrayed in *w.* garments. 4. 4; 7. 9, 13
18. and *w.* garments, that thou mayest clothe thyself
6. 2. And I saw, and behold, a *white* horse. 19. 11
11. there was given them to each one a *white* robe
7. 14. and made them *white* in the blood of the Lamb
14. 14. And I saw, and behold, a *white* cloud
19. 14. *white* horses, clothed in fine linen, *w.* and pure
20. 11. And I saw a great *white* throne
see bright, whiten.

Whited.

Mat. 23. 27. for ye are like unto *whited* sepulchres
Acts 23. 3. God shall smite thee, thou *whited* wall

Whiten.—*A.V.* ¹*white.*

Mk. 9. 3. so as no fuller on earth can ¹*whiten* them

Whole.

Mat. 5. 29. and not thy *whole* body be cast into hell. 30
6. 22. thy *whole* body shall be full of light. *Lu.* 11. 36
23. thy *whole* body shall be full of darkness
8. 32. the *whole* herd rushed down the steep into the sea
16. 26. if he shall gain the whole *world.* *Mk.* 8. 36
Mk. 12. 33. is much more than all *whole* burnt offerings
Lu. 23. 1. And the *whole* company of them rose up
Jno. 4. 53. and himself believed, and his *whole* house
11. 50. and that the *whole* nation perish not
Acts 13. 44. almost the *w.* city was gathered together to hear
1 *Cor.* 12. 17. If the *whole* body were an eye—If the *whole* were hearing, where were the smelling?
Jas. 2. 10. For whosoever shall keep the *whole* law
1 *Jno.* 2. 2. not for ours only, but also for the *whole* world
5. 19. and the *whole* world lieth in the evil one
see all, world.

Whole.—*A.V.* ¹*healed,* ²*saved.*

Mat. 9. 12. They that are *w.* have no need of a physician. *Mk.* 2. 17: *Lu.* 5. 31
9. 21. touch his garment, I shall be made *w.* *Mk.* 5. 28
22. faith hath made thee *whole*. And the woman was made *whole*. *Mk.* 5. 34: *Lu.* 8. 48
12. 13. and it was restored *whole*, as the other
15. 31. they saw the dumb speaking, the maimed *whole*
Mk. 5. 23. that she may be made ¹*whole*, and live [²42
10. 52. thy faith hath made thee ¹*whole*. *Lu.* 17. 19: 18.
Lu. 7. 10. returning to the house, found the servant *whole*
8. 36. possessed with devils was made ¹*whole*
Jno. 5. 6. Wouldest thou be made *whole*?
14. Behold, thou art made *whole*: sin no more. 9, 11, 15
7. 23. I made a man every whit *whole* on the sabbath?
Acts 4. 9. by what means this man is made *whole*
14. 9. seeing that he had faith to be made ¹*whole*
see healed, health, wholly.

Wholesome *A.V.*—*see sound.*

Wholly.—*A.V.* ¹*whole.*

Lu. 11. 36. no part dark, it shall be ¹*wholly* full of light
1 *Th.* 5. 23. God of peace himself sanctify you *wholly*
1 *Tim.* 4. 15. these things; give thyself *wholly* to them
see full.

373

WHORE

Whore *A.V.—see harlot.*

Whoremonger—s *A.V.—see fornicator—s.*

Wicked.—*A.V.* ¹*malicious.*

Mat. 13. 49. and sever the *w.* from among the righteous
 18. 32. Thou *wicked* servant. 25. 26: *Lu.* 19. 22
Acts 18. 14. it were a matter of wrong or of *w.* villany
1 Cor. 5. 13. Put away the *w.* man from among yourselves
2 Pet. 2. 7. distressed by the lascivious life of the *wicked*
 3. 17. being carried away with the error of the *wicked*
3 Jno. 10. prating against us with ¹*wicked* words
 see evil, evil one, lawless, miserable.

Wicked One *A.V.—see evil one.*

Wickedness—es.—*A.V.* ¹*malice,* ²*maliciousness,* ³*naughtiness.*

Mat. 22. 18. But Jesus perceived their *wickedness,* and said
Mk. 7. 22. covetings, *wickednesses,* deceit, lasciviousness
Lu. 11. 39. inward part is full of extortion and *wickedness*
Acts 8. 22. Repent therefore of this thy *wickedness*
Rom. 1. 29. filled with all unrighteousness, *wickedness*
1 Cor. 5. 8. neither with the leaven of malice and *w.*
Eph. 6. 12. against the spiritual hosts of *w.* in the heavenly
Jas. 1. 21. putting away all filthiness and overflowing of ³*w.*
1 Pet. 2. 1. Putting away therefore all ¹*wickedness*
 2. 16. using your freedom for a cloke of ²*wickedness*
 see amiss.

Wide.

Mat. 7. 13. for *wide* is the gate, and broad is the way

Widow.

Mk. 12.43. This poor *w.* cast in more than all. 42: *Lu.* 21. 2, 3
Lu. 2. 37. she had been a *w.* even for fourscore and four
 4. 26. of Sidon, unto a woman that was a *widow* [years
 7. 12. the only son of his mother, and she was a *widow*
 18. 3. and there was a *widow* in that city
 5. because this *widow* troubleth me, I will avenge her
1 Tim. 5. 4. But if any *w.* hath children or grandchildren
 5. Now she that is a *widow* indeed, and desolate
 9. Let none be enrolled as a *widow* under threescore
Rev. 18. 7. I sit a queen, and am no *widow* [years old

Widows.—*A.V.* ¹*women.*

Mk. 12. 40. they which devour *widows'* houses. *Lu.* 20. 47
Lu. 4. 25. many *widows* in Israel in the days of Elijah
Acts 6. 1. because their *widows* were neglected
 9. 39. and all the *widows* stood by him weeping
 41. and calling the saints and *widows,* he presented her
1 Cor. 7. 8. But I say to the unmarried and to *widows*
1 Tim. 5. 3. Honour *widows* that are *widows* indeed
 11. But younger *widows* refuse
 14. I desire therefore that the younger ¹*widows* marry
 16. If any woman that believeth hath *widows*—relieve
 them that are *widows* indeed
Jas. 1. 27. to visit the fatherless and *w.* in their affliction

Wife.

Mat. 1. 6. Solomon of her that had been the *wife* of Uriah
 20. fear not to take unto thee Mary thy *wife.* 24
 14. 3. his brother Philip's *wife.* *Mk.* 6. 17: *Lu.* 3. 19
Mk. 1. 30. Simon's *wife's* mother lay sick of a fever. *Lu.* 4. 38
 12. 19. leave a *w.* behind—and brother should take his *w.*
 20. brethren; and the first took a *wife.* *Lu.* 20. 29
 23. In the resurrection whose *wife* shall she be of them?
 for the seven had her to *wife.* *Lu.* 20. 33

WILDERNESS

Lu. 1. 5. he had a *wife* of the daughters of Aaron
 13. thy *wife* Elisabeth shall bear thee a son
 18. old man, and my *wife* well stricken in years
 14. 20. have married a *w.,* and therefore I cannot come
 17. 32. Remember Lot's *wife*
 18. 29. There is no man that hath left house, or *wife* or
 20. 28. having a *wife*—his brother should take the *wife*
1 Cor. 5. 1. that one of you hath his father's *wife*
 7. 3. Let the husband render unto the *wife* her due: and
 likewise also the *wife* unto the husband
 4. The *w.* hath not power over her own body—but the
 10. That the *wife* depart not from her husband [*wife*
 12. If any brother hath an unbelieving *wife*
 14. unbelieving husband is sanctified in the *wife,* and
 the unbelieving *wife* is sanctified in the brother
 16. For how knowest thou, O *wife,* whether thou shalt
 save thy husband? or how knowest thou, O
 husband, whether thou shalt save thy *wife* ?
 27. bound unto a *w.* ?—loosed from a *w.* ? seek not a *w.*
 34. is a difference also between the *wife* and the virgin
 39. A *wife* is bound for so long time as her husband
 9. 5. Have we no right to lead about a *wife* that is a
Eph. 5. 23. For the husband is the head of the *wife*
 33. severally love each one his own *wife*—and let the *w.*
1 Tim. 3. 2. must be—the husband of one *wife.* 12 : *Tit.* 1. 6
 5. 9. having been the *wife* of one man
Rev. 21. 9. I will shew thee the bride, the *wife* of the Lamb
 see woman.

His Wife.

Mat. 5. 31. shall put away *his wife.* 19. 9 : *Mk.* 10. 11
 32. every one that putteth away *his wife.* *Lu.* 16. 18
 8. 14. he saw *his wife's* mother lying sick of a fever
 18. 25. sold, and *his w.,* and children, and all that he had
 19. 3. lawful for a man to put away *his wife.* *Mk.* 10. 2
 5. cleave to *his wife;* and the twain. *Mk.* 10. 7: *Eph.* 5. 31
 10. If the one of the man is so with *his wife*
 22. 24. his brother shall marry *his wife,* and raise up
 25. no seed left *his wife* unto his brother. *Mk.* 12. 19.
 27. 19. his *w.* sent unto him, saying, Have thou nothing
Lu. 14. 26. hateth not *his* own father, and mother, and *wife*
Acts 5. 1. man named Ananias, with Sapphira *his wife*
 2. kept back part of the price, *his w.* also being privy to it
 7. when *his wife,* not knowing what was done, came
 18. 2. lately come from Italy, with *his wife* Priscilla
 24. 24. Felix came with Drusilla, *his wife*
1 Cor. 7. 2. let each man have *his* own *wife*
 11. and that the husband know not *his wife*
 33. for the things of the world, how he may please *his w.*
Eph. 5. 28. He that loveth *his* own *wife* loveth himself. 33
Rev. 19. 7. and *his wife* hath made herself ready

Wild.—*A.V.* ¹*raging.*

Rom. 11. 17. thou, being a *wild* olive, wast grafted in
 24. that which is by nature a *wild* olive tree
Jude 13. ¹*w.* waves of the sea, foaming out their own shame

Wilderness.—*A.V.* ¹*desert.*

Mat. 3. 1. John the Baptist, preaching in the *wilderness*
 of Judæa. *Mk.* 1. 4 : *Lu.* 3. 2
 3. The voice of one crying in the *wilderness.* *Mk.* 1. 3:
 Lu. 3, 4 : *Jno.* 1, 23 [*Mk.* 1. 12 : *Lu.* 4. 1
 4. 1. Jesus led up of the Spirit into the *wilderness.*
 11. 7. What went ye out into the *w.* to behold ? *Lu.* 7. 24
 24. 26. Behold, he is in the ¹*wilderness* ; go not forth
Mk. 1. 13. he was in the *wilderness* forty days tempted
Lu. 15. 4. leave the ninety and nine in the *wilderness*
Jno. 3. 14. as Moses lifted up the serpent in the *wilderness*

374

WILDERNESS

Jno. 6. 31. Our fathers ate the manna in the ¹wilderness. 50
11. 54. departed thence into the country near to the w.
Acts 7. 30. an angel appeared to him in the wilderness. 38
36. in the Red sea, and in the wilderness forty years. 42
44. the tabernacle of the testimony in the wilderness
13. 18. suffered he their manners in the wilderness
21. 38. led out into the wilderness the four thousand men
1 Cor. 10. 5. for they were overthrown in the w. Heb. 3. 17
2 Cor. 11. 26. in perils in the wilderness
Heb. 3. 8. in the day of the temptation in the wilderness
Rev. 12. 6. And the woman fled into the wilderness. 14
17. 3. And he carried me away in the Spirit into a w.
see desert, deserts.

Wiles.—*A.V.* ¹lie in wait to deceive.
Eph. 4. 14. in craftiness, after the ¹wiles of error
6. 11. be able to stand against the wiles of the devil

Wilfully.—*A.V.* ¹willingly.
Heb. 10. 26. For if we sin wilfully after that we have received
2 Pet. 3. 5. For this they ¹w. forget, that there were heavens

Will.—*A.V.* ¹be so, ²pleasure, ³willingly.
Mat. 6. 10. Thy will be done, as in heaven, so on earth
7. 21. but he that doeth the will of my Father. 12. 50
18. 14. Even so it is not the will of your Father
20. 14. it is my will to give unto this last, even as
21. 31. Whether of the twain did the will of his father?
26. 42. pass away, except I drink it, thy will be done
Lu. 12. 47. which knew not his lord's w., and made not ready
22. 42. nevertheless not my will, but thine, be done
23. 25. but Jesus he delivered up to their will
Jno. 1. 13. nor of the w. of the flesh, nor of the w. of man
4. 34. My meat is to do the will of him that sent me
5. 30. seek not mine own will, but the will of him that
6. 38. not to do mine own will, but the will of him that
39. And this is the will of him that sent me
Acts 13. 22. after my heart, who shall do all my will
21. 14. we ceased, saying, The will of the Lord be done
Rom. 8. 20. was subjected to vanity, not of its own ³will
1 Cor. 7. 37. but hath power as touching his own will
9. 17. If I do this of mine own ³will—not of mine own w.
Eph. 5. 17. but understand what the will of the Lord is
6. 7. with good will doing service, as unto the Lord
Phil. 1. 15. even of envy and strife; and some also of good w.
Heb. 2. 4. gifts of the Holy Ghost, according to his own w.
10. 9. Lo, I am come to do thy will. 7
10. By which will we have been sanctified
Jas. 1. 18. Of his own w. he brought us forth by the word
1 Pet. 3. 17. if the will of God should so ¹w., that ye suffer
2 Pet. 1. 21. For no prophecy ever came by the w. of man
Rev. 4. 11. because of thy ²will they were, and were created
see willeth, willing, wish.

Free Will.
Philem. 14. should not be as of necessity, but of free will

Will of God.—*A.V.* ¹his will.
Mk. 3. 35. For whosoever shall do the will of God
Rom. 1. 10. prospered by the will of God to come unto you
8. 27. intercession for the saints according to the w. of G.
12. 2. the good and acceptable and perfect will of God
15. 32. come unto you in joy through the will of God
2 Cor. 1. 1. apostle of Christ Jesus through the will of God.
1 Cor. 1. 1: Eph. 1. 1: Col. 1. 1: 2 Tim. 1. 1
6. 5. selves to the Lord, and to us by the will of God
Gal. 1. 4. present evil world, according to the w. of our G.
Eph. 6. 6. doing the will of God from the heart

WILLETH

Col. 4. 12. perfect and fully assured in all the will of God
1 Th. 4. 3. For this is the will of God. 5. 18
2 Tim. 2. 26. captive by the Lord's servant unto the ¹w. of G.
Heb. 10. 36. having done the will of God, ye may receive
1 Pet. 2. 15. For so is the will of God, that by well-doing
3. 17. For it is better, if the will of God should so will
4. 2. flesh to the lusts of men, but to the will of God
19. let them also that suffer according to the will of God
1 Jno. 2. 17. but he that doeth the w. of G. abideth for ever
see counsel, desires.

His Will.
Lu. 12. 47. nor did according to his will, shall be beaten
Jno. 7. 17. If any man willeth to do his will
Acts 22. 14. our fathers hath appointed thee to know h. w.
Rom. 2. 18. knowest his will, and approvest the things
9. 19. For who withstandeth his will?
1 Cor. 16. 12. and it was not at all his will to come now
Eph. 1. 5. according to the good pleasure of his will
9. having made known unto us the mystery of his will
11. who worketh all things after the counsel of his will
Col. 1. 9. may be filled with the knowledge of his will
Heb. 13. 21. perfect in every good thing to do his will
1 Jno. 5. 14. if we ask anything according to his will
see mind, will of God.

Will-worship.
Col. 2. 23. have indeed a show of wisdom in will-worship

Will (*Verb*).
Mat. 8. 3. I will, be thou made clean. Mk. 1. 41: Lu. 5. 13
20. 15. lawful for me to do what I will with mine own?
32. What will ye that I should do unto you?
26. 39. not as I will, but as thou wilt. Mk. 14. 36
27. 17. whom will ye that I release unto you? 21: Mk. 15. 9: Jno. 18. 39
Mk. 6. 25. I will that thou forthwith give me in a charger
14. 7. and whensoever ye will ye can do them good
Lu. 4. 6. and to whomsoever I will I give it
12. 49. and what will I come unto you with a rod
Jno. 5. 21. even so the Son also quickeneth whom he will
15. 7. ask whatsoever ye w., and it shall be done unto you
17. 24. I will that, where I am, they also may be with me
21. 22. If I will that he tarry till I come. 23
Acts 18. 21. I will return again unto you, if God will
Rom. 7. 18. to will is present with me, but to do that
9. 18. mercy on whom he w., and whom he w. he hardeneth
1 Cor. 4. 19. But I will come to you shortly, if the Lord will
7. 36. let him do what he will; he sinneth not
39. she is free to be married to whom she will
12. 11 dividing to each one severally even as he will
2 Cor. 8. 11. so there was the readiness to w., so there may be
Phil. 2. 13. God which worketh in you both to w. and to work
Tit. 3. 8. I will that thou affirm confidently
Jas. 4. 15. For that ye ought to say, If the Lord will
Rev. 22. 17. he that will, let him take the water of life
see desire.

Will not.
Mat. 21. 29. And he answered and said, I will not
Mk. 14. 29. Although all shall be offended, yet will not I

Willeth.—*A.V.* ¹listeth, ²will, ³will have.
Mat. 11. 27. to whomsoever the Son ²w. to reveal him. Lu. 10. 222
Jno. 9. 16. So then it is not of him that willeth [10. 222
1 Tim. 2. 4. who ³willeth that all men should be saved
Jas. 3. 4. rudder, whither the impulse of the steersman ¹w.
Rev. 2. 21. she willeth not to repent of her fornication
see wouldest.

WILLING

Willing.—*A.V.* ¹*ready*, ²*will*, ³*willingly*.
Mat. 1. 19. and not *willing* to make her a public example
11. 14. if ye are ³*willing* to receive it, this is Elijah
26. 15. What are ye ²*w.* to give me, and I will deliver him
41. the spirit indeed is *willing*, but the flesh. *Mk.* 14.¹38
Lu. 22. 42. Father, if thou be *willing*, remove this cup
Jno. 5. 35. and ye were *willing* to rejoice for a season
6. 21. They were ²*w.* therefore to receive him into the boat
Rom. 9. 22. What if God, *willing* to shew his wrath
2 *Cor.* 5. 8. *willing* rather to be absent from the body
1 *Tim.* 6. 18. ready to distribute, *willing* to communicate
see accord, desiring, gave, minded, readiness, well pleased, wishing.

Willingly.
1 *Pet.* 5. 2. not of constraint, but *w.*, according unto God
see will, wilfully, willing.

Wilt.
Mat. 8. 2. Lord, if thou *wilt*, thou canst make me clean.
Mk. 1. 40: *Lu.* 5. 12
13. 28. *Wilt* thou then that we go and gather them up?
15. 28. be it done unto thee even as thou *wilt*
17. 4. if thou *wilt*, I will make here three tabernacles
26. 17. Where *wilt* thou that we make ready for thee to
eat the passover? *Mk.* 14. 12: *Lu.* 22. 9
39. not as I will, but as thou *wilt*. *Mk.* 14. 36
Mk. 6. 22. unto the damsel, Ask of me whatsoever thou *wilt*
10. 51. What *w.* thou that I should do unto thee? *Lu.*18.41
Lu. 9. 54. Lord, *wilt* thou that we bid fire to come down
see wouldest.

Win.—*A.V.* ¹*possess.*
Lu. 21. 19. In your patience ye shall ¹*win* your souls
see gain.

Wind—s.—*A.V.* ¹*heat*, ²*spirits.*
Mat. 7. 25. and the *winds* blew, and beat upon that house. 27
8. 26. he arose, and rebuked the *w.* and the sea. *Lu.* 8. 24
27. the *w.* and the sea obey him? *Mk.* 4. 41; *Lu.* 8. 25
11. 7. a reed shaken with the *wind*? *Lu.* 7. 24
14. 24 for the *wind* was contrary. *Mk.* 6. 48: *Jno.* 6. 18:
30. But when he saw the *wind*, he was afraid | *Acts* 27. 4
32. into the boat, the *wind* ceased. *Mk.* 4. 39; 6. 51
Jno. 3. 8 The *wind* bloweth where it listeth
Acts 2. 2. a sound as of the rushing of a mighty *wind*
27. 14. tempestuous *wind*, which is called Euraquilo. 15
28. 13. after one day a south *wind* sprang up
Eph. 4. 14. carried about with every *wind* of doctrine
Heb. 1. 7. Who maketh his angels ²*w.*, And his ministers
Jas. 1. 6. like the surge of the sea driven by the *wind*
11. For the sun ariseth with the scorching ¹*wind*
3. 4. though they are so great, and are driven by rough *w.*
Jude 12. clouds without water, carried along by *winds*
Rev. 6. 13. when she is shaken of a great *wind*
7. 1. holding the four *winds* of the earth, that no *wind*
see four, south.

Window.
Acts 20. 9. And there sat in the *w.* a certain young man
2 *Cor.* 11. 33. and through a *w.* was I let down in a basket

Wine.—*A.V.* ¹*vinegar.*
Mat. 9. 17. new *wine* into old wine-skins—*wine* is spilled
—new *wine* into fresh. *Mk.* 2. 22; *Lu.* 5. 37, 38
27. 34. gave him ¹*w.* to drink mingled with gall. *Mk.* 15.23
Mk. 2. 22. *w.* will burst the skins, and the *w.* perisheth. *Lu.*
Lu. 5. 39. no man having drunk old *w.* desireth new. [5.37
7. 33. Baptist is come eating no bread nor drinking *w.*
10. 34. his wounds, pouring on them oil and *wine*

WISDOM

Jno. 2. 3. And when the *wine* failed—They have no *wine*
9. ruler of the feast tasted the water now become *wine*
10. on first the good *wine*—good *wine* until now
4. 46. Cana of Galilee, where he made the water *wine*
Eph. 5. 18. And be not drunken with *wine*, wherein is riot
1 *Tim.* 3. 8. Deacons—not given to much *wine*
5. 23. but use a little *wine* for thy stomach's sake
Tit. 2. 3. not slanderers nor enslaved to much *wine*
Rev. 14. 8. all the nations to drink of the *w.* of the wrath
16. 19. to give unto her the cup of the *wine*
17. 2. drunken with the *wine* of her fornication. 18. 3
18. 13. frankincense, and *wine*, and oil, and fine flour
see brawler.

Winebibber.
Mat. 11. 19. Behold, a gluttonous man, and a *w. Lu.* 7. 34

Wine-bibbings.—*A.V.* ¹*excess of wine.*
1 *Pet.* 4. 3. lusts, ¹*wine-bibbings*, revellings, carousings

Wine *fat A.V.*—*see winepress.*

Winepress.—*A.V.* ¹*winefat.*
Mat. 21. 33. and digged a *winepress* in it. *Mk.* 12. ¹1
Rev. 14. 19. cast it into the *w.*, the great *w.* of the wrath
20. And the *winepress* was trodden without the city,
and there came out blood from the *winepress*
19. 15. he treadeth the *w.* of the fierceness of the wrath

Wine-skins.—*A.V.* ¹*bottles.*
Mat. 9. 17. put new wine into old ¹*wine-skins*—put new
wine into fresh ¹*w-s.* *Mk.* 2. ¹22: *Lu.* 5. ¹37, ¹38

Wings.
Mat. 23. 37. gathereth her chickens under her *w. Lu.* 13. 34
Rev. 9. 9. sound of their *w.* was as the sound of chariots
12. 14. to the woman the two *wings* of the great eagle

Winked *A.V.*—*see overlooked.*

Winter.
Mat. 24. 20. that your flight be not in the *w. Mk.* 13. 18
Jno. 10. 22. feast of the dedication at Jerusalem: it was *w.*
Acts 27. 12. the haven was not commodious to *winter* in
—they could reach Phœnix, and *winter* there
1 *Cor.* 16. 6. it may be that I shall abide, or even *winter*
2 *Tim.* 4. 21. Do thy diligence to come before *winter*
Tit. 3. 12. Nicopolis: for there I have determined to *w.*

Wintered.
Acts 28. 11. ship of Alexandria, which had *w.* in the island

Wipe-d.—*A.V.* ¹*wipe.*
Lu. 7. 38. and ¹*wiped* them with the hair of her head. 44.
10. 11. we do *wipe* off against you. [*Jno.* 11. 2: 12. 3
Jno. 13. 5. wash the disciples' feet, and to *wipe* them
Rev. 7.17. God shall *w.* away every tear from their eyes. 21.4

Wisdom.
Mat. 11. 19. And *w.* is justified by her works. *Lu.* 7. 35
12. 42. of the earth to hear the *w.* of Solomon. *Lu.* 11. 31
13. 54. Whence hath this man this *wisdom*. *Mk.* 6. 2
Lu. 1. 17. the disobedient to walk in the *w.* of the just
2. 40. the child grew, and waxed strong, filled with *w.*
52. And Jesus advanced in *wisdom* and stature
11. 49. Therefore also said the *wisdom* of God
21. 15. for I will give you a mouth and *wisdom*

376

WISDOM

Acts 6. 3. full of the Spirit and of *w*., whom we may appoint
  10. not able to withstand the *w*.—by which he spake
7. 10. gave him favour and *wisdom* before Pharaoh
22. Moses was instructed in all the *w*. of the Egyptians
Rom. 11. 33. riches—of the *w*. and the knowledge of God!
1 Cor. 1. 17. to preach the gospel : not in *wisdom* of words
  19. I will destroy the *wisdom* of the wise
  20. hath not God made foolish the *w*. of the world?
  21. in the *w*. of God the world through its *w*. knew not
  22. Jews ask for signs, and Greeks seek after *w*. [God
  24. Christ the power of God, and the *wisdom* of God
  30. who was made unto us *wisdom* from God
2. 1. came not with excellency of speech or of *wisdom*
  4. my preaching were not in persuasive words of *w*.
  5. that your faith should not stand in the *w*. of men
  6. we speak *w*. among the perfect—a *w*. not of this world
  7. we speak God's *wisdom* in a mystery, even the *wisdom*
  13. not in words which man's *wisdom* teacheth
3. 19. For the *w*. of this world is foolishness with God
12. 8. to one is given through the Spirit the word of *w*.
2 Cor. 1. 12. sincerity of God, not in fleshly *wisdom*
Eph. 1. 8. made to abound toward us in all *wisdom*
  17. Father of glory, may give unto you a spirit of *w*.
3. 10. made known through the church the—*w*. of God
Col. 1. 9. with the knowledge of his will in all spiritual *w*.
  28. teaching every man in all *wisdom*
2. 3. Christ, in whom are all the treasures of *wisdom*
  23. Which things have indeed a show of *wisdom*
3. 16. word of Christ dwell in you richly in all *wisdom*
4. 5. Walk in *wisdom* toward them that are without
Jas. 1. 5. But if any of you lacketh *w*., let him ask of God
3. 13. shew by his good life his works in meekness of *w*.
15. This *w*. is not a *w*. that cometh down from above
17. But the *wisdom* that is from above is first pure
2 Pet. 3. 15. according to the *wisdom* given to him
Rev. 5. 12. to receive the power, and riches, and *wisdom*
7. 12. Blessing, and glory, and *wisdom*, and thanksgiving
13. 18. Here is *wisdom*. He that hath understanding
17. 9. Here is the mind which hath *wisdom*

Wise.—*A.V.* [1]*case*, [2]*means*, [3]*not*.

Mat. 1. 18. birth of Jesus Christ was on this *wise*.
  2. 6. in no [3]*wise*. 5. 18 : 10. 42: 13. [3]14 : 16. [3]28 : 18. [3]3 :
  Mk. 9. [3]1, [2]41 : Lu. 9. [3]27 : Acts 13. 41 ; 28. [3]26 ;
  Rom. 3. 9 : 1 Th. 4. [3]15 : 5. [3]3 : Rev. 3. [3]5 : 9. [3]6 :
  21. [3]25, 27
5. 20. ye shall in no [1]*wise* enter into the kingdom
10. 16. be ye therefore *wise* as serpents
11. 25. didst hide these things from the *wise*. Lu. 10. 21
24. 45. Who then is the faithful and *w*. servant. Lu. 12. 42
25. 2. five of them were foolish, and five were *wise*. 8.
  4. the *wise* took oil in their vessels with their lamps
  9. the *wise* answered, saying, Peradventure there will
Lu. 10. 19. and nothing shall in any [2]*wise* hurt you
Jno. 21. 1. on this *wise*. Acts 13. 34 : Heb. 4. 4
Rom. 1. 14. both to the *wise* and to the foolish
22. Professing themselves to be *w*., they became fools
12. 16. Be not *wise* in your own conceits. 11. 25
16. 19. I would have you *wise* unto that which is good
27. to the only *wise* God, through Jesus Christ, to whom
1 Cor. 1. 19. I will destroy the wisdom of the *wise*
20. Where is the *wise* ? where is the scribe ?
27. that he might put to shame them that are *wise*
3. 10. as a *wise* masterbuilder I laid a foundation
18. If any man thinketh he is *wise*—let him become a
fool, that he may become *wise*
19. He that taketh the *wise* in their craftiness
20. The Lord knoweth the reasonings of the *wise*
4. 10. We are fools for Christ's sake, but ye are *w*. in Christ

WITHHOLD

2 Cor. 11. 19. bear with the foolish gladly, being *w*. your-
Eph. 5. 15. ye walk, not as unwise, but as *wise* [selves
2 Th. 2. 3. let no man beguile you in any [2]*wise*
2 Tim. 3. 15. able to make thee *wise* unto salvation
    see *man, men, understanding*.

Wisely.

Lu. 16. 8. unrighteous steward because he had done *wisely*

Wiser.

Lu. 16. 8. their own generation *w*. than the sons of the light
1 Cor. 1. 25. the foolishness of God is *wiser* than men

Wish.—*A.V.* [1]*desire*, [2]*will*, [3]*would*.

Acts 25. 22. I also could [3]*wish* to hear the man myself
Rom. 9. 3. For I could *wish* that I myself were anathema
1 Cor. 16. 7. For I do not [2]*wish* to see you now by the way
Gal. 4. 20. I could [1]*wish* to be present with you now
    see *pray*.

Wished.

Acts 27. 29. anchors from the stern, and *wished* for the day

Wishing.—*A.V.* [1]*willing*.

Mk. 15. 15. Pilate, [1]*wishing* to content the multitude
2 Pet. 3. 9. not [1]*wishing* that any should perish

Wist.

Mk. 9. 6. For he *wist* not what to answer [answer him
14. 40. eyes were very heavy ; and they *wist* not what to
Lu. 2. 49. *wist* ye not that I must be in my Father's house?
Jno. 5. 13. But he that was healed *wist* not who it was
Acts 12. 9. and he *w*. not that it was true which was done
23. 5. Paul—I *wist* not, brethren, that he was high priest

Wit *A.V.*—*see (make) known*.

Witchcraft *A.V.*—*see sorcery*.

Withdraw.

2 Th. 3. 6. that ye *withdraw* yourselves from every brother

Withdrawn.—*A.V.* [1]*gone aside*.

Acts 26. 31. when they had [1]*w*., they spake one to another
    see *parted*.

Withdrew.—*A.V.* [1]*departed*, [2]*turned aside*, [3]*went aside*.

Mat. 2. 22. [Joseph] [2]*withdrew* into the parts of Galilee
12. 15. Jesus perceiving it *w*. 14. [1]13 : Mk. 3. 7 : Lu. 5. 16
15. 21. Jesus went out thence, and [1]*w*. into the parts of
Lu. 9. 10. [3]*w*. apart to a city called Bethsaida [Tyre
Jno. 6. 15 [1]*w*. again into the mountain himself alone
Acts 15. 38. [Mark] [1]*withdrew* from them from Pamphylia
    see *drew*.

Wither—ed.—*A.V.* [1]*dried*.

Mat. 12. 10. man having a *w*. hand. Mk. 3. 1, 3 : Lu. 6. 6, 8
13. 6. had no root, they *withered* away. Mk. 4. 6
21. 19. the fig tree *withered* away. 20 : Mk. 11. [1]20, 21
Lu. 8. 6. it *withered* away, because it had no moisture
Jno. 5. 3. them that were sick, blind, halt, *withered*
15. 6. is cast forth as a branch, and is *withered*

Withereth.

Jas. 1. 11. with the scorching wind, and *withereth* the grass
1 Pet. 1. 24. The grass *withereth*, and the flower falleth

Withhold.—*A.V.* [1]*forbid*.

Lu. 6. 29. taketh away thy cloke [1]*withhold* not thy coat also

WITHHOLDETH

Withholdeth *A.V.—see restraineth.*

Without *A.V.—see apart, free, outside.*

Withstand.—*A.V.* ¹*resist.*

Lu. 21. 15. your adversaries shall not be able to ¹withstand
Acts 6. 10. they were not able to ¹withstand the wisdom
   11. 17. who was I, that I could withstand God? [ment
Rom. 13. 2. they that ¹w. shall receive to themselves judge-
Eph. 6. 13. that ye may be able to withstand in the evil day
2 Tim. 3. 8. so do these also ¹withstand the truth
1 Pet. 5. 9. whom ¹withstand stedfast in your faith

Withstandeth.—*A.V.* ¹*resisted,* ²*resisteth.*

Rom. 9. 19. For who ¹withstandeth his will?
   13. 2. resisteth the power, ²withstandeth the ordinance

Withstood.

Acts 13. 8. But Elymas the sorcerer—withstood them
2 Tim. 3. 8. And like as Jannes and Jambres w. Moses
   4. 15. for he greatly withstood our words
       see resisted.

Witness.—*A.V.* ¹*martyr,* ²*record,* ³*report,* ⁴*testify—ied —eth—ing,* ⁵*testimony,* ⁶*witnesses.*

Mat. 23. 31. Wherefore ye ⁵w. to yourselves, that ye are sons
   26. 62. Answerest thou nothing? what is it which
       these witness against thee? 27. 13; Mk. 14. 60
Mk. 14. 55. the whole council sought witness against Jesus
   56. many bare false witness against him, and their
       witness agreed not together. 57, 59
Lu. 22. 71. What further need have we of witness?
Jno. 1. 7. The same came for w., that he might bear w.
   8. that he might bear witness of the light
   15. John beareth witness of him, and crieth, saying
   19. And this is the ²witness of John, when the Jews
   32. John bare ²witness, saying, I have beheld the Spirit
   34. I have seen, and have borne ²witness that this is
   2. 25. any one should bear ⁴witness concerning man
   3. 11. and bear ⁴witness of that we have seen; and ye
       receive not our witness
   26. to whom thou hast borne witness
   28. Ye yourselves bear me witness, that I said
   32. that he beareth ⁴w.; and no man receiveth his ⁵w.
   33. He that hath received his ⁵witness hath set his seal
   5. 31. If I bear witness of myself, my witness is not true
   32. It is another that beareth w. of me—the w. which
   33. he hath borne witness unto the truth [he witnesseth
   34. But the ⁵witness which I receive is not from man
   36. But the witness which I have is greater than that
   37. Father which sent me, he hath borne w. of me
   8. 13. Thou bearest ²w. of thyself; thy ²w. is not true
   14. Even if I bear ²witness of myself, my ²witness is true
   17. in your law it is written, that the ⁵w. of two men is true
   19.35. he that hath seen hath borne ⁴w., and his ²w. is true
   21. 24. This is the disciple which beareth ⁴witness of
       these things—we know that his ⁵witness is true
Acts 1. 22. of these must one become a witness with us
   4. 33. gave the apostles their witness of the resurrection
   10. 43. To him bear all the prophets witness
   13. 22. David to be their king; to whom also he bare ⁵w.
   14. 3. which bare ⁵witness unto the word of his grace
   17. And yet he left not himself without witness
   22. 15. For thou shalt be a witness for him unto all men
   20. when the blood of Stephen thy ¹witness was shed
   26. 16. to appoint thee a minister and a witness
Rom. 1. 9. For God is my witness. Phil. 1. ⁸8 : 1 Th. 2. 5
   2. 15. their conscience bearing witness therewith

WIVES

Rom. 9. 1. I lie not, my conscience bearing witness with me
   10. 2. For I bear them ²w. that they have a zeal for God
2 Cor. 1. 23. I call God for a ²witness upon my soul
   8. 3. I bear ²witness, yea and beyond their power
Gal. 4. 15. I bear you ²witness, that, if possible, ye would
Col. 4. 13. For I bear him ²w., that he hath much labour
Heb. 2. 4. God also bearing witness with them
   10. 15. And the Holy Ghost also beareth witness to us
   11. 2. therein the elders had ⁵witness borne to them
   4. Abel—had w. borne to him that he was righteous,
       God hearing ⁴witness in respect of his gifts [him
   5. before his translation he hath had ⁵witness borne to
   39. these all, having had ³witness borne to them
1 Pet. 5. 1. a fellow-elder, and a w. of the sufferings of Christ
1 Jno. 4. 14. And we have beheld and bear ⁴witness
   5. 7. And it is the Spirit that beareth witness, because
   8. there are three who bear w., the Spirit, and the water
   9. If we receive the witness of men, the witness of God
       is greater: for the witness of God is this, that he
       hath borne ⁴witness concerning his Son
   10. hath the ²witness—hath not believed in the witness
   11. And the ²w. is this, that God gave unto us
3 Jno. 3. when brethren came and bare ⁴w. unto thy truth
   6. who bare witness to thy love before the church
   12. Demetrius hath the ⁵witness of all—we also bear
       ²witness—our ²witness is true   [mony
Rev. 1. 2. who bare ²w. of the word of God, and of the testi-
   5. and from Jesus Christ, who is the faithful witness
   2. 13. in the days of Antipas my ¹witness, my faithful one
   3. 14. These things saith—the faithful and true witness
       see accuse, bare, bear, false, testimony, witnesses.

Witnessed.—*A.V.* ¹*testified—eth.*

Rom. 3. 21. being witnessed by the law and the prophets
1 Cor. 15. 15. because we ¹w. of God that he raised up Christ
1 Tim. 6. 13. who before Pontius Pilate w. the good confession
Heb. 7. 8. of whom it is witnessed that he liveth
   17. for it is ¹witnessed of him, Thou art a priest for ever

Witnesses.—*A.V.* ¹*witness.*

Mat. 18. 16. mouth of two w. or three every word may be
   established. 2 Cor. 13. 1 : 1 Tim. 5. 19 : Heb. 10. 28
   26. 65. what further need have we of w.? Mk. 14. 63
Lu. 24. 48. Ye are ¹witnesses and consent unto the works
   24. 48. Ye are witnesses of these things
Acts 1. 8. and ye shall be my witnesses both in Jerusalem
   2. 32. This Jesus did God raise up, whereof we all are w. 3.15
   5. 32. And we are witnesses of these things. 10. 39.
   7. 58. and stoned him; and the w. laid down their garments
   10. 41. but unto witnesses that were chosen before of God
   13. 31. who are now his witnesses unto the people
1 Cor. 15. 15. Yea, and we are found false witnesses of God
1 Th. 2. 10. Ye are witnesses, and God also, how holily
1 Tim. 6. 12. good confession in the sight of many witnesses
2 Tim. 2. 2. things which thou hast heard—among many w.
Heb. 12. 1. compassed about with so great a cloud of w.
Rev. 11. 3. And I will give unto my two witnesses
       see witness.

Witnesseth.

Jno. 5. 32. the witness which he witnesseth of me is true
       see testifieth.

Witnessing *A.V.—see testifying.*

Wives.

Mat. 19. 8. Moses—suffered you to put away your wives
Acts 21. 5. with w. and children, brought us on our way
1 Cor. 7. 29. that have w. may be as though they had none

WIVES

Eph. 5. 22. *Wives*, be in subjection unto your own husbands. *Col.* 3. 18: 1 *Pet.* 3. 1 [husbands
24. subject to Christ, so let the *wives* also be to their
25. Husbands, love your *wives*. 28: *Col.* 3. 19
1 *Tim.* 4. 7. but refuse profane and old *wives'* fables
1 *Pet.* 3. 1. be gained by the behaviour of their *wives*
7. dwell with your *wives* according to knowledge
see women.

Woe—s.—*A.V.* ¹*alas.*

Mat. 11. 21. *Woe* unto thee, Chorazin! *woe* unto thee, Bethsaida! *Lu.* 10. 13
18. 7. *Woe* unto the world because of occasions of stumbling!—*woe* to that man through whom. *Lu.* 17. 1
23. 13. But *woe* unto you, scribes and Pharisees. 14 [margin], 15, 16, 23, 25, 27, 29
24. 19. But *woe* unto them that are with child. *Mk.* 13. 17
26. 24. but *woe* unto that man. *Mk.* 14. 21: *Lu.* 22. 22
Lu. 6. 24. But *woe* unto you that are rich! [ye that laugh
25. *Woe* unto you, ye that are full now!—*W.* unto you,
26. *Woe* unto you, when all men shall speak well of you!
11. 42. But *w.* unto you Pharisees! for ye tithe mint. 43
44. *Woe* unto you! for ye are as the tombs which
46. *Woe* unto you lawyers also! for ye lade men
47. *Woe* unto you! for ye build the tombs
52. *Woe* unto you lawyers! for ye took away the key
1 *Cor.* 9. 16. for *woe* is unto me, if I preach not the gospel
Jude 11. *Woe* unto them! for they went in the way of Cain
Rev. 8. 13. *Woe, woe, woe*, for them that dwell on the earth
9. 12. The first *Woe* is past: behold, there come yet two *Woes* hereafter
11. 14. The second *Woe* is past: behold, the third *Woe*
12. 12. *Woe* for the earth and for the sea: because the
18. 10. ¹*Woe*, ¹*woe*, the great city, Babylon [devil

Wolf.

Jno. 10. 12. beholdeth the *wolf* coming—and the *wolf*

Wolves.

Mat. 7. 15. but inwardly are ravening *wolves* [*Lu.* 10. 3
10. 16. I send you forth as sheep in the midst of *wolves.*
Acts 20. 29. after my departing grievous *wolves* shall enter

Woman.—*A.V.* ¹*wife,* ²*women.*

Mat. 5. 28. every one that looketh on a *woman* to lust after
9. 20. a *w.*, who had an issue. 22: *Mk.* 5. 25, 33: *Lu.* 8. 43
13. 33. is like unto leaven, which a *w.* took. *Lu.* 13. 21
15. 22. a Canaanitish *woman* came out. *Mk.* 7. 25, 26
23. O *woman*, great is thy faith: be it done unto thee
22. 27. them all the *woman* died. *Mk.* 12. 22: *Lu.* 20. 32
26. 7. a *w.* having an alabaster cruse. *Mk.* 14. 3: *Lu.* 7. 37
10. Why trouble ye the *woman?* for she hath wrought
13. also which this *woman* hath done shall. *Mk.* 14. 9
Lu. 4. 26. of Sidon, unto a *woman* that was a widow
7. 39. who and what manner of *woman* this is
44. And turning to the *woman*, he said unto Simon, Seest thou this *woman?* 50
8. 47. when the *w.* saw that she was not hid, she came
10. 38. a certain *woman* named Martha received him
11. 27. as he said these things, a certain *woman*
13. 11. a *w.* which had a spirit of infirmity eighteen years
12. *Woman*, thou art loosed from thine infirmity
16. And ought not this *woman*, being a daughter of
15. 8. Or what *woman* having ten pieces of silver
Jno. 2. 4. *Woman*, what have I to do with thee?
4. 7. There cometh a *woman* of Samaria
9. Samaritan *woman* therefore saith—askest drink of me, which am a Samaritan *woman?*

WOMEN

Jno. 4. 21. *Woman*, believe me, the hour cometh
27. they marvelled that he was speaking with a *woman*
28. So the *woman* left her waterpot, and went away
39. believed on him because of the word of the *woman*
8. 3. Pharisees bring a *woman* taken in adultery. 4
10. *W.*, where are they? did no man condemn thee?
16. 21. A *woman* when she is in travail hath sorrow
19. 26. *Woman*, behold, thy son!
20. 13. they say unto her, *W.*, why weepest thou? 15
Acts 9. 36. Dorcas: this *woman* was full of good works
16. 14. And a certain *woman* named Lydia
17. 34. and a *woman* named Damaris, and others
Rom. 1. 27. men, leaving the natural use of the *woman*
7. 2. For the *woman* that hath a husband is bound by law
1 *Cor.* 7. 1. It is good for a man not to touch a *woman*
2. let each *woman* have her own husband
13. the *woman* which hath an unbelieving husband
11. 5. But every *woman* praying or prophesying. 13
6. For if a *woman* is not veiled, let her also be shorn—if it is a shame to a *woman* to be shorn
7. but the *woman* is the glory of the man
8. For the man is not of the *woman;* but the *woman* of
9. neither was the man created for the *w.;* but the *w.*
10. cause ought the *woman* to have a sign of authority
11. Howbeit neither is the *woman* without the man, nor the man without the *woman*, in the Lord
12. *woman* is of the man, so is the man also by the *w.*
13. is it seemly that a *woman* pray unto God unveiled?
15. But if a *woman* have long hair, it is a glory to her
14. 35. it is shameful for a ²*woman* to speak in the church
Gal. 4. 4. God sent forth his Son, born of a *woman*
1 *Th.* 5. 3. as travail upon a *woman* with child
1 *Tim.* 2. 11. Let a *woman* learn in quietness with all
12. But I permit not a *woman* to teach
14. but the *woman* being beguiled hath fallen
5. 16. If any *woman* that believeth hath widows
1 *Pet.* 3. 7. giving honour unto the ¹*woman*
Rev. 2. 20. that thou sufferest the *woman* Jezebel
12. 1. a *woman* arrayed with the sun
4. the dragon stood before the *woman*
6. And the *woman* fled into the wilderness
13. he persecuted the *woman* which brought forth
15. serpent cast out of his mouth after the *w.* water
16. the earth helped the *woman*, and the earth opened
17. And the dragon waxed wroth with the *woman*
17. 3. I saw a *woman* sitting upon a scarlet-coloured beast
4. the *woman* was arrayed in purple and scarlet
6. I saw the *w.* drunken with the blood of the saints
7. I will tell thee the mystery of the *woman*
9. seven mountains on which the *woman* sitteth
see man.

Womb—s.

Lu. 1. 31. And behold, thou shalt conceive in thy *womb*
41. the babe leaped in her *womb.* 44
2. 21. so called—before he was conceived in the *womb*
23. 29. the barren, and the *wombs* that never bare
Jno. 3. 4. enter a second time into his mother's *womb*
see fruit, mother.

Women.—*A.V.* ¹*wives.*

Mat. 11. 11. Among them that are born of *w. Lu.* 7. 28
14. 21. five thousand men, beside *w.* and children. 15. 38
24. 41. two *women* shall be grinding at the mill. *Lu.* 17. 35
27. 55. And many *women* were there beholding from afar. *Mk.* 15. 40, 41: *Lu.* 23. 27, 49, 55
28. 5. the angel—said unto the *women*, Fear not
Lu. 1. 42. Blessed art thou among *women*
8. 2. certain *w.* which had been healed of evil spirits
24. 10. the other *women* with them told these things

WOMEN

Lu. 24. 22. Moreover certain *w.* of our company amazed us
24. and found it even so as the *women* had said
Acts 1. 14. continued stedfastly in prayer, with the *women*
5. 14. to the Lord, multitudes both of men and *w.* 8. 12
8. 3. haling men and *w.* committed them to prison. 9. 2
13. 50. Jews urged on the devout *w.* of honourable estate
16. 13. and spake unto the *w.* which were come together
17. 4. and of the chief *women* not a few
12. also of the Greek *women* of honourable estate
Rom. 1. 26. for their *women* changed the natural use
1 *Cor.* 14. 34. Let the *women* keep silence in the churches
Phil. 4. 3. help these *women*, for they laboured with me
1 *Tim.* 2. 9. that *w.* adorn themselves in modest apparel
10. (which becometh *women* professing godliness)
3. 11. ¹*Women* in like manner must be grave
5. 2. the elder *women* as mothers; the younger as sisters
2 *Tim.* 3. 6. take captive silly *women* laden with sins
Tit. 2. 3. that aged *women* likewise be reverent [hands
4. that they may train the young *w.* to love their hus-
Heb. 11. 35. *Women* received their dead by a resurrection
1 *Pet.* 3. 5. the holy *women* also, who hoped in God
Rev. 9. 8. And they had hair as the hair of *women*
14. 4. These are they which were not defiled with *women*
see children, widows, women.

Won *A.V.—see gained.*

Wonder. *–A.V.* ¹*admiration*, ²*marvel.*

Acts 3. 10. they were filled with *wonder* and amazement
13. 41. Behold, ye despisers, and *wonder*, and perish
Rev. 17. 6. I wondered with a great ¹*wonder*
7. angel said unto me, Wherefore didst thou ²*wonder*?
8. And they that dwell on the earth shall *wonder*
see sign.

Wondered.

Mat. 15. 31. multitude *w.*, when they saw the dumb speaking
Lu. 2. 18. And all that heard it *wondered* at the things
4. 22. and *wondered* at the words of grace
24. 41. And while they still disbelieved for joy, and *w.*
Acts 7. 31. And when Moses saw it, he *w.* at the sight
Rev. 13. 3. and the whole earth *wondered* after the beast
17. 6. when I saw her, I *wondered* with a great wonder
see amazed, marvelled, marvelling.

Wonderful.

Mat. 21. 15. and the scribes saw the *w.* things that he did
see mighty.

Wondering.

Lu. 24. 12. Peter—departed to his home, *wondering* at that
Acts 3. 11. porch that is called Solomon's, greatly *wondering*

Wonders.

Mat. 24. 24. and shall shew great signs and *w.* *Mk.* 13. 22
Jno. 4. 48. Except ye see signs and *wonders*
Acts 2. 19. I will shew *wonders* in the heaven above
22. works and *wonders* and signs, which God did by him
43. and many *wonders* and signs were done by the
apostles. 5. 12; 14. 3; 15. 12
4. 30. that signs and *w.* may be done through the name
6. 8. Stephen—wrought great *wonders* and signs
7. 36. [Moses] led them forth, having wrought *wonders*
Rom. 15. 19. in the power of signs and *w.*, in the power
2 *Cor.* 12. 12. by signs and *wonders* and mighty works
2 *Th.* 2. 9. with all power and signs and lying *wonders*
Heb. 2. 4. witness with them, both by signs and *wonders*
see signs.

WORD

Wont.—*A.V.* ¹*ever done.*

Mat. 27. 15. the governor was *w.* to release unto the multitude
Mk. 10. 1. and, as he was *wont*, he taught them again
15. 6. ask him [Pilate] to do as he was ¹*wont* to do
see custom, supposed.

Wood.—*A.V.* ¹*matter.*

1 *Cor.* 3. 12. costly stones, *wood*, hay, stubble
2 *Tim.* 2. 20. vessels—but also of *wood* and of earth
Jas. 3. 5. how much ¹*wood* is kindled by how small a fire!
Rev. 18. 12. and all thyine *wood*—most precious *wood*

Wool.

Heb. 9. 19. with water and scarlet *wool* and hyssop
Rev. 1. 14. and his hair were white as white *wool*

Word.—*A.V.* ¹*nothing*, ²*preaching*, ³*saying*—*s*, ⁴*speech*,
⁵*spirit*, ⁶*words*, ⁷*work.*

Mat. 2. 8. and when ye have found him, bring me *word*
4. 4. bread alone, but by every *word* that proceedeth
8. 8. only say the *w.*, and my servant—be healed. *Lu.* 7. 7
16. and he cast out the spirits with a *word* [*Lu.* 12. 10
12. 32. whosoever shall speak a *w.* against the Son of man.
36. that every idle *word* that men shall speak
13. 19. When any one heareth the *word* of the kingdom.
20, 22, 23 : *Mk.* 4. 16, 18, 20 : *Lu.* 8. 13, 15
21. when tribulation or persecution ariseth because
of the *word. Mk.* 4. 17
22. deceitfulness of riches, choke the *word. Mk.* 4. 19
15. 23. But he answered her not a *word*
18. 16. every *word* may be established. 2 *Cor.* 13. 1
22. 46. And no one was able to answer him a *word*
27. 14. And he gave him no answer, not even to one *word*
28. 8. and ran to bring his disciples *word*
Mk. 2. 2. and he spake the *word* unto them. 4. 33
4. 14. The sower soweth the *word*
15. where the *word* is sown—and taketh away the *word.*
14. 72. And Peter called to mind the *word* [*Lu.* 8. 12
Lu. 1. 37. no ¹*word* from God shall be void of power
38. be it unto me according to thy *word*
2. 29. depart, O Lord, According to thy *word*, in peace
4 32. for his *word* was with authority
36. What is this *word*? for with authority and power he
5. 5. but at thy *word* I will let down the nets
24. 19. a prophet mighty in deed and *word* before God
Jno. 1. 1. In the beginning was the *Word*, and the *Word*
was with God, and the *Word* was God
14. And the *Word* became flesh, and dwelt among us
4. 39. because of the ³*word* of the woman, who testified
41. And many more believed because of his *word*
50. The man believed the *word* that Jesus spake. 2. 22
5. 24. I say unto you, He that heareth my *word*
38. And ye have not his *word* abiding in you
7. 36. What is this ⁶*word* that he said, Ye shall seek me
8. 31. If ye abide in my *w.*, then are ye truly my disciples
37. ye seek to kill me, because my *word* hath not free
43. Even because ye cannot hear my *word*
51. If a man keep my ³*word*, he shall never see death
55. but I know him, and keep his ³*word*
12. 38. the *word* of Isaiah the prophet might be fulfilled
48. the *word* that I spake, the same shall judge him
14. 23. If a man love me, he will keep my ⁶*word*
24. and the *word* which ye hear is not mine
15. 3. Already ye are clean because of the *word*
20. Remember the *word* that I said unto you—if they
kept my ³*word*, they will keep yours also
25. that the *word* may be fulfilled that is written

WORD

Jno. 17. 6. gavest them to me; and they have kept thy *w.*
14. I have given them thy *word;* and the world hated
17. Sanctify them in the truth: thy *word* is truth
20. for them also that believe on me through their *word*
18. 9. that the ³*word* might be fulfilled which he spake
Acts 2. 41. They then that received his *w.* were baptized
4. 29. grant unto thy servants to speak thy *w.* with all
10. 36. The *word* which he sent unto the children of Israel
13. 15. Brethren, if ye have any *word* of exhortation
26. to us is the *word* of this salvation sent forth
14. 3. which bare witness unto the *word* of his grace
15. 7. by my mouth the Gentiles should hear the *word*
17. 11. in that they received the *word* with all readiness
18. 5. Paul was constrained by the ⁵*word,* testifying
20. 32. I commend you to God, and to the *w.* of his grace
33. sorrowing most of all for the⁶*w.* which he had spoken
22. 22. they gave him [Paul] audience unto this *word*
28. 25. departed, after that Paul had spoken one *word*
Rom. 9. 9. For this is a *word* of promise, According to
28. for the Lord will execute his ⁷*word* upon the earth
10. 8. The *word* is nigh thee—that is, the *word* of faith
17. cometh of hearing, and hearing by the *w.* of Christ
13. 9. it is summed up in this ³*word*—Thou shalt love
15. 18. obedience of the Gentiles, by *word* and deed
1 *Cor.* 1. 18. ²*w.* of the cross is to them that are perishing
4. 19. the ⁴*w.* of them which are puffed up, but the power
20. For the kingdom of God is not in word, but in power
12. 8. *w.* of wisdom; and to another the *w.* of knowledge
2 *Cor.* 1. 18. our *word* toward you is not yea and nay
5. 19. committed unto us the *word* of reconciliation
10. 11. what we are in *word* by letters when we are absent
Gal. 5. 14. For the whole law is fulfilled in one *word*
6. 6. But let him that is taught in the *word* communicate
Eph. 5. 26. by the washing of water with the *word*
Phil. 2. 16. holding forth the *word* of life
Col. 3. 16. Let the *word* of Christ dwell in you richly
17. And whatsoever ye do, in *word* or in deed
1 *Th.* 1. 5. our gospel came not unto you in *word* only
6. having received the *word* in much affliction
2. 13. the *word* of the message—as the *word* of men
2 *Th.* 2. 2. be troubled, either by spirit, or by *word*
15. ye were taught, whether by *word,* or by epistle
17. stablish them in every good work and *word*
3. 14. if any man obeyeth not our *word* by this epistle
1 *Tim.* 4. 12. an ensample to them that believe, in *word*
5. 17. those who labour in the *word* and in teaching
2 *Tim.* 2. 17. their *word* will eat as doth a gangrene
4. 2. preach the *word;* be instant in season
Tit. 1. 9. holding to the faithful *word* which is according
Heb. 1. 3. upholding all things by the *word* of his power
2. 2. For if the *w.* spoken through angels proved stedfast
4. 2. but the *word* of hearing did not profit them
5. 13. without experience of the *word* of righteousness
7. 28. but the *word* of the oath, which was after the law
12. 19. intreated that no *word* more should be spoken
27. And this *word,* Yet once more, signifieth
13. 22. brethren, bear with the *word* of exhortation
Jas. 1. 21. receive with meekness the implanted *word*
22. But be ye doers of the *word,* and not hearers only
23. For if any one is a hearer of the *word,* and not a doer
3. 2. If any stumbleth not in *word*   [preached
1 *Pet.* 1. 25. this is the *word* of good tidings which was
2. 8. they stumble at the *word,* being disobedient
3. 1. any obey not the *w.,* they may without the *w.* be gained
2 *Pet.* 1. 19. we have the *word* of prophecy made more sure
3. 7. by the same *word* have been stored up for fire
1 *Jno.* 1. 1. our hands handled, concerning the *W.* of life
2. 5. whoso keepeth his *word,* in him verily hath
3. 18. let us not love in *word,* neither with the tongue

WORDS

Rev. 3. 8. thou—didst keep my *word,* and didst not deny
10. Because thou didst keep the *word* of my patience
12. 11. and because of the *word* of their testimony
see heard, tell, utterance.

Word *of God, or the Lord.*—*A.V.* ¹*commandment of God,*
²*word of God,* ³*word of the Lord.*

Mat. 15. 6. ye have made void the ¹*word of God. Mk.* 7. 13
Lu. 3. 2. the *word of God* came unto John
5. 1. multitude pressed upon him and heard the *w.* of *G.*
8. 11. The seed is the *word of God*
21. which heard the *word of God,* and do it. 11. 28
Jno. 10. 35. gods, unto whom the *word of God* came
Acts 4. 31. they [apostles] spake the *w. of G.* with boldness
6. 2. It is not fit that we should forsake the *word of God*
7. And the *word of God* increased
8. 14. heard that Samaria had received the *word of God*
11. 1. that the Gentiles also had received the *word of God*
12. 24. But the *word of God* grew and multiplied
13. 5. proclaimed the *word of God.* 15. 35: 17. 13: 18. 11
7. Sergius Paulus—sought to hear the *word of God*
44. the whole city—together to hear the *word of God*
46. necessary that the *w. of God* should first be spoken
48. were glad, and glorified the ³*word of God*   [to you
19. 20. So mightily grew the ³*w. of the Lord* and prevailed
Rom. 9. 6. as though the *w. of God* hath come to nought
1 *Cor.* 14. 36. was it from you that the *w. of G.* went forth?
2 *Cor.* 2. 17. not as the many, corrupting the *word of God*
4. 2. nor handling the *word of God* deceitfully
Eph. 6. 17. sword of the Spirit, which is the *word of God*
Phil. 1. 14. bold to speak the *word of God* without fear
Col. 1. 25. given me to you-ward, to fulfil the *word of God*
1 *Th.* 2. 13. even the *word of God*—the *word of God*
2 *Th.* 3. 1. that the *word of the Lord* may run and be
1 *Tim.* 4. 5. sanctified through the *w. of God* and prayer
2 *Tim.* 2. 9. but the *word of God* is not bound
Tit. 2. 5. that the *word of God* be not blasphemed
Heb. 4. 12. For the *word of God* is living, and active
6. 5. and tasted the good *word of God*
11. 3. the worlds have been framed by the *word of God*
13. 7. which spake unto you the *word of God*
1 *Pet.* 1. 23. but of incorruptible, through the *word of God*
25. But the *word of the Lord* abideth for ever
2 *Pet.* 3. 5. earth compacted out of water—by the *w. of G.*
1 *Jno.* 2. 14. are strong, and the *w. of God* abideth in you
Rev. 1. 2. who bare witness of the *word of God*
9. for the *word of God* and the testimony of Jesus
6. 9. them that had been slain for the *w. of God.* 20. 4
19. 13. and his name is called The *Word of God*

Word *of truth.*—*see truth.*

Words.—*A.V.* ¹*saying*—*s.*

Mat. 7. 24. which heareth these ¹*w.* of mine. ¹26: *Lu.* 6. ¹47
28. when Jesus ended these ¹*words.* 19. ¹1: 26. ¹1
10. 14. shall not receive you, nor hear your *words*
12. 37. For by thy *words* thou shalt be justified, and by
thy *words* thou shalt be condemned
24. 35. *words* shall not pass. *Mk.* 13. 31: *Lu.* 21. 33
26. 44. saying again the same *words. Mk.* 14. 39
Mk. 8. 38. ashamed of me and of my *words. Lu.* 9. 26
10. 24. And the disciples were amazed at his *words*
Lu. 1. 20. because thou believedst not my *words*
4. 22. wondered at the *words* of grace which proceeded
24. Let these ¹*words* sink into your ears
24. 8. And they remembered his *words*
11. those *words* appeared in their sight as idle talk
44. These are my *words* which I spake unto you

WORDS

Jno. 3. 34. whom God hath sent speaketh the w. of God
5. 47. his writings, how shall ye believe my words?
6. 63. the words that I have spoken unto you are spirit
68. shall we go? thou hast the words of eternal life
7. 40. the multitude therefore, when they heard these ¹w.
8. 47. He that is of God heareth the words of God
10. 19. division again among the Jews because of these ¹w.
14. 10. w. that I say unto you I speak not from myself
24. He that loveth me not keepeth not my ¹words
15. 7. and my words abide in you, ask whatsoever ye will
17. 8. for the words which thou gavest me I have given
19. 13. When Pilate—heard these ¹w., he brought Jesus
Acts 2. 14. Ye men of Judæa—give ear unto my words
22. Ye men of Israel, hear these words
40. And with many other words he testified
5. 20. speak—to the people all the words of this Life. 24
6. 13. This man ceaseth not to speak words against this
7. 22. Moses—he was mighty in his words and works
10. 22. Cornelius—his house, and to hear words from thee
44. While Peter yet spake these words
11. 14. [Peter] who shall speak unto thee words
13. 42. they besought that these words might be spoken
15. 15. And to this agree the words of the prophets
24. troubled you with words, subverting your souls
18. 15. if they are questions about words and names
20. 35. and to remember the words of the Lord Jesus
26. 25. but speak forth words of truth and soberness
Rom. 3. 4. That thou mightest be justified in thy ¹words
10. 18. And their words unto the ends of the world
1 Cor. 1. 17. preach the gospel: not in wisdom of words
2. 4. preaching were not in persuasive words of wisdom
13. not in words which man's wisdom teacheth
14. 19. I had rather speak five words with my understanding—than ten thousand words in a tongue
Eph. 5. 6. Let no man deceive you with empty words
1 Th. 4. 18. Wherefore comfort one another with these w.
1 Tim. 4. 6. nourished in the words of the faith
6. 3. sound words, even the w. of our Lord Jesus Christ
4. doting about questionings and disputes of words
2 Tim. 1. 13. Hold the pattern of sound words
2. 14. that they strive not about words, to no profit
4. 15. for he greatly withstood our words
2 Pet. 2. 18. uttering great swelling w. of vanity. Jude 16
3. 2. remember the words which were spoken. Jude 17
Rev. 1. 3. they that hear the words of the prophecy. 22. 18
17. 17. until the words of God should be accomplished
19. 9. These are the true ¹words of God
21. 5. Write; for these words are faithful and true. 22. ¹6
22. 7. Blessed is he that keepeth the ¹w. of the prophecy
9. with them which keep the ¹words of this book
10. Seal not up the ¹words of the prophecy of this book
19. if any man shall take away from the words
see saying, sayings, speech, talk, these things.

Work.—*A.V.*¹*do,*²*labour—s,*³*miracle—s,*⁴*shew,*⁵*working.*

Mat. 14. 2. therefore do these powers ⁴work in him
21. 28. Son, go work to-day in the vineyard
Mk. 6. 5. And he could there do no mighty work
9. 39. there is no man which shall do a mighty ³work
13. 34. authority to his servants, to each one his work
Lu. 13. 14. There are six days in which men ought to work
Jno. 4. 34. My meat is to do the will—and to accomplish his
5. 17. My Father worketh even until now, and I work [w.
6. 27. ³Work not for the meat which perisheth
28. must we do, that we may work the works of God?
29. This is the w. of God, that ye believe on him whom
7. 21. I did one work, and ye all marvel
9. 4. We must work the works of him that sent me—the
night cometh, when no man can work

WORKETH

Jno. 17. 4. having accomplished the work which thou hast
Acts 5. 38. if this counsel or this work be of men [given me
13. 2. Separate me Barnabas and Saul for the work
41. For I work a work in your days, A work which
ye shall in no wise believe
14. 26. for the work which they had fulfilled
15. 38. and went not with them to the work [Mark]
Rom. 2. 15. the work of the law written in their hearts
8. 28. love God all things work together for good
14. 20. Overthrow not for meat's sake the work of God
1 Cor. 3. 13. each man's work shall be made manifest—w.
14. If any man's work shall abide [of what sort it is
15. If any man's work shall be burned, he shall suffer
9. 1. are not ye my work in the Lord?
Gal. 6. 4. But let each man prove his own work
10. let us ¹work that which is good toward all men
Eph. 4. 12. unto the work of ministering, unto the building
19. to work all uncleanness with greediness
Phil. 1. 22. if this is the fruit of my ²work, then what I shall
2. 12. work out your own salvation with fear and
13. both to will and to ¹work, for his good pleasure
30. for the work of Christ he came nigh unto death
1 Th. 1. 3. your work of faith and labour of love
4. 11. do your own business, and to w. with your hands
5. 13. exceeding highly in love for their work's sake
2 Th. 1. 11. and every work of faith, with power
2. 7. For the mystery of lawlessness doth already work
3. 10. If any will not work, neither let him eat
11. disorderly, that ⁵work not at all, but are busybodies
12. that with quietness they w., and eat their own bread
2 Tim. 4. 5. do the work of an evangelist, fulfil thy ministry
Heb. 6. 10. God is not unrighteous to forget your work
Jas. 1. 4. And let patience have its perfect work
1 Pet. 1. 17. judgeth according to each man's work
Rev. 22. 12. to render to each man according as his work is
see difficulty, evil, good, word, workest, worketh, wrought.

Workers.—*A.V.* ¹*keepers.*

Lu. 13. 27. depart from me, all ye workers of iniquity
2 Cor. 11. 13. For such men are false apostles, deceitful w.
Phil. 3. 2. Beware of the dogs, beware of the evil workers
Tit. 2. 5. soberminded, chaste, ¹workers at home, kind
see fellow-worker, working.

Workest.—*A.V.* ¹*work.*

Jno. 6. 30. may see, and believe thee? what ¹workest thou?

Worketh.—*A.V.* ¹*causeth,* ²*doeth,* ³*effectual,* ⁴*work.*

Jno. 5. 17. My Father worketh even until now
Acts 10. 35. and worketh righteousness, is acceptable to him
Rom. 2. 9. anguish, upon every soul of man that ²w. evil
10. honour and peace to every man that worketh good
4. 4. Now to him that worketh, the reward is not
5. But to him that worketh not, but believeth on him
15. for the law worketh wrath; but where there is no law
5. 3. knowing that tribulation worketh patience
13. 10. Love worketh no ill to his neighbour
1 Cor. 12. 6. the same God, who worketh all things in all
11. all these worketh the one and the same Spirit
16. 10. he worketh the work of the Lord, as I also do
2 Cor. 1. 6. which ³w. in the patient enduring of the same
4. 12. So then death worketh in us, but life in you
17. worketh for us more and more exceedingly
7. 10. For godly sorrow worketh repentance—but the
sorrow of the world worketh death
9. 11. which ¹worketh through us thanksgiving to God

382

WORKETH

Gal. 3. 5. and *worketh* miracles among you, doeth he it
Eph. 1. 11. who *w.* all things after the counsel of his will
2. 2. that now *worketh* in the sons of disobedience
3. 20. according to the power that *worketh* in us
Phil. 2. 13. for it is God which *worketh* in you both to will
Col. 1. 29. to his working, which *worketh* in me mightily
1 *Th.* 2. 13. of God, which also *worketh* in you that believe
Jas. 1. 3. that the proof of your faith *worketh* patience
20. the wrath of man *w.* not the righteousness of God
25. not a hearer that forgetteth, but a doer that ⁴*w.*
see maketh, working.

Work *Iniquity.—see iniquity.*

Working—s.—*A.V.* ¹*labouring*, ²*operation—s*, ³*strong delusion*, ⁴*workers*, ⁵*worketh*, ⁶*working.*

Mk. 16. 20. the Lord *working* with them, and confirming
Rom. 1. 27. men with men *working* unseemliness
7. 13. might be shewn to be sin, by *working* death to me
1 *Cor.* 4. 12. and we toil, *working* with our own hands
9. 6. have we not a right to forbear *working* ?
12. 6. there are diversities of ²*workings*, but the same God
10. and to another ⁶*workings* of miracles
2 *Cor.* 6. 1. And ⁴*working* together with him we intreat
Gal. 5. 6. but faith ⁵*working* through love
Eph. 1. 19. according to that *w.* of the strength of his might
3. 7. according to the *working* of his power [part
4. 16. according to the *w.* in due measure of each several
28. *working* with his hands the thing that is good
Phil. 3. 21. according to the *working* whereby he is able
Col. 1. 29. I labour also, striving according to his *working*
2. 12. raised with him through faith in the ²*w.* of God
1 *Th.* 2. 9. ¹*w.* night and day, that we might not burden any
2 *Th.* 2. 9. according to the *working* of Satan [of you
11. God sendeth them a ³*w.* of error, that they should
Heb. 13. 21. *working* in us that which is well-pleasing
Rev. 16. 14. for they are spirits of devils, *working* signs
see work.

Workman.
2 *Tim.* 2. 15. a *workman* that needeth not to be ashamed
see labourer.

Workmanship.
Eph. 2. 10. For we are his *workmanship*, created in Christ

Workmen.
Acts 19. 25. together, with the *workmen* of like occupation

Works.—*A.V.* ¹*children*, ²*deeds.*

Mat. 11. 2. John heard in the prison the *w.* of the Christ
19. And wisdom is justified by her ¹*works*
23. 3. but do not ye after their *w.* ; for they say, and do not
5. But all their *works* they do for to be seen of men
Lu. 11. 48. and consent unto the ²*works* of your fathers
Jno. 3. 19. for their ²*works* were evil [reproved
20. cometh not to the light, lest his ²*works* should be
21. to the light, that his ²*works* may be made manifest
5. 20. and greater *works* than these will he shew him
36. the *works* which the Father hath given me to accomplish, the very *works* that I do
6. 28. we do, that we may work the *works* of God? [doest
7. 3. thy disciples also may behold thy *w.* which thou
7. hateth, because I testify of it, that its *works* are evil
8. 39. Abraham's children, ye would do the *w.* of Abraham
41. Ye do the ²*works* of your father
9. 3. that the *works* of God should be made manifest

WORKS

Jno. 9. 4. We must work the *works* of him that sent me
10. 25. the *works* that I do in my Father's name, these
32. for which of those *works* do ye stone me?
37. If I do not the *works* of my Father, believe me not
38. though ye believe not me, believe the *works*
14. 10. but the Father abiding in me doeth his *works*
11. or else believe me for the very *works'* sake
14. 12. the *works* that I do shall he do also ; and greater *works* than these shall he do
15. 24. the *works* which none other did, they had not
Acts 7. 41. and rejoiced in the *works* of their hands
26. 20. turn to God, doing *works* worthy of repentance
Rom. 2. 6. who will render to every man according to his ²*w.*
3. 20. because by the ²*works* of the law shall no flesh
27. By what manner of law ? of *works* ? Nay: but by a
29. justified by faith apart from the ²*works* of the law
4. 2. For if Abraham was justified by *works*
6. God reckoneth righteousness apart from *works*
9. 11. might stand, not of *works*, but of him that calleth
32. they sought it not by faith, but as it were by *works*
11. 6. But if it is by grace, it is no more of *works*
13. 12. let us therefore cast off the *works* of darkness
2 *Cor.* 11. 15. whose end shall be according to their *works*
12. 12. by signs and wonders and mighty ²*works*
Gal. 2. 16. man is not justified by the *works* of the law
3. 2. Received ye the Spirit by the *works* of the law
5. doeth he it by the *works* of the law, or by the hearing
10. For as many as are of the *w.* of the law are under
5. 19. Now the *works* of the flesh are manifest [a curse
Eph. 2. 9. not of *works*, that no man should glory
10. created in Christ Jesus for good *works*
5. 11. no fellowship with the unfruitful *w.* of darkness
Col. 1. 21. enemies in your mind in your evil *works*
2 *Tim.* 1. 9. a holy calling, not according to our *works*
4. 14. the Lord will render to him according to his *w.*
Tit. 1. 16. but by their *works* they deny him
3. 5. not by *works* done in righteousness
Heb. 1. 10. And the heavens are the *works* of thy hands
2. 7. And didst set him over the *works* of thy hands
3. 9. And saw my *works* forty years
4. 3. although the *w.* were finished from the foundation
4. God rested on the seventh day from all his *works*
10. hath himself also rested from his *works*, as God did
6. 1. again a foundation of repentance from dead *works*
9. 14. cleanse your conscience from dead *works* to serve
Jas. 2. 14. if a man say he hath faith, but have not *works* ?
17. Even so faith, if it have not *works*, is dead in itself
18. I have *works* : shew me thy faith apart from thy *works*, and I by my *works* will shew thee my faith
20. O vain man, that faith apart from *works* is barren ?
21. Was not Abraham our father justified by *works*
22. faith wrought with his *works*, and by *works* was
24. Ye see that by *works* a man is justified [faith
25. was not also Rahab the harlot justified by *works*
26. even so faith apart from *works* is dead
3. 13. so let him shew by his good life his *works*
2 *Pet.* 3. 10. the earth and the *works* that are therein
1 *Jno.* 3. 8. that he might destroy the *works* of the devil
2 *Jno.* 11. giveth him greeting partaketh in his evil ²*works*
3 *Jno.* 10. I will bring to remembrance his ²*works*
Jude 15. convict all the ungodly of all their ²*w.* of ungodliness
Rev. 2. 2. I know thy *works*. 19: 3. 1, 8, 15
6. that thou hatest the ²*works* of the Nicolaitans
22. great tribulation, except they repent of her ²*works*
23. give unto each one of you according to your *works*
26. he that keepeth my *works* unto the end, to him will I
3. 2. for I have found no *works* of thine fulfilled
9. 20. repented not of the *works* of their hands. 16. ⁹11

383

WORKS

Rev.14. 13. from their labours; for their w. follow with them
18. 6. double unto her the double according to her works
20. 13. judged every man according to their works. 12
see deeds, evil, great, mighty.

World.—A. V. *earth.*
Mat. 4. 8. sheweth him all the kingdoms of the world.
5. 14. Ye are the light of the world   [Lu. 4. 5
13. 22. and the care of the world. Mk. 4. 19
35. utter things hidden from the foundation of the w.
38. and the field is the world; and the good seed, these
39. and the harvest is the end of the world
40. so shall it be in the end of the world. 49
16. 26. be profited, if he shall gain the whole world,
and forfeit his life? Mk. 8. 36: Lu. 9. 25
18. 7. Woe unto the w. because of occasions of stumbling!
24. 3. sign of thy coming, and of the end of the world?
21. tribulation—not been from the beginning of the w.
28. 20. I am with you alway, even unto the end of the w.
Mk. 14. 9. the whole world, that also which this woman
Lu. 1. 70. prophets which have been since the w. began).
2. 1. that all the world should be enrolled   [Acts 3. 21
20. 35. that are accounted worthy to attain to that world
21. 26. fear, and for expectation of the things which are
coming on the ¹world ʳand the w. knew him not
Jno. 1. 10. He was in the w., and the w. was made by him,
29. Lamb of God, which taketh away the sin of the w.!
3. 16. For God so loved the world, that he gave his only
17. sent not the Son into the world to judge the world;
but that the world should be saved through him
4. 42. is indeed the Saviour of the world. 1 Jno. 4. 14
6. 33. down out of heaven, and giveth life unto the world
51. which I will give is my flesh, for the life of the world
7. 4. If thou doest these things, manifest thyself to the w.
7. The world cannot hate you; but me it hateth
8. 12. I am the light of the world. 9. 5
26. which I heard from him, these speak I unto the w.
12. 19. ye prevail nothing: lo, the w. is gone after him
47. I came not to judge the world, but to save the world
14. 17. Spirit of truth: whom the world cannot receive
19. a little while, and the world beholdeth me no more
22. manifest thyself unto us, and not unto the world?
27. not as the world giveth, give I unto you
30. much with you, for the prince of the world cometh
31. that the world may know that I love the Father
15. 18. If the world hateth you, ye know. 1 Jno. 3. 13
19. If ye were of the world, the world would love—ye
are not of the w.—out of the w.—w hateth you
16. 20. weep and lament, but the world shall rejoice
28. and am come into the world: again, I leave the w.
33. world ye have tribulation—I have overcome the w.
17. 5. the glory which I had with thee before the w. was
6. the men whom thou gavest me out of the world
9. I pray for them: I pray not for the world
14. the world hateth them, because they are not of the
world, even as I am not of the world. 16
15. not that thou shouldest take them from the world
21. that the w. may believe that thou didst send me. 23
24. thou lovedst me before the foundation of the world
25. O righteous Father, the world knew thee not
18. 20. I have spoken openly to the world
21. 25. the world itself would not contain the books
Acts 11. 28. should be a great famine over all the world
15. 16. things known from the beginning of the world
17. 6. These that have turned the world upside down
24. The God that made the world and all things
31. in the which he will judge the w. in righteousness
19. 27. whom all Asia and the world worshippeth
24. 5. among all the Jews throughout the world
Rom. 1. 8. your faith is proclaimed throughout the whole w.

WORLD

Rom. 1. 20. since the creation of the world are clearly seen
3. 6. for then how shall God judge the world?
19. the w. may be brought under the judgement of God
4. 13. or to his seed, that he should be heir of the world
10. 18. And their words unto the ends of the world
11. 12. Now if their fall is the riches of the world
15. casting away of them is the reconciling of the world
1 Cor. 1. 20. where is the disputer of this world?—God
made foolish the wisdom of the world?
21. the world through its wisdom knew not God
27. God chose the foolish things of the w.—weak things
28. and the base things of the world   [of the world
2. 12. But we received, not the spirit of the world
3. 22. Apollos, or Cephas, or the world, or life, or death
4. 9. for we are made a spectacle unto the world
13. we are made as the filth of the world
5. 10. fornicators of this world -go out of the world
6. 2. shall judge the world? and if the world is judged
7. 31. those that use the world, as not abusing it
33. married is careful for the things of the world. 34
11. 32. that we may not be condemned with the world
2 Cor. 5. 19. God was in Christ reconciling the world
7. 10. but the sorrow of the world worketh death [8, 20
Gal. 4. 3. in bondage under the rudiments of the w. Col. 2.
6. 14. through which the world hath been crucified unto
me, and I unto the world
Heb. 1. 6. bringeth in the firstborn into the world he saith
2. 5. not unto angels did he subject the world to come
9. 26. often have suffered since the foundation of the w.
11. 7. through which he condemned the world
38. (of whom the world was not worthy)
Jas. 1. 27. and to keep himself unspotted from the world·
2. 5. God choose—poor as to the world to be rich in faith
3. 6. the tongue is a fire: the world of iniquity
4. 4. the friendship of the world—friend of the world
2 Pet. 2. 5. spared not the ancient world—when he brought
a flood upon the world of the ungodly
20. after they have escaped the defilements of the world
3. 6. by which means the world that then was
1 Jno. 2. 2. not for ours only, but also for the whole world
15. Love not the world, neither the things that are in
the world. If any man love the world
16. of life, is not of the Father, but is of the world
17. And the world passeth away, and the lust thereof
3. 1. For this cause the world knoweth us not
17. whoso hath the w.'s goods, and beholdeth his brother
4. 5. They are of the world: therefore speak they as
of the world, and the world heareth them
5. 4. For whatsoever is begotten of God overcometh
the world—overcome the world. 5
19. of God, and the whole world lieth in the evil one
Rev. 3. 10. that hour which is to come upon the whole w.
11. 15. The kingdom of the w. is become the kingdom of
12. 9. Satan, the deceiver of the whole world [our Lord
see age, ages, earth, evermore, times, worlds.

Foundation of the **World.**—*see foundation.*

In, or into the **World.**

Mat. 24. 14. gospel—shall be preached in the whole w. 26. 13
Mk. 10. 30. and in the w. to come eternal life. Lu. 18. 30
Go ye into all the world, and preach the gospel
Jno. 1. 9. which lighteth every man, coming into the world
10. He was in the world, and the world was made by him
3. 17. God sent not the Son into the world to judge
19. light is come into the w., and men loved the darkness
6. 14. This is—the prophet that cometh into the world
9. 5. When I am in the world, I am the light of the world

WORLD

Jno. 10. 36. whom the Father sanctified and sent *i. the w.*
11. 27. Son of God, even he that cometh *into the world*
12. 46. I am come a light *into the world*
13. 1. having loved his own which were *in the world*
16. 33. *In the world* ye have tribulation
17. 11. I am no more *in the w.*, and these are *in the w.*
18. send me *into the w.*, even so sent I them *into the w.*
18. 37. born, and to this end am I come *into the world*
Rom. 5. 12. as through one man sin entered *into the world*
13. for until the law sin was *in the world*
1 *Cor.* 8. 4. we know that no idol is anything *in the world*
2 *Cor.* 1. 12. we behaved ourselves *in the world*
Eph. 2. 12. having no hope and without God *in the world*
Col. 1. 6. also *in all the world* bearing fruit and increasing
2. 20. as though living *in the w.*, do ye subject yourselves
1 *Tim.* 1. 15. Christ Jesus came *into the w.* to save sinners
3. 16. believed on *in the world*, received up in glory
6. 7. for we brought nothing *into the world*
Heb. 10. 5. when he cometh *into the world*, he saith. 1. 6
1 *Pet.* 5. 9. accomplished in your brethren who are *in the w.*
2 *Pet.* 1. 4. the corruption that is *in the world* by lust
1 *Jno.* 2. 15. Love not the world, neither the things—*in the w.*
16. For all that is *in the world*, the lust of the flesh
4. 1. many false prophets are gone out *into the world*
3. that it cometh; and now it is *in the world* already
4. greater is he that is in you than he that is *in the w.*
9. God hath sent his only begotten Son *into the world*
2 *Jno.* 7. For many deceivers are gone forth *into the world*

This World.—*A.V.* ¹*worldly.*

Mat. 12. 32. it shall not be forgiven him, neither in *this w.*
Lu. 16. 8. the sons of *this w.* are for their own generation
20. 34. The sons of *this world* marry [wiser
Jno. 8. 23. ye are of *this world*; I am not of *this world*
9. 39. For judgement came I into *this world*
11. 9. because he seeth the light of *this world*
12. 25. he that hateth his life in *this world* shall keep it
31. Now is the judgement of *this world* : now shall
the prince of *this world* be cast out
13. 1. he should depart out of *this world* unto the Father
16. 11. because the prince of *this world* hath been judged
18. 36. My kingdom is not of *this world* : if my kingdom were of *this w.*, then would my servants fight
Rom. 12. 2. And be not fashioned according to *this world*
1 *Cor.* 1. 20. where is the disputer of *this world*?
2. 6. a wisdom not of *this w.*, nor of the rulers of *this w.*
8. which none of the rulers of *this world* knoweth
3. 18. If any man thinketh that he is wise—in *this world*
19. For the wisdom of *this w.* is foolishness with God
5. 10. not altogether with the fornicators of *this world*
7. 31. for the fashion of *this world* passeth away
2 *Cor.* 4. 4. the god of *this world* hath blinded the minds
Gal. 1. 4. might deliver us out of *this present evil world*
Eph. 1. 21. every name—not only in *this world*
2. 2. ye walked according to the course of *this world*
1 *Tim.* 6. 17. Charge them that are rich in *this present w.*
2 *Tim.* 4. 10. Demas forsook me, having loved *this present w.*
Tit. 2. 12. righteously and godly in *this present world*
Heb. 9. 1. and its sanctuary, a sanctuary of ¹*this world*
1 *Jno.* 4. 17. because as he is, even so are we in *this world*

Worldly.

Tit. 2. 12. denying ungodliness and *worldly* lusts
see this world.

World-rulers.—*A.V.* ¹*rulers of the darkness of this world.*

Eph. 6. 12. against the ¹*world-rulers* of this darkness

50

WORSHIPPED

Worlds.—*A.V.* ¹*world.*

1 *Cor.* 2. 7. which God foreordained before the ¹*w.* unto our
Heb. 1. 2. through whom also he made the *worlds* [glory
11. 3. the *worlds* have been framed by the word of God

Worm—s.

Mk. 9. 48. their *w.* dieth not, and the fire is not quenched
Acts 12. 23. he [Herod] was eaten of *worms*

Wormwood.

Rev. 8. 11. the name of the star is called *W.*—became *w.*

Worn.—*A.V.* ¹*ware.*

Lu. 8. 27. for a long time he had ¹*worn* no clothes

Worse.—*A.V.* ¹*better.*

Mat. 9. 16. and a *worse* rent is made. *Mk.* 2. 21
12. 45. and the last state of that man becometh *worse* than the first. *Lu.* 11. 26
27. 64. and the last error will be *worse* than the first
Mk. 5. 26. was nothing bettered, but rather grew *worse*
Jno. 2. 10. men have drunk freely, then that which is *w.*
5. 14. sin no more, lest a *worse* thing befall thee
Rom. 3. 9. What then? are we in ¹*worse* case than they?
1 *Cor.* 8. 8. neither, if we eat not, are we the *worse*
11. 17. come together not for the better but for the *w.*
1 *Tim.* 5. 8. denied the faith, and is *w.* than an unbeliever
2 *Tim.* 3. 13. evil men and impostors shall wax *w.* and *w.*
2 *Pet.* 2. 20. the last state is become *worse* with them

Worship.—*A.V.* ¹*devotions.*

Mat. 2. 2. star in the east, and are come to *worship* him
8. me word, that I also may come and *worship* him
4. 9. if thou wilt fall down and *worship* me. *Lu.* 4. 7
10. Thou shalt *worship* the Lord thy God. *Lu.* 4. 8
15. 9. but in vain do they *worship* me. *Mk.* 7. 7
Jno. 4. 20. Jerusalem is the place where men ought to *w.*
22. Ye *worship* that which ye know not: we *worship* that which we know
23. *worship* the Father in spirit and truth. 21, 24
12. 20. certain Greeks among those that went up to *w.*
Acts 7. 43. The figures which ye made to *worship* them
8. 27. eunuch—who had come to Jerusalem for to *w.*
17. 23. and observed the objects of your ¹*worship*—What therefore ye *worship* in ignorance
18. 13. persuadeth men to *w.* God contrary to the law
24. 11. twelve days since I went up to *w.* at Jerusalem
1 *Cor.* 14. 25. he will fall down on his face and *worship* God
Phil. 3. 3. who *worship* by the Spirit of God, and glory in
Heb. 1. 6. And let all the angels of God *worship* him
Rev. 3. 9. I will make them to come and *w.* before thy feet
4. 10. and shall *worship* him that liveth for ever and ever
9. 20. that they should not *worship* devils, and the idols
11. 1. and the altar, and them that *worship* therein
13. 8. And all that dwell on the earth shall *worship* him
12. them that dwell therein to *worship* the first beast
15. many as should not *w.* the image of the beast. 14. 11
14. 7. *worship* him that made the heaven and the earth
15. 4. all the nations shall come and *worship* before thee
19. 10. before his feet to *worship* him—*w.* God. 22. 8, 9
see glory, serve, worshippers, worshippeth.

Worshipped.

Mat. 2. 11. and they fell down and *worshipped* him
8. 2. there came to him a leper and *worshipped* him
9. 18. there came a ruler, and *worshipped* him
14. 33. they that were in the boat *worshipped* him

385

WORSHIPPED

Mat. 15. 25. But she came and *worshipped* him, saying
18. 26. The servant therefore fell down and w. him
28. 9. took hold of his feet, and *worshipped* him
17. And when they saw him, they *worshipped* him
Mk. 5. 6. he saw Jesus from afar, he ran and w. him
15. 19. and bowing their knees *worshipped* him
Lu. 24. 52. they *worshipped* him, and returned to Jerusalem
Jno. 4. 20. Our fathers *worshipped* in this mountain
9. 38. Lord, I believe. And he *worshipped* him
Acts 10. 25. and fell down at his foot, and *worshipped* him
16. 14. one that *worshipped* God, heard us
18. 7. named Titus Justus, one that *worshipped* God
Rom. 1. 25. and *worshipped* and served the creature rather
2 *Th.* 2. 4. against all that is called God or that is w.
Heb. 11. 21. and w., leaning upon the top of his staff
Rev. 5. 14. And the elders fell down and w. 11. 16 : 19. 4
7. 11. they fell on their faces, and *worshipped* God
13. 4. and they *worshipped* the dragon—they w. the beast
16. 2. and which *worshipped* his image. 19. 20
20. 4. and such as *worshipped* not the beast
see served.

Worshipper-s.—*A.V.* ¹*service,* ²*worship.*

Jno. 4. 23. when the true *worshippers* shall worship the Father—the Father seek to be his ²*worshippers*
9. 31. but if any man be a *worshipper* of God
Heb. 9. 9. the conscience, make the ¹*worshipper* perfect
10. 2. because the w., having been once cleansed
see temple keeper.

Worshippeth.—*A.V.* ¹*worship.*

Acts 19. 27. whom all Asia and the world *worshippeth*
Rev. 14. 9. If any man ¹w. the beast and his image

Worshipping.—*A.V.* ¹*served God.*

Mat. 20. 20. the mother—with her sons, *worshipping* him
Lu. 2. 37. ¹*worshipping* with fastings and supplications
Col. 2. 18. by a voluntary humility and w. of the angels

Worthily.—*A.V.* ¹*becometh,* ²*godly sort,* ³*worthy.*

Rom. 16. 2. that ye receive her [Phœbe] in the Lord, ¹w.
Eph. 4. 1. beseech you to walk ³*worthily* of the calling
Col. 1. 10. to walk ³*worthily* of the Lord unto. 1 *Th.* 2. ³12
3 *Jno.* 6. set forward on their journey ²*worthily* of God

Worthy.—*A.V.* ¹*becometh,* ²*meet.*

Mat. 3. 8. Bring forth—fruit ²10. of repentance. *Lu.* 3. 8
11. whose shoes I am not *worthy* to bear. *Mk.* 1. 7 : *Lu.* 3. 16 ; *Jno.* 1. 27 ; *Acts* 13. 25
8. 8. Lord, I am not *worthy* that thou shouldest come under my roof. *Lu.* 7. 6
10. 10. for the labourer is *worthy* of his food
11. village ye shall enter, search out who in it is *worthy*
13. And if the house be *worthy*—but if it be not *worthy*
37. loveth father or mother more than me is not *worthy* of me—is not *worthy* of me. 38
22. 8. but they that were bidden were not *worthy*
Lu. 7. 4. He is *worthy* that thou shouldest do this for him
7. neither thought I myself *worthy* to come unto thee
10. 7. for the labourer is *worthy* of his hire. 1 *Tim.* 5. 18
12. 48. and did things *worthy* of stripes, shall be beaten
15. 19. I am no more *worthy* to be called thy son
20. 35. they that are accounted w. to attain to that world
Acts 26. 20. turn to God, doing works ²w. of repentance
Rom. 8. 18. are not *worthy* to be compared with the glory
Phil. 1. 27. let your manner of life be ¹*worthy* of the gospel of Christ [acceptation. 4. 9
1 *Tim.* 1. 15. Faithful is the saying, and *worthy* of all

WOUNDED

Heb. 10. 29. shall he be judged *worthy,* who hath trodden
11. 38. (of whom the world was not *worthy*)
Rev. 3. 4. shall walk with me in white ; for they are w.
4. 11. *Worthy* art thou, our Lord and our God
5. 2. Who is *worthy* to open the book. 4, 9
12. *Worthy* is the Lamb that hath been slain
16. 6. hast thou given them to drink : they are *worthy*
see corrected, count, counted, honourable, prevail, worthily.

Worthy *of death.—see death.*

Wot.

Acts 3. 17. I *wot* that in ignorance ye did it
7. 40. as for this Moses—we *wot* not what is become of him
Rom. 11. 2. Or w. ye not what the scripture saith of Elijah ?
Phil. 1. 22. then what I shall choose I *wot* not

Would.—*A.V.* ¹*desire.*

Mat. 7. 12. *would* that men should do unto you. *Lu.* 6. 31
23. 37. how often w. I have gathered thy children. *Lu.* 13.
27. 15. release—one prisoner, whom they *would* [34
Mk. 3. 13. and calleth unto him whom he himself *would*
9. 35. If any man ¹*would* be first, he shall be last of all
10. 36. What *would* ye that I should do for you ? 35
Jno. 6. 11. likewise also of the fishes as much as they w.
Acts 18. 14. reason *would* that I should bear with you
26. 29. I *would* to God, that whether with little or with
Rom. 7. 15. for not what I *would,* that do I practise. 19, 21
1 *Cor.* 4. 8. yea and I *would* that ye did reign
7. 7. Yet I *would* that all men were even as I myself
14. 5. Now I *would* have you all speak with tongues
2 *Cor.* 11. 1. *Would* that ye could bear with me in a little
12. 20. find you not such as I *would,* and should myself be found of you such as ye *would* not [poor
Gal. 2. 10. only they *would* that we should remember the
5. 12. I *would* that they which unsettle you *would* even
17. that ye may not do the things that ye *would*
Phil. 1. For I w. have you know how greatly I strive
3 *Jno.* 10. and them that *would* he forbiddeth
Rev. 3. 15. I *would* thou wert cold or hot
see desired, wish.

Would *not.*

Mat. 2. 18. Rachel weeping—And she w. *not* be comforted
18. 30. And he *would not* : but went and cast him
23. 37. under her wings, and ye *would not !* *Lu.* 13. 34
Mk. 9. 30. and he *would not* that any man should know
Lu. 18. 4. And he *would not* for a while : but afterward
19. 27. which *would not* that I should reign over them
Rom. 7. 16. But if what I *would not,* that I do. 20
19. but the evil which I *would not,* that I practise
11. 25. For I *would not,* brethren, have you. 1 *Cor.* 10. 1
1 *Cor.* 10. 20. I *would not* that ye should have communion
2 *Cor.* 12. 20. myself be found of you such as ye *would not*

Wouldest.—*A.V.* ¹*wilt.*

Mat. 20. 21. What ¹w. thou ?—that these my two sons
Jno. 21. 18. and walkedst whither thou *wouldest*—and carry thee whither thou *wouldest* not
Heb. 10. 5. Sacrifice and offering thou *wouldest* not. 8

Wound.—*A.V.* ¹*wrapped.*

Mk. 15. 46. taking him down, ¹w. him in the linen cloth
see bound, death-stroke, stroke, wounding, wrapped.

Wounded.

Lu. 20. 12. they *wounded,* and cast him forth. *Mk.* 12. 4
Acts 19. 16. they fled out of that house naked and *wounded*
see beat, smitten.

WOUNDING

Wounding.—*A.V.* ¹*wound.*
1 *Cor.* 8. 12. ¹*wounding* their conscience when it is weak

Wounds.
Lu. 10. 34. bound up his *wounds,* pouring on them oil
see bound.

Woven.
Jno. 19. 23. without seam, *woven* from the top throughout

Wranglings.—*A.V.* ¹*perverse disputings.*
1 *Tim.* 6. 5. ¹*wranglings* of men corrupted in mind

Wrapped.—*A.V.* ¹*wound.*
Mat. 27. 59. *wrapped* it in a clean linen cloth. *Lu.* 23. 53
Lu. 2. 7. and she *wrapped* him in swaddling clothes. 12
Acts 5. 6. the young men arose and ¹*wrapped* him round
see rolled, wound.

Wrath—s.—*A.V.* ¹*vengeance,* ²*wrath.*
Mat. 3. 7. to flee from the *wrath* to come? *Lu.* 3. 7
Lu. 4. 28. they were all filled with *w.* in the synagogue.
21. 23. and *wrath* unto this people [*Acts* 19. 28
Rom. 2. 5. treasurest up for thyself *w.* in the day of *wrath*
8. obey unrighteousness, shall be *wrath* and indignation
3. 5. Is God unrighteous who visiteth with ¹*wrath* ?
4. 15. for the law worketh *w.*; but where there is no law
9. 22. What if God, willing to shew his *wrath*—vessels
of *wrath* fitted unto destruction
12. 19. Avenge not yourselves—but give place unto *wrath*
13. 4. an avenger for *wrath* to him that doeth evil
5. needs be in subjection, not only because of the *w.*
2 *Cor.* 12. 20. there should be strife, jealousy, *wraths*
Gal. 5. 20. [works of the flesh] strife, jealousies, ²*wraths*
Eph. 2. 3. and were by nature children of *wrath*
4. 26. let not the sun go down upon your *wrath*
31. Let all bitterness, and *wrath,* and anger, and clamour
6. 4. And, ye fathers, provoke not your children to *wrath*
Col. 3. 8. anger, *wrath,* malice, railing, shameful speaking
1 *Th.* 1. 10. Jesus, which delivered us from the *w.* to come
2. 16. but the *w.* is come upon them to the uttermost
5. 9. For God appointed us not unto *wrath*
1 *Tim.* 2. 8. lifting up holy hands, without *w.* and disputing
Heb. 3. 11. As I sware in my *wrath.* 4. 3
11. 27. forsook Egypt, not fearing the *wrath* of the king
Jas. 1. 19. swift to hear, slow to speak, slow to *wrath*
20. the *w.* of man worketh not the righteousness of God
Rev. 6. 16. hide us—and from the *wrath* of the Lamb
17. for the great day of their *wrath* is come
11. 18. thy *w.* came, and the time of the dead to be judged
12. 12. devil is gone down unto you, having great *wrath*
14. 8. drink of the wine of the *w.* of her fornication. 18. 3
16. 19. the cup of the wine of the fierceness of his *wrath*

Wrath of God.
Jno. 3. 36. but the *wrath of God* abideth on him
Rom. 1. 18. For the *wrath of God* is revealed from heaven
5. 9. we be saved from the *wrath of God* through him
Eph. 5. 6. cometh the *w.* of *G.* upon the sons of disobedi.
Rev. 14. 10. drink of the wine of the *w.* of *G.* [ence. *Col.* 3. 6
19. winepress, the great winepress, of the *wrath of God*
15. 1. for in them is finished the *wrath of God*
16. 1. pour out the seven bowls of the *w.* of *God.* 15. 7
19. 15. winepress of the fierceness of the *w.* of *Almighty God*

Wrest.
2 *Pet.* 3. 16. which the ignorant and unstedfast *wrest*

WRITING

Wrestle.—*A.V. see wrestling.*

Wrestling.—*A.V.* ¹*wrestle.*
Eph. 6. 12. For our ¹*w.* is not against flesh and blood

Wretched.
Rom. 7. 24. O *w.* man that I am! who shall deliver me
Rev. 3. 17. and knowest not that thou art the *wretched* one

Wrinkle.
Eph. 5. 27. a glorious church, not having spot or *wrinkle*

Write.—*A.V.* ¹*written,* ²*wrote.*
Mk. 10. 4. Moses suffered to *write* a bill of divorcement
Lu. 1. 3. to *write* unto thee in order, most excellent
16. 6. Take thy bond, and sit down quickly and *w.* fifty
7. Take thy bond, and *write* fourscore
Jno. 1. 45. Moses in the law, and the prophets, did *write*
19. 21. *Write* not, The King of the Jews
Acts 15. 20. but that we *w.* unto them that they abstain
25. 26. Of whom I have no certain thing to *write*—
I may have somewhat to *write*
Rom. 15. 15. But I ¹*write* the more boldly unto you
16. 22. I Tertius, who ²*write* the epistle, salute you
1 *Cor.* 4. 14. I *write* not these things to shame you
5. 11. now I ¹*write* unto you not to keep company
9. 15. I ¹*write* not these things that it may be so done
14. 37. take knowledge of the things which I *w.* unto you
2 *Cor.* 1. 13. For we *write* none other things unto you
2. 9. For to this end also did I *write,* that I might know
9. 1. the saints, it is superfluous for me to *write* to you
13. 10. For this cause I *write* these things while absent
Gal. 1. 20. Now touching the things which I *w.* unto you
Phil. 3. 1. To *write* the same things to you, to me indeed
1 *Th.* 4. 9. ye have no need that one *write* unto you
2 *Th.* 3. 17. which is the token in every epistle: so I *write*
1 *Tim.* 3. 14. These things *write* I unto thee, hoping to
Philem. 19. I Paul ¹*write* it with mine own hand
21. Having confidence in thine obedience I ²*w.* unto thee
Heb. 8. 10. And on their heart also will I *w.* them. 10. 16
2 *Pet.* 3. 1. the second epistle that I *write* unto you
1 *Jno.* 1. 4. these things we *write,* that our joy may be
2. 7. Beloved, I *write* no new commandment *write* I unto you
8. Again, a new commandment *write* I unto you
12. I *write* unto you, my little children. 2. 1
13. I *write* unto you, fathers—I *w.* unto you, young men
2 *Jno.* 12. Having many things to *write* unto you, I would
not *write* them with paper and ink. 3 *Jno.* 13
Jude 3. I was giving all diligence to *write* unto you—I
was constrained to *write* unto you
Rev. 1. 11. What thou seest, *write* in a book. 19
2. 1. To the angel of the church in Ephesus *write*
8. in Smyrna *write.* 12. in Pergamum *write*
18. in Thyatira *write.* 3. 1. in Sardis *write*
3. 7. in Philadelphia *write.* 14. in Laodicea *write*
12. and I will *write* upon him the name of my God
10. 4. I was about to *write*—and *write* them not
14. 13. ¹*Write,* Blessed are the dead which die in the Lord
19. 9. *Write,* Blessed are they which are bidden to the
21. 5. *Write :* for these words are faithful and true
see written.

Writeth.—*A.V.* ¹*describeth.*
Rom. 10. 5. For Moses ¹*writeth* that the man that doeth
the righteousness which is of the law shall live

Writing.
Mat. 5. 31. let him give her a *writing* of divorcement
see written.

WRITINGS

Writings.—*A.V.* ¹*scriptures.*
Jno. 5. 47. But if ye believe not his *writings*, how shall ye
2 *Tim.* 3. 15. from a babe thou hast known the sacred ¹*w.*

Written.—*A.V.* ¹*write,* ²*writing.*
Mk. 11. 17. Is it not *w.*, My house shall be called. *Lu.* 19. 46
15. 26. his accusation was *written* over, THE KING OF THE JEWS. *Mat.* 27. 37; *Jno.* 19. ²19
Lu. 4. 17. [Jesus] found the place where it was *written*
10. 20. rejoice that your names are *written* in heaven
21. 22. that all things which are *w.* may be fulfilled. 18.31
24. 44. fulfilled, which are *written* in the law of Moses
Jno. 2. 17. His disciples remembered that it was *written*
10. 34. Is it not *written* in your law, I said, Ye are gods ?
12. 16. remembered they that these things were *w.* of him
19. 20. *written* in Hebrew, and in Latin, and in Greek
22. Pilate answered, What I have *written* I have *written*
20. 30. Many other signs—which are not *written*
31. these are *written*, that ye may believe that Jesus
21. 25. the which if they should be *written* every one—would not contain the books that should be *w.*
Acts 13. 29. fulfilled all things that were *written* of him
21. 14. to the law, and which are *written* in the prophets
Rom. 2. 15. shew the work of the law *w.* in their hearts
4. 23. Now it was not *written* for his sake alone
15. 4. *written* aforetime were *written* for our learning
1 *Cor.* 4. 6. learn not to go beyond the things which are *w.*
9. 10. Yea, for our sake it was *written*
10. 11. and they were *written* for our admonition
2 *Cor.* 3. 2. Ye are our epistle, *written* in our hearts
3. *written* not with ink, but with the Spirit of the living
7. the ministration of death, *written*, and engraven
Gal. 3.10. continueth not in all things that are *w.* in the book
6. 11. See with how large letters I have *written*
1 *Th.* 5. 1. ye have no need that aught be ¹*w.* unto you
1 *Pet.* 5. 12. I have *w.* unto you briefly, exhorting.*Heb.*13.22
1 *Jno.* 2. 13. I have ¹*written* unto you, little children
14. I have *written* unto you, fathers—I have *written* unto you, young men
21. I have not *written* unto you because ye know not
26. These things have I *written* unto you. 5. 13
Rev. 1. 3. and keep the things which are *written* therein
2. 17. and upon the stone a new name *written*
5 1. a book *written* within and on the back
14. 1. the name of his Father, *written* on their foreheads
17. 5. upon her forehead a name *written*, MYSTERY
8. whose name hath not been *w.*in the book. 20.15 : 21.27
19. 12. a name *written*, which no one knoweth but he
16. on his thigh a name *written*, KING OF KINGS
21. 12. twelve gates—and names *written* thereon
22. 18. the plagues which are *written* in this book. 19
see enrolled, write, wrote.

Is Written.
Mat. 2. 5. In Bethlehem of Judæa: for thus it *is written*
4. 4. it *is written.* 6, 7, 10; 21. 13: 26. 31; *Mk.* 1. 2 : 14. 27 : *Lu.* 3. 4 : 4. 8 : *Jno.* 6. 45; 8. 17 : *Acts* 1. 20:
13. 33; 23. 5; *Rom.* 2. 24 : 3. 10 : 4. 17 : 10. 15 :
11. 26; 12. 19 : 14. 11 : 15. 21 : 1 *Cor.* 1. 19 : 2. 9 :
3. 19 : 10. 7 : 14. 21 : 2 *Cor.* 9. 9 : *Gal.* 3. 10, 13 :
4. 22, 27 : *Heb.* 10. 7
11. 10. This is he, of whom it *is written.* *Lu.* 7. 27
26. 24. even as it *is written* of him. *Mk.* 9. 13 : 14. 21
Mk. 9. 12. and how it *is written* of the Son of man
Lu. 2. 23. (as it *is written*—Every male that openeth
10. 26. What *is written* in the law ? how readest thou ?
20. 17. What then is this that *is written*, The stone
22. 37. this which *is written* must be fulfilled in me

WROTH

Lu. 24. 46. Thus it *is written*, that the Christ should suffer
Jno. 15. 25. that *is written* in their law, They hated me
Rom. 11. 8. according as it *is w.* 1 *Cor.* 1. 31 : 2 *Cor.* 4. 13
1 *Cor.* 9. 9. For it *is w.*—Thou shalt not muzzle the ox.
15. 45. So also it *is written*, The first man Adam
54. that *is written*, Death is swallowed up in victory
1 *Pet.* 1. 16. because it *is written*, Ye shall be holy

Wrong.—*A.V.* ¹*injured,* ²*reward.*
Mat. 20. 13. Friend, I do thee no *wrong*
Acts 7. 24. And seeing one of them suffer *wrong*
26. ye are brethren, why do ye *wrong* one to another ?
27. But he that did his neighbour *wrong* thrust him
18. 14. Gallio—If indeed it were a matter of *wrong*
25. 10. to the Jews have I [Paul] done no *wrong*
1 *Cor.* 6. 7. Why not rather take *wrong ?*
8. Nay, but ye yourselves do *wrong*, and defraud
2 *Cor.* 7. 12. I wrote not for his cause that did the *wrong*, nor for his cause that suffered the *wrong*
12. 13. was not a burden to you ? forgive me this ¹*wrong*
Gal. 4. 12. Ye did me no ¹*wrong*: but ye know that
Col. 3. 25. he that doeth *w.* shall receive again for the *w.*
2 *Pet.* 2 13. suffering ²*wrong* as the hire of wrong-doing

Wrong-doer.—*A.V.* ¹*offender.*
Acts 25. 11. If then I am a ¹*wrong-doer*—I refuse not to die

Wrong-doing.—*A.V.* ¹*evil-doing,* ²*unrighteousness.*
Acts 24. 20. men themselves say what ¹*w.-doing* they found
2 *Pet.* 2. 13. suffering wrong as the hire of ²*wrong-doing*
15. Balaam—who loved the hire of ²*wrong-doing*

Wronged.
2 *Cor.* 7. 2. Open your hearts to us : we *wronged* no man
Philem. 18. But if he hath *wronged* thee at all, or oweth

Wrongfully.—*A.V.* ¹*false—ly.*
Lu. 3. 14. violence to no man, neither exact anything ¹*w.*
19. 8. if I [Zacchæus] have ¹*w.* exacted aught of any man
1 *Pet.* 2. 19. a man endureth griefs, suffering *wrongfully*

Wrote.—*A.V.* ¹*written.*
Mk. 10. 5. hardness of heart he *w.* you this commandment
12. 19. Master, Moses *wrote* unto us. *Lu.* 20. 28
14. 13. tablet, and *wrote*, saying, His name is John
Jno. 5. 46. ye would believe me ; for he *wrote* of me
8. 6. and with his finger *wrote* on the ground. 8
19. 19. Pilate *wrote* a title also, and put it on the cross
21. 24. This is the disciple which—*wrote* these things
Acts 15. 23. and they *wrote* thus by them, The apostles
18 27. and *wrote* to the disciples to receive him
21. 25. touching the Gentiles which have believed, we ¹*w.*
23. 25. And he *wrote* a letter after this form
1 *Cor.* 5. 9. I *w.* unto you in my epistle. 2 *Cor.* 2. 3, 4 : 7. 12
7. 1. Now concerning the things whereof ye *wrote*
2 *Cor.* 7. 12. I *wrote* not for his cause that did the wrong
Eph. 3. 3. unto me the mystery, as I *wrote* afore in few words
2 *Pet.* 3. 15. Paul also, according to the wisdom given—¹*w.*
2 *Jno.* 5. not as though I *w.* to thee a new commandment
3 *Jno.* 9. I *w.* somewhat unto the church : but Diotrephes
see write.

Wroth.—*A.V.* ¹*angry.*
Mat. 2. 16. Then Herod—was exceeding *wroth*
18. 34. And his lord was *wroth*, and delivered him
22. 7. But the king was *wroth* ; and he sent his armies
23. 25. are ye ¹*wroth* with me, because I made a man
Rev. 11. 18. the nations were ¹*wroth*, and thy wrath came
12. 17. And the dragon waxed *wroth* with the woman

WROUGHT

Wrought.—*A.V.* ¹*committed*, ²*done*, ³*mighty*, ⁴*shewed*, ⁵*work*.

Mat. 26. 10. for she hath *w*. a good work upon me. Mk. 14. 6
Mk. 6. 2. what mean such mighty works *w*. by his hands?
Jno. 3. 21. manifest, that they have been *wrought* in God
Acts 4. 16. a notable miracle hath been ²*w*. through them
    22. on whom this miracle of healing was ⁴*wrought*
    5. 12. many signs and wonders *w*. among the people
    7. 36. [Moses] led them forth, having ⁴*wrought* wonders
    15. 12. wonders God had *w*. among the Gentiles. 21. 19
    18. 3. he abode with them and they *w*.; for by their trade
    19. 11. God *wrought* special miracles by the hands of Paul
Rom. 7. 5. the sinful passions—⁵*wrought* in our members
    8. sin—*wrought* in me through the commandment
    15. 18. save those which Christ *wrought* through me
1 Cor. 5. 3. judged him that hath so ²*wrought* this thing
2 Cor. 5. 5. Now he that *w*. us for this very thing is God
    7. 11. what earnest care it *wrought* in you
    12. 12. Truly the signs of an apostle were *w*. among you
Gal. 2. 8. (for he that *wrought* for Peter unto the apostleship—*wrought* for me also unto the Gentiles)
Eph. 1. 20. which he *wrought* in Christ, when he raised him
Heb. 11. 33. subdued kingdoms, *wrought* righteousness
Jas. 2. 22. Thou seest that faith *wrought* with his works
1 Pet. 4. 3. For the time past may suffice to have *w*. the
2 Jno. 8. that ye lose not the things which we have *w*. [desire
Jude 15. works of ungodliness which they have ungodly ¹*w*.
Rev. 19. 20. the false prophet that *w*. the signs in his sight
    see spent.

Y.

Yea.

Mat. 5. 37. But let your speech be, Yea, yea. Jas. 5. 12
    9. 28. They say unto him, Yea, Lord. 13. 51
Acts 5. 8. And she said, Yea, for so much
    22. 27. Tell me, art thou a Roman? And he said, Yea
2 Cor. 1. 17. that with me there should be the yea yea
    18. our word toward you is not *yea* and nay
    19. Jesus Christ—was not *yea* and nay, but in him is *yea*
    20. be the promises of God, in him is the *yea*
Phil. 4. 3. Yea, I beseech thee also, true yokefellow
Heb. 13. 8. the same yesterday and to-day, yea and for ever

Year.

Lu. 2. 41. And his parents went every *year* to Jerusalem
    4. 19. To proclaim the acceptable *year* of the Lord
    13. 8. Lord, let it alone this *year* also, till I shall dig
Jno. 11. 49. Caiaphas, being high priest that *y*. 51: 18. 13
Acts 11. 26. even for a whole *year* they were gathered
    18. 11. And he dwelt there a *year* and six months
2 Cor. 8. 10. the first to make a beginning a *year* ago
    9. 2. Achaia hath been prepared for a *year* past
Heb. 9. 7. the high priest alone, once in the *year*
Jas. 4. 13. we will go into this city, and spend a *year*
Rev. 9. 15. for the hour and day and month and *year*
    see numeral words, year by year.

Year by Year.—*A.V.* ¹*every year*.

Heb. 9. 25. entereth into the holy place ¹*year by year*
    10. 1. can never with the same sacrifices *year by year*
    3. remembrance made of sins ¹*year by year*

Years.

Lu. 1. 7. they both were now well stricken in years. 18
    4. 25. heaven was shut up three *years* and six months
    13. 7. Behold, these three *years* I come seeking fruit

YOU

Acts 20. 31. remembering that by the space of three *years*
Gal. 1. 18. Then after three *years* I went up to Jerusalem
    4. 10. observe days, and months, and seasons, and *years*
Heb. 1. 12. And thy *years* shall not fail   [months
Jas. 5. 17. it rained not on the earth for three *years* and six
2 Pet. 3. 8. one day is with the Lord as a thousand *years*,
    and a thousand *years* as one day
Rev. 20. 2. Satan, and bound him for a thousand *y*. 3, 7
    4. lived, and reigned with Christ a thousand *years*. 6
    5. rest of the dead lived not until the thousand *years*
    see grown, many, numeral words, e.g.—twelve, eighteen, etc.

Yesterday.

Jno. 4. 52. *Yesterday* at the seventh hour the fever left him
Acts 7. 28. as thou killedst the Egyptian *yesterday*?
Heb. 13. 8. Jesus Christ is the same *yesterday* and to-day

Yield.—*A.V.* ¹*bear*.

Acts 23. 21. Do not thou therefore *yield* unto them
Jas. 3. 12. can a fig tree, my brethren, ¹*yield* olives—neither can salt water *yield* sweet
    see present.

Yielded.—*A.V.* ¹*brought forth*.

Mat. 13. 8. good ground, and ¹*y*. fruit, some a hundredfold
    27. 50. again with a loud voice, and *yielded* up his spirit
    see gave (up), presented.

Yield—eth—ing *Fruit.—see fruit*.

Yoke.

Mat. 11. 29. Take my *yoke* upon you, and learn of me
    30. For my *yoke* is easy, and my burden is light
Lu. 14. 19. And another said, I have bought five *y*. of oxen
Acts 15. 10. should put a *y*. upon the neck of the disciples
Gal. 5. 1. be not entangled again in a *yoke* of bondage
1 Tim. 6. 1. Let as many as are servants under the *yoke*

Yoked.

2 Cor. 6. 14. Be not unequally *yoked* with unbelievers

Yokefellow.

Phil. 4. 3. Yea, I beseech thee also, true *yokefellow*

Yonder.

Mat. 17. 20. unto this mountain, Remove hence to *y*. place
    26. 36. Sit ye here, while I go *yonder* and pray

You, *with You, Yours*.

Mat. 17. 17. how long shall I be *with you*? how long shall I bear *with you*? Mk. 9. 19: Lu. 9. 41
    28. 20. to observe all things whatsoever I commanded *you*; and lo, I am *with you* alway
Lu. 24. 44. which I spake unto *you*, while I was yet *with y*.
Jno. 7. 33. Yet a little while I am *with you*. 13. 33
    14. 9. Have I been so long time *with you*
    17. for he abideth *with you*, and shall be in *you*
    20. I am in my Father, and ye in me, and I in *you*
    16. 4. from the beginning, because I was *with you*
1 Cor. 3. 21. glory in men. For all things are *yours*. 22
    16. 10. see that he be *with you* without fear
2 Cor. 12. 14... for I seek not *yours*, but *you*
Col. 2. 5. absent in the flesh, yet am I *with you* in the spirit
1 Th. 3. 4. when we were *with you*, we told *you*. 2 Th. 2. 5
2 Th. 3. 10. when we were *with you*, this we commanded *y*.

YOUNG

Young.
Lu. 2. 24. A pair of turtle doves, or two *young* pigeons
Jno. 12. 14. And Jesus, having found a *young* ass
    21. 18. When thou wast *young*, thou girdedst thyself
Tit. 2. 4. train the *young* women to love their husbands
    see little, younger.

Young *child and children.—see child, little children.*

Young *man and men.—see man, men.*

Younger.—*A.V.* ¹*young.*
Lu. 15. 12. and the *younger* of them said to his father
    13. the *younger* son gathered all together
    22. 26. the greater among you, let him become as the *y.*
Rom. 9. 12. The elder shall serve the *younger*
1 Tim. 5. 1. the *younger* men as brethren. Tit. 2. ¹6
    2. as mothers; the *younger* as sisters, in all purity
    11. But *younger* widows refuse
    14. I desire therefore that the *younger* widows marry
1 Pet. 5. 5. Likewise, ye *younger*, be subject unto the elder

Youth.
Mk. 10. 20. these things have I observed from my *y.* Lu.18.21
Acts 26. 4. My manner of life then from my *youth* up
1 Tim. 4. 12. Let no man despise thy *youth*

Youthful.
2 Tim. 2. 22. But flee *youthful* lusts, and follow after

ZEALOUS

Z.

Zeal.—*A.V.* ¹*fervent mind.*
Jno. 2. 17. The *zeal* of thine house shall eat me up
Rom. 10. 2. witness that they have a *zeal* for God
2 Cor. 7. 7. your longing, your mourning, your ¹*z.* for me
    11. what longing, yea, what *zeal*, yea, what avenging!
    9. 2. your *zeal* hath stirred up very many of them
Phil. 3. 6. as touching *zeal*, persecuting the church
    see labour.

Zealous—ly.—*A.V.* ¹*followers,* ²*forward.*
Acts 21. 20. and they are all *zealous* for the law
    22. 3. being *zealous* for God, even as ye all are
1 Cor. 14. 12. since ye are *zealous* of spiritual gifts
Gal. 1. 14. more exceedingly *zealous* for the traditions
    2. 10. the poor; which very thing I was also ²*z.* to do
    4. 17. They *zealously* seek you in no good way
    18. But it is good to be *z.* sought in a good matter
Tit. 2. 14. a people for his own possession, *z.* of good works
1 Pet. 3. 13. if ye be ¹*zealous* of that which is good?
Rev. 3. 19. and chasten: be *zealous* therefore, and repent

PROPER NAMES.

AARON

Aaron.
Lu. 1. 5. he had a wife of the daughters of *Aaron*
Acts 7. 30. saying unto *Aaron*, make us gods which shall go
Heb. 5. 5. called of God, even as was *Aaron*
7. 11. and not be reckoned after the order of *Aaron*
9. 4. and *Aaron's* rod that budded

Abaddon.
Rev. 9. 11. His name in Hebrew is *Abaddon*

Abel.
Mat. 23. 35. the blood of *Abel* the righteous. *Lu.* 11. 51
Heb. 11. 4. By faith *Abel* offered unto God
12. 24. that speaketh better than that of *Abel*

Abiathar.—*Mk.* 2, 26

Abijah.—*Mat.* 1. 7: *Lu.* 1. 5

Abilene.—*Lu.* 3. 1

Abiud.—*Mat.* 1. 13

Abraham—'s.
Mat. 1. 1. Jesus Christ—the son of *Abraham*. *Lu.* 3. 34
2. *Abraham* begat Isaac. *Acts* 7. 8
17. generations from *Abraham* unto David
3. 9. raise up children unto *Abraham*. *Lu.* 3. 8
8. 11. sit down with *Abraham*, and Isaac, and Jacob
13. 28. Ye shall see *Abraham*, and Isaac, and Jacob
22. 32. the God of *Abraham*. *Mk.* 12. 26: *Lu.* 20. 37: *Acts*
Lu 3. 34. Isaac, the son of *Abraham* [3. 13: 7. 32
13. 16. daughter of *Abraham*, whom Satan had bound
16. 22. carried away by angels unto *Abraham's* bosom
23. seeth *Abraham* afar off
25. But *Abraham* said, Son. 29
19. 10. forasmuch as he also is a son of *Abraham*
Jno. 8. 39. A's. children, ye would do the works of *A.*
40. ye seek to kill me,—this did not *Abraham*
52. *Abraham* is dead, and the prophets
57. fifty years old, and hast thou seen *Abraham?*
58. I say unto you, Before *Abraham* was, I am
Acts 3. 25. covenant which God made—saying unto *A.*

ABRAHAM

Acts 7. 16. tomb that *Abraham* bought for a price in silver
17. promise drew nigh, which God vouchsafed unto *A.*
13 26. Brethren, children of the stock of *Abraham*
Rom. 4. 2. For if *Abraham* was justified by works
3. *Abraham* believed God. 9. *Gal.* 3. 6; *Jas.* 2. 23
9. To *A.* his faith was reckoned for righteousness
Gal. 3. 7. of faith, the same are sons of *Abraham*
8. preached the gospel beforehand unto *Abraham*
9. which be of faith are blessed with the faithful *A.*
14. upon the Gentiles might come the blessing of *A.*
16. Now to *Abraham* were the promises spoken
18. God hath granted it to *Abraham* by promise
4. 22. *Abraham* had two sons, one by the handmaid
Heb. 6. 13. For when God made promise to *Abraham*
7. 1. met *A.* returning from the slaughter of the kings
2. to whom also *Abraham* divided a tenth part of all
4. unto whom *Abraham*, the patriarch, gave a tenth
5. these have come out of the loins of *Abraham*
6. counted from them hath taken tithes of *Abraham*
9. through *Abraham* even Levi, who receiveth tithes
11. 8. By faith *Abraham* 17
1 *Pet.* 3. 6. as Sarah obeyed *Abraham*, calling him lord

Abraham, *with father.*
Mat. 3. 9. We have *Abraham* to our *father*. *Lu.* 3. 8
Lu. 1. 73. The oath which he sware unto *A.* our *father*
16. 24. said, Father *Abraham*, have mercy on me
30. Nay, *father A.:* but if one went unto them from the
Jno. 8. 39. said unto Him, Our *father* is *Abraham* [dead
53. Art thou greater than our *father Abraham*
56. Your *father Abraham* rejoiced to see my day
Acts 7. 2. The God of glory appeared unto our *father A.*
Rom. 4. 1. What then shall we say that *A.,* our *forefather*
12. walk in the steps of that faith of our *father A.*
16. the faith of *Abraham,* who is the *father* of us all
Jas. 2. 21. Was not *Abraham* our *father* justified by works

Abraham, *with seed.*
Lu. 1. 55. Toward *Abraham* and his *seed* for ever
Jno. 8. 33. They answered us, We be *Abraham's seed*
37. I know that ye are *Abraham's seed*; yet [his *seed*
Rom. 4. 13. not through the law was the promise to *A.* or to
9. 7. neither, because they are *Abraham's seed*, are they
11. 1. I also am an Israelite, of the *seed* of *Abraham*

ABRAHAM

2 *Cor.* 11. 22. Are they the seed of *Abraham?* so am I
Gal. 3. 16. to *A.* were the promises spoken, and to his seed
    29. if ye are Christ's, then are ye *Abraham's* seed
Heb. 2. 16. but he taketh hold of the seed of *Abraham*

Aceldama *A.V.—see Akeldama.*

Achaia.

Acts 18. 12. But when Gallio was proconsul of *Achaia*
    27. when he was minded to pass over into *Achaia*
    19. 21. when he had passed through Macedonia and *A*
Rom. 15. 26. Macedonia and *Achaia* to make a certain
    contribution   [of *A.*
1 *Cor.* 16. 15. house of Stephanas, that it is the firstfruits
2 *Cor.* 1. 1. with all the saints which are in the whole of *A.*
    9. 2. that *Achaia* hath been prepared for a year past
    11. 10. stop me of this glorying in the regions of *A.*
1 *Th.* 1. 7. to all that believe in Macedonia and in *Achaia*

Achaicus.—1 *Cor.* 16. 17

Achim.—*Mat.* 1. 14

Adam

Lu. 3. 38. the son of *Adam*, the son of God
Rom. 5. 14. Nevertheless death reigned from *A.* until Moses
    —not sinned after the likeness of *A.*'s transgression
1 *Cor.* 15. 22. For as in *Adam* all die   [life-giving spirit
    45. The first man *A.* became — last *Adam* became a
1 *Tim.* 2. 13. For *Adam* was first formed, then Eve
    14. and *Adam* was not beguiled, but the woman
Jude 14. Enoch, the seventh from *Adam*, prophesied

Addi.—*Lu.* 3. 28

Adramyttium.—*Acts* 27. 2

Adria.—*Acts* 27. 27

Advocate.—1 *Jno.* 2. 1

Æneas.—*Acts* 9. 33, 34

Ænon.—*Jno.* 3. 23

Agabus.—*Acts* 11. 28 ; 21. 10

Agar *A.V.—see Hagar.*

Agrippa.

Acts 25. 13. *A.* the king and Bernice arrived at Cæsarea. 23
    22. *A.* said unto Festus, I also could wish to hear. 26. 32
    24. And Festus saith, King *Agrippa*, and all men
    26. before you, and specially before thee, king *Agrippa*
    26. 1. *Agrippa* said unto Paul, Thou art permitted
    2. I think myself happy, king *Agrippa*, that I am
    19. Wherefore, O king *Agrippa*, I was not disobedient
    27. King *Agrippa*, believest thou the prophets?
    28. *Agrippa* said unto Paul, With but little persuasion

Ahaz.—*Mat.* 1. 9

Akeldama.—*A.V. Aceldama.—Acts* 1. 19

Alexander

Mk. 15. 21. the father of *Alexander* and Rufus
Acts 4. 6. and Caiaphas, and John, and *Alexander*
    19. 33. brought *A.* out of the multitude — *A.* beckoned
1 *Tim.* 1. 20. of whom is Hymenæus and *Alexander*
2 *Tim.* 4. 14. *Alexander* the coppersmith did me much evil

ANTIOCH

Alexandria—an-s.

Acts 6. 9. Libertines and of the Cyrenians, and of the *A.*
    18. 24. Jew named Apollos, an *Alexandrian* by race
    27. 6. ship of *Alexandria* : 28. 11

Alpha, *see Omega.—Rev.* 1. 8 ; 21. 6 ; 22. 13

Alphæus.

Mat. 10. 3. James the son of *Alphæus*; *Mk.* 3. 18; *Lu.*
    6. 15 ; *Acts* 1. 13
Mk. 2. 14. Levi the son of *Alphæus*

Amminadab.—*Mat.* 1. 4 ; *Lu.* 3. 33

Amon.—*Mat.* 1. 10

Amos.—*Lu.* 3. 25

Amphipolis.—*Acts* 17. 1

Amplias, or Ampliatus.—*Rom.* 16. 8

Ananias.

Acts 5. 1. certain man named *Ananias*, with Sapphira
    3. Peter said, *Ananias*, why hath Satan filled thy heart
    5. And *Ananias* hearing these words fell down
    9. 10. certain disciple at Damascus, named *Ananias*;
    and the Lord said unto him in a vision, *Ananias*
    12. hath seen a man named *Ananias* coming in. 22. 12
    13. but *Ananias* answered, Lord, I have heard
    17. *A.*—laying his hands on him said, Brother Saul
    23. 2. the high priest *Ananias* commanded. 24. 1

Andrew.

Mat. 4. 18. Simon who is called Peter, and *Andrew* his
    brother. 10. 2 ; *Mk.* 1. 16 ; *Lu.* 6. 14 ; *Jn.* 1. 40 ; 6. 8
Mk. 1. 29. they came unto the house of Simon and *Andrew*
    3. 18. and *Andrew*, and Philip, and Bartholomew
    13. 3. and John, and *Andrew*, asked him privately
Jno. 1. 44. Bethsaida, of the city of *Andrew*, and Peter
    12. 22. telleth *Andrew* : *Andrew* cometh, and Philip
Acts 1. 13. upper chamber,—and James and *Andrew*

Andronicus.—*Rom.* 16. 7

Anna.—*Lu.* 2. 36

Annas.

Lu. 3. 2. high-priesthood of *Annas* and Caiaphas. *Acts* 4 6
Jno. 18. 13. bound him, and led him to *Annas* first
    24. *Annas* therefore sent him bound unto Caiaphas

Anointed.—*A.V. Christ. Acts* 4. 26

Antioch.

Acts 6. 5. Nicolas a proselyte of *Antioch*
    11. 19. as far as Phœnicia, and Cyprus, and *A.* speaking
    20 who, when they were come to *Antioch* spake
    22. sent forth Barnabas as far as *Antioch*   [in *A.*
    26. brought him unto *A.*—were called Christians first
    27. there came down prophets from Jerusalem unto *A.*
    13. 1. Now there were at *Antioch*, in the church
    14. passing through from Perga, came to *A.* of Pisidia
    14. 19. came Jews thither from *Antioch* and Iconium
    21. they returned to Lystra and to Iconium, and to *A.*
    26. Attalia ; and thence they sailed to *Antioch*
    15. 22. choose men—and send them to *A.* with Paul
    23. brethren which are of the Gentiles in *Antioch*
    30. [Judas and Silas] came down to *Antioch*

ANTIOCH

Acts 11. 35. Paul and Barnabas tarried in *Antioch*
18. 22. [Paul] saluted the church, and went down to *A.*
Gal. 2. 11. when Cephas came to *Antioch*, I resisted him
2 Tim. 3. 11. what things befell me at *Antioch*

Antipas.—*Rev.* 2. 13

Antipatris.—*Acts* 23. 31

Apelles.—*Rom.* 16. 10

Apollonia.—*Acts* 17. 1

Apollos.
Acts 18. 24. Now a certain Jew named *Apollos*
19. 1. while *Apollos* was at Corinth, Paul—came to
1 Cor. 1. 12. I am of Paul; and I of *Apollos*. 3. 4
3. 5. What then is *Apollos* ? and what is Paul?
6. I planted, *Apollos* watered; but God gave the increase
22. whether Paul, or *Apollos*, or Cephas
4. 6. transferred to myself and *Apollos* for your sakes
16. 12. *A.* the brother, I besought him much to come
Tit. 3. 13. Set forward Zenas the lawyer, and *Apollos*

Apollyon.—*Rev.* 9. 11

Apphia.—*Philem.* 2

Appius.—*(Appii-Forum.)*—*Acts* 28. 15

Aquila.
Acts 18. 2. found a certain Jew named *Aquila*
18. and with him [Paul] Priscilla and *Aquila*
26. when Priscilla and *Aquila* heard him, they took
Rom. 16. 3. Salute Prisca and *Aquila*. 2 *Tim.* 4. 19
1 Cor. 16. 19. *Aquila* and Prisca salute you much

Arabia.
Gal. 1. 17. but I went away into *Arabia*
4. 25. Now this Hagar is Mount Sinai in *Arabia*

Arabians.—*Acts* 2. 11

Aram *A.V.*—*see Ram and Arni.*

Archelaus.—*Mat.* 2. 22

Archippus.—*Col.* 4. 17 : *Philem.* 2

Areopagus—ite.—*Acts* 17. 19, 22, 34

Aretas.—2 *Cor.* 11. 32.

Arimathæa.—*Mat.* 27. 57: *Mk.* 15. 43 : *Lu.* 23. 51:
Jno. 19. 38

Aristarchus —*Acts* 19. 29 : 20. 4 : 27. 2 : *Col.*
4. 10 : *Philem.* 24

Aristobulus.—*Rom.* 16. 10

Arni.—*A.V. Aram.*—*Lu.* 3. 33

Armageddon *A.V.*—*see Har-Magedon.*

Arphaxad.—*Lu.* 3. 36

Artemas.—*Tit.* 3. 12

Asa.—*Mat.* 1. 7, 8

Asher.—*A.V. Aser.*—*Lu.* 2, 36 : *Rev.* 7. 6

BALAAM

Asia.
Acts 2. 10. in Pontus and *A.* in Phrygia and Pamphylia
6. 9. and of them of Cilicia and *Asia*, disputing [*Asia*
16. 6. forbidden of the Holy Ghost to speak the word in
19. 10. all they which dwelt in *Asia* heard the word
22. [Paul] himself stayed in *Asia* for a while
26. almost throughout all *A.*, this Paul hath persuaded
27. whom all *Asia* and the world worshippeth
31. the chief officers of *Asia*, being his friends
20. 4. accompanied him as far as *Asia*—and of *Asia*
16. that he might not have to spend time in *Asia*
18. from the first day that I set foot in *Asia*
27. 2. about to sail unto the places on the coast of *Asia*
Rom. 16. 5. Epænetus — firstfruits of *Asia* unto Christ
1 Cor. 16. 19. The churches of *Asia* salute you
2 Cor. 1. 8. concerning our affliction which befell us in *A.*
2 Tim. 1. 15. all that are in *Asia* turned away from me
1 Pet. 1. 1. sojourners of the Dispersion in—*Asia*
Rev. 1. 4. to the seven churches which are in *Asia*

Assassins.—*Acts* 21. 38

Assos.—*Acts* 20. 13, 14

Asyncritus.—*Rom.* 16. 14

Athenians.—*Acts* 17. 21

Athens.
Acts 17. 15. conducted Paul brought him as far as *Athens*
16. while Paul waited for them at *Athens*, his spirit
22. Ye men of *Athens*, in all things I perceive that
18. 1. he departed from *Athens*, and came to Corinth
1 Th. 3. 1. we thought it good to be left behind at *A.* alone

Attalia.—*Acts* 14. 25

Augustan—us, *see Emperor*
Lu. 2. 1. went out a decree from Cæsar *Augustus*
Acts 27. 1. centurion named Julius, of the *Augustan* band

Azor.—*Mat.* 1. 13, 14

Azotus.—*Acts* 8. 40

B.

Baal.—*Rom.* 11. 4

Babylon.
Mat. 1. 11. at the time of the carrying away to *Babylon*. 12
17. carrying away to *Babylon* fourteen generations; and
from the carrying away to *Babylon* unto the Christ
Acts 7. 43. And I will carry you away beyond *Babylon*
1 Pet. 5. 13. She that is in *Babylon*, elect together with you
Rev. 14. 8. Fallen, fallen is *Babylon* the great. 18. 2
16. 19. and *B.* the great was remembered in the sight
17. 5. *BABYLON* THE GREAT, THE MOTHER OF
THE HARLOTS
18. 10. Woe, woe, the great city, *B.*, the strong city [down
21. with a mighty fall shall *B.*, the great city, be cast

Balaam.
2 Pet. 2. 15. followed the way of *Balaam* the son of Beor
Jude 11. ran riotously in the error of *Balaam* for hire
Rev. 2. 14. hast there some that hold the teaching of *B.*

BALAK

Balak.—*Rev.* 2. 14.

Barabbas.—*Mat.* 27. 16, 17, 20, 21, 26 : *Mk.* 15. 7, 11, 15 : *Lu.* 23. 18 : *Jno.* 18. 40

Barachiah.—*Mat.* 23. 35

Barak.—*Heb.* 11. 32

Bar-Jesus.—*Acts* 13. 6

Bar-Jonah.—*Mat.* 16. 17

Barnabas, *see* Paul *and* Saul.

Acts 4. 36. Joseph, who by the apostles was surnamed *B*.
9. 27. But *B*. took him, and brought him to the apostles
11. 22. and they sent forth *Barnabas* as far as Antioch
30. to the elders by the hand of *Barnabas* and Saul
12. 25. And *Barnabas* and Saul returned from Jerusalem
13. 1. prophets and teachers, *Barnabas*, and Symeon
2. Separate me *Barnabas* and Saul for the work
7. Sergius Paulus—called unto him *Barnabas* and Saul
43. devout proselytes followed Paul and *Barnabas*
46. Paul and *Barnabas* spake out boldly, and said
50. stirred up a persecution against Paul and *Barnabas*
14. 12. And they called *Barnabas*, Jupiter
14. when the apostles, *Barnabas* and Paul, heard of it
20. on the morrow he went forth with *B*. to Dorbe
15. 2. Paul and *Barnabas* had no small dissension—appointed that Paul and *Barnabas*
12. they hearkened unto *Barnabas* and Paul rehearsing
22. send them to Antioch with Paul and *Barnabas*
25. unto you with our beloved *Barnabas* and Paul
35. Paul and *Barnabas* tarried in Antioch, teaching
36. Paul said unto *B*., Let us return now and visit
37. *B*. was minded to take with them John also. 39
1 *Cor.* 9. 6. Or I only and *Barnabas*, have we not a right
Gal. 2. 1. I went up again to Jerusalem with *Barnabas*
9. to me and *Barnabas* the right hands of fellowship
13. *Barnabas* was carried away with their dissimulation
Col. 4. 10. and Mark, the cousin of *Barnabas*

Barsabbas.—*Acts* 1. 23 ; 15. 22

Bartholomew.—*Mat.* 10. 3 ; *Mk.* 3. 18 ; *Lu.* 6. 14 ; *Acts* 1. 13

Bartimæus.—*Mk.* 10. 46

Beautiful Gate.—*Acts* 3. 10

Beelzebub.

Mat. 10. 25. called the master of the house *Beelzebub*
12. 24. by *Beelzebub* the prince of the devils. *Mk.* 3. 22 : *Lu.* 11. 15
27. if I by *Beelzebub* cast out devils. *Lu.* 11. 18, 19

Belial—2 *Col.* 6. 15

Benjamin (*Tribe of*).

Acts 13. 21. Saul, the son of Kish, a man of the *tribe of B*.
Rom. 11. 1. of the *tribe of Benjamin*. *Phil.* 3. 5 [thousand
Rev. 7. 8. Of the *tribe of Benjamin* were sealed twelve

Beor.—2 *Pet.* 2. 15

Berœa.—*Acts* 17. 10, 13 : 20. 4

Bernice.—*Acts* 25. 13, 23 : 26. 30

PROPER NAMES.

CÆSAR

Bethabara, *see* Bethany.

Bethany.

Mat. 26. 6. When Jesus was in *B*., 21. 17 : *Mk.* 11. 11 : 14. 3 : *Jno.* 12. 1
Mk. 11. 1. *Bethany* at the Mount of Olives. *Lu.* 19. 29
12. when they were come out from *Bethany* he hungered
Lu. 24. 50. he led them out—over against *Bethany*
Jno. 1. 28. these things were done in *B.* beyond Jordan
11. 1. a certain man was sick, Lazarus of *Bethany*
18. Now *Bethany* was nigh unto Jerusalem

Bethesda.—*Jno.* 5. 2

Bethlehem.

Mat. 2. 1. Jesus was born in *B.* of Judæa. 5 : *Lu.* 2. 4
6. And thou *Bethlehem*, land of Judah
2. 8. [Herod] sent them to *Bethlehem*, and said
16. slew all the male children that were in *Bethlehem*
Lu. 2. 15. Let us now go even unto *B.*, and see this thing
Jno. 7. 42. Christ cometh of the seed of David, and from *B.*

Bethphage.—*Mat.* 21. 1 ; *Mk.* 11. 1 : *Lu.* 19. 29

Bethsaida.

Mat. 11. 21. woe unto thee, *Bethsaida*. *Lu.* 10. 13
Mk. 6. 45. to *Bethsaida*, while he himself sendeth
8. 22. And they come unto *Bethsaida*
Lu. 9. 10. and withdrew apart to a city called *Bethsaida*
Jno. 1. 44. Now Philip was from *Bethsaida*. 12. 21

Bishop.—1 *Pet.* 2. 25

Bithynia.—*Acts* 16. 7 : 1 *Pet.* 1. 1

Blastus.—*Acts* 12. 20

Boanerges.—*Mk.* 3. 17

Boaz.—*Mat.* 1. 5 ; *Lu.* 3. 32

Bosor *A.V.*—*see* Beor.

Bush.—*Mk.* 12. 26. *Lu.* 20. 37

C.

Cæsar.

Mat. 22. 17. give tribute unto *Cæsar*. *Mk.* 12. 14 : *Lu.* 20. 22
21. they say unto him, *C*.—Render therefore unto *C*. the things that are *C*.'s. *Mk.* 12. 16, 17 : *Lu.* 20. 24, 25
Lu. 2. 1. there went out a decree from *Cæsar* Augustus
3. 1. fifteenth year of the reign of Tiberius *Cæsar*
23. 2. and forbidding to give tribute to *Cæsar*
Jno. 19. 12. thou art not *Cæsar's* friend—speaketh against *C*.
15. chief priests answered, We have no king but *Cæsar*
Acts 17. 7 these all act contrary to the decrees of *Cæsar*
25. 8. nor against *Cæsar* have I sinned at all
10. I am standing before *Cæsar's* judgement-seat
11. I appeal unto *Cæsar*
12. Thou hast appealed unto *C*. : unto *C*. shalt thou go
21. him to be kept till I should send him to *Cæsar*
26. 32. at liberty, if he had not appealed unto *Cæsar*
27. 24. Fear not, Paul ; thou must stand before *Cæsar*
28. 19. I was constrained to appeal unto *Cæsar*
Phil. 4. 22. they that are of *Cæsar's* household

394

CÆSAREA

Cæsarea.
Mat. 16. 13. Jesus came into the parts of *Cæsarea* Philippi
Acts 8. 40. all the cities, till he came to *C*. [*Mk*. 8. 27
9. 30. they brought him down to *Cæsarea*
10. 1. a certain man in *Cæsarea*, Cornelius by name
24. on the morrow they entered into *Cæsarea*
11. 11. three men—sent from *Cæsarea* unto me
12. 19. And he went down from Judæa to *Cæsarea*
18. 22. when he had landed at *Cæsarea*, he went up
21. 8. on the morrow we departed and came unto *C*.
16. also certain of the disciples from *Cæsarea*
23. 23. Make ready 200 soldiers to go as far as *Cæsarea*
33. when they came to *C*., and delivered the letter
25. 1. after three days went up to Jerusalem from *C*.
4. answered, that Paul was kept in charge at *Cæsarea*
6. [Festus] went down unto *Cæsarea*
13. Agrippa the king and Bernice—arrived at *Cæsarea*

Caiaphas.
Mat. 26. 57. led him away to the house of *Caiaphas*. 3
Lu. 3. 2. high priesthood of Annas and *Caiaphas*
Jno. 11. 49. *Caiaphas*—said unto them, Ye know nothing
18. 13. Annas—father in law to *Caiaphas*
14. *Caiaphas* was he which gave counsel to the Jews
24. *Caiaphas* sent him bound unto *Caiaphas*
28. They lead Jesus therefore from *Caiaphas* into the
Acts 4. 6. *Caiaphas*, and John, and Alexander [palace

Cain.
Heb. 11. 4. a more excellent sacrifice than *Cain*
1 Jno. 3. 12. not as *Cain* was of the evil one, and slew
Jude 11. for they went in the way of *Cain*, and ran

Cainan.—Lu. 3. 36, 37

Calvary A.V.—see *The skull*. Lu. 23. 33

Cana of *Galilee*.—Jno. 2. 1, 11; 4. 46: 21. 2

Canaan (Land of).
Acts 7. 11. there came a famine over all Egypt and *Canaan*
13. 19. destroyed seven nations in the *land of Canaan*

Canaanæan or *Canaanite*.—Mat. 10. 4; Mk. 3. 18

Canaanitish.—(Woman.)—Mat. 15. 22

Candace.—Acts 8. 27

Capernaum.
Mat. 4. 13. he came and dwelt in *Capernaum*. 8. 5 : Mk. 2.
1: 9. 33 : Lu. 4. 31: Jno. 2. 12 [Lu. 10. 15
11. 23. And thou, *Capernaum*, shalt thou be exalted
17. 24. And when they were come to *C*. Mk. 1. 21
Lu. 4. 23. whatsoever we have heard done at *C*. do also
7. 1. he [Jesus] entered into *Capernaum*
Jno. 4. 46. nobleman, whose son was sick at *Capernaum*
6. 17. were going over the sea unto *Capernaum*
24. got into the boats, and came to *C*. seeking Jesus
59. in the synagogue, as he taught in *Capernaum*

Cappadocia.—Acts 2. 9 : 1 Pet. 1. 1

Carpus.—2 Tim. 4. 13

Castor and *Pollux* A.V.—see *The Twin Brothers*.

Cauda.—A.V. *Clauda*. Acts 27. 16

CHRIST

Cedron A.V.—see *Kidron*.

Cenchreæ.—Acts 18. 18 ; Rom. 16. 1

Cephas.
Jno. 1. 42. thou shalt be called *Cephas*
1 Cor. 3. 22. Whether Paul, or Apollos, or *Cephas*. 1. 12
9. 5. and the brethren of the Lord, and *Cephas*
15. 5. he appeared to *Cephas*; then to the twelve
Gal. 1. 19. I [Paul] went up to Jerusalem to visit *Cephas*
2. 9. James and *Cephas* and John,—reputed to be pillars
11. When *Cephas* came to Antioch, I resisted him
14. I [Paul] said unto *Cephas* before them all

Chaldæans.—Acts 7. 4

Charran A.V.—see *Haran*.

Chios.—Acts 20. 15

Chloe.—1 Cor. 1. 11

Chorazin.—Mat. 11. 21 : Lu. 10. 13

Christ—or the *Christ*.
Mat. 1. 17. carrying away to Babylon unto *the C*. fourteen
2. 4. [Herod] inquired of them when *the C*. should be
16. 16. Thou art *the Christ*. Mk. 8. 29
20. that they should tell no man that he was *the Christ*
23. 10. for one is your master, even *the Christ*
24. 5. shall come in my name, saying, I am *the Christ*
26. 63. tell us whether thou be *the C*., the Son of God
68. Prophecy unto us, thou *Christ*
Mk. 9. 41. cup of water to drink, because ye are *Christ's*
12. 35. scribes that *the C*. is the Son of David ? Lu. 20. 41
14. 61. the high priest asked—Art thou *the Christ*
15. 32. let *the C*., the King of Israel, now come down
Lu. 2. 11. is born—a Saviour, which is *Christ* the Lord
26. see death, before he had seen the Lord's *Christ*
3. 15. concerning John, whether haply he were *the C*.
4. 41. devils—knew that he was *the Christ*
9. 20. And Peter answering said, *The Christ* of God
22. 67. saying, If thou art *the Christ*, tell us
23. 39. Art not thou *the Christ* ? save thyself. 35
24. 26. Behoved it not *the Christ* to suffer. Acts 17. 3
46. Thus it is written, that *the Christ* should suffer
Jno. 1. 20. he [John Bap.] confessed, I am not *the Christ*
25. Why then baptizest thou, if thou art not *the Christ*
41. We have found the Messiah—*Christ*
4. 25. I know that Messiah cometh (which is called *C*.)
29. told me all things—can this be *the Christ*
7. 26. rulers indeed know that this is *the Christ*
27. when *the C*. cometh, no one knoweth whence he is
31. When *the Christ* shall come, will he do more signs
41. This is *the C*.—doth *the C*. come out of Galilee ?
42. *the Christ* cometh of the seed of David
9. 22. that if any man should confess him to be *Christ*
10. 24. If thou art *the Christ*, tell us plainly
11. 27. I have believed that thou art *the Christ* (Martha)
12. 34. heard out of the law that *the C*. abideth for ever
20. 31. may believe that Jesus is *the C*., the Son of God
Acts 2. 31. spake of the resurrection of *the Christ*
36. that God hath made him both Lord and *Christ*
3. 18. God foreshewed—that his *Christ* should suffer
8. 5. Philip went—Samaria and proclaimed unto them
26. 23. how that *the Christ* must suffer [*the C*.
Rom. 5. 6. in due season *Christ* died for the ungodly
8. while we were yet sinners, *Christ* died for us
6. 4. like as *Christ* was raised from the dead
9. knowing that *Christ* being raised from the dead
7. 4. dead to the law through the body of *Christ*

CHRIST

Rom. 8. 10. if *Christ* is in you, the body is dead because of
9. 3. wish that I myself were anathema from *Christ* | sin
5. and of whom is *Christ* as concerning the flesh
10. 4. *Christ* is the end of the law unto righteousness
6. ascend into heaven?—to bring *Christ* down
7. that is, to bring *Christ* up from the dead
17. and hearing by the word of *Christ*
14. 9. to this end *Christ* died, and lived again
15. Destroy not—him for whom *Christ* died
18. herein serveth *Christ* is well-pleasing to God
15. 3. For *Christ* also pleased not himself
7. even as *Christ* also received you, to the glory of God
8. I say that *Christ* hath been made a minister
18. things save those which *Christ* wrought through me
19. I have fully preached the gospel of *Christ*
20. preach the gospel, not where *C.* was already named
29. I shall come in the fulness of the blessing of *Christ*
16. 5. Epænetus—the firstfruits of Asia unto *Christ*
16. All the churches of *Christ* salute you
18. they that are such serve not our Lord *Christ*
1 Cor. 1. 17. For *C.* sent me not to baptize, but to preach
23. but we preach *Christ* crucified, unto Jews a
24. *Christ* the power of God, and the wisdom of God
8. 23. ye are *Christ's*; and *Christ* is God's
4. 1. account of us, as of ministers of *Christ*
10. We are fools for *Christ's* sake
5. 7. passover also hath been sacrificed, even *Christ*
7. 22. called, being free, is *Christ's* bondservant
8. 11. perisheth, the brother for whose sake *Christ* died
12. wounding the conscience—ye sin against *Christ*
21. under law to *Christ*, that I might gain them
10. 4. the rock that followed them : and the rock was *C.*
15. 3. how that *Christ* died for our sins
12. if *Christ* is preached that he hath been raised
15. witnessed of God that he raised up *Christ*
16. hath *Christ* been raised :—if *Christ* hath not. 13, 14
20. now hath *Christ* been raised from the dead
23. *Christ* the firstfruits; then they that are *Christ's*
2 Cor. 1. 5. as the sufferings of *Christ* abound—comfort also aboundeth through *Christ*
2. 12. when I came to Troas for the gospel of *Christ*
3. 4. such confidence have we through *C.* to Godward
5. 16. though we have known *Christ* after the flesh
18. reconciled us to himself through *Christ*
6. 15. what concord hath *Christ* with Belial
10. 7. that he is *Christ's*—even as he is *Christ's*
11. 2. I might present you as a pure virgin to *Christ*
3. simplicity and the purity that is towards *Christ*
12. 10. in distresses, for *Christ's* sake
Gal. 2. 17. is *Christ* a minister of sin ? God forbid
20. crucified with *C.*—but *C.* liveth in me [nought
21. if righteousness is through the law, then *C.* died for
3. 13. *Christ* redeemed us from the curse of the law
16. as of one, And to thy seed, which is *Christ*
24. law hath been our tutor to bring us unto *Christ*
27. baptized into *Christ* did put on *Christ*
29. if ye are *Christ's* then are ye Abraham's seed
4. 19. I am again in travail until *Christ* be formed
5 1. With freedom did *Christ* set us free
2. receive circumcision, *Christ* will profit you nothing
4. Ye are severed from *Christ*, ye who would be
Eph. 2. 12. ye were at that time separate from *Christ*
3. 17. that *C.* may dwell in your hearts through faith
4. 15. into him, which is the head, even *Christ*
20. But ye did not so learn *Christ*
5. 2. walk in love, as *Christ* also loved you
14. from the dead, and *Christ* shall shine upon thee
23. as *Christ* also is the head of the church
24. as the church is subject to *Christ*, so let the wives

CHRIST JESUS

Eph. 5. 25. even as *Christ* also loved the church
32. I speak in regard of *Christ* and of the church
6. 5. singleness of your heart, as unto *Christ*
Phil. 1. 20. *Christ* shall be magnified in my body
3. 7. gain to me—I counted loss for *Christ*
8. count them but dung, that I may gain *Christ*
Col. 2. 3. they may know the mystery of God, even *Christ*
8. rudiments of the world, and not after *Christ*
3. 1. where *Christ* is, seated on the right hand of God
4. When *Christ*, who is our life, shall be manifested
11. but *Christ* is all, and in all
24. of the inheritance: ye serve the Lord *Christ*
1 Tim. 5. 11. when they have waxed wanton against *Christ*
Philem. 6. every good thing which is in you, unto *Christ*
20. joy of thee in the Lord : refresh my heart in *Christ*
Heb. 3. 6. but *Christ* as a Son, over his house
5. 5. So *Christ* also glorified not himself to be made
9. 11. But *Christ* having come a high priest
24. *C.* entered not into a holy place made with hands
28. So *Christ* also, having been once offered
1 Pet. 2. 21. because *Christ* also suffered for you
3. 15. sanctify in your hearts *Christ* as Lord
18. Because *Christ* also suffered for sins once
4. 1. Forasmuch then as *Christ* suffered in the flesh
1 Jno. 2. 22. liar—denieth that Jesus is the *Christ*
5. 1. Whosoever believeth that Jesus is the *Christ*
see also blood, body, grace, preach-ed, anointed, Christ Jesus, Lord.

Christ Jesus, *or* Jesus Christ.

Mat. 1. 1. The book of the generations of *Jesus Christ*
16. was born *Jesus*, who is called *Christ*. 27. 17, 22
18. The birth of *Jesus Christ* was on this wise
Mk. 1. 1. The beginning of the gospel of *Jesus Christ*
Jno. 1. 17. grace and truth came by *Jesus Christ*
17. 3. whom thou didst send, even *Jesus Christ*
20. 31. *Jesus* is the *Christ*, the Son of God
Acts 2. 38. baptized every one of you in the name of *J. C.*
3. 6. in the name of *Jesus Christ* of Nazareth. 4. 10
20. that he may send the *Christ*—even *Jesus*
5. 42. ceased not to teach and to preach *Jesus* as the *C.*
8. 12. name of *Jesus Christ*, they were baptized
9. 34. Peter said—Æneas, *Jesus Christ* healeth thee
10. 36. preaching good tidings of peace by *Jesus Christ*
48. commanded them to be baptized in the name of *J. C.*
16. 18. in the name of *Jesus Christ* to come out of her
18. 5. Paul—testifying to the Jews that *J.* was the *C.* 28
Rom. 1. 1. Paul, a servant of *Jesus Christ.* Ph. 1. 1
6. among whom are ye also, called to be *Jesus Christ's*
8. I thank my God through *Jesus Christ* for you all
2. 16. according to my gospel, by *Jesus Christ*
3. 22. through faith in *Jesus Christ* unto all them
24. through the redemption that is in *Christ Jesus*
5. 15. gift by the grace of the one man *Jesus Christ*
17. life through the one, even *Jesus Christ*
6. 3. baptized unto *C. J.* were baptized into his death
11. alive unto God in *Christ Jesus*
8. 1. no condemnation to them that are in *Christ Jesus*
2. *Christ Jesus* made me free from the law of sin
11. he that raised up *Christ Jesus* from the dead
15. 5. the same mind one with another according to *C. J.*
16. minister of *C. J.* unto the Gentiles
17. glorying in *Christ Jesus* in things pertaining to God
16. 3. Prisca and Aquila my fellow-workers in *C. Jesus*
25. according to my gospel and the preaching of *J. C.*
27. to the only wise God, through *Jesus Christ*
1 Cor. 1. 1. Paul—apostle of *Jesus Christ* 2 Cor. 1. 1 : Eph. 1. 1; Col. 1. 1; 1 Tim. 1. 1.; Tit. 1. 4
2. sanctified in *Christ Jesus*

CHRIST JESUS

1 *Cor.* 1. 4. grace of God which was given you in *C. J.*
    30. *Christ J.*, who was made unto us wisdom from God
  2. 2. not to know anything—save *Jesus Christ*
  3. 11. foundation can no man lay—which is *Jesus Christ*
  4. 15. in *Christ Jesus* I begot you through the gospel
  16. 24. My love be with you all in *Christ Jesus*
2 *Cor.* 1. 19. *Jesus Christ*, who was preached among you
  4. 6. glory of God in the face of *Jesus Christ*
  13. 5. know ye not—that *Jesus Christ* is in you
Gal. 1. 1. Paul an apostle—through *Jesus Christ*. 12
  2. 4. spy out our liberty which we have in *Christ Jesus*
  16. faith in *Jesus Christ*, even we believed on *C. J.*
  3. 1. before whose eyes *Jesus Christ* was openly set forth
  14. might come the blessing of Abraham in *Christ Jesus*
  22. that the promise by faith in *J. C.* might be given
  26. through faith, in *Christ Jesus*. 2 *Tim.* 3. 15
  28. for ye all are one man in *Christ Jesus*
  4. 14. ye received me—even as *Christ Jesus*
  5. 6. in *Christ Jesus* neither circumcision availeth
  24. they that are of *Christ Jesus* have crucified the flesh
Eph. 1. 1. to the saints—and the faithful in *Christ Jesus*
  5. adoption as sons through *Jesus Christ* unto himself
  2. 6. sit with him in the heavenly places in *Christ Jesus*
  7. grace in kindness toward us in *Christ Jesus*
  10. created in *Christ Jesus* for good works
  13. now in *Christ Jesus* ye that once were far off
  20. *Christ Jesus* himself being the chief corner stone
  3. 1. For this cause I Paul, the prisoner of *Christ Jesus*
  21. unto him be the glory in the church and in *Christ J.*
Phil. 1. 1. the saints in *Christ J.* which are at Philippi
  6. will perfect it until the day of *Jesus Christ*
  8. after you all in the tender mercies of *Christ Jesus*
  11. fruits of righteousness, which are through *J. C.*
  19. and the supply of the Spirit of *Jesus Christ*
  2. 5. Have this mind—which was also in *Christ Jesus*
  11. confess that *Jesus Christ* is Lord, to the glory of God
  21. seek their own, not the things of *Jesus Christ*
  3. 3. glory in *Christ Jesus*, and have no confidence in
  8. of the knowledge of *Christ Jesus* my Lord
  12. for which also I was apprehended by *Christ Jesus*
  14. prize of the high calling of God in *Christ Jesus*
  4. 7. shall guard—your thoughts in *Christ Jesus*
  19. according to his riches in glory in *Christ Jesus*
  21. Salute every saint in *Christ Jesus*
Col. 1. 4. having heard of your faith in *Christ Jesus*
  4. 12. Epaphras—a servant of *Christ Jesus*
1 *Th.* 2. 14. churches of God which are in Judæa in *C. J.*
  5. 18. this is the will of God in *Christ J.* to you-ward
1 *Tim.* 1. 1. God our Saviour, and *Christ Jesus* our hope
  14. faith and love which is in *Christ Jesus*. 2 *Tim.* 1. 13
  15 *Christ Jesus* came into the world to save sinners
  16. that in me as chief might *Jesus Christ* shew forth
  2. 5. between God and men, himself man, *Christ Jesus*
  3. 13. boldness in the faith which is in *Christ Jesus*
  5. 21. I charge thee in the sight of God and *Christ Jesus*.
  6. 13; 2 *Tim.* 4. 1
2 *Tim.* 1. 1. Paul an apostle of *Christ J.*—which is in *C. J.*
  9. grace, which was given us in *Christ Jesus*
  10. manifested by the appearing of our Saviour *C. J.*
  2. 1. be strengthened in the grace that is in *Christ Jesus*
  3. hardship with me, as a good soldier of *Christ Jesus*
  8. Remember *Jesus Christ*, risen from the dead
  10. obtain the salvation which is in *Christ Jesus*
  3. 12. godly in *Christ Jesus* shall suffer persecution
Tit. 1. 4. God the Father and *Christ Jesus* our Saviour
  2. 13. glory of our great God and Saviour *Jesus Christ*
  3. 6. Holy Ghost which he poured—through *Jesus C.*
Philem. 1. Paul, a prisoner of *Christ Jesus*. 9, 23.
Heb. 10. 10. offering of the body of *J. Christ* once for all

CHRIST (LORD JESUS)

Heb. 13. 8. *Jesus Christ* is the same yesterday and to day
  21. through *Jesus Christ* ; to whom be the glory
1 *Pet.* 2. 5. acceptable to God, through *Jesus Christ*
  4. 11. all things God may be glorified through *Jesus C.*
1 *Jno.* 1. 3. with the Father, and with his Son *Jesus Christ*
  2. 1. Advocate with the Father, *J. Christ* the righteous
  3. 23. believe in the name of his Son *Jesus Christ*
  4. 2. confesseth that *J. C.* is come in the flesh. 2 *Jno.* 7
  5. 6. came by water and blood, even *Jesus Christ*
2 *Jno.* 3. from God the Father, and from *Jesus Christ*
  20. in him that is true, even in his Son *Jesus Christ*
Jude 1. Judas, a servant of *Jesus Christ*—kept for *J. C.*
Rev. 1. 1. The Revelation of *Jesus Christ*
  5. from *Jesus Christ* who is the faithful witness

Christ (Lord Jesus).

Acts 11. 17. when we believed on the *Lord Jesus Christ*
  15. 26. hazarded their lives for the name of our *L. J. C.*
  20. 21. repentance—and faith toward our *Lord Jesus C.*
Rom. 1. 1. *J. C.* our *Lord*, through whom we received grace
  7. God our Father, and the *Lord Jesus Christ*
  5. 1. peace with God through our *Lord Jesus Christ*
  11. rejoice in God through our *Lord Jesus Christ*
  21. eternal life through *Christ Jesus* our *Lord.* 6. 23
  7. 25. I thank God through *Jesus Christ* our *Lord*
  8. 39. love of God, which is in *Christ Jesus* our *Lord*
  13. 14. But put ye on the *Lord Jesus Christ*
  15. 6. glorify the God and Father of our *Lord Jesus C.*
  30. I beseech you, brethren, by our *Lord Jesus Christ*
1 *Cor.* 1. 2. call upon the name of our *Lord Jesus Christ*
  3. peace from God—and the *Lord Jesus Christ*
  7. revelation of our *Lord Jesus Christ*
  8. day of our *Lord Jesus Christ*
  9. fellowship of his Son *Jesus Christ* our *Lord*
  10. through the name of our *Lord Jesus Christ*
  6. 11. justified in the name of the *Lord Jesus Christ*
  8. 6. one *Lord, J. C.*, through whom are all things
  15. 31. glorying—which I have in *Christ J.* our *Lord*
  57. victory through our *Lord Jesus Christ*
  16. 22 The grace of the *Lord Jesus Christ* be with you.
  Rom. 16. 20 ; 2 *Cor.* 13. 14 ; *Gal.* 6. 18 ; *Ph.* 4. 23 ;
  1 *Th.* 5. 28 ; 2 *Th.* 3. 18 ; *Phil.* 25
2 *Cor.* 1. 2. God our Father, and the *Lord Jesus Christ,*
  Gal. 1. 3 ; *Eph.* 1. 2 ; 6. 23 ; *Ph.* 1. 2 ; 1 *Th.* 1. 1 ;
  2 *Th.* 1. 1, 2 ; 1 *Tim.* 1. 2 ; 2 *Tim.* 1. 2
  3. Father of our *Lord Jesus Christ. Eph.* 1. 3 ; *Col.* 1. 3
  4. 5. we preach not ourselves, but *Christ Jesus* as *Lord*
Gal. 6. 14. the cross of our *Lord Jesus Christ*
Eph. 1. 17. that the God of our *Lord Jesus Christ*
  3. 11. which he purposed in *Christ Jesus* our *Lord*
  6. 24. Grace be with all them that love our *Lord J. C.*
Phil. 3. 20. wait for a Saviour, the *Lord Jesus Christ*
Col. 2. 6. ye received *Christ Jesus* the *Lord*
1 *Th.* 1. 3. patience of hope in our *Lord Jesus Christ*
  5. 9. salvation through our *Lord Jesus Christ*
  23. at the coming of our *L. J. C.* 2 *Th.* 2. 1 ; 2 *Pet.* 1. 16
2 *Th.* 1. 12. grace of our God, and the *Lord Jesus Christ*
  2. 14. glory of our *Lord Jesus Christ*
  16. Now our *Lord J. C.* himself, and God our Father
  3. 6. in the name of our *Lord Jesus Christ. Eph.* 5. 20
  12. command and exhort in the *Lord Jesus Christ*
1 *Tim.* 1. 12. I thank him—even *Christ Jesus* our *Lord*
  6. 3. the words of our *Lord Jesus Christ*
  14. appearing of our *Lord Jesus Christ*
Jas. 1. 1. James, a servant of God, and of the *Lord Jesus C.*
  2. 1. the faith of our *Lord Jesus Christ*
1 *Pet.* 1. 3. Blessed be the God and Father of our *L. J. C.*
2 *Pet.* 1. 8. knowledge of our *Lord Jesus Christ*. 3. 18
  11. eternal kingdom of our *Lord* and Saviour *J. C.*

CHRIST (LORD JESUS)

2 Pet. 1. 14. even as our *Lord Jesus Christ* signified unto me
Jude 4. denying our only Master and *Lord, Jesus Christ*
17. apostles of our *Lord Jesus Christ*
21. looking for the mercy of our *Lord Jesus Christ*
25. through *Jesus Christ* our *Lord*

In or Into Christ, or Christ Jesus.

Acts 24. 24. concerning the faith *in Christ Jesus*
Rom. 6. 11. alive unto God *in Christ Jesus*
9. 1. I say the truth *in Christ*, I lie not
12. 5. we, who are many, are one body *in Christ*
16. 7. apostles, who also have been *in Christ* before me
9. Salute Urbanus our fellow-worker *in Christ*
10. Salute Apelles the approved *in Christ*
1 Cor. 3. 1. unto carnal, as unto babes *in Christ*
4. 10. but ye are wise *in Christ*
15. 10,000 tutors *in Christ*, yet have ye—for *in C. J.*
17. remembrance of my ways which be *in Christ*
15. 18. which are fallen asleep *in Christ* have perished
19. If in this life only we have hoped *in Christ*
22. so also *in Christ* shall all be made alive
2 Cor. 1. 21. he that stablisheth us with you *in Christ*
2. 14. always leadeth us in triumph *in Christ*
17. in the sight of God, speak we *in Christ*. 2 *Cor.* 12. 19
3. 14. which veil is done away *in Christ*
5. 17. Wherefore if any man is *in Christ*
19. God was *in Christ* reconciling the world
12. 2. I know a man *in Christ*, fourteen years ago
Gal. 1. 22. churches of Judæa which were *in Christ*
2. 17. while we sought to be justified *in Christ* [Christ
3. 27. many of you as were baptized *into C.* did put on
Eph. 1. 3. spiritual blessings in the heavenly places *in C.*
10. to sum up all things *in Christ*
12. we who had before hoped *in Christ*
20. strength of his might which he wrought *in Christ*
3. 6. fellow-partakers of the promise *in Christ Jesus*
4. 32. even as God also *in Christ* forgave you
Phil. 1. 13. my bonds became manifest *in Christ*
26. glorying may abound *in Christ Jesus*
2. 1. If there is any comfort *in Christ*
Col. 2. 5. stedfastness of your faith *in Christ*
1 Th. 4. 16. the dead *in Christ* shall rise first
1 Pet. 3. 16. revile your good manner of life *in Christ*
5. 10. called you unto his eternal glory *in Christ*
14. Peace be unto you all that are *in Christ*

Is Christ.

Mat. 24. 23. Lo, here *is* the *Christ*. Mk. 13. 21
Lu. 2. 11. a Saviour, which *is Christ* the Lord
23. 2. saying that he himself *is Christ* a king
Acts 9. 22. Saul—Damascus, proving that this *is* the *Christ*
17. 3. Jesus, whom I proclaim unto you, *is* the *Christ*
Rom. 8. 34. It *is Christ* Jesus that died
1 Cor. 1. 13. *Is Christ* divided? was Paul crucified
11. 3. head of every man *is Christ*
12. 12. are one body; so also *is Christ*
Gal. 2. 17. *is Christ* a minister of sin?
3. 16. And to thy seed, which *is Christ*
Phil. 1. 21. For me to live *is Christ*, and to die is gain
Col. 1. 27. which *is Christ* in you, the hope of glory

Of the Christ.

Mat. 11. 2. John heard in the prison the works *of the C.*
22. 42. What think ye *of the Christ*?

Of Christ.

Rom. 8. 9. if any man hath not the spirit *of Christ*
35. Who shall separate us from the love *of Christ*

CHRISTIAN

1 Cor. 1. 6. testimony *of Christ* was confirmed in you
12. I *of* Cephas; and I *of Christ*
17. lest the cross *of Christ* should be made void
2. 16. But we have the mind *of Christ*
6. 15. bodies are members *of Christ*?—members *of Christ*
11. 1. imitators of me, even as I also am *of Christ*
3. the head *of Christ* is God
2 Cor. 1. 5. the sufferings *of Christ* abound
2. 10. forgiven it in the person *of Christ*
15. we are a sweet savour *of Christ* unto God
3. 3. ye are an epistle *of Christ*
4. 4. light of the gospel of the glory *of Christ*
5. 10. manifest before the judgement-seat *of Christ*
14. the love *of Christ* constraineth us
20. on behalf *of Christ*—on behalf *of Christ*
8. 23. they are the glory *of Christ*
10. 1. meekness and gentleness *of Christ*
5. thought into captivity to the obedience *of Christ*
11. 10. As the truth *of Christ* is in me
13. fashioning themselves into apostles *of Christ*
23. Are they ministers *of Christ*
12. 9. the strength *of Christ* may rest upon me
13. 3. ye seek a proof *of Christ* that speaketh
Gal. 1. 7. would pervert the gospel *of Christ*
10. I should not be a servant *of Christ*
6. 12. may not be persecuted for the cross *of Christ*
Eph. 3. 4. understanding in the mystery *of Christ*
8. the unsearchable riches *of Christ*
19. to know the love *of Christ* which passeth
4. 7. the measure of the gift *of Christ*
12. building up of the body *of Christ*
13. measure of the stature of the fulness *of Christ*
5. 5. inheritance in the kingdom *of Christ* and God
6. 6. as servants *of Christ*, doing the will of God
Phil. 1. 10. void of offence unto the day *of Christ*
29. granted in the behalf *of Christ*
2. 16. whereof to glory in the day *of Christ*
30. for the work *of Christ* he came nigh unto death
3. 18. enemies of the cross *of Christ*
Col. 1. 24. that which is lacking of the afflictions *of Christ*
3. 16. Let the word *of Christ* dwell in you richly
4. 3. a door for the word, to speak the mystery *of C.*
2 Th. 3. 5. love of God, and into the patience *of Christ*
1 Tim. 4. 6. thou shalt be a good minister *of Christ* Jesus
Heb. 3. 14. we are become partakers *of Christ*
11. 26. accounting the reproach *of Christ* greater riches
1 Pet. 1. 11. the Spirit *of Christ* which was in them
4. 13. ye are partakers *of Christ's* sufferings
14. If ye are reproached for the name *of Christ*
5. 1. witness of the sufferings *of Christ*
Rev. 11. 15. the kingdom of our Lord, and *of* his *Christ*
12. 10. the authority *of* his *Christ*
20. 6. they shall be priests of God, and *of Christ*

With Christ.

Rom. 6. 8. if we died *with Christ*, we believe
8. 17. heirs of God, and joint-heirs *with Christ*
Gal. 2. 20. I have been crucified *with Christ*
Eph. 2. 5. quickened us together *with Christ*
Phil. 1. 23. desire to depart and be *with Christ*
Col. 2. 20. If ye died *with Christ* from the rudiments
3. 1. If ye then were raised together *with Christ*
3. your life is hid *with Christ* in God
Rev. 20. 4. reigned *with Christ* a thousand years

Christian—s.

Acts 11. 26. disciples were called *Christians* first in Antioch
26. 28. but little persuasion—make me [Agrippa] a *C.*
1 Pet. 4. 16. if a man suffer as a *C.*, let him not be ashamed

CHRISTS

Christs.
Mat. 24. 24. there shall arise false *Christs*, and false prophets. Mk. 13. 22

Chuza.—*Lu.* 8. 3.

Cilicia.
Acts 6. 9. of *Cilicia* and Asia, disputing with Stephen
15. 23. the Gentiles in Antioch and Syria and *Cilicia*
41. through Syria and *Cilicia*, confirming the churches
21. 39. I am a Jew, of Tarsus in *Cilicia* 22. 3
23. 34. when he understood that he was of *Cilicia*
27. 5. sea which is off *Cilicia* and Pamphylia
Gal. 1. 21. I came into the regions of Syria and *Cilicia*

Clauda A.V.—*see Cauda.*

Claudia.—*2 Tim.* 4. 21

Claudius.—*Acts* 11. 28: 18. 2

Claudius Lysias.—*Acts* 23. 26

Clement.—*Ph.* 4. 3

Cleopas.—*Clopas.*—*Lu.* 24. 18; *Jno.* 19. 25

Cnidus.—*Acts* 27. 7

Colossæ.—*Col.* 1. 2.

Comforter.—*Jno.* 14. 17, 26: 15. 26: 16. 7

Corban.—*Mk.* 7. 11

Core A.V.—*see Korah.*

Corinth.
Acts 18. 1. departed from Athens, and came to *Corinth*
19. 1. while Apollos was at *Corinth*
1 Cor. 1. 2. the church of God which is at C. 2 Cor. 1. 1
2 Cor. 1. 23. I forbare to come unto *Corinth*
2 Tim. 4. 20. Erastus abode at *Corinth*

Corinthians.—*Acts* 18. 8. : 2 *Cor.* 6. 11

Cornelius.
Acts 10. 1. certain man in Cæsarea, *Cornelius* by name
3. angel of God—saying to him, *Cornelius*
17. the men that were sent by *Cornelius*
22. *Cornelius* a centurion, a righteous man
24. *Cornelius* was waiting for them
25. that Peter entered, *Cornelius* met him
30. *Cornelius* said, Four days ago
31. *Cornelius*, thy prayer is heard

Cos, or Coos.—*Acts* 21. 1

Cosam.—*Lu.* 3. 28

Creator.—*Rom.* 1. 25 ; 1 *Pet.* 4. 19

Crescens.—*2 Tim.* 4. 10

Cretans.—*Cretes or Cretians.*—*Acts* 2. 11 : *Tit.* 1. 12

Crete.
Acts 27. 7. sailed under the lee of *Crete*. 13
12. a haven of *Crete*
21. and not have set sail from *Crete*
Tit. 1. 5. For this cause left I thee in *Crete*

DAVID

Crispus.—*Acts* 18. 8 : 1 *Cor.* 1. 14

Cyprus.
Acts 4. 36. Barnabas—a Levite, a man of *Cyprus*
11. 19. travelled as far as Phœnicia, and *Cyprus*
20. some of them men of *Cyprus* and Cyrene
13. 4. they sailed to *Cyprus* 15. 39 : 27. 4
21. 3. when we had come in sight of *Cyprus*
16. bringing with them one Mnason of *Cyprus*

Cyrene.
Mat. 27. 32. found a man of C., Simon by name. Mk. 15. 21 :
Acts 2. 10. and the parts of Libya about *Cyrene* [Lu. 23. 26
11. 20. men of Cyprus and *Cyrene*
13. 1. Lucius of *Cyrene*

Cyrenians.—*Acts* 6. 9

Cyrenius A.V.—*see Quirinius.*

D.

Dalmanutha.—*Mk.* 8. 10

Dalmatia.—*2 Tim.* 4. 10

Damaris.—*Acts* 17. 34

Damascenes.—*2 Cor.* 11. 32

Damascus.
Acts 9. 2. asked of him letters to *Damascus*
8. he drew nigh unto *Damascus*. 8
10. a certain disciple at *Damascus*, named Ananias
19. with the disciples which were at *Damascus*
22. confounded the Jews which dwelt at *Damascus*
27. and how at *Damascus* he had preached boldly
22. 5. [Saul] journeyed to *Damascus*
6. I made my journey, and drew nigh unto D. 26. 12
10. the Lord said unto me, Arise, and go into *Damascus*
11. by the hand of them that were with me, I came into D.
26. 20. declared both to them of *Damascus* first
2 Cor. 11. 32. In *Damascus* the governor under Aretas
Gal. 1. 17. and again I returned unto *Damascus*

Daniel.—*Mat.* 24. 15

David.
Mat. 1. 1. Jesus Christ, the son of *David* [3. 31
6. Jesse begat D. the king. And D. begat Solomon. Lu.
17. from Abraham unto D. are fourteen generations ;
 and from *David* unto the carrying away
20. Joseph, thou son of *David*, fear not
9. 27. Have mercy on us, thou son of D. 15. 22 : 20. 30, 31 :
 Mk. 10. 47, 48 : Lu. 18. 38, 39 [2. 25 : Lu. 6. 3
12. 3. read what D. did, when he was an hungred. Mk.
23. amazed, and said, Is this the son of David ?
21. 9. saying, Hosanna to the son of *David*. 15 [20. 41
22. 42. They say unto him, The son of D. Mk. 12. 35 : Lu.
43. D.—call him Lord. 45 : Mk. 12. 36, 37 : Lu. 20. 42, 44
Mk. 11. 10. Blessed is—the kingdom of our father *David*
Lu. 1. 27. Joseph, of the house of *David*
32. give unto him the throne of his father *David*
69. In the house of his servant *David*
2. 4. to the city of D.—of the house and family of D. 10

[PROPER NAMES.

DAVID

Jno. 7. 42. Christ cometh of the seed of *D.*—village where
Acts 1. 16. by the mouth of *D.* concerning Judas [*D.* was
  2. 25. For *David* saith concerning him
  20. say unto you freely of the patriarch *David*
  34. For *David* ascended not into the heavens
  4. 25. by the mouth of our father *David* thy servant
  7. 45. before the face of our fathers, unto the days of *D.*
  13. 22. raised up *D.* to be their king;—found *D.* the son
  34. the holy and sure blessings of *David*   [of Jesse
  36. For *David*, after he had in his own generation
  15. 16. I will build again the tabernacle of *David*
Rom. 1. 3. of the seed of *David* according to. 2 Tim. 2. 8
  4. 6. *David* also pronounceth blessing upon the man
  11. 9. *David* saith, Let their table be made a snare
Heb. 4. 7. defineth a certain day, saying in *David*
  11. 32. time will fail me if I tell—of *David*
Rev. 3. 7. he that hath the key of *David*
  5. 5. the Root of *David*, hath overcome
  22. 16. the offspring of *D.*, the bright, the morning star
      for city of David, see city.

Death.—*Rev.* 6. 8

Decapolis.—*Mat.* 4. 25: *Mk.* 5. 20: 7. 31

Deliverer.—*Rom.* 11. 26

Demas.—*Col.* 4. 14: 2 *Tim.* 4. 10: *Phil.* 24

Demetrius.—*Acts* 19. 24, 38: 3 *Jno.* 12

Derbe.—*Acts* 14. 6, 20: 16. 1: 20. 4

Devil.—*Rev.* 12. 9: 20. 2

Diana.
Acts 19. 24. which made silver shrines of *Diana*
  27. the temple of the great goddess *Diana*
  28. Great is *Diana* of the Ephesians. 34
  35. the city—is temple-keeper of the great *Diana*

Didymus.—*Jno.* 11. 16; 20. 24: 21. 2

Dionysius.—*Acts* 17. 34

Diotrephes.—3 *Jno.* 9

Dispersion.—*Jno.* 7. 35: *Jas.* 1. 1: 1 *Pet.* 1. 1

Dorcas.—*Acts* 9. 36, 39

Drusilla.—*Acts* 24. 24

E.

Eber—*A.V. Heber. Lu.* 3. 35

Egypt.
Mat. 2. 13. child and his mother, and flee into *Egypt*. 14
  15. Out of *Egypt* did I call my son
  19. appeareth in a dream to Joseph in *Egypt*
Acts 2. 10. in *Egypt* and the parts of Libya about Cyrene
  7. 9. jealousy against Joseph, sold him into *Egypt*
  10 favour and wisdom before Pharaoh king of *Egypt*
    —made him governor over *Egypt*
  11. there came a famine over all *Egypt* and Canaan
  12. Jacob heard that there was corn in *Egypt*

EMMOR

Acts 7. 15. And Jacob went down into *Egypt*
  17. the people grew and multiplied in *Egypt*
  18. there arose another king over *Egypt*
  34. the affliction of my people which is in *Egypt*—
    come, I will send thee unto *Egypt*
  36. wrought wonders and signs in *Egypt*
  39. turned back in their hearts into *Egypt*
  40. led us forth out of the land of *Egypt*
  13. 17. when they sojourned in the land of *Egypt*
Heb. 3. 16. all they that came out of *Egypt* by Moses
  8. 9. to lead them forth out of the land of *Egypt*
  11. 26. greater riches than the treasures of *Egypt*
  27. By faith he [Moses] forsook *Egypt*
Jude 5. having saved a people out of the land of *Egypt*
Rev. 11. 8. spiritually is called Sodom and *Egypt*

Egyptian—s.
Acts 7. 22. Moses was instructed—wisdom of the *Egyptians*
  24. avenged him—smiting the *Egyptian*
  28. as thou killedst the *Egyptian* yesterday
  21. 38. Art thou not then the *Egyptian*, which
Heb. 11. 29. which the *Egyptians*—were swallowed up

Elamites.—*Acts* 2. 9

Eleazar.—*Mat.* 1. 15

Eliakim.—*Mat.* 1. 13: *Lu.* 3. 30

Eliezer.—*Lu.* 3. 29

Elijah—*A.V. Elias.*
Mat. 11. 14. this is *Elijah*, which is to come
  16. 14. Some say—*Elijah. Mk.* 6. 15: 8. 28: *Lu.* 9. 8, 19
  17. 3. appeared unto them Moses and *E.* 4: *Mk.* 9. 4, 5:
  10. *Elijah* must first come. *Mk.* 9. 11, 12 [*Lu.* 9. 30, 34
  17. 11. *Elijah* indeed cometh
  12. that *Elijah* is come already. *Mk.* 9. 13
  27. 47. This man calleth *Elijah. Mk.* 15. 35
  49. let us see whether *Elijah* cometh. *Mk.* 15. 36
Lu. 1. 17. in the spirit and power of *Elijah*
  4. 25. many widows in Israel in the days of *Elijah*
  26. unto none of them was *Elijah* sent
Jno. 1. 21. Art thou *Elijah?*
  25. not the Christ, neither *Elijah*
Rom. 11. 2. what the scripture saith of *Elijah*
Jas. 5. 17. *Elijah* was a man of like passions with us

Elisabeth.
Lu. 1. 5. and her name was *Elisabeth*
  7. *Elisabeth* was barren
  13. thy wife *Elisabeth* shall bear thee a son
  24. *Elisabeth*, his wife, conceived. 36
  40. and saluted *Elisabeth* [Mary]
  41. When *Elisabeth* heard the salutation — and
    Elisabeth was filled with the Holy Ghost
  57. Now *Elisabeth's* time was fulfilled

Elisha.—*Lu.* 4. 27

Eliud.—*Mat.* 1. 14, 15

Elmadam.—*Lu.* 3. 28

Elymas.—*Acts* 13. 8

Emmanuel *A.V.*—see *Immanuel.*

Emmaus.—*Lu.* 24. 13

Emmor *A.V.*—see *Hamor*

ENOCH

Enoch.
Lu. 3. 37. Methuselah, the son of *Enoch*
Heb. 11. 5. By faith *Enoch* was translated
Jude 14. *Enoch*, the seventh from Adam, prophesied

Enos.—Lu. 3. 38

Epænetus.—Rom. 16. 5

Epaphras.—Col. 1. 7. : 4. 12 : Philem. 23

Epaphroditus.—Phil. 2. 25 : 4. 18

Ephesian—s.—Acts 19. 28, 34, 35 : 21. 29

Ephesus.
Acts 18. 19. And they came to *Ephesus*. 19. 1
21. he set sail from *Ephesus*
24. Apollos—a learned man, came to *Ephesus*
19. 17. both Jews and Greeks, that dwelt at *Ephesus*
26. that not alone at *E.*,—this Paul hath persuaded
35. Ye men of *Ephesus*
20. 16. Paul had determined to sail past *Ephesus*
17. from Miletus he sent to *Ephesus*
1 Cor. 15. 32. I fought with beasts at *Ephesus*
16. 8. I will tarry at *Ephesus* until Pentecost
Eph. 1. 1. to the saints which are at *Ephesus*
1 Tim. 1. 3. I exhorted thee to tarry at *Ephesus*
2 Tim. 1. 18. how many things he ministered at *E.*, thou
4. 12. But Tychicus I sent to *Ephesus* [knowest
Rev. 1. 11. to the seven churches ; unto *Ephesus*
2. 1. To the angel of the church in *Ephesus*

Ephraim—Jno. 11. 54

Epicurean A.V.—see Stoic.—Acts 17. 18

Er.—Lu. 3. 28

Erastus.—Acts 19. 22 : Rom. 16. 23 : 2 Tim. 4. 20

Esau.
Rom. 9. 13. Jacob I loved, but *Esau* I hated
Heb. 11. 20. By faith, Isaac blessed Jacob and *Esau*
12. 16. or profane person, as *Esau*

Esli.—Lu. 3. 25

Esrom A.V.,—see Hezron.

Ethiopia—ans.—Acts 8. 27

Eubulus.—2 Tim. 4. 21

Eunice.—2 Tim. 1. 5

Euodia.—Phil. 4. 2

Euphrates.—Rev. 9. 14 : 16. 12

Euraquilo.—A.V. Euroclydon.—Acts 27. 14

Eutychus.—Acts 20. 9

Eve.
2 Cor. 11. 3. the serpent beguiled *Eve*
1 Tim. 2. 13. For Adam was first formed, then *Eve*

Ezekias A.V.—see Hezekiah.

FATHER

F.

Fair Havens.—Acts 27. 8

Father—God.
Mat. 11. 25. I thank thee, O *Father*. Lu. 10. 21 : Jno. 11. 41
26. Yea, *Father*, for so it was well-pleasing. Lu. 10. 21
27. knoweth the Son, save the *F.* ;—*F.* save the Son
13. 43. shine forth as the sun in the kingdom of their *F.*
24. 36. The *F.* loveth the Son but the *Father*. Mk. 13. 32.
28. 19. baptizing them into the name of the *Father*
Mk. 14. 36. Abba, *F.*, all things are possible unto thee
Lu. 9. 26. the glory of the *Father*, and of the holy angels
10. 22. Son is save the *Father*—*Father* is save the Son
11. 2. When ye pray, say, *F.*, Hallowed be thy name
22. 42. *Father*, if thou be willing, remove this cup
23. 34. *F.*, forgive them ; for they know not what they do
46. *Father*, into thy hands I commend my spirit
Jno. 1. 14. glory as of the only begotten from the *Father*
18. Son, which is in the bosom of the *Father*
3. 35. The *F.* hath given all things
4. 21. nor in Jerusalem, shall ye worship the *Father*
23. worship the *Father* in spirit—the *Father* seeks to be
5. 19. but what he seeth the *Father* doing
20. *Father* loveth the Son, and sheweth him all things
21. for as the *Father* raiseth the dead
22. neither doth the *Father* judge any man
23. Son, even as they honour the *Father*—not the *F.*
26. For as the *Father* hath life in himself
36. which the *F.* hath given me—the *F.* hath sent me
37. *Father* hath sent me, he hath borne. 8. 18
45. Think not that I will accuse you to the *Father*
6. 27. for him the *Father*, even God, hath sealed
37. All that which the *F.* giveth me shall come unto me
44. No man can come to me, except the *F.* draw him
45. hath heard from the *Father*, and hath learned
46. seen the *F.*, save he which is from God, he hath
57. living *F.* sent me,—because of the *F.* [seen the *F.*
65. except it be given unto him of the *Father*
8. 16. not alone, but I and the *Father* that sent me
27. They perceived not that he spake to them of the *F.*
28. as the *Father* taught me, I speak these things
41. we have one *Father*, even God
10. 15. as the *Father* knoweth me, and I know the *F.*
17. therefore doth the *Father* love me
29. none is able to snatch them out of the *F.'s* hand
30. I and the *Father* are one
32. many good works have I shewed you from the *F.*
36. whom the *F.* sanctified and sent into the world
38. The *F.* is in me, and I in the *F.* : 14. 10, 11 : 17. 21
12. 26. serve me, him will the *Father* honour
27. *Father*, save me from this hour
28. *Father*, glorify thy name
49. I speak not of myself ; but the *F.* which sent me
50. even as the *Father* hath said unto me, so I speak
13. I should depart out of this world unto the *Father*
3. the *F.* had given all things into his hands
14. 6. no one cometh unto the *F.*, but by me
8. Lord shew us the *Father* and it sufficeth us. 9
9. Philip ? he that hath seen me hath seen the *F.*
10. the *Father* abiding in me doeth his works
11. I am in the *Father*, and the *Father* in me. 10
12. these shall he do ; because I go unto the *F.* 16. 10
13. that the *Father* may be glorified in the Son
16. And I will pray the *F.* and he shall give you. 16. 26
26. the Holy Spirit, whom the *F.* will send in my name
28. go unto the *Father* : for the *F.* is greater than I
31. I love the *F.*,—*F.* gave me commandment. 12. 49

FATHER

Jno. 15. 9. as the *F.* hath loved me, I also have loved you
16. ye shall ask of the *F.* in my name. 16. 23
26. send unto you from the *Father,*—from the *Father*
16. 3. they have not known the *Father,* nor me
15. whatsoever the *Father* hath are mine
17. shall see me: and, Because I go to the *Father*
25. shall tell you plainly of the *Father*
26. I will pray the *Father* for you
27. *F.* himself loveth you.—came forth from the *F.*
28. I came out from the *Father,*—and go unto the *F.*
32. because the *Father* is with me
17. 1. he said, *F.,* the hour is come; glorify thy Son
5. O *Father,* glorify thou me with thine own self
11. Holy *Father,* keep them in thy name
24. *Father,* that which thou hast given me
25. O righteous *Father,* the world knew thee not
18. 11. the cup which the *Father* hath given me
20. 21. as the *Father* hath sent me, even so send I you
Acts 1. 4. to wait for the promise of the *Father* [authority
7. seasons, which the *Father* hath set within his own
2. 33. received of the *F.* the promise of the Holy Ghost
Rom. 6. 4. raised from the dead through the glory of the *F.*
8. 15. spirit of adoption, whereby we cry, Abba, *Father*
15. 6. the God and *Father* of our Lord Jesus Christ.
2 *Cor.* 1. 3 : 11. 31 : *Eph.* 1. 3 : 1 *Pet.* 1. 3
1 *Cor.* 8. 6. there is one God, the *F.,* of whom are all things
15. 24. deliver up the kingdom to God, even the *Father*
2 *Cor.* 1. 3. *Father* of mercies, and God of all comfort
6. 18. And I will be to you a *Father,* and ye shall be to
me sons. *Heb.* 1. 5
Gal. 1. 1. God the *Father,* who raised him from the dead
3. peace from God the *Father.* 2 *Tim.* 1. 2 : *Tit.* 1. 4
4. 6. Spirit of his Son into our hearts, crying, Abba, *F.*
Eph. 1. 17. God of our Lord Jesus Christ, the *F.* of glory
2. 18. access in one Spirit unto the *Father*
3. 14. For this cause I bow my knees unto the *Father*
4. 6. one God and *Father* of all, who is over all
5. 20. the name of our Lord Jesus Christ to God, even
the *Father.* Col. 1. 3, 12 : 3. 17
6. 23. and love with faith, from God the *Father*
Phil. 2. 11. Jesus Christ is Lord, to the glory of God the *F.*
Col. 1. 19. pleasure of the *Father* that in him should all
the fulness dwell
1 *Th.* 1. 1. church of the Thessalonians in God the *Father*
2 *Th.* 1. 2. peace from God the *Father*
1 *Tim.* 1. 2. From God the *Father* and Christ Jesus
Heb. 1. 5. I will be to him a *F.,* and he shall be to me a Son !
12. 9. be in subjection unto the *F.* of spirits, and live
Jas. 1. 17. coming down from the *Father* of lights
27. Pure religion and undefiled before our God and *F.*
3. 9. Therewith bless we the Lord and *Father*
1 *Pet.* 1. 2. to the foreknowledge of God the *Father*
17. if ye call on him as *Father,* who without respect
2 *Pet.* 1. 17. he received from God the *F.* honour and glory
1 *Jno.* 1. 2. the eternal life, which was with the *Father*
3. our fellowship is with the *Father,* and with his Son
2. 1. we have an advocate with the *Father,* Jesus Christ
13. little children, because ye know the *Father*
15. the love of the *Father* is not in him
16. vain glory of life, is not of the *Father*
22. is the antichrist, even he that denieth the *Father*
23. hath not the *F.*:—confesseth the Son hath the *F.* also
24. shall abide in the Son, and in the *Father*
3. 1. what manner of love the *F.* hath bestowed upon us
4. 14. the *Father* hath sent the Son to be the Saviour
2 *Jno.* 3. peace shall be with us from God the *F.*—Son of the
4. as we received commandment from the *Father* [F.
9. the same hath both the *Father* and the Son
Jude 1. that are called, beloved in God the *Father*

His **Father**—*God.*

Mat. 16. 27. glory of *his Father.* *Mk.* 8. 38
Jno. 5. 18. but called God *his* own *Father*
Rev. 1. 6. be priests unto *his God* and *Father*
14. 1. name of *his Father* written on their foreheads

My **Father**—*God.*

Mat. 7. 21. he that doeth the will of *my Father.* 12. 50
10. 32. him will I confess before *my Father*
33. him will I also deny before *my Father*
11. 27. have been delivered unto *my Father.* *Lu.* 10. 22
15. 13. Every plant which *my* heavenly *F.* planted not
16. 17. Revealed it unto thee, but *my Father*
18. 10. behold the face of *my Father* which is in heaven
18. 19. shall be done for them of *my Father*
35. So shall also *my* heavenly *Father* do unto you
20. 23. for whom it hath been prepared of *my Father*
25. 34. Come, ye blessed of *my Father*
26. 29. I drink it new with you in *my Father's* Kingdom
39. O *my Father,* if it be possible, let this cup pass
42. O *my Father,* if this cannot pass away
53. thinkest thou that I cannot beseech *my Father*
Lu. 2. 49. that I must be in *my Father's* house
22. 29. a Kingdom, even as *my Father* appointed
24. 49. I send forth the promise of *my F.* upon you
Jno. 2. 16. make not *my F.'s* house a house of merchandize
5. 17. *My Father* worketh even until now, and I work
40. For this is the will of *my Father*
43. I am come in *my F.'s* name, and ye receive me not
6. 32. *my F.* giveth you the true bread out of heaven
8. 19. know neither me, nor *my F.*:—know *my F.* also
38. I speak the things which I have seen with *my F.*
49. I honour *my Father,* and ye dishonour me
54. it is *my Father* that glorifieth me
10. 18. This commandment received I from *my Father*
25. The works that I do in *my Father's* name
29. *My Father,* which hath given them unto me
37. If I do not the works of *my Father*
14. 1. In *my Father's* house are many mansions
7. ye would have known *my Father* also
20. in that day ye shall know that I am in *my Father*
21. he that loveth me shall be loved of *my Father.* 23
15. 1. I am the true vine, and *my F.* is the husbandman
8. Herein is *my F.* glorified, that ye bear much fruit
10. as I have kept *my Father's* Commandments
15. all things that I heard from *my Father*
23. He that hateth me, hateth *my Father* also. 24
20. 17. I ascend unto *my Father* and your *Father*
Rev. 2. 27. to shivers ; as I also have received of *my F.*
3. 5. I will confess his name before *my F.,* and before his
Rev. 3. 21. and sat down with *my F.* in his throne [angels

Our **Father**—*God.*

Mat. 6. 9. *Our Father* which art in heaven. *Lu.* 11, 2
Rom. 1. 7. peace from God *our Father.* 1 *Cor.* 1. 3 : 2 *Cor.*
1. 2 : *Eph.* 1. 2 : *Phil.* 1. 2 : *Col.* 1. 2 : *Philem.* 3
Gal. 1. 4. According to the will of *our* God and *Father*
Phil. 4. 20. unto *our* God and *F.* be the glory for ever
1 *Th.* 1. 3. Jesus Christ, before *our* God and *Father*
3. 11. *our* God and *Father* himself, and our Lord Jesus
13. unblameable in holiness before *our* God and *Father*
2 *Th.* 1. 1. of the Thessalonians in God *our F.* [comfort
2. 16. God *our F.* which loved us and gave us eternal

Thy **Father**—*God.*

Mat. 6. 4. *Thy Father* which seeth in secret 6. 18
6. shut thy door, pray to *thy Father*—and *thy Father*
18. not seen of men to fast, but of *thy F.*—and *thy F.*
Jno. 8. 19. said, therefore, unto him, Where is *thy Father ?*

FATHER

Your **Father**—*God.*

Mat. 5. 16. glorify *your Father* which is in heaven
45. That ye may be sons of *your F.* which is in heaven
48. therefore shall be perfect, as *your* heavenly *F.* is
6. 1. else ye have no reward with *your Father* [perfect
8. for *your Father* knoweth what things ye have need of. 32: *Lu.* 12. 30
14. *your* heavenly *F.* will also forgive you. *Mk.* 11. 25
15. neither will *your F.* forgive your trespasses. *Mk.*
26. *your* heavenly *Father* feedeth them [11. 26
7. 11. shall *your F.* which is in heaven give good things
10. 29. shall fall on the ground without *your Father*
18. 14. the will of *your Father* which is in heaven
23. 9. call no man *your F.*, for one is *your Father*
Lu. 6. 36. Be ye merciful, even as *your Father* is merciful
11. 13. more shall *your* heavenly *F.* give the Holy Spirit
12. 32. *your F.'s* good pleasure to give you the kingdom
Jno. 8. 42. If God were *your Father*, ye would love me
20. 17. I ascend unto my Father, and *your Father*

Felix.

Acts 23. 24. Paul—bring him safe unto *Felix*
26. Lysias unto the most excellent governor *Felix*
24. 3. in all places, most excellent *Felix*
22. But *Felix*, having more exact knowledge
24. *Felix* came with Drusilla, his wife
25. *Felix* was terrified, and answered
27. *Felix* was succeeded by Porcius Festus;—*Felix* left Paul in bonds. 25. 14

Festus.

Acts 24 27. Felix was succeeded by Porcius *Festus*
25. 1. *Festus* therefore having come
3. Howbeit *Festus* answered
9. But *Festus*, desiring to gain favour
12. Then *Festus*, when he had conferred
13. Agrippa—arived at Cæsarea, and saluted *Festus*
14. *Festus* laid Paul's case before the king
22. Agrippa said unto *Festus*, I also could wish to hear
23. at the command of *Festus* Paul was brought
24. And *Festus* saith, King Agrippa, and all men
26. *Festus* saith with a loud voice, Paul, thou art mad
25. I am not mad, most excellent *Festus*
32. unto *Festus*, this man might have been set at liberty

Fortunatus.—1 *Cor.* 16. 17

G.

Gabbatha.—*Jno.* 19. 13

Gabriel.—*Lu.* 1. 19. 26

Gad.—*Rev.* 7. 5

Gadarenes, *also Gerasenes.*—*Mat.* 8. 28

Gaius.—*Acts* 19. 29: 20. 4: *Rom.* 16. 23: 1 *Cor.* 1. 14: 3 *Jno.* 1

Galatia.

Acts 16. 6. the region of Phrygia and *Galatia.* 18. 23
1 *Cor.* 16. 1. to the churches of *Galatia. Gal.* 1. 2
2 *Tim.* 4. 10. Crescens to *Galatia*
1 *Pet.* 1. 1. of the dispersion of Pontus, *Galatia*

Galatians.—*Gal.* 3. 1

GENTILES

Galilee, *see Cana.*

Mat. 2. 22. withdrew into the parts of *Galilee*
3. 13. Then cometh Jesus from *Galilee.* *Mk.* 1. 9
4. 12. He [Jesus] withdrew into *Galilee*
15. Beyond Jordan, *Galilee* of the Gentiles
18. walking by the sea of *Galilee.* *Mk.* 1. 16
23. Jesus went about in all *Galilee.* *Mk.* 1. 14
25. great multitudes from *Galilee.* *Mk.* 3. 7
15. 29. came nigh unto the sea of *Galilee*
17. 22. while they abode in *Galilee* [of Judæa
19. 1. he departed from *G.*, and came into the borders
21. 11. Jesus, from Nazareth of *Galilee* [16. 7
26. 32. I will go before you into *G.* 28. 7. 10: *Mk.* 14. 28
27. 55. followed Jesus from *Galilee.* ministering unto him. *Mk.* 15. 41: *Lu.* 23. 49, 55
28. 16. the eleven disciples went into *Galilee*
Mk. 1. 28. all the region of *Galilee*
39. synagogues throughout all *G.* preaching. *Lu.* 4. 44
6. 21. high captains, and the chief men of *Galilee*
7. 31. came through Sidon unto the sea of *Galilee*
9. 30. passed through *Galilee*
Lu. 1. 26. unto a city of *Galilee,* named Nazareth
2. 4. Joseph also went up from *Galilee*
39. they returned into *Galilee,* to their own city
3. 1. Herod being tetrarch of *Galilee*
4. 14. Jesus returned in the power of the Spirit into *G.*
31. came down to Capernaum, a city of *Galilee*
5. 17. out of every village of *Galilee*
8. 26. of the Gerasenes, which is over against *Galilee*
17. 11. through the midst of Samaria and *Galilee*
23. 5. beginning from *G.*, even unto this place. *Acts* 10. 27
24. 6. spake unto you when he was yet in *Galilee*
Jno. 1. 43. minded to go forth into *Galilee*
4. 3. departed again into *Galilee.* 7. 1
43. he went forth from thence into *Galilee*
45. when he came into *G.*, the Galilæans received him
47. Jesus was come out of Judæa into *Galilee.* 46, 54
6. 1. to the other side of the sea of *Galilee*
7. 9. he abode still in *Galilee*
41. doth the Christ come out of *Galilee*
52. Art thou also of *G.?*—out of *G.* ariseth no prophet
12. 21. Philip, which was of Bethsaida of *Galilee*
Acts 1. 11. Ye men of *Galilee,* why stand ye
5. 37. rose up Judas of *Galilee* in the days
9. 31. church throughout all Judæa and *Galilee*
13. 31. came up with him from *Galilee* to Jerusalem

Galilæan—s.

Mat. 26. 69. Thou also wast with Jesus the *G.* *Mk.* 14. 70
Lu. 13. 1. the *Galilæans,* whose blood Pilate [*Lu.* 22. 59
2. Think ye that these *G.* were sinners above all the *G.*
23. 6. he asked whether the man were a *Galilæan*
Jno. 4. 45. the *Galilæans* received him [Jesus]
Acts 2. 7. are not all these which speak *Galilæans ?*

Gallio.—*Acts* 18. 12, 14, 17

Gamaliel.—*Acts* 5. 34: 22. 3

Gaza.—*Acts* 8. 26

Gennesaret.—*Mat.* 14. 34: *Mk.* 6. 53: *Lu.* 5. 1

Gentiles, *see Greeks.*—*A. V.* ¹*Heathen.*

Mat. 4. 15. beyond Jordan, Galilee of the *Gentiles*
5. 47. do not even the—*Gentiles* the same
6. 7. praying use not vain repetitions, as the ¹*G.* do
32. After all these things do the *Gentiles* seek
10. 5. Go not into any way of the *Gentiles*
18. for a testimony to them and to the *Gentiles*

GENTILES

Mat. 12. 18. he shall declare judgement to the *Gentiles*
21. in his name shall the *Gentiles* hope
13. 17. let him be unto thee as the ¹*Gentile*   [*Lu.* 18. 32
20. 19. deliver him unto the *G*. to mock. *Mk.* 10. 33
25. rulers of the *Gentiles* lord it over them. *Mk.* 10. 42
Lu. 2. 32. A light for revelation to the *Gentiles*   [the *G*.
21. 24. Jerusalem—trodden down of the *G*.—times of
22. 25. kings of the *G*. have lordship over them
Acts 4. 25. Why did the ¹*Gentiles* rage
27. Pontius Pilate, with the *Gentiles* and the peoples
9. 15. bear my name before the *Gentiles* and kings
10. 45. on the *G*. also was poured out the gift of the
11. 1. *G*. also had received the word of God [Holy Ghost
18. to the *Gentiles* also hath God granted repentance
13. 46. lo, we turn to the *Gentiles*
47. I have set thee for a light of the *Gentiles*
48. as the *Gentiles* heard this, they were glad
14. 2. the Jews—stirred up the souls of the *Gentiles*
5. onset both of the *Gentiles* and of the Jews
27. opened a door of faith unto the *Gentiles*
15. 3. declaring the conversion of the *Gentiles*
7. the *Gentiles* should hear the word of the gospel
12. wrought among the *G*. by them [Barnabas and Paul]
14. how first God did visit the *Gentiles*
17. And all the *Gentiles*, upon whom my name is called
19. from among the *Gentiles* turn to God
23. brethren which are of the *Gentiles* in Antioch
18. 6. from henceforth I will go unto the *Gentiles*
21. 11. deliver him [Paul] into the hands of the *G*.
19. God had wrought among the *Gentiles*
21. Jews which are among the *G*. to forsake Moses
25. as touching the *Gentiles* which have believed
22. 21. send thee [Saul] forth far hence unto the *G*.
26. 17. from the *Gentiles* unto whom I send thee
20. Judæa, and also to the *Gentiles*
Acts 26. 23. light both to the people and to the *Gentiles*
28. 28. salvation of God is sent unto the *Gentiles*
Rom. 1. 13. as in the rest of the *Gentiles*
2. 14. when *Gentiles* which have no law
24. name of God is blasphemed among the *Gentiles*
3. 29. is he not the God of *Gentiles* also? yea, of *G*. also
9. 24. Jews only, but also from the *Gentiles*
30. *Gentiles*, which followed not after righteousness
11. 11. salvation is come unto the *Gentiles*
12. and their loss the riches of the *Gentiles*
13. I speak to you that are *G*.—I am an apostle of *G*.
25. until the fulness of the *Gentiles* be come in
15. 9. the *G*. might glorify God for his mercy;—among
10. Rejoice, ye *Gentiles*, with his people   [the *G*.
11. Praise the Lord, all ye *Gentiles*
12. rule over the *Gentiles*; on him shall the *G*. hope
16. minister of Christ Jesus unto the *G*.,—offering up
18. the obedience of the *Gentiles*   [of the *G*.
27. if the *Gentiles* have been made partakers
16. 4. but also all the churches of the *Gentiles*
1 *Cor.* 5. 1. fornication as is not even among the *Gentiles*
10. 20. things which the *Gentiles* sacrifice
12. 2. Ye know that when ye were *Gentiles*
2 *Cor.* 11. 26. in perils from the ¹*Gentiles* [Paul]
Gal. 1. 16. I might preach him among the *Gentiles*
2. 2. gospel which I preach among the *Gentiles*
8. wrought for me also unto the *Gentiles*
9. we [Paul and Barnabas] should go unto the ¹*Gentiles*
12. Cephas—did eat with the *Gentiles*
14. livest as do the *Gentiles*,—compellest thou the *G*.
15. not sinners of the *Gentiles*
3. 8. God would justify the ¹*Gentiles* by faith
14. upon the *Gentiles* might come the blessing
Eph. 2. 11. ye, the *Gentiles* in the flesh

GOD

Eph. 3. 1. Paul, the prisoner of Christ Jesus in behalf of you
    G. to wit, that the *Gentiles* are fellow-heirs   [*G*.
8. preach unto the *G*. the unsearchable riches of Christ
4. 17. ye no longer walk as the *Gentiles* also walk
Col. 1. 27. glory of this mystery among the *Gentiles*
1 *Th.* 2. 16. forbidding us to speak to the *Gentiles*
4. 5. even as the *Gentiles* which know not God
1 *Tim.* 2. 7. a teacher of the *Gentiles* in faith and truth
2 *Tim.* 4. 17. that all the *Gentiles* might hear
1 *Pet.* 2. 12. your behaviour seemly among the *Gentiles*
    4. 3. wrought the desire of the *Gentiles*
3 *Jno.* 7. went forth, taking nothing of the *Gentiles*

Gerasenes, also *Gadarenes*.—*Mk.* 5. 1: *Lu.* 8. 26, 37

Gergesenes A.V.—see *Gadarenes* and *Gerasenes*.

Gethsemane.—*Mat.* 26. 36: *Mk.* 14. 32

Gideon.—*Heb.* 11. 32

God.

Mat. 1. 23. Immanuel—being interpreted, *God* with us
5. 8. pure in heart; for they shall see *God*
6. 24. ye cannot serve *God* and mammon. *Lu.* 16. 13
30. But if *God* doth so clothe the grass. *Lu.* 12. 28
15. 4. For *God* said, Honour thy father and thy mother
19. 6. What therefore *God* hath joined together *Mk.* 10. 9
22. 21. unto *God* the things that are *God's*. *Mk.* 12. 17: *Lu.* 20. 25
32. I am the *G*. of Abraham,—*G*. of Isaac,—*G*. of Jacob?
    God is not the *God* of the dead, but of the living.
    Mk. 12. 26, 27: *Lu.* 20. 37, 38: *Acts* 3. 13: 7. 32
27. 43. He trusteth on *God*; let him deliver him now
Mk. 2. 7. who can forgive sins but one, even *God*
12. they were all amazed, and glorified *God. Lu.* 7. 16
5. 7. I adjure thee by *God*, torment me not
10. 18. none is good save one, even *God. Lu.* 18. 19
12. 14. of a truth teachest the way of *God*
13. 19. creation which *God* created until now
Lu. 1. 26. Gabriel was sent from *God* unto—Nazareth
37. no word from *God* shall be void of power
47. my spirit hath rejoiced in *God* my Saviour
64. tongue loosed, and he [Zacharias] spake, blessing *G*.
2. 13. heavenly host, praising *God*. 20
28. into his [Simeon] arms, and blessed *God*, and said
5. 21. Who can forgive sins, but *God* alone?
7. 16. *God* hath visited his people
29. the publicans, justified *God*, being baptized
8. 39. how great things *God* hath done for thee
12. 21. treasure for himself, and is not rich toward *God*
24. Consider the ravens—*God* feedeth them
16. 15. *God* knoweth your hearts
18. 1. a judge which feared not *God*. 4
7. And shall not *God* avenge his elect
11. *God*, I [Pharisee] thank thee, that I am not
13. *God*, be merciful to me [Publican] a sinner
20. 16. *God* forbid. *Rom.* 3. 3, 6, 31: 6. 1, 15: 7. 7, 13:
    11. 1, 11: 1 *Cor.* 6. 15: *Gal.* 2. 17: 3. 21
23. 40. Dost thou not even fear *God*, seeing thou art
Jno. 1. 1. the Word was *God*
6. a man sent from *God*, whose name was John
18. No man hath seen *God* at any time
3. 2. thou art a teacher come from *God*—signs that thou
    doest, except *God* be with him
16. For *God* so loved the world, that he gave
17. *God* sent not his Son into the world to judge
21. manifest, that they have been wrought in *God*
34. he whom *God* hath sent speaketh the words of *God*
6. 27. for him the Father, even *God*, hath sealed

PROPER NAMES.]   404

GOD

Jno. 6. 46. seen the Father, save he which is from God
8. 40. the truth, which I heard from God
41. we have one Father, even God
8. 42. If God were your Father,—am come from God
9. 16. Pharisees said, This man is not from God. 33
29. We know that God hath spoken unto Moses
31. We know that God heareth not sinners
10. 33. thou, being a man, makest thyself God
11. 22. whatsoever thou shalt ask of G., G. will give thee
14. 1. ye believe in God, believe also in me
16. 30. we believe that thou camest forth from God
17. 3. that they should know thee the only true God
Acts 2. 17. it shall be in the last days, saith God
22. wonders and signs, which God did by him [Jesus]
36. God hath made him both Lord and Christ
3. 13. the God of our fathers, hath glorified his Servant
18. things which God foreshewed. 21
5. 29. We must obey God rather than men
31. Him did God exalt with his right hand
32. the Holy Ghost, whom God hath given to them
7. 9. Joseph, sold him—and God was with him
25. God—was giving them deliverance. 35
32. I am the God of thy fathers
42. God turned, and gave them up to serve
45. the nations which God thrust out
50. Son of man standing on the right hand of God
10. 15. What God hath cleansed. 28
38. how that God anointed him—God was with him
11. 17. who was I, that I could withstand God?
13. 16. Men of Israel, and ye that fear God
17. The God of this people Israel chose our fathers
14. 27. rehearsed all things that God had done. 15. 4
17. 23. inscription, TO AN UNKNOWN GOD
24. The God that made the world and all things therein
18. 21. I will return again unto you, if God will
23. 4. Revilest thou God's high priest?
Rom. 1. 24. G. gave them up to the lusts of their hearts. 28
3. 4. God forbid : yea, let God be found true
11. There is none that seeketh after God
25. whom God set forth to be a propitiation
29. is G. the G. of Jews only? is he not the G. of Gen-
30. yea, of Gentiles also : if so be that G. is one [tiles also
4. 2. whereof to glory ; but not toward God
17. even God, who quickeneth the dead
8. 3. God, sending his own Son in the likeness
31. If God is for us, who is against us
33. It is God that justifieth
9. 22. What if God, willing to show his wrath
11. 1. Did God cast off his people? 2
8. God gave them a spirit of stupor
21. if God spared not the natural branches
32. God hath shut up all unto disobedience
15. 5. the God of patience and of comfort
13. the God of hope fill you with all joy
16. 26. commandment of the eternal God
1 Cor. 1. 21. world—knew not G., it was G.'s good pleasure
27. God chose the foolish—God chose the weak. 28
3. 6. God gave the increase. 7   [God's building
9. God's fellow-workers : ye are God's husbandry,
6. 13. God shall bring to nought both it and them
8. 4. there is no God but one
6. yet to us there is one God, the Father
9. 10. Is it for the oxen that God careth
10. 5. with most of them God was not well pleased
12. 7. the same God, who worketh all things
18. God set the members each one of them
28. God hath set some in the church
14. 33. God is not a God of confusion, but of peace
15. 28. that God may be all in all

2 Cor. 1. 9. but in God which raiseth the dead
18. But as God is faithful, our word toward you
21. Now he that establisheth us—anointed us, is God
23. But I call God for a witness upon my soul
4. 6. seeing it is God, that said, Light   [himself
5. 19. God was in Christ reconciling the world unto
20. as though God were entreating by us
6. 16. and I will be their God
7. 6. he that comforteth the lowly, even God
9. 7. for God loveth a cheerful giver
11. 11. God knoweth. 12. 2
13. 11. the God of love and peace shall be with you
Eph. 2. 4. God being rich in mercy, for his great love
12. no hope and without God in the world
4. 6. one baptism, one God and Father of all [gave you
32. forgiving each other, even as G. also in Christ for-
5. 1. Be ye therefore imitators of God
Phil. 1. 28. but of your salvation, and that from God
2. 13. it is God which worketh in you
27. but God had mercy on him
Col. 4. 3. God may open unto us a door for the word
1 Th. 2. 10. Ye are witnesses, and God also
4. 6. as the Gentiles which know not God. 2 Th. 1. 8
8. rejecteth not man, but God
2 Th. 2. 4. exalteth himself against all that is called God
—setting himself forth as God
11. for this cause God sendeth them a working of error
13. for that God chose you from the beginning
1 Tim. 1. 17. the only God, be honour and glory   [men
2. 5. there is one G., one mediator also between G. and
5. 6. widow—hath her hope set on God
6. 17. hope set on the uncertainty of riches, but on God
2 Tim. 2. 25. if peradventure G. may give them repentance
Tit. 1. 16. They profess that they know God
Heb. 1. 1. G., having of old time spoken unto the fathers
8. Thy throne, O God, is for ever and over
9. Therefore God, thy God, hath anointed thee
3. 4. he that built all things is God
4. 10. rested from his works, as God did from his
6. 10. God is not unrighteous to forget your work
13. when God promise to Abraham—he sware by
18. it is impossible for God to lie   [himself
7. 17. Wherein God, being minded to shew more
8. 10. And I will be to them a God
10. 7. Lo, I am come—to do thy will, O God
11. 10. city—whose builder and maker is God   [us
40. God having provided some better thing concerning
13. 4. fornicators and adulterers God will judge
Jas. 1. 13. I am tempted of G. : for G. cannot be tempted
2. 19. Thou believest that God is one
4. 8. Draw nigh to G., and he will draw nigh to you. [in G.
1 Pet. 1. 21. believers in G.—your faith and hope might be
2. 5. rejected indeed of men, but with G. elect, precious
19. if for conscience toward G. a man endureth griefs
3. 21. interrogation of a good conscience toward God
5. 5. God resisteth the proud
2 Pet. 2. 4. if God spared not angels when they sinned
1 Jno. 4. 12. No man hath beheld God—God abideth in us
5. 20. This is the true God, and eternal life
2 Jno. 9. abideth not in the teaching of Christ, hath not G.
Rev. 7. 17. and God shall wipe away every tear
17. 17. God did put in their hearts to do his mind
18. 5. God hath remembered her iniquities
21. 3. God himself shall be with them, and be their God
7. I will be his God, and he shall be my son
22. 18. God shall add unto him the plagues
19. God shall take away his part from the tree of life
   see Almighty—Father, Lord God, true.

GOD

Against God.
Acts 5. 39. ye be found even to be fighting *against* God
6. 11. words against Moses, and *against* God ?
Rom. 8. 7. mind of the flesh is enmity *against* God
9. 20. O man, who art thou that repliest *against* God
Rev. 13. 6. opened his mouth for blasphemies *against* God

Before God.
Lu. 1. 6. both righteous *before* God [Zacharias and Elis.]
8. [Zacharias] executed the priest's office *before* God
24. 19. Jesus—mighty in deed and word *before* God
Acts 8. 21. thy [Simon] heart is not right *before* God
10. 4. thine alms are gone up for a memorial *before* God
23. 1. Paul—I have lived *before* G. in all good conscience
Rom. 2. 13. not the hearers of a law are just *before* God
14. 22. The faith—have thou to thyself *before* God
Gal. 1. 20. behold, *before* God, I lie not
1 Th. 3. 13. in holiness *before* our God and Father
Jas. 1. 27. Pure religion and undefiled *before* our God
Rev. 3. 2. no works of thine fulfilled *before* my God
9. 13. golden altar which is *before* God [day and night
12. 10. cast down, which accuseth them *before* our God

Glory of God, or of the Lord.
Lu. 2. 9. *glory of the Lord* shone round about them [not
Jno. 5. 44. *glory* that cometh from the only God ye seek
11. 4. This sickness is not unto death, but for the *g. of G.*
40. if thou believedst, thou shouldest see the *glory of G.*
Acts 7. 55. (Stephen) saw the *g. of G.*, and Jesus standing
Rom. 3. 23. all have sinned, and fall short of the *g. of G.*
5. 2. rejoice in hope of the *glory of God*
15. 7. as Christ also received you, to the *glory of God*
1 Cor. 10. 31. whatsoever ye do, do all to the *glory of God*
11. 7. [man] forasmuch as he is the image and *g. of God*
2 Cor. 1. 20. unto the *glory of God*, through us
3. 18. reflecting as a mirror the *glory of the Lord*
4. 6. *glory of God* in the face of Jesus Christ
15. thanksgiving to abound unto the *glory of God*
8. 19. ministered by us to the *glory of the Lord* [God
Phil. 1. 11. through Jesus Christ, unto the *g.* and praise *of*
2. 11. Jesus Christ is Lord, to the *glory of G.* the Father
Rev. 15. 8. temple was filled with smoke from the *g. of God*
21. 11. holy city, Jerusalem,—having the *glory of God*
23. for the *glory of God* did lighten it
Glorified God, or glorifying God, see glorified, glorifying.

High God
Mk. 5. 7. Jesus, thou Son of the Most *High* God. *Lu.* 8. 28
Acts 16. 17. These men are servants of the Most *High* God
Heb. 7. 1. Melchizedek—priest of God Most *High*

Holy One of God.—Lu. 4. 34: Jno. 6. 70

God of Heaven.
Rev. 11. 13. gave glory to the *God of heaven*
16. 11. blasphemed the *God of heaven*

House of God see House.

God is, or, is not.
Mat. 3. 9. that God *is* able of these stones to raise up. *Lu.*
22. 32. God *is not* the God of the dead [3. 8
Jno. 9. 33. set his seal to this, that God *is* true
4. 24. God *is* a Spirit: and they that worship him
13. 31. God *is* glorified in him [Jesus]
Acts 10. 34. God *is* no respecter of persons
Rom. 1. 9. For God *is* my witness. *Phil.* 1. 8

Rom. 11. 23. God *is* able to graft them in again [1. 18
1 Cor. 1. 9. God *is* faithful, through whom. 10. 13 : 2 Cor.
14. 25. declaring that God *is* among you indeed
33. God *is not* a God of confusion
2 Cor. 5. 5. wrought for us this very thing *is* God
9. 8. God *is* able to make all grace abound unto you
Gal. 3. 20. but God *is* one
6. 7. God *is not* mocked
1 Th. 2. 5. God *is* witness ; nor seeking glory
Heb. 6. 10. God *is not* unrighteous to forget
11. 16. God *is not* ashamed of them—called their God
12. 29. for our God *is* a consuming fire
13. 16. with such sacrifices God *is* well pleased
1 Jno. 1. 5. that God *is* light, and in him is no darkness
3. 20. because God *is* greater than our heart
4. 8. knoweth not God ; for God *is* love

God of Israel.
Mat. 15. 31. multitude—glorified the *God of Israel*
Lu. 1. 68. Blessed be the Lord, the *God of Israel*

Living God.
Mat. 16. 16. Thou art the Christ, the son of the *l. G.* [Peter]
26. 63. I adjure thee by the *living God* [High Priest]
Acts 14. 15. turn from those vain things unto the *living G.*
2 Cor. 3. 3. written—with the Spirit of the *living God*
6. 16. we are a temple of the *living God*
1 Th. 1. 9. from idols, to serve a *living* and true God
1 Tim. 3. 15. the church of the *living God*
4. 10. we have our hope set on the *living God*
Heb. 3. 12. falling away from the *living God*
9. 14. from dead works to serve the *living God*
10. 31. fearful thing to fall into the hands of the *l.* God
12. 22. unto the city of the *living God*
Rev. 7. 2. angel—having the seal of the *living God*

My God, see also Lord my God.
Mat. 27. 46. My God, *my* God, why hast thou forsaken me?
Jno. 20. 17. I ascend unto—*my G.* and your God | *Mk.* 15. 34.
28. Thomas answered—My Lord, and *my God*
Rom. 1. 8. I thank *my G.* 1 Cor. 1. 4 : *Phil.* 1. 3 ; *Philem.* 4.
2 Cor. 12. 21. *my God* should humble me before you
Ph. 4. 19. *my God* shall fulfil every need of yours
Rev. 3. 12. temple of *my God,*—name of *my God,*—city of
my God,—from *my God*

Of God, see also Born of God, Glory of God, Word of God, &c.
Mat. 2. 12. warned *of God* in a dream. 22
4. 4. every word that proceedeth out of the mouth *of G.*
5. 9. peacemakers: for they shall be called sons *of G.*
34. neither by the heaven, for it is the throne *of God*
12. 4. entered into the house *of God*, and did eat the shew bread [David]. *Mk.* 2. 26 : *Lu.* 6. 4
16. 23. thou mindest not the things *of God* [Peter]
21. 12. Jesus entered into the temple *of God*
22. 16. teachest the way *of God* in truth
29. not knowing the scriptures, nor the power *of God*
23. 22. sweareth by the throne *of God* [*Mk.* 12. 24
26. 61. I am able to destroy the temple *of God*
Mk. 1. 24. who thou art, the Holy One *of God*
Lu. 1. 19. I am Gabriel, that stand in the presence *of God*
26. flesh shall see the salvation *of God*
Jno. 1. 13. nor of the will of man, but *of God*
6. 45. they shall all be taught *of God*
7. 17. teaching, whether it be *of God* [*of God*
8. 47. He that is *of God*—words *of God*— ye are not

GOD

Jno. 9. 3. but that the works *of God* should be made mani-
31. any man be a worshipper *of God* [fest
12. 43. glory of men more than the glory *of God*
Acts 5. 39. if it is *of God*, ye will not be able to overthrow
8. 20. thought to obtain the gift *of God* with money
Rom. 2. 29. praise is not of men, but *of God*
3. 3. none effect the faithfulness *of God*
9. 16. but *of God* that hath mercy
13. 1. no power but *of God*—are ordained *of God*
14. 10. we shall all stand before the judgement-seat *of G.*
1 *Cor.* 2. 1. proclaiming to you the mystery *of God*
2. 12. spirit which is *of God*
11. 12. but all things are *of God*. 2 *Cor.* 5. 18
15. 34. some have no knowledge *of God*
2 *Cor.* 1. 20. how many soever be the promises *of God*
2. 17. but as *of God*, in the sight *of God*
Phil. 3. 9. righteousness which is *of God* by faith
1 *Tim.* 4. 4. every creature *of God* is good
1 *Jno.* 3. 10. doeth not righteousness, is not *of God*
4. 1. prove the Spirits whether they are *of God*
2. confesseth that Jesus Christ is come—is *of God*
3. confesseth not Jesus is not *of God*
4. Ye are *of God*, my little children
6. We are *of God* :—he who is not *of God* heareth us not
5. 19. We know that we are *of God*
3 *Jno.* 11. He that doeth good is *of God*

Our God, see also Lord our God.

Lu. 1. 78. tender mercy of *our God*
1 *Cor.* 6. 11. in the Spirit of *our God* [gospel
1 *Th.* 2. 2. we waxed bold in *our God* to speak unto you the
3. 9. we joy for your sakes before *our God* [unto you
11. may *our God* and Father himself—direct our way
13. unblameable in holiness before *our God*
2 *Th.* 1. 1. *our G.* may count you worthy of your calling
Heb. 12. 29. for *our God* is a consuming fire [Christ
2 *Pet.* 1. 1. righteousness of *our God*, and Saviour Jesus
Rev. 4. 11. Worthy art thou, our Lord and *our G.*, to receive
5. 10. them to be unto *our God* a kingdom and priests
7. 10. Salvation unto *our God* which sitteth. 19. 1
12. power and might be unto *our God* for ever and ever
19. 4. Give praise to *our God*, all ye his servants

Thy God, see also Lord thy God.

Heb. 1. 9. Therefore God, *thy God* hath anointed thee

To, or unto God.

Mat. 15. 5. profited by me is given *to God* [*Lu.* 20. 25
22. 21. and *unto G.* the things that are God's. *Mk.* 12. 17 :
Mk. 7. 11. Corban, that is to say, Given *to God*
Lu. 2. 14. Glory *to God* in the highest
38. Anna—gave thanks *unto God*
6. 12. [Jesus] continued all night in prayer *to God*
18. 43. when they saw it, gave praise *unto God*
Jno. 9. 24. Give glory *to God* : we know that this man
13. 3. came forth from God, and goeth *unto God*
16. 2. shall think that he offereth service *unto God*
Acts 4. 19. hearken unto you rather than *unto God*
24. lifted up their voice *to God* with one accord
5. 4. not lied unto men, but *unto God*
26. 18. from the power of Satan *unto God*
20. Gentiles—should repent and turn *to God*
Rom. 6. 10. life that he liveth, he liveth *unto God*
11. but alive *unto God* in Christ Jesus
13. present yourselves *unto G.*—righteousness *unto G.*
17. thanks be *to God*
7. 4. that we might bring forth fruit *unto God*
12. 1. living sacrifice, holy, acceptable *to God*

GREEK

Rom. 14. 11. every tongue shall confess *to God*
12. shall give account of himself *to God*
15. 30. ye strive,together with me in your prayers *to God*
1 *Cor.* 10. 20. sacrifice to devils, and not *to God* [for me
14. 2. speaketh not unto men, but *unto God*
15. 24. when he shall deliver up the kingdom *to God*
2 *Cor.* 2. 15. sweet savour of Christ *unto God*
5. 13. whether we are beside ourselves, it is *unto God*
Phil. 4. 20. Now *unto* our God and Father be the glory
1 *Th.* 1. 9. how ye turned *unto God* from idols
3. 9. thanksgiving can we render again *unto God* for you
Heb. 7. 19. better hope, through which we draw nigh *unto*
25. them that draw near *unto God* through him [*God*
9. 14. offered himself without blemish *unto God*
11. 4. By faith Abel offered *unto God*
5. Enoch—well-pleasing *unto God*
6. for he that cometh *to God* must believe that he is
12. 23. and *to God* the Judge of all
28. we may offer service well-pleasing *to God*
13. 15. let us offer up a sacrifice of praise *to God* con-
Jas. 4. 7. Be subject therefore *unto God* [tinually
8. Draw nigh *to God* and he will draw nigh to you
1 *Pet.* 3. 18. Christ also suffered—might bring us *to God*
4. 6. live according *to God* in the spirit
5. 2. willingly, according *unto God*
Rev. 5. 9. didst purchase *unto God* with thy blood
12. 5. and her child was caught up *unto God*
14. 4. to be the first-fruits *unto God* and unto the Lamb

With God.

Mat. 19. 26. *with God* all things are possible. *Mk.* 10. 27 :
Mk. 10. 27. impossible, but not *with God* [*Lu.* 18. 27
Lu. 1. 30. thou [Mary] hast found favour *with God*
2. 52. in favour *with God* and man [Jesus]
Jno. 1. 1. the Word was *with God.* 2
5. 18. making himself equal *with God. Phil.* 2. 6
Rom. 2. 11. there is no respect of persons *with God*
5. 1. let us have peace *with God* through our Lord Jesus
9. 14. Is there unrighteousness *with God* ? [Christ
1 *Cor.* 3. 19. wisdom of this world is foolishness *with God*
7. 24. called, therein abide *with God* [tion
2 *Th.* 1. 6. righteous thing *with God* to recompense afflic-
Jas. 4. 4. friendship of the world is enmity *with God* ?
1 *Pet.* 2. 20. patiently, this is acceptable *with God*

Your God, see Lord your God.

Jno. 8. 54. of whom ye say, that he is *your God*
20. 17. I ascend unto—my God and *your God*

Godhead.—*Acts* 17. 29 : *Col.* 2. 9

Gog.—*Rev.* 20. 8

Golgotha.—*Mat.* 27. 33 : *Mk.* 15. 22 : *Jno.* 19. 17

Gomorrah, *see Sodom.*—*Mat.* 10. 15 : *Rom.* 9. 29 :
2 *Pet.* 2. 6 ; *Jude* 7

Grecian.

Acts 6. 1. arose a murmuring of the *Grecian* Jews
9. 29. disputed against the *Grecian* Jews

Greece.—*Acts* 20. 2

Greek.—*A.V.* ¹*Gentile.*

Mk. 7. 26. the woman was a *Greek*, a Syrophœnician
Acts 16. 1. his [Timothy] father was a *Greek.* 3

GREEK

Rom. 1. 16. to the Jew first, and also to the *G.* 2. 9, 10
   10. 12. there is no distinction between Jew and *G.* *Gal.* 3
Gal. 2. 3. Titus who was with me, being a *G.* [28: *Col.* 3. 11

Greek *(Language).*

Jno. 19. 20. written in Hebrew, and in Latin, and in *Greek*
Acts 21. 37. And he said, Dost thou know *Greek ?*
Rev. 9. 11. and in the *G.* tongue he hath the name Apollyon

Greeks.—*A.V.* ¹*Gentiles.*

Jno. 7. 35. Dispersion among the ¹*G.*, and teach the ¹*G. ?*
   12. 20. there were certain *Greeks* among those
Acts 11. 20. spake unto the *Greeks* also
   14. 1. both of Jews and of *Greeks* believed. 17. 4, 12
   18. 4. [Paul] persuaded Jews and *Greeks*
   19. 10. heard the word of the Lord, both Jews and *G.*
   17. both Jews and *Greeks*, that dwelt at Ephesus
   20. 21. testifying both to Jews and to *Greeks* repentance
   21. 28. [Paul] brought *Greeks* also into the temple
Rom. 1. 14. I am debtor both to *Greeks* and to Barbarians
   3. 9. Jews and ¹*Greeks*, that they are all under sin
1 *Cor.* 1. 22. and *Greeks* seek after wisdom
   24. both Jews and *Greeks*, Christ the power of God
   10. 32. Give no occasion of stumbling, either to Jews, or
   12. 13. baptized into one body, whether Jews or ¹*G.* [to ¹*G.*

H.

Hades.—*Mat.* 11. 23; 16. 18: *Lu.* 10. 15: 16. 23: *Acts* 2. 27, 31: *Rev.* 1. 18: 6. 8: 20. 13, 14

Hagar.—*A.V. Agar. Gal.* 4. 24, 25

Hamor.—*Acts* 7. 16

Haran.—*Acts* 7. 2, 4

Heber—*see Eber.*

Har-Magedon.—*Rev.* 16. 16

Hebrew—a.

Jno. 5. 2. pool, which is called in *Hebrew* Bethesda
   19. 13. The Pavement, but in *Hebrew*, Gabbatha
   17. a skull, which is called in the *Hebrew* Golgotha
   20. title—written in *Hebrew*, and in Latin, and in Greek
   20. 16. Mary—saith unto him in *Hebrew*, Rabboni
Acts 6. 1. arose a murmuring—against the *Hebrews* [22. 2
   21. 40. Paul—spake unto them in the *Hebrew* language
   26. 14. a voice saying—in the *Hebrew* language, Saul
2 *Cor.* 11. 22. Are they *Hebrews ?* so am I
Phil. 3. 5. a *Hebrew* of *Hebrews* [Paul]
Rev. 9. 11. his name in *Hebrew* is Abaddon
   16. 16. place which is called in *Hebrew* Har-Magedon

Heli.—*Lu.* 3. 23

Hermas.—*Rom.* 16. 14

Hermes.—*Rom.* 16. 14

Hermogenes.—2 *Tim.* 1. 15

HOLY GHOST

Herod

Mat. 2. 1. in the days of *Herod* the king. *Lu.* 1. 5
   3. And when *Herod* the king heard it
   7. Then *Herod* privily called the wise men
   12. they should not return to *Herod*
   13. *Herod* will seek the young child to destroy him
   15. was there until the death of *Herod*
   16. Then *Herod*, when he saw that he was mocked
   19. But when *Herod* was dead
   22. in the room of his father *Herod* [*Lu.* 3. 1, 19: 9. 7
   14. 1. *Herod* the tetrarch heard the report. *Mk.* 6. 14, 16:
   3. For *Herod* had laid hold on John. *Mk.* 6. 17, 18
   6. when *H.*'s birthday came, and pleased *H. Mk.* 6. 21, 22
Mk. 6. 20. *Herod* feared John
   8. 15. the leaven of *Herod*
Lu. 3. 19. evil things which *Herod* had done
   8. 3. the wife of Chuza, *Herod's* steward
   9. 9. And *Herod* said, John I beheaded
   13. 31. for *Herod* would fain kill thee
   23. 7. of *Herod's* jurisdiction, he [Pilate] sent him unto *H.*
   8. when *Herod* saw Jesus
   11. And *Herod* with his soldiers set him at nought
   12. And *Herod* and Pilate became friends
   15. no, nor yet *Herod*: for he sent him back
Acts 4. 27. both *Herod* and Pontius Pilate
   12. 1. *Herod* the king put forth his hands to afflict
   6. And when *H.* was about to bring him [Peter] forth
   11. delivered me out of the hand of *Herod* [guards
   19. when *Herod* had sought for him—he examined the
   21. *Herod* arrayed himself in royal apparel
   13. 1. the foster brother of *Herod* the tetrarch
   23. 35. commanded him [Paul] to be kept in *H.* palace

Herodians.—*Mat.* 22. 16; *Mk.* 3. 6; 12. 13

Herodias.

Mat. 14. 3. put him in prison for the sake of *H. Mk.* 6. 17
   6. the daughter of *Herodias* danced. *Mk.* 6. 22
Mk. 6. 19. And *Herodias* set herself against him
Lu. 3. 19. being reproved by him for *Herodias*

Herodion.—*Rom.* 16. 11

Hezekiah.—*A.V. Ezekias.*—*Mat.* 1. 9, 10

Hezron.—*A.V. Esrom.*—*Mat.* 1. 3: *Lu.* 3. 33

Hierapolis.—*Col.* 4. 13

High Priest.—*Heb.* 3. 1

Holy Ghost.

Mat. 1. 18. she was found with child of the *Holy Ghost*
   20. that which is conceived in her is of the *Holy Ghost*
   3. 11. he shall baptize you with the *Holy Ghost. Mk.* 1. 8: *Lu.* 3. 16: *Acts* 1. 5
   28. 19. Father and of the Son and of the *Holy Ghost*
Mk. 13. 11. it is not ye that speak, but the *Holy Ghost*
Lu. 1. 15. and he shall be filled with the *Holy Ghost*
   35. The *Holy Ghost* shall come upon thee
   41. and Elisabeth was filled with the *Holy Ghost*
   67. his father Zacharias was filled with the *Holy Ghost*
   3. 22. the *Holy Ghost* descended in a bodily form
Jno. 20. 22. Receive ye the *Holy Ghost. Acts* 2. 38
Acts 1. 2. given commandment through the *Holy Ghost*
   8. when the *Holy Ghost* is come upon you
   16. *Holy Ghost* spake before by the mouth of David
   2. 33. received of the Father the promise of the *H. G.*
   4. 8. Peter, filled with the *Holy Ghost*, said unto them

HOLY GHOST

Acts 4. 25. who by the *H. G.*—didst say, Why did the Gen-
31. and they were all filled with the *Holy Ghost* [tiles
5. 3. Satan filled thy heart to lie to the *Holy Ghost*
32. and so is the *Holy Ghost*, whom God hath given
7. 51. ye do always resist the *Holy Ghost*
55. [Stephen] being full of the *Holy Ghost*, looked up
8. 15. prayed for them, that they might receive the *H. G.*
17. hands on them, and they received the *Holy Ghost*
18. the *Holy Ghost* was given, he offered them money
19. I lay my hands, he may receive the *Holy Ghost*
9. 17. thy sight, and be filled with the *Holy Ghost*
31. in the comfort of the *Holy Ghost*, was multiplied
10. 38. anointed him with the *H. G.* and with power
44. *Holy Ghost* fell on all them which heard the word
45. Gentiles also was poured out the gift of the *H. G.*
47. baptized, which have received the *H. G.* as well as
11. 15. the *Holy Ghost* fell on them, even as on us
16. water; but ye shall be baptized with the *Holy Ghost*
24. good man, and full of the *Holy Ghost* and of faith
13. 2 the *H. G.* said, Separate me Barnabas and Saul
4. they, being sent forth by the *Holy Ghost*, went
9. Paul, filled with the *H. G.*, fastened his eyes on him
52. disciples were filled with joy and with the *H. G.*
15. 8. giving them the *H. G.*, even as he did unto us
28. seemed good to the *Holy Ghost*, and to us, to lay
16. 6. forbidden of the *H. G.* to speak the word in Asia
19. 2. Did ye receive the *H. G.* when ye believed?—not
so much as hear whether the *H. G.* was given
6. his hands upon them, the *Holy Ghost* came on them
20. 23. the *Holy Ghost* testifieth unto me in every city
28. in the which the *Holy Ghost* hath made you bishops
21. 11. Thus saith the *Holy Ghost*, So shall the Jews
28. 25. Well spake the *H. G.* by Isaiah the prophet
Rom. 5. 5. shed abroad in our hearts through the *H. G.*
9. 1. conscience bearing witness with me in the *H. G.*
14. 17. righteousness and peace and joy in the *H. G.*
15. 13. abound in hope, in the power of the *H. G.*
16. acceptable, being sanctified by the *Holy Ghost*
19. signs and wonders, in the power of the *H. G.*
1 *Cor.* 6. 19. your body is a temple of the *Holy Ghost*
2 *Cor.* 6. 6. in kindness, in the *H. G.*, in love unfeigned
13. 14. the communion of the *Holy Ghost*, be with you
1 *Th.* 1. 5. in power, and in the *Holy Ghost*
*word in much affliction, with joy of the *Holy Ghost*
2 *Tim.* 1. 14. committed unto thee guard through the *H. G.*
Tit. 3. 5. regeneration and renewing of the *Holy Ghost*
Heb. 2. 4. manifold powers, and by gifts of the *Holy Ghost*
3. 7. as the *H. G.* saith, To-day if ye shall hear
6. 4. and were made partakers of the *Holy Ghost*
9. 8. the *Holy Ghost* this signifying, that the way
10. 15. And the *Holy Ghost* also beareth witness to us
1 *Pet.* 1. 12. the gospel unto you by the *Holy Ghost*
2 *Pet.* 1. 21. spake from God, being moved by the *H. G.*

Holy of Holies.

Heb. 9. 3. tabernacle which is called the *Holy of holies*

Holy One of God ; **Holy and Righteous One.**—*Mk.*
1. 24; *Jno.* 6. 69; *Acts* 2. 27; 3. 14; 13. 35; 1 *Jno.*
2. 20; *Rev.* 16. 6

Holy Spirit.

Mat. 12. 32. whosoever shall speak against the *H. Spirit*.
Mk. 3. 29 ; *Lu.* 12. 10
Mk. 12. 36. David himself said in the *Holy Spirit*
Lu. 2. 25. of Israel : and the *Holy Spirit* was upon him
26. it had been revealed unto him by the *Holy Spirit*
4. 1. Jesus, full of the *Holy Spirit*, returned
10. 21. same hour he rejoiced in the *Holy Spirit*

ISAIAH

Lu. 11. 13. give the *Holy Spirit* to them that ask him ?
12. 10. blasphemeth against the *Holy Spirit*
12. the *Holy Spirit* shall teach you in that very hour
Jno. 1. 33. same is he that baptizeth with the *Holy Spirit*
14. 26. But the Comforter, even the *Holy Spirit*
Acts 2. 4. And they were all filled with the *Holy Spirit*
6. 5. Stephen, a man full of faith and of the *Holy Spirit*
1 *Cor.* 12. 3. can say, Jesus is Lord, but in the *H. Spirit*
Eph. 1. 13. ye were sealed with the *Holy Spirit* of promise
4. 30. grieve not the *Holy Spirit* of God
1 *Th.* 4. 8. but God, who giveth his *Holy Spirit* unto you
Jude 20. most holy faith, praying in the *Holy Spirit*

Holiest *A.V.*—*see Holy of Holies.*

Hosea.—*A. V. Osee.*—*Rom.* 9. 25

Hymenæus.—1 *Tim.* 1. 20 ; 2 *Tim.* 2. 17

I.

Iconium.

Acts 13. 51. [Paul and Barnabas] came unto *I.* 14. 21
14. 1. in *Iconium*, that they entered together
19. came Jews thither from Antioch and *Iconium*
16. 2. the brethren that were at Lystra and *Iconium*
2 *Tim.* 3. 11. things befell me at Antioch, at *Iconium*

Idumæa.—*Mk.* 3. 8

Illyricum.—*Rom.* 15. 19

Immanuel—*A.V. Emmanuel.*—*Mat.* 1. 23

Isaac.

Mat. 1. 2. Abraham begat *Isaac* ; and *Isaac* begat Jacob.
Lu. 3. 34 ; *Acts* 7. 8
8. 11. shall sit down with Abraham and *I. Lu.* 13. 28
22. 32. I am the God of Abraham, and the God of *Isaac*.
Mk. 12. 26 ; *Lu.* 20. 37 ; *Acts* 3. 13; 7. 32
Rom. 9. 7. In *Isaac* shall thy seed be called. *Heb.* 11. 18
10. conceived by one, even by our father *Isaac*
Gal. 4. 28. as *Isaac* was, are children of promise
Heb. 11. 9. dwelling in tents, with *Isaac*, and Jacob
17. Abraham, being tried, offered up *Isaac. Jas.* 2. 21
20. By faith *Isaac* blessed Jacob and Esau

Isaiah—*A.V. Esaias.*

Mat. 3. 3. spoken of by *I.* the prophet. 4. 14 ; 8. 17 ; 12. 17
13. 14. is fulfilled the prophecy of *Isaiah*
15. 7. well did *Isaiah* prophecy of you. *Mk.* 7. 6
Mk. 1. 2. as it is written in *Isaiah* the prophet
Lu. 4. 17. the book of the prophet *Isaiah*
1. 23. way of the Lord, as said *Isaiah. Lu.* 3. 4
12. 38. that the word of *Isaiah* the prophet might be ful-
39. they could not believe, for that *I.* said again filled
41. These things said *Isaiah*, because he saw his glory
Acts 8. 28. [eunuch] was reading the prophet *Isaiah.* 30
28. 25. spake the Holy Ghost by *Isaiah*
Rom. 9. 27. *Isaiah* crieth concerning Israel
29. as *Isaiah* hath said before, Except the Lord
10. 16. For *Isaiah* saith, Lord, who hath believed
20. And *Isaiah* is very bold, and saith
15. 12. again, *I.* saith, There shall be the root of Jesse

ISCARIOT

Iscariot, *see Judas Iscariot.*

Israel.

Mat. 2. 6. Which shall be shepherd of my people *Israel*
20. young child—and go into the land of *Israel.* 21
8. 10. so great faith, no, not in *Israel. Lu.* 7. 9
9. 33. It was never so seen in *Israel*
10. 6. go rather to the lost sheep of the house of *Israel*
23. gone through the cities of *Israel*
19. 28. thrones, judging the twelve tribes of *I. Lu.* 22. 30
Mk. 12. 29. Jesus answered, The first is, Hear, O *Israel*
Lu. 1. 54. He hath holpen *Israel* his servant
80. till the day of his shewing unto *I.* [John Bap.]
2. 25. looking for the consolation of *Israel*
32. And the glory of thy people *Israel*
34. falling and rising up of many in *Israel*
4. 25. many widows in *Israel* in the days of Elijah
27. many lepers in *Israel* in the time of Elisha
24. 21. we hoped that it was he which should redeem *I.*
Jno. 1. 31. he should be made manifest to *Israel*
3. 10. Art thou [Nicodemus] the teacher of *Israel ?*
Acts 1. 6. this time restore the kingdom to *Israel ?*
2. 22. Ye men of *Israel,* hear these words
8. 12. Ye men of *Israel,* why marvel ye at this man ?
4. 27. with the Gentiles and the peoples of *Israel*
5. 31. a Saviour, for to give repentance to *Israel*
35. Ye men of *Israel,* take heed to yourselves
13. 16. Men of *Israel,* and ye that fear God
17. The God of this people *Israel* chose our fathers
23. God—brought unto *Israel* a Saviour
24. John had first preached—to all the people of *Israel*
21. 28. crying out, Men of *Israel,* help
28. 20. because of the hope of *Israel,* I am bound
Rom. 9. 6. they are not all *Israel,* which are of *Israel*
27. children of *Israel* be as the sand of the sea
31. but *Israel,* following after a law of righteousness
10. 19. But I say, Did *Israel* not know ?
21. to *Israel* he saith, All the day long did I spread
11. 2. Elijah—pleadeth with God against *Israel*
7. That which *Israel* seeketh for—obtained not
25. a hardening in part hath befallen *Israel*
26. and so all *Israel* shall be saved
1 *Cor.* 10. 18. Behold *Israel* after the flesh [God
Gal. 6. 16. peace be upon them—and upon the *Israel* of
Phil. 3. 5. of the stock of *Israel,* of the tribe of Benjamin
Rev. 21. 12. the names of—the children of *Israel*
see Children of, Congregation of, Daughters of, Elders of, God of, Holy One of, House of, King and Kings of, Princes of.

Israelite—s.

Jno. 1. 47. Behold, an *Israelite* indeed [Nathaniel]
Rom. 9. 4. my kinsmen—who are *Israelites*
11. 1. For I [Paul] also am an *Israelite*
2 *Cor.* 11. 22. Are they *Israelites ?* so am I

Issachar.—*Rev.* 7. 7

Italian band.—*Acts* 10. 1

Italy.—*Acts* 18. 2; 27. 1, 6; *Heb.* 13. 24

Ituræa.—*Lu.* 3. 1

JEREMIAH

J.

Jacob.—*Israel.*

Mat. 1. 2. Isaac begat *Jacob*; and *Jacob* begat Judah. *Lu.*
3. 34: *Acts.* 7. 8 [dom. *Lu.* 13. 28
8. 11. with Abraham, and Isaac, and *Jacob* in the king-
22. 32. God of Abraham, and the God of Isaac, and the
God of *Jacob ? Mk.* 12. 26: *Lu.* 20. 37: *Acts* 3. 13:
7. 32, 46
Lu. 1. 33. he shall reign over the house of *Jacob* for ever
Jno. 4. 5. parcel of ground that *Jacob* gave to his son
6. and *Jacob's* well was there
12. Art thou greater than our father *Jacob*
Acts 7. 12. when *Jacob* heard that there was corn
14. And Joseph sent, and called to him *Jacob*
15. And *Jacob* went down into Egypt
Rom. 9. 13. *Jacob* I loved, but Esau I hated
11. 26. He shall turn away ungodliness from *Jacob*
Heb. 11. 9. dwelling in tents, with Isaac and *Jacob*
20. By faith Isaac blessed *Jacob* and Esau
21. By faith *Jacob*—blessed each of the sons of Joseph

Jacob.—*Mat.* 1. 15, 16

Jairus.—*Mk.* 5. 22: *Lu.* 8. 41

Jambres.—2 *Tim.* 3. 8

James.—*various.*

Mat. 4. 21. *James* the son of Zebedee, and John. 10. 2: *Mk.*
1. 19: 3. 17 : 10. 35: *Lu.* 5. 10: 6. 14: *Acts* 1. 13
10. 3. *James* the son of Alphæus. *Mk.* 3. 18: *Lu.* 6. 15:
Acts 1. 13
17. 1. Jesus taketh with him Peter, and *James,* and
John. *Mk.* 5. 37: 9. 2: 14. 33: *Lu.* 8. 51: 9. 28
Mk. 1. 29. Simon and Andrew, with *James* and John
10. 41. moved with indignation concerning *James* and
13. 3. Peter and *James*—asked him privately [John
15. 40. the mother of *James* the less. 16. 1 : *Mat.* 27. 56:
Lu. 6. 16. Judas the son of *J. Acts* 1. 13: *Jude* 1 [*Lu.* 24. 10
9. 54. when his disciples *James* and John saw this
Acts 12. 2 And he [Herod] killed *J.* the brother of John
17. Tell these things unto *James,* and to the brethren
15. 13. *James* answered, saying, Brethren
21. 18. Paul went in with us unto *James*
1 *Cor.* 15. 7. then he appeared to *James*
Gal. 1. 19. *James* the Lord's brother. *Mat.* 13. 55 : *Mk.* 6. 3
2. 9. *James* and Cephas and John—reputed to be pillars
12. For before that certain came from *James*
Jas. 1. 1. J., a servant of God and of the Lord Jesus Christ

Jannai.—*Lu.* 3. 24

Jannes.—2 *Tim.* 3. 8

Jared.—*Lu.* 3. 37

Jason.—*Acts* 17. 5, 6, 7, 9: *Rom.* 16. 21

Jechoniah.—*Mat.* 1. 11, 12

Joram.—*Mat.* 1. 8

Jehoshaphat.—*Mat.* 1. 8

Jephthah.—*Heb.* 11. 32

Jeremiah.—*A. V. Jeremias.*

Mat. 2. 17. that which was spoken by *J* the prophet. 27. 9
16. 14. some say John the Baptist—others *Jeremiah*

JERICHO

Jericho.

Mat. 20. 29. as they went out from *Jericho*. Lu. 18. 35: 19. 1
Mk. 10. 46. And they come to *Jericho*—went out from *J.*
Lu. 10. 30. A certain man was going—to *Jericho*
Heb. 11. 30. By faith the walls of *Jericho* fell down

Jerusalem.

Mat. 2. 1. wise men from the east came to *Jerusalem*
3. Herod—was troubled and all *Jerusalem* with him
3. 5. Then went out unto him *Jerusalem*. Mk. 1. 5
4. 25. followed him great multitudes from—*J.* Mk. 3. 8:
5. 35. nor by *J.*, for it is the city of the great King [Lu. 6. 17
15. 1. there come to Jesus from *Jerusalem* Pharisees and
16. 21. must go unto *Jerusalem*, and suffer [scribes
20. 17. as Jesus was going up to *Jerusalem*
18. Behold, we go up to *J.* Mk. 10. 33: Lu. 18. 31
21. 1. when they drew nigh unto *Jerusalem*
10. And when he was come into *Jerusalem*
23. 37. O *Jerusalem, Jerusalem*, which killeth. Lu. 13. 34
Mk. 3. 22. scribes which came down from *Jerusalem*. 7. 7
10. 32. in the way, going up to *Jerusalem*
11. 1. they draw nigh unto *Jerusalem*. 15, 27
11. he entered into *Jerusalem*, into the temple
15. 41. women which came up with him unto *Jerusalem*
Lu. 2. 22. brought him up to *Jerusalem*, to present him
25. a man in *Jerusalem*, whose name was Simeon
38. looking for the redemption of *Jerusalem*
41. his parents went every year to *Jerusalem*
43. the boy Jesus tarried behind in *Jerusalem*
45. they returned to *Jerusalem*, seeking for him
5. 17. Judæa and *Jerusalem*
9. 31. spake of his decease—at *Jerusalem*
53. his face was as though he were going to *J.* 51
10. 30. A certain man was going down from *Jerusalem*
13. 4. offenders above all the men that dwell in *J.?*
22. journeying on unto *Jerusalem*
33. that a prophet perish out of *Jerusalem*
17. 11. they were on the way to *Jerusalem*
19. 11. parable, because he was nigh to *Jerusalem*
28. he went on before, going up to *Jerusalem*
21. 20. when ye see *Jerusalem* compassed with armies
24. *Jerusalem* shall be trodden down of the Gentiles
23. 7. Herod, who himself also was at *Jerusalem*
28. Daughters of *Jerusalem*, weep not for me
24. 13. Emmaus, which was threescore furlongs from *J.*
18. Dost thou alone sojourn in *Jerusalem* and not know
33. returned to *Jerusalem*, and found the eleven
47. unto all the nations, beginning from *Jerusalem*
52. returned to *Jerusalem* with great joy
Jno. 1. 19. Jews sent unto him from *Jerusalem*
2. 13. Jesus went up to *Jerusalem*. 5. 1
23. when he was in *Jerusalem* at the passover
4. 20. *J.* is the place where men ought to worship. 21
45. seen all the things that he did in *J.* Acts 10. 39
5. 2. there is in *Jerusalem* by the sheep gate a pool
10. 22. feast of the dedication at *Jerusalem*
11. 18. Bethany was nigh unto *Jerusalem*
55. many went up to *Jerusalem* out of the country
12. 12. heard that Jesus was coming to *Jerusalem*
Acts 1. 4. he charged them not to depart from *Jerusalem*
8. ye shall be my witnesses both in *Jerusalem*
12. Then returned they unto *Jerusalem*—nigh unto *J.*
19. it became known to all the dwellers at *Jerusalem*
2. 5. there were dwelling at *Jerusalem* Jews, devout
14. all ye that dwell at *Jerusalem*, be this known unto
4. 5. elders and scribes were gathered together in *J.*
5. 16. multitude from the cities round about *Jerusalem*
28. ye have filled *Jerusalem* with your teaching
6. 7. the disciples multiplied in *Jerusalem*

JESUS

Acts 8. 1. persecution against the church—at *Jerusalem*
14. apostles which were at *Jerusalem* heard
25. returned to *Jerusalem*, and preached. 13. 13: 22. 17
26. the way that goeth down from *Jerusalem* unto Gaza
27. eunuch—who had come to *Jerusalem* for to worship
9. 2. he [Saul] might bring them bound to *Jerusalem*
13. evil he did to thy saints at *Jerusalem*
21. in *Jerusalem* made havock of them
26. when he was come to *Jerusalem*. 28: 21. 17
11. 2. when Peter was come up to *Jerusalem* [in *J.*
22. report—came to the ears of the church which was
27. came down prophets from *Jerusalem* unto Antioch
12. 25. Barnabas and Saul returned from *Jerusalem*
13. 27. they that dwell in *Jerusalem*, and their rulers
31. came up with him from Galilee to *Jerusalem*
15. 2. Paul and Barnabas—should go up to *J.* 21. 15
4. And when they were come to *Jerusalem*
16. 4. ordained of the apostles and elders that were at *J.*
19. 21. through Macedonia and Achaia, to go to *Jerusalem*
20. 16. to be at *Jerusalem* the day of Pentecost
22. I go bound in the spirit unto *Jerusalem*
21. 4. that he should not set foot in *Jerusalem*. 12
11. So shall the Jews at *Jerusalem* bind the man
13. also to die at *Jerusalem* for the name of the Lord
31. tidings came—that all *Jerusalem* was in confusion
22. 5. bring them—unto *J.* in bonds, for to be punished
18. get thee quickly out of *Jerusalem* ['Saul]
23. 11. thou hast testified concerning me at *Jerusalem*
24. 11. since I went up to worship at *Jerusalem*
25. 1. after three days went up to *Jerusalem*
3. that he would send for him [Paul] to *Jerusalem*
7. the Jews which had come down from *Jerusalem*
9. Wilt thou go up to *J.*, and there be judged. 20
15. when I was at *Jerusalem*, the chief priests
24. Jews made suit to me, both at *Jerusalem* and here
26. 4. mine own nation, and at *Jerusalem*
10. And this I also did in *Jerusalem*
20. to them of Damascus first, and at *Jerusalem*
28. 17. [Paul] was delivered prisoner from *Jerusalem*
Rom. 15. 19. so that from *Jerusalem*,—I have fully preached
25. I go unto *Jerusalem*, ministering unto the saints. 26
31. my ministration—for *Jerusalem* may be acceptable
1 Cor. 16. 3. I send to carry your bounty unto *Jerusalem*
Gal. 1. 17. neither went I up to *Jerusalem* to them
18. I went up to *Jerusalem* to visit Cephas
2. 1. I went up again to *Jerusalem* with Barnabas
4. 25. Hagar—answereth to the *Jerusalem* that now is
26. the *Jerusalem* that is above is free
Heb. 12. 22. city of the living God, the heavenly *Jerusalem*
Rev. 3. 12. the new *Jerusalem*. 21. 2
21. 10. shewed me the holy city *Jerusalem*

Jesse.—Mat. 1. 5, 6: Lu. 3. 32: Acts 13. 22: Rom. 15. 12

Jesus.

Mat. 1. 21. shalt call his name *J* 25: Lu. 1. 31: 2. 21
2. 1. *Jesus* was born in Bethlehem of Judea
3. 13. Then cometh *Jesus* from Galilee to the Jordan
16. *Jesus*, when he was baptized. Lu. 3. 21
4. 1. Then was *Jesus* led up of the Spirit
17. From that time began *Jesus* to preach
23. *Jesus* went about in all Galilee
7. 28. when *Jesus* ended these words
8. 10. And when *Jesus* heard it, he marvelled
14. when *Jesus* was come into Peter's house
18. when *Jesus* saw great multitudes
34. all the city came out to meet *Jesus*
9. 2. and *Jesus* seeing their faith. Mk. 2. 5

JESUS

Mat. 9. 4. Jesus knowing their thoughts. Mk. 2. 8; Lu. 5. 22;
9. as Jesus passed by from thence, he saw a man [9 47
10. sinners came and sat down with Jesus. Mk. 2. 15
19. Jesus arose, and followed him
22. But Jesus turning—said, Daughter, be of good cheer
23. when Jesus came into the ruler's house
27. as Jesus passed by from thence, two blind men
30. Jesus strictly charged them, saying, See that no man
35. Jesus went about all the cities and the villages
10. 5. These twelve Jesus sent forth
11. 1. when Jesus had made an end of commanding
12. 1. Jesus went on the sabbath-day
15. Jesus perceiving it withdrew from thence
13. 1. On that day went Jesus out of the house
34. All these things spake Jesus in parables
53. when Jesus had finished those parables
14. 1. Herod—heard the report concerning Jesus
12. disciples—they went and told Jesus
13. when Jesus heard it, he withdrew
29. Peter—walked upon the waters, to come to Jesus
31. immediately Jesus stretched forth his hand
15. 1. there come to Jesus from Jerusalem Pharisees
21. Jesus went out thence, and withdrew
29. Jesus departed thence [Tyre and Sidon]
32. Jesus called unto him his disciples
16. 8. Jesus perceiving it said, O ye of little faith
13. when Jesus came into the parts of Cæsarea
21. From that time began J. to shew unto his disciples
17. 1. Jesus taketh with him Peter
4. Peter answered, and said unto Jesus
7. And Jesus came and touched them
8. they saw no one, save Jesus only. Mk. 9. 8; Lu. 9. 36
18. And Jesus rebuked him; and the devil. Lu. 9. 42
19. came the disciples to Jesus apart
25. Jesus spake first to him, saying
18. 1. came the disciples unto Jesus. 26. 17
19. 1. when Jesus had finished these words
26. Jesus looking upon them said to them
20. 17. as Jesus was going up to Jerusalem
25. Jesus called them unto him
30. when they heard that Jesus was passing
34. Jesus, being moved with compassion
21. 6. disciples went, and did even as Jesus appointed
11. This is the prophet, Jesus, from Nazareth of Galilee.
12. Jesus entered into the temple of God [Mk. 10. 47
23. 18. But Jesus perceived their wickedness
42. Jesus asked them a question
23. 1. Then spake Jesus to the multitudes
24. 1. Jesus went out from the temple
26. 1. when Jesus had finished all these words
4. they might take Jesus by subtilty
6. when Jesus was in Bethany
10. But Jesus perceiving it said unto them. Mk. 8. 17
19. disciples did as Jesus appointed them
26. Jesus took bread, and blessed [Gethsemane
36. Then cometh Jesus with them unto a place called
49. [Judas] came to Jesus, and said, Hail, Rabbi
50. they came and laid hands on Jesus. Mk. 14. 53
51. one of them that were with J. stretched out his hand
57. they that had taken Jesus led him away. Lu. 14. 53
59. sought false witness against Jesus. Mk. 14. 55
63. But Jesus held his peace
69. Thou also wast with Jesus. 71: Mk. 14. 67.
75. Peter remembered the word which Jesus had said.
  Mk. 14. 72
27. 1. took counsel against Jesus to put him to death
11. Now Jesus stood before the governor
20. ask for Barabbas, and destroy Jesus
26. but Jesus he scourged and delivered. Mk. 15. 15

Mat. 27. 27. soldiers of the governor took J. into the palace
37. JESUS THE KING OF THE JEWS. Jno. 19. 19
46. Jesus cried with a loud voice. 50; Mk. 15. 34, 87;
  Lu. 23. 46
54. they that were with him watching Jesus
55. women—which had followed Jesus from Galilee [38
57. Joseph, who also himself was Jesus' disciple. Jno. 19.
58. asked for the body of Jesus. Mk. 15. 43; Lu. 23.52;
28. 5. I know that ye seek Jesus. Mk. 16. 6 [Jno. 19. 36
9. Jesus met them, saying, All hail [appointed
16. disciples went—unto the mountain where J. had
18. And Jesus came to them and spake unto them
Mk. 1. 9. Jesus came from Nazareth of Galilee
14. Jesus came into Galilee. Jno. 4. 47; 7. 1 [4. 34
24. J. of Nazareth? art thou come to destroy us? Lu.
25. Jesus rebuked him. Lu. 4. 34
45. Jesus could no more openly enter. Jno. 11. 54
2. 17. when Jesus heard it, he saith unto them
3. 7. And Jesus with his disciples withdrew to the sea
5. 6. And when he saw Jesus from afar. Lu. 8. 28
7. What have I to do with thee, Jesus, thou Son of the
15. they come to J. [unclean spirits] [Most High God?
20. how great things Jesus had done for him. Lu. 8. 39
21. when Jesus had crossed over again in the boat
27. having heard the things concerning Jesus. Lu. 7. 2
30. Jesus, perceiving—power proceeding from him
36. But Jesus, not heeding the word spoken
6. 30. apostles gather themselves together unto Jesus
8. 27. J. went forth, and his disciples, into the villages
9. 2. Jesus taketh with him Peter, and James, and John
4. Elijah with Moses: and they were talking with Jesus
5. Peter answereth and saith to Jesus, Rabbi, it is good
25. when Jesus saw that a multitude came running
27. Jesus took him by the hand, and raised him up
10. 14. when Jesus saw it, he was moved with indignation
21. And Jesus looking upon him loved him
23. Jesus looked round about, and saith unto his dis-
32. and Jesus was going before them [ciples. 27
42. And Jesus called them [disciples] to him
47. J., thou son of David, have mercy on me. Lu. 18. 88
49. Jesus stood still and said, Call ye him. Lu. 18. 40
50. [blind man] sprang up, and came to Jesus
11. 7. they bring the colt unto J. Lu. 19. 35; Jno. 12. 14
33. they answered Jesus and say, We know not
12. 34. when Jesus saw that he answered discreetly
14. 60. high priest stood up in the midst, and asked J.
15. 1. bound Jesus, and carried him away
Lu. 2. 43. the boy Jesus tarried behind in Jerusalem
52. Jesus advanced in wisdom and stature
3. 23. Jesus himself, when he began to teach
5. 8. Peter—fell down at Jesus' knees
12. leprosy: and when he saw Jesus, he fell on his face
19. let him down—couch into the midst before Jesus
6. 11. communed—what they might do to Jesus
7. 4. [elders of the Jews] came to Jesus. 8. 35
6. Jesus went with them [elders of the Jews]
9. when Jesus heard these things, he marvelled
6. 35. in his right mind, at the feet of Jesus
40. as Jesus returned, the multitude welcomed him
41. Jairus—fell down at Jesus' feet [infirmity]
13. 12. when Jesus saw her, he called her [woman with
14. because Jesus had healed on the sabbath
17. 13. saying, Jesus, Master, have mercy on us
18. 37. Jesus of Nazareth passeth by
19. 3. And he [Zacchæus] sought to see Jesus
22. 47. Judas—drew near unto Jesus to kiss him
63. the men that held Jesus mocked him
23. 25. Pilate spake—desiring to release Jesus
25. but Jesus he delivered up to their will

PROPER NAMES. 412

JESUS

Lu. 23. 26. laid on him the cross, to bear it after *Jesus*
42. *J.*, remember me when thou comest in thy kingdom
24. 15. *Jesus* himself drew near, and went with them
19. The things concerning *Jesus* of Nazareth
Jno. 1. 36. [John] looked upon *Jesus* as he walked
41. He brought him unto *Jesus*
42. *Jesus* looked upon him, and said, Thou art Simon
45. We have found—*Jesus* of Nazareth
47. *Jesus* saw Nathanael coming to him
2. 2. *Jesus* also was bidden—to the marriage
11. This beginning of his signs did *Jesus* in Cana
14. and *Jesus* went up to Jerusalem. 5. 1 : 12. 12
22. believed—the word which Jesus had said
24. *Jesus* did not trust himself unto them
3. 22. After these things came *Jesus* and his disciples
4. 1. *Jesus* was making and baptizing more disciples
2. *Jesus* himself baptized not   [than John
6. *Jesus* therefore, being wearied—sat thus by the well
44. *Jesus* himself testified, that a prophet
53. hour in which *Jesus* said unto him, Thy son liveth
54. again the second sign that *Jesus* did
5. 6. When *Jesus* saw him lying
13. for *Jesus* had conveyed himself away
14. Afterward *Jesus* findeth him in the temple
15. it was *Jesus* which had made him whole
16. persecute *Jesus*, because he did these things
6. 1. *Jesus* went away to the other side of the sea
3. And *Jesus* went up into the mountain. 6. 15
11. *Jesus* therefore took the loaves
17. dark, and *Jesus* had not yet come to them
19. they behold *Jesus* walking on the sea
22. *Jesus* entered not with his disciples into the boat
24. multitude saw that *Jesus* was not there—seeking *J.*
42. Is not this *Jesus*, the son of Joseph
64. *J.* knew—who it was that should betray him. 18. 4
7. 14. *Jesus* went up into the temple, and taught
39. because *Jesus* was not yet glorified   [the ground
8. 6. *Jesus* stooped down, and with his finger wrote on
9. *J.* was left alone, and the woman [where are they?
10. *Jesus* lifted up himself and said unto her, Woman,
59. took up stones—to cast at him : but *J.* hid himself
9. 11. *Jesus* made clay, and anointed mine eyes. 14
35. *Jesus* heard that they had cast him out
10. 23. *Jesus* was walking in the temple
11. 6. *Jesus* loved Martha, and her sister, and Lazarus
13. Now *Jesus* had spoken of his death
20. Martha—when she heard that *Jesus* was coming. 17
30. Now *Jesus* was not yet come into the village
31. Mary—when she came where *J.* was—fell down
33. When *Jesus* therefore saw her [Mary] weeping
35. *Jesus* wept
39. *Jesus*—groaning in himself cometh to the tomb
46. told them the things that *Jesus* had done
51. [Caiaphas] prophesied that *Jesus* should die
56. They [Jews] sought therefore for *Jesus*
12. 1. *J.*—six days before the passover came to Bethany
3. anointed the feet of *Jesus*, and wiped his feet
9. they came, not for *Jesus*' sake only
11. many of the Jews went away, and believed on *J.*
16. when *Jesus* was glorified, then remembered they
21. saying, Sir, we would see *Jesus*
13. 1. *Jesus* knowing that his hour was come
3. *Jesus*, knowing that his Father had given all things
21. When *Jesus* had thus said, he was troubled
23. reclining in *Jesus*' bosom one of his disciples, whom
    Jesus loved. 25 : 20. 2 : 21. 7, 20
16. 19. *J.* perceived that they were desirous to ask him
18. 2. *Jesus* oft-times resorted thither with his disciples
7. Whom seek ye? And they said, *Jesus* of Nazareth

Jno. 18. 13. officers of the Jews, seized *Jesus*, and bound him
15. Simon Peter followed *Jesus*—entered in with *Jesus*
19. high priest—asked *Jesus* of his disciples
22. one of the officers standing by struck *Jesus*
28. They lead *Jesus*—from Caiaphas into the palace
19. 1. Pilate therefore took *Jesus*. 17
5. *J.* therefore came out, wearing the crown of thorns
9. [Pilato] saith unto *J.*, Whence art thou? But *J.* gave
13. Pilate—brought *Jesus* out, and sat down
18. on either side one, and *Jesus* in the midst
20. place where *J.* was crucified was nigh to the city
23. when they had crucified *Jesus*, took his garments
25. standing by the cross of *Jesus* his mother
26. When *Jesus* therefore saw his mother
28. *Jesus*, knowing that all things are now finished
30. When *Jesus* therefore had received the vinegar
33. when they came to *J.* and saw that he was dead
40. they took the body of *J.*, and bound it. 38, 42 [*J.* 21. 4
20. 12. where the body of *Jesus* had lain
14. beholdeth *Jesus* standing, and knew not that it was
26. *Jesus* cometh, the doors being shut. 19, 24
31. believe that *Jesus* is the Christ. 1 *Jno.* 5. 1
21. 13. *Jesus* cometh, and taketh the bread
14. the third time that *Jesus* was manifested. 1
23. *Jesus* said not unto him, that he should not die
25. many other things which *Jesus* did. 20. 30
Acts 1. 1. all that *Jesus* began both to do, and to teach
11. this *Jesus*, which was received up from you
16. Judas, who was guide to them that took *Jesus*
2. 22. *Jesus* of Nazareth, a man approved of God
32. This *Jesus* did God raise up. 5. 30 : 13. 33
3. 13. God of our fathers, hath glorified his Servant *J.*
4. 2. proclaimed in *Jesus* the resurrection
13. knowledge of them, that they had been with *Jesus*
27. against thy holy Servant *Jesus*
30. through the name of thy holy Servant *Jesus*
5. 40. not to speak in the name of *Jesus*. 4. 18
6. 14. this *Jesus* of Nazareth shall destroy this place
7. 55. *Jesus* standing on the right hand of God
8. 35. Philip—preached unto him [eunuch] *Jesus*
9. 5. I am *Jesus* whom thou persecutest. 22. 8 : 26. 15
27. [Paul] preached boldly in the name of *Jesus*. 9. 20
10. 38. even *Jesus* of Nazareth, how that God anointed
13. 23. brought unto Israel a Saviour, *Jesus*
16. 7. assayed to go into Bithynia ; and the Spirit of *J*
17. 3. this *J.*, whom—I proclaim unto you, is the Christ
7. there is another king, one *Jesus*
18. because he preached *Jesus* and the resurrection
19. 13. I adjure you by *Jesus* whom Paul preacheth
14. believe on him—that is, on *Jesus*
15. *Jesus* I know, and Paul I know ; but who are ye?
25. 19. and of one *Jesus*, who was dead
26. 9. things contrary to the name of *Jesus* of Nazareth
28. 23. persuading them concerning *Jesus*
Rom. 3. 26. justifier of him that hath faith in *Jesus*
8. 11. Spirit of him that raised up *Jesus*   [is anathema
1 *Cor.* 12. 3. no man speaking in the Spirit of God saith, *J.*
2 *Cor.* 4. 5. ourselves as your servants for *Jesus*' sake [11
10. the dying of *J.*,—life also of *J.* may be manifested.
11. alway delivered unto death for *Jesus*' sake
14. shall raise up in us also with *Jesus*
11. 4. For if he that cometh preacheth another *Jesus*
Gal. his Father had given my body the marks of *Jesus*
Eph. 4. 21. even as truth is in *Jesus*
Phil. 2. 10. in the name of *Jesus* every knee should bow
1 *Th.* 1. 10. raised from the dead, even *Jesus*
4. 14. if we believe that *J.* died,—are fallen asleep in *J.*
Heb. 2. 9. a little lower than the angels, even *Jesus*
3. 1. Apostle and High Priest of our confession, even *J.*

JESUS

Heb. 4. 14. a great high priest—*Jesus* the Son of God. 6. 20
7. 22. hath *Jesus* become the surety of a better covenant
10. 19. enter into the holy place by the blood of *Jesus*
12. 2. looking unto *Jesus*, the author and perfecter
24. and to *Jesus* the mediator of a new covenant
13. 12. *Jesus* also,—suffered without the gate
1 *Jno.* 1. 7. blood of *Jesus* his Son cleanseth us
2. 22. denieth that *Jesus* is the Christ?
4. 3. every spirit which confesseth not *Jesus* is not
15. confess that *Jesus* is the Son of God. 5. 5 [of God
Rev. 1. 9. kingdom and patience which are in *Jesus*
14. 12. they that keep—the faith of *Jesus*
17. 6. the blood of the martyrs of *Jesus*   [timony of J.
19. 10. brethren that hold the testimony of *J.*—the tes-
20. 4. had been beheaded for the testimony of *Jesus*
22. 16. I *Jesus* have sent mine angel

Jesus Christ—*see Christ.*

Jesus, with Lord.

Mk. 16. 19. So then the *Lord Jesus*—was received up into
Lu. 24. 3. found not the body of the *Lord Jesus* [heaven
Acts 1. 21. the *Lord Jesus* went in and went out   [fled
2. 36. both *Lord* and Christ, this *Jesus* whom ye cruci-
4. 33. witness of the resurrection of the *Lord Jesus*
7. 59. saying, *Lord Jesus*, receive my spirit
8. 16. baptized into the name of the *Lord Jesus.* 19. 5
9. 17. the *Lord*, even *Jesus*, who appeared unto thee
11. 20. Greeks also, preaching the *Lord Jesus*   [saved
16. 31. Believe on the *Lord Jesus*, and thou shalt be
19. 13. name over them which had evil spirits the name
17. name of the *Lord Jesus* was magnified[of the *L. J.*
20. 24. ministry which I received from the *Lord Jesus*
35. remember the words of the *Lord Jesus*
21. 13. to die at Jerusalem for the name of the *L. Jesus*
Rom. 4. 24. raised *Jesus* our *L.* from the dead
10. 9. confess with thy mouth *Jesus* as *Lord*
14. 14. I know, and am persuaded in the *Lord Jesus*
1 *Cor.* 5. 4. in the name of our *L. J.*—power of our *L. J.*
5. may be saved in the day of the *Lord Jesus*
9. 1. have I not seen *Jesus* our *Lord* ?
11. 23. how that the *Lord Jesus* in the night—took bread
12. 3. no man can say *J.* is *L.*, but in the Holy Spirit
2 *Cor.* 1. 14. ye also are ours, in the day of our *Lord Jesus*
4. 14. he which raised up the *Lord Jesus*   [I lie not
11. 31. The God and Father of the *L. J.*—knoweth that
Eph. 1. 15. heard of the faith in the *Lord Jesus. Philem.* 5
Phil. 2. 19. I hope in the *L. J.* to send Timothy shortly
Col. 3. 17. do all in the name of the *Lord Jesus*
1 *Th.* 2. 15. who both killed the *L. J.* and the prophets
19. Are not even ye, before our *Lord J.* at his coming?
3. 11. our *Lord Jesus*, direct our way unto you
13. coming of our *Lord Jesus* with all his saints
4. 1. we beseech and exhort you in the *Lord Jesus*
2. what charge we gave you through the *Lord Jesus*
2 *Th.* 1. 7. at the revelation of the *Lord Jesus*
8. to them that obey not the gospel of our *Lord Jesus*
12. name of our *Lord Jesus* may be glorified
2. 8. lawless one, whom the *Lord Jesus* shall slay
Heb. 13. 20. great shepherd of the sheep—our *Lord Jesus*
2 *Pet.* 1. 2. knowledge of God and of *Jesus* our *Lord*
Rev. 22. 20. Amen: come, *Lord Jesus*
21. grace of the *Lord Jesus* be with the saints
see also Lord Jesus Christ, Name of the Lord, Grace of the Lord Jesus Christ.

Jesus for Joshua, see Joshua.

JEWS

Jesus Said, or Saith, or Answered and Said, or Began to Say, or Spake, or Asked—
Mat. 3. 15: 4. 7, 10: 8. 4, 13, 20, 22: 9. 15, 28: 11.
4, 7, 25: 13. 57: 14. 16, 27: 15. 28, 34: 16. 6, 17,
24: 17. 9, 17, 22, 26: 18. 22: 19. 14, 18, 21, 23, 28:
20. 23: 21. 16, 21, 24, 31, 42: 22. 1, 29: 24. 4: 26.
31, 34, 50, 52, 55, 64: 27. 12: 28. 10: *Mk.* 1. 17:
2. 19: 6. 4: 9. 23, 39: 10. 5, 18, 24, 29, 38, 39, 51,
52: 11. 6, 22, 29, 33: 12. 17, 24, 29, 35: 13. 2, 5:
14. 6, 18, 27, 30, 48, 62: 15. 5: *Ln.* 4. 4, 8, 12: 5.
10, 31, 34: 6. 3, 9: 7. 40: 8. 30, 45, 46, 50: 9. 41,
50, 58, 62: 10. 30, 37: 14. 3: 17. 17: 18. 16, 19, 24,
42: 19. 5, 9: 20. 8, 34: 22. 48, 51, 52: 23. 28, 34:
Jno. 1. 38, 43, 48, 50: 2. 4, 7, 19, 22: 3. 5, 10: 4. 7,
10, 13, 16, 18, 21, 26, 34, 48, 50: 5. 8, 17, 19: 6. 5, 10,
26, 29, 32, 35, 43, 53, 61, 67, 70: 7. 6, 16, 21, 28, 33,
37: 8. 11, 12, 14, 19, 25, 28, 31, 34, 39, 42, 49, 54,
58: 9. 3, 37, 39, 41: 10. 6, 7, 25, 32, 34: 11. 4, 9,
14, 23, 25, 39, 40, 41, 44: 12. 7, 23, 30, 35, 36, 44:
13. 7, 8, 10, 21, 26, 27, 29, 31, 36, 38: 14. 6, 9. 23:
16. 31: 17. 1: 18. 1, 5, 8, 11, 20, 23, 32, 34, 36, 37:
19. 11: 20. 15, 16, 17, 21, 29: 21. 5, 10, 12, 15, 18,
21, 22

Jesus (Justus.)—Col. 4. 11

Jesus.—A. V. Jose.—Lu. 3. 29

Jew.

Jno. 3. 25. questioning—John's disciples with a *Jew*
4. 9. thou, [woman of Sychar] being a *Jew*, askest drink
18. 35. Pilate answered, Am I a *Jew* ?
Acts 10. 28. unlawful thing for—a *Jew* to join himself
13. 6. a *Jew*, whose name was Bar-Jesus
18. 2. found a certain *Jew* named Aquila
24. a certain *Jew* named Apollos
19. 14. seven sons of one Sceva, a *Jew*
34. they perceived that he was a *Jew*
21. 39. Paul said, I am a *Jew*, of Tarsus in Cilicia. 22. 3
Rom. 1. 16. to the *Jew* first, and also to the Greek. 2. 9, 10
2. 17. if thou bearest the name of a *Jew*
28. he is not a *Jew*, which is one outwardly
29. he is a *Jew*, which is one inwardly
3. 1. What advantage then hath the *Jew* ?
10. 12. no distinction between *Jew* and Greek. *Gal.*
1 *Cor.* 9. 20. to the Jews I became as a *J.* [3. 28: *Col.* 3. 11
Gal. 2. 14. If thou, being a *Jew*, livest as do the Gentiles

Jews.

Mat. 28. 15. saying was spread abroad among the *Jews*
Lu. 7. 3. elders of the *Jews*, asking him
23. 51. Arimathæa, a city of the *Jews*
Jno. 1. 19. *Jews* sent unto him from Jerusalem
2. 6. after the *Jews'* manner of purifying
13. passover of the *Jews* was at hand. 6. 4: 11. 55
18. The *Jews* therefore answered and said—What sign.
20: 7. 35: 8. 22, 48, 52, 57: 10. 33: 11. 36: 19. 7
3. 1. Nicodemus, a ruler of the *Jews*
4. 9. For *Jews* have no dealings with Samaritans
22. for salvation is from the *Jews*
5. 1. There was a feast of the *Jews.* 7. 2
15. man went away and told the *J.* that it was Jesus
16. for this cause did the *Jews* persecute Jesus
18. therefore the *Jews* sought the more to kill him.
6. 41. The *Jews* therefore murmured   [7. 1
52. The *Jews* therefore strove one with another
7. 11. The *Jews* therefore sought him at the feast
13. for fear of the *Jews.* 19. 38: 20. 19
15. The *Jews* therefore marvelled

PROPER NAMES.   414

JEWS

Jno. 8. 31. Jesus - said to those *Jews* which had believed
9. 18. The *Jews* therefore did not believe　　　[agreed
22. because they feared the *Jews*: for the *Jews* had
10. 19. There arose a division again among the *Jews*
31. The *Jews* took up stones again to stone him
11. 8. Rabbi, the *J.* were—seeking to stone thee　[them
19. the *Jews* had come to Martha and Mary, to console
31. The *J.* then—followed her [Mary], supposing—the
33. and the *Jews* also weeping　　　　　　　　　[tomb
54. Jesus—walked no more openly among the *Jews*
12. 9. common people—*Jews* learned that he was there
11. many of the *Jews* went away, and believed. 11. 45
13. 33. [Jesus] said unto the *J.*, Whither I go, ye cannot
18. 20. temple, where all the *J.* come together　[come
36. I should not be delivered to the *Jews*
38. Pilate—went out again unto the *Jews*
19. 12. the *Jews* cried out—If thou release this man
20. This title therefore read many of the *Jews*
21. chief priests of the *J.*—said to Pilate, Write not
40. as the custom of the *Jews* is to bury
42. There then because of the *Jews*' Preparation. 31
Acts 2. 11. sojourners from Rome, both *J.* and proselytes. 5
6. 1. arose a murmuring of the Grecian *Jews*. 9. 29
9. 23. confounded the *Jews* which dwelt at Damascus
23. the *Jews* took counsel together to kill him
10. 22. Cornelius—well reported of by all the nation of
the *Jews*　　　　　　　　　　　　　　　　　[the *J.*
39. things which he [Jesus] did both in the country of
11. 19. speaking the word to none save only to *Jews*
12. 3. saw that it pleased the *Jews*
11. expectation of the people of the *J.* [tho *Jews*. 14. 1
13. 5. proclaimed the word of God in the synagogues of
43. many of the *Jews*—followed Paul and Barnabas
50. the *Jews* urged on the devout women
14. 4. part held with the *J.*, and part with the apostles
19. there came *Jews* thither from Antioch
16. 3. circumcised him because of the *Jews*
20. These men, being *Jews*, do exceedingly trouble
17. 5. But the *Jews* being moved with jealousy. 13. 45
18. 4. persuaded *Jews* and Greeks [Paul]
12. *Jews* with one accord rose up against Paul
14. Gallio said unto the *Jews*—O ye *Jews*
19. reasoned with the *Jews*
28. he powerfully confuted the *J.* [1 *Cor.* 10. 32: 12. 13
19. 10. both *Jews* and Greeks. 17: 20. 21; *Rom.* 2. 9;
13. Certain also of the strolling *Jews*, exorcists
33. brought Alexander—the *Jews* putting him forward
20. 3. a plot was laid against him by the *Jews*. 19
21. 11. So shall the *Jews* at Jerusalem bind the man
20. thousands there are among the *Jews*
27. *Jews* from Asia—stirred up all the multitude. 24. 18
23. 12. *Jews* banded together, and bound themselves
27. This man was seized by the *Jews*
24. 9. the *Jews* also joined in the charge
25. 7. *Jews* which had come down from Jerusalem stood
6. Neither against the law of the Jews　[round about
9. Festus, desiring to gain favour with the *Jews*. 24. 27
10. to the *Jews* have I done no wrong
26. 2. whereof I am accused by the *Jews*. 7: 22. 30
3. questions which are among the *Jews*
21. the *Jews* seized me in the temple
Rom. 3. 29. Or is God the God of *Jews* only?　[wisdom
1 *Cor.* 1. 22. *Jews* ask for signs, and Greeks seek after
23. Christ crucified, unto *Jews* a stumbling-block
24. them that are called, both Jews and Greeks
9. 20. to the *Jews* I became as a Jew,—might gain *Jews*
2 *Cor.* 11. 24. Of the *Jews* five times—forty stripes save
Gal. 1. 13. in the *Jews*' religion. 14　　　　　　　[one
2. 13. And the rest of the *Jews* dissembled likewise

JOHN

Gal. 2. 14. and not as do the *Jews*, how compellest thou the
Gentiles to live as do the *Jews*?
15. We being *Jews* by nature, and not sinners
1 *Th.* 2. 14. even as did they of the *Jews*
Rev. 2. 9. which say they are *Jews*, and are not.　3. 9
　　　see Gentiles, Greeks, synagogue.

All the Jews.

Mk. 7. 3. and *all the Jews*, except they wash
Acts 18. 2. commanded *all the Jews* to depart from Rome
21. 21. thou teachest *all the Jews*—to forsake Moses
22. 12. well reported of by *all the Jews*
24. 5. mover of insurrections among *all the Jews*
26. 4. My manner of life—know *all the Jews*

King of the Jews.

Mat. 2. 2. Where is he that is born *King of the Jews*
27. 11. Art thou the *King of the Jews*? *Mk.* 15. 2: *Lu.*
　　　　23. 3: *Jno.* 18. 33
29. Hail, *King of the Jews*! *Mk.* 15. 18: *Jno.* 19. 3
37. written, *THIS IS JESUS THE KING OF THE
JEWS. Mk.* 15. 26: *Lu.* 23. 38; *Jno.* 19. 19 [18. 39
Mk. 15. 9. I release unto you the *King of the Jews. Jno.*
12. do unto him whom ye call the *King of the Jews*
Lu. 23. 37. If thou art the *King of the Jews*, save thyself
Jno. 19. 21. Write not, the *King of the Jews*; but, that he
said, I am *King of the Jews*

Jewess.—*Acts* 16. 1: 24. 24

Jewish.—*Tit.* 1. 14

Jewry.—*A. V. Judæa.*

Jezebel.—*Rev.* 2. 20

Joanan.—*Lu.* 3. 27

Joanna.—*Lu.* 8. 3: 24. 10

Job.—*Jas.* 5. 11

Joda.—*A.V. Juda.—Lu.* 3. 27

Joel.—*Acts* 2. 16

John (*the Baptist*).

Mat. 3. 1. In those days cometh *John* the *Baptist*
4. *J.* himself had his raiment of camel's hair.　*Mk.* 1. 6
13. cometh Jesus—unto *John*, to be baptized. *Mk.* 1. 9
14. But *John* would have hindered him
4. 12. heard that *J.* was delivered up. *Mk.* 1. 14: *Lu.* 3. 20
9. 14. the disciples of *J. Lu.* 5. 33: 7. 18: *Jno.* 3. 25 [7. 19
11. 2. *J.* heard in the prison—sent by his disciples *Lu.*
4. Go your way and tell *John* the things. *Lu.* 7. 22
7. Jesus began to say—concerning *John. Lu.* 7. 24
11. hath not arisen a greater than *John* the *Baptist*
12. from the days of *John the Baptist* until now
13. prophets and the law prophesied until *John*
18. For *John* came neither eating nor drinking
14. 2. This is *John the Baptist*; he is risen
3. For Herod laid hold on *John. Mk.* 6. 17
4. *John* said unto him, It is not lawful　[*Mk.* 6. 21, 25
8. Give me here in a charger the head of *John the B.*
10. sent—beheaded *John* in the prison. *Lu.* 9. 9
21. 26. Some say, *John the Baptist. Mk.* 8. 28
17. 13. he spake unto them of *John the Baptist*
21. 25. The baptism of *John*, whence was it? *Mk.* 11. 30:
　　　　Lu. 7. 29: 20. 4
26. all hold *John* as a prophet. *Mk.* 11. 32; *Lu.* 20. 6

JOHN

Mat. 21. 32. *J.* came unto you in the way of righteousness
Mk. 1. 4. *John* came, who baptized in the wilderness
  2. 18. Why do *John's* disciples—fast
  6. 14. *John the Baptist* is risen from the dead. 16
  18. *John* said unto Herod, It is not lawful
  20. Herod feared *J.*, knowing that he was a righteous
Lu. 1. 13. thou shalt call his name *John.* 60, 63   [man
  3. 2. word of God came unto *John*, the son of Zacharias
  15. all men reasoned in their hearts concerning *John*
  16. *John* answered. *Jno.* 3. 27
  7. 20. *John the Baptist* hath sent us unto thee
  28. none greater than *John*
  33. *John the Baptist* is come eating no bread
  9. 7. said by some, that *John* was risen from the dead
  19. And they answering said, *John the Baptist*
  11. 1. teach us to pray. even as *J.* also taught his disciples
  16. 16. The law and the prophets were until *John*
Jno. 1. 6. a man, sent from God, whose name was *John*
  19. And this is the witness of *John.* 32
  28. beyond Jordan, where *John* was baptizing. 10. 40
  35. on the morrow *John* was standing
  40. One—that heard *John* speak, and followed him
  3. 23. *John* also was baptizing in Æuon
  24. For *John* was not yet cast into prison
  4. 1. Jesus was making—more disciples than *J.*   [1. 15
  5. 33. 1e have sent unto *J.*, and he hath borne witness.
  36. the witness that I have is greater than that of *John*
  10. 41. *J.* indeed did no sign : but all things—*J.* spake
Acts 1. 5. *John* indeed baptized with. 11. 16 : 19. 4
  13. 24. when *John* had first preached before his coming
  25. And as *John* was fulfilling his course
  19. 3. And they said, Into *John's* baptism

John *(the Apostle).*

Mat. 4. 21. James the son of Zebedee, and *John.* 10. 2:
       Mk. 1. 19 : 3. 17 : 10. 35 : *Lu.* 5. 10 : 6. 14 : *Acts* 1. 13
  17. 1. Jesus taketh—Peter, and James, and *John. Mk.* 5.
       37 : 9. 2 : 14. 33 : *Lu.* 8. 51 : 9. 28
Mk. 1. 29. Andrew, with James and *John*   [*Lu.* 9. 49
  9. 38. *John* said unto him, Master, we saw one casting.
  10. 41. moved with indignation concerning James and *J.*
  13. 3. Peter and James and *John*—asked him privately
Lu. 9. 49. *J.*—said, Master, we saw one casting out devils
  54. disciples James and *John* saw this
  22. 8. sent Peter and *John*, saying, Go and make ready
Acts 3. 1. Peter and *John* were going up into the temple.
  11. as he [the lame man] beheld Peter and *John* [3. 4
  4. 13. when they beheld the boldness of Peter and *J.*
  19. Peter and *John* answered
  8. 14. they sent unto them Peter and *John*
  12. 2. [Herod] killed James the brother of *John*
Gal. 2. 9. and *John*—reputed to be pillars
Rev. 1. 1. signified it by his angel unto his servant *John*
  4. *John* to the seven churches which are in Asia
  9. I *John*, your brother and partaker with you
  22. 8. And I *John* am he that heard and saw

John *(surnamed Mark).*

Acts 12. 12. house of Mary the mother of *John*
  25. taking with them *John* whose surname was Mark
  13. 5. and they had also *John* as their attendant
  13. *J.* departed from them and returned to Jerusalem
  15. 37. Barnabas was minded to take with them *John*

John *(Jonas, Jona) (Bar-Jona), the father of Peter and Andrew.*

Mat. 16. 17 : *Jno.* 1. 42 : 21. 15, 16, 17

John *(various).—Acts* 4. 6

JOSEPH

Jonah.

Mat. 12. 39. but the sign of *Jonah* the prophet. 16. 4 :
       Lu. 11. 29, 30
  40. *Jonah* was three days and three nights—the whale
  41. repented at the preaching of *Jonah* - greater than
       Jonah is here. *Lu.* 11. 32

Jonam.—*Lu.* 3. 30

Jonas, *see John, the father of Peter and Andrew.*

Joppa.

Acts 9. 36. at *Joppa*—disciple named Tabitha
  38. as Lydda was nigh unto *Joppa*
  42. it became known throughout all *Joppa*
  43. [Peter] abode many days in *Joppa*
  10. 5. And now send men to *Joppa.* 8. 32 : 11. 13
  23. certain of the brethren from *J.* accompanied him
  11. 5. I was in the city of *Joppa* praying

Joram.—*Mat.* 1. 8

Jordan.

Mat. 3. 5. all the region round about *Jordan. Lu.* 3. 3
  6. were baptized of him in—*Jordan. Mk.* 1. 5, 9
  13. Then cometh Jesus from Galilee to the *Jordan*
  15. Toward the sea, beyond *Jordan*
  4. 25. multitudes—from beyond *J. Mk.* 3. 8   [*Mk.* 10. 1
  19. 1. and came into the borders of Judæa beyond *J.*
Lu. 4. 1. Jesus, full of the Holy Spirit, returned from the *J.*
Jno. 1. 28. were done in Bethany beyond *Jordan*
  3. 26. Rabbi, he that was with thee beyond *Jordan*
  10. 40. he went away again beyond *Jordan*

Jorim.—*Lu.* 3. 29

Josech.—*Lu.* 3. 27

Joseph—'s.

Jno. 4. 5. ground that Jacob gave to his son *Joseph*
Acts 7. 9. moved with jealousy against *Joseph*, sold him
  13. *J.* was made known to his brethren ; and *Joseph's*
  14. And *J.* sent, and called to him Jacob [race became
  18. another king over Egypt, which knew not *Joseph*
Heb. 11. 21. Jacob—blessed each of the sons of *Joseph*
  22. By faith *Joseph*, when his end was nigh
Rev. 7. 8. Of the tribe of *J.* [were sealed] twelve thousand

Joseph—'s *(husband of Mary).*

Mat. 1. 16. Jacob begat *Joseph* the husband of Mary
  18. Mary had been betrothed to *Joseph. Lu.* 1. 27
  19. And *Joseph* her husband, being a righteous man
  20. Lord appeared—saying, *Joseph*
  24. *Joseph* arose from his sleep
  2. 13. an angel of the Lord appeareth to *Joseph.* 19
Lu. 2. 4. *Joseph* also went up from Galilee—into Judæa
  16. and found both Mary and *Joseph*, and the babe
  3. 23. being the son (as was supposed) of *Joseph*
  4. 22. Is not this *Joseph's* son ? *Jno.* 6. 42
Jno. 1. 45. Jesus of Nazareth, the son of *Joseph*

Joseph *(various).—A.V.* ¹*Jose.*

Mat. 13. 55. his brethren, James, and *J.* [50 : *Jno.* 19. 38
Mk. 15. 43. *J.* of Arimathea, 45 : *Mat.* 27. 67, 59 : *Lu.* 23
Lu. 3. 24. Jannai, the son of *Joseph.* ¹30
Acts 1. 23. they put forward two, *Joseph* called Barsabbas
  4. 36. *J.*, who by the apostles was surnamed Barnabas

JOSES

Joses.
Mat. 27. 56. Mary the mother of James and *Joses*. *Mk*. 15.
Mk. 6. 3. and brother of James and *Joses* [40, 47

Joshua.—*A.V. Jesus.*—*Acts* 7. 45: *Heb.* 4. 8

Josiah.—*Mat.* 1. 11

Jotham.—*Mat.* 1. 9

Judah.
Mat. 1. 2. Jacob begat *Judah*
3. *Judah* begat Perez. *Lu.* 3. 33 [princes of *Judah*
2. 6. thou Bethlehem, land of *Judah* — among the
Lu. 1. 39. Mary arose—and went—into a city of *Judah*
Heb. 7. 14. our Lord hath sprung out of *Judah*
Rev. 5. 5. the Lion that is of the tribe of *Judah*
7. 5. Of the tribe of *Judah* were sealed twelve thousand

Judas, or Jude *(various).*
Mat. 13. 55. James, and Joseph, and Simon, and *Judas?*
Lu. 3. 30. Symeon, the son of *Judas* [*Mk.* 6. 3
6. 16. *Judas*, the brother of James. *Acts* 1. 13: *Jude* 1
14. 22. *Judas* (not Iscariot) saith unto him, Lord
Acts 5. 37. After this man rose up *Judas* of Galilee
9. 11. inquire in the house of *Judas* for one named Saul
15. 22. *Judas* called Barsabbas, and Silas. 27
32. *Judas* and Silas, being themselves also prophets

Judas Iscariot.
Mat. 10. 4. *Judas Iscariot*, who also betrayed him. 26. 25:
27. 3: *Mk.* 3. 19: *Lu.* 6. 16: *Jno.* 6. 71: 12. 4:
13. 2: 18. 2, 5
26. 14. *Judas I.* went unto the chief priests. *Mk.* 14. 10
47. *Judas*, one of the twelve, came. *Mk.* 14. 43: *Lu.*
22. 47: *Jno.* 18. 3 [*Iscariot*
Lu. 22. 3. Satan entered into *Judas* who was called
48. *Judas*, betrayest thou the Son of Man with a kiss
Jno. 13. 26. the sop, he taketh and giveth it to *Judas*
29. some thought, because *Judas* had the bag
Acts 1. 16. Holy Ghost spake—David concerning *Judas*
25. apostleship, from which *Judas* fell away

Judæa.
Mat. 2. 1. Jesus was born in Bethlehem of *Judæa*. 5
22. Archelaus was reigning over *Judæa*
3. 1. preaching in the wilderness of *Judæa*
5. all *Judæa*. *Mk.* 1. 5: *Lu.* 6. 17: 7. 17 [*Mk.* 3. 7
4. 25. Jerusalem and *Judæa*, and from beyond Jordan.
19. 1. into the borders of *Judæa* beyond Jordan
24. 16. let them that are in *Judæa* flee. *Mk.* 13. 14: *Lu.*
Mk. 10. 1. cometh into the borders of *Judæa* [21. 21
Lu. 1. 5. Herod, king of *Judæa*
65. noised abroad throughout all the hill country of *J.*
5. 17. village of Galilee and *Judæa*
23. 5. teaching throughout all *Judæa*
Jno. 3. 22. Jesus and his disciples into the land of *Judæa*
4. 47. Jesus was come out of *Judæa* into Galilee. 3, 54
7. 1. he [Jesus] would not walk in *Judæa*
3. Depart hence, and go into *Judæa*
11. 7. Let us go into *Judæa* again
Acts 1. 8. ye shall be my witnesses—in all *Judæa*
2. 9. dwellers in Mesopotamia, in *J.*, and Cappadocia
14. Peter—spake forth unto them, saying, Ye men of *J.*
8. 1. abroad throughout the regions of *Judæa*
9. 31. the Church throughout all *Judæa*—had peace
10. 37. which was published throughout all *Judæa*
11. 1. brethren that were in *J.* heard that the Gentiles
29. send relief unto the brethren that dwelt in *Judæa*

LAMB

Acts 12. 19. he went down from *Judæa* to Cæsarea
15. 1. certain men came down from *Judæa* and taught
21. 10. came down from *J.* a certain prophet, named
26. 20. throughout all the country of *Judæa* [Agabus
28. 21. We neither received letters from *Judæa*
Rom. 15. 31. from them that are disobedient in *Judæa*
2 Cor. 1. 16. set forward on my journey unto *Judæa*
Gal. 1. 22. unknown by face unto the churches of *Judæa*
1 Th. 2. 14. churches of God which are in *J.* in Christ Jesus

Judge.—*Acts* 10. 42

Julia.—*Rom.* 16. 15

Julius.—*Acts* 27. 1, 3

Junias or *Junia.*—*Rom.* 16. 7

Jupiter.—*Acts* 14. 12, 13: 19. 35

Justice.—*Acts* 28. 4

Justus.—*Acts* 1. 23: 18. 7: *Col.* 4. 11

K.

Kidron.—*A.V. Cedron.*—*Jno.* 18. 1

King.—*Mat.* 5. 35: 21. 5: 25. 34, 40: *Jno.* 19. 14, 15.
1 *Tim.* 1. 17: 6. 15: *Heb.* 7. 2: *Rev.* 15. 3: 17. 14

King *of Israel.*—*Mat.* 27. 42: *Mk.* 15. 32: *Jno.* 1. 49:
12. 13

King *of Peace, see* peace.

King *of Righteousness, see* righteousness.

King *of Salem, see* Salem.

Kish.—*A.V. Cis.*—*Acts* 13. 21

Korah.—*A.V. Core.*—*Jude* 11

L.

Lamb.
Jno. 1. 29. Behold the *Lamb* of God. 36
Rev. 5. 6. in the midst of the elders, a *Lamb* standing
8. fell down before the *Lamb*, having each one
12. Worthy is the *Lamb* that hath been slain
13. and unto the *Lamb*, be the blessing
6. 1. when the *Lamb* opened one of the seven seals
16. on the throne, and from the wrath of the *Lamb*
7. 9. before the *Lamb*, arrayed in white robes
10. Salvation unto our God—and unto the *Lamb*
14. and made them white in the blood of the *Lamb*
17. for the *Lamb* which is in the midst of the throne
12. 11. overcame him because of the blood of the *Lamb*
13. 8. *Lamb*—slain from the foundation of the world
14. 1. behold, the *Lamb* standing on the mount Zion
4. which follow the *Lamb* whithersoever he goeth—
first-fruits unto God and unto the *Lamb*

LAMB

Rev. 14. 10. and in the presence of the *Lamb*
15. 3. and the song of the *Lamb*
17. 14. war against the *L.*, and the *L.* shall overcome
19. 7. for the marriage of the *Lamb* is come
9. are bidden to the marriage supper of the *Lamb*
21. 9. I will shew thee the bride, the wife of the *Lamb*
14. names of the twelve apostles of the *Lamb*
22. and the *Lamb*, are the temple thereof
23. did lighten it, and the lamp thereof is the *Lamb*
27. they which are written in the *Lamb's* book of life
22. 1. the throne of God and of the *Lamb*. 3

Lamech.—*Lu.* 3. 36

Laodicea.

Col. 2. 1. I strive for you, and for them at *Laodicea*
4. 13. much labour—for them in *Laodicea*
15. Salute the brethren that are in *Laodicea*
16. read the epistle from *Laodicea*
Rev. 1. 11. to the seven churches—unto *Laodicea*
3. 14. to the angel of the church in *Laodicea* write

Laodiceans.—*Col.* 4. 16

Lasea.—*Acts* 27. 8

Latin.—*Jno.* 19. 20

Lazarus.

Lu. 16. 20. a certain beggar named *Lazarus*
23. Abraham afar off, and *Lazarus* in his bosom
24. send *Lazarus*, that he may dip the tip of his finger
25. and *Lazarus* in like manner evil things
Jno. 11. 1. *Lazarus* of Bethany
2. whose brother *Lazarus* was sick
5. Jesus loved Martha, and her sister, and *Lazarus*
11. Our friend *Lazarus* is fallen asleep
14. *Lazarus* is dead. 12. 1
43. cried with a loud voice, *Lazarus*, come forth
12. 2. *Lazarus* was one of them that sat at meat
9. but that they might see *Lazarus* also
10. that they might put *Lazarus* also to death
17. when he called *Lazarus* out of the tomb

Lebbæus *A.V.*—*see Thaddæus.*

Legion.—*Mk.* 5. 9: *Lu.* 8. 30

Levi *(son of Jacob).*

Heb. 7. 9. *Levi*, who receiveth tithes. 5
Rev. 7. 7. Of the tribe of *Levi* (were sealed) twelve thousand

Levi *(Matthew).*

Lu. 3. 24. Matthat the son of *Levi*. 29
5. 27. named *Levi*, sitting at the place of toll. *Mk.* 2. 14
29. *Levi* made him a great feast in his house

Levite—s.—*Lu.* 10. 32: *Jno.* 1. 19: *Acts* 4. 37

Levitical.—*Heb.* 7. 11

Libertines.—*Acts* 6. 9

Libya.—*Acts* 2. 10

Linus.—2 *Tim.* 4. 21

Lion *(of Judah).*—*Rev.* 5. 5

Living One.—*A.V. he that liveth.*—*Rev.* 1. 17

LORD

Lois.—2 *Tim.* 1. 5

Lord

Mat. 7. 21. Not every one that saith unto me, *Lord, Lord*
22. *Lord, Lord*, did we not prophesy by thy name [5. 12
8. 2. *Lord*, if you wilt, thou canst make me clean. *Lu.*
6. *Lord*, my servant lieth in the house sick
8. *Lord*, I am not worthy that thou shouldest come
21. *Lord*, suffer me first to go and bury my father. *Lu.*
25. Save, *Lord*; we perish [9. 59
9. 28. They say unto him, Yea, *Lord*
38. Pray ye therefore the *L.* of the harvest. *Lu.* 10. 2
11. 25. O Father, *Lord* of heaven and earth. *Lu.* 10. 21
14. 28. *Lord*, if it be thou, bid me to come unto thee
30. [Peter] cried out, saying, *Lord*, save me
15. 22. O *Lord*, thou son of David
25. saying, *Lord*, help me [Canaanitish woman]
27. she said, Yea, *Lord*: for even the dogs eat of the
16. 22. Be it far from thee, *Lord* [crumbs
17. 4. *Lord*, it is good for us to be here
15. *Lord*, have mercy on my son: for he is epileptic
18. 21. *Lord*, how oft shall my brother sin against me
26. *L.*, have patience with me, and I will pay thee all
20. 30. *Lord*, have mercy on us. 31 [opened
33. They say unto him, *Lord*, that our eyes may be
21. 3. The *Lord* hath need of them. *Mk.* 11. 3
42. This was from the *L.*, And it is marvellous in our
eyes? *Mk.* 12. 11
22. 43. doth David in the Spirit call him *Lord*, saying
44. The *Lord* said unto my *Lord*. *Mk.* 12. 36: *Lu.* 20. 42:
Acts 2. 34
45. If David then calleth him *L. Mk.* 12. 37: *Lu.* 20. 44
24. 42. ye know not on what day your *Lord* cometh
25. 11. the other virgins, saying, *Lord, Lord*, open to us.
Lu. 13. 25 [talents. 22
20. *Lord*, thou deliveredst unto me five talents,—two
24. *Lord*, I knew thee that thou art a hard man
37. *Lord*, when saw we thee an hungred. 44
26. 22. Is it I, *Lord*?
27. 10. potter's field, as the *Lord* appointed me
28. 6. Come, see the place where the *Lord* lay
Mk. 5. 19. how great things the *Lord* hath done for thee
7. 28. Yea, *Lord*: even the dogs under the table eat
11. 3. The *Lord* hath need of him. *Lu.* 19. 31, 34.
29. The *Lord* our God, the *Lord* is one
13. 20. except the *Lord* had shortened the days
16. 20. preached everywhere, the *L.* working with them
Lu. 1. 6. walking in all the commandments—of the *Lord*
17. to make ready for the *Lord* a people [blameless
25. Thus hath the *Lord* done unto me in the days
28. thou that art highly favoured, the *Lord* is with thee
38. Mary said, Behold, the handmaid of the *Lord*
45. things which have been spoken to her from the *Lord*
46. My soul doth magnify the *Lord*
58. *L.* had magnified his mercy towards her [Elisabeth]
66. For the hand of the *Lord* was with him
68. Blessed be the *Lord*, the God of Israel
2. 11. a Saviour, which is Christ the *Lord*
15. which the *Lord* hath made known unto us
26. death, before he had seen the *Lord's* Christ
29. lettest thou thy servant, O *Lord*
5. 8. I [Peter] am a sinful man, O *Lord*
6. 46. why call ye me, *Lord, Lord*, and do not the things
7. 6. *Lord*, trouble not thyself: for I am not worthy
13. when the *Lord* saw her, he had compassion on her
19. sent them to the *Lord* [to come down
9. 54. *Lord*, wilt thou that we [James and John] bid fire
61. another also said, I will follow thee, *Lord*

LORD

Lu. 10. 17. *Lord,* even the devils are subject unto us
30. Mary, which also sat at the *Lord's* feet
40. *Lord,* dost thou not care that my sister did leave
11. 1. his disciples said unto him, *L.*, teach us to pray
12. 41. *Lord,* speakest thou this parable unto us
13. 8. *Lord,* let it alone this year also, till I shall dig
23. *Lord,* are they few that be saved ?
14. 22. *Lord,* what thou didst command is done
17. 5. apostles said unto the *Lord,* Increase our faith
37. they answering say unto him. Where, *Lord* ?
18. 41. he said, *Lord,* that I may receive my sight
19. 8. Behold, *L.*, the half of my goods I give to the poor
16. *Lord,* thy pound hath made ten pounds. 18, 25
20. *Lord,* behold here is thy pound
20. 37. when he calleth the *Lord* the God of Abraham
22. 33. *Lord,* with thee I [Peter] am ready to go
38. *Lord,* behold here are two swords
49. *Lord,* shall we smite with the sword ?
61. And the *Lord* turned and looked upon Peter
24. 34. The *Lord* is risen indeed, and hath appeared
Jno. 6. 34. *Lord,* evermore give us this bread
68. *Lord,* to whom shall we go
8. 11. [Woman] she said, No man, *Lord*
9. 36. who is he, *Lord,* that I may believe on him ?
38. he said, *Lord,* I believe. 11. 27
11. 2. Mary which anointed the *Lord* with ointment
3. *Lord,* behold, he [Lazarus] whom thou lovest is sick
12. *Lord,* if he [Lazarus] is fallen asleep, he will recover
21. *L.*, if thou hadst been here, my brother had not died.
34. They say unto him, *Lord,* come and see [32
39. *Lord,* by this time he stinketh
12. 38. *L.*, who hath believed our report ?—arm of the *L.*
13. 6. *Lord,* dost thou wash my feet ? [head.
9. *Lord,* not my feet only, but also my hands and my
13. Ye call me Master, and *Lord* [feet
14. If I then, the *L.* and the Master, have washed your
25. on Jesus' breast, saith unto him, *Lord,* who is it ?
36. *Lord,* whither goest thou ?
37. *Lord,* why cannot I follow thee even now ?
14. 5. *Lord,* we know not whither thou goest
8. *Lord,* shew us the Father
22. *Lord,* what is come to pass
20. 2. They have taken away the *Lord* out of the tomb
13. I [Mary Magdalene] have seen the *Lord*
20. disciples—were glad when they saw the *Lord*
25. said unto him, We have seen the *Lord*
21. 7. saith unto Peter, It is the *Lord.* So when Simon Peter heard that it was the *Lord*
12. Who art thou ? knowing that it was the *Lord*
15. Yea, *Lord;* thou knowest that I love thee. 16, 17
20. *Lord,* who is he that betrayeth thee ?
21. saith to Jesus, *Lord,* and what shall this man do ?
Acts 1. 6. *Lord,* dost thou at this time restore
24. Thou, *Lord,* which knowest the hearts of all men
2. 25. I beheld the *Lord* always before my face
36. God hath made him both *Lord* and Christ
47. the *Lord* added to them day by day
4. 24. O *L.*, thou that didst make the heaven and the earth
26. Against the *Lord,* and against his Anointed
29. now, *Lord,* look upon their threatenings
7. 60. *Lord,* lay not this sin to their charge [22
8. 24. Pray ye for me to the *L.*, that none of the things.
9. 5. he said, Who art thou, *Lord* ? 22. 8 : 26. 15
10. Ananias. And he said, Behold, I am here, *Lord*
13. *Lord,* I have heard from many of this man
27. declared unto them how he had seen the *Lord*
10. 4. [Cornelius] said, What is it, *Lord* ?
14. Peter said, Not so, *Lord.* 11. 8
36. tidings of peace by Jesus Christ (he is *Lord* of all)

LORD

Acts 12. 17. how the *Lord* had brought him [Peter] forth
15. 17. residue of men may seek after the *Lord*
16. 15. If ye have judged me to be faithful to the *Lorp*
17. 24. he, being *Lord* of heaven and earth
22. 10. What shall I do, *L. ?* And the *L.* said unto me
19. *Lord,* they themselves know that I imprisoned
Rom. 4. 8. Blessed is the man to whom the *L.* will not
9. 28. for the *Lord* will execute his word [reckon sin
29. Except the *Lord* of Sabaoth had left us a seed
10. 12. for the same *Lord* is *Lord* of all
16. Isaiah saith, *Lord,* who hath believed our report ?
11. 3. *Lord,* they have killed thy prophets
34. who hath known the mind of the *Lord ?* 1 *Cor.* 2. 16
12. 11. serving the *Lord ;* rejoicing in hope
19. I will recompense, saith the *Lord*
14. 5. for the *Lord* hath power to make him stand
6. regardeth it unto the *Lord*—eateth unto the *Lord*
8. Whether we live therefore, or die, we are the *Lord's*
9. that he might be *Lord* of both the dead and the living
11. As I live, saith the *Lord,* to me every knee shall bow
15. 11. Praise the *Lord,* all ye Gentiles
1 *Cor.* 1. 3. in every place, their *Lord* and ours
2. 8. they would not have crucified the *Lord* of glory
3. 5. and each as the *Lord* gave to him
20. The *Lord* knoweth the reasonings of the wise
4. 4. he that judgeth me is the *Lord*
5. judge nothing before the time, until the *Lord* come
19. I will come to you shortly, if the *Lord* will
6. 13. the body—for the *L. ;* and the *Lord* for the body
14. God both raised the *Lord,* and will raise up us
7. 10. I give charge you, not I, but the *Lord.* 12
16. as the *Lord* hath distributed to each man
22. called in the *Lord*—is the *Lord's* freedman
10. 21. ye cannot drink the cup of the *Lord,* and the cup of devils: ye cannot partake of the table of the *L.*
22. Or do we provoke the *Lord* to jealousy ?
26. the earth is the *Lord's,* and the fulness thereof
11. 23. I received of the *L.* that which also I delivered
12. 5. diversities of ministrations, and the same *Lord*
2 *Cor.* 3. 17. Now the *Lord* is the Spirit : and where the Spirit of the *Lord* is, there is liberty
5. 6. at home in the body, we are absent from the *Lord*
8. willing—to be at home with the *Lord*
11. 17. I speak not after the *Lord,* but as in foolishness
Eph. 4. 5. one *Lord,* one faith, one baptism
6. 8. the same shall he receive again from the *Lord.*
Col. 3. 24. [Father
Phil. 2. 11. Jesus Christ is *Lord,* to the glory of God the
4. 5. The *Lord* is at hand
Col. 3. 13. even as the *Lord* forgave you [in love
1 *Th.* 3. 12. the *Lord* make you to increase and abound
4. 6. the *Lord* is an avenger in all these things
16. the *Lord* himself shall descend from heaven
5. 27. I adjure you by the *Lord* that this epistle be read
2 *Th.* 3. 3. *Lord* is faithful, who shall stablish you
16. *Lord* of peace himself give you peace—The *Lord* be with you all
1 *Tim.* 6. 15. King of kings, and *Lord* of lords. *Rev.* 17. 14 :
19. 16 [Onesiphorus
2 *Tim.* 1. 16. The *Lord* grant mercy unto the house of
18. to find mercy of the *Lord* in that day
2. 7. the *Lord* shall give thee understanding in all things
19. The *Lord* knoweth them that are his
22. call on the *Lord* out of a pure heart
24. the *Lord's* servant, must not strive
26. by the *Lord's* servant unto the will of God
3. 11. out of them all the *Lord* delivered me
4. 8. crown of righteousness, which the *Lord*—shall give

LORD

2 *Tim.* 4. 13. the *L.* will render to him according to his
17. the *Lord* stood by me, and strengthened me [works
18. The *Lord* will deliver me from every evil
22. The *Lord* be with thy spirit [the *Lord*
Philem. 16. A brother beloved—both in the flesh, and in
20. let me have joy of thee in the *Lord*
Heb. 1. 10. Thou, *Lord,* in the beginning hast laid
2. 3. at the first been spoken through the *Lord*
7. 14. our *Lord* hath sprung out of Judah
21. the *Lord* sware and will not repent
8. 11. every man his brother, saying, know the *Lord*
10. 30. The *Lord* shall judge his people [the *Lord*
12. 14. sanctification without which no man shall see
13. 6. The *Lord* is my helper; I will not fear
Jas. 1. 7. think that he shall receive anything of the *Lord*
3. 9. Therewith bless we the *Lord* and Father
4. 15. If the *Lord* will, we shall both live, and do this
5. 7. until the coming of the *Lord*
11. seen the end of the *Lord,* how that the *Lord*
14. anointing him with oil in the name of the *Lord*
15. the *Lord* shall raise him up
1 *Pet.* 2. 3. ye have tasted that the *Lord* is gracious
2 *Pet.* 2. 11. railing judgement against them before the *L.*
3. 8. one day is with the *Lord* as a thousand years
9. The *Lord* is not slack concerning his promise
Jude 5. the *Lord* having saved a people out of Egypt
9. The *Lord* rebuke thee
14. Behold, the *Lord* came with ten thousands
Rev. 11. 4. standing before the *Lord* of the earth
8. where also their *Lord* was crucified
15. kingdom of our *Lord,* and of his Christ
14. 13. Blessed are the dead which die in the *Lord*
15. 4. Who shall not fear, O *L.,* and glorify thy name?
17. 14. *Lord* of lords, and King of kings. 19. 16
see Sabaoth, Master, Jesus.

Lord with God.

Mat. 4. 7. Thou shalt not tempt the *Lord* thy God. *Lu.* 4.
10. Thou shalt worship the *Lord* thy God. *Lu.* 4. 8 [12
22. 37. Thou shalt love the *Lord* thy God. *Lu.* 10. 27
Mk. 12. 30. The *Lord* our God, the *Lord* is one—love the
Lord thy God [their God
Lu. 1. 16. children of Israel shall he turn unto the *Lord*
1. 32. *Lord* God shall give unto him the throne
Acts 2. 39. as many as the *L.* our *G.* shall call unto him
3. 22. A prophet shall the *Lord* God raise up among you
Rev. 4. 8. Holy, holy, holy, is the *Lord* God, the Almighty
11. Worthy art thou, our *Lord* and our God
11. 17. We give thee thanks O *Lord* God, the Almighty
Rev. 15. 3. O *Lord* God, the Almighty. 16. 7: 21. 22
18. 8. Strong is the *Lord* God which judged her
19. 6. Hallelujah: for the *Lord* our God, the Almighty
22. 5. the *Lord* God shall give them light
6. the *Lord,* the God of the spirits of the prophets
see Christ, Master, Fathers, God of Israel.

Lord, *see Jesus.*

Lord Jesus Christ, *see Christ, page* 397

In the Lord, on the Lord.

Acts 9. 42. many believed *on the Lord*
14. 3. tarried there speaking boldly *in the Lord*
Rom. 16. 2. Phœbe,—ye receive her *in the Lord*
8. Ampliatus my beloved *in the Lord*
11. household of Narcissus, which are *in the Lord*
12. Tryphœna and Tryphosa, who labour *in the Lord*
Persis—laboured much *in the Lord*

LORD

Rom 16. 13. Salute Rufus the chosen *in the Lord*
22. I Tertius,—salute you *in the Lord* [2 *Cor.* 10. 17
1 *Cor.* 1. 31. He that glorieth, let him glory *in the Lord.*
4. 17. Timothy—faithful child *in the Lord*
7. 22. he that was called *in the Lord*
39. married to whom she will; only *in the Lord*
9. 1. are not ye my work *in the Lord*
2. mine apostleship are ye *in the Lord*
11. 11. the man without the woman, *in the Lord*
Eph. 2. 21. a holy temple *in the Lord*
4. 17. testify *in the Lord*
5. 8. darkness, but are now light *in the Lord*
6. 1. Children, obey your parents *in the Lord*
10. be strong *in the Lord*
21. Tychicus—faithful minister *in the Lord. Col.* 4. 7
Phil. 1. 14. most of the brethren *in the Lord*
2. 29. Receive him therefore *in the L.* [Epaphroditus]
4. 1. stand fast *in the Lord.* 1 *Th.* 3. 8
2. be of the same mind *in the Lord*
10. I rejoice *in the Lord* greatly
Col. 3. 18. as is fitting *in the Lord*
20. well-pleasing *in the Lord*
4. 17. ministry which thou hast received *in the Lord*
1 *Th.* 5. 12. know them—over you *in the Lord*
2 *Th.* 3. 4. we have confidence *in the Lord*
Philem. 16. a brother beloved—*in the Lord*
20. let me have joy of thee *in the Lord*
Rev. 14. 13. Blessed are the dead which die *in the Lord*
see trust, Christ.

My Lord.

Mat. 22. 44. The Lord said unto *my Lord. Mk.* 12. 36:
Lu. 20. 42: *Acts* 2. 34
Lu. 1. 43. mother of *my Lord* should come unto me
Jno. 20. 13. they have taken away *my Lord* [Mary Mag.]
28. *My Lord* and my God [Thomas]
Phil. 3. 8. knowledge of Christ Jesus *my Lord*

Name of the Lord.

Mat. 21. 9. Blessed is he that cometh in the *name of the*
Lord. 23. 39: *Mk.* 11. 9: *Lu.* 13. 35: 19. 38:
Jno. 12. 13
Acts 2. 21. call on the *name of the Lord* shall be saved
8. 16. baptized into the *name of the Lord* Jesus. 19. 5
9. 29. preaching boldly in the *name of the Lord* [Paul]
19. 13. evil spirits the *name of the Lord* Jesus
17. the *name of the Lord* Jesus was magnified
21. 13. die at Jerusalem for the *name of the Lord* Jesus
1 *Cor.* 6. 11. justified in the *Name of the Lord* Jesus
Col. 3. 17. do all in the *name of the Lord* Jesus
2 *Tim.* 2. 19. every one that nameth the *name of the Lord*
Jas. 5. 10. prophets who spake in the *name of the Lord*
5. 14. anointing him with oil in the *name of the Lord*
see call.

Sight of the Lord.

Lu. 1. 15. he [John Bap.] shall be great in the *s. of the L.*
2 *Cor.* 8. 21. things honourable,—in the *s. of the Lord*
Jas. 4. 10. Humble yourselves in the *sight of the Lord*

Spirit of the Lord.

Acts 5. 9. agreed together to tempt the *Spirit of the L.*
8. 39. *Spirit of the Lord* caught away Philip
2 *Cor.* 3. 17. Lord is the Spirit; and where the *Spirit of*
18. as from the *Lord the Spirit* [the *Lord* is

Way—s of the Lord.

Mat. 3. 3. make ye ready the *way of the L. Mk.* 1. 3: *Lu.*
Jno. 1. 23. make straight the *way of the Lord* [3. 4

[PROPER NAMES.] 420

LORD

Acts 13. 10. cease to pervert the right *ways of the Lord*
18. 25. instructed in the *way of the Lord* [Apollos]

Word of the Lord.

Lu. 22. 61. Peter remembered the *word of the Lord*
Acts 8. 25. when they had testified and spoken the *w. of*
11. 16. I remembered the *word of the Lord* [*the L.*
13. 49. the *word of the Lord* was spread abroad
16. 32. they [Paul and Silas] spake the *word of the L.*
19. 10. they which dwelt in Asia heard the *w. of the L.*
1 *Th.* 1. 8. sounded forth the *word of the Lord*
4. 15. this we say unto you by the *word of the Lord*
2 *Th.* 3. 1. that the *w. of the L.* may run and be glorified
1 *Pet.* 1. 25. the *word of the Lord* abideth for ever
see also angel, commandment, fear, glory, hear, power, &c.

The Lord *said*—*Mat.* 22. 44: *Mk.* 12. 36: *Lu.* 20. 42: *Acts* 2. 34: 9. 10: 11. 16

Saith the Lord.—*Acts* 15. 17: *Rom.* 12. 10; 1 *Cor.* 14. 21; 2 *Cor.* 6. 17: *Heb.* 8. 9, 10: *Rev.* 1. 8

Lot.

Lu. 17. 28. came to pass in the days of *Lot*
29. in the day that *Lot* went out from Sodom
32. Remember *Lot's* wife
2 *Pet.* 2. 7. and delivered righteous *Lot*

Lucius.—*Acts* 13. 1: *Rom.* 16. 21

Luke.—*A.V. Lucas.*

Col. 4. 14. *Luke*, the beloved physician. *Philem.* 24
2 *Tim.* 4. 11. Only *Luke* is with me

Lycaonia.—*Acts* 14. 6, 11

Lycia.—*Acts* 27. 5

Lydda.—*Acts* 9. 32, 35, 38

Lydia.—*Acts* 16. 14, 40

Lysanias.—*Lu.* 3. 1

Lysias (*Claudius Lysias*).—*Acts* 23. 26 : 24. 22

Lystra.—*Acts* 14. 6, 8, 21: 16. 1, 2 : 2 *Tim.* 3. 11

M.

Maath.—*Lu.* 3. 26

Macedonia.

Acts 16. 9. a man of *M.*—saying, Come over into *M.*
10. we sought to go forth into *M.* 20. 1, 3 ; 2 *Cor.* 1. 16: 2. 13 ; 7. 5; 1 *Ti.* 1. 3
12. a city of *Macedonia*, the first of the district
18. 5. Silas and Timothy came down from *Macedonia*
19. 21. when he [Paul] had passed through *M.* 1 *Cor.*
22. having sent into *Macedonia* two of them [16. 5
29. Gaius and Aristarchus, men of *Macedonia*
Rom. 15. 26. been the good pleasure of *Macedonia*
2 *Cor.* 8. 1. grace of God which hath been given in the churches of *Macedonia*
9. 2. I glory on your behalf to them of *Macedonia*
4. if there come with me any of *Macedonia*
11. 9. when they came from *M.*, supplied—my want

MARY

Phil. 4. 15. when I departed from *M.*, no church had fellow-
1 *Th.* 1. 7. ensample to all that believe in *Macedonia* [ship
8. word of the Lord, not only in *Macedonia* and Achaia
4. 10. toward all the brethren which are in all *M.*

Macedonian.—*Acts* 27. 2

Madian, *see Midian.*

Magadan or **Magdala.**—*Mat.* 15. 39

Magdalene, *see Mary.*

Magog.—*Rev.* 20. 8

Mahalaleel.—*A.V. Maleleel.*—*Lu.* 3. 37

Majesty.—*Heb.* 1. 3 : 8. 1

Malchus.—*Jno.* 18. 10

Manaen.—*Acts* 13. 1

Manasseh.

Mat. 1. 10. Hezekiah begat *Manasseh* and *M.* begat Amon
Rev. 7. 6. tribe of *Manasseh* [were sealed] twelve thousand

Mark.—*A.V. Marcus.*

Acts 12. 12. John, whose surname was *Mark.* 25 : 15. 37
15. 39. Barnabas took *Mark* with him
Col. 4. 10. *Mark*, the cousin of Barnabas. *Phil.* 24
2 *Tim.* 4. 11. Take *Mark*, and bring him with thee
1 *Pet.* 5. 13. saluteth you ; and so doth *Mark* my son

Market of Appius.—*A. V., Appii forum.*—*Acts* 28. 15

Mars' Hill, *see Areopagus.*

Martha.

Lu 10. 38. certain woman named *Martha* received him
40. *Martha* was cumbered about much serving
41. *Martha, Martha*, thou art anxious and troubled
Jno. 11. 1. the village of Mary and her sister *Martha*
5. Now Jesus loved *M.*, and her sister, and Lazarus
19. Jews had come to *M.* and Mary, to console them
20. *Martha*, therefore, when she heard that Jesus
21. *Martha*, therefore, said unto Jesus. 24
30. Jesus—was still in the place where *M.* met him
39. *Martha*, the sister of him that was dead, saith
12. 2. made him a supper there : and *Martha* served

Mary (*the Mother of our Lord*).

Mat. 1. 16. Jacob begat Joseph the husband of *Mary*
18. When this mother *M.* had been betrothed to Joseph
20. fear not to take unto thee *Mary* thy wife
2. 11. and saw the young child with *Mary* his mother
13. 55. is not his mother called *Mary*? *Mk.* 6. 3
Lu. 1. 27. and the virgin's name was *Mary*
30. Fear not, *Mary* : for thou hast found favour
34. And *Mary* said unto the angel, How shall this be
38. And *Mary* said, Behold the handmaid of the Lord
39. And *Mary* arose in those days, and went
41. when Elizabeth heard the salutation of *Mary*
46. *Mary* said, My soul doth magnify the Lord
56. *Mary* abode with her about three months
2. 5. to enrol himself with *Mary*, who was betrothed to
16. found both *Mary* and Joseph, and the babe [him
19. But *Mary* kept all these sayings
34. Simeon—said unto *Mary* his mother
Acts 1. 14. with the women, and *M.* the mother of Jesus

421 [PROPER NAMES.

MARY

Mary Magdalene.
Mat. 27. 56. among whom was *Mary Magdalene*. *Mk*
   15. 40: *Jno.* 19. 25
61. *Mary Magdalene* was there, and the other Mary
28. 1. came *Mary Magdalene*—to see the sepulchre.
   Mk. 15. 47: *Jno.* 20. 1
Mk. 16. 1. *Mary Magdalene*—bought spices
   9. he appeared first to *Mary Magdalene*   [devils
Lu. 8. 2. *Mary* that was called *M.*, from whom seven
Jno. 20. 11. But *Mary* was standing—at the tomb weeping
16. Jesus saith unto her, *Mary*. She turneth [*Lu.* 24. 10
18. *Mary Magdalene* cometh and telleth the disciples.

Mary *(Various).*
Mat. 27. 56. *Mary* the mother of James and Joses. 61: 28, 1:
   Mk. 15. 40, 47: 16. 1: *Lu.* 24. 10
Lu. 10. 39. sister called *Mary*, which also sat at the Lord's
   42. *Mary* hath chosen the good part   [feet
Jno. 11. 1. the village of *Mary* and her sister Martha
   2. it was that *Mary* which anointed the Lord
   19. many of the Jews had come to Martha and *M.*
   20. but *Mary* still sat in the house
   28. and called *Mary* her sister secretly, saying
   31. The Jews saw *Mary*, that she rose up quickly
   32. *Mary* therefore, when she came where Jesus was
   12. 3. *Mary* therefore took a pound of ointment
   19. 25. his mother's sister, *Mary* the wife of Clopas
Acts 12. 12. the house of *Mary* the mother of John
Rom. 16. 6. Salute *M.*, who bestowed much labour on you

Master *(Jesus).*
Mat. 12. 38. *Master*, we would see a sign from thee
   19. 16. *Master*, what good thing shall I do
   22. 16. saying, *M.*, we know that thou art true. *Mk.* 12. 14
   24. *Master*, Moses said, If a man die. *Mk.* 12. 19
   36. *M.*, which is the great commandment in the law?
   26. 18. The *Master* saith, My time is at hand
Mk. 4. 38. *Master*, carest thou not that we perish?
   5. 35. why troublest thou the *Master* any further?
   9. 17. *Master*, I brought unto thee my son. *Lu.* 9. 38
   38. *M.*, we saw one casting out devils. *Lu.* 9. 49
   10. 17. Good *M.*, what shall I do that I may inherit
      eternal life? *Lu.* 10. 25: 18. 18
   20. *M.*, all these things have I observed from my youth
   12. 32. Of a truth, *M.*, thou hast well said. *Lu.* 20. 39
   13. 1. *Master*, behold what manner of stones   [11
   14. 14. The *M.* saith, Where is my guest-chamber. *Lu.* 22.
Lu. 3. 13. said unto him, *Master*, what must we do?
   5. 5. *Master*, we toiled all night, and took nothing
   8. 24. awoke him, saying, *Master*, *master*, we perish
   45. *Master*, the multitudes press thee and crush thee
   49. Thy daughter is dead; trouble not the *Master*
   9. 33. *Master*, it is good for us to be here
   12. 13. *Master*, bid my brother divide the inheritance
   17. 14. voices, saying, Jesus, *Master*, have mercy on us
   19. 39. Pharisees—said unto him, *M.*, rebuke thy disciples
   21. 7 *Master*, when therefore shall these things be?
Jno. 8. 1. *Master*, this woman hath been taken in adultery
   11. 28. The *Master* is here, and calleth thee
   13. 13. Ye call me *Master*, and, Lord. 14
Eph. 6. 9. both their *M.* and yours is in heaven. *Col.* 4. 1
2 *Pet.* 2. 1. denying even the *Master* that bought them
Jude 4. denying our only *Master* and Lord, Jesus Christ
Rev. 6. 10. How long, O *Master*. the holy and true

Mattatha.—*Lu.* 3. 31

Mattathias.—*Lu.* 3. 25, 26

MOSES

Matthan.—*Mat.* 1. 15

Matthat.—*Lu.* 3. 24, 29

Matthew, *see Levi.*
Mat. 9. 9. he saw a man, called *Matthew*, sitting
   10. 3. Thomas, and *Matthew* the publican. *Mk.* 3. 18:
      Lu. 6. 15: *Acts* 1. 13

Matthias.—*Acts* 1. 23, 26

Medes.—*Acts* 2. 9

Melchi.—*Lu.* 3. 24, 28

Melchizedek.
Heb. 5. 6. priest for ever After the order of *M.* 10: 6. 20:
   7. 11, 17
7. 1. *M.*, King of Salem, priest of God Most High
   10. in the loins of his father, when *Melchizedek* met him
   15. if after the likeness of *M.* there ariseth another priest

Melea.—*Lu.* 3. 31

Melita.—*Acts* 28. 1

Menna.—*A.V. Menan.*—*Lu.* 3. 31

Mercury.—*A.V. Mercurius.*—*Acts* 14. 12

Mesopotamia.
Acts 2. 9. and the dwellers in *Mesopotamia*
   7. 2. Abraham, when he was in *Mesopotamia*

Messiah.
Jno. 1. 41. We have found the *Messiah* (which is
   4. 25. The woman saith unto him, I know that *M.* cometh

Methuselah.—*Lu.* 3. 37

Michael.
Jude 9. *Michael* the archangel, when contending with the
Rev. 12. 7. *M.* and his angels going forth to war   [devil

Midian.—*A.V. Madian.*—*Acts* 7. 29

Miletus.—*Acts* 20. 15, 17: 2 *Tim.* 4. 20

Mitylene.—*Acts* 20. 14

Mnason.—*Acts* 21. 16

Moloch.—*Acts* 7. 43

Moses.
Mat. 17. 3. there appeared unto them *Moses* and Elijah.
   Mk. 9. 4: *Lu.* 9. 30   [9. 33
   4. and one for *Moses*, and one for Elijah. *Mk.* 9. 5: *Lu.*
   19. 7. Why then did *Moses* command to give a bill
   8. *M.*—suffered you to put away your wives. *Mk.* 10. 4
   22. 24. Master, *M.* said, If a man die, having no children
   23. 2. scribes and the Pharisees sit on *Moses'* seat
Mk. 1. 44. cleansing the things which *Moses* commanded
   7. 10. *Moses* said, Honour thy father and thy mother
   10. 3. What did *Moses* command you?   [20. 28
   12. 19. *Moses* wrote unto us, If a man's brother die. *Lu.*
   26. have ye not read in the book of *Moses*
Lu. 2. 22. purification according to the law of *Moses*
   16. 31. If they hear not *Moses* and the prophets. 29

MOSES

Lu. 20. 37. that the dead are raised, even *Moses* shewed
24. 27. beginning from *Moses* and from all the prophets
44. written in the law of *Moses*
Jno. 1. 17. law was given by *Moses*
45. We have found him of whom *Moses*—did write
3. 14. as *Moses* lifted up the serpent in the wilderness
5. 45. there is one that accuseth you, even *Moses*
46. if ye believed *Moses*, ye would believe me
6. 32. It was not *Moses* that gave you the bread
7. 19. Did not *Moses* give you the law
22. For this cause hath *Moses* given you circumcision
  (not that it is of *Moses*, but of the fathers)
23. that the law of *Moses* may not be broken
9. 28. Thou art his disciple; but we are the disciples of *M.*
29. We know that God hath spoken unto *Moses*
Acts 3. 22. *Moses* indeed said, A prophet
6. 11. speak blasphemous words against *Moses*
14. change the customs which *Moses* delivered
7. 20. *Moses* was born, and was exceeding fair [tians
22. *Moses* was instructed in all the wisdom of the Egyp-
29. And *Moses* fled at this saying
31. when *Moses* saw it, he wondered at the sight
32. And *Moses* trembled, and durst not behold
35. This *Moses* whom they refused, saying
37. This is that *Moses*, which said—A prophet
40. as for this *Moses*,—we wot not
44. even as he appointed who spake unto *Moses*
15. 1. Except ye be circumcised after the custom of *M.*
5. charge them to keep the law of *Moses*
21. *Moses* from generations of old hath in every city
21. 21. teachest all the Jews—to forsake *Moses*
26. 22. the prophets and *Moses* did say should come
Rom. 5. 14. death reigned from Adam until *Moses*
9. 15. he saith to *M.*, I will have mercy on whom I will
10. 5. *M.* writeth that the man that doeth [have mercy
19. First *Moses* saith, I will provoke you to jealousy
1 *Cor.* 9. 9. it is written in the law of *Moses*
10. 2. were all baptized unto *Moses* in the cloud
2 *Cor.* 3. 7 look steadfastly upon the face of *Moses*
13. are not as *Moses*, who put a veil upon his face
15. whensoever *M.* is read, a veil lieth upon their heart
2 *Tim.* 3. 8. Jannes and Jambres withstood *Moses*
Heb. 3. 2. as also was *Moses* in all his house. 5
3. counted worthy of more glory than *Moses*
16. all they that came out of Egypt by *Moses*
7. 14. of Judah; as to which tribe *Moses* spake nothing
8. 5. even as *Moses* is warned of God
9. 19. commandment had been spoken by *Moses*
10 28. A man that hath set at nought *Moses*' law
11. 23. By faith *Moses*—was hid three months
24. By faith *Moses*, when he was grown up, refused
12. 21. *Moses* said, I exceedingly fear and quake
Jude 9. the devil he disputed about the body of *Moses*
Rev. 15. 3. they sing the song of *Moses* the servant of God
  see law, book, commanded.

Most High, *see God.*—*Lu.* 1. 32, 35, 76; 6. 35;
  Acts 7. 48

Myra.—*Acts* 27. 5

Mysia.—*Acts* 16. 7, 8

N.

Naaman.—*Lu.* 4. 27

Naggai.—*A.V. Nagge.*—*Lu.* 3. 25

NYMPHAS

Nahor.—*Lu.* 3. 34

Nahshon.—*Mat.* 1. 4; *Lu.* 3. 32

Nahum.—*Lu.* 3. 25

Nain.—*Lu.* 7. 11

Naphtali.

Mat. 4. 13. in the borders of Zebulun and *Naphtali*
15. and the land of *Naphtali*, Toward the sea
Rev. 7. 6. Of the tribe of *N.* [were sealed] twelve thousand

Narcissus.—*Rom.* 16. 11

Nathan.—*Lu.* 3. 31

Nathanael.—*Jno.* 1. 45, 46, 47, 48, 49; 21. 2

Naum *A.V.*—*see Nahum.*

Nazarene—s.—*Mat.* 2. 23; 26. 71; *Mk.* 14. 67; 16 6;
  Acts 24. 5

Nazareth.

Mat. 2. 23. came and dwelt in a city called *Nazareth*
4. 13. leaving *N.*, he came and dwelt in Capernaum
Mk. 1. 9. Jesus came from *Nazareth* of Galilee
Lu. 1. 26. a city of Galilee, named *Nazareth*
2. 4. Joseph—out of the city of *Nazareth*, into Judæa
39. returned into Galilee, to their own city *Nazareth*
51. came to *N.*; and he was subject unto them. 4. 16
Jno. 1. 45. Jesus of *Nazareth.* 18. 5. 7; 19. 19; *Mat.* 21. 11
  Mk. 1. 24; 10. 47; *Lu.* 4. 34; 18. 37; 24. 19; *Acts* 2
  22; 3. 6; 4. 10; 6. 14; 10. 38; 22. 8; 26. 9
46. Can any good thing come out of *Nazareth*?

Neapolis.—*Acts* 16. 11

Nereus.—*Rom.* 16. 15

Neri.—*Lu.* 3. 27

Nicanor.—*Acts* 6. 5

Nicodemus.—*Jno.* 3. 1, 4, 9; 7. 50; 19. 39

Nicolaitans.—*Rev.* 2. 6, 15

Nicolas.—*Acts* 6. 5

Nicopolis.—*Tit.* 3. 12

Niger.—*Acts* 13. 1

Nineveh.—*Mat.* 12. 41; *Lu.* 11. 32

Ninevites.—*Lu.* 11. 30

Noah.

Mat. 24. 37. as were the days of *Noah*, so shall. *Lu.* 17. 26
38. until the day that *Noah* entered—ark. *Lu.* 17. 27
Lu. 3. 36. Shem, the son of *Noah*
Heb. 11. 7. By faith *Noah*, being warned of God
1 *Pet.* 3. 20. God waited in the days of *Noah*
2 *Pet.* 2. 5. but preserved *Noah* with seven others

Nymphas.—*Col.* 4. 15

OBED

O.

Obed.—*Mat.* 1. 5; *Lu.* 3. 32

Mount of Olives, *or* Olivet.

Mat. 21. 1. *m. of O.,* then Jesus sent two. *Mk.* 11. 1; *Lu.*
  24. 3. as he sat on the *mount of Olives. Mk.* 13. 3 [19. 29
  26. 30. sung a hymn—unto the *m. of O. Mk.* 14. 26;
Lu. 19. 37. at the descent of the *m. of Olives* | *Lu.* 22. 39
  21. 37. lodged—that is called the *mount of Olives*
Jno. 8. 1. house : but Jesus went unto the *mount of Olives*
Acts 1. 12. unto Jerusalem from the *mount* called *Olivet*

Olympas.—*Rom.* 16. 15

Omega, *see Alpha.*—*Rev.* 1. 8; 21. 6; 22. 13

Onesimus.—*Col.* 4. 9 : *Philem.* 10

Onesiphorus.—*2 Tim.* 1. 16 : 4. 19

Ozias *A.V.*—*see Uzziah.*

P.

Pamphylia.—*Acts* 2. 10; 13. 13 ; 14. 24 ; 15. 38;
  27. 5

Paphos.—*Acts* 13. 6, 13

Paradise.—*Lu.* 23. 43; *2 Cor.* 12. 4 ; *Rev.* 2. 7

Parmenas.—*Acts* 6. 5

Parthians.—*Acts* 2. 9

Passover.—*Lu.* 22. 1 ; *Acts* 12. 4

Patara.—*Acts* 21. 1

Patmos.—*Rev.* 1. 9

Patrobas.—*Rom.* 16. 14

Paul, *see Saul.*

Acts 13. 9. But Saul, who is also called *Paul*
  13. Now *Paul* and his company set sail
  16. *Paul* stood up, and beckoning with the hand
  43. Jews and of the devout proselytes followed *Paul*
  45. things which were spoken by *Paul*
  46. *Paul* and Barnabas spake out boldly
  50. persecution against *Paul* and Barnabas
14. 9. the same heard *Paul* speaking
  11. when the multitudes saw what *Paul* had done
  12. Barnabas, Jupiter ; and *Paul,* Mercury
  14. apostles, Barnabas and *Paul,* heard
  19. they stoned *Paul,* and dragged him out
15. 2. Paul and Barnabas had no small dissension
  12. they hearkened unto Barnabas and *Paul.* 2
  22. send—to Antioch with *Paul* and Barnabas
  25. with our beloved Barnabas and *Paul*
  35. *Paul* and Barnabas tarried in Antioch
  38. *Paul* thought not good to take with them
  40. *Paul* chose Silas, and went forth

PAUL

Acts 16. 8. Him would *Paul* have to go forth with him
  9. And a vision appeared to *Paul* in the night. 18. 9
  14. the things which were spoken by *Paul*
  17. The same following after *Paul* and us cried out
  18. But *Paul,* being sore troubled, turned
  19. they laid hold on *Paul* and Silas, and dragged
  25. *Paul* and Silas were praying and singing
  28. But *Paul* cried with a loud voice
  29. fell down before *Paul* and Silas, and brought
  36. jailor reported the words to *Paul*
  37. *Paul* said unto them. 19. 4; 21. 39; 22. 25, 29;
    23. 3, 5 ; 24. 10 ; 25. 7, 10 ; 26. 25, 29 ; 27. 30
17. 2. *Paul,* as his custom was, went in to them
  4. persuaded, and consorted with *Paul* and Silas
  10. immediately sent away *Paul*
  13. word of God was proclaimed of *Paul*
  14. brethren sent forth *Paul*
  15. they that conducted *Paul* brought him
  16. while *Paul* waited for them at Athens
  22. *Paul* stood in the midst of the Areopagus
  33. Thus *Paul* went out from among them
18. 5. *Paul* was constrained by the word
  12. the Jews with one accord rose up against *Paul*
  14. when *Paul* was about to open his mouth
  18. *Paul,* having tarried after this yet many days
19. 1. *Paul* having passed through the upper country
  6. when *Paul* had laid his hands upon them
  11. God wrought special miracles by the hands of *Paul*
  13. I adjure you by Jesus whom *Paul* preacheth
  15. and *Paul* I know ; but who are ye ?
  21. *Paul* purposed in the spirit
  26. *Paul* hath persuaded and turned away
  29. Gaius and Aristarchus—*Paul's* companions
  30. when *Paul* was minded to enter in
20. 1. *Paul* having sent for the disciples
  7. *Paul* discoursed with them. 9
  10. *Paul* went down, and fell on him
  13. set sail for Assos, there intending to take in *Paul*
  16. *Paul* had determined to sail past Ephesus
  37. wept sore, and fell on *Paul's* neck
21. 4. these said to *Paul* through the Spirit [feet
  11. [Agabus] taking *Paul's* girdle, he bound his own
  13. *Paul* answered, what do ye, weeping
  18. the day following *Paul* went in with us [himself
  26. *Paul* took the men, and the next day purifying
  29. *Paul* had brought into the temple [Trophimus]
  30. laid hold on *Paul,* and dragged him out of the
  32. and the soldiers, left off beating *Paul* [temple
  37. as *Paul* was about to be brought into the castle
  40. *Paul,* standing on the stairs, beckoned
22. 23. And *Paul* said, But I am a Roman born
  30. brought *Paul* down and set him before them
23. 1. *Paul,* looking stedfastly on the council, said
  3. said *Paul* unto him, God shall smite thee
  5. *Paul* said, I wist not, brethren
  10. fearing lest *Paul* should be torn in pieces
  12. eat nor drink until they had killed *Paul.* 14
  16. *P.'s* sister's son heard of them lying in wait—told *P.*
  17. *Paul* called unto him one of the centurions
  18. *Paul* the prisoner called me unto him [to-morrow
  20. Jews have agreed to ask thee to bring down *Paul*
  31. took *Paul,* and brought him by night to Antipatris
24. 1. informed the governor against *Paul*
  24. Felix came—and sent for *Paul*
  26. hoped—that money would be given him of *Paul*
  27. favour with the Jews, Felix left *Paul* in bonds
25. 4. *Paul* was kept in charge at Cæsarea
  14. Festus laid *Paul's* case before the king
  23. at the command of Festus *Paul* was brought in

PAUL

Acts 25. 19. one Jesus—whom *Paul* affirmed to be alive
26. 1. Agrippa said unto *Paul*—*Paul* stretched forth. 28
24. *Paul*, thou art mad: thy much learning
27. 1. delivered *Paul*—to a centurion named Julius
3. Julius treated *Paul* kindly
24. Fear not, *Paul*; thou must stand before Cæsar
33. *Paul* besought them all to take some food
43. the centurion, desiring to save *Paul*
28. 3. when *Paul* had gathered a bundle of sticks
8. unto whom [Publius] *Paul* entered in, and prayed
15. whom when *Paul* saw, he thanked God
16. *Paul* was suffered to abide by himself
1 *Cor*. 1. 12. I am of *Paul*. 3. 4 [the name of *Paul*
13. was P. crucified for you? or were ye baptized into
3. 5. and what is *Paul*?
22. *Paul*, or Apollos, or Cephas. [*Col*. 4. 18: 2 *Th*. 3. 17
16. 21. The salutation of me *Paul* with mine own hand.
2 *Cor*. 1. 1. *Paul*, an apostle. *Rom*. 1. 1: 1 *Cor*. 1. 1
10. 1. Now I *Paul* myself intreat you [circumcision
Gal. 5. 2. I *Paul* say unto you, that, if ye receive
Eph. 3. 1. I *Paul*, the prisoner of Christ Jesus. *Phil*. 1
Col. 1. 23. whereof I *Paul* was made a minister
1 *Th*. 2. 18. fain have come unto you, I *Paul*
Tit. 1. 1. *Paul*, a servant of God
Philem. 9. being such a one as *Paul* the aged
19. I *Paul* write it with mine own hand
2 *Pet*. 3. 15. as our beloved brother *Paul*—wrote unto you

Paulus, *see Sergius Paulus*.

Pavement.—*Jno*. 19. 13

Peleg.—*Lu*. 3. 35

Perez.—*Mat*. 1. 3: *Lu*. 3. 33

Pentecost.—*Acts* 2. 1: 20. 16: 1 *Cor*. 16. 8

Perga.—*Acts* 13. 13, 14: 14. 25

Pergamum or Pergamos.—*Rev*. 1. 11: 2. 12

Persis.—*Rom*. 16. 12

Peter *(Simon Peter).*
Mat. 8. 14. when Jesus was come into *Peter's* house
10. 2. Simon, who is called *Peter*. 4. 18: *Mk*. 3. 16: *Lu*. 6. 14: *Acts* 10. 5, 18, 32: 11. 13
14. 28. *Peter* answered him and said (or saith). 15. 15:
17. 4: 19. 27: 26. 33, 35: *Mk*. 9. 5: 14. 29: *Lu*. 8, 45: 9. 20, 33: 12. 41: 22. 58, 60: *Jno*. 6. 68:
13. 6, 9, 36, 37: *Acts* 2. 38: 4. 19: 5. 3, 8, 9, 29: 8. 19: 9. 34: 10. 14, 33, 47: 12. 11: 15. 7
29. And *Peter* went down from the boat
16. 18. thou art *Peter*, and upon this rock I will build
21. *Peter* took him, and began to rebuke him. *Mk*. 8. 32
23. said unto *Peter*, Get thee behind me. *Mk*. 8. 33
17. 1. taketh with him *Peter*. 26. 37: *Mk*. 5. 37: 9. 2: 14. 33: *Lu*. 8. 51: 9. 28
24. received the half shekel came to *Peter*
18. 21. *Peter*, and said to him, Lord, how oft
26. 40. and saith unto *Peter*. *Mk*. 14. 37
58. *Peter* followed him afar off. *Mk*. 14. 54: *Lu*. 22. 54
69. Now *Peter* was sitting without in the court.
73. that stood by came and said to *Peter* [*Lu*. 22. 61
75. P. remembered the word which Jesus. *Mk*. 14. 72:
Mk. 8. 29. *Peter*—saith—Thou art. *Mat*. 16. 16: *Lu*. 9. 20
11. 21. *Peter* calling to remembrance saith [privately
13. 3. *Peter* and James and John and Andrew asked him
14. 66. as *Peter* was beneath in the court

PHANUEL

Mk. 14. 70. they that stood by said to *Peter*
16. 7. tell his disciples and *Peter*, He goeth before you
Lu. 5. 8. Simon P., when he saw it, fell down at Jesus' knees
9. 32. *Peter* and they—were heavy with sleep [10. 28
18. 28. *Peter* said, Lo, we have left. *Mat*. 19. 27: *Mk*.
22. 8. he sent P. and John, saying, Go and make ready
34. I tell thee, *Peter*, the cock shall not crow
56. *Peter* sat in the midst of them
61. the Lord turned, and looked upon *Peter*
24. 12. *Peter* arose, and ran unto the tomb. *Jno*. 20. 3
Jno. 1. 41. Bethsaida,—city of Andrew and *Peter*
6. 8. Andrew, Simon *Peter's* brother
13. 6. So he cometh to Simon *Peter*
24. Simon *Peter*—saith unto him, Tell us who it is
18. 10. Simon *Peter* therefore having a sword
11. therefore said unto *Peter*. 17: *Acts* 2. 37
15. Simon *Peter* followed Jesus
16. *Peter* was standing at the door—brought in *Peter*
25. Simon P. was standing and warming himself. 18:
26. kinsman of him whose ear *Peter* cut off. [*Mk*. 14. 67
27. *Peter* therefore denied again
20. 2. She runneth therefore, and cometh to Simon *Peter*
5. the other disciple outran *Peter*
6. Simon *Peter* therefore also cometh [Didymus
21. 2. There were together Simon P., and Thomas called
3. Simon *Peter* saith unto them, I go a fishing
7. So when Simon *Peter* heard that it was the Lord
11. Simon P. therefore went up, and drew the net to land
15. Jesus saith to Simon *Peter*, Simon, son of John
17. *Peter* was grieved because he said unto him
21. *Peter*—seeing him saith to Jesus, Lord. 20
Acts 1. 13. *Peter* and John and James
15. in these days *Peter* stood up in the midst
2. 14. But *Peter*, standing up with the eleven
3. 1. *Peter* and John were going up into the temple
3. seeing *Peter* and John about to go into the temple
4. And *Peter*, fastening his eyes upon him [lame man]
6. *Peter* said, Silver and gold have I none
11 as he held *Peter* and John, all the people ran
4. 8. Then *Peter*, filled with the Holy Ghost
13. when they beheld the boldness of *Peter* and John
5. 15. as *Peter* came by—his shadow might overshadow
8. 14. they sent unto them *Peter* and John
9. 32. as *Peter* went throughout all parts
38. the disciples, hearing that *Peter* was there
40. But *Peter* put them all forth, and kneeled—and when he saw *Peter*, she sat up
10. 9. *Peter* went up upon the housetop to pray
13. came a voice to him, Rise, *Peter*; kill and eat. 11. 7
17. while *Peter* was much perplexed in himself
26. *Peter* raised him [Cornelius] up, saying, Stand up
44. While *Peter* yet spake these words, the Holy Ghost
45. amazed, as many as came with *Peter*
11. 2. when *Peter* was come up to Jerusalem
4. *Peter* began, and expounded the matter
12. 3. he [Herod] proceeded to seize *Peter* also
5. *Peter* therefore was kept in the prison
6. *Peter* was sleeping between two soldiers, bound
7. smote *Peter* on the side, and awoke him
14. knew P.'s voice—told that P. stood before the gate
16. But *Peter* continued knocking
18. stir among the soldiers, what was become of *Peter*
Gal. 2. 7. even as P. with the gospel of the circumcision
8. he that wrought for *Peter* unto the apostleship
1 *Pet*. 1. 1. *Peter*, an apostle of Jesus Christ. 2 *Pet*. 1. 1
see Simon.

Phalec. *A.V.*—*see Peleg*.

Phanuel.—*Lu*. 2. 36

PHARAOH

Pharaoh
Acts 7. 10. gave him [Joseph] favour and wisdom before P.
13. Joseph's race became manifest unto Pharaoh
21. Pharaoh's daughter took him up, and nourished him
Rom. 9. 17. For the scripture saith unto P. [daughter
Heb. 11. 24. Moses—refused to be called the son of P.'s

Pharisee
Mat. 23. 26. Thou blind Pharisee, cleanse first the inside
of the cup
Lu. 7. 36. entered into the P.'s house, and sat down. 37
39. when the Pharisee which had bidden him saw it. 37
11. 37. a Pharisee asketh him to dine with him
18. 10. to pray; the one a P., and the other a publican
11. The Pharisee stood and prayed thus with himself
Acts 5. 34. stood up one in the council, a Pharisee, named
23. 6. Brethren, I am a P., a son of Pharisees | Gamaliel
26. 5. after the straitest sect of our religion I lived a P.
Phil. 3. 5. as touching the law, a Pharisee [Paul]

Pharisees.
Mat. 3. 7. the P. and Sadducees coming to his baptism
5. 20. exceed the righteousness of the scribes and P.
9. 11. Pharisees saw it, they said. Mk. 2. 16; Lu. 5. 30
14. Why do we and the P. fast oft. Mk. 2. 18; Lu. 5. 33
34. P. said, By the prince of the devils casteth he. 12. 24
12. 2. P.—said unto him. Mk. 2. 24; Lu. 6. 2. [11. 47
14. P. went out, and took counsel. 22. 15; Mk. 3. 6; Jno.
33. P. answered him, saying, Master. 16. 1: Mk. 8. 11
15. 12. Pharisees were offended
16. 6. Take heed and beware of the leaven of the P.
11. 12; Mk. 8. 15; Lu. 12. 1
19. 3. Pharisees tempting him, and saying. Mk. 10. 2
21. 45. chief priests and the P. heard his parables
22. 34. Pharisees, when they heard that he had put the
41. while the P. were gathered together | Sadducees
23. 2. scribes and the Pharisees sit on Moses' seat
13. woe unto you, scribes and Pharisees, hypocrites!
15, 23, 25, 27, 29; Lu. 11. 42, 43
27. 62. chief priests and the P. were gathered together
Mk. 7. 1. unto him the Pharisees, and certain of the scribes
3. P., and all the Jews, except they wash. 5. Mat. 15. 1
12. 13. P. and of the Herodians—catch him in his talk
Lu. 5. 17. there were P. and doctors of the law sitting by
21. P. began to reason—Who is this that speaketh
6. 7. P. watched him, whether he would heal. 14. 1, 3
7. 30. Pharisees and the lawyers rejected for themselves
36. one of the P. desired him that he would eat
11. 39. ye Pharisees cleanse the outside of the cup
53. Pharisees began to press upon him vehemently
13. 31. P., saying to him, Get thee out, and go hence
15. 1. the Pharisees and the scribes murmured, saying
16. 14. P., who were lovers of money, heard all these
17. 20. by the P., when the kingdom of God cometh
19. 39. some of the P.—said unto him, Master, rebuke
Jno. 1. 24. And they had been sent from the Pharisees
3. 1. a man of the Pharisees, named Nicodemus
4. 1. P. had heard that Jesus was making and baptizing
7. 32. the Pharisees heard the multitude murmuring—
and the Pharisees sent officers to take him. 45
47. P. therefore answered them, Are ye also led astray?
48. rulers believed on him, or of the Pharisees?
8. 3. the Pharisees bring a woman taken in adultery
13. P. therefore said unto him, Thou bearest witness
9. 13. they bring to the P. him that aforetime was blind
15. the P. also asked him how he received his sight
16. the Pharisees said, This man is not from God
40. Pharisees—said unto him, Are we also blind?

PHYGELUS

Jno. 11. 46. away to the P.—told them the things which
Jesus had done
57. P. had given commandments, that if any man
12. 19. Pharisees—said—Behold how ye prevail nothing
42. because of the Pharisees they did not confess it
18. 3. soldiers, and officers from the chief priests and the
Acts 15. 5. certain of the sect of the P. who believed [P.
23. 6. Paul perceived—one part were Sadducees—other
P.—he cried out—I am a Pharisee, a son of P.
7. a dissension between the Pharisees and Sadducees
8. neither angel, nor spirit; but the P. confess both
9. some of the scribes of the Pharisees' part stood up

Phenice. A. V.—see Phœnix.

Philadelphia.—Rev. 1. 11: 3. 7

Philemon.—Philem. 1

Philetus.—2 Tim. 2. 17

Philippians.—Ph. 4. 15

Philip (Various).
Mat. 10. 3. Philip, and Bartholomew. Mk. 3. 18; Lu.
6. 14; Acts 1. 13 [6. 17
14. 3. sake of Herodias, his brother Philip's wife. Mk.
Lu. 3. 1. his brother Philip tetrarch of—Iturœa
Jno. 1. 43. findeth Philip; and Jesus saith—Follow me
44. Now Philip was from Bethsaida
45. Philip findeth Nathanael, and saith unto him
46. Philip saith unto him [Nathanael], Come and see
48. Before Philip called thee—I saw thee
6. 5. Jesus—saith unto Philip, Whence are we to buy
12. 21. these therefore came to Philip [bread
22. Philip cometh and telleth Andrew; Andrew cometh
14. 8. Philip saith—Lord, show us the Father [and P.
9. dost thou not know me, Philip?
Acts 6. 5. and they chose Stephen—and Philip
8. 5. And Philip went down to the city of Samaria
6. gave heed—unto the things that were spoken by P.
12. when they believed Philip preaching good tidings
13. being baptized, he continued with Philip
29. the Spirit said unto Philip, Go near
30. Philip ran to him, and heard him reading
31. [eunuch] besought Philip to come up and sit
34. eunuch answered Philip
35. Philip opened his mouth
38. down into the water, both Philip and the eunuch
39. the Spirit of the Lord caught away Philip
40. But Philip was found at Azotus
21. 8. entering into the house of Philip the evangelist

Philippi, see Cæsarea.—Acts 16. 12; 20. 6; Phil. 1. 1;
1 Th. 2. 2

Philologus.—Rom. 16. 15

Phlegon.—Rom. 16. 14

Phœbe.—Rom. 16. 1

Phœnicia.—Acts 11. 19; 15. 3; 21. 2

Phœnix.—Acts 27. 12

Phrygia.—Acts 2. 10; 16. 6; 18. 23

Phygelus.—2 Tim. 1. 15

PILATE

Pilate, *or* **Pontius Pilate.**
Mat. 27. 2. delivered him up to *Pilate. Mk.* 15. 1
13. Then saith *Pilate* unto him. 17. 22, 65; *Mk.* 15.
   14: *Lu.* 23. 4: *Jno.* 18. 31, 37; 19. 6, 10, 15
24. when *Pilate* saw that he prevailed nothing
58. went to *P.*, and asked for the body of Jesus. Then
   P. commanded. *Mk.* 15. 43: *Lu.* 23. 52; *Jno.* 19. 38
62. and the Pharisees were gathered together unto *P.*
Mk. 15. 2. *Pilate* asked him [Jesus]. 4: *Lu.* 23. 3
5. insomuch that *Pilate* marvelled. 44
9. *Pilate* answered them. 12: *Jno.* 18. 35; 19. 22
15. *Pilate*, wishing to content the multitude, released
Lu. 3. 1. *Pontius Pilate* being governor of Judæa
13. 1. whose blood *Pilate* had mingled with their sacri-
23. 1. brought him [Jesus] before *Pilate* [fices
6. when *Pilate* heard it he asked
11. Herod—sent him back to *Pilate*
12. Herod and *Pilate* became friends
13. *Pilate* called together the chief priests
20. *Pilate* spake—again, desiring to release Jesus
23. *Pilate* gave sentence
Jno. 18. 29. *Pilate* therefore went out unto them
   33. *Pilate* therefore entered again into the palace
   38. *Pilate* saith unto him, What is truth?
19. 1. *Pilate* therefore took Jesus, and scourged him
4. *P.* went out again, and saith—Behold, I bring him
6. *Pilate* saith—Take him yourselves, and crucify him
8. When *Pilate* therefore heard this saying
12. Upon this *Pilate* sought to release him
19. *Pilate* wrote a title also, and put it on the cross
31. Jews—asked of *P.* that their legs might be broken
Acts 3. 13. denied before the face of *Pilate*
4. 27. both Herod and *Pontius Pilate*, with the Gentiles
13. 28. yet asked they of *Pilate* that he should be slain
1 *Tim.* 6. 13. who before *P. P.* witnessed the good confession

Pisidia.—*Acts* 13. 14: 14. 24

Pollux *with Castor, see The Twin Brothers.*

Pontius Pilate, *see Pilate.*

Pontus.—*Acts* 2. 9: 18. 2: 1 *Pet.* 1. 1

Porcius Festus. *see Festus.*

Potentate.—1 *Tim.* 6. 15

Prætorium.—*Mk.* 15. 16

Preparation.—*Mat.* 27. 62; *Mk.* 15. 42; *Lu.* 23. 54; *Jno.* 14, 31, 42

Prince of Life, *or* **Prince.**—*Acts* 3. 14: 5. 31

Priscilla, *or* **Prisca.**—*Acts* 18. 2, 18, 26; *Rom.* 16. 3: 1 *Cor.* 16. 19: 2 *Tim.* 4. 19

Prochorus.—*Acts* 6. 5

Psalms, *Book of.*—*Lu.* 20. 42: *Acts* 1. 20

Ptolemais.—*Acts* 21. 7

Publius.—*Acts* 28. 7, 8

Pudens.—2 *Tim.* 4. 21

Puteoli.—*Acts* 28. 13

Pyrrhus.—*Acts* 20. 4

ROMANS

Q.

Quartus.—*Rom.* 16. 23

Quirinius.—*A.V. Cyrenius.*—*Lu.* 2. 2

R.

Rabbi.—*Mat.* 23. 7, 8: 26. 25, 49: *Mk.* 9. 5; 11. 21: 14. 45: *Jno.* 1. 38, 49: 3. 2, 26: 4. 31: 6. 25: 9. 2: 11. 8

Rabboni.—*Mk.* 10. 51: *Jno.* 20. 17

Raca.—*Mat.* 5. 22

Rachel.—*Mat.* 2. 18

Rahab.
Mat. 1. 5. Salmon begat Boaz of *Rahab*
Heb. 11. 31 By faith *Rahab* the harlot perished not
Jas. 2. 25. was not also *Rahab* the harlot justified

Ram.—*Mat.* 1. 3, 4

Ramah.—*Mat.* 2. 18

Rebecca.—*Rom.* 9. 10

Red Sea.
Acts 7. 36. wonders and signs in—the *Red* sea
Heb. 11. 29. By faith they passed through the *Red sea*

Rehoboam.—*Mat.* 1. 7

Rephan.—*Acts* 7. 43

Reu.—*A.V. Ragau. Lu.* 3. 35

Reuben.—*Rev.* 7. 5

Rhegium.—*Acts* 28. 13

Rhesa.—*Lu.* 3. 27

Rhoda.—*Acts* 12. 13

Rhodes.—*Acts* 21. 1

Righteous One.—*A.V. Just One.*—*Acts* 3. 14: 7. 52; 22. 14

Roman.
Acts 16. 12. Philippi—a *Roman* colony
22. 25. Is it lawful for you to scourge a—*Roman*?
26. for this man is a *Roman*
27. Tell me, Art thou a *Roman*?
28. Paul said, But I am a *Roman* born   [23. 27
29. was afraid, when he knew that he was a *Roman.*

Romans.
Jno. 11. 48. the *Romans* will come and take away
Acts 16. 21. not lawful for us to receive—being *Romans*
37. beaten us publicly—men that are *Romans*

ROMANS

Acts 16. 38. feared, when they heard that they were *R.*
25. 16. not the custom of the *Romans*
28. 17. delivered prisoner—into the hands of the *R.*

Righteous One.—*A. V. Just One.*—*Acts* 3. 14 : 7. 52 : 22. 14

Rome.

Acts 2. 10. sojourners from *Rome*, both Jews and
18. 2. commanded all the Jews to depart from *Rome*
19. 21. I must also see *Rome*
23. 11. so must thou bear witness also at *Rome*
28. 14. and so we came to *Rome*
16. when we entered into *Rome*, Paul was suffered
Rom. 1. 7. to all that are in *Rome*, beloved of God
15. ready to preach the gospel to you—in *Rome*
2 *Tim.* 1. 17. when he was in *Rome*, he sought me

Root of David.—*Rev.* 5. 5

Rufus.—*Mk.* 15. 21 : *Rom.* 16. 13

Ruth.—*Mat.* 1. 5

S.

Sabaoth (*Lord of*).—*Rom.* 9. 29 : *Jas.* 5. 4

Sadducees, *see Pharisees.*

Mat. 3. 7. Pharisees and *S.* coming to his baptism
16. 1. and *S.* came, and tempting him asked him
6. beware of the leaven of the Pharisees and *S.* 11
12. the teaching of the Pharisees and *Sadducees*
22. 23. *Sadducees*, which say that there is no resurrection. *Mk.* 12. 18 : *Lu.* 20. 27 : *Acts* 23. 8
34. they heard that he had put the *Sadducees* to silence
Acts 4. 1. captain of the temple and the *S.* came upon them
5. 17. which is the sect of the *Sadducees*
23. 6. Paul perceived that the one part were *Sadducees*
7. a dissension between the Pharisees and *Sadducees*

Sadoc.—*Mat.* 1. 14

Salamis.—*Acts* 13. 5

Salem.—*Heb.* 7. 1, 2

Salim.—*Jno.* 3. 23

Salmon.—*Mat.* 1. 4, 5 : *Lu.* 3. 32

Salmone.—*Acts* 27. 7

Salome.—*Mk.* 15. 40 : 16. 1

Samaria.

Lu. 17. 11. was passing through the midst of *S. Jno.* 4. 4, 5
Jno. 4. 7. cometh a woman of *Samaria* to draw water
Acts 1. 8. witnesses—in all Judæa and *Samaria*
8. 1. scattered abroad throughout—Judæa and *Samaria*
5. Philip went down to the city of *Samaria*
9. Simon—amazed the people of *Samaria*
14. heard that *Samaria* had received the word
9. 31. the church throughout—*Samaria* had peace
15. 3. passed through both Phœnicia and *Samaria*

SAUL

Samaritan—s.

Mat. 10. 5. enter not into any city of the *Samaritans*
Lu. 9. 52. entered into a village of the *Samaritans*
10. 33. a certain *Samaritan*, as he journeyed, came
17. 16. giving him thanks : and he was a *Samaritan*
Jno. 4. 9. The *S.* woman therefore saith—drink of me, which
10. Jews have no dealings with *Samaritans* [am a *S.*
39. many of the *Samaritans* believed on him
40. the *Samaritans*—besought him to abide with them
8. 48. that thou art a *Samaritan*, and hast a devil
Acts 8. 25. the gospel to many villages of the *S.*

Samos.—*Acts* 20. 15

Samothrace.—*Acts* 16. 11

Samson.—*Heb.* 11. 32

Samuel.

Acts 3. 24. all the prophets from *S.* and them that followed
13. 20. he gave them judges until *Samuel* the prophet
Heb. 11. 32. of David and *Samuel* and the prophets

Sapphira.—*Acts* 5. 1

Sarah.

Rom. 4. 19. and the deadness of *Sarah's* womb
9. 9. will I come, and *Sarah* shall have a son
Heb. 11. 11. *Sarah* herself received power to conceive
1 *Pet.* 3. 6. as *Sarah* obeyed Abraham, calling him lord

Sardis.—*Rev.* 1. 11 : 3. 1, 4

Satan.

Mat. 4. 10. Get thee hence, *Satan*
12. 26. if *Satan* casteth out *Satan*, he is divided
16. 23. said unto Peter, Get thee behind me, *S. Mk.* 8. 33
Mk. 1. 13. wilderness forty days tempted of *Satan*
3. 23. How can *Satan* cast out *Satan* ?
26. if *Satan* hath risen up against himself. *Lu.* 11. 18
4. 15. straightway cometh *S.*, and taketh away the word
Lu. 10. 18. I beheld *Satan* fallen as lightning from heaven
13. 16. daughter of Abraham, whom *Satan* had bound
22. 3. *Satan* entered into Judas—called Iscariot
31. Simon, Simon, behold, *Satan* asked to have you
Jno. 13. 27. after the sop, then entered *S.* into him [Judas]
Acts 5. 3. Ananias, why hath *Satan* filled thy heart to lie
26. 18. from the power of *Satan* unto God
Rom. 16. 20. God of peace shall bruise *S.* under your feet
1 *Cor.* 5. 5. to deliver such a one unto *Satan* [shortly
2 *Cor.* 2. 11. no advantage may be gained over us by *Satan*
11. 14. *Satan* fashioneth himself into an angel of light
12. 7. a messenger of *Satan* to buffet me [Paul]
1 *Th.* 2. 18. come unto you—*Satan* hindered us [*Satan*
2 *Th.* 2. 9. whose coming is according to the working of
1 *Tim.* 1. 20. Hymenæus and Alexander ; whom I delivered
5. 15. already some are turned aside after *S.* [unto *S.*
Rev. 2. 9. are a synagogue of *Satan.* 3. 9
13. *Satan's* throne is—where *Satan* dwelleth
24. which know not the deep things of *Satan*
12. 9. he that is called the Devil and *Satan*
20. 2. the old serpent, which is the Devil and *Satan*
7. the thousand years are finished, *S.* shall be loosed

Saul, *see Paul.*

Acts 7. 58. at the feet of a young man named *Saul*
8. 1. And *Saul* was consenting unto his death
3. But *Saul* laid waste the church
9. 1. *Saul*, yet breathing threatening and slaughter
4. *Saul, Saul,* why persecutest thou me ? 22. 7 : 26. 14

SAUL

Acts 9. 8. And *Saul* arose from the earth
11. inquire in the house of Judas for one named *Saul*
17. Brother *Saul*—receive thy sight. 22. 13
22. But *Saul* increased the more in strength
24. but their plot became known to *Saul*
11. 25. he went forth to Tarsus to seek for *Saul*
30. to the elders by the hand of Barnabas and *Saul*
12. 25. Barnabas and *Saul* returned from Jerusalem
13. 1. prophets and teachers, Barnabas—and *Saul*
2. Holy Ghost said, Separate me Barnabas and *Saul*
7. [Sergius Paulus] called unto him Barnabas and *Saul*
9. But *Saul*, who is also called Paul

Saul *(son of Kish)*.—*Acts* 13. 21

Saviour.

Lu. 1. 47. my spirit hath rejoiced in God my *Saviour*
2. 11. born to you this day in the city of David a *Saviour*
Jno. 4. 42. and know that this is indeed the *S.* of the world
Acts 5. 31. Him did God exalt—to be a Prince and a *S.*
13. 23. brought unto Israel a *Saviour*, Jesus
Phil. 3. 20. from whence also we look for a *S.* [*Tit.* 1. 3
1 *Tim.* 1. 1. according to the commandment of God our *S.*
2. 3. good and acceptable in the sight of God our *Saviour*
4. 10. the *S.* of all men, specially of them that believe
2 *Tim.* 1. 10. appearing of our *Saviour* Christ Jesus
Tit. 1. 4. God the Father and Christ Jesus our *Saviour*
2. 10. adorn the doctrine of God our *S.* in all things
13. appearing of the glory of our great God and *S.*
3. 4. when the kindness of God our *Saviour*, and his love
6. upon us richly, through Jesus Christ our *S.* [Christ
2 *Pet.* 1. 1. in the righteousness of our God and *S.* Jesus
11. eternal kingdom of our Lord and *S.* Jesus Christ
2. 20. knowledge of the Lord and *Saviour* Jesus Christ
3. 2. Lord and *Saviour* through your apostles
18. grace and knowledge of our Lord and *S.* Jesus Christ
1 *Jno.* 4. 14. sent the Son to be the *Saviour* of the world
Jude 25. to the only God our *Saviour*—be glory, majesty

Sceva.—*Acts* 19. 14

Scythian.—*Col.* 3. 11

Secundus.—*Acts* 20. 4

Seleucia.—*Acts* 13. 4

Semein.—*A.V. Semei.*—*Lu.* 3. 26

Sergius Paulus.—*Acts* 13. 7

Serug.—*Lu.* 3. 35

Seth.—*Lu.* 3. 38

Sharon.—*Acts* 9. 35

Shealtiel.—*Mat.* 1. 12; *Lu.* 3. 27

Shechem.—*Acts* 7. 16

Shelah.—*Lu.* 3. 36

Shem.—*Lu.* 3. 36

Shepherd.—1 *Pet.* 2. 25; 5. 4

Siloam.—*Lu.* 13. 4; *Jno.* 9. 7, 11

Sidon.
Mat. 11. 21. had been done in Tyre and *Sidon. Lu.* 10. 13
22. more tolerable for Tyre and *Sidon. Lu.* 10. 14

SMYRNA

Mat. 15. 21. withdrew into the parts of Tyre and *Sidon.*
Mk. 7. 24, 31
Mk. 3. 8. about Tyre and *Sidon*, a great multitude—came.
Lu. 4. 26. Zarephath, in the land of *Sidon* [*Lu.* 6. 17
Acts 12. 20. displeased with them of Tyre and *Sidon*
27. 3. And the next day we touched at *Sidon*

Silas.
Acts 15. 32. Judas and *Silas*, being—prophets. 22, 27
40. Paul chose *Silas*, and went forth
16. 19. laid hold on Paul and *Silas*, and dragged them
25. about midnight Paul and *Silas* were praying
29. [jailor] fell down before Paul and *Silas*
17. 4. persuaded, and consorted with Paul and *Silas*
10. sent away Paul and *Silas* by night unto Berœa
14. and *Silas* and Timothy abode there still
15. receiving a commandment unto *Silas* and Timothy
18. 5. *Silas* and Timothy came down from Macedonia

Silvanus.
2 *Cor.* 1. 19. preached—even by me and *Silvanus*
1 *Th.* 1. 1. Paul, and *Silvanus*, and Timothy. 2 *Th.* 1. 1
1 *Pet.* 5. 12. By *Silvanus*, our faithful brother

Simeon *(Tribe of)*.—*Rev.* 7. 7

Simeon.—*Lu.* 2. 25, 34

Simon (Peter), *see also* Peter.
Mat. 4. 18. *Simon* who is called *Peter*
16. 17. Blessed art thou, *Simon* Bar-Jonah
17. 25. What thinkest thou, *Simon* ? the kings of
Mk. 1. 16. he saw *Simon* and Andrew the brother of *S.*
29. they came into the house of *Simon. Lu.* 4. 38
30. *Simon's* wife's mother lay sick. *Lu.* 4. 38
36. *Simon* and they that were with him followed [11. 13
3. 16. *Simon* he surnamed *Peter. Lu.* 6. 14; *Acts* 10. 32.
14. 37. *Simon*, sleepest thou ? Couldst thou not watch
Lu. 5. 3. into one of the boats, which was *Simon's*
4. he said unto *Simon*, Put out into the deep
10. were partners with *Simon*—*Simon*, Fear not
22. 31. *Simon*, *Simon*, behold, Satan asked to have you
24. 34. The Lord is risen indeed, and hath appeared to *S.*
Jno. 1. 40. Andrew, *Simon Peter's* brother
41. He findeth first his own brother *Simon*
42. Thou art *S.* the son of John—Cephas, which is—*Peter*
21. 15. *Simon*, son of John, lovest thou me. 16, 17

Simon *(various)*.
Mat. 10. 4. *Simon* the Canaanæan. *Mk.* 3. 18
13. 55. his brethren, James, and Joseph, and *S. Mk.* 6. 3
26. 6. in the house of *Simon* the leper. *Mk.* 14. 3
27. 32. man of Cyrene, *S.* by name. *Mk.* 15. 21; *Lu.* 23. 26
Lu. 6. 15. *Simon* which was called the Zealot. *Acts* 1. 13
7. 40. *Simon*, I have somewhat to say unto thee
44. *Simon*, Seest thou this woman ?
Jno. 6. 71. he spake of Judas the son of *S.* Iscariot. 13. 2, 26
Acts 8. 9. *Simon* by name, which—used sorcery
13. And *Simon* also himself believed [hands
18. *S.* saw that through the laying on of the apostles'
24. *Simon*—said, Pray ye for me to the Lord
9. 43. in Joppa with one *Simon* a tanner. 10. 6, 32
10. 17. inquiry for *Simon's* house, stood—and asked

Sinai.—*Acts* 7. 30, 38; *Gal.* 4. 21, 25

Smyrna.—*Rev.* 1. 11; 2. 8

SODOM

Sodom.
Mat. 10. 15. more tolerable for *Sodom*. 11. 24 ; *Lu.* 10. 12
11. 23. if the mighty works had been done in *Sodom*
Lu. 17. 29. in the day that Lot went out from *Sodom*
Rom. 9. 29. We had become as *Sodom*, and had been
2 *Pet.* 2. 6. turning the cities of *Sodom* and Gomorrah into
Jude 7. Even as *Sodom* and Gomorrah [ashes
Rev. 11. 8. city, which spiritually is called S. and Egypt

Solomon.
Mat. 1. 6. David begat *Solomon*
7. and *Solomon* begat Rehoboam
6. 29. S. in all his glory was not arrayed. *Lu.* 12. 27
12. 42. hear the wisdom of S.;—a greater than S. is here.
Jno. 10. 23, *Solomon's* porch. *Acts* 3. 11 : 5. 12 ; [*Lu.* 11. 31
Acts 7. 47. But *Solomon* built him a house

Son.—*Mat.* 24. 36 : 28. 19 ; *Mk.* 1. 11 : 5. 7 ; 9. 7 :
13. 32 ; 14. 61 ; *Lu.* 1. 32 ; 2. 48 : 3. 22 : 8. 28 :
9. 35 ; 10. 22 ; *Jno.* 1. 18 : 3. 16, 17, 35, 36 : 5. 19,
20, 21, 22, 23, 26 ; 6. 40 : 8. 36 : 14. 14 ; 17. 1 :
Acts 13. 33 ; *Rom.* 1, 3, 9 ; 5. 10 : 8. 3, 29, 32 ;
1 *Cor.* 15. 28 ; *Gal.* 1. 16 : 4. 4, 6 ; *Col.* 1. 13 ;
Heb. 1. 2, 5, 8 : 5. 5, 8 : 6. 7 ; 7. 28 ; 2 *Pet.* 1. 17 ;
1 *Jno.* 1. 3, 7 ; 2. 23, 24 : 3. 23 : 4. 9, 10, 14 : 5. 12,
20 ; 2 *Jno.* 3. 9

Son of God.—*Mat.* 4. 3, 6 : 8. 29 ; 14. 33 ; 26. 63 ;
27. 41, 43, 44 ; *Mk.* 1. 1 ; 3. 11 ; 15. 39 ; *Lu.* 1. 35 :
3. 38 ; 4. 3, 9, 41 ; 22. 70 ; *Jno.* 1. 34, 49 ; 3. 19 ;
5. 25 ; 9. 35 ; 10. 36 ; 11. 5, 27 ; 19. 7 ; *Acts* 8. 37
[margin] ; 9. 20 ; *Rom.* 1. 4 : 2 *Cor.* 1. 19 ; *Gal.*
2. 20 ; *Eph.* 4. 13 ; *Heb.* 4. 14 ; 7. 3 ; 10. 29 ;
1 *Jno.* 3. 8 : 4. 15 : 5. 5, 10, 12, 14, 20 ; *Rev.* 2. 18.

Son of Man—*Christ.*
Mat. 8. 20. Son of *man* hath not where to lay. *Lu.* 9. 58
9. 6. know that the S. of *m.* hath power on earth to forgive sins. *Mk.* 2. 10 ; *Lu.* 5. 24
10. 23. cities of Israel, till the *Son of man* be come
11. 19. The *Son of man* came eating. *Lu.* 7. 34 [6. 5
12. 8. the S. of *m.* is lord of the Sabbath. *Mk.* 2. 28 ; *Lu.*
32. a word against the *Son of man. Lu.* 12. 10
40. so shall the *Son of man* be three days and three
13. 37. He that soweth the good seed is the *Son of man*
41. The *Son of man* shall send forth his angels
16. 13. Who do men say that the *Son of man* is
17. *Son of man* shall come in the glory of his Father
28. see the *Son of man* coming. 24. 30 ; *Mk.* 13. 26 ; *Lu.*
17. 9. until the *Son of man* be risen. *Mk.* 9. 9 [21. 27
12. Even so shall the *Son of man* also suffer. *Mk.* 8. 31
22. The *Son of man* shall be delivered. 20. 18 ; 26. 2 ;
Mk. 9. 31 ; 10. 33 ; *Lu.* 9. 44 ; 24. 7
19. 28. *Son of man* shall sit on the throne of his glory
20. 28. the *Son of man* came not to be—but to minister.
Mk. 10. 45
24. 27. so shall be the coming of the *Son of man*. 37, 39
30. shall appear the sign of the *Son of man* in heaven
44. ye think not the *Son of man* cometh. *Lu.* 12. 40
25. 31. when the *Son of man* shall come in his glory
26. 24. The S. of *Man* goeth—the S. of *man* is betrayed.
45 ; *Mk* 14. 21, 41 ; *Lu.* 22. 22 [62 ; *Lu.* 23. 69
64. the S. of *man* sitting—right hand of power. *Mk.* 14.
Mk. 8. 38. the *Son of m.* also shall be ashamed. *Lu.* 9. 26
9. 12. written of the *Son of man. Lu.* 18. 31
Lu. 6. 22. your name be evil, for the *Son of man's* sake
9. 22. The *Son of man* must suffer many things
11. 30. so shall also the *Son of man* be. 17. 24
12. 8. him shall the *Son of man* also confess

SYNTYCHE

Lu. 17. 22. desire to see one of the days of the *Son of man*
26. so shall it be also in the days of the *Son of man*
30. in the day that the *Son of man* is revealed
18. 8. when the *Son of man* cometh, shall he find faith
19. 10. For the *Son of man* came to seek and to save
21. 36. to pass, and stand before the *Son of man*
22. 48. betrayest thou the *Son of man* with a kiss
Jno. 1. 51. ascending and descending upon the *Son of man*
3. 13. Even the *Son of man*, which is in heaven
14. Even so must the *Son of man* be lifted up
5. 27. Execute judgement because he is the *Son of man*
6. 27. Eternal life, which the *Son of man* shall give
53. Except ye eat the flesh of the *Son of man*, and
62. What then if ye should behold the *Son of man*
8. 28. lifted up the *Son of man* then shall ye know
12. 23. that the *Son of man* should be glorified
34. *Son of m.* must be lifted up ? Who is this S. of *m.*
13. 31. Jesus saith, Now is the *Son of man* glorified
Acts 7. 56. the *Son of man* standing on the right hand

Sopater.—*Acts* 20. 4

Sosipater.—*Rom.* 16. 21

Sosthenes.—*Acts* 18. 17 : 1 *Cor.* 1. 1

Spain.—*Rom.* 15. 24, 28

Spirit of the Lord or God, see also Holy Spirit.
—*Lu.* 4. 18 ; *Acts* 5. 9 ; 8. 39 ; *Rom.* 8. 9, 15 :
1 *Cor.* 2. 11, 14 ; 3. 17 : 6. 11 ; 7. 40 ; 12. 3 :
2 *Cor.* 3. 3, 17, 18 ; *Gal.* 4. 6 ; *Phil.* 1. 20 ; 3. 3 ;
1. *Pet.* 4. 14 : 1 *Jno.* 4. 2.

Spirit of your Father, or Spirit, see also Holy.—Mat.
10. 20 ; 12. 31 ; *Mk.* 1. 10, 12 ; *Lu.* 2. 27 : 4. 1, 14 ;
Jno. 1. 32, 33 ; 3. 5, 6, 8 ; 4. 24 ; 7. 39 ; 14. 17 : 15.
26 ; 16. 13 ; *Acts* 2. 4, 17, 18 ; 6. 3 : 8. 29 ; 11. 12,
28 ; 16. 7 ; 21. 4 ; *Rom.* 8. 2, 10, 11, 16, 23, 26, 27 ;
1 *Cor.* 2. 4, 10, 13 ; 12. 4, 9, 10, 11, 13 ; 2 *Cor.* 1.
22 ; 5. 5 ; 12. 18 ; *Gal.* 3. 2, 3, 5 ; 4. 29 ; 5. 5, 16,
17, 18, 22, 25 ; 6. 8 ; *Eph.* 2. 19, 22 ; 3. 6, 16 ; 4. 3 :
5. 18 ; 6. 17, 18 ; *Phil.* 2. 1 ; *Col.* 1. 8 ; 1 *Th.* 5.
19 ; 2 *Th.* 2. 13 ; 1 *Tim.* 4. 1 ; *Heb.* 9. 14 ; 10. 29 ;
1 *Pet.* 1. 2, 11 : 4. 14 : 1 *Jno.* 3. 24 : 5. 7, 8 ; *Jude*
19 ; *Rev.* 1. 10 : 2. 7, 17, 29 ; 3. 1, 6, 13, 22. 4. 2,
5 ; 5. 7 ; 14. 13 : 17. 3 ; 21. 10 ; 22. 17

Stachys.—*Rom.* 16. 9

Stephanas.—1 *Cor.* 1. 16 : 16. 15, 17

Stephen.
Acts 6. 5. they chose *Stephen*, a man full of faith. 8
9. arose certain of them—disputing with *Stephen*
7. 59. they stoned *Stephen*, calling upon the Lord
8. 2. and devout men buried *Stephen*
11. 19. tribulation that arose about *Stephen* travelled
22. 10. when the blood of *Stephen* thy witness was shed

Stoic, see Epicurean.—*Acts* 17. 18

Straight (Street.)—*Acts* 9. 11

Susanna.—*Lu.* 8. 3

Sychar.—*Jno.* 4. 5

Symeon.—*Lu.* 3. 30 : *Acts* 13. 1 ; 15. 14

Syntyche.—*Phil.* 4. 2

SYRACUSE

Syracuse.—*Acts* 28. 12

Syria.

Mat. 4. 24. the report of him went forth into all *Syria*
Lu. 2. 2. when Quirinus was governor of *Syria*
Acts 15. 23. the Gentiles in Antioch and *Syria*
    41. went through *Syria* and Cilicia confirming
18. 18. sailed thence for *Syria*. 20. 3 : 21. 3
Gal. 1. 21. I came into the regions of *Syria* and Cilicia

Syrian.—*Lu.* 4. 27

Syrophœnician.—*Mk.* 7. 26

Syrtis.—*A.V. quicksands.*—*Acts* 27. 17

T.

Tabitha.—*Acts* 9. 36, 40

Tamar.—*Mat.* 1. 3

Tarsus.

Acts 9. 11. inquire—for one named Saul, a man of *Tarsus*
    30. and sent him forth to *Tarsus*
    11. 25. [Barnabas] went forth to *Tarsus* to seek for Saul
    21. 39. Paul said, I am a Jew, of *Tarsus*. 22. 3

Terah.—*Lu.* 3. 34

Tertius.—*Rom.* 16. 22

Tertullus.—*Acts* 24. 1, 2

Thaddæus.—*Mat.* 10. 3: *Mk.* 3. 18

Theophilus.—*Lu.* 1. 3 : *Acts* 1. 1

Thessalonica.

Acts 17. 1. to *T.*, where was a synagogue of the Jews
    11. these were more noble than those in *Thessalonica*
    13. But when the Jews of *Thessalonica* had knowledge
    27. 2. Aristarchus, a Macedonian of *T.*, being with us
Phil. 4. 16. for even in *Thessalonica* ye sent once [to *T.*
2 *Tim.* 4. 10. Demas—loved this present world, and went

Thessalonians.—*Acts* 20. 4 ; 1 *Th.* 1. 1 ; 2 *Th.* 1. 1

Theudas.—*Acts* 5. 36

Thomas.

Mat. 10. 3. *Thomas. Mk.* 3. 18 ; *Lu.* 6. 15 : *Acts* 1. 13
Jno. 11. 16. *Thomas*—called Didymus. 20. 24 : 21. 2
    14. 5. *Thomas* saith unto him, Lord, we know not
    20. 26. disciples were within, and *Thomas* with them
    27. saith he to *Thomas*, Reach hither thy finger
    28. *Thomas*—said unto him, My Lord and my God

Three Taverns.—*Acts* 28. 15

Thyatira.

Acts 16. 14. Lydia, a seller of purple, of the city of *T.*
Rev. 1. 11. to the seven churches—unto *Thyatira*
    2. 18. to the angel of the church in *Thyatira* write
    24. I say, to the rest that are in *Thyatira*

TYRANNUS

Tiberias.—*Jno.* 6. 1, 23 : 21. 1

Tiberius Cæsar.—*Lu.* 3. 1

Timæus.—*Mk.* 10. 46

Timon.—*Acts* 6. 5

Timothy.

Acts 16. 1. disciple was there, named *Timothy*
    17. 14. and Silas and *Timothy* abode there still
    15. receiving a commandment unto Silas and *Timothy*
    18. 5. when Silas and *T.* came down from Macedonia
    19. 22. having sent into Macedonia—*T.* and Erastus
    20. 4. there accompanied him as far as Asia—*Timothy*
Rom. 16. 21. *Timothy* my fellow-worker saluteth you
1 *Cor.* 4. 17. have I sent unto you *Timothy*. 1 *Th.* 3. 2
    16. 10. if *Timothy* come see that he be—without fear
2 *Cor.* 1. 1. *Timothy* our brother. *Col.* 1. 1 : *Phil.* 1
    19. by us, even by me and Silvanus and *Timothy*
Phil. 1. 1. Paul and *Timothy*, servants of Christ Jesus
    2. 19. hope in the Lord Jesus to send *Timothy*
1 *Th.* 1. 1. Paul, and Silvanus, and *Timothy*. 2 *Th.* 1. 1
    3. 6. when *Timothy* came even now unto us from you
1 *Tim.* 1. 2. unto *Timothy*, my true child. 18 : 2 *Tim.* 1. 2
    6. 20. O *Timothy*, guard that which is committed
Heb. 13. 23. our brother *Timothy* hath been set at liberty

Titus.

2 *Cor.* 2. 13. because I found not *Titus* my brother
    7. 6. comforted us by the coming of *Titus*
    13. joyed the more exceedingly for the joy of *Titus*
    14. our glorying also, which I made before *Titus*
    8. 6. Insomuch that we exhorted *Titus*
    16. earnest care for you into the heart of *Titus*
    23. Whether any inquire about *Titus*, he is my partner
    12. 18. I exhorted *Titus*—Did *Titus* take any advantage
Gal. 2. 1. with Barnabas, taking *Titus* also with me
    3. not even *Titus* who was with me, being a Greek
2 *Tim.* 4. 10. Crescens to Galatia, *Titus* to Dalmatia
Tit. 1. 4. to *Titus*, my true child after a common faith

Titus Justus.—*Acts* 18. 7

Trachonitis.—*Lu.* 3. 1

Troas.

Acts 16. 8. passing by Mysia, they came down to *Troas*
    11. Setting sail therefore from *Troas*
    20. 5. waiting for us at *Troas*. 6
2 *Cor.* 2. 12. when I came to *Troas* for the gospel of Christ
2 *Tim.* 4. 13. The cloke that I left at *Troas* with Carpus

Trophimus.—*Acts* 20. 4 : 21. 29 : 2 *Tim.* 4. 20

Tryphæna.—*Rom.* 16. 12

Tryphosa.—*Rom.* 16. 12

Twin Brothers (The).—*Acts* 28. 11

Tychicus.

Acts 20. 4. and of Asia, *Tychicus* and Trophimus
Eph. 6. 21. *Tychicus*, the beloved brother
Col. 4. 7. All my affairs shall *T.* make known unto you
2 *Tim.* 4. 12. But *Tychicus* I sent to Ephesus
Tit. 3. 12. I shall send Artemas unto thee, or *Tychicus*

Tyrannus.—*Acts* 19. 9

TYRE

Tyre.
Mat. 11. 21. *Tyre* and Sidon. 22: 15. 21; Mk. 3. 8: 7. 24.
  31: Lu. 6. 17: 10. 13, 14
Acts 12. 20. highly displeased with them of *Tyre*
21. 3. we sailed unto Syria, and landed at *Tyre*
7. when we had finished the voyage from *Tyre*

U.

Urbanus—A.V. *Urbane*. Rom. 16. 9

Uriah.—Mat. 1. 6

Uzziah.—A.V. *Ozias*. Mat. 1. 8, 9

W.

Way (The).—Acts 9. 2: 19. 9, 23: 22. 3: 24. 14, 22

Word.—Jno. 1. 1: 1 Jno. 1. 2: Rev. 19. 13

Wormwood.—Rev. 8. 11

Z.

Zacchæus.—Lu. 19. 2, 5, 8

Zachariah.—Mat. 23. 35: Lu. 11. 51

Zacharias.
Lu. 1. 5. priest named *Zacharias*, of the course of Abijah
  12. and *Zacharias* was troubled
  13. Fear not, Z. ; because thy supplication is heard
  18. *Zacharias* said unto the angel

ZION

Lu. 1. 21. people were waiting for Z., and they marvelled
  40. into the house of *Zacharias* and saluted Elisabeth
  59. would have called him *Zacharias*, after—his father
  67. father *Zacharias* was filled with the Holy Ghost
3. 2. word of God came unto John the son of *Zacharias*

Zerephath.—Lu. 4. 26

Zealot.—A.V. *Zelotes*.—Lu. 6. 15: Acts. 1. 13

Zebedee.
Mat. 4. 21. in the boat with *Zebedee*. Mk. 1. 20
  20. 20. came to him the mother of the sons of Z. 27. 56
  26. 37. the two sons of *Zebedee*. 4. 21: 10. 2: Mk. 1. 19:
    3. 17: 10. 35: Lu. 5. 10: Jno. 21. 2

Zebulun.
Mat. 4. 13. in the borders of *Zebulun* and Naphtali
  15. The land of *Zebulun*, and the land of Naphtali
Rev. 7. 8. tribe of *Zebulun* [were sealed] twelve thousand

Zelotes, *see Simon.*

Zenas.—Tit. 3. 13

Zerah.—Mat. 1. 3

Zerubbabel.—Mat. 1. 12, 13: Lu. 3. 27

Zion.
Mat. 21. 5. Tell ye the daughter of *Zion*
Jno. 12. 15. Fear not, daughter of *Zion*
Rom. 9. 33. Behold, I lay in *Zion* a stone of stumbling
  11. 26. There shall come out of *Zion* the Deliverer
Heb. 12. 22. ye are come unto mount *Zion*
1 Pet. 2. 6. Behold, I lay in *Zion* a chief corner stone
Rev. 14. 1. behold, the Lamb standing on the mount *Zion*

APPENDIX I.

OMITTED WORDS OF AUTHORISED VERSION.

This Appendix is inserted by permission from "Ely Lectures on the Revised Version," by Canon Kennedy, D.D.—Bentley, 1881.*

MATTHEW.

1. 25. firstborn
2. 18. lamentation, and
5. 22. without a cause
27. by them of old time
44. bless them that curse you, do good to them that hate you —despitefully use you, and
6. 4. himself
13. for thine is the kingdom, and the power, and the glory, for ever, Amen.
33. of God
8. 32. swine
9. 13. to repentance
35. among the people
10. 3. Lebbæus, whose surname was
18. 9, 43. to hear
44. Again
51. Jesus saith unto them —Lord
14. 30. boisterous
33. came and
15. 4. commanded
8. draweth nigh unto me with their mouth, and
14. of the blind
17. yet
16. 3. O ye hypocrites
4. the prophet
17. 21. Howbeit, this kind goeth not out, but by prayer and fasting
26. Peter
18. 11. For the Son of man is come to save that which was lost
29. at his feet
— all
35. their trespasses
19. 20. from my youth up
29. or wife
20. 6. idle

20. 7. and whatsoever is right, that shall ye receive
16. for many be called, but few chosen
22, 23. and to be baptized with the baptism that I am baptized with?
34. eyes
22. 13. take him away, and
30. of God
23. 8. even Christ
14. Woe unto you, scribes and Pharisees, hypocrites! for ye devour widows' houses, and for a pretence make long prayer; therefore ye shall receive the greater damnation
19. fools and
24. 2. Jesus
25. 6. cometh
13. wherein the Son of man cometh
20, 22. besides them
31. holy
26. 3. and the scribes
24. now
55. with you
59. and elders
60. false witnesses
63. answered and
27. 23. governor
35. that it might be fulfilled which was spoken by the prophet, They parted my garments among them, and upon my vesture did they cast lots
58. body
61. by night
28. 2. from the door
9. as they went to tell his disciples
20. Amen

MARK.

1. 13. there
14. of the kingdom
19. thence
24. Let us alone
31. immediately
42. as soon as he had spoken
2. 2. straightway
17. to repentance
22. new
— spilled
3. 5. whole as the other
15. to heal sicknesses, and
5. 13. Jesus
40. lying
6. 11. Verily I say unto you, It shall be more tolerable for Sodom and Gomorrha in the day of judgment, than for that city
36. bread
51. beyond measure, and wondered
7. 2. they found fault
4. and of tables
8. as the washing of pots, and cups: and many other such like things ye do
12. And *(the erasure of this particle changes the construction of* 11-12, *and renders the added "he shall be free" needless*
16. If any man have ears to hear, let him hear
35. straightway
8. 9. that had eaten
17. yet
26. nor tell it to any in the town
9. 3. as snow
23. believe
24. with tears, Lord
29. and fasting

---

* Appendix III. of the above work consists of "Select Textual Corrections in the Revised Version of the New Text," and shews changes or corrections made in the Revised Version, and words omitted. As the changed words are shewn in the body of the Concordance, the omitted words only are given here.

APPENDIX I.

9. 33. among yourselves
 58. and he followeth not us
 44, 46. Where their worm dieth not, and the fire is not quenched
 45. into the fire that never shall be quenched
 49. and every sacrifice shall be salted with salt
10. 6. God
 21. take up the cross, and
 29. or wife
 46. begging
11. 8. and strawed them in the way
 10. in the name of the Lord
 26. But if you do not forgive, neither will your Father which is in heaven, forgive your trespasses
 29. also
12. 4. they cast stones
 6. also
 22. had her, and
 23. therefore, when they shall rise
 27. God
 — therefore
 30. this is the first commandment
 31. like
 33. and with all the soul
13. 8. and troubles
 14. spoken of by Daniel the prophet
 22. even
14. 19. and another said, Is it I
 22. eat
 24. now
 27. because of me this night
 31. the more
 43. great
 52. from them
 70. and thy speech agreeth thereto
15. 3. but he answered nothing
 7. with him
 28. And the scripture was fulfilled, which saith, And he was numbered with the transgressors

LUKE.

1. 28. blessed art thou among women
 29. when she saw him
 35. of thee
 75. life
2. 9. lo,
 40. in spirit
 42. to Jerusalem
4. 4. but by every word of God
 8. Get thee behind me, Satan: for
 18. to heal the brokenhearted
 41. Christ
5 33 Why do
 38. and both are preserved
 39. straightway
6. 10. whole as the other
 16. also

6. 45. of his heart
7. 10. that had been sick
 11. many of
 31. And the Lord said
 44. of—head
8. 20. by certain which said
 34. and went
 45. and sayest thou, Who touched me?
 48. be of good comfort
 54. put them all out, and
9. 1. his—disciples
 7. by him
 10. desert place belonging to
 54. even as Elias did?
 55, 56. and said, Ye know not what manner of spirit ye are of. For the Son of man is not come to destroy men's lives, but to save them
 57. it came to pass
 — Lord
10. 1. also
 11. unto you
 20. rather
 35. when he departed
 38. it came to pass
11. 2. which art in heaven, Thy will be done as in heaven
 4. but deliver us from evil
 29. the prophet [cries!
 44. scribes and Pharisees, hypo-
 54. that they might accuse him
12. 31. all
13. 19. great
 35. verily
 — the time come when
15. 21. make me as one of thy hired servants.
17. 9. I trow not
 36. Two men shall be in the field; the one shall be taken, and the other left
19. 45. therein, and them that bought
20. 13. when they see him
 14. come
 23. Why tempt ye me?
 30. childless
21. 4. of God
22. 31. And the Lord said
 64. they struck him on the face
 68. me, nor let me go
23. 17. For of necessity he must release one unto them at the feast
 23. and of the chief priests
 38. in letters of Greek, and Latin, and Hebrew
 42. Lord
24. 1. and certain others with them
 42. and of an honeycomb
 40. of Jerusalem
 53. praising and
 — Amen

JOHN.

1. 40. and saith unto
 51. Hereafter

4. 4. the Christ
 43. and went
 51. and told him
5. 3. great
 3, 4. waiting for the moving of the water. For an angel went down at a certain season into the pool, and troubled the water: whosoever then first after the troubling of the water stepped in, was made whole of whatsoever disease he had
 16. and sought to slay him
 27. also
 30. Father
6. 11. to the disciples, and the disciples
 22. when
 — whereinto his disciples were entered
 51. which I will give
 58. your—manner
7. 20. and said
 30. by night
 39. Holy
8. 6. as though he heard them not
 9. being convicted by their own conscience
 10. and saw none but the woman
 20. Father
 59. going through the midst of them, and so passed by
9. 6. of the blind man
 11 the pool of
10. 12. the sheep
 13. the hireling
 26. as I said unto you
11. 41. from the place where the dead was laid
12 1. which had been dead
 4. Simon's son
13. 32. If God be glorified in him
16. 16. because I go to the Father
17. 12. in the world
18. 40. all
20. 29. Thomas
21. 25. Amen

ACTS.

1. 14. and supplication
 19. proper
2. 7. one to another
 30. according to the flesh, he would raise up Christ
 31. his soul
 33. now
 41. gladly
3. 6. rise up and
 22. unto the fathers
 26. Jesus
4. 17. straitly
 24. thou art God
5. 24. the high priest and
6. 3. Holy
 13. blasphemous
7. 30. of the Lord

APPENDIX I.

7. 32. the God (2)
37. the Lord your
8. 37. him shall ye hear
believest with all thine heart, thou mayest. And he answered, and said, I believe that Jesus Christ is the Son of God
9. 5, 6. it is hard for thee to kick against the pricks. And he, trembling and astonished said, Lord, what wilt thou have me to do? And the Lord said unto him
12. in a vision
13. forthwith
19, 26. Saul
10. 6. he shall tell thee what thou oughtest to do
11. unto him
21. which were sent unto him from Cornelius
23. Peter
30. fasting
32. who, when he cometh, shall speak unto thee
11. 22. but he should go
28. Cæsar.
13. 42. the Jews—out of the synagogue, the Gentiles
14. 28. there
15. 11. Christ
18. unto God are all his works
24. saying, ye must be circumcised, and keep the law
34. Notwithstanding it pleased Silas to abide there still
16. 31. Christ
17. 5. which believed not
26. blood
18. 1. Paul
21. I must by all means keep this feast that cometh in Jerusalem; but
19. 4. Christ
10. Jesus
35. goddess
20. 15. and tarried at Trogyllium
24. with joy
25. of God
21. 8. that were of Paul's company
22. the multitude must needs come together
25. that they observe no such thing, save only
22. 20. unto his death
30. from his bands
23. 9. let us not fight against God
30. the Jews—Farewell
31. governor
24. 6-8. and would have judged according to our law. But the chief captain Lysias came upon us, and with great violence took him away out of our hands: Commanding his accusers to come unto thee
25. 16. to die

28. 16. the centurion delivered the prisoners to the Captain of the guard: but
29. And when he had said these words, the Jews departed, and had great reasoning among themselves

ROMANS.

1. 16. of Christ
24. also
29. fornication
31. implacable
3. 22. and upon all
4. 11. also
6. 11. our Lord
12. it in
7. 18. I find
8. 1. who walk not after the flesh, but after the Spirit
34. even
9. 31. of righteousness
32. works of the law: For
10. 15. preach the gospel of peace, and
11. 6. But if it be of works, then is it no more grace: otherwise work is no more work
13. 9. Thou shalt not bear false witness
14. 6. and he that regardeth not the day, to the Lord he doth not regard it
9. rose
21. or is offended, or is made weak
15. 8. Jesus
15. brethren
24. I will come to you
29. of the gospel
16. 18. Jesus
24. The grace of our Lord Jesus Christ be with you all. Amen

I. CORINTHIANS.

2. 13. Holy
3. 3. and divisions
5. 3. as
4. Christ (2)
7. for us
13. therefore
6. 20. and in your spirit, which are God's
7. 5. fasting and
8. 4. other
9. 1. Christ
18. of Christ
22. as
10. 9, 10. also
23. for me, (2)
28. unto idols
— for the earth is the Lord's and the fulness thereof
11. 2. brethren,
21. Take, eat
— broken

11. 29. unworthily
14. 25. And thus
15. 20. and become
47. the Lord
16. 22. Jesus Christ

II. CORINTHIANS.

4. 10. the Lord
5. 12. For
18. Jesus
21. For
7. 16. therefore
8. 19. same
9. 4. boasting
11. 3. so
31. Christ
12. 11. in glorying
13. 2. I write
4. though
14. Amen

GALATIANS.

3. 1. that ye should not obey the truth
— among you?
17. in Christ
5. 19. Adultery
21. murders
6. 15. in Christ Jesus
17. the Lord

EPHESIANS.

3. 9. by Jesus Christ
14. of our Lord Jesus Christ
4. 9. first
5. 30. of his flesh, and of his bones
6. 10. my brethren
12. world

PHILIPPIANS.

4. 13. Christ

COLOSSIANS.

1. 2. and the Lord Jesus Christ
14. through his blood
16. that are (2)
28. Jesus
2. 2. and of the Father
11. of the sins
18. not
3. 18. own
4. 18. Amen

I. THESSALONIANS.

1. 1. from God our Father, and the Lord Jesus Christ
2. 15. own
19. Christ
3. 2. and our fellowlabourer
11. 13. Christ
4. 11. own
5. 27. holy
28. Amen

APPENDIX I.

II. THESSALONIANS.

1. 8. Christ
   12. Christ (1)
2. 4. as God
   16. even
3. 18. Amen

I. TIMOTHY.

1. 1. Lord
   17. wise
2. 3. For
   7. in Christ
3. 3. not greedy of filthy lucre
4. 12. in spirit
5. 4. good and
   16. man or
   21. Lord
6. 5. from such withdraw thyself
   7. and it is certain
   12. also
   17. the living
   21. Amen

II. TIMOTHY.

1. 11. of the Gentiles
4. 1. Lord
   22. Jesus Christ
   — Amen

TITUS.

1. 4. Lord
2. 7. sincerity
3. 15. Amen

PHILEMON.

6. Jesus

HEBREWS.

3. 1. Christ
6. 10. labour

7. 4. even
   21. after the order of Melchisedec
8. 12. and their iniquities
10. 9. O God
    30. saith the Lord
11. 11. and was delivered of a child
    13. and were persuaded of them
    32. and of (3)
12. 20. or thrust through with a dart
13. 6. and

JAMES.

1. 25. he
4. 4. adulterers and
5. 5. as

I. PETER.

1. 7. much
   22. through the Spirit
   — pure
   23. for ever
2. 12. shall
3. 16. as of evildoers
   20. once
4. 1. for us
   3. of our life
   — us
   14. on their part he is evil spoken of, but on your part he is glorified
5. 10. Jesus
   — settle
   11. glory and
   14. Jesus. Amen

II. PETER.

1. 21. holy
3. 10. in the night

I. JOHN.

3. 14. his brother
4. 3. that

4. 3. Christ is come in the flesh
5. 7. in heaven the Father, the Word, and the holy Ghost: and these three are one
   8. and there are three that bear witness in earth
   13. that believe on the name of the Son of God
   21. Amen

II. JOHN.

3. the Lord
9. of Christ
13. Amen

JUDE.

25. wise

REVELATION.

1. 8. the beginning and the ending
   9. Christ (2)
   11. I am Alpha and Omega, the first and the last: and
   13. seven
   18. Amen
2. 7. the midst of
   9. works, and
5. 14. him that liveth for ever and ever
6. 1, 3, 5, 7, and see
7. 5-8 were sealed (except of Judah and Benjamin)
11. 17. and art to come
12. 17. Christ
14. 5. before the throne of God
16. 3, 4, 8, 10, 12, 17. angel
   5. O Lord
   17. of heaven
18. 2. mightily
22. 1. pure
   20. Even so

APPENDIX II.
NEW AND DISUSED WORDS, AND ALTERED SPELLING.
NEW WORDS.

A List of Words used in the Revised Version, and which do not appear in the Authorised. The old words for which they have been substituted are given in the body of the Concordance.

In some cases an entirely new root-word or its inflexions or derivatives have been introduced by the Revisers, as: *decide, decision; snatch, snatcheth, snatching*. In other instances the word is not thus entirely new, but is connected with some word or words in the Authorised Version, as *healeth, healings*; the words *heal, healed, healing*, appearing in the old version. Words of this latter class are printed in italics.

Abidest
Abyss
Accounteth
Accurately
Active
Acts
Actually
Advanced
Affirming
Afflict
Aforepromised
Aim
Amidst
Ancient
Anew
Animals
Announce—d
Anxiety
Anxious
Apparition
Appointeth—ing
Apportioned
Aright
Arisen—ing
Array—ing
Arrive
Ashore
Assassins
Assemble
Attendant
Aught
Autumn (see trees)
Avenging
Awe

Baggage
Bank (trench)
Bankers
Bathed
Bay
Beach
Bearers
Befitting
Believer
Bereaved, bereft
Beseecheth
Besoughtest
Betrothed
Biddeth—ing
Billows
Blowing
Blows
Bond
Bondservant—s
Boon
Bowl—s

Boy
Branded
Break–broken fast
Broke
Broken pieces
Burnished

Carousings
Casting off (nautical)
Causing
Cell
Cellar
Circuit
Citizenship
Clanging
Cleanness
Close sealed
Coast (verb)
Collections
Communicating
Compassions—ate
Completed—ly—tion
Concealed
Conduct (noun)
Confuted
Console
Continency
Convict—eth
Copy—ies
Councillor
Coveting—s
Create
Cross—ed—ing
Crowd
Cruse
Crush
Cushion

Dance
Daring
Dashed—eth
Dawn (noun)
Daybreak
Dazzling
Deal (verb)
Deathstroke
Decide, decision
Defect
Defilement—s
Defineth
Delivereth
Demeanour
Deposed
Despairing

Destroyeth
Destroying (noun)
Destructive
Diadems
Difficulty
Disbelieve—d—eth
Discharged
Discipline
Discoursed
Dishonoured
Disparagement
Dispersion
Dispute—s
Disrepute
Divinity
Doomed
Drag—ged
Drift
Drinker
Dysentery

Earnestness
Effulgence
Embarking
Emperor
Emptied
Enacted
Encounter
Encourage—d—ing—ment
Enmities
Enrol—led—ment
Enslaved
Ensnare
Entice
Epileptic
Erring
Escaping
Exact (adjective)
Exacted—ly
Excellencies
Exercising
Exhortations
Expect—ed—eth
Explain
Extort

Faction—s
Face (verb)
Factious
Failed
Fainthearted
Fainting
Falsehood
Fall off (nautical)

Families
Fashioneth
Fearfulness
Fellow-citizen
Fellow-elder
Fellow-members
Fellow-partakers
Fellow-worker
Fickleness
Fighting
Final
Finishing
Fitting
Flute-players
Forefather
Foregoing
Foresail
Foreshewed
Forfeit
Forgot
Foster-brother
Freedman
Freight
Fullgrown

Gainsaid
Games
Gangrene
Gave way (nautical)
Gear
Genealogy
Gently
Glassy
Glories—ed—est
Glorifieth
Gluttons
Goad
Goal
Goings
Grandchildren
Granting
Gratulation
Griefs
Guard (verb) guards—ed—eth—ians
Guileless

Hades
Handed
Hanging
Hardening
Hardship
Haughty
Hazarding
Healeth
Healings

APPENDIX II.

Hardest
Heavier
Hindrance
Hoisting
Holy of Holies
Holy Ones
Hosts
Hyacinth

Imitate—tors
Implanted
Impostors
Impulse
Indulgence
Inside
Insolent
Insurrections
Interest
Interposed
Interrogation
Intreating
Intrusted
Irksome
Its

Jealousies
Justice

Killedst
Kinswoman

Lascivious
Late, later
Lawlessness
Lawsuits
Lay out (nautical)
Lee (nautical)
Lender
Life-giving
Lighting
Listening
Longing
Lord—ing
Love-feasts
Loving
Lowered—ing

Maidservants
Mantle
Mariners
Marvelling
Meddler
Mere
Mess
Mid heaven
Ministrations
Mirror
Mists
Mockery
Moored

Narrative
Neighbourhood
North-east

Objects (noun)
Occasions
Offereth
Olives (fruit)
Onset
Onward
Overboard

Overflow—ing
Overlooked
Over-ripe
Overshadowing

Pangs
Part (verb) parting
Perfecter
Perishing
Perverted
Pits
Planks
Pleadeth
Plot—s
Portions
Powerfully
Prætorian guard
Precede
Preciousness
Prejudice
Priced
Prison-house
Probation
Proclaim
Proconsul—s
Progress
Prolonged
Promising
Pronounced—eth
Proveth
Proving (noun)
Publishing
Punishing
Pursue—d
Put—ting to sea

Questioning—s
Quit (free from)

Rabble
Race (generation)
Ranus
Reasoneth
Reasonings
Reckonest—ing
Reclining
Refined
Reflecting
Regret
Regular
Rehearsing
Reigning
Reminded
Rendered
Renounceth
Restless
Restoration
Restraineth
Revealing
Revel—ling
Reverent
Reviler—ing
Rid
Riding
Rocky
Roll (noun)
Roused
Rudders
Rusted
Sacred
Saileth

Scatter
Scorching
Seated
Seemly
Seized
Self-condemned
Self-control
Senseless
Separateth—tions
Services
Set—ting sail
Severed
Shameful
Sharers
Shekel, half shekel
Shewn
Shouted
Shrank, shrink
Shudder
Silent
Sinning
Skins (wineskins)
Sluggish
Smiting
Snatch—eth—ing
Sojourner—s
Solid
Somewhere
South-east
Sowing
Spice
Springs
Stablishing
Steep (noun)
Steersman
Stirring
Stored
Story (loft)
Stretchest
Strict
Stroke
Strolling
Stupor
Subjecting
Succeeded
Sum—med (verb)
Sumptuous
Sunrising
Surge
Surmised
Surpasseth
Suspense
Swearers
Swiftly

Tarrieth—ing
Touchings
Tear (noun)
Temple-keeper
Tend
Tenderly
Tents
Torn
Terrors
Thinking
Thresh
Threshing-floor
Throw—ing
Tilled
Toll

Torch
Traced—ing
Trade (noun)
Train
Tranquil
Treasurer
Treated
Trials
Trusteth
Turneth
Tutor

Unapproachable
Unbeliever
Unceasing—ly
Uncertainty
Underneath
Undressed
Unfaithful
United
Unlifted
Unmixed
Unripe
Unseemliness
Unsettle
Unstedfast
Unveiled
Uprightness
Useful
Uttering

Vainglorious
Vauntings
Victorious
Villany
Vinedresser
Vintage
Visiteth
Vote
Vouchsafed

Wallet
Wantonly
Wasting
Watchers
Waterless
Weakened
Weaknesses
Weighed
Weighed anchor
Welcome—d
Wet—ted
Wheel
Whiten
Wickednesses
Wine-bibbings
Wine-skins
Wishing
Withstandeth
Workest
Workings
World rulers
Worn (verb, wear
Worthily
Wounding
Wranglings
Writeth
Writing-tablet
Wrong-doer
Wrong-doing

APPENDIX II.
DISUSED WORDS.

A list of words which appear in the Authorised Version, but which are not used in the Revised. Words now disused, but connected with others occurring in the Authorised Version are printed in Italics.

Abstinence
Abuse
Acceptably
Accomplishment
Acknowledged—eth—
   ing—ment
Addicted
Administered-ration-s
Admired—ation
Advantaged—eth
Adversity
Advice
Affect
Afoot
Alas
Allow- ed—eth
Allure
Appeased
Approach—eth—ing
Ascendeth
Assented
Atonement
Attended
Attentive
Avoid
Awaking

Backside
Banquetings
Barbarous
Baser
Battle
Beateth
Beguiling
Bellies
Benevolence
Bishoprick
Bits
Blaspheming—ously
Blaze
Blessedness
Blindness
Bloody flux
Blotting
Boards
Boisterous
Bondmaid—woman
Bottles
Bottomless pit
Bountifulness
Box
Brawlers
Breaker—s
Briers
Brokenhearted
Brotherly
Brute
Busybody
By and by

Cage
Candle
Canker—ed
Carefulness
Carnally
Carriages
Castaway
Catcheth
Certify
Chargeable
Charity—ably
Chastisement
Circumspectly
Closet—s
Cloven
Comers
Commonly
Commotious
Comparison
Comprehend—ed
Concupiscence
Condemneth
Conference
Conformable
Confound
Confused
Consecrated
Constantly
Consulted—eth
Contemptible
Conversation
Converted
Convince—d—eth
Countries
Courteous
Cousins
Craved
Creditor
Creek
Crimes
Cumbereth
Cunning
Curseth

Damage
Damned—able—ation
Deacon
Dearly
Dearth
Debate—s
Deceivableness
Deceivings
Declaration
Decreed
Deemed
Delicacies
Deliciously
Demanded
Departing (verb)
Depths
Deputy—ies

Derided
Descendeth
Described
Desiredst
Despiseth
Despiteful
Devotions
Diminishing
Dined
Disallowed
Discovered
Discreet
Diseased
Dishonesty
Disposition
Distributing
Ditch
Divorced
Drawback
Dressed—er
Drove
Drowned
Dureth (endureth)

Easter
Edges
Effectually
Elected
Eloquent
Embraced
Emulation—s
Endeavour—ing
Ending
Endued
Engrafted
Ensue
Entangle
Entertain
Equals
Eschew
Estates
Esteemed—ing
Evidence
Evidently
Excel—leth
Exclude
Executioner
Expelled
Experiment
Expired
Express

Fainted
Faults
Feebleminded
Feign
Fellow-helper—s
Fellow-labourer
Finisher
Fleshy
Floor

Flourished
Flux
Fold (verb)
Followers
Foolishly
Forepart
Foresaw
Foretell—told
Forgetful
Forsaketh
Forward—ness
Fragments
Frankly
Freed
Frequent
Fresh
Frustrate
Furtherance

Gains
Garrison
Gatherings
Gay
Gazing
Gendereth
Gnasheth
Grave—s
Greedily
Grudge—ing
Guest

Habitations
Hall
Handwriting
Haters—red
Heaped
Heathen
Hedged
Helm
Hem
Heresy
Hideth
Highway
Hinder-part (stern)
Holiest
Honesty

Illuminated
Immortal
Imparted
Implead
Impute—eth—ing
Incontinent
Inexcusable
Infants
Infidel
Inhabitants—ers
Inordinate
Instantly
Instructor—s
Intruding

APPENDIX II.

Issued

Jangling
Joyful—ness
Judgement-hall

Keeper—est
Kindleth
Kindreds
Kinsfolks

Laded
Lauding
Late (of late)
Laud
Launch
Leaders
Leddest
Let—teth (to hinder)
Lewd—ness
Liberal
Licence
Lightness
Limiteth
Line
Lineage
Lively
Loft
Looking (noun)
Lunatick

Maidens
Mainsail
Malicious
Manifestly
Market—s
Marred
Martyr
Memory
Mischief
Mixed
Moderation
Morsel
Mortality
Motions
Moving
Mused
Musicians
Mutual

Naughtiness
Neglecting
Negligent
Nephews
North-west
Notice
Nourishment

Object
Occupy—iety

Odours
Omitted
Omnipotent
Operation—s
Ornament
Overcharge
Overseers

Pained—fulness
Paps
Partial
Particular—ly
Patterns
Peaceably
Peculiar
Penury
Perceivest
Performed—ance
Perilous
Perjured
Pernicious
Pertaineth
Pillow
Pipers
Plain (level place)
Plainness
Polluted
Powder
Praised—s
Predestinate—d
Preferred
Premeditate
Presently
Press (noun)
Presumptuous
Prevent—ed
Pricks
Professed—ion
Profiting
Proper
Proposed
Prosperous
Pulled—ing
Purged—eth—ing
Purposeth

Quarrel
Quarters
Quickening
Quicksands

Raising
Rear
Receipt
Recommended
Record
Redound
Regarding
Remainest—ing
Remit—ted
Reproachfully

Reprobates
Resemble
Reserve
Resort
Restitution
Revenge—r
Reward—ed

Sacrilege
Sang
Sardine
Savourest
Schoolmaster
Science
Scrip
Seared
Seemed
Shadowing
Shape
Sharpness
Sheepfold
Shipmen
Shipping
Shooteth
Shunned
Sights
Similitude
Skin—s
Sky
Slip
Slumber
Solitary
Sometime—s
Sorrowed
South-west
Spitefully
Spitted
Spoiled
Sporting
Staggered
Stead
Stepped
Stony
Straitly
Strake
Strawed
String
Strived—ings
Stuck
Stuff
Stumblingstone
Subdue
Submitted—ing
Subvert—ed
Succoured
Sucked
Sue
Sundry
Superstition
Supped
Surely
Sweetsmelling

Tales
Talk—est—eth
Taxed—ing
Terrible
Testator
Thankworthy
Thunderings
Tinkling
Toiling
Town
Transforming
Transgresseth
Travelling
Trench
Trieth
Troubles
Trow
Trucebreakers
Trying

Unction
Unrebukeable
Unskilful
Untaken
Untimely
Untoward
Uppermost
Useth
Usurp
Usury

Vagabond
Valiant
Valued
Vanities
Venomous
Verity
Vex
Vial—s
Vigilant
Violent—ly
Vocation
Volume

Wailing (noun)
Wandered
Wanted
Wave
Ware (verb, wear)
Waxing
Weariness
Wholesome
Whore—monger—s
Winefat
Winked
Wit
Witchcraft
Witnessing
Won
Wound (noun)

APPENDIX II.

The following Table shews the instances in which both New and Disused Words are from the same root.

NEW.	DISUSED.	NEW.	DISUSED.
Approveth	Approving	Injury—ies	Injured
Assaulting	Assault—ed	Inspired	Inspiration
Balance	Balances	Mastered	Mastery—ies
Basketfuls	Basketsfull	Mindest	Minding
Bewailing	Bewail	Obeyeth	Obeying
Bewitch	Bewitched	Offenders	Offences, offend—er
Boastful	Boast—ed—ers -ing—s	Palsied -	Palsies
Causing	Causes	Partake—took—eth—ing	Partakest
Cherubim	Cherubims	Persuasive—ness	Persuadest
Coasting	Coasts	Pitiable	Pitiful
Comforting	Comfortless	Pondering	Poudered
Complaint	Complaints	Practise—d	Practises
Concluding	Conclude—d	Precepts	Precept
Continuest	Continuance	Provideth	Providing
Contradicted	Contradicting—ion	Rail—ers	Railer
Correcting—or	Corrected	Rash	Rashly
Corrupting	Corrupteth	Repute—d	Reputation
Countest—ing	Counteth	Requireth	Require—ing
Decaying	Decay—eth	Riotously	Rioting
Delude—ing	Delusion	Rob	Robbery
Different	Differences	Satisfied	Satisfy—ing
Discernings—ment	Discerner—ing	Scoffed -	Scoffers
Dispute—s	Disputation	Secondly	Secondarily
Dreamings	Dreamers	Seduceth	Seduce—ers
Exchanged	Exchangers	Shamefastness	Shamefacedness
Faithfulness	Faithfully	Stoneth	Stonest
Faring	Fared	Store-chamber	Store-house
Fellow-worker	Workfellow	Tearing	Teareth
Flattery	Flattering	Tiles	Tiling
Foreign	Foreigners	Urged—urgent	Urge
Foreknown	Foreknow	Vanishing	Vanish
Fulfilment	Fulfilling (noun)	Variation	Variableness
Greeted	Greet—eth—ings	Warneth	Warning
Grindeth	Grind	Warred	Warreth
Hastening	Hasted—ing	Waver—ed	Wavereth—ing
Headstrong	Heady	Withold	Withholdeth
Heretical	Heretick	Wounding	Wound
Humbleminded	Humbleness	Wrestling	Wrestle

The following Words have been altered in the Spelling.

NEW.	DISUSED.
Ankle	Ancle
Aught	Ought (anything)
Braided	Broided—ered
Chrysoprase	Chrysoprasus
Graft—ed	Graff—ed
Hallelujah	Alleluia
Hoisted	Hoised
Lowring	Lowering
Outrun	Ontrun
Spew	Spue
Sponge	Spunge
Stoic	Stoicks
Incorruptible	Uncorruptible
Veil	Vail

APPENDIX III.

LIST OF READINGS AND RENDERINGS PREFERRED BY THE AMERICAN COMMITTEE,

RECORDED AT THEIR DESIRE.

CLASSES OF PASSAGES.

1. Strike out "S." (i. e. Saint) from the title of the Gospels and from the heading of the pages.
2. Strike out "the Apostle" from the title of the Pauline Epistles, and "of Paul the Apostle" from the title of the Epistle to the Hebrews; strike out the word "General" from the title of the Epistles of James, Peter, 1 John, and Jude; and let the title of the Revelation run "The Revelation of John."
3. For "Holy Ghost" adopt uniformly the rendering "Holy Spirit."
4. At the word "worship" in Matt. ii. 2, etc., add the marginal note "The Greek word denotes an act of reverence, whether paid to man (see chap. xviii. 26) or to God (see chap. iv. 10)."
5. Put into the text uniformly the marginal rendering "through" in place of "by" when it relates to prophecy, viz., in Matt. ii. 5, 17, 23; iii. 3; iv. 14; viii. 17; xii. 17; xiii. 35; xxi. 4; xxiv. 15; xxvii. 9; Luke xviii. 31; Acts ii. 16; xxviii. 25.
6. For "tempt" ("temptation") substitute "try" or "make trial of" ("trial") wherever enticement to what is wrong is not evidently spoken of, viz., in the following instances: Matt. iv. 7; xvi. 1; xix. 3; xxii. 18, 35; Mark viii. 11; x. 2; xii. 15; Luke iv. 12; x. 25; xi. 16; xxii. 28; John viii. 6; Acts v. 9; xv. 10; 1 Cor. x. 9; Heb. iii. 8, 9; 1 Pet. i. 6.
7. Substitute modern forms of speech for the following archaisms, viz., "who" or "that" for "which" when used of persons; "are" for "be" in the present indicative; "know," "knew," for "wot," "wist"; "drag" or "drag away" for "hale."
8. Substitute for "devil" ("devils") the word "demon" ("demons") wherever the latter word is given in the margin (or represents the Greek words δαίμων, δαιμόνιον); and for "possessed with a devil" (or "devils") substitute either "demoniac" or "possessed with a demon" (or "demons").
9. After "baptize" let the marg. "Or, in" and the text "with" exchange places.
10. Let the word "testament" be everywhere changed to "covenant" (without an alternate in the margin), except in Heb. ix. 15—17.
11. Wherever "patience" occurs as the rendering of ὑπομονή add "stedfastness" as an alternate in the margin, except in 2 Cor. i. 6; James v. 11; Luke viii. 15; Heb. x. 1.
12. Let ἀσσάριον (Matt. x. 29; Luke xii. 6) be translated "penny," and δηνάριον "shilling," except in Matt. xxii. 19; Mark xii. 15; Luke xx. 24, where the name of the coin, "a denarius," should be given.
13. Against the expression "the God and Father of our Lord Jesus Christ" add the marginal rendering "Or, *God and the Father*," etc.; viz., in Rom. xv. 6; 2 Cor. i. 3; xi. 31; Eph. i. 3; Col. i. 3; 1 Pet. i. 3. And against the expression "our God and Father" add the marg. "Or, *God and our Father*"; viz., in Gal. i. 4; Phil. iv. 20; 1 Thess. i. 3; iii. 11, 13; Jas. i. 27. And against the expression "his God and Father" add the marg. "Or, *God and his Father*," viz., in Rev. i. 6.
14. Let the use of "fulfil" be confined to those cases in which it denotes "accomplish." "bring to pass," or the like.

MATTHEW.

3. 7. Against "to his baptism" add marg. Or, *for baptism*
10. For "is the axe laid unto" read "the axe lieth at" So in Luke iii. 9.
6. 11. Let the marg. read Gr. *our bread for the coming day, or our needful bread*. So in Luke xi. 3.
27. For "his stature" read "the measure of his life" (with marg. Or, *his stature*) So in Luke xii. 25.
8. 4. Here and in Matt. xxvii. 65; Mark i. 44, for "go thy [your] way" read simply "go"
9. 6, 8. For "power" read "authority" (see marg.⁴) So in Mark ii. 10; Luke v. 24.
10. 39. "life" strike out the marg. So in xvi. 25; Mark viii. 35; Luke ix. 24; xvii. 33; John xii. 25.
12. 23. For "Is this the son of David?" read "Can this be the son of David?" [comp. John iv. 29.]
31. "unto men" strike out the marg.
19. 14. For "of such is" read "to such belongeth" with marg. Or, *of such is* So in Mark x. 14; Luke xviii. 16.
20. 1. For "that is" read "that was"
22. 23. For marg.⁴ read "Many ancient authorities read *saying*."
23. 9. For "Father, which is in heaven" read "Father, *even* he who is in heaven."
23. For "judgment" read "justice" So in Luke xi. 42.
26. 29. For "I will not drink" read "I shall not drink" Similarly in Mark xiv. 25; Luke xxii. 16, 18.
27. 27. For "palace" read "Prætorium" with marg. Or, *palace* [as in Mark xv. 16] So in John xviii. 28, 33; xix. 9.

MARK.

2. 4, 9, 11, 12. "bed" add marg. Or, *pallet* So in vi. 55; John v. 8, 9, 10, 11, 12; Acts v. 15; ix. 33.
7. 4. For "wash" read "bathe" [comp. Luke xi. 38.]
10. 13. For "brought" read "were bringing" So in Luke xviii. 15.
32. "and they that followed," etc., omit the marg.
45. For "For verily," etc., read "For the Son of man also," etc.
11. 24. For "have received" read "receive" with marg. Gr. *received*.
14. 3. For "spikenard" read "pure nard" (with marg. Or, *liquid nard*), and omit marg.⁸ So in John xii. 3.

APPENDIX III.

LUKE.

1. 35. Let the text run "wherefore also the holy thing which is begotten shall be called the Son of God" with the present text in the margin.
   70. For "since the world began" read "of old" Similarly Acts iii. 21; xv. 18.
2. 34. For "and rising up" read "and the rising"
   37. For "even for" read "even unto"
3. 14. For "Do violence to no man," etc., read "Extort from no man by violence, neither accuse any one wrongfully" and omit marg.
   20. For "added yet this above all" read "added this also to them all"
4. 1. For "by the Spirit" read "in the Spirit" and omit the marg.
6. 16. For "was the traitor" read "became a traitor"
8. 3. For "Chuza" read "Chuzas"
   29. For "commanded" read "was commanding"
   33. For "were choked" read "were drowned"
9. 12. For "victuals" read "provisions"
   18. For "alone" read "apart"
   46. For "should be greatest" read "was the greatest"
11. 38. For "washed" read "bathed himself" [comp. Mark vii. 4.]
12. 49. For "what will I," etc., read "what do I desire" (with the marg. Or, how I would that it were already kindled!)
13. 32. "I am perfected" add marg. Or, I end my course
15. 16. For "have been filled" read "have filled his belly" (with the marg. Many ancient authorities read have been filled.)
17. 6. Read "If ye had faith," etc., and "it would obey you."
   11. For "through the midst of" read "along the borders of" and substitute the present text for marg.
18. 5. "lest she wear me," etc., add marg. Or, lest at last by her coming she wear me out
   7. For "and he," etc., read "and yet he," etc., with the marg. Or, and is he slow to punish on their behalf?
19. 29. For "the mount of Olives" read "Olivet" So in xxi. 37; see Acts i. 12.
   42. "day" add marg. Some ancient authorities read thy day.
   "peace" add marg. Some ancient authorities read thy peace.
20. 20. "rule" add marg. Or, ruling power
22. 24. For "is accounted" read "was accounted"
   70. For "Ye say that I am" read "Ye say it, for I am" and substitute the text for the marg.
23. 2. "Christ a king" omit the marg.
   15. "he sent him," etc., add marg. Many ancient authorities read I sent you to him.
   23. For "instant" read "urgent"
   46. Let margin and text exchange places.
24. 30. Read "he took the bread and blessed; and breaking it he gave to them"
   38. For "reasonings" read "questionings"

JOHN.

1. 3, 10, 17. Substitute the marginal rendering for the text.
2. 17. For "The zeal of thine house" read "Zeal for thy house"
3. 20. For "ill" read "evil" So in v. 29.
   29. For "fulfilled" read "made full" [and so xv. 11; xvi. 24; xvii. 13. See "Classes of Passages," xiv.]
5. 27. Substitute the marginal rendering for the text.
7. 8. For "I go not up yet" read "I go not up" and change the marg. to Many ancient authorities add yet.
21, 22. For "marvel. For this cause hath Moses," etc., read "marvel because thereof. Moses hath," etc., and omit the marg.
23. "a man every whit whole" add marg. Gr. a whole man sound.
38. For "out of his belly" read "from within him" (with marg. Gr. out of his belly.)
8. 24, 28. "I am he" omit marg. (and the corresponding portion of marg.) So in xiii. 19.
25. Substitute for the present marg. Or, Altogether that which I also speak unto you
26. "unto the world" omit marg. "Gr. into."
44. For "stand" read "standeth" and omit marg.
52, 53. For "is dead" and "are dead" read "died" [Compare vi. 49, 58.]
58. For "was" read "was born" and omit marg.
10. 8. "before me" add marg. Some ancient authorities omit before me.
12. 43. For "the glory of men . . . the glory of God" read "the glory that is of men . . . the glory that is of God"
14. 1. Let marg. and the text exchange places.
   14. For "shall ask me anything" read "shall ask anything" and let marg. read Many ancient authorities add me.
16. 25, 29. For "proverbs" read "dark sayings"
17. 24. For "I will" read "I desire"
18. 37. For "Thou sayest that," etc., read "Thou sayest it, for I am a king" and substitute the present text for the marg. (comp. Luke xxii. 70.)
21. 7. "was naked" add marg. Or, had on his under garment only.

ACTS OF THE APOSTLES.

2. 47. For "those that were being saved" read "those that were saved" with the text in the marg.
3. 21. For "since the world began" read "from of old"
8. 16. For "he was fallen" read "it was fallen"
13. 18. For "suffered he their manners" read "as a nursing-father bare he them," and in the marg. read "Many ancient authorities read suffered he their manners."
14. 9. "made whole" omit marg.
15. 18. For "from the beginning of the world" read "from of old"
23. 5. "The apostles and the elder brethren" read "The apostles and the elders, brethren," and put the present text into the marg.
17. 22. For "somewhat superstitious" read "very religious" and put the present text in the marg.
19. 31. For "chief officers of Asia" read "Asiarchs" (with marg., i. e., officers having charge of festivals in the Roman province of Asia.)
20. 28. For "God" read "the Lord" (with marg. Some ancient authorities, including the two oldest mss., read God.)
21. 10. For "many days" read "some days"
23. 30. "against the man," etc., add marg. Many ancient authorities read against the man on their part, I sent him to thee, charging, etc.
35. For "hear thy cause" read "hear thee fully"
24. 17. For "many years" read "some years"
25. 3. For "laying wait" read "laying a plot"
26. 28. "With but," etc., add marg. Or, In a little time.

APPENDIX III.

29. " whether with little," etc., add marg. Or, *both in little and in great*, i. e., in all respects
27, 37. Omit marg.*

ROMANS.

1. 17. For " by faith " read " from faith " and omit the marg.
  18. For " hold down " read " hinder "
2. 12. " have sinned " add marg. Gr. *sinned*.
  13. For " a law " read " the law "
  14. For " which have no " read " that have not the " For " having no " read " not having the "
  14, 15. Enclose in a parenthesis.
  15. " their thoughts," etc., add marg. Or, *their thoughts accusing or else excusing them one with another*
  18. In marg.* for " *provest* " read " *dost distinguish* "
  22. Omit the marg.
3. 9. For " in worse case " read " better " and omit the marg.
  21. Begin a paragraph.
  23. " have sinned " add marg. Gr. *sinned*.
  25. " set forth " omit marg.* (" *purposed* ")
   For " by his blood " read " in his blood " (retaining the comma after " faith ") and omit marg.*
  31. Make a paragraph of verse 31.
4. 1. For " according to the flesh, hath found " read " hath found according to the flesh " and put the present text into the margin.
5. 1. For " let us have " read " we have " and in marg.* read Many ancient authorities read *let us have*. So in verses 2, 3 for " let us " read " we " (twice).
  7. Omit marg.* (" *that which is good* ")
6. 7. " justified " add marg. Or, *released*
7. 25. For " I myself with the mind serve " read " I of myself with the mind, indeed, serve "
8. 3. Let marg.* (" *and for sin* ") and the text exchange places.
  5, 6, 9, 13. For " spirit " read " Spirit "
  13. For " mortify " read " put to death " and omit marg.
  24. For " by " read " in " (with marg. Or, *by*)
  26. For " himself " read " itself "
  34. For " shall condemn " read " condemneth "
9. 5. For marg.* read Or, *flesh: he who is over all, God. be blessed for ever*
  22. " willing " add marg. Or, *although willing*
11. 11. Begin the paragraph here instead of at ver. 13.
12. 1. For " reasonable " read " spiritual " with marg. Gr. *belonging to the reason*.
  6. Omit marg.* (" *the faith* ")
  19. Let marg.* (" *the wrath* of God ") and the text exchange places.

1 CORINTHIANS.

1. 18. For " are perishing . . . are being saved " read " perish . . . are saved " and put the present text into the marg.
  19. For " And . . . reject " read " And the discernment of the discerning will I bring to nought "
  20. Omit marg.* (" Or, *have part therein* ")
2. 6. For " the perfect " read " them that are fullgrown "
  8. For " knoweth " read " hath known "
  12. For " is of God " read " is from God "
   For " are freely given to us by God " read " were freely given to us of God "
  13. For " comparing spiritual things with spiritual " read " combining spiritual things with spiritual *words* " and omit marg.¹

14. " natural " add marg. Or, *unspiritual ; Gr. psychical*.
4. 8. For " have reigned " read " have come to reign "
  9. For " and to angels " read " both to angels " and substitute the present text for the marg.
  21. For " meekness " read " gentleness "
5. 10, 11. Let marg.* and* and the text exchange places.
7. 6. For " permission " read " concession "
  21. Let marg.* (" *nay, even if* ") and the text exchange places.
  25. For " faithful " read " trustworthy "
  26. For " the present distress " read " the distress that is upon us "
  31. For " abusing it " read " using it to the full " and omit the margin.
8. 3. For " of him " read " by him "
  8. " commend " add marg. Gr. *present*.
9. 10. " altogether " let " assuredly " be the rendering in the text, and substitute " *altogether* " for the marg.
  27. " have preached " add marg. Or, *have been a herald*
11. 10. Omit marg.* (" *have authority over* ")
  19. For " heresies " read " factions " (with marg. Gr. *heresies*.)
  27. For " unworthily " read " in an unworthy manner "
12. 31. Read " And moreover a most excellent way," etc.
13. 12. Read " then shall I know fully even as also I was fully known " and omit marg.* and *.
  13. Omit marg.* (" *but greater than these* ")
14. 3. For " comfort " read " exhortation "
  33, 34. For " of peace; as," etc., read " of peace. As in all the churches of the saints, let," etc. [and begin the paragraph with " As," etc.].
15. 2. Adopt marg.* for the text (substituting " *the word which* " for " *what* ").
  8. For " as unto . . . time " read " as to the *child* untimely born "
  19. Let marg.* and the text exchange places.
  33. For " Evil company doth corrupt good manners " read " Evil companionships corrupt good morals "
  34. For " Awake up " read " Awake to soberness " and omit marg.¹⁰
  44, 46. " natural " add marg. Gr. *psychical*.
  51. For " We shall not all " read " We all shall not " and put the present text into the marg.

2 CORINTHIANS.

1. 9. For " answer " read " sentence " (with marg. Gr. *answer*.)
  15. For " before " read " first "
  24. Read in the text " for in faith ye stand fast "
2. 14. Begin a new paragraph with this verse.
  15. For " are being saved . . . are perishing " read " are saved . . . perish " and put the present text into the marg.
3. 9. For " is glory " read " hath glory " and let marg.* run Many, etc. *For if the ministration of condemnation is glory*.
  18. Let marg.* and the text exchange places.
   Omit marg.⁷ (" *the Spirit* which *is the Lord* ")
4. 3. For " are perishing " read " perish " and put the present text into the marg.
7. 8, 9. For " I do not regret it, though," etc., read " I do not regret it: though I did regret *it* (for I see that that epistle made you sorry, though but for a season), I now rejoice," etc.
12. 7. Strike out " —wherefore " and add marg. Some ancient authorities read—*wherefore*.

445

APPENDIX III.

GALATIANS.

1. 7. "which is not another *gospel:* only," etc., add the marg. Or, *which is nothing else save that,* etc.
   10. Read " For am I now seeking the favour of men or of God" and for "seeking to please" read "striving to please"
2. 1. Strike out marg.² ("*in the course of*")
   16. For " save " read " but " and omit marg.⁵
   20. For " yet I live ; *and yet* no longer I " read " and it is no longer I that live " and omit marg.²
3. 22. For " hath shut up " read " shut up "
   23. Omit marg.¹ ("*the faith*")
   24. For " hath been " read " is become "
4. 12. For " be " read " become "
   For " I *am as* " read " I also *am become* as "
   16. For " because I tell you " read " by telling you "
   19. Substitute a dash for the comma after " you "
5. 1. Substitute marg.⁷ ("*For freedom*") for the text.
   12. For " cut themselves off " read " go beyond circumcision "
   20. Substitute marg.³ ("*parties*") for the text.
6. 1. "in any trespass " add marg. Or, *by*
   10. " as " add marg. Or, *since*
   11. Let the marg. ("*write*") and the text exchange places.

EPHESIANS.

1. 16. For "and which *ye shew*" read "and the love which *ye shew*" and in marg.⁸ for "insert" read " omit "
2. 2. For " power " read " powers " (with marg. Gr. *power.*)
3. 13. For " ye faint not " read " I may not faint " (with marg. Or, *ye*)
6. 9. For " both " read " he who is both "

PHILIPPIANS.

1. 16. To " the one," etc., add marg. Or, *they that are moved by love* do it.
   17. To " but the other," etc., add the marg. Or, *but they that are factious proclaim Christ*
   22. Read in the text " *if* this shall bring fruit from my work " with marg. Gr. *this is for me fruit of work.*
   Omit marg.⁷ (" *I do not make known* ")
2. 1. For " comfort " read " exhortation "
   6. For " being " read " existing " and omit marg.²
   Let the text run "counted not the being on an equality with God a thing to be grasped " and omit marg.³
   14. For "disputings " read " questionings "
   15. For " may be " read " may become "
3. 8. Substitute marg.⁶ ("*refuse*") for the text.
   9. For " of God " read " from God "
   12. For "apprehend . . . apprehended" read "lay hold on . . . laid hold on", and in marg.¹ for "*apprehend . . . apprehended*" read "*lay hold . . . laid hold on*"
   13. For "apprehended" read "laid hold"
4. 4. Omit marg.⁵ ("*Farewell*")
   19. For "fulfil" read "supply" [Comp. "Classes of Passages," XIV.]

COLOSSIANS.

1. 26. For " from all " read " for "
2. 15. For "having put off from himself" read "having despoiled" and substitute the text for marg.¹

3. 5. For " Mortify " read " Put to death " and omit marg.⁸
   16. For " richly " read " richly ; " and omit the semicolon after " wisdom " putting the present text into the marg.

1 THESSALONIANS.

2. 6. Let marg.¹ run *claimed authority*, and then let the marg. and the text exchange places.
4. 12. For " honestly " read " becomingly "
5. 22. Omit marg.⁴ ("*appearance*")

2 THESSALONIANS.

2. 2. For " is *now* present " read " is just at hand "
   10. For "are perishing" read "perish" with the text in the marg.
3. 2. Omit marg.³ (" *the faith* ")

1 TIMOTHY.

1. 16. For " hereafter " read " thereafter "
   18. Substitute marg.³ ("*led the way to thee*") for the text.
2. 4. Read "who would have all men to be saved"
   15. Let marg.⁷ and the text exchange places.
5. 12. For " faith " read " pledge " (with marg. Gr. *faith.*)
6. 9. For " desire " read " are minded "

2 TIMOTHY.

1. 10. For "incorruption" read "immortality" with marg. Gr. *incorruption.*
2. 26. Read " having been taken captive by him unto his will " ; and let marg.¹¹ run Or, *by him, unto the will of God.* Gr. *by him,* etc.

TITUS.

1. 2. " before times eternal " add marg. Or, *long ages ago*
2. 13. Let the text and marg.⁸ exchange places.
3. 10. For " A man . . . heretical " read " a factious man "

HEBREWS.

1. 7. Omit marg.⁷ ("*spirits*")
   9. To the first " God " add marg. Or, *O God.*
2. 16. Let the text run "For verily not to angels doth he give help, but he giveth help to," etc. (with marg. Gr. *For verily not of angels doth he take hold, but he taketh hold of,* etc.)
   17. For " might be " read " might become "
3. 9. Let marg.⁵ (" *Where* ") and the text exchange places.
   11. " As " add marg. Or, *So* So in iv. 3.
4. 2. Let the text and marg.² exchange places, reading in marg. " Many ancient authorities," etc.
   7. Read " a certain day, To-day, saying in David, so long a time afterward (even as hath been said before), To-day if ye," etc.
6. 1. For " let us cease," etc., read " leaving the doctrine of the first principles of Christ, let us " with marg.³ Gr. *the word of the beginning of Christ.*
   9. In marg.⁴ for " *are near to* " read " *belong to* "
8. 8. " finding fault," etc., add marg. Some ancient authorities read *finding fault* with it *he saith unto them.*
9. 4. Let marg.⁵ and the text exchange places.
   9. For " parable " read " figure " So in xi. 19. Omit ¹ " *now* "
   14. " the eternal Spirit " add marg. Or, *his eternal spirit*

APPENDIX III.

17. Let marg.⁴ and the text exchange places.
10. 1. For "they can" read "can" (and for marg.⁸ read Many ancient authorities read *they can*.)
22, 23. Let the text and marg.¹ exchange places.
23. For "the assembling of ourselves together" read "our own assembling together"
34. For "⁴ ye yourselves have" read "² ye have for yourselves" (and omit marg.⁴, letting marg.² read Many ancient authorities read *that ye have your own selves for a*, etc.)
11. 1. Read "faith is assurance of things hoped for, a conviction," etc.
5. Read in the text "for he hath had witness borne to him that before his translation he had been," etc., with the present text in the marg.
12. 3. For "themselves" read "himself" (and let marg.¹ run Many ancient authorities read *themselves*.)
17. For "rejected (for . . . of repentance)" read "rejected; for he found no place for a change of mind *in his father*" with marg. Or, *rejected (for he found no place of repentance)*, etc. Or, *rejected; for . . . of repentance*, etc.
13. 18. For "honestly" read "honourably"
20. For "the eternal" read "an eternal"
24. "They of" add marg. Or, *The brethren from*

JAMES.

1. 3. For "proof" read "proving"
17. For "boon" read "gift"
3. 1. For "many" read "many *of you*"
4. 4. "adulteresses" add marg. That is, *who break your marriage vow to God.*

1 PETER.

2. 2. In marg.⁶ for "reasonable" read "belonging to the reason."
5. 2. "according unto God" read "according to the *will of* God" (and so in marg. ²). Comp. Rom. viii. 27.

2 PETER.

1. 1. Let marg.⁴ and the text exchange places.
7. For "love of the brethren" read "brotherly kindness" (twice) with marg. Gr. *love of the brethren*.
17. For "came such a voice to him from the excellent glory" read "was borne such a voice to him by the Majestic Glory" and omit marg.⁴
18. For "come" read "borne" and omit marg.⁵
2. 13. For "love-feasts" read "deceivings" and in marg.⁴ read Some ancient authorities read *love-feasts*.

1 JOHN.

3. 19, 20. For "him, whereinsoever . . . because God," etc., read "him: because if our heart condemn us, God," etc. (with the present text in the marg.)
5. 18. Substitute marg.² for the text, and add marg.³ Some ancient manuscripts read *him*.

2 JOHN.

1 (and 5). "lady" add marg. Or, *Cyria*

3 JOHN.

4. dele marg.³
8. For "with the truth" read "for the truth"

JUDE.

1. For "Judas" read "Jude" and add marg. Gr. *Judas*.
4. For "set forth" read "written of beforehand" putting the present text into the marg.
22. Against "And on some," etc., add the marg. Some ancient authorities read *And some refute while they dispute with you.*

REVELATION.

1. 8. Omit marg.⁸ ("*the Lord, the God*")
13. Omit marg.² ("*the Son of man*")
3. 2. For "fulfilled" read "perfected"
4. 6. "of the throne" add marg. Or, *before* [comp. v. 6; vii. 17.]
5. 6. "in the midst of the throne," etc., add marg. Or, *between the throne with the four living creatures, and the elders*
6. 6. "A measure," etc., add marg. [instead of marg.⁴ and⁵] Or, *A chœnix* (i. e., about a quart) *of wheat for a shilling*—implying great scarcity.
11. For "be fulfilled" read "be fulfilled *in number*" and then let the marg. and the text exchange places.
7. 17. "of the throne" add marg. Or, *before* (See iv. 6.)
10. 6. Substitute marg.² (*delay*) for the text.
12. 4. For "stood . . . was . . . was . . . might" read "standeth . . . is . . . is . . . may"
13. 1. "he stood" add marg. Some ancient authorities read *I stood*, etc., connecting the clause with what follows.
8. Let marg.⁶ and the text exchange places. [Comp. xvii. 8.]
14. 6. For "an eternal gospel" read "eternal good tidings"
15. For "over-ripe" read "ripe" with marg. Gr. *become dry*.
15. 2. For "that come" read "that come off"
16. 9. For "the God" read "God"
16. Har-Magedon add marg. Or, *Ar-Magedon*
19. 15. For "of Almighty God" read "of God, the Almighty"
22. 3. For "do him service" read "serve him"

www.ingramcontent.com/pod-product-compliance
Lightning Source LLC
Chambersburg PA
CBHW022133300426
44115CB00006B/170